A GUIDE TO THE ANCIENT WORLD

MICHAEL GRANT

A GUIDE TO THE ANCIENT WORLD

A DICTIONARY OF CLASSICAL PLACE NAMES

THE
H.W. WILSON COMPANY
1986

Library of Congress Cataloging-in-Publication Data

Grant, Michael, 1914–
A guide to the ancient world.

Bibliography: p.
1. Mediterranean Region—Gazetteers. 2. Classical antiquities. I. Title.
DE25.G72 1986 913.8´003´21 86–15785
ISBN 0-8242-0742-4

MAPS BY LILI WRONKER

PRINTED IN THE UNITED STATES OF AMERICA

CONTENTS

INTRODUCTION

Although the Greek and Latin languages are not studied as extensively as they used to be, it seems evident that interest in the classical civilization as a whole, that is to say in its history, literature, archaeology and art, has by no means diminished in recent years but has, indeed, increased. Moreover, despite all pressures in the opposite direction this trend shows no sign of weakening: which is surely to the credit of our age, because of the inexhaustible wealth and interest of that civilization—without understanding it we cannot understand ourselves. It is in these conditions and expectations that the present book has been planned. It is intended to provide information to readers, students and travelers about the most important geographical locations in the ancient Greek, Etruscan and Roman world.

About nine hundred places have been selected, covering—as that world covered—an area extending from the Atlantic Ocean to Pakistan, and from the Sahara to southern Russia. The places I have attempted to describe are mostly cities and towns and other habitation sites, though rivers, mountains and lakes (even if not strictly 'places') have also been included where it has seemed desirable to do so. All these names are marked on the maps, and ancient changes of name, as well as modern equivalents, are noted by cross-references.

The period covered is from the early first millennium BC, when the historic civilization of the Greek city-states emerged—in circumstances which have recently been much clarified—from the ruins of its Bronze Age (Mycenaean) forerunner, until the later fifth century AD, when the western Roman empire fell or was transformed.

Each entry includes data of a historical, geographical, archaeological and (where appropriate) artistic and mythological character. Evidence is taken from the ancient Greek and Latin writers, of whom lists are appended—and, in addition, from the sites themselves, and from excavation reports: including, as far as possible, those recently published, though in such a vast and active field any claim to be fully up-to-date would be imprudent. Inscriptions, too, are employed, and chosen examples—as I feel that a student of numismatics will be excused for adding—of the huge, varied and still not fully published coinage of the Greek and Roman worlds. It has also seemed helpful to show readers where they can turn for additional information, and that has been the guiding principle of the list of modern books and periodicals supplied at the end of the book. At least two words of apology need to be added. First, much has obviously been omitted; the book could have been ten or twenty times longer, but then, I think, it would have lost such claim as it may possess to general utility. Second, and even more pressing, I am only too well aware of my audacity in having attempted such a task at all and conscious of the imperfections of what I am offering. I can only hope that the volume will be useful all the same.

I want to express my gratitude not only to previous encyclopedists, whose work has of course proved invaluable, but to all those members of library and museum staffs and universities and publishing houses who have given me generous assistance. For particular acts of help, and items of information, I owe thanks to the Academy of Sciences of the Soviet Union, Mr. C.H. Annis, Professor Manuel Fernandez-Miranda, Mr. M.W.C. Hassall, Dr. J.G.F. Hind, Mr. Peter Lyner, Mrs. Liz Moore, Dr. A.J.N.W. Prag, Mr. Terry Sandell, Professor A. Snodgrass and Mr. A.D. Spencer. My debt to collaborators in the H.W. Wilson Company is very great. My wife has been my partner in the whole undertaking.

Michael Grant, 1986

MAPS

By Lili Wronker

ASIA MINOR

GREECE

AEGEAN ISLANDS

NORTH AFRICA

SPAIN

EGYPT

ITALY

CENTRAL ITALY

SYRIA

THE BLACK SEA

THE BALKANS

THE EAST

BRITAIN

GAUL

CENTRAL EUROPE

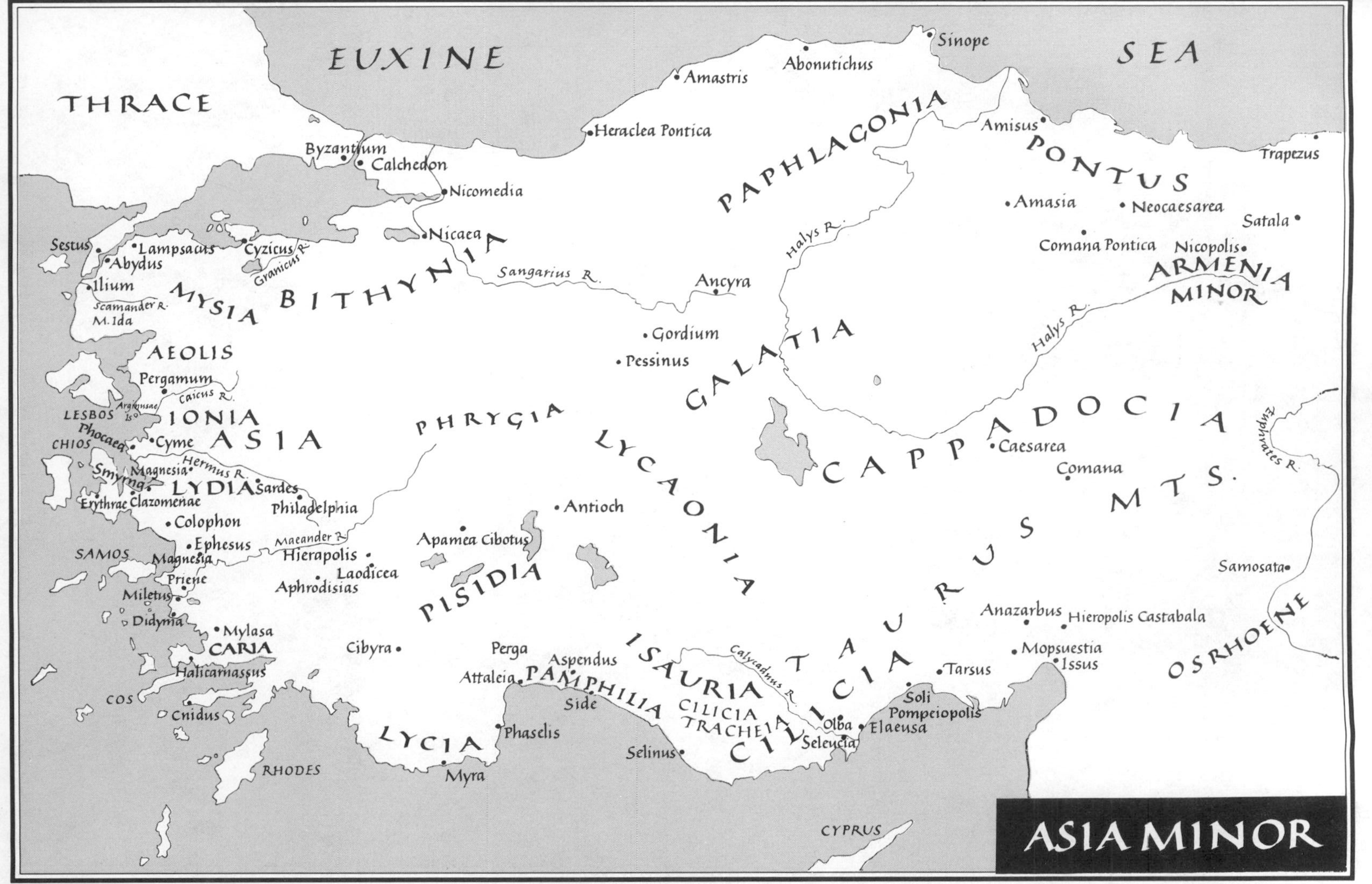
ASIA MINOR
EUXINE SEA
THRACE
Sinope
Abonutichus
Amastris
Heraclea Pontica
Byzantium
Calchedon
Nicomedia
Nicaea
PAPHLAGONIA
Amisus
PONTUS
Trapezus
Amasia
Neocaesarea
Satala
Comana Pontica
Nicopolis
ARMENIA MINOR
Halys R.
Sangarius R.
Ancyra
Sestus
Lampsacus
Abydus
Cyzicus
Granicus R.
Ilium
Scamander R.
M. Ida
MYSIA
BITHYNIA
Gordium
Pessinus
GALATIA
AEOLIS
Pergamum
Caicus R.
Arginusae Is.
LESBOS
IONIA
ASIA
PHRYGIA
LYCAONIA
CAPPADOCIA
Caesarea
Comana
Euphrates R.
Phocaea
Cyme
CHIOS
Hermus R.
Magnesia
Smyrna
LYDIA
Sardes
Erythrae
Clazomenae
Philadelphia
Colophon
Antioch
Ephesus
Maeander R.
Hierapolis
Laodicea
Aphrodisias
SAMOS
Magnesia
Priene
Miletus
Didyma
Mylasa
CARIA
Halicarnassus
COS
Cnidus
RHODES
Apamea Cibotus
PISIDIA
TAURUS MTS.
Samosata
Anazarbus
Hieropolis Castabala
Mopsuestia
Issus
OSRHOENE
Cibyra
Perga
Aspendus
Attaleia
PAMPHILIA
Side
ISAURIA
Calycadnus R.
CILICIA
CILICIA TRACHEIA
Tarsus
Soli Pompeiopolis
Olba
Elaeusa
Seleucia
Selinus
Phaselis
LYCIA
Myra
CYPRUS

MEDITERRANEAN SEA

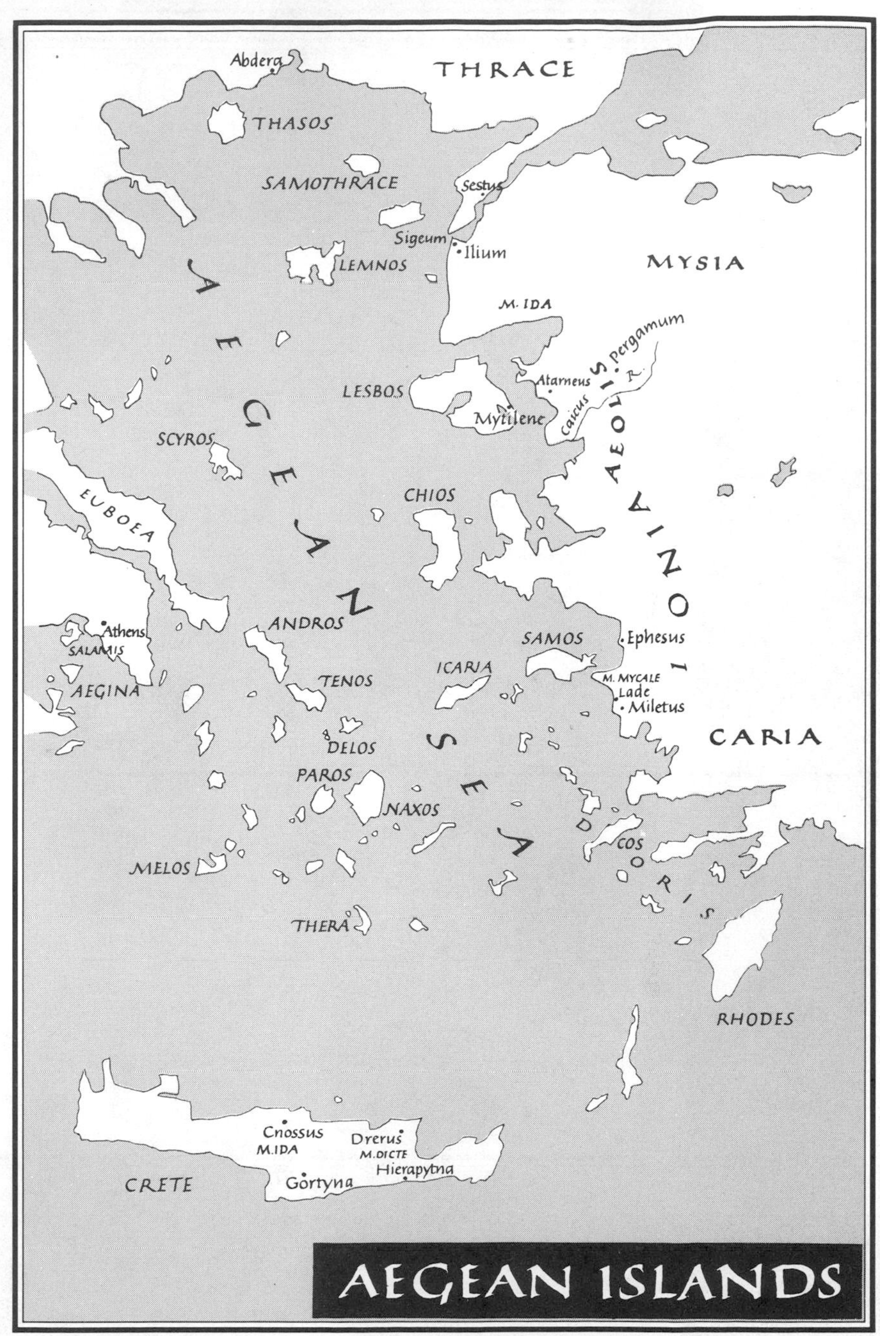
Abdera
THRACE
THASOS
SAMOTHRACE
Sestus
Sigeum
Ilium
LEMNOS
MYSIA
M. IDA
Pergamum
Caicus R.
Atarneus
AEOLIS
LESBOS
Mytilene
SCYROS
AEGEAN SEA
EUBOEA
CHIOS
IONIA
ANDROS
Athens
SALAMIS
AEGINA
SAMOS
Ephesus
ICARIA
M. MYCALE
Lade
Miletus
TENOS
DELOS
CARIA
PAROS
NAXOS
DORIS
COS
MELOS
THERA
RHODES
Cnossus
M. IDA
Drerus
M. DICTE
Hierapytna
Gortyna
CRETE
AEGEAN ISLANDS

GAUL
CALLAECIA
Legio
Asturica
Bracara Augusta
Durius R.
Calagurris
Iberus R.
Osca
Emporiae
Clunia
Numantia
Bilbilis
Caesaraugusta
Ilerda
Barcino
Tarraco
TARRACONENSIS
MAJORICA
Conimbriga
LUSITANIA
Tagus R.
Saguntum
Valentia
BALEARIC IS.
EBUSUS
Olisipo
Emerita
Ilici
BAETICA
Baetis R.
Corduba
Carthago Nova
Italica
Hispalis
Munda
Urso
TARTESSUS
Tartessus
Malaca
Gades
SPAIN

HISPANIA
Utica
Caesarea
Hippo Regius
Bulla Regia
Cirta
Thugga
Bagradas R.
Tingis
Tipasa
Sitifis
Cuicul
Madaurus
Zama Regia
Thamugadi
Lambaesis
Thysdrus
Lix
AFRICA
NUMIDIA
Capsa
Volubilis
MAURETANIA
NORTH AFRICA

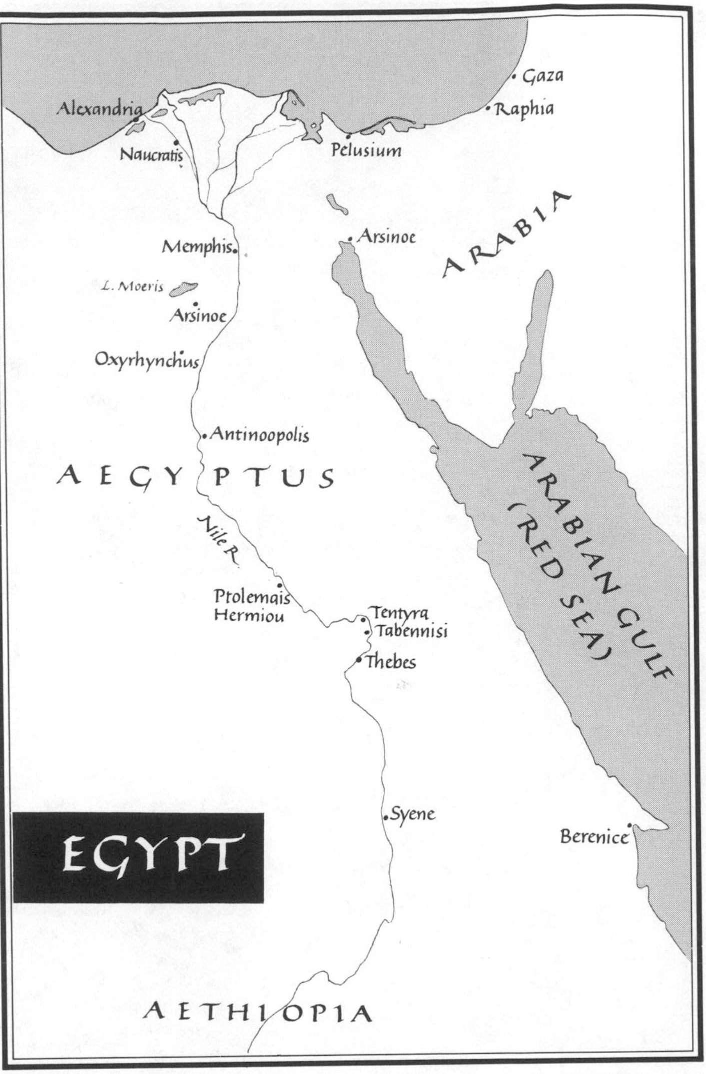

Gaza
Raphia
Alexandria
Naucratis
Pelusium
ARABIA
Arsinoe
Memphis
L. Moeris
Arsinoe
Oxyrhynchus
Antinoopolis
AEGYPTUS
Nile R.
ARABIAN GULF
(RED SEA)
Ptolemais Hermiou
Tentyra
Tabennisi
Thebes
Syene
Berenice
EGYPT
AETHIOPIA

Apollonia
MEDITERRANEAN
Ptolemais
Cyrene
Arsinoe
Euhesperides
SEA
Sabratha
Sugolin
Oea
Lepcis
Magna
CYRENAICA
TRIPOLITANA

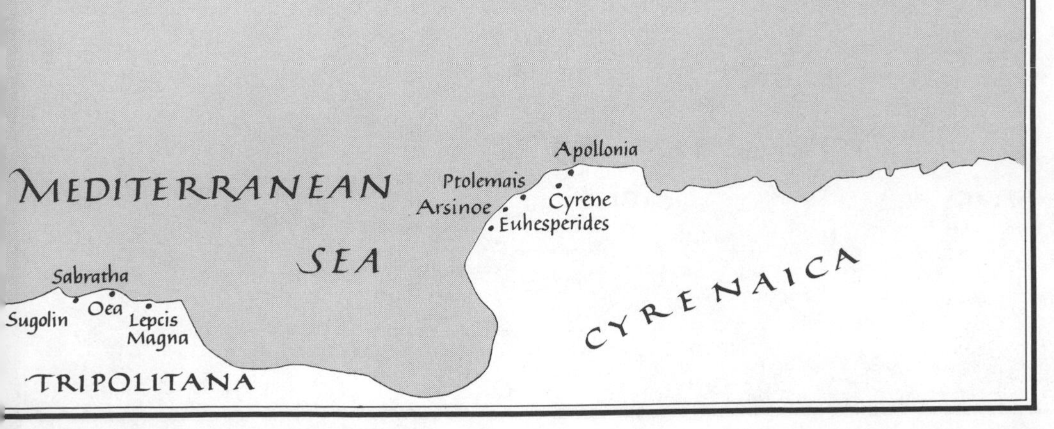

ITALY

RAETIA
NORICUM
PANNONIA
Comum
Mediolanum
Padus R.
Ticinum
Benacus L.
Clastidium
Placentia
Sirmio
Dertona
Trebia R.
Cremona
Verona
LIGURIA
Mantua
Patavium
GALLIA
CISALPINA
Aquileia
Genua
Brixellum
Ateste
Padus R.
Mutina
Adria
Spina
Luna
Misa
DALMATIA
Luca
Ravenna
Pisae
Arnus R.
Faesulae
Rubicon R.
Florentia
Ariminum
ETRURIA
UMBRIA
APENNINUS
ADRIATIC SEA
Volaterrae
Iguvium
Catena Metallifera
Ilva
Arretium
Cortona
CORSICA
Clanis R.
Trasimene L.
Vetulonia
Ancona
Perusia
PICENUM
Alalia
Calusium?
Rusellae
Firmum
Cosa
Volsinii
Vulci
Asculum
Salonae
Graviscae
Tarquinii
Tiber R.
Pyrgi
Veii
Caere
Rome
Tibur
Ostia
LATIUM
Tusculum
SARDINIA
Lavinium
Antium
Fregellae
SAMNIUM
Larinum
Luceria
CAMPANIA
Cumae
Capua
Neapolis
Beneventum
APULIA
Cannae
Aufidus R.
Ausculum
Herculaneum
Pompeii
Stabiae
Caralis
Capreae
Venusia
Posidonia
LUCANIA
Elea
Metapontum
Brundusium
Cape Palinurus
Taras
CALABRIA
Sybaris
AEGATES IS.
Drepanum
Eryx
Motya
Utica
Panormus
Lipara
Lilybaeum
Segesta
Messana
Carthage
Himera
Scylla
BRUTTII
Croton
Selinus
Mylae
AFRICA
SICILY
Naulochus
Tauromenium
IONIAN SEA
Centuripae
Rhegium
Locri Epizephyrii
Acragas
Henna
MT. Aetna
Naxos
Morgantina
Catana
Cape Ecnomus
Philosophiana
Hadrumetum
Gela
Leontini
Megara Hyblaea
Camarina
Syracuse

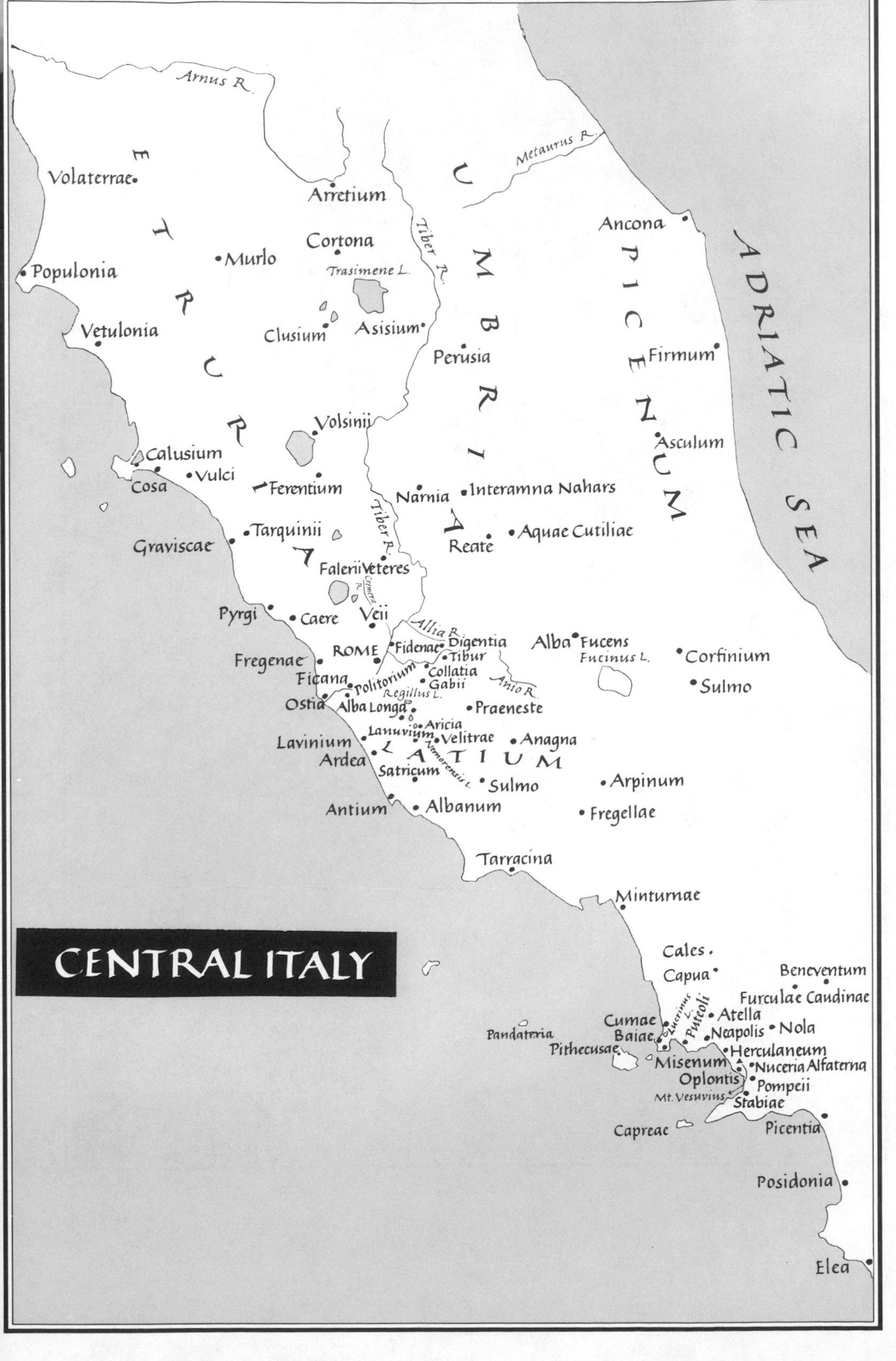
CENTRAL ITALY
ETRURIA
UMBRIA
PICENUM
LATIUM
ADRIATIC SEA
Arnus R.
Metaurus R.
Tiber R.
Trasimene L.
Volaterrae
Arretium
Cortona
Murlo
Populonia
Vetulonia
Clusium
Asisium
Perusia
Ancona
Firmum
Volsinii
Asculum
Calusium
Cosa
Vulci
Ferentium
Narnia
Interamna Nahars
Graviscae
Tarquinii
Reate
Aquae Cutiliae
Falerii Veteres
Cremera R.
Pyrgi
Caere
Veii
Allia R.
ROME
Fidenae
Digentia
Alba Fucens
Fucinus L.
Corfinium
Fregenae
Tibur
Collatia
Gabii
Ficana
Politorium
Regillus L.
Anio R.
Sulmo
Ostia
Alba Longa
Praeneste
Aricia
Lanuvium
Velitrae
Anagna
Lavinium
Ardea
Nemorensis L.
Satricum
Arpinum
Antium
Albanum
Fregellae
Tarracina
Minturnae
Cales
Capua
Beneventum
Furculae Caudinae
Lucrinus L.
Puteoli
Atella
Cumae
Baiae
Neapolis
Nola
Pandateria
Pithecusae
Herculaneum
Misenum
Nuceria Alfaterna
Oplontis
Pompeii
Mt. Vesuvius
Stabiae
Capreae
Picentia
Posidonia
Elea

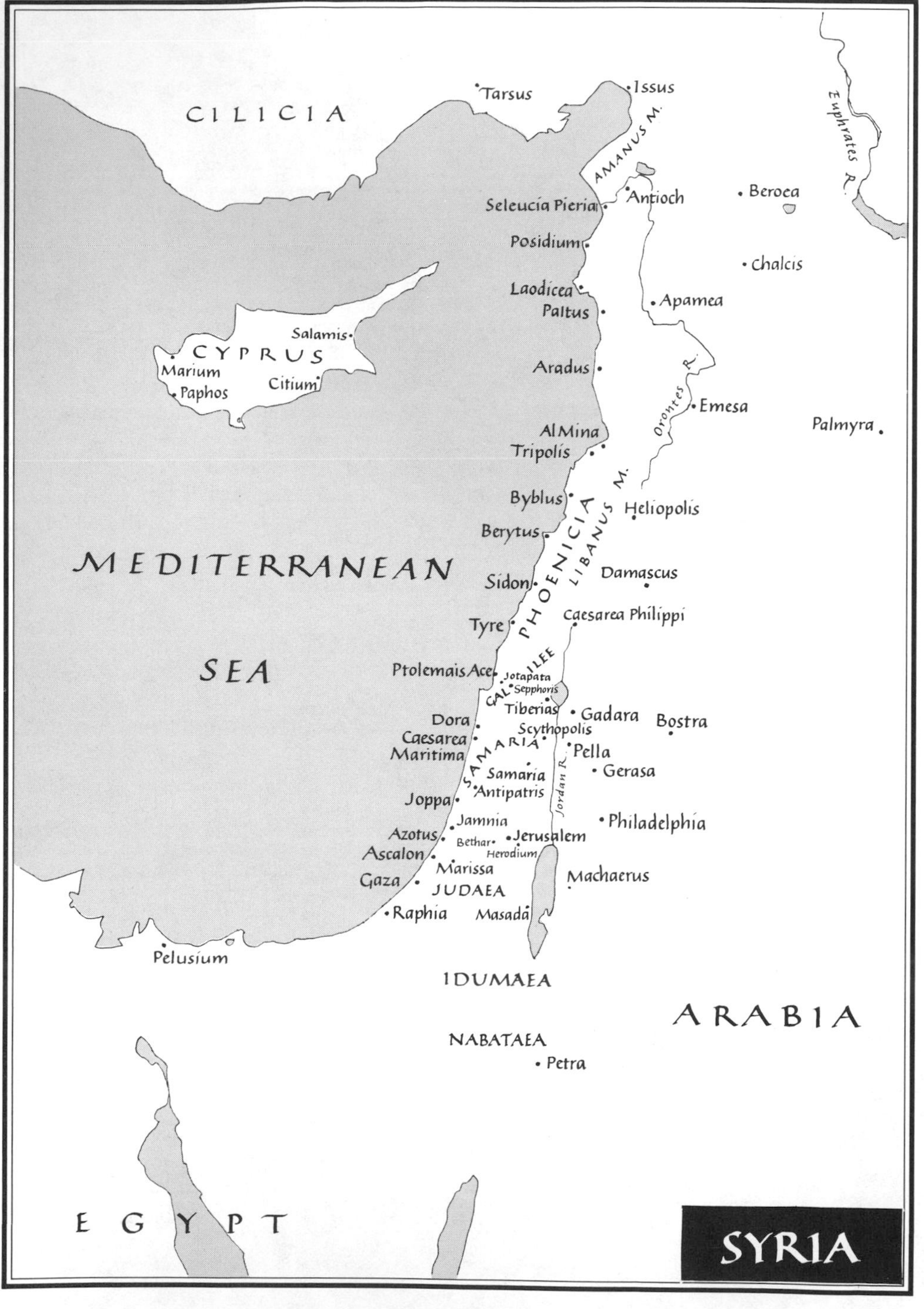
CILICIA
Tarsus
Issus
AMANUS M.
Euphrates R.
Seleucia Pieria
Antioch
Beroea
Posidium
Chalcis
Laodicea
Paltus
Apamea
Salamis
CYPRUS
Marium
Paphos
Citium
Aradus
Orontes R.
Emesa
Palmyra
Al Mina
Tripolis
LIBANUS M.
Byblus
Heliopolis
Berytus
PHOENICIA
MEDITERRANEAN
SEA
Sidon
Damascus
Tyre
Caesarea Philippi
GALILEE
Ptolemais Ace
Jotapata
Sepphoris
Tiberias
Gadara
Bostra
Dora
Scythopolis
Caesarea Maritima
SAMARIA
Pella
Jordan R.
Samaria
Gerasa
Antipatris
Joppa
Jamnia
Philadelphia
Azotus
Bethar
Jerusalem
Herodium
Ascalon
Marissa
Machaerus
Gaza
JUDAEA
Raphia
Masada
Pelusium
IDUMAEA
ARABIA
NABATAEA
Petra
EGYPT
SYRIA

THE BLACK SEA
SCYTHIA
Tyras R.
Hypanis R.
Borysthenes R.
Olbia
Tanais
Tanais R.
MAEOTIS L.
Tyras
SCYTHIA MINOR
DACIA
Panticapaeum
Phanagoria
Hermonassa
Nymphaeum
Neapolis Scythica
Theodosia
Gorgippia
Bosphorus (Cimmerian)
Hypanis R.
Chersonesus
Istrus
Axiopolis
Tomis
Durostorum
Tropaeum Trajani
Danuvius R.
Callatis
MOESIA
EUXINE (BLACK) SEA
Pityus
Dioscurias
CAUCASUS MTS.
Marcianopolis
Odessus
Phasis
Haemus M.
Abonutichus
Sinope
Heraclea Pontica
Amastris
Amisus
Trapezus
Byzantium
Bosphorus (Thracian)
Calchedon
PAPHLAGONIA
Bizye
PONTUS
Tzirallum
Perinthus
Prusias on the Hypius
Amasia
Neocaesarea
Chrysopolis
Halys R.
Lycus R.
Satala
Nicomedia
BITHYNIA
Comana Pontica
Nicopolis
Chersonesus
Euphrates R.
Nicaea
Cyzicus
Abydus
Sangarius R.
Ancyra
ARMENIA
Ilium
Gordium

THE BALKANS
Lauriacum
Ovilava
Vindobona
Carnuntum
Danuvius R.
NORICUM
PANNONIA
Noreia
Virunum
Poetovio
Emona
Siscia
Mursa Major
Cibalae
Bonoia-Malata
ILLYRICUM
DALMATIA
Sirmium
Singidunum
Margum
Salonae
Issa
ADRIATIC SEA
ITALY
Dyrrhachium
Scodra
MACEDONIA
Porolissum
Napoca
Apulum
DACIA
Buridava
Drobeta
Gamzigrad
MOESIA
SUPERIOR
Naissus
Bononia
Ratiaria
Romula-Malva
Oescus
Nova
Serdica
HAEMUS MTS.
MOESIA INFERIOR
Philippopolis
Beroe Augusta Trajana
THRACE
Philippi
Abdera
Hadrianopolis
Caenophrurium
Perinthus
Bizye
Byzantium
Marcianopolis
Odessus
Durostorum
Danuvius R.
Tropaeum Trajani
Callatis
Troesmis
SCYTHIA MINOR
Istrus
EUXINE
SEA
Tyras R.
Hypanis R.
SCYTHIA
Tyras
Olbia

THE EAST

CASPIAN SEA
Artaxa
ARMENIA
Euphrates R.
Tigranocerta
Tigris R.
Samosata
Edessa
Nisibis
Zeugma
Carrhae
Hieropolis Bambyce
Singara
MESOPOTAMIA
ASSYRIA
Hatra
Beroea
Nicephorium Callinicum
Circesium
Dura Europus
Palmyra
SYRIA
Ctesiphon
Seleucia
BABYLONIA
Babylon
Euphrates R.
Tigris R.
ARABIA
Ecbatana
PARTHIAN EMPIRE
Susa
Charax
PERSIS
PERSIAN GULF
Oxus R.
Alexandria Eschate
SOGDIANA
PAROPAMISUS MTS.
Alexandria in Margiana
Bactra
BACTRIA
Alexandria beside Caucasus
ARIA
Alexandria in Aria
Cabura
Indus R.
Taxila
DRANGIANA
ARACHOSIA
Alexandria in Arachosia
Hydaspes R.
INDIA
GEDROSIA
Indus R.

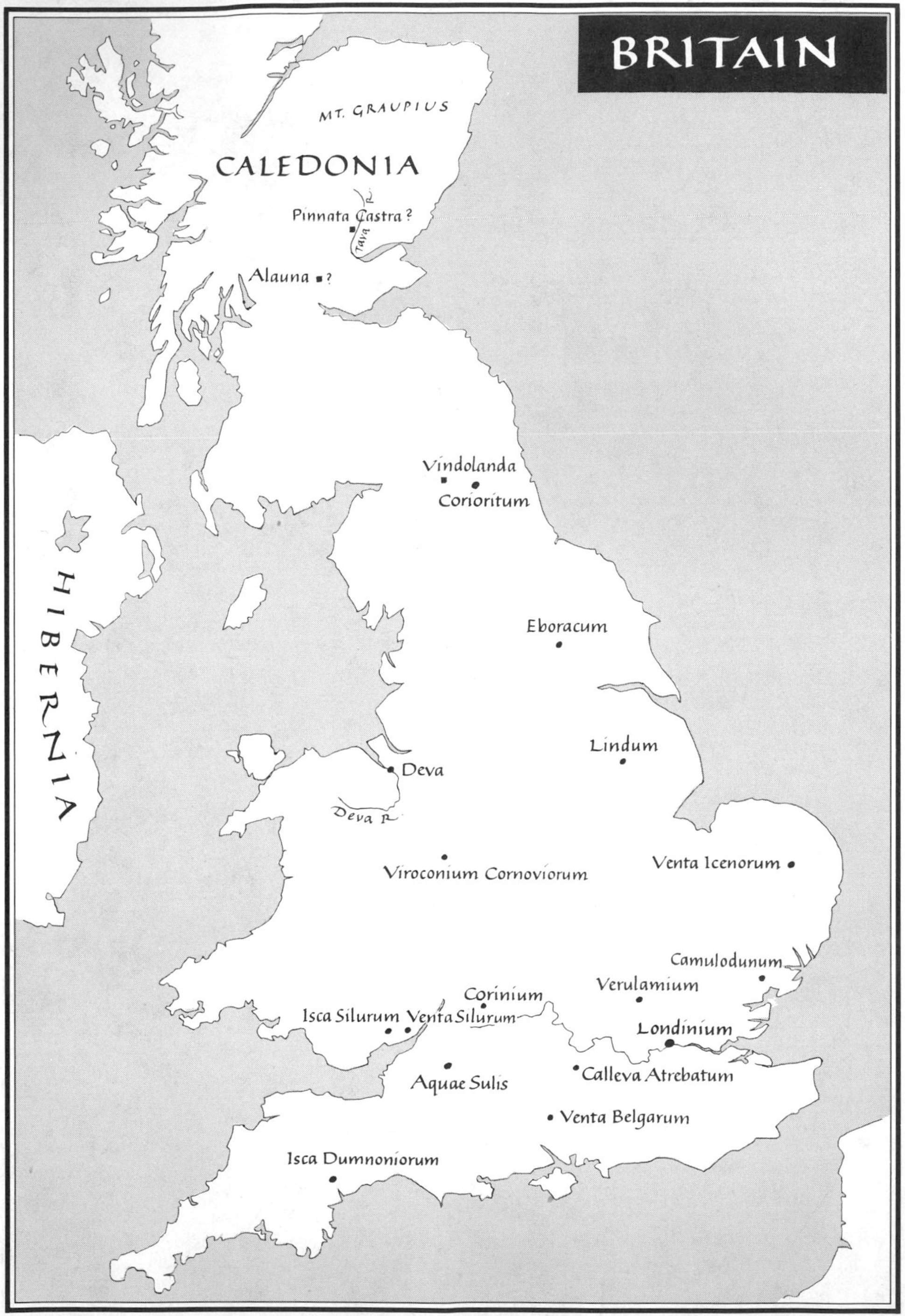
BRITAIN
MT. GRAUPIUS
CALEDONIA
Pinnata Castra ?
Tava R
Alauna ?
HIBERNIA
Vindolanda
Corioritum
Eboracum
Lindum
Deva
Deva R
Viroconium Cornoviorum
Venta Icenorum
Camulodunum
Verulamium
Corinium
Isca Silurum
Venta Silurum
Londinium
Aquae Sulis
Calleva Atrebatum
Venta Belgarum
Isca Dumnoniorum

BRITANNIA
Londinium
FRISII
GERMANIA
INFERIOR
Colonia Agrippinensis
Atuatuca
Rhenus R.
Gesoriacum
BELGICA
Borbetomagus
Samarobriva
Durocortorum
Lutetia Parisiorum
CAMPI CATALAUNII
Argentorate
Moselle R.
GERMANIA SUPERIOR
Cenabum
Alesia
Liger R.
Augusta
Rauricorum
Vesontio
Caesarodunum
Augustodunum
Aventicum
Bibracte
Limonum Pictonum
Liger R.
Genava
Lugdunum
SABAUDIA
Augustonemetum
Ledosus
Augusta Praetoria
Gergovia
Vienna
AQUITANIA
Rhodanus R.
Segusio
Valentia
Burdigala
Uxellodunum
Vasio Vocontiorum
Arausio
Garumna R.
Condatomagus
Carpentorate
Nicaea
Glanum
Antipolis
Arelate
Aquae Sextiae
Tolosa
Baeterrae
Massalia
Forum
Julii
Narbo
HISPANIA
GAUL

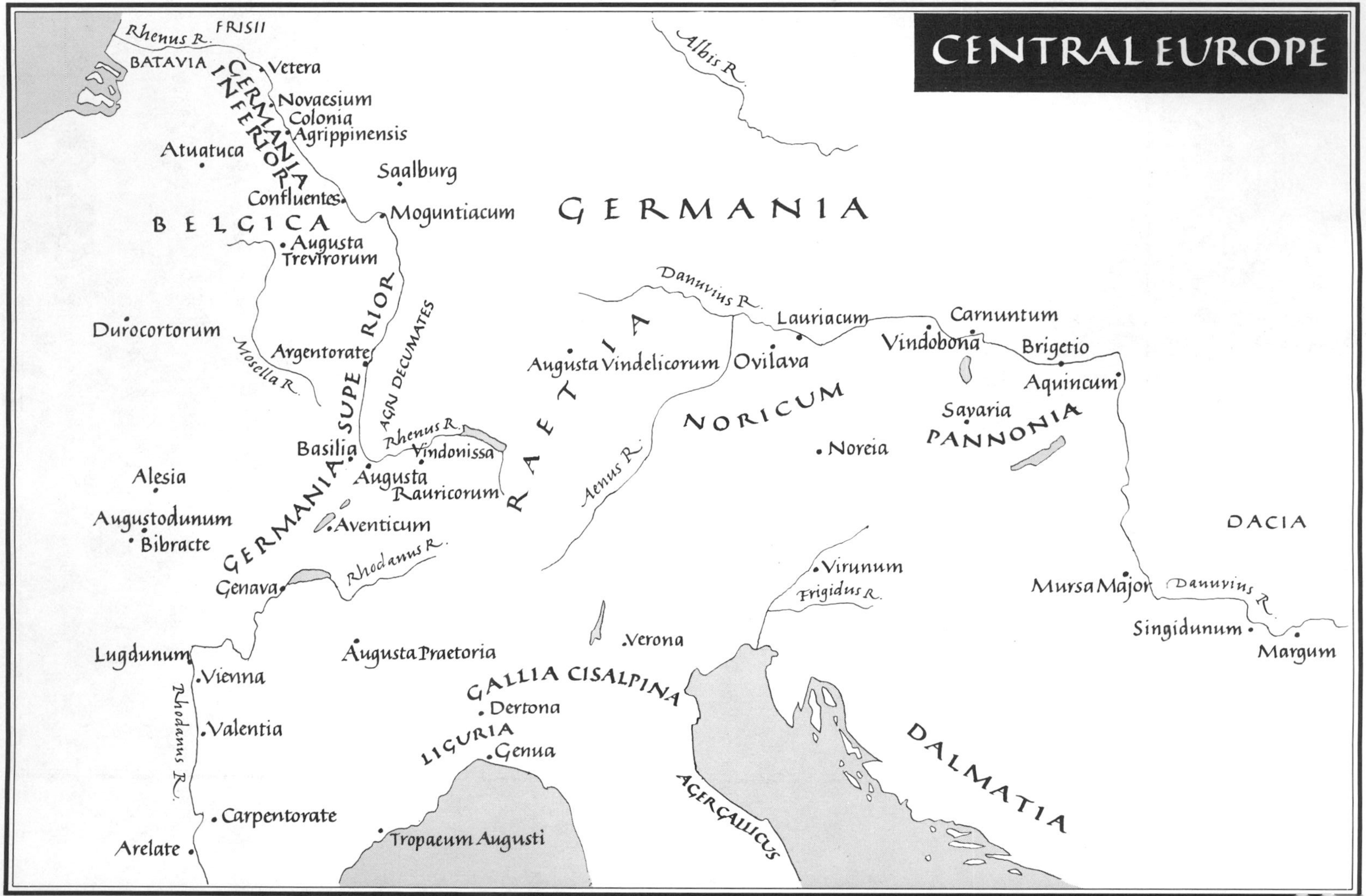

CENTRAL EUROPE

PLACE NAMES

Abdera (Avdira). A city in Thrace (northern Greece); situated on Cape Bulustra (a corruption of the medieval Polystylon), eleven miles northeast of the river Nestos. According to Greek mythology, the foundation of the city went back to Heracles, whose eighth labor was the capture of the man-eating horses of Diomedes, king of the neighboring Bistonians. However, the first attempt to found Abdera, according to Herodotus, was made in the seventh century BC by colonists from Clazomenae (Klazumen) in Ionia led by Tynisias, but they were driven back by the Thracians. In 545 BC the people of another Ionian city, Teos (Sığacık), finding Persian domination intolerable, placed settlers on the site (including the poet Anacreon) and reconstructed the town. It controlled an extensive area—'covered with vineyards and fertile,' according to Pindar. An ear of grain is shown on its fine coins. However, the Abderans were constantly at pains to protect their territory from Thracian incursions. Nevertheless, their city was also a center for trading with the Thracian (Odrysian) rulers of the hinterland, and provided a harbor for the commerce of upper Thrace in general.

When the Persians came to Thrace in 513/512 they took control of Abdera, and did so once again in 492. In 480 it was one of the halting places selected by Xerxes as he marched the Persian army along the northern shores of the Aegean toward Greece. As a member of the first Athenian Alliance (Delian League) established after the end of the Persian Wars, it contributed (from 454 BC) a sum of between ten and fifteen talents, indicating its position as the third-richest city in the League. In 431, at the beginning of the Peloponnesian War against Sparta, it took the lead in an endeavor to enroll Thrace (under the Odrysian ruler Sitalces) and Macedonia in the Athenian cause. Although 'Abderite' later became a synonym for stupidity, Abdera produced two fifth-century thinkers of outstanding distinction, Democritus and Protagoras.

In 376 the city was destroyed by the Thracian tribe of the Triballi, and *c* 346 its remaining inhabitants were incorporated by Philip II in his Macedonian kingdom. After the death of Alexander the Great, Abdera fell successively into the hands of King Lysimachus of Thrace, the Seleucids, the Ptolemies, and then, once again, the Macedonians, whose possession ended in 196 when the

Romans declared it a free state. In 170, however, it was besieged and sacked by Roman and Pergamene soldiers, and never really recovered, although in Roman imperial times it remained, officially speaking, a 'free city,' and in the early Middle Ages was a small Byzantine town and the seat of a bishopric.

The recent excavation of a cemetery (half-a-mile from the site) dating back to the second half of the seventh century BC confirms the city's foundation date given by Herodotus. The uncovering of a Hellenistic 'House of the Dolphins' has now been completed. Other finds are on show in the museum at Kavalla.

Abkhazia *see* Colchis

Abonutichus, Abonou Teichos (Wall of Abonos), later Ionopolis (İnebolu). A small port on the Euxine (Black) Sea coast of Paphlagonia (northern Asia Minor), at the mouth of the river İkiçay. Abonutichus started to issue coinage in the first century BC and achieved city status in the time of the Roman Principate (30 BC; or later?), first under that name and then (from Marcus Aurelius onward, for a time) as Ionopolis. It was the birthplace of one of the most outrageous charlatans of the ancient world, Alexander of Abonutichus, whose career in the second century AD is ruthlessly displayed in Lucian's *Alexander, or the False Prophet.* A successful exploiter of women, Alexander claimed to control a new manifestation of the god Asclepius, in the form of a snake called Glycon (depicted on the city's coinage), with whose assistance he uttered oracles and staged mysteries. His circular shrine has been identified.

Abrit(t)us, Abrittos (Razgrad). A stronghold in Lower Moesia (northeastern Bulgaria), on the road from Marcianopolis (Reka Devnia) to the Danube. Originally a Thracian settlement, it became a Roman fortress in the first century AD and attained urban status in the second. Extensive fortifications have survived, probably dating from the Gothic incursions of the mid-third century.

In 251, these attacks made Abrittus the scene of one of the most catastrophic battles in Roman history. After the king of the Goths, Kniva, had invaded Lower Moesia, the emperor Trajanus Decius arrived in the province and tried to cut off the Goths' retreat. In the ensuing battle, however, Decius and his son Herennius Etruscus, following initial successes, were trapped (as the fifth-century historian Zosimus, despite his partiality for Decius, had to admit) in a bog, where they were killed and the bodies never recovered. This was the first time a Roman emperor had been slain in battle by a foreign foe. The greater part of the imperial army was destroyed. The city walls, erected soon afterward, combine towers of three different shapes.

Abu Serai *see* Circesium

Abydus (Nağara Point). A city in Mysia (northwestern Asia Minor); on the Asiatic bank of the Hellespont (Dardanelles), at the narrowest point of the strait. Abydus, which lies away from the main current and possesses the best harbor in the Hellespont, was first mentioned in the *Iliad*'s catalog of the ships in the

Trojan fleet. The mountains to the southeast contained gold mines, which were said to have been the source of King Priam's wealth, and the region was also rich in horses.

After the Trojan War, Abydus was said to have been settled by Thracians, until *c* 675 BC Miletus established a colony there, by agreement with King Gyges of Lydia (*c* 685–657). Darius I of Persia burned the city down in 512, but in 480 it formed the western end of the double bridge (replacing another destroyed by a storm) by which Xerxes I crossed over the Hellespont to Europe. Shortly afterward, it joined the Delian League, which became the Athenian empire. Never friendly to the Athenians, Abydus revolted in 411, providing a naval base to the Spartans—Athens' enemy in the Peloponnesian War (431–404)—who suffered a defeat off the coast. In 386 the city passed into Persian hands, until liberation by Alexander the Great in 334. In 200 the people of Abydus fought determinedly against Philip V of Macedonia, but were compelled to surrender. Three years later it temporarily became an outpost of the Seleucid monarch Antiochus III. The kingdom of Pergamum, and the Romans, officially regarded it as a free state, and under the Roman empire, despite the exhaustion of the local gold mines, it became an important customs station. Abydus is inaccessible today, since it forms part of a Turkish military zone; extensive remains of buildings and walls were reported by earlier travelers, but have not apparently survived.

The place attained literary fame through the story of Hero and Leander, which was told by the Greek poet Musaeus in the fifth or sixth century AD, but goes back to an Alexandrian tale originating many hundreds of years earlier. Hero was priestess of Aphrodite at Sestus, on the other bank of the Hellespont. Leander, who lived at Abydus, fell in love with her and used to swim by night across the strait to visit her. One night, however, a storm put out the light by which she guided him across, and he was drowned; whereupon she threw herself into the sea.

Abydus *see* Ptolemais

Acanthus, Akanthos (Ierissos). A city on the isthmus that links Acte (*qv*), one of the three promontories of the peninsula of Chalcidice, with the Macedonian mainland. Acanthus was founded by colonists from the island of Andros, and derived prosperity from agricultural produce exported from its harbor. It sided with the invaders during the Persian Wars, supporting first their general Mardonius (492) and then King Xerxes I, whom it helped to dig his canal across the isthmus (though his camels were set upon by lions nearby; a lion is seen savaging a bull on the city's extensive coinage). The Acanthians later formed part of the Delian League (controlled by Athens) and Athenian empire, and initially sided with Athens in the Peloponnesian War (431–404), but under pressure from their oligarchic party went over to the Spartan general Brasidas in 424. Under the Peace of Nicias (421) the city was conceded autonomy but compelled to resume the payment of tribute to Athens. Taken over by the kingdom of Macedonia in the fourth century, it was plundered by the Romans in 200; but its port remained of some significance, and the town continued to survive in imperial times. Although excavations have not been extensive, imposing remains of the acropolis walls are still to be seen. Moreover, the line of Xerxes' canal can be traced, starting at a village a mile and a half to the southeast of Ierissos.

The name of the city is also that of a herbaceous plant, belonging to the perennial family of the Acanthaceae, that was reproduced in stylized form on Corinthian capitals (*spinosus,* 'thorny,' preferred by the Greeks; *mollis,* 'soft,' favored by the Romans).

Acarnania. A region of northwestern Greece, bounded by the river Achelous, the Ionian Sea, and the Gulf of Ambracia. The lower reaches of the Achelous were bordered by a fertile plain, but otherwise the territory was ringed by mountains. The inhabitants ranked as Greeks but (unlike those of neighboring Amphilochia) long remained relatively uncivilized. In the fifth century, if not earlier, the Acarnanians formed their own cantonal league, with its capital at Stratus on the right bank of the Achelous, which issued coinage portraying the personified river-god and his daughter the spring-goddess Callirhoe, mother of the mythical Acarnan.

The Acarnanians were originally called Cephallenians, from the island of that name (Cephalonia), and were subject to Odysseus of Ithaca, according to Homer. Corinthian colonies had been settled in the most favorable coastal locations from an early date, and during the mid-fifth century Corinthian and Athenian commercial interests came into conflict in the area. In 432/31 the members of the Acarnanian League invoked the aid of Athens against Ambracia (Arta) and other colonies, and then in 429/26, after the outbreak of the Peloponnesian War, they renewed the appeal. About 400 a federal coinage made its appearance. In 390, however, the Acarnanians were subjugated by King Agesilaus II of Sparta, remaining under Spartan control until fifteen years later, when they became members of Athens' Second League. They backed Thebes in its successful assertion of power against Sparta, but joined Athens in resisting King Philip II of Macedonia (359–336), of which country, however, they subsequently became dependants.

In 314, prompted by one of Alexander the Great's successors, Cassander—the ruler of Macedonia and most of Greece—they superseded their League by a new federation of recently founded cities. Amid continuous frontier disputes, Acarnania was partitioned in 263/255 between Aetolia and Epirus, but after the collapse of the Epirote monarchy a quarter of a century later it regained its independence and acquired the island of Leucas, which became the federation's principal mint. In 200 the Acarnanians took the losing side of Philip V of Macedonia against the Romans, and lost Leucas in 167, but were allowed to retain their confederacy until the time of Augustus (31 BC–AD 14). *See also* Actium, Stratus.

Ace, Acre *see* Ptolemais

Achaea, Akhaia. (1) A name derived from *Akhaioi,* employed in the *Iliad* to mean 'Greeks,' with particular reference to the followers of Achilles and Agamemnon.

(2) The historical Achaea, which was a narrow territory on the north coast of the Peloponnese between Sicyon and Elis (southeastern Thessaly, across the Gulf of Corinth, was known as Achaea Phthiotis). Descended from Late Bronze Age migrants from the Argolid, the Achaeans of the northern Peloponnese sent colonists to south Italy and remained neutral in the Persian and Peloponnesian Wars.

(3) An ancient Achaean confederacy was revived in 280 by the union of four cities, to which the remaining Achaean communities were soon added. They were joined in 251 by Sicyon (the birthplace of the statesman Aratus) and then by Arcadian cities, including Megalopolis (the birthplace of the historian Polybius). Eventually including almost the whole of the Peloponnese and part of central Greece as well, the Achaean confederacy became the principal power in Greece, until conflict with the Romans resulted in its dissolution (146) and the assignment of its territory to the Roman province of Macedonia.

(4) In 27 BC Achaea—extended in significance to comprise the greater part of Greece—became a senatorial province on its own account (apart from the years between AD 15 and 44 when it was temporarily reunited with Macedonia). Nero announced the 'liberation' of Greece (67), but this was cancelled a few years later by Vespasian. Epirus and Thessaly were subsequently detached from Achaea, the former to become a province on its own account and the latter to form part of Macedonia. In the later empire Crete and the Cyclades (Insulae) were also taken away from Achaea to become separate provinces.

Acragas, Agrigentum (Agrigento). A city near the southwestern coast of Sicily. After earlier occupation by native Sicans, the Greek city—taking its name from a river on its east side, while the river Hypsas (Santa Anna) bounded it to the west—was founded *c* 580 BC by colonists of Rhodian and (in smaller numbers) Cretan origin from Gela, led by Aristonoos and Pystilos. The extensive site (praised by Polybius) occupied a large, basin-like plateau two miles from the sea, surrounded on three sides by low cliffs, and dominated from the north by a ridge rising to two peaks, one of which was the acropolis. In its early years Acragas was ruled by an oligarchy, which was superseded *c* 571 by the autocratic rule of the 'tyrant' Phalaris, who vigorously extended his territory, overpowering native towns in the interior. He was said to have roasted his political opponents alive in a hollow brazen bull. From the latter part of the same century Acragas became rich from the production of grain, the export of wine and olives (which were sent to Carthage, according to Timaeus and Diodorus), and the breeding of cattle.

The great period of the city, when its population may have reached a total of 100,000, was the reign of Theron (488–472), who expanded its territory as far as the north coast of Sicily. In so doing, he came into conflict with the Carthaginians, who controlled the western part of the island; but they suffered an historic, decisive defeat by the forces of Acragas and Syracuse at the battle of Himera (480). The years that followed were a period of conspicuous wealth and grandiose building for the Acragantines. Pindar, who lived at their court, declared the place to be the 'fairest of mortal cities,' and eulogized its ruler. Simonides of Ceos, too, was a visitor, and repaired relations between Acragas and

Syracuse, which had deteriorated since Himera. After expelling Theron's son Thrasydaeus, Acragas adopted a semi-aristocratic and then a democratic form of government, under the guidance of its most famous citizen, the philosopher, scientist, poet, orator, statesman, mystic and supposed miracleworker Empedocles. The chariots of Acragas were victorious in the major Greek games; in 412 the Olympic sprint winner Exaenetus was escorted into the city by three hundred chariots, and honored by magnificent coins.

Neutral in the struggle between Athens and Syracuse in the Peloponnesian War, Acragas was besieged and sacked by the Carthaginians in 406, a disaster from which it did not fully recover. Refounded by Timoleon (sent by the Corinthians to Sicily) in 338, it regained a certain local importance under the autocrat Phintias (289–279) but soon afterward it fell a victim to the rivalry between the Romans and Carthaginians, who sacked the city in succession (262/1, 255/4); the Romans sold 25,000 of its inhabitants into slavery. Finally, in 211/210, it was once more besieged and occupied by the Romans (who again sold many of its people as slaves) and disappeared from the political scene. However, after repopulation by Roman colonists under the name of Agrigentum (197), it enjoyed a considerable economic recovery. By the time of Cicero's speeches against Verres, the former governor of the island (70), its people had regained much of their wealth. Diodorus emphasizes the riches they derived from vineyards, olives and racehorses; and in the imperial period they developed textile and sulphur industries, and possessed an important commercial harbor.

Traces of a settlement going back to pre-colonial times have come to light. The splendor of the city in the classical Greek epoch is displayed by a series of Doric temples, forming an almost continuous sacred area (now an archaeological zone) lining the ridge at the southern end of the site. No less than nine such shrines were built between 480 and 400, a figure exceeded only by Athens. The best preserved is a temple conventionally, though inaccurately, ascribed to Concord; its correct designation is unknown. It owes its survival to conversion into a church (St. Gregory of the Turnips) in early Christian times; similarly, the fourth century AD church of Santa Maria dei Greci was built over a temple attributed to Athena. Recent excavations have revealed a shrine of the underworld (chthonic) divinities, and a temple of Asclepius was erected near mineral springs outside the walls.

Acre *see* Ptolemais Ace (Judaea)

Acropolis *see* Athens

Acte, Akte (Athos), Mount. The easternmost of the three promontories of the peninsula of Chalcidice, in northern Greece, which extends downward from Macedonia to the Aegean Sea. Acte is thirty miles long and six-and-a-half miles wide at its broadest point, and has a mountainous spine culminating in a pyramid-shaped peak that rises sheer from the sea to a height of 6,667 feet. According to Aeschylus, the mountain was sacred to Zeus. One legend recounts that it was the stone flung at Poseidon by a giant named Athos; another story tells how Poseidon separated it from the peninsula in his struggle with the giant. As

Thucydides reports, Acte was colonized by Chalcis in Euboea (probably in the eighth century BC), though its non-Greek population remained considerable.

In 492 the Persian fleet invading Greece under Mardonius was wrecked off the headland by a storm, with the loss of three hundred ships and twenty thousand men. Before his campaign of 480 to avoid the passage around this dangerous cape, Xerxes dug a canal, from sixty-five to a hundred feet in breadth and six to ten feet deep, through the narrow neck of the promontory, which at this point measured a mile and a half across. Deinocrates of Rhodes subsequently offered to carve the mountain into a gigantic bust of Alexander the Great. During the Middle Ages Christian hermits came to the peninsula, and the theocratic republic of monks, which has given Athos the name of the Holy Mountain (Ayion Oros), began to take shape (the monastery of the Grand Lavra dates from 963).

Acte *see* Attica, Chalcidice

Actium, Aktion (Akra Nikolaos). A flat, sandy promontory on the coast of Acarnania in northwestern Greece, on the southern side of the strait leading from the Ionian Sea into the Ambracian Gulf. Actium belonged originally to the Corinthian colonists of Anactorium, who founded the worship of Apollo Actius and the Games named the Actia before 575 BC. By the early third century the temple was the federal shrine of the Acarnanians. The harbor was used to exploit local pearl fisheries.

When Antony (Marcus Antonius) and Octavian (the future Augustus) disputed the mastery of the Roman world in 31 BC, Actium was the site of Antony's camp, and gave its name to the naval battle (September 2nd) fought just outside the gulf in which Antony and Cleopatra were decisively defeated. After breaking out with only a small portion of their fleet, they escaped to Egypt, where they committed suicide in the following year. Actium was, in consequence, celebrated by Augustus and all who supported him—notably Virgil and Horace—as the decisive landmark inaugurating the empire-wide principate that he now proceeded to establish. He commemorated his victory by founding Nicopolis on the other side of the strait, and establishing Actian Games there, a quadriennial festival that transformed the earlier Actia and ranked equally with the Olympic Games. A new Actian era was also introduced.

Adamklissi *see* Tropaeum Trajani

Adiabene *see* Assyria

Adria *see* Atria

Adrianople *see* Hadrianopolis

Adriatic Sea. The term was used interchangeably with 'Ionian Sea' to denote the waters between Italy and the Balkan peninsula. Later, it became convenient to call the northern and southern parts of this gulf the Adriatic and Ionian Seas respectively, with their division at the Straits of Otranto (although the Adriatic coast north of that point was also described as the Ionian Gulf).

Aea *see* Colchis

Aegae, Aigai (Vergina). In the region of Pieria in Macedonia, south of the river Haliacmon. Aegae was said to have been a residence of the god Poseidon, and the surrounding area was known as the Garden of Midas—an historical being proverbial for his wealth, and worshipped at the foot of Mount Bermion—because of its vines, orchards and roses. The city replaced Lebaea, the capital of the kings of Macedonia until Archelaus (413–399 BC) established himself at Pella instead. Aegae has now been convincingly identified with Vergina, where, in addition to a large prehistoric necropolis, an imposing number of rectangular and barrel-vaulted tombs of *c* 340–320 have come to light. Their grandeur and artistic excellence suggest that they were built to house the ashes of the Macedonian royal family, and one grave, the Great Tomb, is believed to have contained the remains of the ruler Philip II (359–336): a conclusion confirmed by examination of the skull, which reveals a grave head-wound corresponding to Philip's known loss of an eye. (The tomb also covers a smaller mound housing additional graves.)

Some of these burial places were adorned by wall paintings—including a Rape of Persephone and a Lion Hunt—that provide a unique contribution to our knowledge of this rarely preserved ancient Greek art. The grave goods include a ceremonial parade-shield, ornamented with ivory (and now restored), in addition to caskets sheathed in gold and silver plate (one containing remnants of cloth), and a superbly executed crown of gold leaves. Ivory heads from the same site represent Alexander the Great and, apparently, his father Philip II and his mother Olympias.

The ruins of an ancient city extend between Vergina and the town of Palatitsa, about a mile and a half to the west. On a small plateau between the acropolis and a cemetery stand the remains of a royal palace of the third century, containing large peristyle courts, double-storeyed colonnades and circular halls. A hundred yards north of the palace, the theater in which Philip II was murdered (336) has now been located; a statue-base is inscribed with the name of his mother Eurydice. A three-aisled early Christian basilica came to light in 1982.

Aegates Islands (Egadi) off the western extremity of Sicily. The principal islands were Aegusa or Bucinna (Favignana)—the easternmost of the islands—and Phorbantia (Levanzo) and Hiera (Marettimo).

In 241 BC, during the twenty-third year of the First Punic War, a newly raised Roman fleet under the consul Gaius Lutatius Catullus defeated a new Carthaginian fleet under Hanno in the waters between Aegusa and Hiera. Hanno's vessels, carrying mercenaries, foodstuffs and money, had set sail from north Africa to western Sicily early in March, before the winter storms ended. Anchoring off

Hiera, he awaited a favorable wind to enable him to cross over to Sicily, where he proposed to land his soldiers (under the command of the experienced Hamilcar) so that they could engage the Romans in battle. Meanwhile Lutatius, learning of Hanno's arrival and correctly conjecturing what he had in mind, anchored his own fleet off Aegusa. On March 10th, the Carthaginian squadron (consisting of two hundred and fifty ships according to Diodorus, four hundred according to Eutropius and Orosius) set sail for the Sicilian shore. Lutatius, despite the unfavorable wind, confronted them, and the Carthaginians, weighed down by their heavy cargo, were overwhelmed. Fifty of their ships were sunk and seventy captured with their crews. This proved the decisive victory that at long last brought the First Punic War to an end. The peace terms that Carthage was compelled to accept included the evacuation of Sicily, which thus became Rome's first overseas province.

Aegean Sea, Aigaion (Turkish Ege). The sea between Greece and Asia Minor (Asiatic Turkey), with Crete as its southernmost point. It includes a remarkable number of islands, including, especially, the Cyclades, Northern and Southern Sporades, and large islands adjoining Greece (Euboea) and western Asia Minor (Lesbos, Chios, to the south; Samos and Rhodes to the southeast; while Crete lies in the Cretan Sea). The name Aegean is variously derived from the city of Aegae in Aeolis (Nemrud Kalesi) or from the Amazonian queen Aegea or Theseus' father Aegeus, both of whom were believed to have drowned themselves in the sea. The term Aegean Civilization is sometimes used for the Bronze Age cultures of the region (Minoan, Cycladic, Helladic [including Mycenaean] and Troadic [Trojan]).

Aegiale, Aegialeia *see* Sicyon

Aegina, Aigina. A mountainous, volcanic Greek island in the Saronic Gulf, midway between Attica and the Peloponnese. This geographical position is the reason for its importance in Mediterranean commerce from the earliest periods. It was believed that the island, formerly known as Oenone, was colonized successively by Argives, Cretans and Thessalians (Myrmidons, after whom it took the name Myrmidonia); the last-named settlement seems to have been established about the thirteenth century BC, then abandoned a century or two later.

The island was supposedly conquered *c* 1100 BC by the Dorian Greeks under Deiphontes, a descendant of Heracles in the fifth generation. But then we are told that, after a period of abandonment, it received further immigrants, perhaps from Epidaurus; their settlement may be attributed to *c* 950–900. Aegina was a member of the Amphictyony of Calauria (Poros), a maritime council representing the principal cities on the Saronic and Argive Gulfs; and under the rule of a stable mercantile oligarchy, it became, in the seventh century, a Greek sea-power of the first order. Its silver coinage (from *c* 550), with the design of a turtle, circulated extremely widely; and the Aeginetans also developed the oldest system of weights and measures known to the classical world, and produced pottery and bronze ware which became well-known throughout the Mediterranean area. There was often rivalry between Aegina and Samos, notably at the trading port of Naucratis (Kom Gieif) in Egypt.

But, above all, it was Athens that resisted the commercial supremacy of the Aeginetans. Already in the early years of the sixth century its statesman Solon passed laws designed to restrict Aeginetan trading, which caused the island to ally itself in turn with Sparta and Thebes in the hope of checking the Athenians' rising power; and in 506 the long struggle against them began. In 490 the Aeginetans took no part in the Greek resistance to Darius I culminating in the battle of Marathon, and two years later they won a naval victory against Athens. (They also constructed a new port at about this time.) Indeed, the great Athenian fleet that defeated Xerxes I at Salamis in 480 had ostensibly been raised to deal with the Aeginetans, because of the sympathy they had shown toward the Persians. In the event, however, the Aeginetans did contribute a squadron to the Greek fleet that confronted Xerxes at Salamis, and their bravery in the battle won them 'the first prize for valor.' In the following year, too, they fought beside their Athenian rivals at Plataea. But Aegina's special glory was its inspiration of at least seven of the finest odes of Pindar, including the eighth *Pythian*.

Nevertheless, the Athenian statesman Pericles called the island the 'eyesore of the Piraeus,' and war broke out between the two states in 459. It ended with the capture of Aegina by the Athenians, followed by its compulsory enrollment in the Athenian confederation (Delian League) to which it was obliged to contribute thirty talents annually. But resentment remained strong, and the Aeginetans played a substantial part in persuading Sparta to enter the Peloponnesian War against Athens (431). As a result, the Athenians deported the island's entire population and apportioned the land among their own people, while Sparta gave a new home to the exiled inhabitants at Thyrea; though in 424 the Athenians captured that town too, and transferred the refugees to Athens. In 405, however, when the Peloponnesian War had finally gone in favor of the Spartans, they were allowed back to their island under a Spartan governor.

From 322 to 229 Aegina was under Macedonian control, and then belonged to the Achaean League until 211, when it was taken over by the Romans and attached to the Aetolian League (which enslaved its inhabitants), only to be sold, in the following year, to Attalus II of Pergamum—a transfer which introduced a new period of prosperity. After the Pergamene kingdom was annexed by Rome (133), Aegina went with it. During the 30s, Mark Antony assigned the island to the Athenians. In AD 267 the city suffered a destructive siege from German (Herulian) invaders.

Traces of Thessalian Bronze Age settlement have come to light on the slopes of Mount Elia. But the principal monument of the island is the temple of Aphaea (a pre-Greek goddess, assimilated to Athena), on the highest point of Cape Colonna, a pine-clad hill above the sea. The building, of which part survives today including a number of columns and fine pediment sculptures in varying styles (now to be seen in the Munich and Athens museums), dates from 520–478 BC (starting a decade after a fragmentary Temple of Apollo). In the late Roman period it was destroyed and replaced by a massive fortress. Remains of two earlier shrines on the site have also been discovered, and portions of all three altars can be seen. The sacred area also contains a theater and stadium. A further sanctuary, in the district of Mesagro, was built over a Mycenaean site in the seventh century.

Aegospotami, Aigos potamoi (or potamos). A place with an open beach bearing the name of a stream (the Karaova Suyu) that descends into the sea at that point; on the east coast of the Thracian Chersonese (Gallipoli [Gelibolu] peninsula), facing the Hellespont (Dardanelles), at a point where its channel is two miles wide.

The decisive and final engagement of the Peloponnesian War was fought there in 405 BC; Xenophon offers a graphic description. The Spartan Lysander, with the aid of large subsidies from his Persian friend Cyrus II, had mustered two hundred ships and moved them, together with his land forces, to the Hellespont, where he captured Lampsacus (Lapseki, on the Asian coast opposite Aegospotami). An Athenian fleet of a hundred and eighty ships under Conon and Philocles proceeded to Aegospotami, where they offered battle on four successive days. But their challenges met with no response from Lysander; and during the afternoons the Athenian crews foraged ashore for their evening meal. On the fifth day, however, after both fleets had acted precisely as before and the Athenian crews had disembarked, Lysander led his fleet at full speed across the channel, and the Athenians were taken completely by surprise, losing one hundred and seventy-one of their ships in the subsequent battle. Tens of thousands of prisoners were captured, and by November Lysander was blockading the Piraeus. In April of the following year Athens surrendered.

Aegosthena, Aigosthene (Porto Germano). The northernmost town in the territory of the Greek city of Megara. Inaccessibly located on the slopes of Mount Cithaeron, in a deep inlet of the Gulf of Corinth, the place possessed a fort and sanctuaries of Poseidon and Heracles and the legendary prophet Melampus, in whose honor an annual festival was held.

After the coup of 379 BC in which Theban exiles had bloodily liberated their city from its pro-Spartan government, the Spartan king Cleombrotus, having failed to reverse this situation, disbanded his army at Aegosthena. In 371 the Thebans won a great victory over the Spartans at Leuctra in Boeotia. When news of the disaster reached Sparta, its king Archidamus marched north, collecting allied contingents on his way. At Aegosthena, as Xenophon describes, he encountered the survivors from the battle. Shocked by their demoralization and the heavy loss of life, Archidamus decided to turn back to Sparta; his action marked the triumphant ascendancy of Thebes and the Boeotian League. Along with Megara, Aegosthena formed part of the Achaean League in 244, and after a brief period of cession to Boeotia reentered the League after Rome's victory over Philip V in the Second Macedonian War (197).

Aegosthena's fortification system, erected between the fifth and third (?) centuries BC, is one of the best preserved examples of Greek military architecture. It comprises a massive polygonal wall, protecting the acropolis, and an encircling city-wall, both equipped with large square towers. The wall-bases and towers were partly filled with earth as a protection against battering rams. But in 1981 the upper part of the almost completely preserved southeastern tower collapsed in an earthquake. Two watchtowers at a higher level were examined by archaeologists in the following year.

Aegyptus, Aigyptos (Egypt). After twenty-six dynasties of independent kings had been succeeded by two periods of Persian domination (525–404, 343–332), Alexander the Great occupied Egypt, visiting the traditional capital Memphis but founding the new city of Alexandria which became the capital of the country, although retaining, with its Greek character, a distinct mode of existence. After his death the house of Ptolemy I Soter ruled Egypt for nearly three hundred years. The Ptolemies derived vast wealth from the fertility of the Nile valley and from their elaborately organized kingdom, and controlled an empire of substantial but fluctuating size, in competition with the Seleucids and other Hellenistic powers. During the later part of the period internal weaknesses caused the country to fall increasingly under Roman domination, and Cleopatra VII's attempt to revive its fortunes by association first with Julius Caesar and then Mark Antony eventually failed and terminated in her suicide (30). This was followed by the Roman annexation of Egypt, though it became (owing to its vast and diversified resources, and its importance to the Italian grain supply) a province of a special kind, controlled not by a senatorial governor but by a prefect of equestrian rank, personally dependent on the emperor. (For the southern frontier of the province, *see* Aethiopia.) In AD 69 it was an invitation from the prefect of Egypt, Tiberius Julius Alexander, that prompted Vespasian to make his successful bid for the purple. Avidius Cassius, after quelling a revolt against Marcus Aurelius (172), included Egypt among the territories which he rebelliously controlled for three months (175); and the abundant and hugely varied provincial coinage, issued at Alexandria, reflects the temporary seizure of the country by subsequent usurpers from time to time, including the prefects Mussius Aemilianus (*c* 260) and Domitius Domitianus (295–7). During the later empire the country was subdivided into the provinces of Aegyptus Jovia, Augustamnica, Arcadia and the Lower and Upper Thebaid. This last-named area became the birthplace of monasticism, producing Paul of Thebes who fled to the desert in 250, Saint Antony who gathered his followers near Mount Quolzoum, and Saint Pachomius who established a monastery at Tabennisi, an island in the upper Nile (*c* 320). *See also* Alexandria, Antinoopolis, Arsinoe, Memphis, Naucratis, Nile, Oxyrhynchus, Pelusium, Ptolemais, Syene, Tabennisi, Tentyra, Thebes. For the earliest period, *see* Naucratis.

Aelia Capitolina *see* Jerusalem

Aemiliavum *see* Condatomagus

Aenaria *see* Pithecusae

Aenus, Ainos (Enoz). A city on the coast of Thrace, on the east bank of the mouth of the river Hebrus (Maritza, Meriç); now in European Turkey. It was known to the Thracians as Poltyobria, after their legendary King Poltys, but the name Aenus already appears in Homer's *Iliad,* in connection with the Trojan War. The place was also called Apsinthus. In the seventh century BC it was resettled by colonists from Mytilene (Lesbos) and Cyme (Namurt Limanı, Aeolis). Their city occupied a high ridge overlooking a useful harbor (now silted up) at the mouth of the river. Its geographical position gave the place considerable commercial importance, for Aenus not only possessed lucrative fisheries of its own, but also enjoyed access, through its control of the Hebrus valley, to the rich grain, fruit and timber-producing lands of central and eastern Thrace, and, in addition, commanded a trade route between the Aegean and the Black Sea.

In the fifth century, when its extensive coinage, bearing the head of Hermes, was first issued, Aenus was a member of Athens' Delian League, to which it contributed twelve talents in 454. This sum, however, was subsequently diminished, because Aenus' prosperity had suffered, first from the rise of the Odrysian kingdom in Thrace and, secondly, from the diversion of much of its commerce into the hands of the Athenians themselves. Nevertheless, according to Thucydides, the people of Aenus supplied *peltasts* (light infantry) to Athens at Pylos in 425, during the Peloponnesian War, and were still allies of the Athenians during the Sicilian expedition ten years later. From 341 onward Aenus was successively under the control of the Macedonian, Egyptian and Pergamene monarchies, until in 185 it was pronounced a 'free city' by the Romans. During the later Roman empire it became the capital of the small province of Rhodopa. The ancient habitation center is supposed to have been on the same site as the modern town; the castle of the Gattilusi was erected on the site of the acropolis.

Aeolian Islands *see* Lipara

Aeolis, Aiolis, the northern portion of the west coast of Asia Minor, from the entrance of the Hellespont (Dardanelles) to the mouth of the river Hermus (Gediz Çayı). Aeolis took its name from the mythical Aeolus, son of Hellen, but writers of the fifth century BC attributed the Aeolic settlement to the descendants of Orestes, the son of Agamemnon, king of Mycenae, and there remained Aeolian families that claimed this origin. However, the speech of the country resembled the dialects of Boeotia and Thessaly, and it appears to have been from those regions that the first immigrants came (perhaps in the eleventh century BC), planting their initial settlements on the island of Lesbos, and then along the mainland coast as well.

Owing to the presence of a native people, the Mysians, to the north, it was not until a considerably later stage that the Troad was occupied, mainly by people from Mytilene, the principal city of Lesbos. In the south, Cyme occupied a key position, and was believed to have been the mother city of many small towns in the region, planted on projecting peninsulas or set on hills beside the lower Hermus valley. The Aeolian cities were loosely grouped together in a league, probably religious in origin. Its members were originally said to have been twelve—on the pattern of the Ionian confederacy—but the number was reduced to eleven when Smyrna (İzmir) fell into Ionian hands and became regarded as part of Ionia instead. *See also* Cyme, Lesbos, Mytilene.

Aethalia *see* Ilva

Aethiopia, Aithiopia, was a name applied by Greeks to any region in the far south, including (according to Aeschylus) even India. The Aithiopes are mentioned on Bronze Age Pylos tablets. Homer describes them as 'people of burnt out faces,' the furthest of humankind, whose banquets the gods visit. But from the time of Herodotus, who distinguished between straight- and woolly-haired races (in east and west respectively), the name was especially related to the lands south of Egypt, extending into Nubia (northern Sudan) and Abyssinia (now the state of Ethiopia). Its inhabitants lived on millet and barley (from which they made a drink) and used butter and tallow instead of olive oil. In the fourteenth century BC the Kingdom of Egypt extended southward as far as Napata, just below the Fourth Cataract (near Karima in the Sudan). According to the *Iliad,* Memnon, a mythical King of Aethiopia, helped the Trojans in their war against the Greeks. From *c* 750 Napata was capital of the Nubian kingdom of Kush (itself often known as Aethiopia), and its monarch Taharko (690–664) extended his control over Egypt. But Napata fell to an Egyptian force, strengthened by Greek and Carian mercenaries, in *c* 591/590; whereupon the capital, probably under King Aspelta, or, according to another view, later, was transferred to Meroe (Baharawiga), south of the Nile's junction with the Astaboras (Atbara); Mussawarat es-Sufra and Naqa, far to the south, were important Meroitic religious centers. By the time of Ptolemy II Philadelphus (283/2–246) the Greeks knew the Nile as far up as Meroe. Its kingdom, ruled by a series of monarchs bearing the title Katake (Candace), dominated the middle Nile valley; and although the worship of both Egyptian and indigenous gods (for example Apedemek) continued, a partial process of Hellenization had taken place. Shortly after the annexation of Egypt in 30 BC by Octavian (Augustus), Meroitic forces, on the orders of a determined one-eyed queen, poured north across the frontier on the First Cataract, but were pursued back by Gaius Petronius (23–22), who destroyed Napata. He also stormed the stronghold of Primis (Kasr Ibrim, on a steep hill on the east bank of the Nile, seventy-five miles south of the Second Cataract), but subsequently refortified, garrisoned and provisioned it, relieving a further attack three years later. The sequel was Rome's occupation of the Dodecaschoenus, 'twelve measures of land' dedicated to the temple of Isis at Philae, between the First and Second Cataracts. This border remained intact until incursions from the frontier people of the Blemmyes in the later third century AD, after which the Dodecaschoenus was abandoned. It was probably in the same century that Heliodorus of Emesa (Homs) wrote his romantic novel the *Aethiopica* about mythical personages of the country. About 320–50 Meroe was sacked by the rulers of the Aethiopic state of Axum (Aksum) in Tigre (northern Ethiopia), which was founded in the first century AD and (as Rufinus records and coins confirm) became Christian as early as the first half of the fourth century, as a result of the missionary endeavors of St. Frumentius in the reign of King Ezana, who was the first Axumite King to call himself King of Aethiopia.

Meanwhile, however, Primis, now well outside the range of the eastern Roman (Byzantine) empire, recovered impressively from its earlier destruction, as excavations on the site—originally 228 feet above the Nile plain, and now an island on Lake Nasser—have revealed. Its great eastern gate is one of the most important examples of military engineering in Africa, and several large houses of late Roman or early Byzantine date, with water cisterns and plastered living rooms, are now uncovered. Owing to the heat and dryness of the area more than 20,000 textile fragments, as well as basketry, rope, leather, wood and papyrus manuscript fragments in seven languages, have been preserved. From the early medieval period Primis was an episcopal see.

Aetna, Aitne (Etna). A volcanic mountain lying between Tauromenium (Taormina) and Catana (Catania) in northeast Sicily, still the highest active volcano in Europe, a little less than 11,000 feet in height. Aetna was held to be the forge of Hephaestus (Vulcan) or the Cyclopes, or was identified with the mountain beneath which the imprisoned Titan, Enceladus, perpetually struggled to free himself. Empedocles (*see* Acragas) was said to have thrown himself into the crater so that his disappearance would create the belief that he was a god, but his action was detected when the volcano cast up one of his bronze sandals.

The native population (Sicans) were believed to have migrated westward because of the volcano's activity. Eruptions of 479, 425, 396, 141, 135, 126, 122, 50, 44, 38, and 32 BC and AD 40 are recorded. The earliest of these phenomena was described by Pindar and Aeschylus, while its successor in 396, when lava flows reached the sea, was said to have prevented the Carthaginian general Himilco from attacking Syracuse. The eruption of 122 BC destroyed Catana. It had been renamed Aetna in 476 BC when Hiero I of Syracuse deported the Catanaeans and repeopled their city with Syracusans and Peloponnesians. But in 461 these, in turn, were also expelled to Inessa (Poira) on the southern slopes of the mountain, which likewise assumed the name of Aetna.

The *Aetna* is a Latin didactic poem six hundred and forty-four lines long, probably dating from the first century AD, which describes and professes to explain the eruptions of the volcano, attributed by the unknown author to the action of wind operating at high pressure in subterranean channels.

Aetolia, Aitolia. A region of northwestern Greece bounded on the north and east by the spurs of Mount Parnassus and Mount Oeta, on the west by the middle and lower reaches of the river Achelous, and on the south by the western approaches of the Corinthian Gulf. 'Old Aetolia' comprised the seacoast from Achelous to Calydon, and its annex (Epictetus) extended eastward to the border of Ozolian Locris. Inland, the country included the rugged southern continuation of the Pindus range, descending into the fertile central Aetolian plain.

The coastal towns, especially Pleuron and Calydon, figure prominently in myth and legend and were known to Homer (Aetolus, Oeneus, Althaea, Meleager and Deianira are all ascribed to the region). The subsequent history of Aetolia, however, was not maritime but centered on the interior. In the fifth century some of the tribesmen still lived under their chieftains in unfortified villages, and were scarcely regarded as Greeks. But when the Peloponnesian War broke out they were able to form a common front against invasion by the Athenian general Demosthenes, whom their archers and slingers repulsed (426).

By 367, at latest, the Aetolians had formed themselves into a federal league, headed by an annually elected General or President and comprising a primary Assembly which was convened for two regular annual meetings at their cult center on the hilltop of Thermum. This confederacy came to form one of the principal political units of Hellenistic times. Gaining possession of Naupactus and then Delphi (*c* 300), it protected the shrine from invasion by the Gauls (279)—as Pausanias described—and subsequently, by a victory over the Boeotians (245), won control of all central Greece, following up this achievement by interventions in the Peloponnese. The Aetolians also acquired a bad reputation as pirates and encouragers of piracy. In the Second Macedonian War (200–197) they supported Rome against the Macedonian King Philip V, contributing largely to the Roman victory at Cynoscephalae by means of their cavalry. When, however, the Romans seemed to display insufficient gratitude, the Aetolians retaliated by inviting the Seleucid Antiochus III the Great into Greece (192). After defeating him, the Romans punished the Aetolians by restricting their territory to their own homeland and compelling them to accept a treaty which officially accepted them as allies but in fact brought their independence to an end. In 27 BC Augustus included Aetolia in the province of Achaea. *See also* Calydon, Thermum.

Africa. The name of a Roman province. When the Romans obliterated the Carthaginian empire after the Third Punic War, they allowed most of its continental African territories to pass under the control of the client kings of Numidia, but annexed the most fertile region for themselves as a new province of Africa, comprising five thousand square miles of what is now the northern part of Tunisia. Its capital was Utica (Bordj bou Chateur), Carthage having been destroyed. In the civil war between Julius Caesar and the followers of Pompey, the former, after his victory at Thapsus in 46 BC, added the kingdom of Numidia to the province, and his plan to revive and colonize Carthage was carried through by Octavian (Augustus), who made it the capital of Africa; the province now extended from the river Ampsagas (Rummel) to Cyrenaica and—uniquely among provinces governed by proconsuls—was garrisoned by a legion. In the reign of Gaius (AD 37–41), this legion, together with the administration of Numidia, was handed over to an imperial official (*legatus*). Under Nero (54–68), according to Pliny the Elder, half the province was owned by six landowners. Punic (Carthaginian) long continued to be a common spoken language.

Africa was of immense importance to Italy as a granary, and Carthage became the second city of the west after Rome itself. Christianity expanded more rapidly than in any other western province, producing Tertullian, Cyprian and Augustine. Septimius Severus (193–211), who came from Lepcis Magna in Tripolitania, made Numidia into a separate province. Africa was the scene of the short-lived reigns of Gordianus I and II Africanus (238). In the later empire the old proconsular province, reduced in size, was united with five other provinces, extending from Mauretania Caesariensis to Tripolitana, to form the administrative diocese of Africa. The region witnessed the rebellions of Domitius Alexander (308), Firmus (379) and Gildo (397–8), before succumbing in the following century to Gaiseric the Vandal. *See also* Carthage, Hadrumetum, Hippo Regius, Lepcis Magna, Madaurus, Oea, Sabratha, Sugolin, Thapsus, Thugga, Thysdrus, Utica.

Ager Gallicus. In 232 BC the tribune of the people Gaius Flaminius, championing the peasant middle classes, proposed that the *ager Gallicus* (*et Picenus*?), the region of eastern Italy recently confiscated from the Gallic tribe of the Senones, should be divided into small allotments and distributed to poor Roman citizens. He forced this measure through the Roman Assembly in the face of determined opposition from the senators, whose wishes and interests he had disregarded. In consequence, historians of aristocratic sympathies argued that the measure not only 'demoralized' the people but also, because it so greatly irritated the Gauls—against whom it was intended as a measure of self-defence—precipitated their invasion of 225.

Agilkia *see* Syene

Agri Decumates. The name given to the region of southwestern Germany forming a reentrant or 'duck's beak' (Württemberg, Baden and Hohenzollern) between the upper Rhine and upper Danube. The name, *Decumates* (to which the only classical reference is in Tacitus' *Germania*) probably derives from a pre-Roman term. Its meaning, however, was forgotten, and has subsequently been much disputed; the most probable suggestion is that it translates a Celtic word meaning 'ten' and indicating early occupation by a tribe consisting of ten cantons. The area was at one time occupied by the Celtic tribe of the Helvetii, which immigrated gradually about 200 BC. Subsequently it passed into the hands of the German tribe of the Suebi, and after their departure for Bohemia (Boiohaemum) soon after 9 BC was populated by homeless Gauls. The Romans gradually annexed the region in the Flavian period, particularly under Vespasian and Domitian between 74 and 98, in order to shorten communications between the Rhine and Danube armies; it was linked with the provinces of Upper Germany and Raetia, possessing frontier fortifications that extended along the line Rheinbrohl-Arnsburg-Inheiden- Schierenhof-Gunzenhausen-Pförring. However, the Agri Decumates were evacuated by Gallienus (*c* 259–60), in the face of invasions by the German tribal group of the Alamanni and of secession by the western usurper Postumus on the Rhine. It is possible that part of the territory was recovered by Aurelian (270–75), but if so this reoccupation was only temporary.

Agrigentum *see* Acragas

Agrippia Caesarea *see* Phanagoria

Ahmetbeyli (Claros) *see* Colophon

Aï Khanum *see* Seleucia (?) on the Oxus

Aix-en-Provence *see* Aquae Sextiae

Akar Çayı *see* Ipsus

Akbaşı *see* Sestus

Akko *see* Ptolemais (Judaea)

Akra Nikolaos *see* Actium

Aksu *see* Perga

Aksum *see* Aethiopia

Alalia, Aleria. Town on the east coast of Corsica. About 565–560 BC a group of Greek settlers from Phocaea (Foca) in Ionia founded a town on the site, and they were joined some twenty years later by additional colonists from the same city, when this was under siege from the Persians. Situated beside a large bay (now filled in) which enjoyed protection from the northeast wind, Alalia looked out over the alluvial plain of the river Tavignano, commanding access to the interior of the island and to lakes rich in fish and salt. Moreover, the colonists dominated the approaches to Caere (Cerveteri) and other ports of mainland Etruria, which was only eighty miles away by sea, and possessed goods, and particularly supplies of copper and iron, which the Alalians were eager to acquire. In order to oppose, however, what they regarded as threatening competition from Alalia, Caere decided to throw in its lot with Carthage, which was endeavoring to establish a firm foothold in Sardinia; and about 535 an important naval confrontation took place between these two allies and the Alalians. This engagement, fought somewhere off the coast of Corsica (or perhaps Sardinia), and known as the 'battle of Alalia,' was won by the Alalian fleet. But the Alalians lost many prisoners to the Caeretans—who allegedly stoned them to death—and suffered so much damage in the fight that, according to Herodotus, the survivors decided to evacuate their colony altogether and settle in southwest Italy instead. In fact, however, as archaeological discoveries indicate, they were not so wholly excluded from Corsica (or even from Alalia) as Herodotus suggests. But it does seem that henceforth the Greek inhabitants of the port were joined by Etruscans; by the turn of the century it contained Etruscan workshops (and graffiti) and Etruscan chamber tombs. Diodorus reported that the Etruscans actually founded a colony on the island—perhaps at or near Alalia itself—known as Nicaea or Victory Town (a Greek name that hints at a Greek presence among the new settlers). At all events, excavations show that throughout this whole period, and later, Alalia remained a cosmopolitan maritime center of some importance.

After a brief period of Carthaginian rule, the Romans took the city (known to them as Aleria, the name it still bears today) in 259. During the civil war between Marius and Sulla it sided with the former, and was forced to receive a military colony by Sulla in 81. Julius Caesar and Augustus introduced additional settlers, and the town assumed the name of Colonia Veneria Julia Pacensis Restituta Tertianorum Aleria. Augustus posted a detachment of the Misenum fleet at the port, which remained the administrative capital of Corsica (initially part of the province of Sardinia, and later a separate province). However, its prosperity suffered from the rival development of Ostia (*qv*).

Excavations of the Roman colony have brought to light buildings adjoining the forum, including a temple that dates from the time of Hadrian and was probably dedicated to Rome and Augustus. Elsewhere in the city a private bathing establishment has been brought to light; it may have been attached to the governor's residence.

Alaşehir *see* Philadelphia (Lydia)

Alauna (?), a locality in Caledonia (Scotland) mentioned in Ptolemy's *Geography* and tentatively identified with Ardoch (Braco) in Perthshire, ten miles north of Stirling (though others prefer to locate it at Watercrook or Maryport).

The remains of Ardoch are the best preserved of any Roman stronghold in Scotland. They comprise two intersecting forts, of which one may have been built by Cnaeus Julius Agricola (*c* AD 83), and the other, more extensively preserved, under Antoninus Pius (*c* 140) to serve as an outpost—later reconstructed and strengthened—of the Antonine Wall. A complicated system of protective ditches has been preserved on two sides. The garrison consisted of auxiliaries, probably including a detachment of cavalry. Ardoch was a station on the road between two other fortresses, Camelon and Strathmore.

Alba Fucens (Albe). A town in central Italy situated on an oblong hill (3,315 feet high) between the peaks of the Ceraunii Mts. (Velino) and the Fucine Lake, at the intersection of the Via Valeria Tiburtina, which linked Rome to the Adriatic, and another road that led from southern Etruria to Campania by way of the river Liris (Liri). This crossroads position, dominating five valleys, gave the place major strategic importance. After defeating the tribe of the Aequi, Rome established a Latin colony, 6,000 strong, at Alba Fucens in 303 BC, and used it as an advanced base in the Second Samnite and Second Punic Wars. During the second century the place served as a fortress in which dethroned princes were incarcerated, including Syphax of Numidia, Perseus of Macedonia and Bituitus of the Arverni (Gaul). The Social War (91–87 BC), in which Alba Fucens was besieged by the rebels but relieved by a Roman force, inaugurated a period of great prosperity, in which the city provided a market for a large agricultural area and a fishing industry. The third and fourth centuries AD were periods of decline.

The hill of Alba Fucens, together with two other hills (San Pietro and Pettorino) separated by a valley, were enclosed by a massive wall of irregular polygonal limestone blocks, dating mostly from the third century BC, but modified in the second and early first centuries. Despite its hilly situation, the town provides a classic example of grid planning, mainly of first century date. Monuments include a porticoed forum, rectangular basilica, assembly center (*comitium*), circular market, bathing establishment, elaborate and grandiose Sanctuary of Hercules, temple of Apollo (second century BC), amphitheater (presented by Tiberius' adviser Macro, praetorian prefect AD 31–37), theater, shops (including a wineshop and a fuller's establishment), and houses of various epochs with mosaic floors and painted walls.

Albanum (Albano Laziale) and **Alba Longa** (Castel Gandolfo). On the western slope of the crater enclosing Lake Albanus (Albano) in Latium, about twelve miles southeast of Rome. According to legends preserved by Livy and Dionysius of Halicarnassus, after Aeneas (a refugee from Troy) had founded Lavinium, his son Ascanius, thirty years later, went from there to establish Alba Longa, from which in turn, after a long line of Alban kings, Romulus and Remus went forth to found Rome itself. The earliest tombs in the necropolis beside the town seem to date from about 1100 BC; Alba Longa influenced the Latin communities round about—apparently as the head of a local league—and there may be some truth in the tradition that a number of them were its offshoots. Alba Longa eventually lost its primacy in Latium, allegedly through its destruction by the Romans; this eclipse can perhaps be dated to the end of the sixth century when its principal families (Julii, Tullii, Curiatii, Quinctii [or Quinctilii], Cloelii, Geganii, Servilii) migrated or were transported to Rome, while others moved to neighboring Bovillae and maintained Alban cults and memories at its shrines. Cemeteries with Early Iron Age tombs have come to light; but Alba Longa itself was not rebuilt.

Its name, however, was preserved by Albanum, to the south of Castel Gandolfo. This was the location of an imperial villa going back to a residence of Pompey and greatly developed by Domitian (AD 81–96); it occupied the site of the present Villa Barberini and possessed a huge domain, the fertile *ager Albanus,* which extended in an arc from Castrimoenium (Marino) to Aricia (Ariccia) and apparently incorporated the whole lakeside. Domitian's immense and palatial mansion, of which considerable remains survive, was at least three storeys high and possessed a private theater and an abundance of terraces, pavilions and fountain buildings, including a grotto beside the lake in which fragmentary high-relief sculptures (notably figures of Polyphemus and Scylla) have been found. Albanum later became the site of a camp (Castra Albana) constructed by Septimius Severus for the Second Parthian Legion (created in AD 193), a step of historical significance because it was the first time that a legion had been stationed within Italy itself; it served as a protection for the emperor, and provided the nucleus of a future strategic reserve. Remains of the camp (partly brought to light by bombing in 1944) include fortifications, an amphitheater, two baths, a large water reservoir, an aqueduct and a cemetery. In the fourth century, the camp ceased to be occupied, and Civitas Albanensis, the forerunner of the modern town of Albano Laziale, came into existence.

Alban stone (*lapis Albanus*) is a greenish-grey volcanic stone extensively used as a building material at Rome and in its neighborhood. Alban wine was also well-known.

Albanus, Mons. The name given to the Alban Hills (Vulcano Laziale, Colli Albani), and particularly to their dominating peak, the Alban Mount (Monte Cavo, 3,115 feet, named after the Latin community Caba), thirteen miles southeast of Rome, overlooking Lake Albano (see Alba Longa). The volcano has been inactive in historical times; but its earlier eruptions had guaranteed the future prosperity of the area by covering the clay plain for miles around with layers of new soil containing phosphates and potash. Early in the first millennium BC, when the Bronze Age was becoming the Iron Age, the Indo-European-speaking peoples who tended herds on the Alban Mount—and then began to cultivate the soil—became the Latins, a loosely federated group of communities sharing the common sanctuary of Jupiter Latiaris on the mountaintop.

When Rome, after the destruction of Alba Longa, gained control of this shrine, its consuls used to lead a procession to it for an annual celebration (the *feriae Latinae*). Triumphs *in monte Albano* were also celebrated by generals who had not been allowed a Triumph at Rome (for example Gaius Papirius Maso in 231, and Marcus Claudius Marcellus in 211 BC); these ceremonies were unofficial, and held at the personal expense of the commander concerned. Remains of the Via Triumphalis can still be seen, as well as of Roman villas, temples and theaters. Because of the healthy coolness of these hills in hot weather, they provided the Romans with a favorite summer resort.

Albis (Elbe), River. The longest and most important navigable waterway in the eastern part of Germany. Tacitus attributes it to the tribal land of the Hermunduri. The Albis was known by the time of Julius Caesar, and in the course of the German expeditions under Augustus its banks were reached by his stepson Drusus senior (Nero Drusus) in the fourth and last of his campaigns, undertaken in 9 BC, shortly before his death. As a result of this achievement, Augustus wrote in his political testament, the *Res Gestae Divi Augusti,* 'the provinces of the Gauls, the Spains, and Germany, bounded by the Ocean from Gades to the mouth of the Albis, I reduced to a state of peace.' It was his intention to replace the long, right-angled Rhine-Danube frontier by the much shorter Elbe-Danube line (perhaps as a preliminary to even more extensive expansion).

This project, by incorporating the greater part of Germany, would have had an incalculable effect on the subsequent course of European history. But it was frustrated by two developments. First, the conquest of Boiohaemum (Bohemia), which was required by the plan, had to be called off owing to the outbreak of a rebellion in Illyricum (AD 6). Secondly, three years later, the destruction of Varus' three legions by Arminius, of the tribe of the Cherusci, made the territories between the Rhine and the Elbe untenable. When the emperor Tiberius' nephew and adoptive son Germanicus (the son of Drusus senior) made a further attempt to subjugate these regions—described by Tacitus—he set up a trophy in AD 16 with an inscription asserting that he had conquered the nations between the Rhine and the Elbe. But, although he was granted a Triumph, he retreated, leaving this conquest unattained.

Alcala del Rio *see* Ilipa

Aleria *see* Alalia

Alesia (above Alise-Sainte-Reine, Côte d'Or, France). A hill-fort town on the summit of Mons Alisiensis (Mount Auxois) belonging to the Mandubii, a client tribe of the Aedui. Alesia was the scene of the most famous and decisive event of Julius Caesar's invasion of Gaul (described in his own *Gallic War*), the siege of his enemies led by Vercingetorix (52 BC). A leader of the tribe of the Arverni, Vercingetorix inspired a revolt against the Roman conquest and was acclaimed king of his tribe, as his father had been before him, and commander-in-chief of the confederate army. After initial successes, he suffered a serious defeat and retreated into Alesia. Caesar invested the fortress with a siege wall ten miles in perimeter; outside this wall he constructed further lines of circumvallation in order to ward off Gallic relieving forces. When these arrived, they were beaten off, and a sortie by Vercingetorix likewise failed. He finally had to surrender owing to lack of supplies, and was compelled to walk in Caesar's Triumph (46), after which he was put to death.

Alesia consisted of huts made of dry stone and mud. Traces of the Gallic fortifications, supplementing the natural strength of the position, have been found by the combined use of vertical and oblique air photography, and Caesar's account of his siege works has been amplified by excavations. Subsequently, under Roman rule, a Gallo-Roman town was established on the same hilltop plateau. An important group of buildings of first and second century AD has been brought to light, including a three-apsed basilica, a theater, houses incorporating shops, and the establishments of bronze, silver and iron workers to whom the town owed its prosperity. Nearby (at Croix-S-Charles) a large sanctuary was constructed around a curative spring, dedicated to Apollo Moritasgus. The town suffered damage in 197 (not earlier as has sometimes been stated), and again in the 260s, eventually falling into decay. However, a eucharistic service made of lead, found in a well, is attributable to a fourth-century date, and thus provides one of Gaul's earliest pieces of archaeological evidence testifying to the cult of a saint.

Alexandria in Egypt. When Alexander the Great seized Egypt from the Persians, he planned the foundation of the new city of Alexandria, the first known city to bear the name of its founder rather than that of a god or mythical hero. It was established, Strabo records, on the site of the fishing village of Rhacotis (the name of Alexandria remained Rakoti in Coptic); it needed remarkable foresight to imagine in this poor village the spectacular city of the future. Most of Alexander's colonies were located and planned with a military purpose, and no doubt he had in mind, when selecting the site of Alexandria, that existing harbors in the Delta could not accommodate a large fleet. However, the foundation was also, and primarily, prompted by commercial motives, so that it could take the place of Tyre in Phoenicia, which he had destroyed. Alexandria faced both ways, and was defensible from either side: it was linked to the interior of the country by Nile canals debouching in Lake Mareotis (Maryut), and to the north it had two fine harbors opening on to the Mediterranean.

On his departure from Egypt, Alexander appointed Cleomenes, a Greek from Naucratis (Kom Gieif), as financial administrator of Egypt, responsible for building and populating the new city. The latter aim was largely achieved by transferring the citizens of Canopus, northeast of Alexandria, to the site. On the death of Alexander in 323, Egypt was taken over by Ptolemy I Soter, the son of Lagus, who had the body of Alexander buried at Memphis (Mit Riheina) until a worthy tomb could be erected for him at Alexandria. Ptolemy I had Cleomenes assassinated, and was crowned King of Egypt in 304, founding the Lagid dynasty, which lasted two hundred and seventy-four years. During his reign Alexandria was largely constructed and adorned with many of its most famous buildings. They employed as their symbol and guide the Pharos lighthouse (now Kait Bey fort), planned by Sostratus of Cnidus during this period, and completed under Ptolemy I's son and successor Ptolemy II Philadelphus to become one of the Seven Wonders of the World. The city's harbors were able—unlike any others in the Delta—to accommodate the large ships of the epoch.

Ptolemy I moved his capital from Memphis to Alexandria, where he began the construction of royal palaces, comprising a cluster of Greek pavilions, halls and living rooms arranged around elegant parks. He also developed a new cult of Serapis (derived from Osor-hapi, already worshipped at Rhacotis), in order to give the Greek community its own patron god, and began the construction of a huge temple in his honor upon an eminence overlooking Alexandria. Moreover, it was Ptolemy I who, acting on the advice of Aristotle's pupil Demetrius of Phaleron, established the Museum. This foundation, including a large dining room, a crescent-shaped portico and a colonnaded, tree-lined garden, was designed to house a group of scholars, and rapidly developed into an increasingly impressive center of state-subsidized learning, the most important of all centers of Greek culture.

Nearby, but more or less separate, was the Library, which later equalled and then eclipsed the Museum in fame. Also initiated by Ptolemy I, but more particularly developed by his son, the Library contained by far the greatest quantity of books that had ever been collected, perhaps numbering as many as half a million volumes. The Chief Librarians, like the Directors of the Museum, were a succession of eminent scholars appointed by the king; the second of them was also a famous poet, Apollonius Rhodius (*c* 295–*c* 215 BC), and his assistant was another, Callimachus of Cyrene (*c* 310–*c* 240 BC). The literary atmosphere stimulated in Alexandria by these cultural institutions also attracted Theocritus of Syracuse (*c* 310–*c* 250 BC), pioneer of bucolic poetry. It was understandable that the whole poetic movement of Hellenistic Greece should be described as Alexandrian.

With remarkable speed Alexandria became the largest of all Greek cities. Centered on a principal avenue wider than any in the world, it extended over a rectangular area four miles long and three-quarters of a mile wide, and comprised, before 200 BC, approximately 500,000 inhabitants. These included the descendants of the Greek and Macedonian settlers; the city was careful to preserve its Greek traditions, and for a long time maintained links with the city-states of the homeland. The Greeks of Alexandria, although not represented by their own assembly or a council (or if they possessed the latter they soon lost it), enjoyed their own privileged organization (*politeuma*). The extensive Jewish community also maintained an autonomous organization, which was directed by *presbyteroi* or elders (according to the Letter of Aristeas) under a president. But over and above these civic units, Alexandria was also the home of many thousands of Egyptians, and people of countless other races. It was a place of uniquely cosmopolitan character, a center that invited people of all races and beliefs to share in its endlessly varied and vigorous activities.

The city also became enormously rich, developing a highly controlled command economy that made vast fortunes by exporting the surpluses of Egypt, and trading throughout the near and middle east, of which it became the principal port. This maritime commerce came naturally to Alexandria, because, despite its contacts with the interior of Egypt by way of the Nile, it never quite belonged to the country. The city was not so much its center as its superstructure. People spoke of traveling from Alexandria 'to Egypt.' It was also the capital of an empire. For the Ptolemies were not kings 'of Egypt,' but rulers, in undefined terms, over territories that at one time extended along the coast of Asia Minor. Southern Syria and Lebanon (Coele Syria) were fought over with the Seleucids no less than five times, until the region was finally lost to them in 200. Thereafter the powers of the Ptolemaic kingdom gradually shrank, as it became first overshadowed by Rome and then virtually its client, until its last monarch Cleopatra VII made a final bid to revive its fortunes by political and amorous alliances first with Julius Caesar and then with Antony (Marcus Antonius.) But the bid failed, and in 30 BC, after Antony and Cleopatra had committed suicide in Alexandria, their conqueror Octavian, the future Augustus, annexed Egypt as a very special and personally controlled province of the Roman empire. Alexandria, enlarged by a new suburb named Nicopolis (Victory City), remained the capital of the new province (even if often described as Alexandria 'ad Aegyptum'), and although its political independence had gone it still witnessed important events. Under Gaius (AD 37–41) and his successor Claudius, for example, there were serious riots between Greeks and Jews; and it was in Alexandria that Vespasian had himself proclaimed emperor in 69. Caracalla, when mocked by the inhabitants, massacred a considerable number of young people (215); Aurelian, to avenge an attempt at independence made by the city after his defeat of Zenobia, queen of Palmyra—one of a number of usurpers represented on the city's abundant provincial coinage—destroyed the royal quarter (272), and Diocletian inflicted even more violent destruction after a further revolt (294/5).

Meanwhile, however, Alexandria, although now only the capital of the small province of Aegyptus Jovia, had entered a period of new and extraordinary activity as a center of Christian theological debate. Tradition had it that St. Mark had come there in person and converted Alexandrians to Christianity. In the third century the Alexandrian School of Christian learning produced the outstanding figures of Clement and Origen. It was at Alexandria that the dissident beliefs of Arianism were formulated, and it was there that the towering, combative Athanasius the Great (328–76) served as bishop. In 415 the learned Hypatia, influential as teacher of the pagan Neoplatonist philosophy, was lynched at Alexandria by a crowd of angry Christians, at the instigation of their bishop Cyril, subsequently sainted.

Ancient Alexandria is difficult to reconstruct, since nearly all the buildings have been destroyed and debris has covered the old levels. According to reports that have not yet been fully confirmed, remains of the Ptolemaic palaces have been discovered in the eastern section of the harbor area. The exact locations of the Museum and Library within the royal quarter are still not known, however, nor are the sites of the tombs of Alexander and the Ptolemies (though the former has been tentatively identified at Bab-el-Charki). Excavations have revealed other tombs, often interestingly decorated and elaborately cut out of the rock, in various parts of the city and its neighborhood, notably at Anfushy (second to first centuries BC), Wardian, Shatby, Moustafa Pasha, Kom-el-Shugafa (Hill of Tiles; late first or second century AD), and Hadra (now destroyed). A theater constructed of marble has been found beside the railroad station. The so-called 'Pompey's pillar' is a column erected by Diocletian; excavations around its base have revealed the foundation deposits of the Temple of Serapis (Serapeum), dating from the time of Ptolemy III Euergetes (246–221 BC), who restored or completed the building. Late Roman houses have been discovered at Kom-el-Dikkeh, and at Qusur al-Rubaiyyat archaeologists have uncovered the Monastery of Kellia, dating back to the fourth century AD.

Alexandria (Ghazni, Afghanistan). A town in the land of the Paropamisadae, south of the Paropamisus Range (Hindu Kush). Founded in 329 BC by Alexander the Great. After its loss by the Seleucids to the Parthians, this Alexandria was successively in the hands of Indo-Greeks, Scythians, and then Indo-Greeks again (under their kings Amyntas [*c* 100–75 BC] and Hermaeus Soter [*c* 40–30]) before its final loss to the Greek world a few years later.

Alexandria Among the Oreitae *see* Gedrosia

Alexandria Beside Caucasus (Begram or Jebal Seraj or Opian Charikar, Afghanistan). Situated on the west bank of the united Panjshir-Ghorband rivers near their confluence, facing (and possibly united with) the native Kapisa on the east bank. Known as Yonaki ('the Greek town'), it was founded, according to Arrian and Curtius, by Alexander the Great (*c* 329). Its descriptive cognomen, 'Beside Caucasus,' was due to its location south of the Paropamisus (Hindu Kush) range, which the Macedonians mistakenly described as 'The Caucasus.' Situated in a corridor between these heights and the Koh-i-Baba range, the town was situated at a road intersection and served as a focus of communications between Arachosia, Bactria and India.

Alexandria Beside Issus *see* Issus

Alexandria Charax *see* Charax

Alexandria Eschate, or Alexandria on the Tanais (Leninabad, formerly Khojend). A town in Soviet Central Asia, in the borderland of Sogdiana (now Tajikistan), on the river Jaxartes (Syr Darya)—named the Tanais after the Don by Alexander the Great—at the point where it turns sharply to the north, and a number of important roads meet. Founded by Alexander *c* 327 to settle Macedonian and Greek soldiers and inhabitants of the region and control the pass over the Tian Shan range to Kashgar, it was known as Eschate, 'the farthest,' because it was the most remote (and also the northernmost) of Alexander's foundations. It was later refounded by the Seleucid monarch Antiochus I.

Alexandria in Arachosia; Alexandropolis (Old Kandahar in Afghanistan). Founded by Alexander the Great in 329 BC (according to Isidorus of Charax); the modern name is a corruption of 'Alexander.'

Alexandria in Aria *see* Aria

Alexandria in the Land of the Fish-Eaters *see* Gedrosia

Alexandria in Margiana. Six towns were said to have been created by Alexander the Great in 328 in the oasis of Merv (Turkmenistan in Soviet Central Asia), but only this one is recorded (by Curtius, Isidorus, Charax and Strabo). It was refounded by Antiochus I Soter under the name of Antiochia, but severely damaged by nomads *c* 293. The city was bisected, according to Pliny the Elder, by the river Margus (Murghab) (canalized into Lake Zotha), and had a circumference of eight and three-quarter miles. This was where the Parthians brought the Roman prisoners captured in the battle of Carrhae (53 BC). The oasis, surrounded by deserts, grew large vines and bunches of grapes. Excavations have been undertaken recently.

Alexandria of the Arachosians *see* Arachosia

Alexandria (?) on the Oxus *see* Seleucia(?) on the Oxus

Alexandria Troas *see* Ilium

Allia, River (Fosso Maestro). A stream that rises in the Crustuminian mountains (named after the town of Crustumerium) and flows into the Tiber about eleven miles from Rome. The scene of the gravest military disaster in the early history of the Romans, when in *c* 390/387 BC their army, consisting of two legions—perhaps the largest force they had ever put into the field—was overwhelmed by invading Gauls (Senones) about 30,000 strong, i.e., outnumbering them twofold, under the command of their king Brennus. Diodorus locates the engagement on the west bank of the Tiber, but Livy and Plutarch are probably correct in ascribing it to the east bank, with the Romans' right wing, forming their reserve, standing on the Crustuminian slopes. The Gauls routed this force on the hill slopes and drove the main Roman army back to the Tiber. Three days later the Gauls arrived in Rome itself. The priests and Vestal Virgins had fled to Caere. Only the Capitol resisted; the rest of the city was plundered and burned.

The date of the engagement, July 18th, was remembered ever afterward as a day of evil omen. The event was also encrusted with legends. It was said that a little before the battle an unknown divine seer, Aius Locutius ('sayer and speaker'), bade a certain Marcus Caedicius tell the city's magistrates that the Gauls were on their way; and after their departure a precinct and shrine were dedicated on the Via Nova where the voice had been heard. It was also recounted that the Gauls, when they arrived in Rome, found those senators who had been too old to fight seated on their ivory chairs like gods on their thrones, awaiting their fate in serene patience. Many stories gathered round the name of the Roman leader Camillus, who allegedly drove the Gauls out of the city.

Al Mina (ancient name unknown). A commercial port in northern Syria (now the Turkish province of Hatay), at the mouth of the river Orontes (Nahr el-Asi). There are traces of Bronze Age (Mycenaean) occupation and commerce at a nearby hill site (Sabouni), but the main settlement and trading post (*emporion*) was established in *c* 825–800 BC. Cypriots and Phoenicians played a part, but the principal role was enacted by seamen and businessmen from Chalcis and Eretria in Euboea, who acquired gold and ivory, etc. in the near east and, from the eighth century onward, dispatched these objects from Al Mina (via the Eretrian colony of Corcyra [Corfu]) to other Euboean trading stations at Pithecusae (Ischia) and Cumae (Cuma) beside the Gulf of Cumae (Bay of Naples) in Campania (southwest Italy), where they were exchanged with the Etruscans for copper and iron. Other Greek coastal settlements in north Syria include Posidium (Ras-el-Bassit) and Tell Sukas (Paltus).

Al Mina seems to have been destroyed in *c* 700, in the course of a Cilician revolt against Assyrian domination, but was rebuilt with a stronger Greek element than before, demonstrated by the presence of Corinthian ware (perhaps brought partly by Aeginetans) and by pottery from various eastern Greek centers as well. During the later seventh century there was further rebuilding, followed by a period of inactivity, perhaps resulting from Babylonian conquest. From *c* 520, however, under Persian rule, a new town was built, and imports from Greece, especially Athens, became increasingly extensive, until Al Mina was eclipsed by the founding of Seleucia in Pieria by Seleucus I Nicator (301). Excavations at Al Mina have revealed a series of single-storeyed warehouses constructed of mud brick on stone foundations around courtyards, and adjoined by shops and workshops.

Al Mina *see* Tripolis

Alpheus, River. The largest river in the Peloponnese (southern Greece). Rising in southern Arcadia near Asea (Frangovrysis)—according to one fictitious tradition the source is shared with the river Eurotas—it flows past Olympia to the Ionian Sea, through which its waters were believed to pass, rising again in the fountain of Arethusa on the island of Ortygia at Syracuse in Sicily. This belief was explained by a frequently told mythological tale. This recounted how Arethusa, nymph of a spring of Elis in the Peloponnese, was bathing, wearied from hunting, in the Alpheus, when the river-god fell in love with her. She fled from his clutches to Ortygia, where the goddess Artemis hid her in the ground and let her gush out from it in the form of a fountain; but Alpheus flowed under the sea to Ortygia and joined her.

Al-Tantura *see* Dora

Altınbaşak *see* Carrhae

Amanus (Gavur Dağları). A mountain range (the southern extension of the Taurus [Toros]) at the northwestern extremity of Syria (now the Turkish Hatay), bordering Asia Minor. The Amanus is crossed by the Syrian Gates (Beilan Pass). The range formed part of the territory of the Syro-Hittite state of Samal in the late second and early first millennia BC. Alexander the Great fought the second of his great battles with the Persians at its foot (*see* Issus).

When Pompey the Great had suppressed the Seleucid kingdom, his general Lucius Afranius cleared the passes of brigands (64 BC), and Pompey recognized Tarcondimotus I as ruler of a client state of Amanus, with his capital at Hieropolis-Castabala. Cicero, as proconsul of Cilicia (51–50), campaigned against the brigands on the mountains—loudly proclaiming his achievements—but they subsequently inflicted a reverse on Quintus Caecilius Metellus Pius Scipio, which he too, however, treated as a victory by assuming the title of *imperator*. Tarcondimotus three times took the losing side in Roman civil wars, supporting Pompey against Caesar, Cassius against Antony and Octavian, and Antony against Octavian (the future Augustus): he issued coinage under the title 'Philantonios' and lost his life in the Actium campaign (31). Thereafter the victor deposed Tarcondimotus' son Philopator I (despite the latter's attempt to move over to the winning side), but restored another son, Tarcondimotus II, eleven years later. Tarcondimotus II was succeeded by Philopator II (probably his son) who died in AD 17, whereupon the territory was incorporated into the Roman province of Syria-Cilicia—with the approval, according to Tacitus, of the majority of its population.

Amasia, Amaseia (Amasya). A city in Pontus (northern Asia Minor); on the western edge of the Pontic mountains. Situated in a deep gorge between two towering, fortified crags (incorporated in its fortifications), the place commands the fertile middle valley of the river Iris (Yeşil Irmak) and the principal roads of the country, including the ancient trade route between Tarsus and Amisus (Samsun). The god Hermes was revered as the creator of the city.

When King Mithridates I (Ktistes, 'the Founder' (301–266 BC), a partially Hellenized Persian, gained control over Pontus and asserted himself against major Hellenistic monarchs, he established his capital at Amasia, where his immediate successors continued to live. Some of the most remarkable and realistic coin portraits in the entire Greek series are those of Mithridates III (*c* 220–185) and Pharnaces I (185–169). Pharnaces transferred his residence to Sinope (Sinop), but Amasia remained of particular importance to the royal house owing to its proximity to the shrine of the chief Pontic deity Zeus Stratios (see below) and its possession of memorials to the earlier monarchs of the dynasty. It was the birthplace of Mithridates VI Eupator (*c* 120–63), the greatest of the Pontic kings, who posed the most dangerous challenge the Romans had ever encountered in the east.

Captured by the Roman commander Lucullus in 70, Amasia was granted city status by Pompey the Great (*c* 64), who gave it a large and fertile territory in his new province of Bithynia-Pontus. Subsequently the Romans placed the city, according to Strabo, under 'kings'—that is to say, under a client prince, appointed by Antony—but Augustus annexed it to his province of Galatia in 2 BC, from which it reckoned a new civic era, becoming the capital of the district of Pontus Galaticus. Under Trajan (AD 98–117), Amasia was incorporated in the new, enlarged province of Cappadocia—which included Pontus—receiving the titles of metropolis, *neokoros* (an honorific appellation relating to the conduct of the imperial cult) and 'first city.' The city's importance grew with the development of roads to the eastern frontier, and it successively assumed the names of Hadriana, Severiana, Antoniniana (after Caracalla, 211–17) and Alexandriana (after Severus Alexander, 222–35). In the provincial reorganization of Diocletian (284–308), it became the capital of the new province of Helenopontus.

The Augustan geographer Strabo, who was born at Amasia, describes it with pride, attributing to it the finest features that a city and fortress could possess. One of the overlooking heights (Harşene Kalesi) still displays a tower and part of a wall of Hellenistic date. At the foot of the cliff, a terrace supported by masonry of the same period marks the location of the royal palace. The memorials of the early monarchs take the form of freestanding shrines (*heroa*) carved out of the rock. The city of Roman times is depicted on a coin of Severus Alexander which displays one of these rock-cut tombs incorporated in the imposing city-walls (shown on another, recently published, piece, undergoing reconstruction). The same coin also shows a temple, probably dedicated to the imperial cult, in the foreground, and high at the rear appears a similar building which is probably the shrine of Zeus Stratios (although in fact this stood some distance back, on the high plateau at Büyük Evlia). The great monumental altar of Zeus Stratios likewise appears as a local coin-type, accompanied by a tree or a flower. One of the city's two bridges connected it with suburbs on the east bank of the Iris, where the modern town is located.

Amastris (Amasra). A coastal city of Pontus (northern Asia Minor), situated on a rocky peninsula joined to the mainland by a narrow isthmus, which provided two harbors. The river Parthenius (Filyos) entered the Euxine (Black) Sea not far off, and a small stream, the Meles, debouched beside Amastris itself. It was founded *c* 300 BC by a queen of that name—widow of Dionysius of Heraclea Pontica (Ereğli), of which she became the ruler after his death—on the site of a town named Sesamus (mentioned by Homer), a Milesian colony that became the acropolis of a new city absorbing three other small colonies, Cromna (near Kurucaşile), Cytorus (formerly a market of Sinope [Sinop], now Kidros), and Tium (Filyos), which soon seceded. The forests in the hinterland provided ships' timber and valuable boxwood. From *c* 265/260 Amastris formed part of the kingdom of Pontus until its capture by a Roman force under Gaius Valerius Triarius (not Lucullus, as Appian records) in 70. Pompey the Great confirmed its status in 64, and it inaugurated its era from that date. Pliny the Younger, Trajan's representative in Bithynia-Pontus, described it as 'a handsome and well-equipped city,' though its local rivulet had become a smelly sewer. Remains of a Roman temple and a three-storey warehouse have survived, in addition to the four ancient moles which protected the larger of the two harbors; harbor buildings are also to be seen at Cytorus. Coins of Amastris honor Homer and a number of deities, including Zeus Strategos and Dionysos Sebastos, and the river-gods Parthenius and Meles.

Ambiani *see* Samarobriva

Ambracia (Arta). A city situated north of the Gulf of Actium on low mountain spurs overlooking a bend of the fertile lower reaches of the river Arachthus, and commanding the only entry by land from southern Greece into Epirus. Colonized in the later seventh century BC by Gorgos, son of the Corinthian tyrant (autocrat) Cypselus, it developed into an independent state under a democratic government, with a fortified port Ambracus (Phidhokastra) on the bank of a lagoon beside the gulf. Ambracia took part in the Persian Wars. During the Peloponnesian War, it took the side of the Spartans; but its attempts to control the Gulf of Actium caused conflict with neighboring Acarnania and Amphilochia, whose forces, with the assistance of the Athenian general Demosthenes, inflicted a severe defeat on the Ambracians at Olpe in 426. This engagement, noted by Thucydides, was Athens' first military victory of the war. During the winter, however, Sparta's ally Corinth succeeded in sending 300 heavily-armed infantry (hoplites) to Ambracia to secure it against further Athenian attack.

In the following century the Ambracians were members of the first Corinthian League (395), set up in opposition to Sparta. An attempted siege by Philip II of Macedonia in 342 was frustrated by the Athenian orator Demosthenes, but Philip, after his victory over Athens and its allies at Chaeronea (338), occupied and garrisoned Ambracia. When Pyrrhus I (297–272), at the expense of Macedonia, began to make his kingdom of Epirus into a large-scale state, he took possession of the city and made it his capital, spending lavishly on its enlargement and adornment. After the fall of the Epirote monarchy it issued coinage showing an obelisk, the sacred conical stone of Apollo Agyieus. Ambracia became an object of contention between Macedonia and the Aetolian League, of which it was a member from 230/229. But in 189 it fell to the Roman general Marcus Fulvius Nobilior, suffering severely at his hands, yet subsequently gaining recognition of its 'freedom.' However, the foundation of Nicopolis by Octavian (the future Augustus) to celebrate his victory over Antony and Cleopatra at Actium in 31 BC meant the eclipse and partial incorporation of Ambracia, although it continued to survive as a city into the second century AD. Parts of its wall are still extant, enclosing a perimeter of three miles according to Livy, and the foundations of a temple of the early fifth century BC have been uncovered, as well as remains of the capital of Pyrrhus.

Ameria *see* Cabeira

Amida (Diyarbakır, in southeastern Turkey). Situated near the right bank of the Tigris, at the uppermost limit of its navigation, on a spur at the bend of the river. In the reign of Constantius II (AD 337–61), a large fortress was created at Amida, to serve as a frontier-station of Roman Mesopotamia, and to protect the provinces of Armenia that lay to its northwest. At first it was garrisoned by a single legion, but this was reinforced by six more in the face of attack by the Sassanian (Persian) King Shapur (Sapor) II in 359. A detailed eyewitness account of the siege by Ammianus Marcellinus, who was an officer of the garrison, has survived.

The city was retaken by Julian the Apostate (363), and in the same year his successor Jovian doubled the population by introducing refugees from Nisibis (Nusaybin), which he had ceded to the Persians under a treaty. An inscription of 367/375 commemorates the erection of an additional rampart. The walls that are still to be seen at Diyarbakır today (and are among the finest examples of medieval military architecture) follow the pattern of the original fourth-century walls. They are made of black basalt: 'black the walls,' the saying went, and "black the hearts of the men of Amida.'

Amisus (Samsun). In Pontus, on the northern coast of Asia Minor; situated between the deltas of the rivers Halys (Kizil Irmak) and Iris (Yeşil Irmak), at the head of the only effective trade route into the interior. Amisus was founded in the mid-sixth century BC by colonists from Miletus (Balat) or Phocaea (Foca) in Ionia (western Asia Minor). The ancient city (Kara Samsun) stood on a large headland northwest of the modern town, bounded on two sides by the Euxine (Black) Sea and partially cut off from the mainland by a ravine, so that it constituted a peninsula, and virtually, an island.

In the middle of the fifth century the place received colonists (cleruchs) from Athens, who renamed their settlement Piraeus and developed it into an important commercial center drawing on the resources of the hinterland; in the absence of a natural harbor, two moles were constructed to provide an anchorage beneath the promontory. After a period of Persian rule, during which the city's democratic constitution was suspended, it was declared free by Alexander the Great, reassuming the name of Amisus. In about the middle of the third century BC, however, it had become part of the kingdom of Pontus, perhaps annexed by Mithridates III (*c* 250–c 220). Amisus was enlarged and adorned, particularly by Mithridates VI Eupator the Great (120–63), who constructed a fortified subsidiary town, under the name of Eupatoria. During his wars with the Romans, Lucullus destroyed Eupatoria (71) and burned and plundered large parts of Amisus itself, but subsequently restored and liberated the city and extended its territory; its rights were subsequently confirmed by Pompey the Great (64) who gave it a new constitution, and then again by Julius Caesar. Antony (Marcus Antonius) placed Amisus under an autocrat ('tyrant') named Strato, whose removal by Octavian, the future Augustus, was signalized by the adoption of a new civic era dating from 32/31. Controlling a large strip of land, which included the fertile plain of Themiscyra (Terme) and was extended westward to the Halys, Amisus remained (as its coinage stresses), a free city, loosely attached to the province of Bithynia-Pontus, and then to Cappadocia (when it incorporated Pontus), until the time of Diocletian (AD 284–305), who attached it to the new province of Helenopontus, part of the administrative diocese of Pontica.

A coin of Hadrian (131/2) shows an altar and temple of Zeus in front of three towering peaks, and an issue of Caracalla (211–17) depicts a temple of Demeter. Other pieces depict a variety of deities. Attempts to find their shrines have yielded no results because the site of Amisus is an inaccessible Turkish military zone today, although a sanctuary has come to light a mile and a half inland, the remains of city-walls and towers have been reported, and a large signed mosaic of Achilles and Thetis is now to be seen.

Amman *see* Philadelphia (Rabbath-Ammon)

Amphiareum *see* Oropus

Amphipolis. A town that was first Thracian and then Macedonian (northern Greece), occupying a plateau upon a spur of Mount Pangaeus, at a crossing point beside the east bank of the river Strymon (Struma) which, as it approaches its estuary, two and a half miles away, encloses the town on its north, west and south sides (hence Amphi-polis, the surrounded city), while on the east side—comprising a series of natural terraces—a wall protected the passage leading to the mountain.

Originally the place was an Edonian (Thracian) settlement, named Ennea Hodoi (Nine Roads). In 497 BC Histiaeus, the autocratic ruler (tyrant) of Miletus, and his son-in-law Aristagoras endeavored to settle colonists, but the Edonians drove them off. A similar attempt by the Athenians in 465 likewise ended in failure. Finally, however, in 437 BC, using the trading port of Eion as its base, a party of Athenians and Greeks from other cities, under the leadership of Hagnon, son of Nicias, succeeded in establishing a colony. Amphipolis owed its importance partly to its strategic location—commanding a vital bridge across the Strymon and communications with northern Greece and the Thracian coast—and partly to its proximity to the gold and silver mines of Mount Pangaeum, and to lands yielding rich agricultural produce and extensive supplies of wood.

During the Peloponnesian War, however, the Spartan general Brasidas captured the city without encountering resistance, helped by treason among the colonists (424). We learn from the historian Thucydides how he himself held the Athenian command in Thrace, but failed to reach Amphipolis in time—only succeeding in the rescue of Eion—and was consequently sent into exile because his failure meant a grave loss of timber for shipping. Two years later an attempt by another Athenian leader, Cleon, to recapture the city proved equally unsuccessful, and in the battle both Cleon and Brasidas were killed. Brasidas was buried in the city, and venerated as hero and founder by annual games and sacrifices.

The Peace of Nicias between Athens and Sparta (421) provided for the restoration of Amphipolis to the Athenians. Yet the city remained virtually independent—issuing coins with magnificent full-face heads of Apollo—until 357, when it was occupied by Philip II of Macedonia, who employed it as one of the royal mints for his famous gold issues. Alexander the Great used the Strymon estuary as a naval base for his expedition to Asia in 334, and his three most famous admirals, Nearchus, Androsthenes, and Laomedon all came from Amphipolis, which also served him as a major mint. During the Hellenistic period it remained a Macedonian city and fortress. After the battle of Pydna between the Romans and the Macedonian monarch Perseus (168), however, the victorious Roman general Lucius Aemilius Paullus, surnamed Macedonicus, convened a meeting of selected Romans and Greeks at Amphipolis to decide the future fate of the royal territories. The country was divided into four districts, and Amphipolis was declared the capital of one of them.

In 146, however, the arrangement was dissolved, and Macedonia became a province of Rome. Amphipolis retained its prosperity, becoming a station on the Via Egnatia (*c* 130) which extended across the Balkans from the Adriatic coast to Byzantium. In 48, after his victory at Pharsalus, Julius Caesar pursued his defeated enemy to the city, only to find that he had already set sail for Egypt. Another distinguished visitor, according to the *Acts of the Apostles*, was St. Paul.

A round tower built to protect the east flank of the long wall of Thucydidean times has now been uncovered, and many hundreds of wooden stakes and beams have disclosed the location of the Strymon bridge. The 'Lion of Amphipolis,' reconstructed and re-erected, formed part of a funeral monument that may have been built in honor of Alexander the Great's admiral Laomedon. Excavations have also uncovered a Hellenistic necropolis (containing more than four hundred graves), dwellings dating back to the fourth century BC, and Roman houses, including one with a floor mosaic depicting the Rape of Europa. Remains of a temple of Clio and of a later Roman portico (*stoa*) have also come to light, in addition to Christian basilicas, containing fine and varied polychrome mosaics. An early hexagonal church has now been completely revealed, in addition to a complex of fifth-century buildings, including one surmounted by a two-storeyed hexagonal lantern.

Amphissa. The principal city of Western (Ozolian) Locris near Delphi in central Greece. Claiming to derive its name from a legendary hero Amphissos, son of Apollo, or from Amphissa, who was the granddaughter of Aeolus and was loved by Apollo, this 'greatest and most illustrious city of the Locrians,' as Pausanias called it, dominated the route between Mounts Pindus and Parnassus to the sea. It was used as a refuge by the Delphians and Phocians during the Persian invasion of 480 BC. During the Peloponnesian War between the Athenians and Spartans, it supported the expedition of the Spartan commander Eurylochus against the port of Naupactus, which lay to its west (426).

In the Third Sacred War (356), Amphissa sided with the Thebans against the Phocian separatists who had seized Delphi, but was subjugated by the Phocian commander Onomarchus in 353. Independent again after his defeat and death in the following year, Amphissa, instigated by Thebes, acted against the Athenians by proposing that they should be fined by the authority controlling the sanctuary of Delphi (the Delphic Amphictyony), but the Athenian orator Aeschines countered by accusing Amphissa of sacrilegiously encroaching on sacred Delphian territory. This became the cause of a Fourth Sacred War (also known as the Amphissan War), in which Philip II of Macedonia captured the city and destroyed its walls (338). However, it recovered, and in 279 beat off a siege by the Aetolian confederacy, so that it was able, in the following year, to send a force of four hundred heavily-armed infantrymen (hoplites) to defend Delphi against invading Gauls. Subsequently, Amphissa became part of the Aetolian League, and successfully resisted a siege by a Roman force. But after the eclipse of the League by the Romans, the city passed into Roman hands. When Octavian (the future Augustus) defeated Antony at Actium (31) and founded Nicopolis to celebrate his victory—drawing in settlers from neighboring Greek communities—Amphissa was occupied by Aetolian refugees (who did not want to settle in Nicopolis) and henceforth claimed to be no longer Locrian but Aetolian.

The city has been identified on the site of the medieval baronial castle of Salona, where a well-preserved section of the wall, dating back to the fourth century BC, has come to light. A circular baptistry of the fourth century AD, with fine mosaics (suggesting a long local tradition), has also been discovered. Pausanias saw a Temple of Athena, and the tombs of Amphissos and Amphissa and of another founder figure, the hero Andraemon, and his wife Gorge.

Ampurias *see* Emporiae

Amyclae *see* Sparta

Anagnia (Anagni). A town in Latium, forty miles east-southeast of Rome; situated at a height of 1,510 feet above the valley of the river Trerus (Sacco), which it dominated. Anagnia was the capital of the Hernici (meaning 'men of the rocks' in Oscan—though their territory was fertile). According to legend, a man of Anagnia, Laevius Cispius, brought help to the Roman King Tullus Hostilius (*c* 673–642 BC). The Hernici made a defensive alliance with Rome in about 486 and subsequently fought on its side against the Aequi and Volsci. In 387 and 362, however, they opposed the Romans; but the alliance was revived in 358. In 306, we learn from Livy, Anagnia led all the Hernican towns, except three, into war against Rome. They were defeated, however, and brought into subjection, and in the end so completely Latinized that their own language is no longer identifiable.

During the third century the town was plundered by Pyrrhus of Epirus, and then in the second Punic War by Hannibal. In the following century it was a *municipium* with full citizen rights. Cicero possessed an estate there, and during the Second Triumvirate (42–31), according to Servius, Antony established a mint, but if that is true, its products have not been identified with certainty. Vitellius' general Fabius Valens and Commodus' mistress Marcia were born at Anagnia.

Tombs and well-preserved polygonal walls of the fourth century BC are to be seen, and the remains of three sanctuaries (one dedicated to Venus Libitina) probably belong to the same period. The artificial terrace of the forum is of late Republican date, and so is a votive deposit, apparently connected with the worship of Ceres. The temples of the region were still well-known in the time of Marcus Aurelius. Septimius Severus had a residence (the Villa Magna) in the neighborhood. Below the city was the Compitum Anagninum (Anagnian Cross-Roads), of which traces have been discovered on the Via Latina and Via Labicana.

Anape *see* Gorgippia

Anazarbus (Anavarza). A city in Cilicia (southeastern Asia Minor), on the right bank of the the Sumbaş Çayı, a tributary of the river Pyramus (Ceyhan) on its middle reaches; Anazarbus was named after a nearby mountain. In the first century BC it probably belonged to Tarcondimotus, the prince of Amanus who controlled the hinterland of the eastern Cilician plain. But after his defeat and death, fighting on Antony's side (31), the victorious Augustus, when visiting the city in AD 19, refounded it with civic status under the new name of Caesarea By Anazarbus. A new era was inaugurated to celebrate the occasion. Gaining in importance and prosperity, the city became during the third century AD an assiduous rival of the provincial capital Tarsus, granting an honorary magistracy (*demiourgos*) to the emperor Elagabalus (218–22), so that Tarsus retaliated by conferring the same honor on his successor Severus Alexander. Under the provincial reorganization of Diocletian (284–305), Anazarbus was the capital of the province of Cilicia Secunda.

The imposing crag, more than six hundred feet high, on which the acropolis was built, dominated the city, which lay at the foot of its precipitous face; the fortress-crowned rock appears on local coins of Claudius, accompanied by a head of Zeus. Parts of the city walls are still to be seen, and—just outside them—the amphitheater, in which the Christians Tarachus, Probus and Andronicus were martyred. Portions of a theater, stadium and large necropolis have also survived, and at the end of the main street, which, like the thoroughfare crossing it, was flanked by continuous colonnades, there stands a fine triumphal arch, probably dating from the time of Septimius Severus (193–211). An aqueduct dedicated to Domitian in 90 extends in a northwesterly direction across the plain to the headwaters of the Sumbaş Çayı; this, or a second aqueduct serving the city, is depicted on a coin of Severus Alexander (222–35), together with the sluicegate or settlement tank that surmounted it. Beside Domitian's aqueduct are the traces of a large Corinthian temple, which may be the building illustrated on a coin issued under Marcus Aurelius and Lucius Verus (161–69). Other religious buildings shown on the coinage include a shrine of which a model is set on a carriage drawn by elephants (Julia Maesa, 218–23), a temple of the City Fortune (Severus Alexander (222–35), and a tripartite structure apparently surmounted by the orb of the Sun (Maximinus I and his son Maximus, 235–38).

Under the Byzantine empire Anazarbus became an archbishopric, renamed Justinianopolis after its reconstruction following a sixth-century earthquake.

Ancona. A city in Picenum (Marche) on the east coast of Italy. Its name comes from the Greek *ancon,* elbow joint, referring to the shape of its port, which provides the only good harbor (natural but artificially improved) on the central part of the eastern coast. The site forms an impressive arc on two spurs of a promontory descending from the massif of Mount Cunerus (Cunero). Founded in about 390 BC by Greek refugees fleeing from Dionysius I of Syracuse, Ancona was very productive of wine and wheat. In 268 it was taken over by the Romans, who employed it as a fleet station in their Illyrian War of 178; and it was also used by Lucius Cornelius Cinna as the mustering point of his eastern expedition against his rival Sulla in 84. Meanwhile Ancona had developed a flourishing Mediterranean trade. When Caesar crossed the Rubicon in 49, at the outset of his Civil War against Pompey the Great, Ancona was one of the first cities that came over to his side.

After the subsequent battles of Philippi (42) and Actium (31), it received drafts of Roman colonists. Under the principate, it became the main Italian port for Dalmatia. Trajan, before starting on his second expedition to the Danube (105), improved and enlarged the harbor, erecting a new mole to which his triumphal arch (115) on the quay still bears witness. There are also well-preserved remains of an amphitheater; and the substructures of a temple, presumably dedicated to Venus, whom Catullus and Juvenal describe as the city's patron deity, lie underneath the ancient cathedral of San Ciriaco on the Monte Guasto promontory. The contents of Picene, Hellenistic and Roman tombs are displayed in the Museo Nazionale delle Marche.

Ancyra (Ankara, now the capital of Turkey). A city in central Asia Minor, lying around a steep crag that formed its acropolis. In accordance with the tradition (preserved by Pausanias) that Ancyra was founded by the mythical Phrygian king Midas, archaeological evidence confirms occupation by the Phrygians, who conquered and settled in the central and western parts of the peninsula toward the end of the second millennium BC. Situated at the junction of east-west and north-south trade routes, Ancyra became the second metropolis of Phrygia (after Gordium), and its museums today contain rich material from that epoch.

Following a period under Persian control, the place was occupied and visited by Alexander the Great in 333 BC, and subsequently belonged to the empires of Antigonus I Monophthalmos and the Seleucids; its commercial importance increased as that of Gordium waned. The Gauls who invaded the peninsula from 278 onward seem to have built in a new town on the same site, which later in the same century became the capital of one of their three (Galatian) tribal groups, the Tectosages. In 189 Ancyra was temporarily occupied by the Roman general Cnaeus Manlius Vulso, and early in the following century became part of the territories of Mithridates VI Eupator of Pontus, until he was defeated by the Romans under Pompey. In 64/63, Pompey, in the course of his reorganization of the country, confirmed Ancyra's position as the center of an enlarged Tectosagan dominion. Antony gave Galatia and adjoining territories to the client king Amyntas, and when Augustus, on the death of Amyntas, annexed the country in 25 the city became the capital of the new Roman province, and prospered. Under the provincial reorganization of Diocletian, it remained the capital of Galatia Prima.

Of the various surviving remains from the Roman period—including baths and a late 'Column of Julian'—the most important is the Temple of Rome and Augustus, erected in the emperor's honor during his lifetime by the Council of the three Galatian tribes. On its walls is a bilingual (Latin and Greek) inscription known as the Monumentum Ancyranum, which comprises by far the best preserved text of Augustus' famous political testament the *Res Gestae Divi Augusti,* offering an official interpretation of his actions throughout his career, together with a list of the honors that the senate and Roman people had conferred on him. The temple also contains a second inscription, containing a list of the high priests of the *koinon* (provincial organization) of Galatia in the reign of Tiberius (AD 14–37).

Ancyra was visited by St. Paul, whose *Epistle to the Galatians* was written to strengthen the faith of its Christian inhabitants. He may have founded a church there (though its first attestation dates from 192). An inscription records a visit to the city by Hadrian, probably in 117. About 269 it passed into the hands of the secessionist Palmyrene empire of Zenobia, but three years later Aurelian entered its gates without opposition. In 324 it figured prominently in an attempt to suppress the Arian heresy, when a meeting of bishops held at Antioch arranged for a church council to be held at Ancyra—whose bishop Marcellus was strongly anti-Arian. But Constantine the Great, who did not want either of the extreme factions to triumph completely, transferred the meeting to Nicaea (İznik). In 362 the powerful non-Christian community of Ancyra gave a triumphal welcome to Julian the Apostate when he visited the place. (This city is to be distinguished from another of the same name, the chief center of Abbaitis in Mysia or western Phrygia.)

Andriace *see* Myra

Andros. The most northerly and second-largest island of the Cyclades archipelago in the Aegean Sea, Andros is twenty-five miles long and ten miles across, and lies six miles southeast of Euboea and two miles north of Tenos. Its origins were variously attributed to two mythical heroes from whom it was said to have derived its name, one the son of Eurymachus or Anius and the other (according to Diodorus and Pausanias) the recipient of the island from Rhadamanthys, the son of Zeus and Europa.

The Andrians regarded themselves as Ionian Greeks, although they may also have possessed an admixture of Thracian blood. Dependent on the Euboean city of Eretria in the eighth century BC, they sent colonists, in the following century, to Acanthus, Stagirus, Argilus and Sane (jointly with Chaleis) in Macedonia, and these settlements prospered. In 490, however, Andros submitted to the Persian invasion of Darius, and ten years later it supplied ships to Xerxes I, earning harassment from the Greek fleet. Although subsequently enrolled in the Athenians' Delian League it remained on bad terms with them, and between 450 and 446 was obliged to admit Athenian colonists (cleruchs); this was one of the first occasions on which Athens planted settlements on the territory of its allies. However, Andros revolted in 411, and was attacked by an Athenian fleet.

In 378/7 it entered the Second Athenian League, though not wholeheartedly. After Philip II of Macedonia had defeated the Greek city-states at Chaeronea in 338, the island came under his kingdom's control, and during the Hellenistic period became a bone of contention between the Macedonians and Ptolemies. In 200, during Rome's second Macedonian War, it was captured by a combined

Roman, Pergamene and Rhodian fleet, and ruthlessly plundered. It remained a possession of Pergamum until that state was annexed by Rome in 133, whereupon Andros may have belonged, at first, to the new Roman province of Asia Minor, though it was subsequently, and more logically, attached to Macedonia-Achaea, and then, after those countries had been divided into two provinces, to Achaea.

The principal centers, in ancient times, were located in the western part of the island. Among them was Palaeopolis, the capital, which contained a number of temples, including a shrine of Dionysus who was the principal deity of the islanders (and appeared on their earliest sixth-century coinage). A walled settlement at Zagora, to the southeast of Palaeopolis, had been important in the ninth and eighth centuries BC, but was abandoned thereafter, though its temple remained in use until after 500. Andros is notable for an important *Hymn to Isis* that was found on its territory.

Anio (Aniene). A river of central Italy, about seventy miles in length. Rising from two springs in the Simbruini mountains (from *sub imbribus,* under the rain) of the Sabine country—of which it provided the border with Latium—it flowed west-southwest past Sublaqueum (Subiaco) through a narrow valley beside Tibur (Tivoli), where there was a famous and spectacular waterfall nearly seventy feet high, now changed by landslides. Then the river descended after further cascades and numerous twists to the level of the Roman Campagna, where it joined the Tiber near the antique town of Antemnae, halfway between Rome and Fidenae (Castel Giubileo). It was navigable below Tibur and fed two aqueducts, the Anio Vetus (272 BC) and the Anio Novus (AD 38–52), which supplied the needs of Rome, as the river still does today. Nero created a group of artificial lakes in the upper course of the Anio near Sublaqueum (Subiaco), where he built a villa, of which considerable remains survive, indicating occupation until the late imperial epoch. In 472 the German general welcomed the new western emperor Olybrius at his camp beside its banks.

Ankara *see* Ancyra

Ankore *see* Nicaea

Annaba *see* Hippo Regius

Ano Englianos *see* Pylos

Ansedonia *see* Cosa

Antalya *see* Attaleia

Anthela *see* Thermopylae

Anti-Apennines, Mounts. A series of Italian mountain ranges and hills forming a lower extension of the Apennines behind the coastal plain (Maremma) which borders on the Tyrrhenian Sea. It contained the Metal-Bearing Chain of hills (Catena Metallifera [*qv*], prolonged into the island of Ilva [Elba]), and extended downward to Mounts Amiata and Tolfa: the three mountain groups providing the metallic wealth that gave the Etruscan cities their prosperity and power. The other, northern extremity of the Anti-Apennines, across the river Arnus (Arno), was bordered by their continuation or appendix the Apuan Alps, rising behind other Etruscan settlements that eventually provided the Romans with very important quarries of marble (Luna [Luni], Massa-Carrara).

Antigoneia *see* Antioch, Mantinea, Nicaea

Antinoopolis, Antinoe, Antenon, Hadrianopolis (Sheikh Abadeh). A city in middle Egypt, a hundred and eighty miles south of Cairo, situated upon the east bank of the Nile opposite Hermopolis Magna (Ashmunein). Built on the ruins of an ancient Egyptian town—either Besa or Nefrusi, containing sanctuaries of the divinities Bes and Hathor respectively—Antinoopolis was founded by Hadrian (AD 130), as Pausanias reports, in memory of his beloved Antinous, who had drowned himself in the Nile not far from the place.

The new settlement, 'the city of the Antinoeis, the new Hellenes,' was colonized by Greeks or Hellenized Egyptians from various centers, including people (chosen by lot) from Ptolemais (El-Manshah) and a number of ex-soldiers, and was granted a privileged Greek constitution based on that of Naucratis (Kom Gieif). Developing, before long, into a prosperous urban complex, and benefiting from porphyry quarries adjoining a road built by Hadrian to the Red Sea coast, the city became the capital of the late imperial province of the Upper Thebaid and the seat of Catholic and Monophysite bishoprics. The stones of many of the ancient buildings (still standing in 1800) were removed to build a sugar factory at Roda, but the remains of a theater and other structures have recently been discovered.

Antioch by Daphne. Antiochia, in northern Syria; the modern Antakya in the Hatay, southeastern Turkey. Antioch was situated at the edge of a large and fertile plain between Mount Silpius and the left bank of the river Orontes (Nahr el-Asi) where it cut through to the sea, so that the city stood at a focal point of communications with both south and east. Excavations have revealed traces of a pre-classical settlement, but the city was founded in about 300 BC by Seleucus I Nicator, founder of the Seleucid dynasty, who named it after his father Antiochus and populated it with 5,300 Athenian and Macedonian ex-soldier settlers (transferred from Antigonus I Monophthalmos' short-lived foundation of Antigoneia); at the same time Seleucus renamed the Orontes after the Macedonian river Axius. Antiochia by Daphne, which owed this name to its suburb of Daphne, famous for a shrine of Apollo (among other royal gods), became the capital of the Seleucid empire's western territories, supplanting Seleucia in Pieria, which became its harbor (except during a brief intermission from 241–219, when the port passed into the hands of the Ptolemies). Antioch was soon the principal center of northern Syria and one of the greatest cities in the world.

Its growth took place in stages. Laid out from the start according to the regular gridiron plan frequently found at contemporary Hellenistic towns, it at first only occupied a small strip beside the river; but the original plan already envisaged considerable enlargement, which was duly achieved. A new walled quarter, containing numerous handsome temples, was added by the founder's son Antiochus I Soter (281–261). Seleucus II Callinicus (246–226) created a third walled quarter on an island in the Orontes, which was linked with the main city by five bridges and adorned by a four-faced arch at the intersection of its two principal streets. In about 170 Antiochus IV Epiphanes built a fourth quarter, giving it the name of Epiphania, so that Antioch became known as the Tetrapolis (four cities).

Enriched with many fine monuments and statues, including the famous Tyche (Fortune) of Eutychides (early third century), Antioch became a model of wealthy urban sophistication, blending a vast cosmopolitan range of different populations, including numerous Aramaeans and a substantial Jewish community whose privileges were said to go back to Seleucus I. Since, however, the city was the Seleucids' western residence, its people, who were reputedly dissolute, played a prominent and tumultuous part in the dynastic revolutions that disfigured the reigns of the later rulers, as Seleucid power and influence gradually shrank but Rome expanded. After an interval during which the Armenian monarch Tigranes I the Great incorporated the city in his territories (83–66), it was annexed by Pompey the Great and became the capital of the Roman province of Syria (64). Then, in 49/8 Caesar granted its administration autonomous status, and new eras were reckoned from both these dates.

During the Roman Principate many easterners migrated from Antioch to Rome, so that the satirist Juvenal complained that the Orontes had flowed into the Tiber. It was here that Mucianus, governor of Syria, planned the rebellion that led to the accession of Vespasian (AD 69). The city was also the principal base for recurrent military operations against the Parthians in Mesopotamia. One of the emperors who used it for this purpose, Trajan, gave the Antiochenes funds for sumptuous rebuilding after one of the numerous earthquakes that afflicted the area (115), like Hellenistic and Roman rulers before him and other Roman and Byzantine emperors in subsequent centuries.

During the civil wars of the later second century, its adherence to the pretender Pescennius Niger (193–98) brought about its degradation by the victorious Septimius Severus, but in 201 it was restored to its former rank, and received the honorary title of colony from his son and successor Caracalla. At some point during the 250s or 260s—perhaps at the beginning of the sole reign of Gallienus (260), during Valerian's captivity—the city fell briefly into the hands of the Sassanian (Persian) monarch Sapor (Shapur) I (who deported a large number of the inhabitants to Susiana). Soon afterward, it formed a vital part of the territories first of the usurpers Macrianus and Quietus (260–61) and then of the breakaway Palmyrene monarch Zenobia (271): the first of the major battles in which Aurelian defeated her armies was fought nearby.

Despite many such disturbances, however, Antioch continued to derive great wealth from its position on the great commercial route from Asia to the Mediterranean, and from the exploitation of wine, olive oil and other natural resources abundantly available in its extensive hinterland. After Rome and Alexandria, it was the third city of the empire; and after Alexandria and Seleucia on the Tigris (Tell Umar), the third city of the east. Under the provincial reorganization of Diocletian, it became not only the capital of the administrative diocese Oriens but also a residence of one of the four tetrarchs who shared the rulership of the empire. In the fourth century St. John Chrysostom estimated its population as 200,000, excluding children and slaves.

Antioch played a major part in the propagation of Christianity. Soon after the Crucifixion of Jesus, St. Peter and St. Paul visited the city. In spite of much persecution (including the martyrdom of St. Ignatius, bishop of Antioch, in 107 and the destruction of churches by Diocletian), Christianity became and remained extremely strong. After it became the official faith under Constantine I, the bishops of Antioch were very influential personages who made known their theological views (often markedly different from the doctrines of Constantinople and Alexandria) in no uncertain fashion. In 325 Arius, whose opinions were held to be derogatory to the divinity of the Son, was condemned by a synod at Antioch; a further important meeting took place there in 340. In the following year Constantine's son Constantius II dedicated a magnificent basilica, the Golden Octagon, which his father had begun. Antioch was also a preeminent center of eastern monasticism. Nevertheless, its inhabitants remained notorious for the disturbances that accompanied their chariot racing and other spectacles; and they received Constantius' pagan successor Julian the Apostate (in whose reign [362] the temple at Daphne was burned down) with disrespectful mockery, for which he retaliated in his satirical treatise the *Misopogon* (Beard-Hater).

At the same time, however, the city displayed a highly active intellectual life, of which the leader was the Greek rhetorician Libanius (314–*c* 393). From his writings, and those of his pupil St. John Chrysostom, and the works of Strabo, Julian, Euagrius, Procopius and Malalas, it is possible to reconstruct the principal topographical features of the urban area, which occupied, at the period of its greatest expansion, the whole plain between the Orontes and the mountains. The Hellenistic gridiron plan, revealed by aerial photographs, can still be traced in the modern town, whose main street follows the axis of the ancient city. But the depth of successive strata has made excavation problematical. However, the course of the wall has been reconstructed, and a few houses, an amphitheater, two hippodromes, and several baths have been uncovered. One of the bridges leading to the (now vanished) island has also survived, and excavations have revealed traces of twin Hellenistic arches. A wealth of late antique art has also come to light; but little else remains of the magnificent palace quarter and churches dating from the periods of Diocletian and Constantine respectively. At the pleasure resort of Daphne, however, a theater and several villas and baths have been excavated.

Antioch in Mygdonia *see* Nisibis

Antioch in Pisidia, Antiochia (Yalvaç). A city in south-central Asia Minor; more accurately described as 'toward Pisidia,' since it lay within the borders of Phrygia, in a fertile region sometimes known as Pisidian Phrygia. Established by the Seleucids on a plateau with seven eminences above the river Anthius, separated from the Sultan mountains by a two-hundred-foot-deep defile, Antioch gained additional importance from the foundation on a nearby hill (Karakuyu) by the Attalids of Pergamum of a sanctuary of Men Askaenus. Established in the second century BC, it possessed numerous temple serfs and extensive estates and became one of the most important hilltop sites of Asia Minor.

The city was declared free by the Romans after their victory over Antiochus III the Great (188 BC). When, however, they annexed the Galatian kingdom of Amyntas (25), Antioch formed part of the new province of Galatia that was founded in its place, and became a Roman colony, under the name of Caesarea—either immediately or some five years later—receiving as settlers the retired soldiers of two legions whose standards appear on an inauguratory coinage. A second issue under Augustus is inscribed PARENS, referring either to the emperor or to the colony itself; if the latter, the term is intended to indicate its seniority over other Augustan colonies in Pisidia, with which Antioch was linked by a series of military roads designed to maintain control of the mountainous country. Subsequent coinages, which continued until Claudius II Gothicus (AD 268–70), depict busts or figures of the river Anthius and of Men Askaenus (MENSIS) in addition to various other deities, including a female GENIVS who is identified with FORTVNA. There are also references to the Victory, Courage (VIRTVS) and Concord of emperors. From the time of Septimius Severus onward the larger bronze denomination (*sestertius*) displays the letters SR (*senatus Romanus*), apparently referring to some form of monetary control or initiative by the Roman senate. In the later empire Antioch became capital of a new province of Pisidia.

Excavations have revealed an Augustan Forum (the Augusta Platea) with a semicircular rock-cut rear wall, and a colonnaded street (the Tiberia Platea), approached by a monumental, triple-arched Propylon of the mid-first century AD, on the site of which the Monumentum Antiochenum (a fragmentary version of the *Res Gestae Divi Augusti, see* Ancyra) was discovered. A temple of fine architectural quality has been tentatively identified as a shrine of Augustus. By the end of his dynasty Antioch was already a large and imposing city (St. Paul and Barnabas were among its visitors), and a second major period of construction—marked by the city gate (AD 212)—extended between the epochs of Septimius Severus and Constantine the Great. Other finds include a small theater and a fourth-century Christian basilica; and, in the neighborhood, substantial remains of an aqueduct can be seen. The Sanctuary of Men has been shown to consist of a temple on a stepped podium within a large walled enclosure.

Antiochia *see also* Ace, Alexandria in Margiana, Aradus, Charax, Edessa, Gadara, Nisibis, Ptolemais Ace, Tarsus

---

Antipatris, formerly Aphek and Capharsaba (Afek, Ras-al-Ain, eleven miles northeast of Tel Aviv). A very ancient settlement in Judaea (now Israel) on the borderland between the plain of Sharon and the hills of Samaria. It bore the additional names of Pegae, 'the springs' and Arethusa (after a famous spring at Syracuse in Sicily), because it adjoined the one perpetual stream that flows from the Judaean hills into the Mediterranean, named Aujeh 'the Crooked.' Aphek-Capharsaba possessed an early Hellenistic fort which, according to Josephus, was captured by the Jewish (Hasmonaean) ruler John Hyrcanus I (*c* 132). The town was rebuilt *c* 63 by Pompey the Great and subsequently refounded by Herod the Great (37–4), who renamed it after his father Antipater. It served as a halfway house on the road between Jerusalem and Herod's greater foundation, Caesarea Maritima; thus St. Paul stopped here after his arrest (guarded by an escort of four hundred and seventy soldiers).

Antipatris was converted into a model agricultural settlement and became the center of a thickly populated area. Its coinage, showing a temple of Ashtoreth-Astarte (assimilated to Tyche-Fortuna), seems to have been limited to Elagabalus (AD 218–222), who probably advanced it to civic status. The city was still referred to as a road station at the end of antiquity. A mausoleum of imperial date with a courtyard and forecourt has been uncovered.

Antipolis (Antibes). A city on the southern coast of Gaul (France), in the territory of the Ligurian tribe of the Deciates. Its name has been thought to describe its position 'opposite' Nicaea (Nice), but may instead be a rationalization of a Ligurian name. Antipolis possessed a harbor protected by a small promontory. Inhabited since the beginning of the first millennium BC, it subsequently became a commercial outpost of Massalia (Massilia, Marseille) or of Phocaea (Foca) in Ionia, which colonized it. Greek pottery from the sixth century BC onward has come to light, and more numerous and longer inscriptions than have been found at any other site in southern France, including a lead curse tablet, a victory monument (at Biot), and pieces of pottery inscribed with the names of deities and their worshippers.

Polybius records that in 154 BC, in response to an appeal by Antipolis, the Roman consul Quintus Opimius drove off attacking Ligurians; and thereafter it came under the protection of Rome, which converted southern Gaul into the province of Gallia Narbonensis in 121 BC, with the exception of the free city of Massilia. When Marcus Aemilius Lepidus (shortly to become a member of the Second Triumvirate) was governor of Narbonensis (44–43), Antipolis struck a bronze coin with a Greek inscription bearing his name; the issue probably celebrates him as a founder or refounder (*ktistes*), on the grounds that he had admitted the city to the 'Latin right' (half-citizenship, under which the annually elected functionaries became Roman citizens) which we know from Pliny the Elder that Antipolis obtained. The port area was enlarged in Roman times, and coin-finds indicate that the place was still of substantial importance in the third and fourth centuries AD.

Beneath the cathedral and the Grimaldi castle nearby, excavations have revealed traces of the acropolis which probably contained the principal temple; remains of houses and cisterns are also preserved. In the lower town, traces of a theater, amphitheater, ramparts, baths, harbor jetties and aqueducts are to be seen; and wrecked ships have been found in the adjoining sea. There is evidence of the shrine of an earth cult at Vaugrenier nearby.

Antium (Anzio). A town on the coast of Latium (Lazio), thirty-one miles south of Rome, on a peninsula jutting out into the Tyrrhenian Sea. According to legend, the place was founded by Antias, the son of Odysseus and Circe. Cremation and inhumation burials going back to the eighth and seventh centuries BC resemble those of the Alban hills and of Rome. The small port of Antium, protected from the northwest winds, was the only natural harbor of any value in Latium, and when the tribe of the Volsci came down from the central Italian mountains in the sixth century and established themselves on the middle reaches of the Liris (Garigliano)—looting and raiding Latin and Roman territory almost every year—they made the place into their principal coastal stronghold.

It is possible, to judge from Livy, Dionysius of Halicarnassus and the *Fasti Triumphales,* that Rome captured Antium on a number of occasions during the fifth and early fourth centuries BC. But if so it was always lost again, and had to be retaken in 338, when Gaius Maenius captured its port and ships, setting up their prows (together with his own statue) on the speaker's platform (hence called *rostra* [beaks]) in the Roman Forum. Although the Volscians continued their piratical activities thereafter, Maenius' victory meant the termination of their independent power (so that they gradually succumbed to Romanization). Moreover, in the same year a colony of Roman citizens—perhaps the second after Ostia—was established at Antium, apparently augmented by native settlers; and in 317 the town was granted autonomous local government.

In the civil wars of the early first century BC it was sacked by Marius, but subsequently became a fashionable resort which contained the villas of many wealthy Romans, in addition to famous temples. It was the birthplace of the historian Valerius Antias (who magnified its early history) and of the emperors Gaius (Caligula, AD 37–41) and Nero (54–68), who possessed a residence there, constructed a new harbor with two piers built out on two small promontories, and added a further draft of settlers taken from retired soldiers of the praetorian guard. Almost all the other emperors of the first century, too, owned mansions at Antium; and so did Septimius Severus (193–211). Subsequent epochs, however, witnessed gradual decline, until the barbarian invasions of the fifth and sixth centuries AD led to its virtual abandonment.

Traces of Volscian fortifications and of the Roman port and storehouses are still to be seen. There are also remains of a theater, an aqueduct and a number of villas, including one that rose above a series of terraces facing the sea and may have belonged to an imperial owner. The Villa Spigarelli is built over another ancient mansion that occupied an equally impressive site and contained wall paintings and mosaics. Antium contained a famous Temple of Fortune, whose site has not yet been identified; the heads of the Fortune Antiates (Victor and Felix) appear on the coins of Quintus Rustius (19 BC), an Augustan moneyer who came from the city. A shrine of Aesculapius is also recorded. The statue of Apollo Belvedere, now in the Vatican, was found at Antium; also a calendar of Roman Republican date, the *Fasti Antiates.*

Anxur *see* Tarracina

Aosta *see* Augusta Praetoria

Apamea (Qalaat al-Mudik). A city in Syria situated on a plateau at the edge of the Jebel Zawiye, formed into a peninsula by the river Orontes and a large lake, which spreads into broad marshes and extensive cattle- and horse-pasturing meadows. Formerly called Chersonesus and Pharnace and then Pella (a Macedonian military colony), it subsequently (like other cities elsewhere) took the name of Apamea, the Iranian wife of the first Seleucid monarch Seleucus I Nicator (312–281), who was probably the city's founder—though some attribute its establishment to his son Antiochus I Soter (281–261) instead. Apamea became an important citadel and military headquarters of the Seleucid kings, in which they kept their treasury; and they bred and maintained their cavalry horses in the adjoining plain. The city was the birthplace of Eunus, who led a formidable slave-rebellion in Sicily in 135–133, and of the greatest polymath of the ancient world, the philosopher Posidonius (*c* 135–51/50).

Pompey the Great, in the course of his annexation of Syria (64), destroyed the fortress, but it recovered to become, after his death, the formidably defended headquarters of his follower Quintus Caecilius Bassus who, after killing Sextus Caesar, a kinsman of the dictator Julius (46), resisted Julius' generals until, after the latter's death, the beleaguered troops went over to his murderer Cassius. In the subsequent Civil War between Octavian (the future Augustus) and Antony (32–30), it sided with the latter, and was punished by the victor accordingly. Claudius (AD 41–54) restored the city under the name of Claudia Apamea, whereupon it issued its only coinages of Roman imperial date, showing the city-goddess seated above the river-god Orontes or Axius (see Antioch) and the heads of Zeus, the Sun and the Moon. The usurper Saturninus was besieged in Apamea by the army of Probus (276–82) and killed by his own soldiers. During the later empire it was the center of famous philosophical schools.

The principal surviving remains include a city gate, a theater, a broad colonnaded avenue of the second century AD, a large building on the forum, resembling a basilica, which was named after the goddess Tyche (Fortune), and a late fourth-century Jewish synagogue with an extensive floor mosaic, subsequently overbuilt by a huge Christian church, one of several that have been found in the city. Most of the discoveries at Apamea have been moved to the museums at Damascus and Brussels.

Apamea Cibotus, formerly Celaenae, Kelainai (Dinar). A town in southern Phrygia (west-central Asia Minor), situated on the river Marsyas, which joined the Maeander in its suburbs. The place stood on an eminence overlooking the junction of the west-east road from Ionia to central Asia and the north-south road from northern Phrygia down to the Pamphylian coast. It was named Celaenae by the early fifth century BC, during the period of Persian occupation, when Xerxes I made it into a fortress; but Greek names were already making an appearance. The pretender Cyrus the Younger (d. 401) had a hunting park near Celaenae, and Alexander the Great passed through the city on his expedition through Asia Minor and made it the capital of his satrapy of Phrygia, under Antigonus I Monophthalmos.

Like a number of other towns, it was renamed Apamea, after Apama the wife of Seleucus I Nicator (312-281)—creator of the Seleucid dynasty. This change of name accompanied its refoundation, undertaken by his son Antiochus I Soter (281-261), who reorganized the native town as an autonomous community, and moved it down to the fertile plain. It became famous because of the treaty signed by Antiochus III the Great with the Romans (188). After his disastrous defeat at their hands at Magnesia ad Sipylum (Manisa) in the previous year, Antiochus had fled to Apamea, where he agreed to evacuate nearly the whole of Asia Minor, so that the Seleucids ceased to be a major Mediterranean power.

Apamea came under the control of the kings of Pergamum, who employed it as a mint but allowed autonomy to its local authorities, symbolized by a city council and a gymnasium. Together with certain other regions of Phrygia, it became part of the Roman province of Asia *c* 120/116 (after Rome, annexing the Pergamene state [133], had temporarily assigned the city to the kingdom of Pontus). In the early first century it was largely destroyed by one of a series of earthquakes (the frequency of which caused the inhabitants to worship Poseidon, the patron of such upheavals), but was soon rebuilt with the assistance of the Pontic King Mithridates VI, in exchange for adherence to his cause against Rome. Subsequently, however, Apamea returned into the hands of the Romans, who assigned the region to the province of Asia (except for a brief period [56-50] when it came under the proconsuls of Cilicia, for whom, including Cicero [51-50], it coined).

Official Roman assizes were held in the city, and the substantial benefits derived from the influx of population on these occasions are vividly described by Dio Chrysostom (*c* AD 40-after 112). In trading activity, too, Apamea ranked second only to Ephesus in the entire province. In this connection it bore the additional name or nickname of Cibotus, 'the Chest,' from the containers in which goods arriving by caravan routes from the east were packed for forwarding to the seaports on the west coast of Asia Minor. Five such chests appear on coins of Hadrian (117-38). On an issue of Septimius Severus (193-211), however, a depiction of one of these chests contains two figures and is labelled *Noe* (Noah), referring to an alternative interpretation of 'Cibotus' as Noah's Ark. This remarkable coin design bears witness to the existence of an influential Jewish community at Apamea, of which something had been heard as early as Republican times.

Apennines, Mounts *see* Appenninus; also Anti-Apennines

Aphek *see* Antipatris

Aphrodisias (Geyre). A city in Caria (southwestern Asia Minor). Situated on a plateau at a height of about 1,800 feet on the western slopes of the Salbacus (Baba Dăgı) range, above the fertile valley containing the sources of the river Morsynus, a tributary of the Maeander (Büyük Menderes). A second small river, the Timeles (a tributary of the Harpasus), also rises in the region. The place had been an important settlement at least as early as the Copper (Chalcolithic) Age, and continued to exist throughout the Bronze Age. One of its early names was Ninoe, perhaps related to Nin, a Mesopotamian (Akkadian) designation for the moon-goddess: the mythical Ninus and Semiramis have been identified on local reliefs, and the name Aphrodisias was probably intended as a translation of Ninoe, equated with Aphrodite, whose temple was the city's principal shrine. The city was also known, at one period, as Megalopolis.

As Appian reports, it enjoyed favorable relations with Rome in the time of Sulla (who regarded Aphrodite-Venus as his protector) and again under Julius Caesar (who claimed to be her descendant). During the later first century BC, it was joined to the neighboring town of Plarasa in a union combining the two cities into a single community (*sympoliteia*), on which the Roman senate, at the instigation of Antony, conferred freedom and immunity from taxes (*c* 35).

Republican and triumviral inscriptions discovered at Aphrodisias are very varied and informative. Octavian (the future Augustus, 31 BC–AD 14) granted additional civic honors, including the inviolability of the temple of Aphrodite. Imperial support continued to be forthcoming, and in the earliest centuries AD the city enjoyed considerable renown as a religious and cultural center. It was the birthplace of the medical writer Xenocrates, the novelist Charito, and the Peripatetic (Aristotelian) philosopher Alexander who dedicated his work to Septimius Severus (193–211) and Caracalla (211–17). But its outstanding distinction lay in the field of sculpture, of which, benefiting from the proximity of marble quarries, it became one of the outstanding producers in the entire Greco-Roman world; the sculptors of its original and varied output, including numerous portraits, have been identified from several dozen signatures on works at Rome and elsewhere.

Promoted to be the capital of a new province of Phrygia-Caria, Aphrodisias was surrounded by powerful walls, 12,000 feet in circumference, begun in the 260s under the threat of Gothic invasion. Within these walls, the city was constructed on an axially aligned gridiron plan. Substantial remains include fortifications, a recently discovered Sebasteion (shrine of the imperial cult) that has proved particularly rich in architectural features and sculpture, a large and a small theater, an elaborately decorated pagan basilica, a stadium, a gymnasium, extensive baths including an imposing circular apsed hall, and a considerable part of the colonnade surrounding the marketplace. Recent investigations have made it possible to reconstruct the elaborate gateway (*tetrapylon*) of the *agora,* transformed into a *nymphaeum* (fountain building) in the fifth century AD. Excavations in the neighborhood have also produced an unusual number of fragments of the most important economic inscription of ancient times, the Edict of Maximum Prices which Diocletian promulgated and exhibited in provincial capitals.

Owing to the shrine of Aphrodite—of which fourteen columns, as well as the monumental precinct gateway, are still to be seen—paganism continued to be popular in early Christian times. Nevertheless, Aphrodisias became the seat of a bishopric (at least from 325), and was sometimes known by the new name of Stavropolis (city of the cross). In this late imperial period, according to Hierocles, the city was the capital of a province of Caria; and *c* 350 it was fortified with a new circuit wall against threats of Persian attack.

Aphrodisias *see* Seleucia on the Calycadnus

Apollonia (Pojani). A city beside the Ionian Sea in southern Illyricum (now Albania), near the mouth of the river Aous (Vijosë), on a site in the widest and richest part of the Albanian plain, commanding a route across Mount Haemus (the Balkan Range). Located within the territory of the Taulantii, the place was named after a temple of Apollo on the hill of Sthyllas. It was established in 588 BC by settlers from Corcyra (Corfu), with the assistance of its mother-city Corinth, taking the name of Gylaceia from the Corinthian who presided over the foundation, and issuing coins (from *c* 400) which displayed first Corcyraean and then Corinthian affinities.

Equipped with an oligarchic constitution, Apollonia grew quickly in size and prosperity until by 350 it was able to overcome one of its neighbors, Thronium, dedicating a votive offering at Olympia in honor of the victory. During the Hellenistic period the city's resources and strategic importance attracted the attention of Macedonian, Illyrian and Epirote (Molossian) kings, as well as of the Corcyraeans; and at the beginning of the third century it was incorporated in the kingdom of Pyrrhus of Epirus. After his death in 272, however, it sought an alliance with Rome (260), and in 229 came under Roman protection.

Apollonia became the terminal of one of the two branches of the Via Egnatia that crossed the Balkans (*c* 130). Julius Caesar made it his headquarters for the campaign of Dyrrhachium against Pompey (48), and three years later gave orders that an army should be gathered there for his proposed expedition against the Parthians, which was prevented by his murder. When his adoptive son Octavian (the future Augustus) learned of his death and decided to avenge it, he was studying in the famous school of rhetoric at Apollonia, which Cicero described as a dignified and noble city (*urbs gravis et nobilis*). Subsequent coins honor Nero (AD 54–68) as founder (refounder) and patron of Greece.

The monetary issues of Apollonia also laid stress on an adjoining nymphaeum (fountain building), dedicated to Pan and the Nymphs, of whom three are shown dancing around its sacred fire. This edifice, like temples of Apollo and Zeus, depicted on coins of Caracalla (211–17) and his mother Julia Domna respectively, can no longer be seen. Partially surviving monuments include a temple of Aphrodite (on the acropolis), a smaller theater at its foot, a Hellenistic portico containing a small sanctuary nearby, the rectangular colonnaded monument of the superintendents of public games, a gymnasium, a bathhouse, a library (?), shops, a triple Roman arch, and shrine-like tombs. Important discoveries include an archaic frieze of fighting warriors from the acropolis temple, the Meleager of Scopas (in the museum at Tirana), copies of the Ludovisi Ares (of which the original is in the National Museum [Terme] at Rome) and a work by Praxiteles.

Apollonia, later Sozusa (Marsa Susa), a city in Cyrenaica (Libya). Founded, according to Strabo, by settlers from the island of Thera (Santorini). Archaeological discoveries suggest a foundation date of *c* 600 BC—that is to say, a generation or two after the establishment of Cyrene (Shahat), for which it provided a natural harbor. In the third century BC, when two philosophers, Ecdemus and Demophanes, remodeled the constitutions of the cities of Cyrenaica, Apollonia was elevated to the status of a city, and became a member of the federal Libyan Pentapolis, growing in importance as Cyrene and Ptolemais (Tolmeta) waned. Generally known, in Christian times, as Sozusa, it became the capital of the province of Upper Libya in the sixth century, and succumbed to the Arabs in the seventh.

Although the ancient harbor facilities have disappeared beneath the sea, excavations on land have revealed a number of buildings including a Hellenistic temple and theater outside the walls. These fortifications, too, were Hellenistic, probably dating from the early third century BC, but rebuilt in Byzantine times; the main city-gate and a round tower have been excavated. An early Roman villa and late Roman baths (destroyed in an earthquake of AD 365), and a number of Byzantine edifices, have also come to light.

Apollonia *see* Panticapaeum

Appenninus (Appennino, Apennines). A series of mountain chains forming the backbone of the Italian peninsula. The name, of Celtic origin, originally denoted only the northernmost of the three sections of the complex, extending from the Maritime Alps to Ancona; this includes the Ligurian, Tuscan (Tosco-Emiliano), and Umbrian Apennines. The central (Roman or Umbro-Marchigiano and Abruzzi) Apennines extend southward as far as the river Sagrus (Sangro) and include volcanic peaks (notably the Alban Hills) and crater lakes (*e.g,* Lake Volsiniensis [Bolsena]). The southern (Neapolitan, Lucanian, Calabrian) Apennines (together with the Sila mountains) form a series of isolated blocks rather than continuous ranges. Volcanic regions in this sector include Mount Vesuvius and the Campi Phlegraei (Phlegraean Fields, behind Puteoli [Pozzuoli]), as well as the Lipara (Aeolian) Islands.

Apsinthus *see* Aenus

Apuan Alps *see* Anti-Apennines

Apulia (Puglia). A region of southeastern Italy that took its name from the Apuli, a Samnite Oscan-speaking tribe inhabiting the land around the promontory of Mt. Garganus (Gargano) extending into the Adriatic Sea. The name Apulia later included regions occupied by other peoples, notably the Daunii (who spoke the same language, but possessed a distinctive material culture, especially in the seventh to fifth centuries BC), and the Messapian-speaking Peucetii. Greek writers used the name Iapygia as a synonym for Apulia (or sometimes with particular reference to Calabria in the heel of Italy). Although lacking Greek colonies, Apulia was considerably Hellenized by the end of the fourth century BC, under the influence of Taras (Tarentum, Taranto).

Between 326 and 317 the territory came under the control of Rome; and the first coins of Ausculum (Ascoli Satriano), Teate (later Teanum Apulum, now Chieti), Canusium (Canosa) on the river Aufidus (Ofanto) and Luceria (the capital, colonized 315/314; now Lucera) were issued early in the following century.

By that time, the Via Appia (312) was opening up the western borderlands of the region, where the Latin colony of Venusia (Venosa) was founded in 292 as a Roman military station, much to the displeasure of the Tarentines, who saw it as a threat. The Apulians remained loyal to Rome in its wars against King Pyrrhus of Epirus (280–275).

The southern part of the region contains numerous hills, including Mount Vultur (Vulture), an extinct volcano whose summit commands an imposing view. But the northern and coastal plains produced wine and oil, and the Romans developed the breeding of migrant cattle and horses. However, devastations during the Second Punic War (218–201), in which many Apulians revolted to Hannibal, contributed to the ruin of their country, and large-scale sheepfarming damaged the prosperity of the towns; so that they proved willing to join the Italian rebellion against Rome (Social War, 91–87). Thereafter, Apulia somewhat faded from view; Strabo described it as deserted, but Columella praised its grain from firsthand knowledge, and at the end of the first century AD its wool was still among the best. Canusium regained importance as a station on the Via Trajana between Beneventum (Benevento) and Barium (Bari), where it joined the coastal road. During the later empire and Middle Ages the name of Apulia was extended to comprise a territorial unit including the former Calabria (of which the name was transferred from the heel of Italy to its toe, the territory of the Bruttii).

Apulum (Alba Iulia). The principal town of Dacia (Rumania), named after the tribe of the Dacian Apuli (unconnected with the Italian people of the same name), and situated at the confluence of the rivers Marisus (Mureş) and Ampelum (Ampoi) on the main road from Tibiscum (Jupa) and Sarmizegethusa to Napoca (Cluj) and Porolissum (Jac, Moigrad), in a fertile landscape not far from the Transylvanian gold mines. Following Trajan's conquest of Dacia (107) Apulum was permanently garrisoned by a legion, and a civilian settlement (*canabae*) on low ground north and east of the camp became a *municipium.* Under Hadrian (117–38) Apulum was the capital of Upper Dacia (Transylvania with a western extension) and then, after that province had been further subdivided into Apulensis and Porolissensis, the capital of the former. In the time of Marcus Aurelius (161–80) it was the capital of the reunited Three Dacias. Toward the end of the century a second civilian settlement south of the camp, possessing a harbor on the Marisus River, was granted the rank of a colony. An inscription of 253 in honor of Volusianus (the son of Trebonianus Gallus) calls it the *Colonia Aurelia Apulensis Chrysopolis.*

Apulum was the mint of provincial bronze coinage for eleven years, from Philip (246) to Gallienus (257), displaying the name of Dacia and a figure of its personification carrying legionary standards. Finds collected in Alba Julia's museum bear witness to extensive manufacturing activities and the existence of commercial corporations. Inscriptions and sculptural remains suggest that Aesculapius and Salus (Hygiea) were the patron divinities of the city, but inscriptions also record cults of Persian deities and of the Celtic Bussumarus, the Punic Tanit and the Asian Dolichenus and Sabazius. Two Roman cemeteries have been located by recent excavations.

Aquae Cutiliae (Cutilia). A spa near Reate (Rieti) in the Sabine country of central Italy. Its sulphurous waters were drunk as a purgative, according to Pliny the Elder; Strabo reports that patients bathed in them as well. According to Suetonius and Dio Cassius, unwise use of the spring, which was regarded as a cold-water cure, contributed to the death of Vespasian (a native of Reate) in AD 79.

Aquae Sextiae (Aix-en-Provence, Bouches-du-Rhône, southern France). The place derives its name from its hot springs and from the name of Gaius Sextius Calvinus, who established a town there in 122 BC in the territory of the Celto-Ligurian tribe of the Salluvii (Salyes), whose principal center at Entremont nearby he had destroyed (Livy, Velleius, Strabo). The first Roman foundation in Transalpine Gaul—leading irrevocably to the subsequent creation of a province in the area—Aquae Sextiae was designed as a fortress dominating the roads leading from Massalia (Massilia, Marseille) to the river Druentia (Durance), and from the Rhodanus (Rhône) to the borders of Italy. The principal event in local history was a decisive battle beneath Mont Sainte Victoire in BC 102, in which the Roman general Gaius Marius overwhelmed an invading force of Germans (Teutones), killing more than a hundred thousand of them and freeing Italy from all fears of barbarian attack.

The presence of a Roman garrison attracted business, and Julius Caesar, after conquering Massilia, which had sided with his enemy Pompey the Great in the Civil War (49), gave part of the defeated city's territory to Aquae Sextiae. At the same time, too, he may have added an award of Latin rights (conferring citizenship upon elected civic officials) which was later exchanged for full Roman citizenship—probably in the reign of Augustus—with the title of Colonia Julia Augusta; or perhaps it was only then that the place obtained Latin status. In the later fourth century AD it became the capital of the province of Narbonensis Secunda. A gate, and stretches of road, the ruins of five aqueducts, and remains of three substantial houses (*villae urbanae*) have survived. The baptistery of the cathedral of Saint-Sauveur dates from *c* 400.

Aquae Sulis (Bath). A town in the county of Somerset, southwestern England. The Roman settlement, founded *c* AD 75, stood at the intersection of several roads, at a point where the river Avon was crossed by the Fosse Way. But it owed its existence and significance, then and later, to its hot springs, which reached the surface through three vents.

Attracting visitors as early as the fifth millennium BC, the principal Sacred Spring (from which water emerged at 116° F) was surrounded in Roman times by a major complex of buildings. These included an exceptionally large bathing establishment that incorporated the Circular, Great and East Baths; the temple of the Celtic deity Sulis (assimilated to Minerva), dating from the third quarter of the first century AD, and represented by a famous Gorgon pediment; and a circular temple of the time of Hadrian (AD 117–38), now reconstructed on the basis of four sculptured blocks found a century ago.

In the third century, Solinus, noting Aquae Sulis as one of the natural wonders of the world, records that coal was burned on the temple altar—and coal ash has been found in the precinct. The ruins of the deserted site were described in an eighth-century poem. The waters have recently been found to be contaminated by bacteria and unfit for use. Excavations on the southern part of the precinct continue, and thirty Roman villas have been discovered within a ten-mile radius of the city.

Aquileia. A city in northeastern Italy, at the eastern extremity of the Venetian plain, seven miles from the head of the Adriatic, beside the river Natiso or Natissa (now the Natisone canal). Occupying a fertile site that controlled routes across the Julian Alps, Aquileia was seized in 186 BC by Gauls from across the Alps. Five years later, however, they were ejected by the Romans, whose board of three commissioners, Publius Cornelius Scipio Nasica, Gaius Flaminius, and Lucius Manlius Acidinus established a Latin colony (in which the elected civic functionaries became Roman citizens) of 3,000 settlers. The colony was designed to exploit gold mines nearby and to act as a customs station and a springboard for Roman expansion in other parts of Cisalpine Gaul (northern Italy) with which it was linked by its river and by Viae Aemilia Altinate (175), Annia (153) and Postumia (148). Aquileia served as a base for wars against the Istri in 178/7, and then, after reinforcement by a further 1,500 colonists in 169, fulfilled a similar role in the successful campaigns of the consul Gaius Sempronius Tuditanus against the Taurisci, Iapudes and Liburni (129); the two first-named tribes attacked the city again in 52. When Julius Caesar expanded the borders of Italy northward, Aquileia became part of the homeland. It exchanged Latin for Roman status in or about the time of Augustus.

Assisted by a large harbor at the wide rivermouth, commerce, industry and agriculture, together with the natural strategic importance of the site, gave Aquileia much prosperity. It grew with even greater rapidity after the Romans, in the early years of the Principate, extended their frontier northward to the Danube, so that the city became an emporium for the trade of Danubian lands, and a center from which vital lines of communication radiated to the north and east. The working of iron (from Noricum) by the Aquileians, and their importation of amber (from the Baltic) and manufacture of glass, remained unchallenged. Their long period of peace, however, was interrupted by a siege conducted by invading Germans (Marcomanni and Quadi) in 168, which was successfully beaten off by Marcus Aurelius. Then in 238, after Balbinus and Pupienus had gained the support of the senate and of Italy against Maximinus I Thrax, this was the first place, in the 'War of Aquileia,' to offer strong resistance to the invading army of Maximinus, whose discontented soldiers murdered him outside its walls: and Pupienus proceeded immediately to the city, where the leaderless army acclaimed him. In the subsequent years of the century, however, Aquileia suffered severely from barbarian invasions owing to its geographical position.

Nevertheless, it continued to gain in importance, becoming one of the strategic points of Gallienus' Italian defence system (260–68), the capital of the administrative region Venetia-Istria, the center of a flourishing school of bronze and marble portrait sculpture, and a late imperial mint. One of the world's largest cities, with a population of 70,000–100,000 inhabitants and a port on the island of Ad Aquas Gradatas (Grado), Aquileia earned the name of *Roma*

Secunda, the next city after Rome itself. When Constantine II and Constans I, two of the sons of Constantine I the Great, came into conflict with one another, Constantine II was killed on the banks of the river Aussa (Ausa), a little to the west (340). The episcopate or patriarchate of Aquileia had been founded by their father, and its cathedral, built at the same time by the first bishop Theodore—one of many early Christian basilicas in the city—was the scene of an historic church council, attended by St. Ambrose and St. Jerome. The city was captured and razed to the ground by Attila the Hun in 452. Its surviving inhabitants fled to the neighboring lagoons of Venice, which was thus launched on its historical career; while Aquileia declined into a malaria-stricken village, although remaining a bishopric until 568, when the Lombard invasion caused the see to be transferred to Ad Aquas Gradatas, which became known as Nova Aquileia.

The old Aquileia, in the course of the centuries, became a quarry for construction materials, so that little more than its foundations have been preserved. The forum of the imperial period (on a different site, apparently, from its Republican forerunner) is partially excavated. Inscriptions record the worship of more than thirty divinities—including a number of local origin—but few of their shrines have been located; an imperial palace, too, existed, but has not been found. However, remains of an amphitheater, a circus, three thermal establishments, and a number of storehouses still survive. An imposing quayside on the Natiso, a small inner harbor, has also been discovered. A series of fine mosaics including a pavement in the cathedral (displaying the story of Jonah) goes back to the city's original foundation.

Aquincum (Budapest) in Pannonia (Hungary). A fortress and township situated on the right bank of the Danube at an important crossing (noted by the *Itinerarium Antonini Augusti*), where waterways and land routes met, Aquincum was the center of the Eravisci—a tribe of Celtic origin but Illyrian culture—and became, under Tiberius (AD 14–37) at latest, a Roman military camp manned by auxiliaries (Obuda, Old Buda). From the time of Domitian (81–96) the garrison consisted of a legion. During the reign of Trajan, Aquincum became the capital of the province of Lower Pannonia (106). The civilian settlement (*canabae*) which developed as a separate entity two miles from the camp was raised to the rank of *municipium* by Hadrian (124) and to colonial status perhaps under Septimius Severus (193–211), in the course of his improvements to the road system of the province. In this period, the place was one of the cornerstones of the imperial frontier defence system; and two fortresses, Transaquincum and Contra-Aquincum, were constructed face-to-face on the opposite side of the river.

Aquincum was overrun by marauders *c* 260, but thereafter made a modest recovery. In the following century, however (by which time the provincial capital was elsewhere), it came under continual attacks from the Sarmatians, and was so severely damaged, according to Ammianus Marcellinus, that Valentinian I, engaged in strengthening the fortifications across the Danube, could not find sufficient winter quarters for his troops (374/5). Twenty years later the garrison was transferred to Gaul, and shortly afterward the city was abandoned by its Roman administrators, although the surviving population did not leave with them. In the early Middle Ages Buda developed from the legionary camp of Aquincum, and Pest from the fortress of Contra-Aquincum.

The legionary commander's residence (of second-century date) has been identified in front of the main gate of the fortress, and a bathhouse can be seen beneath a modern building. There is also a military amphitheater. The civilian settlement possessed another, and also displays remains of a basilica, bathhouses, a meat market, the building of a trading corporation, rows of shops, numerous houses and villas, a gladiators' barracks, and waterworks and walls. The deities whose temples have been located include Mithras and Fortuna; three early churches were built over pagan shrines. On an island in the Danube, opposite Óbuda, there are traces of a large palace of the Roman provincial governor, built by Hadrian in 107 when he held that office before becoming emperor. Among the objects displayed in the museum are the bronze portions of a portable organ.

Aquitania (Aquitaine). The territory of the Aquitani, extending from the river Garonne to the Pyrenees in southwestern Gaul (France). The Aquitani differed from other Gauls in language, customs and appearance, preserving various primitive elements resembling features of Iberian culture, or peculiar to themselves. They were divided into a number of small tribes which during the Gallic wars of Julius Caesar were defeated by Publius Licinius Crassus, the son of the triumvir (56 BC). In Caesar's description of Gaul, Aquitania is an area bordered to the south by the Pyrenees and to the north by the river Garumna (Garonne). When, however, Octavian (subsequently Augustus) completed the subjugation of the area in 38 and 27, he created a new province of Aquitania——with its capital at Burdigala (Bordeaux)—which extended northward to include the Celtic tribes up to the river Liger (Loire).

During the third century AD the original Aquitanian tribes, now reduced to nine, were detached to form the separate province of Novempopulana, based on Elusa (Eauze), later superseded by Civitas Auscorum (Auch). The province of Aquitania now lay to its north, and in the later empire was subdivided into Aquitania Prima and Secunda, with their capitals at Avaricum (Bourges) and Burdigala. It was as a result of this fragmentation, in Christian times, that the archbishops of the Ausci, Avaricum and Burdigala competed for the primacy of Aquitania. In the later fourth century the poet Ausonius described it as a wealthy country; it produced grain and wine and exported Pyrenean marble. Soon after 400, however, this situation was transformed by the invasions of the Visigoths, who in 417 were recognized as a federate state in Aquitania Secunda (together with parts of Novempopulana and Narbonensis Prima); a proportion of the Roman properties in the area came under their control, and they replaced Catholicism by Arianism. In 475 the Visigothic monarch Euric declared national independence; but in 507 the victory of Clovis at Vouillé (near Limonum Pictonum [Poitiers]) made the whole of Aquitania part of Frankish territory instead.

Arabia. Knowledge of the country among the Greeks began in the time of Alexander the Great, whose admiral Hieron of Soli sailed down the Persian Gulf (324/3), while Anaxicrates proceeded down the Red Sea through the Gulf of Bab el-Mandeb to the southern coast of Arabia. In Hellenistic times the Seleucid monarchs planted settlements along the coast of the Persian Gulf between the mouths of the Euphrates-Tigris and Gerrha (in the Hofhuf oasis) in the west of the Arabian peninsula (where they arranged trade agreements). The Egyptian King Ptolemy II Philadelphus sponsored explorations of the Red Sea and punished the hostile and active Nabataeans of northwestern Arabia (Petraea) by concluding a commercial treaty with the Lihyanites of Dedan to their south and thus tapping the route which led through Medina and the Nabataean capital Petra to Syria.

In the southern region, Arabia Eudaemon (Felix)—of which a civilization of the second millennium BC has now been discovered in the interior of North Yemen—the geographer Eratosthenes (*c* 275–194 BC) noted a fourfold division between the kingdoms of the Minyans, Sabaeans, Qatabanians and Hadhramautites. Subsequently the Sabaeans (producers of myrrh and frankincense and cinnamon who, like another people, the Himyarites, copied the Athenian coinage from the third through the first centuries BC) gained the ascendancy over the others. The Roman emperor Augustus sent an expedition under the governor of Egypt, Aelius Gallus, to conquer the region (25–24). But, as Strabo suggests, it totally failed; the blame was placed on the duplicity of Syllaeus, chief minister of the Nabataean state, which for the previous forty years had been a client kingdom (often at odds with neighboring Judaea). Nevertheless, Roman naval supremacy in the Red Sea was secured not long afterward by the reduction of Arabia Eudaemon and the establishment of friendly relations with the southern Arabian rulers.

In Arabia Petraea Augustus' grandson Gaius Caesar conducted operations against nomads threatening the Roman frontier (AD 1). But subsequently Trajan decided that nothing less than the annexation of the Nabataean kingdom was necessary for the protection of his border defences and trade routes. This task was carried out *c* 106 by Aulus Cornelius Palma Frontonianus, as inscriptions confirm, and was followed *c* 111–12 by the constitution of the Roman province of Arabia, with its capital at Bostra (Busra Eski Sham), where a legion was stationed. Under Diocletian (289–305) the frontier was greatly strengthened, as excavations at El-Lejjun, a major garrison fortress east of the Dead Sea, confirm. At this period the province underwent enlargement, but was subsequently divided, so that while Bostra remained the capital of a diminished Arabia, the remainder of its former territory was incorporated in Syria Palaestina, and later (by about 358) became part of the separate province of Palaestina Tertia Salutaris (perhaps after a short career under the name of Arabia Secunda), consisting principally of Sinai. *See also* Bostra, Nabataea, Petra.

Arachosia. A large part of what is now southern Afghanistan (Seistan), bounded on the north by Bactria and the Cabura (Kophen, Kabul) valley (the land of the Paropamisadae) and on the south by Gedrosia (Baluchistan). Arachosia was a satrapy of the Persian (Achaemenid) empire, from which excellent cavalry was recruited and elephants and ivory were exported. After Alexander the Great had invaded the Persian dominions and defeated Darius III Codomannus at Gaugamela (331), Barsaentes, satrap of Arachosia, was one of the two men who, supporting the rival claims of Bessus to the Persian throne, stabbed Darius to death. Then he returned to his own country to mobilize additional troops. But Alexander pressed on into Arachosia, where he may have founded Alexander of the Arachosians—the site of recent discoveries—at or near the royal residence (Shahr-i-Kohna, Old Kandahar). Subsequently Arachosia formed part of a huge province given by Alexander to one of his Macedonian supporters, Sibyrtius. When the king died, the territory passed to Seleucus I Nicator, but its eastern section probably constituted part of the territories that he ceded to the Indian emperor Chandragupta Maurya in exchange for war elephants (301); and *c* 260 Kandahar passed into the hands of Chandragupta's grandson Asoka.

Soon afterward, what had now become the furthest parts of the Seleucid kingdom, including western Arachosia, were divided between the Greek kingdom of Bactria (256/5) and the Parthian empire (*c* 247); the major Parthian routes as far as Arachosia are described by Isidorus of Charax. Later, the Bactrian monarch Demetrius I (*c* 200–185) seems to have retaken part of the Arachosian land originally ceded to Chandragupta Maurya back from the Mauryan empire (which was now failing), and to have founded the Greek colony of Demetrias in the territory he had conquered—apparently the first such settlement established by a Bactrian monarch (another was called Euthydemia after his father). In the later second and first centuries BC this and other huge regions of central Asia were disputed between Indo-Greek kings and Scythians, and then, as the former gradually vanished, passed definitively out of the Greek sphere, becoming the western territories of the Indo-Scythian (Kushan) empire.

Aradus, formerly Arvad (Ruad), situated on an island two miles southwest of its mainland port Antaradus (Tartus) on the coast of Phoenicia near Tripoli. Founded by exiles from Sidon, Aradus was the principal city of northern Phoenicia, under the rule of hereditary kings who employed its harbor (consisting of two bays separated by a natural mole) for eastern trading, derived their water supply from an abundant fresh spring in the sea—reached by a tunnel—and presided over a league of mainland communities. After submitting, as Arrian recounts, to Alexander the Great in 333/2 (from which a new era was reckoned) and providing him with a royal mint, the local dynasty was abolished by the Seleucid Antiochus II in 259, the year from which a subsequent era was dated; temporarily adopting the name of Antiochia in Pieria, the city became the 'free' associate of other towns (its former dependencies) in a Seleucid-sponsored federation. In *c* 90 however (after an earlier treacherous attempt) it succeeded in destroying one of these neighbors, Marathus (Amrit), and displayed its commercial strength, during this period, by issuing a stream of silver coinage. Captured by Antony after vigorous resistance, and deprived of some of its territorial possessions, Aradus issued coins with his and Cleopatra's heads (38/7, 35/4).

The city remained prosperous in imperial times, depicting Astarte (Ashtoreth, Aphrodite) on its coinage, accompanied by smaller portraits of the emperors. The novelist Charito mentioned a temple and a large colonnaded marketplace, but these have not been found. Aradus derived much of its revenue from a great shrine of Zeus Baetocaeces in the hills of the adjoining mainland—and remained resolutely pagan. For this reason Constantine the Great weakened its authority by depriving it of Antaradus, which was granted the status of a separate city. The ancient jetty of Antaradus has survived; at Aradus itself the principal remains are those of the rampart encircling the island. *See also* Tripolis.

Arausio (Orange). Situated in the interior of southern Gaul (Vaucluse, France), five miles east of the river Rhodanus (Rhône). Its hill (Saint-Eutrope) rises three hundred feet above the plain, dominating the route across the river. In pre-Roman times Arausio was one of the centers of the tribal confederation of the Cavares, who, according to Strabo, constituted the strongest and most Romanized political unit of southern Gaul.

Not long after the annexation of the region by the Romans (as their province of Gallia Narbonensis), Arausio became the scene of one of the worst military disasters in their history. As Livy's *Epitome* informs us, the armies of the bickering Roman consuls Cnaeus Mallius Maximus and Quintus Servilius Caepio were cut to pieces, one after another, by the invading German host of the Cimbri (105 BC). This catastrophe threw Italy wide open, and it was not for another four years that the invaders were beaten back. During the campaign the Romans occupied the hill of Arausio, and in 35/33 Octavian (the future Augustus) founded a colony of ex-legionaries there, on land taken from the Tricastini (a tribe of the former Cavares federation). The name of the new settlement, *Firma,* reflects its role as a military stronghold.

New methods of photography have revealed the perimeter and street plan of the city and the configuration (centuriation) of its rural lands. The most important surviving monuments comprise an arch of the reign of Tiberius (*c* AD 26), decorated with reliefs depicting battle scenes, and a theater of later date of which the stage wall was described by Louis XIV as 'the handsomest wall in my realm.' There are also the remains of large temples, and of three tablets inscribed with successive surveys of Arausio's territorial possessions.

Arbela *see* Gaugamela

Arcadia. The mountainous central area of the Peloponnese (southern Greece), bounded by the Argolid, Elis, Achaea, Laconia and Messenia. The most prosperous regions of Arcadia were its eastern plains (containing important towns) and the valley of the river Alpheus. By the middle of the sixth century the country had accepted subordinate alliances with the Spartans, who felt that they needed to control Arcadian towns (notably Tegea) in order to safeguard their access to the isthmus of Corinth. However, the Arcadians were also able to form a loose union of their own, mainly for cult purposes, which met at the religious center of Heraea (Ayios Ioannis) and issued coinage (*c* 470?–*c* 418) on the occasion of the Arcadian Games. Strong in manpower—so that they were in great demand as mercenaries—they remained glad to exploit any weakness on the part of the Spartans, and united (except for the city of Mantinea) to fight them *c* 469 at Dipaea in Arcadia; but the battle resulted in a decisive Spartan victory, against great odds.

During the Peloponnesian War Athens formed an alliance with Mantinea, Argos and Elis, which the Spartans soon brought to an end (418). In 370–362, under the guidance of the Theban leader Epaminondas, the cities of Arcadia set a precedent for Greek federalism by establishing a political league (growing out of an earlier religious union) based on the new, strategically located city of Megalopolis, which they created by the amalgamation of more than forty villages; but although control over Olympia was temporarily established (365), the federal experiment was frustrated by particularism, though it was still in existence, or had been restored, in 320/310.

In the Hellenistic Age Megalopolis supported the Macedonians while the other Arcadian cities rebelled against their domination (331, 323, 266). Thereafter, the cities divided their allegiance between the Achaean and Aetolian Confederacies; at Cynaetha (Kalavrita), for example, where factions influenced by social upheavals fought bitterly for years about redistributions of land, the two Leagues competed to encourage violence among the local contestants. From *c* 250 the Arcadians were members of the Achaean League, in which they played an important part; and after Rome had defeated and suppressed the Achaeans, Arcadia, like the rest of Greece, became part of the Roman province of Macedonia (146) until Greece was detached under the name of Achaea, to form a separate province in 27. But in Roman times Arcadia fell into decline and was almost deserted.

Among eminent Arcadians was the poetess Anyte of Tegea (*c* 300), the Achaean League's soldier-statesman Philopoemen of Megalopolis (*c* 253–182), and the historian Polybius (*c* 200–after 118) who came from the same city. *See also* Mantinea, Megalopolis, Orchomenus, Stymphalus, Styx, Tegea.

Arcadia *see* Aegyptus

Arčar, Arcsar *see* Ratiaria

Ardea. A town of the Latin tribe of the Rutuli, in Latium (Lazio), twenty-three miles south of Rome, beside the Via Ardeatina. According to myth, Ardea was founded by the son of Ulysses (Odysseus) and Circe or Danae. Its legendary associations exerted a major influence on Roman tradition. Virgil records a story that Juno stirred up the Rutulian prince Turnus of Ardea, son of Daunus and the romantic enemy figure of the *Aeneid,* to stir up hostility against Aeneas and his Trojans, so that Latinus should give his daughter Lavinia in marriage to Turnus instead of to Aeneas. The hostility between Turnus and Aeneas may reflect early tensions between Ardea and its neighbor Lavinium (Pratica di Mare).

Ardea is now about seven miles from the sea, but in early times it had a flourishing harbor (Castrum Inui, at the mouth of the Fosso dell'Incastro) which served as a port for Latium. Ardea itself was an early Iron Age center (ninth–eighth centuries BC) which developed into one of the most prominent Latin cities and became a member and federal sanctuary of a (or the) Latin League. According to legend, the last of the Roman kings, Tarquinius Superbus, was at Ardea, besieging the town, when he learned of the rebellion against him at Rome which brought the monarchy to an end (*c* 510).

Shortly afterward (*c* 508), Ardea was ascribed to the sphere of influence of the Romans in their first treaty with Carthage, if this is authentic. However, soon after the middle of the following century Ardea and Aricia were both free enough to quarrel over the allegiance of the little town of Corioli, and the Romans were called in to arbitrate; whereupon they adjudicated the disputed place to themselves. In *c* 442 Ardea remained important enough to sign a separate treaty with the Romans, who reinforced it with settlers (as a *colonia Latina*) to provide a barrier against the Volscians. When Marcus Furius Camillus, conqueror of Veii, went into exile, it was to Ardea that he went, and from Ardea that he returned to Rome to drive out the Gauls (*c* 387/6). But a Samnite raid *c* 315 caused the town to decline, a process that was accelerated by the civil wars between Marius and Sulla in the early first century. By the time of Augustus (31 BC–AD 14) only traces of the ancient Ardea survived, but numerous villas in the neighborhood (and possibly a colony under Hadrian AD 117–38) kept its memory alive. A herd of imperial elephants was also maintained nearby.

The original citadel lay at the end of a plateau rising above two valleys and protected by sixty-foot-high cliffs and a tufa wall. The defences of the later, expanded settlement have likewise left important remains. In addition, there are traces of early temples (subsequently rebuilt), one of which—adorned by paintings now in the Museo della Villa Giulia at Rome—appears to have been dedicated to the city's patroness Juno. The worship of Castor and Pollux, too, was important. A sanctuary, or sacred zone, on the adjacent Colle del Noce has now been discovered. Excavations have also brought to light one of the earliest surviving pagan basilicas, probably attributable to the early first century BC.

Ardoch *see* Alauna

Arelate (Arles). A city in southern Gaul (Gallia Narbonensis), situated on a rocky hill spur overlooking marshland—the place-name means 'near the marshes' in Celtic—in the Camargue plain where the river Rhodanus (Rhône) divides to form its delta, in the territory of the Salluvii tribe. Phocaean colonists from Massilia (Massalia, Marseille)—fifty-five miles to the east—established two market settlements on the site or in the neighborhood, Theline and Rhodanusia (as we learned from Pseudo-Scymnus and Avienus respectively), but they were destroyed by the Ligurians in 535 BC.

Reviving during the fourth century, the place gained new importance from the *Fossae Marianae,* canals linking Arelate with the Golfe de Fos which were dug by order of Gaius Marius in 104. Julius Caesar, after employing the town as a naval base in his successful campaign against Massilia (49), entrusted Tiberius Claudius Nero, three years later, with the foundation of a colony, which was located opposite the earlier habitation center and given the name of Colonia Julia Arelate Sextanorum (referring to the veterans of the sixth legion who were settled there), and was granted a considerable part of the former territory of Massilia. After substantial enlargement by Augustus—when the Via Julia Augusta from Italy (13–12 BC) joined up with the Via Domitia—the city derived commercial significance from its position as a port of trans-shipment for vessels between the Rhodanus and the sea, under the supervision of five corporations (the *navicularii Arelatenses*).

Under a reorganization of late imperial times, it became the capital of the province of Narbonensis—and was subsequently chosen by Constantine the Great and his successors as their part-time residence. In 313 Constantine established an imperial mint at Arelate, and in the following year he selected it as the meeting-place of the first representative Synod of Christian bishops in the Roman west. His son Constantius II, celebrating his thirtieth anniversary (*tricennalia*) at the place (354), gave it the name of Constantia; it was now the most prosperous city of Gaul. In 409 it was seized by the usurper Constantine III, who made it his capital. But in 411 he was besieged by Constantius (III), on behalf of the emperor Honorius, and forced to capitulate. Shortly afterward other pretenders, Jovinus and his brother Sebastianus, employed Arelate as one of their mints; and after their removal Constantius had to proceed there once again to suppress Priscus Attalus, who had been set up by the Visigoths (for the second time) as a puppet Roman emperor.

It was also in this period that the praetorian prefecture of the Gauls (one of the major administrative divisions of the empire) transferred its capital from Treviri (Augusta Trevirorum) to Arelate: whereupon the bishops of the latter city did their best to assert their supremacy over other bishops of the area, and indeed over the whole of Gaul, although without complete success. In 418 Honorius made a move toward the decentralization of the western empire by enacting that a representative assembly for the administrative diocese of the Seven Provinces (southwest and central Gaul) should meet every autumn at Arelate, to debate matters of public interest. In the course of the edict, addressed to the praetorian prefect of Gaul, the emperor paid a remarkable tribute to the amenities of the city and the extent and variety of the foreign goods that poured into its harbor. However, the decision to create the assembly did not lead to very impressive effects. In 427 the Visigoths laid siege to the place, but in the treaty that followed three years later it remained in Roman hands. Then in 455 a Romano-Gallic nobleman Avitus, persuaded, Sidonius Apollinaris suggests, by the Visigothic King Theodoric II, was invested with the purple at Arelate before proceeding to Rome to assume, briefly, the imperial authority. A second siege of the city by the Visigoths was repelled in 457: but in 476 it succumbed to their monarch Euric (who had asserted his total independence) and was laid waste and annexed.

The most important extant monuments date from the early imperial and Constantinian periods. In the first category are remains of the forum and buildings surrounding it, in addition to a sumptuous theater, a well-preserved amphitheater with a capacity of 21,000 spectators (fortified in the Middle Ages), and a circus outside the city beside the Rhodanus. The Constantinian buildings include massive baths (La Trouille), of which an enormous vaulted apse is preserved. On the opposite (right) bank of the river there was a substantial seaport suburb (Trinquetaille), approached by a bridge. A battery of water mills has been discovered at Barbegal nearby.

Arezzo *see* Arretium

Argentorate (Strasbourg). A city in what is now Alsace (eastern France, on the German frontier), two miles west of the Rhenus (Rhine). The city originated on an island between two branches of that river's tributary the Helella (Ill). Originally the capital of the German tribe of the Triboci, it was known to the Romans as Argentorate (or Argentoratum), silver fort. Augustus' stepson Drusus senior (Nero Drusus, died 9 BC) may have established a garrison of auxiliaries there. From soon after AD 16 until 43 a fortress existed, forming part of the military command (subsequently province) of Upper Germany; it was occupied by a legion, and then by legionary detachments, who constructed the first basalt wall (to supplement an earthen bank). After destruction in the Gallo-German rebellion of 69–70 Argentorate resumed its role as a legionary headquarters in *c* 80 (shortly before the elevation of Upper Germany to the status of a province).

Further serious damage followed in 235, for during the third and fourth centuries the place was severely exposed to German invasions, which led the inhabitants of its adjoining civilian settlement (*canabae*) to abandon their quarter and crowd into the fortress for protection. The most famous event in local history, recounted by Ammianus Marcellinus, took place in 357, during the reign of Constantius II, when Julian (later the Apostate), whom he had appointed as his deputy with the title of Caesar, routed a large confederacy led by the kings of the tribal group of the Alamanni, thus reasserting Roman control over the upper Rhine and freeing Gaul from the danger of German invasions. In the later fifth century, however, the place fell into the hands of the Franks, who gave it its present name.

Arginusae. The name of three small islands off the Aegean (western) coast of Asia Minor, opposite the southern end of the island of Lesbos. Tthe principal event in the islands' history, described by Thucydides, Xenophon and Diodorus, took place in 406 BC toward the end of the Peloponnesian War, when the Athenian navy won its last victory against the Spartans. An Athenian fleet under Conon had been blockaded by superior forces under Callicratidas in the harbor of Mytilene (Lesbos). But by ruthless conscription of their last resources of manpower and money the Athenians contrived to raise a new flotilla of one hundred and ten triremes, manned by 22,000 men and reinforced by forty vessels from subject allies. Learning that this naval force was approaching, Callicratidas sailed from Cape Malea at midnight in order to surprise the enemy fleet at dawn; and the Athenians put out to sea to confront him. Callicratidas himself was killed early in the action, and after sustaining heavy losses the whole of the Spartan right wing, of which he had been the commander, broke and fled southward; and then the left wing, under a Theban general Thrasondas, fled as well. The Athenians set up a trophy on the headland of Cynossema (Kilidülbehar) after which the battle is sometimes named; it had been the greatest engagement between Greek and Greek during the course of the war.

On the Spartan side seventy-five ships were sunk; among the victors thirteen went to the bottom, and twelve were put out of action. But a gale sprang up from the north, and the eight generals in command of the Athenian fleet retired to shelter without being able to rescue the survivors from their disabled, waterlogged ships. Athens was appalled by a casualty list of 5,000, and six of the generals (including the son of Pericles) were tried before the Assembly for negligence and put to death. Not for the first time, politics had ruined what the navy had achieved; and in the following year the last Athenian fleet was destroyed at Aegospotami, so that Athens was obliged to capitulate in 404.

Argos. A city in the southern part of Argolis (the Argolid), a territory, approximately triangular in shape, in the northeastern part of the Peloponnese (southern Greece) based on a central plain and flanked on the northeast and northwest by mountains and on the south by the sea. This is the country of the Bronze Age fortress centers of Mycenae and Tiryns, and of the Mycenaean kingdom of Agamemnon in Homer's *Iliad* in which the whole region is called Argos (' the plain'; the name was also sometimes used to denote the whole of the Peloponnese or even the whole of Greece).

The city of Argos was situated in the southern part of this plain. Occupied since prehistoric times, the place attained great importance in the Bronze Age, as recent excavations have emphasized. Argos was described in the Homeric poems as the kingdom of Diomedes, who acknowledged the overlordship of Agamemnon. In the Dorian invasion toward the end of the second millennium BC it came, according to legend, under the control of Temenus, a descendant of the hero Heracles. When a group of hamlets amalgamated to form an urban center beneath the citadel, it replaced Mycenae as the principal city of Argolis, reaching its peak under King Pheidon (early seventh century, rather than mid-eighth?), who seems to have won a decisive victory over the Spartans at Hysiae in Thyreatis that enabled him to take control of the Olympic Games. The possessor of a fleet of warships, Pheidon made Argos the most formidable state in the Peloponnese (throughout which his iron coinage [?] and system of weights and measures were accepted), if not, indeed, in the whole of Greece. But the power of Argos fell as that of Sparta rose, and thereafter, although it remained the largest Peloponnesian city, its role in Greek history was secondary.

About 494, at Sepeia in the Argolid, its army was heavily defeated by the Spartans, who, according to Plutarch and Pausanias, were only kept out of the city of Argos by its women, rallied by the poet Fetesilla. In 480/79 the Argives remained neutral in the Persian War (with a bias in favor of the Persians), but subsequently, after the introduction of a kind of a democratic government, they allied themselves with Athens against Sparta in 461. During the earlier part of the Peloponnesian War between those states they remained neutral. A subsequent alliance with Athens, Mantinea and Elis was short-lived because of military defeat (418), followed by oligarchic revolution. A federal union with Corinth, imposed by force (392), was frustrated some five years later by the dictation of Persian terms in the King's Peace (Peace of Antalcidas).

After welcoming the subsequent rise of Thebes, the Argives again suffered from aggression from the Spartans, against whom they appealed to Philip II of Macedonia. In the Lamian War (323/2), however, they sided with the Greeks against the Macedonian Antipater, only to suffer capture from other successors of Alexander in 317 and 303. Argos was the scene of the death, during a night attack, of Pyrrhus, king of Epirus (272), against whom it had joined forces with Sparta. Thereafter it once again became subject to Macedonia, but in 229 joined the Achaean League, remaining a member (with brief intermissions of Spartan control, 225,196) until Rome destroyed the League and annexed Greece as part of its new province of Macedonia (146). In the reign of Trajan (AD 98–117), Argos resumed the issue of coins, continuing these mintages until the reign of Gallienus, when the city was temporarily captured by German invaders (267). It suffered capture again in 395, but continued to be important in Byzantine times.

The remains of a prehistoric site on Aspis ('shield,' because of its shape) hill have been uncovered, and of temples of Pythian Apollo and Athena Oxyderces on the neck of land between this hill and another, Larissa, which was the citadel—dominating the landscape by its cone—and contained a shrine of Zeus and one of the first theaters in Greece, of the later fourth century BC. At a lower level, buildings adjoining the marketplace (agora) have been identified, including a further theater (of which the investigation is continuing), a council chamber, and a large portico erected in the fifth century. The later part of the same century witnessed Argos' outstanding contribution to the arts, the sculpture of Polyclitus. It was he who was chosen to execute the cult statue of Argos' divine patron Hera at her sanctuary the Heraeum—six miles north of Argos—when it was reconstructed by Eupolemus to replace an early seventh century building burned down in 423 (itself the successor of a Mycenaean shrine). Another Argive temple, dedicated to Aphrodite, of which the excavation has been completed, was rebuilt in the first or second century AD. Two large bathhouses have now been restudied.

Aria. A territory in what is now western Afghanistan, watered by the rivers Arius (Heri, Hari) and Murghab, and bordered by Parthia to the west, Margiana and Bactria to the northeast, Drangiana to the south. After his victory at Gaugamela against the Persians and the subsequent death of their King Darius III Codomannus (330), Alexander the Great pursued his would-be successor Bessus—who had proceeded to Bactria—through Aria. Alexander rapidly reached its royal residence, Artacoana, and having, as he believed, subdued the country, founded the colony of Alexandria in Aria (Herat) nearby, on the river Arius (330). Then he proceeded on his way, having appointed a Persian, Arsames, as the satrap of the region (Drangiana was subsequently added to his governorship). In 329, however, according to Arrian and Diodorus, Alexander sent Stasanor, of the royal house of Soli in Cyprus, to supersede Arsames, who had proved disloyal. After Alexander's death, Antipater reportedly replaced Stasanor by his brother (?) Stasander, but he was removed by Antigonus I Monophthalmos in 316.

Subsequently Aria formed part of the Seleucid empire until it came under the control of the breakaway Parthian realm (*c* 247). However, the second and greatest founder of the Greco-Bactrian state, Euthydemus I (*c* 235–200), captured Alexandria in Aria on his southwestern frontier, thus strengthening his position against his Parthian neighbors. Subsequently Aria came under Parthian rule again, and passed in the third century AD to the Sassanian Persians, although subject, at the end of the classical period, to barbarian incursions.

Aricia (Ariccia). A town in Latium (Lazio), on a spur at the edge of fertile volcanic depression at the foot of Mons Albanus, where the outer slopes of the craters of Lakes Albanus (Albano) and Nemorensis (Nemi) meet. Aricia was said to have been founded in mythical times, allegedly by settlers from Alba Longa (Castel Gandolfo, a short distance to the north) or by a Sicilian named Archilochus; at all events, from about the seventh century BC onward the leadership of the Latin communities began to pass to it from Alba Longa. Aricia was one of the places which exerted the largest influence on the legends of Rome (sixteen miles to the northwest), recounted by Livy and Dionysius of Halicarnassus. Toward the end of the sixth century the Aricians were said to have organized resistance to the last Roman king, Tarquinius Superbus, and to have helped Aristodemus the Effeminate, the Greek ruler of Cumae (Cuma) in Campania, to repel attacks by the Etruscans (*c* 505). Aricia was also, by tradition, assigned a role in the myth-encrusted battle of Lake Regillus between the Romans and the Latins (*c* 496), although the latter were stated to have been under the leadership of Tusculum, which may, by this time, have succeeded Aricia as the head of the Latin confederation opposed to Rome.

In 446 the rulers of Aricia and Ardea were locked in a quarrel regarding boundaries, in which the Romans mediated to their own advantage. Aricia was finally subdued by Rome in the Latin War (338), after which it was apparently granted second-class citizenship (*civitas sine suffragio*); the chief officials (magistrates) of the town, and of the *municipium* into which it was subsequently converted, retained the ancient title of dictator. In the civil wars of the early first century BC, Aricia was sacked by Gaius Marius (87) and reconstructed by the victorious Sulla. It was the birthplace of the Roman political agitator Publius Clodius Pulcher (d. 52) and of Augustus' mother Atia. Horace describes the place as the first stopping-point on a journey to Brundusium (Brindisi).

In the days of Aricia's headship of the Latin League one of its leading shrines, the Grove of Ferentina, served as the meeting place of the confederacy. Even more famous, however, was the nearby Temple of Diana Nemorensis (imitated from the shrine of Artemis Tauropolos in Tauris [Crimea]), in the woods surrounding the lake; its priest, the *rex nemorensis,* was, by custom, a runaway slave who gained this 'royal' office by murdering his predecessor. Egeria, the legendary consort and adviser of the Roman king Numa Pompilius (in origin probably a water-goddess) was worshipped in association with Diana, and so was the Italian god Virbius, identified with the mythical Greek huntsman Hippolytus—loved by Diana—who was raised from the dead by Aesculapius (Asclepius). Remains of the massively terraced temple are still to be seen; and surviving traces of the fortifications of Aricia itself include three successive periods of construction.

Arikamedu *see* India

Arime *see* Pithecusae

Ariminum (Rimini). A city on the Adriatic coast of the Ager Gallicus (formerly occupied by the Gauls, now Emilia-Romagna), between Ancona and Ravenna.

At first an Umbrian town, it was made a Latin colony in 268 BC and became an important stronghold in the line of defence against the danger of renewed Gallic aggression; Polybius, Livy and Strabo describe its position, and show how it dominated the bottleneck between the Apennines and the sea. Possessing a substantial harbor at the mouth of the river Ariminus (Marecchia), the city also became the terminal point of the great nothern highway from Rome, the Via Flaminia (220); and when Hannibal invaded Italy shortly afterward, it remained loyal to the Romans. Subsequently its road links were given even greater importance by the construction of the Via Aemilia from Ariminum to Placentia (Piacenza) (187, with subsequent extensions) and the Via Popillia to Aquileia (132).

Roman citizenship, with the title of *municipium,* was conferred on Ariminum in 89/88. Sacked by Sulla for supporting the cause of his enemy Marius, it was subsequently Caesar's point of departure for his invasion of Italy, at the outset of the Civil War against Pompey the Great (49). After Caesar's death, its lands were confiscated for the colonization of ex-soldiers (41). During the following decade, the triumvir Octavian (the future Augustus) employed the place temporarily as his headquarters in his wars against the Illyrians, and at about the same period it was granted the title of *colonia.* During the civil war between Vitellians and Flavians in AD 69 it was occupied by the latter. It became an episcopal see from at least the fourth century, and in 359 housed an ecclesiastical council.

The principal monuments of Ariminum are an Arch of Augustus (marking the junction of the Via Flaminia and the Via Aemilia, and inspiring the fifteenth century facade of the Tempio Malatestiano), and the Bridge of Augustus (completed by Tiberius, 14–37) on which the Via Aemilia entered the city. There are also fragmentary remains of an amphitheater, probably dating from the time of Hadrian (117–38). Recent excavations have revealed important building activities during the middle and later empire, especially in the private sector.

Armenia. A mountainous country to the northeast of Asia Minor, named, according to Greek tradition, after Armenus of Armenium in Thessaly. The geographer Strabo describes Armenia as bounded to the west and south by the river Euphrates and Cappadocia and Commagene, to the north by Colchis and Albania and Iberia, and to the east by Media Atropatene. The Armenians were invaders, speaking an Indo-European tongue, who occupied the area after the collapse of the kingdom of Urartu shortly before 600 BC. But they became subject first to Cyaxares, king of Media, and then to the Achaemenid Persian monarch Cyrus II the Great (*c* 550 BC). Xenophon describes the proud and powerful Armenian aristocracy, the people's high standard of living (with plenty of meat and barley wine), and their partly subterranean houses.

The country subsequently formed part of the empire of Alexander the Great (331) and his Seleucid successors (301). After the defeat of the Seleucid King Antiochus III the Great by the Romans (190/89), his satraps Artaxias and Zariadres revolted and established themselves, with Roman support, as independent kings of Greater Armenia (the major plateau east of the Euphrates) and Sophene (immediately east of that river) respectively, building their capitals at Artaxata

(Artashat), and Carcathiocerta (site uncertain). Tigranes II the Great (*c* 94–56) gave the country a unity that lasted five hundred years, founding a new capital at Tigranocerta; but the huge empire he added, including extensive acquisitions from the Parthians, could not be maintained, since, first, Lucullus captured Tigranocerta (Farkin; 69), and then Pompey the Great compelled Tigranes to abandon Syria and his other conquests and become a subject ally of Rome (66).

This Roman supremacy, however, was continually contested by Parthia, throughout a series of dynastic changes culminating in the treaty of Rhandeia (AD 63) arranged by Nero's general Corbulo, according to which it was agreed that Tiridates I, an Arsacid (member of the Parthian royal house), should occupy the Armenian throne, with the status of a vassal of Rome. Meanwhile Lesser Armenia (to the west of the Euphrates) had remained a Roman client state under a succession of different royal houses, until Vespasian (69–79) incorporated it into the Roman province of Cappadocia. Trajan also annexed Greater Armenia (114), but his successor Hadrian withdrew the Roman frontier to the Euphrates. Statius Priscus, a general of Marcus Aurelius and Lucius Verus, occupied Artaxata, and built a 'new city' Caenepolis (Vagarshapat, now Etchmiadzin; 163) which soon became the capital of the country.

Caracalla's attempt to annex Armenia in 216 proved unsuccessful, and after the Parthian empire had succumbed to the Sassanian Persians, their monarch Shapur II placed a vassal of his own, Artavasdes, on the Armenian throne (*c* 252). Diocletian's Caesar Galerius, however, forced the Persians to leave (287), confirming Tiridates III's claim to the kingship under Roman protection. His subsequent conversion to Christianity by St. Gregory the Illuminator (*c* 300)—who built his cathedral at Caenepolis directly over the Roman fort—made Armenia the first land to adopt the new religion officially, and thereby he created a permanent rift between his dynasty and the Persians.

However, after Tiridates III had been murdered by the baronial aristocracy (336/7), their discontent with a later monarch, Arsaces III, led to the division of the country into two states dominated by the east Roman and Persian rulers respectively (387). The former section was divided into the Roman provinces of Armenia Prima (Minor) and Secunda and Sophene (Gentes), and the latter became a Persian province in 428. Nevertheless, national unity was strengthened, in the cultural sphere, by St. Mesrop's invention of the Armenian alphabet (*c* 410), and by the creation of a national Christian literature, of which the fifth century was regarded as the Golden Age. Armenia is the oldest Christian nation to have survived into modern times. *See also* Artaxata, Tigranocerta.

Armenia Minor (Lesser Armenia) *see* Armenia

Arnus (Arno). The principal river of Tuscany, one hundred and fifty miles long, second only in importance to the Tiber in central Italy. It rises on the slopes of Mount Falterona and in its upper course flows through the former lake basin of the Casuentini (Casentino). Near Arretium (Arezzo) it turns west, traverses a second ancient lake basin, and after a narrow gorge (at Incisa) enters a third basin, that of Florentia (Florence). Thereafter, the river completes its lower course toward the sea, in an almost due westerly direction, receiving from the north the waters of its tributary the Umbro (Ombrone Pistoiese), and from the south those of the Pesa, Elsa and Era.

The Arnus played an extremely important (though until recently little understood) part in the northern expansion of the Etruscans. From *c* 600, or earlier, certain of their city-states, and particularly Volaterrae (Volterra), maintained a line of trading posts or markets up to and beyond the river, including particularly Pisae (Pisa) at its mouth, where in ancient times it was joined by the Auser (Serchio). The Arnus basin was difficult to exploit, not only because of sudden floods and droughts, but owing to the waterlogged swamps which extended widely on both its banks; according to legend the services of Heracles himself had been needed in order to drain them. But the Etruscans, too, were highly skilled irrigators, and created effective drainage systems. By this means, the Volaterrans advanced up to the Arnus along a broad front, making especially abundant use of its tributaries, beside which numerous Etruscan sites and artifacts have come to light. Particularly large concentrations of finds occur around Artemium (Artumena, Artimino) just north of the river, beside its junction with the Umbro. Moreover, by the sixth or fifth century BC, there was an Etruscan city at Faesulae (Fiesole), presiding over a major route from the Arnus to the north. Its finds again display Volaterran influence, and these reappear at Etruscan sites such as Poggio di Colla in the intensively cultivated Mugello valley.

After Volaterrae had gradually lost its independence to the Romans, the Arnus valley, too, passed into their hands. But in many areas its marshlands still remained intractable. In the Second Punic War (218–201), for example, when Hannibal invaded Italy, we learn from Polybius that it took him four days to cross these bogs, and in the course of doing so he lost an eye in an accident.

Arpinum (Arpino). A town in northeastern Latium (Lazio), in the valley of the Liris (Liri, Garigliano). Arpinum first belonged to the Volscians and was then conquered by the Samnites and subsequently by the Romans, who granted it second-class status (*civitas sine suffragio*) in 305/3 and full citizenship in 188 BC. Like other Italian cities, it was granted the rank of a city (*municipium*) in 90/89.

Arpinum became famous because Gaius Marius (*c* 157) and Cicero (106) were born in its territory. Marius' birthplace was the village of Cereatae, and Cicero's was said to have been a villa (later owned by the poet Silius Italicus) a mile north of Arpinum, at the Insula Arpinas (Isola di Liri, between the rivers Liris and Fibreno), where traces of the house believed to have been Cicero's still exist beneath the church of San Domenico. His treatise On Laws (*De Legibus*) is staged at Arpinum. The tradition that Augustus' general Marcus Agrippa was also born there is uncertain.

The most noteworthy remains of the place are early megalithic walls, still attaining, at certain points, a height of ten feet, and a width of six—the most impressive defensive system of the kind still surviving in Italy. These walls, penetrated by a pre-Roman gate (the Porta dell'Arco) and another gate of Roman construction, encircled the acropolis, which was known in medieval times as the Civitas Ciceroniana and subsequently as Civita Vecchia.

Arretium (Arezzo). A city in central Italy that was at first an Etruscan settlement founded by Clusium (Chiusi), thirty miles away. The place, which Strabo described as the farthest inland of all the cities of Etruria, stood on a fertile plateau that overlooks the northern extremity of the Clanis (Chiana) valley and is close, on the other side, to the southward curve of the Arnus (Arno). The villages on the site seem to have been amalgamated into a town during the sixth century BC, when an acropolis was established on a low eminence within the area covered by the modern habitation center. When the power of Clusium waned *c* 500, Arretium became independent, and continued to develop an important industry of bronze work, encouraged by strong commercial contacts with the Gauls of northern Italy, whom the Arretines supplied with arms. But the most famous example of their work is the Chimaera now in the Museo Archeologico at Florence, dating from *c* 400.

The assertion by Dionysius of Halicarnassus that Arretium joined other Etruscan cities in offering help to the Latins against the Roman King Tarquinius Priscus (*c* 616–579 BC) is probably anachronistic. Latin inscriptions at Tarquinii known as the *elogia Tarquiniensia* seem to indicate that a man of that city known as Aulus Spurinna intervened at Arretium, perhaps *c* 358–351, to help put down an uprising of slaves. And Livy reports that in 302 a Roman commander stepped in to prevent the expulsion of the wealthy, powerful and originally royal family of the Cilnii. It was no doubt because of social discontents of this kind that the Arretines turned willingly to Rome, into whose hands their city passed peacefully and permanently, by treaty or prolonged truce, during the third century BC despite a setback in 294 when a Roman relieving army was defeated by besieging Gauls (Senones).

In 205, toward the end of the Second Punic War, Arretium contributed large quantities of metals, wheat and agricultural implements to Scipio Africanus' victorious expedition to north Africa. Before or after 200, the city became the first terminal of the Via Cassia from Rome, and the starting point of the Via Flaminia Minor (187) leading across the Apennines to Bononia (Bologna). In the Civil Wars of the early first century its people supported the cause of Marius against Sulla and were punished by loss of territory, and by the imposition of a colony of ex-soldiers. Nevertheless, the city recovered, and under Augustus became the best-known of all Etruscan centers because of its mass production of the red pottery known as 'Arretine'—often stamped with graceful decorations in low relief—which flooded the markets of the Roman world for nearly a century. It was also famous as the birthplace of Maecenas, minister of Augustus and patron of literature, who claimed descent from the royal house of the Cilnii.

Although parts of an early wall (*c* 300 BC) are still to be seen, the preservation and excavation of important monuments has been hindered by the development of a medieval and Renaissance town on the same site.

Arsameia (Eski Kahta). In Commagene (southeast Turkey), on the river Nymphaeus (Kahta Çayı), a tributary of the Euphrates. Refounded by Arsames (Arschama)—from whom, according to one view, the Seleucid royal family traced its descent—over a very ancient settlement on the road between Melitene (Malatya) and Samosata (Samsat), Arsameia became a military strong point and the site of a mausoleum and cult center (*hierothesion*) built by King Antiochus I Theos Dikaios Epiphanes Philoromaios Philhellen of Commagene (69–before 31) in honor of his father King Mithridates I Callinicus. Above a rock-cut inscription is a relief (now re-erected) on which Mithridates I is seen clasping the hand of Artagnes, a Persian deity whom the Greeks identified with Heracles.

A mile outside the town is a Roman bridge erected by four Commagenian cities in honor of Septimius Severus (*c* AD 200); and further on, beside the Nymphaeus, stands a mound that provided the burial place for royal women. Antiochus I set up a similar center in his father's honor at a second Arsameia on the Euphrates, the modern Gerger. For his own tomb, *see* Commagene.

Arsinoe (Ardsherud). An Egyptian port at the northern end of the Sinus Heroopoliticus (Gulf of Suez), established by Ptolemy II Philadelphus (283–246 BC), son of the founder of the Ptolemaic dynasty of Egypt, who gave it the name of his late sister and wife Arsinoe II Philadelphus (d. 270). Capital of the Heroopolite nome (district), the town was the terminal point of a canal leading from the Pelusiac arm of the Nile delta, and was also connected by road to Aila (Aelana, now Akaba), at the head of the Gulf of Akaba (or Elat). Despite shoals and east winds, it became one of the principal harbors of Egypt.

During the reign of Cleopatra VII (51–30), ruling under the protection of her Roman lover Antony, the place, as we know from Strabo, temporarily assumed the new name of Cleopatris. A little to its west, Trajan (AD 98–117) established a garrison in Clysma, at the end of a new canal leading from Babylon (Baboul) at the southern apex of the Nile delta.

Arsinoe (Cyprus) *see* Marion

Arsinoe. A town in Egypt, formerly Shedet and Crocodilopolis (Medinet-el-Fayum). The principal town of the large oasis of the Fayum—twenty-four miles west of the Nile—of which the name comes (in Coptic) from an Egyptian word meaning 'sea': This referred to Lake Moeris (described by Herodotus and at first known to the Greeks as Limne, 'the lake'), which in ancient times occupied an extensive area of the Fayum depression and is now represented by the much shrunken Birket el-Qarun at the edge of the oasis. A radio-carbon date of 4440 BC has been obtained for the early occupation of the region.

Beside the lake stood the Egyptian town of Shedet, dedicated to the crocodile god Sebek (Suchus), whose earthly representative, a living crocodile, was fed on grain and meat and wine and received worship, bedecked with jewels and fed by priests, in a local temple (of which ruins remain): so that the Greeks called the place Crocodilopolis. King Ptolemy II Philadelphus (283–246 BC) established a colony of ex-soldiers in the place, gave it the name of his late sister and wife Arsinoe II Philadelphus (d. 270), and made it the capital of the Arsinoite nome (district); at a later date it was temporarily renamed Ptolemais Euergetis (after Ptolemy VIII Euergetes II, 164–116). In Roman times the place became one of the four assize centers of the imperial governorship of Egypt.

Arsinoe was the primary source of the papyri that became a major export of the area, and numerous examples (inscribed in Greek, Coptic and Arabic) have been found, including the Moeris Lake Papyrus displaying a geographical plan of the nome. The Fayum was also one of the principal centers of one of the most noteworthy artistic achievements of the Roman imperial world, represented by skillfully highlighted funerary portraits of men and women executed in tempera or encaustic (pigmented beeswax usually applied by a hot *spatula* or *cauterium*) on wooden panels inserted in mummy cases and preserved by the completely dry climate. These portraits were among the precursors of the Christian Coptic art of the future; already in the second century Arsinoe was becoming an important center of the new religion, and subsequently its territory housed more than 10,000 monks.

Arsinoe, formerly Taucheira (Tocra, Tawqrah). A member of the group of five cities of Cyrenaica (Libya) known as the Pentapolis; on the coast between Berenice (Benghazi) and Ptolemais (Tolmeta). The name Taucheira, recorded by Herodotus, is probably Libyan, but pottery found on the site shows the existence of a Greek settlement as early as the 720s BC, very soon after the traditional date of the foundation of Cyrene itself. After the conquest of Cyrenaica by Ptolemy II Philadelphus of Egypt (283–246 BC; or his son Ptolemy III Euergetes, 246–221), the town was renamed Arsinoe after the second queen of that name, wife of the second Ptolemy and mother of the third. Like Arsinoe (Ardsherud) at the head of the Sinus Heroopoliticus (Gulf of Suez), it was temporarily renamed Cleopatris by Cleopatra VII (51–30).

Arsinoe had a poor harbor but a fertile hinterland favored by numerous wells, so that it survived as the last fortified Byzantine stronghold in Cyrenaica. Excavations and air photographs have enabled the successive plans and dimensions of the ancient city to be identified.

Arsinoeia *see* Ephesus

Artacoana *see* Aria

Artaxata (Artashat). A city in Armenia; situated in the folds of Mount Ararat in the Armenian Soviet Socialist Republic twenty miles southwest of Erivan. A royal center founded by Artaxias I in 188 BC, on the advice, according to Plutarch and Strabo, of the exiled Carthaginian Hannibal (defeated by the Romans in the Second Punic War), who was reputedly present at its construction. Strabo also records that the town was established on an elbow of land resembling a peninsula, and was protected on nearly every side by the river Araxes (Aras).

Nevertheless, Artaxata was captured by the Romans on several occasions in the course of their invasions of Armenia. After Pompey the Great had defeated the Armenian King Tigranes I the Great, Tigranes lost his greatly expanded kingdom but was allowed to remain as client monarch at Artaxata (66 BC). In the reign of Nero, it was burned down by Corbulo (AD 58), but was rebuilt by Tiridates I (who became Rome's protegé) under the temporary name of Neronia. Trajan entered Artaxata in 114, and an inscription referring to one of his legions has been found on the site. When Statius Priscus invaded Armenia in 163, during the joint reigns of Marcus Aurelius and Lucius Verus, he built Caenepolis ('New City,' later Vagarshapat), 20 miles away, and this soon became the new capital. This development, and the existence of several previous royal residences at other locations, suggest that Artaxata may have acquired a reputation for unhealthiness.

Artemisium, Artemision. A promontory on the northwest coast of the Greek island of Euboea, taking its name from a temple of Artemis Proseoia which, to judge from architectural fragments, was probably situated at the modern village of Potaki, near Pevki Bay.

The place derives its importance from a naval engagement in the Persian War (480). As Xerxes I moved southward into Greece, winning over Thessaly and most of the central portion of the country, the allied command of the Greek city-states opposed to him (under Spartan generalship, influenced by the Athenian Themistocles) posted its land forces at the pass of Thermopylae on the mainland, and its navy off Artemisium forty miles to the east-northeast. Xerxes' fleet, after waiting for the army to secure the Gulf of Pagasae, and then moving down past the inhospitable coast of Thessaly, lost half his battle fleet in late summer storms and three naval engagements. After three days, however, he compelled the Greek fleet, also severely damaged, to withdraw southward from Artemisium—having learned, meanwhile, that the land force of the Greeks at Thermopylae had been outflanked and its rear guard under the Spartan King Leonidas destroyed.

Central Greece was now totally lost, and Athens would have to be evacuated. Yet the battle of Artemisium had stimulated the morale of the Greeks, since they had shown their superiority, man for man and ship for ship, and could be proud that, with only a part of their naval forces, they had succeeded for a time in holding up the Persian fleet. They awarded the prize of valor to the Athenians, who according to the poet Pindar had 'laid the bright foundation of freedom' at Artemisium.

Artemium (?) (The Latin name is deduced from the modern Artimino; the Etruscan name was probably Artumena, derived from a local cult of Artumes [Artemis].) An Etruscan city just north of the borders of Etruria proper, beside the junction of the river Arnus (Arno) with one of its northern tributaries the Umbro (Ombrone Pistoiese). Artemium commanded the valley of this stream, an important route to northern Italy; and it also controlled an adjacent ford, crossing the Arnus toward the south. Finds on its lofty defensible hill (Piaggerina) include Greek and Etruscan pottery ranging from the seventh to fifth centuries BC. Moreover, at nearby Comeana, a grandiose Etruscan tomb of *c* 600 has been discovered, as well as two others at Quinto Fiorentino to the east.

Artemium, which was probably founded by Volaterrae (Volterra), may well have been, at this period, the principal Etruscan township in the entire Middle Arno area, as well as a key-point on the route of explorers and traders to the north. It was subsequently superseded by Faesulae (Fiesole), but a recent emendation of a passage in Cicero's *Letters to Atticus,* which seems to refer to *Artemini,* suggests that the place was still in existence in his time.

Arverna *see* Augustonemetum

Ascalon (Ashkelon). An ancient coastal city of Philistia, now in the south-western corner of Israel, adjacent to the Gaza Strip. Although its harbor facilities, between two chains of petrified sand dunes, were not extensive, Ascalon possessed ramparts crowning a semicircle of cliffs and a hinterland amply supplied with wells and productive of vines, olives and fruit trees. After many turbulent centuries of changing ownership it passed successively into the hands of the Assyrians, Babylonians and Tyrians, and came under the control of Alexander the Great after his conquest of Tyre. Thereafter it tenuously preserved a measure of autonomy under the conflicting auspices of the Ptolemies and Seleucids near whose borders it stood.

Although a center of Hellenism—well-known as the birthplace of writers, philosophers, and artists—it diplomatically opened its gates to the Jewish (Hasmonaean) ruler Jonathan Maccabaeus (147), but started to reckon a new era from 104/3 BC, when the Egyptian King Ptolemy IX Soter Lathyrus rescued it from the domination of another Judaean ruler. In consequence, although the city persistently remained free, it placed the Egyptian monarch's head—and his Ptolemaic eagle—on its coins, and subsequently honored Ptolemy XII Auletes (80–51) in the same way, inaugurating a further civic era in 58. During the civil war between his children Ptolemy XIII and Cleopatra VII, Ascalon placed the head of Cleopatra on its coinage (49–47). When Caesar, arriving in Egypt in 48 and taking the side of Cleopatra, found himself besieged in Alexandria, the force sent to relieve him was blocked at Ascalon; but the Idumaean chieftain Antipater, who had important family connections in the place, arrived with his titular ruler John II Hyrcanus to clear the way. In 38/7 Ascalon revived its silver coinage once again with Cleopatra's head, as a hostile gesture to the pro-Parthian, anti-Roman Antigonus, who had seized control of Judaea. In the immediately following years, however, Antony reasserted Roman authority; but when the region was disputed between his two mutually hostile protegés Cleopatra and Herod the Great of Judaea, and Antony felt obliged to accept Cleopatra's claim to annex numerous coastline centers, Ascalon was exempted, and remained free.

After Cleopatra and Antony succumbed to Octavian (the future Augustus) in 30, he still permitted the city to retain the status of an independent enclave. Herod, who retained his power after Antony's death, could probably have incorporated it into his dominions, but its association with his family caused him to respect its independence. However, Josephus informs us that he built a royal palace and baths there, and traces of colonnaded buildings survive. Following Herod's death in 4 BC, and the distribution of his kingdom among his sons, Augustus gave Ascalon (or at least its royal palace) to Salome, his daughter by Elpis; but it subsequently passed, as a 'free city,' under the general supervision of the Roman province of Judaea when this was established in AD 6.

The city prospered from the production of onions and of a popular wine—which is still drunk today—and its harbor (Maiumas Ascalon), two miles to the south, was evidently improved and enlarged, since its bronze coins depict galleys, apparently of substantial size. Aplustres (the curved sterns of ships) and tridents also appear on the coinage, in the hands of a figure tentatively identified as Derceto, the goddess of a famous local sanctuary.

Ascalon retained its prominence in the later Roman empire, and was described by Eusebius in the fourth century AD as the most famous city of Palestine. It remained hostile to Christianity until the time of Julian thc Apostate (361–63), but Christian basilicas and a "Well of Peace" were constructed later. The remains of a synagogue have also been discovered.

Ascoli Piceno *see* Asculum Picenum

Ascoli Satriano *see* Ausculum Satrianum

Ascra, Askra, a small township or village in Boeotia (central Greece), on the northwestern slopes of Mount Helicon. Its exact location has been disputed, but the presence of a tower (mentioned by Pausanias) and the discovery of Mycenaean and Greek pottery suggest that it was situated on the slope of Askra Pyrgos or Pyrgaki ('tower') hill, near the modern Panayia and not far from the city of Thespiae to which Ascra belonged. According to a legend described by the unknown Heseginous, quoted by Pausanias, it was founded by Oeoclus (the son of Poseidon and Ascra) and by Aloeus' sons, the giants Otus and Ephialtes, who piled Pelion on Ossa.

Ascra was also (according to his own testimony) the birthplace of Hesiod, who is often coupled or contrasted with Homer as the principal representative of the earliest epic poetry (*c* 700 BC). He indicates that his father, a trader of Cyme (Namurt Limanı) in Aeolis (western Asia Minor), had turned his back on the unprofitable dangers of the sea in order to settle at Ascra, 'a miserable village, awful in winter and worse in summer, good at no time'—although this description of its climate is much exaggerated, and, according to Athenaeus, the place was at least famous in antiquity for its beetroot. There Hesiod and his brother Perses, after their father's death, quarrelled over the succession to his estate, a situation that inspired the hard picture of the farmer's year and severe sermon on justice provided in his *Works and Days*—a unique source of information about social conditions in early archaic Greece.

At some unknown date the people of Thespiae were said to have destroyed Ascra. It was inhabited, however, in the days of Plutarch (before 50–after 120 AD). But according to the traveller and geographer Pausanias, who wrote during the middle years of the second century, 'in my time one tower and nothing more was left of Ascra to remember it by.'

Asculum Picenum (Ascoli Piceno). In Picenum (Marche), eastern Italy; situated amid impressive mountains in the center of the valley of the river Truentus (Tronto), at its confluence with the Castellano. It was said to have been founded by the Sabines but became the principal city of the Piceni.

An ally of the Romans in 299 BC, it suffered conquest at their hands in 268; whereupon its captors forcibly transferred the population to Apulia, at the same time extending the Via Salaria (running from Rome to Reate [Rieti] and later to Amiternum [San Vittorino]) so that it led to Asculum Picenum and then to the Adriatic. The 'Social War' (between Rome and its Italian subject-allies or *socii*) broke out in 91 at Asculum, when its people killed a visiting praetor and all other Romans in the city; but then the city succumbed, after a two-year siege, to Cnaeus Pompeius Strabo, whose success marked the termination of the northern part of the war; thousands of missiles dating from the siege have been discovered in the neighborhood. After the infliction of severe punishment, however, Asculum subsequently, as we learn from Cicero, acquired the status of a *municipium*. It sided with Julius Caesar in his Civil War with Pompey the Great (49), and after his death received a colony of ex-soldiers from the triumvirs (or Augustus), together with an addition to its territory.

Strabo emphasized the defensible qualities of the site. Its citadel was located on a rocky terrace isolated on three sides by streams and closed off on the other side by a hill. The two main streets of the ancient city, the *decumanus maximus* and *cardo maximus*, correspond to the modern Corso Mazzini and Via Malta respectively, the forum being at their intersection. The church of San Gregorio Magno incorporates the remains of an ancient temple ('of Vesta'), and a theater and amphitheater have also been identified. A bridge of the first century BC, the Ponte di Cecco, bringing the Via Salaria across the river Castellano, was blown up in 1944, but the Ponte Solesta (of Augustan date), across the Truentus, has been restored and is still in use.

Ashdod *see* Azotus

Ashkelon *see* Ascalon

Asia was the name of the great province formed by the Romans in western Asia Minor when they annexed the kingdom of King Attalus III of Pergamum in 133 BC, extending their control or supervision to the numerous rich and ancient city-states in this extensive and, in most parts, highly civilized region. The province, with its capital at Pergamum, originally comprised Mysia (with the Troad), Aeolis and Ionia together with the islands belonging to these territories; and Lydia, farther inland, was also incorporated. Another region that was included was Caria, though perhaps not at once. The greater (northern) part of Phrygia was also absorbed into Provincia Asia in 116, though between 56 and 50 certain areas of south Phrygia belonged to the province of Cilicia, and in 25 eastern Phrygian territories were added to a newly created province of Galatia.

The Asian province was so ruthlessly exploited by Roman governors and financiers that a large part of its population responded to the call of Mithridates VI Eupator of Pontus to revolt (88–84), collaborating, it was said, in the massacre of 80,000 Italian residents in a single day. Arbitrary Roman exactions continued to be frequent until the time of Augustus, when prosperity was restored. In the administrative division of the Roman provinces between emperor and senate, Asia and Africa were the principal senatorial provinces, entrusted to senior proconsuls of consular rank. Ephesus overtook Pergamum as Asia's most important city, though it is uncertain whether it also became the official capital of the province. Provincial unity was expressed in the Commune Asiae, a general assembly of the cities of the province, which provided for the official worship of Rome and Augustus under the direction of the Chief Priest of Asia.

The *Acts of the Apostles* offer a vivid picture of conditions in Asia during the mid-first century AD, and Dio Chrysostom and Aelius Aristides testify to its great prosperity in the century that followed, during which 168 of its cities issued their own local bronze coinage. In the third century, however, Asia suffered severely from Gothic invasions. Phrygia-Caria became a separate province before 259, and in the later empire the former Asian province was subdivided into no less than seven smaller provinces (Asia, Lydia, Caria, Hellespontus, Insulae, Phrygia Pacatiana, and Phrygia Salutaris), which were grouped together with adjoining territories to form the administrative diocese of Asiana. This region, together with the more easterly diocese of Pontica which comprised most of the remaining portions of Asia Minor, provided the principal reservoir of manpower and financial resources to the Byzantine empire centered on Constantinople.

Asisium (Assisi). In Umbria, on the western slopes of the Apennines. It became a Roman city (*municipium*), though inscriptions show that its chief annually elected officials retained the old Umbrian title of *Marones.*

Asisium was the birthplace of the Augustan elegiac poet Propertius (between 54 and 47 BC), whose family were local notables—by far the most eminent personage that the place produced, until the contrasted figure of St. Francis. Most of the city was destroyed by the Goth Totila (Baduila) in AD 545.

The remains of a temple, traditionally ascribed to Minerva, are incorporated in the church of Santa Maria. The foundations of a small shrine dedicated to Castor and Pollux (the Dioscuri) have also been found, in the neighborhood of the colonnaded forum, where traces of a tribunal can be seen. There are also remains of a theater and amphitheater. The acropolis hill displays a series of terraces supported upon massive travertine substructures. The town was surrounded by a powerful wall consisting of rectangular blocks of limestone.

Aspalathus *see* Salonae

Aspendus, Aspendos (Belkis). A city in Pamphylia (southern Asia Minor), eight miles inland on the navigable river Eurymedon (Köprü Çayı or Pazar Çayı), which provided it with an important harbor. Strabo indicates that the founders of Aspendus came from Argos; and an Argive element may have remained among the mixed multitude of Greeks who, according to tradition, colonized Pamphylia after the Trojan War, under the leadership of Amphilochus, Calchas and Mopsus. The alleged descent from these leaders seems to be echoed in the earliest designation of the city inscribed on its coins, Estvediys, since this is apparently derived from the name of Asitawandas, founder of the recently discovered city of Karatepe in Cilicia, for whom a bilingual inscription claims descent from Mopsus. It is possible, however, that the principal Greek settlement did not take place until the seventh century BC. Its population derived revenue from salt-pans beside an adjacent lake, and from olives in the hills behind.

Although Aspendus possessed two easily defensible hills, their fortifications evidently failed to keep out Croesus, king of Lydia (*c* 560–546). When he, in his turn, was defeated by the Persians, the city passed into their hands, but seems to have retained a considerable degree of independence. Its fifth century silver coinage (the series bearing the name of Estvediys) was based on the Persian standard, and circulated far and wide over a prolonged period, prompting extensive barbarous imitations; these pieces depicted a heavy-armed infantryman (hoplite), a branch of soldiery for which the city was famous.

In 469 Cimon engaged the Persians by sea and then by land at the mouth of the Eurymedon, winning victories that were probably the occasion of Aspendus' enrollment in the Delian Confederacy sponsored by Athens. But there is no evidence that the city ever paid tribute, since it seems to have preferred Persian rule, and in 411, during the Peloponnesian War, provided a Persian base to the satrap Tissaphernes. On the arrival of Alexander the Great in 333, its leaders offered to surrender, but then declined his terms after all; rather than face a siege, however, they eventually submitted, paying a fine because they had supplied horses to the king's Persian enemies. Occupied by King Ptolemy I Soter of Egypt, Aspendus was later subject to the Seleucids until 189 BC, when Cnaeus Manlius Vulso, after concluding peace with the Seleucid monarch Antiochus III the Great, exacted tribute from the city, as the price of an alliance with Rome. From 102 until *c* 44, together with the rest of Pamphylia, Aspendus probably belonged to the province of Cilicia, of which the deputy governor Gaius Verres, according to Cicero, looted the city unmercifully. But Strabo, two or three generations later, described it as populous, and it issued its own bronze coinage from the beginning of the Principate until after the middle of the third century AD.

On the flat top of the larger of the two hills are the remains of numerous structures that lined the marketplace (*agora*). But by far the most important monument of Aspendus is its theater, built on the smaller hill. This is the best preserved Roman theater in Asia Minor, and has a claim to be the finest anywhere in the world. It was constructed *c* AD 160 by a local architect Zeno, and dedicated to the local gods and to the imperial family of Antoninus Pius. The stage building is immense, its back wall being three hundred and sixty feet long and eighty feet high. The auditorium has a diameter of three hundred and eighteen feet, and contains forty rows of seats providing accommodation for an audience of seven thousand five hundred. The acoustics of the building are still impressive. Another important Roman monument, of which substantial traces survive, is the aqueduct that brought the city's water supply across a marshy stretch of country, from thirty miles away in the mountains to the north.

Assus, Assos (near Behramkale). A city on the south shore of the Troad (northwestern Asia Minor) that occupied the terraces of a steep volcanic cone rising sharply from the sea and overlooking the plain of the river Satnioeis (Tuzla). The double 's' of its name, and Strabo's indication that the whole region was once inhabited by the tribe of the Leleges, point to a non-Greek origin. However, Strabo and Alexander Polyhistor, depending on earlier writers, record a subsequent settlement by Greek (Aeolian) colonists from Methymna on the island of Lesbos (which is 7 miles away), presumably in the eighth or seventh century BC. The larger of the town's two (artificially created) harbors was used by ships in order to avoid the strong currents off the west coast of the Troad—across which vessels were also conveyed from Assus by land. In the sixth century the city came under the control of Lydia, and after the fall of the last Lydian monarch Croesus it became part of the Persian province of Phrygia and the Hellespont, and provided the Persians with wheat. After the Persian Wars, however, it was a member of the Delian League presided over by Athens.

In 365 Assus staved off a combined land and sea attack by the Persian satrap Autophradates and King Mausolus of Halicarnassus. It was at this time under the control of a banker named Eubulus, who established his capital at Atarneus (Kale Ağılı or Dikili, forty-five miles to the southwest), and was succeeded by his former eunuch-slave Hermias (*c* 355–341). A Platonist (and the recipient of the master's Seventh Epistle), Hermias admitted his fellow Academicians Erastus and Coriscus of Scepsis to a share of his power and encouraged them to found a philosophical school at Assus. There, after the death of Plato (348), they were joined by Aristotle (who married Hermias' niece, adopted his daughter Pythias and gave him political advice), as well as by Xenocrates and Callisthenes, and later Theophrastus as well. Assus was the birthplace of Cleanthes (331), who became head of the Stoic school.

The city suffered from the competition of Alexander Troas (founded by Antigonus I, 310) and lost its position as a land portage terminal, concentrating henceforth on agriculture instead. It became subject in turn to the Seleucids, the kings of Pergamum (241–133) and then Rome's province of Asia. The ship which took St. Paul to Italy called at its port. The local coinage of Assus continued into the third century, during which Gothic invasions were deterred by its strong walls. Spanning a circumference of two miles, they go back, in part, to archaic times; in their reconstructed form, they enabled Eubulus to resist the Persians and Mausolus. Still in an excellent state of preservation, and including towers that are preserved to a height of nearly sixty feet, they are the most complete city-walls surviving anywhere in the Greek world. On the separately fortified acropolis, remains have been found of a splendid temple of Athena dating from about 530 BC. Sculptures from the site are now at Paris, Istanbul and Boston, but architectural traces are scanty, though enough to bear witness to the employment of the Doric Order, which is exceptional in Asia Minor, where the Ionic Order was habitual.

Assyria (now part of northern Iraq and southeastern Turkey) is the Greek form of a geographical name 'country of [the god, city] Ashur,' used in pre-Greek texts to denote the homeland of the Assyrian people on the Upper Tigris, bounded on the north and east by the Masius range (Tur Abdin) and the Kurdish hills. This was the central region of the Assyrian empire (destroyed by the Babylonians in 612 BC). In consequence, Herodotus, Xenophon and later writers apply the name 'Assyria' to the entire territory between the Iranian-Armenian mountains and the Syro-Arabian desert; and confusions with 'Syria' also occur.

After the conquests of Alexander the Great, part of the Assyrian homeland—the district of the two Zab rivers—was incorporated in the Seleucid empire, and then became a vassal kingdom (later a province) of the Parthians, in which capacity (under the name of Adiabene [Azerbaijan] which had strictly been applicable to a more northerly region) it was frequently convulsed by dynastic disputes and Partho-Roman wars. In AD 116 Trajan annexed the region (together with southward extensions) as the Roman province of Assyria, but immediately after his death in the following year it was abandoned by his successor Hadrian. In 195 Septimius Severus sent an expedition across the Tigris into Adiabene-Assyria, and assumed the title Adiabenicus. No permanent annexation, however, was achieved, and in 216 his son Caracalla, after advancing to the eastern borders of Adiabene, likewise achieved no lasting success. At about this period Syriac-speaking Christianity was introduced into the country. When the Parthian empire began to succumb to the Sassanian Persians in the late 220s, Adiabene was one of the territories, according to an Armenian tradition, that their own King Chosroes I first endeavoured to defend against the new power, but in vain, since the country was soon incorporated in the Persian dominions.

Asturica (Astorga). A city in northwest Spain; the place took its name from the tribe of the Astures, who were suppressed by Augustus and his generals (26–19 BC). Incorporated in the province of Hispania Tarraconensis, it was rebuilt (by legionaries) in Romanized guise under the name of Augusta, and fulfilled a considerable role as a mining town for gold, chrysocolla (a silicate of copper used for dyeing) and minium (sulphide of mercury or cinnabar). Asturica was also a communications and horse-breeding center. Pliny the Elder describes it as a splendid city (*urbs magnifica*). A house of early imperial date, with paintings of Pompeian style, has been discovered, as well as a prison, sewers and inscriptions mentioning mining personnel and deities, including non-Roman gods, such as Grannus and Apollo Sagatus.

Asturica was a bishopric by the mid-third century AD, and was subsequently represented in Spanish ecclesiastical councils. Its medieval walls are built over fortifications of late Roman date.

Astypalaea *see* Samos (There was also an island of that name between Cos and Amorgos.)

Atarneus (Kale Ağılı or Dikili). A city near western Asia Minor, opposite the island of Lesbos, usually regarded as belonging to Mysia, though sometimes to Lydia and Aeolis. Occasionally heard of in the fifth and early fourth centuries BC, Atarneus was the capital of the autocrat ('tyrant') Hermias (*c* 355) who became virtually independent of Persia and the head of an independent state of considerable naval, military and financial strength. For his cultural interests, and the philosophers whom he attracted to his princedom, *see* Assus. Advised by Aristotle, he negotiated an agreement with King Philip II of Macedonia, but in 344 was treacherously arrested by a representative of the Persian King Artaxerxes III Ochus and killed.

The design displayed on the city's earliest fourth-century coins was a coiled-serpent, sacred to Dionysus. Atarneus possessed a fertile territory and had access to gold mines and precious stones. Pliny the Elder described it as insignificant and deserted, probably (it would seem from Pausanias) because of a plague of mosquitoes.

Atella (near Orta di Atella). In Campania (southwest Italy), between Capua (Santa Maria Capua Vetere) and Neapolis (Naples). Founded in about the fourth century BC (on an Iron Age site) it was one of the cities of the Campanians (a blend of Samnite invaders and the indigenous population) which, threatened by fresh waves of Samnite invasion, sought Roman intervention in 343 BC. Shortly afterward, however, it fell out with the Romans, coming under their control five years later, and receiving a second-class form of citizenship (*civitas sine suffragio*). From about 250 it issued its own bronze coinage with the inscription *Aderl,* its name in the Oscan language.

During the Second Punic War, Atella was the first of the Campanian cities to defect from Rome to Hannibal after his victory at Cannae, in 216. Recovered by the Romans in 211, it was severely punished by the confiscation of a large part of its territory, the execution of the leaders of the rebellion, and the removal of the remaining inhabitants to Calatia (near Maddaloni), their place being taken by immigrants from Nuceria Alfaterna (Nocera Superiore). Atella coined no more, but thanks to the fertility of its territory recovered rapidly, so that Cicero in 63 was able to describe it as one of the most important places in Campania. Under Augustus, it gained the rank of *municipium*; Tacitus records the existence of an amphitheater in the reign of Tiberius (AD 14–37). Remains include houses, baths and tombs of Republican date, a large bathhouse of the second century AD, and a subterranean painted mausoleum of the same period at nearby Caivano.

The place's principal claim to distinction rests on the dramatic form to which it gave a name, the Atellan Fables (*fabulae Atellanae*), a designation that indicates either that this form of entertainment originated at Atella or that the developments that it underwent there were sufficiently important to have impressed and influenced the Romans. These Fables were rustic farces on a rough stage, performed in the Oscan language, to which they owed the alternative designation of Oscan Games (*ludi Osci*). Owing certain elements to the Greek culture that had pervaded large parts of southern Italy (Magna Graecia), they displayed stock characters including the foolish old gentleman (Pappus), the cunning swindler (Dossennus), the clown (Maccus) and the glutton (Bucco or Manducus). They represented a significant transition between the simple song-and-dance sketches of the past and the mature Latin drama of the future.

Ateste (Este). A city in Venetia (Cisalpine Gaul, northeast Italy), at the southern extremity of the Euganean hills, twenty-one miles south-southwest of Patavium (Padua). In ancient times the place occupied a strategic position beside the river Atesis (which is now nine miles away), enjoying easy access to land routes. At an early date, therefore, it became the focus of civilization in eastern Italy north of the Padus (Po)—and gave its name to one of the principal

Iron Age cultures of the region. This was developed by an invading people, apparently of Danubian origin, who settled at first in the adjacent hills and then, in about the ninth century BC, moved down to the river and founded Ateste, which became the capital of the Veneti and remained for eight hundred years the most important commercial and artistic center of Venetia.

Like their contemporaries in many other territories, the population buried the ashes of their cremated dead in urnfields (open cemeteries). The majority of the finds from the Atestine cemeteries, in which four successive periods have been distinguished, consist of pottery—including elaborately ornamented cinerary urns—and bronze work, notably large buckets (*situlae*) of sheet bronze, richly decorated with distinctive geometric and figured engravings and reliefs. Although, in contrast to the adjoining port of Atria (Adria), Greek imports are few, the exported products of Ateste not only reached the head of the Adriatic but were taken across the Alps to Carniola and the Tyrol. Inscriptions, which begin to appear in the fourth century, are written in north Etruscan characters, but their language is the Indo-European dialect known as Venetic.

The Atestine Veneti began to decline when the Gauls invaded northern Italy in the fourth and third centuries, and in the years around 200 they passed peacefully under the control of Rome. By this time, Ateste had begun to be eclipsed by the growth of Patavium (Padua; with which boundary disputes occurred in the second century, requiring settlement by Roman intervention), and despite the establishment of a colony of ex-soldiers by Octavian (Augustus) after the battle of Actium (31) the city never regained its importance. Indeed, after the third century AD, it is not heard of again. Such few remains of Roman Ateste as have survived come mostly from tombs and villas in the neighborhood.

Athens is situated in the southeastern part of the plain of Attica, three miles from the sea. The Athenians claimed that they were the indigenous ('autochthonous') inhabitants of the country (though in fact there had been a pre-Hellenic population): the fabulous King Erechtheus was said to have been the son of Gaia (Earth) and to have been brought up by Athena from whom (after a contest between her and Poseidon) the city took its name. On the precipitous hill known as the Acropolis stood an olive tree allegedly planted by Athena to commemorate the contest.

Archaeological evidence confirms that the Acropolis was a center of Mycenaean power. Moreover, Athens apparently survived the political upheavals that accompanied the downfall of that civilization toward the end of the second millennium BC and the invasions of the Dorians (who were said to have tried in vain to take the place (*c* 1065?); instead it was occupied by Ionian Greeks (held by Athenian tradition to be the founders of all other Ionian communities elsewhere). According to legend, Athens was ruled at that time by King Codrus, who died in battle—or sacrificed his life—to save his country, and was succeeded by his son Medon, who in turn was followed by his descendants until the eighth century. It seems to have been at about that time, and in the epoch that followed, that the various communities of Attica gradually amalgamated (synoecized) to form the city of Athens, a process attributed by legend to a single act of King Theseus, son of Aegeus (or of Poseidon). The population of the new foundation was grouped in four tribes (*phylai*).

The power of the kings, however, gradually succumbed to attacks from the old aristocratic families (*eupatridai*), who provided the members of the Council later known as the Areopagus, and the three chief magistrates known as archons (elected at first for ten years and then annually). From about the mid-seventh century the concentration of land and wealth in relatively few hands, and the reduction of the indebted peasantry to virtual serfdom, provoked a series of social crises and disorders. The failure of Cylon to seize power was followed by the legislation or 'constitution' of Draco (*c* 621/620), but further civil strife led to the election of Solon as chief archon, with the power to create laws, in 594/3 or 592/1 (though some prefer a later date). His measures, known as the *Seisachtheia* (shaking off of burdens), included the release of peasants from serfdom by the cancellation of all debts for which land or liberty was the security, and the redemption of all who had been sold into slavery, and the prohibition of all borrowing on the security of the person. Solon also invested the popular Assembly (Ecclesia) with certain legislative powers, and made it into a judicial body under the title of the Heliaea—so that for the first time the people (or a panel selected from it by lot) acted as jurors and judges. Moreover, if the tradition is correct—although some regard it as anachronistic—Solon also established Athens' new, historic Council, the *Boule,* comprising a hundred members from each tribe.

These moves, later hailed as the beginnings of democracy, accompanied the development of the Athenian state into an international force. Its widely recognized commercial and artistic evolution was signalized by the production of superb vases in the black-figure style (from *c* 600). At the same time, Athens, utilizing its ports on the sandy beach of Phaleron and in the deep-water inlets of Piraeus and Zea (on either side of the Munichia promontory), was beginning to display imperial ambitions, signalized by the settlement of Sigeum on the Hellespont (Dardanelles) in 600, the conquest of the island of Salamis (soon after 600) and the introduction of the first silver coinages of the city, displaying family badges or devices (*c* 575 or rather later).

Nevertheless, the rapid transformation of society provoked further disturbances, which were exploited by Pisistratus so as to establish himself as autocratic ruler ('tyrant') in 561, 556 and 546. He maintained a network of alliances, purified Delos as the center of Ionian religion, and expanded his possessions overseas to Rhaecelus (later Aenea) on the Thermaic Gulf and Sigeum in the Troad (northwestern Asia Minor). The black-figure pottery attained new heights of commercial importance and artistic beauty, and was replaced from *c* 530 by the brilliant red-figure technique. After Pisistratus' death in 527, his sons Hippias and Hipparchus took over his power; and it was at this time that the famous, long-lived and very widely circulated silver coins with the head of Athena, and her owl, began to be issued.

In 514, however, Hipparchus was assassinated by Harmodius and Aristogeiton (revered as heroes), and four years later his brother Hippias was expelled by an aristocratic revolution supported by Sparta. At Athens, this overthrow of the Pisistratids was followed by an internal struggle for power in which Cleisthenes emerged victorious (508/7), defeating invasions from Sparta, Chalcis (Euboea) and Boeotia (506). He then took measures to ensure the development of democracy. His ten new, artificial tribes, replacing the four old Ionian tribes and each representing in itself a cross-section of the various elements in the state, brought about the rapid eclipse of the nobles; and Cleisthenes subordinated the Boule and Areopagus alike to the Ecclesia, which henceforth met regularly and possessed the authority to deal with any important state question. (Aristotle's statement, however, that it was Cleisthenes who also introduced ostracism—a method of banishing for five years any prominent citizen who had made himself unpopular—is perhaps anachronistic.)

In 498 Athens sent a fleet of twenty ships to support the unsuccessful revolt of the Ionian Greeks against Persian rule. This was the pretext for the historic invasions of Greece by the Persians, in whose defeats at Marathon (490), Salamis (480, under the guidance of Themistocles), Plataea, and Mycale (479) Athens played a leading part. Encouraged by Sparta's reluctance to commit itself to foreign wars, the Athenians profited by these successes to establish, under their own leadership, the Delian League (478/7), on whose behalf Cimon crushingly defeated the Persian land and sea forces at the mouth of the river Eurymedon (467). In 449 the Peace of Callias excluded the Persians from western Asia Minor. These events, accompanied by measures of coercion directed against the allies, helped to bring about a gradual conversion of the Delian League into an Athenian empire, strengthened by the construction of Long Walls to their ports the Piraeus and Phaleron (456, 445) and culminating in the transfer of the League's treasury to Athens in 454/53. Meanwhile, in the earlier 450s, the Athenians had also gained control of a land empire on the Greek mainland, but this was disrupted by Thebes (447) and Sparta; though Pericles, who remained Athens' dominant statesman for many years (d. 429), concluded a thirty-year peace with Sparta in 446/48. This peace left the Athenians' hands free to reduce recalcitrant allies, notably Samos (440/39), and lasted until 431 when mutual jealousies caused the outbreak of the Peloponnesian War against Sparta and Thebes. After twenty-seven years, the war ended with the complete defeat of Athens, the temporary replacement of its democratic government by a narrow oligarchy (repeating a pattern foreshadowed in 411), the demolition of its Long Walls, and the dissolution of its empire.

The fifth century had been the Golden Age of Athenian civilization. A period of extraordinary prosperity was ushered in by the discovery of a rich vein of silver at Laurium. The city's coins, weights, measures and exports were accepted over a very large area. Financed by the contributions of the empire, Pericles masterminded the incomparable buildings of the Acropolis. Important writers and thinkers, notably Herodotus and Anaxagoras, were encouraged to visit or reside at Athens, and a unique literary efflorescence was marked by the names of the tragedians Aeschylus, Sophocles and Euripides, the comic dramatist Aristophanes, and Thucydides the historian of the Peloponnesian War. Socrates, too, was the first person to apply serious critical thought to problems of morality and the conduct of life, until his questionings were brought to an end by execution at the hands of the restored democracy in 399 (the 'Poros building' in which he spent his last days, immortalized by Plato, has now been identified).

Athens quickly recovered its independence after the Peloponnesian War, rebuilding its Long Walls and its fleet. But its endeavor, in association with other states, to overthrow the Spartan supremacy was terminated by the inglorious King's Peace or Peace of Antalcidas (387), which abandoned the Greek cities of Asia Minor to Persia. A Second Athenian Confederacy (377) was crippled by revolts (357–354), and efforts to check the rising power of Philip II of Macedonia were crushed at the battle of Chaeronea (338), after which Athens was compelled to join a new Hellenic League under Macedonian control. An attempt, after the death of Philip's son Alexander the Great, to oust the Macedonians resulted in a further defeat in the Lamian War (323–322). However, during the fourth century Athens had remained in the forefront of cultural life. Plato and Aristotle (an immigrant from Macedonia) laid the basis for all future philosophy, Demosthenes (who led the resistance to Philip) raised oratory to supreme heights, Menander's New Comedy exerted an immense influence on future European drama, and Praxiteles endowed sculpture with a new and more subtle dimension. After 300, the philosophers Epicurus and Zeno, the founders of Epicureanism and Stoicism respectively, established their schools in the city.

A new move by the Athenians, in conjunction with Peloponnesian allies, to oust the Macedonians ended with their defeat in the Chremonidean War (266–262). But in 229 the Macedonian garrison departed, and the city recovered its independence, continuing to retain ostensible freedom after Greece had passed into Roman hands (146). In 88–86, however, Athens supported Mithridates VI Eupator of Athens against the Romans, and was sacked and partly destroyed by Sulla. Its citizens pleaded their glorious past; but Sulla retorted that he was there to punish rebels, not to be given lessons in ancient history. Nevertheless, Athens retained much of its intellectual prestige and continued to be a center of philosophical education. Cicero and Horace were among those who studied at its educational institutions. In the second century AD, the city enjoyed another revival under Hadrian and the Antonines, exemplified by the career of their friend the wealthy sophist Herodes Atticus. In 267 the city's sack by the German Heruli, despite brave resistance led by the historian Dexippus, caused very severe damage. Julian the Apostate (361–63) was a lover of Athens, and its philosophical schools were still frequented until their closure by the Byzantine emperor Justinian I in 529. There is literary and archaeological evidence for fourteen Christian basilicas at Athens during the fifth and sixth centuries.

Fragments of a wall dating back to the Mycenaean epoch can still be seen on the Acropolis. But its great temple of Athena, the Parthenon, was probably begun in limestone during the sixth century BC and replanned in marble after the battle of Marathon (490); the unfinished Doric shrine was burned by the Persians in 480. Pericles renewed the project in 447, and the reconstruction of the building was entrusted to the architects Ictinus and Callicrates and the sculptor Phidias, many of whose masterpieces are to be seen in the British Museum. His great gold and ivory statue of Athena was dedicated in 438 BC, but transported in AD 426 to Constantinople, where it did not survive. The adjoining, complicated, Ionic temple known as the Erechtheum was completed in 407. On its southern Portico of the Korai (maidens), six sculptured female figures (Caryatids) replaced the usual columns. The temple itself contained a primitive wooden image of Athena or its replica. Also to be seen on the Acropolis are the Propylaea (Gateway) and small Ionic Temple of Athena Nike (Wingless Victory), completed in 437/432 and *c* 420 respectively.

Built into the southern side of the hill is the Roman Theater of Dionysus, on the site of the structure in which the great Athenian dramatists had staged their plays. Nearby stands the Odeon of Herodes Atticus (AD 161). At the foot of the Acropolis the Mint (*c* 400 BC) has now been located, and to the northwest lies the marketplace (agora), containing administrative edifices, temples, and porticos, including the recently discovered Stoa Poikile (painted Stoa *c* 470–460) frequented by the philosophers, and a long portico that was erected by Attalus II of Pergamum (159–138) and has now been reconstructed as an Agora Museum. Overlooking the agora is the most complete surviving Greek temple (*c* 449–440 BC), dedicated to Athena and Hephaestus and erroneously known as the Theseum. Other buildings in the area include the little octagonal Tower of the Winds (a water clock of the second century BC), a Roman market, and the Library of Hadrian.

To the north of the agora, on the outskirts of the city, are remains of the Ceramicus (Potter's Quarter) and Dipylon Gate (fourth century BC). Southeast of the Acropolis rise the immense Corinthian columns of the Temple of Olympian Zeus, completed by Hadrian after earlier projects in the sixth and second centuries BC had been discontinued.

Athos, Mount *see* Acte

Atria, Hadria (Adria). A coastal city in Cisalpine Gaul (northeastern Italy) on the northern side of the delta of the river Padus (Po); the Adriatic Sea was named after the place. Atria was originally settled by the (Illyrian?) Veneti. Subsequently, like Spina, it became remarkable because immigrants and traders from Greek and Etruscan city-states lived and worked there together from *c* 520/510 BC, apparently in amicable cooperation. The Etruscans built a canal from an adjacent mouth of the Padus to improve Atria's commercial contacts. Nevertheless, archaeological evidence from the site suggests that Greeks (especially from Aegina) were predominant, so this was probably their principal port in the upper Adriatic, whereas Spina played a similar role for the Etruscans.

When the Gauls invaded Italy from *c* 400 onward, Atria fell into the hands of the tribe of the Boii; the iron chariot of one of their chieftains, together with the skeletons of its two horses, is to be seen in the local museum. The Via Popillia (132) linked Atria with Ariminum (Rimini) and Aquileia, and it became a Roman *municipium*. But by the early years of the Roman Principate the sea had already receded eight miles from the town, which had consequently lost its importance.

Attaleia (Antalya). A coastal town of Pamphylia (southern Asia Minor). Since its harbor, though small, is the best on the coast, there may have been a pre-Greek settlement. The Greek city was founded by Attalus II Philadelphus of Pergamum (160/159–138 BC), whose colonists perhaps included Athenians (since they are honored as kinsmen on later local coins).

Although retaining autonomy after the creation of the Roman provinces of Asia and Cilicia, and probably furnishing ships to Lucullus during Sulla's campaign against Mithridates VI of Pontus (85), Attaleia subsequently supported the pirate chief Zenicetes—who seized control of the area—and after his suppression by Publius Servilius Vatia Isauricus (77) was punished by annexation accompanied, according to Cicero, by losses of territory. When Pompey the Great assembled his fleet to deal with the remainder of the pirates ten years later, Attaleia served as his base.

A visit by Hadrian in AD 130 gave an opportunity for substantial construction, and the most impressive of the city's seven gates, and parts of the towered wall that extends between them, date from this occasion. A frcc-standing, two-storeyed tower (Hidirlik Kulesi) was perhaps employed to house artillery, or may have formed the base of a lighthouse. A road led inland from Attaleia into Pisidia, where it joined a major route, the Via Sebaste. The place became a Roman colony in the late third century AD, and achieved greater importance in Byzantine times. (There were other Attaleias in Mysia and Lydia, the present Dikili and Selçuklu respectively.)

Attica. A triangular promontory of about a thousand square miles forming the easternmost part of central Greece, separated from Boeotia (to the north) by Mounts Parnes and Cithaeron and from Megara (to the west) by Mount Ceratus. Attica is also bounded by the Euboean channel to the east, by the Aegean Sea to the southeast and by the Saronic Gulf to the southwest. Its southern extremity is Cape Sunium, and its original name was Acte, denoting a piece of land juttings out into the sea. Four lines of mountains—from east to west, Laurium [source of Attica's principal resource, its silver mines], Pentelicus, Hymettus and Aegaleos—divide the territory into three plains, the Mesogeia (growing vines, olives and figs), the Pedia (in which Athens is situated), and the Thriasian plain (with its chief town at Eleusis).

Despite the union of Attica in the eighth and seventh centuries BC under the Athenians, power and wealth in the territory remained regionally based until Pisistratus and Cleisthenes broke the influence of these local baronies and associations (*see* Athens). When the Peloponnesian War started in 431, the Athenians were unable to prevent annual invasions of Attica by destructive Spartan armies, and had to withdrew behind their city walls; and the subsequent occupation of Decelea, on the foothills of Mount Parnes, as a permanent Spartan garrison on Attic soil (413) made a considerable contribution to the eventual Athenian defeat. *See also* Athens, Brauron, Cithaeron, Decelea, Eleusis, Hymettus, Ilissus, Marathon, Oropus, Pentelicus, Piraeus, Salamis, Sunium.

Atuatuca, Aduatuca. The place of this name, which may have been on the site of the modern Casterat on the Meuse (Mosa, Meuse, Maas) south of Maastricht, lay in the territory of the Eburones, clients of the Atuatuci, who lived between the Rhenus (Rhine) and the Mosa.

At the time of Julius Caesar's occupation of Gaul, Atuatuca was a fortress of the German tribe of the Atuatuci, descended from the Cimbri and Teutones whose invasions the Romans had repelled at the end of the previous century. Caesar established a winter camp on the site, garrisoned by one and a half legions under the command of Quintus Titurius Sabinus and Lucius Aurelius Cotta. In 54 BC the Eburones, led by Ambiorix, attacked the camp and massacred most of the Roman troops, together with their commanders. A number escaped and found their way back to the camp, and there, in despair, committed suicide, but a few others escaped through the forest to bring news of the disaster to Caesar's lieutenant Labienus. Caesar replaced the lost soldiers by bringing in three fresh legions, including one borrowed from Pompey. He employed these to exterminate the Eburones, systematically devastating the country so that any who had managed to survive should die of starvation. Ambiorix himself, however, evaded the manhunt.

Augustus repopulated the area—which now belonged to the province of Gallia Belgica—by moving in the tribe of the Tungri, who probably came from across the Rhine, and established a new center, on a hilltop overlooking the river Jeker, under the name of Atuatuca Tungrorum (the modern Tongres or Tongeren). For a short time, Atuatuca Tungrorum probably housed a military garrison, but after its withdrawal the place still remained an important center of road communications and trade. Its grid of streets bordered by wooden houses dated from the time of Claudius (AD 41–54), as did a large aqueduct. After destruction during Civilis' Gallo-German revolt (69–70), the city was quickly rebuilt, and the second century witnessed the construction of walls embracing an impressive circumference. In the same period, an earlier temple was replanned and enlarged on Roman lines.

About 275/6 the town was captured and plundered by the Franks, and subsequently its fortifications were rebuilt to cover a smaller perimeter. Under the reorganization of Diocletian, Atuatuca Tungrorum became part of the province of Germania Secunda, and from this time onward reassumed an increasingly military character (to which recently revealed late imperial defences bear witness), although Maastricht eclipsed it as the economic, political and religious center of the region. The fall of Colonia Agrippinensis (Köln) to German invaders in 457/ 8 meant the loss of Atuatuca as well.

Aufidus (Ofanto). The principal river of Apulia and southern Italy, a hundred and three miles in length. Rising near the Tyrrhenian Sea, it flows into the Adriatic, past Canusium (Canosa di Puglia) and Cannae, where, in 216 BC, during the Second Punic War, the Romans suffered their gravest defeat from Hannibal. The poet Horace, who was born in Venusia (Venosa) nearby, often mentions the river. It is only a feeble stream in summer, and probably always was. But Horace writes of its savage violence in wintertime, describing it as bull-like (*tauriformis*), with reference to the roar of its waters, which could be heard, he said, a long distance away (*longe sonans*).

Augsburg *see* Augusta Vindelic(or)um

Augst *see* Augusta Rauricorum

Augusta *see* Londinium

Augustamnica *see* Aegyptus

Augusta Praetoria (Aosta). A two-mile wide valley in the Val d'Aosta (Cisalpine Gaul, northwestern Italy), flanked by high mountains. Standing at the Italian end of the Great and Little St. Bernard Passes over the Pennine and Graian Alps respectively, at the confluence of the rivers Duria Major (Dora Baltea), a tributary of the Padus (Po) and another stream, the Buthier, the place belonged to the Gallic tribe of the Salassi, who controlled the mining industry of the valley (including gold and iron); it was here that Augustus' general Aulus Terentius Varro Murena encamped in 25 BC when engaged in subjugating this recalcitrant people. As a sequel, in order to maintain the control thus established and assure communications with Gaul, the emperor replaced the camp by a military colony consisting of 3,000 retired praetorian guardsmen to whose branch of the army the new settlement owed its name. It became and remained the capital of the region; inscriptions record that the Salassi, at least later, gained civic rights in the community.

The center of modern Aosta preserves the Roman plan almost without change. Today's higher ground level has buried some of the Roman monuments, but those still visible are mostly of Augustan date. They include the arched rear wall of a theater or Odeon (originally roofed because of the climate), eight arcades of the amphitheater (unusually located within the city itself) and town walls, which make Augusta Praetoria one of the best preserved of all Roman fortified cities: although damaged, they survive for almost their whole rectangular length together with two gates (including the triple, two-curtained Porta Praetoria) and a famous single-spanned Arch of Augustus adorned, on each face, with Corinthian columns supporting a Doric entablature.

Augusta Rauricorum (Augst). A city on the south bank of the Rhine, eight miles above Basilia (Basel in Switzerland), in the territory of the Celtic tribe of the Raurici. A Roman colony was planned by Julius Caesar to prevent incursions into the newly conquered regions of Gaul (Gallia Comata) from the east, and established after his death by Lucius Munatius Plancus, proconsul of that country, who allotted the settlers land between the Rhenus (Rhine) and the Jura Mountains.

The site may not, however, have received extensive buildings until *c* 15 BC, when it assumed new importance during the conquest of the central Alps and regions beyond by Augustus' stepsons Tiberius and Nero Drusus (Drusus senior). In the course of these campaigns, its strategic position in Upper Germany, as the terminus of roads from Gaul and Italy to the Rhine frontier, justified the presence of a garrison, maintaining close communications with other such posts at Augusta Praetoria (Aosta) and Augusta Vindelicorum (Augsburg). Legionary detachments were subsequently stationed at Augusta Rauricorum at various times, and the inhabited area was considerably enlarged in the second century AD, only to suffer destruction from invading Alamanni in 259–60. Thereafter the population must have been considerably diminished, as the lower town was abandoned and only the highest part (Kastelen) retained its fortifications. About the time of Diocletian, however, this fortress was succeeded by a riverside strongpoint some four hundred yards to the north, constructed by a newly raised legion and given the name of Castrum Rauracense (Kaiseraugst).

The original Augusta Rauricorum had covered an approximately rectangular area measuring about seven hundred by four hundred yards and comprising fifty-two blocks (*insulae*). The extensive surviving remains include a forum, a market (the 'Neben Forum'), a theater apparently converted at one stage into an amphitheater, another amphitheater (made of wood), a three-aisled basilica or meeting hall (imitating Trajan's Basilica Ulpia at Rome) and a *curia* (place of assembly for the local governing body) in the shape of a three-quarter circle. Houses, a bath for men and a bath for women, and workshops have also been uncovered, as well as industrial installations comprising scalding tubs and smoke chambers for the processing of meats and sausages, which, according to Varro, was a Gallic speciality.

Temples include a shrine dedicated to Jupiter and a Septizodium dedicated to the seven planets (in the Ergolz Meadow); most of these sanctuaries, it would seem from recent excavations, were based on Celtic rather than Roman models. Fragments of steles (sculptured slabs) depicting the locally worshipped Dea Nehalennia have also been discovered. A treasure of silverware from Castrum Rauracense is in the Augst museum.

Augusta Taurinorum (Torino, Turin). A city in Gallia Cisalpina (northwestern Italy), at the foot of the Mont Genèvre pass over the Cottian Alps; situated on the left bank of the river Padus (Po), which became navigable at this point, at its confluence with the Durias Minor (Dora Riparia). The chief center of the tribe of the Taurini, the place is probably identical with the Taurasia which, according to Appian, was captured by Hannibal in 218 BC, at the beginning of the Second Punic War. It gained importance from its position on the Via Fulvia from Placentia (Piacenza) to the Alps (159).

The settlement of a Roman colony is likely to date from *c* 29/28, three or four years before a force sent by Augustus conquered the Salassi to the north. After Vitellius' victory in the Civil War of AD 69, a legion that he moved out of Augusta Taurinorum owing to its disorderly conduct left fires that consumed part of the colony. The rectangular symmetry of the ancient urban plan was retained by the medieval and modern city. The Porta Principalis Sinistra (Palatina) is an unusually fine surviving example of a city gate.

Augusta Trevirorum or Treverorum (Trier [Trèves] in northwest Germany). A city situated in a region of Gallia Belgica that possesses rich natural resources, at a point where the river Mosella (Moselle) widens and where three routes spread out to reach the Rhenus (Rhine) at Colonia Agrippinensis (Köln), Koblenz (Confluentes) and Moguntiacum (Mainz). The settlement originally belonged to the Treviri, a Gallic tribe (containing a strong German admixture), which furnished cavalry to Julius Caesar but gave him a good deal of trouble. A huge sacred precinct in the Altbach Valley, together with other sanctuaries in the region, constituted an important tribal religious center.

Noting the strategic advantages of the place, which natural mountain barriers protected from attack, Augustus refounded it in 16 BC (the bimillenary has recently been celebrated) as Augusta Trevirorum, perhaps granting the community the honorary title of *colonia,* although this rank more probably dates from

Claudius (AD 41–54). The first river bridge, it now appears, was erected *c* 44 (replaced *c* 140, with alterations *c* 185). The city became the headquarters of the fiscal authorities of the province of Gallia Belgica and of the military commands of Upper and Lower Germany, remaining a civilian community but operating as a supply center for the armies on the frontiers. Commerce flourished, extensive pottery was manufactured, and an important school of native sculpture developed.

During the joint reign of Valerian and Gallienus (253–60), the latter apparently refortified Augusta Trevirorum; he also issued coinage there (257), thus inaugurating the city's long career as one of the principal mints of the empire. When Postumus, three years later, established a breakaway empire of western Europe, he chose the city as his capital and the headquarters of his praetorian guard. But shortly after the collapse of this secessionist state the place suffered crippling damage from attacks by Franks and Alamanni (*c* 275). Nevertheless, it soon resumed its former importance, and when Diocletian instituted the tetrarchy—according to which the administration of the empire was divided between two Augusti and two Caesars—the Caesar Constantius I, entrusted with the western provinces, established his imperial seat at Augusta Trevirorum (293), which soon became known simply as Treviri (Treveri) or Treviris.

His steps to create a resplendent palace quarter were extended by his son Constantine I the Great (306–37), who likewise resided at Treviri for a time: his birthday celebrations there in 310 were the theme of a contemporary eulogy (one of a number of Latin Panegyrics delivered at the place). In 328 he again took up his residence at Treviri to supervise military operations against the Alamanni. The city continued to be frequented by his sons, and closed its gates against the troops of Decentius Caesar, brother of the usurper Magnentius (335). Renewed prosperity came in the time of Valentinian I (364–75), who made Treviri his headquarters for prolonged operations against the Germans; his son and successor Gratian was there when his father died. They both issued great gold medallions at the local mint, commemorating the Glory of the Romans and Triumph over Barbarian Nations, and Theodosius I, on his accession (379), likewise coined there with the type of a phoenix, inscribed PERPETVETAS.

Possessing a population of about 80,000 inhabitants, Treviri was now not only the capital of the province of Belgica Prima, but also the seat of the Praetorian Prefecture of Gaul (covering western Europe), a major center of Christianity north of the Alps, and the site of great state factories (for arms, weaving, and gold and silverware). In 406/7 it was sacked and burned by the German invaders (Vandals) who had broken across the Rhine, and at least two devastations by the Franks followed shortly afterward. Coins show that the city subsequently acknowledged the usurpers Jovinus and Sebastianus set up by the Burgundians and Alans (411–13), and then recognized Priscus Attalus too, after his second proclamation as emperor by the Visigoths. In view of all these disturbances the Praetorian Prefect of the Gauls moved his residence southward to Arelate (Arles). Later in the fifth century Treviri fell into Frankish hands: probably the last representative of Roman authority was Arbogastes (475–76).

The remains of the ancient town—the most remarkable Roman complex in northern Europe—include an amphitheater with a capacity of 20,000 (*c* 108), public baths (Barbarathermen), temples, and two very important buildings of a later date. One is the Aula Palatina (otherwise known as the Basilica), started by Constantius I and completed by Constantine the Great (305–10) as the Hall of Audience or Throne Room of their palace. It is an apsed structure, of which the dramatic interior is matched by an imposing external wall displaying two tiers of massive rounded windows framed by arcade-like projections. The other major monument is the massive Porta Nigra, the Roman city-gate *par excellence,* designed to proclaim imperial might. It probably dates from the early years of Constantine's reign. The same period witnessed the construction of elaborate and novel Imperial Baths (Kaiserthermen), and grandiose churches, of which remains have been incorporated in subsequent reconstructions: two of them were superimposed on the palace, of which the coffered ceiling has survived, displaying portraits of Constantine's mother Helena and wife Fausta. What seems to have been an imperial summer palace, likewise of fourth century date, has been discovered at Welschbillig, seven miles northwest of Augusta Trevirorum.

Augusta Vindelicorum or Vindelicum (Augsburg) in Raetia (Bavaria, southern Germany). A military (possibly legionary) camp was established near the later town, at Oberhausen, northwest of the river Virdo (Wittach), after the northern campaigns of Tiberius and Nero Drusus (Drusus senior) under Augustus (from *c* 15/9 BC). When the garrison left, *c* AD 14 or 16/17, the occupied area had expanded to the city's subsequent triangular site at the junction of the Virdo and the Licca (Lech). By the time of Claudius (41–54) at latest, Augusta Vindelicorum became the capital of the province of Raetia, linked by roads to Italy and the Danube; it was raised to the status of *municipium* in the reign of Hadrian (117–38), which was the period of its greatest prosperity. Extensively damaged by the invasions of the Alamanni in the later third century, the place nevertheless remained the capital of Diocletian's province of Raetia Secunda, and became, in medieval times, the seat of a bishopric.

The legionary camp has yielded extensive finds of coins and pottery. The subsequent city is hard to reconstruct since the Roman remains lie as much as twenty feet below the present ground level. But considerable remains of the city-wall have survived, perhaps datable to the epoch of Hadrian.

Augustodunum (Autun). A city overlooking the left bank of the Arroux, a tributary of the Liger (Loire) in Gallia Lugdunensis (Saône-et-Loire). Augustodunum was the chief city of the Aedui, founded by Augustus to replace their former capital Bibracte. Succeeding to a prehistoric site—now revealed by air photography—the new foundation stood on the major routes linking Lugdunum (Lyon) with the valleys of the Liger and Sequana (Saône) and with the towns of the Senones and the Parisii, and is shown by its remains to have enjoyed impressive wealth. Already in AD 21, as Tacitus indicates, it was a prosperous city, enjoying a high educational standard, which contributed greatly to the Romanization of the area. In 269, however, Augustodunum was besieged and captured by Tetricus, ruler of the breakaway empire of the west established by Postumus, and suffered severe damage.

Constantius I Caesar, one of the rulers of the tetrarchy established by Diocletian, was urged to take steps to restore its former status. This plea was made by Eumenius, a rhetoric teacher of Greek origin who was born at Augustodunum and became Constantius' most influential secretary (*magister memoriae*) and then director of the school (Scholae Maenianae) which was a prominent center of Gallo-Roman culture. In 297 in the presence of the provincial governor, Eumenius delivered a speech (preserved as the ninth in a collection of Latin Panegyrics) in which he flattered the four emperors and solicited their approval for the reconstruction of the war-damaged school of his city. It now bore the name of Flavia Aeduorum; in the early fourth century the free population of the city has been estimated at 50,000, including children. However, the reduced perimeter of its later walls bears witness to partial depopulation.

The earlier Augustan fortifications have remained intact at various points, together with gates, including the well-preserved Porte S. André, which displays flanking towers and a pilaster-framed, arcaded upper gallery. Another monument is one of the largest surviving theaters of the Roman world, possessing a diameter of nearly four hundred and fifty feet, and perhaps dating from the latter half of the first century AD. A second large theater, incorporating many of the features of an amphitheater (probably the 'amphitheater' of ancient and Renaissance accounts), has also now been found. In addition, there are ruins of some of the numerous temples referred to by Eumenius and others. His school was in the middle of the city, near the forum; it seems to have included spacious colonnades, adorned with maps of the empire on their rear walls.

Augustonemetum, later Arverna (Clermont-Ferrand in the Auvergne). A city founded by Augustus on a small hill in the basin between the Tiretaine valley and Limagne plain to replace Gergovia as the capital of the formerly dominant tribe of the Arverni, in the province of Aquitania. The tribe's principal temple on the Puy-de-Dôme, dedicated to Mercurius Dumias, was famous for a valuable statue by the Greek sculptor Zenodotus. Augustonemetum (as the place came to be called after AD 14) grew until its devastation by the Alamanni in the third century, after which it declined. Under the reorganization by Diocletian it became part of the province of Aquitania (or Aquitanica) Prima in the administrative diocese of the Seven Provinces.

In the fifth century, under the name of Arverna (or Arvernis), the city became famous as the bishopric of the Latin poet and letter writer Sidonius Apollinaris. A rich and well-connected native of Lugdunum, who played a prominent part at the courts of emperors and Visigothic kings, he acquired the property of Avitacum in Arvernian territory. He also became prefect of Rome, but in 469 returned to Gaul, where he entered the priesthood and became bishop of Arverna. In this capacity, he helped his brother-in-law Ecdicius (son of the emperor Avitus) to confront a series of sieges by the Visigothic King Euric with stubborn resistance, which lasted four years and only came to an end when the western ruler Julius Nepos ceded the Visigoths the Auvergne and recognized their Gallic and Spanish conquests—only one year before the western empire came to an end in Italy itself. Expressing bitterness over this surrender, Sidonius was arrested and detained for a time in the fortress of Liviana near Carcaso (Carcassonne).

Aulis, a small hilly promontory on the west bank of the Euripus, the narrowest part of the channel that separates mainland Greece from the island of Euboea. To the south lies a deep bay, and to the north a small landlocked harbor.

According to legend, it was here that the Greek fleet collected before setting sail for Troy. But the winds were unfavorable, and the men starved and the ships rotted, until the prophet Calchas disclosed that the Greek commander-in-chief Agamemnon must sacrifice his own daughter Iphigenia to the goddess Artemis, in order to appease her displeasure. The deed was immortalized by the *Agamemnon* of Aeschylus, and Euripides' *Iphigenia at Aulis.* The girl's death formed an essential link in the terrible chain of cause and effect which brought down the house of Agamemnon. The poet Pindar asked whether his murder, at the hands of his wife Clytemnestra, was prompted by what he had done—or by her infatuation for her lover Aegisthus. Throughout subsequent centuries, similar questions have been asked: could Agamemnon have somehow avoided sacrificing his daughter at Aulis, or could he not?

Remains of a Mycenaean settlement and cemetery have been found on the promontory. King Agesilaus of Sparta sacrificed at Aulis before setting out for Asia in 397 BC. The place belonged to Thebes until 387, and then to Tanagra. It depended for its living on potters' workshops, fisheries, and the Sanctuary of Artemis Aulideia, where excavations have revealed a base that may have been used to support a thousand-year-old plane tree mentioned by Pausanias. Nearby was a large hotel for pilgrims.

Ausculum Satrianum, also known as Asculum (Ascoli Satriano). A city in Apulia (Puglia, southeastern Italy) eighteen miles south of Foggia. In the fourth and third centuries BC the indigenous town issued bronze coins, with designs inscribed first in Oscan and then in Greek, including an ear of grain, greyhound, horse's head, boar, head of Heracles and figure of Victory. It was at Ausculum that King Pyrrhus of Epirus, during his invasion of Italy, inflicted his second defeat on the Romans in 279 BC, but thereafter he transferred his forces to Sicily. The city's territories were redistributed by Gaius Gracchus (123/2), plundered during the Social War in which Rome faced a rebellion of its allies (91–87), and again redistributed by Julius Caesar. Local discoveries indicate that the modern town occupies the same site as its ancient forerunner.

Autocratoris *see* Sepphoris

Autun *see* Augustodunum

Avaricum (Bourges, Cher, France). The name of the town was taken from the river Avara (Yèvres), one of a number of tributaries of the river Cher meeting in the marshland below the plateau containing the town, which was connected to terra firma by a land isthmus. Avaricum was the chief center of the tribe of the Bituriges, and during Julius Caesar's invasion the proposal by the Gallic leader Vercingetorix that the place should be evacuated and destroyed was successfully resisted by its inhabitants (52). In consequence he was unable to protect it from Caesar, who stormed its defences after a siege of twenty-seven days and slaughtered the entire population.

A succession of Roman towns, attaining considerable expansion and prosperity, has been disclosed by excavations. Ravaged by German invasions in AD 256–57, Avaricum was compelled to build a rampart, which covered a circumference of 5,500 feet and included forty-six towers.

Avarinos *see* Pylos

Avdira *see* Abdera

Aventicum (Avenches, Vaud, Switzerland). Named after the spring-goddess Aventia, the place was situated beside the marshy plain of the river Braye, near the western end of Lake Morat. Aventicum was founded *c* 16–13 BC by Augustus in the province of Gallia Belgica (later Upper Germany) as the administrative center of the Celtic tribe of the Helvetii, to replace their fortified headquarters on Mount Vully at the northeastern end of the lake; they probably gained certain rights in the new town. Aventicum was garrisoned by a military post guarding roads and a harbor. During the Civil Wars of AD 69 it paid dearly for supporting Vitellius against Vespasian, but the latter restored it with the title of Latin colony, planting a settlement of ex-soldiers entrusted with the defence of the military route from Italy to the Rhine. The city was sacked by the Alamanni in 259–60, but the site was not abandoned, and housed an episcopal see in the sixth century.

Its numerous ancient remains include the temple known as La Grange du Dîme (perhaps dedicated to Mercury or to Celtic goddesses, the Matronae), which before Roman times may have formed part of a larger sanctuary comprising other shrines as well. One of these (Le Cicognier) was rebuilt in the second century AD as part of an elaborate architectural complex, including a theater designed for 9,000 spectators. Trajan's temple of Jupiter (Capitolium), it now seems, was built on the site of first century forum baths. One of these thermal establishments is known from an inscription to have included a building for ball games (*sphaeristerium*). The amphitheater had a capacity of 8,000 spectators. Three forts on the river Aare guarding the approaches to the city may date from the time of Valentinian I (364–75).

Avernus. A lake in a crater with a circumference of five miles near Puteoli (Pozzuoli) in Campania (southwest Italy). Its name, of which the derivation is uncertain, was imaginatively derived from the Greek *aornos* (birdless), owing to the belief (described by Lucretius, Virgil and Nonius Marcellus) that any bird that flew over the lake fell into its waters, killed by the mephitic exhalations that rise from them. These vapors, and supposed bottomless depth of Avernus (it is in fact less than two hundred feet deep), and its situation among dark, gloomy woods rising steeply from its banks, combined to inspire the belief that it led down to the underworld; people would not drink its waters, because they believed they came from the infernal river Styx: Artemidorus calls it the Lake of Acheron (Acherusia). The Cimmerians who were, historically speaking, an Iranian military race of the Eurasian steppes (*see* Scythia), but according to Homer lived in eternal darkness near the land of the dead, were said to have made their homes beside the lake; and Strabo, who reports this, adds that Avernus had also been regarded by earlier writers as the location from which Odysseus descended to Hades (*Odyssey, XII*), or visited an oracle of the dead in the vicinity; and Virgil selects a cave on its banks as the place where Aeneas, too, made his descent.

During the Second Punic War Hannibal visited Avernus—in the course of a reconnaissance of the port of Puteoli (Pozzuoli)—and offered a sacrifice there. The lake had no natural outlet until the time of Octavian (the future Augustus), when the architect and engineer Lucius Cocceius Auctus linked it by a canal to the Lucrine Lake, which Agrippa was converting into a naval anchorage, the Portus Julius. Auctus also cut down the adjoining forest, and constructed an unprecedentedly ambitious tunnel, three quarters of a mile in length and wide enough for chariots to pass through on their way to Cumae (Cuma) on the coast. The tunnel has partially survived, under the name of the Grotta di Cocceio or della Pace (damaged in the Second World War, and now closed), but the canal vanished and Avernus became landlocked again. On its east bank are the ruins of enormous ancient baths, including an octagonal structure probably dating from the time of Hadrian (AD 117–138), with a circular interior surmounted by a dome (now fallen) that spanned one hundred and twenty feet. Propitiary sacrifices to the infernal deities continued even after the empire had become Christian.

Axiopolis, formerly Heraclea, Herakleia (Cernavoda), was situated on a double hill (Sofia) beside the right bank of the lower Danube in Scythia Minor (the Dobrogea in southeastern Rumania). Occupied and fortified in the Bronze and Iron Ages, the site dominates not only the Danube route but also the road leading eastward to Tomis (Constanţa) upon the Euxine (Black) Sea. During the fifth and fourth centuries BC the settlement's cemeteries contained both native (Celtic) material and products of the Greek Euxine cities, testifying to close relations between the two communities. The stronghold of Heraclea was probably established by Alexander the Great during his northern expedition (335).

In Roman times, the fortress provided a base for the naval forces protecting the lower Danube, and was the seat, as we learn from inscriptions, of a corporation (*collegium*) of Danubian sailors. Axiopolis, as it was now called, honored the dynasty of the Severi (AD 193–217). It possessed overlapping forts dating from the times of Constantine the Great (306–37) and Justinian I (527–65). Ease of communication with Tomis was important, and in the fifth or sixth century a great rampart (*vallum*) of earth and stone was constructed between the two cities to protect what was now the flourishing province of Scythia. At the same period the inhabited zone was heavily refortified.

Axius, Axios (Vardar). A principal river of Macedonia, rising in the Šar Mountains (Yugoslavia) and flowing through Paeonia down into the Thermaic Gulf (northern Greece). The district of Bottiaea, which formed part of the coastal plain, extended between the Axius and Haliacmon. One of the important routes that converge on the area came down from the Danube via the Margus (Morava) and Axius valleys.

Axum *see* Ethiopia

Ayaş *see* Elaeusa

Ayion Oros *see* Acte

Azotus, the successor of Ashdod, later known also as Shephelah (Minet el-Kalah), a city of Philistia and then Judaea and Syria Palaestina (southwestern Israel) not far from the ancient coastal road (Way of the Sea, Ways of Horus). An exporter of fish and fabrics, the place was served by three small harbors—Ashdod-yam (Tell-Mor), Minet Isdud, and Nebi Yunis, now amalgamated to form the country's largest seaport. After a long and convulsed history in which it fell successively into the hands of Egyptians, Philistines (who established an important center of the worship of their god Dagon), Israelites and Assyrians, in the seventh century BC it withstood a twenty-year siege from King Psammetichus II of Egypt, recorded by Herodotus. Nehemiah, in the later fifth century, cursed the Jews who had married wives from Ashdod, women who spoke a mixture of languages.

In the Hellenistic period a new, maritime town was founded under the name of Azotus Paralius (By the Sea)—the ancient center, three miles from the coast, being described, by way of distinction, as Azotus Mesogeius (Inland). This inland Azotus was captured and sacked by the Jewish (Hasmonaean) ruler Judas Maccabaeus in 163, and destroyed in 148 by Jonathan Maccabaeus, who burned down the temple of Dagon and established a settlement of Jews. Pompey the Great restored the city's autonomy (64/3), and Herod the Great (37–4) settled ex-soldiers at Azotus Mesogeius and gave the territory to his sister Salome; subsequently it was a possession of Livia, the wife of Augustus, and then of Tiberius, her son and successor, before becoming part of the province of Judaea. In the course of the First Jewish Revolt (AD 66–73) it was captured by the future emperor Vespasian. From the time of Hadrian (117–38) the province was known as Syria Palaestina, and in the later empire Palaestina Prima. During this period Azotus was the seat of a bishopric.

At the Hellenistic and early Roman town of Azotus Mesogeius remains of large public buildings, and private houses as well, have been excavated. Traces of the later Roman and Byzantine periods are scantier in this inland town, suggesting that its coastal counterpart had by then become more important.

Azov, Sea of *see* Mareotis, Lake

B

Baalbek *see* Heliopolis

Babylon is situated on a branch of the river Euphrates a little to the north of the modern town of Hillah (southern Iraq), on a somewhat swampy site where there is a narrow land isthmus between the Euphrates and Tigris. Capital of the empire that bore its name, Babylon continued to prosper after its conquest by Cyrus II the Great of Persia (539), who made it his winter residence and the headquarters of the satrapy of Babylonia. Herodotus visited and described its sights in about 450.

During his conquest of the Persian empire, Alexander the Great entered Babylon without encountering resistance (331), and established a mint; but his plan to rebuild its religious pyramid (ziggurat) and make it the capital of his empire was suspended by his death (323). Two years later Seleucus became governor of the city, which suffered devastation, however, during the conflicts of the period and lost its position, as a major entrepôt of commerce between east and west, to the newly founded Seleucia on the Tigris. Nevertheless, the historic temple of Marduk at Babylon was lavishly restored by the Seleucid monarchs, who also revived the theocratic administration of the shrine in an attempt to gain popular goodwill. They also constructed a Greek theater in the city.

When the Parthians broke away from the Seleucid empire (*c* 247), Babylon passed into their hands, and remained important enough to have its own city-governor. Its scholars also played a significant part in the development of Hellenistic science. Eudoxus of Cnidus (*c* 390–340) had already familiarized the Greeks with the star-worship and astrological practices of the ancient Babylonians, and now Hipparchus of Nicaea (*c* 190-after 126), the greatest astronomer of antiquity, employed records of eclipses preserved by the school of astronomy which still flourished at Babylon. But when Strabo wrote about the city, and Trajan visited it in AD 116, there was little left to see.

Babylonia *see* Babylon, Mesopotamia

Bactra-Zariaspa (Vahlika, Balkh, Wazirabad). A city in northern Afghanistan, on the borderline between highlands and plateau, situated about 1,250 feet above sea level beside the river Bactra (Balkh), which was formerly a tributary of the Oxus (Amu Darya), but is now drawn off into irrigation channels. Bactra-Zariaspa gained importance from the fertility of the adjacent plain and the proximity of routes linking Iran with central Asia, India and China. The place was the headquarters of the Persian satrapy of Bactria, annexed by Alexander the Great. After his death it passed into the hands of Seleucus I Nicator.

When, however, Diodotus I (*c* 256–248) and II (*c* 248–235) made Bactria into a kingdom independent of the Seleucids, Bactra-Zariaspa became the capital of their state, and after the Bactrian and Indo-Greek states had succumbed to eastern invaders, it was the capital of the Kushan empire, or at least of its northern portions. Subsequently, during the Middle Ages, it was the principal city of Khurasan; and its fame as a center of government and learning gained it the title of 'mother of cities.'

Bactria. A flat territory between the Paropamisus (Hindu Kush) mountains and the river Oxus (Amu Darya); now part of northern Afghanistan. Bactria suffers from a severe climate, but stands at the commercial crossroads of Asia; an abundance of abandoned water channels bears witness to the fertility of its agricultural and pastoral lands, and a profusion of mounds recalls its reputation as the 'country of a thousand cities.' In the sixth century BC Bactria, with its capital at Bactra-Zariaspa (Balkh), became a province of the Achaemenid Persian empire; Herodotus describes its soldiers in the army of Darius I (521–486).

When Alexander the Great had defeated the Persian King Darius III Codomannus (336–330), the Bactrian satrap Bessus tried to organize resistance in the east, but without success. However, a serious rebellion of 13,000 Greek mercenary settlers (initiated in Alexander's lifetime and resumed after his death) showed that secessionist tendencies were already at work, impelling Seleucus I (if not Alexander before him) to establish a colony at Aî Khanum. Then, *c* 256, Diodotus I Soter, the Seleucid governor of Bactria (and probably also of Sogdiana to its north), became virtually independent of the Seleucid ruler Antiochus III Theos, and his son Diodotus II (*c* 248–235) in due course replaced the coin-portraits of Antiochus (from whose dominions he was now separated by a newly independent Parthian state) by his own head, and assumed the title of king.

Almost all our information about most of the forty monarchs of this remarkable Hellenistic monarchy and its Indo-Pakistani offshoots is derived from coins. The second and greatest founder of the Bactrian state was Euthydemus I Theos (*c* 235–200)—from western Asia Minor—who incorporated Aria (to the southwest) in his dominions and probed eastward as far as Sinkiang. Subsequently, too, with the help of his 10,000 cavalry, he resisted an invasion by the Seleucid Antiochus III the Great, and obliged him to conclude a treaty. Euthydemus' son Demetrius I (*c* 200–185) annexed part of Arachosia (to the south) from the failing Indian (Mauryan) empire, and his successors profited from its collapse to set up Greek rule east of the Khyber pass, extending ultimately over the whole of northern Pakistan. Thus Eucratides I the Great (*c* 170/165–155) and his famous son Menander Soter Dikaios (*c* 155–140/130) controlled the entire area comprising Bactria and the new Indo-Greek territories. Soon afterward, however, Bactria was invaded by Sacae (Scythians) and permanently detached from the Hellenistic world (while the Yüeh-Chih occupied Sogdiana). A palatial sanctuary of the river-god of the Oxus has recently been discovered at Takhti-Sangin.

Baecula. A town in south-central Spain; usually identified with the modern Bailen, north of the river Baetis (Guadalquivir) in the province of Jaén, though an alternative attribution to Betula, south of the river, has now been suggested.

Baecula was the site of a significant battle between the Romans and Carthaginians during the Second Punic War. In 208 BC Scipio Africanus, after his capture of Carthago Nova (Cartagena) in the previous year, marched westward in the hope of occupying the southern part of the peninsula, but was confronted at Baecula by Hasdrubal Barca. Defeated by an outflanking movement of Scipio (a tactic he later perfected), Hasdrubal succeeded in extricating between one half and two-thirds of his force—and withdrew to the Pyrenees in order to continue the struggle in Italy. The Carthaginians sent reinforcements to Spain but were forced to evacuate the country altogether in the following year.

Baeterrae, formerly Besara (Béziers). A town in southern Gaul (Hérault, France), on the river Orobis (Orb), not far from the coast. Inhabited by Iberians, gradually Celticized, and maintaining early commercial contacts with Massalia (Massilia), the place belonged to the territory of the Longostaletes, a branch of the Volcae Tectosages. In the 120s BC it was incorporated in the Roman province of Gallia Narbonensis, forming a station on the Via Domitia from the Rhodanus (Rhône) to the Pyrenees. In *c* 36/35 Baeterrae received a colony of ex-soldiers, known as Septimanorum since they had belonged to the seventh legion.

The city was easily defensible, and derived prosperity from lucrative farming of its fertile land, as well as from copper and lead mines and the proximity of the ports of Agathe (Agde) and Narbo (Narbonne); Mela included it among the richest cities (*urbes opulentissimae*) of the province (*c* AD 40/45). After suffering devastation, however, in the German invasions of *c* 276, its inhabitants felt obliged to erect fortifications. By this time Baeterrae had its own bishopric, and in 356 it was the meeting place of a church council. In 406/9 it was overrun by Vandals and Alans and in 412/413 passed into the hands of the Visigoths.

There are remains of the walls as well as of an amphitheater, an aqueduct that brought water from a distance of eighteen miles, and a sanctuary on the outskirts of the city dedicated to native gods, including Ricoria, the Matronae, the Menmandutiae, the Digines (identified with Castor and Pollux, the Dioscuri) and a native version of Mars. Baeterrae has also yielded an unusually extensive group of portrait busts of the family of Augustus (now in the museum at Toulouse).

Baetica. The southern part of Spain. After their expulsion of the Carthaginians in 206, the Romans in 197 created two separate commands (entrusted to praetors), one consisting of a narrow eastern coastal strip (Nearer Spain, Hispania

Citerior, later Tarraconensis), and the other comprising the southeast coast and the Baetis (Guadalquivir) valley (Further Spain, Hispania Ulterior). In 27 most of the latter region was made into the senatorial province of Baetica by Augustus, who also, at some later date, instituted a new province of Lusitania in the west of the peninsula. Divided into four judicial regions or *conventus* (Gades, Corduba, Astigi, Hispalis), Baetica was a highly Romanized region, sending numerous exports to Rome.

In the course of the German invasions during the last century of the western empire, the province was occupied in AD 410 by the Siling Vandals under their King Fredbal, but seven years later he was captured by the Visigothic monarch Wallia and sent to the Roman emperor Honorius, and during the two years that followed his Siling subjects were almost exterminated. Soon afterward, however, another group of Vandals, the Asdings, together with the Alans who had joined forces with them as one nation, migrated southward from Callaecia (Galicia) and settled in Baetica, but moved on to north Africa in 429. Then the king of the Visigoths, Euric (466–84), from his capital at Tolosa (Toulouse) in southern Gaul, established his rule in Baetica as well as other parts of Spain except the northwest. Apart from temporary annexations by Theoderic the Ostrogoth (507) and the Byzantine emperor Justinian I (who reconstituted a southern Spanish province in 550), Baetica remained in Visigothic hands until Arabs from north Africa landed in 711. *See also* Baecula, Baetis, Corduba, Gades, Hispalis, Ilipa, Malaca, Munda, Tartessus, Uccubi, Urso.

Baetis (Guadalquivir). The principal river of southern Spain (sometimes known as the **Tartessus**), rising in what is now the province of Jaén and flowing into the Atlantic north of Gades (Cadiz). During the Second Punic War Publius Cornelius Scipio was defeated and killed by the Carthaginians near the upper course of the river (211), though later, in 208, his son Scipio Africanus won the victory—at Baecula (Bailen or Betula) not far from its banks—which drove Hasdrubal Barca from Spain.

After Roman annexation, its rich valley became the nucleus of the province of Further Spain (Hispania Ulterior, later Baetica), of which the cities of Hispalis (Seville) and Corduba (Cordoba) lay on its lower and middle reaches, navigable by large sea-going and river-going ships respectively (smaller sea-going vessels could sail up as far as Ilipa [Alcalá del Rio]. During the Civil War between Julius Caesar and the sons of Pompey the Great the cities of the Baetis valley, with the single exception of Ulia (Montemayor), took the side of the latter until the battle of Munda, to the east of the river, destroyed their cause (45).

Bagradas, formerly Bagrada (Medjerda). The principal river of the central portion of north Africa (now in northern Tunisia), rising in the Medjerda Mountains and debouching into the Gulf of Tunis. The valley was rich in cereals.

During the native rebellion (the Truceless War), led by Matho and Spendius, against the Carthaginians following their defeat by the Romans in the First Punic War, Spendius camped at the only bridge over the Bagradas between Carthage and Utica, but was severely defeated by Hamilcar Barca (240 BC). Spendius was captured and crucified, but in the following year Matho compelled Hamilcar to withdraw to the mouth of the river to protect the communications of the capital. The revolt was not put down until 237. After the final defeat of the Carthaginians in the Third Punic War the Bagradas came within the new Roman province of Africa (146).

Bahnasa *see* Oxyrhynchus

Baiae (Baia). A city in Campania (southwest Italy); situated on an inlet toward the western end of the Gulf of Cumae (Bay of Naples), and separated by a neck of land from Cumae (Cuma, on the Tyrrhenian Sea), of which it may originally have been a dependency. It owed its name, according to legend, to Baios the navigator of Odysseus.

Situated on a hillside sloping down to the shore, the place became a highly fashionable resort for wealthy Romans in the first century BC onward, because of its medicinal springs (already exploited from *c* 200, or earlier) and mild climate and attractive surroundings. Owners of houses in the neighborhood included Marius, Cicero, Pompey the Great, Julius Caesar, and the emperors Gaius (Caligula), Nero and Severus Alexander. Gaius (AD 37–41) had a famous bridge of boats constructed from Baiae to Puteoli (Pozzuoli) for an extravagant parade. Nero (54–68), whose palace possessed its own oyster beds and fishing-lakes (depicted on glass bottles), used the pretext of the annual festival of Minerva at Baiae to invite his mother to dinner there, before arranging for her murder at Bauli nearby (59); and he allegedly poisoned his aged aunt Domitia in order to inherit her Baiae estates, on which he constructed a handsome gymnasium. Hadrian died in the neighborhood in 138. A large part of the region was imperial property.

Cicero identified Baiae with every sort of luxurious entertainment and loose living. Horace praised its alluring charms; and descriptions of its villas are provided by Seneca and Martial. Excavations have revealed a vast group of buildings, extending over two centuries, which have been identified as portions of a palace constructed by one of the emperors; three rooms, the 'Stanze di Venere,' are notable for their stuccoed vaults. Adjoining monumental complexes have been interpreted as separate but coordinated thermal establishments: the institutions which made Baiae, in the late Republic and early Principate, the most important and famous medicinal bathing resort in the Mediterranean world, equipped with every curative, residential and recreational amenity. These buildings have, in modern times, been named the Baths of Sosandra, Venus and Mercury. The so-called Baths of Sosandra (or Acque della Rogna) are on three levels, united by grand staircases and ramps. A 'Temple of Venus' is externally square but internally circular, and a large 'Temple of Mercury' has a circular plan both within and without. The nearby 'Temple of Diana' displays an octagonal exterior. Like other parts of the so-called Baths, these three 'temples,' or the first two of them, have generally been identified as portions of the thermal establishments mentioned above, but it has lately been suggested that they instead formed part of the imperial palace. Recent finds include a well-preserved statue of Dionysus, discovered under water, and an unusual assemblage of plaster statuary, comprising casts of Greek bronze originals, intended for copyists at work on marble reproductions.

Baiae, like neighboring Puteoli, experienced (as it still does) the gradual earth movements known as bradyseism (slow earthquake), and since Roman times the sea has moved more than a hundred yards inland. These encroachments and other seismic disturbances, together with the fevers which (according to Cicero) had already been present in Republican times, eventually caused Baiae's decline and ruin, although the use of its therapeutic waters continued without intermission until modern times.

Bailen *see* Baecula

Bakir Çayı *see* Caicus (River)

Baláca *see* Pannonia

Balad Sinjar *see* Singara

Balat *see* Miletus

Balda *see* Paltos

Balearic Islands (Baliares, later Baleares), known as Gymnesiai by earlier Greek travelers because their inhabitants went naked (*gymnos*) in summer. The islands were also known as Aphrodisiades, Hyasousai, and Choirades. The most important of them were Majorica (earlier Kromyoussa and Columba, later Insula [Balearis] Major, now Mallorca [Majorca]), Minorica (earlier Meloussa and Nura, later Insula Minor, now Menorca [Minorca]), and Ebusus (now Iviza or Ibiza).

As a whole range of recent excavations confirms, the two largest islands exhibited extremely vigorous Bronze Age and Iron Age cultures, manifested by three distinctive types of monument found especially on Minorica, the *naveta* (a megalithic chamber tomb shaped like an upturned boat, *c* 1800–1200), the *talayot* (a tower, first round and then square [*c* 850], containing one and then two corbelled cells, also to be seen on Majorica), and the *taula* (a T-shaped structure sometimes attaining a height of twelve feet). This native civilization persisted far into historic times. Meanwhile the Iberian settlements—notably Tuci on Majorica and Sanisera on Minorica—were supplemented by townships displaying Carthaginian influence, brought largely by Balearic troops who served as mercenaries in Carthaginian armies (480, 409) and returned with Punic customs, exemplified by the child necropolis at Cas Santamarier (Son Onis) on Majorica. Settlements of Carthaginian type were Bocchori and Guium (or Guintum) on Majorica, and Mago and Jamo on Minorica. During the Second Punic War, however, Majorica favored Rome; after the War, the islands passed by treaty to the Romans, and were effectively brought into the province of Hispania Citerior (later known as Tarraconensis; Nearer Spain) in 123/2 by Quintus Caecilius Metellus, who took the name of Balearicus, settled 3,000 Italians at Palma and Pollentia (Pollensa) on Majorica, and celebrated a triumph in 121.

Under Augustus, famine caused by a plague of rabbits required military intervention. In the first century AD the islands were employed as places of banishment. Vespasian gave the cities Latin rights (under which their elected officials became Roman citizens). Diocletian (284–305) created a separate Balearic province. In about 416 persecutions of the Jews in Minorica are recorded. The Vandals, who had first attacked the islands in 411, were in possession of them by 467. Balearic wine was regarded as comparable to the best Italian products; and the islands were also well-known for their snails and dye works.

Ebusus and the smaller Ophiussa (Colubraria, now Formentera), the two islands known as the Pityussae ('pine-islands'), lay to the west of Majorica and Minorica and to some extent led a life of their own. On Ebusus, the fortified city of the same name, rising above its port, was established *c* 654/3 BC by the Phoenicians (Carthaginians), whose cemetery at Ereso on the Puig de Molins (Windmill Hill) contains more than 5,000 tombs dating from the fifth to the second centuries BC, in addition to terracottas, including busts of Demeter and Persephone. Unlike Majorica, Ebusus showed sympathy to Carthage during the Second Punic War, which resulted, however, in the supersession of the defeated Carthaginians. Ebusus possessed a harbor at Portus Magnus on the north coast, and under Augustus and Tiberius (and possibly a little later as well) issued its own local bronze coinage. Under the reorganization of Diocletian the Pityussae were united with the rest of the Balearic group to form the separate province bearing its name.

The Ebusans, according to Pliny the Elder, were fond of a fish called *salpa,* elsewhere considered unfit to eat; and its soil, he added, possessed the property of destroying poisonous snakes. In this respect it presumably differed from the other of the two Pityussae islands, of which the name, Ophiussa (Colubraria), means 'snake-land.'

Balhisar *see* Pessinus

Balkh *see* Bactra-Zariaspa

Balkıs *see* Zeugma

Balkız *see* Cyzicus

Bambyce *see* Hieropolis (Syria)

Banasa (Sidi Ali bou Djenoun). In southwestern Mauretania Tingitana (Morocco), on the left (south) bank of the Oued Sebou, in the fertile Rharb plain. A Mauretanian village established for some centuries—producing a characteristic form of painted pottery, inspired by Carthaginian and Iberian wares—Banasa, under the name of Valentia, received a colony of ex-soldiers from Octavian (Augustus; in 33–25 BC—during the interval between the reigns of the Mauretanian kings Bocchus and Juba), and was resettled as Colonia Aurelia by

Marcus Aurelius (161–80). In 284/5, however, after destruction by native tribesmen, the place was abandoned, and the frontier of Diocletian's small province of Tingitania withdrawn to Lixus (Larache) farther north.

The plan of the city, first apparent from photographs taken during World War II, recalls a military camp, bearing witness to the importance of Banasa at the center of the defensive frontier line. The forum and adjacent buildings are relatively well preserved. Bakeries and private houses, of Roman and Mauretanian design, have also been unearthed. But the principal significance of Banasa derives from the discovery of two legal texts. One is the so-called Tabula Banasitana, of the time of Marcus Aurelius, which indicates the grants of Roman citizenship to a Berber chief and his family, defining the conditions under which such non-citizens could be granted the franchise, and throwing light on the workings of the imperial council and government; and the other inscription is an edict of Caracalla (216) exempting the inhabitants of Banasa from taxation.

Banoštor *see* Bononia-Malata

Banyas *see* Caesarea Philippi

Barce *see* Ptolemais

Barcino (Barcelona) on the coast of Catalonia, northeastern Spain. Traditions of Greek and Phoenician (Carthaginian) origin are dubious; more probably the town was founded by the native (Iberian) tribe of the Laietani, who issued a silver coinage there at the end of the second century BC, inscribed BARKENOS. Then, after passing from Carthaginian into Roman hands, and becoming part of the province of Nearer Spain (Hispania Citerior, later Tarraconensis), the place received colonial privileges, as inscriptions have confirmed, during the later Republic and then again from Augustus; the colony bore the names Pia Faventia and then Julia Augusta, and its territory extended from the river Baetulo (Besós) to the Rubricatus (Llobregat). In the second century AD Barcino's excellent harbor, and its strategic position on the road between Tarraco (Tarragona) and Narbo (Narbonne), endowed it with considerable importance.

In 265 the city was destroyed by the Franks and Alamanni, but the powerful fortifications that were subsequently built (and have now been partially restored) enabled it to supersede Tarraco as the most important city in eastern Spain. For a brief period in 409–11 Barcino became a mint, employed by the usurper Maximus, a puppet of the general Gerontius. In 414 Ataulf, under pressure from Roman armies in Gaul, led his Visigoths southward to Barcino, but in the following year he was murdered there in his stables. 'Barcinona,' however, became the Visigothic capital; its seizure in 444 by a Roman adventurer Sebastianus (the son-in-law of the general Bonifatius) was only short-lived.

Remains of the ancient town, including numerous inscriptions, can still be seen. Traces of a Roman temple have recently been uncovered, and in the patio of the archiepiscopal palace portions of a house have come to light: dating back to Augustan times, it was reconstructed *c* 100 and modified three centuries later. Large Roman villa-farms have been excavated to the north, northeast and northwest of the city.

Basilia (Basel in Switzerland). On the left bank of the Rhenus (Rhine), on a spur between that river and the Birsig. A walled settlement in the territory of the Raurici (*see* Augusta Rauricorum). In connection with the German campaigns of Tiberius and Nero Drusus (Drusus senior), the stepsons of Augustus, in 15 BC, a small fort was constructed at Basilia, and it was again garrisoned in the first century AD and gained new importance after the collapse of the Upper German frontier in the mid-third century.

The place became a significant link in the Rhine defence system of Valentinian I, who after operations against the Alamanni built a fortress at Robur (near Hüningen) nearby (374). Early in the following century the bishop of Augusta Rauricorum moved his see to Basilia, and under the secular power of the episcopate the importance of the town continued to increase.

The Münster hill has yielded ancient finds dating from Raurican times; excavations have revealed a two-storeyed granary with two rows of columns, belonging to the late Roman fortress.

Basilicata *see* Lucania

Basiliko *see* Sicyon

Bassae, Bassai ('the glens'). In southwestern Arcadia (Peloponnese, southern Greece). The site (Styli, 'pillars') is on a high ridge southeast of the city of Phigalia. The place was occupied by a sanctuary, of which the most noteworthy element is a temple of Apollo, one of the best preserved Greek shrines.

Its dating has been the subject of much discussion, but it now appears that three successive edifices (*c* 625–575, 500 BC) preceded the present building, which was constructed in the later fifth century (with subsequent adjustments). According to Pausanias, the temple was erected by the Phigalians and dedicated to Apollo (Epikourios, 'the Helper') to thank him for averting the plague that afflicted Athens in 430. He adds that the architect was Ictinus, who designed the Parthenon, but it is now believed (partly on the evidence of pottery fragments) that the work was carried out (or at least completed) by a younger assistant, *c* 420 or later. The structure is curiously elongated, and provides the earliest known example of the Corinthian capital in ancient architecture—though the specimen in question is now lost. The principal glory of the building, however, was its sculptured frieze which (according to a formula that was a novelty in that epoch) encircled the interior of the inner sanctuary (*cella*); it depicted battles of Greeks against Amazons, and Lapiths against Centaurs.

A French architect rediscovered the ruined site in 1765, but was later murdered by brigands; further expeditions took place in 1811–1812, after which the British Museum acquired the frieze at an auction at Zacynthus (Zante). The shrine of Apollo lies beneath the peak of Mount Kotilios; higher up was the precinct of Kotilion, dedicated to Artemis Orthia and Aphrodite, whose sanctuaries were erected at the same time as Apollo's first temple. Unexplored parts of the region have lately been examined by air photography.

Bassit, Basit *see* Posidium

Batavia. The country of the German tribe of the Batavi (an offshoot of the Chatti); the 'Island of the Batavians,' almost a hundred miles long, lies between the Old Rhenus (Rhine) and the Vatialis (Waal), but with extensions down to the mouths of the Mosa (Meuse, Maas) and Scheldt Rivers (the district of Betuwe in the Netherlands preserves their name).

They assisted Augustus' stepson Nero Drusus (Drusus senior) in his invasion of Germany in 12 BC, and their territory remained part of the Roman empire after other trans-Rhenane lands were evacuated in AD 9. They again helped Nero Drusus' son Germanicus in 16, and by the middle of the century were organized into auxiliary regiments of the Roman army under their own chiefs, in addition to providing members of the emperors' personal German bodyguard. In 69, however, one of their leaders, Gaius Civilis, of royal descent, led them into fomenting a major Gallo-German revolt against Rome that scored impressive successes before it was finally stamped out. Subsequently they faded from history; in 275/6 their territory was abandoned by the Romanized population to the Franks (later repulsed temporarily by Constantius I, who concluded a treaty with their chieftain Gennobaudes [288]).

Bath *see* Aquae Sulis

Bedriacum or Betriacum (Tornata), a small village in north Italy, north of the Padus (Po), commanding a road junction of the Via Postumia halfway between Cremona and Mantua (Mantova). It has given its name to two decisive battles that took place during the Civil Wars of AD 69. In the first (April), the generals of Vitellius defeated those of Otho, who committed suicide after the battle. In the second engagement (October) Antonius Primus, acting on behalf of Vespasian, defeated the Vitellians in equally conclusive fashion, thus launching the Flavian dynasty. But neither engagement took place in the immediate vicinity of Bedriacum, and they are better described as the First and Second Battles of Cremona. A number of excavations have taken place in recent decades.

Begram *see* Alexandria Beside Caucasus

Behramkale *see* Assus

Beit-Shan, Beit-Shean *see* Scythopolis

Belevi *see* Ephesus

Belgica, Gallia. After Julius Caesar had conquered the northern and central parts of Transalpine Gaul (Gallia Comata, 'long-haired,' as opposed to Narbonensis [S. France] and Cisalpina [N.Italy]), Augustus divided it into three provinces (Aquitania [S.E.], Lugdunensis [center and N.W.], and Belgica [N.E.]).

The most important center of Gallia Belgica proper was Augusta Trevirorum (Trier). At first, however, the region immediately west of the Rhine, comprising the military commands of Upper and Lower Germany, also came, officially, under the administration of Gallia Belgica. When, however (following the withdrawal of the frontier to the Rhine in AD 9), the fortresses on that river were converted into important permanent camps, the two commanders in question became virtually autonomous, until eventually their commands became separate provinces of Upper and Lower Germany (*c* AD 90), although as far as financial administration was concerned the new units still came under the authorities of Gallia Belgica. In the reorganizations of Diocletian and Constantine, Belgica was divided into two provinces, Prima and Secunda.

Belgorod Dniestrovsky *see* Tyras

Belgrade (Beograd) *see* Singidunum

Belkis *see* Aspendus, Cyzicus

Benacus (Garda). The largest of the Italian lakes, thirty-two miles long and ten miles wide at its greatest breadth, approaching the Alps to the north and flanked by Brixia (Brescia) and Verona to the southwest and southeast respectively. The river Sarca feeds the lake from the north, and from its southern extremity the Mincius (Mincio) flows out to the Padus (Po). The lakeside was a favorite residence of the poet Catullus (d. *c* 54 BC), who immortalized the promontory of Sirmio (Sirmione) at its southern extremity. In AD 268 the emperor Claudius II Gothicus opposed the invading Alamanni by advancing with his legions to the lake, where he defeated them so severely that only half their number succeeded in retreating across the Alps; whereupon, having freed Italy from the threat of devastation, he assumed the title Germanicus Maximus.

Beneventum, formerly Malventum (Benevento). A city in western Apulia (southern Italy), forty miles east-northeast of Neapolis (Naples), at the junction of the rivers Calor (Calore) and Sabato, amid a half-circle of mountains. Reputedly founded by Odysseus' companion Diomedes (according to a legend that may reflect origins traceable to Illyricum, with which Diomedes was associated), the place became the chief center of the Hirpini (a branch of the Samnite peoples), who knew it as Malies, later Malventum. Fragments of pottery have recently provided the first clear evidence of this pre-Roman habitation.

It was at Malventum that the Romans fought their last battle against King Pyrrhus of Epirus (275 BC) which, although indecisive, impelled him to withdraw southward, on his way back to his homeland. Seven years later, a Latin colony was founded at the place: together with Ariminum (Rimini), established at the same time, it was the most distant from Rome of any colony that had so far been created. At the same time, regarding Malventum as an ill-omened name (sounding like 'bad air'—although it was an Illyrian word meaning 'mountain town'), the Romans changed its name to the more auspicious Beneventum ('happy event'). A key communications center located on a number of important roads, including the earliest extension of the Via Appia—Rome's principal route to south Italy—Beneventum became a military base that remained staunchly loyal during the Second Punic War (218-201) and Social War (91-87), gaining colonial rights under the Second Triumvirate (41), which were later confirmed by Augustus. Subsequently the Via Trajana (AD 109) replaced the Via Appia as the main road between Beneventum and Brundusium (Brindisi).

The most important of Beneventum's Roman monuments is the Porta Aurea, Trajan's triumphal arch—one of the finest and best-preserved of its kind—erected at the point where the Via Trajana entered the city, and adorned with a scheme of reliefs celebrating the emperor's various activities in Italy and the provinces. The city also contains other Roman remains including a theater (begun by Hadrian [117-38] and enlarged by Caracalla [211-17] and a bridge (still surviving, though much repaired) over which the Via Trajana, a little beyond the arch, crossed a tributary of the Calore. The museum contains sculptures from a temple of Isis. Beneventum was partially destroyed by Attila the Hun in 452.

Benghazi *see* Euhesperides

Berenice (Cyrenaica) *see* Euhesperides

Berenice (Madinet el-Haras, below Ras Benas). A port on the west coast of the Red Sea, six hundred miles southeast of the Nile delta: known as 'Berenice of the Trogodytes' (not the Troglodytes, or cave dwellers, as was commonly stated), the name vaguely given to various primitive black peoples of this and other African territories. The city was founded by Ptolemy II Philadelphus (283-246 BC) and named after his mother Berenice I, the wife of Ptolemy I Soter. In the first and second centuries AD, under Roman rule, it became the principal Egyptian landing place for goods from Arabia, India and east Africa. They were carried northward by camel caravan to Leukos Limen (White Harbor, now Kuseir), and then west across the desert hills to Coptos (Keft) on the Nile, along a road made or remade by Ptolemy II and provided with water cisterns (to collect such rainwater as fell) and military posts, which supervised the collection of taxes.

Elephants brought to Berenice from remoter Red Sea regions, and from Somaliland, on specially constructed boats were also transported along the same roads; having discharged the elephants, the boats left the port carrying cargoes of grain for outlying coastal stations. In 30, after the defeat of Antony and Cleopatra VII by Octavian (the future Augustus), Cleopatra's son Ptolemy XV Caesar—known as Caesarion and claimed by the queen to have been fathered by Julius Caesar—was dispatched to Berenice so that he could escape to the east.

But Octavian sent messengers who decoyed him back to Alexandria, where he was put to death.

The harbor of Berenice was protected from pirates by a fortification. A temple in the city was dedicated to the Egyptian god Khnem by the emperor Tiberius (AD 14–37). At Sakait nearby, a temple carved out of the rock was dedicated to Serapis and Isis, and sacrifices were offered to the goddess of the local emerald mines. *See also* Pella (Jordan).

Berezan *see* Olbia

Bergama *see* Pergamum

Beroe Augusta Trajana. In northern Thrace (now Stara Zagora in Bulgaria, between Sofia and Bourgas). Originally a Macedonian town named Beroe (or Beroea), the place was situated in a fertile plain beside the foot of the Balkan range (Mt. Haemus), at a crossroads of north-south and east-west routes. The population of Beroe was mainly Greek, coming from Ionia and northern Macedonia. In AD 46 it formed part of the new Roman province of Thrace. The additional names Sebaste Traiane (Augusta Trajana), found on inscriptions and local coins from the later second century onward, indicate the receipt of privileges not, it appears, from Trajan (because the place is not mentioned by the geographer Ptolemy) but from his successor Hadrian (AD 117–38). In 250 Trajanus Decius, in his war against Kniva King of the Goths, was surprised by the enemy while resting his men and horses, and suffered such a grave defeat that he could barely make his escape northward to the Danube. During the first Civil War between Constantine I the Great and Licinius (314 or 316), the two rivals confronted each other with large armies at Beroe, but came to a temporary agreement without fighting. The war was resumed, however, in 324.

During the second half of the fourth century AD Beroe was the second center of Thrace in size and splendor, after Philippopolis (Plovdiv). A bishopric of the city was mentioned at the Council of Serdica (Sofia) in 344, and Pope Liberius, enemy of the Arians, whom he deemed heretics, lived there in exile from 355 to 358. When the Visigoths rose against the eastern emperor Valens, his western colleague Gratian sent Frigeridus to build a fortress near Beroe, while another of his generals, Sebastianus, destroyed a Visigothic force on its way to a fortified camp between that city and Hadrianopolis (Edirne) (377): but this did not save Valens from destruction at Hadrianopolis in the following year. After the disaster, Beroe was again threatened by the Visigoths. But it survived, and subsequently became an important Byzantine military headquarters. Remains of the ancient city have increasingly come to light, including fortifications (169) and an Augusteum (235). A military gateway with three towers appears on a coin of Caracalla (211–17).

Beroea, Berrhoia (Verria). In the Macedonian territory of Bottiaea, near the left bank of the river Haliacmon, at a crossroads on the eastern foothills of Mount Bermion (Vermion). The place was allegedly named after the daughter of the mythical king Beres, during the Macedonian settlement of these hillsides *c* 700 BC. A passage in Thucydides suggests that Beroea was of military importance in 432, when it was attacked by an Athenian force during the rebellion of Potidaea. It was here that the Macedonian army deserted Demetrius I Poliorcetes in favor of Pyrrhus of Epirus (288).

After the defeat of Macedonia's King Philip V at Pydna (168), Beroea was one of the first cities that went over to the Romans. From the time of Augustus onward it enjoyed prosperity as the seat of the Council (*koinon*) of Macedonia, which issued its own coins from AD 44 onward, mostly designed for the great provincial shrine at Beroea. According to an inscription, one of the Council's officials, Gaius Popillius Python, was sent to the emperor Nerva (96–98), before whom he successfully advanced the city's claims to the titles of Metropolis and Neokoros (protector of the imperial temple). Five gold medallions of Caracalla (211–17), found at Aboukir in Egypt, were prizes in games held at Beroea. Subsequently, the city's name appears on the three final mintages of the Council issued in honor of the celebration of further games under Gordian III in 242, a visit by Philip the Arab in 244, and another series of games two years later.

Recent archaeological finds confirm the activity of the town in the fifth century BC. Other ancient remains include substantial portions of Roman roads. Works by a family of Beroean sculptors have been discovered over a wide area of ancient Greece. Notable in Christian history as the place to which St. Paul withdrew after his expulsion from Thessalonica (Salonica), Beroea soon became the seat of a bishopric, and a large early Christian basilica has now been uncovered. During the Byzantine period the city continued to prosper, ranking second only to Thessalonica among Macedonian centers.

Berytus (Beirut). A harbor town on the coast of Phoenicia, between Byblos (Jebeil) and Saida (Sidon), at the foot of Mount Libanus (Lebanon). In Hellenistic times Berytus was a mint of Ptolemy II Philadelphus (289/288–246 BC), and Ptolemy V Epiphanes (205–180), and then of the Seleucids (after receiving the name of Laodicea in Phoenice, probably from Seleucus IV, 187–175). Their coinage continued until the reign of Antiochus VIII Grypus (121–96). The merchants of Berytus travelled far and wide, forming a rich community, for example, at Hellenistic Delos. The city celebrated a new era dating from 81/80 BC, which was intended to signalize its return to Ptolemaic allegiance (under Ptolemy XI Nothos). Subsequently, Berytus coined with the head of Cleopatra VII in 32–31, just before she and Antony were defeated by Octavian (the future Augustus) at Actium.

In 14 Augustus established a Roman colony of ex-soldiers there, to the south and west of the former Hellenistic town, and entrusted it with a large territory, including, initially, the great shrine of Heliopolis (Baalbek). The abundance and variety of the colony's long-lasting bronze coinage bears witness to its commercial prosperity (in competition with Tyre), based on the export of wine and manufacture of textiles, including silk, of which the raw materials were brought in from China. From the third century AD onward the city also became famous for its school of Roman law (in addition to academies of rhetoric and medicine), which, although Berytus was only a Latin island in a Semitic ocean—and although its students were notoriously dissolute—played a large part in the development of the empire's judicial doctrine, counting Ulpian among its professors and Eusebius and Ammianus Marcellinus among its students. This activity continued until the time of the Byzantine emperor Justinian I, when the city was ravaged by an earthquake (551).

The Hellenistic town had lain south of its port, and the Roman city spread further to the south and west. It was presented with lavish buildings by the Jewish monarchs Herod the Great, Agrippa I and II and Queen Berenice, but very few of these splendors survived, even before the recent bombardments. However, a pagan basilica three hundred feet in length has been found, including its Corinthian portico, which has been reerected in front of the museum; and baths, a hippodrome and villas have also been uncovered. The podium of a large temple can be seen upon the 'high place' of the city (Deir el-Qalaa).

Besançon *see* Vesontio

Bethar, Bether (Bittir, known to local Arabs as the 'Jewish ruins'). In Judaea (Israel), seven miles south-southwest of Jerusalem, guarding the entrance to the Wadi Sorek. Guidebooks wrongly identify the place with Beth-zur, mentioned in the Book of Joshua; the 'Hills of Bether' may, however, figure in a disputed passage of the *Song of Songs.*

During the reign of Hadrian, as Eusebius records, the Second Jewish Revolt against the Romans, known to the Jews as the Second Roman War, terminated in the prolonged siege of the Jewish leader Bar Kosiba—known as Bar Kochba, son of a star—inside Bethar (134/5; not for three and a half years as tradition maintained). Bethar was a town large enough to have a council (Sanhedrin) of its own, and its population was no doubt swollen by refugees; it occupied a good defensive position protected on three sides by ravines and on the fourth by a ditch. The Romans sealed off the town with a two-and-a-half mile circumvallation—of which traces can still be seen—supported by two siege camps capable of accommodating a legion and half a legion respectively. The Roman army also built a ramp on which battering rams were erected. But treachery was suspected among the besieged Jews, who put to death Bar Kosiba's uncle, allegedly backed by members of the Samaritan sect. Finally the town fell, and many of its defenders were massacred. The numbers of those who died were magnified still further in Jewish literature, which alleged that their blood flowed down to the sea (since this was forty miles away, the siege has instead been ascribed by some, over-literally, to a second Bethar, close to the shore).

Eusebius seems to suggest that Bar Kosiba was captured and executed after the place had been overrun, although an alternative tradition maintained that he was killed while the siege was still in progress. His body, another story recounted, had a snake coiled around it when it was shown to the emperor, who cried out: 'If his God had not killed him, who could have overcome him?' After Bethar had fallen, Hadrian was hailed *imperator* by his troops for the second time.

Beziers *see* Baeterrae

Bibracte (Mont Beuvray). A town in central Gaul (France). Bibracte, which dominates the surrounding countryside, provides access to the Sequana (Saône) and Liger (Loire: the two rivers after which the modern Department is named) and to the Yonne, was the capital of the Aedui, the Gallic tribe that occupied most of modern Burgundy. Julius Caesar, during his invasion of Gaul, was given valuable assistance by the Aedui. But their support proved less than wholehearted, and in 52 BC their principal town Bibracte was selected for the meeting of a 'council of all Gaul' which appointed Vercingetorix as commander-in-chief of the armies resisting the Roman invasion.

Remains of the Gallic settlement have come to light, including the traces of a temple—probably dedicated to the goddess for whom the city was named. Houses, both of Gaulish and of Roman type, have also been discovered, as well as shops—on either side of the main road—and centers of metalworking and enamelling industries, which probably formed the staple activity of Bibracte. Its wall extended for three miles around the mountain. After resistance to Caesar had collapsed, the inhabitants were transferred to Augustodunum (Autun), a new town in the plain, seventeen miles to the east-southwest. Inscriptions at Augustodunum kept the name of the goddess Bibracte alive, but at Bibracte, too, her temple continued to be frequented, especially on the occasion of annual fairs.

Bhir *see* Taxila

Bichvint *see* Pityus

Bilbilis (Calatayud). A city in northeastern Spain, on a rocky height, at the junction of the river Birbilis (Jiloca) with the Salo (Jalón), which flows on to join the Iberus (Ebro) forty miles to the northeast. Of elongated shape climbing irregularly up the mountainside, Bilbilis was originally an Iberian town. It was the scene of fighting during the Roman civil war between Quintus Sertorius and Sulla's general Quintus Caecilius Metellus Pius, whose capture of the place in 74 BC helped to pave the way for Sertorius' eventual defeat.

Bilbilis, which had already served as an Iberian mint, coined as a Roman *municipium* under Augustus and Tiberius. But it was chiefly notable as the place where the poet Martial (*c* AD 40–104) was born and where he retired from Rome to die, on a rural property presented by a patron Marcella. He describes his hometown as 'renowned for horses and armor,' 'excellent in steel for war,' and 'proud of its gold and iron'—which the river Salo was famous for tempering. Ausonius (d. 395) mentions the site as desolate and abandoned. Excavations have revealed a temple and hydraulic works; a theater has now been completely uncovered.

Birten *see* Vetera

Bithynia. A region of northwestern Asia Minor. The name originally referred to the peninsula of Chalcedon (Kadıköy), but was extended to a much larger region adjoining the Propontis (Sea of Marmara), the Thracian Bosphorus and the Euxine (Black) Sea, and reaching southward to Mount Olympus (Keşiş Dağı) in Mysia. The country was divided into two sections by the river Sangarius (Sakarya), the flatter western part containing the majority of the inhabitants. The Bithynians, records Scylax of Caryanda, were formerly Mysians, but received their new name from Thracian Thynians or Bithynians—in the fourth century BC, according to Xenophon, the north coast was still called Thrace in Asia—who fought continually against the Greek colonists on their coast and became nominal, recalcitrant subjects of the Persian empire in the sixth century BC. In the fourth century, according to Xenophon, the northern Bithynian coastland was still called Thrace in Asia. The Bithynian leader Zipoetes (328–280) avoided submission to Alexander the Great, successfully resisted his successor Lysimachus, and assumed the title of king (297), repelling Seleucus I Nicator, founder of the Seleucid empire. Nicomedes I (280–255) took the perilous step of inviting the Gauls (Galatians) into Asia Minor. Nevertheless, his kingdom, ruled from Nicomedia (İzmit), survived, and increasingly assumed the appearance of a Greek state. It achieved its maximum dimensions, political power and trading wealth under Prusias I Cholus (the Lame) (*c* 230–182). In spite of the presence of the Carthaginian Hannibal (d. 183/2) as a refugee at his court, Prusias avoided a breach with the Romans. Successive monarchs increasingly fell under their influence, until Nicomedes IV Philopator bequeathed them his kingdom in 75/4. It was annexed as a Roman province and united with Pontus in 63.

In the second century AD, twenty-nine Bithynian cities issued their own bronze coinage. However, to put a stop to their mismanagement of their own affairs, the emperor Trajan dispatched Pliny the Younger to the territory as special commissioner (*c* 110–12), and their subsequent correspondence included a famous exchange of letters about the local Christian community. Under Hadrian, Bithynia enjoyed marked imperial favor as the native country of Antinous, whom he loved. There was intense rivalry between Nicomedia and Nicaea (İznik), both of which claimed to be the first city of Bithynia; but the latter displayed its leading role when it became the location of Constantine I the Great's historic Christian Council in 325.

Bithynia possessed useful harbors and land communications, and enjoyed varied agricultural crops, extensive pasturage, abundant supplies of timber, and quarries of fine marble.

Bittir *see* Bethar

Bizye (Vize). A city in Thrace, equidistant between Byzantium (İstanbul, to its southeast) and Hadrianopolis (Edirne, to its northwest). It was the home of the mythological King Tereus, whose wife Procne, as punishment for the seduction of her sister Philomela, served him up their son at a feast, whereupon they escaped his vengeance by turning into a nightingale and a swallow, or vice versa. A sacred precinct of local Thracian divinities seems to go back to the years before 500 BC. In the third century, if not earlier, Bizye became the capital of Astice, the country of the Thracian people of the Astae, whose lands extended between the Propontis (Sea of Marmara) and the Black Sea; a burial tumulus containing gold, silver and bronze articles is attributable to one of their kings. The claim that Bizye had been founded by Greek colonists from Mesembria (Nessebur) seems to have been fictitious.

At one time client kings dependent on the inland Odrysians, the rulers of the Astae reemerged in the first century BC as the second most powerful family in Thrace, united by marriage with the kings of the Sapaci (on the Thraco-Macedonian border), who also, for a time, controlled the Bessi in the interior of the country. In this period Bizye enjoyed considerable prosperity, becoming, in the later years of the century, the capital of King Cotys of the Astae (who married a daughter of the king of the Sapaci, bearing the same name). When the Bessi, conquered by Marcus Lollius (19/18), broke away from the control of the Astae, Augustus reunited the country under the Astican royal house, which continued to rule (after a temporary division) until the Romans decided upon annexation in AD 44/6; inscriptions found at Bizye illustrate the dynasty's complicated relationships. Under the reorganization of the province by Trajan (98–117), the city assumed the additional name of his family Ulpia. In the later empire it was included in the province of Europa, and in 431 a bishop of Bizye is recorded, enjoying authority over other ecclesiastical centers in the region.

Substantial remains of the ancient fortifications have survived, mostly of imperial date but going back to Hellenistic times. The main gateway is shown on a coin of Antoninus Pius (138-61), and an issue of Philip I (244–49) offers a remarkable view of the city within the circuit of its walls, which are studded with seven towers.

Black Sea *see* Euxine Sea

Bodrum *see* Halicarnassus, Hieropolis Castabala

Boeotia. A district of 1,119 square miles in central Greece bordering upon Attica to the southeast (across Mounts Cithaeron and Parnes), the Gulf of Corinth to the south and the Gulf of Euboea to the east, Locris to the north, and Phocis to the west. The strategically located, relatively fertile Boeotian heartland consisted of the plains of Thebes and Orchomenus (on Lake Copais, now drained), which produced good grain and olives and bred horses. The importance of the country in the Bronze Age is reflected in an extraordinary wealth of myths, mainly relating, as far as we are aware of them, to Thebes, since most of the mythology of Orchomenus is lost: the principal foundation story relates to Cadmus, son of Agenor of Tyre, and sower of the dragons' teeth that sprouted the first Theban aristocracy.

Twenty-nine small towns of the Boiotoi (and their names) are preserved in the *Iliad*'s catalog of the Achaeans (which may owe its origin to the region), but in classical times the independent cities numbered about a dozen, dominated in varying degrees by Thebes, which became the administrative center of a Boeotian League, issuing its first federal coinage in the later sixth century BC. Although Boeotia was famous for musicians and poets, notably Hesiod of Ascra and Pindar of Cynoscephalae, its inhabitants tended to be a self-contained agricultural people who did not share in the overseas expansion of Greece, and sided with the enemy in the Persian Wars, after which their victorious Greek compatriots disbanded the Boeotian League. It was reconstituted, however, *c* 447/6 to take Sparta's side against Athens in the Peloponnesian War (431–404), and after a further revival became for a brief period, under Theban leadership, the dominant power of Greece (371–362).

But the defeat of the Boeotians together with their Athenian allies at Chaeronea (338) at the hands of Philip II of Macedonia meant the end of their real independence; and although they devised an effective new federal government (no longer dominated by Thebes) they remained henceforth in a position of virtual subordination either to Macedonia or, at times, to the Aetolian Confederacy (245) or its Achaean counterpart. It was on Boeotian territory, at Cynoscephalae, that the Roman army of Flamininus defeated King Philip V of Macedonia (197). Writing of a period some five years later, Polybius, the Greek historian, paints a bleak picture of the class antagonism and demoralization by which Boeotia was racked. When the Achaeans decided to fight Rome, the Boeotians joined them, and after the collapse of the Achaean cause, followed by the Roman annexation of Greece (146), their League was dissolved, although it was later permitted a formal revival, mainly in order to carry out religious functions.

From now onward however, the country was insignificant and impoverished. Its most distinguished son in Roman imperial times was the philosopher and biographer Plutarch of Chaeronea (before AD 50–after 120). *See also* Chaeronea, Cithaeron, Copais, Coronea, Cynoscephalae, Delium, Leuctra, Orchomenus, Plataea, Tanagra, Thebes, Thespiae.

Boğaziçi *see* Bosphorus (Thracian)

Bologna *see* Bononia

Bolsena *see* Volsinii (Novi)

Bône *see* Hippo Regius

Bononia (earlier Felsina, now Bologna). In Cisalpine Gaul (northern Italy), a little to the north of the Apennines. The considerable group of villages clustered together on the site in the early first millennium BC was located on rising ground above a very fertile and densely populated plain between the Aposa and Ravone rivers at the mid-part of the valley of the Rhenus (Reno)—at that time a southern tributary of the Padus (Po), which furnished access to the Adriatic Sea at Spina and Verucchio. The Rhenus provided the villages with their principal southward communication, by easy passes into other valleys and onward to the river Arnus (Arno) and Etruria; and it was under Etruscan impulses that they were merged to become the city of Felsina not long after 800.

By 730 the new center was already at the height of its expansion. Like the city-states of the Etruscan homeland, it owed its power and prosperity to metals, since iron could be extracted from the adjoining mountainsides and copper was also exploited. Felsina stood at the meeting point of two trade routes that led to sources of metals across the Alps, and developed a major metalworking industry. A find of *c* 700 comprised 18,481 bronze objects that were apparently valued according to weight and thus functioned as forerunners of coinage. About one hundred years later the place became a center for the production of large bronze *situlae* (buckets), analogous to products of Slovene and Alpine territories, and principally intended for cremated ashes. A large series of gravestones shaped like horseshoes and engraved with reliefs (from *c* 510) display certain Etruscan analogies, and in general Felsina became a city of the Etruscans—and their principal center in northern Italy. The site of this urban settlement has not been located, though objects of a non-funerary character have come to light in a sanctuary dating from the sixth to the fourth centuries.

The Felsinans maintained an independent government until *c* 350, when they succumbed to invading Gauls, one of whose tribes, the Boii, gave the place its new name of Bononia. In 196 it fell to the Romans, who planted a Latin colony of 3,000 settlers (189), and linked it with Placentia (Piacenza) on the Po and Ariminum (Rimini) on the coast by the Via Aemilia (187); it was also joined to Aquileia by the Via Aemilia Altinate (175). In 43 Antony, Octavian (the future Augustus) and Lepidus met on a small island (or peninsula) on an adjacent tributary, the Lavinus (Lavino), in order to form the formal Second Triumvirate which established them as rulers of the Roman world. Bononia subsequently received a settlement of ex-soldiers from Antony, to whom (as its patron) the city remained loyal during the Civil War that followed; his enemy, Octavian, meticulously acknowledged the scruple, by exempting citizens from the general oath of allegiance to his cause. Moreover, after his victory, he renewed the colony, of which an inscription honors him as the parent: an altar and priesthood were established to his divinity in his lifetime.

In AD 53 the young Nero made his public début by a speech urging Claudius to restore and enlarge the colony, severely damaged by a fire. In 69 Vitellius gave one of the legions of his defeated rival Otho the task of building amphitheaters at Bononia and Cremona. Bononia continued to be an important road junction and nucleus of agricultural and manufacturing activity, with densely populated suburbs. It became a bishopric, and survived an attack by the Visigoth Alaric in 410. Its Roman remains are not particularly important, since the same site has always been employed: the central part of modern Bologna is built over the right-angled street plan of the Roman city. But a theater has now been found under the Via Massimo d' Azeglio, and there are remains of a twelve-mile aqueduct that brought water into the city.

Bononia (Vidin). Fortress on the Danube in Upper Moesia (northwestern Bulgaria). Its name suggests the presence of a Celtic element in its original Thracian population. Facing the territory of the hostile Dacians across the river, Bononia became a frontier stronghold; then, after the Roman annexation of Dacia (AD 105), it was a rear base and auxiliary garrison, but resumed the role of frontier post (in the new province of Dacia Ripensis) when the old Dacia was evacuated by Aurelian (271). Parts of the town's walls and towers have survived. Bononia was destroyed by the Huns (442), but restored by the Byzantine emperor Justinian I a century later.

Bononia Malata (Banoštor). A fortress on the Danube in Lower Pannonia (Yugoslavia). To judge from its first name, it began as a Celtic, or partly Celtic, settlement. Facing the territory of the hostile Jazyges across the river, Bononia Malata became linked to a fort on the opposite bank, Onagrinum, by a bridge, and served as the Danubian port of Sirmium (Sremska Mitrovica). The remains of houses from the first to the fourth centuries AD have been uncovered, as well as baths and an early Christian church. In the later empire, according to the *Notitia Dignitatum,* the stronghold was garrisoned by legionary detachments, until the province crumbled soon after 400. Objects from the migration period have been found.

Borbetomagus (Worms). In western Germany, on the left bank of the Rhine (eleven miles northwest of Mannheim), forming part of the territory of the Mediomatrici. At the time of Julius Caesar it was the capital of the Vangiones, known as Civitas Vangionum. Under the Principate, the place was an important frontier post of the Roman command, and later province, of Upper Germany (Germania Superior), and then—after the reorganization of Diocletian and Constantine—a fortified stronghold of the province of Germania Prima.

The most important moment in the history of Borbetomagus came in AD 413, when the German tribe of the Burgundians (who had crossed the Rhine and occupied the region in 406/7) were formally recognized by the western Roman emperor Honorius as a federate state, with this city as their capital. These were the Burgundians of the Nibelungenlied, which also preserves the name of their King Gunther (Gundahar), who had first settled his people on the west bank of the Rhine. When, however, Gunther invaded the province of Belgica Prima in 435, in defiance of the Romans, their general Aetius (on behalf of his youthful emperor Valentinian III) induced his allies the Huns to kill the monarch and annihilate his army; it was said that 20,000 Burgundians fell, though the figure must be exaggerated. The kingdom of the Burgundians based on Borbetomagus was now at an end, though their survivors were subsequently transported to Sabaudia (Savoy; 443). Later the Huns used the city as a base of operations against their former associates the Romans, and after their ejection it passed into the hands first of the Alamanni and then of the Franks (*c* 496).

Bordeaux *see* Burdigala

Bordj bou Chateur *see* Utica

Borgo Montello *see* Satricum

Borysthenes *see* Olbia

Bosphorus or Bosporus, Cimmerian. A kingdom extending on either side of the Maeotic Channel (Straits of Kerch), which ran between the Euxine (Black) Sea and the Sea of Maeotis (Azov), separating the Tauric Chersonese (Crimea) from the Caucasus. The name Bosporus ('cow's ford') is derived by Aeschylus from the story of Io, whose mythical wanderings brought her to the place, transformed into a cow, after Hera had resented Zeus' love for her. Colonists from Miletus settled in the eastern portion of the Tauric Chersonese at Panticapaeum (Kerch) in about 600 BC and at Theodosia (Feodosija) in the second half of the sixth century.

The foundations of the Bosphoran state were laid in the 480s when the Archaeanactids, the ruling house of Panticapaeum—of Milesian or Mytilenean origin—unified their compatriots, on either side of the narrows, for protection against non-Greek neighbors. Then in 438 Spartocus I, a Thracian or Thraco-Maeotian mercenary commander, established a powerful, wealthy, highly centralized, and long-lasting state, ruled by members of the Hellenized minority which dominated the local populations, depending for its wealth on the community's metal-working skills, on abundant fisheries (herring, sturgeon, tunny, for which elaborate salting facilities existed), and on exports of grain from the vast Russian interior. Paerisades I (349/8 or 344–311/10) repelled the Royal Scyths of the Crimean hinterland and exercised suzerainty as far as the mouth of the Tanais (Don) and the foothills of the Caucasus, and Spartocus III (304/3–284/3) assumed the title of King of the Bosphorus. Under the threat, however, of a rebellion among the Bosphoran cities, led by a Scythian called Saumacus, Paerisades V felt obliged to appeal to Mithridates VI Eupator of Pontus, who thereupon proceeded to annex the kingdom (*c* 109). After the Romans had suppressed Mithridates, they gave the Bosphorus (now augmented by the important Greek commercial center of Chersonesus [Sevastopol], colonized by Heraclea Pontica [Ereğli] in 421) to his son and betrayer Pharnaces II who later resisted Caesar unsuccessfully at Zela (46) and lost his life.

Asander (46–16), recognized by Augustus, built a wall across the northern isthmus of the peninsula and extended his power along the shore of the Sea of Maeotis as far as the Tanais. Thereafter the kingdom continued its existence for another three hundred and fifty years—with a brief interval of Roman annexation in AD 62–8—as a strategically and commercially important client state of the emperors, who established a naval base at Charax (near Yalta). The kingdom's marks of honor (*timai*), ivory chair, crown and shield, are depicted on the royal coinage—which included the only gold issues produced by any client princedom. The Bosphorus enjoyed renewed economic prosperity in the second and third centuries, while becoming, eventually, more Sarmatian than Greek in character; but in the 250s and 260s the Goths invaded the greater part of the Chersonese, using Bosphoran vessels to launch piratical raids on the Euxine coast; and Panticapaeum fell to Gothic and Alan attacks. However, the coinage of the Bosphoran monarchs continued until Rhescuporis VI (or VII) (303/4–341/2). Subsequently part of their dominions was annexed by the Byzantine empire, whose ruler Justinian I (527–65) built long walls to keep a branch of the Huns out of the territory. *See also* Gorgippia, Hermonassa, Maeotis, Nymphaeum, Panticapaeum, Phanagoria, Theodosia.

Bosphorus or Bosporus, Thracian (Boğaziçi), is the narrow strait, seventeen miles in length, that joins the Euxine (Black) Sea to the Propontis (Sea of Marmara) and separates Europe and Asia at their nearest point. The Bosphorus is noted for its abundance of migratory fish, seasonally passing to and from the Euxine Sea. Thus a dolphin is one of the coin-types of the two most important cities at the southern end of the strait, Calchedon (Kadıköy) on its Asiatic bank and Byzantium (Istanbul) facing it on the European side. Standing upon the dolphin on the issues of Calchedon is an ear of corn, but at Byzantium the coin-type is a cow, referring to the wanderings of Io in the form of that animal which gave the Thracian Bosphorus (like its Cimmerian counterpart; *qv*) its name.

The Bosphorus played a prominent strategic part in the civil wars between Constantine I the Great and Licinius I. In AD 314 or 316 Licinius came to terms with Constantine, because of fears that his rival would use his fleet to blockade the strait. When hostilities were resumed in 324, Constantine outwitted Licinius' colleague Martinian, who failed to prevent him from crossing over to the Asiatic bank, where Constantine landed at Riva at the northern end of the Bosphorus; the subsequent battle of Chrysopolis (Üsküdar) sealed Licinius' fate. When, immediately afterward, Constantine decided to convert Byzantium into the great new city of Constantinople, the supreme strategic and commercial advantages of the Bosphorus proved a dominant factor guiding his choice.

Bostra (Busra Eski-Sham). Situated in the Transjordanian plain of Auranitis (Hauran, now in Syria), at the head of the desert route from central Arabia, the town of Bostra belonged to the kingdom of the Nabataean Arabs, attaining increased importance and prosperity as a caravan market under their king Rabbel II (AD 71–106), in whose reign it apparently replaced Petra as the Nabataean capital. After the subsequent annexation of the kingdom by Trajan, the place remained the capital of the new Roman province of Arabia—under the name of Nova Bostra Trajana—becoming the headquarters of the legion that formed the provincial garrison and the terminal of Trajan's great road to the Sinus Aelanites (Gulf of Elat or Akaba). Bostra was probably made a colony by Elagabalus (218–22), under whose successor, Severus Alexander, Latin replaces Greek on its coinage. Issues depict the cults of Tyche, Ammon and Dusares and the Actian-Dusarian Games; though meanwhile the city also developed into a prominent center of Christianity, at which the first known Arab bishop, Beryllius, wrote his *Didascalia,* and Origen took part in important synods. When Zenobia set up a secessionist empire of the east, Bostra was sacked (*c* 271). Under the reorganization of Diocletian (284–305), however, it remained the capital of the truncated province of Arabia, and became a keypoint on his military road to the Euphrates.

The ancient town, constructed of black basalt, displays a large three-bayed, pilastered, monumental arch, and an exceptionally well-planned and well-preserved Roman theater (its stage building decorated by Corinthian columns of pink Egyptian granite). There is also an elaborate bathing establishment, and a massive rectangular residence known as Trajan's Palace. In the later Roman and Byzantine periods (until the Arab conquest in 637) the place became a prominent Christian center, possessing a sixth century cathedral and basilica of fine architectural quality.

Boulogne *see* Gesoriacum

Bounomos *see* Pella

Bourges *see* Avaricum

Bracara Augusta (Braga). A city in the southern part of Callaecia (Galicia; but now in northern Portugal, capital of the province of Minho). Situated in a region dotted with hilltop towns built in the eighth and seventh centuries BC by Celts who intermarried with the local Iberians, the town was supposedly founded in 296 by the Bracari, a tribe that fiercely resisted the Roman general Decimus Junius Brutus when he raided northward in 137 from the Lusitanian territory that had been conquered two years earlier; Brutus assumed the title of Callaicus.

The region was loosely attached to the Roman province of Further Spain (Hispania Ulterior), but after a series of rebellions Augustus extended Nearer Spain (Hispania Citerior, Tarraconensis) to the northwest coasts of the peninsula, refounding Bracara with the title of Augusta as one of the judicial districts (*conventus*) of the province. It also became an important economic and communications center, and produced a distinctive form of pottery. More than a dozen coin-hoards dating from the fourth century AD have been found. In 411 Bracara Augusta became the capital of the German (Suebian) king of Callaecia, who was saved from his Vandal enemies by a Roman force some years later. But the city fell to Theoderic II, king of the Visigoths, in 456, after a siege of three weeks culminating in savage acts of plunder. The conversion of the Visigoths from Arianism to orthodox Catholicism at two synods held at Bracara in 563 and 572 marked the beginning of a long career of ecclesiastical preeminence.

Archaeological evidence of pre-Roman occupation is insignificant. Roman monuments of which traces still exist include a sanctuary dedicated to the native god Tongoenabiagus, built around a fountain. Inscriptions bear witness to other Roman temples, and refer to a market that can no longer be located.

Branchidae *see* Didyma

Brauron (Vraona). Situated beside a small bay on the east coast of Attica, it was a flourishing fortified settlement from the Neolithic to the later Bronze Age. According to Greek myth Brauron was the place to which Orestes and Pylades escaped from Mycenae after murdering Clytaemnestra, together with Iphigenia who became the chief priestess of Brauron. It was reputedly one of the twelve independent townships united under the leadership of Athens (twenty-four miles distant); tradition maintained that the amalgamation was carried out by the Athenian hero Theseus.

The settlement was abandoned *c* 1300 BC, but from the later eighth century the place regained its importance as the location of a sanctuary of Artemis, 'the home of the maidens.' Her cult statue was stated by Euripides to have been brought from Tauris (Crimea) by Iphigenia and Orestes; but Pausanias queries the legend. Iphigenia herself was also believed to be buried at the shrine. The cult of Artemis Brauronia was chiefly for women, and at her annual festival young girls between the age of five and ten, who were dedicated to her service and known as *arktoi* (bears), performed a bear-dance dressed in saffron robes (perhaps bearskins at an earlier period).

Excavations have revealed remains of the sanctuary, of which the most sacred feature was a spring until *c* 500, when a temple was erected. Only its foundations are now to be seen; but objects dedicated to the goddess have come to light, including pieces of bone and wood preserved by the mud. The shrine was probably destroyed by the Persians in 480 BC, but an impressive Doric portico of *c* 430–420 indicates that it was subsequently reconstructed. However, the flooding of the river Erasinus in the fourth or third century brought its existence to an end. In recent years there have been skillful excavations on the waterlogged site.

Brescello *see* Brixellum

Brettioi *see* Bruttii

Brigetio (Ö-Szöny in Hungary, in the province of Komarom). Situated on the right bank of the Danube, to the west of its great bend, and northwest of Aquincum (Budapest). A Roman military fortress on the northern frontier of the province of Pannonia established by Augustus. The first camp for auxiliary troops must have been built in the first century AD. When Trajan divided Pannonia in two, Brigetio belonged to the Upper province, and for a time became a legionary garrison (*c* 100–106), in addition to providing support for the Danube fleet (with the assistance of a camp across the river, named Celemantia Isa [Leanyvár in Czechoslovakia]).

Destroyed in the Marcomannic Wars of Marcus Aurelius (*c* 169–72), Brigetio was later rebuilt, and transferred by Caracalla (211–17) to the province of Lower Pannonia. It was now one of the leading economic and cultural centers of the frontier region, and the civil settlement adjoining the camp received urban status as a *municipium* and subsequently as a *colonia* (although an alternative view maintains that it was instead the larger, military community that received these honors). In the tetrarchic period, in or after the time of Diocletian (284–305), Brigetio was destroyed again. Its subsequent reconstruction was less impressive. Tile-stamps indicate that Valentinian I (364–75) carried out some work on the site. The final abandonment and destruction of the city occurred later in the same century.

Excavations reveal a succession of buildings, including various walls and gates, the residence of the military commander, the centers of professional guilds, and shrines and altars dedicated to Roman and Pannonian and oriental gods and goddesses. Worship was especially devoted to healing divinities, and an inscription refers to a curative spring (Fons Salutia). An aqueduct brought the waters of the warm springs of Tata to Brigetio.

Brilessos *see* Pentelicus

Brindisi *see* Brundusium

Britannia (Britain). Tin was worked in Cornwall (in the southwest) from the Bronze Age, but the country first became known to the Greeks not as early as the sixth century BC, as has sometimes been supposed, but some two hundred years afterward, when Pytheas of Massalia (Massilia, Marseille) apparently visited Cornwall and a tin depot at Ictis (St. Michael's Mount). The latest of a series of waves of Celtic invaders, comprising a group of the Gallic Belgae, overran southeastern Britain in the early part of the first century BC, and Julius Caesar felt impelled to try to round off his conquests in Gaul by invading the island in 55 and 54 BC. Thereafter its southern tribes were regarded as vassals, though they did not see themselves in this light. Preparations for definitive conquest were made by Gaius (Caligula) in AD 40, but first carried out by his successor Claudius, whose general Aulus Plautius overran the 'Lowland Zone' (43-47), captured the Belgic capital Camulodunum (Colchester)—in the presence of the emperor—and created the new province of Britannia, a region extending from the Abus (Humber) estuary to the Sabrina (Severn).

It may have been after the rebellion of Boudicca (Boadicea) of the Iceni (East Anglia) in AD 60 that the provincial capital was transferred from Camulodunum to Londinium (London); or perhaps this occurred somewhat later. Under Domitian, Agricola (78-85) advanced far into Caledonia (Scotland), but Hadrian's Wall (122) established a Tyne-Solway frontier, temporarily extended by the Antonine Wall (of Antoninus Pius, *c* 142) between the Firth of Forth and the Clyde. Britannia exported grain, cattle, tin, gold, silver, iron, hides, slaves and hunting dogs. After disturbances and attempted usurpations under Commodus (180-92), Clodius Albinus, governor of the province, made an attempt to gain the throne, crossing over to Gaul and thus throwing the frontier open to Caledonian incursions. Septimius Severus, after defeating Albinus (197), penetrated deep into their country, but was only able, or content, to reestablish the frontier of Hadrian's Wall (209-11). He also divided the Roman part of the island into two provinces, Upper and Lower Britain, with their capitals at Londinium (London) and Eboracum (York) respectively.

A revolt under Probus (276-82) was put down by his Mauretanian general Victorinus. In the same period Saxon piracy prompted the construction of forts and signal stations along the eastern and southern coasts. In *c* 286 Carausius, admiral of the well-equipped fleet protecting the country (the Classis Britannica), declared himself emperor—issuing coinage at Londinium, Camulodunum and perhaps elsewhere—but his successor Allectus was removed by Constantius I on behalf of the central authority (296/7). The two provinces, elevated to the status of an administrative diocese with its capital at Londinium, were now further subdivided into four (Prima, Secunda, Maxima Caesariensis and Flavia

Caesariensis)—increased to five by Constans I who created the additional province of Constantia (Valentia), with its capital at Eboracum, *c* 343. After heavy attacks by the Caledonians in the 360s order was restored with difficulty, and new forts constructed by Theodosius the Elder (father of the emperor Theodosius I).

Attempting to usurp the imperial throne, the Roman governors Magnus Maximus and Constantine III (383–88, 407–11) crossed over to Gaul with most of their troops. Denuded of the garrison, and cut off from the central administration by German invasions of Gaul, the Romano-British population gradually passed under the control of Saxon immigrants who, after enrolling (early in the fifth century) as 'federated' troops, introduced groups of their compatriots (including Angles and Jutes) in their wake, so that the country came under German domination in the 440s. *See also* Aquae Sulis, Camulodunum, Eboracum, Isca Dumnoniorum, Isca Silurum, Lindum, Londinium, Venta Icenorum, Venta Silurum, Verulamium.

Brixellum (Brescello). In northern Italy, on the south bank of the Padus (Po), which can be crossed at that point. Augustus made it into a Roman colony, settled by ex-soldiers. In the Civil War of AD 69, when the decisive First Battle of Cremona (or Bedriacum) was about to be fought between the generals of Otho and Vitellius, Otho himself did not take part in the engagement, having withdrawn across the Padus to Brixellum with a considerable number of troops. Tacitus believed, no doubt correctly, that his absence weakened the morale of his soldiers, and contributed to their subsequent total defeat.

When news of the disaster was brought to Otho at Brixellum, efforts were made to persuade him to await the imminent arrival of reinforcements from Moesia, who might well have been able to reverse and restore the situation. But he could feel no hope, and decided to put an end to the blocdshed by taking his own life (April 16th, 69). To his nephew his last words were these: 'Don't forget that your uncle was an emperor—and don't remember it too often either.' At Brixellum, Vitellius was shown his rival's modest grave, and observed: 'a little grave for a little man.'

Brundusium, Brundisium, formerly Brentesion (Brindisi). On the east coast of what was in ancient times Calabria (and is now part of Puglia), in southeastern Italy. Traditions of early Greek colonists from Cnossus (Crete) and then Taras (Taranto)—involving the names of Theseus or Iapyx—are uncorroborated, but further legends associating the foundation with Diomedes (who was believed to have come from Thrace) tend to confirm the alternative supposition that the place (which is the nearest Italian town to the Adriatic coast) originally belonged to the Messapians or their scarcely distinguishable neighbors the Calabrians, who immigrated in the early Iron Age from the Balkans. The name Brentesion is derived from the Messapian *biendos* (stag), since the adjoining twin-branched bay seemed to resemble a stag's antlers.

About 440 BC Brundusium established treaty relations with Thurii (the former Sybaris [Sibari]). In 246, during the First Punic War, the Romans planted a Latin fortress-colony there, with the intention of closing the Adriatic to Carthaginian shipping; the new foundation caused alarm to the Illyrians (and helped to provoke subsequent wars with them). By 244, and probably earlier, the Via Appia had been extended to its terminal point at Brundusium, which became the regular port of embarkation for Roman armies crossing the Adriatic. It was also the birthplace of the Latin dramatist Pacuvius (*c* 220–136).

Following the Italian rebellion (Social War) in the early first century, Brundusium, like other towns, was given the rank of *municipium* (89/88). After the outbreak of Civil War in 49, Caesar pursued Pompey the Great to its harbor, but his enemy skillfully evaded attempts to blockade him and escaped across the Adriatic to Epirus. In 40 Antony besieged the city, when Octavian (the future Augustus) tried to prevent him from landing in Italy; and it was by the subsequent Treaty of Brundusium that they and their fellow member of the Second Triumvirate, Lepidus, temporarily settled their differences. Three years later the poet Horace undertook the journey which became the theme of his 'Journey to Brundusium' (*Satires* I, 15). In 19 Virgil died there, on his way back from Greece.

According to Pliny the Elder, Brundusium obtained its revenue from oysters, vines and bees, and Strabo praises its fruit (despite shallow soil) and its wool. Since the modern town is built over its ancient counterpart, remains are meager.

Bruttii, formerly Brettioi, named after the tribe of the same name who inhabited the mountainous southwestern peninsula (toe) of Italy, now known as Calabria (in ancient times Calabria was Italy's heel). The inhabitants became known by the Oscan name of Brettioi ('slaves,' 'runaways') after breaking away from the Lucanians to whom they were subject (356), and establishing an independent regime at Consentia (Cosenza); they captured Hipponium (Vibo Valentia) and Terina (Catanzaro), two of the numerous Greek cities near the coast, and resisted attacks first from Taras (Tarentum, Taranto) and then from Syracuse. Their principal products were ships' timber and pitch.

Becoming partially Hellenized, and issuing numerous and varied coins with Greek inscriptions, the Bruttians sided with Pyrrhus of Epirus against the Romans, who celebrated six Triumphs at their cost (278–272) and annexed half of the Sila forest, although permitting them to retain a mint. After the Bruttians had defected to Hannibal during the Second Punic War, and had been subsequently brought to order (216–213), they were deprived of further territory, ringed around with Roman colonies, and, according to Appian, virtually reduced to slavery. In *c* 131 the Via Appia received an extension, probably known as the Via Annia, which passed through Consentia on its way to the coastal city of Rhegium (Reggio di Calabria). During the later empire Bruttii was united with Lucania as a single region.

Budapest *see* Aquincum

Bulda *see* Paltos

Bulla Regia (Hammam Daradji). A town in the Bagradas (Medjerda) valley in northern Africa (Tunisia). It passed from the control of Carthage into the hands of Numidian princes—who established one of their royal residences there—and then became part of the Roman province of Africa, obtaining the successive statuses of free city from Augustus, *municipium* from Vespasian, and Roman colony from Hadrian.

Bulla Regia profited from its strategical commercial location and from the abundance of grain in its territory, and benefited from the accession of the African emperor Septimius Severus (193–211), during whose reign at least one important provincial governor came from the city. Its archaeological remains are very substantial, including a forum, several temples, baths (still standing to an impressive height), a theater, and a number of private houses, some of which display an underground storey, to counteract the summer heat.

Burdigala (Bordeaux). A port of Aquitania (southwestern Gaul) on the left (west) bank of the river Garumna (Garonne), sixty miles from its mouth, above its junction with the Duranius (Dordogne). Burdigala was the chief town of the Celtic tribe of the Bituriges Vivisci from about the third century BC. After conquests by Julius Caesar's general Publius Licinius Crassus (56), it became the capital of Augustus' province of Aquitania, and was later granted the rank of *municipium,* probably in the time of Vespasian (AD 69–79). Thereafter it grew in size and prosperity, profiting from its vineyards, which were almost as famous as they are now. But German devastations in the later third century caused severe setbacks, involving a shrinkage in the dimensions of the city.

Nevertheless, recovery soon followed, and under the provincial reorganization of Diocletian and Constantine Burdigala remained the capital of the newly constituted province of Aquitania Secunda and became the residence of the governor-general (*vicarius*) of the administrative diocese of Gaul. The poet Ausonius, who was born there during the first half of the fourth century, described it as a square walled city and one of the principal educational centers of Gaul. It was also the scene of a Church Council in 384. However, its defences were overrun by the Vandals in 409 and by the Visigothic monarch Ataulf in 413; before moving on to Spain two years later, he devastated its buildings and set them on fire. But when Wallia, the next king but one, was invited back to Gaul by the Romans in 417, Burdigala—together with the rest of Aquitania Secunda, and the two provinces lying to its south—was made part of his federated kingdom.

The Garumna was connected to the inland port by a channel (represented by the Navigère gate); and a tributary, the Devèze, was likewise canalized to supply the city with water. Ausonius also refers to the fountain of Divona, of which the twelve bronze mouths poured forth water from a sacred spring. A huge amphitheater, of which remains survive (the Palais Gallien), dates to *c* 200 or earlier.

Burgaz *see* Cnidus

Burgundia, the land of the Burgundiones (Burgundians), a German tribe who came originally from the southern coasts and islands of the Baltic (notably Bornholm, which was originally Burgundarholm), and after a period in the Vistula valley migrated westward in the third century AD to the upper and middle reaches of the river Moenus (Main), where they first came into conflict with the Romans *c* 279.

Extending their rule in the region between the river Nicer (Neckar) and the Taunus mountains, they crossed the Rhenus (Rhine) in 406 and were recognized as federates by the usurper Constantine III in the following year. In 413, with the encouragement of Honorius, they established a kingdom in the Roman province of Germania Prima—with its capital at Borbetomagus (Worms)—of which the destruction by the Huns in 435–37, prompted by Rome, is reflected in the *Nibelungenlied.* In 443 the Roman general Aetius transferred the survivors to Sabaudia (Savoy), where their state gradually expanded its frontiers to include the area that came to be known as Burgundy, and continued to exist until its annexation by the Franks in 534. *See also* Borbetomagus, Sabaudia.

Buridava, Boridava (Stolniceni), situated in Dacia (later Dacia Apulensis, now Rumania), on the banks of the river Aluta (Olt). The name is Geto-Thracian, and the settlement was the chief trading center of the tribe of the Buri. It played an important part in the Dacian wars of Trajan (AD 101/2, 105/6). The names of military units preserved on brick and tile stamps include that of the personal guard (*pedites singulares*) of the governor of Lower Moesia, who established his headquarters at Buridava in preparation for the second of Trajan's campaigns.

The fortress housed an auxiliary garrison and became an important station on the eighteen-foot-wide military road to the north of the province, also deriving profits from sheep raising and the export of salt down the Aluta to the Danube. Excavations have revealed the outlines of the ancient town, which included a substantial stone camp, apparently constructed by Hadrian (117–38), adjoining a civilian settlement that includes a large bathing establishment.

Busra Eski Sham *see* Bostra

Buthrotum (Vatzindro, Butrinto). A town of Epirus (now Albania), situated on a low hill at the end of a narrow channel flowing from a lake into the Adriatic Sea, opposite Corcyra (Corfu). Dating back to prehistoric origins—as finds on the site confirm—it owed its foundation, according to legends (preserved by Virgil), to Priam's son Helenus, who settled in Epirus with Hector's widow Andromache after the fall of Troy. The center of a tribal union, Buthrotum possessed fine harbors, which served as fishing centers and ports of call on the coastal route, and enabled the place to flourish in Hellenistic times. Julius Caesar planned to found a colony there, settled by ex-soldiers. But Cicero's friend Atticus, who was patron of the region, complained to the dictator about the confiscations which the scheme would necessitate. So Caesar agreed to waive the plan—provided that the wealthy Atticus provided cash compensation. The unfortunate prospective settlers, we learn from Cicero, were not told of the change of plan when they set out across the Adriatic; Caesar explained that once they arrived he would settle them elsewhere, and presumably he did.

Nevertheless, Augustus established a colony at Buthrotum, to which a varied series of monetary issues (in his reign alone) bears witness. Some of the pieces refer to a *colonia Augusta* and others to *colonia Julia*; the latter designation alludes either to a settlement before the emperor assumed the title of Augustus in 27 BC or to the earlier project initiated, even if not carried out, by Julius Caesar. One coinage honors Salus (well-being) and Concordia, and another depicts a three-arched bridge. Large portions of the city's acropolis and fortifications have been recently excavated, and well-preserved remains of a theater have survived on a peninsula at the maritime end of the channel linking the sea to the lake.

Büyük Menderes (River) *see* Maeander

Byblus (Jebeil). A coastal city of Phoenicia (Lebanon), at the foot of Mount Libanus (Lebanon). Already occupied in the fourth millennium BC, the place was described as the oldest city in the world by Philo of Byblus (AD 64–141), who claimed (authentically, as is now believed) to be drawing on the work of Sanchuniathon, a Phoenician of the later second millennium BC. According to one tradition Cinyras, king of Cyprus and founder of its cult of Aphrodite, ruled over Byblus as well. It was a center of the cult of Cinyras' son Tammuz-Adonis—whom Aphrodite loved—and possessed close relations with the Egyptians, who believed that the goddess Isis had come there to find the body of Osiris, slain by Typhon; connections were also maintained with Bronze Age Cretans and Greeks (who derived their name for papyrus, *biblion*, from the city). Byblus played a leading part in the development of the alphabet. About 1800 (?) a simpler script than the old Egyptian hieroglyphic (pictorial) appeared, consisting of eighty syllabic signs interlarded by characters depicting natural objects in a stylized fashion. Byblus was also in the forefront when a completely alphabetic script developed in about the tenth century.

It became a dependency of the Achaemenid Persians, under whose rule local autonomous princes issued silver coins in the fourth century. Then the city submitted to Alexander (who employed its mint) and came under Seleucid rule. Autonomous coins of the first century BC, describing Byblus as 'holy' in Phoenician script, depict Isis, Harpocrates, Cronos and Tyche. Pompey the Great freed it from autocratic rule by beheading its ruler (64/63). Threatened by Ituraeans from the hinterland, it rebuilt its fortifications with the aid of King Herod the Great of Judaea (37–4).

Ancient remains include traces of walls, and paved streets, a temple, a basilica, an apsed *nymphaeum* (fountain building) containing statuary, and a recently excavated habitation center of the second century AD containing fine mosaics (of Atalanta and Meleager, and Acme and Charis). Another mosaic pavement, representing Dionysus (Bacchus), has been found in the theater. Coins of Macrinus (AD 217–18) depict an imposing sanctuary of Astarte-Aphrodite adjoining a porticoed courtyard, of which the walls have been opened up by the artist to display a balustraded altar surmounted by a conical stone (*baetyl*).

Byzantium, later Constantinople (İstanbul). A Greek colony at the southern end of the Thracian Bosphorus on its European side, occupying a promontory bordering upon the elongated natural harbor of the Chrusokeras (Golden Horn) to the north and the Propontis (Sea of Marmara) to the south. The habitation area at first occupied only the eastern tip of the promontory, that is to say the easternmost of the seven hills of the later city.

The foundation date of Byzantium was variously assigned to 668, 659 and *c* 657 BC, and the founders probably came from Megara, though other groups from central Greece and the Peloponnese are likely to have participated. Fortified by walls regarded in antiquity as among the strongest in any Greek land, the colony owed its origin and subsequent prosperity to its unrivalled facilities for trapping tunny migrating from the Euxine (Black) Sea to the Mediterranean, its access to the Euxine grain trade and its location at the shortest crossing point from Europe to Asia. Byzantium was under Persian rule from the time of the Scythian expedition of Darius I (512), when Mandrocles threw a bridge of boats across the Bosphorus, until the Ionian Revolt (500–494), and after the collapse of the revolt until the city's 'liberation' by the Spartan king Pausanias in 478. In the following year, however, the Athenians achieved his expulsion, and Byzantium became a member of their Delian League. But it rebelled in 440 and again in 412, after Athens' defeat at Syracuse during the Peloponnesian War, only to be retaken by Alcibiades in 408.

Following the final collapse of the Athenians at Aegospotami in 405, Byzantium came under Spartan domination, but was brought back into alliance with the Athenians—under a democratic constitution—in 389, serving as a member of their confederacy from 378/7 to 357 and then again (after a rebellion) in 340/339 when its inhabitants resisted Philip II of Macedonia in a famous siege, reputedly through the intervention of the goddess Hecate whose crescent they placed on their coins (it subsequently became the symbol of Islam). During the reign of Alexander the Great the city was no longer able to resist domination by the Macedonian kingdom, of which the subsequent decline, however, enabled it to reassert its independence. Financially ruined by the need to buy off invading Gauls (270) and pay them tribute, its leaders began to impose a toll on all ships passing through the Bosphorus—a measure which the Rhodians, by forcible means, annulled in 219.

When the Roman province of Bithynia-Pontus was established in the first century BC, Byzantium remained a free city loosely attached to it, but was subsequently subjected to tribute. Owing its sufferings in Thracian wars, however—including a period of subordination to the Thracian monarchy—the emperor Claudius accorded its people tax remission for five years. During the civil strife toward the end of the second century AD, the Byzantines took the side of Pescennius Niger against Septimius Severus, who, after successfully concluding a prolonged siege (193–96) of the city, destroyed its buildings and fortifications and executed its principal leaders. In view of the strategic value of the place, however, it was soon magnificently restored by Severus, who doubled its circumference; and Games entitled Antoninia Augusta (after Caracalla, 211–17) received celebration on its coins. In the last year of Gallienus (268, or possibly after the accession of Claudius II Gothicus in that year) a German fleet, manned by Goths and Heruli, captured the city, but were defeated in a naval battle and forced to withdraw.

During the civil wars following the abdication of Diocletian (305) the defences of Byzantium were strengthened, and after it had figured prominently in Constantine the Great's struggle with Licinius I he decided that it should be the location of his great projected city Constantinopolis (324). In addition to its possession of an excellent harbor, the new foundation could be defended by land and sea, and was accessible to the vital industrial centers of heavily populated coastal Asia Minor and Syria, and within reach of the grain-producing lands of Egypt and south Russia as well. Although Rome lost none of its ancient privileges, and at first Constantinople, designated the 'New Rome', ranked beneath it, Constantine fully intended that his new creation should in due course become the metropolis of the empire.

Six years after the rebuilding began, the refounded and greatly enlarged city, adorned with numerous works of art from pagan temples, received its formal inauguration (330). As at Rome, there was a free issue of bread, distributed in 332 to 80,000 persons. In 340 the founder's son Constantius II, who carried out his father's plan to make Constantinople his capital, inaugurated its senate, together with a hierarchy of imperial officials modeled on Rome; henceforth one of the annual consuls of the empire was normally inaugurated at the new city. In 359 its first prefect took office.

When Valentinian I divided his dominions into western and eastern empires, he gave the eastern section to his brother Valens, who ruled at Constantinople and endowed it with magnificent buildings.

In 381 the Council of Constantinople declared that its bishop 'should have the primacy of honor after the bishop of Rome, because it was the New Rome,' and in 451 the Council of Chalcedon gave him patriarchal authority over extensive areas. The year 425 witnessed the establishment of a university, of which the professors, appointed by the Senate, were granted a monopoly of higher education. The climax of the city's growth and splendor was reached in the early years of Justinian I (527–65), in whose reign the population probably attained half a million. This figure was diminished by more than half by the great plague of 542. Nevertheless, Constantinople continued its existence as the capital of the Byzantine empire until 1453 (with only the brief intermission of crusaders' ['Latin'] rule, 1204–61), and for the most of this period it was by far the most important political, commercial and cultural center in all Europe.

Archaeological evidence for ancient Greek Byzantium—before it became Constantinople—is scarce, because so much building has continued on the site ever since. Almost certainly the acropolis of the Megarian colonists was within the perimeter of the later Ottoman Seraglio, and their marketplace (*agora*) was near Aya Sofya Square. Little remains of the grandiose rebuilding and enlargement of the city by Septimius Severus. Moreover, the immense architectural enterprises begun by Constantine the Great and carried out by his successors are again only poorly represented, although we have texts that provide numerous valuable topographical indications. It appears that, inside a greatly expanded perimeter, Constantine erected the buildings appropriate to an imperial metropolis. In the center of an elliptical forum was placed a radiate statue of the emperor upon a porphyry column, still standing (the 'Burnt Column'). Nearby were senate house, hippodrome (built by Septimius Severus and enlarged by Constantine) and the Great or Sacred Palace which remained the residence of subsequent rulers for eight hundred years. Nothing is left, except in later, altered form, of Constantine's conically roofed, cross-shaped Basilica of the Holy Apostles—an Apostles' Martyrium and his own intended mausoleum, later replaced by the mosque of Sultan Mehmet II the Conqueror—or his Church of the Holy Peace (St. Irene) on the site of Aphrodite's temple, or the Church of Holy Wisdom (St. Sophia, Aya Sofya), dedicated by Constantius II (360); both St. Irene and St. Sophia were superseded after a fire by Justinian's buildings still to be seen today. The aqueduct of Valens, however, remains standing, for more than half a mile of its length.

Theodosius I (379–95) erected the Golden Gate, the chief ceremonial entrance to the city—comprising three arches (the central opening being a triumphal arch reserved for the emperor)—which was later flanked by square marble towers, and is quite well preserved today. He and Arcadius (395–408) also added new fora, of which details are unknown. But it was Theodosius II (408–50) who provided the most impressive of Constantinople's ancient monuments: its fortifications, which replaced those of Constantine and doubled the perimeter of the city. Despite earthquakes and dilapidations, the land walls erected in 413 and doubled in 447 still stand, extending for more than four miles from the upper reaches of the Golden Horn to the Propontis (Sea of Marmara). In the late 430s a single seawall was added, of which the sections on the Propontis are well preserved, although those along the Golden Horn have vanished. Land and seawalls together were equipped with about four hundred towers.

C

Cabeira *see* Neocaesarea

Cabura *see* Paropamisadae

Cadiz *see* Gades

Caenepolis *see* Armenia, Artaxata

Caenophrurium (Simekli, Çorlu). A coastal town or village in southeastern Thrace (now European Turkey), not far from the Propontis (Sea of Marmara); situated near the eastern borders of Caenice (to which it owes its name, 'garrison of the tribe of the Caeni'), which was one of the fifty regions (*strategiai*) of Thrace listed by the geographer Strabo. Its capital was probably at Aprus (near İnecik).

In AD 275 the emperor Aurelian, on his way to conduct a campaign against the Persians, stopped at Caenophrurium. While there, he detected his secretary Eros in a lie, and threatened him with punishment. In the hope of protecting himself, Eros informed a number of senior officers of the praetorian guard that their ruler had destined them, together with himself, for execution. The officers, bearing in mind Aurelian's reputation as an iron disciplinarian—and perhaps, in some cases, prompted by guilty consciences—accepted the report of Eros as authentic, and one of their number, a Thracian named Mucaper, struck the emperor down, thus robbing Rome of the man who had been largely responsible for its military recovery from the disasters of previous decades.

Caenopolis, Caenepolis *see* Armenia, Artaxata

Caere, the Etruscan Cisra or Chaisr(i)e (now Cerveteri). One of the principal cities of Etruria, situated near its southern extremity (now in Lazio). From about the ninth century BC the site was occupied by a group of villages, or perhaps by a single village, with others scattered nearby; it extended along the outermost spurs of the metal-rich Tolfa mountains, overlooking the coastal plain of the Tyrrhenian Sea, which was three-and-a-half miles away. The valleys of two streams bordered the habitation site on either side, meeting to form the little river Vaccina. At least part of the Tolfa range had come under Caere's control (passing out of the hands of Tarquinii) by the early seventh century BC; and by this time its villages had already been amalgamated into a single city.

Before long, it extended its power and ownership further to the northwest and north, incorporating a number of considerable inland settlements. Moreover, it succeeded Tarquinii as the principal Etruscan naval and sea-trading power, possessing no less than five identifiable ports at Pyrgi (Santa Severa), Castellina, Punicum (Santa Marinella), Alsium (Palo) and Fregenae (Fregene). Being the southernmost of the Etruscan maritime cities, Caere was the nearest to the Greek markets and colonies of Campania, notably Cumae (Cuma), from whose alphabet the Etruscan script was adapted.

But concern prompted by the establishment of a Greek (Phocaean) colony at Alalia (Aleria) in Corsica, dominating the sea approaches to Etruria, inspired Caere to oppose the new foundation, in alliance with its trading partners and rivals the Carthaginians. Following upon the 'Battle of Alalia' (*c* 535), the Caeritans massacred the surviving members of the Greek crews; and subsequently they themselves, it appears from Diodorus, established a settlement of their own in Corsica—at Alalia or nearby.

Bilingual inscriptions, in Greek and Punic, of their king Thefarie Velianas (*c* 500), incised on sheets of gold leaf found at Pyrgi, indicate that the connection with the Carthaginians still, for a time, remained strong. But hostile relations with their Etruscan neighbor Veii threw the rulers of Caere into the arms of Rome, which under its Etruscan monarchy and early Republic used their harbors and fleets for its overseas trade (true, Rome's arch-enemy in Virgil's *Aeneid,* Mezentius, was a Caeritan—but he was a Caeritan whose own city had rejected him). Helped by its friendship with Rome, Caere enjoyed, as excavations show, a very powerful cultural and commercial influence—perhaps extending in some cases to political control—as far afield as various regions in Latium and Campania. However, its interests in the latter region were severely threatened, first by Aristodemus of Cumae (who repelled an Etruscan expedition in 525/24), and then by Syracuse, whose forces extensively plundered the Caeritan coastlands *c* 453.

Meanwhile the keynote of the city's foreign policy remained its alliance with the Romans. Thus, toward the end of the fourth century, when its neighbors and compatriots, the people of Veii, were locked in a deadly struggle with Rome, it failed to support them, and they succumbed. Moreover, when *c* 387 the Gauls under Brennus temporarily occupied Rome, Caere gave asylum to the sacred objects evacuated from the city, and helped hasten Brennus' departure. In response, Rome granted it special privileges, and the two states sent joint colonies to Sardinia and Corsica (*c* 378/77, 357/54). Yet *c* 353 the Caeritans at last became impatient of Rome's increasing domination, and protested or rebelled. However, their gesture was brought to order, and they were deprived of their coastland territory (in favor of Roman colonists) by the terms of a hundred-year treaty or truce. Their independent days were now over, but Roman nobles were still sent to Caere to study the Etruscan language and literature—and perhaps to learn Greek as well.

The greatly increased wealth brought in by the export of metals during the early days of the city's existence is demonstrated by the lavish burial furniture of its graves, notably the gold jewelry (now in the Vatican) from the Regolini-Galassi tomb. The Banditaccia cemetery too, consisting of earth grave-mounds heaped upon plinths of rock or stone, provides a unique memorial of Etruscan civilization in the late seventh and sixth centuries. From *c* 550–540 the Caeritans also became well-known for their working of hammered sheet-bronze; and they inaugurated an impressive school of widely exported ceramics. This was developed through the initiative of Ionian refugees from Persian aggression, who became an important and welcome element in the life of the city, frequenting a temple dedicated to the Greek goddess Hera.

Caere had already produced significant sculptors, and now, in 520, some of the greatest masterpieces of the age were created to adorn the lids of the sarcophagi of its dead: notably life-size figures of a husband and wife reclining on a banqueting couch, now to be seen at Rome (Villa Giulia Museum) and Paris (the Louvre). After 400 Caere became a prolific producer of 'red-figure' pottery. However, from the third to the first century only poor graves are evident, mostly reusing earlier tombs; and by early imperial times Strabo reports that this once mighty city was little more than a village. Nevertheless, buildings of the Roman epoch, including a theater and an Augusteum, have been identified.

Caerleon *see* Isca Silurum

Caerwent *see* Venta Silurum

Caesaraugusta, formerly Salduie or Salduba or Saldubia (now Zaragoza [Saragossa]). A town in northeastern Spain, on the right bank of the river Iberus (Ebro). The pre-Roman town, belonging to the tribal territory of the Sedetani, possessed its own mint and provided a cavalry contingent to the Roman troops of Cnaeus Pompeius Strabo (father of Pompey the Great) fighting Italian rebels in the Social War, a contribution which earned the community Roman citizenship (89 BC). About seventy years later Augustus refounded it as a colony for retired legionary soldiers, discharged after his and Agrippa's wars against the Cantabrians in the north of the peninsula.

An important bridgehead, river port and crossroads, Caesaraugusta was the headquarters of a large judicial district of the province of Hispania Tarraconensis (Citerior, Nearer Spain), and the principal commercial and military station of the Iberus valley. The geographer Mela described it as having been one of the most important cities of the interior, and Strabo testifies to the part it played as a center of Romanization. The colony is notable for the production, under Augustus, of the most extensive bronze coinage of any local mint in the entire peninsula; and the series continued under Tiberius (AD 14–37), depicting an equestrian statue of that emperor and two temples dedicated to the cult of the deified Augustus. The issues came to an end in the time of Gaius (Caligula,

37–41). The perimeter of ancient Caesaraugusta has been identified by clearing the riverbank, and an important part of the ancient wall—reconstructed in the third century after damage from German invasions—is now uncovered. Thereafter economic development continued. There are important Roman villas at Sadaba and Rienda (Artieda de Aragón) in the neighborhood.

Caesaraugusta was one of the first cities of Spain to which Christianity penetrated, and had a bishop of its own by the middle of the third century. Prudentius names eighteen martyrs of the persecutions who came from the place. In 380, during the reign of Gratian, it housed a Church Synod which condemned the Priscillianist heresy. Constantine III (407–11), when he usurped the imperial title in Gaul, established his son Constans at Caesaraugusta as his deputy in Spain, with the rank of Caesar. In 453 it was one of the cities captured by the Visigoth Euric.

Caesarea, formerly Iol, in Mauretania (now Cherchel in Algeria, sixty-two miles west of Algiers). Iol was originally a small trading port founded by the Carthaginians, and in the time of Julius Caesar became the capital of Bocchus II, king of part of Mauretania. After his death (33 BC) his kingdom was annexed by Rome, and granted by Augustus in 25 to Juba II (son of Juba I of Numidia) who married Cleopatra Selene (daughter of Cleopatra VII of Egypt). Establishing his residence at Iol, Juba II made it a splendid Greco-Roman city, under the name of Caesarea—a name that sometimes appears on his abundant silver coinage, together with heads of Africa and representations of a temple and grove (LVCVS) in honor of Augustus.

After the death of Juba II (AD 23) and disturbances following the murder of his son and successor Ptolemy (40), the city became, under Claudius, the capital of a new province of Mauretania Caesariensis, receiving a colony of ex-soldiers (44). Caesarea was the birthplace (164) of the emperor Macrinus. With a population estimated at 100,000, it had become one of the largest centers of north Africa, and one of its principal harbor towns and naval and auxiliary bases. But the city was captured and plundered in the rising of Firmus against Valentinian I (372)—put down by Theodosius the Elder, father of the emperor Theodosius I—and again by the Vandals in 429 during the course of their occupation of north Africa. When Belisarius drove them out (535/4), Caesarea became the capital of the Byzantine province of Mauretania Secunda.

Excavations have uncovered a unique rectangular amphitheater (converted from the theater of Juba II), in which Saint Marciana was martyred. Archaeologists have also now traced the development of the water supply of Caesarea, developing from a simple canal of late first century date to its amplification (with bridges) in about the time of Hadrian (117–38), followed by continuous repairs until destruction by tribesmen in the course of the fourth century. Walls protecting a lighthouse on an adjacent island display an equally complex history of successive rebuildings. The Cherchel and Algiers museums contain excellent mosaic pavements, as well as statues that in many cases reflect the artistic tastes of Juba II.

Caesarea, formerly Mazaca and then Eusebeia (Kayseri) in Cappadocia (Asia Minor). A city situated immediately to the north of the sacred Mount Argaeus (Erciyeş), which appears frequently on its coins. After Cappadocia had become an autonomous state in 301 BC, thereafter gaining complete independence, its rulers established their capital at Mazaca, renamed Eusebia in honor of Ariarathes V Philopator (163–120), who promoted Greek culture as far as he could in a backward country. After the city's sack by Tigranes I the Great of Armenia (77), its inhabitants were deported, but freed by the Roman general Lucullus eight years later.

Subsequently reconstructed by Pompey the Great, Mazaca became the capital of Augustus' client king Archelaus (36 BC–AD 17)—who changed its name to Caesarea in 13/9 BC—and then of the new Roman province of Cappadocia established by Tiberius, from whose time onward it served as a very prolific mint, exceptionally issuing an extensive silver coinage (of which the largest known hoard has, for the most part, recently passed into the hands of the Metropolitan Museum, New York). After the capture of Valerian by the Persians, Caesarea, after a heroic defence, fell into their hands through treachery, but was subsequently recovered. In the later empire, shrunk in size, it remained the capital of a smaller province of Cappadocia Prima, otherwise consisting mainly of imperial estates.

According to Strabo, the region supplied timber, stone and fodder, but the city itself stood in barren, untilled territory. Recent excavations have somewhat increased its sparse surviving remnants; they include large imperial baths (despite difficulties in procuring water). When the site was finally abandoned, a church reputedly built by St. Basil became the center of a new medieval town, of which the circuit, described by Procopius as once again diminished, was given walls by Justinian I.

Caesarea *see also* Antioch in Pisidia, Cyme, Phanagoria, Tralles

---

Caesarea by Anazarbus *see* Anazarbus

Caesarea Maritima, formerly the Tower of Strato (Stratonis Turris). On the Mediterranean coast of Judaea (now Israel), northwest of Jerusalem. Stratonis Turris, named after a circular stone tower erected by Strato I, king of Sidon in Phoenicia (*c* 370–358)—and now, it is believed, uncovered by archaeological investigations—was a small Phoenician naval station enabled by its modest anchorage, and by the agricultural wealth of the Sharon plain in its hinterland, to achieve a reasonable prosperity in the third and second centuries BC.

Captured by the Jewish (Hasmonaean) monarch Alexander I Jannaeus in 103, it was annexed to the Roman province of Syria in 63, but restored by Octavian (the future Augustus) to Herod the Great of Judaea in 30. The port he constructed at Caesarea was one of his most remarkable achievements: he started to build it in 22—on the site of Hellenistic harbor works that have now been discovered—and completed the work twelve years later, under the official name of 'Caesarea Beside the Augustan Harbor.' This great harbor, twenty fathoms deep, protected by a seawall and a breakwater, and larger (according to Josephus) than the port of Piraeus, was entered from the north, the quarter from which the wind blows least severely; its construction shows advanced technology incorporating a sluice system and making use of hydraulic concrete.

Herod also built a Temple of Rome and Augustus, of which the outlines have been tentatively identified. Air photography and excavation have revealed a theater as well (the earliest of its kind in Judaea; it was reconstructed in the second century AD). In addition, Herod equipped the city with an amphitheater, hippodrome and Mithraeum (recently located within a large granary complex); and a fine stretch of the city wall, with two circular towers, has been uncovered. Caesarea possessed two aqueducts (of which portions have survived), bringing water from the springs at the foot of Mount Carmel, eight miles to the northeast. It also developed its own purple-dyeing industry, and rapidly became a busy trading center, as well as an important royal custom post.

When Judaea was annexed by the Romans (AD 6), Caesarea Maritima became the capital, official mint and principal garrison-town of the new province, and an inscription put up by Pontius Pilatus, the best known of all its prefects (later known as procurators), has been found there. It was at Caesarea that St. Peter baptized a Roman centurion and St. Paul was imprisoned for two years. In about 60, tension between the Greco-Syrian majority of the inhabitants, and the large Jewish minority which resented its lack of citizenship, led to riots; Nero decided against the demands of the Jews. Further disturbances (66), culminating in the massacre of the Jewish population, helped to spark off the First Jewish Revolt (First Roman War). Vespasian, proclaimed emperor at Caesarea (69), raised it to the rank of a colony, and it remained the capital of the province, which was henceforth governed by legates of much higher rank than before (and following the Second Jewish Revolt under Hadrian [132–38]was renamed Syria Palaestina). Caesarea also became an important center of both Jewish and Christian learning. Origen settled at the place in 231, and his *Exhortation to Martyrdom* describes the effect of the persecutions of Christians upon its life (235). It was the birthplace of the historians Eusebius (*c* 260) and Procopius (*c* 500), and continued to flourish in Byzantine times.

Caesarea Philippi, formerly Panion, Panium, Panias (now Banyas in Syria). A town situated on the slope of Mount Panion (Hermon) where the principal source of the river Jordan flows from a cave. Originally known, perhaps, as Baal-gad or Baal-hermon, the town and mountain of Panion owed this Greek name (which was also the designation of the whole district) to the worship of the god Pan. It was the site of the decisive battle in which the Seleucid monarch Antiochus III the Great defeated Ptolemy V Epiphanes of Egypt, with the result that Judaea (Palestine) passed into the former's hands (200 BC).

The town was later presented by Augustus to Herod the Great of Judaea, who built a temple in honor of the emperor. After Herod's death (4 BC), it became capital of the princedom or tetrarchy of the late king's son Philip, who enlarged it under the name of Caesarea Philippi, depicting upon his coins the shrine of Pan, of which remains dating from the Roman period have survived. Jesus visited the region, and it was there, according to the Bible, that he charged St. Peter with his mission. A later Jewish prince Agrippa II, to whom the Romans granted the tetrarchy in 53, subsequently renamed the city Neronias in honor of Nero

(54–68). But coins show that at least from the later second century onward it was generally known as Caesarea Panias, or Caesarea Beneath Panion.

Caesarodunum, Altionos, Civitas Turonum, Turoni (Tours, Indre-et-Loire). A town in west-central Gaul, beside a crossing of the river Liger (Loire), just above its confluence with the Caris (Cher), at an important meeting of roads running down their valleys and converging on the main route to the Atlantic. Capital of the small tribe of the Turones, the place played an important part in native resistance during the Gallic Wars of Julius Caesar (whose name it subsequently incorporated) in its new designation Caesarodunum. After the creation of the Roman province of Gallia Lugdunensis, it again fulfilled a prominent role in the Gallic revolt under Tiberius (AD 21).

Destroyed by a German attack in 275, the town was equipped with fortifications; and—in the later empire—reverting to the name of Civitas Turonum or Turoni, it became the capital of the province of Lugdunensis Tertia. Its greatest distinction in ancient times, however, was owed to the episcopate of the Pannonian St. Martin of Tours (372–97), who also founded a monastic community, Majus Monasterium (Marmoutier), outside the city. During the centuries that followed, St. Martin's fame as a dominant ecclesiastical figure and missionary and miracleworker brought thousands of famous pilgrims to his shrine. In the late 430s or 440s, the city was threatened by an invasion of rebellious Aremorici (from Britanny), and after various subsequent vicissitudes came under the control of the Franks under Clovis, whose investiture as a Roman consul took place in the town (508). St. Gregory of Tours, the great historian of the Franks, was the bishop of Turoni and died there in 594.

The Romans moved the city from the right to the left bank of the Liger. Its principal well-preserved monument is an amphitheater dating back to the second century AD, which is one of the largest in the empire. Portions of the massive third century wall have also survived, and recent discoveries include a fourth century building complex and rampart beneath the medieval castle.

Cagliari *see* Caralis

Caicus (Bakır Çayı). The principal river of Mysia (northwestern Asia Minor), situated in a valley containing rich agricultural land. The port of Elaea (Reşadiye) stood at the mouth of the river—southeast of the island of Lesbos—and higher up in the valley were Pergamum (Bergama) in Mysia and Stratonicea (Eskihisar) in Lydia. The Persian kings Darius I and Xerxes I granted land in the region to immigrant exiles from Greece. When Agesilaus of Sparta invaded Persian Asia Minor in 396 and 395 BC, he inaugurated the second of these campaigns by marching up the Caicus valley to the plateau of Phrygia. The Attalid kingdom of Pergamum owed much of its prosperity to the wheatlands on either side of the river, annexed by Eumenes I in 262/61. The lower course of the stream was diverted by a canal constructed in the time of Augustus (31 BC–AD 14).

Caistor-by-Norwich *see* Venta Icenorum

Calabria. In ancient times, this was the name applied to the southeastern promontory or 'heel' of Italy, inhabited by Messapians and other tribes before it passed into Roman hands in the third century BC. When Augustus divided Italy into regions, he joined Calabria to Apulia to form one of them. Although lacking in water, Calabria, according to Strabo, had been remarkably fertile, and was especially famous for its wool; but by his day all except two of its thirteen towns (Tarentum [Taras] and Brundusium [Brindisi]) had dwindled into villages. When the invading Lombards seized Calabria in the late seventh century AD, the Byzantine administrators of the parts of Italy that still remained under their control transferred its name to the southwestern promontory (toe) of Italy, that had formerly been known as the land of the Bruttii.

Calagurris (Calahorra). A town in northern Spain (now the province of Logroño), beside the left bank of the river Cidacos near its junction with the Iberus (Ebro). Mentioned by Livy in connection with Rome's Celtiberian Wars (188/87 BC), it strongly supported the free-lance Sertorius by resisting the government troops of Pompey the Great and Lucius Afranius (76). The town assumed the additional names of Nassica (still unexplained) and Julia, the latter on the occasion of its establishment as a *municipium* in 29/28 by Octavian (Augustus), under whom the local mint issued a considerable series of bronze coins; and we learn from Suetonius that, like Caesar before him, he recruited Calagurritans for his personal bodyguard.

The city was the birthplace of the rhetorician Quintilian (*c* AD 30–35) and possibly also of the greatest Christian Latin poet, Prudentius (348). By the end of the fourth century, however, Ausonius recorded the virtual abandonment of the site. A circus capable of accommodating 20,000 spectators has partially survived, and there are remains of an aqueduct and a twenty-arch bridge that crossed the Iberus on the way to Virovesca (Briviesca).

Calatafimi *see* Segesta

Calatayud *see* Bilbilis

Calchedon, Kalchedon (or Chalcedon, Chalkedon; now Kadıköy). A city in Bithynia (northwestern Asia Minor), across the Thracian Bosphorus from Byzantium (Constantinople, Istanbul). The etymology of the name is uncertain, but the place, which has yielded prehistoric remains (Fikirtepe), may originally have been a Thracian settlement. The Greek city was established by colonists from Megara, traditionally in 685 BC. It was known, Herodotus observes, as 'the city of the blind,' because its founders missed the much superior site of Byzantium, colonized only seventeen years later; though the truth rather was that the emigrants from Megara did not at first feel strong enough to seek a footing among the dangerous peoples on the European side of the strait, despite the vulnerability of Calchedon to unfavorable currents.

Deriving revenue from the copper mines and semiprecious stones of the adjacent island of Chalcitis, Calchedon became, after the Persian Wars, a member of Athens' Delian League, and in 416 its forces attacked and defeated the native Bithynians. The city passed into Persian hands in 387, but helped the Romans against Philip V of Macedonia, earning its liberation after they had defeated him. Xenocrates, head of the Platonic Academy (339–314/12), was born at Calchedon. The city was attached, still as a free community, to the Roman province of Bithynia (74); but in the following year, during the Third War against Mithridates VI of Pontus, Marcus Aurelius Cotta was forced to barricade himself inside its walls, where he could not prevent the Pontic fleet from capturing sixty of his ships. A prolonged local coinage of the imperial epoch includes issues honoring Hadrian's Bithynian companion Antinous as a hero (*heros*), and depicting him riding on a griffin. It was at Calchedon that the defeated emperor Macrinus was captured by the forces of Elagabalus (218).

During the reigns of Valerian and Gallienus the city was more than once laid waste by the Goths (*c* 258, 267). Nevertheless, Constantine the Great (306–37) was alleged to have seriously considered it as a possible capital before his choice finally fell on Byzantium. It also figured prominently in his civil wars against Licinius, who, as Constantine approached Byzantium by sea in 324, crossed over to Calchedon and appointed a co-emperor, Martinian, to stop his enemy from crossing, but in vain. However, the most important event that took place in Calchedon in ancient times dates from the following century. This was the Fourth Ecumenical Council of 451 (during the reign of the eastern emperor Marcian): the meeting of bishops which, amid immense and lasting controversy, formulated a doctrine—still accepted as authoritative by Christian churches—describing Jesus Christ as complete in his humanity and divinity alike.

Caledonia, the name used by Tacitus for the land of the Celtic Caledonii in the Scottish highlands, and by Ptolemy for the inhabitants of the Great Glen southwest of the Beauly Firth. Other writers are vaguer, whereas Dio Cassius divides non-Roman Britain between the Caledonii and Maeatae.

Agricola defeated the Caledonii at Mons Graupius (Bennachie?) in AD 84, but without conquering them decisively. After the construction of Hadrian's Wall (Tyne-Solway) and Antonine Wall (Forth-Clyde, later abandoned), Septimius Severus renewed the attack on them (209–11), but again without lasting results, though tenuously dependent client kingdoms were later established in Dumbarton and Lothian. The Picts, a people, apparently, of mixed Celtic and non-Celtic race (though the Romans used the name inexactly), are first heard of *c* 297, and became a serious threat in the fourth century, when, based on Strathmore, they began to control much of central and eastern Scotland; while at the same time immigrants from Ireland not only occupied the maritime regions of Britain from south Wales to the Solway Firth, but planted colonies on the coasts of Argyllshire which developed *c* 500–50 into principalities, later unified to form Dalriada (the name of their homeland Ulster), in which St. Columba founded his monastery at Iona *c* 563. These settlers were known as Scotti, and became so numerous and powerful that they gave their name to the whole country.

Cales (Calvi Vecchia). A city in Campania (southwest Italy), near its borders with Latium, occupying a long narrow plateau, nearly surrounded by the Rio dei Lanzi and other streams, at the foot of a spur of Mount Maggiore. Founded, according to an erroneous etymological comparison, by the Greek mythological hero Calais, son of Boreas, Cales was in fact a settlement of the Aurunci, a tribe identified with the Osci or Ausonii, after whom the whole of Italy was sometimes named. But recent excavations have also made it apparent that the place became one of the foremost centers of Etruscan expansion into this territory: an important tomb has been dated *c* 635/25, which appears to have been the time when an Etruscan ruler can first be identified at the city.

In 335 Marcus Valerius Corvus captured the place, celebrating a Triumph, and the Romans made it the location of their first Latin colony in Campania, establishing 2,500 settlers there; situated on the Via Latina, it also became the seat of a financial official, the quaestor for south Italy. For several centuries to come, Cales' distinctive black-glazed pottery on a red base, imitating metalwork, enjoyed a very extensive circulation throughout the peninsula and even far beyond it. The inhabitants of the place also produced sculpture, wine and agricultural implements, and issued plentiful bronze (*aes grave*) coins, depicting a wine cup; silver issues followed. During the Second Punic War Livy records Cales as one of the twelve communities that, after suffering heavy losses, refused the Romans further aid against Hannibal (209), thus incurring severe punishment later. Reinforced, however, in 184, it became prosperous once again, receiving *c* 89 the status of *municipium* (exchanged for the rank of Roman colony in the second century AD).

The city's fortifications display successive reconstructions and, in particular, restorations of the epoch of Sulla (81/80 BC). It was in his time, too, that an earlier theater was enlarged, and a central bathing establishment constructed. Another dates from the second century AD, when the late Republican amphitheater was also rebuilt. The city suffered virtual destruction at the hands of the Vandal Gaiseric (429-77).

Callaecia, Gallaecia (Galicia), occupies the northwestern corner of the Iberian peninsula, taking its name from the tribe of the Callaeci (Callaici), whose origin was disputed. Famous, according to Strabo, for their ability as warriors—and for the abundance of various metals on their territory—they were attacked in 138/37 BC by Decimus Junius Brutus, who celebrated a Triumph for the victories he had won over them (and over the Lusitani). These successes, followed up by a naval expedition of Julius Caesar (governor of Further Spain) in 60, made the Callaeci more or less accessible to the influence of Roman arms and trade. They were linked, at this stage, with the province of Further Spain, but after Augustus' generals had penetrated and subjugated their strongholds in 25 he enlarged Nearer Spain (Citerior, Tarraconensis) instead, to include this north-western region of the country. Under the reorganization of Diocletian and Constantine Callaecia became a separate province, extended eastward to include Legio (Leon), which became its capital. In 411 German invaders, the Suevi, formed a Callaecian kingdom which was destroyed by the Visigoths in 585.

Callatis, Kallatis (Mangalia in Rumania). A city on the west coast of the Euxine (Black) Sea, situated in an area of fertile grain-land. To judge by an early name Acervetis or Carvatis, Callatis was originally inhabited by a branch of the Thracian tribal group of the Getae. Settlers from Heraclea Pontica (Ereğli in northern Asia Minor) of Megarian origin—Dorians, that is to say, rather than Ionians like other settlers in the region—founded a Greek colony, though not, it would seem, in the later sixth century BC, as has been supposed, but one hundred and fifty years later, when its silver coinage first appears.

Long independent (except perhaps for a brief early period under Athenian control), and deriving profitable revenue from its agriculture, Callatis opposed determined though unsuccessful resistance to Lysimachus, one of Alexander's successors who had established a kingdom in Thrace (313/10). After regaining its freedom, the city suffered a severe defeat from Byzantium (*c* 260?), and, in addition, like other Greek communities, came under prolonged pressure from Scythian chieftains in the interior. During the first century it sided with Mithridates VI Eupator of Pontus against the Romans, to whose general Lucullus it fell by siege in 72; about two years later a treaty was concluded with the city (though this has alternatively been attributed to *c* 114–107). About 50 Callatis was captured by the Dacian king Burebistas, who was murdered, however, *c* 44.

An inscription of AD 2 at Callatis is dedicated to a Roman commander Publius Vinicius, possibly the first governor of Moesia, to which Callatis henceforth belonged; when the province was divided into two by Domitian (85/6), it became part of Lower Moesian territory, but was by this time eclipsed by the rival city of Tomis (Constanţa), twenty-seven miles to the north. However, after the tribe of the Costoboci had broken across the Danube (*c* 170–72), Callatis equipped itself with fortifications, resuming its local coinage. But frequent invasions during the ensuing century continuously weakened its strength and ability to resist, though a recovery became apparent under Diocletian (284–305) and his successors.

The earlier city is mostly under the sea, of which the level has risen by over six feet. But its importance is reflected by mounds containing rich grave-gifts in chambered tombs. Several hundred late classical and Hellenistic terracotta figurines have been published, pointing to a local manufacture that reached its peak in the third century BC. Underwater archaeology has revealed part of the harbor, and stretches of fortifications of the second and third centuries AD. Cults of Demeter and Dionysus have also been noted, and a Christian basilica of Syrian type, forming part of a series of reconstruction programs dating from early Byzantine times.

Calleva Atrebatum (Silchester in Hampshire, southern England, eight miles southwest of Reading). Calleva was a prosperous town of the Belgic tribe of the Atrebates, whose King Commius penetrated to the place; a certain Eppillus coined there in AD 5–10. The town was taken by Epaticcus, king of the Catuvellauni (the most powerful of the Belgic peoples) *c* 25, but after the Roman invasion of 43 reverted to the Atrebates, under Cogidubnus who had become a Roman client; it served as their cantonal capital, and its position as an important road junction stimulated rapid development. Protection of the inhabitants (estimated at about 2,000) was provided by a polygonal earthwork enclosing a perimeter of two hundred and thirty acres, reduced at the beginning of the second century to about one hundred.

The street plan—the most fully known in Roman Britain—divided Calleva into about forty blocks. Public buildings that have now been identified include a basilica (beside the forum, showing a pre-Flavian occupation layer over pre-Roman post-holes), bathing establishments, a poorly preserved amphitheater and at least three square Romano-Celtic temples, in addition to another of polygonal shape. A large official residence, numerous houses and shops, and a variety of local industries (notably metal-working) have also come to light. Calleva was a center for the manufacture of jet, which was in demand for its rarity, value and magic powers. Town walls are also visible, and earlier complicated inner and outer earthen defences have been revealed by air photography and recently described. A small Christian church is perhaps datable to the fourth century, when Calleva continued to flourish. It became a garrison for German mercenaries, and in a final phase the habitations of the last Callevans were separated from those of Saxon settlers by an earthwork.

Calusium, Kalousion(?) (Orbetello). On the coast of Etruria (Tuscany), opposite the protruding promontory and peninsula of Mount Argentarius (Argentario). Today, after prolonged erosion, the Argentario is joined to the mainland at either side by a pair of sandbars. These form the sides of an enclosed lagoon, on the mainland bank of which an Etruscan town was located, upon a spit by the modern Orbetello. This site has been identified with the 'Calusium' named by Polybius (which may be the maritime 'Clusium' mentioned by Virgil—the famous Clusium lies far inland).

In antiquity both of the isthmus sandbars that joined the Argentario to the mainland were penetrated by channels linking the sea with the lagoon, which consequently formed an excellent harbor. The existence of an active Etruscan settlement, inhabited continually from the eighth century BC onward, is demonstrated by adjoining cemeteries and confirmed by recent discoveries of houses dating from the fifth to the third centuries on the Doganella site. A sphinx of volcanic stone—one of the local discoveries—indicates, by its style, the influence of the major Etruscan city-state of Vulci, to whose sphere the port evidently belonged. Fragments of amphoras found in one of these isthmus channels show that for a period the place remained an active harbor and commercial center after the beginning of Roman domination, but as time went on, owing to the silting of the lagoon, it lost its importance, which was transferred to the colony of Cosa (Ansedonia) four and a half miles away.

Calvi Vecchia *see* Cales

Calydon, Lakydon (Kourtaga). A Greek city in Aetolia near the north coast of the Gulf of Patrae (Patras), at the entrance of the Gulf of Corinth. Calydon possessed extraordinary importance in Greek myth. These stories centered around the house of King Oeneus, husband of Althaea and father or reputed father of Tydeus, Deianira and Meleager. Tydeus was the father of the Homeric hero Diomedes; Deianira married Heracles, murdered him with a poisoned robe, and committed suicide (*see* Sophocles' *Women of Trachis*); Meleager, in the company of a great array of heroes, slew the monstrous Calydonian boar sent by Artemis (a favorite theme of archaic and classical art), and gave its head to Atalanta whom he loved, thus precipitating a massive quarrel in which he killed one, or more than one, of his uncles—Althaea's brothers—and himself met his death.

Calydon did not play a conspicuous part in ancient history. However, its remains, the most important in Aetolia, include splendidly decorated temples of Apollo (?) and Artemis in the sacred precinct of Laphrion, dating back to the end of the seventh century BC and reconstructed at subsequent periods. The temple of Artemis contained a famous gold and ivory statue of the goddess by Menaechmus and Soidas of Naupactus (460), mentioned by Pausanias. Massive Hellenistic fortifications have partially survived. The Heroon (or Leonteion, after Leon its owner), a rectangular, colonnaded edifice of *c* 100, includes a room decorated with at least eleven large medallions depicting the legendary history of Calydon. During the civil wars of the first century it was occupied by Pompey the Great, and in 30 its inhabitants were transferred to Nicopolis, the new foundation of Octavian (Augustus), who had defeated Antony off nearby Actium in the previous year.

Camarina, Kamarine (near Scoglitti) on the southern coast of Sicily. Situated upon a low promontory thirteen miles south of Hybla Heraea (Ragusa), in fertile country between the mouths of the rivers Hippares (Camarina) and Oanis (Rifriscolaro), Camarina was a colony founded by the Syracusans in 599/8 BC on a previously uninhabited site. It stood close to their border with the territory of Gela, and was continually affected by the power struggles between the two cities. According to the historian Philistus, Camarina established an alliance with the native Sicels in the interior. Destroyed in 553/2 by the Syracusans, it was partially rebuilt (and recolonized) by Gela in 492 and again in 461 (after a second destruction, this time by Geloans in 484). Pindar's Fourth Olympian Ode celebrates the victory of Psaumis the Camarinaean in the chariot race of 452. After Camarina had joined an anti-Syracusan coalition in 427–424, an agreement with the Geloans confirmed its control over an extensive territory, including Morgantina (Serra Orlando). The later fifth century witnessed the production of beautiful coinage—signed by the artists Euaenetus and Exacestides—depicting the nymph Camarina, the river-god Hipparis, and the tutelary deity Athena.

When the Athenians attacked Syracuse in the Peloponnesian War (415), Camarina vacillated, declaring its neutrality but then coming over to the side of the Syracusans; but they abandoned the city to Carthaginian invaders in 405. Displaced to Syracuse, and then Leontini, the citizens of Camarina returned in 396, but continued to pay tribute to Carthage. In 339, however, Timoleon, a Corinthian who had assumed authority at Syracuse and beaten off the Carthaginian menace, reconstructed and recolonized the city, inaugurating a final period of prosperity. But it proved brief, since a body of Campanian mercenaries known as the Mamertines, who had seized Messana (Messina), destroyed much of Camarina in 275, and the Romans repeated this action in 258, reducing its inhabitants (according to Diodorus) to slavery. The town survived, however, on a diminished scale, until Strabo, in the early years of the Principate, reported its site as abandoned.

Topographical study reveals a story of repeated destruction and rebuilding. The city walls, dating from the mid-sixth century BC, enclosed a circumference of nearly four miles, within which a fifth-century right-angled grid plan is discernible. Remains of the temple of Athena, of that period, can still be seen, and traces of dwellings dating back to the fourth century (House of the Merchant, House of the Inscription) and the second and first centuries (House of the Altar). The agora has recently been identified on a bluff overlooking the sea—adjacent to a Temple of Athena above which a small church was later erected—while underwater excavations have revealed harbor installations, of Hellenistic date, at the mouth of the Hipparis, and a sunken ship of the time of Septimius Severus (AD 193–211) containing columns of *giallo antico* marble. Large necropoleis of various epochs surround the city on three sides.

Camirus *see* Rhodes

Campania. A region of southwest Italy, between the Apennines and the Tyrrhenian Sea, extending from the (fluctuating) boundaries of Latium, first to the promontory of Surrentum (Sorrento), and then as far as the river Silarus (Sele). The volcanic soil of the territory was very fertile, but it was for purposes of trading that the first of many Greek markets—subsequently cities—were founded. The earliest of these colonists, in the eighth century BC, were Euboeans who settled first on the island of Pithecusae (Ischia), off the northwestern end of the Gulf of Cumae (Bay of Naples), and next at Cumae (Cuma)—later a major maritime city-state—whose merchants then settled in Neapolis (Naples, *c* 600), the mother city of Pompeii and Herculaneum.

Some of the city-states of Etruria largely owed their affluence to trading with Campanian centers, and recent research has revealed an extremely powerful Etruscan presence—alongside that of the Greeks—in the region from the eighth and seventh centuries onward, not at Cumae, which remained Greek, but at cities including Capua (Santa Maria Capua Vetere; a major road-center), Nola, Cales (Calvi), Fratte di Salerno, and Picentia (Pontecagnano). The Greeks in the area severely defeated the Etruscans in 474, but Cumae and Capua were overrun in the 420s by Italic (Sabellian) invaders, who merged with the native population, imposing their Oscan language. Confronted, however, by fresh Sabellian incursions, these Campanians—as they were now called—sought Roman protection (*c* 343), which very soon meant Roman control, including limited forms of citizenship.

During the Second Punic War (218–201) a number of towns refused to give the Romans further aid, or seceded to Hannibal, incurring severe punishment, followed by the foundation of further colonies (94; more were added in 59). During the last two centuries BC Puteoli (Pozzuoli), situated on the Gulf of Cumae, which was also filled with rich pleasure resorts, became the principal port of the Romans. However, after a damaging earthquake in AD 61, these places suffered terrible destruction from the eruption of Vesuvius in 79, which destroyed Pompeii, Herculaneum, Stabiae (Castellamare di Stabia) and Oplontis (Torre Annunziata). About 285 Campania, which had been combined with Latium to form a single Italian region since the beginning of the Principate, became the name of a district or province comprising these two territories. Later, however, the designation was restricted to Latium, where the area subsequently known as the Campagna Romana is situated.

Campi Catalaunii, Catalaunian Plains. A region in Champagne (central France), settled by the Gallic tribe of the Catalauni, centered on Châlons-sur-Marne (Durocatalaunum). It was here that Aurelian eliminated the breakaway Gallo-Roman empire in AD 273, defeating the army of Tetricus, who deserted his own troops and changed sides while the fighting still continued.

But the most famous event in the history of the region was a second battle in 451, when Aetius—the leading general of the western emperor Valentinian III—and his Visigothic ally Theoderic I confronted Attila, king of the Huns, and the forces of his numerous German subjects. Although Theoderic, together with huge numbers of soldiers on either side, lost his life, the result was a very heavy defeat for the Huns, who evacuated Gaul; after an abortive push into Italy, Attila died four years later, and his enormous empire fell apart. The exact site of the historic engagement is uncertain. It has been designated the 'battle of Châlons,' because Jordanes and Hydatius ascribe it to the Catalaunian Plains; it took place, according to one suggestion, in the area northeast of Châlons, on the way to the Forest of Argonne. But the term 'Catalaunian Plains' could refer vaguely to almost any part of the territory of Champagne. In the Law of the Burgundians, the engagement is described as *pugna Mauriacensis,* which have led some to locate it south of Châlons, in the neighborhood of Troyes.

Campi Phlegraei *see* Puteoli

Campus Serenus *see* Tzirallum

Camulodunum (Colchester). A town of southeastern Britannia (England), in an agricultural district ten miles from the coast of Essex. Named after the Gallo-British god Mars Camulus, and situated on a promontory bounded on three sides by marshy valleys, the pre-Roman town at Lexden Heath belonged to the tribe of the Trinovantes, but was occupied *c* AD 10 (for the second time) by the Catuvellauni—the most powerful Belgic people—under their King Cunobelinus (perhaps the legendary Old King Cole), who before his death in 42 made Camulodunum his capital fortress and mint (the Great Lexden Barrow was the grave of a member of his family); the place was now the leading commercial port of Britain. The emperor Claudius was present at its capture by his general Aulus Plautius in 43, whereupon it briefly became a legionary headquarters: some six years later Publius Ostorius Scapula fôunded a colony of ex-soldiers, which at first served as the capital of the British province. During the rebellion of Boudicca (Boadicea), queen of the Iceni, in 60, Camulodunum was destroyed, but was subsequently reconstructed, under the name of Victricensis, to become once again, until 70, a legionary headquarters (of which the outline has been discovered) and—although the provincial capital had been moved to Londinium (London), fifty miles to the southwest—still ranked as one of the principal towns of Roman Britain, covering an area of a hundred and ten acres.

Its earthwork defences were supplemented in the second century by a stone wall, of which the greater part, over a mile long, survives, together with the western (Balkerne) Gate, which had originally been a triumphal arch. Other important remains include those of the Temple of Claudius (under the later Norman castle; the subject of a recent full report) and of other shrines, of Celtic type, in the suburbs, where there is also a theater of very unusual plan (now explored), which was perhaps the tribal meeting place of the Trinovantes after the establishment of the colony. Camulodunum may have been one of the mints of Carausius and Allectus, Roman officers who usurped the imperial throne in Britain (*c* 287–96), although the attribution is disputed. In the later empire Camulodunum formed part of the province of Maxima Caesariensis in the administrative diocese of the Britanniae. One of the three British bishops at the Council of Arelate (Arles) in 314 was either from Camulodunum or Lindum (Lincoln).

Çan Çayı *see* Granicus

Cannae. A town on the right bank of the river Aufidus (Ofanto) in Apulia (Puglia), southeast Italy, five miles northeast of Canusium (Canosa), of which it was a dependency. Discoveries on and around the site go back to prehistoric times, but the place is famous for the defeat inflicted on the Romans by Hannibal during the Second Punic War (216 BC). Cannae was at this time a small fortress and important supply base. The battle took place on a smooth local plain in the neighborhood; whether this was on the left or right bank of the Aufidus—which has often changed its course—remains uncertain, but the course of events can be reconstructed from the accounts of Polybius and Livy. Two inexperienced consuls, Lucius Aemilius Paullus and Gaius Terentius Varro, had been entrusted with the joint command of the largest force Rome had ever put into the field, numbering perhaps 48,000 infantry and 6,000 cavalry. In a supreme effort to end the war at a single blow, they engaged Hannibal's 35,000 infantry and 10,000 cavalry, believing that their numerical superiority would prove decisive. However, the prevailing hot sirocco wind blew blinding sand clouds into the Romans' faces, and they found themselves hopelessly trapped by a pincer movement of the Carthaginians' light troops on either flank and cavalry in the rear. After savage resistance, the consuls' army was almost wholly destroyed, thus incurring its gravest catastrophe of the war and the bloodiest defeat any Roman army ever suffered. Hannibal's unprecedented envelopment of a larger force by a smaller one was copied by the German general Von Schlieffen during the First World War, in 1914.

Excavations of the Roman town (including part of the wall) suggest that Cannae continued to serve as a satellite of Canusium as late as the fourth century AD.

Canusium, Kanousion (Canosa). A city situated on the borders of Daunia and Peucetia, regions of Apulia (Puglia) in southeast Italy. Canusium lay beside the right bank of the river Aufidus, fifteen miles from its mouth. According to Hellenizing myth (and false etymology) the city was founded by the hero Diomedes, and named after his hunting dogs (*canes*). Although a township of the Daunians—who in the seventh and sixth centuries made Geometric pottery, formerly attributed to Rubi (Ruvo)—its development under Hellenistic influences is illustrated by archaeological finds and by coins with Greek inscriptions; Horace describes the place as bilingual in Greek and Latin at his own epoch.

Canusium submitted to Rome in 318 BC, but preserved the right to issue coinage, and manufactured fine polychrome vases. Its prosperity was largely based on the cleaning and dyeing of wool. During the Second Punic War the city admitted Roman survivors from the disastrous battle of Cannae nearby (216). However, it sided against Rome in the Social War (allies' rebellion), taking in the defeated Samnite general Trebatius (89), and thus incurring Roman retribution. Nevertheless, like other Italian cities, Canusium became a *municipium*. It was a station on the Via Trajan (AD 109) between Beneventum (Benevento) and Brundusium (Brindisi) and a colony of Antoninus Pius (138-61) or Marcus Aurelius (161-80), and was enlarged—as we learn from Philostratus—by the Athenian sophist Herodes Atticus (consul in 143), who provided an aqueduct to remedy the shortage of water, on which Horace had remarked. Procopius notes that in the sixth century it was Apulia's most important city.

Remains of Neolithic and Bronze Age occupation, and of the Daunian habitation site, have been discovered. Later finds include parts of the city wall and towers (incorporated in medieval fortifications), the Arco Romano (perhaps a funerary monument), Hellenistic and Roman temples, tombs of the fourth century BC (Ipogei Lagasta) and of the Augustan age and second century AD, a Roman bathhouse, and a Roman bridge across the Aufidus, rebuilt in the Middle Ages.

Capisa, Kapisa *see* Alexandria Beside Caucasus, Paropamisus

Cappadocia. A country in east-central Asia Minor. The name had once been applied to a much larger region extending from the Euxine (Black) Sea to the Taurus (Toros) Mountains and from Lake Tatta (Tuzgölü) in the center of the peninsula to the Euphrates. Subsequently, however, the term was employed for the southern part of this territory, namely Greater Cappadocia (part of the northern area being described as Pontus Cappadocicus). Thus defined, Cappadocia was a massive, rugged, isolated tract of broken mountain masses and some tableland (notably the high fruit-bearing plain of Melitene and the large plain of Cataonia) which suffered from extreme temperatures, but produced numerous horses, sheep and mules, as well as red ochre, stone, onyx and alabaster (in the west), and silver and lead (in the Taurus).

After Assyrian, Phrygian and Cimmerian penetration, the Achaemenid (Persian) conquest (585 BC) installed a satrap ruling at Mazaca (the later Caesarea, now Kayseri) and an Iranian nobility exercising feudal control over extensive areas, while other considerable territories were under priestly domination, notably the lands surrounding the shrine of Ma at Comana. The Persian satrap Ariarathes I, who claimed descent from the Achaemenid royal house, evaded Alexander the Great's attempts to supersede him, but was killed in 322 and replaced by the late king's former secretary Eumenes of Cardia.

In 301, however, Ariarathes II recovered control—nominally as a vassal of the Seleucids: but then the third ruler of the same name (*c* 250–220) declared himself king. He and his son, however, remained Seleucid allies until the defeat of Antiochus III the Great by the Romans (189/8), of whom henceforth the Cappadocian monarchs became clients. Cities were few and culture was backward, but Ariarathes V Eusebes Philopator (163–130) promoted Hellenization as much as he could.

After a period of chaos during Rome's wars against Mithridates VI of Pontus, the country was restored and financed by Pompey (64/63). But in 36 Antony removed Ariarathes X Eusebes Philadelphus, because he had displayed Parthian sympathies, and replaced him by Archelaus Philopatris Ktistes (of a different family), who ruled until the time of Tiberius, when Cappadocia was annexed as a Roman province (AD 17) and its extensive royal properties were taken over by the emperor. Destined to become extremely important because of its strategic frontier location, the country was merged with Galatia by Vespasian (72)—to watch over Armenia and Persia, and dominate Pontic brigands—until Trajan formed a new united province of Cappadocia and Pontus (107/113). Cappadocia was invaded by Sapor I of Persia in 251/2 and again some years later. From the time of the eastern emperor Valens (364–78) there were two Cappadocian provinces, Prima and Secunda.

Capreae (Capri). A mountainous island off the lower extremity of the Gulf of Cumae (Bay of Naples) in Campania (southwest Italy). Comprising an area of four square miles, and formed of a single block of limestone, it includes a high western portion (containing Monte Solaro, 1,932 feet, overlooking the town of Anacapri) and a lower eastern portion (where the principal town Capri is situated). The island has provided late Neolithic finds—notably in a famous sea-cave, the Blue Grotto—and, according to a legend preserved by Virgil, was occupied by the Teleboi from Acarnania (northwest Greece) at the time of the Trojan War. In historical times Capreae had Greek occupants, and from 326 BC belonged to Neapolis (Naples). It was well known for its *ephebia,* an organization to which wealthy young people belonged. Gradually Romanized, the island became a favorite resort of Augustus, who made it independent of the Neapolitans, ceding them Aenaria (Pithecusae, now Ischia) instead.

In AD 27 his successor Tiberius gave Capreae fame by settling there for the last decade of his reign, controlling the imperial government from the island in order to stay away from the irritations of Rome. It was from Capreae that he arranged the suppression of the conspiracy of Sejanus (31). His isolation and seclusion gave rise to stories of extraordinary debauchery, recorded by Tacitus and Suetonius. According to tradition, there were twelve early imperial residences on the island—perhaps dedicated to the twelve major deities. But the only identifiable remains are those of the Villa Jovis, mentioned by Suetonius (revealing complex structures that formed part of a large estate on the rocky northeastern tip of the island), the Villa Damecuta on the promontory that juts out from Anacapri (buried by cinders in the eruption of Vesuvius in 79), and the Palazzo al Mare near the principal port (Marina Grande). After the time of Tiberius, Capreae was employed as a place of exile for disgraced imperial personages, notably Crispina and Lucilla, the wife and sister of Commodus (182).

Capsa (Gafsa). A city in north Africa (southern Tunisia), situated in an oasis on a pass between two hills, at a point where roads from various directions converge. Occupied by an ancient settlement (which gave its name to a prehistoric culture), Capsa supported King Jugurtha of Numidia and his Gaetulian allies (to whom it lay close) in their war against the Romans (112–104 BC). In 107 one of the first actions of the new Roman commander Gaius Marius was to undertake a spectacular desert march to seize Capsa, which he then destroyed, massacring its inhabitants. Having raised the spirits of his troops by this achievement, he next felt able to launch a general attack on enemy strongholds.

Capsa revived to become a *municipium* under Hadrian (AD 117–38) and subsequently a *colonia.* Its principal ancient remains are three large-walled water basins placed over springs and connected to one another by underground channels.

Capua, formerly Volturnum and Capeva (Santa Maria Capua Vetere, not the modern Capua, which is the ancient Casilinum). Situated in the interior of Campania (southwest Italy), twenty miles inland from Cumae (Cuma) and sixteen miles from Neapolis (Naples), Capua stood on level ground in the middle of very fertile agricultural territory, beside a ford of the river Volturnus or Vulturnus (Volturno)—on an important north-south route—and near another river as well, the swampy Clanius (Regi Lagni).

These names (like Capeva) are both Etruscan, and although legend ascribed the establishment of the city to Capys, a companion of Aeneas, it was in fact founded, or refounded, by the Etruscans—as Velleius Paterculus recorded—on the site of an earlier (Iron Age) settlement. Recent excavations have revealed an unbroken development from at least *c* 800 BC, including an eighth-century necropolis beside a sanctuary of Artumes (Artemis, Diana) on nearby Tifata. It was at about this time that the place became an urbanized city-state, dominating a wide surrounding area and making early contacts with the neighboring Greek centers Pithecusae (Ischia) and Cumae; the latter became a hostile rival and yet at the same time contributed largely to Capua's adoption of a Greco-Etruscan rather than purely Etruscan culture. This blend is reflected in the bronze work and silverware for which the place became and remained famous, exporting its products far and wide. Iron came from Populonia in Etruria in the form of partially smelted blooms. After the weakening of Etruscan power in Campania in 474—at the hands of Cumae and Syracuse—Capua was captured *c* 425 by the invading Sabellians or Samnites (who took Cumae soon afterward), and became the principal city of the Campanian people that gradually evolved from the invaders' descendants.

Menaced by new Sabellian invaders (*c* 343), Capua supported the rebellion of the Latins and other allies against Rome some three years later. In 338, therefore, the Romans confiscated a rich part of their territory (the *ager Falernus*) and distributed it to Roman citizens, granting to the Capuans themselves an inferior form of the franchise (*civitas sine suffragio*), though they preserved their native Oscan langugage and the Oscan name of their state officials (*meddices*). After their connection with Rome had been strengthened by the Via Appia, which linked the two cities in 312, Capua, still relying on its metalworking industries, and exporting its famous perfumes made of wild roses and olive oil, became the second city in Italy, notorious, according to Athenaeus, for its people's arrogance and luxurious living. During the Second Punic War, however, shaken by the Romans' defeat at Cannae (216)—and still unwilling to acknowledge their supremacy as an Italian power—Capua seceded to Hannibal (who reputedly intended to make it the capital of Italy), but was recaptured after a short siege (212-211) and deprived of its political rights, losing its territory to newly settled colonists (194) and small farmers.

In 73 it was the starting point of the slave revolt of Spartacus (member of a famous local school of gladiators), who defeated two Roman armies before his suppression two years later. Subsequently, Capua received drafts of ex-soldier settlers from Julius Caesar (200,000 in number settled there in 59 on Pompey the Great's behalf) and then again, in 43 from Antony and in 36 and later from Octavian (Augustus), assuming the titles Concordia Julia Valeria and Julia Felix Augusta. Under the dynasty of Vespasian (69-96)—it has recently been discovered—the city became a Colonia Flavia. In the fourth century AD Ausonius pronounced it the eighth-greatest city in the empire, remarking that at one time it had been a second Rome. But it was sacked by Gaiseric the Vandal in 456, and nearly destroyed by the Saracens in 840. Among the numerous and varied results of local excavations (including recent examinations of the early levels), a continuous series of bronzes, architectural terracottas and vases have emerged. Traces of numerous temples are also to be seen, including a fine early painted Mithraeum, of the second and early third centuries AD. But Capua's most impressive surviving monument is its amphitheater, the successor (in the second century AD) of the arena from which Spartacus and his fellow gladiators made their escape, a building second only to the Colosseum in dimensions and grandeur. Tombs outside the city, on the road to Caserta, include one that is the largest in Campania.

Caralis, Carales, Karalis (Cagliari). A city in Sardinia, at the head of the gulf of the same name at the center of the south coast. Although a Greek story claimed the mythical Aristaeus as its founder, the name seems Carthaginian. The commercial and civic life of the ancient settlement, the heir to prehistoric villages, centered around the lagoon of Santa Gilla, which was at that time accessible to ships and formed part of the harbor. After Rome had annexed Sardinia and Corsica and converted them into a province, Caralis in due course (despite a rising in 177 BC), became its capital, serving also as the principal point of the road system of the island. It obtained the rank of *municipium,* probably from Octavian (the future Augustus). A temple dating back at least to the third century BC has been identified on the site. A fuller's shop with a pavement of Republican date, and an amphitheater of the second century AD on the flank of the acropolis (Castello) hill, and the so-called House of Tigellius—in reality a group of three houses—are also to be seen. A large and luxurious public bath containing fine statues has now been excavated near the forum; and the city is still provided with water by an aqueduct dating from the first century AD. Outside, the Sant' Avendrace and Bonaria hills contain pit-tombs dug into the rock. During the vicissitudes of Sardinia in the fifth century, Caralis became a naval base for operations against the Vandals and Goths. In this period, the Christian basilica of San Saturnino (or Santi Cosma e Damiano) was erected, between the Castello and Bonaria hills.

Cardia, Kardia (near Bulair). At the head of the Gulf of Melas on the west side of the Thracian Chersonese (Gelibolu, Gallipoli), at its narrowest point. Founded by colonists from Miletus, (Balat)—perhaps supplemented by Clazomenae (Klazümen)—in the late seventh century BC, it received a draft of Athenian settlers under the leadership of Miltiades the Elder (560), who strengthened the defences and built a wall across the isthmus. After a temporary interruption by the Persian king Darius I (493), Cardia remained under the control of the Athenians, serving as one of their naval bases in the Peloponnesian War against Sparta (431–404).

In the fourth century, however, the city became the focus of a bitter struggle between Athens and Macedonia. In 352/1 it joined the Macedonian king Philip II, and during the reign of his son Alexander the Great came under the autocratic rule ('tyranny') of a certain Hecataeus. Cardia was the birthplace of Eumenes, Alexander's secretary, who became one of the principal Greek leaders after the king's death, and of Hieronymus, who wrote an important history of the same period. After Alexander's death, however, Lysimachus, who had gained control of Thrace, destroyed the city, removing its population to his new capital Lysimachia. But the elder Pliny, writing in the first century AD, indicated that by his time Cardia had regained some of its earlier importance.

Caria, Karia. A region in the extreme southwest of Asia Minor, extending upward to the river Maeander (Büyük Menderes), and bordering on Ionia, Lydia, Phrygia and Lycia. The Greeks who settled Cnidus and Halicarnassus (Bodrum) on the coast believed that the Carians' predecessors in the country, whom they subsequently employed as domestic slaves, came from the adjacent islands. But the Carians themselves claimed to be indigenous, and retained their non-Indo-European language throughout classical times. Their men served as mercenaries, especially in Egypt, and after subjection to King Croesus of Lydia and then to the Persians, joined the Ionian revolt against the domination of the latter (499–494), ambushing a Persian army, and subsequently helping the Athenian Cimon to win the battle of the river Eurymedon against the same foe (467).

By this century, if not earlier, the Carians possessed a loose and mainly religious national organization, based on the sanctuary of Zeus Karios at Mylasa (Milas); while a league known as the 'nation of the Chrysaoreis,' comprising all the villages of Caria, conducted regular meetings—from what date is unknown—at the Temple of Zeus Chrysaoreus near Stratonicea (Eskihisar). In

414/3, during the Peloponnesian War, the Athenians unwisely supported a revolt against the Persians in Caria, led by Amorges. The Persian satrap of Caria, Hecatomnus (395–377), had his capital at Mylasa, and commanded the Persian fleet in operations against Cyprus. His son Mausolus (377/6–353) moved his residence to Halicarnassus, where he ruled as a virtually independent sovereign and briefly elevated Caria to a central role in Mediterranean history, expanding his territory into Lycia and Ionia, enforcing suzerainty over the Greek islands, and pursuing a policy of Hellenization, supported by trade and manufacture. His sister Ada was deposed (340) but reinstated by Alexander the Great.

After various complicated vicissitudes under his successors, Caria belonged for long periods to the Ptolemaic empire. It suffered from a grave earthquake in 227, and lost much of its territory to the Rhodians as their reward for supporting Rome against the Seleucid Antiochus III the Great (188). In 168, however, Caria was declared by the Romans independent of Rhodes, and in 133, or perhaps a few years later, it became part of the new Roman province of Asia, with the exception of cities that were still recognized as 'free.' By the time of Strabo Carian had become a dead language, studied by antiquaries. A new province of Phrygia and Caria was detached from Asia before AD 259, and in the later empire Caria became a separate province on its own account. *See also* Aphrodisias, Cnidus, Halicarnassus, Mylasa, Stratonicea.

Carnuntum (between Petronell and Deutsch-Altenburg in Austria, twenty-five miles from Vindobona [Vienna]). Situated at the crossroads of two major commercial thoroughfares (the amber road to the Baltic, and a route along the Danube), Carnuntum was at first a mixed settlement of Illyrians and Celts. Incorporated in Augustus' new Roman province of Noricum (16 BC), it received a camp, originally measuring some 1,500 by 1,200 feet, which became the base for Tiberius' attacks against the Marcomanni (AD 6); some eight years later, it was garrisoned by a legion. At this juncture Carnuntum was transferred to the province of Pannonia, and when that was subdivided by Trajan (*c* 103) it became the capital of Upper Pannonia (Pannonia Superior). Hadrian, during a visit in 124, reconstructed the civilian settlement (*canabae*) adjoining its military counterpart with the status of a *municipium.*

For two years (172–74) Carnuntum was the headquarters of Marcus Aurelius, who made it the starting point of his retaliatory strike against the Marcomanni and wrote the second book of his *Meditations* in the fortress. Septimius Severus, governor of Upper Pannonia, was hailed emperor there (193), and not long afterward the city was raised to colonial rank. Finds indicate that it was the mint and capital of the short-lived usurper Regalianus (260–61). After the tetrarchy established by Diocletian (284–305) had broken down, Carnuntum achieved special fame as the location of the conference held by him and his colleagues and successors to decide the future of the empire (308); the altar set up to Mithras on this occasion has been preserved. Valentinian I hastened to the city in 375 to launch a counteroffensive against the Germans, but according to Ammianus, found it abandoned and crumbling to pieces. He ordered that its buildings should be restored, but destruction by invaders came some twenty years afterward, at the latest.

Excavations at the military settlement have revealed walls, a large forum and an amphitheater. A second, even larger amphitheater, appears at the civilian settlement, of which other notable monuments are a huge gate (Heidentor) and a building complex, measuring 440 by 350 feet and enclosed by walls and porticos, which contained an impressive audience hall and was perhaps the governor's palace. The extent of the city itself is not yet known, but archaeological investigations confirm both that it was rebuilt in the period of Diocletian, or shortly afterward, and that it ceased to exist, at least as a major center, before 400.

Carpentorate, later Forum Neronis (Carpentras, Vaucluse). In southern Gaul (Gallia Narbonensis), to the east of the river Rhodanus (Rhône) on the left bank of the Auzon. The name of the place may have been derived from a local god Carpentus, or possibly from *carpentum,* a two-wheeled covered gig (*cf* French *charpente*). It was the capital of the tribe of the Memini, whose name was incorporated in the designation of the *colonia Julia Meminorum,* founded by Octavian (Augustus), though this was later changed temporarily to Forum Neronis. The communications of Carpentorate included a road link with the great coastal routes from Italy to Spain. Excavations have disclosed that the settlement of the Memini was on a hill more than a mile to the west of the later foundation. In the Roman city a triumphal arch is to be seen. During the fifth century AD Carpentorate was destroyed by the Ostrogoths, Franks and Burgundians.

Carpow *see* Tava

Carrhae (Haran; now Altıbaşak). A city in northern Mesopotamia (now the southeastern region of Asiatic Turkey), twenty-five miles southwest of Edessa (Urfa), near the river Bilechas, a tributary of the Euphrates. According to Jewish tradition, the patriarch Abraham lived at Haran in the course of his migration from Ur to Canaan. It possessed a famous temple of the moon-god Lunus (Sin) and was a provincial capital of the Assyrian empire, serving as a fortress and important commercial center. Under the Seleucid dynasty it possessed a Macedonian military colony, and subsequently passed within the boundaries of the Parthian empire.

When the Roman triumvir Marcus Licinius Crassus invaded Parthian Mesopotamia in 53 BC, Carrhae was the scene of his catastrophic defeat by 'Surenas,' a Parthian noble of the Suren family whose personal name has not come down to us. Learning that the Parthians were upon him, Crassus formed his men into a square, which was overwhelmed by showers of arrows discharged with various trajectories. Abandoning 4,000 wounded, Crassus withdrew to Carrhae, but was compelled by his desperate troops to go out and negotiate with the enemy, who killed him at Sinnaca nearby. About 10,000 Romans escaped, but more than 30,000 were captured or killed.

Carrhae was temporarily recovered by Trajan (AD 114–17), to form part of a new Roman province of Mesopotamia, and then again by Lucius Verus, the colleague of Marcus Aurelius (162–65). It was probably at the latter date that the city was granted colonial status (under the name of Lucia Aurelia). Then the city received additional honors (under the designation of Antoniniana) from Caracalla—who was murdered, however, while on his way there to worship at the temple of Lunus (217). Carrhae, of which another title was Philoromaios, lover of the Romans, continued to issue coinage—apart from a brief Parthian reoccupation under Maximinus I (235–38)—until Gordian III (238–44). After the Sassanian Persians has taken over the Parthian empire, Diocletian's Caesar Galerius was severely defeated by them in the neighborhood of the city (296) but completely reversed the situation by a subsequent victory. The fortress fell to the Moslems in 629. Coins of imperial date depict the tripartite shrine of a celestial deity, presumably Lunus; and an early Christian basilica, the Great Mosque, and the present citadel were all built on the sites of pagan temples. The site has recently been elucidated by surface investigations and recovery excavations.

Cartagena *see* Carthago Nova

Carthage. A city in north Africa (Tunisia), situated on a peninsula projecting seaward from the Gulf of Tunis, linked to the mainland by an isthmus less than three miles wide (at one point). The city stood at the narrow waist of the Mediterranean, only seventy-five miles wide, and was in easy reach of lucrative purple mollusc (*murex*) beds. A southward-facing bay behind a small headland provided a spacious and sheltered port, which has now have been identified. This was later supplemented by two artificial harbors. The ancient citadel (the Byrsa) was constructed on a low hill overlooking the sea. The most important of the colonies of the Phoenicians (developed from trading posts) in north Africa, the 'New City' of Carthage (Kart-Hadasht), was established by settlers from Tyre (es-Sur)—traditionally in 814 BC, although a date some two generations later is often preferred. The legend of Dido, described in various ways by Virgil and others, celebrates the foundation.

During the seventh century, however, Carthage became independent of Tyre and began to bring other Phoenician settlements in the western and central Mediterranean under its control, in addition to subduing the native tribes of north Africa. About 535, supported by the Etruscan city-state Caere, the Carthaginians defeated a Greek (Phocaean) fleet at a naval battle named after Alalia in Corsica, and subsequently extended their authority in Sardinia, Spain, and (western) Sicily, where struggles with the Greeks continued for centuries. Friendly relations with Rome terminated in the First Punic War (264–241), resulting in Carthage's defeat and surrender of Sicily, followed (after rebellions) by the loss of Sardinia and Corsica as well. Hamilcar's subsequent establishment of a second Carthaginian empire in Spain (237–39) led to the Second Punic War (218–201), of which the principal event was Hannibal's prolonged, often victorious, but eventually unsuccessful invasion of Italy. Large-scale operations also took place in Spain, which the Carthaginians finally lost, together with the war. Their subsequent revival, however, provoked the Romans into launching the Third Punic War (149–146), resulting in the destruction of Carthage and the annexation of its principal territory as the new province of Africa, which assumed immense importance as the granary of Rome.

After an abortive attempt by Gaius Gracchus to establish a Roman colony on the derelict site (under the name of Junonia), this was achieved, in accordance with a plan of Julius Caesar, by Lepidus in 42/40. Octavian (Augustus) drafted a further batch of settlers in 28; air photography has revealed an elaborately organized colonial countryside. The city was now the capital of the province (producing a short-lived free-lance ruler, Clodius Macer, in AD 68). In the second century, Carthage became an outstanding cultural and educational center, particularly well-known for its orators and lawyers; it ranked as the 'Rome of Africa,' the second city of the west and the second or third of the entire empire in the size of its population, which amounted to more than 300,000. It was adorned with many new buildings, Commodus (180–92) established a new fleet (the Classis Herculea) at its port, and Septimius Severus (193–211) celebrated his 'indulgence' to the city on the imperial coinage. In 238, however, in protest against the oppressive regime of Maximinus I, Gordianus I Africanus and his son instituted a rebellion at Carthage, which was recognized by the Roman senate but immediately suppressed by the governor of Numidia. In 296/7 the Tetrarchy of Diocletian, in connection with frontier operations, instituted a mint at the city, which was also used during the brief usurpation of Domitius Alexander against Maxentius (308).

Carthage played a leading part in the early history of Christianity, being the birthplace of Tertullian (*c* 160–240) and the episcopal see of St. Cyprian (*c* 200–58). In *c* 311–14 a quarrel concerning the bishopric prompted the establishment of the Donatist heresy, which remained the dominant church of the region for the rest of the century. It was condemned, however, by five hundred and seventy bishops meeting at the Synod of Carthage (in the Baths of Gargilius) in 411, through the advocacy of St. Augustine; whereupon one of its supporters, Heraclianus, proclaimed himself emperor there (following other damaging *coups d'état* toward the end of the preceding century) but was put to death (413). Although walls were constructed *c* 425, invading Vandals under Gaiseric (Genseric) seized Carthage almost without resistance, thus inflicting an almost fatal blow upon the western empire. It now became the capital of an independent Vandal state until recovered by Belisarius (553), on behalf of the eastern (Byzantine) emperor Justinian I, under whom the city experienced a major revival, until it fell to the Arabs in 697. One of a number of new studies of the site has investigated its complex, long-distance trading operations during the fifth, sixth and seventh centuries.

Since the edifices of all the different epochs of the city's life provided subsequent builders with an inexhaustible supply of stone, what remains of the ancient town is limited. Nevertheless, for the past decade or more, international excavation has been active, in a remarkable variety of different sectors, although up to now scarcely one-fiftieth of the area between the walls has been investigated—and the locations of the earliest settlement and harbor still remain uncertain. However, the old Carthaginian sacrificial area (*tophet*) and cemeteries can be seen, and a prolonged series of reconstructions of the circular harbor on the neighboring Ilot d'Amirauté (from *c* 200 BC onward) have now been revealed. There are also a number of fragmentary Roman monuments in the city. The most impressive of these is the symmetrically designed, vaulted, thermal establishment of Antoninus Pius (AD 138–61) on the seashore, which was fed by an eighty-two-mile long aqueduct from Zaqui (Zaghouan) and stands today in an archaeological park. The 'Theodosian Wall' dates from *c* 425. The best preserved of several early churches is the remarkable and complex Basilica of Damous el-Karita, north of the forum, dating back in part to the time of Saint Augustine (354–430). The mosaics of Bigua monastery are of the later fifth century. The new Musée Romain et Paléochrétien has now been opened at Dermech.

Carthago Nova (Cartagena, Murcia). A city on the southeastern, Mediterranean coast of Spain; situated on a promontory bounded by a bay (protected by an island) and by a large lagoon. Formerly Mastia, capital of the Iberian tribe of the Mastieni, it was refounded by Hasdrubal as Kart Hadasht (New City), and made the capital of the Carthaginian empire of Spain—the nearby Baebelo silver mines providing three hundred pounds of the metal a day. It was also a principal base for operations against the Romans (228/6 BC). During the Second Punic War its surprise and capture by Scipio Africanus the Elder, after a brief siege (209), paved the way for the expulsion of the Carthaginians from the peninsula, after which Carthago Nova became part of the Roman province of Nearer Spain (Hispania Citerior).

The historian Polybius visited the city in 133, and reported that 40,000 silver miners were at work, earning huge sums for Rome. Also in the area were extensive salt-pans (for curing), and plantations of esparto grass (employed to make ships' ropes, baskets and sandals); the place also became famous for its mackerel-fishing and the odoriferous fish sauce known as *garum.* Receiving Latin rights (*ie* citizenship for its elected officials) from Julius Caesar, the city subsequently attained colonial status—probably under the Second Triumvirate—and until the reign of Gaius (AD 37–41) issued its own coinage, which records honorific grants of office to Kings Juba II (25 BC–AD 23) and Ptolemy (AD 23–40). Its population has been estimated at 30,000, and Strabo described it as well-fortified and prosperous. From this time onward, however, it took second place—among Spain's Mediterranean ports—to Tarraco (Tarragona), after which the province was now named. In the reorganization of Diocletian and Constantine, however, it became the capital of a separate province, Carthaginensis, and from *c* 400 was the see of a bishopric. In 425 it was looted and severely damaged by the Vandals, but recovered to become the capital of the short-lived Byzantine province of southern Spain (552–*c* 615).

Ancient Carthago Nova was served by an aqueduct carried by the bridge spanning the channel between its bay and lagoon. It is still possible to detect traces of Scipio's camp outside the city, and within its boundaries columns and walls of the forum, and remains of streets and of the amphitheater can be seen.

Carystus, Karystos (Paleochora). At the southwestern extremity of the central Greek island of Euboea, a mile inland from an extensive bay. The prehistoric population, of which traces occur in finds (from Neolithic times onward), belonging, according to Homer's *Iliad,* to the Abantes—perhaps of Thracian origin—after whom the whole of the island was sometimes named. In 490, during the Persian Wars, the Carystians refused to give troops and hostages to Darius

I, who forced them to surrender; but in 480 they contributed to the fleet of Xerxes I. Some five years later Athens forced them to become members of the Delian League, but during the Peloponnesian War they joined other Euboean cities in rebellion (411). Carystus backed Athens against the Macedonians in the unsuccessful Lamian War (323/2), but supported the Macedonian king Philip V against the Romans, whose fleet, with their Pergamene allies, captured the city in 198.

It was declared 'free' by the Romans two years later, however, and sent ships to help them when their Italian allies rebelled in the Social War (91-87). Under Nero (AD 54-68) and Trajan (98-117), its earlier local coinage was briefly resumed, and a new peak of prosperity was reached under Hadrian (117-38), owing to Roman demand for the greenish Carystian marble. The region was also a source of asbestos. Its most impressive monument is an ancient sanctuary of Hera, the 'Dragon's House,' on neighboring Mount Oche, which was roofed by four superimposed layers of corbelled blocks and has been found to contain pottery of many different periods.

Casale *see* Piazza Armerina

Casale di Conca *see* Satricum

Cassandrea *see* Potidaea

Castalia *see* Delphi

Casteggio *see* Clastidium

Castel di Decima *see* Politorium

Castel Gandolfo *see* Alba Longa

Castel Giubileo *see* Fidenae

Castellamare *see* Stabiae, Velia

Castellamare del Golfo *see* Segesta

Castellum Rauricense *see* Augusta Rauricorum

Casterat *see* Atuatuca

Castiglione *see* Gabii

Castra Augustoflaviensia *see* Margum

Castra Regina *see* Raetia

Castra Vetera *see* Vetera

Catalaunian Plains *see* Campi Catalaunii

Catana, Katane (Catania). A city in northeastern Sicily, beside the sea and the mouth of the little river Amenanus (now disappeared) and ten miles north of the Symaethus (Simeto); it is also not far from the southern extremity of Mount Aetna (Etna), at the beginning of a fertile volcanic plain. According to tradition, Catana was settled *c* 729 BC by colonists from the Sicilian city of Naxos (itself a colony of Chalcis in Euboea). Gaining independence, Catana adopted a legal code drawn up by its renowned and almost legendary citizen Charondas, who probably lived in the sixth century. In 476/5 Hiero I of Syracuse expelled its inhabitants to Leontini (Lentini), giving Catana the new name of Aetna and populating it with Dorian mercenaries; but in 461 they were driven out, and the old name was revived.

In their Sicilian expedition, during the Peloponnesian War, the Athenians used Catana as a base for operations against Syracuse (415). But in 403 the Syracusan ruler Dionysius I captured the city, which from then onward formed part of the dominions of Syracuse, with brief intermissions of subjection to Carthage (under Mago and Himilco, 396) and occasional periods of independence (for example, after liberation by Timoleon, 339). Catana opened its gates to the invader Pyrrhus of Epirus (278), and was captured by the Romans near the outset of the First Punic War (263). Subsequently it suffered severe damage in the First Slave Revolt (*c* 135), in an eruption of Etna (121), and from the depredations of the governor Verres (73–71), although, according to his enemy Cicero, Roman rule had in general brought prosperity to the place. Afflicted again by the civil war between Octavian (the future Augustus) and Sextus Pompeius (36), Catana received colonial status from the former (21) and overtook Messana (Messina) as the most populous city of the region. In AD 251 it was the scene of the martyrdom of St. Agatha, patron of the city.

Part of ancient Catana was lost beneath a lava flow in 1669, but surviving remains include a recently excavated Roman theater (reconstructed from an earlier Greek structure), graves of numerous periods, and a great variety of informative inscriptions. But the city's most important monuments are its coins, including a superb series of the fifth century BC, bearing the names both of Catana and of Aetna.

Catena Metallifera, Colline Metallifere (Metal-Bearing Range). Part of the Anti-Apennine Mountains in northwest Etruria (Tuscany, western Italy), producing the metals that attracted Greek traders from southwest Italy (Campani) and thus brought about the rise of the Etruscan city-states and created their wealth. The Catena Metallifera provided the only considerable supplies of copper and iron in the central Mediterranean region, and many traces of their

Etruscan workings can still be seen. The two main nuclei, the Massetano (centered on Massa Veternensis, now Massa Marittima) and the Campigliese (from Campiglia Marittima; also producing tin and alum, used for dyeing) were situated in the immediate hinterland of Populonia, opposite the island of Aethalia (Ilva, Elba), which was also rich in metals.

Caucasus (Kavkaz). A range of mountains (also known as the Caspian range) extending between the Euxine (Black) and Caspian Seas (in a broader sense the term Caucasus is used to include regions to the north and south as well). The mythical hero Prometheus was said to have been imprisoned on a Caucasus mountainside, and the land of Colchis (to the southwest) was the goal of the Argonauts' quest for the Golden Fleece. After a prolonged and at times brilliant prehistory, in which the route beside the Caspian already played a major part in migrations from central to southwest Asia—and an east-west road became frequented as well—the Black Sea coast of the Caucasus was colonized by the Greeks between the eighth and sixth centuries BC. Herodotus knew of the great size of the range and the diversity of its peoples (later stressed in further detail by Strabo and Pliny the Elder; *see also* Dioscurias. For the northwestern area, *see* Bosphorus [Cimmerian], Phanagoria).

Alexander the Great's conquest of the Persian empire freed the southern fringes of the Caucasian region, but Iberia (Georgia), through which ran the Dariel pass or Caucasian Gates (also misleadingly known as the Caspian Gates), came under the control of Mithridates VI of Pontus until his defeat by Pompey the Great (65); thereafter the little Iberian state was a Roman client from time to time, though Nero's proposed expedition to annex it never materialized. Albania (Shirvan) to the east was often loosely dependent upon Rome; the reorganization of Cappadocia by Vespasian (AD 69–79) was intended to dominate Albania and Iberia alike. As for Colchis bordering on the Euxine coast, parts of its maritime strip were more or less permanently under Roman and, later, Byzantine supervision and control. The ample Caucasian forests were especially prized for shipbuilding. (Alexandria by the Caucasus [*qv*] has nothing to do with the Caucasus mountains; it is in the Paropamisus [Hindu Kush], and owed its name to a confusion between the two ranges).

Caudine Forks *see* Furculae Caudinae

Celaenae *see* Apamea Cibotus

Cenabum, Genabum, in north-central Gaul. The geographer Strabo indicates that the river Liger (Loire) flows past Cenabum, 'at about the middle of the voyage'—that is to say, the journey from Augustonemetum (Clermont-Ferrand) to the coast. Cenabum has been identified both with Gien and with Orléans (forty miles to its west-northwest); the original center may have been at the former. The town was part of the territory of the Carnutes, whose massacre of the Roman garrison placed there by Julius Caesar, during his Gallic War (54 BC), sparked off the general uprising led by Vercingetorix against the Romans. Arriving rapidly, Caesar burned and devastated Cenabum. It was rebuilt later, however, and after a time of further pillaging, we hear of a town named Aurelianum, capital of the *civitas Aurelianorum,* from which Orléans received its name. The designation may have been connected with the emperor Probus (Marcus Aurelius Probus, 276–82), and the town's fortifications probably date from this period (at which Aurelianum had evidently superseded Cenabum). In 451 the city was besieged by Attila the Hun. Its bishop Anianus (St. Aignan) went to seek assistance from the western Roman general Aetius, but the town fell. However, Attila withdrew, and evacuated Gaul after his defeat at the Campi Catalaunii.

The most impressive finds of the region are six large animals of hammered bronze (including a horse dedicated to the god Rudiobus) and a number of statues of remarkable style from Neuvy-en-Sullias, nineteen miles upstream.

Cenchreae *see* Corinth

Cennatis, Cennateis *see* Olba

Centuripae, Kentoripe. A town in Sicily, on a strategically located hillcrest nineteen miles southwest of the crater of Etna and twenty-one miles northwest of Catana. A native Sicilian (Sicel) town, gradually Hellenized in the fifth and fourth century BC, Centuripae was continually fought over by Syracuse and its enemies, siding with the Athenian expedition against the Syracusans (414–413) but frequently, though rebelliously, under their domination. Timoleon liberated the city from an autocratic regime (339).

The city became noteworthy for some of the finest and most highly distinctive pottery of Hellenistic times, extending from the fourth to the first centuries BC. The scenes painted on these vases depict figures (often displayed in relief) upon a red or rose-pink background, displaying subtle variations of polychrome coloring, and delicate light and shade effects. Numerous locally manufactured terracotta figurines have also been found in adjoining cemeteries.

After submission to Rome during the First Punic War (263), the loyalty and strategic importance of Centuripae gained it the rank (unusual in Sicily), in 241, of a non-taxpaying community (*civitas libera et immunis*). Cicero, deploring exploitation by the governor Verres (73–71), pays high and perhaps somewhat exaggerated tribute to the city's grandeur and prosperity, based on the large-scale production of wheat on its fertile soil. In spite of restoration by Augustus and some rebuilding in the second and third centuries AD its subsequent history was one of decline. Extensive Roman architectural remains include a late Hellenistic house of unusual design, and an imposing monumental building of Augustan date (Mulino Barbagallo) containing an internal colonnade.

Cephissis (Lake) *see* Copais

Cercinitis, Kerkinitis. On the northwest coast of the Tauric Chersonese (Crimea). Situated in a region populated first by the tribe of the Satarchae and then by Scythian nomads, Cercinitis seems to have received a Greek colony in the fifth century BC from Heraclea Pontica (Ereğli) in northern Asia Minor. The place is mentioned by Hecataeus and Herodotus. The latter refers to its location on the river Hypakiris; but the urban settlement is probably identifiable with the site later known as Eupatoria (Yevpatorya: see below) on Lake Donuslav (the name 'Kerkinitis' seems to refer to a lake), where recent excavations have uncovered fourth- and third-century burials, and fortified settlements nearby. Situated in a fertile agricultural zone, Cercinitis supplied much of the Tauric Chersonese with grain, and enjoyed active relations with the natives of the interior. After apparently becoming a colony and appendage, from the early fourth century, of the city of Chersonesus (Sevastopol), Cercinitis issued coins of its own from *c* 300, but in the mid-second century was conquered by the partially Hellenized Royal Scyth princedom (based on Neapolis [Simferopol]), and remained in its hands, apart from a brief period of detachment by Mithridates VI Eupator (120–63), to whom Cercinitis owed the new name of Eupatoria. Continuing excavations have uncovered a house approximately contemporary with the foundation of the Greek colony, stone city-walls of the fourth and third centuries, and a number of rich graves of the same period. By about the fourth century AD the place was abandoned.

Cernavoda *see* Axiopolis

Cerveteri *see* Caere

Cerynia, Keryneia (Mamusia). A Greek town in the mountainous interior of Achaea (northern Peloponnese), near the small city of Helice, beside the river Cerynites (Calavryta). In *c* 460 BC, according to Pausanias, the inhabitants gave refuge to the people of Mycenae, driven out of their hometown. From the fourth century onward Cerynia was one of the independent cities of the Achaean League.

Cerynia owed its fame to the mythical Cerynian Hind with golden antlers and bronze hoofs that roamed the neighboring hills. There were, reputedly, five such animals, of which four drew the chariot of Artemis, to whom they were sacred; the capture of the fifth hind was the third (or according to another version, the fourth) labor of Heracles, who wounded the beast with an arrow and brought it to Eurystheus at Mycenae. Portions of the town walls of Cerynia are still to be seen, and remains of its theater.

Cetis *see* Olba

Chaeronea, Chaironeia. The northernmost city of Boeotia (central Greece), strategically located in the narrow Cephisus plain between Mounts Acontium and Thurium, astride the main invasion route from the north. Chaeronea belonged to Orchomenus until at least 424 BC. In the fourth century it was a member of the Boeotian League.

The place is famous for three important battles that were fought on its plain. The first took place in 338, when Philip II of Macedonia totally crushed the

Boeotians, Athenians and their allies, thus bringing to an end the classical epoch of truly independent city-states. The site of the battle is marked by the great mound in which the Macedonian dead were buried, and by the marble Lion of Chaeronea (now re-erected) which has been believed, since ancient times, to belong to the funeral monument of the Sacred Band of Thebans who fell to a man (skeletons found on the site have been identified as theirs).

Subsequently, in 245, the Boeotians suffered an equally decisive defeat at Chaeronea, this time at the hands of the Aetolian League, so that they never again played a leading part in Greek politics. And in 86 the hundred-thousand-strong invading army of Mithridates VI of Pontus, under the command of Archelaus, was routed at Chaeronea by the Roman general Sulla. In Roman imperial times, it was the birthplace and home of the philosopher and biographer Plutarch (after AD 50–after 120), whose family had long been established in the city.

Chalcedon *see* Calchedon

Chalcidice. A peninsula of Macedonia (northern Greece) that extends southward into the promontories of Pallene (Cassandra), Sithonia (Longos) and Acte (Athos). The northwestern part of the peninsula was known as Bottice, after the Bottiaeans who had occupied it by the early seventh century BC, following their expulsion from western Macedonia. Meanwhile, in the previous century, Greek cities had begun the establishment of a number of colonies in the region, to which they gave the name of Chalcidice; the last and most important of these settlements was Potidaea (*c* 600). After temporarily submitting to Xerxes I (480) —who had dug a one-and-a-half mile canal through Acte three years earlier— the people of Chalcidice joined the Delian League under Athenian leadership, but revolted in 433/31 and established a league of their own, issuing a fine and widely distributed federal coinage at their capital Olynthus.

At the request, however, of some of their neighbors, who were alarmed by their growing power, Sparta intervened to make the Chalcidians their subject-allies (382–379). They were able to transfer their allegiance to the Second Athenian Confederacy, but in 356 concluded an alliance with Philip II of Macedonia, who crushed them eight years later, destroying Olynthus. But the city recovered, together with others in the area, and the Chalcidice seemed to have enjoyed a quasi-autonomous position in the Macedonian kingdom. Some of its cities continued to maintain their existence during the Roman empire, notably Cassandrea (founded in 316 BC, on the site of Potidaea), which successfully resisted a Gothic assault in AD 268. *See also* Acanthus, Olynthus, Potidaea, Stagirus, Torone, Uranopolis.

Chalcis. The principal city of Euboea (off the eastern coast of central Greece), dominating the narrowest part of the Euripus channel separating the island from Boeotia on the mainland. According to legend Chalcis was colonized by Cothus the Athenian after the Trojan War. Recent research has clarified the extremely important role played by Chalcis in the emergence of Greece in the early first millennium BC, during and after the so-called Dark Age. Its imposing location made it one of the first of the new Greek cities that became able to resume the overseas trading suspended after the end of the Mycenaean epoch. The exports of Chalcis (and its neighbor Eretria) circulated widely throughout the eastern Mediterranean, offset by the influx of abundant jewelry. One of the principal centers of these exchanges was Al Mina on the north Syrian coast (founded *c* 825–800 BC), the focus of lively trading activities in which, for at least a century, Chalcis and Eretria played a leading part.

Moreover, the Chalcidians were famous for their metal-working, which attained great importance when iron became the basis of technology in Greece. In consequence, they were particularly eager to acquire the metals of Etruria; and in order to achieve this aim, joined by Eretria and the small Euboean town of Cyme, they established important trading posts in southwest Italy, first on the island of Pithecusae (Ischia) and then at Cumae (Cuma), which maintained commercial contacts with Etruria (thus contributing substantially to the rise of the Etruscan city-states). Chalcis and Eretria also began the colonization of the Macedonian promontories of Chalcidice in the course of the eighth century.

Shortly before 700 (?), however, the two cities became locked in a violent and prolonged dispute over the rich Lelantine plain that lay between them—the earliest Greek war that can be regarded as fully historic, in which both sides mustered a number of allies. With the help of Thessalian cavalry, Chalcis won one major battle, possibly two, in this Lelantine War, but its final outcome is not certain, and from then onward its commercial supremacy was increasingly overtaken by Corinth. In *c* 506 it was obliged to cede a substantial part of the plain to 4,000 Athenian colonists (cleruchs). Subsequently, however—although it had supported the Athenians in the Persian War against Xerxes I—it revolted against them in 446, but met with ill success, remaining tributary until a further rebellion in 411.

Philip II of Macedonia garrisoned Chalcis in 338 as one of his principal strongpoints, and under subsequent Macedonian rule it retained major strategic importance as one of the principal 'fetters' or 'keys' by which his kingdom controlled Greece. At the same time, too, it became a leading commercial center of the Hellenistic world. Like other Euboean cities, Chalcis was 'liberated' by Flamininus in 197. Its decision, however, to support the Achaean League in its struggle with Rome earned it partial destruction (146). Yet by 86 it had recovered sufficiently to serve as the base for another enemy of the Romans, Archelaus, the general of Mithridates VI Eupator of Pontus, between his successive defeats at Chaeronea and Orchomenus.

Under Augustus (32 BC–AD 14), Chalcis coined with the head of the nymph Chalcis and the portraits of two proconsuls of Achaea, Lucius Rufinus and Mescinius. But the principal coin-type of imperial times is Hera, whose statue, on a coin of Septimius Severus (AD 193–211), is shown seated on a sacred conical stone (shown separately on other coins). During the third century, Chalcis resumed its leadership of Euboea. The traces of its ancient wall can be seen from air photographs.

Chalcis Beneath Lebanon. Earlier known to Polybius as Gerrha; later Ain-Jarr and now Mejdel Anjar (in Lebanon); a city at the foot of Mount Anti-Libanus (Anti-Lebanon) in Hollow Syria (Coele-Syria).

In 88 BC Chalcis Beneath Lebanon received a quasi-monastic group of refugee Jews, like those of the more famous Damascus Community. By this time the city had for some years been the capital of a succession of tetrarchs (client-princes of the Romans), whose control extended over fluctuating areas of Massyas and Abilene as far as the sanctuary of Heliopolis (Baalbek)—to which they owed their additional title of chief priest. The state, which dated its era from 117 or 114, is likely to have been founded by Mennaeus, who gave the city its Greek name, although it retained its native character. Coins were subsequently issued by Mennaeus' son Ptolemy (*c* 85–40), Ptolemy's son Lysanias (40–*c* 35)—who ruled a large area but was put to death by Cleopatra VII of Egypt—and Zenodorus (*c* 35–20, probably a member of the same royal house), who leased his princedom from Cleopatra, and then had it confirmed but subsequently diminished and finally abolished (for gross misgovernment) by Augustus.

The region then passed into the hands of Herod the Great of Judaea (d. 4 BC). Subsequently, after a period of Roman rule, his grandson of the same name became king of Chalcis (AD 41–48), assuming the designation Philoklaudios in honor of the emperor Claudius, and receiving the 'guardianship' of the Jerusalem temple and its treasury. When Herod of Chalcis died, his kingdom seems to have been treated as an imperial estate, but the royal title and supervision passed to his nephew Agrippa II—later transferred to a larger kingdom based on Caesarea Philippi (Panias, Banyas). (Chalcis Beneath Lebanon is to be distinguished from Chalcis By Belus [Kinnesrin] in northern Syria).

Chalons *see* Campi Catalaunii

Charax, Spasinou Charax. Situated on an artificial elevation between the rivers Tigris and Choaspes (perhaps Kerhah, Kharkeh: *see also* Susa) at the point where they meet, near the Persian Gulf (and the modern frontier between Iraq and Iran). Pliny the Elder describes its foundation by Alexander the Great, who was said to have brought settlers from the royal city of Durine (and some invalid soldiers), but the evidence for this Alexandria is uncertain. A colony, however, was founded by the Seleucid Antiochus IV Epiphanes (175–164 BC) under the name of Antiochia, but after this settlement had been destroyed (not for the first time) by flooding, it was restored by Hyspaosines (*c* 127–124)—son of a local Arab ruler Sagdodonacus—after whom it took the name of Spasinou. Charax, serving as a port for caravans from the interior until the recession of the Gulf, put an end to this activity.

Kings of Characene, whose capital was Spasinou Charax issued coins from the later second century BC to the third century AD; the later issues bear the head not only of the local monarch but of his Arsacid (Parthian) patron. The kingdom of Characene came to an end *c* AD 224–28, when the Parthians were superseded by the Sassanian Persians. The most famous citizen of Spasinou Charax was Isidorus, who wrote an important geographical work, with special reference to Parthian territories, *c* 25.

Charikar *see* Alexandria ad Caucasum

Charybdis. The name given to a stretch of sea on the western side of the northern entrance to the Fretum Siculum (Strait of Messana, now Messina), adjoining Cape Pelorus (Peloro) According to tradition, Charybdis was a whirlpool (though none is now to be seen in the area) which sucked in and spewed out water three times a day. The whirlpool was thought of as a female monster—the daughter of Poseidon and Gaia—whom Zeus had thrown into the sea. In conjunction with another monster Scylla, who inhabited a cave opposite, it was believed that Charybdis destroyed every ship that tried to pass through the strait: 'between Scylla and Charybdis' signified avoiding an evil, only to fall into a greater one. The legendary vessel Argo, manned by the Argonauts, escaped both monsters; but the ship of Odysseus, after he had lost six sailors to Scylla, was wrecked by Charybdis, from which the hero himself was saved only by clinging to a fig tree that grew over the whirlpool.

Cherchel *see* Caesarea (Iol, Mauretania)

Chersonesus, Chersonesos, Cherronesos (near Sevastopol). A city on the west coast of the Tauric Chersonese (Crimea). Founded *c* 422/421 BC by colonists from Heraclea Pontica (Ereğli) in Pontus (northern Asia Minor) and from Delium in Boeotia (central Greece), it became the principal Tauric urban settlement, benefiting from its position at the north end of the shortest span of the Euxine (Black) Sea, and deriving wealth from its vines, which had to be covered over in winter. Chersonesus absorbed a number of native serfs, as burials now suggest. Although its semi-isolated site restricted inland trade, it also colonized Cercinitis on the northwest coast, and enlarged its territory to include the Mayachny peninsula six miles to its west—probably the 'Old Chersonese' of Strabo, a refuge against hostile natives behind a double line of walls.

After a long period of independence, the prosperity of Chersonesus declined during the second century, when it came under attacks from the Scythian king Palak, appealing for help to Mithridates VI Eupator of Pontus (120–63) who drove the marauders off. Thereafter the city formed part of the kingdom of the Cimmerian Bosphorus, but was declared free by the Romans, inaugurating a new era in 36 BC and issuing coins of its own (including gold), of which a dated series extends from AD 37 to 95.

The city was laid out on a symmetrical grid plan. Its defences, rebuilt in the third and fourth centuries AD against Gothic and other incursions, are among the most important ancient monuments of the northern Euxine area. As recent excavations have revealed, large numbers of tombstones were incorporated in their construction, displaying inscriptions, reliefs of medical instruments (on the graves of two doctors of the fourth century BC), and traces of polychrome decoration. Other remains include a mint (fourth century BC), at least one theater (*c* 200), establishments for making wine, pottery workshops, a glass-making factory (third/fourth century AD), cisterns for salting fish, Roman baths, and a large barrack building for the Roman garrison. On a peninsula outside the walls traces of numerous fortified grain-producing areas and vineyards have been uncovered. A scientific analysis of the wheat (mostly soft-grained), barley (less common) and other grains, and of grape seeds found on these allotments has now been undertaken.

Chersonesus *see* Apamea

Chersonesus, Cnidian *see* Cnidus

Chersonesus, Tauric *see* Bosphorus (Cimmerian).

Chersonesus (Chersonesos), Thracian (Gelibolu, Gallipoli). A narrow peninsula—Chersonesus means 'land island'—extending down from Thrace to the Troad (northwestern Asia Minor), from which it was separated by the Hellespont (Dardanelles) that links the Propontis (Sea of Marmara) to the Aegean. Occupied in the eighth and seventh centuries BC by colonists from Miletus (Balat) in Ionia and elsewhere, the Thracian Chersonese passed into the hands of Miltiades the Elder of Athens, who fortified the Bulair isthmus (*c* 560 BC); and after the stormy career of his nephew and namesake (*c* 550-489)—the hero of Marathon—the peninsula remained in the hands of the Athenians (with a Spartan interlude, 404-386) until 338, when it passed under the control of Philip II of Macedonia. Ravaged by the Thracians, and disputed between Hellenistic rulers, the Chersonese was taken over by the kingdom of Pergamum (189), who converted most of the region into state property, an arrangement retained after Roman annexation (133). *See also* Cardia, Lysimachia, Sestus.

Chester *see* Deva

Chesterholm *see* Vindolanda

Chiana *see* Clanis (River)

Chichester *see* Noviomagus

Chios. A Greek island, thirty miles long (from north to south) and from eight to fifteen miles broad, five miles from the coast of Ionia (western Asia Minor). Its early inhabitants were reputed to have included Lydians and Carians. However, Chios was settled by Ionians at about the end of the second millennium BC (perhaps followed by Abantes from Euboea *c* 875) and claimed to have been the birthplace of Homer, an assertion which, although already disputed in antiquity, gained the support of Semonides of Amorgos. Chios was admitted into the Ionic League in the eighth century, and its principal town of the same name, in a rich and beautiful plain on the east side of the island, had a democratic regime by the sixth century (though in later years democratic and oligarchic governments alternated). In the sixth century Glaucus was believed to have developed ironworking on the island, which was the center of flourishing schools of metalworkers and stone-cutters, and produced a famous family of artists described by Pliny the Elder.

Incorporated into the Persian empire by Cyrus II the Great (559–529), Chios joined the Ionian revolt led by its ally Miletus (Balat), contributing a hundred ships to fight in the disastrous battle of Lade (Batmas; 495). Brought to order and devastated, the Chians fought on the Persian side against their fellow Greeks at Salamis (480), under the leadership of an autocratic ruler ('tyrant') Strattis. However, they subsequently joined the Delian League sponsored by Athens, until induced to secede during the Peloponnesian War (412). At this time they were the largest slave-owners in the Greek world, with the single exception of the Spartans. In 384 they joined the Second Athenian Confederacy, but again seceded in 357. About 346 the island came under the control of the Carian state, founded by Mausolus of Halicarnassus (Bodrum), but was betrayed to the Persian admiral Memnon, from whose control it passed, amid various vicissitudes, into a League established by Alexander the Great.

A recently discovered inscription provides for the establishment of a festival of Rome and the honoring of Romulus and Remus. If, as has been suggested on epigraphic grounds, this inscription belongs to the 220s, it precedes Rome's generally recognized influence in the region; but the dating has been disputed. At all events, in the years that followed, Chios supported the Romans in their Macedonian and eastern wars, enjoying free and allied status. The city was sacked in 86 by Zenobius, a general of Mithridates VI of Pontus, and its inhabitants were deported, but Sulla returned them to their homes. The island's coinage of the Roman imperial epoch (which exceptionally bears a series of denomination marks) preserves a strongly autonomous appearance, depicting Homer but not the emperors—although a holiday was instituted to honor the birthday of Tiberius' nephew and adoptive son Germanicus (AD 18).

Surviving remains include archaic Greek houses excavated at the capital of the island, Hellenistic dwellings at its well protected port of Delphinion, a sanctuary of Athena over another harbor town (Emporion, dating from the late eighth and seventh centuries BC), and a large polygonal wall at New Emporion (Pindakas) on a nearby hill. From early times the island was famous for its sweetish wine, for which Ariusia, in its southern region, became especially well-known; the jars of Chios (notably painted pots of the seventh and sixth centuries BC, formerly, but mistakenly, regarded as Rhodian) bear witness to a large share in the Egyptian and Euxine (Black) Sea wine trade. The island also produced figs, white mastic gum and fine cloth. In the Roman empire the high standard of living among the people of the island was proverbial: 'from boyhood I lived like a Chian,' says a character in the *Satyricon* of Petronius.

Chiragan *see* Tolosa

Chiusi *see* Clusium

Chrysaoris *see* Stratonicea

Chrysopolis (Üsküdar, Scutari). On the Asiatic side of the Thracian Bosphorus, opposite Byzantium (Constantinople, Istanbul). Deriving its name, according to legend, from Chryses, the son of Agamemnon and Chryseis, it was a dependency of neighboring Calchedon (Kadıköy), the first Greek colony established on this coast. In the late fifth century BC, during the Peloponnesian War, the Athenians employed Chrysopolis to collect tolls from ships crossing the staits. Xenophon came there at the end of the famous Retreat of the Ten Thousand, before returning to Europe (400).

In AD 268 a fleet of German (Gothic and Herulian) marauders captured Chrysopolis as well as Byzantium. During the following century, the place momentarily took the center of the world stage, during the final stage of the second civil war between Constantine I the Great and Licinius (324). Eluding Licinius' colleague Martinian, who had been told to prevent him from crossing over into Asia, Constantine traversed the strait and pressed on to Chrysopolis, where a decisive battle sealed the fate of Licinius, and put an end to his bid for the Roman world.

Chrysopolis *see* Apulia

Cibalae (Vinkovci in Yugoslavia). In Pannonia (later Lower Pannonia), on a tributary of the Save, between that river and the Danube. A prehistoric site, the place became a Roman *municipium* and then colony, probably in the times of Hadrian (AD 117-38) and Septimius Severus (192-211) respectively. It was situated at the intersection of roads leading to the great military bases of Sirmium (Sremska Mitrovica), Siscia (Sisak), Mursa Major (Osijek) and Aquincum (Budapest).

During the first of the two civil wars between Constantine I the Great and Licinius (*c* 316), a major battle was fought a few miles from Cibalae (probably at Vukovar). Although Licinius' army of 35,000 men was encamped in a wide plain, Constantine, with 30,000 troops, advanced through a defile (between a hill and a swamp) to meet him, and after a ferocious engagement the forces of Licinius fled, with a loss, it was said, of 20,000 lives, and the entire heavy equipment of the army. A subsequent engagement at Campus Ardiensis in Thrace proved indecisive, and the two men temporarily came to an agreement, according to which Licinius ceded Illyricum (except Thrace) to his rival. Recent excavations at Cibalae have yielded a number of discoveries, including hydraulic installations.

Cibyra (Horzum). A city in southern Phrygia (west-central Asia Minor; sometimes described as Cibyra Major, to distinguish it from another place of the same name in Cilicia [Güney Kalesi]). The people of Cibyra claimed to be of Spartan origin, but according to Strabo they were the descendants of Lydians and later Pisidians who had transferred the city to a new site; its people spoke four languages. Constructed on a ridge overlooking the broad and fertile plain of the river Indus (Horzum Çayı), Cibyra derived its revenue from the working and embossing of iron, and from its location on a strategically and commercially important route linking the western and southern coastal cities of the peninsula. A large region, including numerous villages, came under its political control.

Strabo indicates that the place owed its success to excellent laws and an effective government, which he defines as a 'tyranny' (autocracy) of a moderate character; in 189 BC, however, its ruler, a certain Moagetes, was described as cruel and treacherous. At some time during the same century, Cibyra took the lead in forming a federation (Tetrapolis) with three other cities (Bubon, Balbura [Katara] and Oenoanda [İnceveliler]) in the river plain and the mountains to its east and south. Cibyra also began to issue its own coinage, and concluded a treaty of friendship and alliance with Rome, erecting a statue of the goddess Roma. In 84 BC, however, this arrangement was brought to an end by Lucius Licinius Murena, who broke up the Tetrapolis, dispossessed the ruler of the city (again named Moagetes), and annexed its entire territory to the province of Asia (interrupted by a brief attachment to Cilicia), so as to control the important road on which it lay.

Italian businessmen soon flocked to this important trading center, to which numerous inscriptions—and a reference by Horace—bears witness. Cibyra was refounded by Augustus or received a new constitution, adopting the name Sebaste (Augusta) in his honor. In AD 23, however, it was severely damaged by an earthquake. As a relief measure Tiberius remitted taxation for three years, in recognition of which Cibyra assumed the additional name of Caesarea, instituted Caesarean Games, and inaugurated a new era (24/25). Further assistance in rebuilding was provided by Claudius (41-54), two of whose governors of Lycia, Quintus Veranius and Titus Clodius Eprius Marcellus, were honored by portraits on the local coinage. At a subsequent stage this also depicted 'The Rome of Hadrian' (Rome Hadriane), to celebrate that emperor's visit to Cibyra (129), on whose people, according to an inscription, he conferred 'great honors.' During the later empire the city belonged to the province of Caria, in which its bishopric enjoyed precedence. Of its city center very little survives today, but a theater and Odeum are fairly well preserved, and there are remians of a stadium and an early Christian church.

Cierus *see* Prusias on the Hypius

Cilicia. Usually understood to signify the extreme southeastern maritime strip of Asia Minor, together with its hinterland, comprising a wild and mountainous western portion 'Rough' or 'Rugged' Cilicia (Tracheia, Aspera) with abundant timber for ships, and an eastern plainland rich in flax, vines, olives, date palms and grain. This was 'Smooth' or 'Level' Cilicia (Pedias, Campestris), including the estuaries of the rivers Cydnus (Tarsus), Sarus (Seyhan) and Pyramus (Ceyhan).

Cilicia was named after the mythical Cilix, who settled there after searching for his sister Europa at the bidding of their father Agenor, King of Tyre or Sidon. After the Trojan War, according to another legend possessing some historical foundation, parts of the coastland were settled by Greeks known as Cilices (originating, according to Homer, from the Troad, in the northwestern part of the peninsula), led by Mopsus the seer and later reinforced during the age of colonization. After Assyrian domination in the eighth century BC, the Cilicians were ruled by a line of native kings bearing the name of Syennesis, who subsequently became clients of the Persians. After Alexander the Great had entered the country through the Cilician Gates of the Taurus (Toros) Mountains unopposed (333), the country was long disputed between the Ptolemies and Seleucids (and mainly in the hands of the latter), while the priestly dynasty of thc Teucrids ruled at Olba (Uğura).

In the latter part of the second century the piracy that raged throughout the eastern Mediterranean had its principal bases on the coast of Cilicia Tracheia; to deal with the menace, therefore, the Romans created a 'province' known as Cilicia—it is mentioned in a recently discovered law of 100. Of fluctuating dimensions, this province included portions of the southern coast that lay west of Cilicia proper, but did not incorporate Cilicia Pedias until 64—three years after Pompey the Great had suppressed the pirates. In 56, the province was temporarily extended to cover a huge inland area (extending up into Phrygia), so that it now protected the province of Asia completely from the east side and spared it the necessity of a garrison. Thereafter, while parts of Cilicia Tracheia were entrusted to a variety of native dynasts, Pedias was merged with the province of Syria, until in AD 72 Vespasian united the two regions to form a single Cilician province. Thirty-nine of its cities issued coinage in the early second century AD. Under the reorganization of Diocletian and Constantine this province was subdivided into three, Cilicia Prima, Cilicia Secunda (extending into the north-western corner of Syria, now the Turkish Hatay) and Isauria (comprising Cilicia Tracheia). *See also* Anazarbus, Elaeusa, Hieropolis-Castabala, Issus, Mopsuestià, Olba, Seleucia on the Calycadnus, Selinus, Soli Pompeiopolis, Tarsus.

Cimbri. A German tribe from north Jutland (where their name is still preserved by Himmerland [Aalborg]). Toward the end of the second century BC overpopulation and a shrinking coastline impelled them to emigrate southward, with the Teutones and Ambrones. After suffering a repulse from the tribe of the Scordisci near Singidunum (Belgrade) and gaining a victory over a Roman force at Noreia (near Klagenfurt; 113), their combined horde, numbering perhaps half a million persons, moved westward into Gaul, where they won further victories over Roman armies in the Rhodanus (Rhône) valley and near Tolosa (Toulouse (109,107), and then again at Arausio (Orange) (105), where Quintus Servilius Caepio and Cnaeus Mallius Maximus lost 80,000 men.

Next, after an abortive detour into Spain, they returned to Gaul and split up again into their two main tribal groups, the Cimbri and Teutones. Gaius Marius destroyed the Teutones at Aquae Sextiae (Aix-en-Provence; 102), and in the following year the Cimbri, who had travelled eastward and entered Italy by the Brenner Pass, drove back Quintus Lutatius Catulus near Tridentum (Trento), but were annihilated by the combined forces of Marius and Catulus at Campi Raudii near Vercellae (Vercelli) in the valley of the Padus (Po).

Cimmerian Bosphorus *see* Bosphorus (Cimmerian).

Cimmerians *see* Scythia

Circesium (Abu Serai). In Mesopotamia (now eastern Syria), on the left bank of the Euphrates at its junction with the Chaboras or Aborras (Khabur). Originally a Seleucid foundation, Circesium stood at the border of Osrhoene, on the often-disputed boundary of the Roman and Parthian dominions; Septimius Severus made the fortress part of his great Euphrates bulwark, under an Osrhoenian client-king (195), and it was subsequently incorporated by Caracalla (211–17) in the province of Mesopotamia. It was near Zaitha, four miles from this fortress, that Gordian III was murdered by his own troops in 244.

Situated on the main frontier route through Bostra (Busra esh-Sham) and Palmyra to Petra, Circesium became the capital and frontier station of Diocletian's province of Osrhoena, and was equipped by him, according to Ammianus Marcellinus, with new fortifications, covering a triangular perimeter. Julian the Apostate (361–63) found a garrison of 6,000 men in the fortress, and left 4,000 more—in addition to a pontoon bridge across the Chaboras. When the Persian king Chosroes I invaded the empire in 540, he decided that Circesium was too strong to assault, and passed it by.

Cirta, later Constantina (Constantine). The principal town of Numidia (north Africa; now Algeria). The name is derived from *kirtha,* a Phoenician word for city. A fortress perched high on a diamond-shaped plateau surrounded on three sides by a precipitous ravine—through which runs the river Ampsaga (Oued Rummel)—Cirta was first an important Carthaginian settlement, then a town of the Numidian Massyli, and subsequently one of the capitals of Syphax, king of the Massaesyli, in the later third century BC. After Syphax sided with Carthage against the Romans, and was captured in the final stages of the Second Punic War (203), Cirta came into the hands of his Massylian neighbor Masinissa, and was the location of his meeting with Sophonisba, the defeated king's wife whom he loved, and, according to Livy, furnished with poison to save her from captivity at Rome. Masinissa encouraged the settlement of Italian businessmen, and so did his son Micipsa (148–118), who built up Cirta into a fine fortified town, settling a colony of Greeks there and establishing a local military force. But Micipsa's son Jugurtha, when he seized the place from his brother Adherbal (112), had many of the merchants massacred, thus precipitating his war against Rome.

The Numidian king Juba I joined the Pompeians in their civil war against Julius Caesar, who after defeating them at Thapsus (Ed-Dimas, 46) gave the city and territory of Cirta (promoted to Latin status) to his friend Publius Sittius of Nuceria Alfaterna (Nocera Superiore) in Campania (46), whose head appears on rare coins issued by a community in the region. After a brief period under Juba II (30–25; before his transfer to Mauretania) Cirta was attached to the Roman province of Africa by Octavian (the future Augustus) and became a Roman colony.

Benefiting from its position on an important crossroads, the city now became the center of a confederation including three other colonies of the area; its territory also comprised a number of outlying fortresses. In the second century AD its wheat, marble and copper brought prosperity to its citizens, of whom the most famous was Fronto (*c* 100–166), the foremost orator of his day and tutor to the future emperors Marcus Aurelius and Lucius Verus. Cirta subsequently became the capital of Septimius Severus' new province of Numidia (203), and a new stage in its construction and amplification began. Severely damaged by the usurper Domitius Alexander in his war against Maxentius (308), the city was restored by Constantine the Great with the new name of Constantina (313). It already, by this time, possessed a considerable Christian community, and became the center of an ecclesiastical district. Three early basilicas and a circular baptistery (now restored) can be seen, and a medieval wall, which is largely constructed out of Roman material.

Cisalpine Gaul *see* Gallia Cisalpina

Cithaeron, Kithairon. A mountain range in central Greece separating Attica and the Megarid from Boeotia. Cithaeron was rich in religious observances, including a cult of Zeus, the festival of the Daedala in honor of Hera, and the mystic rites of Dionysus. It was here, according to myth, that Pentheus was torn to pieces by Bacchants for spurning his worship, and Actaeon, because he had seen Artemis bathing, was turned into a stag and killed by his own hounds. In the Theban mythological cycle, preserved by the tragic drama of Sophocles, it was on Cithaeron that Oedipus was exposed as an infant, and found by a shepherd looking after his sheep on the mountain's summer pastures. In historical times numerous forts on its heights and slopes guarded the frontiers of Attica.

Citium, Kition. One of the principal cities of ancient Cyprus, situated on its southeast coast. Remains go back to the Bronze (Mycenaean) Age, but *c* 800 BC, under the name of Keti, Citium was colonized by Phoenicians from Tyre (Es-Sur), and subsequently, as an independent city, became the center of Phoenician power and trading on the island, with easy access to the rich copper deposits near Tamassus (Politiko). After a period as capital of the Assyrian province of Cyprus (709–*c* 668), it habitually took the Persian side against the Greeks, and was besieged in 450/49 by the Athenian Cimon, who died there. Its greatest distinction was to have been the birthplace of Zeno (335–263), founder of the Stoic school of Greek philosophy, who was probably of Phoenician origin. Citium served as a mint of Alexander the Great, but in 312 its King Pumiathon was executed by the orders of Ptolemy I Soter of Egypt, under whose dynasty the city became gradually Hellenized. An earthquake of AD 79 caused serious damage, but Nerva (96–98) sponsored works of restoration. Citium remained important throughout ancient times, and possessed a bishopric from at least the fourth century.

Substantial remains of the Mycenaean (and later) walls survive, but the most important building is the large temple of Astarte (Ashtoreth); it was erected within a courtyard surrounded by wooden columns (with surviving stone bases), shortly before 800 BC, on the site of a Mycenaean shrine. During the five centuries of its existence (until Ptolemy burned the town's Phoenician sanctuaries) it experienced at least four major reconstructions. Massive chamber tombs of archaic date are to be seen in the western necropolis, and a Hellenistic bathhouse has lately been uncovered at Chrysopolitissa.

Cittadella *see* Cannae

Civita Castellana *see* Falerii Veteres

Civitalba *see* Sentinum

Civitas Ambianorum *see* Samarobriva

Civitas Turonum *see* Caesarodunum

Clanis (Chiana). A river of central Italy that played a major part in the development of Etruria. From its source near Arretium (Arezzo), it ran through a broad valley beside Clusium (Chiusi), and after receiving the Pallia (Paglia) tributary flowed into the Tiber beside Volsinii (Orvieto). Clusium, which became an Etruscan city-state of imperial dimensions, owed much of its wealth to the fertility of the valley of the Clanis, particularly in grain, as ancient writers (Columella, Livy, Strabo) emphasize.

The Clusines provided large-scale irrigation to limit the floodwaters of the river, as an elaborate system of trenches, tunnels and conduits still testifies. The Clanis was a considerable and even navigable stream in ancient times, but after the valley became marshy and malarial, from the Middle Ages onward, its character has been transformed by modern hydraulic engineers, who have directed what remains of its waters (the Canale Maestro di Chiana) into the Arnus (Arno). According to Tacitus and Dio Cassius, this diversion had been planned in AD 15, but was abandoned after a protest from the Florentines. (The Clanis probably gave its name to two rivers in the regions of Campania settled by the Etruscans, the Clanis or Glanis [Liri] and Clanius [Regi Lagni; *see* Capua]).

Claros *see* Colophon

Clashing Rocks *see* Symplegades

Clastidium (Casteggio). A town in north Italy (Cisalpine Gaul), seven miles south of the river Padus (Po),of which it controls the crossing to Ticinum (Pavia). About 232 BC the Insubrian Gauls, having established their Cisalpine capital at Mediolanum (Milan)—thirty-six miles to the north—came into conflict with the Romans. Ten years later the battle of Clastidium was fought, in which the consul Marcus Claudius Marcellus killed the Gallic chieftain Viridomarus with his own hand. This was the first authentically historical occasion of the winning of *spolia opima,* spoils offered by a Roman general who had slain an enemy leader in single combat (it was also the only occasion on which these *spolia* were ever won, since Octavian, the future Augustus, rejected a similar claim in 29). The poet Naevius celebrated Marcellus' achievement in an historical play entitled *Clastidium.*

At the outset of the Second Punic War (218), the town was betrayed into Hannibal's hands. When the Romans reasserted their control toward the end of the century, they made it a dependency of Placentia (Piacenza). The Via Postumia (148), spanning the northern part of Italy, passed through the place. There are remains of Roman bridges over two streams in the vicinity.

Claudiopolis *see* Cyrene

Clazomenae (Klazümen, near Urla). A city in Ionia (western Asia Minor), on the south coast of the Gulf of Smyrna (İzmir) twenty-three miles west of the city of that name. Recent excavations have fixed the phases of occupation and limits of the site from the Bronze Age onward. Clazomenae was one of the twelve cities of the Ionian League. Its founders were said to have come from Cleonae and Phlius in the Peloponnese and to have settled on the original (mainland) site of Clazomenae—after failures to establish themselves elsewhere. In about 600 BC the inhabitants successfully repelled an assault by the Lydians under Alyattes, but succumbed to his son Croesus (*c* 560–546). During the later sixth century they gave their name to a series of East-Greek black figure vases and developed a distinctive art form, consisting of painted terracotta sarcophagi (produced also at Smyrna), the subject of a recent comprehensive study.

It was through fear of Persian invasion, according to Pausanias, that the Clazomenians decided—probably at the time of the Ionian Revolt (499–494)—to move to their subsequent site on a small island four hundred yards from the coast (adjoined by eight other cultivable islands). Nevertheless, the city could not avoid passing under Persian control, only emerging to become a member of the Delian League directed by Athens; it was during this period that Clazomenae produced its most famous son, the philosopher Anaxagoras (*c* 500–428). In 412 it revolted from the Athenians and in the fourth century, according to Strabo, its people engaged in war against a mainland town (Chytrion or Chiton) which was, according to one view, located on Clazomenae's original mainland site. By thc King's Peace (Peace of Antalcidas) of 387 the city was allocated to the Persians, but issued coins (sometimes signed) with superb almost full-face portraits of Apollo. Alexander the Great, according to Pliny the Elder and Pausanias, built a causeway joining the island town to the mainland (334).

Brutus held court at Clazomenae in 43, after the murder of Caesar, but the city subsequently honored Augustus as 'founder' (*ktistes*), because of relief measures undertaken after an earthquake in 12. In addition to the usual heads of rulers and their wives, coins of the imperial epoch displayed heads of Rome and its Senate personified , and portraits of Anaxagoras as well. Clazomenae was well-known for its fish-paste.

Cleopatris *see* Arsinoe

Clermont-Ferrand *see* Augustonemetum

Clitumnus (Clitunno). A river of Umbria (central Italy), flowing into the Tinia (Teverone, Topino) and thence into the Tiber. Virgil's *Georgics* refer to the white sacrificial oxen feeding on its banks. Beside the springs (Sacraria, Fonti del Clitunno), four miles south of Trebiae (Trevi), where the river gushes out in a sudden flow, was a shrine of Jupiter Clitumnus, who gave out oracles on leaves and foretold the future by lots. Other deities were worshipped there also. The temple is believed (though not with universal agreement) to lie beneath the church of San Salvatore, mainly constructed from ancient materials in the fifth or sixth century AD.

Pliny the Younger, who gives details of the site, describes its attraction for ancient tourists; a special society, the Hispellates, was entrusted by Augustus with operating an inn and baths at no charge. The crystal-clear water of the springs were praised by Byron and Carducci.

Clunia (Peñalba de Castro). A town in north-central Spain, north of the river Durius (Douro). Its name, which first appeared as *Clounioq* and then as *Clunia* on its coins, is probably Celtic; the place belonged to the Celtiberian tribe of the Arevaci. During the civil war between Sertorius and Pompey the Great (commanding the governmental troops), Clunia, after hesitating between the two sides, chose the former and was besieged by Pompey (75 BC), but subsequently fell into the hands of Sertorius' general (and eventual murderer) Perperna. It was again attacked by Quintus Caecilius Metellus Nepos, governor of Nearer Spain, during his campaign against the tribe of the Vaccaei (56–55), who, together with the Arevaci, were reduced by Lucius Afranius *c* 53.

During the early Principate Clunia was a *municipium* and district capital in Nearer Spain (Hispania Tarraconensis). It had its moment of fame in AD 68 when the provincial governor Servius Sulpicius Galba, who had allowed himself to be hailed 'legate of the senate and Roman people' in defiance of Nero, retired there in despair on receiving news that his principal potential ally, Vindex, had lost his army and his life fighting against a loyalist army at Vesontio (Besançon). Shortly afterward, however, the freedman Icelus arrived with the news that Nero was dead, and that Galba had been accepted as his successor by the senate and the praetorian guard; whereupon his soldiers at Clunia (including a newly recruited legion) likewise acclaimed him as emperor. When Galba arrived in Rome, he commemorated the place where he had assumed the purple by the issue of a large brass coin (of which the authenticity has been wrongly placed in doubt) indicating by its inscription HISPANIA, CLVNIA SVL (*picia*), that he had conferred on the city his own family name Sulpicia: its personified figure is depicted presenting the *palladium,* emblem of empire, to Galba.

By the time of Hadrian, Clunia had attained colonial rank. It was destroyed by the Franks and Alamanni during the third century, and again, after devastation, in the fifth. Excavations have revealed a large forum, one or more basilicas, a theater, houses, and an underground sewer (Cueva de Roman).

Clusium, formerly Clevsin (Chiusi). A city in the interior of Etruria, perched on a rocky volcanic spur above the important river Clanis (Chiana, now scarcely existent), whose potentially rich valley was cleared by impressive drainage operations. In about 700 BC the Umbrian villages on the plateau, and throughout the surrounding region, were absorbed into the new Etruscan city-state. Although far distant from the coastline that brought other Etruscan communities their prosperity, surviving cemeteries have made it clear that within a century of its foundation Clusium had become the most important city of northeastern Etruria, and was growing continually wealthier. It was evolving, too, at the same time, a distinctive art form, consisting of large terracotta cremation urns with lids fashioned into generalized, but vivid, shapes and features of human heads. Clusium also produced distinctive sculpture, in relief and in the round, and glossy black (bucchero) pottery; and it sent colonists who founded the cities of Arretium (Arezzo), Cortona, Perusia (Perugia) and Volsinii (Orvieto).

The Roman writer Varro has left a fantastic account of the tomb of the sixth-century Clusine king Lars Porsenna beside the city, which has not yet been found, though an enormous grave of different appearance (the Poggio Gaiella) can be seen three miles from its walls. Lars Porsenna (both words may represent titles rather than personal names) appears to have attained more widespread power in the Italian peninsula than any other Etruscan before or after his time. In all likelihood, it was largely due to him that the influence of Clusium accomplished a unique, comprehensive double expansion, to the north beyond the Apennines and to the south into Campania. Livy and other Latin writers also immortalized his attack on Rome: according to Roman patriotic saga, his onslaught on the Sublician Bridge was thwarted by Horatius Cocles, but Tacitus, Pliny and Dionysius of Halicarnassus were aware of an alternative, and probably more reliable, tradition indicating that for a time he occupied the city, and became its ruler.

During the early Roman Republic, relations between the two states remained close, and—according to accounts which may well have an historical basis—it was because of Rome's favorable response to a Clusine appeal against the Gauls (which resulted in the death of their chieftain) that it was attacked by them and captured (390 or 387). However, the defences of Clusium were subsequently threatened by the Romans when their forces penetrated the Ciminian Forest into Volsinian territory (310), and in 295 the two states came to blows. On the whole, however, the absorption of the Clusines into the Roman world during the century that followed was conducted peacefully. At this epoch, a large district found their city was in the hands of only about twenty families, with whom the Roman ruling class was no doubt careful to cultivate friendly relations.

Cnidus, Knidos. A coastal city of Caria (southwestern Asia Minor), opposite the islands of Nisiros and Telos. Leaving aside an earlier foundation attributed to the mythical Triopus, the original settlement, established by the Spartans early in the first millennium BC, has been located (despite some disagreement) at Datça, situated on a broad sheltered bay on the southern coast of the long Cnidian Chersonese (Reşadiye peninsula), twenty miles east of its foreland (Cape Krio). The later city, however, lay at the western extremity of the peninsula (Burgaz), upon an imposing series of terraces rising from the water's edge to an acropolis and linked to an adjoining (residential) island by moles which thus created two harbors, one military and one commercial. Annexing Triopium, the people of Cnidus belonged to a group of island and mainland communities known as the Dorian Hexapolis. They earned revenue from their widespread export of wine (used also to make vinegar), as well as the production of onions, medicinal oils, and reeds for pens. They were also a sea-going people who colonized Corcyra Nigra (Korčula) in the Adriatic and the Lipara (Aeolian) islands north of Sicily.

After the Delphic oracle had advised against the construction of a defensive canal, the Cnidians were obliged to submit to Persia (after 546). Following the Persian defeat at Mycale (479), they joined the Delian League under the leadership of Athens, from which, however, they revolted in 412, during the Peloponnesian War. Cnidus was the birthplace of Ctesias, physician and historian of Persia, and of the outstanding mathematician, astronomer and geographer Eudoxus (*c* 390–340). During this period the oligarchy in power was replaced by a democratic government. After the death of Alexander the Great, the city came under the domination of the Ptolemaic dynasty, for whose first two kings the Cnidian Sostratus designed and completed (279) the lighthouse (Pharos) of Alexandria. The early second century was a period of Rhodian control. From 129 the Romans conceded Cnidus 'free' status.

Cnidus celebrated festivals in honor of its patron goddess Artemis Hyacinthotropus. However, the head of the goddess Aphrodite Euploia (inherited from the Phoenicians) appears earlier and more regularly on its coinage (the only fairly extensive Greek monetary series in Caria). The recently examined circular temple of Aphrodite, of which the gardens are described by Pseudo-Lucian, stood on a lofty terrace, and housed the renowned statue by Praxiteles (*c* 364), which had been rejected by Cos because of its nudity. Coins issued under the Roman Principate depict the statue; the goddess is represented as if about to enter a bath, naked and seen from the front, with her head in profile, holding a robe under an urn. A Doric temple dedicated to Apollo Carneios may have been the site of the Dorian games celebrated in the city, a continuation of an ancient festival of Triopian Apollo, attended by representatives from neighboring cities. Other partially preserved and excavated buildings include a council chamber (formerly believed to have been an Odeon), a Doric portico (perhaps designed by Sostratus), a theater, a stadium, and a small temple of the second century AD.

Cnossus, Knossos. A city of northern Crete, on the west bank of the river Kairatos. After its unparalleled Bronze Age splendors, the city, reconstructed by Greeks slightly to the north of the destroyed Minoan palace, recovered a considerable degree of importance in the early first millennium BC, and remained the most important city of the island; it possessed ports at Amnisus (Karteros, reputedly the harbor of the legendary Minos) and Katsamba and Heraclion (Herakleion, the modern capital of Crete). Cnossus is frequently mentioned by Homer, and was reported by Scymnus to have colonized the Aegean islands of Peparethos and Icos, to which Strabo more questionably adds Brundusium (Brindisi) in south Italy.

In the fifth century Cnossus began to issue coinage depicting the Minotaur and its labyrinth. It made a treaty with its western neighbor Tylissus, but was frequently at war with Lyttus (Xidas), which it seized in 346 and destroyed in 221/19, during an expansionist drive. Its people were also intermittently engaged in strife with Gortyna, which after Cnossus (because of its resistance to Roman occuaption) had been destroyed by Quintus Caecilius Metellus, known as Creticus (69/67), took its place as the capital of the island (henceforth united with Cyrenaica as a Roman province). However, Cnossus may have served as a mint for more than one Roman admiral during the civil wars of the later first century BC, and after Octavian (the future Augustus) had established a colony of ex-soldiers there in 36, with the title of *Nobilis,* continued to issue bronze coinage on its own account for a time.

Traces of classical Greek and Hellenistic temples have survived, and of a Roman basilica, small amphitheater, and houses, including the large 'Villa of Dionysus' named after a floor mosaic depicting the heads of Dionysus and Maenads framed in medallions.

Coblenz *see* Koblenz

Coele Syria *see* Syria

Colchester *see* Camulodunum

Colchis. The region at the eastern extremity of the Euxine (Black) Sea (the western part of the Soviet Republic of Georgia), including the valley of the Phasis (from which the pheasant takes its name, now the Rioni): bounded by Iberia (E.), Armenia and Pontus (S.) and the Caucasus Mountains (N.). The Greeks regarded Colchis as a country of magic and wealth, embodied in the legend of the argonauts, who sailed there to capture the Golden Fleece from Aeetes, King of Aea ('the land,' identified with Colchis), as later recounted in the *Argonautica* of Apollonius Rhodius.

Several Greek colonies were established in Colchis by the Milesians. Although handicapped by fever, prevalent in their marshy lowlands, the Colchians sold the Greeks a variety of products—including iron (from its alleged inventors the Chalybes), timber, which they brought down the mountain rivers, and hemp and linen cloth: while Phasis—perhaps Simagre, eleven miles east of Poti, destroyed *c* 450 BC, but later reconstructed—their city or market town and earliest mint (from *c* 500) was the terminal of a commercial route to central Asia. Remarkable discoveries at Vani, sixty miles from the coast (sometimes identified with the capital of Aeetes) and at Pichvnari (six miles north of Kobaleti) and rich finds of gold jewelry in the valley of the River Kvirila and at Absar, show the wealth of Colchian culture during the late fifth, fourth and third centuries BC, and testify to its links with both the Greek and the Scytho-Iranian worlds; while another city, Dioscurias (later Sebastopolis, now Sukhumi), was noted for its polyglot cosmopolitanism (it was said that seventy languages could be heard in its market).

It is disputed whether the state of Colchis, succeeding to a Kingdom of Qulha destroyed *c* 720, was established in the sixth century or only as late as the third. After a period of rule by local chieftains, it came, reluctantly, under the control of Mithridates VI Eupator of Pontus (*c* 111–110). Following his defeat by Pompey the Great (66), a Roman client, Aristarchus, was placed on its throne; not long afterward, however, Mithridates' son Pharnaces II seized the country, but was expelled by Caesar (48). Colchis was then incorporated in the Roman province of Bithynia and Pontus. Emperors of the second century AD, however, entrusted it to a series of local dynasts; Hadrian's governor of Cappadocia, Arrian, described its coastal forts (134).

In the final period of antiquity, Colchis became part of the independent state of Lazica, which abandoned its initially friendly relations with Rome and attracted the interference of the eastern emperor Marcian (456) because of its strategic position as a barrier against both the Transcaucasian tribes and the Persians. *See also* Dioscurias, Phasis, Pityus.

Collatia (near Osteria d'Osa or Lunghezza). A town in Latium (Laxio) ten miles east of Rome, commanding the crossing of the river Anio (Aniene) and the road between Veii and Gabii (Castiglione). The story that Collatia was founded by the Silvii, the legendary royal house of Alba Longa (Castel Gandolfo) descended from Aeneas, points to a period when Collatia was under Alban domination. Tradition recorded its destruction by Rome's king Tullus Hostilius (665 BC), but it was subsequently restored by the Tarquins.

The place became famous for the part it was said to have played in the downfall of the Roman monarchy (*c* 510/9). According to the saga, recounted by Livy, Dionysius of Halicarnassus, and others, it was the scene of the tragic death of the heroine Lucretia, whose violation by Sextus Tarquinius, son of King Tarquinius Superbus, impelled her to plunge a dagger into her breast. It was at her own home that she died, because her husband Lucius Tarquinius Collatinus was governor of Collatia, to which he owed his name. Lucretia's funeral, the story went on, roused the people of the town, and they marched on Rome to drive the king out, led by Lucius Junius Brutus, who became one of the first pair of consuls of the new Republic that was now inaugurated. The other consul was Collatinus, who allegedly was forced to retire from the office because of his Tarquinian name. He may have been an authentic, dimly remembered personage of the transitional period between the monarchy and the Republic around whom legends subsequently clustered. Pliny the Elder, writing in the first century AD, reported that the town of Collatia had vanished without a trace.

Colonia Agrippinensis or Agrippinensium, formerly Oppidum Ubiorum (Köln, Cologne). The place was founded on the south (left) bank of the Rhenus (Rhine) in 38 BC to house the tribe of the Ubii, whom Marcus Agrippa, on behalf of Octavian (the future Augustus), had transferred from the right bank at their own request. This Oppidum Ubiorum became a fortress of the military command of Lower Germany (Germania Inferior), garrisoned by two legions (until the reign of Tiberius, AD 14–37) and containing an Altar of Rome and Augustus—serving the imperial cult of the territory, in place of an earlier Altar of the Ubii—which has not been located.

In 50 Claudius refounded Oppidum Ubiorum as a military colony bearing the names of the altar and of his wife Agrippina the Younger (Colonia Ara Augusta Agrippinensis). The headquarters of the Rhine fleet (Classis Germanica) were a small distance upstream, and an important commercial harbor developed between the city and the river. In 69 the colony was compelled to join the Gallo-German rebellion of Civilis, but when the rising seemed doomed, its inhabitants murdered all the Germans stationed in the city and burned to death a further contingent outside the walls, after first making them drunk. When Lower Germany was made a separate province by Domitian (*c* 69), Colonia Agrippinensis became its capital, continuing to prosper as the principal center of trade and industry in the Rhineland. The glassware it produced was exported throughout all western and northern Europe.

The German wars of the mid-third century inflicted severe damage on the city. In 260 Saloninus Caesar, the second son of Gallienus, was stationed at the stronghold—under the supervision of a general named Silvanus—when Postumus, probably governor of the Lower German province, rebelled and after a successful siege of the city murdered them both, setting up a rival empire of the western provinces. One of his base silver coinages bears the name of Colonia Agrippinensis, to which his principal mint apparently was transferred from Augusta Trevirorum (Trier) in 267, remaining there under the further secessionists who succeeded him (268–73). The reign of Probus (276–82) witnessed a brief rebellion by Bonosus, commander of the Rhine fleet, and Proculus, who may have been his associate. In 310 Constantine I the Great erected a bridge across the river, leading to another fortress, Divitia (Deutz), on the opposite bank. Following a twenty-eight day usurpation by the local infantry commander Silvanus, Colonia Agrippinensis was captured by the Franks in 355 (they were driven out by Julian in the following year), and again after the withdrawal of the frontier troops in 463—becoming the residence of the Frankish king Childeric (d. 481) a few years later.

A modern street, the Hohestrasse, lies exactly over the ancient main thoroughfare (*cardo maximus*). Excavations at other points have uncovered two whole areas of the ancient city, including the military headquarters or *praetorium,* bathhouses, temples of Jupiter Capitolinus and Mercury-Augustus and Mithras, a subterranean shrine of indigenous deities known as the Matronae, a large Roman villa from which a Dionysiac floor-mosaic and a recently discovered second-century wall painting survive, and the church of St. Gereon of which the origins go back to the mid-fourth century. For the past ten years excavations have been proceeding on a river island. One of the best-preserved Roman villas in Germany lies three miles west of Colonia Agrippinensis, at Mügerdorf.

Colonus, Kolonos (Kolokythou). A small district (deme) of Attica, situated a mile-and-a-half north of the Athenian Acropolis (in the neighborhood of Plato's Academy). The deme included a flat hill containing the sanctuary of Poseidon Hippios ('of horses') and Athena Hippia, after which the area was sometimes known as Kolonos Hippios (as opposed to Kolonos Agoraios, which lay to the west of the city's marketplace). The Athenian Assembly that set up the revolutionary, oligarchic committee of the Four Hundred in 411 BC, during the Peloponnesian War, met at the shrine of Poseidon.

But Colonus is particularly famous for its prominent role in Greek mythology. It was the place where Theseus and Pirithous descended to the Underworld, crossing the bronze threshold. Above all, it was here that Oedipus found refuge and was buried, according to the *Oedipus at Colonus* of Sophocles, the most famous man the district produced. He pays a glowing tribute to Colonus' beauty, in which its modern successor, the suburb Kolokythou, is deficient.

Colophon, Kolophon (Değirmendere). A Greek city of Ionia (western Asia Minor), situated eight miles from the sea on a group of three hills, at the edge of a fertile plain between Smyrna (İzmir) and Ephesus (Selçuk). According to Strabo, its founders came from Pylos in Messenia; and potttery of the Mycenaean period has been found. The city, though noted for its naval and particularly its cavalry forces, came successively under the control of the Lydians and then of the Persians, subsequently alternating between Persian and Athenian allegiance. Colophon colonized Myrlea (later Apamea, now Mudanya) in Bithynia (northern Asia Minor) and Siris in southern Italy (*c* 680–652). Moreover, at some date before the fifth century, the Colophonians planted a fort at Notium (on a promontory above the adjacent anchorage of Claros), but suffered increasingly from encroachments by this former dependency. Final disaster came when their attempt to resist one of Alexander's successors, Lysimachus, proved unsuccessful, and he compelled the entire population to migrate to Ephesus. After his death in 281, they were reestablished on their old site, but never became important again. The Colophonians, on whom freedom was conferred in Rome's treaty with the Seleucid Antiochus III the Great (188), did not come from the old city but from New Colophon, as Notium was now called. Colophon was famous, Strabo commented, for its extravagant living, comparable to the notorious luxury of the people of Sybaris (Sibari) in south Italy. A legend also attributed the invention of spindles for weaving wool to the daughter of one of the dyers in the city. It was the birthplace of the elegiac poet and musician Mimnermus (seventh century BC). But it owed its greatest fame to the control of the sanctuary of Apollo of Claros, eight miles to the south (near Ahmetbeyli). The cult, located in a grove, was famed for its oracle, described by the *Homeric Hymn to Apollo* and by the early imperial historian Tacitus, in whose time, as recent excavations suggest, it was entering on its most flourishing period. The often reconstructed temple, which contained a colossal seated statue of Apollo between standing figures of Artemis and Leto, was built over a crypt (still in an excellent state of preservation) containing the well where the priest-prophet of the shrine drank the water of inspiration. A series of inscriptions list the delegations that came to the holy place in order to consult the oracle, especially from inland Asia Minor and the Euxine (Black) Sea coast.

The two cities of Colophon placed heads of Apollo on their coinages, and an issue of imperial date naming the Council (*koinon*) of Ionia displays personifications of the thirteen cities of the Ionian League standing in a semicircle before the temple of Clarian Apollo, in front of which a bull and a flaming altar are to be seen.

Columnae Herculis *see* Gades

Comana, later Hierapolis (now Şar), in Cataonia (Cappadocia, eastern Asia Minor). The place was situated in the valley of the river Sarus (Seyhan), at the eastern end of the main pass through the western Anti-Taurus ranges. In Hellenistic times the two Comanas, in Cappadocia and Pontus, were the principal cult centers of the great earth- and mother-goddess Ma (identified with the warrior-deity Enyo by the Greeks, and with Bellona by the Romans). These sanctuaries possessed autonomous status under their own chief priests, who were generally related to the royal houses of their countries, and ranked second to the king; there were also numerous temple serfs and prostitutes.

Strabo reports that as many as 6,000 servants (including numerous Persians) worked for the shrine at Cappadocian Comana, in addition to a considerable lay population around the sanctuary and in the adjacent fertile valleys, which contained the priestly estates. After receiving city status from King Archelaus of Cappadocia (or perhaps from the Romans, after *c* AD 80) Comana became a Roman colony under Caracalla (211-17)—because of its location on the chief military road to the eastern frontier—and continued to receive further honors until the empire became Christian. The city was known as Chryse (the Golden), to distinguish it from Comana Pontica. Surviving remains include a theater and numerous inscriptions.

Comana Pontica (later Hierocaesarea, now near Gümenek) in Pontus (northern Asia Minor). Situated beside fortified hills in the valley of the river Iris (Yeşil Irmak), between Zela (Zile) and Neocaesarea (Niksar). In Hellenistic times this Comana and the place of the same name in Cappadocia (from which it derived) were the two principal cult-centers of the goddess Ma, enjoying similar status, and possessing equally large staffs of temple serfs. Comana Pontica was also a center of commerce. It became an autonomous client principality in Pompey's settlement of Pontus (64) under its priest-king Archelaus, whom Caesar replaced by Lycomedes.

The place was attached to Pontus Galaticus, a region of the Roman province of Pontus and Bithynia, in AD 34, from which it reckoned a new era, ceasing to be a sacerdotal state and becoming a city of the empire under the name of Hierocaesarea. It remained the center of a considerable territory, but gradually declined in importance toward the end of the imperial epoch. Its coins under the Principate sometimes display a head or figure of Enyo (Ma), wearing a radiate crown and holding a shield and a club. A gate with a baroque broken pediment appears on an issue of Septimius Severus (AD 198).

Comeana *see* Artemium

Commagene. A territory in the extreme north of Syria (now southeastern Turkey) situated on the southern slopes of the Taurus (Toros) range, and extending to the river Euphrates. After successively becoming an Assyrian province and a dependency of Persia, it reemerged in history as a client-state of the Seleucids under Arsames II, who founded two fortified cities both named Arsameia (Eski Kahta and Gerget; *c* 230). About 162 a subsequent satrap, Ptolemaeus, declared himself independent; later Samosata (Samsat; founded by King Samos *c* 150) became the royal capital. One of the subsequent rulers, Antiochus I Theos, rewarded by Pompey the Great for deserting Mithridates VI of Pontus, was deposed by Antony in 38 for his support of a Parthian invasion; extensive remains of his massive dynastic mausoleum on top of the Nemrud Dağı (mountain) have come to light, consisting of a tumulus surrounded by courtyards—one of which is adorned by reliefs depicting the kings and his ancestors and indicating that the royal house adhered to an ostensibly Hellenized version of the Zoroastrian religion.

On the death of Antiochus III in AD 17 Tiberius made the kingdom into a Roman province, divided into four city territories. But it reverted to the status of a client kingdom (with an enlarged sphere of influence, to judge from its coins) under Antiochus IV Epiphanes 'the Great' (38, 41–72). After his removal, however—for alleged Parthian sympathies —the country was incorporated in the province of Syria as an autonomous federal unit (*koinon*). But Hellenization remained superficial; even in the capital Samosata, the future Greek writer Lucian (*c* 120-after 180) did not speak Greek as a boy (his mother tongue was probably Aramaic). A grandson of the last kings of Commagene, Gaius Julius Antiochus Epiphanes Philopappus, became a benefactor of Athens, building a monument still named after him. (114–16). *See also* Arsameia, Samosata, Zeugma.

Comum (Como). A city of Cisalpine Gaul (north Italy), at the southwestern extremity of Lake Larius (Como). Settled by the Insubrian Gauls, but plagued by incursions by Rhaetian tribesmen, Comum was occupied by the Roman general Marcus Claudius Marcellus in 196 BC, receiving colonists in 89 (later reinforced), and 59, with Latin rights (conferring citizenship on its annually elected officials) and the full Roman franchise respectively. The second of these settlements—known as Novum Comum—carried out by Julius Caesar under a law enabling him to organize such foundations at his own discretion, comprised a draft of 5,000 colonists (including 500 Greeks). But the colony created a *cause celèbre* in 51, when one of the consuls, named, like the original captor of the city, Marcus Claudius Marcellus, had a man of Novum Comum flogged—a penalty from which Roman citizens were exempted by law—in order to show his contempt for Caesar's action: this helped to widen the gulf between conservatives and Caesarians which became civil war two years later.

Under Augustus the city became a *municipium*. It was chiefly famous as the birthplace of the historian and scientist Pliny the Elder (AD 23/4–79) and his nephew and adoptive son Pliny the Younger (*c* 61–112), author of literary letters and a *Panegyric* of Trajan. In their time, the place was well-known for its iron industry, although there were no mines nearby. Traces of the bath building, with library, erected by the younger Pliny have survived, in addition to walls of Republican date and other fortifications indicating that Comum was a place of military importance in the later imperial epoch.

Condatomagus, later Aemiliavum (Millau). A town in Aquitania, southwestern Gaul (Aveyron, France), situated on the left bank of the river Tarnis (Tarn), downstream from its junction with the Dourbie. In the first century AD Condatomagus was one of the principal production centers of stamped pottery in the Roman empire, known as La Graufesenque Ware after the plain on which the town was situated. Subsequently Condatomagus was eclipsed as a pottery center by Ledosus (Lezoux), but still retained some commercial importance. A fort of the Iron Age and Roman epoch has been excavated at La Grinède overlooking the plain and valley.

Condeixa-a-Velha *see* Conimbriga

Confluentes, Ad Confluentes (Koblenz). A Roman fortress town, at the confluence of the rivers Rhenus (Rhine) and Mosella (Moselle), on the borders between the commands (later provinces) of Lower and Upper Germany. An auxiliary garrison was stationed at the fortress from the time of Tiberius (AD 14–37) or Claudius (41–54). Confluentes was destroyed in the Gallo-German revolt of 70, but may have been subsequently rebuilt. Although no longer situated on the frontier, which was moved forward to include the Agri Decumates (the reentrant between the upper Rhine and upper Danube), the city remained an important communications center; and an adjacent civilian settlement continued to exist.

Following German invasions shortly after the mid-third century, the Agri Decumates were evacuated, and Confluentes, which had suffered destruction (*c* 259/60), again became a frontier town. It was reconstructed with massive fortifications by Maximian (286–305), and again by Constantius II (337–61) or his successor Julian the Apostate (361–63), only to fall to the Franks during the fifth century. Abundant remains of a bridge of late imperial date across the Mosella have been recovered from the riverbed, including thousands of wooden piles with iron tips.

Conimbriga (Condeixa-a-Velha) in Lusitania (Beira, Portugal). The name is derived from the pre-Celtic tribe of the Conii, whose settlement dates from the seventh century BC. Situated on a triangular spur, Conimbriga was probably captured by Decimus Junius Brutus Callaicus in 138, and then became swiftly and thoroughly Romanized. Under Vespasian (AD 69–79) or Domitian (81–96) it became a *municipium,* with the surname of Flavium, but probably ceased to be under Roman control at the beginning of the fifth century, when it became the property of the tribe of the Cantabri. Thereafter the city was twice attacked by the Suevi in 465 and 468 and (according to Idatius) partly destroyed, subsequently passing into the hands of the Visigoths.

Conimbriga is the largest site to have been excavated in Portugal. Remains of the Augustan and Flavian fora, an aqueduct, and of four public bathing establishments can be seen. But the most important discoveries are luxurious houses that were built around large colonnaded (peristyle) courtyards with central pools, and contained extensive and lavish floor mosaics, displaying mythological, animal and hunting scenes. The mosaics in the House of the Fountains are particularly notable. A hoard of 4,304 coins has recently been discovered.

At the end of the ancient epoch another town nine miles to the north, Aeminium on the river Munda (Mondego), took over the name of Conimbriga, and became the modern Coimbra.

Constanța *see* Tomis

Constantia *see* Salamis

Constantine *see* Cirta

Constantinople *see* Byzantium

Copais. A large lake that covered most of the western plain of Boeotia (central Greece), fed by the river Cephisus (after which the lake was sometimes known as Cephissis) and other streams, and taking its name from the town of Copae (meaning 'oars') near its northeast corner. A cave on the adjacent slopes of Mount Ptoon was occupied continuously from the Palaeolithic to the Bronze Age, and there was also an important Bronze Age (Mycenaean) fortress at Gla (later an island).

Lake Copais was early subjected to extensive drainage and clearance operations, generally, though conjecturally, attributed to the Minyans, one of whose principal centers was Orchomenus, on the west side of the lake; drainage wells, perhaps dating back to prehistoric times, have now been excavated two miles from its bank. According to legend, the outlets of Lake Copais were blocked by Heracles, who was claimed by Thebes (which lay to the southeast) as one of its heroes: the story may reflect hostile action taken by the Thebans during their wars against Orchomenus. Despite repeated efforts at irrigation, notably by Crates of Chalcis, an engineer of Alexander the Great, the surrounding land always remained swampy. The comic dramatist Aristophanes reported that the lake was famous for its eels. Its reeds furnished the Boeotians with their musical instrument the *aulos* resembling a clarinet or oboe. *See also* Haliartus, Orchomenus.

Copia *see* Lugdunum, Sybaris

Corbridge *see* Corioritum

Corcyra, Kerkyra, Korkyra (Corfu). The northernmost island of the Ionian archipelago off the northwest coast of Greece, separated by a narrow channel from the mainland (now Albania). Comparatively heavy rainfall provides a much more luxuriant vegetation than that of the other islands of the group. According to Thucydides, Corcyra was believed to be Homer's Scheria, the legendary home of the Phaeacians, although it does not seem likely that the poet intended to identify Scheria with any real place.

Corcyra was originally inhabited by people with Illyrian and Apulian connections. In the early eighth century BC, however, when the Euboean cities of Chalcis and Eretria took the lead in widespread maritime commercial exchanges, the Eretrians, perhaps joined by Liburni from the Illyrian mainland, established a commercial post on a peninsula the east coast of the island. Their settlement, at first named Drepane, possessed two harbors, one on the sea and the other on a deep lagoon; and the traders owned holdings on the mainland opposite, enabling them to control the strait. Corcyra lies at a point where the Adriatic Sea is almost at its narrowest, and the Euboeans regarded the island as a staging point to Italy, and particularly to Campania from which they could reach out to Etruria and acquire its metals.

About 733 colonists from the rapidly rising commercial center of Corinth arrived, and later expelled the Eretrians. The new settlers established a community under the name of Palaepolis (just north of the modern city), situated between two harbors and surmounted by an acropolis (Analepsis). These colonists claimed that the name Corcyra was itself of Corinthian origin—derived from a corruption of the name Gorgo, the demon conquered by the Corinthian hero Bellerophon (although it has also been argued that the word was of Illyrian origin). However, Corcyra soon became involved in ferocious strife against its mother city Corinth, whose fleet it defeated heavily at Sybota (*c* 664?). In spite of this clash, Corcyraeans and Corinthians were still able to combine forces to colonize Epidamnus (later Dyrrhachium, Durrës) on the Adriatic coast (*c* 625). But in 435 a struggle for the control of this joint colony again brought Corcyra and Corinth into open conflict; and this contributed strongly to the subsequent outbreak of the Peloponnesian War.

In that conflict, Corcyra supported Athens, and Corinth took the side of Sparta. In 427 and 425 the pro-Athenian democrats at Corcyra massacred the oligarchic opposition, but in 410 the city terminated the Athenian alliance, only to renew the link in 375 after a period under the hegemony of the Spartans, whose efforts to recapture the island in 373 were beaten off. The Corcyraeans then once more abandoned the Athenian cause (360), only to embrace it again twenty years later, in the hope of keeping the Macedonians out; which, however, proved impossible. The island was fought over by Alexander the Great's successors and passed under the domination of Agathocles of Syracuse (*c* 300) and Pyrrhus of Epirus (195). Coins of the period show the forepart of a ship, referring to galley races held on the occasion of religious festivals. In 229 the Romans liberated Corcyra from the Illyrian queen Teuta and made it a naval base, subsequently attached to the province of Macedonia.

Corcyra's most important surviving monument is a gigantic relief of a Gorgon from the Doric temple of Artemis (*c* 585). There was also another, older sanctuary, dedicated to a protective deity of the region, and subsequently surrounded by other shrines. The mosaic pavement of the Christian basilica of Haghia Kerkyra, built over the remains of a Hellenistic Council chamber, is inscribed with an epigram of archbishop Gavianus of the fifth century AD.

Corduba (Cordoba). A city of southern Spain, on the right bank of the river Baetis (Guadalquivir) and the southern slopes of the Sierra de Cordoba. Originally a native town (to judge from its Iberian name), it was refounded by Marcus Claudius Marcellus in 152 BC and became the capital of Further Spain (Hispania Ulterior, later Baetica) and a center of Roman life and culture. Elevated to colonial status, perhaps by Gnaeus Pompeius, Pompey the Great's elder son (*c* 46/5)—who issued coins at the city displaying his father's head—it was punished by Julius Caesar after the Pompeians' defeat at the battle of Munda (45), and 20,000 of its inhabitants were massacred. Augustus settled a draft of ex-soldiers at the colony, under the new name of Patricia, and it remained the most completely Romanized center in the entire peninsula.

Corduba Patricia derived great prosperity from its location on the Baetis (then navigable up to the city) and on the Via Augusta (the new commercial highway to northern Spain), and earned extensive revenue from its grain, oil, wool, and mines. It was the birthplace of the rhetorician Seneca the Elder (*c* 55 BC–AD 37/41), of his son of the same name who achieved renown as a philosopher, scientist and minister of Nero (*c* 4 BC/1 AD–AD 65), and of the poet Lucan (AD 39–65) whose father was the elder Seneca's brother. During the second century AD Corduba was rivalled by Hispalis (Seville) and Italica (Santiponce). But its bishop Ossius (Hosius; d. 357) was the most powerful western churchman of his age, and an intimate counsellor of Constantine the Great. After passing into Visigothic hands, the city was temporarily recovered by Justinian I (*c* 550–84).

The modern network of streets is largely superimposed on the Roman plan, and a large temple and bathhouse have been identified. But the most remarkable remains are those of a bridge across the river Baetis; it was originally built by Julius Caesar after his victory over the Pompeians, and its foundations are still to be seen under a subsequent Moorish construction.

Corfinium (Corfinio). A town in central Italy (Abruzzo), controlling an important bridgehead across the river Aternus (Aterno). It was the chief town of the tribe of the Paeligni, who became allies of Rome before 300 BC. At the time of the Italian rebellion against the Romans (Social War, 91–87), the construction of a city, according to Diodorus, had recently been completed, including a forum and Council chamber.

It was now that Corfinium had the first of its two moments of fame, when the rebels gave it the name of Italia and made it the capital of their federation (90). However, they were quickly obliged to move their headquarters further south. Corfinium's second and equally transitory moment came in 49, during the first stage of the civil war between Julius Caesar and Pompey the Great, when Lucius Domitius Ahenobarbus barricaded himself with the city, hoping to hold up Caesar's southward advance; but after a week he capitulated.

During the early Principate, Corfinium, reinforced by new settlers, became an important communications center since it was here that two important roads of Claudius (AD 41–54) met, an extension of the Via Valeria—from Rome to the Adriatic Sea, known as the Via Claudia Valeria—and the Via Claudia Nova. Two aqueducts, mainly subterranean, have been traced.

Corinium Dobunnorum (Cirencester in Gloucestershire, England). On the main road from Londinium (London) to Glevum (Gloucester). Recent excavations have shown that the first site was a farm, followed by a Roman military presence which soon took the form of an auxiliary fort (*c* AD 49). Above the fort the central buildings of early Corinium have been discovered, representing the first stages of the civil settlement that developed into the tribal capital of the Dobunni (after 60). The forum and basilica date from shortly before 100, and an amphitheater southwest of the town was erected in the early years of the following century. The course of the river Churn was diverted into an artificial channel, which came to be employed as part of second- and-third century defences. As an inscription shows, Corinium became the capital of the province of Britannia Prima in the fourth century, and occupation continued well into the fifth.

Corinth, Korinthos. The isthmus city, controlling communications between the northern part of Greece and its southern peninsula (the Peloponnese) and between the Gulf of Corinth (leading to the Adriatic or Ionian Sea) to the west and the Saronic Gulf (Aegean Sea) to the east. The ancient settlement lay on the slopes of a lofty acropolis (Acrocorinth), six miles west of the isthmus, two miles inland from the Gulf of Corinth and its harbor town of Lechaeum, and eight miles from a second harbor, Cenchreae, on the Saronic Gulf.

The site was occupied since Neolithic times, but during the Later Bronze Age was temporarily eclipsed by Korakou on the coast, which may well be the 'wealthy Corinth' of Homer's *Iliad,* subject to the kings of Mycenae. Corinth was also identified with the epic city of Ephyra, associated in Greek mythology with Sisyphus (compelled eternally to roll a stone up a hill, from which it then rolled down again) and Bellerophon (rider of the winged horse Pegasus), whose links with southern Asia Minor reflect eastern commercial relations. As the Mycenaean civilation collapsed, Dorians, supposedly led by Aletes, occupied the region in about the eleventh century BC, and after 750 the city-state of Corinth was formed by the union (synoecism) of eight villages.

The Corinthians quickly exported their Geometric pottery, planting colonies on the Ionian islands of Ithaca (*c* 750?) and Corcyra (Corfu, *c* 733) and at Syracuse (traditionally contemporary with Corcyra). During the same century they annexed the northern part of the isthmus (the southern Megarid) to safeguard their harbor traffic, building the temple and sanctuary of Poseidon (Kiras Vrysi, *c* 700; recently excavated), whose Isthmian Games became a Panhellenic festival in 581/80. Just north of the isthmus, there were important shrines of Hera at Peiraeum (Perachora), taken over by Corinth *c* 750–725. Potters began to develop the Protocorinthian style of ceramics, inspired by near-eastern contacts, and these and the other Corinthian wares that followed enjoyed a virtual monopoly over an extensive area for a century and a half to come. The long, low warships that appear on some of the early vases provide an indication of the fighting power that backed this commercial drive.

From *c* 747, the traditional date of the abolition of the monarchy, Corinth was ruled by the Dorian oligarchy of the Bacchiad clan of two hundred families, one of whose members, Eumelus, concluded a long tradition of epic poetry; his works are now lost. But then, perhaps after a naval defeat at the hands of Corinth's colony Corcyra (*c* 664?), the Bacchiads were supplanted by Cypselus, Periander and other members of the family who ruled as autocrats or 'tyrants' (*c* 658/7-583/1 or later). It was at this time that Corinth attained the height of its prosperity and power, sailing both seas—the Aegean and the Adriatic (the latter via the Corinthian Gulf)—hauling ships across the isthmus on a stone carriage way, establishing additional colonies, dispatching artists and craftsmen as far afield as Etruria in western Italy, and issuing silver coins (from *c* 575), known as *poloi* (colts) because of their representation of the winged horse Pegasus, that formed the principal medium of monetary exchange throughout the Mediterranean world.

The autocracy was replaced by a constitutional administration that governed well but could not prevent Corinth from being outstripped by Athens as a commercial power, from about 550 onward. The Corinthians fought with distinction in the Persian Wars, but were heavily defeated by the Athenians on land and sea in 460; and disputes between the two powers over Corcyra and Potidaea contributed largely to the outbreak of the Peloponnesian War (431), in which Corinth sided with Sparta, to whose League it had long belonged. However, the final failure of Athens in the war did not place any lasting revival within the reach of the Corinthians, who entered into a series of short-lived alliances with stronger states (notably in the 'Corinthian War' against Sparta in 392-386, when the city was temporarily absorbed by Argos) and underwent violent internal convulsions and outbreaks of strife between oligarchs and democrats which meant that the city could play little part in external politics. Nevertheless, when Sicilian Greeks sought assistance against their own autocracies and their Carthaginian neighbors, Corinth sent out Timoleon (344), who ruled successfully at Syracuse. Shortly afterward, the Corinthians attempted to block encroachments from Philip II of Macedonia. After his victory over the Greek city-states at Chaeronea (338), however, he placed a garrison in Acrocorinth, and employed the city as the headquarters of a new Panhellenic League of Corinth, under his own direction; and it was there that he and his son Alexander declared war against the Persians.

While remaining a center of industry and trade—and gaining, incidentally, a widespread reputation for commercialized sex—Corinth also retained its position as a key fortress, not infrequently changing hands. In the second century it became the capital of the Achaean League, and after the League's armies had been defeated by the Romans it suffered annihilation at the hands of Lucius Mummius 'Achaicus' (146), who shipped its art treasures to Italy. On the centenary of its destruction, however, Julius Caesar founded a colony for ex-soldiers on the site, named, as its coins show, 'Praise of Julius' (*Laus Julii*); the new settlement resumed its role as a commercial entrepot, and became the capital of the province of Achaea. St. Paul passionately addressed its Christian community (*c* AD 50/51). The coinage of the Corinthian colony recorded a visit (*adventus*) and speech (*adlocutio*) of Nero, who made an unsuccessful attempt to cut a canal through the isthmus; and a later issue recorded a new colonial title Flavia, owed to a refoundation by Domitian (81-96). Other coinages offer numerous and varied designs of local significance, including the lighthouse of Lechaeum and the harbor at Cenchreae and a wealth of references to the city's famous myths, cults and monuments.

One such monument is the sacred fountain of Pirene (on the rock of Acrocorinth), the principal source of the water supply of Corinth, originally opened, according to legend, by Pegasus' stamping hoof, and shown on coins of Septimius Severus (193–211). Beside the fountain, a small temple, rebuilt during the fourth century BC, has come to light. More important is the shrine of Apollo Pythios on 'Temple Hill,' of which seven columns still stand, dating back to a sixth-century reconstruction of an earlier building (*c* 700). There were also Corinthian sanctuaries of Zeus, Athena Hellotis, Demeter and Persephone (Kore), Asclepius, and Aphrodite (on Acrocorinth). The remains of a very large Doric portico (the South Stoa, perhaps of the 320s BC) and traces of a Hellenistic race course and sports complex (replacing previous structures). Later, the Romans rebuilt the city in a lavish fashion: at least three basilicas can be traced, as well as three magnificent public baths, a theater (enlarging its Greek forerunner), an amphitheater, and private dwellings including a large villa of the third century AD (near the shore) which was furnished with a sophisticated water supply.

About 268 Corinth was partially destroyed by the Goths and Herulians when they overran Greece. Earthquakes of 365 and 375 did further damage (repeating an upheaval in 79). After all these disasters, the forum was replanned and repaired. But the Visigoths under Alaric struck again in 395, and in 521 the city was destroyed by a further earthquake, which the historian Procopius saw as proof that God was abandoning the empire.

Corioritum (?) (Corbridge; not Corstopitum as has been supposed, which was Corchester). A Roman stronghold near the northern frontier of Britannia (Northumberland), situated on the north bank of the river Tyne where it was bridged by the road leading from Eboracum (York) up into Caledonia (Scotland). An original timber fort with turf ramparts, probably dating from the governorship of Cnaeus Julius Agricola (*c* AD 79), was burned down, but subsequently reconstructed—probably in connection with the building of Hadrian's wall—receiving a garrison (*c* 139–60) and substantial new buildings, including granaries, used during the campaigns of Septimius Severus (208–11). Altogether six successive forts, lying on top of each other, have now been revealed by excavations. There are also temples and recorded cults of the local Apollo Maponus and the Syrian Jupiter Dolichenus, whose worship suggests that the place had become an important market center for foreigners.

Outside the military area, on the way to a bridge, over the Tyne, excavations have revealed an extensive storehouse and works depot, and a large corridored building that may have been an official rest house. In its ornamental pool was found a notable piece of sculpture, the Corbridge Lion, originally part of a tombstone, adapted to become the coping stone of a water tank. Many edifices were restored or partially reconstructed by Constantius I (*c* 297) and Valentinian I (369). Gold coins and rings and silver plate reflect continued prosperity in the later fourth century, until the Romans left *c* 410 (or perhaps a little later).

Çorlu *see* Tzirallum

Coronea, Koroneia (near Kutumala). A city in Boeotia (central Greece), on a height at the entrance of a valley leading to Mount Helicon. The city presides over the gap between the west bank of Lake Copais and the hills, so that its occupants dominated the communications between western and eastern Boeotia. The names of an adjoining river, Curarius (Coralius), and of a temple dedicated to Athene Itonia, both bear witness to early settlement from Thessaly.

In historical times Coronea was the scene of two important battles. In 447 BC an Athenian army under the command of Tolmides was defeated by Boeotian oligarchs holding Orchomenus and supported by exiles from Locris and Euboea. The second engagement took place in 394 BC during the so-called 'Corinthian War' between Agesilaus II of Sparta and the combined forces of Thebes, Athens, Argos and Corinth, which united to check the Spartans' claims to supremacy (encouraged by their victory in the Peloponnesian War, 404). Marching back to Greece after operations against the Persians, and receiving reinforcements on the way, Agesilaus reached Coronea almost without any resistance. In the battle that followed, the right wing of each army routed the left wing of its opponent, but although the engagement ended in a technical Spartan victory it was in fact a defeat, since Agesilaus had to evacuate central Greece and return to the Peloponnese. Sparta's claims to hegemony were eventually shattered by the Thebans in 371. During the Third Sacred War, however, the Phocian Onomarchus defeated the Boeotian army and captured Coronea (352), subsequently using it as a base for devastations of Boeotia; but after Philip II of Macedonia brought the war to an end the Thebans massacred all the male population of Coronea and sold the rest as slaves. During the Hellenistic period the Coroneans were generally hostile to the Romans, but in 170 the Roman senate voted against the destruction of the city.

The head of a Gorgon that appeared on coins of Coronea during the fifth and fourth centuries BC recalled the worship of Athena Itonia, whose temple was the place where national Pan-Boeotian festivals were celebrated. It was told that one night the goddess appeared before her priestess Iodama, with the Gorgon's head on her tunic, whereupon Iodama was transformed into stone. The custom of lighting a fire on her altar every day was still maintained when Pausanias visited Coronea in the second century AD.

Corsica, the Greek Cyrnus (Kyrnos). A Mediterranean island off Etruria (Tuscany), north of Sardinia. The early inhabitants, who built circular monuments (*torri*) during the Bronze Age, were believed to have been of mixed Ligurian and Iberian origin. From about 600 BC, however, Corsica was the scene of rivalry between Greeks, Carthaginians and Etruscans.

It was about that time that Greeks from Phocaea (Foca) in Ionia (western Asia Minor) founded the colony of Alalia (Aleria) in the eastern part of the island to dominate the trade routes. The Carthaginian commander Malchus' subsequent attempt to subjugate Sardinia (*c* 550) prompted a clash with the Phocaeans (aided by the Etruscan city Caere) off the coast of Corsica or Sardinia, known as the battle of Alalia (*c* 536); in the engagement the Phocaeans, although victorious, suffered such heavy losses that, even if they did not have to evacuate Alalia completely as Herodotus reports, the balance of power shifted in favor of Carthage. However, the Etruscans were not excluded from the island since a colony known as Nicaea (Victory Town), probably founded after the battle, was ascribed by Diodorus to settlers from Caere—though its name suggests the presence of a Greek component as well. Sicilian Greeks raided the coast in 453 and 384, but Carthaginians had become dominant by the end of the century.

During the First Punic War, however, they lost Alalia to the Romans (259), who subsequently annexed Corsica to their new province of Sardinia (227), though the recalcitrant interior was not reduced to order until *c* 163, and then only nominally. However, the Romans settled colonies at Colonia Mariana and Alalia (*c* 93 or 86–79), and under the Principate (when, at some juncture, the island became a separate province) considerable portions of its territory flourished, producing cattle, timber, honey and granite; although the philosopher Seneca the Younger lamented bitterly when Corsica became his place of exile (AD 43–49). After the mid-fifth century, however, despite a naval victory by the western Roman general Ricimer (456), it was annexed by the Vandal king Gaiseric, subsequently passing under Ostrogothic rule for a short period before enrollment in the western provinces briefly reconquered by Justinian I (552).

Cortona, earlier Kurtun. A city in eastern Etruria (Tuscany) eighteen miles east of Arretium (Arezzo), situated on a hill dominating the plain between the river Clanis (Chiana) and Lake Trasimene. The story that Cortona was founded by Corythus, the son of Zeus and father of Dardanus, and Theopompus' supposition that it was the place where Odysseus died, are only two out of a number of myths prompted by the city's future importance. In fact, it originally comprised a group of Umbrian villages that first made themselves apparent in the seventh century BC, when large monumental mound-tombs were constructed in the vicinity. The legend that the philosopher Pythagoras came to the place *c* 531 (perpetuated by the name, 'Tanella di Pitagora,' imaginatively given to a Hellenistic mausoleum) resulted from a confusion with Croton (Crotone) in south Italy.

In about the fifth century, the villages at Cortona were amalgamated into a single Etruscan city on the initiative of Clusium (Chiusi) from which, however, it soon asserted its freedom of action. Equipped with an imposing wall (covering a two-mile circumference), the new foundation was strategically located at the center of a network of roads; and it was also within easy reach of the Tiber. It inhabitants manufactured magnificent bronze work, notably the richly ornamented and complex fifth-century lamp that is now in the local museum. In 310, according to Livy, Cortona was one of the principal cities of Etruria; but a treaty with Rome, at this juncture, virtually signalized the termination of its independence. In AD 405 it was one of the Italian cities that succumbed temporarily to the invasion of Radagaisus the Ostrogoth.

Corupedium, Ķorou (or Kourou) Pedion: A plain beside the river Hermus (Gediz Çayı) in Lydia (western Asia Minor), near Magnesia ad Sipylum (Manisa). It was here, between the north bank of the Hermus and its tributary the Phrygius (formerly Hyllus) that the last important battle between the successors of Alexander the Great took place. The rival commanders were Lysimachus and

Seleucus I (Nicator). When Lysimachus' oppressive policies weakened his rule in northern and western Asia Minor, Seleucus, moving against him from Syria (282 BC), rapidly penetrated the peninsula. Lysimachus, with his Macedonian army, came south to meet him, and in February, 281 the two great armies clashed at Corupedium. Lysimachus was defeated and killed; and the whole of Alexander's Asian empire was at Seleucus' feet. But he too died in the following year, and the dynasty that he founded never retained more than partial control of Asia Minor.

Coryphasium *see* Pylos

Cos, Kos. An island of the southern Sporades group—now the Dodecanese—off the coast of Caria (southwestern Asia Minor). Cos was occupied in the later Bronze Age, and according to tradition its first rulers were Thessalian. During or after the collapse of the Mycenaean (Bronze Age) civilization the island was colonized by Dorians (perhaps from Epidaurus), and it was under Dorian (Heraclid) leadership that Homer's *Iliad* records its participation in the Trojan War. Cos became a member of the religious and political union known as the Dorian hexapolis. At the end of the sixth century it passed under Persian control, from which it emerged after the battle of Mycale (479, concluding the Persian Wars) to join Athens' Delian League. Toward the end of the Peloponnesian War, however, the island fell to the Spartan Lysander.

In 366, after internal upheavals, the various towns of the island (notably Astypalaea) were amalgamated into a single capital city, on the northeastern coast. One of the leaders of the rebellion of Athens' allies in the Social War (357–355), Cos later passed successively into the hands of Mausolus of Caria, Alexander the Great, and the Ptolemies (309–260). Philetas, founder of the Hellenistic poet-scholar tradition, was born at Cos, like his pupil Ptolemy II Philadelphus (309/8); and Theocritus, creator of bucolic poetry, lived for a time on the island and places some of his *Idylls* in its setting, notably the *Harvest-Home,* which describes a walk in the noonday heat of high summer. Next, the island came under the control of the Macedonians (whose king Antigonus II Gonatas defeated the Egyptians off their island in 258) and then of the Rhodians, entering into the Roman orbit early in the second century BC and then becoming a 'free' community attached to the province of Asia, with a brief interruption when it was sacked by Mithridates VI of Pontus. About 41/40 to 31 Cos was ruled by a 'tyrant' (autocrat) Nicias, who enjoyed Antony's support, and issued coins displaying his own diademed portrait; an epigram of Crinagoras mentions his death. Influenced by his physician Gaius Stertinius Xenophon, who came from Cos, the emperor Claudius (AD 41–54) granted its inhabitants immunity from taxation. In 142 an earthquake shattered its buildings (as had already happened in 6 BC), but their reconstruction was assisted by Antoninus Pius. In the later empire Cos became part of the Province of Insulae (The Islands). It suffered from two further severe earthquakes, in 469 and 554.

From the fourth century BC onward, the coinage of the Coans had laid particular stress on Heracles, from whom their founders were reputedly descended. But thereafter the emphasis was shifted to Asclepius,the god of healing, whose cult, it was claimed, had been brought from Epidaurus. His sanctuary, the Asclepieum, stood near the capital city of the island beside a gushing stream of medicinal water. But it was only after the death of Hippocrates (399), the embodiment of an ideal physician whose great and long-lived medical school took the name of the Asclepiads, that the monumental buildings of the cult were erected. In the fourth century, Apelles painted Aphrodite Anadyomene (Rising from the Sea) for the Asclepieum, thus earning the designation of 'the Coan' (although Colophon was his birthplace). The final form of the sanctuary, achieved with the assistance of the Attalid kings of Pergamum, was characteristic of the Hellenistic conception of shrines comprising huge architectural precincts. On the uppermost of four terraces rose the six-columned Doric temple of the god, while another, Ionic, shrine and altar stood on the terrace beneath, and at the level below that, various rooms for the sick were to be found; the lowest level of all contained baths.

Within the city itself traces of another Hellenistic temple and colonnades are to be seen, together with a theater, Odeon and stadium, and baths of Roman imperial date. Outside the walls was the port, in which a temple of Aphrodite Pandemos and Pontia struck the eye of all who arrived by sea. The site of the earlier chief town, Astypalaea, is marked by polygonal walls, and there are various Hellenistic buildings in other parts of the island. It also contains a series of early Christian basilicas, constructed during the years between the two earthquakes (469–554), and decorated with handsome mosaic floors. Cos was famous for its manufacture of tussore silk of the wild silkworm, first mentioned by Aristotle (d. 322), but probably older. It became greatly sought after in lieu of the true silk of the Chinese *bombyx mori,* which could not yet be obtained in the west, and was, besides, too expensive for most pockets; its threads were wound, whereas those at Cos were carded. The island also produced all types of fruits, and especially grapes, which were dried to make raisins, but after mixture with seawater made famous white wine.

Cosa (Ansedonia). A town situated on steep grey cliffs overlooking the Tyrrhenian Sea, four-and-a-half miles southeast of the Etruscan maritime city of Orbetello (Calusium?). Although Cosa, too, had an Etruscan name (Cusithe), its surviving remains date back to the foundation of the Latin colony in 273 BC, comprising lands which were probably distributed among about 2,800 families, of whom half lived in the town. The colony fulfilled an important role in the service of Rome's military and naval strategy and agricultural expansion. However, in the course of some unexplained assault in the 60s, it was sacked, burned and depopulated. Partially reconstructed under Augustus, the place continued to exist as a local cult and festival center until the third century AD. In the following century its forum became the center of a large estate. When Rutilius Namatianus passed by Cosa in 416 he found its buildings in ruins.

Excavations have thrown vivid light on the structure and character of a Republican colony. Cosa was protected by massive, irregular, polygonal fortifications, rising to a height of forty feet, and pierced by three gates. On the loftier of twin summits stood the citadel, containing temples of the Capitoline Triad (Jupiter, Juno, Minerva) and Mater Matuta (?). On a saddle between the two heights was the forum, entered through a triple archway, lined with colonnades on two sides, and surrounded by public buildings (senate, basilica, baths, theater-like assembly) and shops and offices. The colony's residential blocks, lining the slopes, consist of houses that were at first, in the third century BC, uniformly designed, but later constructed according to freer plans, based on covered halls or open courtyards.

The colony's port, Succosa, in a sea lagoon providing an inner and outer harbor, lay in the lee of the eastern isthmus (leading to Mount Argentarius); and the neighboring Lake Buriano also had an ancient outlet to the sea. The elaborate feats of Roman hydraulic engineering undertaken to prevent silting and flooding are still visible today (the Tagliata Etrusca [not Etruscan], Canale della Tagliata and Spacco della Regina).

On the top of a hill close to Cosa (Setta Finestre) are the ruins, now largely uncovered, of a large late Republican villa, containing atrium, peristyle, many wall paintings and polychrome mosaics and marble floors—one of the very few such villas that have been excavated outside Campania. Many of its walls were built of mud on low stone bases. Associated with the villa was an extensive working farm and industrial area, including a great barn, many storerooms, an oil mill and oil press, three grape presses and a vat, and twenty-seven pigsties around a large open courtyard. The villa and farm were apparently abandoned in the mid-second century AD.

Cremera (Valchetta or Fossa di Formello in Lazio, west-central Italy). A stream flowing in a deep gully past the Etruscan city of Veii, of which a dependency, Fidenae (Castel Giubileo), controlled the point where the Cremera flowed into the Tiber, close to Rome. Fidenae still seems to have belonged to the Veientines *c* 477–475, when the clan of the Fabii, who dominated the Roman Republic at this time, and conducted frontier cattle raids, set up a fort near the offending outpost, cutting its communications with Veii. In the Battle of the Cremera that followed—an event much embroidered by legend—the Veientines won a total victory, reputedly killing three hundred members of the Fabian clan and leaving only one youth alive. The Romans did not secure control of Fidenae until 435 BC.

Cremna *see* Pisidia

Cremni *see* Panticapaeum

Cremona. A town on the north bank of the river Padus (Po) in Cisalpine Gaul (north Italy). A settlement (according to the elder Pliny) of the Gallic tribe of the Cenomanni, it was the first colony founded by the Romans on the further side of the Padus (218 BC), as a bulwark against hostile Gauls, notably the Insubres and Boii. In the Second Punic War, which began at that time, Cremona loyally supported Rome against Hannibal, but suffered such severe losses that additional colonists were dispatched in 190. The place became an important river ford and station on the Via Postumia (148) between Placentia (Piacenza) and Mantua (Mantova). In 41 BC its lands were seized and distributed to ex-soldiers.

For the two great battles fought near Cremona of AD 69, the Year of the Four Emperors, *see* Bedriacum. After the second of these engagements, the troops of the victorious Vespasian sacked the city and destroyed it by fire. But it was reconstructed soon afterward, and retained a military garrison, whose parade ground can still be traced; among the items to be seen in the museum is part of a legionary's strongbox. Subterranean vaults beneath the cathedral preserve the floor mosaic of an early Christian basilica.

Crenides *see* Philippi

Crete. An island of the Aegean, to the south and southeast of Greece. After its Minoan (Bronze Age) glories, the tradition remained that the world's first sea power had been that of a Cretan king, Minos. During the historical epochs of antiquity the island was still populous—containing, according to the *Iliad,* ninety cities, and according to the *Odyssey* a hundred (in which many languages were spoken). Yet it remained outside the mainstream of events: although the beginnings of Greek art were attributed to the legendary Cretan Daedalus, Phoenician craftsmen showed remarkable activity on the island in the eighth and seventh centuries BC (*see* Ida), the Cretans were among the earliest receivers of the north Semitic alphabet, and the aristocratic constitutions and social systems of the Cretan city-states attracted keen outside interest. These ways of life closely resembled (and according to Strabo decisively influenced) the totalitarian system of Dorian Sparta, because despite the mixed racial origins of the populations of Crete (confirmed by the *Odyssey*), its ruling classes, like those of Sparta, were descended from Dorian immigrants; although, in contrast to that city, a number of the island states issued coins of exceptionally fine design.

Heavily fortified and often loosely banded together in a Cretan League (of which Cnossus, Lyttus and Gortyna disputed the leadership), these cities spent a great deal of time attacking one another. As a result of this disturbed history, Cretans were very prominent among the Greek males of Hellenistic times who sought employment abroad as mercenary soldiers; and the island also gained a reputation as a center of piracy, second only to Cilicia. Such activities were encouraged by Philip V of Macedonia, who, setting himself up as a protector of the Cretans (216), encouraged them to ravage the fleets of his rival Rhodes.

Subsequently, these pirates supported King Mithridates VI of Pontus against the Romans, whose general Quintus Caecilius Metellus 'Creticus' captured and annexed the island (68/67), attaching it to Cyrenaica as a joint province, with Gortyna as its administrative capital. The Cretan League, reestablished as a provincial council, issued its own coins, with both local and Roman types, and under imperial rule the island enjoyed a prolonged period of uninterrupted peace and prosperity. *See also* Cnossus, Drerus, Dicte, Gortyna, Ida, Lyttus.

Crocodilopolis *see* Arsinoe (Fayum)

Croton (Crotone). A Greek city on the east coast of the toe of Italy, in the territory of the Bruttii (the modern Calabria), situated beside the mouth of the river Aesarus (Esaro), on a headland which forms and flanks two adequately protected harbors. Originally a town or village of the Messapians, the place was settled *c* 710 BC by Achaeans under the leadership of Myscellus of Rhypae (Kumari); it controlled the important sanctuary of Hera Lacinia, on the promontory of Cape Lacinium (Colonna) seven miles to the southeast. As the new city prospered, its territory extended over the fertile plains to the south, and its people founded colonies at Caulonia (*c* 675) and Terina.

Croton became especially famous for its successes in the Olympic Games, at which, during the later sixth century, its legendary citizen Milo, the best-known of all Greek athletes, was six times victorious in wrestling (and six times in the Pythian Games of Delphi as well). Croton also gained renown because the philosopher Pythagoras of Samos settled there *c* 531, establishing a religious society under whose administration the city, despite a severe defeat on the river Sagra (Allaro?) by Locri Epizephyrii and Rhegium (Reggio di Calabria), collaborated with its rival Sybaris (Sibari) and with Metapontum (Metaponto) to destroy Siris (Siri) *c* 530. Then Croton launched a successful attack upon Sybaris itself (*c* 510, allegedly through the prowess of Milo), thus becoming the most important power in southern Italy.

Soon afterward, the Pythagorean administration of the city was replaced by a democracy, which in the later years of the fifth century issued plentiful and exceptionally artistic coinage, perhaps under the influence of the great painter Zeuxis who was working there at the time. However, it lost its independence to Syracuse under Dionysius I (406–357), and again (after Lucanian and Bruttian attacks) under Agathocles (299). Damage was also caused by the invasions of Pyrrhus of Epirus (280–278, 275). Roman rule followed, but in the Second Punic War Croton revolted in 216 and became the base employed by Hannibal for the conduct of his final retreat from Italy. A Roman colony (194) did not succeed in reviving the city's fortunes.

In recent years archaeological investigations have confirmed the traditional foundation date, and uncovered a north-south road dating from the seventh century BC; the line of the town walls has been established, and the location of the citadel is now known. The remains of the harbors (improved by a canal) have come to light, and it is clear that there was extensive building in the years before 300. Excavations have revealed the plan of the sanctuary of Hera Lacinia, which originated in the seventh century, although the existing remains are those of a shrine dating from the second quarter of the fifth, subsequently adorned by a famous painting of the goddess by Zeuxis. Numerous fragments bear witness to the high quality of the marble decoration. Various buildings of the temple precinct have also been revealed. After a visit, Hannibal set up a bronze plaque, but the shrine's magnificent treasures were robbed by Dionysius I and Pompey the Great. Nevertheless, Livy testifies to the great reputation that the holy place continued to enjoy.

Ctesiphon (Taysafun). A city on the east bank of the river Tigris in Mesopotamia (central Iraq), sixty miles southeast of Baghdad. When the Parthian Arsaces I broke away from the Seleucid empire (*c* 247 BC) and his second century successors incorporated Babylonia in their territories, Ctesiphon—formerly, according to Polybius, a Seleucid military camp—was refounded as an important fortress opposite the Seleucid city Seleucia on the Tigris (which formerly flowed between the two cities and not, as now, through the middle of Ctesiphon); it also became the winter residence of the Parthian (monarchs), who appreciated its healthy air. The two cities were temporarily occupied by Trajan in AD 116, sacked by Avidius Cassius, the general of Marcus Aurelius and Lucius Verus, in 165, and captured and plundered again by Septimius Severus in 197.

Ctesiphon prospered, however, when it became the principal city of the Sassanian Persians, who superseded the Parthians (226) (despite temporary occupations by Carus [283] and by Galerius [296]). Extensive suburbs were added, including Asfanabr, site of the gigantic vaulted hall the Taq-e-Kisra, probably begun in the third century and completed in the sixth; its strong, airy, subtly curving vault can still be seen.

Cufino, Mount *see* Ecnomus

Cuicul (Djemila). A city in a mountainous region of northwestern Numidia (Algeria), situated on a rocky spur between two streams, the Guergour and the Betame, above the main road between the Roman provinces of Africa and Mauretania. Formerly a Berber fort, and then dependent on Cirta (Constantine), Cuicul was made a Roman colony by the emperor Nerva (AD 96–98). It owned fertile wheat-growing land, and in the second century, enlarged by the immigration of Romanized Berbers, became an imposing city. Under the rule of the African Septimius Severus (193–211) and his son Caracalla (211–17) it produced a number of their principal advisers and governors.

Important remains survive. The town plan has become clear from recent excavations; in contrast to the camp-like regularity of other towns, it is improvised to fit the cliff-top site. The forum and adjacent public buildings, including a market, can be seen. Houses with splendid and distinctive mosaic pavements, of which the most famous is a hunting scene from the 'House of Bacchus,' testify to continuous occupation from the second to the fourth or fifth century. At the height of the city's prosperity, before and after 200, its dimensions were enlarged to include new areas outside the old walls and extended up the slopes of an adjacent hill. These quarters contain a theater, large baths of the reign of Commodus (AD 180–92), arches of different epochs, and temples of Saturn and the Severan dynasty, close to an extensive additional forum. An earthquake in 365 caused major damage, but new buildings were very soon erected. A Christian quarter contains two basilicas, a baptistery and a palace for the bishops, one of whom attended the Carthage Council in 256. In the fifth century the city declined, though a bishopric still existed in 553.

Cumae, formerly Cyme (Cuma). A city on the coast of Campania (southwestern Italy), beyond the northern extremity of the gulf that was given its name (or was known as the Crater: now the Bay of Naples). The lofty isolated acropolis of Cumae, adjoining beached bays and a sheltered harbor (at the former outlet from Lake Acherusia [Fusaro]), had been inhabited by a native population since about the tenth century BC. About 750 it became a Greek trading post manned by merchants originating from Euboea who had settled on the nearby island of Pithecusae (Ischia). Most of the traders were from Chalcis, under the leadership of Megasthenes, whose fellow leader Hippocles came from the neighboring small Euboean town of Cyme (Paleokastri?) which gave the new market its name.

The trading post was converted into a regular colony that asserted its independence *c* 730/25. The highly fertile soil of the adjacent Campanian plainland encouraged a flourishing commerce in grain; and Italy's cultivation of the olive and vine may have been inaugurated by the Cumaeans—and taught by them (like the Greek alphabet) to the Etruscans. Cumae played a preeminent part in the new commercial relations between the Greeks and the Etruscan city-states, largely based on the Cumaeans' importation of Etruscan iron and copper in exchange for gold brought by Cumae from the markets of its fellow Euboeans in northern Syria. Profits were also derived from the shellfish that abounded in the Lake Avernus and especially Lake Lucrinus.

By means of these various activities Cumae rapidly became a major political power, colonizing Zancle or Messana (Messina) in Sicily (*c* 725), Neapolis (Naples) and Dicaearchia (Puteoli). It was also famous for its Sibyl, who, as Virgil recounts, delivered oracles (on behalf of Apollo, replacing Hera), and allegedly bargained with the Roman king Tarquinius Priscus (*c* 616–579). Beneath the acropolis the Sibyl's cave can still be seen, containing vaulted chambers, galleries, bays, doors and baths (cisterns) cut into the rock. But the first known historical personage of the city was its 'tyrant' (autocrat) Aristodemus the Effeminate, who twice defeated expeditions from one or more Etruscan states (*c* 524, and *c* 504 at Aricia [Ariccia]), although he later granted asylum to Rome's expelled King Tarquinius Superbus. A third Etruscan attack was repelled, with Syracusan aid, at sea off Cumae (474), celebrated by Pindar. However Cumae, like Capua, was overwhelmed by native Italian (Sabellian) invaders in the 420s. In 338 it came under the control of the Romans, loyally supported them in their wars, and in 180 abandoned Oscan for Latin as its official language.

As the port of Puteoli (Pozzuoli) rose, Cumae declined. However, in 37/36 it received a substantial new harbor, in the bay between the acropolis and the promontory (linked with Lake Acherusia) as an element in Marcus Agrippa's massive naval complex, the Portus Julius. Agrippa joined Cumae to Lake Avernus by a remarkable tunnel, while another passed under the acropolis to the beach; and then the city's population was replenished by a colony of ex-soldiers, probably in the reign of Claudius (AD 41–54). There was still extensive building activity in the first and second centuries AD, embellishing Cumae with villas, temples and an amphitheater; so that the poet Juvenal was exaggerating when he described the place as empty.

Cunaxa. On the left bank of the Euphrates, perhaps Kunish near Felluja, forty miles north of Babylon (now in Iraq). Cunaxa was the scene of a battle in 401 BC between the Persian monarch Artaxerxes II and his brother Cyrus the Younger, who had mobilized a substantial body of Greek mercenaries, ostensibly for operations in Asia Minor, but in reality to fight against his brother the king, as was clear when he led them across the Euphrates.

They came unexpectedly upon Artaxerxes at Cunaxa, and battle was joined. The Greek heavily armed troops on Cyrus' right, under the Spartan Clearchus, routed the opposing left wing, but a strong Persian cavalry contingent threatened their rear and Cyrus' left wing's inner flank: whereupon Cyrus charged Artaxerxes' center with his bodyguard and wounded him, but lost his own life, and his army was decisively defeated. The Greek mercenaries, however, as one of their number Xenophon described, succeeded in closing ranks and escaping; and so began their historic Retreat of the Ten Thousand (*Anabasis*) to the Black Sea.

Curia *see* Raetia

Curium, Kourion. On the southwest coast of Cyprus, situated on a promontory overlooking the sea and the river Kouris. The region had been inhabited in the Neolithic and Bronze Ages and was subsequently settled, according to Herodotus, by colonists from Argos. It became one of the kingdoms of the island, subject—after transfer onto a new site—to King Sargon of Assyria (673 BC) and subsequently to the Persians, in whose favor its king Stasanor betrayed a Greek rebellion (498). But a subsequent monarch (probably the last) named Pasicrates took a fleet to assist Alexander the Great in his siege of Tyre (332). Curium flourished in Hellenistic and Roman times, but suffered badly in a series of earthquakes in the fourth century AD culminating in its burial by volcanic lava in 365. One of the city's Christian bishops was martyred under Diocletian (284–305); another, at the Council of Ephesus (431), helped to assert the claims of the Cypriot Church to the independence (autocephaly) that it retains.

Monuments uncovered during past decades included a stadium, a basilica and sanctuary of Apollo, houses paved with fourth- and fifth-century mosaics, and, above all, a fine theater, of which the surviving (and partially reconstructed) remains, of Roman date, were imposed on a Hellenistic building of the second century BC, and show signs of adjustment to serve as an amphitheater. Very recently ambitious attempts to uncover the buildings buried by the eruption of 365/7 have been initiated. The extensive finds in these operations, which include furniture and perfectly preserved skeletons, have raised hopes of major future developments.

About 2 miles west of Curium was the vast, complex precinct (now cleared and restored) of a sanctuary of Apollo Hylates, which began its existence in the eighth century BC, owes its surviving remains to a reconstruction in the first century AD, and continued to be frequented until the fourth-century earthquakes.

Cutilia *see* Aquae Cutiliae

Cyme, Kyme (Namurtköy). A Greek city beside the coast of Aeolis (western Asia Minor), twenty-five miles north of Smyrna (Izmir), occupying twin hills above two streams (one named Xanthus) between the mouths of the rivers

Caicus (Bakir Çayı) and Hermus (Gediz Çayı). Tradition ascribed the foundation of the place to an Amazon named Cyme, but according to Strabo it was colonized by Greeks after the Trojan War. He described it as the largest and most important of the Aeolian cities, of which, together with Lesbos, it ranked as the metropolis. The people of Cyme reputedly colonized Cebren (Akpinarköy) in the Troad and Side (Selimiye) in Pamphylia and had a share in nearly thirty other settlements as well. When the father of the poet Hesiod migrated to Boeotia in the eighth century BC, it was from Cyme that he had come.

Although its people were said to dislike seafaring—their unwillingness to collect harbor-tolls for the first three centuries of the city's existence earned them a reputation for stupidity—they contributed ships to the European expedition of the Persian king Darius I (512), and then again to Xerxes I in the year of Salamis (480). Thereafter the city belonged to the Delian League, under Athens' guidance, during the rest of the fifth century, and to the Second Athenian League in the fourth. The historian Ephorus (*c* 405–330) came from Cyme and wrote its history. Subsequently it was under the successive control of Seleucids, Pergamenes, and Romans. A late Hellenistic inscription honors a benefactor Archippe: 'when she fell ill the population was in agony.'

In the reign of Tiberius a severe earthquake ruined the city (AD 17), which thanked him for his relief measures by assuming the name of Caesarea. Its coinage, which had been more or less continuous since the seventh century BC, resumed under Nero (AD 54–68) and continued until Gallienus (253–68). These pieces displayed varied designs, including Homer and his mother Critheis (believed to have come from Cyme), the river-gods Hermus and Xanthus, and the heads of a legendary prophetess the Sibyl (claimed by the city through etymological association with Cumae) and of the Amazon, after whom the city was named. Little remains of the ancient city, but two moles can be detected at its harbor, which has recently been excavated. *Seel also* Cumae

Cynaetha *see* Arcadia

Cynoscephalae, Kynoskephalia (meaning 'Dog's Heads'). A range of hills in Thessaly (northern Greece) in the region of Scotussa (now Mavrovouni, about seven miles west of Volos). In 364 the Theban general Pelopidas attacked King Alexander of Pherae (Thessaly) on the ridge, and his army won a decisive victory against greatly superior forces, bringing the Thessalian princedom to an end, although Pelopidas himself lost his life.

In 197 Cynoscephalae was the scene of another and a more famous battle, in which the Roman general Titus Quinctius Flamininus, supported by troops of the Aetolian League, defeated Philip V and terminated the Second Macedonian War. To the alarm of the Greek states, the Roman legion had got the better of the less flexible Macedonian phalanx (largely owing to an outflanking movement undertaken, on his own initiative, by an unknown Roman officer). This was the first of many Roman military successes in the east that sealed the ultimate downfall of the Hellenistic world.

Cynossema *see* Arginusae

Cynthus, Mount *see* Delos

Cyprus. An island in the eastern Mediterranean fifty miles south of Rough Cilicia (Tracheia, Aspera; southeastern Asia Minor). Between its mountains the central plain of Mesaoria was thickly forested and provided wood for shipbuilding and the smelting of copper ores from the island's mines. After receiving important Mycenaean (Achaean) settlements in the Later Bronze Age, Cyprus was the object of strong Syrian (*c* 1000) and then Phoenician penetration (*c* 800). After subsequent Assyrian overlordship (from 709) a brief period of independence was followed by subordination to Egypt (from the 560s) and then to Persia (545). From the late sixth century onward coinage was issued by at least six city kings (first in Cypriot and then in Greek), and issues by two Phoenician monarchs followed. The Greek cities of the island joined the Ionian Revolt (498–496), but the Phoenician communities remained loyal to Persia. The island provided ships to Xerxes I's fleet (480), but after a revolt led by Evagoras of Salamis (386–374) and another rebellion in which the nine kings of the island participated (351), all its states declared for Alexander the Great (333), helping him to capture the Phoenician city of Tyre. Following vicissitudes under his successors Cyprus passed into the hands of Ptolemy I Soter of Egypt, gaining independency briefly under Ptolemaic princes (107–89, 80–58).

The island was annexed on behalf of Rome by Cato the Younger—whose integrity in the matter was praised, though the king committed suicide on his arrival—and it was attached to the province of Cilicia. Julius Caesar made it a dependency of Arsinoe IV and Ptolemy XIV, half-sister and half-brother of Cleopatra VII, who eliminated them and took the island over. When her regime was destroyed in 31/30 by Octavian (the future Augustus), Cyprus became a separate province. The Roman governors, and then the island Council (*koinon*), issued coinage, mainly displaying types of Salaminian Zeus and the temple of Aphrodite at Paphos (which had replaced Salamis as the capital). Barnabas, a Jewish convert to Christianity, was born in Cyprus and returned there twice as a missionary, on one occasion in the company of St. Paul (AD 46). The years 115–17—the final period of Trajan's reign—witnessed a massive rebellion of the Jews in Cyprus, in common with members of the Diaspora elsewhere: they annihilated the non-Jewish inhabitants of Salamis, destroying the city, and after the revolt had been put down a decree was issued forbidding any Jew ever to set foot in the island again on pain of death. An earthquake at the beginning of the fourth century caused widespread destruction and famine. *See also* Citium, Curium, Marium, Paphos, Salamis, Soli.

Cyrenaica or Cyrene, Kyrene (now the eastern portion of the Libyan state), extending from the Gulf of Syrtes Major (Sirte) in the west to the borders of Egypt in the east. Being isolated from that country by deserts, it was nearer to the Greek world. Whereas the interior was dominated by tribes of pastoral Berbers, the northern coastal strip was later known as the Pentapolis, from its possession of five Greek cities, all situated on the coast except Cyrene (the earliest, *c* 630 BC) and Barce. From the seventh century agricultural expansion was rapid.

Alexander the Great's seizure of Egypt gave him virtual control of Cyrenaica, and in 332 Ptolemy I Lagus came in person to enforce his succession, yet the local Greeks never wholly acquiesced in their subjection to the Ptolemies. About 312/9 they revolted, and again *c* 306, after which the king's half-brother Magas was installed as Egyptian viceroy; but in 274 he declared himself independent and assumed the royal title, reigning, as viceroy and king, for a total of fifty years. Shortly after his death coins show the cities as a Republican League (*koinon*)—modeled on the Achaean confederacy, as Polybius and Plutarch suggest—but Ptolemy III Euergetes (246–221) reasserted Egyptian control by marrying Magas' daughter Berenice. Later, however, the Romans settled a dynastic quarrel by detaching Cyrenaica once again, setting up Ptolemy VIII Euergetes II ("Pot-Belly") as its ruler (163–145). Later, he returned to the Egyptian capital Alexandria, but his will restored the independence of the Cyrenaican territory, which was allotted to Ptolemy Apion (116).

He in his turn left it to the Roman state (96), which at first only claimed for itself the royal domains and a tax on the medicinal plant silphium—a chief product of the country—but in 74 created a province of Cyrene, with which Crete was amalgamated seven years later. In 34, however, Antony gave Cyrenaica back to Ptolemaic rule, and it was conferred by Cleopatra VII upon her infant daughter Cleopatra Selene, though a Roman garrison remained. In the subsequent wars between Antony and Octavian (the future Augustus), the local commander Lucius Pinarius Scarpus is shown by his coins to have prudently changed sides from the former to the latter (31). Cyrene (with Crete) resumed Roman provincial status, but in AD 115, during the reign of Trajan, a large-scale rebellion of Cyrenaican Jews—under a certain Andreas or Lukuas—caused immense human and material losses, eliminating cultivators and reducing the territory to ruins. Under the reorganization of the later empire it was converted into two provinces, Upper Libya and Lower Libya (Marmarica), with their capitals at Ptolemais (Tolmeta) and Paraetonium (Mersa Matruh) respectively. An earthquake in 365 caused widespread destruction. *See* Cyrene, Euhesperides.

Cyrene, Kyrene (Shahhat). A Greek city in the territory named after it (or known as Cyrenaica). Herodotus describes—and his account, though containing legendary elements, is backed up by a later inscription—how in the 630s BC, acting on the advice of the Delphic oracle, a small group of Greeks was compelled by famine to leave the Aegean island of Thera (Santorin), and set sail for the north coast of Africa. After unsuccessful settlements on the islet of Platea (in the Gulf of Bomba) and at Aziris (Wadi el-Chalig, near Darnis [Derna]), their new leader Aristoteles, the first Battus, perhaps a native African title, transferred his people eight miles inland.

The site he selected for them lay on a spur, later two spurs of an elevated limestone plateau, to the south of a perennial spring named after the nature-goddess Cyrene, whom mythologists declared to have been a bride of Apollo. Under subsequent members of its leader's dynasty, alternately named Battus and Arcesilaus, the city flourished for eight generations, deriving rich profits from its grain, wool, oil, horses and the medicinal plant silphium—valued as a foodstuff for people and animals, flavoring and laxative, and regarded as a cure for all ills—which figures prominently on local coins (it died out early in the Christian era). A port was established at Apollonia (Marsa Sousa), and a new draft of colonists—including people from the Rhodian city of Lindus—introduced by Battus II (*c* 583–560) established the city's supremacy over a wide region (according to Herodotus) by defeating the Egyptians and Libyans at a place named Irasa, though strained relations with the Libyans of the hinterland continued for a long time thereafter and were exacerbated by internal factions.

After repelling an attack from Egypt, Cyrene passed into the hands of its monarch Cambyses (525) and then under Persian domination (*c* 515), from which it regained its independence some forty years later. In about 400 the Battiad monarchy came to an end, and a democratic form of government took its place. Despite the disturbed history of the territory in Hellenistic times (*see* Cyrenaica), and an assertion of independence by the port of Apollonia, the Ptolemaic city of Cyrene was at this epoch one of the major intellectual centers of the world. Its medical school was renowned, and it was the birthplace of the poet Callimachus (*c* 305–240), the geographer Eratosthenes (*c* 275–194), Aristippus, who founded the Cyrenaic school of philosophy (forerunner of the Epicurean school), and Carneades (214/13–129/8), the head of the Platonic Academy.

Augustus' five Edicts of Cyrene (7–6, 4 BC), discovered on the site, are of major historical importance; four of them refer to juridical arrangements in the province of Crete and Cyrenaica. The Jewish revolt of AD 115 devastated the city, but Hadrian undertook large-scale reconstruction. It was not until the following centuries that a final process of decline set in, due to the attacks of hostile desert tribesmen and a series of disastrous earthquakes. The city duly rebuilt its shattered walls, but henceforth they enclosed a much smaller perimeter. Something of these various defences can be seen, and excavations have also revealed an ancient but repeatedly rebuilt, and now partly restored, temple of Apollo—yielding famous statues of the god and of Venus, now in the British Museum and at Rome—a massive shrine of Zeus (destroyed by the Jewish insurgents in 115), a marketplace (*agora* or forum) surrounded by public buildings, and a grandiose rectangular porticoed enclosure (recently reconstructed) known as the Caesareum, which was dedicated to Rome and Augustus and formed part of a larger complex. An extramural Sanctuary of Demeter and Persephone (at Wadi Bel Gadir) dating from 600 BC to AD 262, has been uncovered, and a varied array of cemeteries extend outside the wall on every side. On the site of Apollonia, too (which became the capital in Byzantine times), archaeologists have made extensive discoveries, although most of the harbor constructions are now beneath the sea.

Cyrnus *see* Corsica

Cythera, Kythera (Kithira). An island off Cape Malea, the easternmost of the three southern promontories of Greece. From *c* 2000 BC there was a Minoan (Cretan) colony on the island, which possessed rich deposits of the purple shell (*murex*) as well as a twenty-one acre town, now submerged, on the adjoining mainland peninsula of Onugnathos [Elafonisi]). The harbors of Cythera included Scandia (mentioned in Homer's *Iliad*), which is probably the modern Kastri. In *c* 550 Argos, whose possession of Cythera seemed a threat to the Spartans ('it was better sunk beneath the sea,' said their statesman Chilon), had to cede them the island (in one of two bloody battles referred to by Herodotus), but Athens seized it from 424 to 421—during the Peloponnesian War—and again from 393 to 386. Lost to Sparta once more in 195, it was given back to the Athenians by Augustus in 21.

The ancient city of Cythera was on the height now called Paleocastro, where traces of a wall can be seen. A renowned sanctuary of Aphrodite or Cythera or Urania, probably of eastern (Phoenician) origin, stood on the slopes of the hill. For it was at Cythera, according to one version recounted by Hesiod (who was aware that other islands made similar claims), that Aphrodite rose from the foam (*aphros*) of the sea, which had gathered around the severed organ of her father Uranus (Heaven). On the coins of Cythera her head is crowned by a flying figure of Eros.

Cyzicus (Balkız, Belkis). A city of Mysia (northwestern Asia Minor) on the southwestern shore of the Propontis (Sea of Marmara), occupying part of a hilly island Arctonnesus (Kapi Dağı) which was converted into a peninsula (containing part of the city) by the construction of two parallel dykes and accumulations of sand. Settled *c* 679 BC (the earlier date, *c* 756, given by Eusebius, is unlikely) beside the river Aesepus, Cyzicus was a colony of the Milesians, reputedly the first settlement established by that people, who selected it because of its defensible site and access to two fine harbors on either flank (later linked by a canal), in contrast to the unwelcoming northern coast of the Propontis. Part of the city was on level ground and part on the slopes of a hill, Arctonorus ('bear-mountain').

Served by two roads, and enjoying an administration renowned for its efficiency, Cyzicus rapidly became an important stopping point on the route between the Euxine (Black) Sea and the Aegean, and its electrum (pale gold) coins—on which the tunny-fish, a vital foodstuff, regularly appears—were the most important monetary issues of the eastern Greek world during the sixth and fifth centuries.

After joining the Ionian revolt against the Persians (500–494), Cyzicus became a member of Athens' Delian League (and its largest contributor in the region), and during the Peloponnesian War was the scene of a naval victory won by Alcibiades against the Spartans (410). In the fourth century it passed from Persian hands (387) into the Second Athenian Confederation (until 357/5). In Hellenistic times the city continued to enjoy considerable commercial importance; it came under the control of the Seleucids (281) and later supported the Pergamene king Eumenes II (183), whose mother Apollonis came from Cyzicus.

When the Romans created the province of Asia (133), it became a 'free' city, receiving additions to its already extensive lands because of stalwart resistance to King Mithridates VI of Pontus (74). During the early Principate, however, Cyzicus twice fell into disgrace. First, in 20 BC, it was deprived of its freedom for five years and lost certain possessions, apparently after some Roman citizens (probably trade rivals) had been killed on its territory. Then in the reign of Tiberius, according to Suetonius, a similar offense was committed again (in AD 25) and resulted in a definitive loss of the privilege. Nevertheless, the city's harbors and lagoon were dredged and new canals opened under Gaius (37–41), as inscriptional evidence shows, and local coinage continued until Claudius II Gothicus (268–70). Its types include heads of the mythical founder, Cyzicus, the river-god Aesepus, temples of Hermes and Hadrian and Caracalla, and a number of elaborate architectural views depicting the sanctuary of Demeter, whose Mysteries constituted the city's most important cult. Strabo also refers to a temple of Dindymene (Cybele), allegedly founded by the Argonauts, on Mount Dindymus which rose above the Arctonorus.

D

Dacia (Rumania). A large country north of the Lower Danube, centering on the high plateau of Transylvania (completely encircled by mountains), but extending in a wider sense westward to the river Pathisus or Tisia (Tisza, Theiss), eastward to the Hierasus (Sereth), and northward to the vicinity of the Vistula. A people of Thracian stock, with German and Sarmato-Scythian components, who came under Celtic influence in the fourth century BC, the Dacians developed the gold, silver and iron mines of the Carpathians. 'The Dacians keep to the mountains,' observed Florus; they tended upland, circular sheepfolds in the high Carpathian pastures, and the shape of these sheepfolds was echoed in the sanctuaries of their towns. These included complex stone calendrical monuments based on their observations as pastoralists and incorporated their system for marking these observations.

Eager to assimilate more advanced techniques and customs, the Dacians traded with the Hellenistic Greeks (who confused them with another Thracian people, the Getae), and imported their wine. In association with other tribal groups, they fought against Roman generals before and after the end of the second century, but first became a major power under Burebista (*c* 60), who united their various elements and enforced his domination beyond the Pathisus and as far as Thrace and the Euxine (Black) Sea, where the Greek coastal cities came forcibly under his control. Provoked by Burebista's offer of assistance to his enemy Pompey the Great, Julius Caesar, we learn from Suetonius, was planning a large-scale operation against him at the time of his murder. Burebista, too, died soon afterward, and his empire broke up; but Octavian (the future Augustus) sought a marriage alliance with one of his successors, Cotiso, before his civil war against Antony (31–30). In 14 Cnaeus Cornelius Lentulus destroyed the Getic (Geto-Thracian, Geto-Dacian) settlements in the southeastern part of the country.

After continuing from time to time to make assaults upon the Roman frontiers, the Dacians were reunited under Decebalus, who heavily defeated two of Domitian's generals (AD 85–86). The emperor improved his situation by a victory at Tapae (in southwest Transylvania, west of the Dacian capital Sarmizegethusa), but was obliged (by an internal crisis) to come to an agreement, under which he recognized Decebalus as a client ruler. Provoked, however, by his independent conduct, Trajan reduced the Dacians and their allies and conquered Transylvania and the Banat in the First and Second Dacian Wars (101/2, 105), graphically depicted on the spiral frieze of the Column in his forum at Rome. This was the last Roman conquest to bring massive financial gains, derived from enormous booty and the rapid exploitation—assisted by new roads—of the country's gold mines, centered on Ampelum (Zlatna); wooden writing tablets have been found in the mining district at Alburnus Minor (Roşia Montana). In 119/20 Hadrian divided the conquered area into two provinces, Upper Dacia (comprising Transylvania with a western extension; its capital was at Apulum [Alba Julia]) and Lower Dacia (Wallachia [Oltenia and Muntenia], garrisoned by auxiliaries, with its capital at Romula Malva [Reşca], so that the new province came to be known as Dacia Malvensis). However, *c* 124—or at least before 133, as the discovery of an inscription has indicated—Upper Dacia was further subdivided into a pair of provinces, Apulensis and Porolissensis (to the north), with their capitals at Apulum and Napoca (Cluj) respectively. A massive immigration into Dacia from other provinces swelled the new cities, and there was also an influx of trained miners. During the German Wars under Marcus Aurelius (*c* 168), the three provinces were constituted a single military area.

In 271, however, the emperor Aurelian, although a great conqueror elsewhere, decided that Dacia's vulnerability to German invasions made it untenable, so that it became the first Roman province to be abandoned. Fifth-century cemeteries at Sintana de Mureş, Apahida and Sameseni in Transylvania suggest the growth of mixed communities of Dacians, Sarmatians, and Daco-Rumanians. The language of Latin origin, still spoken by Rumanians today, has continued to survive uninterruptedly throughout the centuries—as Rumanians argue, despite Hungarian dissent. *See also* Apulum, Napoca, Porolissum, Romula Malva and Sarmizegethusa. (In the early third century, to the confusion of historians, two provinces named Dacia [Ripensis and Mediterranea] were established in the territory that had formerly been known as Upper Moesia [*see* Moesia], productive of soldiers, generals and emperors.)

Dalmatia. The northwestern region of the Balkan peninsula, together with its islands (now forming the coastal territory of Yugoslavia), separated from the interior by the Dinaric Alps. The territory took its name from the Delmatae (Dalmatians), an Illyrian (Indo-European-speaking) tribe influenced by Celtic culture. In the fourth century BC the Greeks settled colonies on the coast and the islands, while the Dalmatians came under the control of the Illyrian kingdom (*see* Illyricum). The Greek cities appealed to Rome against Dalmatian encroachments, and a long series of conflicts ensued, in the course of which the Romans destroyed the tribal capital Delminium (Županac).

Dalmatia was subsequently incorporated in the Roman province of Illyricum, though not with any effectiveness until after heavy fighting during the civil war between Caesar and the Pompeians (49–47), followed by major operations by Octavian (the future Augustus) in 34–33, and then further military action in 16 and 11–9 (when Tiberius was in command). Soon afterward, however, followed the great Illyrian revolt (AD 6–9), which although initiated in Bosnia, came to be known as the Dalmatian War. At its termination Illyricum was divided into two administrative parts; the upper province, with its capital at Salonae (Solin), was also known as Dalmatia.

In 42 one of its governors, Lucius Arruntius Camillus Scribonianus, persuaded his two legions to launch a rebellion against the emperor Claudius, which lasted four days. Two-and a-half-centuries later, under Diocletian, the southeastern corner of Dalmatia was detached to form part of a new province of Praevalitana, forming part of what had now become the administrative diocese of Dacia. At the very end of antiquity Dalmatia assumed great importance as a fighting ground between military adventurers on the border between the western emperors and their often unfriendly eastern colleagues. About 461 Marcellinus, withdrawing his allegiance from the west, was appointed the eastern monarch Leo I's commander-in-chief in the region (*magister militum Dalmatiae*), but, according to Damascius, set himself up as an independent ruler. The title passed to his nephew Julius Nepos, who with Leo's support seized the western throne (474). Upon his ejection in the following year he returned to Salonae. In 476 his successor in Italy, Romulus Augustulus, abdicated and the country became a German kingdom. But Nepos, with the ostensible (though only passive) support of the new eastern emperor Zeno, continued to proclaim himself as Augustus, until his death six years later, so that Dalmatia, during this period, was harboring the last of all the Roman emperors in the west.

Damascus (Esh-Sham). A city in southern Syria, beyond the Anti-Lebanon range. The only city of the country that has always been of significance—remaining the capital of the Syrian state today—it lies on the edge of the eastern desert beside two rivers (the ancient Abana [Chrysoroas] and Pharpar, now the Barada and A'waj respectively) and at the meeting point of roads running west (to Berytus, now Beirut) and northeast (to Palmyra) and south. After a prolonged and animated earlier history, the state of Damascus, under the control of the Aramaeans, first became politically important in the early first millennium BC, when its monarchs, supported by a wealth of copper, a fine chariot force, famous fruit orchards and the fertile wheat crops of Bashan played a leading role in the complex power struggles of the region. In 732, however, the kingdom was destroyed by the Assyrians; and it subsequently became a Persian garrison city.

After Alexander the Great had defeated the Persians at Issus (333), Damascus was occupied by his general Parmenio (and employed as a royal mint). By the end of the century, it had been incorporated in the Seleucid empire, though overshadowed by the new foundation of Antioch on the Orontes (Antiochia by Daphne [Antakya]). After a period under Egyptian control, however, it became the capital of the Seleucid monarchs Demetrius III Philopator (95–87) and Antiochus XII Dionysus (*c* 87–84)—under whom it issued coins bearing the new name of Demetrias. The *Zadokite Fragment* or *Damascus Document* refers to the migration of an austere, quasi-monastic group of Jews to the city, which may have taken place at this period: however, the reference to Damascus in the document could also be purely metaphorical.

Threatened with capture by predatory Ituraean Arabs, the city placed itself under the protection of the Nabataean Arab Kingdom, ruled by Aretas III Philhellen (85). Nevertheless, it was occupied in 65 by the troops of the Roman general Aulus Gabinius, acting on behalf of Pompey the Great, who moved into the city shortly afterward, and made it a member of a league of ten cities (Decapolis), loosely attached to the new province of Syria. The Greek historian Nicolaus, who became the chief minister of Herod the Great of Judaea, was born at Damascus *c* 64. Granted by Antony to Cleopatra VII of Egypt, the city passed into the hands of Octavian (Augustus)—obtaining in the process, however, Ituraean territory down to Mount Hermon (31/30)—but was subsequently ceded by Gaius (Caligula) to Aretas IV of Nabataean Arabia (*c* AD 37). It was in his hands when Damascus experienced its most influential happening of classical times: the sudden conversion of St. Paul to Christianity. Paul, a strict Pharisaic Jew, had been sent to bring the adherents of the recently crucified Jesus back to their own faith. Instead he claimed that, outside the gates of Damascus, a blinding vision had felled him to the ground, and he arose an utterly believing Christian.

After the city had been reincorporated into Roman Syria in 62, its people, according to Josephus, killed 10,000 Jews at the outset of the First Jewish Revolt (66). Damascus was the birthplace of Apollodorus, the most famous of all architects of the imperial epoch, who designed the great projects of Trajan (98–117). From the second century AD the city prospered (especially from the export of fruits to Italy), receiving the title of 'metropolis' from Hadrian (117–38) and colonial rights from Severus Alexander (222–35). Under the reorganization of Diocletian (284–305), who established arms factories in the city, it became the capital of the province of Phoenice Libanensis.

The shrine of Zeus Damascenus—the Semitic storm-god Hadad—was the largest of all Syrian sanctuaries. It consisted of a temple built in the middle of two concentric courts. The turreted wall of the inner court has survived as the wall of the Omayyad mosque, and remains of the massive rampart of the outer enclosure are extant. The main features of the ancient town plan can also be partially seen; its principal axis is the 'Street Called Straight' mentioned in the *Acts of the Apostles*, which comprised three sections with slightly different orientations. A coin of Macrinus (217/18) shows a temple of the city's Fortune (Tyche-Astarte) with a shell decoration, foreshadowing the Islamic *mihrab* on its pediment. Issues of Philip I the Arab (244–49) and his wife Otacilia Severa, under whom the city's colonial coinage with Latin inscriptions started, depict a model of the same sanctuary of Tyche, displaying her turreted bust inside and fitted with carry-bars at the base—together with another shrine overlooking a river-god in a grotto, and a temple on a high podium over a spring, with an altar in front of its steps. Theodosius I (379–95) and Arcadius built a church in honor of St. John.

Dana *see* Tyana

Danuvius (Ister, Danube), River. The 'Danubian Culture' (from *c* 4500) was the first farming culture of much of central and eastern Europe (developing into regional 'Danube II' branches early in the fourth millennium). As a result of the conquests of Augustus (31 BC–AD 14), the Danube became, along its entire course, the frontier of the Roman empire, bordering on the provinces of Raetia, Noricum, Pannonia and Moesia. Near the northwestern corner of Raetia, the frontier made a right-angled turn northward, following the Rhenus (Rhine) to the North Sea. To cut off this reentrant and thus shorten the imperial boundaries, Vespasian and Domitian moved beyond the Upper Danube to annex the Agri Decumates (AD 74–98). Trajan also advanced across the Lower Danube to create the province of Dacia (Rumania) in 105. But both territories were subsequently abandoned, by Gallienus (*c* 260–68) and Aurelian (271) respectively.

Throughout the Roman Principate countless military operations were undertaken to prevent German and other invaders from crossing the river, particularly during the second and third centuries, and again in the fifth, when the erosion of the frontier on the middle and lower reaches of the Danube heralded the downfall of the western empire. Diocletian (284–305) built new fortified landing bases at intervals along the north bank, but Constantine I the Great returned to the traditional river frontier (*c* 332–34). *See also* Aquincum, Axiopolis, Bononia, Bononia Malata, Brigetio, Carnuntum, Dacia, Drobeta, Durostorum, Moesia, Noricum, Novae, Oescus, Pannonia, Raetia, Ratiaria, Singidunum, Viminacium, Vindobona.

Daphne *see* Antioch by Daphne

Dar Buk-Ammarah *see* Sugolin

Datça *see* Cnidus

Daulis *see* Phocis

Dead Sea *see* Masada

Decelea, Dekeleia (Tatoi). A small town in Attica on a pass over the eastern end of Mount Parnes, commanding the plain that led southward to Athens and northward toward Euboea. It was said to have been one of the twelve Attic cities induced by the legendary King Theseus to combine in the formation of a new state with Athens as its capital.

Decelea played a prominent part in the latter stages of the Peloponnesian War between the Athenians and Spartans, since it was occupied by the Spartan King Agis II from 413 to 404 BC as a permanent base on Attic soil, threatening the crops and silver mines on which Athens depended. The Spartans appealed, for propaganda purposes, to a traditional friendship between their own city and Decelea, whose mythical founder Decelus was believed to have disclosed to the Dioscuri (Castor and Pollux) where Theseus had hidden their sister Helen (at Aphidnae). But Decelea was in fact selected by the Spartan government for strategic reasons—on the traitorous advice of the Athenian Alcibiades—because its site was so well placed to damage the Athenians, not least by severing their links with their silver mines at Laurium and their port on the Euboean Strait at Oropus. Remains of a fortified enclosure on a wooded hill (Paleokastro) have been plausibly identified as Agis' camp.

Değirmendere *see* Colophon

Deir El-Medina *see* Thebes (Egypt)

Delium, Delion (Dhilesi). In Boeotia (central Greece), on the Euboean Strait; founded by settlers from Tanagra. The site of a sanctuary of Apollo (shrine of Delos, after which the place took its name), Delium was also the location of the most important battle of the Archidamian War (431–421), the first part of the Peloponnesian War between Athens and Sparta described by Thucydides. In a three-pronged endeavor to conquer Boeotia, of which the capital, Thebes, was one of Sparta's principal allies, the Athenians intended to fortify Delium as a permanent naval base on enemy territory. The Athenian Hippocrates captured the place without resistance, completing its fortification; but since the other forces comprising the triple invasion had failed to achieve their objectives, the Theban commander Pagondas caught up with his retreating army about a mile south of Delium. Each force had about 7,000 heavy infantry (hoplites), but the Athenians could not match the 10,000 Boeotian light troops, since their own had gone ahead. Hippocrates, nevertheless, turned to fight, and his right wing did well. But his left wing was rolled up and caused a general rout, in which he himself and nearly a thousand troops were killed. The Boeotians then used an enormous blow pipe to set the palisades of Delium on fire, and those members of the garrison who could not escape were captured or killed. The Athenian attempt to put Boeotia out of the war had totally failed.

Delos. A small infertile island, short of water, about three miles long and between a mile and half a mile across, in the Aegean archipelago of the Cyclades, of which it was regarded as the center and origin. Its loftiest point is the steep and rocky Mount Cynthus, three hundred and fifty feet high, the site of settlements dating back to the third millennium BC. According to Thucydides, it had been occupied by sea rovers from Caria (southwestern Asia Minor), who were supposedly driven out by King Minos of Crete. Before the end of the second millennium BC colonists from the mainland of Greece had made their appearance, and by the time of Homer's *Odyssey* Delos was already renowned as the birthplace of Apollo and Artemis. One of the numerous myths relating to the theme told how it had drifted through the Aegean until moored by Zeus so that the wandering Leto could give them birth: a story told, with variations, by the *Homeric Hymn to Apollo* and Callimachus' *Hymn to Delos.*

The island became the seat of a great Ionic festival to which the Ionian states, including Athens, sent a delegation every year to celebrate the supposed birthday of Apollo. After a period between *c* 700 and *c* 550, during which it apparently belonged to the island of Naxos, Pisistratus asserted Athenian control, 'purifying' the sanctuary by clearing away the graves that surrounded it. In 478/477, when Athens formed a maritime confederacy to ensure Greek independence from the recently defeated Persians, it was known as the Delian League because its common treasury was located on the island until 454 (or somewhat earlier). In 426 the Athenians reorganized the site and festival on an even more grandiose scale, rebuilding the temple soon afterward (*c* 418/417). After the Peloponnesian War (431-404) had ended in their defeat, Sparta gave the Delians their independence—subsequently interrupted by a further period of Athenian domination (378/7-314).

Later, they joined the League of the Islanders, probably sponsored by the Ptolemies of Egypt. Hellenistic monarchs vied with one another to institute new federal festivals and construct grandiose buildings, and it was not long before Delos became the headquarters of the grain and slave trans-shipment trades of the Aegean, and a center on which numerous foreign businessmen and bankers converged, including numerous Italians. However, its leaders made the mistake of supporting King Perseus of Macedonia against the Romans (171-168). In consequence, they handed the island over to Athens, which deported its inhabitants and replaced them by its own colonists (cleruchs), whose trade benefited from the destruction of Corinth (146). To assist them and damage Rhodes—which had incurred Roman displeasure—Delos was made a free port; so that an even larger cosmopolitan population flocked to its markets, which enjoyed a new period of great prosperity.

At some date unknown, however, a slave rebellion broke out, and in 87 Menophanes, a general of Mithridates VI of Pontus, punished Delos for supporting the Romans against his master by inflicting wholesale destruction. In 69 it was sacked once again, by pirates who favored Mithridates. From these blows the island never recovered, as a center either of commerce or of a cult. True, it was exempted from Roman taxation by the Lex Gabinia Calpurnia (58), and the religious observances were maintained in some fashion; but Pausanias described Delos as almost deserted, except for a few Athenian officials.

Excavations have added substantially to our knowledge of Greek and Greco-Roman civilization. The landing place of Delos is seen to have been equipped with the earliest artificial harborworks of which we have any knowledge in the Greek world, including a massive mole three hundred feet long dating back to the eighth century BC. Behind the harbor, approached by a monumental avenue flanked by porticoes, four temples are to be seen. They included a shrine of Artemis (perhaps dating back to before 800, on the site of a Mycenaean building); and the sanctuary of Apollo—begun in the fifth century and completed in the third—which stood at the center of the precinct and contained three temples dedicated to the god; the earliest, dating from the later sixth century, was unequalled at the time for its splendor in the entire Greek world.

Also visible are the famous Terrace of Lions (containing nine sculptured figures of that animal, of which four still stand on the way to the precinct), a Pillared (Hypostyle) Hall of the late third century BC—perhaps a corn exchange—containing nine rows of five columns each, the long, narrow Hellenistic 'Sanctuary of the Bulls' (apparently designed to house a warship, in commemoration of some naval victory) and two other edifices of the same epoch, the so-called Agora of the Italians (the largest building in Delos) and the 'Establishment of the Poseidoniasts'—merchants, shippers and warehousemen from Berytus (Beirut) in Phoenicia. Some of their warehouses, as well as docks, quays, a stadium, a gymnasium, temples of oriental deities and a synagogue, can likewise be traced. There are also remains of numerous houses, many with admirable mosaics, which have provided vital evidence for residential conditions during the last centuries BC—revealing also the works, especially portraits, of Delian sculptors (successors of an ancient school), who helped to form the tastes of the Romans. The theater, on the lower slopes of Mount Cynthus, has an auditorium supported by massive substructures. On the summit of the mountain was a sanctuary of Zeus and Athena, beneath which remains of a primitive cave-temple and of prehistoric curvilinear huts have come to light.

Delphi. Situated in the territory of Phocis (central Greece), on a spectacular site on the steep lower southern slopes of Mount Parnassus, overlooked by the towering Phaedriades (Shining Rocks) above; the Gulf of Corinth lies six miles away, 2,000 feet below. Continuously inhabited from the later Bronze Age (at first at Lycoria, near the Corycian Cave), the place was believed by Greeks to be the middle point of the earth, because Zeus had released two eagles, one from the east and one from the west, and bidden them fly toward the center, which proved to be Delphi. Its mythical founder was Delphus, son of Poseidon by the nymph Melaine.

It derived incalculable renown and influence from its possession of the greatest of all temples and oracles of Apollo. According to the *Homeric Hymn to Apollo*, the god seized an earlier oracle of Gaia (the Earth) at Delphi—then named Pytho and corresponding to an archaeologically attested late Mycenaean goddess—by slaying the female serpent (Python) that guarded the prophetic spring (Cassotis); thereafter he uttered his own oracles, through a priestess (Pythia) seated on a tripod at the edge of a chasm, from which a vapor (*pneuma*) emerged. It was supposedly under the inspiration of this vapor that, in response to enquiries transmitted to her through a male prophet, the Pythia, 'in possession by the god'—having drunk the waters of Cassotis and undergone purification at the Castalian spring or springs, gushing forth from the Phaedriades—gasped out a disconnected series of words, which the priests reformulated and interpreted in hexameter verse. But there is no chasm traceable today (the hole may have been a gap in the temple pavement exposing a small spot of undisturbed sacred soil beneath). Consequent doubts about the authenticity of the vapor have prompted alternative explanations; but the suggestion, for example, that the priestess drugged herself on potassium cyanide, derived from the laurel leaves that she chewed, is unconvincing. Some have therefore preferred to ascribe the entire phenomenon to clever stage management, aided by an effective information system; and it is true that the prophecies—conservative but adaptable to circumstances—often (though not always) showed a considerable amount of political good sense: as Aeschylus, in his *Oresteia*, intended to demonstrate. However, due weight must also be given to the probability of emotional suggestion and mediumistic, ecstatic trance, for which widespread parallels have been noted in other civilizations.

There was a tradition that the first priests were Cretans from Cnossus, who had disembarked at Cirrha (Xeropigadi) beside the fertile Crisaean plain on the Gulf of Corinth, and introduced the cult of Apollo Delphinios (dolphin) at Delphi, which thus assumed its name. The sanctuary was already known to the *Iliad*, and by 700 had become famous throughout the Greek world. Its growing wealth attracted the envy of Cirrha, which, however, in the course of the First Sacred War (*c* 590), was destroyed by the Thessalians and other forces, acting on behalf of the Amphictyonic League. This was a group of twelve peoples, north and south of the Gulf, who chose Delphi (in place of Thermopylae) as their federal sanctuary. The Amphictyonic Council reorganized the Pythian Games (in 586/5 or 582/1) and elevated them to Panhellenic status, adding a chariot race to their musical contests. The oracle was now at the height of its prestige, directing national policies (in Etruscan as well as Greek city-states) and receiving consultation whenever a colony was sent out.

In 548, after the temple had been destroyed by fire, it was rebuilt by the Athenian family of the Alcmaeonids, with the aid of funds gathered throughout the Greek world. Preserved, supposedly by a miracle, from attack by the Persians (480)—whose victory it had wrongly anticipated—Delphi continued to receive rich gifts from numerous Greek communities. The Second Sacred War (448) was precipitated by the Phocians' seizure of the place. Liberated by the Spartans, it was given to Phocis once again by the Athenians under Pericles, but regained its independence in or before 421. Continued quarrels between Delphi and Phocis (which committed systematic robberies), and further disputes between the Amphictyony and the Locrians (Third and Fourth Social Wars, 356–346 and 340–338), encouraged the intervention of Philip II of Macedonia, who took over the Phocians' two seats on the Amphictyonic Council.

In 278 the Aetolian Confederacy claimed and gained a great deal of credit for repelling an invasion of Delphi by the Gauls, exploiting the occasion to become its protecting power. The kings of Pergamum (Bergama) showed the shrine munificent favor, but it was the Romans who, in 191, replaced the Aetolians as its controllers. Plundered by the Thracians (91) and by Sulla (86), the Delphians received assistance from Augustus (31 BC–AD 14), who reorganized the Amphictyony. By the time of Claudius (51), however, the site was impoverished and half-deserted, and Nero was said to have carried five hundred statues away. But with encouragement from the phil-Hellene Hadrian, vigorous attempts to revive the city and sanctuary were made by Plutarch, priest of Pythian Apollo at Chaeronea (105–26) and a member of the Amphictyonic Council, which now proceeded to issue coins in honor of Antinous, the youth Hadrian loved.

About 170 Pausanias, visiting Delphi, found the sanctuaries dilapidated, but despite depredations still filled with works of art. The bronze tripod-support of intertwined serpents dedicated by the Greek cities after the battle of Plataea (479 BC) was removed by Constantine the Great to Constantinople (İstanbul), where it can still be seen. Julian the Apostate (AD 361–63) sent his physician Oribasius to restore the temple, but the only utterance of the oracle was a lament for its bygone glory. It was closed down by Theodosius I (379–95), as part of his campaign in favor of Christianity. The monuments still to be seen are divided into two zones, on either side of the Castalian spring. To its west was the temple of Pythian Apollo, of which six corroded columns have been reerected. The building was reconstructed at various times, loaded with a variety of precious offerings, and adjoined by the 'Treasuries' of various cities (*e.g.* Sicyon, Siphnos, Athens, Thebes, Syracuse) on the Sacred Way. Nearby are a holy grave, theater and stadium. A zone of monuments further to the east contained the shrines of Athena Pronaia (built over a Bronze Age sanctuary) and Artemis and other deities, a Treasury of Massalia (Marseille), another in Doric style, a marble rotunda (Tholos) of the fifth century BC, and a gymnasium.

Demetrias. A Greek town in the district of Magnesia (eastern Thessaly), at the head of the Gulf of Pagasae (Gulf of Volos), at or near the base of a peninsula slightly to the northeast of the ancient Pagasae (which it partially absorbed), southeast of the modern Volos. Standing at the only practicable entrance to Thessaly by sea, the city was founded *c* 293 BC by Demetrius I Poliorcetes as an amalgamation (synoecism) of seven or eight small towns or villages (named by Strabo), to which, as we learn from inscriptions, five more were subsequently added. Demetrius made good use of an excellent site, which became a center of commercial activity. But above all, as his powerful fortifications and the ship's prow on the new foundation's coins indicate, the place was intended to be a Macedonian fortress and military harbor, one of the principal 'fetters of Greece.'

During the years 196–191, however, Demetrias passed successively into the hands of three other powers, including Rome, which made it leader of a Magnesian League. Philip V of Macedonia regained control in 191, but after his son Perseus had been defeated by the Romans (167), it came under Roman control once more, remaining the head of the Magnesian League. Its walls, however, were partly demolished, but a hundred and eighty-two projecting towers of the acropolis (Palatia) can still be seen, as well as remains of a shrine of Apollo on the neighboring saddle, and at the foot of the acropolis a temple of Artemis Iolkia, a Sacred Market (identified by inscriptions), a theater, and a large building with a central colonnaded court, questionably identified as the Macedonian palace. Neleia (Pefkakia, Magoula), one of the communities originally incorporated in Demetrias, possesses an early Christian basilica altered or enlarged at two or three different epochs.

Demetrias *see also* Damascus, Sicyon

Demre *see* Myra

Dendera *see* Tentyra

Dertona (Tortona). A town of Cisalpine Gaul (north Italy), on the Olubria (Scrivia), a southern tributary of the Padus (Po). Dertona occupied a highly strategic position, controlling the passage between the Ligurian Alps and the Po basin, and thus helping to confine the Ligurian tribes to their native mountains. It was also a particularly important communications center, becoming not only a station on the Via Postumia (148 BC) between Placentia (Piacenza) and Genua (Genoa), but also the terminal of the Via Aemilia Scauri (109). This reached the Ligurian coast a little to the west, joining up with the road that later became the Via Julia Augusta and led westward along the south coast of Gaul. Like the road, Dertona assumed the name Julia, testifying to a colonial foundation by Caesar or Octavian (Augustus)—perhaps replacing a colony of 109, though Velleius Paterculus is ambiguous on this point. Numerous mosaics, architectural fragments, and imposing funeral monuments bear witness to the city's position as a major regional center.

In AD 461, however, it suddenly gained a more sinister prominence, when the emperor Majorian was murdered there. His heavy defeat by the Vandals off the coast of Spain had lost him the support of the dominant German general Ricimer. When, therefore, Majorian returned overland to Italy, Ricimer sent officers who met him at Dertona, tore the purple off his back, and cut off his head.

Deva (Chester). A Roman town in Britannia (Cheshire, England), taking its name from the river Dee, of which it stood at the mouth (and lowest practical crossing), on a sandstone ridge, possessing a harbor navigable by seagoing ships, and commanding a ford and major routes between Wales and the north. Earlier occupation may be assumed, but the legionary stronghold dates from the time of Vespasian (*c* AD 74–78). Timber construction was replaced by stone under Trajan (*c* 100–102). The dimensions of the fortress are exceptionally large. It stood between two powerful and threatening tribes, the Brigantes and Ordovices, and became a strategically important, basic element in the frontier defences when the route up the western marches and along the North Wales coast was linked, across the Pennines, with Eboracum (York).

The civil settlement had become an independent community by the early third century. In about 300, however, Deva suffered damage, and its walls were rebuilt on a more substantial scale, perhaps by Constantius I Chlorus. Soon afterward it formed a link in the defences of the west coast against pirates from Hibernia (Ireland), forming part of the province of Flavia Caesariensis within the administrative diocese of the Britanniae. Before 400, however, the site was abandoned, perhaps in the time of Magnus Maximus (383–88).

Buildings identified in the original camp include the commander's residence (*praetorium*), and the administrative building (*principia*) together with its shrine, barracks, storehouses and workshops. Outside the walls are officers' baths (probably built in stone from the outset, in the 70s AD), stables, and a spacious (and partly excavated) amphitheater, as well as granaries near the harbor gate.

Dia *see* Naxos

Dicaearchia *see* Puteoli

Dicaeopolis *see* Segesta

Dicte, Dikte. A mountain in Crete, variously identified with Mount Lassithis, southeast of Cnossus, or—more probably—Mount Modi, at the eastern extremity of the island, overlooking a shrine of Dictaean Zeus (on the site of the Minoan city of Paleokastro; the word 'Dictaean' appears on a tablet from Cnossus of Mycenaean date). The site provides remains dating back to the seventh and sixth centuries BC. It was here that the famous *Hymn to Dictaean Zeus* was found.

One of the conflicting myths regarding the birthplace of Zeus, followed by Diodorus and Apollodorus, indicated that he was born to Rhea at Dicte—inside a cave (identified with the sanctuary at Psychro) according to the latter authority, although this detail may be due to a confusion with another story ascribing his birth to a cave in the center of the island (*see* Ida). The ancients were likewise not agreed whether Zeus was nursed and reared—and guarded by the Curetes—on Dicte (Apollodorus, Virgil, Servius, Vatican mythographers) or Ida (Callimachus, Lactantius, Placidus).

Didyma or Branchidae (Didim). An oracular sanctuary of Apollo in Ionia (western Asia Minor), on a plateau of the peninsula of Miletus (Balat), ten miles south of that city. Didyma was under the control of the priestly clan of the Branchidae, who claimed descent from Branchus, a Carian youth loved by Apollo. In pre-Ionian times, according to Pausanias, the oracle had been located at a spring sacred to a local goddess. Situated in a precinct in which pottery of the seventh century BC has now been discovered, Apollo's shrine enjoyed an enormous and widespread reputation, to which witness is borne, for example, by dedications from the Egyptian pharaoh Necho II (*c* 610–595) and Croesus of Lydia (*c* 560–546). A Second Temple, of which the initial work dated from about Croesus' time, was burned down by a Persian monarch, probably Darius I after the collapse of the Ionian Revolt (494); in 480 the Branchidae—together with the temple treasures—were removed by Xerxes I to Sogdiana in central Asia, where their descendants were later massacred by Alexander the Great.

However, the oracle was revived, under the administration of Miletus, and with the aid of Seleucus I Nicator a great Third Temple was begun *c* 300, though its construction continued, at intervals, for the next six hundred years. The remains of these successive developments, with their unusual design incorporating a raised stage-like chamber and crypt, provide one of the most imposing extant monuments of the ancient world; the younger Pliny ranked it as the second of all Greek shrines in splendor, after the Artemisium in Ephesus (Selçuk), which was ignored by Strabo—together with a temple at Acragas (Agrigento)—when he described the Didyma temple as the largest in existence. Its cult statue of Apollo Philesios, a work of Canachus of Sicyon that was stolen by the Persians, was especially famous. Approached by an impressive Sacred Way from Miletus which was lined by statues of seated figures, and has now been partially cleared, the sanctuary also included other shrines, and a number of additional buildings, as well as a grove and water installations that evidently played an integral part in the cult. In addition to the shrine of Apollo, five sanctuaries of other deities at Didyma are epigraphically attested.

The Megala Didymeia, instituted *c* 200 BC, became one of the major Games of the ancient world. As for the oracle, it remained very active in the third century AD, ranking only below Claros in Asia; but then there were plunderings, of which the signs can still be seen. The cult was brought to an end by the Christianizing policy of Theodosius I (378–95), although he reconstructed the habitation center of Didyma, including a large and complex bathing establishment, which has now been revealed by excavation.

Digentia (Licenza). In Latium (Lazio, western Italy), northeast of Tibur (Tivoli) and Rome, at the foot of Mount Lucretilis (Colle Rotonda). A low wooded hill above the road, offering views of the Sabine hills, displays the remains of a compact and fairly well-preserved Roman villa comprising twelve rooms, two courtyards, a bathing establishment and a colonnaded court with a pool; mosaic pavements with black and white geometric designs are to be seen. The building has been plausibly identified with the villa presented to Horace by Maecenas, minister of Octavian (the future Augustus), in 33/32 BC, and celebrated by the poet in his *Odes, Epodes* and *Satires.* Above the house is a waterfall which is known as the Fonte Oratina and is believed to have been the spring celebrated by Horace as the Fons Bandusiae; this had been the name of a fountain in the neighborhood of his birthplace Venusia (Venosa).

Dikili *see* Atarneus

Dimetoka *see* Granicus

Dinar *see* Apamea Cibotus (Phrygia)

Diocaesarea *see* Olba, Sepphoris

Dionysia *see* Naxos

Dioscurias, later Sebastopolis (Sukhumi). A Greek city on the eastern Euxine (Black) Sea coast of Colchis (the autonomous Republic of Abkhazia in Soviet Georgia), on the southern slopes of the Caucasus near the mouth of the small river Besletka. An earlier native settlement of the second and early first millennia BC, frequented by local tribes, was superseded *c* 540 by a colony sent from Miletus (Balat), geographically the remotest that it ever established. Thenceforth the city of Dioscurias (if, as seems probable, it possessed that status) became busily engaged in the import of wares from many parts of Greece, and the export of local salt and of Caucasian timber, linen, and hemp. It was also remarkable for the seventy languages spoken in its bazaars—or some said three hundred, but Strabo was skeptical about this estimate.

Although the sea made serious inroads upon the territory of its Greek quarter, the place continued to flourish until its conquest by Mithridates VI Eupator in the later second century. Under Augustus (in Greek, Sebastos) it assumed the name of Sebastopolis. But its greatness was past, and in the first century AD Pliny the Elder described the site as deserted. This must, however, have been an exaggeration, since the town was still noted as extant by Arrian, who was governor of Cappadocia under Hadrian in the 130s. The remains of towers and walls of Sebastopolis have been found underwater; on land the lowest levels so far reached by archaeologists are of the first and second centuries AD.

Diospolis *see* Neocraesarea

Diospolis Magna *see* Thebes (Egypt)

Dipaea *see* Arcadia

Diyarbakır *see* Amida

Djemila *see* Cuicul

Dnieper, River *see* Borysthenes

Dodona, Dodone. A city in Epirus (northwest Greece), at the foot of Mount Tomaros (Olytsikas), fourteen miles south of the modern Janina. It was famous for its holy place and oracle of Zeus (Naios), which went back at least to *c* 1200 BC. In Homer's *Iliad,* Achilles prayed to Zeus of Dodona, and speaks of the Selli, its priests, who 'had unwashed feet and slept on the ground': a description which seems to recall some earlier cult of a deity of the earth, with which contact had to be maintained. In the *Odyssey,* Odysseus consulted the oracle in order to learn the will of Zeus from a sacred oak; and Hesiod, too, mentions Dodona. In the eighth century Zeus was worshipped there in association with the goddess Dione—a female equivalent to his own name. When Herodotus visited the place three hundred years later, he found that the Selli had been replaced by three priestesses, known as 'doves.' Applicants to the oracle wrote their questions (mostly requiring the answer 'yes' or 'no') on thin sheets of lead; these were subsequently folded and placed inside a jar, which was taken charge of by one of the priestesses. Examples of their answers have survived, dealing with national, professional and domestic problems. It was also believed that the oracle rang out its messages on a brazen gong (an offering from the people of Corcyra), or conveyed them through the murmur of a sacred spring. Eventually Dodona was eclipsed by the oracle of Apollo at Delphi.

Never of very spectacular appearance—partly because of its isolated location—the sanctuary, to judge from recent archaeological reconstructions, does not seem to have displayed durable buildings until the fourth century BC, from which the first of several stages of pre-Roman construction can be dated. The most important restorations and enlargements were the work of King Pyrrhus of Epirus (297–272), who made the precinct into the religious center of his expanded kingdom and developed the festival of the Naia in relation to the cult.

Dodona was successively sacked and destroyed by the Aetolians (219/218), the Romans (167), and the troops of Mithridates VI Eupator of Pontus (88 BC). Nevertheless, Hadrian visited the place in AD 132 and the festival lasted at least until the following century. When the empire became Christian, the oaks were cut down and a basilica erected, before or after 500; a bishop of Dodona was present at the Church Council of Ephesus in 443.

In addition to the shrine of Zeus, Dodona possessed additional temples, apparently dedicated to Aphrodite and Dione, as well as a Council house (Bouleuterion) and an adjacent guesthouse that, as recent excavations have suggested, was destroyed in 167 BC and then repaired, only to suffer destruction once again on a later occasion. But the most impressive and best-preserved monument is the theater (on the way up to the acropolis), dating from the epoch of Pyrrhus and transformed into an amphitheater in the time of Augustus.

Don, River *see* Tanais

Dora, earlier Dor (Al-Tantura). A coastal city of northern Judaea (Israel) south of Mount Carmel, standing on the ancient coast road (the Ways of Horus or Way of the Sea) and possessing two harbors, separated by a cliff. After occupation by Late Bronze Age inhabitants, and then, in the later second millennium BC, by one of the so-called 'Sea Peoples,' Dor remained independent of Israel. Later, however, it became an Assyrian provincial capital (*c* 734), before passing to the Persians, who gave it to King Eshmunazar of Sidon *c* 450. The city was besieged by the Seleucid Antiochus III the Great in 219, and again in 139/8 by Antiochus VII Sidetes, who failed in an attempt to trap his rival Trypho there (though Trypho committed suicide shortly afterward). Subsequently Dora and nearby Stratonis Turris (the later Caesarea Maritima) came under the control of a prince named Zoilus, but Dora, as we learn from Josephus, passed into the hands of the Jewish (Hasmonaean) ruler Alexander I Jannaeus (103–76), remaining a powerful fortress.

After Pompey the Great's reduction of Judaea to client status, the city reckoned a new era from his grant of autonomy (64), and was rebuilt by Aulus Gabinius (*c* 56/55). On the eve of the First Jewish Revolt or Roman War (AD 66–73) the pagan inhabitants forcibly erected the emperor's statue in the synagogue. After the revolt, Dora for a time issued coins with Greek inscriptions (since its hybrid Phoenician culture had been considerably Hellenized), adopting a title that claimed maritime importance (*nauarchis*) and displaying the head of a mythical founder Dorus. Septimius Severus (193–211) attached the city to Phoenicia, and under the later empire it formed part of the province of Palaestina Prima. But Eusebius (*c* 260–340), and then the pilgrim Paula, described its buildings as ruined: it recovered, however, to become the seat of a Byzantine bishopric.

Excavations have revealed uninterrupted occupation since the second millennium BC; extensive remains dating from Hellenistic and later times include a large Roman temple and theater near the coast.

Doris. The smallest and northernmost region of central Greece, comprising the headwaters of the river Cephissus and containing four small towns (the Dorian Tetrapolis). Its command of the main north-south road between the neighboring regions of Oetaea and Phocis and its membership of the Amphictyony—the body that controlled Delphi—gave the territory a certain importance. But its prestige was mainly due to the belief that it was the mother country of the original, legendary Dorian invaders of the Peloponnese: probably it was true that a group of them had passed that way.

In 457 and 426 the Spartans, who (as their poet Tyrtaeus confirms) accepted this view that Doris was their land of origin, sent armies to help its people against the encroachments of the Phocians and Oetaeans respectively. In the fourth century the territory fell into the hands first of the Phocian general Onomarchus and then of Philip II of Macedonia. Its Tetrapolis still existed in 196.

Dougga *see* Thugga

Draco, River *see* Orontes

Drangiana, Drangiane. An eastern Iranian territory (now forming part of Sistan, of which the greater part is in southwestern Afghanistan). Named after the tribe of the Drangae, who derived profit, according to Strabo, from the tin found in the country, though its wine was poor. Under Persian control they served in the army of Xerxes I (486–465 BC), wearing uniforms like those of the Medes. Alexander the Great, during his conquest of the Persian empire, entered Drangiana (330), which formed part of an Arachosian satrapy under Barsaentes (later put to death). Entering the royal residence Phrada (Nad Ali, Faranj?), he executed Philotas (general of his Companions) for alleged complicity in a plot; and when he left he refounded the city, which (then or later) assumed the name of Prophthasia, 'Anticipation,' with reference to the detection of the conspiracy. Alexander moved on to the region of the Hamun-i-Helmand, adjoining the outflow of the river Etymandrus (Helmand) into a lake, where he found—and exempted from tribute—a primitive and allegedly innocent tribe, known as the Benefactors, because they had supplied provisions to the Persian king Cyrus II.

Alexander detached Drangiana from the still unconquered satrapy of Arachosia, merging it with Aria (to its north); the territory subsequently passed into the hands of the Seleucids, and then, despite menaces of Parthian encroachment, passed under the control of Euthydemus I Theos (*c* 235–200), second founder of the Greco-Bactrian state. But when the Sacae (Scythians) overran vast portions of the region about 120, Drangiana was one of the lands that succumbed to them. At the beginning of the Christian era a description of the middle Etymandrus valley was provided by Isidorus of Charax.

Drepanum, Drepanon or Drepane (Trapani). A coastal town at the western extremity of Sicily (in front of Mount Eryx), supposedly owing its name, meaning 'sickle,' to the narrow spit of land on which it is situated: this derivation is doubtful, however, because in ancient times the promontory was an archipelago.

Possessing a harbor on its south side protected by an islet (Colombaia), Drepanum was of native Sican origin. It became the trading port of the city of Eryx (Monte San Giuliano), but *c* 260 BC, soon after the beginning of the First Punic War, was taken and fortified by the Carthaginian general Hamilcar, who moved part of the population of Eryx into the fortress. In 249, as Polybius and Diodorus record, the Roman consul Publius Claudius Pulcher suffered a serious reverse (at the hands of Adherbal) as he entered the harbor, losing ninety-three of his hundred-and-twenty-three ships—the first and only defeat that the Romans suffered at sea during the war. Pious persons ascribed this defeat to his insistence on engaging the enemy in spite of unfavorable religious omens. For when he had learned, before the battle, that the sacred chickens refused to eat, he reportedly had them dropped overboard, remarking 'Well, if they won't eat, let them drink.' In 249 the Romans launched a prolonged attempt to recapture Drepanum by siege, and in 242 a new fleet under Gaius Lutatius Catulus still failed to take the place, though its provisions were running low; but in the following year his victory off the Aegates (Egadi) Islands terminated the war, and the city surrendered. During the Roman period its wealth and influence were eclipsed by Lilybaeum (Marsala).

Drerus, Dreros. A small city in northeastern Crete, on one of the southern spurs of Mount Kadiston, to the west of the Mirabello Gulf. From the eighth to the sixth centuries BC, Drerus was one of the most important city-states in the island. A group of archaic inscriptions includes the earliest complete constitutional law yet discovered in Greek lands, of the later seventh century BC; the document is at pains to prevent illegal extension of office by the city's administrators (*kosmoi*), which could have resulted in the establishment of an autocracy (*tyrannis*). During Hellenistic times the Drerians were allies of Cnossus and enemies of Lyttus, to whose people, according to an inscription of *c* 220, the youths (*epheboi*) of Drerus swore that they would do 'all manner of harm.' A century later, however, the town had apparently become a dependency of Cnossus (or possibly of Lyttus).

The site has yielded remains of a building of importance to architectural history, one of the earliest known temples of the Geometric (Iron) Age, dating from the eighth century BC. It was probably dedicated to Apollo Delphinios, who, together with Athena Poliouchos, was Drerus' principal divinity; the excavation of the shrine was prompted by the discovery of statues of hammered bronze plating (originally intended as facings for wood), representing Apollo, Artemis and Leto (*c* 650–640). Not far from the temple is a group of later rooms identified as the government building (*prytaneion*). Another structure may have been a meeting place for local associations (*hetaireiai*).

Drizipara *see* Tzirallum

Drobeta (Turnu Severin). A city in Dacia (Olteṇia, Rumania) on the north (left) bank of the Danube, near the Iron Gates. Formerly a tribal center, it was captured by Trajan during his Dacian wars of conquest, and was the place he selected for his celebrated river bridge (from Pontes [Kostol] on the south bank), constructed by the great architect-engineer Apollodorus of Damascus (*c* AD 104), and depicted on the emperor's column at Rome and on his coins. Two thousand four hundred feet in length, the bridge possessed a wooden floor resting on wooden arches and twenty stone piles, of which remains are still to be seen (structures belonging to its terminal section are covered by the railway). Hadrian (117–38), under whom Drobeta formed part of the province of Lower Dacia (later Dacia Apulensis), raised the city to the rank of *municipium* (with the title of Aelium), and Septimius Severus (193–211) made it a colony.

Inscriptions show that the ex-soldiers and merchants who lived in the town included people from numerous countries, worshipping many foreign deities, notably Jupiter under the alien name of Zbelsurdos. Even after the abandonment of Dacia by Aurelian (271), Drobeta remained an important Roman bridgehead; and in the fourth century it was rebuilt and provided with massive defences, gates and towers, as the terminal of the Oltenian system of fence and palisade fortifications. In the 440s, however, the place was totally destroyed by Attila's Huns; when Justinian I, in the following century, built a fort on its ruins, he called it by a new name, Theodora.

Dubravica *see* Margum

Dura, later Dura-Europus (Qalat es-Salihiya) in eastern Syria. Situated above a steep cliff overlooking the right bank of the Middle Euphrates, on a plateau between two steep ravines, the place is only accessible from the west. Its Semitic name Dura presupposes a pre-Greek settlement and caravan center. The supplementary, and characteristically Macedonian, name Europus was added when the place was refounded as a frontier fortress and Greek military colony by Nicanor, probably a general of Seleucus I Nicator, toward the end of the fourth century BC.

Under subsequent Parthian rule (from *c* 114), it was the most important riverside station on the Royal Road from Syria to Babylon, and developed considerable commercial and agricultural prosperity. Although Greek cultural influences by no means vanished, a process of orientalization became perceptible, as the tidy Greek town-plan was gradually converted into a crowded bazaar quarter. Very briefly incorporated in the Roman empire when Trajan formed his province of Mesopotamia across the river (AD 116), Dura Europus was again occupied by the generals of Lucius Verus in 165 and obtained colonial status under Septimius Severus (193–211), becoming a powerfully fortified strongpoint on the eastern boundary of the frontier province of Syria. But after a rapid decline in its prosperity, it was besieged and destroyed by the Sassanian Persian king Sapor (Shapur) I *c* 257.

Excavations on the site, although uncovering less than half of its total area, have added enormously to our knowledge of the life, culture and art of the region during the successive periods of the city's existence. A remarkable mixture of Semitic, Greek, Parthian and Roman civilizations has been revealed. There were strong links with Palmyra to the west, indicated by a temple of its gods and by Palmyrene inscriptions. Both Jewish and Christian places of worship are to be seen; a house-synagogue with paintings in exceptionally good condition (transferred to the National Archaeological Museum at Damascus) has thrown remarkable and unexpected light on aspects of contemporary Judaism.

The governor's palace occupied an impressive location above the Euphrates. Beneath it stood a citadel, furnished with three gates and three towers, guarding the river bank. Massive Hellenistic walls are to be seen, and Roman and Parthian baths and military equipment; and numerous parchments and papyri have come to light. The papyri (now at Yale University) include portions of a Seleucid legal code, numerous Greek contracts, and Roman military documents. Most of the inscriptions found at Dura Europus are Greek; in addition to Palmyrene, Latin, Pahlavi, Middle Persian, Parthian, Safaitic, Aramaic and Syriac are also represented.

Durocortorum, later Remi (Reims). A city in the interior of northern Gaul (Department of Marne, on the northern border of Champagne, France), situated on flat ground beside the swampy valley of the Vesle, a tributary of the Axona (Aisne). There had been a Celtic settlement on the site, but it is not certain whether this was the Durocortorum Remorum (mentioned by Caesar) which formed the capital of the independent Remi—Rome's principal allies in the region—since that may have been ten miles away at Vieux Reims. After the Roman conquest, a city was built for the Remi at the place which later became Reims itself, and its location as a principal communications center of northern Gaul earned it the position of the capital of the province of Gallia Belgica. The main-town plan is recognizable, and its gates can be traced, including the fairly well preserved Porte Mars. Architectural fragments, floor mosaics and wall paintings indicate a high level of prosperity.

During the German invasions of the third quarter of the third century AD, however, Durocortorum suffered severely at least once, and perhaps on two or even three occasions. Nevertheless, under the reorganization of Diocletian (284–305), the city, henceforth known as Urbs Remorum or Remi, retained its metropolitan position as capital of the new province of Belgica Secunda. By this time it was already a Christian bishopric, and the chapels of Saints Sixtus and Saint Clement date from *c* 300. The latter building later became the basilica of St. Remigius (Remi) who, according to tradition, baptized the Frankish king Clovis.

Durostorum, later Dorostolum (Silistra). In Lower Moesia, on the right bank of the Danube (on the borders of the Dobruja in northeastern Bulgaria, formerly part of the Rumanian Dobrogea). The place-name—preserved in the old Bulgarian Drastar—is probably of Thracian origin.

Durostorum was a Roman military camp shortly before or after the beginning of the Christian era. Following Trajan's conquest of Dacia, across the Danube, it became the garrison of a legion (AD 105/6) and a local headquarters of the river customs authority. Antoninus Pius established an adjacent civilian settlement (*canabae*), to which Marcus Aurelius gave municipal status, after the place had suffered severely in an invasion by the German tribe of the Costoboci (170). In 238 it was again devastated by another tribe, the Carpi, who deported part of its population as slaves. The garrison of Durostorum was implicated in the short-lived revolt of Regalianus, governor of Upper Pannonia (238). Under the later empire, it became capital of the province of Scythia, and increased substantially in importance.

It was a center of Christianity in the Dobruja, and the focal point of the activities of Saint Dasius. It was thc custom of the Roman soldiers, on the occasion of the annual Saturnalia festival, to dress a young man as King Saturn, give him a splendid escort, and on the thirtieth day make him kill himself on the god's altar. In 303, however, during the joint reign of Diocletian and Maximian, a Christian named Dasius refused to accept the position (because he disapproved of the debaucheries accompanying the celebrations) and was beheaded. The most famous son of Durostorum, however, was Aetius, the greatest general of the later western empire, who was born there shortly before 400. The city possessed important buildings and artistic monuments, including a fine painted grave which survives; to the east and southeast are remains of fortifications.

Dyrrhachium, Dyrrhachion, formerly Epidamnus, Epidamnos (Durrës). A Greek city on the Adriatic coast in southwestern Illyria (now Albania, nineteen miles west of Tirana). Founded *c* 627 BC by Corinth and Corcyra (Corfu) under the name of Epidamnus, it began from *c* 300 to be generally known as Dyrrhachium (originally the name of the headland on which the city was located, taken from the tribe of the Dyrrhachii and, according to mythology, from Dyrrhachus the son of Ionius); indeed, this latter designation had already appeared on the tribe's coinage some two centuries earlier. Possessing a good harbor on an isthmus, Dyrrhachium shared with Apollonia the control of the Myzeqija, the widest and richest part of the central Albanian coastal plain. The city's active trade with the Illyrians in the interior was organized by an annually appointed or reappointed seller (*poletes*).

After the death of Alexander the Great, it passed into the hands of Cassander (d. 297) and Pyrrhus of Epirus (d. 272). In 229 it came under the dominant influence of the Romans—after they had broken a siege by Illyrian tribesmen—and subsequently served as a base for Roman armies in the Balkans, becoming the terminal of the northern branch of the Via Egnatia which spanned the Balkan peninsula (*c* 130).

Dyrrhachium's moment of notoriety came during the civil war between Pompey the Great and Julius Caesar (49–48), when Pompey made it his principal base. In the course of an elaborate campaign of attempted encirclements, Caesar endeavored to blockade the enemy fortress, but the attempt was a disastrous failure, and he recoiled inland to the Thessalian plain. This, however, proved Pompey's last success before catastrophe overtook him at Pharsalus.

When Antony and Octavian (the future Augustus) had crushed Caesar's assassins at Philippi (42), veterans were settled at Dyrrhachium, which assumed the designation of Colonia Julia Veneria (after Venus, the alleged ancestress of Caesar and tutelary deity of the colony); the founder was a certain Quintus Paquius Rufus, who celebrated the occasion by an issue of coinage, which was resumed following a further draft of colonists by Augustus in the second decade

BC. In the later empire the city became the capital of the province of New Epirus (Epirus Nova). The modern town is constructed over the ancient site and finds are relatively sparse.

E

Ebora, Ebura (Evora). A Roman city in the interior of Lusitania (Portugal), situated sixty miles east of Olisipo (Lisbon) but also connected with the south coast by a road; it stands on a low hill among rolling plains. Celtic Ebora may have been the headquarters of Quintus Sertorius' secessionist activity against the Roman government (*c* 80 BC). It received Latin rights (conferring Roman citizenship on its annually elected officials) and the titles of Liberalitas Julia from Julius Caesar or Augustus, under whom it issued a single coinage, probably celebrating his appointment as chief priest (*pontifex maximus,* 12 BC). Vespasian (AD 69–79) added the rank of *municipium.* Inscriptions show a large number of families of Roman and Italian origin. A bishop of Ebora attended the Church Council of Iliberis (Elvira, *c* 300).

The place is noteworthy for one of the best preserved temples in the peninsula—although its façade has disappeared—which is known, without good reason, as the 'Temple of Diana,' and dates from the second or third century AD. A frieze from another Roman temple is to be seen in the local museum.

Eboracum or Eburacum (York). A city in northern England, on a ridge which crosses the Vale of York and provides a favorable line of communications. Furthermore, its location at the confluence of the Ouse and Foss—both tidal in ancient times—provided good defences and easy access to the sea. Eboracum was a stronghold of the Brigantes, the largest tribe in Britain. Whether the Romans (who created the province of Britain in AD 43) established a base there before the seventies is uncertain, but following dissensions in the tribal royal house the Roman governor Quintus Petillius Cerealis (71–74) undoubtedly did so; and either in his time or under Cnaeus Julius Agricola (*c* 78–85) Eboracum became the garrison of a legion (moved from Lindum [Lincoln]). Hadrian (117–38) visited the city, and Septimius Severus rebuilt it as the capital of a new province of Lower Britain; it may also have become a Roman *municipium* or colony at the same time. Severus died while he was there (211). So did Constantius I (306), and it was at Eboracum that his son Constantine the Great was proclaimed emperor. It was now the capital of Britannia Secunda, within the administrative diocese of the Britanniae, and under Constans I (*c* 343) may have become the capital of a fifth British province of Valentia.

The civil settlement (*canabae*) adjoining the camp lay east of the Ouse, and beside its west bank was a business quarter which became a *colonia* before 237, and possessed an episcopal see by 314, when a bishop of Eboracum was the leading British representative at the Council of Arelate (Arles). Recent excavations show a succession of timber buildings, probably dating from the earliest period of Roman occupation. But the principal surviving monument of the fortress consists of its walls (including a multiangular tower), rebuilt in 107/8—as an inscription records—and again *c* 200, and then once more *c* 300, under Constantius I, when various impressive stone bastions were constructed (probably replacing wooden towers), as well as a monumental turreted gate overlooking the river. The city probably contained large imperial palaces of the same epoch, but they have not survived.

Ebro, River *see* Iberus

Ebusus *see* Balearic Islands

Ecbatana, Epiphaneia (Hamadan). A major city of northern Media (now west-central Iran), at a height of 6,000 feet beneath the summit of Mount Alwand, dominating a broad and fertile plain (Qareh Su) and forming the crossroads of important routes. Traditionally founded, as Herodotus reports, by Deioces, a semi-legendary king of the Medes in the eighth century BC, it became the capital of the Median empire and then the summer capital of the Achaemenid Persian kings. Alexander the Great captured Ecbatana in 330 and, according to Strabo, looted a huge sum from its treasury. It was subsequently employed as a summer residence by the Seleucid monarchs, to whom it owed the new name Epiphaneia. Then it passed into the hands of the Arsacids (Parthians)—who maintained the custom of residing there during the summer—and subsequently became part of the Sassanian (Persian) empire.

Ecnomus, Eknomon. A hill in southern Sicily (Poggio Sant'Angelo or Monte Cufino), rising just above the coast. Phalaris, autocrat ('tyrant') of Acragas (Agrigento) (*c* 570/65–554/549 BC), possessed a fortress in the neighborhood, and Agathocles of Syracuse was defeated there by the Carthaginians (311). The town of Phintias (Licata) was founded beneath the hill and named after its founder, the ruler of Acragas (282/80).

In the waters off the adjacent Cape Ecnomus, the Romans, under Lucius Manlius Vulso and Marcus Atilius Regulus, won an important naval victory over the Carthaginian fleet early in the First Punic War (256). This enabled them to carry the war to north Africa, but not with initial success. In 249 the Carthaginian admiral Carthalo forced a Roman flotilla onto the shore near the cape.

Ed-Dimas *see* Thapsus

Edessa. A town at the entrance of the pass leading from the plain into Upper Macedonia (northern Greece), beside waterfalls of the river Voda—a branch of the Lydias (Loudhias)—on the edge of a semicircular plateau and backed by the northeastern foothills of Mount Bermium (Vermion).

The first inhabitants of the place were Bryges (Thracians). But then its strategic fortifiable location caused it to play an important part in Macedonian history: recent excavations of the Longos site reveal continuous occupation from *c* 700 BC onward. Subsequently Edessa became a station on Rome's Via Egnatia (*c* 130) extending across the Balkan peninsula. Although little of the acropolis has survived, important remains of the lower town are still extant, including walls going back to the fourth century BC; an early Christian basilica is also to be seen. From the Middle Ages until the present century the place was known by the Slavonic name of Vodena (after the river Voda).

Edessa, later Antiochia by the Callirhoe (Urfa). In northwestern Mesopotamia (now southeastern Turkey). Its river was the Scyrtus ('Leaper,' Daisan), a tributary of the Euphrates, and another tributary, the Balissos or Belichos (Beliç), had its source nearby. After long prehistoric existence under the designation of Urhai (Orrhoe), which is echoed by the modern name of Urfa (and gave the district the ancient designation of Osrhoene), the place was refounded as a military colony by Seleucus I Nicator (*c* 303/2), under the Macedonian designation of Edessa. Its coins under Antiochus IV Epiphanes (175–164) temporarily substituted the name of 'Antiochia by the Callirhoe' after a local spring (Rosas, Birket Ibrahim) filled with sacred carps, of which the waters flowed into the Scyrtus. Subsequently the city passed under Parthian rule, but *c* 132 became the capital of an independent kingdom of Osrhoene, enlarged by Pompey the Great (*c* 64).

Thereafter Edessa oscillated between dependency on Parthia and Rome. Caputured and sacked by Trajan in AD 116, it started its regal coinage under the Nabataean king Vaël (163), a Parthian client, who was displaced in 166/7 by Mannus VIII Philoromaeus, set on the throne by Avidius Cassius, the general of Lucius Verus and Marcus Aurelius. Mannus' successor Abgar IX the Great (*c* 177/79–212/14, with brief intermission), depicted with his family on a floor mosaic in a recently excavated hypogeum (subterranean tomb), was permitted by Septimius Severus to retain Edessa and part of his kingdom when Osrhoene became a Roman province (195). In his time Edessa was noteworthy for its most famous son, the king's friend Bardesanes (Bar-Daisan), who was converted to Christianity—in a form condemned as heretical because of its astrological fatalism and suspected dualism; he also has a claim to be regarded as the creator of Syriac literature, to which Arab civilization owed so much. The local bishop Palut took a stand against Bardesanes' theological aberrations. But the latter's church, which possessed an episcopal see of far-reaching importance, claimed as its founder one of the seventy-two disciples of Jesus named Addai, believed to have been sent to Edessa in response to a letter written by King Abgar the Black (*c* 9–46) to Jesus himself, whose alleged reply promising the city freedom from conquest was widely circulated. Meanwhile Caracalla had made Edessa a colony (*c* 215), and died nearby two years later. But the city reverted to royal rule under Abgar X (242–44), who issued coins displaying himself in the company of the emperor Gordian III; and the city, in his reign, provides our earliest surviving Syriac document on perishable material, a deed of sale found at Dura-Europos. The starving garrison of Edessa determinedly defended itself against the Sassanian Persian Sapor (Shapur) I (260) and subsequently the fortress was allotted an arms factory by Diocletian (284–305), who established it as the capital of his province of Osrhoene, which had become famous for its archers and horsemen. It served as the principal base of Constantius II (337–61) during the Persian wars at the end of his reign. When Jovian ceded Nisibis (Nusaybin), with other cities, to the Persians in 363, Saint Ephraim, the most famous of the Syrian literary fathers, settled at Edessa until his death there ten years later. But its renowned theological 'School of the Persians' was frowned on by eastern emperors because of its continued adherence to the teaching of Nestorius (d. 451), regarded as unsound on the unity of the two natures of Christ; so that they compelled some of its teachers to emigrate to Persia in 457, and closed the school down altogether in 489. *See also* Hieropolis Bambyce.

Edirne *see* Hadrianopolis

Egadi Islands *see* Aegates

Egesta *see* Segesta

Egypt *see* Aegyptus

Eion. A city in western Thrace, later Macedonia (northern Greece); at the estuary of the river Strymon (Struma), on the edge of marshy country. Eion was used as a base during the Persian invasions of Darius I and Xerxes I, who constructed river bridges above the town (480). In 476, its Persian governor Boges, in the face of an Athenian attack, threw all his treasure into the river, set fire to his palace, and killed his harem and himself; whereupon the Athenians entered the city and established a colony, which they employed as a starting point for naval expeditions to Thrace.

It gained greatly in significance after the foundation of Amphipolis (437), twenty-five miles up the river, which it served as a port. In 424, during the Peloponnesian War, both Amphipolis and Eion were threatened by a Spartan army under Brasidas. The Athenian general Eucles, at Amphipolis, appealed for help to the historian Thucydides, who was in command of a fleet at Thasos. Thucydides, with seven ships, arrived in time to save Eion, but Amphipolis had fallen a few hours earlier, and he was sent into exile, from which he did not return until twenty years had passed and the war was over.

Eisenstadt-Gölbesacken *see* Pannonia

Elaeus(s)a, later Sebaste (Ayaş). A city on the coast of Rough Cilicia (Cilicia Tracheia [Aspera], southeastern Asia Minor), situated on a shallow bay with an island (now a peninsula) in the center, providing a protected harbor. Founded in the second century BC (or perhaps the first, when it began to issue coinage), Elaeusa was given by Antony to King Tarcondimotus I of the Amanus and then *c* 20–17 to Archelaus I Philopatris of Cappadocia, who built a palace on the island—at which he often resided—and issued coins at Elaeusa, changing its name to Sebaste (Augusta). After his death in AD 17, and the annexation of Cappadocia by the Romans, a son of Archelaus may have succeeded him at Elaeusa, which subsequently, however, became the property (and mint) of Antiochus IV of Commagene (38–72). After his death, the city was loosely attached to a new Roman province combining the two Cilicias (Rough and Smooth [Pedias, Campestris]) and continued to issue abundant coinage, proclaiming its freedom and maritime distinction (*nauarchis*). Elaeusa was still prosperous in the fifth century AD, although its harbor silted up soon afterward.

Surviving remains include a theater and an aqueduct, and a temple of the Roman period at the high western extremity of the bay. This building was subsequently converted into a church; another, too, exists on the island. There is also an enormous number of tombs around Elaeusa, mostly dating from the second century AD onward and clustering thickly, in particular, along the coast road. Fortresses in the vicinity may have been outposts of the priestly kingdom of Olba (Uğura).

El-Araisch *see* Lixus

Elatea *see* Phocis

Elba (Island) *see* Ilva

Elbe, River *see* Albis

Elche *see* Ilici

El-Djem *see* Thysdrus

Elea, earlier Iele, later Velia (near Castellamare di Velia). A Greek city on the coast of Lucania (southwest Italy), near its border with Campania; situated on a previously uninhabited site on the edge of a spur of the Apennines, between two rivers (the Palistro and the Fiumarella Santa Barbara). When a naval engagement against the Carthaginians and Etruscans, the Battle of Alalia (*c* 535 BC), had weakened the hold of the Greeks (colonists from Phocaea [Foca] in Ionia) over Corsica, a party of them left the island, and after a stop at Rhegium (Reggio di Calabria) settled at Elea (named Iele on its earliest coins). The colonization was celebrated in epic verse by the exiled philosopher Xenophanes of Colophon, but soon the new city became famous for its own great Eleatic school of philosophy, led by Parmenides (born *c* 515)—who reputedly gave the colony its constitution—and then by his friend and pupil Zeno (born *c* 490). For Elea, according to Diogenes Laertius, though an inconsiderable city, was capable of producing great men.

Enjoying access to two harbors, the place became prosperous from fishing and trade, and maintained close relations with Massalia (Marseille), which, in consequence, was sometimes regarded, perhaps with a measure of truth, as its colonizer (they shared the same Phocaean origin). A member of the league of Italian Greeks defeated by Dionysius I of Syracuse (388–386), Elea, now known as Velia, subsequently became a faithful ally of Rome, furnishing it with a stronghold against the Carthaginians. Among the Romans who owned a villa nearby were Gaius Trebatius Testa, a friend of Cicero, who, during a visit to Testa, conducted an important political conversation with Brutus, another local householder (44). Augustus' doctor Antonius Musa advised Horace to take the curative waters of Velia, and the city had a well-known medical school, supposedly based on the principles of Parmenides.

Excavations have now revealed remains of the original colony, with polygonal masonry and unbaked brick structures. There are remains of two, or three, circuits of walls—one of the gates (the Porta Rosa) has survived—and traces of a number of temples, including a large Ionic shrine on the acropolis, from which the dwelling quarters were moved to the lower town in the early fifth century BC. Traces of a colonnaded marketplace (agora) area can also be seen. Like other sections of the city, the agora shows signs of a number of reconstructions, which have prompted the theory that Elea-Velia suffered unexplained disasters in the third century BC and the first and late fifth centuries AD. But in any case, the absence of useful agriculture, isolation from important roads, and the silting up of the place's two harbors must all have contributed to its decline.

Elephantine *see* Syene

Eleusis (Elefsis). The most important center in Attica after Athens and the Piraeus; situated on a landlocked bay at the head of the fertile Thriasian plain, in a strategic position opposite the island of Salamis and at the junction of roads leading from Athens, the Peloponnese and northern Greece. Dating back to the Early Bronze Age, Eleusis took advantage of its naturally strong acropolis to remain independent of Athens, under its own kings; it was perhaps not until after *c* 675 that it became subject to the Athenians. It was devastated by Xerxes I's Persians in 480/79, by invading Transdanubian tribesmen (Costoboci) in AD 170, and by Alaric's Visigoths in 395—from whose depredations it never recovered.

Eleusis owed its enormous fame to the Mysteries in honor of Demeter and her daughter Persephone (Kore, the Maiden), which were already celebrated in the Mycenaean (Late Bronze) Age and, although the evidence for unbroken continuity is insecure, achieved Pan Hellenic status at about the time when the *Homeric Hymn to Demeter* was written (*c* 600 BC). The story was that Demeter, distraught owing to the seizure of her daughter by Hades (Pluto), came to Eleusis. There she was found seated beside the well by the daughters of the local king and taken into the royal household, where, to the accompaniment of miracles, she befriended the king's son Demophon. Revealing her identity, she retired to the temple built for her, until Zeus conceded that Persephone might return to the upper world for two-thirds of the year, thus restoring its fertility. Thereupon, before returning to Mount Olympus with her daughter, she revealed to the king of Eleusis 'the conduct of her rites and all her Mysteries.' Their character remained secret, so that Aeschylus, according to Aristotle, had to seek sanctuary when it was thought he had revealed them in a play. It appears, however, that the mystic, nocturnal, torchlight ceremonies enacted the rape of Persephone, and the arrival of Demeter at Eleusis in search for her, and that they culminated in a thanksgiving, accompanied by the tossing of the torches into the air. To the west of the city was the Rharian plain, where Demeter was said to have sowed the first seeds of corn, and the field of Orgas, planted with trees sacred to her and to her daughter. Belief in the afterlife was exalted by the cult.

At Eleusis itself, a *megaron* (porched house) of Mycenaean date (*c* 1500–1100 BC) seems to have been her first shrine. During the epoch that followed it was succeeded by a circular or apsed building, which in turn was replaced by a rectangular edifice soon after 600. In the second half of the same century, under the rule of Pisistratus of Athens, the precinct began to approximate to its final form, within a fortified, square-towered enclosure wall. The Telesterion (Hall of Initiation) was rebuilt on a square plan, with its roof held up by twenty-two columns, and tiers of rock-cut steps around three of the sides to provide seats for initiates. Within the building was a small storehouse for sacred relics, the Anaktoron or Holy of Holies. The cult was administered by two Athenian lay families, the Eumolpids and Kerykes.

After destruction by the invading Persians (480)—whose breach in the wall has been traced—the Athenian statesman Cimon embarked on major repairs and enlargements, followed by others undertaken by Pericles, under whom (after a false start by Ictinus, designer of the Parthenon) a new Telesterion—with forty-two columns—was planned by three other architects. The precinct was again expanded in the course of the fourth century, when a portico, known as the Stoa of Philo, was constructed, and a Temple of Hades built beside the Sacred Way, within a cave that was believed to be the entrance to the Underworld, through which the god had carried Persephone down to his realm.

About 50 BC the Lesser Propylaea was built by two Romans to fulfill vows made by their uncle Appius Claudius Pulcher, the author of a work on divination procedures dedicated to Cicero. The emperor Hadrian (AD 117–38) set up two triumphal arches identical with those he had erected at Athens. Marcus Aurelius, after the German incursion, gave orders for the construction of a Greater Propylaea, imitating its ancient Athenian counterpart. A temple was also built to the memory of his aunt Faustina the Elder, who had been deified (AD 141) and was hailed as the New Demeter.

Elikore *see* Nicaea

Elis, Walis ('valley'). A territory and city-state in the northwest of the Peloponnese (southern Greece). The nucleus of the region was Hollow Elis, in the basin of the river Peneus. According to tradition, it was settled by Dorians from Aetolia (on the north side of the Gulf of Corinth), under a certain Oxylus. The Eleans planted a colony at Buchetium on the Gulf of Ambracia (Arta) *c* 700 BC and two other colonies in Epirus in the 660s. They also annexed the regions to the south of Elis itself, notably Pisatis, which extended down to the river Alpheus. Within Pisatis was Olympia, and Elis gained control of the Olympic Games in about the sixth century, if not before (Strabo believed it had controlled them from the very beginning in 776).

Although little concerned with politics, the oligarchy that governed the territories under Elean control generally maintained relations of friendship and alliance with Sparta. But these were twice broken, first in 471, when the local ruling oligarchy gave way to a democracy, which founded the city of Elis, and then again in 420 (during the Peloponnesian War), when the Eleans sided with an anti-Spartan league owing to friction concerning the district of Triphylia, which lay to the south of Pisatis—so that it bordered on Sparta's dependency of Messenia—but had been annexed by Elis (with the exception of Lepreum) at about the middle of the century.

In the 360s the independence of Triphylia from Elis was sponsored by the Arcadian League. After coming under Macedonian rule in 322, however, the Eleans regained the territory through an alliance with the Aetolian Confederacy (245); but they lost it again after the campaign of Philip V of Macedonia (217). In 191 they were compelled to enter the Achaean League; whereupon their independence came to an end, although they won Triphylia back from the Romans in 146 and continued to maintain their prestige as neutral presidents of the Olympic Games.

The coins of Elis in imperial times are chiefly notable for two issues of Hadrian displaying figures of the Olympian Zeus of Phidias; these are the most faithful reproductions of that statue to have survived. Rescue operations on the site have securely fixed the boundaries of the city, and recent excavations have uncovered the 'South' or 'Corcyrean' Portico (Stoa) and Hellenistic buildings.

Elisavetovskaya *see* Tanais

El-Lejjun *see* Arabia

El-Manshah *see* Ptolemais Hermiou

El-Musheneq *see* Machaerus

El-Nahnasa *see* Oxyrhynchus

Elymais *see* Susa

Elysium, Elysion. A mythological concept that has no physical location. According to Homer it was a beautiful meadow at the western extremity of the earth, on the banks of the river Oceanus; Hesiod speaks of the Islands of the

Blest (*makaron nesoi*) beside Oceanus. It was in these idyllic surroundings that those favored by Zeus enjoyed a life of bliss after death. Among them were his son-in-law Menelaus and his son Rhadamanthys: who, according to Pindar, acts as the assessor of Cronus, presiding over those who have three times passed blamelessly through life. In later myth, notably Virgil's *Aeneid*, the Elysian Fields were situated in the Underworld (Hades), and regarded as thc dwelling place of those selected for special favor by the judges of the dead.

Emerita (Merida). A Roman city in the interior of Lusitania (now in western Spain). Situated on the right bank of the river Anas (Guadiana) at its confluence with the Alba Regia (Albarregas)—where traces of a river port have been discovered—it was founded in 25 BC by Publius Carisius, a general of Augustus, as a colony with extensive territory, and the name of Augusta, for veterans discharged after the Cantabrian Wars (reinforced and enlarged by further drafts under Otho, AD 69). It also became the capital of the Lusitanian province. Emerita was linked to the north by Augustus' road leading up to the Tagus, and its southern communications were assured by bridges across its own two rivers. Both these structures survive in substantial sections; fifty-seven of the sixty-four granite arches of the larger bridge, across the Anas, are still extant.

Other outstanding Roman monuments include an aqueduct (Los Milagros, 'the marvel,' bringing water from a reservoir three miles away), of which thirty-seven piers and ten three-tiered arches are preserved. There are also remains of temples of Mars, Concordia Augusta, Serapis, Mithras and the imperial cult (the last-named, in which many Roman sculptures have been found, was formerly known as the temple of Diana); a theater, constructed by Augustus' general Agrippa and rebuilt by Hadrian (AD 117–38), which accommodated 6,000 spectators and still shows a well-preserved (though partly restored) stage wall; an amphitheater with 15,000 seats; a circus accommodating no less than 30,000; and fortifications, including a monumental gate that Carisius illustrates on his coins. The Arch of Trajan (98–117; Arco de Santiago) is also to be seen. These fine structures are all the more remarkable because the district possessed no great natural wealth of its own. A remarkable cosmological mosaic dates from the mid-second century AD.

Later, the Christian community of Emerita became very important, and it was an episcopal see from *c* 250. In the following century, a luxurious house was converted into a Christian basilica and baptistery. At this period Emerita was said to have ranked as the ninth city in the empire. A find of 1,400 fourth- and fifth-century coins at Torrecaños (Guareña) in the neighborhood has recently been published, as well as a catalog of the important glass collection in the local museum.

Emesa (Homs). On the river Orontes (Nahr el-Asi) in Syria; a market town and caravan station built on volcanic basalt, at the point where the road from Palmyra (Tadmor) to the sea passed through a gap in the mountains. In the early 60s BC, during the final disintegration of the Seleucid kingdom, its monarch Antiochus XIII Asiaticus (whose claim to the throne had been recognized by the Roman general Lucullus) was kidnapped by Sampsiceramus, one of a line of princes controlling Emesa; and Pompey the Great confirmed Sampsiceramus' rulership of the city (*c* 63), although their friendship caused Cicero to make fun of Pompey as an oriental potentate. After the defeat of Antony by Octavian (the future Augustus) at Actium (31), the latter executed another king of Emesa, Alexander, for inciting Antony to kill his brother Iamblichus, whose son was restored in 20. In the seventies AD, however, the dynasty came to an end, and its principality was absorbed into the Roman province of Syria.

Emesa was famous for its temple of El-Gabal (called Heliogabalus by the Greeks and Romans; the site is now occupied by the Great Mosque), to which, according to Herodian, all the neighboring princes sent rich gifts every year. The shrine, which is depicted on several series of local coins, contained a huge black conical stone, probably a meteorite, which was believed to have been sent down from heaven by Zeus. The successive chief priests, who wore spectacular costumes, belonged to a family known as the Bassiani (from a Syrian title *Basus*), descended from the former native dynasty. The daughter of one of these priests, Julia Domna, became the second wife of Septimius Severus (193–211), and one of the most remarkable of Roman empresses; she arranged for Emesa to be exempted from tribute. After their son Caracalla had been displaced by a coup (217), his successor Macrinus was overthrown by Domna's sister Julia Maesa, who placed her own fourteen-year-old grandson, the current high priest of Emesa, on the Roman imperial throne, with the designation of Marcus Aurelius Antoninus (which had also been the names of Caracalla): but we know him as Elagabalus, because his four-year reign (218–22) witnessed the importation to Rome of the Emesan cult stone, and the elevation of the god (described on coins as *Deus Sol Elagabalus*) to the supreme position in the imperial cult. His cousin Severus Alexander (222–35), who succeeded him, sent the stone back to Emesa. It was the birthplace of the novelist Heliodorus, author of the *Aethiopica*, who may have lived at about the same time.

During the latter years of the century, the rise of the princes of Palmyra caused the partial eclipse of Emesa, and its history was turbulent. In 253/4 gold coins depicting the holy stone were issued by the chief priest of the time, Uranius Antoninus, who while holding out against the Persian king Sapor (Shapur) I momentarily asserted his own independence. In 262 a further usurpation of the purple, by Macrianus and Quietus, came to an end when Odenathus of Palmyra, acting for the central Roman government, attacked Emesa and put Quietus and his praetorian prefect to death. When, shortly afterward, Odenathus' widow Zenobia abandoned Palmyra's previous loyalty to Rome, the emperor Aurelian routed her general Zabdas near Emesa (273), which forced her army to fall back to final defeat at Palmyra. Emesa subsequently became an important Christian center. The principal monument surviving until recent times, a tall, two-storeyed funerary tower, has been destroyed and replaced by the railway station.

Emona, Aemona (Ljubljana, Laibach). A Roman city on or beyond the northeast frontier of Italy (now the capital of Slovenia, Yugoslavia), at the junction of the rivers Ljubljanica and Gradaščica in the upper valley of the Savus (Sava). According to legend, the place was founded when the fleeing Argonauts wintered there. After prehistoric settlement, it belonged to the Illyrians (from whose language it derives its name) and then, in the second and first centuries BC, to the Celtic tribe of the Taurisci. Under Octavian (Augustus), Emona served as a legionary base and river port; it became a colony for ex-soldiers either in 34/33 BC or during the reign of Tiberius (*c* AD 15), when its legion was transferred to Carnuntum. In the second century AD Emona was attached to Italy (as Ptolemy recorded), but also, in view of its position on the principal road across the Julian Alps, possessed economic ties with Upper Pannonia. Under the reorganization of Diocletian (284–305) it seems to have been attached to the new district or province of Venetia Histria.

The ancient topography of the city is now clarified. Its fortified *Porta Praetoria* has been excavated and preserved, in addition to a residential block (Jakopičev Art). Emona was the seat of a bishopric, and part of a Christian center—including an octagonal baptistery—has been uncovered, dating back to the end of the fourth century, when St. Jerome was corresponding with friends in the city. Alaric the Visigoth camped at Emona (408), and it was probably destroyed in the middle of the century by Attila the Hun.

Emporiae, formerly Emporion (Ampurias). On the northeast coast of Spain, at the end of the Gulf of Rosas on the Costa Brava. Shortly after 600 BC Greeks from Phocaea (Foca) in Ionia (western Asia Minor)—followed before the end of the century by settlers from the Phocaean colony of Massalia (Massilia, Marseille)—occupied the island of Palaia Polis or Palaeopolis, 'Old City' (San Martin d'Ampurias, now attached to the mainland), where they constructed a Temple of Ephesian Artemis. Then a trading post (Neapolis) was established on a mainland promontory just across the strait, using the mouth of the river Clodianus (Fulvia) as a harbor. This settlement, soon achieving the dimensions of a city, received fresh drafts of colonists and reached the height of its importance from the fifth to the third centuries as Massalia declined. Its inhabitants benefited from their manufacture of flax and other agricultural products, and from their location on the great military highway from the north to the south of the Iberian peninsula.

Becoming an ally of Rome, Emporiae was the landing port for Roman troops during the Second Punic War (218–211) and again (after the creation of the province of Hispania Citerior, Nearer Spain) in 195, when Marcus Porcius Cato established a military camp near the town. The adjacent native settlement of Indica, occupied by the native Indigetes, was separated from the Graeco-Roman city by a wall which, according to Livy, both sides vigilantly manned against one another, although contacts, if not always peaceful, were frequent and close. As a *municipium,* established by Julius Caesar in 45 BC, Emporiae recommenced the issue of coinage (with designs that made no reference to Rome), but after Augustus replaced it by Tarraco (Tarragona) as the capital of the province (now named Hispania Tarraconensis), it went into eclipse, a process accelerated by the combined effects of the silting of its port, a Frankish invasion in AD 265, and the rise of a rival city, Barcino (Barcelona).

The Greek settlement of early days was overlaid by the much larger Roman city; the centers of both can be traced as a result of excavations. The principal temple was dedicated to Asclepius (Aesculapius), and there were shrines of Serapis and of Rome and Augustus. A porticoed *agora* or forum has also come to light, in addition to shops and houses and a cistern for filtering water through charcoal and sand.

Enkomi *see* Salamis (Cyprus)

Enna *see* Henna

Enoz *see* Aenus

Epano Englianos *see* Pylos

Ephesus (Selçuk). A city of Ionia (western Asia Minor) which in ancient times stood on the south side of the long narrow estuary of the river Cayster (Küçük Menderes), though silt has driven the coastline increasingly farther to the west. Amazon founders were cited, but the population also claimed descent from Ionian colonists led by Androclus—son of the legendary Athenian king Codrus—who was alleged to have driven out the pre-Greek inhabitants (Carians and Leleges) before the end of the second millennium BC.

The initial monetary issues ascribed (despite some dissent) to Ephesus, in the seventh century, display the earliest inscription on any coin, 'I am the badge of Phanes.' Ephesus maintained itself against Cimmerian invaders (migrating from south Russia) *c* 650, but during the following century was obliged to accept the suzerainty of Croesus of Lydia and then of the Persian king Cyrus II. Among the natives of the city, in these periods, were the satirical poet Hipponax and the philosopher Heraclitus. When the Ionians rebelled against the Persians, its people slaughtered the inhabitants of Chios (their commercial rivals) after the Greek defeat at Lade (495).

From *c* 454 the Ephesians paid tribute to Athens, but in 412, during the Peloponnesian War, they joined the general revolt against its domination and sided with Sparta. After a time, they sought to abandon this allegiance, but their city was ceded to the Persians by the King's Peace or Peace of Antalcidas (387), passing into the hands of Alexander the Great in 333. After further vicissitudes, it was conquered and replanned by Lysimachus, who imported numerous new citizens and launched the city—under the name of Arsinoeia—on its Hellenistic career of wealth and prosperity (294), exemplified by the earliest issue of the later widespread *cistophori* (silver tetradrachms showing the sacred Dionysiac chest) shortly before 200. Handed over by the Romans to Pergamum (189), Ephesus was granted freedom in the will of the kingdom's last monarch, Attalus III (133), and retained this status under the Romans, who made it the capital of their province of Asia. In 88, however, it joined other cities of the region in massacring Roman citizens at the instigation of Mithridates VI of Pontus, thus incurring heavy punishment from Sulla; and twice, subsequently, it took the losing side in Roman civil wars.

Nevertheless, in imperial times it rivalled Pergamum in importance, serving as the residence of the emperors' financial representatives (procurators) in the province. It was here that the population, egged on by the silversmiths, delivered their famous protest against St. Paul, described in the *Acts of the Apostles*; the *Letter to the Ephesians*, traditionally ascribed to his hand, forms part of the New Testament. According to one version, Ephesus was also the last home of the Virgin Mary, who had supposedly been lodged nearby by the apostle St. John In AD 431 the Third Ecumenical Council, held at Ephesus, reconfirmed her worship as *theotokos*, the Mother of God.

By this time, however, the city was long past its zenith. Severely damaged by the Goths *c* 262, it had suffered gravely from silting, which made its harbor almost useless. In earlier times, however, Ephesus had put its commanding position, at the western end of the Cayster trade route into the Asiatic interior, to remarkable use. Strabo called it the greatest business center of the entire peninsula, sending ships to all quarters of the known world, and 'growing richer every day.' Aristides described the city as the bank of Asia.

But it owed by far its greatest distinction to its Temple of Artemis, preserving, in amended form, an ancient cult of the Anatolian mother-goddess, whose memory was perpetuated by her curious cult statue, displaying twenty-four breast-like, egg-shaped, protuberances and animals carved in high relief. After an earlier shrine had been destroyed by the Cimmerians, the Artemisium was reconstructed, with the aid of Croesus of Lydia, by the Cretan architects Chersiphron and Metagenes, who started work *c* 560 BC. In 356 their temple was burned down, but subsequently rebuilt—and endowed with masterpieces by the greatest living Greek artists—after the assistance of Alexander the Great had been refused. The appearance of the shrine can be reconstructed from several coin-types, and especially from a recently discovered piece of Maximus (AD 236/8). Attacked again *c* AD 253 and 262/3 (or 267) by Gothic invaders, it suffered complete destruction after the empire had become Christian. Thereafter its site was wholly sunk in swamps, so that in the nineteenth century it took six years even to discover where it had been—thirty feet beneath the surface.

The three earliest Greek settlements were, first, on the northeastern slope of Mount Pion (Panayır Dağı), second, beside the Artemisium, and, third, in the valley and on its adjoining broad slopes between Mounts Pion and Coressus (Bülbül Dağı). The last-named site was also the location of the Hellenistic and Roman city. Its surviving monuments are among the most impressive and extensive of the classical world. Excavations have revealed the straight West Road of Lysimachus, paved with marble and lined with colonnades, which formed a grandiose entry from the harbor, and was crossed at right angles by the equally imposing Marmorean Way, leading south to the Library of Celsus and Temple of Isis and north to the Gymnasium and Stadium. Beside this crossroads rise the walls of one of the largest of all ancient theaters—the building in which the uproar against St. Paul took place. Archaeologists have also uncovered the street of the religious brotherhood of the Curetes, which leads steeply up the valley to the plateau south of Mount Pion.

The buildings adjoining the street include the Prytaneum (Town Hall); a small theater (Odeon); an arched and richly ornamented Temple of Hadrian (AD 117–38); the Heroum of Titus Julius Celsus Polemaeanus (consul in 92) which was converted into a library by his son and has recently had its facade reconstituted; a *nymphaeum* (house of fountains); and the lately revealed, elaborate 'Baths of Varius,' rebuilt at the end of the fourth century AD by the wealthy Christian lady Scholastica, of which the important floor mosaic, like others, is being conserved by new methods. Residential blocks, likewise uncovered, offer unique insight into the domestic architecture and mural painting of the eastern Roman empire.

The Council Church at Ephesus, the location of the Third Ecumenical Council (see above), is a triple-aisled columnar basilica of the fourth century AD, built over earlier structures. It was also known as the Church of St. Mary, but the House of the Blessed Virgin (Mereyemana), a famed center of pilgrimage since its supposedly miraculous discovery, is at Panayia Kapulu, five miles south of Selçuk, on a sacred site of the fertility cult going back to early pagan times. At Selçuk itself is the Church of St. John, originally a mausoleum on the apostle's believed grave, replaced in the sixth century by a domed basilica that has now been excavated and restored. On the north slope of the Panayir Dağı was a pilgrim church, with catacombs, constructed over an earlier burial area known as the Grotto of the Seven Sleepers, the place where seven or eight soldiers were believed to have fallen into a miraculous sleep during Trajanus Decius' persecution of the Christians in 250, from which they awakened in the time of Theodosius II (408–50), bearing witness to the Resurrection of the Dead. The Grotto has been recently excavated.

Between Ephesus and what is now the town of Koz Pinar lies the village of Belevi; its ancient name is unknown. In its vicinity, two important tombs are to be seen. One is a great mausoleum, consisting of a cube of rock surmounted by a rectangular marble chamber; it is approached through a Corinthian colonnade, above which winged lions were set in pairs. This structure is now ascribed to the fourth century BC, when the territory was under Persian control. The second tomb is dug out of the top of a hill, penetrated by a fifty-foot tunnel which leads to two burial chambers. Although its date is uncertain, once again attribution to the fourth century seems plausible. The proximity to the Artemisium of Ephesus suggests a hero-cult, perhaps dedicated in the 330s to Pixodarus Euangelus of Halicarnassus (Bodrum), the brother of Mausolus, whose Mausoleum at that city certain features of these buildings recall.

Epidamnus *see* Dyrrhachium

Epidaurus. A Greek city in the Argolid (northeastern Peloponnese) on the rocky hill of a small peninsula (Acte, Nisi) within a recess of the Saronic Gulf. Homer's *Iliad* reports its participation in the Trojan War. First occupied by Carians from southwestern Asia Minor (hence, according to Strabo, its early name Epicarus), and then settled by Ionian Greeks, Epidaurus subsequently passed into the hands of Dorians, coming, it was said, from Argos. A natural stronghold, enclosed by high mountains, it belonged in the seventh and sixth centuries BC to a religious league (Amphictyony) based on a cult of Poseidon on the island of Calauria; but shortly before 500 its ruler Procles married his daughter Melissa to Periander of Corinth, who killed her and annexed the city.

The Epidaurians paid a religious tax to Argos but remained independent, and at one time (according to Herodotus) controlled the island of Aegina, which subsequently, however, was hostile. After participation in the Persian Wars (480–479) the city consistently sided with Sparta, but became a member of the Achaean League (243) and later came to be recognized as a friend and ally by Rome. Epidaurus was renowned for a sanctuary dedicated to the healing god Asclepius (Aesculapius), of whom it claimed, with the support of Delphi (despite competition from elsewhere) to have been the birthplace and to possess the oldest cult. This Asclepieum, located in a valley six miles from the city—the site of four-yearly Panhellenic Games and horse races—superseded a shrine and festival of the god's father Apollo (Malos or Maleatas) on nearby Mount Kynortion, of which recent excavations indicate Mycenaean origins and a revival of the cult in the later seventh century BC.

Finds at the Asclepieum do not go back to very early times, but the cult enjoyed a vigorous upsurge from *c* 380/75, when poetry and music contests were added to the Games and a great new temple was built by the architect Theodorus. It offered therapy based on psychosomatic principles, and became the model for similar shrines in many parts of the Mediterranean world, attracting innumerable offerings and monuments. The gold and ivory statue of Asclepius, made by Thrasymedes of Paros in the first half of the fourth century, is reproduced on coins, but has not survived; of the temple itself—which was looted by Sulla in 87 and pirates in 67—nothing has survived but foundations. But numerous other structures connected with the sanctuary offer more extensive remains, including a dormitory, a hostel with four courtyards, and the physiological department for curative bathing. Restorations of the time of Antoninus Pius (AD 138–61) are evident. Today, however, the most notable building of Epidaurus is its theater, the best preserved in Greece, constructed of local limestone *c* 300 by Polyclitus the Younger of Argos, and famous in antiquity for its harmonious proportions. Despite enlargements in the second century, the auditorium still retains remarkable acoustic properties today. Another, smaller, theater (odeum) has also been discovered. A circular building (*tholos*), of which the interior was decorated with painted panels by Pausias, was likewise designed by Polyclitus. When there was a serious outbreak of plague at Rome in 293 BC, the Senate sent envoys to Epidaurus asking for the dispatch of the serpent sacred to Asclepius. In AD 395 Alaric's Visigoths raided the sanctuary. During the sixth century the replacement of the pagan healing god by Christ and the saints was signalized by the construction of a five-aisled Christian basilica. New studies of the principal buildings of Epidaurus are now published, and the underwater remains of the harbor have been photographed by balloon-borne camera.

Epiphaneia *see* Ecbatana

Epirus. A territory that now lies partly in northwestern Greece and partly in southern Albania. Epirus comprises four high mountain ranges, parallel to the coast and enclosing narrow valleys that provide pasture but not very much grain. Bronze Age shepherds and hunters brought Indo-European river-names, and Mycenaean remains have been found at the oracular shrines of Zeus at Dodona and of the Dead beside the river Acheron. In the early Iron Age three main groups of Doric-speaking tribes emerged in Epirus, the Chaones (north-west), Molossi (central, around Dodona), and Thesproti (southwest). Far more developed, however, were the maritime colonies, founded by Greek city-states, notably Corcyra (on an adjacent island) and Ambracia (Arta on the mainland, beside the southern border of Epirus).

As to the Epirotes themselves—famous for their splendid horses and cattle—it was the Molossi who first unified the greater part of the country, in a confederacy under their king Alexander I (342–330), brother-in-law of Philip II of Macedonia. Then Pyrrhus I (297–272), establishing his capital at Ambracia, placed Epirus on the world stage by expanding his kingdom in every direction and launching an invasion of Italy and Sicily, where he confronted the Romans and Carthaginians (280–275). But his successors became involved in endless internecine wars, and *c* 232 the monarchy came to an end. The federal Epirote League, which later replaced it, split up, and the Molossi, in opposition to neighboring tribes, fatally decided to support the losing cause of Perseus of Macedonia against Rome. In consequence, a Roman army devastated the country and deported 150,000 of its inhabitants into slavery (167). Those who remained were subsequently attached to the new province of Macedonia (146).

After his victory over Antony at Actium (31), Octavian (the future Augustus) depopulated most of the Epirote cities (including Ambracia) in order to find inhabitants for his new foundation of Nicopolis, which henceforth dominated the southern part of the country. When he subsequently made Achaea into a separate province (27), it included most of Epirus. In the first or second centuries AD, however, Epirus became a province on its own account, developing urban life in the interior (as a new city-name, Hadrianopolis, testifies). The reorganization of Diocletian (AD 284–305) subdivided this province into two, an Old (southern) and New (northern) Epirus, with their capitals at Nicopolis and Dyrrhachium (Durrës) respectively. *See also* Actium, Ambracia, Buthrotum, Dodona, Dyrrhachium, Nicopolis, Sybota.

Erchomenos *see* Orchomenus

Ereğli *see* Heraclea Pontica, Perinthus

Eretria. A city on the Aegean island of Euboea, situated at the central point of its west coast, where the channel widens from the narrow strait of the Euripus, which divides the island from Boeotia and Attica. Eretria was settled in the Bronze Age; Strabo records that it had been formerly called Melaneis, and that after the Trojan War it was settled by Aielus from Athens, taking its name from a marketplace in that city; although he also points out, first, the existence of an earlier local place name Arotria, and, second, an alternative derivation from Eretrieus of Macistus in Triphylia (Peloponnese). 'Old Eretria,' which Strabo likewise mentions, may perhaps have been the same as Lelanton (*qv*), identified with Lefkandi nearby, where a foundry of *c* 900 BC has been discovered.

Together with its northern neighbor Chalcis, Eretria played a leading part in the renewed diffusion of Mediterranean trading and expansion that followed. According to Strabo, the city (strengthened by settlers from Elis) could put many troops into the field, and ruled over Andros, Teos, Ceos and other islands. But its most important enterprise was the foundation of a colony on Corcyra (Corfu), with outposts on the mainland opposite, which guaranteed domination of the straits. In the later eighth century Chalcis and Eretria began the colonization of the Chalcidice (Macedonia). But Eretria also joined forces with Chalcis and Cyme (probably another place on the island, not the city of Aeolis in western Asia Minor) in founding Pithecusae (Ischia) and Cumae (Cuma) in Campania (southwest Italy); their intention was to secure copper and iron from Etruria in exchange for gold imported by the Euboean states from trading stations such as Al Mina and Posidium (Ras-el-Bassit) in Syria. But a prolonged and disastrous war with Chalcis toward the end of the eighth century BC—in which the possession of the Lelantine Plain, which lay between the two cities, was at stake—ended in the virtual exhaustion of both contestants.

Eretria's support of the Ionian Revolt against Persia (499/8) brought down on it the vengeance of Darius I, whose generals Datis and Artaphernes besieged and burned the city shortly before the battle of Marathon (490). It was soon rebuilt, however, and (although Themistocles compared its people to the octopus or cuttle-fish that was their emblem, 'because they had a sword but no heart') it became a member of the Athenian-controlled Delian League and then the Athenian empire. In the course of the Peloponnesian War, however, the Euboean cities launched a general revolt against the Athenians, uniting in a league under the leadership of Eretria (411). Once again it became a member of an Athenian League (the Second, 378/7); and once again it revolted (349), but thereafter, following various political oscillations, spent the third century under Macedonian control. During these periods Eretria remained the most important and prosperous city of Euboea; it was the birthplace of the renowned painter Philoxenus (later fourth century), and the center of a school of philosophy under Menedemus (died *c* 265). During the Second Macedonian War, however, it suffered destruction at the hands of the Romans and their Pergamene allies (198) from which it never wholly recovered, though it was recognized as 'free' (except for a brief period of attachment to Athens under Augustus) and still continued to issue coinage in Roman imperial times.

Recent excavations have cast much light on the town plan of ancient Eretria, in which the drained deltaic mouths of a local river were employed as roads from early times. Attic pottery of *c* 875–825 comes from the nucleus of the early settlement, and incineration tombs beginning at about the same epoch have been brought to light. Walls date back to the eighth century and from *c* 700 (when a new defensive complex was created). There has been a unique discovery of a hoard from a goldsmith's shop of the latter period. Successive temples of Apollo Daphnephorus—despite chronological controversies—seem to have started with a wooden shrine of the eighth or seventh century, destroyed by the Persians in 490; fragments of a fine pediment of Theseus abducting the Amazon Antiope (in the Chalcis museum) belong to its reconstruction, perhaps in the 470s. A mid-fourth-century Doric temple of Dionysus has also been located. Rich finds in an unusual Heroon (shrine of heroes) go back to the eighth century and culminate in splendid Hellenistic edifices; a 'House of Mosaics' contains three panels of polychrome pebble floor mosaics of mid-fourth-century date. Eretria also provides one of the best-known examples of a Hellenistic theater.

Erice *see* Eryx

Erymanthus, Erymanthos. A high range of mountains in northwestern Arcadia (Peloponnese, southern Greece), after which the Erymanthian Boar was named. It was the Fourth Labor of Heracles to trap this beast in deep snow on the mountain and bring it back alive to Eurystheus, king of Mycenae. The highest peak of the range is Mount Olonus. A river Erymanthus flowed south from the mountains to join the Alpheus, and this was also the earliest name of the Arcadian city of Psophis.

Erythrae, Erythrai (Ildırı). A town in Ionia (western Asia Minor), on the coast opposite the island of Chios, beside a river named by its coins as Axos and Aleon (of which the waters, according to Pliny the Elder, caused hair to grow on the body). The town was said to have been inhabited by Lycians, Carians and Pamphylians, and later by settlers from various parts of Ionia under Cleopus or Cnopus, a descendant of the legendary Athenian King Codrus (the coinage also names a mythical warrior Erythrus as founder).

The possessor of abundant grazing and a hundred miles of rugged coastline, containing purple fisheries (hence the city's name, 'crimson'), Erythrae became a member of the Panionian (Ionian League) and subsequently came under the domination of Lydia and Persia, against which, in the Ionian revolt, it sent eight ships to the battle of Lade (494). It joined and left Athens' Delian League, and rebelled against renewed Athenian domination in 412, during the Peloponnesian War. A sixteen-line decree emanating from Athens, which has recently been discovered, indicates that in 394–386 this and other Ionian cities were free of Persian influence. In the fourth century Erythrae became friendly with Mausolus and Hermias, rulers of Halicarnassus (Bodrum) and Atarneus respectively. Alexander the Great planned to cut a canal through its peninsula. After subsequent association with the Pergamene kingdom, it became a free city attached to the Roman province of Asia (133).

The podium of its sanctuary of Athena Polias, revealed by recent excavations, dates back to the eighth century. The building was destroyed in 545, and reconstructed *c* 530. The shrines of Heracles (Ipoctonus, slayer of an insect that destroyed the vines, whose cult-image, according to Pausanias, floated in on a raft from Tyre) and of Tyche (Fortuna)—both depicted on coinages of Roman imperial date—and the grotto of the Sibyl of Erythrae (a prophetess second only to the Sibyl of Cumae) have not been identified with certainty. But the landward fortifications are well preserved, and a theater has been excavated. An unusual floor-mosaic of third-century date has also been preserved.

Eryx (Erice). A city in northwestern Sicily, on a mountain of the same name (San Giuliano), eight miles northeast of Drepanum (Trapani). Founded by a native people, the Elymians, Eryx still displays walls going back to the eighth century BC, and reconstructed in later epochs. A dependency of Acragas (its coins would suggest) in the sixth century and of Segesta during the fifth, Eryx was subsequently occupied by the Carthaginians, with a brief intermission during the invasion of Pyrrhus of Epirus, 278/79. During the First Punic War, however, in 259, its inhabitants were evacuated and transferred to Drepanum (Trapani). In the further course of the war, the deserted town of Eryx passed temporarily into the hands of the Romans (249–244), who resumed their occupation on a permanent basis after hostilities were over.

They regarded Eryx with conspicuous favor because (as Virgil later stressed) its people, like themselves, traced their origins back to Troy through Aphrodite or Venus, the patron goddess of the city (derived from the Carthaginian Astarte) and mother of Aeneas. The cult of Venus Erycina was introduced to Rome at about the beginning of the Second Punic War (218–201), and in 181 a Roman temple was built in her worship, at which a 'day of whores' was celebrated each year—suggesting that ritual prostitution was also a feature of the original sanctuary at Eryx. This shrine on the Erycian acropolis, of which the podium and part of the precinct enclosure survive, was naturally held in great honor. A body of Roman troops was appointed to watch over its security, and the principal cities of Sicily were ordered to contribute toward its lavish upkeep.

Together with an elaborately jewelled bust of the goddess, the temple is depicted on a Roman *denarius* of *c* 57 BC (issued by the moneyer Gaius Considius Nonianus). On this coin the acropolis, on which the shrine stands, is surrounded by a wall with towers on each side and a gate in the center (a fine ring of walls can still be seen on the site, going back to Carthaginian times). The *denarius* recalls that the Roman commander Sulla's final victory in his civil war against the Marians took place near the temple of Venus Erycina at the capital (82); and the designs are apparently intended to express the moneyer's sympathy with the claim of his family's patron Pompey the Great to have succeeded Sulla as the special favorite of Venus. The Eryx temple, which at this time again belonged to Segesta, was restored by the emperor Claudius (AD 41–54).

Eski Antalya *see* Side

Ethiopia *see* Aethiopia

Etruria. A region of western Italy comprising the modern Tuscany together with the northern part of Lazio, down to the Tiber. For its city-states and towns, *see* Arretium, Caere, Calusium, Clusium, Cortona, Perusia, Populonia, Tarquinii, Veii, Vetulonia, Volsinii, Volaterrae, Vulci. Certain of these states also extended their power, influence and culture to northern centers (Artemium, Faesulae, Misa, Pisae, and, further north, Atria, Felsina [Bononia], Spina) and to the south (Capua, Picentia, Praeneste, Rome, Salernum). Benefiting from active trading exchanges with Greek markets—and then colonies—at Pithecusae and Cumae, the Etruscan city-states were at their greatest in the seventh and sixth centuries BC. After one of them, Veii, succumbed to the Romans soon after 400, the others, too, gradually passed under Roman control. In the later imperial epoch Etruria (under the name of Tuscia) was combined with Umbria to form a single Italian region.

Euboea, Euboia (Evvia). The largest island, after Crete, of the Aegean archipelago, a hundred and six miles long and between four and thirty miles wide, separated by a channel (reaching its narrowest point in the Euripus) from Attica and Boeotia (central Greece). Inhabitants of Euboea during the Bronze Age, the Abantes (Thracians from Abae in Phocis, according to Aristotle), are mentioned in the list of Greek ships in Homer's *Iliad*; mention is also made of Dryopes and Ellopes, although in historical times the population was Ionian.

For the island's history in the Iron Age and Persian Wars, *see* Chalcis and Eretria. Its cities revolted from the Athenian empire in 446 and again in 411 (during the Peloponnesian War) and subsequently changed hands on numerous occasions, though a League of Euboean states, formed in the later fourth century BC, maintained its existence until dissolved by the Romans for aid given to the Achaean Confederacy (146); at the same time the island was severely punished, made liable to tribute, and attached to the Roman province of Macedonia-Achaea (and from 27 onward to Achaea). In the second century AD Dio Chrysostom depicts the southern part of Euboea as desolate and deserted.

Euhesperides, later Berenice (Benghazi). A city situated on the coast of Cyrenaica (Libya), on the eastern shore of the Gulf of Syrtes Major (Sirte, Sidra). About 549 (?) BC colonists from Cyrene settled on a low hill forming a promontory that overlooked the north bank of a lagoon (Sebkh es-Selmani) connected with the sea. Air photography has revealed the ground plan of Euhesperides and the perimeter of its walls, and archaeologists have shown that most of its houses were made of mud bricks resting on stone foundations. The floors of these dwellings displayed what may be the earliest tessellated (as opposed to pebble) mosaics so far discovered.

But the lagoon was already drying out in antiquity (it is now a salt marsh), and in 247/6 Ptolemy III Euergetes of Egypt founded a new city farther to the southwest, once again on a low headland; it stood between the lagoon and the sea, and on its south side a shallow inlet served as a harbor. Excavations in what is now the Sidi Khrebish cemetery have uncovered a large quarter inhabited from the time of Ptolemy III onward for fourteen hundred years; forty sculptural and one hundred and fifty-nine terracotta fragments from the site have been published. An inscription of the first century BC alludes to civil disturbances and attacks by pirates, and reconstructions testify to damage in the Jewish Revolt (AD 115). By 153/4 the city was struggling for status, since the emperors favored Cyrene instead. A new defensive wall bears witness to threats from Marmaric tribesmen, whose rebellion was quelled *c* 268.

According to some versions the mythological Garden of the Hesperides, the nymphs who guarded the Golden Apples, was located in the region, where natural hollows have been thought to provide a suitable setting for the story. One of these hollows, four miles east of Berenice, contains an underground pool and river (Jokh el-Kebir), which may have been regarded as an entrance to the infernal regions, so that it would account for the name of Euhesperides' river-god

Lethon—like the underworld river Lethe—who is depicted on its coins. Lake Tritonias, shown to the stranded Jason and his Argonauts by the Hesperides (transformed into trees), is identified by some modern scholars with a lagoon (Buhayrat Bu Zazirah) three miles north of the city.

Eumolpia *see* Philippopolis (Thrace)

Eupatoria *see* Amisus, Cercinitis

Euphrates (Firat). The greatest river of western Asia, and the most westerly of the Two Rivers of Mesopotamia, the other being the Tigris. The section of the Euphrates forming the borderline between Mesopotamia (Osrhoene) and Syria became the frontier between the Roman and Parthian empires in 64 BC, and was continually fought over in subsequent years. Trajan's attempt to subjugate the valley of the Euphrates down to its mouth in AD 115–17 proved only transitory, but the Romans long remained masters of territories in northwestern Mesopotamia. *See* Circesium, Dura Europos, Osrhoene, Samosata, Zeugma.

Euripus strait, separating Euboea from central Greece. *See* Chalcis, Eretria, Euboea

Europus *see* Dura

Eurymedon, River *see* Aspendus

Eusebia *see* Tyana

Euxine Sea. The Greek name for the Black Sea—a euphemistic term, meaning 'friendly to travelers.' In mythology, the sea was famous for the story of the Argonauts, told in the epic poem of Apollonius Rhodius (third century BC), but probably first developed through the influence of maritime explorations by Miletus (Balat) in Ionia (western Asia Minor), which pioneered the colonization of its coast, from the eighth and more abundantly from the seventh century onward. For Greece the western and northern Euxine shores and hinterlands provided their main source of grain supplies for several centuries, receiving olive oil and wine in exchange. The earliest surviving account of the sea is by Herodotus. A fourth-century survey bearing the name of the (sixth century) Scylax of Caryanda gives more details about its southern shores and Arrian of Bithynia (second century AD) describes its entire coastline.

Evora *see* Ebora

Evvia *see* Euboea

Evvia

Exeter *see* Isca Dumnoniorum

F

Faesulae, formerly Visul (Fiesole). On a hill northeast of Florentia (Florence). After early Iron Age settlement, Faesulae was colonized by one of the Etruscan city-states, probably Volaterrae (Volterra), with which it was linked by a cross-country route and possessed cultural and artistic connections. The leading town of a rich agricultural zone extending southeastward along the Middle Arnus (Arno), Faesulae succeeded Artemium or Artumena (Artimino) and Quinto Fiorentino (Poggio del Giro) as the most important Etruscan center in the region. For it stood not only on the road from Volaterrae but also on a major northward thoroughfare from the Arnus across a principal Apennine pass, and was utilized as a springboard for further northerly Etruscan expansion, employing a route that led up into the intensely cultivated Mugello valley, where there was another settlement at Poggio Colla. Faesulae was also the headquarters of a quarrying and stone-carving industry, and became a full-fledged Etruscan city (and city-state) in the sixth or fifth century BC.

It supported Rome during the Second Punic War (218–201) and subsequently benefited from the extension of the Via Cassia to nearby Florentia (Florence). However, it joined the Italian rebels in the Social War, when it was defeated by Lucius Porcius Cato (89); and subsequently the city had to receive a colony of Sulla's ex-soldiers, which caused unrest among the expropriated landowners (as Cicero's comments on the Catilinarian conspiracy confirm). Nevertheless the height of Faesulae's prosperity was still to come, in the time of Augustus (31 BC–AD 14). Thereafter it was gradually eclipsed by Florentia. But in 406 it became the scene of an important event when the west Roman commander Stilicho repulsed the invasion of the Ostrogoths under Radagaisus, who, after his supplies had been cut off, was captured and executed; the victory earned Stilicho a triumphal arch at Rome.

Traces of a wall of the fifth century BC have come to light but the major part of the surviving fortifications of Faesulae dates from some two hundred years later. The temple of an Etruscan healing deity has been excavated, including annexes probably intended for pilgrims. Destroyed by fire, this shrine was rebuilt in the time of Augustus, to which the theater and baths also belong; but the baths also show traces of subsequent reconstruction, extending into the third century AD.

Falerii Veteres, Old Falerii (Civita Castellana). The chief town of the region of the Falisci in central Italy (now part of Lazio), which extended from a bend of the river Tiber to the west and to Lakes Sabatinus (Bracciano) and Ciminius (Vico) and the Ciminian Forest in the east. The towns of this Faliscan territory were perched on platforms of volcanic rock rising above the deep valleys of the Tiber's tributaries. In the eighth and seventh centuries BC the Faliscans already possessed an original and diversified culture of their own. Shortly afterward, however (if not earlier), they became subject to powerful influences from neighboring Etruria, so that—although their language was Indo-European, and they did not speak Etruscan—it was customary (as Livy and the elder Pliny record) to regard them as Etruscans. Moreover, they forged close links with the Etruscan city-state of Veii, which at least once, following a procedure known as the 'Sacred Spring' rite, sent colonists to the Faliscan town of Capena, famous for its sanctuary of the goddess Feronia. But the most important of the small group of Faliscan towns was Falerii Veteres. Like the city-states of neighboring Etruria, which it equalled in power in the seventh century BC, it stood on a defensible plateau bounded by ravines, through which flowed two tributaries of the Tiber, the Treia and the Maggiore. A number of foundation legends (often revealing Greek influences) included a story, told by Servius, that the same man, Halaesus, founded Falerii and Veii. During the sixth century Falerii enjoyed close relations with Rome. But when, like other Faliscan cities, it had sided with Veii against the Romans (*c* 396), it was besieged by them and, despite successful resistance, was compelled, together with Tarquinii, to agree to a treaty or truce in 358. Following two subsequent rebellions it was destroyed in 241, whereupon its surviving inhabitants were resettled at Falerii Novi (Santa Maria di Falleri), a site selected by the Romans because it was situated in the plain and could never be fortified against them. Falerii Novi was made a Roman colony by Gallienus (AD 260–68).

Fanum Fortunae (Fano). A city of eastern Italy in the territory known as the Ager Gallicus on the coast of Umbria (Marche), at the mouth of the river Metaurus (Metauro). Fanum Fortunae achieved importance because of its location on the Via Flaminia from Rome (220 BC); and it was also a staging point on the coastal thoroughfare joining the Via Aemilia (187), the road which opened up northern Italy. First mentioned in Caesar's *Civil War* as a place occupied by his troops after their crossing of the Rubicon (49), Fanum Fortunae received a colony of ex-soldiers from Octavian (the future Augustus), together with the name of *Colonia Julia* (later *Flavia*) *Fanestris.* The colony was equipped with fortified walls, punctuated by handsome gates, one of which, the three-arched and two-storeyed Arco di Augusto, still survives. But the temple of Fortune, which presumably gave the city its name, has not been traced.

Farkin *see* Tigranocerta

Fayum *see* Arsinoe

Feodosiya *see* Theodosia

Ferentium (Ferento, Acqua Rossa). A town in Etruria (now northern Lazio), four miles north of Viterbo, and southeast of Lake Volsiniensis (Bolsena). Situated in a territory scarred by deep ravines, Ferentium was an Etruscan foundation of some regional significance; and the considerable extent of its non-funerary remains (rare in Etruria) made it an important source for Etruscan art and architecture of the archaic period. Some 1,500 terracottas of the sixth century BC have been found within a single temple, and other discoveries include abundant decorative architectural terracottas belonging to private houses. It appears that the town was destroyed *c* 500, no doubt by a more powerful Etruscan neighbor.

After the Romans had secured control of the area *c* 265 BC, they constructed a new town slightly to the northeast of the original settlement. It was the birthplace of the emperor Otho (AD 69) whose family tomb has been discovered; and Flavia Domitilla, the wife of Vespasian, was probably also born at Ferentium. Its theater is one of the best preserved in Italy, probably going back to the late Republican period. Subsequently, however, the place dwindled into a village. (It is to be distinguished from Ferentinum [Ferentino], a town of the tribe of the Hernici, southeast of Rome.)

Ficana (near Acilia). An early Latin settlement between Rome and Ostia, on the northeastern extremity of Monte Cugno, part of a range of hills overlooking the plain on the left (south) bank of the Tiber. The site appears to have been continually occupied from the Late Bronze Age into the Iron Age, when a fortification system was developed (*c* 700 BC) supplementing natural defences (steep slopes) by an earthwork and ditch. A little earlier, the first permanent dwellings had been erected, consisting of huts, the oldest of which displays a curious elongated form, followed by substantial buildings in the mid-seventh century, constructed on foundations of cut tufa.

According to a tradition preserved by Livy and Dionysius of Halicarnassus, Ficana was one of the Latin towns captured and destroyed by the Roman king Ancus Marcius toward the end of the same century. This cannot be confirmed, but there does seem to have been some rebuilding after a fire at about that time. A necropolis of *c* 650–600 has been discovered, and the bodies of children were found buried beneath the huts (adults had to be buried outside the settlement). This practice continued after 600, when Ficana had assumed more modest dimensions. The middle years of the Roman Republic, however, witnessed a certain amount of replanning—perhaps in connection with a revival of the town's importance in relation to the Roman colony at Ostia—and extensive remains from this period, too, have come to light.

Fidenae (Castel Giubileo). In Latium (Lazio), west-central Italy. Situated on a hill overlooking the east bank of the Tiber (at a point where the river could be crossed) it became the first station on the Via Salaria, five miles north of Rome;

and it was the same distance, across the river, from the Etruscan city of Veii, which stands on a stream (the Valchetta, Cremera) meeting the Tiber just opposite Fidenae. It was a Latin town, founded, according to tradition, by the kings of Alba Longa. But its entry into the sphere of influence of the Veientines perhaps *c* 500 seemed to the Romans an intolerable affront, in view of its strategic and sensitive position.

The offending outpost still belonged to Veii *c* 477–475 when a member of the dominant Roman clan of the Fabii set up a frontier fort nearby—which an expedition from Veii promptly destroyed. But *c* 435 or *c* 425 the Romans seized control of Fidenae, probably converting it into a colony of the Latin League (an action attributed by legend to Romulus). This was an action leading inexorably to their decisive war against Veii, which resulted in the latter city's destruction (*c* 396). After the retreat of the invading Gauls (*c* 387) Fidenae rebelled against the Romans and suffered destruction at their hands, the stones of its buildings being used to construct the so-called Servian Wall around Rome (*c* 378). Nevertheless, the town continued to exist on an unimportant scale, possessing its own wooded amphitheater, which collapsed in AD 27 with serious loss of life, though the figures of 20,000 or even 5,000 casualties, quoted by Suetonius and Tacitus respectively, are evidently exaggerated.

Fiesole *see* Faesulae

Filosofiana *see* Philosophiana

Firmum Picenum (Fermo). A city of Picenum (Marche, east-central Italy) situated on a hill overlooking the Adriatic, four miles distant, on which it possessed a coastal fort (Castellum Firmanorum or Firmanum). A stronghold of the tribe of the Piceni in the early Iron Age, Firmum became a Latin colony in 264 BC, remained loyal to the Romans in the Second Punic and Social Wars, and supported Julius Caesar in his civil war with Pompey the Great (49), but in the further civil strife after Caesar's death took the side of the Republicans against Antony; as a punishment for which ex-soldiers were sent to settle at the place, with Roman colonial rights. Firmum decayed under the Principate, and fell to Alaric the Visigoth in AD 408.

Large rectangular blocks of the original colony's walls can still be seen, as well as the traces of a theater, but the most noteworthy surviving structure is a chain of cisterns (*piscina epuratoria*); more than twenty have been explored. The cathedral stands on the site of an early Christian church (itself replacing a pagan temple), of which a fifth century mosaic pavement survives.

Fishbourne, *see* Noviomagus

Florentia (Firenze, Florence). A city at the northeastern extremity of Tuscany, on the north bank of the Arnus (Arno) near its junction with the Mugnone. Neolithic objects of *c* 3000 BC have come to light, and a large necropolis (beneath the Piazza della Repubblica) dates from the ninth to the sixth century; Corinthian imports appeared *c* 600. Although the principal cities of the region in Etruscan times had been at Artemium (Artimino) and Faesulae (Fiesole), finds show that Florentia also attracted early attention (although the prehistoric site has not been identified) because of its favorable location at a river crossing and at the junction of north-south and east-west land routes, converted by the Romans into the Via Flaminia (220) and an extension of the Via Cassia respectively.

Subsequently the place became a Roman colony, perhaps through the initiative of Octavian (the future Augustus). In the reign of Tiberius (AD 14–37), according to the historian Tacitus, a Florentine mission visited Rome with the request that the river Clanis (Chiana) should not be diverted into the Arnus, since flooding would result; and they won their appeal. The city prospered in the second century, and during the later empire became the seat of the governor (*corrector*) of the district or province of Tuscia et Umbria. Procopius (born *c* 500) describes it as a considerable fortress.

The town-plan of Florentia resembled that of a Roman camp. Discoveries include the traces of brick-faced fortifications with round towers and three gates, a theater of the first century AD, an amphitheater of *c* 100, a private house, two bathing establishments, a sanctuary of Isis (second century), and the forum with its triple-shrined Temple of Jupiter Capitolinus, displaying two phases of construction and later transformed into the church of Santa Maria di Campidoglio. It is believed, however, that the most important remains of the city will be found beneath the Piazza Signoria, when this is more fully excavated; the service gallery of a bathing establishment has recently come to light. Beneath the Cathedral, originally known as Santa Reparata but later called Santa Maria del Fiore, are abundant remains of mosaic pavements and columns belonging to an earlier basilica of the fourth or fifth century. But to a Florentine living a thousand years later the adjacent baptistery was the supreme witness of the city's noble Roman origins. An eleventh- and twelfth-century enlargement of an earlier edifice, it has yielded coins of Honorius (395–421) and is believed by many to reproduce the shape of a building of about that period initiated by St. Ambrose, who also dedicated the first Basilica of St. Lawrence (San Lorenzo), consecrated in 393 and serving as the city's cathedral until replaced by Santa Reparata five centuries later. Another early church rebuilt in the thirteenth century, probably on fifth-century foundations, was dedicated to St. Ambrose himself; and Santa Felicita, across the river, dates back to about the same time.

Foça *see* Phocaea

Foce di Sele *see* Posidonia

Forchia *see* Caudine Forks

Formella, Fosso di *see* Cremera, River

Formiae (Formia). A Roman city on the Tyrrhenian (west) coast of Italy, situated in Latium (Lazio) on the Gulf of Caieta (Gaeta) eighty-eight miles southeast of Rome. Originally an Ausonian or Volscian harbor (though legend ascribed its foundation to Laestrygones or Greeks—from whose word *hormos,* anchorage, its name was dubiously said to have been derived), the place owed its prosperity to an abundant water supply, the marketing of wine (the famous Caecuban), and the production of olives and various fruits; its position on the Via Appia from Rome to Capua (312 BC) also provided a great impetus.

In 295 the territory of Formiae was plundered by Samnites; but in 188 it was promoted from partial (Latin) to Roman citizenship. However, further plunderings followed, at the hands of pirates (66) and Sextus Pompeius (43), the younger son of Pompey the Great. Yet Formiae continued at all times to be a resort for rich Romans and a favorite location for their seaside mansions, a number of which have left conspicuous remains. Among those who frequented the place were Pompey the Great and Cicero, who was assassinated near his Formian villa by soldiers of Antony after his proscription by the Second Triumvirate (43). But suggested identifications of his residence (the Villa Rubino) or tomb (the Tomba di Cicerone) are purely conjectural.

Forum Julii (Fréjus). A city on the southeast coast of Gaul (Var, France), near the Italian border; situated at the mouth of the river Argenteus (Argens). The place belonged to the tribe of the Oxybii, and traces of their pre-Roman settlement have been found. The name Forum Julii suggests that it was Julius Caesar who created a market town there, probably as a supply center during his campaign against Massalia (Massilia, Marseille, 49 BC); it was situated on an extension of the Via Aurelia, which passed through the main street.

Then Octavian (the future Augustus), after his victory against Antony at Actium (31), settled a colony of ex-soldiers at the place. He also sent the warships captured at Actium as a contribution to the major naval base that he now proceeded to associate with his new colony; hence its name *colonia Pacensis Classica,* from *classis,* fleet. The fleet was still there in AD 69, but the base gradually became less important, not least because the harbor (now entirely dry) was already beginning to silt up; although the place retained a degree of prosperity. Its most distinguished natives were the poet Gaius Cornelius Gallus (born *c* 69 BC; a friend of Augustus and Virgil) and Cnaeus Julius Agricola (father-in-law of the historian Tacitus, and hero of his *Agricola,* born AD 40).

Noteworthy remains of the port and fortifications survive. There are also a theater and an amphitheater, as well as an exceptionally well-preserved aqueduct, and excavations are adding new discoveries. Forum Julii became the seat of a bishopric at the end of the fourth century, and the earliest remains of the episcopal baptistery date from not long afterward.

Fosso Regina *see* Allia

Frattaminore *see* Atella

Fregellae (Opri). A city in Latium (Lazio), seventy miles southeast of Rome, in the territory of the Hernici; situated on the river Liris (Liri) near its junction with the Melfa and other streams, and controlling a route to the Tyrrhenian Sea. In 328 BC the Romans blocked further northwestward expansion by the powerful Samnite group of peoples by establishing a Latin colony at the strategic site of Fregellae (328). This act (confirmed by recent excavations) precipitated the Second Samnite War (328–321), which (despite a temporary evacuation of Fregellae) was won by Rome and paved the way for the decisive Third War (298–290).

Served by the ancient Via Latina, the colony remained firmly loyal in Rome's wars against Pyrrhus of Epirus (280–275) and Hannibal (the Second Punic War, 218–201). In the second century, however, when its population had become largely de-Romanized by mass immigrations of Samnites and Paeligni, the city took the lead among Italian communities clamoring for full Roman citizenship, and in 125 actually took up arms in support of its claim. Rome's response was to wipe it out of existence, establishing a new colony in its place at nearby Fabrateria Nova (La Civita, near Falvaterra).

Fréjus *see* Forum Julii

Frigidus (Vipacco, Vipava, Wippach). A tributary of the river Aesontius (Isonzo), spanning what is now the Yugoslav-Italian border. In AD 394 the banks of the river were the scene of a decisive battle in which Theodosius I defeated and killed the usurper Eugenius, whose Frankish general Arbogast then committed suicide. The battle was regarded as a historic victory for the Christian church, since Theodosius was conspicuously devout, whereas Eugenius, although likewise a Christian, had allied himself with the powerful group of pagan Roman senators under the leadership of Nicomachus—and Arbogast had been an enthusiastic pagan. Early medieval sites in the region have been excavated.

Frisii, a Germanic people whose name is perpetuated by Friesland, a northern province of the Netherlands, but whose territory (together with its islands) extended southward as far as the Rhenus (Rhine) and northward to the Amasia (Ems). In 12 BC, during the reign of Augustus, the Frisians were subjugated by his stepson Nero Drusus (Drusus junior) and made liable to the payment of a tax consisting of ox hides. In AD 28, in protest against extortionate demands, they revolted, and the governor of Lower Germany, Lucius Apronius, was unable to put them down. In 47, however, according to the historian Tacitus, Corbulo—who later became a renowned general—compelled them to give hostages, live inside a reservation, and accept a stable government including a senate, administrative officers and laws of their own.

To enforce these arrangements, he established a fortified post in their territory. But not long afterward the Roman troops were withdrawn to the left bank of the Rhine; whereupon the Frisians attempted a further rebellion (58). In 69, too, during the Gallo-German uprising of Civilis, they were mobilized by the Canninefates (their southern neighbors across the Rhine) to launch an attack on a Roman camp from the sea; and they helped the Canninefates and Civilis' Batavian compatriots to win a land battle not far from the Rhine.

In the third century Frisian military units (*cunei Frisiorum*) served in the Roman army in Britain; and *c* 286–96 Frisia played an important part in the struggle waged by the central Roman government against Carausius and Allectus, who had usurped the purple in Britain—although there is some doubt about the relations between, and relative positions of, the Frisii and the Franks, who had extended their power as far as the Frisian coasts and islands.

Nevertheless, the Frisians still had a very important future ahead of them. During the fifth century the insufficiency of farmland on their marshy coasts caused some of them to join the Anglo-Saxon migrations to England. But those who stayed behind spread eastward as far as the Visurgis (Weser), gained control of the islands named after them, and expanded southward into the Rhine hinterland (Frisia Magna) as well. Constructing their dwellings on "torps" (artificial hillocks), and building a port at Dorestad (Wyk te Duurstede) on the Vatialis (Waal) mouth of the Rhine, these Frisians became a major maritime trading power at the outset of the medieval epoch.

Fucinus Lacus (Fucine Lake, Conca del Fucino). Situated in the territory of the Marsi, with their capital Marruvium (San Benedetto dei Marsi) beside its eastern bank, this was the largest lake in central Italy, covering an area of 38,000 acres. It possessed no visible outlet and was subject to sudden fluctuations in size, often flooding the surrounding countryside (for example in 137 BC).

In consequence, the emperor Claudius, pursuing an unrealized plan of Julius Caesar, attempted to drain the lake by digging a tunnel to connect it with the river Liris (Liri) between three and four miles to the south. Thirty thousand men worked on the project for eleven years, and its completion was accompanied by imposing celebrations in the emperor's presence (AD 52), which proved, however, according to the possibly exaggerated account of Tacitus, a dangerous fiasco (and weakened the position of the emperor's adviser Narcissus) because the waters got out of control and endangered the spectators. Repairs by Trajan (98–117) and Hadrian (117–38) proved equally ineffective. In the nineteenth century, however, the entire lake bed was drained and reclaimed for agricultural production.

Furculae Caudinae, Caudine Forks. A narrow defile in Samnium (south-central Italy) where the Samnites under Gavius Pontius inflicted a shattering defeat on the Roman consuls Titus Veturius and Spurius Postumius in 321 BC, during the Second Samnite War. The consuls advanced into the valley only to find it blockaded at both ends, whereupon, after vainly attempting to force their way out, they capitulated to avoid starvation. Pontius accepted their surrender on the condition that the entire defeated army should pass under a 'yoke' of spears, and six hundred Roman knights were handed over as hostages. The Romans did not win the war for another seventeen years, and a third war (298–290) was needed to bring final victory.

Three main sites have been suggested for the battle. The pass between Arienzo and Arpaia (subsequently flanked by soaring medieval castles) is the most likely—especially as it still contains a locality named Forchia.

G

Gabii (Torre di Castiglione, near Osteria dell'Osa). An ancient Latin city on the eastern shore of the small crater lake of Castiglione, which was probably drained in antiquity as it is now. The site was a strategic one, linked to Rome—twelve miles to the west-southwest—by the Via Gabina, and on the way to Praeneste (Palestrina) and Campania.

Gabii played an extremely important part in Roman legend and saga. Founded, according to Virgil, by Alba Longa, it was the place to which King Numitor was said to have sent the twins Romulus and Remus to receive their education. There was also a story that Rome's last king, Tarquinius Superbus, toward the end of the sixth century BC seized the town after his son Sextus had treacherously executed its leaders: an action the youth took because his father, when asked what should be done about Gabii, had silently switched off the heads of the tallest poppies in his garden with his stick. After the king's expulsion from Rome and the establishment of the Republic, Sextus withdrew to Gabii, where he was later assassinated. Then the Romans, it was believed, made a treaty of alliance with the city (493); and the alleged text of this agreement was discovered in the time of Augustus. It was inscribed, according to Dionysius of Halicarnassus, on a wooden shield covered with the hide of a sacrificial ox and kept in the Temple of Semo Sancus. The discovery was celebrated by *denarii* issued by one of the state moneyers. Roman tradition likewise called attention to the ancient association with Gabii by the adoption of its distinctive form of clothing, the *cinctus Gabinus,* a way of draping the toga that left both arms free. However, Gabii stood in a peculiar relationship with the capital, its land (according to Varro) being neither 'Roman' nor 'foreign' but 'dependent upon its own auspices.' These signs of its early significance have been confirmed by recent excavations, which reveal a rich and important cult center of the seventh and sixth centuries BC—which literary traditions of early shrines of Apollo and Juno evidently reflect.

During the years before and after 100 BC, the volcanic tufa stone of Gabii (*lapis Gabinus*)—hard and fireproof, but flaky—was widely employed for construction at Rome, to which it was transported on the river Anio (Aniene). By the 50s, however, according to Cicero, the place itself had shrunk to a mere village; the poets of the Augustan age spoke of its proverbial desolation. But they were exaggerating—or a recovery took place after their time—because in the second century AD Gabii was a flourishing *municipium* with fine buildings, including a lavish bathhouse.

Gadara (Umm Keis, Mukes). A city to the east of the river Jordan, southeast of Lake Gennesaret or the Sea of Galilee in Galaaditis (Gilead), which formed part of northeastern Judaea or southwestern Syria (Coele-Syria, 'Hollow Syria,' in a loose sense of the term) and now belongs to the state of Jordan. Gadara owned well-known hot springs in the nearby river Hieromax (Yarmuk).

Excavations indicate occupation since the seventh century BC. A third-century foundation by the Ptolemies has also been conjectured, but subsequent Seleucid suzerainty (notably in the time of Antiochus III the Great, 223–187) is demonstrated by the city's surnames Antiochia and Seleucia, to which Stephanus of Byzantium bears witness. During this period Gadara attained remarkable distinction as a major center of Greek culture and Hellenization, including among its natives the Epicurean philosopher and epigrammatist Philodemus, the love poet Meleager, and the satirist Menippus.

Conquered by the Jewish (Hasmonaean) king Alexander I Jannaeus (*c* 100), it was freed by Pompey the Great *c* 64 (temporarily assuming the name of Pompeia), and became a member of the league of Greek cities known as the Decapolis (all situated beyond the Jordan, except Scythopolis [Bethshan]), which retained autonomy in the new Roman province of Syria. Augustus returned Gadara to the Jewish kingdom of Herod the Great (who made it the capital of his province of Peraea), though when Marcus Agrippa and then the emperor himself (20) visited Syria, the city's leaders took the opportunity to complain against Herod and appeal to be withdrawn from his rule, on the grounds that he had confiscated their property and desecrated their temples. Their protest was in vain, but they gained their wish after Herod's death (4 BC), when Gadara was incorporated in the Roman province of Syria. In AD 66, however, it suffered destruction by the Jews at the beginning of their First Revolt.

Subsequently, the city renewed its coinage at least until the reign of Gordian III (238–44), and an inscription assigns it the rank of a colony, named after Valentinian I (364–78) or III (425–55). Its history is peculiarly difficult to reconstruct owing to confusions with other towns of the same name, notably the capital of Peraea (Es-Salt) and the settlement that replaced the ancient Gezer, otherwise known as Gazara; the Biblical story of the Gadarene swine, for example, does not necessarily refer to this city.

Gades, formerly Gadir, Gadeira (Cadiz). On the southwestern (Atlantic) coast of Spain, south of the mouths of the river Baetis (Guadalquivir). The small island (Isla de Léon) and a larger island (now a peninsula), which contained the city of Gades, partially enclosed and protected two extensive harbors on inner and outer bays toward the north. Phoenicians from Tyre (Es-Sur) founded an independent settlement under the name of Gadir (fortress), traditionally *c* 1100, although some favor a somewhat later date; it served as an entrepot for trading in tin and silver, and maintained important fisheries.

Toward the end of the sixth century the place passed into Carthaginian hands. Its ports provided Hamilcar Barca with his first base when he began to establish the second Carthaginian empire in Spain (237), for which he issued coinage at Gades with Phoenician inscriptions. But when that empire was lost, this, like other cities, was taken over by the Romans (206), receiving favorable terms. One of its natives was Lucius Cornelius Balbus, of Carthaginian origin—Julius Caesar's extremely influential minister, and the nephew of his banker. Rome's first foreign-born consul (in 40), Balbus established a New City to supplement the old town at Gades, so that henceforth the urban complex as a whole was known as the Twin (Didyme). Under Augustus, when the place became the terminal of the Via Augusta (the ancient Heraclean Way from Gaul to Italy), it resumed its earlier role as a mint, striking large medallic bronze pieces in honor of the emperor and Balbus and Marcus Agrippa—as 'patron and parent' of the *municipium,* which he presumably founded (*c* 19)—as well as for Augustus' grandsons Gaius and Lucius and his stepson Tiberius.

Strabo enlarges on the importance of Gades at this time, noting the large and numerous merchant vessels it fitted out for Mediterranean and Atlantic traffic alike, and remarking that it possessed as many as five hundred Roman knights (*equites*), a number only equalled by the single Italian city of Patavium (Padua). A new harbor town (Portus Gaditanus) established by Balbus on the opposite side of the bay enabled the city to maintain and enlarge its intensive trading activities; its fish sauce (*muria*), rich milk, its dancing girls—the Puellae Gaditanae—gained special renown. In the second century AD, however, the commercial importance of Gades was eclipsed by Italica (Seville), and when Avienus arrived two hundred years later he found it derelict.

The Greeks, who had first visited the place to study the movement of the tides—to them, a novel phenomenon—attributed the dwelling place of Geryon, the monstrous triple-bodied king of Erytheia (or Erythraea) slain by Heracles to the Gaditan islands, and identified Melkart and Baal with Heracles and Cronos (Saturn). The temple of Heracles, of which nothing is now to be seen, was one of the outstanding shrines of the ancient world, regarded by the Iberians and Libyans—according to Strabo—as the site of the Pillars of Heracles, representing the furthest point of the hero's exploration (although Greeks ascribed this landmark to the Fretum Gaditanum [Straits of Calpe-Gibraltar]). The temple was visited by Hannibal and Fabius Maximus, but its treasures were plundered by the Carthaginian Mago in 206. When Julius Caesar, too, came to the sanctuary (in 60), his future power was allegedly foretold by the priests (who alone were allowed to enter the temple, with its wholly Semitic ritual). But he objected to the customary human sacrifices in the Temple of Moloch and put a stop to them. The excavation of five cemeteries in the neighborhood of the city has recently continued.

Gafsa *see* Capsa

Galatia. A large territory in central Asia Minor. The name was used to designate the regions invaded in the early third century BC by the Celts (Gauls) from Europe, who after a great deal of raiding and looting were finally (*c* 230) limited to an area (mostly barrren uplands) extending from the river Sangarius (Sakarya) in the west to beyond the Halys (Kızıl İrmak) in the east, and already containing a wide variety of native populations. The Galatians, comprising a military aristocracy about 20,000 strong, were organized into three tribes, the Tolistobogii (or Tolistoagii) and Tectosages and Trocmi, centered on Blucium (Pessinus [near Balhisar] was also in Tolistobogian territory), Ancyra (Ankara), and Tavium (Büyük Nefez Köy) respectively. These tribes sent delegates to a religious and legal council of the Galatian people at Drynemetum (unidentified). After they had sided with the Seleucid king Antiochus III the Great against the Romans, their general Cnaeus Manlius Vulso overran their territory, carrying off a huge quantity of loot (189); and after Rome's first war against Mithridates VI of Pontus, Galatia became its protectorate (85).

Cicero's speech *On Behalf of Deiotarus* tells of the Galatian prince of that name who changed sides from Pompey the Great to Julius Caesar and became, amid fluctuating fortunes, ruler of the whole of the country, changing sides, once again, to the victorious Antony and Octavian (the future Augustus) before Philippi (42); he died two years later. Another Galatian, Amyntas, successfully transferred his allegiance from Antony to Octavian (31); but his death six years later was followed by the creation of a Roman Provincia Galatica (later known as Galatia), which embraced substantial adjoining regions and received a number of Roman colonies (including Antioch in Pisidia [Yalvaç], Lystra [Hatunsaray], and Cremna [near Gürmeği]) to keep down brigands and protect communications. Coins were issued in the name of a central Galatian Council (*koinon*). St. Paul's *Epistle to the Galatians* (*c* AD 52–55) bears witness to the early foundation of Christian communities.

After a series of minor enlargements of the province, the extensive territories of Cappadocia and Lesser Armenia were incorporated in 72, but detached again *c* 107–13; and further adjustments followed. Under the reorganizations of late imperial times the province was subdivided into Galatia Prima and Galatia Salutaris (in the administrative diocese of Pontus) and Pisidia and Lycaonia (in the diocese of Asiana). At the time of St. Jerome, the Galatians were still speaking their own Celtic language. The products of the territory, according to Pliny the Elder, included wool and red kermes dye from insects in oak trees. *See also* Ancyra, Antiochia in Pisidia, Lycaonia, Pessinus, Pisidia, Tavium.

Galicia *see* Callaecia

Galilee. The northern region of Judaea (Israel, Palestine)—bounded to the east by the river Jordan and Lake Gennesaret (the Sea of Galilee), to the north by the Leontes (Litani), to the west by Phoenicia, and to the south by Samaria. The territory consists of two parts: Upper Galilee, which is hilly, and Lower Galilee, which is fertile and contains no high hills.

After a long Biblical history the Jewish (Hasmonaean) ruler Simon Maccabaeus transported the Galilean Jews to Judaea, leaving Galilee to those who were willing to live under Seleucid (Syrian) rule (*c* 163). John Hyrcanus I, however (134–104), extended his authority onto Galilean soil, and forcible conversions to Judaism were imposed. In 54/3 the country revolted in favor of

Aristobulus II, the dispossessed brother of John Hyrcanus II, and a further serious rising had to be dealt with by the youthful Herod the Great (son of the Judaean chief minister Antipater), who had been installed, with Caesar's backing, as governor of Galilee (47). Herod's over-forceful methods caused his temporary exile, but Antony reinstated him in 42, with the title of prince (tetrarch), and subsequently Galilee formed part of his kingdom (37).

When he died in 4 BC, Galilee and Peraea passed into the hands of his son Herod Antipas, who almost immediately had to deal with a local rebellion led by a certain Judas, the son of Ezekias (Hezekiah). This uprising compelled the Roman officer entrusted with its suppression to appeal to the governor of Syria, Varus, who crucified 2,000 insurgents and sold many others as slaves. When Rome annexed the regions south of Galilee as the province of Judaea in AD 6, a further uprising broke out in the new province, led by a Judas from Gamala in Gaulanitis (Golan) (perhaps the same as the earlier rebel of that name) who was known as 'the Galilean'—which virtually meant anarchist—and came to be celebrated by a series of subsequent revolutionaries as their forerunner. As for Herod Antipas, he gave his first residence Sepphoris (Saffuriyeh) the new name of Autocratoris ('emperor's city'), and then built a new capital, Tiberias (after the emperor Tiberius). At a time when numerous Galilean holy men professed various forms of unorthodox Judaism, his reign witnessed the missions of John the Baptist (in Peraea), whom he executed, and of Jesus (of Nazareth in Galilee), whom he expelled.

After Antipas' subsequent demotion by the Romans (39) his kingdom passed to his nephew Agrippa I, and then after Agrippa's death (44) to the Roman province of Judaea; though Nero (54–68) transferred two fishing towns on the Sea of Galilee to the late king's son Agrippa II. When the First Jewish Revolt broke out in 66, it was to Galilee that the historian Josephus was ordered to proceed to command an insurgent force. But by summer 67 Vespasian was in the territory, whereupon Josephus, besieged at Jotapata (Jefat), surrendered to the Romans. Vespasian also won a naval battle on the Sea of Galilee, celebrated on his coins.

The devastation following the Revolt meant that henceforth Galilee, rather than the ruined ancient core of Judaea, was destined to become the center of Jewish territory and religion and scholarship. It held more or less aloof from the Second Revolt (132–35) and (although some of its cities issued strongly pagan coinages) possessed increasingly numerous synagogues and rabbinical schools. The Jewish Nasi (prince, or spiritual leader) Simon II received Roman recognition for his reconstituted Council at Usha in Galilee, from which it moved in the early third century to Tiberias. Subsequently, the most famous of all his successors, the patriarch Judah I ha-Nasi (135–219)—regarded as the principal architect of the *Mishnah*—likewise resided at Galilee, first at Beth-Shearim and then at Sepphoris (renamed Diocaesarea), where, with the support of Romans, he maintained considerable state. The foundations of the 'Jerusalem' Talmud were laid at Tiberias. In the later empire (*c* 400) Galilee came within the province of Palaestina Secunda. *See also* Jotapata, Sepphoris, Tiberias.

Gallia Cisalpina (northern Italy). The country was named after the various tribes of the Gauls (Celts) who migrated into Italy, mostly by way of the Brenner Pass, from about 400 BC onward. Although repelled by the Veneti, they pushed back the Ligurians, Etruscans and Umbrians; and one marauding band of Insubrian Gauls, under Brennus, defeated a Roman army beside the river Allia (Fosso Maestro) and briefly captured Rome itself (*c* 387). In 222, however, Marcus Claudius Marcellus defeated and personally killed the Insubrian invader Viridomarus at Clastidium (Casteggio).

Cisalpine Gaul, under the name of Gallia Togata, subsequently became an immensely prosperous and powerful center of Romanization. In 89 the Transpadane region received Latin rights (under which city officials became Roman citizens), while the Cispadane part of Cisalpine territory received the full franchise. Subsequently the two areas were united to become a separate province, but then, after full Roman citizenship had been extended to the Transpadane lands, were incorporated into Italy. The tribes occupying the Alpine foothills were conquered under Augustus and their territory converted into small new provinces. In the later empire northern Italy became the administrative diocese of Italia Annonaria, including the districts or provinces of Venetia-Histria, Liguria, Aemilia, Flaminia-Picenum Annonarium and Alpes Cottiae (much enlarged). *See also* Aquileia, Atria, Augusta Praetoria, Augusta Taurinorum, Bedriacum, Benacus, Bononia, Brixellum, Clastidium, Comum, Cremona, Dertona, Genua, Mantua, Mediolanum, Mutina, Padus, Parma, Patavium, Placentia, Ravenna, Sirmio, Spina, Ticinum, Ticinus, Trebia, Verona.

Gallia Transalpina (approximately France). In support of their ally Massalia (Massilia, Marseille), when it was threatened by a Celtic coalition, the Romans intervened and annexed a belt of territory between the Alps and the Cebenna mountains (Cévennes; 121 BC), which subsequently, in enlarged form, became the province of Gallia Narbonensis. Julius Caesar, in the course of his Gallic Wars (58–51), annexed the rest of the country, which was known as Gallia Comata (long-haired) and was divided, in the time of Augustus, into the three provinces of Belgica, Lugdunensis and Aquitania (together with small Alpine provinces: see Gallia Cisalpina). Upper and Lower Germany were at first military districts attached administratively to Belgica, but under Domitian (*c* AD 90) they, too, became separate provinces. Rebellions in the country include those of Vindex against Nero in 68, the Gallo-German revolt of Civilis in 69/70, and the uprising of guerrillas (Bagaudae) under Aelianus and Amandus (283–86).

In the administrative diocese of the Gauls established during the later empire, Belgica was subdivided into two provinces, and Lugdunensis into four (Prima, Secunda, Tertia and Senonia), while Narbonensis and Aquitania were reorganized as the Septem Provinciae (Narbonensis Prima and Secunda, Viennensis, Aquitania Prima and Secunda, Novempopulana and Alpes Maritimae; the other two small Alpine provinces were incorporated in Italia Annonaria). Gaul enjoyed energetic cultural activity in later antiquity, but during the fifth century suffered severely from a revival of the Bagaudae and succumbed piecemeal to German invaders, the lead being taken by the Visigoths, who in 418 were recognized as federates in the west of the country and in 475 declared their independence of the Romans, only to be superseded in turn (and restricted to

Spain) by Clovis, king of the Franks (507). *See also* Alesia, Antipolis, Aquae Sextiae, Aquitania, Arelate, Arverna, Augusta Trevirorum, Bibracte, Burdigala, Caesarodunum, Campi Catalaunii, Carpentorate, Cenabum, Durocortorum, Forum Julii, Garumna, Genava, Gergovia, Gesoriacum, Glanum, Liger, Ligugé, Limonum Pictonum, Lugdunum, Lutetia Parisiorum, Massalia, Mosella, Narbo, Nemausus, Rhodanus, Rotomagus, Samarobriva, Valentia, Vasio Vocontiorum, Vienna.

Gallipoli *see* Chersonesus (Thracian)

Gamzigrad. Seven miles west of Zaječar in eastern Yugoslavia, near the Bulgarian border. The site of a Roman fortress, of which the anicent name is unknown; it must have played an important part in the defences of the province of Dacia Ripensis, founded south of the Danube by Aurelian (AD 271), and evidently served as the administrative center for adjacent mines and quarries. Recent excavations have uncovered an exceptionally large and luxurious residence, plausibly identified with a palace of the emperor Galerius (d. 311), who was born in the province.

The plan of the mansion, which bears marked resemblances to Diocletian's palace at Spalatum (Split) near Salonae (Solin), centers on a long audience hall with an apse at its eastern end, approached along two spacious corridors and adjoined by two colonnaded courtyards, an apsed dining room, and a suite of baths. The walls were decorated with paintings, rich stucco-work and porphyry and other marble veneers, and the floor mosaics in one room display hunting scenes comparable to those at Philosophiana (Piazza Armerina) in Sicily.

Gamzigrad was surrounded by powerful freestanding walls of which the west gate and a tower have been uncovered. Massive outer fortifications of the adjoining township, including six round towers, also exist in an excellent state of preservation; they may date from the epoch of Constantine the Great (306–37).

Gandhara. A territory in ancient India (roughly equivalent to the northwest frontier province of modern Pakistan), southeast of the Paropamisus (Hindu Kush) mountains, situated between the rivers Indus, Acesines (Chenab) and Hydaspes (Jhelum), and extending westward into and around the valleys of Peshawar and Cabura (Kophen, Kabul, in eastern Afghanistan). After the country had spent some two centuries under Persian (Achaemenid) rule, its monarch Omphis (Ambhi) submitted to Alexander the Great (327 BC), who was reputedly impressed by the Indian sages he encountered at his capital Taxila. Further south, Alexander defeated and reinstated another Indian monarch, Porus (Parvataka or Parvatesha).

Before the end of the fourth century, however, western Gandhara and other territories conquered by Alexander were ceded by one of his successors, Seleucus I Nicator, to the Indian emperor Chandragupta Maurya (Sandracottus) in exchange for war elephants. After Bactria, too, had broken away from the Seleucids (256/5), some of its monarchs during the early second century (Antimachus I Theos, Pantaleon, Agathocles Dikaios) secured control of various parts of Gandhara, minting coins at Taxila and Charsadda (Pushkalavati). Pieces issued at Charsadda are inscribed in Greek and Brahmi, while issues of Demetrius III Aniketos display inscriptions in Greek and Prakrit (written in the Kharosthi script). The greatest of all these Indo-Greek kings, Menander Soter Dikaios (*c* 155–140/30), established the capital of his substantial empire at Sacala (Sialkot), where he was born. *See also* Taxila.

But the Indo-Scythian leader Azes I (*c* 57–35) captured Taxila, and after temporary recovery by Hermaeus Soter (from *c* 40), a tribal chief of the Yüeh Chih, Kudjula Kadphises I, at about the beginning of the Christian era, regained control of the entire region, incorporating it into his rising Kushan empire. The most powerful of its monarchs, Kanishka—in the later first or second century AD—issued coins depicting the deities not only of Persia and Brahminical India but of Greece and Rome as well; and the flourishing school of sculpture and architecture that developed in Gandhara showed a strong impact of provincial Greco-Roman artistic style and imagery.

Garray *see* Numantia

Garumna (Garonne). A river of southwestern Gaul, entering the Cantabrian Sea (Bay of Biscay) by way of the Gironde estuary, into which the Duranius (Dordogne) also debouches. In the Augustan epoch the Garumna flowed, throughout its entire course, inside the province of Aquitania; but under the reorganization of Diocletian (AD 284–305) the border between the provinces of Aquitania Secunda and Novempopulana passed close to the river.

When the government of the western Roman empire authorized Wallia, king of the Visigoths, to set up a federated state in western Gaul (418), the two major cities on the banks of the Garumna, Burdigala (Bordeaux) and Tolosa (Toulouse), were handed over to him and remained in the hands of the independent Visigothic state that came into existence later in the century (475).

Gaugamela (Gomal). In northern Mesopotamia (Iraq); northwest of Arbela (Erbil), northeast of Nineveh, and across the Tigris from the modern city of Mosul. Gaugamela received its name, which means 'Camel's House,' from the Achaemenid Persian king Darius I, who allocated it for the maintenance of the camel that had carried his baggage through the deserts of Scythia (512 BC).

Gaugamela was the scene of a major battle in the war between Alexander the Great and Darius III Codomannus (331). Although the course of the battle is very uncertain, it seems that Darius chose the flat plain as their battlefield because of his superior strength in cavalry, but when an opening became visible in the Persian left center Alexander charged into the gap, causing the opposing center to break and flee, with Darius in the lead. The engagement has often been regarded as an outstanding example of penetration tactics. Although Alexander failed to follow up the pursuit—owing to the need to rescue his left wing under Parmenio—the victory proved decisive. Darius' treasure and royal chariot were captured at Arbela, and he himself, a refugee, was killed by one of his own commanders in the following year.

Gaulanitis. A district in Bashan to the east of the Upper Jordan valley, now the borderland between Israel and Syria; the Golan Heights perpetuate its name. In Biblical times, too, Golan had been the name of this limestone plateau (and a town it contained, later Gaulana); it contained an upper and a lower region, Beth-Maacah (mainly pasturage) and Geshur (rich and fertile). In the Greek period, like the rest of eastern Palestine, Gaulanitis was regarded as part of Coele-Syria (Hollow Syria); but *c* 83–80 the Jewish (Hasmonaean) king Alexander I Jannaeus captured Gaulana and two other cities of the region (Gamala [Jamle?] and Seleucia [Seluqiye?]).

In 47 Julius Caesar's kinsman Sextus Caesar, governor of Syria, included Gaulanitis in the command of the young Herod the Great, and after Herod had become king, he recovered it (in 20) from Zenodorus, the ruler of Chalcis Beneath Lebanon (Mejdel Anjar), to whom it had been temporarily assigned. After Herod's death Gaulanitis became part of the territory of his son Philip (4 BC), who established his capital (Caesarea Philippi) in the neighboring region of Panias. The rebel leader Judas 'the Galilean' may have come not from Galilee but from Gamala. On Philip's death (AD 34), Gaulanitis, like the rest of his kingdom, was incorporated into the Roman province of Syria, but it later returned to Jewish rule under Agrippa I (AD 37–44) and II (53–after 90s), though Gamala rebelled against the latter during the First Jewish Revolt (66). In the later empire (*c* 400), when the number of its inhabited sites had steadily increased to a maximum total, Gaulanitis became a political unit (*clima*) attached to the province of Palaestina Secunda (with the exception, perhaps, of a border strip detached to Arabia).

Gavur Dağları *see* Amanus

Gaza. A city at the southwestern extremity of Philistia and Judaea (now the center of an Arab strip administered by Israel); occupying a key position three miles from the Mediterranean on the vital coastal road (Ways of Horus, Way of the Sea) leading from Egypt to Syria and Mesopotamia. After enjoying limited independence under Persian rule, Gaza was stormed after a long siege by Alexander the Great (332 BC), who first partially destroyed the place but then ordered its repopulation, probably endowing it with a Greek constitution, one of the first to be introduced around the fringes of Judaea. In 312 Gaza was the scene of a victory of Ptolemy I Soter over Demetrius the Besieger (Poliorcetes), but after 200 it passed into Seleucid hands, as its new name Seleucia showed. Besides trading in the popular wine of the region, and serving as a large-scale slave market, the city's port, Maiumas, was used by the Nabataean Arab kingdom as a harbor for the export of spices, brought by land caravans from Arabia. For a time the city was in the hands of the Nabataeans; but then it was captured by the Jewish (Hasmonaean) ruler Jonathan and devastated by Alexander I Jannaeus (96).

When Pompey the Great, however, overran Judaea, he declared Gaza a free city—whereupon it introduced a new era (61)—and another Roman general, Aulus Gabinius (57–55), founded a new town on an adjacent site. It was granted to Herod the Great in 37, and he gained control of it again after its temporary loss to Cleopatra VII of Egypt (*c* 35–30); the governor of his southern territories described his province as 'Idumaea and Gaza.' After the death of Herod's son Archelaus (AD 6), Gaza became a free city, issuing coinage for the occasion. The city prospered during the Roman Principate, especially in the second and third centuries AD, acquiring the status of a Roman colony and a new civic era (128), as well as a famous school of rhetoric and philosophy, and a reputation as a flourishing center of Hellenic culture. Following the Second Jewish Revolt (132–35), the rebel prisoners of war were sold in thousands at Gaza, where 'Hadrian's market' was spoken of for centuries.

Its principal temple was dedicated to Marna ('Lord,' the Baal of Gaza), but there were also shrines of the principal Greco-Roman divinities. Remains of synagogues in both the city and its port have come to light. Although reputedly included in a missionary journey undertaken by St. Peter himself, the Gazans stubbornly stood against Christianity—the temple of Marna being considered a leading stronghold of paganism—so that Constantine chose to show favor to their port Maiumas instead, granting it independence under the name of Constantia. There was an episcopal see at Gaza, but for generations the rival cries 'Marna' and 'Jesus' were heard, until in 402 Bishop Porphyrius, as we learn from his life by Marcus the Deacon, was ordered by the eastern emperor Arcadius to destroy Marna's shrine. Nevertheless, the renown of Gaza's Greek learning continued to increase, although it still possessed many inhabitants who did not know the language.

Gazipaşa *see* Selinus (Cilicia)

Gediz Çayı *see* Hermus, River

Gedrosia (Baluchistan [southern Pakistan] and southeastern Iran). Strabo indicates that the territory was well-watered by rains in the summer but that they failed in winter. Its coastal regions are known as Las Bela (east) and Makran (west), the latter term perhaps being related to 'Maka' on a Persian inscription at Behistun and to the 'Mykians' described by Herodotus as forming part of a Persian satrapy.

In 330/29 the satrap of the day capitulated to the victorious Alexander the Great, and the territory was reorganized. After further successes (against the Indians) Alexander performed the remarkable feat of leading his main army overland throughout both parts of coastal Gedrosia, from east to west (325): Las Bela (where he had left an Alexandria [Rhambacia] in the territory of the Oreitae west of the Indus mouth) and then desolate Makran (the site of another Alexandria [Mashkid?] 'in the land of the Fish-Eaters'). Meanwhile the flotilla of Nearchus coasted along the shore, and Craterus, in charge of elephants and casualties, marched through the northern regions of Gedrosia—both rejoining him at the entrance of the Persian Gulf, in the hinterland of which he founded a further Alexandria (Galashkird). Later the country passed into the hands of the Parthians, and subsequently fell to the Kushans.

Gela ('cold stream'). A city in southern Sicily, west of the mouth of the river Gelas (Gela). Situated on a long, low, narrow, steep-sided, sandy hill—already inhabited by Sicans during the Bronze Age (second millennium BC)—the Greek city was founded *c* 690/88 (not earlier) by colonists from Crete and Lindus (Rhodes). After prolonged struggles with the native population over the control of the fertile inland plain—suitable for breeding excellent cavalry horses—the settlers succeeded in pushing into the interior, where they subjugated native settlements, and expanded along the coast, on which they founded Acragas (Agrigento) (582).

Gela's autocratic ruler ('tyrant') Hippocrates (*c* 498–491/90), succeeding his brother Cleander, created an empire that rose to be Sicily's strongest state, severely defeating the Syracusans at the river Helorus (Eloro). His cavalry commander (*c* 490–478), son of Deinomenes who gave his name to the dynasty, occupied and established his residence at Syracuse, destroyed Camarina and Megara Hyblaea, and in alliance with Theron of Acragas defeated a great Carthaginian army at Himera (Imera; 480). Under his viceroy (and successor) Hiero I Gela's inhabitants greatly diminished in number, but the city was repopulated in 466, refounded Camarina in 461, and remained a leading artistic and cultural center; Aeschylus died there in 456. In 424 it was the scene of a peace conference in face of the menace from the Athenians, whose attack on Syracuse during the Peloponnesian War (415–413) the Geloans helped to oppose. In 405, however, their city was captured and destroyed by the Carthaginians (its population being transported to Leontini [Lentini]), and remained deserted until the Corinthian Timoleon reconstructed its buildings and imported new colonists (338). But Agathocles of Syracuse used Gela as a base against the Carthaginians and massacred 4,000 of its inhabitants (311), and in 280 Phintias of Acragas removed those who remained to the new city named after him (now Licata), where they retained the name of Geloans.

The area of ancient Gela to the west of the acropolis is occupied by the modern town, but on the acropolis itself (Molino a Vento) the foundations of archaic and fifth-century temples can be seen, the former dedicated to Athena. The shrine of Demeter Thesmophoros near the mouth of the river Gelas has disclosed thousands of votive objects. But the surviving stretch of Timoleon's walls are the city's outstanding monument and, indeed, one of the most important relics of the ancient world on the island.

Gelibolu *see* Chersonesus (Thracian)

Genava (Genève, Geneva). A city beside the Lake of Geneva (Lac Leman), on the left bank of the Rhodanus (Rhône). Transferred from the site of a prehistoric lake settlement built on piles, Genava became a walled town of the tribe of the Allobroges, situated on a promontory (Cité) at the beginning of the Swiss plateau, surrounded on three sides by stretches of water: namely the lake, the river (already spanned in pre-Roman times by a bridge), and its tributary the Arve. It was in this frontier region of the province of Gallia Narbonensis (southern France) that Julius Caesar warded off an attempted invasion by the Helvetii (58 BC). Genava was assigned to the territory of Vienna (Vienne), but gained Roman citizenship in AD 40. Two factors contributed to its prosperity. Its harbors handled abundant lake and river traffic causing the establishment of a toll station; and it was a place where the main roads from Italy and Gallia Narbonensis met. It became an autonomous *civitas* in the third century.

The Roman town consisted of three main quarters: an official center on the hill, with principal forum and temples; a residential quarter on the plateau beyond; and a business area associated with the two harbors. Adjoining the forum was the colonnaded official mansion of the local commander, dating from the later fourth century AD, when the place (then in the province of Viennensis) also became an episcopal see. In the mid-fifth century Genava came under the control of the Burgundians (443), whose kings resided there until their transfer to Lugdunum (Lyon; 470). Air photography (with a gyroscope) has revealed the outlines (centuriation) of the agricultural allotments around the city.

Genua (Genoa). A coastal city of Liguria (Cisalpine Gaul, northwest Italy). Finds indicate an early trading post at which the Ligurian inhabitants maintained connections with the Phoenicians (Carthaginians) and Greeks and Etruscans, and at least by the fourth century BC a settled community resided on a hill overlooking the harbor (Santa Maria di Castello).

At the beginning of the Second Punic War (218) Genua was already under Roman control, but suffered destruction from Hannibal (205). Rebuilt by the praetor Spurius Cassius, it was used during the second century as a base against the Ligurians, and formed a station on the Via Postumia leading to Aquileia (148) and on the Via Aemilia Scauri to Vada Volterrana (109). An inscription records that in 117 a boundary dispute with neighbors was settled by Roman adjudicators. Strabo refers to the city's exports (cattle, hides, timber and honey) and imports (olive oil and Italian wine: the local wine, mixed with pitch, was unpleasantly harsh). Genua became of greater importance in the later empire, when it was included in the province of the Cottian Alps.

Georgia *see* Colchis

Gerasa, Antiochia on the Chrysorrhoas (Jerash in Jordan). Situated about thirty miles north of Philadelphia (Amman), in a well-watered section of the highlands of Galaaditis (Gilead), twenty miles east of the river Jordan. Already settled in the Bronze and Iron Ages, the village was transformed into a town, perhaps by Alexander the Great (to whom Iamblichus ascribes its colonization), but more decisively by Antiochus IV Epihanes (175–164), who gave it the name of Antiochia on the Chrysorrhoas (Barada), a tributary of the Jabbachos (Jabbok).

Occupied by the Jewish (Hasmonaean) monarch Alexander I Jannaeus *c* 83, the city subsequently became part of Pompey the Great's province of Syria (64). Sacked by the Jews at the outset of their First Revolt in AD 66 (one of their principal leaders, Simon the son of Gioras, came from the place), Gerasa suffered further destruction and massacre at the hands of Vespasian's lieutenant Lucius Annius. Nevertheless, Vespasian replanned the city—which at this juncture, if not earlier, joined a group of cities known as the Decapolis—and developed its fortifications. The inhabitants of the place derived a lucrative revenue not only from agriculture and mining, but also from their caravan trade with the Nabataean Arabs, especially after Trajan's conversion of the Nabataean kingdom into the province of Arabia (106), to which Gerasa, too, was allotted. It has been estimated that the city's population attained a figure of between ten and fifteen thousand. Hadrian's visit in 128/29 was celebrated by the erection of a large five-bayed triumphal arch (*c* 130). Gerasa became a Roman colony during the early third century, probably in the reign of Elagabalus (218–22).

It possessed a large temple of Zeus, but local coinage identifies Artemis (Diana) as the city's principal patroness identified with its Fortune (Tyche). Her immense, walled precinct of mid-second-century date, rising on an elaborately terraced hillside, is one of the most important religious monuments of the Roman imperial age in the near east—just as Gerasa as a whole provides outstanding remains of a rich Greco-Roman city. Its secular architecture includes three theaters, colonnaded streets, and a remarkable oval agora or forum (*c* 300). Many of the buildings display a peculiar rich ornamentation that in some respects anticipates baroque styles. In the late fourth century Gerasa became a great Christian metropolis with more than a dozen churches, including the three-aisled Cathedral (later fourth century), a Church of the Prophets and Apostles and Martyrs (460), and a basilica dedicated to the martyred St. Theodore (484); while numerous additional shrines were added under Justinian I (527–65) and later.

Gergovia (Gergovie). In central southern Gaul (Puy-de-Dôme, France), on a plateau nine hundred feet high, overlooking the valley of the river Elaver (Allier): a settlement of the tribe of the Arverni, from whom the Auvergne takes its name. During Caesar's Gallic war Gergovia was one of the strongholds of the Arvernian national leader Vercingetorix (52 BC). Seeing that the fortress could not be taken by direct assault, Caesar attempted to capture it by blockade, but his six legions proved insufficient; moreover, Vercingetorix himself was not far off, and after some of Caesar's troops had got out of control in an unsuccessful surprise attack, he was forced to abandon the siege and retreat. The revolt now spread dangerously; though it was crushed at Alesia (Alise-Sainte Reine) later in the year.

A small Gallo-Roman town continued to exist at Gergovia until after the middle of the first century AD, but was eclipsed and partly depopulated by the foundation of Augustonemetum (Clermont-Ferrand) four miles away. A temple of Celtic type, however, remained in use for a time. It has been excavated, together with the ditches of Caesar's two camps and a blast furnace of modest dimensions.

Germania, the home of innumerable tribes, was brought forcibly to the notice of the Romans by the invasions of the Teutones and Cimbri, who after the latter had destroyed a Roman army at Arausio (Orange) in 105 BC were overwhelmed by Marius near Aquae Sextiae (Aix en Provence) and Vercellae (Vercelli) respectively (102, 101). In 58 Julius Caesar routed Ariovistus, king of the Suebi, who had invaded Gaul in 71. The classic description of the various peoples is in Tacitus' *Germania.*

The name meant the following to the Romans: (1) the military commands (from the time of Augustus when the first legionary fortresses were established in 16/13), later converted into provinces (under Domitian, *c* AD 90), of Upper and Lower Germany, generally bordering on the Rhine (although Lower Germany was for a short time extended into Frisia); (2) the Agri Decumates in the reentrant between the upper Rhine and upper Danube, annexed by Vespasian (from 74) and Domitian and evacuated *c* 263; (3) 'Free' Germany, extending for an indefinite distance beyond the Rhine and the Danube. The most notable attempts to annex substantial portions of this vast 'free' region were made by Augustus and Marcus Aurelius (170–80), in both cases without lasting success. German invasions became more and more formidable under Aurelius, and immensely destructive in the third century, though Probus (276–82) succeeded in recovering most of the territory that had been lost.

In the later empire, Upper and Lower Germany were renamed Germania Prima and Secunda, though Germania Prima was smaller than its predecessor, since the southern part of Upper Germany was transferred to the new province of Maxima Sequanorum. Successive German breakthroughs on the Rhine frontier (together with internal problems) contributed decisively to the eventual downfall of the western empire; Germania Secunda came under Frankish rule by the mid-fifth century at the latest. *See also* Agri Decumates, Albis, Argentorate, Augusta Rauricorum, Borbetomagus, Colonia Agrippinensis, Frisia, Haltern, Moguntiacum, Mosella, Rhenus, Teutoburgensis (Saltus), Trajectum, Vesontio, Vindonissa, Visurgis.

Germanicia *see* Ptolemais Ace

Geroevka *see* Nymphaeum

Gerrha *see* Chalcis Beneath Lebanon

Gesoriacum, Bononia (Boulogne-sur-Mer). A coastal town of Gallia Belgica (Pas-de-Calais, France) on the Fretum Gallicum (English Channel). The urban settlement represented an amalgamation of two sites, skirting the east bank of the river Liane: the upper city (Ville-Haute) of Bononia, a Celtic name, and the lower city, Gesoriacum, that developed around an expanding port—very probably the Portus Itius from which Caesar sailed for Britain in 54 BC (though Wissant has been suggested as an alternative). An important lighthouse—partially preserved until the eighteenth century—was constructed at Gesoriacum by the emperor Gaius (Caligula) in AD 40. His plan to employ the port as a base for the invasion of Britain came to nothing; but in 43 it was from here that Claudius' fleet sailed to conquer part of the island. Henceforth it was the normal port of embarkation across the Channel and the headquarters of the British fleet (classis Britannica).

After Carausius, commander of this fleet, had usurped the purple in Britain and northern Gaul (*c* 287), he suffered a fatal blow when Constantius I Chlorus successfully blockaded Gesoriacum by constructing a great mole across its harbor (293). Following Constantius' final reduction of the secessionist empire, the upper city (which had remained loyal) became the principal habitation center, so that the name of Bononia henceforth prevailed; it also became known as Oceanensis. The last ancient mention of the place occurred in 407 when another usurper, Constantine III, landed there in order to seek the imperial throne, denuding Britain, from which he came, of its garrison, and thus paving the way for the virtual abandonment of Bononia as well. The complex fortifications of the two later imperial towns, Bononia and Gesoriacum, enclosing a perimeter half the size of the earlier city, are still partly visible.

Geyre *see* Aphrodisias

Ghazni *see* Alexandria (Paropamisadae)

Ghighen *see* Oescus

Giardini Naxos *see* Naxos (Sicily)

Gibraltar, Straits of *see* Gades

Glanum, Glanon (near Saint-Rémy-de-Provence). A city in Narbonese Gaul (Bouches-du-Rhône, southern France), between the river Rhodanus (Rhône) and its tributary the Druentia (Durance), sixteen miles northeast of Arelate (Arles). Occupied continually since the Chalcolithic (Copper) Age, Glanum became a small Ligurian, Celticized commercial center, well-known for its healing spring and pool, dedicated to the god Glanis and to deities known as the Mothers of Glanum (Matres Glanicae), of whom later statues survive. Imported pottery and coins show that the inhabitants already traded with the Greeks of Massalia (Massilia, Marseille) from the sixth century BC, and from *c* 200—under the influence of the Massalians, who wanted to strengthen their commercial links with the interior—a Greek settlement was established at Glanum, minting its own coinage with the design of a bull (found also on Massalian issues), which seems to have ceased, however, before or after the establishment of the Roman province of Gallia Narbonensis (121).

The considerable settlement that subsequently grew up—benefiting from its proximity to the main road from Italy—at some stage suffered considerable damage, at the hands either of local tribesmen (Salyes) or of German invaders (Cimbri, Teutones, Ambrones). But it was subsequently reconstructed and, after a temporary setback caused by Massalia's defeat by Caesar (49), reemerged not long afterward as the city of Glanum Livii, with Latin rights (conferring Roman citizenship on its elected officials) and unprecedented prosperity. About AD 270, however, it was plundered and destroyed by German invaders. Later, a walled town was constructed at Saint-Rémy.

Certain Gallic survivals are apparent, and both the Greek and Roman towns have left important remains. A council chamber, colonnaded courtyard and peristyle houses go back to the second century BC; while the larger Glanum of late Republican and Augustan date has left the earliest triumphal arch of Gallia Narbonensis (probably *c* 20 BC), an elaborate mausoleum of about the same period dedicated by three Julii to their parents, a temple of Rome and of the house of Augustus, a temple dedicated by Marcus Agrippa to the healing deity Valetudo, a shrine of Hercules, and a monumental complex that may be identifiable with the forum. A sanctuary of the eastern goddess Cybele is also to be seen, with an adjacent House of Attis that probably housed her priests.

Gonnus, Gonnos (Gonni). The principal town of the tribe of the Perrhaebi, who lived on the northern border of Thessaly (eastern Greece). The ridge on which the acropolis of Gonnus stood, occupied since Neolithic times, protruded from the lower flank of Mount Olympus, not only commanding mountain passes leading into Macedonia, but also overlooking the river Peneus and valley of Tempe, through which Xerxes came in 480 BC. The place played a particularly important part in the wars fought by Rome against Macedonia (197, 171) and the Seleucid monarch Antiochus III the Great (191). It also continued to be of some significance thereafter, but declined under Roman rule.

Since Hellenistic times the town had been extended to two adjoining hills fortified by walls with projecting towers. Recent excavations have continued the uncovering of a temple of Asclepius, which displays two phases of construction, and evidently remained in use during the Roman epoch.

Gordium, Gordion (Yassihüyük). In western central Asia Minor near the confluence of the rivers Sangarios (Sakarya) and Tembris (Porsuk); the place was situated on the 'Royal Road,' a natural route from the central plateau of the peninsula to the Aegean. A Bronze Age (Hittite) center, Gordium became the capital of Phrygia in the ninth or eighth century, attaining a high and grandiose degree of civilization under King Midas (*c* 738–695), named after a mythical forerunner whose relations with the gods formed the subject of many well-known Greek stories. Palatial tombs and painted pottery go back to the Phrygian epoch; and at this period Gordium was a famous center of weaving, and spread the knowledge of textiles to Greece and the near east.

After destruction by Cimmerian invaders from Scythia (in 690/5) and successive periods of Lydian and Persian domination, Alexander the Great, when he visited Gordium in 333, was shown the chariot of Gordius, legendary founder of the Phrygian monarchy; and the oracle told him that any man who loosed the 'Gordian knot' of cornel bark binding the yoke to the pole would rule over the whole of Asia. All previous attempts to perform this feat had failed, but in front of a large Macedonian and Phrygian audience Alexander succeeded, either by slicing the knot in two with his sword or by removing the pole pin. In the early third century Gordium received a settlement of Galatian immigrants, but was found deserted by the Roman general Cnaeus Manlius Vulso in 189 BC. In Strabo's time it was a small village.

Gorgippia (Anapa). A Greek city on the Taman peninsula (south Russia), just south of the Cimmerian Bosphorus (Kerch Strait) which separates the Kuban from the Tauric Chersonesus (Crimea). Originally known as the Harbor of the Sindians, after the North Caucasian or Indo-Iranian people who lived in the hinterland—their necropolis at Rassvyet, eight miles away, has been excavated—the place was settled by the Greeks first as a market (sixth century BC) and then as a city, taking its name from a member of the Spartocid dynasty that ruled the kingdom of the Cimmerian Bosphorus, of which Gorgippia became the most southeasterly major town. Before and after 300, it attained considerable commercial importance; and during the first century it enjoyed a second period of prosperity that lasted for two hundred years. Destroyed by the Goths in the 260s AD, it made a partial recovery, though this did not prove long-lived.

The population of Gorgippia contained a strong native element, but Greek inscriptions indicate a largely Hellenized ruling class, which derived prestige from impressive festivals comprising athletic competitions in honor of Hermes. A number of burials of the fifth century BC have now been discovered, and many more from the following century onward, extending over a period of at least five hundred years. The wealth of the city came from its wheat trade, but excavations have also revealed two wine-making establishments, a potter's kiln, and evidence of a bronze and marble sculpture industry in the first and second centuries AD. A description of the topography of ancient Gorgippia has now been published. In the surrounding region no less than eighty settlements and burial grounds, mostly of the fourth and third centuries BC, have been located.

Gortyna, Gortyn (between Ayi Deka and Mitropoli). A city of south-central Crete, in a dominant position at the northern extremity of the rich Mesara plain, occupying both banks of the river Lethaeus (Ieropotamos, Mitropolitanos). References in Homer's *Iliad* and *Odyssey* suggest the hypothesis of a late Bronze Age or early Iron Age walled settlement. The establishment of the historical city, which superseded Bronze Age Phaestos as the principal center in the area, was variously attributed to Minos of Crete or to colonists from Laconia (of whose town Amyclae the Gortynian cult-name Amyclaios is reminiscent) or to Gortys the son of Rhadamanthys or of Tegeates, the founder-hero of Tegea in Arcadia (where the name of Gortys is found).

Inscriptions from Gortyna date from the seventh century BC. This was the reputed epoch of its musician and lawgiver Thaletas, who emigrated to Sparta. But by far the most important of these documents is the so-called Code of Gortyn (*c* 450)—a series of laws relating to personal and family subjects, which display advanced thinking on individual rights (especially those of women, debtors and slaves) and constitute our most valuable source of pre-Hellenistic Greek legislation.

By the third century, when the political situation of the island was unstable (*see* Crete), Gortyna—its walls, long vanished, partly rebuilt by Ptolemy II Philadelphos—had taken over Phaestos and its port of Matala, becoming one of the most powerful cities on the island. A long period of hostilities with Cnossus that ensued was ended by the annexation of Crete by the Romans (68/67), whereupon Cnossus, which had been their enemy, suffered destruction, but Gortyna, which had supported them, was selected as the capital of the new Roman province of Crete and Cyrene.

There are surviving remains of temples of Athena Poliouchos (on the acropolis) and Apollo Pythios (said to have been the most important shrine in the city). Another holy place was dedicated to a group of Egyptian deities; and a cult statue from a temple of Asclepius, too, has been found. Also to be seen are recently uncovered fortifications (attributed to Ptolemy IV Philopator of Egypt, 221–205); a theater; two *nymphaea* (fountain houses); an odeum restored by Trajan; and a building, begun in the same reign, which was apparently the residence of the imperial governor, and was enlarged in the later fourth century (after earthquake damage) to include a large Christian basilica. For at this time Gortyna became the ecclesiastical metropolis of the island; and new road surfaces were also constructed.

Gortyna's port on the south coast was Leben, later Lebena (Ledas), the site of an important sanctuary of Asclepius (an offshoot of his shrine at Balagrae in Cyrenaica, of which the surviving remains are of the second century AD). Lebena subsequently possessed a large Christian basilica, dating from before 400.

Gragnano *see* Stabiae

Granicus (Çan Çayı). A small river of northwestern Asia Minor, running through the Adrasteia plain into the Propontis (Sea of Marmara), a little to the east of the Hellespont (Dardanelles). It was beside this stream, perhaps at the modern Dimetoka (identified by some with the ancient Didyma Teiche), that Alexander the Great won his first major victory over the Persian forces of Darius III Codomannus (334 BC). Arrian and Diodorus offer conflicting accounts of the battle. But it seems clear that, although lacking adequate funds—and command of the sea—Alexander inflicted very heavy losses on the troops of the local satraps and their Greek mercenaries (handicapped by a divided command) in a cavalry melée, during the course of which he incurred great personal danger but succeeded in unhorsing a son-in-law of Darius. His success meant that the whole of Asia Minor now lay open to him and that the next serious resistance he encountered could only be offered at the furthest southeastern extremity, at Issus.

Graupius, Mount. In Caledonia (Scotland); the site of an important battle in AD 83 described in Tacitus' *Agricola*, where the historian's father-in-law and hero Cnaeus Julius Agricola, governor of Britain, was said to have won his crowning victory against an army of Caledonian tribes united under the leadership of Calgacus (while a Roman fleet was simultaneously circumnavigating the island).

The location of the battlefield has long been disputed. But the discovery of a series of campsites, including some that display a recognizable Agricolan pattern, has suggested a location east of the Moray Firth, not far from the coast, and an attribution to Bennachie has now been proposed, near a large camp found by air photography at Durno. Tacitus felt extremely indignant that Agricola, soon after his success, was recalled by the emperor Domitian, who, despite the general's achievements, evidently did not feel that the Roman conquest of Caledonia had been brought appreciably nearer, or was possible.

Graviscae (Porto Clementino). A seaport of Etruria (now northern Lazio), occupying a large, roughly rectangular site between the rivers Marta and Mignone. Graviscae was one of the chief harbor towns of the city-state of Tarquinii before the end of the seventh century BC, though its Etruscan name is unknown, and its Etruscan harbor lies buried under silt.

It was particularly notable for its substantial community of Greek traders, whose existence is detectable from *c* 600. Their presence prompted the construction of shrines first of Aphrodite (the Etruscan Turan) and then, about four decades later, of Hera (Uni) (to whom many Greek dedications have come to light) and of Demeter (of whom 5,000 cultic lamps have been discovered). Most of the Greeks whom Tarquinii permitted to maintain this trading post came from the coastal and island city-states of Asia Minor at a time of Persian pressure: and Athenians and Aeginetans later made their appearance as well. After 480, however, when relations between the Etruscan city-states and Greek south Italy were deteriorating, the Greek presence at Graviscae seems to have come to an abrupt end, and the shrines dwindled into a modest Etruscan sanctuary.

A Roman colony, probably comprising about 2,000 settlers, was established in 181—although they did not trouble to change the ill-sounding name, which was believed, according to an unconvincing etymological interpretation of Cato the Elder, to be derived from *gravis aer,* unhealthy air. Late Roman life is represented by an imposing country mansion, including a large *nymphaeum* (fountain house) and an apsed marble-paved hall. The urban residential area suffered from an extensive fire, which can be ascribed (by a hoard of gold coins) to the Visigothic invasions of 408–10. But a bishop of Graviscae was still recorded in 504.

Guadalquivir, River *see* Baetis

Gubbio *see* Iguvium

Gümenek *see* Comana Pontica

Gylaceia *see* Apollonia (Illyricum)

Gythium, Gytheion. A coastal town of the Peloponnese (southern Greece). Situated at the head of the Laconian Gulf in a small fertile plain at the mouth of the river Gythius, the town was reputedly founded by Apollo and Heracles, reconciled after their quarrel over the Delphic tripod. It was on the small island of Cranae (Marathonisi), a hundred yards from the shore, that Paris, visiting from Troy, was said to have had his first fateful encounter with the Spartan queen Helen, which caused the legendary Trojan War; and it is there, too, at a place of sacred asylum, that objects dating back to the late Bronze (Mycenaean) Age have come to light.

After the Dorian invasion, Sparta, which lay twenty-eight miles inland, treated Gythium as a settlement of *perioeci* (second-class citizens) and used the place as its principal port and arsenal. It was plundered in 456/445 by the Athenian admiral Tolmides and occupied by the Thebans from 369 to *c* 363. King Nabis of Sparta lost the city briefly to the Roman general Flamininus (195–192), whom the Gythians hailed as their savior. Subsequently, however, they passed under the control of the Achaean League, until the Roman annexation of Greece in 146; whereupon they were made members of a Laconian (later 'Free' Laconian) League. Although Marcus Antonius Creticus taxed Gythium heavily (72–71) to assist his operations against pirates (and its citizens had to borrow the sums they had to pay, at an exorbitant rate of interest), it was under the Romans that the place enjoyed its greatest prosperity.

Gythium has supplied two inscriptions from AD 15/16 that make an important contribution to our knowledge of emperor worship. One of them reproduces a letter of Tiberius in which he politely rejects the creation of a cult in his own honor, observing, however, that his late adoptive father Augustus merits such worship, and that his mother Livia will reply on her own behalf when she receives further information. Nevertheless, Gythium instituted a festival in which honors were paid to all three of them, and to their liberator Flamininus as well. Gythium issued coinage under the dynasty of Septimius Severus (193–211)—depicting Apollo and Heracles and a variety of other deities—and appears to have prospered until the fourth century AD. Its theater is fairly well-preserved.

H

Hadria *see* Atria

Hadriane *see* Mopsuestia, Neocaesarea, Olba, Tarsus

Hadrianopolis (Egypt) *see* Antinoopolis

Hadrianopolis, formerly Uscudama (?) (Edirne, Adrianople). A city in Thrace (European Turkey) on both banks of the river Tonzos (Tunca), at its confluence with the Hebrus (Meric, Maritza, Evros), which was navigable downstream from this point. Originally an Odrysian (Thracian) settlement, the place was incorporated in the Roman province of Thrace (AD 46) and refounded by Hadrian *c* 125 under the name of Hadrianopolis, becoming an important station on the roads from Byzantium to Lower and Upper Moesia. It was protected by fortifications, which have partly survived; coins of Gordian III (238–44) depict a city gate with conically roofed towers. A large villa has been discovered nearby at Ivailovgrad.

In the later empire, Hadrianopolis became the capital of the new province of Haemimontus. During the second civil war that Licinius fought against Constantine the Great, he suffered a decisive defeat at Hadrianopolis (324), which gave Constantine the rulership of the whole empire. Even more famous, however, was the crushing defeat inflicted by the Visigoths on the eastern emperor Valens in 378. Admitted within the imperial boundaries by Valens, the Visigoths under Fritigern, exploited by Roman provincial governors, had rebelled and started to devastate the Balkans. Valens hurried from Asia to deal with the emergency, and moved to the attack at Hadrianopolis. But the Visigoths, after a successful flank attack by their horsemen, gained an overwhelming victory. Two-thirds of the Roman army fell, including the emperor himself, whose body was never found. This defeat breached the frontiers irreparably, although in the long run it was not the eastern but the more vulnerable western empire (whose forces had not reached Valens in time) that the battle of Hadrianopolis doomed.

It was also, according to some scholars, a landmark signifying the increasing importance of cavalry in relation to infantry.

Hadrumetum (Susah, Sousse in Tunisia). A coastal city sixty miles south of Carthage, situated on Hammamet Bay and on the fringe of the fertile Sahel strip. Hadrumetum was founded by the Phoenicians or Carthaginians. Its sanctuary and tombs, dating from the sixth century BC onward, testify to its important position within the Carthaginian territories of North Africa; with Tacape (Gabes), it was the principal seaport of the Lesser Syrtes (Sidra).

The city was attacked by Agathocles of Syracuse during his invasion of Africa (310), and provided the base for Hannibal's unsuccessful defensive campaign at the end of the Second Punic War, terminating in the battle of Zama (202). For having sided with the Romans in the Third Punic War (149–146), the Hadrumetans were rewarded with the status of a free city, alongside which a community of Roman citizen traders soon began to form. But during Caesar's civil war with the Pompeians (46), Hadrumetum opposed him, with the result that it was heavily fined, and obliged to accept a colony of ex-soldiers, settled by Lepidus in 42–40. He gave this settlement the title of *Concordia,* to which at the time of a refoundation by Trajan (AD 98–117) the further designation *Frugifera* ('Fruitful') was added.

This title referred to the agricultural wealth of the city, which it derived from the export of olive oil, augmented by profits from horse breeding and shipping. The prosperity of Hadrumetum reached its height under the dynasty of Septimius Severus (193–211), himself of North African origin. The town was also a center for the administration of imperial estates in the eastern part of the province of Africa and, later, in the new province of Valeria Byzacena, of which it became the capital under the reorganization of Diocletian (284–305). Bishops of Hadrumetum are recorded at church councils from the third to the seventh centuries. Traces of various public buildings have come to light, and ancient houses uncovered by excavation reveal rich mosaics, of which the most famous offers a well-known, although more or less imaginary, portrayal of Virgil.

Haemus, Haimos. The ancient (originally Thracian) name of the Balkan Range (Stara Planina, 'high mountains,' in Bulgarian). The chain extended from the river Timacus (Timok) to the Euxine (Black) Sea. In Roman imperial times the Haemus range formed the border between the provinces of (Lower) Moesia and Thrace, and then, under the reorganization of Diocletian (AD 284–305), between Moesia Secunda to the north and Thracia and Haemimontus to the south. The historian Ammianus Marcellinus is a valuable source of information about these mountains. *See also* Beroe Augusta Trajana, Serdica.

Haimanova Mogila *see* Scythia

Haliacmon, Haliakmon. One of the three rivers (together with the Lydias and Axius) that form Macedonia's Thermaic Gulf. The Haliacmon flows eastward from Upper Macedonia (Elimiotis, Elimea) into the gulf between Bottiaea (north) and Pieria (south). *See also* Aegae, Beroea.

Haliartus, Haliartos. A city in Boeotia (central Greece), twelve miles west of Thebes, on the southern shore of Lake Copais (now drained). Its acropolis controlled traffic between northern and southern Greece. Dating back to the Bronze (Mycenaean) Age, Haliartus passed in historical times into the Boeotian League under the control of the Thebans. At the beginning of the Corinthian War, in which Boeotia combined with Athens, Corinth and Argos to combat the supremacy of Sparta (394), the Spartan general and statesman Lysander was surprised and killed at Haliartus. From 338 to 146 the important shrine of Poseidon at nearby Onchestus, in Haliartian territory, was the federal sanctuary of the Boeotian League. During Rome's Third Macedonian War (171–168) Haliartus sided with Perseus, King of Macedonia, whereupon the Roman general Gaius Lucretius razed the city, sold 2,500 of its citizens as slaves, and gave its territory to Athens, which repopulated the place with its own colonists.

As neighboring tombs show, the city was still occupied in Roman times, but it remained insignificant. When Pausanias visited Onchestus he found it in ruins, among which, however, the shrine and statue of Poseidon 'and the grove that Homer praises,' survived. On the acropolis of Haliartus walls of various periods can be identified, in addition to a Temple of Athena of the sixth century BC, and foundations of an earlier shrine. Heraclides Criticus, a geographer of the third century BC, describes the inhabitants of the city as slow-witted.

Halicarnassus (Bodrum). A city in Caria (southeastern Asia Minor), on the north coast of the Ceramic Gulf; its acropolis (Göktepe) overlooked a large sheltered harbor commanding the sea route between the mainland and the island of Cos. According to its later inhabitants, Halicarnassus was founded by colonists from Troezen in the Argolid on territory inhabited by the non-Greek Leleges. The settlers, who may have arrived *c* 900 BC, seem initially to have occupied the 'island,' a small rocky peninsula that was later separated from the Carian mainland by an artificial canal.

The historian Herodotus, who (like an epic poet Panyassis) came from Halicarnassus, described how the town was originally a member of the league of six Dorian cities (Hexapolis) of the region, but came to be expelled from the league's Triopian Games because its victorious athlete Agasicles had taken his prize (a tripod) home instead of dedicating it to Apollo. By Herodotus' time (the fifth century), however, Halicarnassus had become Ionian rather than Dorian, although many of its citizens possessed names that were neither Ionian nor Dorian Greek but Carian. After subjection to Persian rule in the later sixth century, the city was ruled by Queen Artemisia I, who took part in the battle of Salamis (480) and, according to Herodotus, was esteemed by the Persian monarch Xerxes I as one of his wisest advisers. A subsequent member of her dynasty, however, was expelled in favor of a republican constitution, with the support, it was stated, of Herodotus himself. By this time Halicarnassus had joined Athens' Delian League and empire, serving the Athenians as an important naval base during the Peloponnesian War when their other allies revolted (412).

The place became of major significance as capital of the new and powerful principality of Mausolus (377–353), which had to be reckoned with throughout the eastern Mediterranean world; he transferred the populations of six Lelegian communities to Halicarnassus, founding new towns, notably Theangela, in the places where they had formerly dwelt. His sister, widow and successor Artemisia II (d. 350) repelled an attack by the Rhodians and captured Rhodes itself. Thereafter, following several rapid changes of rulership, Alexander the Great, with considerable difficulty, seized the much damaged town of Halicarnassus (334), where he reinstated Ada, the sister of Mausolus and Artemisia II, and left her in charge.

After Alexander's death, the city belonged to a succession of different Hellenistic states—with brief intervals of freedom—until the formation of the Roman province of Asia (133–129). During the first century BC it was the birthplace of the rhetorician and historian Dionysius of Halicarnassus. It suffered devastation from Verres (80) and then again from Brutus and Cassius (43). Under the Principate, it did not greatly flourish. However, the local mint resumed the issue of coins. Some display a figure of Zeus Ascraeus (of the oak trees), who was worshipped at Halicarnassus; and the bald and bearded head of Herodotus is also displayed.

The city had, on one occasion, played a leading role in the history of Greek architecture and art. This distinction was owed to the tomb of Mausolus, which has brought the term 'Mausoleum' into modern languages. Before his death the king had already started work on the building, which was subsequently continued by Artemisia II and Ada. Surmounted, according to Pliny the Elder, by a twenty-four-step pyramid, the colonnaded Mausoleum ranked as one of the Seven Wonders of the World. Its sculptors, Scopas, Timotheus, Leochares and Bryaxis, were among the greatest of the age, and played a major part in giving direction to the Hellenistic art that lay ahead. Mausolus himself, whom a statue that surmounted the monument is often believed to represent, was interpreted by his Greek portrait-artist as a foreigner whose foreignness is deliberately indicated. This and other sculptures from the Mausoleum are now in the British Museum, while, on the site itself, excavations have been resumed; they disclose that the precinct was never completed.

Apart from substantial stretches of the city wall, not much else of ancient Halicarnassus survives, since it lies buried beneath the modern town; but its theater is currently being restored. The architectural writer Vitruvius compares the whole site of the town to the semicircular auditorium of a theater, with the agora by the harbor representing the stage (orchestra); on its left horn was Hermes' temple and on the summit of the Acropolis a shrine and statue of Ares. Nearby, Vitruvius adds, was a secret harbor hidden by the hills, to which the king could issue secret orders. In 1958/9 the first of a group of shipwrecks, eventually totalling fifteen (from the first century AD onward), was discovered near the island of Yassı Adası (Lodo) off the west coast of the Halicarnassus peninsula. Recent archaeological investigations have also thrown much light on the Lelegian princedoms in the hinterland.

Halieis (Porto Cheli). Situated on a useful harbor near the southern end of the Argolid peninsula (northeastern Peloponnese), Halieis was occupied from the early years of the first millennium BC. After a period under Spartan influence, it was settled *c* 470 by refugees from Tiryns (overrun by Argos), who probably established themselves alongside the previous inhabitants.

For the next century and a half the port served as an important naval base in struggles between the major Greek city-states. After repelling an attack by an Athenian force in 460, Halieis was captured by the Spartans some time before the Peloponnesian War. During the war (431–404), however, the town underwent further raids from the Athenians, resulting in an agreement that gave them the use of its acropolis and harbor (423). In the fourth century Halieis was allied with the Spartans (at least until 370/369), issuing coinage under the name of 'the Tirynthians.' Before 300 the locality was gradually abandoned—perhaps after destruction by one of Alexander's successors—although occupation was partly resumed in late Roman times. The population of the place had never exceeded 4,000. They supplemented their (sparse) agricultural resources by fishing and exporting salt: the name of the city means 'salty places,' with reference to local pans. Another export was purple dye derived from the sea snail *murex,* abundantly found in these waters.

A complex series of fortifications is to be seen upon the acropolis of Halieis, as well as on other parts of the site. The city also provides a significant example of an ancient town that has been largely submerged owing to subsequent changes of the coastline; so that its excavation has provided opportunities for the most modern techniques of shallow-water archaeology. In particular, at the east end of the bay some five hundred yards from the town itself, a Sanctuary of Apollo—who often appears on the local coinage—has been found about six feet under the sea. Its nucleus is a long, narrow, three-chambered temple dating back to *c* 675 BC, from which metalwork, pottery, and a statue of the god have been recovered. The shrine was reconstructed early in the fifth century, probably when the Tirynthians arrived, but underwent serious damage not long afterward—perhaps in the course of the Athenian attack in 460—and was never restored, although the altar in front of the building was reerected on a grander scale.

A second, adjoining temple has now been ascribed to *c* 600; it employed titles of Laconian type, *i.e.* belonging to a period when Spartan influence was strong. A third structure may have housed competitors in Games that took place in the small stadium (identified nearby). Or perhaps it served as dining quarters for guests attending religious festivals; many drinking cups have been found in an adjacent well. Considerable progress has also been made in reconstructing successive phases of the town plan, including a number of housing units and a building that contained coin blanks and has accordingly been identified as the local mint.

Haltern (ancient name unknown). A Roman fortress in west Germany, on the northwest bank of the river Luppia (Lippe), thirty-two miles beyond Vetera (Xanten on the Rhenus [Rhine]). Haltern was a legionary and auxiliary base in the reign of Augustus, during a brief period from shortly after the death of Nero Drusus (Drusus senior) in 9 BC (when it perhaps replaced a base at Oberaden) until the abandonment of Trans-Rhenane positions following the obliteration of Varus' army at the Saltus Teutoburgensis (*qv*) in AD 9.

The buildings at Haltern were constructed of wood and protected by an earthen and wooden defence system. They include a field camp, later superseded by the Great Camp, in which it is possible to identify the commander's residence (*praetorium*), administrative office (*principia*), barrack blocks, and medical center (*valetudinarium*). A small fort on an adjacent hill (St. Annaberg) may not have been Roman; but it was Romans who constructed the fortified harbor installations, more than once reconstructed and expanded, on an adjacent tributary of the Luppia.

Halys (Kızıl Irmak). The modern name means Red River, but the ancient name signifies Salt River, from the salt springs on its upper reaches. The longest river in Asia Minor, it rises in the northeast of the peninsula and proceeds in a great loop into the center of the country and then northward to the Euxine (Black) Sea, at a point west of Amisus (Samsun). During the sixth century BC the Halys separated the Lydian kingdom from the Persian empire. In Roman times it flowed through the provinces of Lesser Armenia, Cappadocia, Galatia and Pontus (subdivided, under Diocletian, into Paphlagonia and Helenopontus).

Hamadan *see* Ecbatana

Haran *see* Carrhae

Hatra (Al-Hadr). A city in Mesopotamia (Iraq), situated in an oasis fed by a stream parallel to the right bank of the Tigris (fifty miles south of Mosul). Constructed by the Parthians on a circular plan, Hatra flourished from before the Christian era as a formidably fortified caravan city, standing on the route that led northward from the Persian Gulf. By the end of the first century AD it had asserted a degree of independence from the Parthian empire under its own Arab rulers of the Sanatruq dynasty.

Hatra's most remarkable achievement was to withstand sieges from both Trajan (116) and Septimius Severus (198,199), on whose troops the defenders hurled down jars filled with insects and 'Hatran fire,' a burning bituminous naphtha. Subsequently, however, the fortress became, for a brief period, a dependency of Rome: a group of three dedications of 235 and the immediately following years records the presence of Roman troops. Then, however, it fell for a time into the hands of Shapur I, whose Persian (Sassanian) dynasty had replaced the Parthians. When the historian Ammianus Marcellinus visited the site in 363 he found it deserted.

The imposing complex of temples at Hatra, and the eclectic virtuosity of its sculptors, display a significant synthesis of Iranian, Greek and Roman elements, a blend that is conspicuously illustrated by a colossal temple and sanctuary of the sun-god Shamash (Shemesh), which was under construction in 77.

Hatunsaray *see* Lystra

Heba *see* Rusellae

Helicon. A mountain range in Boeotia (central Greece), between Lake Copais and the Corinthian Gulf. Helicon was renowned as the abode of the Muses, whose sanctuary and supposed grave—belonging to the city of Thespiae, and reputedly consecrated by early Thracian settlers—stood on one of its eastern summits (the Zagora). Nearby were the sacred springs Aganippe and Hippocrene, the latter—reputedly created by the tread of the winged horse Pegasus—providing inspiration to poets.

The mountain slopes have revealed remains of an Ionic shrine, a theater, and statues of the Muses; other sculptural works were taken away by Constantine I the Great (AD 306–37) to decorate his new city of Constantinople. The poet Hesiod, who came from neighboring Ascra, tended sheep on Helicon in his boyhood. Pausanias describes the fertility of its slopes, and the miraculous healing properties of its herbs, and the absence of any poisonous plants or snakes.

Heliopolis (Baalbek) in Lebanon. A city situated in the Orontes (Bekaa) valley between the Libanus (Lebanon) and the Anti-Lebanon ranges. Of prehistoric origins, the place became the religious center of an Ituraean principality which was established in the first century BC and had its civil capital at Chalcis Beneath Lebanon (Mejdel Anjar). From *c* 16–13 Heliopolis was attached by Augustus to the Roman citizen colony of Berytus (Beirut), but subsequently became a flourishing colony on its own account, gaining ground at the expense of Berytus, after the latter had opposed Septimius Severus in his civil war against Pescennius Niger (194/6). The coinage of Heliopolis includes the design of three crowns, described as the prizes of the sacred contests held at the city (the Certamina Sacra Capitolina Oecumenica Iselastica Heliopolitana).

Other coins depict the Temple of Zeus (Jupiter Optimus Maximus, assimilated to Baal), which gave the city its fame. This huge shrine, perhaps inaugurated by Augustus, formed part of a spectacular and elaborate precinct, set on an artificial vaulted terrace and constituting a major masterpiece of composite axial planning. It was joined in the later second century AD by another grandiose temple which is the best preserved of any in the Greco-Roman world. Richly decorated with colossal fluted pilasters and a double tier of niches, it may have been dedicated to Dionysus (Bacchus), for the performance of whose mystic ceremonies its platform perhaps served as a stage; another view ascribes the shrine to Venus-Atargatis.

A neighboring area, in which broad colonnaded streets have been cleared, contains a third temple, which, although much smaller, is equally important to the history of architecture. This elegant so-called Temple of Venus is circular, but the circle is broken by five concave niched recessions between columns; the baroque design earned an imitation by Francesco Borromini (1599–1667). A temple of Hermes, too, stood on top of a hill outside the city walls; the great flight of steps leading up to it is shown on a coin of the Roman emperor

Philip I (244/9). Excavations in an adjoining suburb have disclosed villas of the third and fourth centuries, paved with fine mosaics in classical and orientalizing styles.

Hellespont (Çanakkalc Boğazı, Dardanelles). The narrow strait between Thrace and the Troad (northwestern Asia Minor) leading from the Aegean Sea to the Propontis (Sea of Marmara). The Hellespont began to receive Greek colonists in the later eighth century BC. It was crossed by the Persian King Xerxes I in 480 BC and again by Alexander the Great in 334. It also played a decisive part in the civil war between Constantine I the Great and Licinius in AD 324. Licinius had massed his fleet of three hundred and fifty ships at the Hellespont under Abantus, but Constantine destroyed the fleet and forced the narrows, thus cutting off Licinius' stronghold of Byzantium (Istanbul) from supplies by sea, and precipitating his downfall, which placed the entire empire in Constantine's hands. The strait derives its modern name, the Dardanelles, from Dardanus (Maltepe or Kusköy) on its Asiatic bank.

The Hellespont is overlooked by Troy, the scene of Homer's *Iliad.* But it is also famous in mythology for the love story of Hero and Leander, told by the poet Musaeus, who probably lived in the later fifth century AD. Hero was the priest of Aphrodite at Sestus on the European bank; Leander, who lived at Abydus on the Asian side, fell in love with her and used to swim across the Hellespont by night, until a storm put out the light by which she was accustomed to guide him, and he drowned; whereupon she, too, threw herself into the sea. During the later Roman empire there was a province of Hellespontus, comprising Mysia and districts to its east. *See also* Abydus, Cardia, Lampsacus, Sestus, Sigeum, Troy.

Henna (Enna). A city on a wide rocky plateau of central Sicily—of which it was described as the navel—Henna was protected on every side by steep cliffs. An early native (Sicel) settlement was followed by Hellenization under the control first of Gela (seventh century BC) and later of Dionysius I of Syracuse (*c* 397). After a period of Carthaginian rule, and temporary liberation by Pyrrhus of Epirus (277), Henna passed into the hands of the Romans (258), but its attempt to revolt against them in the Second Punic War was suppressed by a mass slaughter of its citizens in the theater (214), followed by the abolition of its 'free' status. In 135 Henna became the headquarters of the first great Slave Revolt against the Romans, to which numerous inscribed lead sling-shots found in the neighborhood bear witness; it was not until three years later that the consul Publius Rupilius succeeded in capturing the city. Cicero visited it in order to gather evidence of the lootings of the proconsul Verres (73–71), and eloquently described the fertility and beauty of the area. About 43, the town was raised to the status of *municipium* by Lucius Munatius Plancus, one of whose freedmen's names appear on its coins. But not very long afterward Strabo described its population as sparse.

Henna owed its renown to a sanctuary of Demeter (Ceres) and Persephone or Kore (Proserpina). Its coins honored Demeter in the fifth century BC, and it is recorded that revered statues of the two goddesses and of Triptolemus, to whom Demeter gave the gift of grain, stood in the shrine; though only small traces of the building now remain. The *Homeric Hymn to Demeter* (*c* 600) told how Hades (Dis, Pluto) had leapt out in his chariot and seized Persephone, bearing her off to the underworld, where she henceforward had to spend a third of every year. According to a poetic tradition perpetuated by Cicero and Diodorus Siculus, this fateful act, marking the transition from summer to winter, took place in the neighborhood of Henna, on the shores of Lake Pergusa (where tombs dating back to the eighth century have been found): 'Not that fair field/ Of Enna,' as Milton recounted, 'where Proserpin gathering flowers/ Herself a fairer flower by gloomy Dis/Was gathered.'

Heraclea, Herakleia (Policoro). A coastal city of Lucania (Basilicata, southeastern Italy), situated on the Gulf of Taras (Tarentum, Taranto) at the mouth of the river Aciris (Agri). Excavations have uncovered a large pre-Greek community of the later eight century BC, followed by the arrival of Greek settlers soon after 700; but the place was definitively colonized in 443/2, by Taras and Thurii (the former Sybaris [Sibari]), becoming a dependency or, probably, a replacement of the neighboring town of Siris, of which the harbor, at the mouth of the river of the same name (now the Sinni), was blocked by shoals. The purpose of the colonization was to form an outpost against the growing power of the native Lucanians in the interior.

In the early fourth century BC Archytas of Taras chose Heraclea as the seat of the general assembly of the League of Italian Greeks, but Alexander of Epirus, during his invasion of the country (*c* 333–330), moved the center of the confederation to Thurii because of his hostility to the Tarantines. It was at Heraclea that Pyrrhus of Epirus won his first costly ('Pyrrhic') victory over the Romans (280), who shortly afterward detached the city from Taras, granting it a favorable treaty.

Heraclea owes its greatest importance, however, to the discovery of a bronze tablet inscribed with the drafts of four laws that were under preparation at the time of Julius Caesar's death (44), and were given the force of law by Antony shortly afterward. The third of these drafts, containing the so-called *Lex Julia municipalis,* establishes the qualifications for office (magistracy) and membership of governing councils in communities of Roman citizens outside the capital, excluding gladiators, bankrupts, cashiered soldiers, and servants of proscriptions, but admitting exiles whose former rights have been restored. The law also provides that censuses in Rome were to be accompanied or followed by similar procedures in other Italian communities, which should then forward the results to the capital.

The local coinage of Heraclea emphasizes Athena, but a sanctuary of Demeter and Kore (Persephone) has been found outside the city. An elaborate potters' quarter has also come to light, containing many vases of the fourth and third centuries BC, when Heraclea was a leading center for the production of the wares.

Heraclea (Cernavoda) *see* Axiopolis

Heraclea on Latmus. A Carian town (though on the Ionian coast) in southwest Asia Minor, situated on a lower ridge of Mount Latmus (Beş Parmak), where it descends to an inlet of the Aegean Sea (subsequently converted by the silt of the river Maeander [Büyük Menderes] into the inland Lake Bafa). Under its earlier name of Latmus, the place was first a center of the non-Greek Leleges and then a member of Athens' Delian League in the fifth century BC. Subsequently it was taken over by King Mausolus of Halicarnassus (377–353), who created a new city half a mile away under the name of Heraclea.

The place was famous for the myth of Endymion, who was loved by the Moon; according to one version he was a Carian (though Elis also claimed him), and his tomb was shown on Mount Latmus. One of the Scipios confirmed the city's freedom, but in the mid-first century BC it was in debt to a Roman banker. Its leaders voted honors to Augustus (31 BC–AD 14) and his grandson Gaius Caesar, although at the time, according to Strabo, it was only a minor town (*polichnion*) and place of anchorage. Its territory, according to Diodorus, was known as Latmia.

Recent surveys have yielded important discoveries. Traces of the Lelegian and early Greek walls of Latmus have come to light; and the four-mile circuit of Heraclea's subsequent fortifications, probably constructed by Mausolus and studded with sixty-five towers, constitute one of the most important surviving Greek defensive systems. The town plan is symmetrical and rectangular. Above and behind the habitation area stood a temple of Athena (identified by an inscription), dating from the third century BC. Other Hellenistic sites include an unusually shaped sanctuary of Endymion, an agora (flanked on one side by two levels of shops), a council chamber (*bouleuterion*), a theater, and a wrestling school (*palaestra*). The Roman period provides a bathing establishment and fountain-building (*nymphaeum*) attached to a temple on its shore. Early Christian monuments include a basilica outside the walls. The bronze coins of Heraclea, during the imperial epoch, are hard to distinguish from those of another Carian city of the same name (Heraclea Salbace), but an issue of Caracalla depicting a temple of Tyche (Fortune) seems to belong to the Latmian city.

Heraclea Pontica (Ereğli). A coastal city of Bithynia (later Pontus) in northwestern Asia Minor, on the southern coast of the Euxine (Black) Sea; situated on a theater-shaped site on a headland overlooking a natural harbor (the first of any importance east of the Thracian Bosphorus) in the territory of the Mariandyni, whom the colonists subjugated as helot-serfs. Claiming Heracles as its founder (he was said to have reached the underworld through a cave on the Acherusian promontory [Baba Burnu] nearby), the place was colonized *c* 560–558 BC by the Megarians (not the Milesians, as Strabo recorded) with Boeotian assistance. Its democratic government, prospering from a rich agricultural hinterland and sea fisheries, soon controlled the coast as far east as Cytorus (Kidros) and established colonies of its own on the European coast of the Black Sea, at Callatis (Mangalia) and Chersonesus (Sevastopol) in the Tauric Chersonese (Crimea).

However, Leucon I, one of the monarchs of the Cimmerian (Tauric, Crimean) Bosphorus (*c* 389/8–349/8), became involved in serious warfare with Heraclea Pontica. In 364/3 civil strife within the city led to autocratic rule by Clearchus (a protégé of the lower classes and pupil of Plato and Isocrates) and his colorful dynasty, under which Heraclea flourished; his son Dionysius (337/6 or 333/2–305) extended the city's territory, supported Antigonus I Monophthalmos who was one of Alexander the Great's successors, and assumed the title of king. Dionysius' Persian widow and successor Amastris married another of Alexander's successors, Lysimachus of Thrace (302), but later—after he had abandoned her—returned to Heraclea and founded a town named after herself (formerly Sesamus, now Amasra). Before long, however, she was murdered, and *c* 289/8 or 281 Heraclea introduced a democratic government. In Hellenistic times, Bithynian and Pontic kings and Galatian immigrants gradually weakened the city; but with the assistance of a treaty with Rome (after 188) it remained free, until Bithynia was annexed by the Romans in 74. Soon afterward, in collusion with Mithridates VI of Pontus, the Heracleans massacred some Italian businessmen, thus earning subsequent devastation and destruction by Marcus Aurelius Cotta, after a two years' siege described by their local historian, Memnon.

Heraclea received a settlement of ex-soldiers from Julius Caesar (or from Antony in accordance with the late Caesar's plan), though it is doubtful whether an official colony was established; and Antony presented the rest of the city to a Galatian chieftain Adiatorix, whom Octavian (the future Augustus) subsequently executed for slaughtering Roman citizens in his territory. Heraclea's coinage under the Principate describes it as 'metropolis' (of the coastal cities of the region) and 'mother of the city-colonies' and defines its location as 'in Pontus,' indicating that it now belonged to the Pontic section of the combined province of Pontus and Bithynia. In the later empire, however, it was the border town between the provinces of Bithynia and Paphlagonia (later Honorias).

A coin of Gallienus (253–68) shows a lighthouse with three receding storeys, and another piece, dating from the reign of Gordian III (238–44), depicts a stadium with a temple at one end. A shrine of Rome appears on an issue of Philip I (244–49). Certain temples could still be seen at Heraclea by nineteenth-century visitors; but they have now disappeared, and it is not even certain whether the Roman colony stood on the site of the Greek harbor city or beneath the modern town, which lies on the slopes of the citadel hill.

Heraclium, Heracleion *see* Crete, Herculaneum, Pithecusae

Heraea *see* Arcadia

Herat *see* Alexandria (Artacoana)

Herculaneum, Herakleion or Heraclanon (Ercolano beside Resina). A small city in Campania (southwestern Italy), about five miles from Neapolis (Naples) on its bay (in ancient times, the Gulf of Cumae); constructed on a spur projecting from the lower slopes of Mount Vesuvius, beside the coast road. Strabo indicates that Herculaneum, like Pompeii, was successively dominated by

Oscans, Etruscans, Samnites and Romans. A tradition of the Greeks, however, ascribed the foundation of the town to their own mythical hero Heracles (Hercules), and archaeological evidence suggests the dominant influence of neighboring Greek cities, first Cumae (Cuma) and then Neapolis.

About 400, Herculaneum, like other towns of the region, was—as Strabo suggested—occupied by the Samnites, but subsequently, in common with the rest of Campania, came under Roman control (during the last decade of the fourth century). Herculaneum, together with Pompeii, joined the Italian rebellion against Rome known as the Social War (91–87), but was subjugated by the troops of Sulla (89) and became a Roman *municipium*.

Although its population did not exceed four or five thousand, Herculaneum was a favored resort; its promontory running out to the sea, observes Strabo, was excellently placed to catch the southwestern breezes. But the city suffered severely in an earthquake in AD 62, and was totally destroyed by the eruption of Vesuvius in 79. The entire town was buried by a torrid, treacly mass now identified, in technical terms, as a pyroclastic flow of ignimbrite (misinterpreted as a flow of mud), which later solidified into a compact layer attaining a height, at certain points, of sixty feet. Although presenting excavators with severe problems, this covering hindered looters from penetrating much of the site (though see below), and ensured the preservation of wooden frameworks and furniture, cloth and foodstuffs, which makes Herculaneum unique among sites of the classical world.

Its gradual rediscovery during the eighteenth century was of decisive importance in the history of archaeological excavation, just as the monumental eight volumes of *Le antichità di Ercolano* (1757–92), produced by the Royal Herculaneum Academy of King Charles III of Naples, influenced furniture, interior decoration, costume and jewelry throughout Europe for half a century. Prominent among the early discoveries was 'the Villa of the Papyri' adjacent to the city (but now inaccessible, though its renewed uncovering is promised), which contributed a whole library of carbonized ancient Greek papyrus rolls—principally the works of the Epicurean Philodemus of Gadara (*c* 110–40/35 BC)—as well as numerous statues, including a collection of bronzes that is without parallel in the ancient world.

Within the city itself, the array of public buildings is remarkable for so small a place, including a basilica and theater (already robbed, through shafts and tunnels, in the eighteenth century), part of the colonnaded forum, an unusually grand sports ground (*palaestra*) with swimming pool, and two bath houses, one of which is exceptionally well preserved. But the most remarkable feature of Herculaneum consists of its houses—as in Pompeii, but those at Herculaneum are in many cases better preserved. They also display greater variety in construction and design; upper storeys, confidently constructed, are still to be seen, and inner courts display extensive lighting. These houses range from noble mansions with wall paintings, mosaics, terraces and gardens, overlooking the bay, through middle class but still elegantly decorated residences, to the House of Opus Craticium (*a graticcio*) with walls of wood, mortar and rubble, containing small, separate, and separately accessible apartments.

Although scarcely half of the city has been uncovered—the rest lies, perhaps forever, beneath the closely packed town of Resina, and none of the temples (so prominent at Pompeii) have yet come to light—it is possible to discern a different way of life from that of the sister city. The town plan of Herculaneum displays complete regularity; traffic was evidently much less dense; and shops play a less prominent part. Herculaneum possessed its industries, notably fishing, but it was primarily a residential and not a commercial town. Recent excavations have identified the ancient coastline—close by the city. On what was once the beach, the remains of an overturned boat have been revealed, together with skeletons of persons who lost their lives in the eruption, now undergoing examination by new scientific methods that throw light on the physical condition of the victims.

Hermia *see* Seleucia on the Calycadnus

Hermonassa (Tamansk). A coastal city in the Soviet Union, situated at the most southerly part of the Taman peninsula, beside the entrance to the Cimmerian Bosphorus (Strait of Kerch) which separates the east coast of the Euxine (Black) Sea from the Tauric Chersonese (Crimea). Well placed to exploit the early importance of the Taman Gulf (and the estuary of the river Kuban), Hermonassa was founded in the early sixth century BC by colonists who probably came from Miletus in Ionia (western Asia Minor). Its inhabitants reached the height of their prosperity *c* 300 BC.

Recent excavations, of an exceptionally fruitful character, have uncovered streets and numerous buildings, including extensive remains (together with a necropolis) from the early sixth century down into the fifth—when a change in building layout occurred. An important official edifice of the fourth century, with an internal colonnaded courtyard, has also been revealed; and there is another large public building too. Mentioned by Strabo and Pliny the Elder, the city was again redesigned and largely rebuilt in the second century AD; a winery of the years before and after 300 has come to light. (This Hermonassa is to be distinguished from another town of the same name on the coast of eastern Pontus [northeastern Asia Minor]).

Hermus (Gediz Çayı). The second largest river (after the Maeander [Büyük Menderes]) running into the Aegean Sea on the west coast of Asia Minor. Rising on the sacred mountain of the Dindymene mother goddess (Murat Dağı) in Phrygia, the Hermus entered the sea beside Phocaea (Foca)—as it does again today, by deliberate diversion, after having followed another course for centuries. The Pactolus (Sart Çayı)—rich in gold—and Hyllus (Kum Çayı) are among its tributaries. In Roman times, the reclining river-god Hermus was shown on the coinage of Aeolian, Lydian and Phrygian cities.

Herodium (Jebel el-Fureidis in Israel). A fortification seven miles south of Jerusalem, and four miles south east of Bethlehem. Herodium was one of a chain of massive fortress-palaces built by the Jewish monarch Herod the Great, a client of Rome; its construction was begun in 24 BC, and it was finished by 15, when Herod showed his creation to Augustus' lieutenant Marcus Agrippa.

Standing on top of a mountain that rises 2,489 feet above sea level and was elevated further by a massive artificial mound, the stronghold was circular in shape, surrounded by double walls equipped with four towers: some believe that Herod was (and is) buried in the still-unexcavated north tower. The adjacent palace includes a colonnaded and pilastered hall, a large dining hall with adjoining rooms, and a bathing establishment in the Roman manner with painted stucco walls and mosaic floors. Josephus, who offers a detailed account of the complex, describes numerous further constructions at the foot of the hill, including residential apartments, baths, storehouses, plastered cisterns, and pools which, since there is no source of water nearby, were supplied by aqueducts from the neighborhood of Bethlehem.

In the First Jewish Revolt (First Roman War, AD 66–73), Herodium was garrisoned by insurgents and held out until 72, two years after the fall of Jerusalem and its Temple. During the Second Revolt (132–35), it once again became a major fortress, employed (as letters from Wadi Murabbaat reveal) as a center where the rebel leaders stored the grain and taxes they collected. The palace court was, at this juncture, converted into a synagogue or place of assembly, and archaeologists have identified what is believed to have been a ritual bath. After the insurrection was over, Herodium was abandoned, until, during the fifth century, Christian monks established a chapel among the ruins. Rooms in the palace have yielded graffiti in Hebrew, Aramaic, Greek and Latin, ranging in date from the time of Herod the Great to the Byzantine epoch.

Hesperides, Garden of the. Named after the three (or seven) Nymphs who, according to Greek mythology, guarded a tree of golden apples (given by Gaia [Earth] to Hera on the latter's marriage), with the assistance of the dragon Ladon. The eleventh Labor of Heracles was to obtain some of these apples; but they were later returned, it was believed, to the Garden of Hesperides, and subsequently employed on a number of mythical occasions. The Garden was variously located (1) on the western borders of the river Oceanus, in a far northern land of the Hyperboreans, (2) in the Atlas mountains or the region of the Pillars of Heracles (Straits of Gibraltar), (3) in western Cyrenaica at Al Kuwayfiya (*see* Berenice, Euhesperides).

Hibernia, Ierne (Ireland). The island was first known to Greeks through sailors from Massalia (Marseille). Then their compatriot Pytheas, toward the end of the fourth century BC learned more about the country from his circumnavigation of Britain; so that the geographical account offered by Eratosthenes (*c* 275–194) was approximately correct. Strabo, on the other hand, placed Hibernia north of Britain. He describes its inhabitants as heavy eaters (or herb-eaters?), cannibalistic and incestuous. Mela agreed about their undesirable character, but praised their pastures.

An Irish prince took refuge with Cnaeus Julius Agricola, governor of Britain (*c* AD 82), who did not, however, employ this opportunity to cross over into Ireland—perhaps because his emperor, Domitian, would not let him: although subsequently Agricola was heard to say—with dubious accuracy—that it could have been conquered by a small force. Roman trade with Ireland remained small; few imported objects are found there, except coins. The island early showed signs of division into its historic four quarters (Ulster, Munster, Leinster and Connaught), of which the last named was the most important in Roman times, until superseded by Niall of the Nine Hostages (d. 405) at Tara in Meath (a separate central area bordering on each of the four main regions).

Numerous Irish emigrants, known as Scotti, began to settle in Wales, western England, and especially western Scotland (Dalriada), from at least the fourth century onward. Conversely, *c* 431, a Roman churchman named Palladius came from England for a brief stay in Ireland. Shortly afterward, St. Patrick too—apparently a single, historical individual, and not two or more different persons as has been suggested—came to Ireland from his home on the northwestern borders of England. He composed a *Confession* and a *Letter (Corioticus)*, and is thus the only author of this date, working outside the western imperial frontiers, of whose writings examples have survived. St. Patrick introduced the Latin tongue and the Roman episcopal type of church to the Irish, although conformity to Rome was not effectively enforced for two and a half centuries to come.

Hierapolis, formerly Hieropolis. In Phrygia (west central Asia Minor), situated at a height of 1,200 feet above sea level. Its modern name, Pamukkale ('Cotton Castle'), is owed to the whiteness of the cliffs formed by the calcium-oxide bearing hot waters of the Chrysorrhoas (Çoruh Su) flowing down from the Çal Dağı mountain to the plain of the river Maeander (Büyük Menderes) below. Founded, as recently discovered inscriptions show, by the Seleucids from Syria (and not by the Attalids of Pergamum, as has been supposed), the place was probably named after Hiera or Hiero, the wife of the mythical Telephus. But the name Hierapolis, 'holy city,' also seemed relevant to the much frequented local sanctuary of the Plutoneion or Charonion. Sacred to the earth mother Cybele (or to Leto), this was believed to be an entrance to the underworld; it is described by Strabo as a hillside cave, fronted by a fenced enclosure filled with a vapor (carbon dioxide gas), which exercised lethal effects on all except the priestesses of the goddess—who survived by holding their breath. The hot springs of the Chrysorrhoas, producing water that 'congealed into stone,' were incorporated into a bathing establishment of which considerable portions have survived.

Destroyed by severe earthquakes in AD 17 and 60, Hierapolis was imposingly rebuilt, with substantial enlargments, under Domitian (81–96). A large and well-preserved theater (restored under Septimius Severus, in 205–10) has now been cleared; its podium is adorned by a sculptured frieze more than a hundred and eighty feet long. A C-shaped precinct round the temple of Apollos Helios-Lairbenos has also been uncovered, and there are two avenues of tombs; one of them contains the remains of a certain Flavius Zeuxis, whose epitaph indicates that he made seventy-two voyages to Italy. Extensive local coinage of the imperial epoch (which replaces the name of Hieropolis by Hierapolis) often refers to the pagan religious festivals held by the city, known as the Olympian, Pythian and Actian Games and the Games by the Chrysorrhoas.

As recorded by the Pauline *Epistle to the Colossians,* Hierapolis became the seat of an early Christian church, especially associated with St. Philip, who was said to have been executed at the place; the shrine of his martyrdom (*martyrium*), which has now been excavated, dates from the early fifth century. This, it now appears, was an epoch of extensive rebuilding in the city, including a second restoration of the theater. During the two following centuries, however, Hierapolis lost its importance.

Hierapytna (Ierapetra). A city on the coast of Crete, on a low-lying and not easily defensible site west of Cape Erythraeum, at the southern end of the narrowest part of the island. It was colonized early in the first millennium BC by Dorians, but many of the inhabitants were of earlier Cretan stock. The founder was said to have been a certain Cyrbas, whose name (reflected in an earlier designation of the city itself, Cyrba—another was Camirus) indicates a connexion with Rhodes. Treaties, recorded by inscriptions, reveal the active role of Hierapytna in Hellenistic times. Its strong (and sometimes piratical) fleet, based on a useful double harbor, joined the forces of other Cretan cities—supported by Macedonia—against Rhodes, whose dependencies Cos and Calymnus they attacked (204–201); but then the Hierapytnians changed sides. Subsequently they destroyed their neighbor Praesus (*c* 145/140), fought prolonged wars against another town, Itanus, and were the last Cretans to hold out against the Roman conquest by Quintus Caecilius Metellus Creticus (*c* 68).

The coinage of Hierapytna resumed briefly in the time of Tiberius (AD 14–37), under whom silver pieces honored Zeus Cretagenes and the deified Augustus; issues under Gaius (Caligula, 37–41) revived a design of the fourth century BC displaying an eagle and a palm tree. A colossal statue of Hadrian (117–38) trampling a barbarian, now in the Istanbul museum, was found at Hierapytna. The city evidently prospered in the imperial epoch, and Servius (*c* AD 400) reported that in his day it was one of the only two of the former hundred towns of Crete that still survived (the other being Cnossus). Hierapytna became the seat of a bishopric. Traces of an ancient theater and amphitheater can still be seen, but a mental effort is needed to picture the harbors, inner (now marshland) and outer (under the modern town).

Hierocaesarea *see* Comana Pontica

Hieropolis (Al-Manbej). A city in a fertile area of Cyrrhestice (in northern Syria), west of the river Euphrates. Under the names of Mabbog and Bambyce it had presumably been a Syrian sanctuary from ancient times, as is suggested by its name *hiera polis,* holy city: this designation was probably owed to Seleucus I Nicator (d. 281 BC), who refounded and partially Hellenized the place (taking it over from the priestly dynasty of Abd-Hadad), and under the new (temporary) name of Edessa made it an important station on the main road between Antioch and Seleucia on the Tigris. The local cult, devoted to the Syrian nature-goddess Atargatis (Astarte, Ashtoreth), was described by Pseudo-Lucian, *On the Syrian Goddess*, as orgiastic; phallic ex-votos were offered, and gigantic phalli set up in front of the temple and climbed by worshippers once a year. The shrine was looted by Crassus on the way to his disastrous encounter with the Parthians at Carrhae (53). Subsequently Hieropolis served as a bastion of Roman defences against the Parthians and their Persian successors. During the later empire, it became the capital of the province of Euphratensis.

Hieropolis (Phrygia) *see* Hierapolis

Hieropolis Castabala, Kastabalon (Bodrum). An inland city of eastern, 'Smooth' Cilicia of the Plain (Pedias, southeastern Asia Minor), on the river Pyramus (Ceyhan); the principal center of the district of Castabalis. Mentioned, under the name of Kastabalon, as a place where Alexander the Great made a stop before the battle of Issus (333 BC), the town issued coins for the Seleucid king Antiochus IV Epiphanes (175–163) with the name of Hieropolis on the Pyramus, and became, in the first century BC, the capital of the kings of Amanus (*qv*), but was incorporated into the Roman province of Syria-Cilicia early in the reign of Tiberius (AD 17). Its coinage of the third century AD reverts to the original place-name of Castabala.

Some of these coins honor Artemis Perasia, the pre-Greek goddess to whom the city owes its designation as holy (*hiera*), depicting her on a throne beneath which an eagle is perched. Only the foundations of her temple have survived, but a colonnaded street can be traced, and substantial portions of a theater (for the most part free-standing) are still to be seen, in addition to plaster-lined concrete reservoirs. Hieropolis Castabala became a Christian bishopric, and remains of two fifth-century churches are preserved.

Hierosolyma *see* Jerusalem

Himera (Imera). Beside the north coast of Sicily—the only Greek colony on this shore with the exception of Mylae. Himera was founded *c* 649/8 BC on the coastal plain to the west of the river Himera (Grande or Imera Settentrionale), at a site adjoining two hills, by settlers from Zancle (Messana, Messina) of Euboean origin, who were joined in this enterprise by another Euboean group and by the Myletidae (probably a clan of Syracusan refugees from Mylae [Milazzo]). The lyric poet Tisias, better known as Stesichorus ('choral master'), lived at Himera, probably in the first half of the sixth century; his fable of the horse which, driven off his pasturage by a stag, appealed to a man for assistance but could not get rid of him, was said to have been a warning to the Himerans not to call in Phalaris, the Greek autocrat (tyrant) of Acragas, for help against its non-Greek neighbors. The rising prosperity of Himera is shown by its coinage, displaying the emblem of a cock, the harbinger of day (*hemera*), from which the name of the city was believed to have been derived (erroneously, since the word is not of Greek but of native Sicilian derivation).

In the early fifth century, when these issues originated, the city was dominated by a certain Terillus, who was expelled by Theron of Acragas (Agrigento) (483), fled to his son-in-law Anaxilas of Rhegium (Reggio di Calabria), and appealed to the Carthaginians for help. They responded with the most formidable force that had ever invaded the island—intended, according to Herodotus, to effect its complete conquest—and the subsequent battle of Himera, at which Theron and his son-in-law Gelon of Syracuse confronted the invaders, was one of the historic engagements of antiquity. The Carthaginians, under their commander Hamilcar, were preparing to besiege Theron at Himera, but Gelon decided to attack them before they could join forces with Anaxilas, and broke the siege by a trick, inserting cavalry into the enemy's stockade under the pretence that they came from Carthage's ally Selinus (Selinunte). Gelon's troops burned the ships on the beach, and the entire Carthaginian army was killed or captured, Hamilcar himself being among those who fell.

Seventy years were to pass before Carthage tried to conquer Sicily again. When this happened, in 409, Himera (independent of Acragas since 461) was obliterated by Hamilcar's nephew Hannibal—as an act of revenge—and left deserted. Its refugees were settled seven miles away at Thermae Himeraeae (Termini Imerese), which its inhabitants sometimes described as Himera; it was the birthplace of Agathocles, ruler of Syracuse (361), and became a Roman colony under Augustus.

At the old Himera, near the mouth of the river beside the harbor, a large Doric shrine has been excavated; known today as the 'Temple of Victory,' it may have been erected to celebrate the triumph of 480. Uphill on the plain, another sanctuary, comprising three early temples, has come to light; one of these buildings, richly embellished with terracotta decorations, seems to have existed from *c* 550 to *c* 409. Parts of the city walls have also been discoverd, as well as residential blocks, bearing witness to two periods of urban planning and reorientation, in the early and then the middle fifth century BC; both of these successive designs adhered to a strictly geometrical, right-angled plan, replacing an older, irregular configuration. A local antiquarium has recently been opened.

Hippo Regius, formerly Hippou Akra (Hippone, a mile and a half from Annaba, Bône). A coastal city of Numidia (near the northeastern extremity of Algeria), covering two hillocks overlooking a rich, flat plain and a deep, sheltered bay beside the mouth of the river Ubus (Seybouse), which has now radically changed its course. Of early origin, Hippo was a harbor town of the Carthaginians, from whom, after the Second Punic War (218-202 BC), it passed into the hands of the kings of Numidia, becoming their second residence and thus acquiring the designation of Regius, 'Royal' (which distinguishes it from Hippo Diarrhytus or Zarytus [Bizerta], though confusions between the two cities occur in our sources). After Julius Caesar's victory over his Pompeian enemies at Thapsus (46 BC), Hippo Regius shared, for the future, the varying administrative arrangements of the rest of Numidia (*qv*). It prospered from vines, olives and above all grain, and became the second port of Africa.

Hippo Regius was probably the hometown of the biographer Suetonius (born *c* AD 69), but owes its undying fame to the bishopric of St. Augustine (395–430), of which we learn a great deal from his writings. When he had arrived there earlier as a priest, he was accustomed to leave his duties, from time to time, to preside over the Monastery in the Garden, which he had founded; after he had become bishop, the monastery continued to attract his friends, while he himself, now residing in his episcopal palace, established an austere routine (from which female visitors were excluded). His church, baptistery and chapel were all nearby; a large basilica and baptistery of a slightly earlier date have been identified on the site.

But Augustine's Hippo, too, contained villas of the rich, decorated with opulent mosaic floors overlaying similar layers that reflect successive stages of opulent construction. Excavations have also revealed public buildings from the previous stages of the city's existence, including edifices surrounding the forum, which was reconstructed in the time of Vespasian and contained fine statues; several bathing establishments, too, have yielded sculptural works. The theater at Hippo Regius is one of the largest in Africa, and the museum possesses a unique bronze trophy of an officer's cuirass and cloak of about the time of Julius Caesar.

Hippocrene *see* Helicon

Hispalis, later Romula (Seville). In southern (Further) Spain (Baetica), on the left bank of the river Baetis (Guadalquivir), fifty-four miles from the sea. An old Iberian and then probably Phoenician settlement, Hispalis received a settlement of ex-soldiers from Julius Caesar under the name of Colonia Julia Romula (45 BC). Subsequently it became an important trading and ship-building port, accessible to sea-going ships and fed by a fertile hinterland. During the second century AD it eclipsed the old harbor town of Gades (Cadiz) and rivalled Corduba (Cordoba). Hispalis possessed a Christian bishop from *c* 300, if not earlier. During the fifth century, it fell into the hands of the Visigoths (411), Vandals (428), and Suebi (441), and then the Visigoths again.

A town plan of Hispalis has now been reconstructed and published. A large part of its fortifications is traceable. Julius Caesar's colony occupied the highest zone to avoid floods. An early Christian baptistery has been uncovered outside the wall (Los Reales Alcazares). Adjoining the building was a pool (*piscina*), which was reshaped at the end of the fifth century, not long after its initial construction.

Hispania (Spain and Portugal). The basic population consisted of Iberians (who came from Africa, in early Neolithic times) and Celts (arriving from the north, in the late Bronze and Iron Ages). Phoenicians from Tyre (Es-Sur) settled at Tartessus and Gades (Cadiz), and Greeks from Phocaea (Foca) and Massalia (Massilia, Marseille) established coastal colonies. Most of these settlements vanished, however, in the later third century BC, when the Carthaginians, reviving the Phoenician heritage, established a powerful empire in the south and east of the country, founding Carthago Nova (Cartagena) in 228. During the Second Punic War they lost this empire to the Romans (206), who established army commands and conducted a prolonged series of military operations culminating in the fall of the native chieftain Viriathus' stronghold Numantia in 133. It was during this phase that two Roman provinces were created, Hispania Citerior (Nearer Spain) covering the principal route south to Carthago Nova, and Hispania Ulterior (Further Spain) including the Baetis (Guadalquivir) valley and southeast coast.

Spain was the scene of two important victories of Julius Caesar in his civil wars against the Pompeians (Ilerda [Lerida] 49, Munda 45). Augustus finally divided the whole of the peninsula into three provinces, Citerior (subsequently known as Tarraconensis, extending to the north and west coast), Baetica (Ulterior, highly Romanized), and a new province of Lusitania (Portugal and part of western Spain). Municipalization, colonization and the spread of Latin rights (under which the leaders of city administrations became Roman citizens) gradually proceeded—especially under Vespasian, AD 69–79—and during the years to come the older territories reached the height of their economic development. They sent more senators to Rome than any other territory except southern (Narbonese) Gaul, and produced Latin writers of the caliber of the two Senecas, Lucan and Martial. In the later third century, however, Frankish invasions exacted a heavy toll.

Diocletian (284–305) and his successors created new provinces of Carthaginensis, Callaecia (Galicia) and the Balearic Islands within the administrative diocese of the Hispaniae (in which Mauretania Tingitana [Tingitania] was also included). A powerful Christian church, emerging at the Council of Illiberis (Elvira, 300/306), came to be dominated by Bishop Ossius (Hosius) of Corduba (Cordoba), a close adviser of Constantine I the Great; the outstanding Christian Latin poet Prudentius (348–after 405) also came from Spain. In the early fifth century, during the reign of Honorius, the country underwent a complicated series of imperial usurpations (Jovinus, Sebastianus, Maximus), resisting or conniving with successive waves of German invaders, in the course of which Suebi, Vandals and Alans crossed the Pyrenees and were given lands in the west and southwest.

The Visigoths, too, entered Spain, in order to slaughter the Vandals and Alans, but withdrew, for the time being, to occupy lands the Romans had given them in southwestern Gaul. The Vandals, for their part, sailed over to North Africa (429), while the Suebi extended their power in the northeast of the Iberian peninsula. In *c* 468, however, the Visigoths under Euric defeated the Suebi (whose state finally came to an end in 585), and when compelled by the Franks to evacuate Gaul created their own powerful kingdom in Spain instead. *See also* Baecula, Baetica, Baetis, Balearic Islands, Barcino, Bilbilis, Bracara Augusta, Caesaraugusta, Calagurris, Callaecia, Carthago Nova, Clunia, Corduba, Emerita, Emporiae, Gades, Hispalis, Iberus, Ilerda, Ilici, Italica, Lucus Augusti, Lusitania, Malaca, Osca, Tagus, Tarraco, Tartessus, Valentia.

Histiaea, later Oreus (Orei). A city on the northwest coast of Euboea (eastern Greece), overlooking the narrows between the island and Thessaly. Occupied by Abantes (of Thracian orgin) and then by Ellopians from Thessaly (and according to another version by Athenians), Histiaea has yielded Bronze Age and early Iron Age remains, and Homer's *Iliad,* referring to the fertile adjoining plain, calls the place 'rich in vines.'

In 480 BC, after the battle of Artemisium, Histiaea was sacked by the Persians, but subsequently joined Athens' Delian League. After the revolt of the Euboeans against Athens in 447/6, it received exceptionally severe treatment (owing to the massacre of an Athenian crew), its population being deported to

Macedonia and replaced by a colony of a thousand or two thousand Athenians. Although now known as Oreus, after an old, hilly locality in the neighborhood (now Molos), the new settlement may have stood on the same site as its predecessor; Strabo locates it on a high rock at the foot of Mount Telethrius in the Drymus (woodland) beside the river Callas. After the end of the Peloponnesian War (404) the exiles returned, under the auspices of Sparta, but joined the Second Athenian League in 357/6. Next they passed under Macedonian control (with a brief interval of independence, *c* 313) until the outbreak of hostilities between Rome and Philip V, when their city was twice captured by combined Roman and Pergamene forces (207,199). The Roman garrison was removed five years later, and the remarkable abundance of the subsequent Histiaean coinage (imitating Macedonian types, and depicting grapes) suggests a period of renewed prosperity.

The two citadels attributed to the ancient city by Livy have been identified; their duality has given rise to the present plural name Orei (Oreoi). The foundations of a large marble temple are also traceable.

Histria *see* Istrus

Homs *see* Emesa

Hvar *see* Pharos

Hydatos Potamoi *see* Seleucia in Pieria

Hyele *see* Elea

Hymettus. Mountain range in Attica bordering the Athenian plain to the east and south. Hymettus is constructed of two kinds of marble, white (Pentelic) and grayish-blue (Hymettian), both worked extensively in ancient times. It was also famous for its honey, and for the source of the river Ilissus (*qv*) upon its slopes. The mountain housed cults of Zeus (Hymettios and Ombrios), Apollo (Hymettes, Ersos and Proopsios), the Nymphs and Graces, and Pan.

Hyria *see* Seleucia on the Calycadnus

I

Ialysus *see* Rhodes

Iberus, Hiberus (Ebro). The second-largest river in Spain, and the only one of its five major rivers to debouch into the Mediterranean. It flows for five hundred and sixty-five miles through the northeastern part of the country to its delta near Dertosa (Tortosa), southwest of Tarraco (Tarragona), and was navigable for two hundred miles, as far inland as Vareia (near Logroño).

When the Carthaginians were developing their Spanish empire in the later third century BC, Hasdrubal (son-in-law of Hamilcar) advanced up the east coast in the direction of the river. In 226 he was met by Roman envoys, and 'the treaty of the Ebro' was concluded, according to which he agreed not to cross to the north bank of the river with an armed force. It was also, perhaps, understood that the Romans would not interfere with Carthaginian conquests south of the Iberus. But whether this was so or not, they chose to regard Hannibal's capture of Saguntum (Sagunto, south of the river) as a provocation, and the Second Punic War (218–201) ensued. During its course, Cnaeus Cornelius Scipio defeated Hasdrubal Barca (brother of Hannibal) in a naval engagement off the river mouth (217), and Cnaeus' nephew Scipio Africanus the Elder won a brilliant victory near the upper reaches of the Iberus (207), which removed a dangerous threat to his flank and led the way to the total elimination of Carthaginian power from Spain.

An important phase of the civil war between Quintus Sertorius and the Roman government hinged on Sertorius' efforts, temporarily successful, to prevent Pompey from crossing the Iberus (76). Subsequently, it was beside one of its tributaries, the Sicoris (Segre), that Caesar won the decisive victory over his Pompeian enemies at Ilerda (Lerida) (49). *See also* Caesaraugusta, Calagurris.

Ibiza *see* Ebusus

Icaria, Ikaria, Ikaros (Nikaria). An Aegean island of the Sporades group, west of Samos. The island, and the Icarian Sea which lies to its south, derive their names from the mythical Icarus, son of Daedalus. When King Minos, according to mythological tradition, refused to allow Daedalus, constructor of the labyrinth, to leave Crete, and imprisoned him and his son, Daedalus was believed to have constructed artificial wings of feathers, wax and linen for them both, and they succeeded in escaping. But Icarus flew too close to the sun, and fell into the sea that was given his name. According to Pausanias, his tomb was on the island of Icaria.

The principal town of Oene (Kampas), on the north coast of the island, and Thermae on its southwest coast, were members of Athens' Delian League; remains of both these places and of Drapanon and Nas (where there was a temple of Artemis Tauropolos) have survived. From the second century onward Icaria belonged to Samos.

Ichnussa *see* Sardinia

Ictis *see* Britannia

Ida, Ide. The highest range in central Crete; 'around the mountain' according to Strabo, 'are the best cities of the island.' According to Greek mythology it was in a cave on this mountain that the nymph Ida, a daughter of Melisseus, helped her sister Adrasteia to nurse the infant Zeus secretly on the milk of the goat Amaltheia, while the semi-divine Curetes gave him protection by dancing around him and clattering their weapons so that his cries should not be heard. (Another version associates the events of Zeus' infancy with Mount Dicte instead.) The 'Idaean Dactyls,' 'Fingers of Ida,' were wizards who served Adrasteia; Apollonius Rhodius describes them as Cretans, but alternative ancient versions attributed them to the other Mount Ida, in northwestern Asia Minor.

A variety of Bronze Age remains and early votive offerings have been found in two large caves on Mount Ida in Crete. Before 700 BC, highly decorated bronze shields and tympana (tamburines) were made or inspired by Phoenician craftsmen for dedication in the holy place, and the workshop that made them continued to operate until the mid-seventh century BC.

Ida, Ide (Kaz Dağı). A mountain range in the northwestern extremity of Asia Minor, of which the projecting spurs rise between the Propontis (Sea of Marmara) and the Aegean—jutting forward to the Hellespont (Dardanelles); the southern portion of the range is the Troad. Ida, described as 'many fountained' by the *Iliad,* was the source of Troy's river Scamander (Xanthus). It was here, according to the myth, that the Judgement of Paris took place. When Hera, Athena and Aphrodite competed for the Golden Apple to be won by 'the most beautiful,' Zeus commanded them to present themselves to Paris, who was looking after his flocks on the slopes of Ida, so that he could decide which of the goddesses was the loveliest. He awarded the apple to Aphrodite, who as a reward caused Helen, wife of Menelaus of Sparta, to fall in love with him, thus precipitating the Trojan War; Antandrus beside the Gulf of Adramyttium (Edremid) was the reputed site of the fateful decision.

Zeus and Cybele were worshipped on the summit of the mountain. It was rich in timber (fir and oak), which as Thucydides and Strabo pointed out, was much in demand for shipbuilding. This resource was particularly appreciated by the Hellenistic kings of Pergamum. *See also* Ida (Crete).

Idrias *see* Stratonicea

Idumaea (now in southern Israel) derived its name but not its location from Edom, whose people, the traditional enemies of the Israelites, were driven out of their homeland (Mount Seir, south of the Dead Sea and bordering on the Red Sea) by the Nabataean Arabs in the fourth century BC and settled in the southernmost regions of Judah (Judaea), henceforward known as Idumaea.

About 129, the Hasmonaean ruler John Hyrcanus I occupied the country and forcibly converted its inhabitants to Judaism, ordering that they should undergo circumcision, although Jewish public opinion never wholly recognized them as co-religionists. The commercial centers of Adora (Adoraim, Dura) and Marisa (Tel Maresha, Tell Sandahanna) were removed from Jewish control by Pompey the Great, who organized them as cities (*c* 64). The country moved into world history, however, when its native hereditary chieftain Antipater (whose father had been the Hasmonaean governor) became the most important Jew of his time, influencing Roman decisions regarding local problems (62,55) and, above all, winning conspicuous favor from Julius Caesar by sending troops to help him at Alexandria (48).

Then his son Herod the Great became the king of Judaea, as a client of Antony (40), and when Herod gained control of Idumaea three years later, the territory was incorporated in his state as one of its provinces. An attempt by an Idumaean noble, Costobarus, to secede and assert his independence (with the support of Cleopatra VII of Egypt) was crushed *c* 34, and the country remained under Herod's control until his death (4 BC): whereupon it passed first to his son Archelaus, and then to the Roman province of Judaea (AD 6).

During the first Jewish Revolt (First Roman War, 66–73), large numbers of Idumaeans evacuated their homeland (to escape Vespasian's retribution) and poured into Jerusalem, where they joined up with extremist political elements. Before the Second Revolt (132–35), the great Rabbi Akiba, unlike many other Jewish leaders, showed a policy of studied liberalism toward the Idumaean and Egyptian descendants of proselytes, because, it was believed, he foresaw the fatal effects that divisions would exercise upon the forthcoming rebellion—although, alternatively, his motives may have been wholly religious. From *c* 400 Idumaea was part of the Roman province of Palaestina Prima.

Iele *see* Elea

Ierapetra *see* Hierapytna

Ierne *see* Hibernia

Iglița *see* Troesmis

Iguvium (Gubbio). A stronghold in Umbria (central Italy), occupying what Silius Italicus rightly described as a damp, misty and unhealthy site on the western slope of the Apennines. The latest researches have ascribed its foundation to the eleventh or tenth century BC. Iguvium issued its own coins after 300, but lost its importance when the Via Flaminia from Rome to the north (220) passed it by; nevertheless it achieved the status of a 'federated' community, and then of a *municipium.*

The place owes its importance to the discovery (in 1444) of the nine (now seven) bronze Iguvine tablets (*c* 200–80s BC), which are inscribed both in Latin and Umbrian—thus providing our major source of information for the latter language. These texts, which contribute uniquely to our knowledge of ancient Italian religion, record the proceedings of a priestly community, the Atiedian Brethren, and describe their rituals, indicating the names of three religious triads or trinities.

Ildırı *see* Erythrae

Ilerda (Lerida). A town in northeast Spain, at the foot of a hill on the west bank of the river Sicoris (Segre), a tributary of the Iberus (Ebro). It was named after the tribe of the Ilergetes (of whom the Surdaones, in the immediate neighborhood, may have been a branch), and issued silver coins imitating those of the Greek cities of Emporion (Ampurias) and Massalia (Marseille) but inscribed in Iberian characters. In the Second Punic War the chieftains of Ilerda, Indibilius and Mandonius, supported the Carthaginians against the Romans, until they were captured in 205 BC.

It was here, in 49, that Julius Caesar inflicted a decisive defeat on Pompey the Great's generals Afranius and Petreius. After running short of provisions and becoming perilously cut off by the spring rise of the river, he turned the tables on his enemies and forced them into a position in which they, instead, were compelled by lack of food to capitulate. This meant that the whole of Spain fell into Caesar's hands. Under Augustus Ilerda coined with the title of *municipium.* It derives importance from its location on the road from Tarraco (capital of the province) to Osca (Huesca). The town was frequently mentioned by Ausonius (d. AD 395), and became a Visigothic bishopric. An ancient Roman temple, converted into the church of San Lorenzo, was incorporated into an Islamic mosque.

Ilipa (Alcalá del Río). A town in southwest Spain, eight miles from Hispalis (Seville), on the right bank of the Baetis (Guadalquivir). It became a station for river shipping, and was known for rich agriculture and fisheries (illustrated on its coinage) and famed for its exceptionally rich silver mines, hence its additional designation of 'Magna.'

Ilipa was the scene of the decisive battle in the Spanish campaigns of the Second Punic War (206 BC). Scipio Africanus, with 45,000 infantry and 3,000 cavalry, was outnumbered by the forces of his Carthaginian opponents Hasdrubal (son of Gisgo) and Mago; yet, by placing his best (Roman) troops on the wings, he contrived to outflank them. His victory, made possible by his own recently introduced revolutionary training methods, was overwhelming; and he cut off the survivors' retreat. The result was the immediate, total elimination of Carthaginian power from Spain. Many centuries later, Ilipa reappeared as a Visigothic bishopric.

Ilissus, Ilissos. A small river that has its sources in two springs on the slopes of Mount Hymettus, and descends through the stony plain of Attica past Athens to its southeast and south; before the Phaleron marsh was drained in this century, the stream did not reach the sea. According to Greek mythology, it was while playing or resting beside the Ilissus (or, on another version, upon the Areopagus that Oreithyia, the daughter of King Erechtheus, was carried off to Thrace by Boreas, god of the north wind. The Ilissus was also the legendary site of the death of the Athenian king Codrus, at the hand of Dorian invaders; he was said to have offered his death to save his country.

The spring of Callirhoe was converted into a large fountain house, the Enneacrounos, by the Athenian ruler Pisistratus in the sixth century BC. A temple of *c* 430–420 (of which drawings were made before its destruction in the AD 1770s) and an altar to the Muses stood beside the Ilissus. Plato's *Phaedrus* contains a passage expressing admiration for the natural beauties of the stream and its setting, which Ovid also praises in his *Art of Love*. Today, however, all that remains is a covered channel or drain, supplying the fountains in the Palace Garden at Athens.

Ilium, Ilion, Troia (Troy, Hisarlik). A town in the Troad (northwestern Asia Minor), situated on an elevation overlooking the junction of the rivers Scamander (Menderes) and Simois and the southern region of the Hellespont (Dardanelles). The significance of the place in the Bronze Age, and the glories and tragedies of the Trojan War, depicted in Homer's *Iliad,* are reflected by the discovery of numerous successive sites dating back to the second millennium BC. A gap of more than four hundred years separates the destruction of the last of them from the resettlement of the site by Aeolian Greeks (perhaps from Lesbos, with some Rhodian participants) shortly before 700 ('Troy VIII'). During a period of relative insignificance, Ilium derived its only importance from its (still modest) temple of Athena Ilias, visited by the Persian monarch Xerxes I (*c* 480). A later visitor was Alexander the Great (334), who, according to Strabo, adorned the temple with votive offerings, and gave the town city status and immunity from taxation. The center of a religious Federation (*synedrion*) of the Troad (from at least 305), and of an Ilian Festival and Games, it also benefited from the favor of one of Alexander's successors, Lysimachus, and began to issue silver and bronze coinage.

Ilium was subsequently visited by the Seleucid monarch Antiochus III the Great, who offered sacrifices to Athena (192). Two years later Gaius Livius Salinator, mindful of the city's connexion with Rome as the place of origin of Aeneas, inaugurated cordial relations, confirming its privileges. Nevertheless, not long afterward, Demetrius of Scepsis found the locality greatly neglected.

Ilium became part of the Pergamene kingdom, but under subsequent Roman rule, during the First Mithridatic War (85), it was sacked by the disorderly troops of Gaius Flavius Fimbria.

However, the city was rebuilt by Sulla, and accorded respect by many subsequent Roman leaders. Julius Caesar was even said by Suetonius to have thought of migrating to Ilium, and its imperial visitors included Augustus (though he planned to fine its citizens for failing to help his daughter Julia when she was in danger of drowning), Germanicus (AD 17), Hadrian (who rebuilt the temple of Ajax in 124) and Caracalla (who held contests in memory of Achilles in 214). Meanwhile the local mint issued a long series of bronze coins celebrating the legendary traditions of the place and depicting its monuments, including the shrine of Athena Ilias (under Marcus Aurelius, 161–80). About AD 257, Ilium was plundered by the Goths, but when Constantine I the Great (306–37) became emperor it was said to have been one of the sites that he considered as a possible future capital before deciding on Byzantium (Constantinople) instead. Julian the Apostate came to Ilium in 355 before ascending the throne, and his letters mention a Christian bishop.

The early Greek settlers had repaired older walls and founded two modest sanctuaries, dating from the mid-seventh century, of which traces have survived. Remains of theaters and a wrestling school, of Hellenistic and Roman times ('Troy IX'), can also be seen, and the plan of the enlarged Sanctuary of Athena has been reconstructed. Strabo ascribes it to Lysimachus, to whom he likewise attributes the city's first wall, and the existence of the wall in early Hellenistic times has been confirmed by excavations.

Lysimachus was also active at Alexandria Troas, located on a sea-lagoon, seventeen miles south of Ilium. Founded *c* 310 BC by Antigonus I Monophthalmos—who resettled the previous inhabitants of five other towns at the place—under the name of Antigonia, the settlement was enlarged by Lysimachus and renamed Alexandria. It became a Roman colony under Augustus (*c* 20 BC), but an earlier coin attributable to the city bears the title 'Colonia Julia' and portrays Julius Caesar (described as PRINCEPS FELIX), who had presumably inaugurated the colony—in connexion with his known favor toward Troy and its legends. Hadrian showered benefactions on Alexandria Troas, and the wealthy Athenian Herodes Atticus (d. *c* AD 177), at great expense, gave it an aqueduct, which has not survived. The colony's monetary issues, resuming at about the same time, concentrate largely on the cult of Apollo Smintheus, whose temple lay south of the city walls.

Illyricum, Illyria. The northwestern part of the Balkan peninsula (roughly corresponding with modern Yugoslavia and northern Albania), settled by Greek colonists on the coast but otherwise inhabited by the Illyrians, who were of mixed race but spoke an Indo-European tongue, though they never wrote it down.

Divided into seven groups of peoples, they were severely shaken by incursions of Cimmerians and Thracians (*c* 650 BC), and their fleets were driven back by the navies of Greek Corcyra and its mother city Corinth (*c* 625). After numerous further vicissitudes, however, the Illyrians created a strong (often piratical) kingdom of their own in the third century, under Agron of the Ardiaei, who from his capital at Scodra (Shkodër) controlled the greater part of the coast. His widow Teuta and Demetrius of Pharos (Hvar) clashed with Rome in the First and Second Illyrian Wars (229–219); so did Gentius (*c* 180–168), who allied himself with Perseus of Macedonia and shared his defeat by the Romans.

Although part of the eastern Dalmatian coast of the Adriatic now came under Roman control, sporadic operations continued at intervals to be conducted by consuls and proconsuls; no regular province seems to have been created until *c* 118. The composite province allocated to Julius Caesar in 59 included Illyricum, which became the scene of various military operations during his ensuing Civil War with Pompey the Great. Octavian (35–33) and his stepson Tiberius (13–9) fought hard campaigns in the country, resulting in the establishment of a much larger province extending from Istria to the river Drilo (Drin) and from the Adriatic to the Savus (Save), with its administrative capital at Salonae (Solin). After the extension, soon afterward, of the Roman empire to the Danube, Illyricum was subdivided into Upper and Lower provinces (later known as Dalmatia and Pannonia respectively). But the name of Illyricum continued to be loosely applied to a much wider area; thus under the reorganization of Diocletian, the administrative diocese of Illyricum (Pannoniae) included no less than seven provinces: Dalmatia, Pannonia Prima, Pannonia Secunda, Savia, Valeria, Noricum Ripense and Noricum Mediterraneum. Scodra became the capital of another province, Praevalitana. Furthermore, in later times, one of the great administrative divisions of the empire controlled by praetorian prefects—usually four in number—was the prefecture of Illyricum (originally united with the prefecture of Italy [including Africa], and forming part of the eastern empire from *c* AD 395). After the Pannonias had been overrun by the Germans in the fifth century, Dalmatia enjoyed for a time a peculiar, quasi-independent position.

Illyricum possessed a number of palatial country houses with farms attached (*villae rusticae*), notably Tasovčići—the estate of the Papian family in Dalmatia—and Ljušina (near Bosanska Krupa), which possessed two dozen rooms, including an apsidal chamber, round three sides of an open courtyard. *See also* Dalmatia, Pannonia, Pharos, Salonae, Scodra.

Ilva, formerly Aithalia, Vetalu (?) (Elba). An island, eighty-six square miles in area, seven miles from the coast of Etruria (Tuscany, western Italy). Ilva possessed useful agriculture and fisheries, but being virtually an extension of the Catena Metallifera (*qv*) on the mainland, it principally owed its fame and prosperity to its wealth of metals. The name Ilva is Ligurian, but (like other islands possessing mineral wealth) it was also called Aithalia from the smoke (*aithalos*) rising from its metalworkings; late Bronze Age (Mycenaean) tablets of the thirteenth century BC seem to refer to *Aitaro,* and subsequently the Etruscans, who occupied a considerable number of sites on the island, probably called it Vetalu, or perhaps Eitale.

In their time iron was replacing copper as the principal export, and its abundant availability, mostly near the east coast and in open-cast mines, attracted Greek traders, at least from the eighth century BC; for fragments of iron attributable to that date, and originating from Ilva, have been found on the Campanian island Pithecusae (Ischia), the Greek market that fulfilled a pioneer role in developing commercial relations with the metal-rich Etruscan communities. Much of the prosperity of Etruscan Populonia, on the mainland opposite, was derived from Ilva, and both alike seem to have belonged to the powerful city-state of Vetulonia from about the seventh century onward.

It was in order to plunder Ilva's large supplies of iron that a Syracusan fleet attacked the island (as well as Corsica) in 454/3. Not long afterward Populonia took over much of the smelting of this metal from the islanders, who no longer had sufficient wood-coal at their disposal. About 250 Rome gained control of Ilva, but it continued to flourish, at least for a time, supplying granite as well as metals to the mainland. Virgil celebrates its 'inexhaustible mines,' referring less to the the present than the past. The foremost of several Roman towns was Fabricia on the north coast of the island (Portoferraio, 'Iron Harbor,' formerly Feraia, from the iron mines nearby); and large Roman villas have come to light at Grotto di Portoferraio and Cavo di Rio Marina.

Imera see Himera

Inarime see Pithecusae

Inchtuthil see Pinnata Castra

India (the regions now known as Pakistan are particularly relevant). The 'Indus Civilization' had been fully developed *c* 2300 BC, and in the third and fourth centuries BC Persian ideas were being transmitted as far as the Ganges valley. Alexander the Great, in his Indian expedition of 327–325 BC, extended the frontiers of his empire as far as and beyond the Indus, securing the submission of Omphis (Ambhi), whose capital at Taxila (Sirkap) controlled Gandhara; and he also defeated Porus (Parvataka or Parvatesha), king of the Paurava, in the 'battle of the Hydaspes' (Jhelum). Alexander then moved southward, founding Nicaea (Mong?) on the west bank of the Hydaspes, Bucephala (Jelalpur?) on its east bank (named after his horse), Alexandria in India (Multan?) at the junction of the Indus and Acesines (Chenab), and another Alexandria (Portus; the Indian Patala) at the Indus mouth. He also planned yet another foundation at Rhambacia to the west of the estuary (*see* Gedrosia; and *see also* Alexandria for other cites of the same name. The Indian exploits of Alexander inspired a series of stories—detailed in the *Dionysiaca* of Nonnus of Panopolis (fifth century AD)—extending the mythical eastern conquests of the god Dionysus to that country.

About 303 BC, Seleucus I Nicator (sending a mission under Megasthenes, whose *Indica* was the fullest account of the country so far known to the Greeks) ceded a large part of Alexander's conquests east of Kandahar to Chandragupta Maurya (Sandracottus)—who had conquered the whole of north India—in exchange for elephants Seleucus needed in order to defeat his own Greek enemies elsewhere. But as the Mauryan empire collapsed in the early second century, rulers of the Greco-Bactrian state (which had broken away from the Seleucids in 256/5; *see* Bactria) gradually reoccupied these Indian territories and created Indo-Greek principalities, which were grouped together into a united kingdom by Eucratides I 'the Great' (Maharajasa) (*c* 170/165–155). His successor Menander Soter Dikaios (*c* 155–140/130), establishing his capital at Sacala (Sialkot), controlled an enormous empire.

Although subsequently subdivided into a bewildering variety of principalities, the Indo-Greek civilization survived the barbarian takeover of Bactria, achieving moments of glory under Strabo I Epiphanes (*c* 130–75), Amyntas Nicator (*c* 100–75) and finally Hermaeus Soter (from *c* 40). By his time the Scythians (Sacae) and Indo-Scythians had taken Gardez and Taxila respectively, but Hermaeus reconquered other substantial areas as far as the Indus, until the Yüeh Chih crossed the Oxus (Amu Darya) and penetrated his western territories. Finally, at about the beginning of our era, one of the tribal chiefs of the Yüeh Chih, Kudjula Kadphises I, obliterated the Indo-Greek state or states altogether, incorporating the entire vast region into the Kushan empire.

In the reign of Augustus (31 BC– AD14) organized knowledge of the monsoon brought Roman trade into direct and regular contact with the Indian peninsula, so that many ships came straight from Arabia to the main southwestern port of Muziris (Cranganore), to be loaded with pepper. Thus huge hoards of Roman silver coins (Augustus-Claudius) (no doubt constituting payment for Indian exports of the same commodity), and of beryls for Roman women's earrings, have been found in Coimbatore, between Mysore and Travancore. There was also an important land route from the Roman empire to India, at the eastern extremity of which a remarkable commercial center and land and sea terminal has been excavated at Arikamedu (Pondicherry); although Strabo records that by his time only a few merchants had sailed as far as the Ganges. *See also* Gandhara, Paropamisadae, Taxila.

İnebolu see Abonutichus

Inessa see Aetna

Interamna Nahars (Terni). A city in the Sabine country of central Italy (now Umbria), forty-five miles north of Rome. Necropoleis in the Nar valley date back to the early Iron Age (tenth to seventh centuries BC), and an inscription gives the city the legendary foundation date of 673/2.

In 83/2 Interamna was put up for auction by Sulla, as a penalty for having supported his Marian enemies in the civil war. A more permanent hazard was its situation beside the confluence of the rivers Nar (Nera) and Velinus (Serra), since the two streams, although producing exceptionally fertile soil, created a continual danger of floods. The famous Falls of Terni (Cascata delle Marmore), still to be seen today, originate from a channel cut by Manius Curius Dentatus, conqueror of the Sabines (271 BC), by which the waters of the Velinus were thrown over a precipice into the Nar, to drain the Veline lake and prevent inundation—with unsatisfactory results, however, which later prompted furious objections from Reate (Rieti) (54 BC, AD 15).

Interamna became a flourishing *municipium* which lay, we are told by Tacitus, a little way off the Via Flaminia leading to the north, although an earlier northward route may have passed through the city, and an alternative road did so later. In AD 193, when the senate abandoned the transient emperor Didius Julianus in favor of Septimius Severus—who had invaded Italy from the north—a delegation consisting of one hundred of its members was sent to Interamna to convey good wishes to the invader. Severus, surrounded by a bodyguard of six hundred, had each of the envoys searched for concealed arms, but on the next day presented them with monetary gifts and gave them permission to enter Rome in his entourage. In 253 a battle at Interamna Nahars (or, according to another source, at Forum Flaminii near Fulginia [Foligno]) brought about another forcible change of rulers, when Aemilius Aemilianus, governor of Lower Moesia, rose against Trebonianus Gallus (who had been emperor for the past two years) and marched on Italy. In the engagement that followed, Gallus' soldiers abandoned and killed their leader and his son, and transferred their allegiance to Aemilianus. Later in the same year, however, when Valerianus, commander of the Rhine army, likewise rebelled, Aemilianus, too, was assassinated by his troops, a few miles away from the site of his predecessor's murder.

The most important monument of the ancient city is its amphitheater, constructed, according to an inscription, in the time of Tiberius (14–37). Terni is not justified, however, in claiming to be the birthplace of the great historian Tacitus, or his supposed descendants the emperor Tacitus (275/6) and his brother or half-brother Florianus (276). The historian came from elsewhere, and the *Historia Augusta's* attribution of the third-century pair to the city seems full of fabrications; nor are they likely, for that matter, to be descended from the historian at all. Interamna Nahars (Sabinorum) has to be distinguished from other cities of the same name (or sometimes known as Interamnia and Interamnium) belonging to the tribes of the Aurunci, Praetuttiani and Volsci.

Iol *see* Caesarea

Iolcus, Iolkos (near Volos). A city in the district of Magnesia (Thessaly, eastern Greece), near the head of the Gulf of Pagasae (Bay of Volos), beside the river Anaurus (now dry) and beneath Mount Pelion. Iolcus was famed in mythology as the home of Jason (son of Aeson and grandson of Aeolus), said to have been deprived of the throne by his half-brother Pelias, who then induced him to go and fetch the Golden Fleece from Colchis. Iolcus, which possessed ports at Neleia (Cape Pefkakia?) and Pagasae, was reputed to have been the starting point of the expedition of the Argonauts, which is the theme of many ancient legends, embroidered by the *Argonautica* of Apollonius Rhodius.

Excavations (at the western end of the town of Volos) have shown that Iolcus had a Mycenaean-style palace—the northernmost structure of this kind known to us—from which, in the late Bronze Age, Mycenaean influence apparently spread inland into the rest of Thessaly. The palace was burned *c* 1150 BC, but the habitation center retained a certain prosperity at the beginning of the first millennium. Later, however, it suffered eclipse first from Pagasae and then from Demetrias, though retaining a temple and festival of Artemis Iolkia. Strabo records that by his time the town had long since been razed to the ground.

Ionia. The central section of the west coast of Asia Minor, bounded by Aeolis to the north and Caria to the south, and including important adjoining islands. Its coastline and territory extended from beyond the river Hermus (Gediz) to the north, past the Cayster (Küçük Menderes) to the Maeander (Büyük Menderes). Our main sources for the origins of the Ionians are Strabo and Pausanias. It was early, and rightly, maintained, that Ionia had been colonized by migrants from the Greek mainland, taking refuge from the Dorians and other invading tribes; the first of these migrations had taken place at least by 1000 BC. But probably the movements extended over a number of generations; the claim that the legendary Ion, son of Xuthus (or Apollo) and Creusa, led a single colonizing movement—settling for a time, on the way, in Athens where the four tribes were named after his four sons—was probably a later Athenian invention. The Ionians were a major branch of the Greek people who lived in many Hellenic lands. Yet their dialect is a form of speech first known to us from the Homeric poems of Ionia in western Asia Minor, and that is the territory to which the future history of the Ionians mainly belonged.

Before 700 its occupants had formed a religious league, the Panionion, with its sanctuary of Poseidon Heliconius on a spur of Mount Mycale (Samsun Dağı), replacing his shrine at Melia (south of Ephesus), which the Ionians destroyed owing to its inhabitants' unwillingness to accept absorption. In about the third quarter of the seventh century (like the Lydians) they were issuing coinage (*staters*) of pale gold (*electrium*), displaying various designs and conforming with a number of different monetary standards.

In due course twelve city-states emerged: on the mainland, from north to south, Phocaea, Clazomenae, Erythrae, Teos, Lebedus, Colophon, Ephesus, Priene, Myus, and Miletus, and the islands of Chios and Samos. Rapid and fruitful development followed. In the seventh century Miletus and Phocaea (Foca) led an unparalleled burst of overseas colonization. Milesians also founded pre-Socratic philosophy, and other Ionian philosophers of extraordinary distinction followed in the footsteps of these pioneers at home and abroad. The Lydian kings, however, and especially Croesus (*c* 560–546), brought the Ionians under their own control, from which they passed into the hands of the Persians, only to launch a major, five-year-long revolt, that was crushed at Lade, an island off Miletus (495).

After the battle of Mycale (479) had liberated them from Persian domination, the Ionian city-states became members of Athens' Delian League and Athenian empire—in which Lesbos, Chios and Samos (until its revolt in 441) retained privileged status, as contributors of ships—but following Athens' defeat in the Peloponnesian War they were brought under Persian control once again by the King's Peace or Peace of Antalcidas, prompted by Sparta (387). In 334, with the exception of Miletus, they adhered to the cause of Alexander the Great; thereafter they veered uneasily between Ptolemaic pressure by sea and Seleucid supremacy by land, until the kingdom of Pergamum became their suzerain.

By the will of the last Pergamene monarch Attalus III his state was bequeathed to the Romans (133), who incorporated its territories, including Ionia, in their new province of Asia. A century of grievous Roman extortions and depredations followed, until a new era of prosperity began under Augustus. During the Principate Ephesus, Smyrna, Miletus and Samos were among the empire's most resplendent cities; and in the second century AD Pausanias wrote: 'Ionia enjoys the finest of climates and its sanctuaries are unmatched in the world. The wonders of Ionia are numerous, and not much short of the wonders of Greece itself.' Under the reorganization of Diocletian (AD 284–305), the former province of Asia was subdivided into six provinces, of which one, retaining the name of Asia, comprised Ionia, Aeolis and part of the Troad.

Ionian Islands *see* Ithaca

Ionian Sea. Either (1) a synonym of the Adriatic Sea, or (2) the southern continuation of that sea, south of the Strait of Otranto, between the heel of Italy and northwestern Greece: the sea in which the Ionian Islands—Corcyra (Corfu), Leucas, Cephallenia (Cephalonia), Ithaca, Zacynthus (Zante) etc.—are located. Etymologically as well as geographically, the Ionian Sea has nothing to do with the Ionians or Ionia: its 'o' is not long (*omega*) but short (*omicron*), and its name was derived by Aeschylus from the mythical Io who swam from one coast to the other (though a later, alternative version instead derived the word from the Illyrian Ionios, son of Dyrrhachos).

The most remarkable crossing of the sea in historical times inaugurated the civil war between Antony and Octavian (the future Augustus) in 31 BC, when Octavian's admiral Marcus Agrippa sailed across, from west to east, much earlier in the year than naval opinion had considered practicable; and not even by the direct route, since he successfully made a long detour to Mothone in southern Greece. Antony's military position never recovered from this daring move, and his defeat at the battle of Actium was its logical outcome.

Ionopolis *see* Abonutichus

Ipsus. In central Phrygia (west-central Asia Minor), somewhere in the neighborhood of Synnada (perhaps the Roman Iullae, on the plain of the lower Akar Çayı). The scene of one of the decisive engagements of the ancient world (301 BC), 'the Battle of the Kings,' fought between the successors of Alexander the Great: on the one side was Antigonus I Monophthalmos, aiming (with the assistance of his son Demetrius I Poliorcetes) to take over for himself Alexander's entire conquests; and confronting him were his rivals Lysimachus and Seleucus. Some 75,000 soldiers fought in the battle. After a successful cavalry charge, Demetrius continued to press ahead, thus exposing the flank of his father's infantry, which was routed by Seleucus' elephants; while Antigonus himself, waiting in vain for his son to return, was overwhelmed by a shower of missiles and perished. With him died the last possibility of a united Greek empire, and the epoch of separate Successor States had begun.

Ireland *see* Hibernia

Irenopolis *see* Sepphoris

Isaccea *see* Noviodunum

Isauria. A mountainous territory in the southern hinterland of Asia Minor, east of Pisidia, north of Pamphylia, and northwest (or sometimes inclusive) of 'Rough' Cilicia (Cilicia Tracheia, Aspera). In 325 BC the Isaurians murdered Alexander the Great's governor Balacrus, and were punished by Perdiccas, who destroyed their largest settlement Isaura Vetus (Zengibar Kalesi). Thereafter, their villages lived an independent existence, mainly by banditry and piracy which, according to Diodorus, filled Isaura Vetus with silver and gold. Subjugated in 76/5 by Publius Servilius Vatia, who assumed the title of Isauricus, the country was successively included in Rome's province of Cilicia (where the cities on the lower Calycadnus [Göksu] were known as the Isaurian Decapolis), in the client kingdom of Galatia (whose monarch fortified Isaura Vetus), and then, after the annexation of that kingdom (25), in the Galatian province (in which the stronghold attained the rank of a city).

Fortresses were constructed by the Romans at various epochs to keep the turbulent populations in check, and in the later empire two new provinces of Lycaonia (including the former Isauria) and Isauria (Rough Cilicia) were established, in which the civil powers were vested in a military governor. During the fourth century AD Ammianus Marcellinus still described the Isaurians as a menace to their neighbors, and when St. John Chrysostom was exiled by the eastern emperor Arcadius (404), his letters reported that the region was once again distressed by their slaughtering and looting, which continued over a period of three years and caused the ignominious defeat of the east Roman general Arbazacius.

Later in the same century, however, the Isaurians moved onto the center of the world stage when Leo I the Great (457–74) enrolled this hardy, native mountaineering people into his army as a deliberate counterweight to its powerful foreign (German) element. Leo I amalgamated Isaurian villages into the new city of Leontopolis, while those that remained were merged with Isaura Vetus, subsequently known as Colonia Isauria. This policy of developing national Isaurian troops was entrusted to Zeno, himself an Isaurian chieftain (originally named Tarasicodissa), who became Leo's son-in-law and then, after a transitory interval, his successor (474–91): whereupon he firmly persisted in the military enhancement of the Isaurians, who provided two of his principal generals, Cottomenes and Longinus. Anastasius I (493–518), however, put a stop to this brief ascendancy, deporting numerous Isaurians from their homeland and sending them to Thrace.

Isca Dumnoniorum (Exeter). A town in the territory of the tribe of the Dumnonii (Devonshire, southwest England), on a river bearing their name (the Exe). After the invasion of Britain under Claudius (AD 43–48), the place was furnished with a military fort, which was garrisoned shortly afterward by a legion. But *c*

80 this unit was moved to Isca Silurum (Caerleon), whereupon the fortress of Isca Dumnoniorum was replaced by an open civilian settlement, which became—or remained—the administrative center of the Dumnonii. When Britain was divided into two by Septimius Severus (193–211), Isca Dumnoniorum belonged to the upper province (Britannia Superior), and after the fourfold (later fivefold) division of the administrative diocese of the Britanniae in the later empire the town became part of Britannia Prima.

Remains of both its successive phases, military and civilian, are to be seen. The original military headquarters has been located in the center of Exeter. Extending over forty acres (a larger area than had been thought), it included a stone bath house which, after the legion had gone, became the municipal administrative center, adjoining a forum; and new public baths were built nearby. The southwestern defences of the legionary fortress (*c* 55/60–75) and early town (*c* 80–180/200) have now been investigated; the first rampart and ditch (with stone gates) were replaced by a strong stone wall enclosing a hundred-acre perimeter. The presence of coins minted at Alexandria in Egypt bears witness to overseas trade. By 375, however, the forum was no longer in use, though the municipal building continued to be employed, on an impoverished scale, until the Saxons arrived in the fifth century.

Isca Silurum (Caerleon). Situated in the territory of the Silures (southeast Wales), on a river of the same name (Usk). Isca was made the headquarters of a legion (moved from Isca Dumnoniorum [Exeter] by Sextus Julius Frontinus during his conquest of Wales in AD 74/75; perhaps part of the legion had already been there from *c* 56). Originally built of timber banked up with clay, the defences of Silurian Isca were strengthened with stonework (99/100), and after a period of decline were again repaired under the Severi and Valerian (253–60); though before the end of the third century, and probably earlier, the legion had gone. Its allocation to provinces corresponded with that of Isca Dumnoniorum (*qv*). Isca Silurum was traditionally believed to have been the seat of an archbishopric, but this is unlikely.

Surviving remains of the stronghold, which has been carefully explored, include the legionary commander's residence (*praetorium*), administrative headquarters (*principium*), with internal colonnades, barrack-blocks, hospital (with operating theater), cook-houses, latrines, large drill-hall, heated baths, and building for athletics and wrestling (*palaestra*). An adjoining civilian settlement (*canabae*), which remained small because the town of Venta Silurum [Caerwent] was not far away, is shown by inscriptions to have included temples of Diana, Mithras and Jupiter Dolichenus. An amphitheater (no doubt for purposes of military training) and bathing establishment are just outside the fortress wall, and wharves have been excavated on the river.

Ischia, Island *see* Pithecusae

Issa (Vis). An island (with a town of the same name) off the coast of Dalmatia (Yugoslavia). After coming into the hands of the Liburnians (famous seafarers), it was colonized by Dionysius I of Syracuse (406–367 BC), as part of his plan to control the Adriatic (Ionian) Sea. The large bronze coins of the local mint, imitating the products of various Sicilian cities, date from this period.

During the third century Issa founded Tragurium (Trogir) and Epetium (Stobreč) on the mainland, and dominated the entire region. But this position brought it into conflict with the rising power of the Illyrian queen Teuta, who besieged the city as part of a bid to reduce all the Greek harbor-towns on the Adriatic (230). In the following year, however, a Roman fleet took Issa over, and Teuta was reduced to tributary status. In the civil war between Pompey the Great and Julius Caesar (49–48), the Issans sided with the former and their city was penalized by the victorious Caesar, becoming a dependency of the new Roman colony at Salonae (Solin). As a result of recent excavations, the remains that can now be seen include an amphitheater, baths, and a Hellenistic wall and necropolis.

Issus (now in the Hatay, the southern appendix of Turkey in Asia). A small town of 'Smooth' Cilicia of the Plain (Pedias, Campestris) on its eastern extremity, at the head of the Gulf of Issus (Gulf of İskenderun), possessing a mooring-place in a narrow, flat coastal strip (of which the contours have now greatly changed) controlling the road from Asia Minor into Syria. In the early fourth century BC Issus struck its own coins, first with Greek inscriptions and then (from *c* 385 BC) with the city's name in Greek accompanied by the name of the Persian satrap Tiribazus in Aramaic; though he and his successors also coined at the place on their own account, without indicating its name.

In 333 this coastal strip—between Issus and Myriandrus (Iskenderun)—was the scene of the Battle of Issus, the second of the three great land confrontations in which Alexander the Great defeated the Persian armies of Darius III Codomannus—who himself took part in the fighting for the first time. After a prolonged and complex struggle, Alexander's heavy Macedonian phalanx swung left, attacked the enemy's Greek mercenaries (who had sought to exploit a gap) in the flank, and cut them down, at the same time as a cavalry force, which he had transferred to the left wing, put its Persian opponents to flight. A fierce melee (recorded by subsequent Greek painters and mosaicists) took place round the chariot of Darius, who turned his horse and fled; his mother, wife and son were seized in the Persian camp and kept as prisoners. The victory left the heartlands of the Persian empire, Syria, Mesopotamia (Iraq) and Iran, wide open to Alexander. Not long afterward he founded a Greco-Macedonian colony Alexandria Beside Issus near the battlefield; it issued coinage on his behalf, ascribing him the title of king. This Alexandria reckoned a new era from its reorganization by Pompey the Great (67/6). Fragments of its buildings remain.

During the civil war between the emperor Septimius Severus and his rival Pescennius Niger, the decisive engagement was fought in the plain of Issus (AD 194), where Niger's forces were routed when a sudden storm blew up in their faces, and unforeseen attacks by Severus' cavalry outflanked them from the hills and fell on their rear.

İstanbul *see* Byzantium

Ister, River *see* Danube

Istrus, Istros, later Histria, Histropolis. A Greek city of the Dobrogea (Rumania), just south of the delta of the Danube (Ister, from which it takes its name), situated at the end of an island or peninsula—or a low hill on the coastal plain—in a gulf that later became the Sinoe sea-lagoon, and is now a landlocked lake.

Originally a settlement of the Getae—a Thracian tribal group akin to the Dacians who fished in the river mouths—Istrus was colonized during the seventh century BC (in 657 according to Eusebius, or perhaps a little later) by settlers from Miletus in Ionia (western Asia Minor). These colonists set up a dynasty of ruling-class families that retained power even after the adoption of a democratic constitution. Placing their defences in the hands of a citizen militia, augmented by mercenaries and the population of the hinterland (with whom a *modus vivendi* was established, revealed by a cluster of mud-brick native houses outside the walls), the people of Istrus began to trade extensively throughout the eastern Mediterranean world, as well as sending wine, oil and other Greek goods (contained in locally made pottery) far into the interior of Europe. The city was sacked shortly before 500, probably by Scythian marauders. From the fourth century onward, however, it issued plentiful silver coinage, displaying a sea-eagle seizing a dolphin, a design found also at Sinope (Sinop) on the Euxine (Black) Sea coast of Asia Minor. But Istrus suffered destruction again before the end of the century, probably at the hands of one of Alexander the Great's successors, Lysimachus, and was ravaged yet again by the Dacian king Burebistas (*c* 60–44).

Incorporated by Augustus into the new Roman province of Moesia (and then into Lower Moesia from the time of Domitian, *c* AD 85/86), the city greatly expanded its territorial possessions during the first and second centuries AD. New fortifications were constructed under Hadrian (117–38), and there is epigraphic evidence for large estates penetrating deep into the hinterland. In about the middle of the third century Istrus suffered a devastating Gothic irruption, but was rebuilt and received new walls from Probus (276–82). Becoming, in the later empire, part of the new province of Scythia, it was provided with new walls once again, in the time of Constantine I the Great (306–37). Although they now enclosed a smaller perimeter, the place continued to fulfil an important role, not so much, any longer, in maritime activity—owing to the gradual silting up of its harbor—but in frontier control, and in the region's agricultural development. The fortifications were reconstructed by Anastasius I (493–518), but an Avar invasion of 595 caused the abandonment of the extramural settlement, and prompted the creation of a multiple ditch system of landward defences. A generation later Slav pressure deprived the city of its commerce altogether.

Excavations have borne witness to several stages of construction. Discoveries beside the lagoon, going down to depths of between ten and thirteen feet, have revealed a remarkable collection of early sacred buildings, including an archaic temple of Aphrodite (rebuilt in the Hellenistic epoch), a fifth-century BC sanctuary of Zeus Polieus, and fragments of a third-century shrine dedicated to a Thracian divinity whom the Greeks called the 'Great God.' Parts of a Hellenistic rampart can also be seen, and traces of the various successive Roman defences; the well-preserved walls of Probus hastily incorporated a varied collection of architectural materials, including columns and inscribed stones.

The final epoch of Istrus, extending between the fourth and sixth centuries AD, is represented by three separate zones: an official quarter including pagan basilicas and subsequent Christian buildings, a business district comprising shops and industrial works, and a residential area containing large and luxurious houses, one of which contains a private chapel and may have been the residence of a bishop. To the west of the city lies a huge cemetery, going back to very early dates; it includes Greek burials of many periods and the tombs of Getic chieftains, whose remains are surrounded by relics of both animal and human sacrifice. A corpus of Istrian inscriptions has lately been published.

Italica (Santiponce). A city of Hispania Baetica (southern Spain), five miles northwest of Hispalis (Seville). The Roman settlement was established by Scipio Africanus the Elder in 206 BC, during the Second Punic War, to accommodate wounded survivors of the battle of Ilipa and serve as an outpost against the Lusitanians. It received municipal status from Augustus (if not earlier) and was the birthplace of Trajan (AD 98–117) and hometown of Hadrian (117–38), who elevated it to the rank of colony under the titles of Aelia Augusta, and virtually created a new city. Italica's flourishing exportation of olive oil is illustrated by numerous fragments of amphorae on the waste dump of Monte Testaccio at Rome. Although damaged by German invasions (in the 250s or 260s), the city continued to exist, and was the ancestral home of Theodosius I the Great (378–95); its serious decline began in the fifth century.

Recent excavations have enabled the site of the forum of Italica to be completely reconstructed. Its amphitheater, with capacity for 25,000 spectators, seems to have been the fourth largest in the empire. A theater (likewise outside the wall) has also been recently excavated. There are two impressive bathing establishments (the 'Palaces' and 'Baths of the Moorish Queen'), served by an aqueduct bringing water from Tucci (Escacena del Campo). A group of impressive private residences, with courtyards and mosaics, has also come to light, and many other mosaics have been uncovered in a burial ground to the north of the city. The museum at Seville contains a collection of portrait busts found at Italica, including a number of representations of imperial personages.

Ithaca (Ithaki, Thiaki). One of the Ionian islands off the northwest coast of Greece, fifteen miles long and much narrower in width. It was the home of Odysseus at which his wanderings terminated, according to the *Odyssey* of Homer; the identification of the Homeric Ithaca with this island, although sometimes doubted in the past, is now generally regarded as correct. Homer speaks of a sea power formed by Ithaca and three other islands.

Bronze Age remains have come to light on a hill at Pelikata overlooking Polis Bay in the north of the island; and in a collapsed cave (grotto sanctuary of the Nymphs) beside the bay itself, pieces of at least twelve tripod cauldrons of the eighth century BC have been found (Odysseus reputedly had thirteen, and a clay mask bears a dedication to him). Near the adjacent village of Stavros beside the northernmost point of the island, in the neighborhood of Exoghi, a two-roomed tower (the 'School of Homer') is constructed of archaic polygonal masonry. A wall of similar material is to be seen enclosing a sanctuary of an unknown deity on Mount Aetos at the central isthmus; and on the slopes of the same mountain there was a sanctuary with Bronze Age and early Iron Age and imported Corinthian contents and offerings, and terracottas from later epochs as well; although Ithaca played no part in the history of classical Greece.

Vathy, the modern capital of the island, has been identified with the port of Phorcys where Odysseus landed, but it remains a mystery why the shores of this excellent harbor are (as far as can be detected at present) devoid of antiquities.

Ithome *see* Messene

Ivailovgrad *see* Hadrianopolis

Iviza *see* Ebusus

İzmir *see* Smyrna

İzmit *see* Nicomedia

İznik *see* Nicaea (Bithynia)

J

Jac *see* Porolissum

Jaffa *see* Joppa

Jamnia, formerly Jabneel, 'God buildeth' (Yavneh), in western Judaea (Israel). The northernmost of the Philistine cities, with a harbor (Minet Rubin) at the mouth of the river Rubin, Jamnia stood in a fertile and abundantly populated district. During the periods of Persian, Ptolemaic and Seleucid control, it formed part of Idumaea, and was for a time the capital of that province's governor. The Hellenistic history of the town is known from Josephus and *I Maccabbees*. The rebel leader Judas Maccabaeus (167–161 BC) defeated the Seleucid army of Gorgias near Jamnia, where he was the military commandant, but Gorgias subsequently defeated the local Jewish home guard, who had disobeyed Judas' order not to attack.

The town was annexed to the Jewish state by Simon Maccabaeus (142–135) but freed by the Romans under Pompey the Great (*c* 63) and repopulated by Aulus Gabinius (57–55). It was subsequently returned to the Judaean kingdom of Herod the Great (37–4), and after his death was bequeathed to his sister Salome who, when she died, left the place to Livia, the wife of Augustus; after her death (AD 29) it became an imperial property in the province of Judaea. In 35 the Roman agent (*procurator*) Herennius Capito, who was in charge of these estates, arrested the Jewish prince Agrippa I, claiming that he owed money to the Roman treasury; but Agrippa escaped. In 40 trouble broke out between the Jewish and Greek Jamnians, which triggered serious rioting at Alexandria in Egypt. During the First Jewish Revolt (66–73) Vespasian reduced and garrisoned the city, but after the destruction of Jerusalem and its Temple (70) he granted the request of Rabbi Johanan ben Zakkai that he should be permitted to found a settlement for refugees at Jamnia, including an academy which, under its religious leaders (Tannaim), became the country's principal center of Jewish self-perpetuation and study, closely associated with a national council

(Sanhedrin). Under Gamaliel II five hundred boys studied the Torah in the school, and five hundred studied Greek. Although the Jewish leadership subsequently moved to Galilee, Jamnia remained an important, if small, town in late Roman times, becoming the seat of a Christian bishop.

Jebal Seraj *see* Alexandria Beside the Caucasus

Jebeil *see* Byblus

Jebel el-Fureidis *see* Herodium

Jerusalem, Hierosolyma, later Aelia Capitolina, the holy city of Jews, Christians and Moslems. It stands on the ridge that separates the Mediterranean from the Dead Sea, at a point where this west-east route crosses one of the two principal north-south routes of the country. The Old City, possessing access to the Gihon spring, is bounded by the Hinnom and Kedron valleys to the west and east respectively, between them runs a central valley, the Tyropoeon.

The earliest town, occupied by the Jebusites (of uncertain, non-Jewish, origin) was captured by King David (*c* 1000 BC), whose son Solomon extended the site and built the first Temple (*c* 960). After the subsequent division of the united Jewish monarchy into Northern and Southern kingdoms, Jerusalem, the capital of the southern state, was captured in 597 by Nebuchadrezzar II of Babylon, who deported most of the population ten years later. About 530, the Persians, who had succeeded the Babylonians, allowed a group of exiles to return, and the (Second) Temple and walls were gradually rebuilt.

After Alexander the Great had allowed the city to retain its privileges, it passed into the hands first of the Ptolemies and then of the Seleucids (200). Antiochus IV Epiphanes (175–163) built a new citadel (the Acra), and was prompted by his desire for imperial religious uniformity to attempt to Hellenize the Jews, rededicating their Temple of Olympian Zeus. Such unwise measures caused a major uprising, which led to the reconsecration of the Temple (164) and the establishment of an independent Jewish state under the Hasmonaean (Maccabean) dynasty. In 63, however, Pompey the Great captured Jerusalem, which, after a series of puppet regimes and upheavals, was stormed by Gaius Sosius (37) and became the capital of the prosperous client kingdom of Herod the Great, who rebuilt the Temple; though in the subsequent Roman province of Judaea (AD 6), Jerusalem relinquished the role of capital to Caesarea Maritima. The crucifixion of Jesus has been variously attributed to 30 and 33. In the suppression of the First Jewish Revolt (First Roman War), the city was besieged by the Romans and almost totally destroyed, and its Temple obliterated (AD 70); henceforward a legion was stationed there. Hadrian, on the occasion of a near-eastern visit, refounded Jerusalem (130), which, after the Second Revolt (132–35)—prompted largely by the emperor's prohibition of circumcision—no Jew was permitted to enter; the city became a Roman colony, Aelia Capitolina, either in 130 or *c* 135. The conversion to Christianity of Constantine I the Great (306–37) inaugurated a new period of prosperity, founded as before on the pilgrim traffic, which now, however, served the new official faith. Theological disputes gave Bishop Juvenal (421–58) a chance to advance his position *vis-à-vis* the sees of Antioch and Caesarea Maritima.

The small post-Exilic town of the sixth and fifth centuries BC had gradually increased in size until the age of Herod the Great, who became Jerusalem's most active builder of all time. His revived Temple doubled the area of the precinct. The Moslem Dome of the Rock now stands on the massive platform (the Haram al-Sharif) which Herod built for the purpose; some of the splendid masonry of its retaining supports (notably the Wailing Wall) can still be seen, and a new reconstruction of the whole complex has now been made possible. To the west Herod constructed a luxurious palace, of which a tower is still visible, and to the north was his fortress the Antonia, named after Antony who had preceded Augustus as his patron. According to Josephus, the king also erected a theater and amphitheater, probably outside the walls, which he strengthened. Further walls were erected when Agrippa I (41–44) extended the perimeter of the city.

Hadrian's Aelia Capitolina established the topography of the present Old City, of which the street plan is shown on a sixth-century mosaic from Madaba (Medaba in Jordan). According to this picture, Hadrian's column stood just outside the city. The main gate and guard tower have recently been excavated. The tower, which is now mainly underground, was eighteen feet wide and thirty-six feet high—the tallest Roman structure to have survived in Israel. The munificent endowments of Jerusalem under the Christian empire are represented by the Church of the Holy Sepulchre on the Hill of Golgotha, where parts of the Constantinian building can still be seen. The end of Christian Jerusalem came with the Arab conquest in 637.

Joppa (Jaffa). Situated in the central sector of the coastal plain of Judaea (now adjoining Tel Aviv to its south), the ancient city was built on a rock hill one hundred and sixteen feet high, which juts out onto the Mediterranean. A natural breakwater formed an anchorage on the north side of the promontory. In the second millennium BC Joppa was already an active harbor town on the Way of the Sea (the Ways of Horus), the coastal route from Egypt through the Levant. Later the township passed successively into the hands of the Philistines, Israelites, kings of Judah, Assyrians and Persians, who gave it to the rulers of Sidon (Saida). According to Greek mythology, the place was founded by King Cepheus, who named it after his wife Iopia (Cassiopeia). As a sacrifice to a sea monster, it was believed, their daughter Andromeda was chained to a rock in the harbor, but the hero Perseus killed the monster and saved her.

After a brief period of independence, Joppa was captured by Alexander the Great, who employed it as a mint, as did the Ptolemies later on. Next, after oscillating repeatedly between Ptolemaic and Seleucid domination, the city passed during the second century into the hands of the newly independent Hasmonaean (Maccabean) state, of which it became the principal port, receiving a draft of Jewish colonists and resuming coinage. In 138 Simon defeated a Seleucid attempt to regain control; but Pompey the Great occupied Joppa, and granted it autonomy (63). Nevertheless, this proved shortlived, since the town was subsequently in the possession of Cleopatra VII of Egypt and then of Herod the Great of Judaea (37–4), who found its population so hostile, however, that he transferred his main port to Caesarea Maritima. Subsequently Joppa belonged to the Roman province of Judaea (AD 6). The *Acts of the Apostles* refer to St. Peter's stay at the house of Simon the Tanner.

During the First Jewish Revolt (First Roman War, AD 66–73), Vespasian attacked and destroyed the town, refounding it with the title of Flavia and introducing a Roman garrison. Nevertheless, the Jewish community slowly revived, as a number of tombs of the ensuing half-century indicate. Three inscriptions refer to a certain Judah, inspector of weights and measures under Trajan (98–117). Coins were issued in the reign of Elagabalus (218–22), displaying a figure of Athena. The ancient mound of Joppa was excavated between 1955 and 1966. Part of the wall goes back to the Persian period, and a large fortress of Hellenistic date has been traced, as well as sparse remains of the Roman epoch.

Jotapata (Jefat), nine miles south of Sepphoris (Saffuriyeh) in Galilee (now northern Israel), built on precipitous cliffs and surrounded on three sides by ravines. It was the place where Josephus, the greatest of all named Jewish historians, abandoned his compatriots during their First Revolt against the Romans (the First Roman War) and joined the enemy.

This happened in AD 67, after a moderate group of insurrectionary leaders, temporarily in the ascendancy, sent the evidently reluctant historian (who had regarded the uprising as a hopeless prospect) to take command of rebel troops in Galilee. Rent, however, by internal political divisions, and alarmed by the impending approach of the Roman general Vespasian, Josephus' army melted away and took refuge behind the fortifications of Jotapata. Vespasian saw the stronghold as no better than a prison for the rebels; but Josephus stresses the efficiency with which he conducted the defence of the town, pouring boiling oil on the besiegers, dressing his messengers in sheepskins to disguise them as dogs, and plastering the gangways with a boiled mash of the clover-like herb fenugreek, on which the Roman soldiers slipped and slithered. As the defenders' situation, however, gradually deteriorated—after the siege had lasted for forty-seven days—Josephus decided, he tells us, to desert his post along with certain of his friends, and leave his force to its fate. Ignoring, therefore, the suicide pact he had concluded with his men, he surrendered to the Romans, who welcomed him as a collaborator. Immediately after his defection Jotapata was taken, with an estimated loss of 40,000 dead and 1,200 prisoners. Vespasian ordered the city to be destroyed and had all its forts burned to the ground. When a report of its fate reached Jerusalem, the news was at first received with incredulity, but then lamentations continued for thirty days. However, Jotapata recovered sufficiently to earn mention of its Jewish population, including priests, up to at least the third century.

Judaea (1) the Greek equivalent of Judah, the most southerly of the three traditional main divisions of the ancient Holy Land or Palestine (the other divisions were Samaria and Galilee), (2) the name given in Hellenistic times to the whole land and state and by the Romans, in the first instance, to their province in the region (AD 6–41, 44–135).

Judaea (2) passed from Persian control (538–332 BC) into the hands of Alexander the Great, and later came under the control first of the Ptolemies and then of the Seleucids (200). The attempts of Antiochus IV Epiphanes to suppress the Jewish faith (see Jerusalem) led to rebellion and the creation of an independent Hasmonaean (Maccabean) Kingdom, which was, however, brought under Roman domination by Pompey the Great in 63. Herod the Great, resisting encroachment by Cleopatra VII of Egypt, ruled the country as the client first of Antony (37–31/30) and then of Augustus (31/30–4); the birth of Jesus is believed to date from the last year or two of Augustus' life. Herod's kingdom was then divided between his sons Archelaus (Judaea-Judah, Samaria, Idumaea), Herod Antipas (Peraea, the scene of the emergence of John the Baptist, and Galilee, where Jesus' mission was for the most part conducted), and Philip (the north).

After Archelaus' deposition in AD 6 his territory became the Roman province of Judaea, under governors (*praefecti*, then procurators) including Pontius Pilate (26–36), during whose tenure Jesus was crucified. The kingship of Marcus Julius Agrippa I (41–44) was only a brief intermission in this provincial status, though subsequently Agrippa II (49/50–before 93/4) was permitted to rule over outlying parts of the country. The two Jewish Revolts or Roman Wars (66–73, 132–35) had devastating effects, displacing the center of Judaism first to Jamnia (Yavneh) and then to various towns in Galilee. The province, upgraded in status (70) and garrisoned by a second legion (*c* 130), was given the name of Syria Palaestina (135), and in the later empire a number of smaller provinces were created: Palaestina Prima, Palaestina Secunda (the north), Arabia (Transjordan), and Palaestine Tertia or Salutaris (the Sinai Peninsula and parts of the Negev)—a region which now received Christian settlements, for instance at Eleutheropolis (Beit Jibrin) and Nessana (Auja el-Hafir).

Although Aramaic was current speech in Judaea, and Greek, too, was extensively spoken during the classical period, the Jews retained their own Hebrew language—employed for the Mishnah (second century AD); the two Gamaras ('completions'), the Jerusalem (or Palestinian) and Babylonian Talmud, belonging to the fourth and fifth centuries, are composed in western and eastern Aramaic respectively. *See also* Antipatris, Ascalon, Azotus, Bethar, Caesarea Maritima, Gadara, Galilee, Gaza, Herodium, Idumaea, Jamnia, Jerusalem, Joppa, Jotapata, Machaerus, Panium, Pella, Samaria, Scythopolis, Sepphoris, Tiberias, Trachonitis.

Juliopolis *see* Tarsus

K

Kabul *see* Paropamisus

Kadıköy *see* Calchedon

Kaine Polis, Kainopolis *see* Artaxata

Kaiseraugst *see* Augusta Rauricorum

Kalamontari *see* Lelanton

Kale *see* Myra

Kale Ağılı *see* Atarneus

Kalpak *see* Orchomenus (Arcadia)

Kandahar *see* Alexandria in Arachosia

Kapisa *see* Alexandria Beside Caucasus, Paropamisus

Karadağ *see* Cynoscephalae

Karaova Suyu *see* Aegospotami

Karavostasi *see* Soli

Karnak *see* Thebes

Kasr Ibrim *see* Aethiopia

Kato Paphos *see* Paphos

Kayseri *see* Caesarea (Cappadocia)

Kazanluk *see* Seuthopolis

Kaz Dağı *see* Ida (Troad)

Keboussie *see* Seleucia in Pieria

Kemer *see* Parium

Kemerhisar *see* Tyana

Kephalari *see* Mieza

Kephalovrysi *see* Thermum

Kerch, Kertch *see* Panticapaeum

Khirbet Fahil *see* Pella (Jordan)

Khojend *see* Alexandria Eschate

Kınık *see* Xanthus

Kithira *see* Cythera

Kitros *see* Pydna

Kızıl Irmak *see* Halys (River)

Koblenz *see* Confluentes

Koca Çayı *see* Xanthus (River)

Köln *see* Colonia Agrippinensis

Kolokythou *see* Colonus

Kom Gieif *see* Naucratis

Kopanos *see* Mieza

Kophen *see* Paropamisus

Koprinka *see* Seuthopolis

Kostolac *see* Viminacium

Kouklia *see* Paphos

Ksar Pharaoun *see* Volubilis

Küçük Menderes (River) *see* Cayster

Kunish *see* Cunaxa

Kurtun *see* Cortona

L

Lacedaemon *see* Laconia, Sparta

Laconia, Lakonike. The southeastern district of the Peloponnese (southern Greece), bounded on the south and east by the Aegean Sea, on the west by Messenia, and on the north by Arcadia and the Argolid. Laconia contains two mountain chains, Parnon to the east and Taygetus to the west, terminating, on either flank of the Laconian Gulf, in Cape Malea (adjacent to the island of Cythera) and Cape Taenarum (Matapan) respectively, and separated by the plain of Sparta (Lacedaemon), through which flowed the river Eurotas and its tributaries.

In the later centuries of the second millennium BC Laconia was a flourishing Mycenaean kingdom, of which the history is reflected, according to the mythological fashion, in the epic poems of Homer, which display Menelaus as its ruler; the kidnapping of his wife Helen by Paris was the cause of the Trojan War. After the Dorian invasions, traditionally attributed to the descendants of Heracles, Eurysthenes and Procles in 1104, Sparta gradually emerged as the leading city of the region, successively annexing various territories (including Gytheum and Las which became its harbors) and reducing their inhabitants to the status of helots (slaves) or of subordinate, though technically independent, 'dwellers round about' (*perioikoi*). About 540, the northern frontier of Laconia was fixed, after long disputes with the Arcadians and Argives. Euripides described the territory as 'possessing much arable land, but not easy to cultivate, for it is hollow (low-lying), surrounded by mountains, rugged, and difficult for enemies to invade.'

Throughout the classical Greek period the history of Laconia is the history of Sparta, but in 195 the towns on the coast subject to Sparta were liberated by the Romans, and became members of the Achaean Confederacy, under whose domination the whole of Laconia subsequently fell. After the suppression of the Confederacy and annexation of Greece by the Romans (146) the various Laconian cities established a 'Lacedaemonian' League of their own, which Augustus converted into a 'League of the Eleuthero-Laconians' (Free Laconians), independent of Sparta. It comprised twenty-four members, of whom only eighteen remained by the second century AD. Among the coastal towns of Laconia, other than Gythium, were Boiae (Neapolis) and Asopus (Plitra) to the south—the latter adjoined an important regional sanctuary of Apollo Hyperteleates (at Finiki) —and Prasiae (near Leonidion) and Zarax (Yeraka) to the east. In 395 Alaric's Visigoths ravaged Laconia, and later it was overrun by Slavs. *See also* Sparta.

Lade, an island about two miles long, off Miletus in Ionia (western Asia Minor); it is now attached to the coast, and lies more than a mile inland. Lade was the scene of the decisive naval battle (495 BC) that sealed the fate of the Ionian Revolt against the Persians (500–494). In the final phase of the operations in Asia Minor the Persian navy, recruited from Phoenicia, Cyprus and Egypt, encountered the Ionian fleet—under the command of Dionysius of Phocaea—off Lade. On the Ionian side, however, the Samians and Lesbians and others fled, and Dionysius departed for Phoenician waters. This victory enabled the Persians to blockade and capture Miletus, and soon afterward the revolt was at an end.

A second engagement off Lade, in 201, was fought between Philip V of Macedonia and the Rhodians. The sequence of events is disputed, but it appears that Philip, after a reversal at the hands of the combined fleets of Rhodes and Pergamum near Chios, first invaded Pergamene territory and then, off Lade, engaged the Rhodians, who, compelled to face him unaided, suffered a defeat, whereupon they joined the Pergamenes and Egyptians in appealing to Rome. The Romans responded favorably, and the Second Macedonian War that followed brought them a decisive victory over Philip.

Lagina *see* Stratonicea

Lalassis, Lalasseis *see* Olba

Lambaesis (Lambèse, Tazzoult) in Numidia (Algeria), on the northern slopes of Mount Aurasius (Aurès). Under Titus, in AD 81, a legionary contingent built a camp there, which was subsequently renewed and then greatly enlarged to become the headquarters of the Third (Augustan) Legion, the principal force in North Africa, probably in the time of Trajan (98–117).

From Lambaesis the legion was able to control the route that led north from the Sahara, and could send reinforcements, along military roads, to strengthen the auxiliary garrisons of Numidia and Mauretania. In 128 Hadrian visited the fortress, and addressed the troops. The greater part of his speech has survived, and can be seen in Algiers museum; it was found in a camp built by the soldiers for the imperial visit. When the province of Numidia was created in 197/8, Lambaesis served as its capital, and an adjoining civilian settlement (on rising ground south of the camp) was granted the status of *municipium*. Gordian III (238–44) raised it to a colonial rank, at the same time disbanding the legion, which had turned against his grandfather and uncle (238); the unit was reinstated, however, at its former quarters by Valerian (253). Named in subsequent secular and Christian texts, the place became the capital, in the later empire, of the province Numidia Militiana (southern Numidia).

Lambaesis is the finest surviving example of a Roman fortified camp. It contains a four-faced arch (*arcus quadrifrons*, wrongly known as the *praetorium*) and a three-bayed triumphal arch of the time of Septimius Severus (193–211); legionary barracks and headquarters and storerooms; a semicircular temple and two chapels dedicated to Aesculapius, Salus, Jupiter Valens and Silvanus; a Capitolium (246, restored 364–67) enclosed by a rectangular portico, in addition to other temples; several sets of baths, and large latrines; walls with platforms (serving as artillery emplacements) and monumental gates. Outside the walls stands an amphitheater, equipped with machinery for admitting animals into the arena. Married quarters constructed after the army reforms of Septimius Severus developed into a substantial town. Lambaesis was completely surrounded by cemeteries; they include two mausolea rising to a height of two storeys, one of which contained the remains of a legionary commander of the time of Severus Alexander (222–35). The local museum houses a collection of inscriptions that throw remarkable light on Roman army life.

Lamia. The chief city of Malis (central Greece), situated on the foothills of Mount Othrys—west of the Malian Gulf (Gulf of Lamia) and northwest of Thermopylae—and dominating the principal route leading southwards from Thessaly. Lamia was of little or no significance until after 400 BC, when it benefited from the elimination of the Spartan colony at Heraclea in Trachis; the coins its mint now issued show the wounded Philoctetes, the central figure of plays of that name by Sophocles and other tragedians, who attributed his origins to Malis.

Lamia gave its name to the Lamian War of 323/2 BC in which, after the death of Alexander the Great, a number of Greek states sought to shake off Macedonian domination. The Athenian commander Leosthenes, supported by troops from Aetolia, Thessaly, Phocis, Locris, and Delphi, besieged the Macedonian Antipater in Lamia, but was killed, and in the absence of a siege-train the city held out throughout the winter until relief arrived; whereupon the allied states—with which Antipater insisted on dealing separately—felt obliged to come to terms.

Before and after 200 Lamia reached the height of its prosperity as a member of the Aetolian League, serving as a headquarters of the forces of the Seleucid Antiochus III the Great in the war which, in association with the Aetolians, he waged against Rome (191). In the following year, however, the city was captured by Manius Acilius Glabrio and attached by the Romans to the district of Phthiotis in the puppet Thessalian Confederacy which they had established. In late imperial times the town became an episcopal see, under the name of Zitouni. Traces of ancient walls and tombs have been found, and the medieval Catalan castle is built on Greek and Roman foundations.

Lampsacus, Lampsakos (Lapseki). A city of the Troad (northwestern Asia Minor). Its strategic situation at the eastern entrance to the Hellespont (Dardanelles), together with the possession of a good harbor, guaranteed economic success and historical significance. In contradiction to Strabo's statement that its founders came from Miletus, other writers, like the Lampsacenes themselves, believed that they had come from another Ionian city, Phocaea (Foca). During the sixth and fifth centuries BC Lampsacus fell successively under the control of the Lydians, the Persians (whose King Artaxerxes I assigned it *c* 464 to the Athenian exile Themistocles), the Delian League controlled by Athens, the Spartans (who used it as an operational base in 405, at the end of the Peloponnesian War and then the Persians once more. During the first half of the fourth century its earlier coinage (first electrum and then silver) was replaced by a famous series of gold staters, displaying a winged horse, which, together with Persian issues, constituted for a time the principal gold coinage of most of the Mediterranean world.

Free again for a short period, *c* 362 Lampsacus fell once more under Athenian control (355). Then came a resumption of Persian domination (340) (exercised by Memnon, governor of the Troad), from which it was detached by Alexander the Great (334), becoming one of his mints. Its prosperity continued during the Hellenistic Age, in which it shared the vicissitudes of other cities of the Troad (*qv*), allying itself with the Romans *c* 190 and receiving autonomy, but suffering from the depredations of their governor Verres (80). According to Appian, Lampsacus received a draft of Italian settlers from Julius Caesar, and they may (although this is a matter of discussion) have constituted a formal Roman colony, to which a series of coins describing some foundation as Gemina (twin with Parium) has been tentatively attributed. In 35, however, Sextus Pompeius, fleeing to Asia Minor after his defeat by Octavian (the future Augustus) and Agrippa at Naulochus, obtained control of the place by treachery, and after his suppression and death shortly afterward nothing more was heard of the colony, if it had ever existed.

Under the Principate, however, Lampsacus continued to prosper, issuing coinage with Greek inscriptions until the time of Gallienus (AD 253–68). One of its most frequent coin-types was a statue (sometimes in a temple) of the ithyphallic garden-god Priapus, who is described as 'Hellespontine' by Virgil, since one of the leading seats of his worship was located at Lampsacus. Nevertheless, in Christian times the city possessed a bishopric, and its harbor played an important part in the Middle Ages. Remains of walls and other structures are mostly overgrown or have vanished.

Lanuvium (Lanuvio) in Latium (Lazio, western Italy). An ancient Latin city at the southern extremity of the Alban Hills, nearly twenty miles southeast of Rome. According to mythology, the place owed its foundation to Diomedes. An independent member of the Latin League, Lanuvium participated in the Cassian Treaty between the Latin communities and Rome (*c* 493). When the Romans dissolved the League (338), they granted Lanuvium Roman citizenship as a *municipium*. The famous actor Quintus Roscius Gallus, a client of Cicero, came from its territory, and another of his clients Titus Annius Milo, the gangster politician who murdered his political enemy Publius Clodius Pulcher, was a native and municipal official (*dictator*) of Lanuvium. The city suffered, according to Appian, in the Civil Wars, but resumed its prosperity during the Principate, when it was the birthplace of the emperor Antoninus Pius (86).

Its most important remains are to be found on the acropolis, to the north of the ancient (and modern) town. This citadel was surrounded by a tufa wall; its gates, one embellished by a marble equestrian group (partly preserved), were guarded by substantial ramparts. There are also traces of a temple, revealing three successive constructional phases (*c* 500, *c* 300 and third century BC). This may be the famous shrine of Juno Sispes (Sospita) Mater Regina, in whose cult Rome participated; the goddess is depicted, wearing a goatskin cloak, holding a shield and hurling a spear, and accompanied by a snake, on the coins of Roman Republican moneyers, who are probably of Lanuvian origin. Not far from the acropolis are the remains of a number of Roman villas, one of which is conjecturally identified with the home of Antoninus Pius (AD 138–61).

Laodicea in Phoenice *see* Berytus

Laodicea on the Lycus (Ad Lycum), Laodikeia (Eski Hisar, near Denizli). In southwestern Phrygia (Asia Minor), near its borders with Lydia and Caria. Situated on a low flat-topped hill bounded by two streams, the Kapros and Asopos, Laodicea occupied the site of an older settlement (named Rhoas or Diospolis, according to Pliny the Elder: the latter designation corresponding with the position of Zeus [genitive: Dios] as the chief local deity), dominating the valley of the Lycus (Çürüksu Çayı) a few miles east of its junction with the Maeander (Büyük Menderes), beside an important trade route. The story, recorded by Stephanus of Byzantium, that the town was founded by the Seleucid Antiochus I Soter (281–261 BC) in response to a dream, and named after his sister Laodice, appears to be erroneous. Instead, the foundation, perhaps accompanied by an influx of colonists, was apparently the work of Antiochus II Theos in honor of another Laodice who was his cousin and wife, between 261 and 253. Laodicea became famous for the softness and raven-black color of its wool, and, according to Strabo, owed its distinction to the fertility of its territory and the wealth of some of its citizens. When Achaeus, a general of Antiochus III the Great, proclaimed his independence (220), it was at Laodicea that he was crowned; later the city served as a mint for the Attalid kings of Pergamum.

After its inclusion in the Roman province of Asia, it became a center where the proconsul held his assize courts. It opposed Mithridates VI of Pontus in Rome's First Mithridatic War (88–85) and was defended against the king's besieging army by Quintus Oppius, reckoning a new era from 84. From 56 to 50 Laodicea was temporarily detached to form part of the military province of Cilicia. In 40, under the leadership of Zeno, one of its prominent citizens, its people resisted the Parthians and their ally the Roman renegade Labienus. Laodicea suffered severe damage from earthquakes under Augustus (*c* 20 BC), Tiberius (AD 17) and Nero (60), but was given financial assistance to assist its recovery. A new era was dated either from 123 or 130, both years in which Hadrian visited the city. The status of *neokoros* (a privilege mainly related to the imperial cult) was granted by Commodus, withdrawn after his death (192), but restored by Caracalla (211–17). In the later empire Laodicea was the capital of the province of Phrygia Pacatiana. Christianity had been introduced by Epaphras, a companion of St. Paul, though in *Revelations* the Laodiceans were upbraided for their lukewarmness, for which they became a byword. Nevertheless, theirs was one of the 'Seven Churches of the Apocalypse.'

Remains of two theaters, a stadium that also served as an amphitheater (dedicated to Vespasian in AD 79), and a small council chamber (?) are to be seen; also a bath building (?) flanked by a tower serving as the terminal of an aqueduct from a spring in Denizli, and a *nymphaeum* (fountain building), which has been recently excavated. The abundant local monetary issues of Laodicea unusually include portraits of two local dignitaries of early imperial times, Sitalcas and Pytheas. Several other city officials who are named on the coinage belonged to the prominent local family of the Zenonidae, descended from Zeno who had resisted the Parthians in 40 BC; they include Claudia Zenonis and Julia Zenonis, high priestesses in the time of Domitian (AD 81-96), Publius Claudius Attalus, who sponsored coinages under Antoninus Pius (138-61) and Marcus Aurelius (161-80) in his capacity as high priest. Uncommon reverse types on these issues include the city-goddess standing between wolf and boar (representing the river-gods Lycus and Kapros) and seated between standing figures of Phrygia and Caria. The emperor Caracalla (211-17) is also depicted sacrificing in front of a temple, and standing before a shrine beside an agora crowded with people.

Laodicea on the Sea (Ad Mare), Laodikeia (Latakia). Situated on the coast of Syria, occupying a rocky cape flanked on its west and south sides by the Mediterranean (where an excellent harbor was available east of the modern port), and on the east side by a pair of hills. Originally a Phoenician town, named Ramitha or Mazabda, the place was refounded by Seleucus I Nicator (301-281 BC) and named after his mother Laodice. Thanks to its favorable location, extensive middle-eastern trade, wealth in crops, linen, and exportation of wine (which went as far as Egypt), Laodicea achieved an importance scarcely inferior to that of Antioch, in association with which, together with Seleucus' other foundations of Apamea (Qalaat al-Mudik) and Seleucia Pieria, it formed a Tetrapolis, which issued coinage in the second century BC as 'Brother Peoples.'

After achieving independence shortly before 100, Laodicea was brought under Roman rule by Pompey the Great (*c* 63), but received autonomy and the name of Julia on the occasion of Caesar's visit to Syria (47). After his death, his supporter Dolabella told a soldier to kill him to avoid capture by Cassius. The city's freedom was confirmed by Augustus. It was sacked by Pescennius Niger during his civil war with Septimius Severus (AD 193/4), but restored by the latter (in contrast with the degradation of Antioch) and granted the status of a Roman colony, enjoying a subsequent period of great prosperity.

The sanctuaries mentioned by ancient authors and inscriptions (including a shrine of Athena at which human sacrifices were said to have been offered) have disappeared, and so have an amphitheater (except for a few traces), a stadium, baths, and a two-storeyed lighthouse illustrated on a second-century coin. But colonnades and a monumental arch can still be seen, and it is possible to trace the perimeter of the ancient habitation center and to discern the plan of its colonnaded streets beneath the modern town. Coins of imperial date depict the armed statue of Artemis Brauronia, which Seleucus I brought from Susa in Persia to Laodicea, and celebrate an imperial benefaction of grain to its citizens (*aeternum beneficium*).

Lapseki *see* Lampsacus

Larache *see* Lix

Larinum (Larino), an Italian town due east of Rome, fourteen miles from the Adriatic situated on Mount Arenio (Arone) and dominating the valley of the Biferno; it was at one time in Daunia, and is now in Molise. The inhabitants were closely related to the neighboring Oscan-speaking tribe of the Frentani, from which, however, they retained their political independence. A center of the wool trade, Larinum during the third century BC issued bronze coins with Greek and Italian inscriptions and Campanian, Apulian and local designs.

It was involved in some of the military operations of the Second Punic War (218–201 BC), but gained undying notoriety from the trial of a member of one of its leading families, Aulus Cluentius Habitus (66), accused of murdering his stepfather Statius Abbius Oppianicus but successfully defended by Cicero. The orator's speech *Pro Cluentio* casts a unique and lurid light on a small Italian town during the first century BC, where the citizens (even allowing for a certain exaggeration) appear to have led lives of unceasing acquisitiveness resulting in frequent violent crimes and assassinations.

A bronze tablet found at Larinum, and published in 1978, carries part of a decree of the Roman senate in AD 19 embodying measures directed against public performances on stage or in the arena by members of the senatorial class and *equites* (knights). The inscription thus confirms and corrects accounts by Suetonius and Tacitus of partly comparable enactments.

Larissa, Larisa, the principal city and capital of Thessaly (northeastern Greece), dominating the large and fertile East Thessalian plain (Pelasgiotis) from its acropolis situated on a low hill protected by the river Peneus. Though inhabited since Palaeolithic times, the place did not appear in the Homeric Catalog of Ships, but compensated for this deficiency by the accumulation of myths round the nymph Larissa (who fell into the Peneus while playing ball) and above all round the wealthy aristocratic family and ruling house of the place, the Aleuadae, who claimed the Children of Heracles, leaders of the Doric invasion, as their ancestors, and traced their line back to a golden-haired cowherd named Aleuas the Red, who was supposedly descended from one of these Heraclids, Thessalos, and was said to have been courted by a dragon.

It was he to whom the original organization of the Thessalian League was attributed, continuing under successive Aleuadae holding the office of *tagos*. The first of them to assert his authority over the whole of Thessaly probably lived during the later seventh century BC. Eurylochus, who *c* 590 took part in the First Sacred War fought for the possession of the revenues of Delphi, was probably an Aleuad *tagos*; and the earliest known poem by Pindar honored a young protégé of the same house (498). During the invasion of Greece by Xerxes I (480), the Aleuadae of Larissa supported him, but the other Thessalian states dissented and sought briefly, and ineffectively, with the aid of their Greek allies, to defend the valley of Tempe. For subsequent political developments, *see* Thessaly.

The fine and varied coinage of Larissa begins in the early fifth century with coins displaying the sandal of the mythical hero Jason, which he was said to have lost while crossing the river Anauros. In the second half of the century, despite internal conflicts, Larissa remained prosperous and culturally ambitious, welcoming the rhetorician Gorgias and the physician Hippocrates, who died there in 399. Toward the end of the Peloponnesian War (431–404) an oligarchy had gained control of the city, but following its defeat by Lycophron, the autocratic ruler (tyrant) of Pherae (404), the Aleuadae, with the help of the Persian prince Cyrus the Younger, suppressed internal strife and reestablished themselves (402). They maintained resistance to the growing power of Pherae, but after the temporary loss of Larissa (before 374), called in first Thebes and then Macedonia (357/6) to help them. In 344, however, the Macedonian King Philip II annexed Thessaly and expelled a tyrant, Simus, whom he had earlier set up at Larissa. Thenceforward the city remained in the hands of the Macedonian kings (at whose court its leaders often played an important part) until its liberation by the Romans (196), who reinstated it as capital and mint of a new Thessalian confederacy and enlisted its people's assistance against the Seleucid Antiochus III the Great and then against Perseus of Macedonia.

A large inscription of *c* 151/50 BC that has recently come to light indicates that the city supplied grain to Rome. It continued to flourish during the Principate, and in the later empire became the capital of the province of Thessalia. The surviving traces of the ancient city are insignificant, though two groups of rich tombs of the later seventh or early sixth century have now been found at the adjacent villages of Ayios Yeoryios, and sparse remnants of a Hellenistic council house (?) and theater can be seen in the town center. (This Larissa in Pelasgiotis must be distinguished from a second town of the same name, bearing the cognomen Cremaste, in another Thessalian district, Phthiotis).

Larissa *see* Argos, Tralles

Larnaca *see* Citium

Lassois, Mount *see* Vix

Latium (the southern part of the modern district of Lazio). A region of western Italy extending from the Tyrrhenian Sea inland (as far as the Apennines) and from the river Tiber to Campania (where its border was moved from Circaeum [Circeo] to Sinuessa [Le Vagnole]). A well-watered region consisting of plains furrowed into gullies and undulating folds, Latium was inhabited first by various prehistoric peoples and then, as the first millennium BC began, by roving groups of people of mixed race who spoke an Indo-European language and were descended from people connected with the Mycenaean civilization.

Some of these immigrants settled on the Alban Mount, at a time when nomadism was gradually giving way to irrigated agriculture; while others came to live beneath the mountain at Alba Longa (Castel Gandolfo), which was famous for the story, of uncertain authenticity, that it was the parent city of Rome. The small Latin communities (gradually merging into a few larger city-states) formed confederations for religious purposes, based on the Alban Mount (where they performed the worship of Jupiter Latiaris) and on the territory of Aricia (Ariccia) (where the 'League of Ferentina' was centered on a shrine of Diana Nemorensis [of Nemi]). Other groupings centered on Lavinium and Ardea.

The last-named town, and Rome, Alba Longa, Praeneste (Palestrina), Gabii (Castiglione), Ardea, Antium (Anzio) and Politorium (Castel di Decima) were all key points on the routes between the Etruscan city-states and Campania, and themselves became Etruscanized in varying degrees. But the power of the Etruscans in Latium gradually weakened, especially after their defeat by a combined force of Latins and Campanians from Cumae (*c* 506/4)

By this time the Romans had already established a considerable ascendancy in Latium, but the fall of the Roman monarchy caused this domination to be contested—in so far as the historical facts can be disentangled from legend—at the battle of Lake Regillus (Pantano) fought *c* 496 between Rome and what had become known as the Latin League. About 493, the Romans and the League concluded a defensive treaty (the *foedus Cassianum*) against menacing Volsci and Aequi. Gradually, however, Rome resumed the extension of its power throughout Latium, until in 338 it incorporated the smaller towns and reduced the larger cities to a subject status which, however, permitted them to retain their autonomy and continue the establishment, in association with Rome, of 'Latin colonies' drawn from all the peoples of the territory.

Depopulation, however, was soon started by the magnetic pull of Rome and the upheavals of its third-century warfare. During the Second Punic War twelve colonies objected to Roman demands for continuous military service (209), although the Latins as a whole remained loyal. But the abuse of powers by Roman commanders cast a heavy strain on this loyalty, and in 125 Fregellae (Opri) rebelled. The Latins took no major part in the rebellion of allies known as the Social War (91–87), accepting Roman citizenship under the Julian Law (89). Meanwhile the term 'Latium' had gained a fresh life outside as well as inside the territory bearing that name, indicating, in this new sense, the Latin right (*ius Latii*) which gave Roman citizenship to those holding annual offices (magistracies) in the various communities.

As for Latium itself, although Tibur (Tivoli), Praeneste and Antium became fashionable resorts, and opulent villas abounded, the combination of civil wars, large slave-run estates and fevers continued to depopulate the ancient towns, which the Augustan poets (with some exaggeration) described as derelict, and Pliny the Elder, too, in some cases records as having wholly disappeared. Agriculture was superseded with pasturage, and by the end of the ancient period Latium had assumed the deserted guise that it retained until recent years. *See also* Alba Longa, Albanus (Lake, Mount), Allia, Anagnia, Antium, Ardea, Aricia, Arpinum, Collatia, Digentia, Ficana, Fidenae, Gabii, Lanuvium, Lavinium, Nemorensis (Lake), Ostia, Politorium, Praeneste, Regillus (Lake), Rome, Satricum, Terracina, Tibur, Tusculum, Velitrae.

Latmus *see* Heraclea on Latmus

Lattikiye *see* Laodicea on the Sea (Syria)

La Turbie *see* Tropacum Augusti

Laurentum *see* Lavinium, Politorium

Lauriacum (Lorch, beside Enns) in Noricum (Upper Austria). Lauriacum was the terminal of the route leading northward from Aquileia on the Adriatic. It was also strategically placed on the road leading from west to east beside the Danube; and the terrace on which it was built overlooked the junction of the Danube with its southern tributary the Ivesis (Enns), while across the river the valley of the Aist afforded penetration into the interior of Germany. Originally a Celtic settlement, Lauriacum passed into the hands of the Romans when they occupied Noricum in 15 BC. In the middle of the first century AD its auxiliary garrison was protected by earthworks and a double trench, and adjacent civilian quarters (*canabae*) had also come into existence.

After the destruction of the post of the Marcomanni in 170/71 Marcus Aurelius stationed a legion at Albing nearby, but owing to this camp's vulnerability to flooding Septimius Severus built a new fortress at Lauriacum (*c* 205). Under his son Caracalla the civilian town that had arisen two hundred yards to the west of the stronghold received the rank of *municipium,* but thereafter the place suffered from destruction by the Alamanni, and was burned down in the times of Gallienus (253–68) and Aurelian (270–75). In the later empire it belonged to the province of Noricum Ripense. Enjoying a certain revival during the following century, Lauriacum was visited by Constantius II (341), and subsequent temporary residents included Valentinian I, when he was reorganizing the frontier defences (374), and then Gratian (378). Eugippius, in his life of Abbot (St.) Severinus (d. 482), tells how at the very end of the western empire the place—by now the seat of a bishopric—was finally given up to the Germanic invaders, and its population (including numerous refugees from elsewhere) was moved down the Danube to Faviana (Krems) and entrusted to the king of the German tribe of the Rugii.

Most of the legionary camp of Lauriacum has been brought to light; of rhomboid shape, it included all the normal features (including a *valetudinarium,* sick bay), and was surrounded by a six-foot-thick wall with trenches and thirty-six towers. The first major building period of the civilian town, which has also been excavated, dates from the Severan epoch. A commercial forum has been located (the main forum, believed to be in the neighborhood of the church of St. Lorenz, is not yet uncovered), and there are remains of a large bathing establishment, private houses and two dozen cemeteries. The successive strata of Germanic invasions and subsequent reconstructions can be identified. Christianity—Florian was martyred during the persecutions of Diocletian in 304—is represented by a small basilica built over the sick bay of the legionary camp, while the original church of St. Lorenz was likewise of early date.

Laurium, Laurion. A district of low hills in the southeastern corner of Attica in Greece, extending north from Cape Sunium for a distance of nearly eleven miles. The greater part of the region is barren, but there were early discoveries, particularly on the east side, of rich deposits of ore, including *galena,* which yielded silver and made Laurium one of the largest mining arcas in the Greek world. The exploitation of these deposits, which may have started in the middle of the second millennium BC, continued (or resumed) not long after 1000, though still limited, at this stage, to surface operations. In view, however, of the growing need for greater quantities of silver to provide Athens with its coinage, deep mining led to the discovery of rich beds of ore, notably at Maronea (*c* 483). The mines were regarded as state property and were leased to private citizens—employing very numerous slaves and condemned criminals as miners—by Athenian officials known as 'sellers' (*poletai*).

Thereafter programs continued until operations were halted during the Peloponnesian War by the establishment of a hostile Spartan fort at Decelea in central Attica (413). The mines were reopened *c* 335, with encouragement from an earlier writing by Xenophon. However, development was once again hampered in the third century, this time by the low price of silver. Nevertheless, exploitation continued ruthlessly, until the slave miners rose in revolt (*c* 135/3 and *c* 104–100). By the time of Strabo (early first century AD) the men no longer went underground but were reworking the slag heaps on the surface; Pausanias (*c* 150) speaks of Laurium as the place where the Athenians 'had once possessed' silver mines.

Countless remains of the ancient industry can still be seen, though many have not been sufficiently cleared or examined. The mines themselves vary from simple and crude passages to complicated arrangements of deep galleries linked to the surface by shafts that are sometimes three hundred feet deep. There are also washing tables (with nearby water storage cisterns), notably an elaborate series of installations in the Agrileza district, high up in the Laurium valley, where careful excavations since 1978 have revealed an elaborate works-compound comprising a circular roofed section and a courtyard. Another round building, of uncertain function, had been found in 1971 at Pountazeze Bay, and rescue operations of the same date at Gaîdhouromandra Bay revealed a complex in which argentiferous ore was processed in the fourth century BC; while a powerfully walled building at Megala Pafka was found to contain a bank of furnaces. Traces of a defence system have also come to light in the region.

Lavinium (Pratica di Mare). An ancient city in Latium (Lazio), seventeen miles southeast of Rome. Lavinium belonged to the Latin League and became its federal sanctuary during the sixth century BC; it was also mentioned in the first treaty between Rome and Carthage, as described by Polybius (508). Easy access to the sea gave it early contacts with the Greek world, which lent its cults a Greek (not Etruscan) character. At the conclusion of Rome's war with the Latins in 338, the town, which had remained loyal to the Romans, probably became a *municipium.* During the civil wars of the early first century it appears to have suffered gravely from the troops of Gaius Marius. Situated close to the ancient town of Laurentum (Casale Decima)—which was linked to Rome by the Via

Laurentina—Lavinium belonged to the *Laurens ager,* Laurentine territory, and later became identified with Laurentum itself, under the name of Laurolavinium.

According to the myth told by Virgil and Livy and others, Lavinium was founded by Aeneas, a fugitive from Troy, because he had been told to establish the settlement at the place where he would see a sow with thirty young; and it was at Lavinium that the prodigy duly appeared (it is depicted on a medallion of Antoninus Pius, AD 138/9, together with the walls of the city). Aeneas named his new foundation after his wife Lavinia, daughter of Latinus, who was the legendary king of the 'Aborigines,' or Latins, and ruled at Laurentum. It was from Lavinium, according to this tradition, that Aeneas' son Ascanius, thirty years later, founded Alba Longa, from which, after many generations, Romulus and Remus went forth to found Rome itself. Although, therefore, there is no direct, incontrovertible evidence for the veneration of Aeneas at Lavinium until the late fourth century, the place enjoyed enormous renown in subsequent times for the part it had supposedly played in the foundation of Rome. This role was celebrated by an important cult of the (supposedly Trojan) Penates (household gods)—from which the Romans borrowed their own national rites of the same deities—and a sanctuary of the hearth-goddess Vesta, which was closely linked with the cult of the Penates at Lavinium and with Vesta's own worship at Rome. Another deity who received reverence locally was Indiges—a designation for worshipped ancestors—who was identified both with Jupiter and with Aeneas, and whose burial place, under the name of Jupiter Indiges, was shown beside the river Numicus, not far off.

Excavations have confirmed the supposition that Lavinium was the most impressive of the archaic religious centers of Latium. Several extra-urban sanctuaries are now known. One (near the little church of Santa Maria delle Vigne) contains a series of thirteen large altars, carefully aligned, ranging in date from the sixth to about the second century; discoveries on the site include not only votive terracottas but an inscription of *c* 500 testifying to the worship of the Dioscuri (Castor and Pollux), who were identified locally with Lavinium's deified ancestors, or with its Penates. Bronze statuettes of young men (*kouroi*) and women (*korai*) have also been found. However, the claim that a mound tomb of the seventh century, about a hundred yards distant, should be identified with a hero's shrine of Aeneas—seen six hundred years later by Dionysius of Halicarnassus—has now been discounted. A second, 'eastern' sanctuary that has recently been examined contains vast, rich and varied material from about the sixth century down to the end of the third, including a votive deposit from which numerous large statues have emerged and have been, or are being, restored. Most of the figures dated from the second half of the fourth century, though some, in severe style, may go back to the years before 500. At least four of these images, probably of fifth-century date, are striking and original representations of Minerva (Athena Tritonia), fully armed; they were probably buried when a temple of the goddess suffered destruction. Various stretches of the city wall have also come to light, and it has been deduced that Lavinium expanded in the course of the sixth century, when its older sections assumed the functions of an acropolis, from which various objects of all dates have been recovered.

Lebanon, Mount *see* Libanus

Lechaeum *see* Corinth

Ledosus (Lezoux) in eastern Aquitania (Puy-de-Dôme, Auvergne), south-central Gaul. A village forming one of the principal centers of the pottery industry in the Roman empire. Early in the Principate, Italian wares (notably those from Arretium [Arezzo]) lost their primacy, first to Condatomagus (Graufesenque) and then to Ledosus, where (expanding a much earlier trade, exemplified by recent finds of Italian bronzes) potters from the time of Tiberius (AD 14–37) imitated products imported from Italy and sold their handiwork in Gaul, Germany and Britain. These copies consist mainly of terracottas with low relief decoration (*terra sigillata*), but also include bowls, jugs, relief plaques and architectural ornaments. After a subsequent reduction of activity, the workshops of Ledosus revived in the course of the second century and maintained their activity until the fourth.

Lefkandi *see* Lelanton

Lefkas *see* Leucas

Lefkhadia *see* Mieza

Legio (León). A city in northern Spain, in the northwestern part of the Spanish inland plateau (the Meseta), on the southern flank of the Cantabrian mountains. The city was established at the confluence of the rivers Bernesga and Toŕio, on a small hill adequately supplied with water. The name 'Legio' refers to the Roman garrison of the place, consisting of the Seventh Legion (Legio VII Gemina), which was the main military force controlling the potentially troublesome northern regions of the province of Nearer Spain (later known as Hispania Tarraconensis), and keeping a watch over the region's mines. As inscriptions discovered at Villaĺis confirm, the legion was raised in AD 68 by Galba (at first under the name of VII Galbiana) and was permanently stationed at Legio either from *c* 72 or (if, as seems possible, it first served in Upper Germany) some two years later.

Legio, which had the rectangular plan of a Roman camp, apparently reached its greatest size in the time of Trajan (98–117). Discoveries have been limited, because the ancient town lies under its modern successor. But a double set of walls is largely preserved, and a bathing establishment, apparently dating from the time of Antoninus Pius (138–61), has been identified beneath and beside the cathedral; it seems to have formed part of the residence of the legionary commander. At Marialba, outside the city, an apsed church of the Martyrs has come to light. Constructed in two stages, *c* 350 and *c* 400, it is the most important early Christian building in northern Spain.

Leja *see* Trachonitis

Lelantine Plain (Kalamontari) The coastal plain in western Euboea (off central Greece), the most fertile part of the island; it faces the narrows of the Euripus channel, which was used by vessels coasting in the Aegean so as to avoid the rocks and currents of the eastern Euboean coast. The plain was named after the Lelanton stream or torrent—the town of Lelanton (*qv*) is perhaps identifiable with Lefkandi—and belonged to Boeotia's sphere of influence during the Mycenaean age. Its importance, however, dates from the transitional years between that period and the ensuing historical epoch. For the Lelantine plain, which contained curative fountains and mines exceptionally yielding both copper and iron, extended between the cities of Chalcis and Eretria—the leaders of Greek recovery and expansion during this early Iron Age—forming a bone of contention between them. The result was the earliest Greek war that can be regarded as historical (shortly before 700 BC ?). This Lelantine War involved various allies of the two participants, and Thucydides writes as if many or most of the Greek states played a part. One important engagement took place on land, where the cavalry of Pharsalus (in Thessaly) won the day for its allies the Chalcidians. But the war proved disastrous to both sides. Eretria ceased to be a leading power, and Chalcis, too, eventually lost its maritime supremacy to Corinth. By the time of Strabo the copper and iron resources of the plain were exhausted.

Lelanton, Lelantium (?)—the possible ancient name for the modern village of Lefkandi; though an alternative identification of Lelanton with Old Eretria (*see* Eretria) must not be discounted. Lefkandi was a city between Chalcis and Eretria on the island of Euboea, in the central part of the island's west coast (beside the strait), with the Lelantine Plain as its hinterland. The township was flourishing in the mid-twelfth century BC (when a late Mycenaean settlement on the Xeropolis ridge faced the mainland) and then attained an unusual degree of prosperity during the transitional period following the Mycenaean epoch, the so-called Dark Age of Greek history on which recent excavations at Lefkandi have cast exceptional light. It was one of the first places in Greece to obtain luxury goods from the Near East; beads of faience, glass and blue frit (a material for glassmaking) are found with tenth-century cremations.

Also of tenth-, and early ninth-, century date are important burials at Toumba, a prominent hillock overlooking the sea to the west and the Lelantine Plain to the north. Numerous burial grounds located in the area include a particularly rich site (only partially saved from modern bulldozers) that has yielded gold jewelry, imports from Attica, and Near Eastern products, including an Egyptian ring (exceptional at this period). Close by is a sophisticated apsidal building of the later tenth century, of most unusual size—36 by 149 feet. Constructed of mud-brick on a stone foundation, it overlaid two very richly furnished tombs, of which one proves to be the hero's grave (*heroon*), in Homeric style, of a warrior whose bones and ashes (wrapped in strips of cloth which are remarkably well preserved) were buried in an amphora, decorated with reliefs. The other grave contained the remains of a woman laden with gold jewelry, and the skeletons of three or four horses.

A foundry (indicating expertise in Near Eastern metalworking techniques) dates from *c* 900. Thereafter cemetery offerings become increasingly rich in gold and other imported luxuries, profiting, it may be supposed, from (still unidentified) Euboean markets in northern Syria, the forerunners of Al Mina and Posidium (Ras-al-Bassit). Those two settlements were founded *c* 865, and it was at just about that time, for reasons that are not clear, that burials abruptly cease at Lefkandi: though life of a kind continued there until its destruction *c* 700, which may have been an outcome of the Lelantine War between Chalcis and Eretria (sse Lelantine Plain). Perhaps Lefkandi may be the 'Old Eretria' referred to by Strabo, and in this case it is possible to conjecture that its inhabitants evacuated their site at this juncture in order to move to 'New Eretria'. *See also* Eretria, Lelantine Plain.

Lemnos. An island in the northeastern Aegean, containing a volcano that was reputed to be the force of Hephaestus (Vulcan), but had become extinct in historical times. Although rugged, the island was fertilized by its lava, and grew a considerable quantity of wheat. It displays remains of a Bronze Age culture (connected with Troy) at Poliochni on the east coast—the site of seven successive building phases—and is described in the *Iliad* as a provisioning center for the Achaeans during the Trojan War.

Herodotus describes the early inhabitants of Lemnos as 'Pelasgians,' a term used for northern, immigrant elements as opposed to Greeks. He tells how they had been obliged to emigrate from Athens (an unlikely tale intended to justify the later Athenian claim to the island), and how they had vengefully returned to kidnap and murder Athenian women and children at Brauron in Attica, thus giving rise to the Greek description of acts of violence as 'Lemnian deeds.' However this may be, the Hellenization of Lemnos had reached an advanced stage by the eighth century BC.

But the influence of the far-off Etruscans also seems to have been present. For a gravestone (stele) of the early sixth century, found at Camina in the southeastern part of the island (and now in the National Museum at Athens), displays not only a relief of a warrior somewhat reminiscent of sculptures from northern Etruria but also a long inscription which, although indecipherable, displays letters and language possessing evident Etruscan affinities. And Thucydides, too, testifies to 'Tyrsenians' (Etruscans) on Lemnos. These cryptic pieces of evidence do not, as has sometimes been supposed, justify the view that the earliest Etruscans were immigrants from the east, but suggest that one of their city-states later possessed a trading post or market on the island. Moreover, the Lemnians, like (other) Etruscans, had a reputation as kidnappers and pirates (*see above*). Their island lay close to the approaches to the Euxine (Black) Sea, where Etruscan pots and bronzes have been found near the Russian coast.

The Athenian Miltiades the Younger, ruler of the Thracian Chersonese (Gallipoli peninsula), seized Lemnos *c* 500 and planted colonists there, and with brief intermissions of rule by Persia, Sparta (404–393), and Hellenistic monarchies the island remained in the hands of the Athenians, whose ownership the Romans confirmed (166). The principal Lemnian city, Hephaestia, stood on a peninsula beside the north coast, above a nearly landlocked harbor; excavations have revealed pre-Greek, archaic and classical material, and a Greco-Roman theater remains above ground. The soil in the neighborhood, notably at Mosychlos (near Repanidhion), includes a quantity of 'Lemnian earth,' highly esteemed for curative purposes, and extracted on only one day in each year, to the accompaniment of religious ceremonies. Across the bay, at Chloe (Khloi), was a terraced sanctuary of the non-Hellenic Cabiri, whose worship was centered on the island of Samothrace. On the west coast traces exist of another town Myrina (Mirina, Kastron), which stood on a rocky promontory flanked by two good anchorages, and possessed a shrine of Artemis.

Leninabad *see* Alexandria Eschate

Lentini *see* Leontini

León *see* Legio

Leontini, Leontinoi (Carlentini, near Lentini). A Greek city in Sicily, at the southern extremity of the Campi Leontini (Piana di Catania), the largest stretch of fertile plain in the eastern part of the island. Leontini lay six miles inland to the south of the river Terias (San Leonardo, or Lentini). According to mythology, Xuthus the son of the wind-god Aeolus reigned at Leontini; Heracles passed through the place, and it was the home of cannibal giants, the Laestrygones.

Enjoying an excellent water supply, the site was occupied since very early times, and when settlers (originating from Chalcis in Euboea) from the recently established Sicilian colony of Naxos (Punta di Schiso) arrived in 729 BC under the leadership of Theocles, they found native Sicels in possession. There are differing reports of what happened next. According to Thucydides the Chalcidians drove out the Sicels by force. Polyaenus (second century AD), however, had learned of an alternative story that the colonists swore an agreement to live in peace alongside this indigenous population, but subsequently admitted Megarian settlers (who later colonized Megara Hyblaea) on the condition that they turned the Sicels out. Archaeological evidence suggests that the two communities did exist for a time alongside one another.

About 615 or 609, Panaetius, with the help of oppressed classes, became the first 'tyrant' (autocratic ruler) of a Sicilian city-state. At this time Leontini was one of the richest Sicilian communties. Its coinage, which began at about the turn of the century, often depicts a lion (*leon*). This was a play on the name of the city, but the lion was also the symbol of Apollo, who was worshipped at Leontini with special devotion. Another coin-type was a grain of wheat in which the neighborhood abounded, thus providing the inhabitants with their prosperity.

Leontini was captured by Hippocrates of Gela *c* 494; and later a local 'tyrant' (autocrat), Aenesidemus, gained power. This despotic regime, however, was eliminated in 466. Thereafter the city repeatedly sought to evade Syracusan encroachment by contracting alliances with Athens. In 433/2, for example, such an understanding was reached, with Rhegium (Reggio di Calabria) as an additional adherent. Then in 427, during the Peloponnesian War, the most distinguished of Leontini's citizens, the sophist and rhetorician Gorgias, led a delegation to Athens—a landmark in the history of the art of rhetoric, which he introduced to that city. After occupation by the Syracusans five years later, Leontini supported the Athenian expedition against them in 415. However, with a brief intermission in 405–403, when it celebrated an alliance with Catana on its coinage, the city passed once again, and remained, under the control of Syracuse. During the Second Punic War between the Romans and Carthaginians the Syracusan monarch Hieronymus was murdered at Leontini (214), which was then sacked and annexed by the Romans. Losing its political privileges, it suffered in the Second Sicilian Slave War (104), but still derived prosperity from its fertile soil, to which Cicero bears witness. By the time of the later Roman empire, however, it had diminished in size.

At the entrance to the ancient city, which as recent excavations show, was first established on the hill of San Mauro, part of a fortified circuit of mid-seventh century date, and the remains of the south gate (described by Polybius as the Syracusan Gate), have been discovered, and several hundred yards of later fortifications of various epochs (sixth, fifth, third centuries) have come to light. Temples, too, have been located in the San Mauro and Metapiccola hills. A plateau on the Metapiccola summit has yielded remains of rectangular huts of the pre-Greek Sicel village. Sicel cemeteries, farther down, contain tombs in the form of small artificial caves.

Leontopolis *see* Isauria, Nicephorium

Lepcis (or Leptis) **Magna** (Lebda). A coastal city in the Roman province of Africa (now Libya), the easternmost of the three cities that give the region its name of Tripolitan(i)a (the others were Oea [Tripoli] and Sabratha). Situated between the Greater and Lesser Gulfs of Syrtes (Sirte, Gabes), beside a natural harbor at the mouth of the Wadi Lebda, Lepcis Magna was founded by the Carthaginians, not later than 500 BC and perhaps a good deal earlier.

Under Roman rule it continued to flourish, deriving prosperity from the olives and grain in its hinterland and from ivory brought by camel caravans across the Sahara from central Africa. The issue of coinage under Augustus (31 BC–AD 14) suggests that he reorganized and transformed the city (though without granting it citizenship), and inscriptions of the same period bear witness to a priest (*flamen*) of the cult of the deified Julius Caesar (8 BC). These inscriptions are written in neo-Punic, but were followed by Latin counterparts recording a 'patron' of the city and a certain Annobal Rufus, son of Himilcho Tapapus, who combined the offices of *flamen* and chief civic official (here known, in the Carthaginian fashion, as *suffete*).

In AD 69 Tacitus records strained relations between Lepcis Magna and another of the Three Cities, Oea. Lepcis Magna received Roman colonial status from Trajan (98–117)—it is uncertain whether this involved a veteran settlement—and Septimius Severus (193–211), who was a native of the place, confirmed and increased its privileges. It became the seat of a bishop in the third century, but its territory suffered devastation from the tribe of the Austuriani in 363/5; though the city, protected by walls of the late third or fourth century, held out successfully against their attacks. Further destruction, however, came from the Vandal conquest *c* 455. Decline was accelerated by disastrous winter floods and by the encroachment of sand dunes, which finally covered the town—but preserved its buildings, which thus constitute one of the most remarkable Roman sites in the world.

The substantial remains of the Augustan city include a colonnaded marketplace (*macellum*) with two circular halls (8 BC), a theater (AD 1–2, partly reconstructed), and the Old forum (with adjacent temples). A temple of Rome and of the deified Augustus (adorned with extensive imperial statuary) dates from the time of Tiberius (14–37). A large amphitheater (linked to a hippodrome by a cutting) was built into a quarry (56). A shrine to the Great Mother (Magna Mater) is a product of the Flavian epoch (72); and a massive bath building is attributable to the reign of Hadrian (127), while the local senate house (*curia*) belongs to the same period.

But it is the constructional activity of Septimius Severus, the greatest of its native sons, that gave the city its lavish distinction. These buildings include a four-way triumphal arch (following others of Vespasian [69–79] and Trajan [98–117]) set across the junction of the main street and the coast road, and dedicated on the occasion of Severus' visit in 203. He also created a new colonnaded street, running beside a second forum, which measured one thousand by six hundred feet and was flanked by porticos and shops and a huge three-aisled basilica. This commercial and judicial meeting hall, dedicated by Caracalla (216) in replacement of an earlier building (and converted into a church in the sixth century) is one of the finest and best preserved of such edifices in the entire Roman world. Its marble pilasters were richly carved with reliefs illustrating the exploits of Dionysus (Bacchus, Shadrap) and Hercules (Melkart), the patron deities of Lepcis Magna and the Severan house respectively. Severus also reconstructed the harbor on a grandiose scale, though the scheme was apparently unproductive owing to silting. The vaulted Hunting Baths, of third-century date, have survived almost intact, beneath the sand dunes; a wall painting suggests that they belonged to a corporation of hunters who supplied wild beasts to the amphitheaters of Africa and Italy.

Lerida *see* Ilerda

Lerna (Myli, 'the Mills'). A coastal town six miles south of Argos in the Peloponnese, at the foot of Mount Pontinos which runs out into a foreland. Lerna possessed a dozen springs (surrounded by marshes), including the source of the Pontinos stream, and the Amymone spring feeding the Halcyonian Lake (regarded as an entrance to the underworld), and the spring of Amphiaraus. A hill adjoining the marshland contained a Neolithic settlement and a palatial early Bronze Age residence. In historic times the place was known for its shrines of Demeter Prosymna, Dionysus Saotes (with accompanying Mystery cult), and Poseidon. The foundations of a small Greek temple can be seen on a small hill adjoining the Amphiaraus spring.

But Lerna was chiefly famous for the second of Heracles' mythological Labors, in which he overcame the Hydra, a water serpent with the body of a god and a hundred (or five hundred) heads, of which one was said to be immortal. The monster lived at the Amymone spring beneath a plane tree, and was allied with a giant crab. When Heracles tried to kill the Hydra with his sword, he had to call his nephew Iolaus to cauterize the stumps of its necks with a firebrand, because whenever one head was lopped off two others immediately grew up. After disposing of the mortal heads, he chopped off the immortal one and buried it under a rock on the road from Lerna to Eleusis. He then cut open the serpent's body and took possession of its poison in order to anoint his arrows.

Lesbos (recently often called Mitillini). The largest of the Greek islands off the West (Aegean) coast of Asia Minor, at the entrance to the Gulf of Adramyttium (Edremid). Its southern coasts possessed two inlets with very narrow mouths cutting deep into the hills, the Gulfs of Pyrrhaeus Euripus (Kalloni) and Hiera (Yera). The island, of which the northern part consists of volcanic stone, abounds in hot springs. A significant Bronze Age settlement at Thermi, on the east coast, had close links with Troy; and Old Methymna (to the north), Pyrrha and Kourtir (on the Pyrrhaean Gulf to the south) have provided abundant Mycenaean remains. From *c* 1100 (?) a chief element in the population was provided by Aeolian immigrants, who traced their ancestry back to Lesbos, the mythological grandson of the wind-god Aeolus. The fertile soil and favorable climate of the island sustained a Pentapolis (group of five cities) comprising Mytilene (SE)—which, although far the strongest, never completely dominated the others—Methymna, Eresus (SW, famous for its wheat), Antissa (NW), and Pyrrha.

The aristocratic classes of these towns colonized the adjacent coast of Asia Minor (Troad) before 700, participated in the construction of Naucratis (Egypt), and in the late seventh and early sixth centuries enjoyed an extraordinary intellectual and cultural efflorescence represented by the poets Terpander (from Antissa), Arion (from Methymna), Alcaeus (from Mytilene) and Sappho (from Eresus and Mytilene) and by the construction of early 'Aeolic' (or 'proto-Ionic') temples at Mytilene and Nape (in Methymnan territory). Lesbos fell under the rule of the Persians, but after joining the unsuccessful Ionian revolt against their domination was liberated after the Persian defeat at Mycale in 479, and joined the Delian League (sponsored by Athens) and the Athenian empire that took its place. (*See* Mytilene for the subsequent history of that city). During the Peloponnesian War Methymna alone remained loyal to Athens, but the entire island was occupied by the Spartans after their victory at Aegospotami (405). After further oscillations between Athenian, Spartan and again Athenian allegiance (392, 385, 369), Lesbos came into the hands of the Persians once again, and then was successively dominated by Alexander the Great (332), Antigonus I Monophthalmos, and the Ptolemies. Theophrastus (*c* 370–288/5) came from Eresus, and so did Phaenias (*fl* 320), another pupil of Aristotle who himself (like Epicurus) resided for a time on the island. In 196 (or perhaps 190) Mytilene, Methymna, Eresus and Antissa formed a Lesbian League (*isopoliteia*), of which the federal sanctuary and assembly and council meeting place may have been at Mesa (near Pyrrha).

In 191 Lesbos passed under the control of the Romans, who destroyed Antissa (because of its alliance with the Macedonian King Perseus) and gave its territory to Methymna (167/6). Lesbos joined the cause of Mithridates VI of Pontus against the Romans, who subequently extended their control over the whole island. The Lesbian League coined under Marcus Aurelius (AD 161–80) and Commodus (180–92). At an uncertain epoch of the middle or later Principate (early third century?), Longus wrote his novel *Daphnis and Chloe,* which offers a vivid romantic picture of pastoral life on the island. In the late empire it belonged to the province of Insulae (the Islands). From the fifth century there is evidence of bishops of Mytilene and Methymna.

Lesina *see* Pharos

Lesser Armenia *see* Armenia

Leucas, Leukas (Lefkas). An island of the Ionian Sea, opposite the coast of Acarnania (northwestern Greece), to which in ancient times it was originally joined by a sandbar, so as to form a peninsula. Leucas was inhabited in Neolithic and (more extensively) Bronze Age times and may be identified with Homer's Dulichium (not with Ithaca, the home of Odysseus, as was earlier suggested: Telemachus' statement that 'there is no room for horses to exercise on Ithaca, nor are there any meadows' could not apply to Leucas). The island was colonized by the Corinthians *c* 625 BC and remained loyal (unlike Corcyra [Corfu]) to its mother city, issuing coinage on the Corinthian model from soon after 500. The early settlers, colonizing the town of Leucas in the northeast of the island, nearest the mainland, cut through the sandbar to enable ships to pass through, but in the fifth century, according to Thucydides, they had to be hauled across the bar.

In the Persian Wars the Leucadians provided contingents to the Greek fleet at Salamis (480) and to the army at Plataea (479). During the Peloponnesian War (431–404) they assisted Corinth (the ally of Sparta) against Athens. After a shortlived alliance with the Athenians against Philip II of Macedonia, they passed into the hands of a succession of Hellenistic monarchs (Cassander, Agathocles of Syracuse, Pyrrhus of Epirus), but *c* 250 joined the Acarnanian League and became its capital. In 197 the Romans besieged and captured the city and annexed the island, but thirty years later detached it from the Acarnanians with the status of a free community. The figure which appears on its coinage from this period has been identified with Aphrodite Aineias, whose sanctuary stood on a small island beside the northern end of the sandbar joining Leucas to the Greek mainland. In the first century the sandbar was penetrated by a new channel, and a bridge (now under water) was constructed to the mainland. Agrippa seized the island in the civil war against Antony (culminating in the battle of Actium, 31), and in the Principate it was attached first to the new city of Nicopolis and then to the province of Epirus (AD 67).

Prehistoric material has been discovered at Nidri on the east coast. At the city of Leucas portions of the walls of the acropolis and lower town have survived, as well as part of the theater. Remains of lookout towers exist in various parts of the island, and foundations of a Doric temple have been uncovered in the south. There is also a Temple of Apollo (plundered by pirates, and mentioned by Strabo) on Cape Leucatas (Leuce Petra, the White Rock), at the extreme southwest tip of the island, which derives its name from the 2,000-foot white limestone cliff terminating the promontory. It was from here that the priests of Apollo propelled themselves into space, buoyed up—it was said—by live birds and feathered wings, and this was the legendary Leap, 'believed to put an end to the longings of love' (Strabo), from which Sappho threw herself to her death. Criminals, too, were hurled from these heights; Strabo records that, if they survived the ordeal, they were rescued in boats.

Leucophrys *see* Magnesia on the Maeander

Leuctra, Leuktra (now three villages collectively known as Lefktra, formerly Parapoungla). A small town in Boeotia (central Greece), belonging to the city of Thespiae four miles to the northwest. Leuctra, situated on one of the low hills on the fringe of the Theban plain, was famous for the battle which, in 371 BC, destroyed the tradition of Spartan military invincibility. In that year the Persian King Artaxerxes II had insisted that the Greek city-states should swear obedience to the King's Peace or Peace of Antalcidas (387), and the Thebans' request that they should be allowed to sign for the Boeotian League as a whole was rejected. Thereupon King Cleombrotus I of Sparta was instructed by the Persians to attack Thebes unless it agreed to disband the League, which it had no intention of doing. With his army of 11,000 Spartans and allies he confronted 6,000 Boeotians under Epaminondas in the plain of Leuctra. The battle was won by the Boeotian left wing, exceptionally standing forty shields deep and headed by the Sacred Band, whose charge Pelopidas led at the double; the Spartan line was rolled up by sheer superior weight, and Cleombrotus fell mortally wounded.

In spite of this loss and many other casualties, the surviving Spartans wanted to renew the battle. But their allies were unwilling, and they therefore concluded a truce to take up the dead. On the battlefield Epaminondas set up a trophy—replaced at the beginning of the third century by a monumental bronze trophy that was depicted on Boeotian coins. A thin, domed round tower discovered in the neighborhood has been identified, with some probability, as the base of this trophy; and parts of a frieze and trapezoidal blocks, discovered nearby, have now been placed in position on the reconstructed tower. A nearby tumulus may be the Spartan burial place. Pausanias described the battle as 'the most famous ever won by Greeks over Greeks.'

Lezoux *see* Ledosus

Libanus (Lebanon, Lubnan), Mount. A region extending for about thirty miles from north to south behind Berytus (Beirut) in Phoenicia (Lebanon). Between Mount Libanus and the ranges of Anti-Libanus and Hermion (Hermon) lies the narrow cleft of Coele Syria (Hollow Syria)—in its mere restricted sense of the Bekaa valley (see Syria)—containing the upper reaches of the Orontes (Nahr el-Asi) and Leontes (Litani) rivers and the cities of Heliopolis (Baalbek) and Chalcis Beneath Lebanon (Mejdel Anjar).

Mount Libanus provided a hinterland of great economic importance, watering the narrow coastal belt with the moisture stored in its snowcaps and sucked down by the west winds coming off the sea; the famous cedars and other trees, on its slopes provided abundant fuel for metalworking, and for export abroad. After Seleucid domination the Libanus mountains became part of the Roman province of Syria and, later, Phoenice (bordering on another province, Phoenice Libani, to the east).

Libya (1) In Homer's *Odyssey* Libya was a narrow stretch of land in the northwestern part (or beyond the western border) of Egypt. (2) It became the Greek name for the continent of Africa (regarded as a separate continent from the fifth century BC onward, with its frontier along the Nile or to the west—and then east—of Egypt). (3) In the Ptolemaic dominions Libya constituted a region (nome) on the Mediterranean coast, to the west of the Nile delta (subsequently known as the Mareote nome). (4) In the later Roman empire it provided the names of two provinces, Libya Superior (Cyrenaica, the northeastern portion of the modern state of Libya), and Libya Inferior (northwestern Egypt, corresponding with parts of the Homeric and Ptolemaic Libyas). The eastern emperor Valens (364–68) grouped these two provinces with Egypt in the administrative diocese of Aegyptus, which was detached from the diocese of Oriens.

Liger (Loire). The longest river in Gaul (France), rising in the Cevenna (Cevennes) Mountains not far west of Lugdunum (Lyon) and extending for six hundred and thirty-four miles to its estuary in the Bay of Biscay. The tribes of the Carnutes (reduced by Julius Caesar in 53 BC) and Turones bestrode its middle reaches. The cities along its course included Nevirnum (Nevers), Cenabum or Civitas Aurelianorum (Orléans), Caesarodunum (Tours), Juliomagus (Angers) and Condevicnum (Nantes, where an inscription refers to river sailors, *nautae Ligerici*). In the early Roman Principate the Liger came within the province of Gallia Lugdunensis, and in the later empire it flowed successively through Lugdunensis Prima, Lugdunensis Senonia and Lugdunensis Tertia, eventually forming the boundary between the last-named province and Aquitania Secunda.

Ligugé *see* Limonum Pictonum

Liguria. The northwestern coastal strip of Italy on the Ligurian Gulf (Gulf of Genoa), extending into a mountainous hinterland, and originally comprising large additional areas of northern Italy (Cisalpine Gaul) and southeastern Transalpine Gaul (France). The Ligurians, described as 'aboriginal,' were a tough, mixed people of undeterminable language, who came under Iberian,

Celtic, and to a limited extent Greek influences. In the third century BC Polybius, Livy, and others indicate a measure of Greek penetration along the coasts and in the hinterland, from the river Rhodanus (Rhône) down as far as the Arnus (Arno).

Roman campaigns between 238 and 117 BC against the Ligurians (who supported the Carthaginian Mago at the end of the Second Punic War, *c* 205–203, and were denounced by Massalia [Massilia, Marseille] as pirates in 154 and later) gradually subjugated their various tribes, which were included in the provinces of Transalpine (Narbonese) and Cisalpine Gaul (see Gallia). Subsequently Liguria, comprising the elongated coastal area now known by that name together with territories extending northward as far as the Padus (Po), became a region of Augustan Italy; but in the later empire the name was transferred to a district or province to the north of the Po, including Mediolanum (Milan) and sometimes combined with Aemilia (Emilia), whereas the land south of the river, including the present Liguria, became the district or province of the Cottian Alps (the previous designation of a small Alpine princedom and province farther to the west). The emperor Pertinax was born in Liguria in AD 126. *See also* Genua.

Lilybaeum, Lilybaion (Marsala). A city at the western extremity of Sicily, flanked on two sides by the sea and on the land side by a ditch or canal, and equipped with three harbors. An attempt at Greek settlement by colonists from Cnidus (Reşadiye) in Caria (southwestern Asia Minor), under the leadership of Pentathlus (*c* 580 BC), proved unsuccessful, and the place instead became a principal outpost of the Carthaginians in the island. Its significance increased when they made it their principal Sicilian port in place of Motya (Mozia), sacked by Dionysius I of Syracuse (397/6). Subsequently Dionysius made a less successful attack on Lilybaeum (368/7), and Pyrrhus of Epirus, too, during his invasion of Sicily, failed to capture the city (277/6). But at the end of the First Punic War it fell to the Romans (241), after resisting their siege for nine years.

Thereafter Lilybaeum formed part of the Roman province of Sicily, and was the seat of one of its two financial officials (quaestors), a post held by Cicero (76–75) who described it as an impressive city (*splendidissima*)—from which the predatory governor Verres was able to steal many works of art. During the fifties and forties a series of at least eight other officials, probably (in most cases) occupying the same quaestorial office, issued bronze coinage at Lilybaeum with Latin inscriptions, and a Greek piece was minted by Lucius Sempronius Atratinus, Antony's admiral who brought a squadron to the assistance of Octavian against Sextus Pompeius (the son of Pompey the Great) in 36. Augustus subsequently gave Lilybaeum the rank of a citizen community (*municipium*), an occasion for which it minted its last monetary issue. Retaining significance as the principal Sicilian port for Africa, it was made a Roman colony by Pertinax (AD 193) or Septimius Severus (193–211), with the title of Colonia Helvia Augusta. An earthquake caused destruction in 365 and the city was burned by Vandal invaders in 440.

Excavation has been limited because part of the ancient town is covered by its modern successor. But Carthaginian and later graves (including painted and stuccoed shrine-like tombs of the first and second centuries AD) have been explored. Massive defences of the fourth century BC—restored during the civil war between Octavian and Sextus Pompeius—can also be traced, and recently parts of two Carthaginian or Greek warships of the later third century BC have been located in the Stagnone, a lagoon north of the city, and recovered for reconstruction. Traces of the Carthaginian town buildings (Via delle Ninfe) and cemetery (of the later fourth to third century BC) have also now been found, and remains of Roman edifices of the early second century AD. Mosaics extending over a wide period have also come to light; some of the later examples belong to a luxurious residential complex at the western extremity of the city (Cape Boeo), including a bathing establishment with numerous rooms, which indicates that some rebuilding took place after the earthquake in 365. One of the city's wells, at the Sibyl's Cave (so-called owing to a legend that the Cumaean prophetess with that title was buried there), was believed to confer divine powers on those who drank its waters.

Limonum (or Lemonum) **Pictonum,** at one time Pictavi(s) (Poitiers). An inland city of western Gaul (France). Occupying the slopes of a steep rock spur between the valleys of the river Clain and its tributary the Boivre, it commands the 'Gate of Poitou,' a forty-four-mile gap between the Massif Central and the Massif Armoricain, thus providing a channel of communications between the north and south of the country. Originally named Limonum or Lemonum, in the fourth century BC the place took the name of Pictavi(s), having become the chief city of the Celtic tribe of the Pictones (or Pictavi), whose territory must have extended to the Bay of Biscay, because in 56 Julius Caesar commandeered their ships. In 52 some of the Pictones supported the uprising of Vercingetorix against him, and in the following year the leader of their pro-Roman party Duratius was besieged by a large nationalist Gallic force under Dumnacus, leader of the Andes (Andecavi); but Dumnacus was completely defeated and compelled to retire.

Subsequently Limonum became a road junction in the Roman province of Aquitania and prospered from the sale of wine, oil and fish, the construction of ships, and the mining of silver-bearing lead at Melle (Deux Sèvres). The town was sacked by German invaders in 276. In the later empire it belonged to Aquitania Secunda, and resumed the name of Pictavi. The prominent anti-Arian leader St. Hilarius (d. 367) became its bishop. His disciple St. Martin of Tours inaugurated regular western monasticism by founding a community of hermits at Ligugé, south of Pictavi (360), and another, the Monasterium Majus (Marmoutier), on the outskirts of the city (372). After passing into the hands of the Visigoths, Pictavi became a Frankish possession following the victory of Clovis at Vouillé nearby (507).

Parts of the amphitheater, one of the largest in Gaul, have survived, in addition to sections of three aqueducts that provided an ample supply of water. The larger of two public baths displays lavish marble, stucco and mosaic embellishment. Dedications reveal the existence of a temple of the Celtic god Adsmerius, equated with Mercury. Portions of a powerful rampart built after the raid of 276, and equipped with circular towers, can still be seen. In the Baptistery of S. Jean, described as the oldest building of Christian Gaul, the font and the lower levels of the walls are of fourth-century date.

Lincoln *see* Lindum

Lindioi *see* Gela

Lindos *see* Rhodes

Lindum (Lincoln). A city in the northeastern part of Britannia (England), deriving its name from a Celtic word signifying a marshy place, although the major part of the town stood on an escarpment north of the river Witham, which flows through a gap in the limestone ridge known as the Lincoln Edge or Cliff.

In pre-Roman times Lindum belonging to the tribal territory of the Coritani. After the Roman conquest it achieved importance as the meeting point of two major routes, the Fosse Way and Ermine Street, leading south and north respectively. Already, perhaps, an auxiliary fort in the late 40s AD, it seems to have become a legionary fortress in the sixties, housing first one legion and then another until *c* 74/76. About 90, a colony was established on the same hilltop site, and continued until the end of the Roman period to fulfil a significant role as a communications center. From the time of Septimius Severus (193–211) Lindum belonged to the province of Lower Britain (Britannia Inferior), and in the later empire to Flavia Caesariensis.

At the northern extremity of the Upper Colony—which occupied the site of the fortress—stands the Newport Arch, which consisted of a carriageway flanked by two footways, and still spans the street. It forms part of a system of fortifications which is largely visible and has been extensively studied. After 48/60, it has been concluded, the legionary fortress possessed earth and timber defences flanked by a ditch; next, *c* 71, the gate towers were enlarged, and timber towers were added to the ramparts. Stone walls were built *c* 100, and stone fronts added to the timber gate towers; then *c* 210–30 the gates were solidly reconstructed with flanking towers. Further adjustments took place after 300. The Upper Colony was enlarged by the creation of a Lower Colony to the south. The earliest defences of this Lower Colony, which consisted of a rampart fronted by a stone wall and a system of ditches, were built in the late second or early third century.

Within the Upper Colony a massive colonnade has been preserved (in a house at Bailgate). Recent excavations have also conclusively located the site of the forum, on the site of the former church of St. Paul-in-Bail. Sections of an aqueduct approaching the northeastern corner of the hilltop site have also been brought to light. Suburbs extended along Ermine Street and perhaps along the Fosse Way as well. During the 1970s, 1,624 Roman coins were found at sixteen sites in the city, and since then similar discoveries have continued to be made.

Lindus *see* Rhodes

Lipara, also known as Meligunis (Lipari). The largest of the Aeolian Islands (Aioliai Nesoi; Aeoliae or Liparaeae or Vulcaniae Insulae; now known as the

Eolie or Lipari group), Lipara lies twenty miles off northeastern Sicily. The other principal islands of the group are Hiera Hephaesti (or Thermessa or Terasia or Vulcani; now Vulcano, with Mount Vulcanello at its northern extremity), Didyme (Salina), Phoenicussa (Filicudi), Ericussa (Alicudi), Euonymos (Panarea), and Strongyle (Stromboli; a volcano).

Lipara has been described as a 'prehistorian's paradise' because of a continuous series of occupations from the earliest times. A ship wrecked in the seventeenth century BC has recently been found in its bay. Subsequently the island may have served as a staging point for the Mycenaeans on the way to their trading posts at Pithecusae (Ischia) and the neighboring island of Vivara. The term 'Ausonian Culture,' sometimes applied to the Late Bronze Age civilization of the Aeolian islands, is derived from a story (reported by Diodorus) asserting that Liparus, the mythical founder of Lipara—succeeded by his son-in-law Aeolus the wind god, at whose (preexisting) shrine the earliest Greek settlers worshipped—was the son of Auson and king of the Ausonians, who lived in middle and lower Italy; the southern coast of the peninsula stood on the 'Ausonian Sea,' though the Ausonians were, according to an alternative definition, limited to Campania; and, by way of contrast, the term was also extended to the whole of Italy. A later version of the Aeolian islands' 'Ausonian Culture' continued into the Iron Age, with Calabrian and Campanian links and trading activity in obsidian (volcanic black glass), which existed in large quantities at Lipara and was highly prized in antiquity. The island also possessed mines of valuable styptic earth (which checked bleeding).

About 580 BC, a group of emigrants from Cnidus (Reşadiye) in Caria (southwest Asia Minor) and from Rhodes, under the leadership of Pentathlus, driven out of Lilybaeum (Marsala) by Phoenicians and native Elymians, established themselves in the Aeolian archipelago. Pausanias did not know if the islands were previously uninhabited, or if the people the colonists found there were ejected. Diodorus records an implausible story that a few descendants of Aeolus' Greek settlers were present to welcome the newcomers. Archaeological investigation has so far provided no evidence of inhabitants immediately preceding Pentathlus' colonists, but has confirmed the date of *c* 580 for his settlement (rather than 628, proposed by Eusebius). The site they chose at Lipara was on a defensible hill beside the sea (in the area now known as Castello or La Cittade); and they crossed over to the other islands by boat, in order to use their soil for cultivation.

Maintaining a communistic way of life, subsequently followed by a modifed form of collectivism, the inhabitants of Lipara waged constant struggles against the Etruscans for the control of the Tyrrhenian Sea, denouncing them and being denounced in return, as pirates. Early in the Peloponnesian War (427) they allied themselves with Syracuse and withstood a combined assault by troops from Athens and Rhegium (Reggio di Calabria). In 394 Lipara fell briefly to the Carthaginians, but subsequently formed an alliance with Dionysius I of Syracuse. The last of all known important Greek vase painters, in *c* 340, is known as the 'Lipara Painter,' because his works are found and were apparently made on the island (and appear also on neighboring shores). The city of Lipara prospered, but fell by treachery in 304 to Agathocles of Syracuse, who robbed it of its valuables (which subsequently went down in a storm at sea). Lipara later issued coins celebrating an alliance with Tyndaris (off Cape Tindaro), but then succumbed to the Carthaginians, and during the First Punic War (264–261) provided them with a naval base, until the city was captured by the Roman commander Gaius Aurelius in 252.

During his Civil War with Sextus Pompeius (the son of Pompey the Great) in 37/36, Octavian (the future Augustus) employed Lipara as an important fleet station and mint, issuing bronze pieces bearing the signatures of more than a dozen of his officers and repeating the type of Hephaestus (Vulcan) (the principal local deity, together with Poseidon [Neptune]) which had already appeared on local coinage. The head of Augustus appears on a coin which, although inscribed in Greek, refers to *duoviri,* the principal officials of a Roman *municipium,* which at this juncture Lipara evidently became—probably after the deportation of Pompeian supporters. During the empire the island served as a place of exile and a bathing resort. A Christian bishop Agatho is recorded during the persecutions of Valerian (254).

Excavations on the acropolis of the city present a unique stratigraphical series owing to the constant augmentation of volcanic dust. In addition to the remarkable light thus thrown on Sicilian prehistory, rich discoveries in the cemetery known as the Contrada Diana (now an Archaeological Park) dating from the archaic period until the Roman resettlement in the second century BC, have contributed substantially to our knowledge of Italiot and especially Sicilian pottery, and to our evidence for the terracotta industry in which Lipara evidently excelled. A tract of the city wall of the Greek settlement, dating from the later fifth and fourth centuries, has been cleared, as well as a rampart that was built to strengthen the defences in the first century. Remains of Roman houses, built over earlier structures, have come to light, and the Greco-Roman street grid can now be reconstructed.

Outside the city, a sanctuary of Demeter and Persephone has been uncovered, consisting of an altar open to the sky within an enclosed precinct, in which numerous dedicated objects (ex votos) were unearthed. Among a number of wrecked ships brought to the surface in the area is the Capistrello wreck (*c* 300) off the southeast coast of the Lipara island, brought up by a new type of saturation diving equipment and found to contain a cargo of amphorae and pottery. Underwater archaeological activity around the other Aeolian Islands is also continuing, in addition to excavations on land.

Lix, Lixos, Lynx, Lixa (El-Araisch, Larasch). A city in western Mauretania, located on a low eminence above the marshes round the right bank of the river Lix (Lukkus), near its mouth two miles away in the Atlantic Ocean. Pliny the Elder records that this was one of the supposed sites of the Garden of the Hesperides, and that a local sanctuary of Heracles (Melkart), who was believed to have slain the giant Antaeus in the neighborhood, was even older than his shrine at Gades (Cadiz) across the Straits of Gibraltar. However, the earliest traces of habitation so far reported at Lix do not go further back than *c* 600 BC, and even thereafter occupation may have been sporadic for some time to come. The city that eventually emerged owed its prosperity to salt works. It seems to have been destroyed during the first century BC, either during the exile of Quintus Sertorius in Mauretania (*c* 80) or in the course of the Civil Wars between the Pompeians and Julius Caesar (*c* 47), who was supported by the western Mauretanian King Bogud.

The appearance of coinage—which depicts bunches of grapes and fishes, and presents the city's name both in Neo-Punic and Latin (LIXS, LIX)—can be related to its elevation to the status of *municipium* either in 38 (together with Tingis [Tangier]) or *c* 31–25, when the area came temporarily under direct Roman control. Lix subsequently became part of the territory of Juba II, Rome's client king of Mauretania (25 BC–AD 23), and then belonged to his son Ptolemaeus (AD 23–40), after whose removal by Gaius (Caligula) the city became involved in disturbances and was sacked. But when Claudius created a new Roman province of Mauretania Tingitana (to the west of Mauretania Caesariensis), Lix was probably granted colonial status; it recovered rapidly, achieving the height of its prosperity during the second and third centuries, when the salt industry was revived. In the mid-third century, however, the town was plundered once again, and although subsequently rebuilt—within a smaller perimeter—did not resume its former scale of activities. During the fourth century, however, after the creation of the province of Tingitan(i)a, it served as the garrison of a cohort.

The oldest structures of which traces remain go back to the fourth and subsequent centuries BC. A spacious sanctuary on the acropolis, perhaps the shrine of Heracles-Melkart, mentioned by Pliny, includes a large temple standing in a colonnaded courtyard that was probably erected by Juba II, one of the city's principal builders. A small amphitheater and a group of fish-salting and fish-sauce factories belong to the same epoch, while a number of wealthy houses, and additional salt workshops, date from the second and third centuries AD.

Ljubljana *see* Emona

Locri Epizephyrii, Lokroi Epizephyrioi (Locris in the West). A Greek city on the Ionian Sea near the southern extremity of Bruttii (now Calabria), the toe of Italy. Locri Epizephyrii was refounded by the Greeks on a native (Oenotrian, *i.e.* probably Sicel) site on the Zephyrian promontory (Cape Bruzzano) early in the seventh century BC. The colonists were men from Locris (*qv*) on the mainland of Greece, probably for the most part Opuntians (East Locrians), with an admixture of Ozolians (West Locrians), Spartans and fugitive slaves. After three or four years the settlers moved twelve miles northward nearer to the coast (to Gerace Marina which has now been renamed Locri). The members of the oligarchy that ruled Locri Epizephyrii, known as the Hundred Houses, were reputed to have been excellent rulers; the city was famous for its lawgiver Zaleucus (*c* 650?) who, although his career is encrusted in legend, seems to have produced Europe's earliest legal code (notorious for its severity) and acted as arbitrator between social factions.

Locri Epizephyrii defeated Croton (Crotona) in the battle of the Sagras (Sagra), soon after the middle of the fifth century, founded its own colonies (Hipponium where Vibo Valentia was later established [*c* 650], Medma or Mesma [Rosarno], Mataurus or Metaurus [near Gioia Tauro; perhaps the birthplace of the poet Stesichorus] and Torre Galli [*c* 600–550]). Locri also maintained friendly relations with the Syracusans. This was particularly important owing to its persistent friction with the rival city of Rhegium (Reggio di Calabria), whose autocrat (tyrant) Leophron attacked them in 477/6; the Locrians vowed to prostitute their virgin daughters at the festival of Aphrodite if they succeeded in defeating him. The Ludovisi Throne (*c* 470) at the National Museum (Terme) in Rome, adorned with reliefs of the highest quality, and the related Boston Throne, may have come from Locri Epizephyrii. Pindar praised their city in two of his Olympian odes. During the Athenian invasion of Sicily in the Peloponnesian War (415–413) the Locrians were on the side of Syracuse, whose later ruler Dionysius I married a Locrian and joined them in the suppression of Rhegium (390–387); so that Locri gained substantial acquisitions of territory and became the principal city-state of Bruttii.

During the fourth century Plato came to Locri to study, and its native sons included a number of philosophers and the famous physician Philistion. In 356 it welcomed Dionysius II of Syracuse, only to eject him four years later—thereupon issuing, for the occasion, a coin inscribed Peace (Eirene). During the war between Rome and Pyrrhus of Epirus (280–275), Locri changed sides on a number of occasions, and served as a mint for both sides. In an effort to propitiate the Romans it issued a coin celebrating its loyalty (Pistis) toward them, and its envoys reminded the Roman senate of the sanctity of their temple of Persephone or Kore (Proserpina), whose cult was related to the worship of Aphrodite. In the Second Punic War the Epizephyrian Locrians surrendered to Hannibal (216), but had to capitulate to an officer of Scipio Africanus the Elder eleven years later. During the second century Locri appears from Polybius, who knew it well, to have remained a city of note, allied to Rome, and Cicero and Statius bore witness to its wealth during the first centuries BC and AD. In the fifth century AD, although diminished in size, it was still counted by Proclus among the most important towns of South Italy.

Its earlier city wall, erected in the fourth and third centuries BC, had encircled an area that was not wholly occupied by buildings; two main urban complexes have been identified, at Centocamere and Caruso. Hillslopes provided the site for a Hellenistic theater, rebuilt in Roman times, and a Doric temple has been found nearby. Votive objects and dedicatory inscriptions bear witness to the temple of Persephone, which flourished in the sixth and fifth centuries and is to be sought on the top of the Mannella hill. Another shrine, going back to the end of the seventh century and reconstructed in the fifth, is to be seen at Marasa; and a temple archive containing 37 inscribed bronze tablets, of the late fourth or early third century, has been discovered in a cylindrical stone chest not far away. Early cemeteries were augmented by a necropolis of Roman times.

Locris. A name borne by two territories in central Greece, inhabited by Greek peoples speaking an Aeolian dialect; the two regions were separated by Doris and Phocis (which were probably the remnants of early Dorian and other invasions splitting an originally united Locris):

(1) East (Opuntian, Eoian) Locris, on the mainland coast of the Euboean strait, between Boeotia and Malis. The population of East Locris was believed

to have been of pre-Greek (Lelegian) origin, but—despite the survival of certain matriarchal customs—was Hellenized at an early date; its mythical heroes were Patroclus, the comrade of Achilles, and Ajax the Less, son of Oileus. The capital of the East Locrians, where their aristocratic assembly of the 'Hundred Families' held its meetings, was Opus. This ruling class controlled a serf population (*woikiatai*).

It was the East Locrians who in the early seventh century BC led the colonization of Locri Epizephyrii (*qv*) in south Italy; and they vigorously assisted the Greek cause in the Persian Wars. Nevertheless, they were compelled to cede Thermopylae to Thessaly and Daphnis to Phocis. Their territory then consisted of Opuntian Locris round Opus and Hypocnemidian (later Epicnemidian) Locris, 'under' and 'on' the slopes of Mount Cnemis (Knimis)—the name of the mountain means a greave, which appears on the fifth century silver coinage of the city of Thronium. After his victory over the Greek city-states at Chaeronea (338), Philip II of Macedonia transferred the principal coinage of East Locris from the city of Opus, which fell under his displeasure, to the (East) Locrians and Hypocnemidian Locrians in general.

Following the death of Alexander the Great, the East Locrians fell to Cassander and then to Demetrius I the Besieger (Poliorcetes), but the Epicnemidians subsequently joined the Boeotian League and then became independent, forming the Federation of the Eoioi (which subsequently split into two); Thronium issued bronze coinage with Aetolian types (279–168), and Opus resumed its issues after the 'liberation' of Greece by the Roman general Flaminius (197). East Locris was involved in Greek hostilities against Rome (146), suffered depredations from Sulla (86), and in the civil war between Pompey the Great and Julius Caesar (49–48) sided first with the former and then with the latter. Opus coined again briefly under the emperors Galba (AD 68/9) and Otho (69).

(2) West (Ozolian) Locris, southwest of Mount Parnassus, included the valley of Amphissa and the northern shores of the Corinthian Gulf, from Naupactus to the neighborhood of Crisa. The West Locrians probably played a subsidiary part in the colonization of Locri Epizephyrii in south Italy led by the East (Opuntian) Locrians (see above). Backward, disunited, and burdened with an unsavory reputation for piracy, the West Locrians lost Naupactus to Athens (*c* 460); and although relations with East Locris were generally close, differences appeared in the Peloponnesian War (431–404), when most of the western group favored the Athenian side, whereas the easterners—later joined by Amphissa—sided with the Spartans. Owing to the strategic importance of the Amphissa valley, West Locris, by now united in a federation (*koinon*)—based on the town of Physcus—played an important part in the Third Sacred War (355–347), in which it joined forces with Thessaly and Boeotia against Philomelus' Phocian separatists. Amphissa was destroyed by Philip II of Macedonia in 338, but later recovered. In Hellenistic times a western subdivision of the Ozolian Locrians joined the Aetolian League, and under Roman rule belonged to the territory of the Roman colony Patrae. *See also* Amphissa.

Loire (River) *see* Liger

Londinium (later Augusta, now London) near the Tamesis (Thames) in Britannia (England). Bronze Age pottery has been discovered near St. Paul's Cathedral (belonging to a farmstead or hamlet), though otherwise evidence for pre-Roman occupation is scanty. But the site interested the Romans at an early date because it lay at the lowest point of the Thames which was reachable by land transport from the major British harbors and by ships from the ports of Gaul, and it was also at the lowest point at which a harbor and a bridge could be constructed. Whether Julius Casear crossed the Thames here in 54 BC remains conjectural, but Romans arrived on the site not long after the beginnings of the invasion of Aulus Plautius in AD 43: they were probably engaged in pursuit of King Caratacus of the Catuvellauni after his defeat in the area of Durobrivae (Rochester). Flat semi-marshland extended for up to half a mile alongside the Thames, but on the north bank there were several low, flat-topped hills divided by tributaries such as the Fleet and the Walbrook.

Aulus Plautius, while awaiting the arrival of the emperor, presumably established a fort, which recent archaeological evidence tentatively locates in the Westminster area. A ford may have been used there, and it seems very possible that the town itself was in existence by *c* 50. Southwark, on the other side, was early developed as a suburb.

Tacitus reports that when Boudicca, queen of the Iceni in East Anglia, sacked Londinium in 60, the place had already become an important and populous trading center, the meeting point of roads to the north (known to the Saxons as Ermine Street), northeast, northwest and west. Probably, too, it had become, or soon became, the headquarters of the financial chiefs (procurators) of the province, since in the early sixties one of them, Julius Classicianus, who had died in office, was buried at Londinium. The town seems to have been created a *municipium* by the time of Hadrian (117-38), and subsequently became an honorary colony. Moreover, by the second century, if not earlier, it was the capital of the province, and subsequently, after the reorganization of Septimius Severus (193-211), it remained the capital of the new province of Britannia Superior. A town wall—apparently the first—was built of Kentish ragstone in the early third century, enclosing an area which made Londinium the fifth-largest town in the west. The usurpers Carausius (287-93) and Allectus (293-96) issued coinage at its mint, and Constantius I Chlorus, who destroyed this secessionist state, depicted the gate and a kneeling personification of the city on gold medallions commemorating his victorious entry.

During the early fourth century, Londinium became the capital of Maxima Caesariensis—one of the four (later five) provinces into which the former Britannia was now divided—and was the seat of the governor-general (*vicarius*) of those provinces; a Christian bishop, too, is recorded at the Council of Arelate (314). Coinage continued to be issued at its mint until *c* 325, and was resumed by the pretender Magnus Maximus (383-88), whose issues described the city as Augusta, a designation it had received earlier in the century (perhaps together with the conferment of colonial rank).

From the later fourth century onward, however, very little is known of Londinium; but it would appear that, despite the construction of new fortifications in the 390s (recently discovered), its surviving population shrank considerably. When three further usurpers briefly controlled Britain between 406 and 411, and the last of them, Constantine III, withdrew its remaining garrison to the continent, Londinium may have called in German mercenaries to settle in the city and assist in its defence. Not long afterward, however, the organization of its town life had apparently declined into a haphazard day-by-day existence, in which a semirural farming population occupied the shell of the city—changing gradually from a Roman to a Saxon culture—and homeless squatters lived in the abandoned rooms of what had once been elegant houses.

The earliest buildings of Londinium were almost all of clay and timber, and burned easily when set alight by Boudicca. A first bridge lay six hundred yards upstream from London Bridge, beside an openwork landing stage; the site of the landing stage north of Thames Street, and beneath it, has been investigated. A timber and stone courtyard building is dated to *c* 75 by tree-ring analysis of its oak piles, and the same epoch witnessed the erection of a governor's palace (?) in Cannon Street, in addition to a stone fort (Cripplegate) and public baths (Higgin Hill). Wooden tablets bear witness to the activities of the provincial finance officer (procurator), and illustrate the commercial life of the city, which included the importation and distribution of Gaulish terracotta and Rhineland glass.

Many of the buildings of Londinium were destroyed in a serious fire during the reign of Hadrian (*c* 120–30). From his reign (not thirty years earlier, as had been supposed) dates the forum on the summit of Cornhill. A massive oak-based quay (New Fresh Wharf) of late second century date has been found to have replaced the earlier landing stage. A temple of Mithras, built near the east bank of the Walbrook (near the Mansion House) has yielded important marble sculptures—including heads of Serapis and Minerva and statues of Mercury, Bacchus and Pan—which were probably buried in the time of Constantine I the Great (306–37), amid fears of Christian persecution. A large bath structure in lower Thames Street formed part of a private residence (*c* 200). A rubbish pit of about the same date at Southwark has yielded the remains of four hundred and fifty-two animals (of which twenty per cent are non-domesticated red deer, roe deer, hare, wild boar, badger and woodcock), and another pit has yielded traces of fourteen fruits and vegetables.

Lorch *see* Lauriacum

Luca (Lucca). A city in western Italy, situated on the river Auser (Serchio), thirteen miles from the Tyrrhenian Sea. In early times the region was inhabited by a Ligurian population, but as the Etruscan influence expanded northward the Ligurians kept mainly to the hills, and even if there was originally a Ligurian settlement of theirs in or near Luca (as is uncertain, though a pre-Etruscan ritual burial has been uncovered at Buca della Fate, Massarosa), numerous recent discoveries—including fine gold jewelry and coins, see below) in the surrounding area make it virtually certain that it was an Etruscan city (amalgamating earlier villages) in the sixth and fifth centuries BC. Thus the poet Lucan attributes his Etruscan seer Arruns to Luca; it was probably an outpost or market town of Volaterrae (Volterra), the principal city-state of northwestern Etruria. Volaterran objects have been found in the neighborhood, as well as artifacts from Rusellae (Roselle), Caere (Cerveteri) and Latium.

In the early phase of the Second Punic War (218–202) Livy describes Luca as a base of the Roman general Tiberius Sempronius Longus, retreating before Hannibal; presumably it already offered a river crossing, and may have housed a garrison from this time, or not long afterward. The town became a Latin colony (possessing rights at Rome) in 180 (for walls dispelling doubts on this point, see below). The status of a Roman *municipium* was conferred in 90, and a passage in Strabo refers to Luca's large population, including numerous *equites* (knights); although the authenticity of this assertion has been questioned.

In 56 the city gained fame when the members of the First Triumvirate, Pompey the Great, Julius Caesar and Crassus (his presence has been unjustifiably doubted) met there to patch up differences and confirm their partition of the Roman world. Luca was selected for this purpose because at that time it lay just outside Italy in Cisalpine Gaul (a fact obscured by the changed course of its borderline, the river Auser, which now flows past the city on its northern and no longer on its southern side), since Caesar, whose proconsular sphere included Cisalpine Gaul, would have risked prosecution—for serious offences his political enemies claimed he had committed—if he moved outside that region into Italy.

Luca had become important because of its position on an extension of the Via Cassia (continuing to Florentia [Florence]) and because of its accessibility to roads along the coast (Via Aurelia, Via Aemilia Scauri) and northward through the Apennines and Apuan Alps. The town also controlled the Bientina area that lay to its southeast and had earlier attracted the interest of the Etruscans (and of people long before them); its flooded marshlands were drained and cultivated, and in the lowest area no less than fifty pre-Roman and Roman settlements have been discovered, ranging from the third century BC to after AD 200. Attached to the Seventh Region of Italy (Etruria) by Augustus, who granted it Roman colonial status, Luca during the later empire formed part of the province or district of Tuscia et Umbria, and possessed a state-owned factory for the production of swords.

Five Etruscan find sites in the immediate neighborhood—including Pozzuolo (Gattaiola) which displays a continuous stratigraphy from *c* 500 to *c* 250 BC—and has yielded a find of Etruscan coins of the early third century, a potsherd inscribed ETALE (Aethalia, Elba), and fragments of haematite and iron slag that may be of Elban origin—indicating the presence of villages later amalgamated into an Etruscan city, which probably lies beneath the subsequent Roman town. The rectangular plan of the latter can be reconstructed from surviving portions of a towered wall made of great square stone blocks, dating back to the Latin colony of the second century BC. Remains of the forum survive (under the Piazza San Michele and church of San Michele in Foro), and the shape of the amphitheater of the later first century AD (or after)—together with a recently disinterred block of seats—has been preserved by medieval houses, while parts of the substructure of a theater (Piazza delle Grazie) can also be seen. The origins of the Christian baptistery attached to the Church of San Giovanni are believed to go back to the fifth or sixth century.

Lucania (corresponding to most of the modern region of Basilicata, together with the districts of Salernum [Salerno] and Consentia [Cosenza]). A mountain region of southern Italy, bounded by Campania, Apulia (Puglia) and Bruttii (Calabria). Its earliest known inhabitants were Oenotri (a term vaguely applied by the Greeks to peoples throughout southern Italy: perhaps here Sicels) and Chones (Illyrians). From *c* 700, however, the Greeks began colonizing the fertile shorelands of Lucania, establishing settlements on the east coast (Gulf of Taras [Tarentum, Taranto]) at Metapontum (Metaponto), Heraclea (Policoro) and Sybaris (Sibari, replaced by Thurii) and on the west coast (Tyrrhenian Sea) at Posidonia (Paestum), Elea (Velia), Pyxus (Buxentum, Policastro) and Laus (near Cirella). The most important inland town was Potentia (Potenza).

The territory received its name from the Lucanian people, an Oscan-speaking (Sabellian) southern branch of the Samnites. These Lucanians conquered most of the interior in about the mid-fifth century BC, and a generation or two later began to reduce their Greek neighbors, becoming partially Hellenized themselves. Their principal enemy was Taras, which appealed first to Archidamus III of Sparta (*c* 342) and then to Alexander I of Epirus (*c* 333). In 326 the Lucanians formed an alliance with Rome, but underwent military intervention from Lucius Cornelius Scipio Barbatus in 298, and in 291 were so seriously provoked by the Roman colonization of Venusia (Venosa) that they promptly supported the Epirote king Pyrrhus when he invaded Italy (281). Reduced to subjection by Rome, they again supported its enemy during the Second Punic War (216), and during the subsequent hostilities suffered depredations—from Hannibal and the Romans alike—from which they never recovered, although the Via Popillia (132), traversing the country from north to south, opened it up to traders. Thereafter an unhealthy geographical location, and the extension of large slave-operated estates, and the Italian rebellion against Rome known as the Social War (91–87; in which they suffered massacres at the hands of Sulla) all contributed to hasten their decline, so that the Lucanians as a separate nation eventually ceased to exist.

Their territory, together with Bruttii, formed the third Region of Augustus' Italy, and remained a province or district of Italian Suburbicaria in the later empire. When Diocletian arranged that he and his colleague Maximian should abdicate from the throne in AD 305, it was to Lucania that Maximian, reluctantly and temporarily, retired. The western emperor Libius Severus (461–65) was a Lucanian by birth.

Luceria (Lucera). An inland town of southeast Italy, occupying a key hilltop site on the northwestern border of Apulia (Puglia), where the plains of that region meet the highlands of Samnium. The mythological founder of Luceria was Diomedes, who was said to have carried a sacred image of Pallas Athena, the Palladium rescued from Troy, to the site. In historical times Luceria became a Samnite fortress, and during the Second Samnite War, after earlier vicissitudes, was captured by the Romans and made a Latin colony (enjoying rights at the capital) in 314, receiving 2,500 settlers; after heavy fighting in 294, its possession enabled Rome to fasten an iron grip on the southeastern regions of the peninsula. The earliest heavy bronze coinage of the city, displaying a variety of designs, dates from this period.

During the Second Punic War (218-201), Luceria became a Roman winter headquarters, and its lands were devastated by Hannibal. Subsequently however, according to Cicero, it became one of the most important cities of Apulia. Pompey the Great briefly paused there during his retreat from Caesar at the outset of the Civil War (49). After receiving, probably, a Roman veteran colony during the triumviral period (43-32), Luceria formed part of Augustus' Third Italian Region, and attained considerable prosperity during the Principate. In the later empire it was on the northern border of the province or district of Apulia et Calabria.

Built over structures of Republican date—which themselves had overlaid earlier tombs—the amphitheater, according to an inscription, was built in honor of Augustus and of the *colonia* of Luceria. Temples of Athena (Minerva) and Apollo are known to have existed, and an abundant votive deposit testifies to a shrine of the underworld divinities. The remains of a circus and theater have disappeared.

Lucotocia *see* Lutetia

Lucrine Lake (Lago Lucrino or Maricello). A shallow half-salt lagoon near Baiae (Baia), beside the northwestern shore of the Gulf of Cumae (Bay of Naples). Described by Strabo as a 'gulf,' it is separated from the sea by a narrow spit containing the Via Herculanea, over which, according to a mythological tale, Heracles (Hercules) drove the oxen of Geryon across swampland. (Another story called the Lucrine Lake the Acherusian Lake [entrance to Acheron, in the underworld], a name which was more generally attached to Lake Avernus, *qv*). In the early first century BC Gaius Sergius Orata, known as the 'Golden Trout,' developed a fishing (bass) and oyster industry on the Lucrine Lake that became profitable and famous. He also experimented in hypocaustic (heating) arrangements at one of the villas in which the area abounded. These villas included the 'Academia' or 'Cumanum' of Cicero, in which he wrote parts of the *Academica* and *Republic* and entertained Caesar. Soon afterward hot springs were discovered on the site, and the mansion became imperial property.

During the wars of Octavian (the future Augustus) against Sextus Pompeius (son of Pompey the Great) in 37-36, Octavian's admiral Agrippa constructed a great harbor, the Portus Julius, by cutting canals that linked the Lucrine Lake with the Gulf of Cumae to its south and Lake Avernus (Averno) to its north. The Lucrine Lake, which has largely disappeared beneath Monte Nuovo—a hill which was thrown up by an earthquake in 1538—was much more extensive in ancient times than it is now; although too shallow for large ships, it was suitable for the training of oarsmen.

Horace, Juvenal and Martial celebrated the luxurious amenities of the region. Beside the banks of the lake the traces of two swimming pools are to be seen, and a little to the south there are the so-called Stoves of Nero (Stufe di Nerone, or di Tritoli), sweat baths cut out of the rock to facilitate the therapeutic use of vapors emanating from the volcanic soil.

Lucus Asturum, Lucus Augusti (Lugo). In the territory of the Astures (Asturia, (Asturias), which formed part of upland Callaecia (Galicia) in northwestern Spain (Hispania Tarraconensis). Situated on the river Minius (Miño, Minho), the town was founded by Augustus after his reduction of Asturia and the rest of Callaecia (*c* 25 BC), when he brought the hill tribes down to his new valley settlements. The ancient urban plan, detectable under the modern town, mirrors the design of the original military encampment, round which a civilian settlement was gradually formed.

The Roman fortifications, although restored and altered, remain the most complete and best preserved of any in the western provinces outside Rome itself. The walls are one-and-a-third miles in length, eighteen feet thick, and between thirty and forty feet high, with eighty-five closely spaced semicircular towers (still in existence, except for their upper storeys), designed to accommodate archers and missile throwers. The walls were also fronted by ditches and equipped with single-arched entrance gates furnished with portcullises and drawbridges. These defences were devised to meet the Gothic invasions of Spain recorded from AD 260 onward, and provide a remarkable example of a massive constructional undertaking designed to protect what was only a small town. Military planning, advice and manpower were no doubt forthcoming from neighboring Legio (León), which, like Asturica Augusta (Astorga), was another of the walled bastions devised to meet the barbarian threat.

The bridge over the Minius dates from the time of Trajan (98–117), although very little of the original structure survives. There are also remains of baths, water tanks and conduits, and an inscription records a temple to the Carthaginian Dea Caelestis, who was equated with Venus.

Lugdunum or Lugudunum (Lyon, Rhône, France). Situated at the confluence of the rivers Rhodanus (Rhône) and Arar (Saône). In pre-Roman times there were two settlements, one of Fourvière hill above the right bank of the Arar—centered on a sanctuary of the Gallic god Lug—and the other in the plain at Condate, beside the point where in ancient times the two rivers met.

A Roman colony was founded on the Fourvière hill in 43 BC by Lucius Munatius Plancus, governor of Further Gaul (Gallia Comata), who issued a coinage inscribed with the colony's three titles, Copia ('plenty') and Felix and Munatia. Under Augustus (31 BC–AD 14) the city became the capital of his province of Gallia Lugdunensis, the hub of the country's road system, the seat of the provincial council of sixty Gallic communities, and the federal center of the cult of Rome and Augustus, of which the joint altar, serving the two Gauls, is depicted on Augustan coinage; only two columns, of Egyptian granite, survive. Lugdunum became a preeminent imperial mint, protected by a city cohort (*cohors urbana*), until the reign of Gaius (Caligula, AD 37–41) or later.

Claudius was born at the city in 10 BC. Strabo credited it with the largest population of any town in Gaul after Narbo (Narbonne), and Seneca the Younger testified to its magnificence and importance, only briefly impeded by a fire in AD 65 and involvement in the Civil Wars of 68–69, which exacerbated longstanding rivalries with neighboring Vienna (Vienne). There is evidence of widely varied commercial and industrial activities at Lugdunum, which was not only a major clearing house of wheat, wine, and oil and lumber, but a large manufacturing center for export to the Rhineland and elsewhere.

The city's immigrants from the east rapidly introduced oriental pagan cults; and it took an early lead in the persecution of its Christian community (177). During the civil war (196–97) between Septimius Severus (whose son Caracalla was born at Lugdunum) and Clodius Albinus (who made it his provisional capital) its buildings suffered partial destruction. In the breakaway state established by Postumus in western Europe, Lugdunum probably served as a mint for the regional emperors (or usurpers) Laelian and Marius (268), and although plundered soon afterward (and again in the early fourth century) it retained this monetary role on many occasions after the central empire had resumed control, although in the later period—when power shifted to Augusta Trevirorum (Trier)—it was merely the capital of the small province of Lugdunensis Prima. In 470 the Burgundians took over the city.

The theater of Lugdunum, the oldest in Gaul, was built under Augustus in 16–14 BC and enlarged by Hadrian (AD 117–38), a major inspirer of local construction—as current excavations continue to reveal—to whose reign a smaller theater (Odeon) is also attributable, as well as the amplified version of the amphitheater dating back to Tiberius (AD 19), in which Christian martyrs later met their deaths. Hadrian also converted the Altar of Rome and Augustus into a Temple of Rome and the Augusti, and restored and enlarged the Augustan Old Forum (Forum Vetus, from which Fourvière takes its name), while a second forum was built by Antoninus Pius (138–61) on the nearby La Sarra plateau.

Beside the Old Forum stood two temples, the largest of which was perhaps the Capitolium (dedicated to the Capitoline Triad, comprising Jupiter, Juno and Minerva); while other shrines that have now been located were devoted to the worship of Mercury, Cybele (now confirmed), the Matres Augustae, a river-goddess, and Mars. The peristyled, frescoed Villa of Egnatius Paulus bears the alternative name of the Villa of the Mosaics because of its polychrome floor consisting of ninety-one panels with geometric designs (one of more than a hundred magnificent mosaics excavated in the Lugdunum region). At the Condate settlement an industrial quarter has disclosed bronze foundries, potteries and glassmaking factories. Supplementary urban centers have been discovered on the Canabae island (Ainay, Place Bellecour) and ports (Choulans and then Saint Georges). Aqueducts of Augustan (two), Claudian and Hadrianic date have also been traced, the last named connected with reservoirs by advanced hydraulic arrangements making use of siphoning techniques.

In addition to several pagan necropoleis, there are Christian cemeteries, the earliest of which (on Saint-Irénée hill) was the burial place of the leading theologian Irenaeus, bishop of Lugdunum *c* 178–202, who was interred there together with two martyrs. The Basilica of the Maccabees (*c* 390), described by Sidonius Apollinaris, has disappeared, but remains of a number of fourth and fifth century churches and monasteries survive, including one that lies beneath the Cathedral of Saint Jean and formed part, according to recent excavations, of a complex of episcopal buildings. (This Lugdunum [Lyon] is to be distinguished from Lugdunum Convenarum [Saint-Bertrand-de-Comminges, Haute-Garonne]).

Lugo *see* Lucus Asturum

Luna ('Moon', known to the Greeks as the Harbor of Selene; now Luni). A town near the coast of northwestern Italy, five miles south of the estuary of the river Macra or Macras (Magra), which is often described by ancient historians as the border between Etruria and Liguria; the hinterland, of variously defined dimensions, continued to be known as the Lunigiana. Livy recorded that the territory of Luna had earlier been under Etruscan occupation, and coastal finds at Viareggio and Massarosa, on the way from the river Arnus (Arno), have tended to confirm his assertion. Strabo also recorded an Etruscan port a little further north, in the Gulf of La Spezia, but he may have intended to refer to Luna, which possessed a deep natural harbor, or series of harbors, on the Tyrrhenian Sea (although the encroaching coastline has now made it hard to detect them).

Amid rivalry between competing Roman noble factions, Luna became a Roman colony in 177 BC, receiving 2,000 settlers. Its function was to exercise control over the coastal zone, so as to deprive the Ligurians of bases for their traditional piracy and block their expansion to the south, while facilitating the northward expansion of the Romans themselves. The Via Aurelia, the great coastal highway from Rome, leading to its extension the Via Aemilia Scauri (109), formed one of the main streets of the town (the *decumanus maximus,* crossing the *cardo maximus,* which led to the harbor). Nevertheless, air photography suggests a gradual depopulation (Lucan describes the place as having been derelict in 49 BC), which was halted when Octavian (the future Augustus) drafted a new group of colonists.

The city derived its wealth and fame from nearby marble quarries, in the Apuan Alps (above modern Carrara). Strabo describes both white and mottled bluish-grey varieties (pink and green species are also now found), and refers to the ease with which they could be exported by sea. This marble was widely employed at Rome for architectural purposes, and Strabo was already able to record the use of the finer varieties by sculptors (forerunners of Michelangelo, who used the same quarries). Strabo also records that the river Macra was employed for the transportation of wooden constructional beams. The wine of Luna was considered the best in Etruria by Pliny the Elder, and he and Martial also refer appreciatively to its large cheeses.

Inscriptions bear witness to civil and religious activities throughout the Principate, although during the fourth century the unhealthy atmosphere of the place began to take its toll. Remains of halls and other buildings with rich architectural decorations have been uncovered beside the colonnaded forum, as well as the polygonal substructures of a temple now identified as the Capitolium. Only traces survive of the theater, but the large adjacent amphitheater, perhaps of the first century BC, is still quite impressively preserved. The ruins of the three-apsed cathedral of Santa Maria are superimposed on an earlier Roman building.

Lunghezza *see* Collatia

Lusitania. A region in the western part of the Iberian peninsula, comprising Portugal as far north as the river Durius (Douro, Duero) and the district of Emeritanus (now Spanish Estremadura). The warrior tribe of the Lusitani, between the Tagus and Durius, were probably Celts, whose relationship to the Iberians in the south is obscure. In the early first millennium BC the Phoenicians (and later their Carthaginian descendants) maintained a commercial presence, setting up coastal trading posts which exploited the copper mines in the area (among which Vipasca [Aljustrel] became well-known).

After the Second Punic War the Roman province of Further Spain (Hispania Ulterior) was gradually extended into southern Lusitania, but after hostilities that began in 194 a general rising under Viriathus (*c* 147–139) was only defeated with difficulty after the Romans had procured his assassination. Decimus Junius Brutus (later Callaicus), setting up his headquarters at Olisipo (Lisbon), marched northward through the central part of the country, crossed the Durius, and triumphed over the Lusitani and Callaeci. About 80, the Roman commander Quintus Sertorius, resisting the government of Sulla, was summoned back to his former Spanish province by the Lusitani, and held out for eight years. Pompey the Great (73–72) and Julius Caesar (60) incorporated the area up to the Tagus into the Roman province of Further Spain, and Augustus created a new province of Lusitania, governed from Emerita (Merida), where he established a Roman colony in 25 BC. The future emperor Otho, sent out as the province's governor after Nero had fallen in love with his wife Poppaea (AD 58), sided with Galba's revolt (68). The region between Pax Julia (Beja) and Ebora (Evora) was rich in wheat, while the valley of the Tagus abounded in horses and farms; and extensive mining continued.

The last century of the empire saw the establishment of three bishoprics, dependent on the see of Emerita. After the Germans had crossed the Rhine and the Pyrenees, one of their peoples, the Alans, temporarily occupied Lusitania (409–29), while Suebi settled between the Minius and the Durius *c* 411, eventually merging with the urban Hispano-Romans, notably at Portucale (Oporto). Soon after the middle of the fifth century, however, the Suebian monarchy was suppressed by the Arian Visigoths (a process that was repeated, after a Suebic recovery, a century later). *See also* Conimbriga, Ebora, Emerita, Tagus.

Lutetia (or Lucotocia or Lutecia) **Parisiorum** (later Parisii, now Paris). The chief city of the Celtic tribe of the Parisii, who occupied a defensible but flood-threatened island (the Ile de la Cité, then half the size that it is now) on the river Sequana (Seine) in the third quarter of the third century BC. They controlled the local tin trade from the British Isles, and in the first century were issuing a gold coinage of high quality. When Quintus Labienus, with four legions, advanced on Lutetia during Julius Caesar's Gallic War (52), the Gauls burned the town and destroyed the wooden bridges that had linked it with the two sides of the river. Lutetia was subsequently reconstructed and extended onto the Left Bank, becoming part of the province of Gallia Lugdunensis; its prosperity depended on a lumber industry and a local guild of sailors (*nautae Parisiaci*)—whose monument, the 'Pilier de Nantes,' proclaimed their loyalty to Tiberius and depicted both Celtic and Roman gods. An early tombstone of a cavalryman has suggested speculation that there may have been a Julio-Claudian fort.

Suffering in the civil wars at the end of the second century AD, Lutetia was devastated and burned by German invaders *c* 275. In the later empire, it was included in the province of Lugdunensis Senonia, and became an important military base under the name of Parisii. Julian the Apostate was proclaimed emperor there in opposition to Constantius II in 360. Five years later Valentinian I was on his way to the city when he received news of the eastern revolt of the rival emperor Procopius, and was still at Parisii when he learned of its suppression. It may have been under Saint Marcellus, the ninth bishop (*c* 360–436), that a first wooden Christian church was built on the island. After the abdication of the last western Roman emperor in Italy (476), Syagrius still held out for ten years in northern Gaul, but Parisii fell *c* 493 to Clovis, king of the Franks, who made it his capital.

The island has yielded only insignificant remains, its topography and ground level having been completely changed when a wall made of quarried stone and recut blocks was erected round its circumference to ward off invasions. On the Left Bank, around the main street (*cardo maximus*), identified buildings include the forum (Rue Soufflot, replacing a circular structure of the first century AD); a first century (?) amphitheater (the Arènes); a small theater; three bathing establishments, of which the best preserved (*c* 200) with remarkable vaults that are still standing is under the Musée de Cluny; and not only a pagan but a Christian cemetery (currently yielding important discoveries), which suggests that the Left Bank, after the third century invasions, had not (as was often supposed) been left uninhabited. Moreover, it is now believed that during the later empire some construction began on the Right Bank.

Lycaonia, Lykaonia. A section of the southern central tableland of Asia Minor, fluctuating greatly in delimitation but generally thought of as bounded by Galatia, Cappadocia, Isauria, Pisidia and Phrygia. Subject to severe extremes of heat and cold and only a moderate rainfall, the country is described by Strabo as a region of high plains, offering pasturage to sheep and wild asses. The Lycaonians, a wild and lawless people, of uncertain linguistic affinities, originally came from the mountainous regions around Laranda (Karaman) north of the Taurus (Toros) range, but in the time of Persian suzerainty (from which, despite sporadic punitive measures, they remained largely independent), they were already conducting raids over a wilder area and settling in the land that came to bear their name.

More or less subdued by Alexander the Great's general Perdiccas after the king's death (322), they became subject to the Seleucids (280–189)—who established their Lycaonian capital in the plain at Iconium (Konya, originally reckoned as part of Phrygia)—and then belonged to the Attalid kings of Pergamum (189–133). The Attalids' successors the Romans, after granting the territory to the kingdom of Cappadocia (and removing other districts from the kingdom of Pontus in 119 or 116), gave the mountainous southern area to a brigand chief named Antipater (50–*c* 36) and then to his supplanter Amyntas (36–25), by favor of Antony, who also allotted Amyntas most of the plain.

From 25 this plainland formed part of the new Roman province of Galatia, established by Augustus (who founded colonies of veterans at Lystra [Hatunsaray] and Parlais [Beyşehir]). The uplands, however, were ruled by Cappadocian and then Commagenian princes until AD 72, when they were incorporated in an enlarged province of Galatia-Cappadocia (subsequently divided again by Trajan, 98–117). Most of Lycaonia—excluding Iconium (by this time known as Claudiconium) and the Seleucid foundation of Laodicea the Burnt (Catacecaumene, Combusta, by this time Claudiolaodicea; now Ladık)—was added by Antoninus Pius (138–61) to Cilicia, where seven cities were formed into a federation (centered on Laranda, and issued local coinages, especially under Marcus Aurelius (161–80).

The resources of the region included the abundant salt of Lake Tatta (Tuz Gölü, Salt Lake)—employed in remedies for the eyes—and cinnabar from Sizma, and the smelting of copper and lead which presumably gave 'Burnt' Laodicea its name. A passage in *Acts of the Apostles* shows that the native language was still spoken, at least in the mid-first century AD. In *c* 371 Lycaonia became a separate province, with its capital at Iconium, and two of its communities west of Lake Tatta, Gdammaua and Psibela, were raised to city rank as Eudocias (421/443) and Verinopolis (457/479) respectively.

Lycia, Lykia. A district of southern Asia Minor, occupying the protruding shores and mountainous hinterland between Caria and Pamphylia. The Lycians, who spoke two dialects belonging to the Hittite-Luvian group, are frequently mentioned in Hittite, Egyptian and Ugaritic tablets of the fourteenth and thirteenth centuries BC, by which time they were established not yet on the south but on the west coast of Asia Minor. According to Greek mythological tradition, their country was originally called Milyas and its people were known as Termilai ('Trmmili' in Lycian), but they took their new name from the Athenian Lycus, son of Pandion and came to the country from Crete, led by Sarpedon, who together with Glaucus, according to Homer's *Iliad,* was their commander against the Greeks in the Trojan War.

The Greek colonization of the west coast pushed them toward the southeast and restricted their occupation to the region later known as Lycia, where they remained independent until overrun by the Persians *c* 540, despite a determined resistance at Xanthus (Kınık). Under Persian rule, the local dynasts soon began to issue varied and abundant silver coinages on which the names of the princes are given in the Lycian alphabet, combining Greek (Rhodian) and Anatolian characters; the uniformity of these coinages suggests that some sort of a federation of the Lycian city-states was already in existence.

Liberated by the Athenians under Cimon *c* 468, they temporarily joined the Delian League under Athenian leadership, until Persia reestablished its rule. For a time their country formed part of the dominions of Mausolus of Halicarnassus (Bodrum) 377–353); but then they submitted to Alexander the Great. After his death, control passed successively to Antigonus I Monophthalmos, the Ptolemies, and the Seleucid monarch Antiochus III (197), after whose defeat in 190/188 the Romans granted the territory to Rhodes; although the recalcitrant Lycians soon succeeded in reasserting their freedom (164). The innumerable tombs found in the country displayed a highly distinctive architecture, gradually modified by Hellenism. The Lycian League was established (or confirmed) on a regular basis, issuing federal coinage in the names of the various cities, with the design of a lyre representing Apollo, who, together with his sister Artemis, was the principal divinity of the inhabitants.

The League attracted admiration for the excellence of its institutions. In the early Principate, according to Strabo, it was presided over by an elective Lyciarch and included twenty-three cities, of which the names appear in abbreviated form on its coins issued by two monetary districts called after the two major mountain-ranges of the country, Cragus (which comprised a city of the same name and eight promontories) and Massicytes. These mintages include two large bronze pieces, issued at Tlos (Düver) and probably Myra (Demre) respectively, which commemorate the confirmation of Lycia's freedom by Octavian (the future Augustus) in 30/29 BC. Under Claudius (AD 43), the country was annexed and united with Pamphylia as a single province. The governor's residence was the harbor town of Patara (Kelemiş). A proliferation of local coinage occurred under Gordian III (238–44) and his wife Tranquillina, when numerous city mints were briefly in operation. *See also* Xanthus.

Lydia. An inland territory in western Asia Minor, bounded (with indeterminate and fluctuating borders) by Mysia, Phrygia, Caria, Aeolis and Ionia, and centred on the valleys of the lower Hermus (Gediz) and Cayster (Kücük Menderes). That is to say, Lydia extended along the two principal routes from the coast into the interior of the peninsula, and thus lay open to both Greek and Anatolian influences. The country also possessed important natural wealth.

The Lydians, whose race and language are obscure, do not receive a mention in the Homeric poems, but under the Mermnad dynasty (*c* 700–550) they established a powerful kingdom, with its capital at Sardes (Sart). This Lydian kingdom is likely to have been the initiator of coinage, probably in the reign of King Ardys (*c* 652–625). Lydia was also a major innovator in music, so that Greeks—notably Plato and Aristotle—spoke of 'Lydian' and 'mixo-Lydian' modes. King Croesus (*c* 560–546) extended his empire throughout Asia Minor, but was then overthrown by the Persians, who made Lydia their principal satrapy in the west, responsible for dealing with Greek cities on the coast.

Conquered by Alexander the Great, the territory then became part of the Seleucid kingdom, passing into the hands of Pergamum in 190/188 and forming part of the Roman province of Asia from 133. By the beginning of the Christian era, to judge from a corrupt passage of Strabo, the Lydian language had disappeared, at least from the lowlands. However, during the first three centuries of the Principate, numerous rich and thoroughly Hellenized cities of Lydia issued abundant bronze coinage with Greek inscriptions. In the later empire Lydia became a separate province. *See also* Magnesia Beside Sipylus, Philadelphia, Sardes, Thyatira, Tralles.

Lynx *see* Lixus

Lysimachia, Lysimacheia (near Baklaburnu, in European Turkey). A city on the isthmus joining the Thracian Chersonese (Gallipoli peninsula) to the mainland of Thrace, on the south coast of the Melas (Black) Gulf (Gulf of Saros). The settlement was founded and fortified by one of Alexander the Great's successors, Lysimachus, in 309, near the site of the ancient towns of Cardia and Pactye, which he destroyed—bringing their population into Lysimachia, which was intended to command the Chersonese and the passage of the Hellespont (Dardanelles). Its first coins depicted the young Heracles, in a lion's skin.

After the defeat and death of Lysimachus (281) the city came under the control of Seleucus I Nicator; but he was murdered there by Ptolemy I Soter's son Ptolemy Keraunos (Thunderbolt) in the same year. In 279/278 Lysimachia fell to the invading Celts (Galatians), but they were driven out shortly afterward. An inscription of slightly later date recently discovered at Ilium (Troy) records a treaty between Lysimachia and a Seleucid monach, either Antiochus I Soter (281-261) or Antiochus II Theos (261-246).

In about the middle of the third century the place passed briefly under Egyptian influence and then became a member of the Aetolian League. Occupied by Philip V of Macedonia in 202-200, it shortly afterward suffered destruction at the hands of the Thracians, but was rebuilt by the Seleucid Antiochus III the Great (195), who collected the scattered citizens, redeemed those who had been enslaved, and brought in new settlers. During the campaign that led to Antiochus' defeat by the Romans, Lysimachia was seized by Lucius Cornelius Scipio (later Asiaticus), but handed over to the kingdom of Pergamum. About 144, it was captured and destroyed by the Thracians, under King Diegylis, for a second time. According to Pliny the Elder (d. AD 79), the site was deserted in his day.

M

Macedonia, Makedonia. The central part of the Balkan peninsula, north of Greece, west of Thrace, and south of Illyricum and the Danubian territories. From all of these regions important routes converged on the Macedonian plain (formed by the rivers Haliacmon, Lydias and Axius) at the head of the Thermaic Gulf. This fertile plain, enclosed by a great double horseshoe of hills and mountains (containing wild clans under their own princes), remained the nucleus of the country, although its territorial boundaries fluctuated. The Bronze Age culture of Macedonia, little influenced by the Mycenaean civilization, was superseded *c* 1150 by a northern people, apparently followed before long by Dorian invaders, whose descendants, mixed with various other races but speaking a form of Greek, formed the core of at least the upper class of later times. The Macedonians were not mentioned by Homer, but a Greek myth, reproduced by Hesiod, referred their origins to Macedon, the son of Zeus and of Thyia, the daughter of Deucalion; and their Argead dynasty claimed Argive descent.

About 640 Perdiccas I, of this dynasty, pushed eastward from his homeland on the Haliacmon and captured the Macedonian plain from the various peoples who occupied it, moving his capital from Lebaea (unidentified) to Aegae (Palatitsa, Vergina). Although subsequent kings expanded their dominion, Amyntas I, after the expedition of Darius I into the Balkans (512) was obliged to become a Persian vassal, and his successor Alexander I had to accompany Xerxes I against the Greeks (480), although he secretly provided them with help. Alexander organized a national army, comprising both infantry and cavalry, and issued a fine coinage from silver mines acquired at Mount Dysoron (the Krousia Mountains). His son Perdiccas II (*c* 450–413) played off the Athenians against the Spartans in the Peloponnesian War—selling shipbuilding lumber to both sides—and was the father of Archelaus (413–399), who modernized the kingdom and introduced Greek artists to his new capital at Pella.

Philip II (359–336) enormously strengthened, expanded and enriched the state, issued a renowned coinage after acquiring the gold mines of Pangaeum (356), and gained control of Greece by defeating its coalition at Chaeronea (338); whereupon he established a Pan-Hellenic League of Corinth, under his own control. His son and successor Alexander III the Great (336–323) overthrew the Persian empire and carried Macedonian arms to the Nile and the Indus. From the confused Succession Wars that followed his death emerged the Antigonid monarchy of Macedonia, stabilized by Antigonus II Gonatas (284/3–239).

But Philip V (221–179) fought two wars against the Romans, whose victory at Cynoscephalae (197) confined him to Macedonia; and a second defeat suffered by his son Perseus at Pydna (168) caused the Romans to abolish the Macedonian kingdom and replace it by four autonomous Republics. In 146, however, these in turn were transformed into the Roman province of Macedonia, governed from Thessalonica (Salonica), traversed by the Via Egnatia from Thrace to the Adriatic (*c*130), and enlarged by unification with Achaea, that is to say Greece (27).

A Macedonian confederation with an imperial cult and priests made its appearance under Claudius (AD 41–54), who inaugurated a provincial coinage lasting until the time of Philip (244–49). Toward the end of the empire the province was divided into two, Macedonia Prima and Secunda (Salutaris). *See also* Acanthus, Acte, Aegae, Amphipolis, Axius, Beroea, Edessa, Haliacmon, Olynthus, Pangaeum, Pella, Philippi, Pydna, Strymon, Thessalonica, Torone, Uranopolis.

Machaerus, Machairos (Mukawar in rabbinical literature, now El-Musheneq in Jordan). A fortress east of the Dead Sea, built by the Hasmonaean (Maccabean) king of the Jews Alexander I Jannaeus (103–76 BC) at the southern extremity of Peraea on territory recently conquered by John I Hyrcanus (129–104). Erected on a rocky eminence surrounded by ravines on every side, Machaerus guarded the frontier against the Nabataean Arabs and kept watch on the local population. After partial destruction by Pompey the Great in 64/63, it was retaken by the Hasmonaeans in 57 but seized again from them by Aulus Gabinius in the following year.

It was rebuilt between 25 and 13 on a far more imposing scale by Herod the Great as a combined fortress and palace that presided over a civilian settlement lying below. Josephus described the impregnability and luxury of the stronghold, and noted the numerous rain-water cisterns erected at appropriate points. Machaerus was subsequently incorporated in the Roman province of Judaea, perhaps from the inauguration of the province in AD 6 (to judge from the numerous coins of Roman governors found on the site). Here John the Baptist was brought for execution after his arrest by Herod's son Antipas, prince of Galilee and Peraea (4 BC–AD 40).

Following the deposition of Antipas, Machaerus became part of the territories of his nephew Agrippa I (41–44), and on his death was absorbed into the Roman province of Judaea. During the First Jewish Revolt or First Roman War (AD 66–73) it was one of the last rebel fortresses to hold out, but finally surrendered to Lucilius Bassus after a long siege and was destroyed. Remains of the various buildings, walls, Roman siege works and an aqueduct can be seen.

Machuza *see* Mesopotamia

Madaurus, Madauros (Mdaourouch). An inland city of Numidia (eastern Algeria), situated on undulating land 3,280 feet above sea level. Founded in the third century BC with a mixed Berber and Phoenician population, it belonged toward the end of the century to Syphax, chief of the Numidian tribe of the Masaesyli and then to King Masinissa (d. 148). When the Romans formed the province of Africa (146) they employed Madaurus to keep a watch over the powerful tribe of the Musulamii.

During the Flavian dynasty (AD 69–96) the town received a draft of ex-soldiers and the status of a Roman colony (Colonia Flavia Augusta Veteranorum Madaurensium). Its olive groves were notable, and so were its numerous schools. Madaurus was the birthplace of the novelist Apuleius (*c* 123), who belonged to a rich local family. Bishops are known from 348, and St. Augustine (354–430) studied there, though paganism, too, long continued to flourish.

The colonnaded forum is flanked by a basilica of the late imperial epoch. Nearby are the remains of a theater that probably dates from the time of the Severan dynasty (193–235). Large and small bathing establishments, for summer and winter use respectively, belong to the same period. The former stands next to a second pagan basilica, and there is also a fifth century Christian basilica-church in the district, in addition to another outside the town.

Maeander, Maiandros (Büyük Menderes). One of the principal rivers of Asia Minor, the Maeander rises in Phrygia, and flows successively through a plain, a narrow defile, a deep canyon, and a flat fertile valley (dividing Lydia from Caria), before reaching the Aegean Sea in the Latmian Gulf near Priene.

Extensive changes in its direction and estuary have now left the harbor of Miletus and adjacent island of Lade landlocked. The tortuous course of the Maeander in its lower reaches was proverbial, so that the Greeks used its name to describe a winding pattern. Its southern tributaries, from the east to west, included the Lycus (Çürüksu Çayı), Marsynus (or Marsyas), Harpasus (Ak Çay), and another Marsyas (Çina Çayı). Recent discoveries suggest Greek penetration of the Maeander valley at a much older date than has been supposed, during the archaic period and even earlier. *See also* Apamea, Magnesia on the Maeander, Miletus, Priene, Tralles and Tripolis.

Maeotis, Maiotis, Lake (the Sea of Azov). Joined to the Black Sea by the Cimmerian Bosphorus (Strait of Kerch), separating the Tauric Chersonese (Crimea) from the northern reaches of the Caucasus.

The southern and eastern shores of Lake Maeotis belonged to the Bosphoran kingdom, but Greeks from Ionia, attracted by the fisheries, established colonies at Panticapaeum (Kerch) and Phanagoria (Fanagori) on either side of the strait. The Greeks subsequently founded another settlement beside the northeastern extremity of Maeotis, at Tanais (Nedvigovka) by the mouth of the river of the same name (the Don). Nevertheless, Greek geographers remained hazy about the river, and greatly exaggerated the size of Lake Maeotis (which some believed to be linked to the Caspian Sea by an underground passage). *See also* Bosphorus (Cimmerian), Hermonassa, Panticapaeum, Phanagoria, Tanais.

Maepheracta *see* Tigranocerta

Magdalensberg *see* Noreia

Magharadjek *see* Seleucia in Pieria

Magnesia Beside Sipylus (Manisa). A city of Lydia (inland western Asia Minor) lying in the fertile valley of the river Hermus (Gediz), beneath Mount Sipylus (Manisa Dağı), the slopes of which, according to mythology, Niobe after the slaying of her children by Apollo and Artemis was turned into a stone. The place was founded at an early date by the Aeolian Magnetes of eastern Thessaly, at a point where the roads from the interior of the peninsula and from the Propontis (Sea of Marmara) converge on the way to Smyrna (İzmir).

Magnesia Beside Sipylus was the scene of a decisive battle of 190 BC, in which Lucius Cornelius Scipio Asiaticus defeated the Seleucid monarch Antiochus III the Great, who was subsequently, under the Treaty of Apamea (188), compelled to evacuate the whole of Asia Minor. After a period of Pergamene (Attalid) rule, Magnesia passed into the Roman province of Asia (133), sided with Rome in its wars with Mithridates VI of Pontus, and was subsequently granted the status of a free community. It coined *c* 30 with the portrait of the proconsul Marcus Tullius Cicero, the orator's son. In AD 17 the city suffered severe damage from an earthquake, but received imperial relief, celebrating Tiberius on its coinage as 'founder.' An extensive range of coinage, extending to the time of Gallienus (253–68), displays personifications of Magnesia, Hermus and Sipylus and references to local games described as Hadriana Antoneia Enmonideia (the meaning of which is unknown); while an issue of Valerian (253–60) records the city's 'alliance' with Smyrna.

Pausanias came from this area, and refers extensively to local buildings and traditions. He also alludes to monuments bearing the mythological names of the Throne of Pelops and Tomb of Tantalus, which have been tentatively identified a few miles from the city, the former being a large rock cutting in the form of an altar or seat. The 'Rock of Niobe,' in the Çaybaşı district, was believed to be her petrified figure.

Magnesia on the Maeander (ad Maeandrum, near Ortaklar). The only major inland city of Ionia (western Asia Minor), situated in the rich valley of the lower Maeander (Büyük Menderes), although it was closer to its small tributary the Lethaeus. Magnesia was colonized by the Magnetes of eastern Thessaly, who were Aeolians (so that the city was not admitted into the Ionian League). The mythical founder was a hero Leucippus, represented as a warrior on horseback. The original site of the settlement is not known. It was captured by Gyges, king of Lydia (*c* 685–657 BC), and soon afterward underwent destruction at the hands of his killers, who were invading Cimmerians from south Russia; the phrase 'the sufferings of the Magnesians' became proverbial. However, their city was soon rebuilt by the Lydians.

When they succumbed to Persian invasion, Magnesia came under the control of the new masters (*c* 530), and was later (*c* 464) presented by Artaxerxes

I to the exiled Athenian Themistocles, to provide him with a home and with bread. The first coin the local mint ever issued bears his name. The city was captured by the Spartan Thibron in 400/399 and moved to a new location under Mount Thorax and beside the Lethaeus, on the site of an ancient village called Leucophrys, which is also the name by which Xenophon describes the new city. After passing into thc Roman province of Asia, this transplanted Magnesia remained loyal to Rome during the Mithridatic Wars, was rewarded with the status of a free community and continued to flourish during the Principate.

Its remains are inundated every winter by the Lethaeus, and little can now be seen, other than traces of a theater and stadium outside the city center. The place was famous for its temple of Artemis Leucophryene (originally an Asian goddess), a masterpiece of the famous and influential architect Hermogenes (*c* 200), who apparently erected it on the foundations of an earlier building. The new temple was larger than any Asian shrine except those at Ephesus and Didyma, and contained an exceptional number of internal columns; now, however, it lies in total ruin. There are remains of a small Ionic temple of Zeus Sosipolis in the agora. One of the agora walls bears inscriptions relating to a new festival of Artemis instituted to celebrate a miraculous epiphany *c* 220, followed by a declaration by Delphic Apollo asserting the sacred inviolability of the city. The facade of the shrine is reproduced on a coin of the reign of Trajan (AD 98–117) showing a figure of Artemis, crowned by two victories, and a pedimental window at which her epiphany was no doubt reenacted.

Other coinages show her sanctuary in 'alliance' with the Artemisium at Ephesus, local temples of Leto (?) and Dionysus, figures of numerous other deities including Isis and Helios Serapis, a sacred flaming beacon tower, and personifications of the valleys (*kolpoi*) of Magnesia in the form of three water nymphs surrounding a naked male figure seated on a rock. Under Gordian III (238–44) the city acclaimed itself as the 'seventh in Asia.'

Mainz *see* Moguntiacum

Maiumas *see* Gaza

Majorica *see* Balearic Islands

Malaca (Málaga). A city on the south coast of Spain, founded by the Phoenicians on the Guadalmedina river soon after 500 BC, and occupied by their colonists, described by the ancient authors as Libyphoenicians. Providing a market for the tribesmen of north Africa, they made use of their large harbor to develop substantial fishing and fish-sauce and salt-meat industries; some derive the city's name from *malac,* to salt, though *malaka,* trading post, is an alternative etymology.

A period of Carthaginian suzerainty followed in the third century BC. After the defeat of the Carthaginians in the Second Punic War (218–201), the town came under Roman control, but maintained the status of a treaty community (*civitas foederata*), loosely attached to the province of Further Spain (Hispania

Ulterior, later Baetica). In the first years of the Principate Malaca was the only non-Roman and non-Latin (peregrine) city in Spain to continue to issue money without any reference whatever to Rome or to the imperial house, inscribing its coins in Punic characters. Its transfer by Vespasian (AD 69–79) to the status of Latin city (in which the annually elected officials obtained Roman citizenship) is recorded by a bronze tablet (the Lex Malacitana), which gives details of the legislation involved. In the 170s, during the reign of Marcus Aurelius, a group of African raiders attacked Malaca and a wide surrounding area, but were suppressed by the governor of Lusitania in 179. A bishop of Malaca was present at the Council of Illiberis (Elvira) *c* 310/315. Traces of ancient Malaca are scarce, but a theater of the Augustan period is in a good state. Elsewhere in the provinces there are remains of large Roman villas at Faro de Torrox and Rio Verde (Marbella).

Malis. A small district of eastern Greece spanning the mouth of the river Spercheius at the head of the Malian Gulf, bordered by Thessaly (Achaea Phthiotis) and Mount Othrys to the north, Oetaea and Mount Oeta to the south, and the Aenianes to the west. The Malians belonged to the Amphictyony (*see* Delphi), of which the earliest center, at Anthela, lay within their territory; but according to Herodotus their first capital was Trachis. Said to be old-fashioned people, they maintained an antique tradition of light-armed soldiery. During the Persian invasion of 480 they were compelled to join the army of Xerxes I, and it was a Malian, Ephialtes, who informed him of the mountain path that enabled his troops to trap the Greeks at Thermopylae, on the south side of the Malian Gulf.

In the Peloponnesian War, under pressure from the Oetaeans, Malis took the side of Sparta, but the military colony Heraclea Trachinia—which was established by the Spartans in 399, and eclipsed its northern neighbor Trachis—soon came into conflict with the Malians. After the capture of Heraclea by Boeotians and Argives in the Corinthian War (394), and its destruction by Jason of Pherae in 371, another city, Lamia (north of the Spercheios) became the capital and only important city of Malis, issuing coins in the names both of the Lamians and the Malians. Malis took the side of Sparta against Thebes, became a member of the League of Corinth founded by Philip II of Macedonia (338), and subsequently belonged to the Aetolian Confederation (*c* 235). In 189, however, it was merged with Achaea Phthiotis (part of Thessaly) and retained that status throughout the Principate.

Mallorca *see* Balearic Islands

Malta *see* Melita

Malventum *see* Beneventum

Mamertina *see* Messana

Mangalia *see* Callatis

Manisa *see* Magnesia Beside Sipylus

Mantinea. A city in southeastern Arcadia (central Peloponnese, southern Greece). Praised for its beauty in Homer's *Iliad,* it consisted of five separate villages (round an oracular sanctuary of the Arcadian god Poseidon Hippios) until their amalgamation (synoecism) into a city on the river Ophis (*c* 500). Mantinea sent five hundred men to help the Spartans hold Thermopylae against the Persians (480), but in the following year its contingent arrived too late for the battle of Plataea.

The relations of the Mantineans with their southern neighbor Tegea were constantly hostile, because of disputes over boundaries, exacerbated by the behavior of the river Helisson (a tributary of the Alpheus) which continually flooded the territory through which Mantinea flowed. During the Peloponnesian War Mantinea, at this time governed by a moderate democracy, joined a coalition of Argos, Athens and Elis against the Spartans (420), but after the Spartan King Agis II had dismayed the population of Mantinea by diverting the water from Tegean territory onto their own, a Spartan victory in the neighborhood caused the coalition to collapse (418). The Spartans took the city *c* 385 by damming the Ophis, so that its waters caused the sun-dried brick walls to collapse; and then they forced the inhabitants to dismantle their walls and live in villages (that is to say, the property-owning upper class had to stay on their farms).

After Spartan power had been broken by Thebes (371), however, Mantinea was reconstituted and joined the Arcadian League, in rivalry, as always, with Tegea. It was the scene of the last victory of the Theban Epaminondas over the Spartans (362). But after the battle he died of his wounds, the Arcadian League was dissolved, and Mantinea returned to its Spartan allegiance. Subsequently it joined first the Achaean and then the Aetolian Confederations (*c* 230/229), and after temporary occupation by Cleomenes III of Sparta became a member of the Achaean League for the second time, whereupon the local supporters of Cleomenes slaughtered the Achaeans who had settled in the city. In 223/2 the Macedonian King Antigonus III Doson captured and destroyed Mantinea, transporting its population to Macedonia or selling them into slavery, and superseding it by a new foundation on the same site with the name of Antigoneia, which resumed membership of the Achaean League.

After the Romans had established control (146), Mantinea took the side of Octavian (the future Augustus) in his civil war against Antony culminating in the battle of Actium (31). Strabo, who was alive in AD 21, included it among cities no longer existent; but this appears to have been an exaggeration, since Pausanias, in the following century, was still able to describe the place, and Hadrian paid it a visit (125), restoring its ancient name and receiving official worship from its inhabitants, along with his youthful friend Antinous (d. 130). Moreover, the city's coinage was revived by Septimius Severus (193–211) and Caracalla (211–17). (In the latter's reign a Jewish synagogue received mention in an inscription). Thereafter the name of Mantinea continued to appear in geographers' lists.

The stone bases of its reconstructed inner and outer walls, with more than a hundred towers and nine or ten gates, are preserved; excavations have uncovered the colonnaded agora and remains of a theater—originally dating from the fourth century BC, but remodelled on several later occasions.

Mantua (Mantova). A city of Cisalpine Gaul (northern Italy), surrounded on three sides by the river Mincius (Mincio)—a northern tributary of the Padus (Po)—which was probably navigable for part of its length in ancient times. Mantua stood on the northernmost of two or three islands in the river, at a point where it was broadening into a small lake.

In his *Aeneid*, Virgil, who came from the nearby village of Andes, describes the city as 'rich in ancestry, yet not all of one stock: three races are there, and under each race four peoples, and she herself head of the people, her strength from Etruscan blood.' He is apparently saying that the place controlled, or had amalgamated, twelve adjacent centers or villages, of which the inhabitants were divided among three different peoples, namely the Etruscans, Venetians and Umbrians (identified by some with a people named the Sarsinates from Perusia [Perugia]). Recent investigations have uncovered houses, apparently Etruscan, of the fifth century BC (at Castellazzo della Garolda and Forcella)—and the poet's assertion that the Etruscan element was dominant may well be correct, even if somewhat colored by his own partly Etruscan origin: his *cognomen* Maro is Etruscan, the family name Vergilius is commoner in Etruria than elsewhere, and the name of his mother, Magia, may be Etruscan as well. However, the tradition that Mantua rather than Felsina (Bononia, Bologna) was the principal Etruscan community in north Italy seems unwarranted; although the Mantuans sought to substantiate this assertion by tracing their foundation back to the mythological heroes Manto (said to be derived from Mantus, an equivalent of dis Pater) and Ocnus and Tarchon (an Etruscan name), and claiming that the city had been settled by colonists from Thebes in central Greece.

When the Gauls invaded northern Italy, giving it their name (Gallia Cisalpina), in the early fourth century BC, Mantua was protected from their assaults by its marshes, although perhaps only for a time, since the neighboring necropolis of Carzaghetto is exceptionally rich in Celtic material (otherwise scanty in Cisalpine Gaul). By 200 the city had reached an amicable understanding with the Romans, who subsequently made Cisalpine Gaul into a province, first extending Latin rights—which conferred the Roman franchise on local officials (89)—throughout the region, and then granting full citizenship to Mantua and other Transpadane cities (49). In 42 the province was incorporated into Italy; but after Antony's and Octavian's victory over Brutus and Cassius at Philippi ex-soldiers from the victorious army were presented with farmlands taken from Mantua and Cremona, amid lamentations from Virgil. Nevertheless, the elder Pliny recorded that in his time Mantua was the only Etruscan city remaining in existence across the Po. In the fifth century AD it suffered from the ravages first of Alaric the Visigoth and then of Attila the Hun.

Maracanda *see* Sogdiana

Marathon (Plasi). A place on the northeastern shore of Attica, seventeen miles northeast of Athens. Objects from the Neolithic to the Roman periods have been found at a number of sites in the vicinity, but recent excavations have confirmed that the ancient town was at a location named Plasi (not at Marathona). It commanded part of a coastal plain fertile in barley, about two miles wide and five miles long. According to mythology, Marathon was founded by a hero of the same name, and was the place where Theseus slew the wild bull that had ravaged the area for two decades, thus inaugurating his life-long friendship with Pirithous. According to the *Heraclidae* of Euripides, when the children of Heracles took refuge from Eurystheus in the temple of Zeus, Theseus refused to give them up. Possessing, in addition, cults of Heracles, Dionysus, Pan, Delian Apollo, and the hero Echetlaus, Marathon was a member of an ancient religious group of four communities known as the Tetrapolis (comprising also Oenoe, Probalinthus and Tricorythus).

The Athenian ruler Pisistratus landed in the neighborhood when he arrived from the north to seize Athens for the second time (546). But the fame of Marathon rests on the battle fought when the generals of the Persian King Darius I invaded the country in 490. The Persian fleet, based on Eretria in Euboea, landed a force of perhaps 24,000 infantry, archers and a few cavalry (*see* below) on the beach: whereupon the Athenians decided to send eight or nine thousand heavy-armed infantry (hoplites) to confront them. They were reinforced by about a thousand Plataeans, though the Spartans (to whom the runner Pheidippides had been dispatched to appeal for help) could not join them for six days, allegedly (or genuinely) because of a religious festival. Although half of the ten Athenian generals wanted to await their arrival, the polemarch (civil commander-in-chief) Callimachus gave his casting vote in favor of an attack, the conduct of which was apparently entrusted to the influential Miltiades; though tendentious Athenian legends have befogged the whole story. It seems, however, that in the absence of the enemy's cavalry (which may already, although this is not certain, have taken ship toward Athens), the Greek wings outflanked and routed their center, thus deciding the outcome. The Persians lost 6,400 men (against Athenian losses of only 192); but their fugitives evaded pursuit, and were picked up by their fleet. This then moved onward toward Athens; but the Athenian troops from Marathon arrived in time to prevent the ships from landing a Persian force, and they sailed away. The first phase of the Persian Wars was over; the victory had been won by the hoplite middle class, unlike Salamis, ten years later, which was won by the lower-class oarsmen. The tomb of the Athenians and the trophy (Herakleion) have been located; an alleged identification of the Plataean tomb (Vrana), however, seems unacceptable.

The most distinguished native of Marathon was Herodes Atticus (*c* AD 101–77), writer, sophist, orator and Roman consul, whose property has been located (by inscriptions) at Nisi nearby.

Marcianopolis (Reka Devnia). A city in Lower Moesia (northeastern Bulgaria). It was founded by Trajan (AD 98–117)—who gave it the name of his sister Marciana—eighteen miles inland from the Black Sea coast, on a site endowed with abundant springs where roads met from the port of Odessus (Varna), from Durostorum (Silistra) on the Danube, and from Nicopolis ad Istrum (Nikup) to the west.

Originally a settlement of the Thracians (of whom inscriptions show traces), Marcianopolis was occupied by Hellenized immigrants from Asia Minor, who imported Greek and oriental cults. It became the capital of the Roman province of Lower Moesia, and issued coinage, with Greek inscriptions, from Commodus (AD 180–92) onward. These coins depict temples, a triumphal arch surmounted by four figures on pedestals (Macrinus, 217–18), and—after devastation by the Goths in 238—three city gates (Gordian III, 238–44), one with three arches, another elaborately crenellated, and a third which is flanked by conical roofed towers and appears in a bird's-eye view of the fortress-city surrounded by its massive wall. With the help of these defences, a second Gothic attack was repelled (248), although the local coinage does not seem to have continued after that date.

Becoming the capital of Moesia Secunda, Marcianopolis reached the height of its power in the fourth century, when the eastern emperor Valens established his winter quarters there in the course of his campaigns against the Visigoths and other invading peoples in 367/9. In 376/7, however, an imperial force under Lupicinus was routed by a Visigothic army near the city, which was then ravaged and burned by a new set of rebellious Visigothic chieftains, amid scenes of slaughter. Enough was left of the stronghold, however, for a mass of fleeing Roman soldiers to take refuge within its walls. A short time later the whole district was temporarily lost when Valens himself suffered a disastrous defeat and lost his life at Hadrianopolis (Edirne, 378). In 447 Marcianopolis was attacked by Attila the Hun.

Mareshah *see* Marissa

Margiana *see* Alexandria in Margiana

Margum (Orašje, near Dubravica). A fortress-city in Upper Moesia (eastern Yugoslavia), situated on the Danube, at the point where it is joined by its important and strategic tributary, the Margus (Morava). The town lay between Singidunum (Belgrade) and Viminacium (Kostolac), on a site that had been extensively inhabited in the Neolithic and Bronze Ages.

The geographer Ptolemy mentions Margum as the winter quarters of a legion in AD 169, and it was about the same time that it became a Roman citizen community, under the name of *municipium Aurelium Augustum,* engaging in sustantial trading activities and housing a customs station. After the evacuation of Dacia—just across the river—by Aurelian (271), the city became an imperial frontier post. In 285 one of the decisive battles of the epoch was fought in its neighborhood. An Illyrian soldier Diocles (the future Diocletian) had risen against the emperor Carinus, who in the middle of a prolonged and fiercely contested battle was assassinated by one of his own officers, whose wife he had seduced. Diocletian thus came to the throne, and was free to carry out the sweeping reorganizations of the empire that followed; in the course of these readjustments, Margum was assigned to the province of Moesia Prima.

During the fourth century a fortress was built on the left bank of the Danube opposite the city, known as the Castra Augustoflaviensia. About 400, Margum was serving as a base for river naval patrols. It was also the seat of a bishop, who in 441/2 had to surrender the city to Attila's Huns. Nevertheless, it recovered, to become an important military headquarters at the beginning of the following century. Parts of a number of Roman houses have been uncovered, displaying wall paintings, mosaic floors and a house with an underground heating system (hypocaust).

Margus (River) *see* Margum

Marissa, formerly Moresheth-gath (Tel Maresha, Tell Sandahana). A town in southwestern Judaea (Israel), at the entrance to the hill country. It formed part of Idumaea, after the Edomites moved into the area from Edom in the fourth century BC. Then it received Sidonian colonists from Ptolemy II Philadelphus (289/8–246), serving the Egyptians as the Hellenized capital of western Idumaea and the center of their slave trade. Subsequently it passed into Seleucid hands.

Judas Maccabaeus, founder of the Jewish (Hasmonaean) kingdom (167–160 BC), ravaged the place, and it was annexed, together with the rest of Idumaea, by John Hyrcanus I (135–104), who compelled the population to become Jews and accept circumcision. After the conquest of Judaea by Pompey the Great (*c* 63), he restored Marissa to its former inhabitants, and it was rebuilt under the direction of Aulus Gabinius (57). In 40, however, it was destroyed by Parthian invaders, and when Idumaea came under the rule of Herod the Great (37–4) it remained insignificant. Later, the town successively belonged to the Roman provinces of Judaea, Syria Palaestina, and Palaestina Salutaris.

The rectangular Hellenistic settlement, encircled by a wall equipped with towers, has been excavated; and wine and olive presses in the neighborhood provide the clues to its prosperity. It comprised twelve blocks, of which one formed the administrative and military center (consisting of a large open court surrounded by offices) and another was a market quarter comprising a paved market and a colonnaded inn. In the other residential blocks most of the houses were built around a central courtyard. Other discoveries include small lead figures (employed in witchcraft) and more than fifty limestone plaques inscribed with incantations and invocations. The languages in which they are written include Hebrew, Greek and an unidentified tongue, and the personal names mentioned are Semitic, Egyptian, Greek and Roman. The cemetery contains two important painted graves of the mid-third century BC, reminiscent of contemporary Ptolemaic tombs in Egypt, with added Edomite and Phoenician motifs.

Marium, Marion, later Arsinoe (Polis tes Chrysochou). A city three miles from the northwestern shore of Cyprus, situated on two low plateaus dominating a small coastal plain and Chrysochos Bay. A settlement already existed during the Bronze Age and at the beginning of the Iron Age (early first millennium BC).

Coins were issued by King Sasmaus the son of Doxandrus between 575 and 550, when Cyprus was under Persian control. After the Athenian Cimon had liberated Marium shortly before his death (450/449), two other local monarchs,

Stasioecus I and Timocharis, struck further coinage. These issues display the names of the kings and the place-name 'Marieus', using the Greek language but employing a syllabic script which may be akin to the ancient Linear B and Linear A writings of Bronze Age Crete. At about the same period the *Circumnavigation* (*Periplus*) of Pseudo-Scylax describes the city as 'Hellenic.' It derived its wealth (exemplified by finds of rich jewelry in tombs) from copper mines at Limne, and conducted an active commerce with Athens, exemplified by large quantities of Attic pottery; these exports and imports passed through a harbor (west of the modern town) which was protected by a massive breakwater. After the death of Alexander the Great, Stasioecus II, the last king of Marium, sided with Antigonus I Monophthalmos against Ptolemy I Soter of Egypt, who razed the place to the ground and transferred its inhabitants to Paphos. However, Ptolemy II Philadelphus rebuilt it *c* 270 under the name of his wife, Arsinoe, who was also his sister. This new city flourished in the Hellenistic and Roman eras, and in early Christian times became the seat of a bishop.

The earliest town of Marium was founded on the more easterly of the two plateaus (Peristeries east of Polis tes Chrysochou), where cemeteries of early Iron Age date have been uncovered. During the Persian period the habitation area spread to the western eminence (Petrerades, north of Polis), which also became the location of Arsinoe. The local gymnasium, mentioned in an inscription, has not yet come to light. But a sanctuary—tentatively ascribed to Zeus and Aphrodite, whose heads appeared on the coins of Stasioecus II—can be identified on a small ridge between the two hills. Hellenistic and Graeco-Roman cemeteries have been found to the south of Polis.

Marmara, Sea of *see* Hellespont

Marmaraereglisi *see* Perinthus

Marsa Susa *see* Apollonia (Libya)

Marsala *see* Lilybaeum

Marseille *see* Massalia

Martyropolis *see* Tigranocerta

Marzabotto *see* Misa

Masada. A precipitous, isolated height in Judaea (now Israel) rising 1,300 feet above the west coast of the Dead Sea. A small fort was built there by one of the Jewish (Hasmonaean) monarchs, either Jonathan Maccabaeus (160–143 BC) or Alexander Jannaeus (103–76). In 42 Masada was temporarily captured by Malichus from Antipater, the father of Herod the Great, but in 40 Herod employed it as a refuge for his family during his absence in Rome when the Parthians were invading the country. After Herod had established himself on the throne (37), he completely reconstructed the 'eagle's nest' of Masada as the southernmost of his chain of frontier fortresses, combined with luxurious residential quarters.

In AD 66, early in the First Jewish Revolt (First Roman War), an extreme zealot faction of the rebels captured the place from its Roman garrison, and held out until May 73—three years after the fall of Jerusalem. A force of seven thousand Roman troops under Flavius Silva had surrounded the wall (which possessed a hundred and ten towers and three gates) with a circumvallation, not less than eight siege camps, and an earth ramp (still visible) surmounted by a siege tower. When, with the help of a battering ram, the Romans finally broke through after a siege lasting six months, the thousand Jewish defenders, under the leadership of a certain Eleazar ben Yair, set the buildings on fire and then committed suicide, with the exception of two women and five children. Thereafter the fortress was reoccupied by a Roman force until at least 111, which is the date of the latest coin finds.

Excavations have added to Josephus' elaborate description of Masada. At the northern edge of the lofty, boat-shaped plateau, natural terraces of rock were employed as the foundations of a palace, constructed on three levels and decorated with elegant wall paintings. At the western edge of the plateau stood a much larger and more lavish palace, consisting of three units: the monarch's personal residence, a block of workshops and servants' accommodation, and a series of storerooms capable of housing great quantities of weapons and food. The residential and workshop complexes are grouped round central courts; the residential court opens through a colonnaded entrance into a large hall, at the back of which stood the king's throne.

Masada also contains a public bathing establishment, two further groups of storerooms (mentioned by Josephus) and a two-chambered structure which has been plausibly identified as a synagogue—if so, the earliest in existence. A group of twelve cisterns, supplied by two aqueducts from neighboring seasonal watercourses (*wadis*) and sparse rain, confirm Josephus' account of the abundant water supply available to the occupants. Finds dating from the siege during the First Revolt include more than two dozen skeletons, arrows, a gold breastplate, remains of clothing and sandals and food, fragments of pottery (*ostraca*) inscribed with personal names and references to tithes, religious and secular scrolls (including fragments of the earliest known copy of *Ecclesiasticus*), and a letter in Aramaic.

Massalia, Massilia (Marseille, Bouches-du-Rhône). A port on the southern Mediterranean coast of Transalpine Gaul in the Gallic Gulf (Golfe du Lion). Massalia was founded *c* 600 BC by colonists from Phocaea (Foca) in Ionia (western Asia Minor), travelling in flotillas of fifty-oared ships (there is also some evidence for transient earlier, Rhodian, business men in the region). On a small steep limestone peninsula, beside a sheltered basin, the Phocaeans settled on three low hills—within a perimeter of only a mile and a half—presiding over a small plain and over the excellent harbor of Lacydon (Vieux Port). Protected by a marsh, flanked by streams, and situated forty miles from the mouth of the

Rhodanus (Rhône)—far enough to escape its silt—the site was obtained from King Nannus, of the Ligurian tribe of the Segobriges, whose daughter Gyptis married the Greek colonists' leader Phocis.

Throughout the sixth century the Massalians gradually received increasing imports from Ionia and other regions of eastern Greece. Before long they also began to penetrate the interior of Gaul by taking over the traffic that passed north beside the Rhône (itself not easily navigable above the delta). Thus, in exchange for grain, amber and tin, Greek wine amphoras and luxury goods found their way far inland—notably to Vix (Mont Lassois) overlooking the Seine—and Gauls (evolving the La Tène culture) learned from the colonists how to cultivate the fields, and how to grow the vine and olive. Moreover, the Massalians bestrode and dominated the sea route between Spain and Italy; thus along the Mediterranean coast of Gaul, Carthaginian outposts were superseded by a network of Massalian settlements, including Monoecus (Monaco), Nicaea (Nice), Antipolis (Antibes) and Agathe Tyche (Agde)—the earliest—and the white limestone promontory of Leucate.

From there the line of Massalia's colonization was extended to Spain, where settlements were established at Ampurias (Emporiae), Hemeroscopium (near the south cape of the Gulf of Valencia), Alonae (near Cape Nao) and Maenace (Torre del Mar, the remotest of all western Greek colonies). Moreover, the Massalians ventured beyond the Straits of Gibraltar into the Atlantic Ocean, and explored the west African coast. They recorded victories over the Carthaginians in the sixth and fifth centuries, although the success of their mother city Phocaea in the naval Battle of Alalia (*c* 535) was so costly that Phocaean-Massalian influence in Corsica suffered a setback.

Governed by an extreme oligarchy, later replaced by a council of 600—presiding over a constitution much admired for its stability and Ionian laws—the city (from the fifth century onward) struck silver and bronze coinage with the heads of its principal deities Artemis of the Ephesians and Apollo of Delphi (where the Massalians maintained a treasury). From an early date—traditionally the sixth century—Massalia had come to an agreement with the Romans that was later developed into an official alliance. Its ships gave help to Rome during the Second Punic War (218–201), acquiring increased importance in the west after the fall of Syracuse in 210, and its rulers' appeal for help against the marauding Salluvii (125) led before long to the establishment of the Roman province of Gallia Narbonensis (Transalpine [southern] Gaul).

Gaius Marius' Rhône canal from Arelate (Arles) to the sea brought Massilia (as the Romans called it) considerable income from tolls. Cicero's shady client Milo retired to the city in 52, thanking the orator for his failure to deliver his speech in his favor, which enabled him to retire to Massilia and enjoy its red mullets. It retained its independent authority until 49, when, having taken the side of Pompey the Great in his Civil War against Julius Caesar, it was besieged and captured by Caesar's troops. It was saved from destruction by its ancient repute and long pro-Roman record, but was stripped of its fleet, war machines, treasure and most of its territory and dependencies. Thereafter, although retaining federal status and autonomy, and a high reputation for Greek culture and education (Tacitus' father-in-law Agricola was one of those who studied there), Massilia ceased to possess any political importance and gradually continued to decline, although an eminent physician, Crinas, rebuilt its city wall in the time of Nero (AD 54–68).

In 310 the emperor Maximian, who had been induced to abdicate reluctantly together with his senior colleague Diocletian (305), made a second attempt to return to power, once again proclaiming himself Augustus but soon taking refuge from Constantine I the Great in Massilia, where he was besieged, forced to capitulate by his own men, and found dead in suspicious circumstances shortly afterwards. The Visigoth Ataulf failed to capture the city in 413, receiving a severe wound at the hands of the Roman commander Bonifacius, and four years later its bishop successfully defied an attempt by Pope Zosimus to subordinate him to the episcopate of Arelate (Arles); although excommunicated, he remained in his see. Despite subsequent Visigothic rule, Massilia was reported by Agathias to have retained its Greek character until Frankish domination began in 536.

Of the earlier Greek periods of the city only traces (especially pottery) have been discovered. The tongue of land beside the ancient harbor has been excavated, revealing port constructions and warehouses of the first century BC and first and second centuries AD. A gate flanked by two square towers probably belongs to the last of these periods; and so do certain surviving stretches of the walls, although other portions and traces are of Republican and late imperial dates. Religious buildings traceable by excavations or finds include a shrine of Cybele and early Christian churches.

Mauretania. The north African territory north of the Atlas mountains and the Sahara, extending between the river Ampsaga (Wadi el-Kebir)—the border with Numidia and its Massyli—and the Atlantic. Its inhabitants, mostly seminomadic Berber herdsmen, were collectively known to the Greeks as Maurusii and to the Romans as Mauri (loosely though misleadingly translated as 'Moors'), although in a more restrictive sense the Mauri dwelt west of the river Mulucha (Moulouya), while the regions to its east belonged to the Masaesyli.

Grain and olives were grown in a few plains, and from the sixth century BC Phoenicians (followed by Carthaginians) established trading stations along the Mediterranean and Atlantic coasts, and the language at the Mauretanian royal court at Siga (Tafna) was Punic. During the Second Punic War, however, the king of the Masaesyli, Syphax—who resided at Siga—initially fought against Carthage. But in 212 he was won over to its cause by his Carthaginian wife, Saphanbaal (Sophonisba), who committed suicide when her husband was overthrown by Masinissa with Roman help (203). Between 108 and 105 King Bocchus I of Mauretania sided with the Romans against his son-in-law Jugurtha of Numidia, parts of whose territory he was allowed to annex.

During the Civil War between Julius Caesar and the Pompeians (49–46), the Mauretanian kings Bocchus II and Bogud (in the eastern and western parts of the country respectively) supported Caesar, and the former was rewarded with additional territory. After Caesar's death, at the suggestion of Antony's brother Lucius Antonius, Bogud attacked the representatives of Octavian (the future Augustus) in Spain but lost his kingdom to Bocchus II (*c* 38), dying as an exile in Antony's service in 31. Meanwhile, after Bocchus, too, had died in 33, Octavian annexed the whole of Mauretania and established half a dozen military colonies on its territory.

In 25, however, it reverted to the status of client kingdom under the learned and artistic Juba II (married to Cleopatra Selene the daughter of Cleopatra VII of Egypt), who established his capital at Iol Caesarea (Cherchel). But his son Ptolemaeus, who succeeded him in AD 23, was executed by Gaius (Caligula) at Rome (40), and, after a subsequent revolt of the Mauri, led by Aedemon, had been put down, Mauretania was converted by Claudius into two Roman provinces, Tingitana in the west and Caesariensis in the east, with their capitals at Tingi (Tangier) and Iol Caesarea respectively. The principal exports from these territories were purple dyes and valuable woods; and the Mauretanians were highly regarded by the Romans as soldiers, especially light cavalry. They produced one of Trajan's best generals, Lusius Quietus, and the emperors Macrinus (217-18) and Aemilian (253).

The number of citizen colonies rose to eighteen—seven in Tingitana and eleven in Caesariensis—and there were also citizen communities of municipal rank. Unrest occurred in a number of reigns, and Antoninus Pius had to deal with a general tribal revolt (*c* 145-50). Further serious difficulties with Atlas tribesmen known as Quinquegentanei (in the south of Caesariensis), requiring the presence of the emperor Maximian (*c* 297), resulted in a retraction of the frontier in both provinces; and in the subsequent reorganization, a new province, Mauretania Sitifensis, was carved out of the eastern part of Caesariensis, whereas Tingitana or Tingitania, as it was now called, was attached to the administrative diocese of Spain. A Quinquegentanian prince Firmus, with the help of dissident Christians (Donatists), led a dangerous revolt in the 370s, and his brother Gildo repeated the process in 397.

When Gaiseric and his Vandals arrived in Africa in 429 they occupied the Mauretanias, agreeing in 435 to pay an annual tribute to Rome. In 442, however, it was decided that they should be allowed to occupy the province of Africa, while the Mauretanian territories were to revert to Roman control; but little more than a dozen years later Gaiseric overran these territories again without encountering resistance, and the emperor Majorian (457-61) had to acquiesce to their loss.

Mavroyouni *see* Cynoscephalae

Mazaca *see* Caesarea (Cappadocia)

Mecone *see* Sicyon

Medinet Habu *see* Thebes

Mediolanum (Milano, Milan). A city of Cisalpine Gaul (northern Italy), situated on the Olonna (Olona), a small northern tributary of the Padus (Po) near the center of what is now the Lombard plain. The Etruscan outpost of Melpum (Melzo) had been a short distance to the east, near another tributary the Addus

(Adda). The earliest settlement known on the site of Mediolanum was founded by the Insubres (*c* 396), a Gallic tribe which gave Mediolanum its Celtic name, meaning 'plain.'

The town first came under Roman control for a brief spell in 222 and permanently in 194, after which Romanization followed. It obtained Latin rights (granting Roman citizenship to its annually elected officials) in 89 and the rank of *municipium* in 49 when the fertile, prosperous, populous Transpadane region obtained the Roman franchise. The city's colonial status may date from Hadrian (AD 117–38); it was the birthplace of the emperors Didius Julianus (193) and Geta (211/12).

Mediolanum was the principal city of north Italy, and a major communications junction where roads from Gaul, Raetia and Illyricum met. During the third century it became one of the greatest political and military centers of the west, as the growing menace of German invaders invested the region with increased significance. A decisive step occurred when Gallienus, during his sole reign (260–68), set up a mobile, cavalry-based group of reserve armies with its headquarters at Mediolanum, which thus became a focal point of the new defensive system; although the commander of the new force, Aureolus, led a revolt against Gallienus (which after the latter's assassination was overcome by Claudius II Gothicus). Mediolanum was now endowed with an imperial mint—which henceforward fulfilled a massive role—and shortly afterward became the capital of the province or district of Aemilia-Liguria. Then Diocletian's colleague Maximian (286–305) completed the city's fortifications, and made it not only the capital of the administrative diocese of Italia Annonaria but the main imperial residence of the western empire, supplanting Rome. It also became the seat of one of the praetorian prefects (usually four in number) who acted as the rulers' deputies throughout the empire.

Already possessing a Christian community, as inscriptions have confirmed, from the third century onward, it became famous for the 'Edict of Milan' by which Constantine I the Great and Licinius accorded the faith official recognition (313). In the following year a bishop of Mediolanum, Mirocles, attended the church Council of Arelate (Arles); and subsequently the place became an ecclesiastical headquarters of the highest importance. When Valentinian I and Valens created a more or less permanent division between the western and eastern empires (364), Mediolanum became the western imperial capital. It was also the scene of the episcopate of St. Ambrose, who led the Catholic struggle against the Arian heresy and paganism, acting independently not only of the Roman papacy but of the emperor Theodosius I (379–95), with whom he conducted a historic trial of strength. In 404, however, Theodosius' son Honorius moved his residence to the more easily defensible Ravenna. Mediolanum fell to Attila the Hun in 452 and to Odoacer the Herulian in 476.

The rectangular plan of the Roman city can be detected, and there are traces of a theater and amphitheater; remains from the first century BC have now been found in the Piazza del Duomo at a depth of twelve feet. A Gallienic reconstruction remains largely hypothetical, but from the time of Maximian there remains a stretch of the city wall, which, together with a twenty-four-sided brick-faced tower (the Torre di Ansperto), was constructed to bring within the fortifications a new palace quarter, including baths and an adjoining circus: it is hoped to uncover the palace itself as part of a projected Archaeological Park. Another bathing establishment seems to be of Constantinian date. Ausonius (*c* 388) also refers to temples, but in his own epoch the major constructions were churches. These—succeeding a cult center with floor mosaics going back to the third century—still convey a unique impression of the magnificent ecclesiastical architecture of the age, and the leading position of Mediolanum in this development. This preeminence is dislayed by five very large early churches—the Church of the Apostles (later San Nazaro), San Giovanni in Conca, the Duomo (cathedral, on the site of an earlier building dedicated to Santa Tecla), San Lorenzo (which was probably the palace church) and San Simpliciano (named after its founder, who was Ambrose's successor).

Medjerda *see* Bagradas

Megalopolis. A city of Arcadia in the central Peloponnese (southern Greece), situated in a plain beside the river Helisson, two and a half miles from its junction with the Alpheus (of which the Helisson was one of seven tributaries). Megalopolis, the 'Great City,' was founded by the Theban general Epaminondas in 369/368 BC as a stronghold to defend the southern Arcadians against Sparta. It was also the seat of the 'Ten Thousand,' the Assembly of the Arcadian League; this federal capital, on the north bank of the river, was given the additional name of Oresteia. Most of the borderland communities were incorporated—including (according to Pausanias) forty villages completely abandoned for the purpose of this amalgamation. The new city which thus came into existence was one of the largest in the Peloponnese, and possessed the most extensive territory in Arcadia. Coins were issued at its mint bearing the heads of Zeus Lycaeus and the figure of Pan seated on a rock, and displaying the name of Arcadia in a monogram.

However, after the death of Epaminondas at Mantinea (362) and the subsequent disintegration of the Arcadian League, the inhabitants of Megalopolis were only with difficulty, by the intervention of the Theban Pammenes, prevented from returning to their former homes. Persistent Spartan hostility prompted an appeal to Athens (352)—which, although supported by the orator Demosthenes, proved fruitless—and drove the Megalopolitans into friendship with Philip II of Macedonia. When the Spartans and other Greeks rebelled against Alexander the Great's regent Antipater (331), Megalopolis successfully resisted them in the course of a long siege; and its small surviving population also withstood another Macedonian claimant to Greece, Polyperchon (318).

In the third century, with a brief intermission (251–244), the Megalopolitans were under the autocratic rule of local 'tyrants,' the last of whom, Lydiadas, brought the city into the Achaean League (235), retaining his leadership, for most of the time, until the Spartan king Cleomenes III killed him in battle (227). In 223 Cleomenes plundered Megalopolis, but in the following year its eminent citizen Philopoemen, the Achaean statesman, restored the city. Similarly, after the Roman annexation (146), another distinguished native of the place, the historian Polybius, intervened constantly to mitigate its lot: a necessary task, since a comic poet quoted by Strabo declared that 'the Great City is a great desert.'

In imperial times it received a new bridge and portico, during the reigns of Augustus (31 BC– AD 14) and Domitian (AD 81–96) respectively. By the time of Pausanias (*c* 150), however, it lay for the most part in ruins. Nevertheless, it resumed the issue of coinage from Septimius Severus (193–211) to Elagabalus (218–22); some of these pieces celebrate the Lycaean Games, in honor of Zeus Lycaeus.

Pausanias' description has greatly assisted excavators, who have uncovered the agora, part of the sanctuary of Zeus (the rest has been washed away by the Helisson), and two extensive porticos. South of the river are extensive remains of the theater—which Pausanias described as the largest in Greece; it was equipped with a long Doric portico, which served both as a backdrop to the stage and as the entrance to a large rectangular colonnaded council house identified as the Thersilion (named after the architect) of the Ten Thousand. But this building was destroyed by Cleomenes III of Sparta, and never reconstructed.

Megalopolis (Pontus) *see* Sebasteia

Megara. Situated on the northern part of the Isthmus of Corinth between the Peloponnese and the rest of Greece, Megara lay in the narrow but fertile White Plain, the only lowland part of its district (the Megarid). It possessed a good harbor (Nisaea) to the east, on the Saronic Gulf of the Aegean Sea, as well as another (Pegae)—less conveniently accessible—to the west, on the Gulf of Corinth.

The city, which already existed in the Bronze Age, is one of the few in Greece to bear a Greek name (*Megara,* 'Big Houses'). It was believed to have owed its walls to the hero Alcathous—assisted by Apollo—and to have belonged later to Athens; it was at the Scironian Rocks, a pass penetrating Mount Geraneia, that the Athenian hero Theseus was said to have killed a brigand named Sciron. But then came Dorian immigrants (probably from Argos), who brought about the union (synoecism) of a number of villages to form the new city. In the eighth and seventh centuries BC Megara developed an extensive woollen industry, and played a prominent part in trade and colonization, founding Megara Hyblaea in Sicily, Calchedon (Kadıköy) and Byzantium (İstanbul) on the Thracian Bosphorus, and Heraclea Pontica (Ereğli) on the Euxine (Black) Sea.

But Megarian trade was supplanted by the activity of Athens and Miletus and particularly neighboring and hostile Corinth, and the authority of the local landowning aristocracy gave way to the autocratic government of Theagenes (*c* 640–620). Racked by internal strife, Megara had had to cede Perachora (its western region) to the Corinthians, and lost the offshore island of Salamis to the Athenians (*c* 600). The sixth-century elegiac poet Theognis, a nostalgic supporter of the old aristocratic order, was a Megarian; but the theory that comic drama originated among the people of this city (whose gaiety, the *megarensis risus,* was proverbial) cannot be confirmed. Shortly before 500 Megara joined Sparta's Peloponnesian League, and then fulfilled an active role in the Persian Wars. In 460, threatened by a Corinthian attack, it appealed to the Athenians, who helped its citizens to build Long Walls between their capital and Nisaea. In 446, however, as the ambitions of their allies became more evident, the Megarians massacred the Athenian garrison; and Pericles' retaliatory Megarian

Decree (*c* 432), placing an embargo on the city's Aegean and Pontic trade, was one of the contributory causes of the Peloponnesian War between Athens and Sparta. In this conflict, Athens occupied Nisaea (424), but Megara played some part in the Peace of Nicias, which briefly suspended the war (421).

Shortly after 400 the Megarian school of philosophy was founded by a certain Eucleides. At a time when the Megarians were banned from Athens, he was said to have attended the Athenian lectures of Socrates disguised as a woman; in consequence, he is portrayed with female veil and earring on later coins of Megara. During the greater part of the fourth century, as Isocrates confirms, the city prospered, avoiding political adventures, attending to commercial business, and producing fine sculptors; its coins show the head of Apollo Agraeus, whose temple, together with that of Artemis Agrotera, was attributed to the mythical Alcathous. But then Megara fell successively under the control of Alexander the Great's successors Cassander, Ptolemy I (308) and Demetrius I Poliorcetes the Besieger (307), and became part of the Macedonian kingdom. From 243 it belonged to the Achaean League (with intervals of Boeotian and, again, Macedonian allegiance), and suffered destruction, first, when the League was defeated by the Romans (146), and then, once more, when the Megarians took the side of Pompey the Great against Julius Caesar (48). During the Principate their city was attached to the Boeotian League, but revived its own local coinage in the second and third centuries AD. In addition to the traditional figures of Apollo and Artemis, these pieces display (under Septimius Severus, 193–211) the eastern motif of a statue of Demeter carried in a processional shrine on a horse-drawn wagon. In the later third century the city was severely damaged by German invaders and suffered final destruction.

Until recently, excavations had yielded little but a large fountain house, but now more than fifty further investigations have taken place. City defences in two areas are ascribed to the fourth century BC, and numerous houses have revealed distinctive basement or semi-basement chambers, apparently reached by movable ladders; these rooms may have been employed for family cult practices. Part of the main road through the city, leading from Athens to Corinth, has also been located.

Megara. The city of the Megareis Hyblaioi (the form Megara Hyblaea is modern), was situated on the east coast of Sicily, fourteen miles north of Syracuse. The founders came from Megara on the Isthmus of Corinth; the traditional date of their settlement, 728, has been queried owing to the discovery of earlier pottery, which has suggested a possible dating to *c* 750 instead. The immigrants had successively attempted to settle at Trotilum (above La Bruca bay), Leontini (Carlentini near Lentini, from which the Chalcidians expelled them) and Thapsus (off the Gulf of Augusta) before settling at their final location a few miles further to the north. This was the site of a former Neolithic village on a low plateau beside the river Cantera, given them by the native (Sicel) monarch Hyblon, whose name they perpetuated in that of their own new city. Although defenceless, the place was well-watered; it occupied a small coastal plain, and short beaches, behind a promontory, provided an anchorage.

Megara Hyblaea colonized Selinus (Selinunte) *c* 651 or *c* 628. But although possessing its own local pottery industry—which produced wares of fine quality—and able, as finds show, to import wine and oil, it was dominated by the proximity of Syracuse, whose ruler Gelon destroyed the town in 483. During the Peloponnesian War the Syracusans fortified the ruins (at that time unoccupied) against the Athenian expedition. Restored by Timoleon—the Corinthian leader of Syracuse—*c* 340 Megara Hyblaea prospered and issued coinage. In the Second Punic War, however, it suffered extensive destruction at the hands of Marcus Claudius Marcellus (214). Only a few scattered houses and farms were in time built over the site, but new fortifications were constructed during the campaigns of Octavian (the future Augustus) against Sextus Pompeius, son of Pompey the Great (*c* 37/6).

Excavations have shown that the original settlement covered a relatively large zone, though not all the houses were built close together. They were rectangular, single-roomed stone structures, and some of them possessed storage pits for grain. These first buildings—which go back to the late eighth century—were constructed, for the most part, according to a regular plan, which represents one of our earliest known examples of Greek town planning. Shortly before 600, they were augmented by a trapezoidal agora, and flanked by a portico and several shrines. Beside the agora are the foundations of another large portico dating from the epoch of Timoleon, a Doric temple (probably dedicated to Aphrodite) and a bathing establishment of the later third century BC; although the Hellenistic city was smaller than its predecessors. The various cemeteries of Megara Hyblaea include a series of imposing monumental tombs beside the main road to Syracuse. Powerful fortifications were created in haste against the Roman menace. Local finds include a surprising quantity of sculpture.

Mejdel Anjar *see* Chalcis Beneath Lebanon

Meligunis *see* Lipara

Melita, Melite (Malta). The largest of the group of Libyan (Maltese) islands, seventeen miles long and nine miles wide—the two next in size are Gaudus (Gozo) and Cuminum (Comino)—strategically situated between Europe and Africa, in the narrow channel which links the western and eastern portions of the Mediterranean Sea. Occupied since the Neolithic period—when a startling and unique series of megalithic temples were erected—Melita became a Phoenician trading post in about the ninth century, and a colony *c* 600. Subsequently passing into the hands of the Carthaginians, it was annexed at the beginning of the Second Punic War by the Romans (218), who placed the islands under the administration of the governor of Sicily.

Issuing bronze coins of its own with Punic and Greek inscriptions, Melita was called prosperous by Cicero, and Diodorus described the elegance of its houses. It was plundered, however, by Verres, the governor of Sicily, in 73–71, and the Civil Wars at the end of the Roman Republic caused a series of disturbances. In 46 Cicero wrote to a friend that he had persuaded Julius Caesar to pardon Aulus Licinius Aristoteles, a Melitan who had long and loyally supported the Pompeian cause; and after Caesar's murder the island was probably occupied first by the subordinates of Brutus and Cassius (who perhaps, it would seem from a monetary issue, planted a military colony there) and next by Pompey's son Sextus Pompeius, after whose defeat an officer of Octavian (the future Augustus), named Gaius Arruntanus Balbus, produced a coinage with the city's name in Greek and his own in Latin.

St. Paul was shipwrecked off the coast of the island *c* AD 60, and according to tradition its Christianity dates from that time. By the early second century Melita and Gaudus were granted the status of citizen communities (*municipia*), and enjoyed prosperity as producers of fine textiles and olive oils and honey; while Cuminum takes its name from the cumin seed. The islands were also well-known for a breed of lap dogs. It has been surmised that in the fifth century Melita succumbed to the Vandals.

Among villas of various dates, a large town house (now in Rabat, a suburb of Mdina, as the Arabs later called the Roman city) dates back to the third and second centuries BC and received extensions and decorations in the Augustan period (the Roman Villa Museum is now established on the site). Outside the city walls are catacombs of the fourth and fifth centuries AD, which closely resemble those of Rome. At Grand Harbor, which faced northeast and replaced the Carthaginian harbor on Marsascirocco Bay, wharves and storehouses and large baths have been located. Temples were founded on the sites of prehistoric and Carthaginian shrines. Circular defensive towers built at the approaches to the city have been attributed to a wide range of different dates.

Melos. A Greek island, one of the southernmost of the Cyclades archipelago, in the Aegean Sea between Laconia (southern Peloponnese) and Asia Minor. Melos was approximately circular until an early eruption of its volcano created an indentation providing the largest and deepest harbor in the Aegean. From Neolithic times onward, as the site of Phylakopi abundantly illustrates, the island was famous for its monopoly of obsidian (grey to black volcanic glass, found on at least two sites; it was flaked into tools or ground into vessels or statuary), and in consequence played a prominent part in the Bronze Age Minoan and Mycenaean civilizations. During the Dorian migrations, Melos was colonized from Laconia, and became a Spartan colony. The Chora plain was densely settled from the eighth to sixth centuries BC. A local coinage, at first depicting a ewer and then a pomegranate (*melon*), was initiated after 600.

In 480/79 the island sent contingents to help the Greek cause against the Persians at Salamis and Plataea. However, it remained neutral at the outset of the Peloponnesian War between Athens and Sparta (431)—although its people dispatched gifts to the Spartans. What happened next is the principal tragic event of Melos' ancient history. In 426 the Athenians sent a large force to devastate its territory, and in the following year Athens assessed it for tribute. But the island insisted on maintaining its neutrality. In 416, therefore, a further large army of the Athenians and the allies arrived, accompanied by envoys who announced Athens' refusal to accept this neutral status. The debate that followed is one of the highlights of Thucydides' narrative. The Melians' appeal to natural justice was rejected, and after a long siege their resistance was overcome (415), whereupon, by a decree of the Athenian Assembly, all the male inhabitants of the place were put to the sword, its women and children enslaved, and its territories occupied by five hundred colonists from Athens. (It was at this juncture that Athens launched its overconfident expedition to Sicily).

However, the city was liberated *c* 400 by the Spartan Lysander, its survivors came back, and its mint became active once again. Subsequently Melos passed into the hands of the Macedonians and then the Romans, whose emperor Commodus (AD 180–92) it portrayed on a local coinage.

Remains of the Greco-Roman city that succeeded the imposing Bronze Age settlements include traces of the acropolis, a theater, and a portico. Archaic Melos has yielded a rich haul of vases, jewels and gems, and excellent marble statues, notably male nudes (*kouroi*) of the mid-sixth century BC; and more than a hundred 'Melian' reliefs—terracotta wall decorations (or sides of wooden chests) of fifth-century date—have survived. There is a fine fourth-century statue of Asclepius (British Museum) and a third-century Poseidon (National Museum, Athens). But by far the most famous object discovered on the island is a statue of Aphrodite, the 'Venus of Milo,' a Hellenistic masterpiece of second century date that was found (in pieces) at Clima in 1820 and taken to the Louvre.

Memphis (Mit Riheina). A city in Lower Egypt on the Nile, twenty miles south of the modern Cairo; the first capital of the united territories of Lower and Upper Egypt, where Mena or Menes (*c* 3000 BC) founded a fortress named Mennofer (the White Wall). In Greek mythology Memphis was the home of Proteus, who, according to the *Helen* of Euripides, removed Helen (with her treasure) from Troy and kept her safe until Menelaus finally came to claim her. The historian Herodotus, giving details of the city and its monarchs, mentions a shrine of Aphrodite the Refugee (that is to say, Helen) within the court of Proteus' palace. The Greeks regarded Memphis as the central repository of Egyptian wisdom, vested in the high priests of Ptah, under whose guidance leading Greek thinkers including Eudoxus of Cnidus, Democritus of Abdera, and Plato were believed to have studied.

In 332, when Alexander the Great had conquered Egypt and returned from the oasis of Ammon (Siwa), he was crowned Pharaoh at Memphis in the temple of Hephaestus (with whom Ptah was identified), and after his death in 323 his embalmed body was kept at the city by Ptolemy I Soter until his tomb at Alexandria was ready to receive it. Ptolemy I moved his political capital to Alexandria but Memphis remained the principal religious center. The Ptolemaic god Serapis (Sarapis), who was derived from the sacred bull Apis worshipped at Memphis and identified after its death with the god Osiris (as Osor-Hapi), rivalled the preeminence of Ptah; yet it was at the temple of Ptah-Hephaestus that the Ptolemies celebrated their coronations, at least until *c* 171.

When Strabo visited Memphis after the Roman annexation of Egypt (31), he described it as a city of mixed race, second only to Alexandria in size. At that time visitors were still shown the Hephaestieum, as well as temples of Aphrodite-Astarte (Selene?) and Apis; the bullfights in Apis' honor were abolished by Theodosius I in AD 389. During this last period of antiquity Memphis was the capital of the province of Arcadia (earlier Aegyptus Herculia) within the administrative diocese of Egypt (comprising Egypt and Libya).

The Serapeum is to be seen just to the north of an early Step Pyramid. Ranged along the underground passages of the shrine were the sarcophagi of twenty-four bulls, each in a separate chamber. The approach to the building was lined by a long row of sphinxes, and an adjoining exedra (semicircular recess) displayed statues of ten Greek poets and philosophers arranged by Ptolemy I around a figure of Homer.

Menderes, Büyük (River) *see* Maeander

Menderes, Küçük (River) *see* Cayster

Menderes Suyu *see* Ilium

Merida *see* Emerita

Meroe *see* Aethiopia

Merv *see* Alexandria in Margiana

Mesopotamia (Iraq and southeastern Turkey); the territory between the rivers Tigris and Euphrates. Ancient writers usually drew its southern border to the north of Babylonia. The Achaemenid Persian king Cyrus II the Great gained the country from the Babylonians following the destruction of their kingdom in 539 BC, and Alexander the Great took it over after defeating Darius III Codomannus at Gaugamela in 331. After Alexander's death, Seleucus I Nicator made his new Mesopotamian foundation, Seleucia on the Tigris, the eastern capital of his empire (*c* 300). In 141/140 the southern part of the country, together with Babylonia, was overrun by the Arsacid Parthians (and only threw off their rule, very briefly, *c* 140 and *c* 130). For subsequent events, *see* Parthia.

In AD 115 Trajan made the northwestern portion of the territory into a Roman province of Mesopotamia, which Hadrian, however, evacuated immediately after his accession two years later; but the province was revived by Marcus Aurelius and Lucius Verus (165) and Septimius Severus (197–99), with its frontier at Singara (Jebel Sinjar). The Sassanian Persians, taking over the Parthian empire, overran Mesopotamia in 233 and 258, but the Palmyrene leader Odenathus reconquered its cities from 262 to 267 on behalf of the Romans, as their supreme commander in the east, although after the revolt of his widow Zenobia (271), the Persians seem to have reassumed at least partial control. Carus' reoccupation ended with his death (283), but Galerius, Diocletian's Caesar, won a victory (after an initial setback) which returned the country to Roman hands (298). Two provinces were established, Mesopotamia and Osrhoena.

During the third century the extensive 'Babylonian' Jewish communities of Mesopotamia, numbering more than a million persons and continually increasing in size, had begun a prolonged period of extraordinary efflorescence. Their first important academy, founded *c* 212, was at Nehardea on the Euphrates (which had earlier been the center of a transitory Jewish state [*c* 20–35]). A second academy was founded in 219 at Sura, further downstream, and after the destruction of Nehardea by Sapor (Shapur) I in 262, it was replaced by Pumbeditha, beside a canal. A further center was Machuza (Mahoza) near the banks of the Tigris.

The great power conflict for the country was resumed, over an extensive period, by the Roman emperor Constantius II (337–61) and the Persian king Shapur II, to whom Jovian was obliged, in 363, to cede the border territories, including Singara and Nisibis (Nusaybin). In 421/22 the Romans failed to take the northeastern sector back, and it became a rallying point for the Nestorian 'heretics' after their official condemnation by the church (431); while another group, the Monophysite Christians of Edessa (Urfa)—which was still within the empire—likewise failed to accept a ruling directed against their doctrines. The Babylonian Talmud was compiled by the Jewish academies during the same century. *See also* Amida, Carrhae, Circesium, Edessa, Euphrates, Hatra, Nicephorium Callinicum, Nisibis, Osrhoene, Seleucia on the Tigris, Singara, Tigris.

Messana, Messene, earlier Zancle (Messina). A coastal city at the northeastern end of Sicily upon the straits which bear its name and separate the island from Italy. The place lay in a narrow plain between the foothills of the Peloritan mountains (beside Cape Pelorus [Peloro]), named after Zancle's mythical founder, and the long, narrow, curved spit of land or sand bar called Peloris or Pelorias—hence the name Zancle, meaning sickle in the tongue of the previous native inhabitants. This spit provided a natural harbor, as well as three lakes of volcanic origin abounding (we are told by Solinus) in game and fish.

It is now known that the origins of Zancle go back to the fifth millennium BC; and it was later a Bronze Age center. According to Thucydides, the site was subsequently settled by Greek pirates from Cyme (Cumae) in Campania (southwestern Italy)—to judge from finds, this occurred *c* 750–725. They were joined by settlers from Chalcis and other cities of Euboea (Strabo's assertion of colonization from the Aegean island of Naxos does not seem to be accurate). Colonists were soon sent from Zancle to Mylae (Milazzo), and later also to Himera (Imera); and others participated in the foundation of Rhegium (Reggio di Calabria). But in 490/489 the autocratic ruler ('tyrant') of that city, Anaxilas I, prompted a party of his supporters from Samos and Miletus to capture Zancle. Settling a group of Messenians (from the Peloponnese) in the city, he changed its name to Messene—modified, after 461, to the Doric form Messana when Syracusan (Dorian) and other ex-mercenaries arrived, whereupon the Samians were expelled. Regaining its independence and becoming an ally of Syracuse, Messana was destroyed in 397/6 by the Carthaginian Himilco, but was rebuilt by the Syracusans under whose control, with intervals of domination by local autocrats, it remained until *c* 288/84. At that juncture Campanian mercenaries and raiders in Syracusan employment, calling themselves Mamertini (men of Mamers, the

Oscan Mars), seized the city and made it their capital (under the name of Civitas Mamertina). When Hiero II of Syracuse later tried to suppress them, they appealed both to the Carthaginians and Romans (at one stage placing the armed god Adranos, the Punic Adar or Moloch, on their coins). The resulting rivalry between the two empires precipitated the First Punic War (264–241).

After the war Messana was a prosperous ally (*civitas foedera*) of Rome, but during the civil strife following the death of Julius Caesar it became the military headquarters of Sextus Pompeius (42), the son of Pompey the Great, and was sacked in 36 by his victorious enemy Octavian (the future Augustus). Sextus had struck a military coinage at Messana, displaying its famous lighthouse (recalled by the modern village Faro); and an Augustan issue celebrated its subsequent elevation to the rank of a Roman citizen community (*municipium),* before 12 AD.

New discoveries in the Viale Boccetta have documented Zancle's remote origins, and Bronze Age finds have come to light near the harbor. A sanctuary of the eighth or seventh century has been located at the top of the harbor spit, and part of the habitation area can be traced at the point where the spit joins the mainland; recent excavations have shown that the early colony was more extensive than had been supposed. Coins show that its principal deities were Pan and Poseidon. A large chamber tomb of third-century Messana is excellently preserved, and it is thought that the Hellenistic acropolis has been located on Montepiselli hill.

Messene, earlier Ithome (the modern Ithomi and Mavromati, not Messini). A lofty, defensible height (2,646 feet) standing isolated within the plain of Messenia (*qv*), in the southwestern Peloponnese. Ithome was the stronghold of the Messenians in their struggles against the Spartans, notably the First Messenian War of the eighth century BC in which it was believed to have held out for twenty years (*see* Messenia).

In the Third War (Helot Revolt, from *c* 469 or 464), the fortress again resisted, for a duration of about eight years, after which the Athenians gave the defeated garrison a refuge at Naupactus, north of the Corinthian Gulf (456). When Messenia recovered its independence in 369 with the help of the Theban general Epaminondas, he founded the city of Messene, on the slopes of Mount Ithome, to be its capital, inviting all Messenian citizens abroad to become citizens of the new community. Unable on its own account to stand up against Sparta, it sided with Philip II of Macedonia (344), to whose descendant, Philip V, the fortress was described by Demetrius of Pharos (d. 214) as one of the two horns to hold down the cow, that is to say, to control the Peloponnese (the other horn being Corinth).

Messene twice adhered to the Aetolian League—from which, however, it suffered damage—and twice also to its Achaean counterpart, revolting unsuccessfully from the latter in 183/2 and passing into Roman hands in 146. In imperial times, from the later second to early third century AD, it revived the issue of coinage, with the portrait of the mythical Triopas' daughter Messene, of whom there was a temple in the city with a gold (gilt?) and marble statue. Other coins depict Zeus Ithomatas and Demeter, both of whom had already appeared on the earliest coinages, being the principal deities of the mountain. Today, however, Messene is principally notable for its walls of the fourth or third centuries BC. Flanked by thirty-three two-storeyed towers rising to a height of more than thirty feet, they are the best preserved fortifications in Greece, fitted with exceptional precision; according to Pausanias they were the strongest defences in the entire Greek world. The colonnaded courtyard, once regarded as an agora, has now been identified (on the basis of inscriptions) as a sanctuary of Asclepius and Hygiea; at its center a Hellenistic shrine has been excavated, replacing a fourth-century building. Other temples, too, have been located in addition to a theater, stadium, monumental gateway (*propylon*) and council chamber.

Messenia. The southwestern region of the Peloponnese (southern Greece), bordered to the north by Elis and Arcadia and to the east by Mount Taygetus and Laconia, which was dominated by Sparta. Extensive development in the Mycenaean (Bronze) Age is reflected by the remains of Pylos, believed by some to be the palace of the Homeric Nestor, who, according to the *Odyssey,* received a visit from Telemachus, searching for his father Odysseus.

After the Dorian conquest, according to Greek legendary tradition, Messenia passed under the control of Kings Cresphontes and Aepytus, whose territory was centered on the upper Pamisus valley near Mount Ithome. About 740–720(?), however, came the First War against the land-hungry Spartans, who annexed at least the central plain, allegedly causing the Messenian leader Aristodemus—who had offered his daughter to the underworld gods in response to a Delphic oracle—to kill himself on her grave. In the Second War (*c* 650–620?) the Messenian Aristomenes, after a victory and a subsequent defeat, was believed to have fled after the fall of his stronghold Eira (though his dating is problematical), and the whole territory became Spartan; most of its inhabitants were reduced to the status of helots or serfs. After further revolts in *c* 490 and *c* 469 or 464 the country was liberated by Epaminondas the Theban, who founded Messene in *c* 369 as its new capital, designed to keep a check on Sparta. Messenia also possessed towns at Cardamyle (Kardamili) and Thalamai (Koutophari), of which the latter adjoined a well-known sanctuary of Ino-Pasiphae (at Svina). For the subsequent history of the territory *see* Messene; and *see also* Mothone, Pylos.

Metapontum, Metapontion (Metaponto). A Greek city in Lucania (southeast Italy), on the coast of the Ionian Sea (Gulf of Taranto). Metapontum was situated between the mouths of the rivers Bradanus (Bradano) and Casuentus (Basento), which in ancient times flowed only six hundred yards apart, thus providing a site that could be defended on either side against the dense native (Messapian) population of the hinterland. The Greek colony was founded by Achaeans (under pressure from Sybaris [Sibari], which wanted a buffer against Taras [Tarentum, Taranto]) under the leadership of a certain Leucippus (or, according to other accounts, by men from Pylos; and Daulius of Crisa and Metabus are also described as leaders). The foundation probably took place in the later eighth century BC, since Eusebius' date 773 seems too early—though according to an alternative theory, the Achaeans followed earlier Greeks, who had colonized the site because their earlier settlement at nearby Incoronata had been destroyed.

Near the mouth of the Casuentus, the Metapontines possessed an artificial harbor (which is now completely silted up, and lies a thousand yards inland from the receded coastline). The region was famous for the fertility of its farmland, which it celebrated by depicting ears of corn upon its coins, of which the first (incuse) specimens have now been dated as early as 550. Metapontum possessed its own Treasury at Delphi, full of valuable objects. During the later years of the sixth century, the city was the refuge and burial place of the philosopher Pythagoras—whose pupil Aristeas urged the inhabitants to maintain their worship of Apollo with reverence. The Metapontines supported the Athenians in their expedition against Syracuse (415–413), and allied themselves with the invading Alexander of Epirus (332), whom was buried nearby. In 303/2 Metapontum was captured by Cleonymus of Sparta (to whom it had appealed against the Lucanians), and in 278 surrendered to the Romans, who were fighting against Pyrrhus of Epirus.

Then, after various vicissitudes during the Second Punic War—in which for a time it was the headquarters of Hannibal and his army—its population was evacuated by the Romans in 207. Although this did not mean the final abandonment of the town, its dissolution was well under way when Cicero made a pilgrimage to the house of Pythagoras in 50. By the mid-second century AD, only a theater and walls were still more or less complete.

Air photographs, supplemented by trial investigations, have revealed the plan of ancient Metapontum, based on broad east-west avenues. Its dimensions were expanded in the fifth century to create a new agora in a zone outside the original center, now under study and excavation. Flanked by a recently discovered assembly hall (*ecclesiasterion*) of the sixth and fifth centuries (evidently superseding an earlier wooden structure), the agora also adjoined a frequently modified temple of Apollo Lykeios (from which fine reliefs can be seen in the Museum at Potenza). Not far away from these buildings are the foundations of two other temples, one of which dates back to the years before 600 BC. But the most substantial remains are those of another shrine a mile outside the city, dating from the later sixth century and probably dedicated to Hera, though its popular name is the 'Knights' Table' (Tavole Paladine). Another sanctuary, dedicated to Zeus Aglaios, has recently been uncovered beside a spring four miles from the walls. Numerous other cults are also attested by literary sources and local coinages, one of which, of the fifth century BC, refers to Games held in honor of the Greek mainland river-god Achelous (*Acheloio aethlon*). A theater, reconstructed in the third century, provides the first known example of an auditorium made out of an artificial mound supported by a retaining wall.

The territorial possessions of Metapontum outside the city were distributed in the sixth and fifth centuries BC among allotments divided latitudinally by boundaries three hundred and eighty yards apart and longitudinally by drainage ditches every two hundred and twenty four yards. More than two hundred farm buildings have been located in the area between the river Casuentus and another nearby stream, the Chalicandrum (Cavone).

Metaurus (Metauro). An Italian river that rises in the Etruscan Apennines and flows for sixty-eight miles into the Adriatic Sea just south of Fanum Fortunae (Fano).

In 207 BC it was the scene of one of the decisive battles of the Second Punic War (218-201). Hannibal, whose invasion of the peninsula had already lasted eleven years, was in southern Italy, watched by one of the Roman consuls, Gaius Claudius Nero. Hannibal's brother Hasdrubal, who had come from Spain to bring reinforcements, found himself confronted by the army of the other consul, Marcus Livius Salinator, beside the Metaurus. Learning from a captured dispatch rider that the Carthaginian brothers intended to meet in Umbria, Nero boldly proceeded north, by forced marches, in order that his and his colleague's combined armies might engage and defeat Hasdrubal before Hannibal discovered that the two consuls had joined forces. Although the subsequent course of events is controversial, it seems likely that Hasdrubal withdrew inland up the Metaurus valley by night, with the intention of crossing the river; but before (or perhaps after?) he had done this he was compelled to fight. The engagement, however, came to a decisive end when a determined attack delivered by both Roman commanders outflanked his left wing.

Hasdrubal's army was destroyed, and he perished on the battlefield. Speedily returning to southern Italy, Nero acquainted Hannibal with the news by flinging his brother's head into his camp at Larinum (Larino). Hannibal was then compelled to retreat into Bruttii (the modern Calabria), without any hope of replenishing his forces; and Rome's final victory was in sight.

Methone *see* Mothone

Mezitli *see* Soli

Mieza (Eisvoria or Kephalari). A town in Emathia (western Macedonia). After numerous other suggestions it has now been identified with a site between the modern town of Naousa (once famous for its vineyards) and the villages of Lefkhadia and Kopanos, eleven miles north of Beroea ([*qv*], Verria). Plutarch writes of a *nymphaeum* (fountain building) at Mieza—one of the numerous springs of the area—where Aristotle taught Alexander and his fellow pupils for three years from 343/2 BC. According to Pliny the Elder, the place also possessed a group of stalactitic caves known as the Corycideum.

A richly painted and stuccoed vaulted grave of considerable architectural and artistic importance, the 'Great Tomb,' has been discovered at Kephalovrysi, three miles east of Mieza. The metopes of its two-storeyed pedimental façade, painted with centaurs engaged in battles, are surmounted by a continuous frieze displaying other paintings of martial scenes, while four single figures are depicted in the lower intercolumniations. The upper counterparts of these spaces, above the frieze, are decorated with seven false windows. Behind the façade are a lofty anteroom and smaller burial chamber, both arched. A further third-century tomb, which has long been known, displays a painting of a Macedonian horseman spearing a barbarian foot soldier; another of *c* 200, which is likewise painted, provides inscriptions of three dead brothers and their families. Cemeteries from the fifth and fourth centuries have recently been excavated near Naousa and Kopanos respectively, and houses with mosaic floors, a bathhouse, and workshops have also been uncovered in the area, which has, in addition, yielded an inscription recording deeds of purchase and sales of property, and the remains of an early Christian basilica.

Milan *see* Mediolanum

Milas *see* Mylasa

Milazzo *see* Mylae

Miletus, Miletos (Balat). The southernmost of the major cities of Ionia (western Asia Minor)—near its border with Caria—situated in ancient times at the mouth of the rich valley of the river Maeander (Büyük Menderes), but now five miles from the sea. According to Ephorus, the settlement was founded by Sarpedon from Milatos (Mallia) in Crete (or from Lycia?), a claim which may be substantiated by the discovery of successive strata of Bronze Age (Minoan and Mycenaean) occupation, culminating in a late efflorescence at the end of the Mycenaean epoch. About 1200 however, as excavation has shown, the fortifications of the town were wrecked beyond repair. In Homer's account, the people of Miletus (the only place on the whole Ionian coast mentioned in his poems) were apparently Carians. According to later Greek tradition, they lost the city (and their wives) to Ionian settlers under Neleus or Neileos (whose grandfather had come to Athens from Pylos); and it is demonstrable, from archaeological evidence, that Ionian colonists arrived from across the Aegean, probably before 1000 BC.

Subsequently Miletus became the most important, and probably the largest, city in Ionia. It derived renown from the neighboring shrine of Apollo at Didyma (*qv*), and extended its possessions twenty or thirty miles up the river valley. During the seventh and sixth centuries, despite perpetual rivalry with Samos, Milesians sailed from one or another of their four natural harbors (one in a bay to the east of the habitation area, and the others filling inlets to its west) to found many colonies—estimated to number more than sixty—on the Black Sea and its approaches, between the Hellespont (Dardanelles) and Tauric Chersonese (Crimea). Miletus also had much to do with the Greek penetration of Egypt, possessing representatives at the Fort of the Milesians and Naucratis; and its shipowners and businessmen engaged in a large-scale wool trade with Sybaris (Sibari) in southeastern Italy.

Miletus' coinage (at first of *electrum,* pale gold) started as early as the seventh century. But from that time onward the city not only suffered from grave internal strife between rich and poor—represented by the factions of wealth (Ploutis) and Cheromacha (Labor) respectively—but was often at war with the kings of Lydia in the hinterland. One of these, Alyattes, made peace with Thrasybulus, at that time (*c* 600) the autocratic ruler ('tyrant') of the city. Later, however, Miletus seems to have acknowledged the suzerainty of the Lydian monarch Croesus, though maintaining a privileged and prosperous position; its population at this time perhaps amounted to 60,000. After Croesus' fall at the hands of the Achaemenid Persians (546), Miletus, too, came under Persian domination. In 499, however, under the direction of Aristogoras, the son-in-law of its last tyrant Histiaeus, it led the Ionian Revolt, which five years later, following a naval defeat off Lade (*qv*) terminated in the capturc and sack of the city, whereupon its male survivors were removed to the mouth of the Tigris, and all the women and children were enslaved; Phrynichus' tragedy relating to the disaster caused great distress at Athens, and he was fined. The Milesian school of Pre-Socratic philosophy (Thales, Anaximander, Anaximenes) had belonged to the sixth century; Hecataeus, the forerunner of Greek history, advised against the Ionian revolt.

After the Persian defeat by the Greeks at Mycale (479), Miletus joined Athens' Delian League, but in the middle years of the century the Athenians imposed a garrison on its inhabitants. During the Peloponnesian War it rebelled in favor of Sparta (412), but then came successively under the rule of Persian satraps (386) and Mausolus of Caria (*c* 350). It was during the fourth century that Apollo of Didyma became the principal type of the local silver coinage. In 334 the Milesians opposed Alexander the Great on his southward march, submitting only after a siege, whereupon he established a royal mint in the city. During the two centuries that followed, the principal Hellenistic kingdoms—Antigonids, Seleucids, Ptolemies, Attalids—competed for influence over Miletus.

After the creation by the Romans of their province of Asia (133), it suffered seriously during their wars against Mithridates VI of Pontus (120–63), and then again in the civil strife that accompanied the fall of the Republic. St. Paul visited the city *c* AD 51. Subsequently, although Miletus, where the harbor increasingly suffered from silting, had become eclipsed by the grandeur of Ephesus and Pergamum, second-century emperors continued to spend large sums adorning its streets with new buildings. Apollo of Didyma remained prominent on its coinage, and successful resistance to a Gothic siege in 263 was attributed to the god's miraculous intervention.

The earliest city extended northward along a peninsula from the lofty Kalabaktepe (where the 'tyrants' may have built their acropolis) to the Lion Harbor, centering round a temple of Athena. After the Persian Wars the habitation center was displaced in a northeasterly direction to the head of that harbor, where the North Agora was built, flanked by shrines of Asclepius and Apollo (the Delphinium); another recently uncovered temple area, at Humeitepe, has been tentatively ascribed to Demeter. The new city built at this time displayed the right-angled regularity associated with the name of the famous town planner, Hippodamus, himself a Milesian.

The most impressive surviving building is a theater, perhaps the finest in Asia Minor, dating from the third century BC but rebuilt by the Romans with a capacity of at least 15,000. The South Agora of Hellenistic times, the largest known agora of the entire Greek world, further indicates the massive scale on which the public edifices of the city were laid out at this period, when shrines of the Ptolemaic god Serapis and of king Eumenes II of Pergamum—one of the city's greater builders—can also be identifed, in addition to a gymnasium of Eumenes, and a stadium and palaestra that were perhaps likewise attributable to his generosity. A western agora belongs to the end of the Hellenistic epoch.

During the Roman imperial epoch even more magnificent architectural enterprises followed. The reign of Hadrian (AD 117–38) witnessed the construction of a grandiose north gateway to the South Agora, now in the Pergamon Museum in East Berlin. Outside the gateway was a council house, set in a colonnaded courtyard; and an elaborately decorated three-storey *nymphaeum* (fountain building) stood nearby. A bathing establishment to the south of the agora was the gift of Faustina the Younger, the wife of Marcus Aurelius, after her vist to the city in 164. The city's earliest churches of the fourth, fifth and sixth centuries AD have now been investigated, and mosaics belonging to the bishop's palace ware preserved.

Millau *see* Condatomagus

Minorica (Minorca) *see* Balearic Islands

Minturnae (Minturno). Situated a mile from the coast of western Italy, in the Caecuban plain beside the north (and later also the south) bank of the river Liris (Garigliano)—which separated Latium from Campania—Minturnae was originally a settlement of the tribe of the Aurunci, and was captured by the Romans during their conquest of that tribe in 313 BC. In 295 a Roman colony was established on the site, astride the Via Appia (312) which was Rome's principal route to southern Italy. The story of Gaius Marius' refuge from Sulla's henchmen in the nearby marshes (88) became legendary. Subsequently the colony was renewed by Augustus (31 BC–AD 14) and Gaius (AD 37–41), and expanded by Hadrian (117–38). It possessed a bridge over the Liris, the Pons Terinus (of which wooden piles and concrete rubble have been discovered), and was served by what was evidently a busy and complex harbor, the Portus Lirensis.

Strabo praises the plain of Minturnae, despite its swampiness, for tree vines that 'produce the best of wines.' He also refers to a much revered sanctuary near the mouth of the Liris, dedicated to the sea-goddess Marica, mother of Latinus, and frequented from the sixth century BC onward numerous coins found beneath its waters may have been offerings from her pilgrims. The forum and Capitolium of the Republican colony have been excavated. The former was converted into a portico (behind a theater with accommodation for 4,600 persons, now restored) when a new imperial forum was constructed, by which time the Capitolium had been superseded by three new temples; one of them was partly constructed from reused stones bearing a long series of dedicatory inscriptions of the Sullan and post-Sullan epochs.

Water was brought to the city by a well-preserved aqueduct which came from the Auruncan mountains seven miles away, and terminated in a distribution chamber incorporated in the western city gate. This gate formed part of a wall with square and polygonal towers which, before 207 BC, extended the area—surrounded by a limestone fortification—constituting the original camplike colony. Arches of a bathing establishment and remains of an amphitheater are also to be seen.

Miriofiton *see* Olynthus

Mirobriga or Merobriga (Santiago do Cacém). A town in southwestern Lusitania (Alentejo, Portugal), thirteen miles from the Atlantic. Little is known of the history of Mirobriga, but recent excavations have revealed one of the largest sites in the country. Pliny the Elder refers to its people as Celts, and their hill fort has been located and dated by finds of pottery of the fourth century BC. Two superimposed pre-Roman temples have been identified, in addition to Roman shrines of the mid-first century AD known today as the Temples of Venus (an apsidal structure) and Aesculapius, although the latter, situated on the acropolis, was, in fact, probably dedicated to Jupiter. It stood beside the forum, which was also adjoined by a multi-storeyed market building cut out of the rock.

There are remains of private houses, of inns and of an elaborate waterworks, and well-paved streets bordered by shops lead down to two bathing establishments in a natural hollow at the foot of the acropolis. Beside the baths is a stream traversed by a Roman bridge. Mirobriga possesses the only ancient circus to have been discovered in the country so far, which was famous for horse-breeding in ancient times. The town's buildings are also notable for fine wall paintings with intricate geometrical designs. (This Mirobriga is to be distinguished from two other places of the same name in the Iberian peninsula, Mirobriga Vettonum [Ciudad Rodrigo] in northeastern Lusitania [western Spain] and Mirobriga Turdulorum [Capilla] in northern Baetica [south-central Spain]).

Misa (Marzabotto). An Etruscan center in the plain of the river Renus (Reno), seventeen miles south-southwest of the regional capital Felsina (Bononia, Bologna), which it linked with the homeland of Etruria, controlling the Apennine pass and its trade. The town was probably founded not long after 550 BC as part of the northern expansion program of one or more of the city-states of northern Etruria, among which Volaterrae (Volterra) and Clusium (Chiusi) were the most prominent. However, Misa was occupied by the Gallic tribe of the Boii in the fourth century BC, and thereafter gradually declined into little more than a village.

Although the site was partly destroyed by a change of course of the river Renus and a landslide, its remaining traces provide an unusual, revealing picture of an Etruscan habitation center. After small-scale beginnings before 500, the following century witnessed the creation of a carefully oriented rectangular grid based on a wide central street (leading from north to south) flanked by drainage channels and fronted by metal and ceramics workshops. This main street was crossed at right angles by secondary roads, of which the northernmost led to a hillside terrace (Misanello). This terrace contained at least three temples constructed of stone in their lower parts and wood and unbaked bricks above, and surmounted by roofs of brightly painted tiles. The principal cemeteries were subsequently supplemented by a Gaulish necropolis.

Misenum (Miseno). A lofty promontory in southwestern Italy (Campania), comprising three volcanic craters and forming the northwestern extremity of the Gulf of Cumae (Bay of Naples). According to Virgil, the locality was named after the Trojan Misenus, the trumpeter of Aeneas. The man had aroused the jealousy of the sea-god Triton, and when the Trojans landed near Cumae, he was dragged into the waves and drowned, whereupon Aeneas buried him on the promontory—a story that may originate from its shape, which does somewhat resemble that of a tumulus. Strabo also reported a story that the mythical Laestrygones of the *Odyssey* dwelt at Misenum.

A pair of harbors behind the cape—inner and outer, to the west and east respectively—was utilized for centuries by the Greek city-state of Cumae, situated just beyond the Gulf. Hannibal ravaged the port in 214 when Cumae opposed him. In the later Republic, however, Misenum was a center of numerous magnificent villas, notably the residence of Marius which was purchased by the luxurious Lucius Licinius Lucullus for a very large price, adorned with artistic treasures and famous gardens and equipped with fish ponds (for another villa of Lucullus, *see* Neapolis). The 'Treaty of Misenum' between Octavian (the future Augustus) and Antony and Sextus Pompeius in 39 is a misnomer, because the meeting took place further along the Gulf, at Puteoli (Pozzuoli), However, the town harbors of Misenum achieved major and lasting importance early in the reign of Augustus when they became a principal naval base of the reorganized Roman fleet (Ravenna occupying a similar role in eastern Italy). The required conversion of the port, accompanied by the construction of new breakwaters and of a fresh-water reservoir of unparalleled size (the Piscina Mirabilis), was undertaken by Augustus' admiral Marcus Agrippa (in conjunction with the Portus Julius which he had earlier created out of the neighboring lakes Avernus and Lucrinus). The outer harbor of Misenum served the active vessels of the Roman navy and provided room for training exercises, while its inner counterpart (to which it was linked by a canal crossed by a wooden bridge, recorded by inscriptions) was designed for the reserve fleet and for repairs, and offered refuge from storms.

The Villa of Lucullus later passed into imperial hands, and Tiberius died there in AD 37. Meanwhile a town had grown up beside the port and villas of Misenum; it was elevated to the rank of a Roman colony, probably in the reign of Claudius (41–54), which also witnessed an enhancement of the status of the prefects of the local fleet (subsequently known as the Classis Praetoria Misenenesis). One of these officers was Pliny the Elder, who set out across the bay from his residence there to witness the eruption of Vesuvius (79), and perished. The port long maintained its naval character, although it fell into disuse toward the end of the ancient epoch.

The locations of the ancient buildings at Misenum are hard to identify owing to subsequent quarrying; in particular, this has made it impossible to find the Villa of Lucullus although we know that it stood on the promontory itself, among scented gardens known as the 'Elysian Fields.' However, traces of ancient buildings in the whole area are very extensive. Remains of a theater show a passage cut through the hill for easy access from the port, and a recently discovered group of buildings dedicated to the imperial cult includes a tripartite Temple of Augustus in which statues of emperors and deities have been found.

Misis *see* Mopsuestia

Mit Riheina *see* Memphis

Mitrovica *see* Sirmium

Mitylene *see* Mytilene

Miyafarkin *see* Tigranocerta

Modena *see* Mutina

Moesia. Originally the territory of the Moesi, a Thracian people living south of the Danube in what is now eastern Serbia (Yugoslavia). Later the name of Moesia was extended to the entire area south of the river from its tributaries the Drinus (Drina) and Margus (Morava) as far as the Euxine (Black) Sea. After various encounters with the Romans, the Moesi were among a number of tribes subdued by Marcus Licinius Crassus, a general of Octavian (the future Augustus), who advanced the imperial frontier to the Danube, in 30–28 BC.

The newly conquered regions—extending across what are now Bulgaria and southeastern Rumania—were at first loosely attached to the province of Macedonia, but *legati* of Moesia are found in the first decade AD and the region probably became a fully organized province (with its southern border running approximately along Mount Haemus, the main Balkan range) under Tiberius (*c* 15); however, the territory was grouped together with Macedonia and Achaea in a single governorship-general until 44. The governor of Moesia also supervized the Black Sea shore north of the Danube, studded, like the Moesian coast itself, by Greek colonies as far as the Cimmerian Bosphorus (Straits of Kerch). Moreover, by the third quarter of the first century, if not before, the Moesian governor commanded a fleet (the Classis Moesia). Otho's representative, in 69, repelled an incursion by the tribe of the Roxolani.

In 86 Domitian divided the province in two, Upper (western, Malvensis) and Lower (eastern) Moesia (with its capital at Tomis [Constanţa]), with the river Ciabrus (Tsibritsa) as their boundary. After the Dacian Wars of Trajan (105/6), both provinces received trans-Danubian appendages bordering on the newly annexed areas in Dacia (Rumania). Moesia prospered under the Antonines and Severi, and later became a principal breeding ground for Roman soldiers and emperors. But one of its governors, Pacatianus, revolted against Philip the Arab in 248/9, thus opening the way for incursions by varied groups of German tribesmen; and a further rebellion of Ingenuus, based on Pannonia, against Gallienus in 260 was joined by Moesia and its legions, which were also involved in an uprising by the Upper Pannonian governor Regalianus which followed immediately afterwards.

Then, after the evacuation of Dacia under Aurelian (271), the border region between Upper and Lower Moesia—or Moesia Prima and Secunda, as they later came to be called—was converted into two new provinces, confusingly known as Dacia Ripensis (with its capital at Serdica, now Sofia in Bulgaria) and Dacia Mediterranea (*i.e.* southern, not Mediterranean Dacia: ruled from Naîssus, now Niš, in Yugoslavia). Diocletian (284–305) incorporated these provinces into an administrative diocese of Moesia. In Dacia Ripensis, a compact area of Latin settlements, Galerius, who was Diocletian's Caesar (deputy), constructed an imperial palace—now excavated—at Gamzigrad (near Zaječar in eastern Yugoslavia); and he also built the town of Romulianum, in honor of his mother Romula.

Soon afterward, under Constantine I the Great (306–37), these two Dacian provinces and Moesia Prima and two other provinces carved out of it, Dardania and Praevalitana, were made into the administrative diocese of Dacia, whereas Moesia Secunda and its offshoot Scythia (the Dobrogea) became attached to the diocese of Thrace or the Thraces.

In this Scythian province, more than thirty early Christian basilicas have come to light. During the late third and early fourth centuries, Moesia, at least in its western regions, suffered less permanent damage and depopulation than Pannonia, and the pastoral peoples in the hills retained their Romanized traditions long after the cities in the valleys had ceased to exist. *See also* Abrittus, Axiopolis, Bononia, Callatis, Durostorum, Gamzigrad, Haemus, Istrus, Marcianopolis, Margum, Naissus, Novae, Odessus, Oescus, Ratiaria, Singidunum, Tomis, Troesmis, Tropaeum Trajani, Viminacium.

Moguntiacum or Mogontiacum (Mainz). A city and fortress on the left bank of the river Rhenus (Rhine), opposite its junction with the Menus (Main). The name of the place, derived from a Celtic deity Mogon or Mogontia, presupposes a pre-Roman settlement.

Under Augustus (15–12 BC) a fortified legionary camp was built half a mile from the Rhine as a base for the invasion of 'Free Germany,' into which the site commanded important routes. In 9 BC Tiberius erected a funeral monument at Moguntiacum in honor of his late brother, Nero Drusus (Drusus junior). On January 1st, AD 69, the two legions of its garrison overthew the statues of Galba, thus launching the civil war, and were joined soon afterward by their fellow soldiers in Lower Germany, who set up their governor Vitellius as emperor. Later in the same year the Gallo-German rebellion of Civilis, after his first attack had been repelled by Dillius Vocula, destroyed the city, together with all other strongholds as far as the sea. Under Domitian (81–96), the timber fortress was replaced by stone, while a civilian settlement grew up beside it. In 83–85 Moguntiacum was Domitian's base for his operations against the German tribe of the Chatti, and, for the same purpose, a fort was constructed across the river (at Kastel), linked to the town by a bridge. After the rebellion of his governor Lucius Antonius Saturninus in 89, the garrison of two legions was reduced to one; but when the two German commands were converted into provinces a year or so later, Moguntiacum became the capital of Upper Germany, of which it stood at the northern extremity.

In 234 the emperor Severus Alexander, after German incursions had compelled him to concentrate a large western army on the Rhine, established his headquarters at the city, spanning the river with a pontoon bridge (later replaced by a permanent bridge—shown on a lead medallion—of which the piers were seen and described in modern times, though subsequently destroyed). However, Alexander's undignified attempts to pay off the Germans caused his soldiers to murder him and his mother, Julia Mamaea, at the camp (235). When Postumus (260–68) set up a secessionist empire of the western provinces, one of his senior officers, Laelianus, declared himself emperor at Moguntiacum. Postumus took the city by siege and put Laelianus to death, but his refusal to allow his own men to engage in looting caused him to be assassinated shortly afterward. In 286–88 Maximian, joint emperor with Diocletian, successfully averted a mass attack on Moguntiacum by Alamanni and Burgundians.

In about 355 (some say earlier) the place became a citizen community, with the rank of *municipium,* and at about the same time or perhaps not before the reign of Valentinian I (364–75), the town walls—originally dating from the third century—were reconstructed to follow a new course, embracing part of the area of the military fortress that had been abandoned. At this period the city was the capital of the province Germania Prima and the headquarters of the *dux Moguntiacensis,* the military commander of a sector of the Rhine frontier; it was also the seat of a bishopric. When, however, the Germans crossed the frozen river *en masse* at the end of 406, Moguntiacum was the first place to fall; it was looted and many of its inhabitants, who had taken refuge in a church, were massacred. The city remained in the hands of the Burgundians, who shortly afterward encouraged the surviving population to proclaim a Gallo-Roman named Jovinus as dissident Roman emperor (411–13).

The arches of a first-century aqueduct (the Römersteine) can be seen at Mainz-Zahlbach, and fragments from various other buildings have been found incorporated in subsequent constructions.

Moigrad *see* Porolissum

Mont-Beuvray *see* Bibracte

Montesarchio *see* Caudine Forks

Montmaurin *see* Tolosa

Mopsuestia ('the Hearth of Mopsus') or Mopsus (Misis). A city of Smooth Cilicia (Pedias, Campestris) in southeastern Asia Minor, on the right bank of the river Pyramus (Ceyhan), at an important crossing where it flows past the foothills. The legendary founder of the settlement was the diviner Mopsus, whose migration to Cilicia after the fall of Troy, at the head of 'mixed multitudes of peoples,' was recorded by many tales.

Liberated from Persian control by Alexander the Great, the town was renamed Seleucia on the Pyramus by the Seleucid monarch Seleucus IV Philopator (187–175 BC), and coined as such under Antiochus IV Epiphanes (175–163), but did not retain the name for long. In 96 Seleucus VI Epiphanes was killed at Mopsuestia, which suffered devastation. In 68/67 the city adopted a new era to celebrate the ejection, by the Romans, of the Armenian monarch Tigranes I the Great who had occupied Cilicia fifteen years earlier. In imperial times, when Mopsuestia's position on the main road from Antioch to Tarsus brought it prosperity, local coinage labelled its citizens with a remarkable variety of surnames in honour of successive emperors, notably Hadrianoi, Antoninianoi, Alexandroi, Decianoi, Valerianoi and Gallienianoi. Other pieces show the circular Altar of Mopsus (or a model) in the hands of the city-goddess; and we read of the city's 'Holy Ecumenical Games,' in competition with similarly named festivals at other Cilician centers. A coin of the time of Valerian (253-68) depicts the Pyramus bridge (an imperial gift) terminating in massive arches at either end. Remains of the bridge are still to be seen, in addition to the ruins of a theater, stadium and colonnaded street. A large basilica, containing important mosaics, attests the status of Mopsuestia as an episcopal see; the building may have been in existence at the time of the city's famous and controversial bishop, Theodore of Antioch (342–408).

Morava, River *see* Margum

Morgantina, Murgantia (Serra Orlando, three miles from Aidone). A Greek city in east-central Sicily, lying on a ridge at the junction of the island's central plateaus with the fertile Catana (Catania) plain; watered by the upper course of the river Symaethus (Simeto) and its tributaries. The original Sicel hut village goes back to the third millennium BC, and the city's subsequent name was owed to the immigration, recorded by Strabo, of a people known as the Morgetes from south-central Italy *c* 1200 (?). Greek settlers, probably from Catana and Leontini (Carlentini near Lentini), arrived *c* 500 and created an urban community. However, Sicel occupation also continued, and the mixed burial rites, noted in an excavated tomb, have been ascribed to cultural amalgamation, perhaps as a result of intermarriage. Nevertheless, the main role of the city was to form a Greek outpost on the fringe of the Sicel hinterland, dominating the roads to the south and northwest as well as eastward to Catana.

Severe damage inflicted by the Sicel king Ducetius (459) caused a temporary decline, and subsequently Morgantina remained under the domination of the Syracusans until they ceded it to Camarina (425). In 397 Dionysius I restored the influence of Syracuse, whose leader Timoleon undertook the refortification of the city in the 350s, followed by rebuilding and resettlement by other Syracusan rulers, Agathocles (317–289) and Hiero II (275–215). From the middle of the third century, when their coins depict a god Alkos (perhaps identifiable with Apollo), the Morgantinans enriched themselves from their grain-producing surroundings and their skilful production of terracotta figurines. During the Second Punic War, however, when the Roman general Marcus Claudius Marcellus captured Syracuse (211), he sacked Morgentina and handed it over to Rome's Spanish allies. Subsequent repairs were only on a modest scale; then slave revolts (*c* 139–132, 104–100) caused further suffering, and by the time of Augustus, according to Strabo, the town had virtually ceased to exist.

The original settlement stood on a steep isolated acropolis ridge (Mount Cittadella). The later habitation area, at the midpoint of a ridge in a hollow between two low hills, displays a town plan that goes back to the second quarter of the fifth century. But the zone is chiefly notable for an exceptional agora of the time of Agathocles; this was built on a slope, with flights of steps forming three sides of a polygon and serving as seats for public meetings addressed from a podium that has recently been discovered. The remaining side of the agora was flanked by a long stuccoed and painted portico. However, the whole complex was abandoned before completion. Other public buildings included at least four temples of Demeter and Persephone (Kore) as well as another sanctuary dedicated to the gods of the underworld, a theater of the third century BC, and numerous dwellings of the same time or later. The 'House of Ganymede' contains a mosaic—representing Ganymede being carried off by the eagle of Zeus—that dates from *c* 250 and is therefore one of the earliest tessellated mosaics to have been discovered so far. Traces of two large public granaries, built in the fourth and third centuries, have also been unearthed.

Excavations outside the city at San Francesco Bisconti have now revealed an unusual group of shrines that date from the mid-sixth century and the two centuries that followed, and are arranged on at least three different levels of the hillside. Like so many other local monuments, this sanctuary shows signs of destruction by fire, presumably in 211. Objects from the site of Morgantina have now been lodged in a museum at nearby Aidone. During the later Roman empire, a great residence was erected five miles from the city, near Philosophiana (*qv*) and the modern Piazza Armerina.

Mosella (Moselle, Mosel), river. A left-bank tributary of the Rhenus (Rhine) in Gallia Belgica and Germania Superior (northeastern France and western Germany). The great Roman city and base of Augusta Trevirorum (Trier) lay on the Mosella. In AD 58, during the reign of Nero, Lucius Antistius Vetus, military commander of Upper Germany, planned to build a canal linking the Mosella with the Arar (Saône), so that goods arriving from the Mediterranean up the Rhodanus (Rhône) and Arar could pass through the Mosella into the Rhine, and so onward to the North Sea. But the governor of Gallia Belgica, Aelius Gracilis, prevented Vetus from importing the required military workmen into his province ('that would be currying favor in Gaul, and would worry the emperor').

The Mosella was immortalized by a poem of Ausonius (*c* 310–95) bearing its name. Arriving from Bingium (Bingen) and catching his first sight of the river at Noviomagus (Neumagen), he gives an account of its main features, aspects of its navigation, and the fish its waters contained. He also describes its vine-clad banks, the pleasure it gave to the local inhabitants, the country mansions that lined its course, and the tributaries that increased its dimensions on the way to the Rhine.

Mothone or Methone, identified with Homer's 'vine-clad Pedasus,' one of the seven cities promised by Agamemnon to Achilles (although some authorities believed that Pedasus was Corone instead). Mothone was a harbor town on the peninsula of Messenia (southwestern Peloponnese, southern Greece), beside the rocky islet of Mothon. A dependency of Sparta, who gave it to refugees from

Nauplion (Nauplia) in the Argolid, Mothone was unsuccessfully besieged by the Athenians at the outset of the Peloponnesian War (431 BC). Philip II of Macedonia (359–336) removed the town from Spartan rule and attached it to Messenia. In the second century it was issuing its own coinage and became a member of the Achaean League, until annexation by Romc (146).

In 31, during the course of the civil war between Antony and Cleopatra VII in the east and Octavian (the future Augustus) in the west, Mothone played a decisive role in history. Antony's forces and fleets were extended along a series of strong points lining the east coast of Greece from Corcyra (Corfu) in the north to Mothone in the south, where his commander was the exiled Mauretanian king Bogud. Contrary to all expectation, Octavian's admiral Agrippa crossed the Ionian Sea as early as March (when the milder weather had scarcely begun) and employed not the direct route but a long diagonal passage bringing him to Mothone, which he immediately captured, killing Bogud and stationing a garrison in the town. From this base he could harass Antony's other naval stations, and it was now only a matter of time before Octavian himself arrived and the decisive victory at Actium was won.

Mothone was granted the status of a free city by Trajan (AD 98–117). A mole, first constructed in this time or a little later, reinforced the bar that ran out to Mothon island, and protected the harbor. This semicircular port, surrounded by colonnades, is depicted on a coin of Geta, the son of Septimius Severus (193–211), showing a statue at the entrance and a galley about to come in. Other coins of the same period depict a number of deities, including Athena Anemotis, whose temple Pausanias saw: he also visited a shrine of Artemis, and noted an unusual spring of water mixed with pitch.

A number of the many wrecks found off the coast have been investigated by underwater archaeologists, including two of the Roman imperial period containing fragments of columns and sarcophagi.

Motya (Mozia). A city on an islet (San Pantaleo) off the west coast of Sicily, to which it was joined by a mile-long artificial causeway across a shallow lagoon. Colonized by the Phoenicians shortly before 700 BC—the site, as has now been discovered, of a Bronze Age settlement—Motya became one of the naval, military and commercial strongholds of the Carthaginian empire, undergoing, however, at the same time, considerable Greek influence, as is shown by its coins (from the fifth century onward) which combine Punic (later Greek) inscriptions with Greek designs. A famous Carthaginian ship, found in the waters of Motya, has now been taken to the museum at Marsala. Diodorus describes at length how in 397 Dionysius I of Syracuse besieged and captured the city (by the employment of advanced siege equipment), inflicting massacres and crucifixions; whereupon the survivors fled to found Lilybaeum (Marsala), five miles away on the mainland.

The entire perimeter of Motya island, extending for about a mile and a half, was surrounded by walls equipped with about twenty square towers, which seem to date from the early sixth century but were subsequently reinforced. In the northern part of the island (and notably on the Cappidazzu site), remains of Phoenician sacred buildings dating from before 700 have been uncovered.

In the fifth century the growing population required a new mainland necropolis in the Birgi district, linked to the island by a stone-paved rubble causeway.

Motya itself, at the time of its siege by Dionysius I, contained many lofty buildings. After its capture, however, the site was never built over again in its entirety (to the advantage of archaeologists). Nevertheless, remains of a habitation center of limited dimensions, including a large three-naved building, confirm that life did not altogether cease; and a fine Greek marble statue of a youth may also postdate Dionysius' destruction, although this is disputed. The *Cothon* or harbor basin has been carefully examined. It apparently originated in a natural depression, which was subsequently lined with stone and connected with the lagoon by a channel, cut shortly after 500 and flanked by wide quays. However, the channel was allowed to silt up a century later.

Mukawar *see* Machaerus

Munda. A town in Hispania Ulterior (Baetica, southern Spain), south of Ucubi (Espejo) and northeast of Urso (Osuna). The scene of the final, decisive battle of the civil war between Julius Caesar and the Pompeians in 45 BC. Led by Cnaeus Pompeius (elder son of the late Pompey the Great), with the assistance of his brother Sextus and the experienced Labienus, the Pompeians at first controlled most of the cities of the Baetis (Guadalquivir) valley. But Caesar, joined by reinforcements, encroached on this territory, and Cnaeus Pompeius decided to make a stand in a strong position between Munda and Urso. A long, grim struggle was fought before Caesar's Tenth Legion pushed back the opposing left wing, which was then assailed in the flank and rear by the cavalry of Caesar's Mauretanian ally King Bogud.

Labienus fell fighting, Cnaeus Pompeius was hunted down, and only Sextus escaped to take refuge with a Spanish tribe (subsequently reemerging in Sicily). At the news of Munda the Roman senate hailed Caesar as Liberator, and on his return to the capital he celebrated a Triumph.

Mungersdorf *see* Colonia Agrippinensis

Murgantina *see* Morgantina

Murlo is the name of the modern village beside an Etruscan religious and political center (on the Poggio Civitate site), of which the ancient name is unknown. Its remains lie in northeastern Etruria (north-central Italy), just beyond the river Umbro (Ombrone), and between two of its tributaries, upon a wooded ridge forming an extension of the hills known as the Catena Metallifera, from which metals were readily available. Although discoveries at Murlo show connections with various different parts of Etruria, they most nearly resemble the products of the city-state of Clusium (Chiusi), which was linked to the place by a route beside the Umbro and was probably its master.

A large stone building may have been the residence of the local prince or of Clusium's governor; it comprised four wings round a colonnaded central court a hundred and eighty feet square, and dates from *c* 650 and *c* 575 BC, when rebuilding took place after a fire. To this second stage of the palace belong a remarkable group of nearly life-size male and female statues that stood on the apex and acroteria (lateral terminations) of its pediment; more than a dozen of these figures, wearing broad-brimmed hats, have come to light. Friezes have also been discovered, showing banqueting scenes, horse races, and the figure of the local chief, holding a curved horn and accompanied by his wife (seated on a throne): both are attended by slaves. Murlo abruptly ceased to exist *c* 530. Like another town, Ferentium (Ferento, Acquarossa), it may well have been destroyed by the aggressive rising power of Clusium, jealous of the autonomy of its offshoot.

Mursa Major (Osijek). A town in Lower Pannonia on the right bank of the river Dravus (Drave), near its junction with the Danube, at the crossing of two important strategic routes. Brought into existence by Hadrian (*c* AD 133), on or near a legionary fortress site, the settlement was probably a Roman colony.

It was the scene of two important military engagements. About 260, Ingenuus, with help of the legions of Moesia (*qv*), rose against Gallienus in Pannonia, probably after learning that the emperor's father had been captured by the Persians; but Gallienus and his cavalry commander Aureolus crushed him at Mursa Major. Then, during the following century, after the usurper Vetranio had proclaimed himself emperor at the same city (at this time part of the province of Pannonia Secunda), another pretender to the purple, Magnentius, confronted the emperor Constantius II as the latter moved against him from the east (351). Magnentius, marching from Aquileia, established himself at Mursa Major in the rear of Constantius' army, thus forcing him to give battle; but after a long struggle Magnentius' right wing was routed by the imperial heavy cavalry, and he suffered a total defeat—the first reverse, it is believed, that armored horsemen had ever inflicted on legionaries. Magnentius reportedly lost 24,000 men and the victorious Constantius 30,000; it was the bloodiest battle of the century, and severely weakened the empire's military strength.

During the conflict, the bishop of Mursa Major, Valens, an enthusiastic follower of the Arian interpretation of Christianity (regarding the Son as subordinate to the Father) which was favored by Constantius II, predicted the outcome of the battle and was rewarded by domination of the next Church Council. Subsequently, however, the town was overrun by the Visigoths (380) and then, in the middle of the fifth century, sacked by the Huns (followed later by the Avars and Slavs).

The appearance of Mursa Major can be partly reconstructed from seventeenth-century prints and sketches. The place contained a number of important buildings, and a series of terracotta and bronze workshops; an inscription refers to a street lined by fifty shops and fronted by double colonnades. Cults of Jupiter, Hercules, Silvanus, Mercury, Cybele, Osiris, Isis, Danuvius and Dravus are recorded. Outside the walls there was a stadium and a chapel of the Christian martyrs, alluded to by Zosimus and Sulpicius Severus respectively. There is also a reference to a synagogue. The riverbed still contains fragments of stone that belonged to an ancient bridge.

Murtana *see* Perga

Mussawarat Es-Sufra *see* Aethiopia

Mutina (Modena). A city of Cisalpine Gaul (north Italy), south of the river Padus (Po). Situated twenty-three miles northwest of the Etruscans' northern capital Felsina (Bononia, Bologna), Mutina too had an Etruscan name, and finds of Etruscan objects occur in its neighborhood. Subsequently the place passed into the hands of the Gallic tribe of the Boii, and then came under Roman control in 218 BC.

Deriving importance from its position on the Via Aemilia (187) leading from Ariminum (Rimini) to Placentia (Piacenza) (after which the district Emilia-Romagna is still named), Mutina became a Roman citizen colony in 183, but was sacked by the Ligurians in 177. Thereafter, however, it was immediately restored, and prospered from its wine, wool, and fruit. In 78 Marcus Junius Brutus (father of Caesar's assassin), who supported the revolutionary Marcus Aemilius Lepidus (father of the triumvir), was driven into Mutina by government forces under the young Pompey (later the Great) and after a considerable siege, surrendered on terms: whereupon Pompey had him murdered. It was also at Mutina, in 72, that Spartacus, the leader of the slave revolt, routed an army led by Gaius Cassius, governor of Cisalpine Gaul.

But the city's most famous moment came in 43, after the assassination of Caesar, when the twenty-year-old Octavian (the future Augustus) began to emerge as a rival to Antony, and gained the support of the senate. While Antony was besieging Decimus Junius Brutus (who had been appointed governor of Cisalpine Gaul) at Mutina, the two consuls and Octavian defeated him in two battles at Forum Gallorum (Castelfranco) between Mutina and Bononia, and he fled with difficulty across the Alps. But the battle was chiefly historic because both consuls were killed, so that Octavian was left in sole control of the armies of the Republic.

A local ceramics industry is recorded by Pliny the Elder, and funeral monuments attest continuing prosperity. In AD 377 Frigeridus, general of the emperor Gratian, selected Mutina as one of the places of exile where the survivors of the defeated German tribe of the Taifali—notorious, according to Ammianus Marcellinus, for pederasty—were sent to settle and work in the fields. The site of an ancient amphitheater has been located beneath the Chamber of Commerce.

Muziris *see* India

Mycale, Mykale, Mount (Samsun Dağı). A mountain range, reaching a height of 4040 feet, in southwestern Ionia (western Asia Minor), with its extremity at Cape Trogilion, opposite the island of Samos. On an acropolis beside its northern slopes, overlooking the narrow strait, stood the township of Melia or Melie (Kaletepe or Çanlı), a Carian settlement which was destroyed—probably by its neighbors—*c* 700 BC and replaced by a hilltop shrine of Heliconian Poseidon (at Otomatiktepe), which became the federal sanctuary and festival center of the twelve leading Ionian cities and was renamed the Panionion, under the control of the rulers of Priene (Turunçlar) in whose territory it lay. Important political decisions were taken there in 546 and 497, but after the collapse of the Ionian Revolt in 494 the festival was transferred to Ephesus.

The waters of Mycale were the scene of the final engagement of the Persian Wars (479), fought on the same day (tradition alleged) as the land battle of Plataea. Apart from an abortive intervention during the Ionian Revolt, this was the first time that the mainland Greeks had launched a direct attack on Persian territory. The commander of the Greek fleet of 45,000 sailors and 5,000 heavy-armed marines was the Spartan king Leotychidas, who sailed from Samos to Mycale, effected a landing, and broke into the stockaded camp of the Persians and their allies on the south side of the promontory. The enemy lost 40,000 dead, and the people of Miletus butchered the fleeing survivors. This decisive victory liberated Ionia and gave the Greeks supremacy throughout the Aegean.

Toward the end of the Peloponnesian War (431–404), Persian rule was reestablished. But when it came to an end in the middle of the following century (and Priene was rebuilt at the foot of Mount Mycale), the Panionion was reconstructed; remains of its sixty-foot altar have come to light and a Bouleuterion (Council Chamber) has been traced on the slope. The Panionian festival, too, was restored to its original location, but in imperial times was transferred (together with the federal cult of the emperors) to the principal Ionian cities.

Mycenae, Mykenai. A town situated on foothills in the northeast corner of the Argive plain (in the Argolid, northeastern Peloponnese), at a point dominating road communications. The foundation of Mycenae was attributed to the mythical hero Perseus; a water cistern, deep in the rock, was known as his spring, and he was venerated at a shrine outside the city on the way to Argos. After attaining supreme importance as the principal center of Late Bronze Age civilization in Greece during the later second millennium BC—displayed by spectacular and famous architectural remains—Mycenae lost its position to Argos and became insignificant.

Eighty Mycenaeans fought against the Persians at Thermopylae (480) and another contingent at Plataea (479), but in about 468 their acropolis was destroyed by the Argives, who revived the town, however, during the third century, repairing its walls and extending them to enclose a habitation center at a lower level. However, Mycenae subsequently resumed its process of decay, and by the time of Strabo, nothing was to be seen of the place; Pausanias, too, in the second century AD, refers to its state of ruin, though finds of tombs and lamps indicate sparse continued occupation, probably by a few shepherds.

On the acropolis, parts of a seventh-century temple wall, and of sixth-century fortifications, and the foundations of another sanctuary dating from the Argive reconstruction—and dedicated either to Athena or Hera—have survived. In the lower town there are traces of a Hellenistic theater (cut into a Bronze Age grave, the 'Tomb of Clytemnestra'); and houses, baths, cisterns, and a number of inscriptions have also been uncovered.

Mylae, Mylai (Milazzo). A city of northeastern Sicily, at the isthmus of a narrow peninsula extending four miles northward into the sea (terminating in the Capo di Milazzo). Bronze and Iron Age tombs have been uncovered, as well as traces of an early habitation center. According to Greek mythology, the oxen and flocks of the sun-god Helios, described by the *Odyssey,* grazed in the fields of Mylae, of which the fertility was praised by Theophrastus.

The place was colonized *c* 717/16 BC by Zancle (Messana, Messina) and remained one of its dependencies and strongholds. In 426, during the Peloponnesian War, the Athenian commander Laches occupied the place before launching an attack on Messana. In 403 Rhegium (Reggio di Calabria) made an abortive attempt to settle Mylac with refugees from Naxos and Catana (Catania), destroyed by Dionysius I of Syracuse. In 315 it was captured by one of his successors, Agathocles.

The waters off Mylae were the scene of two important naval battles. In the first, during the First Punic War (260), the consul Gaius Duilius grappled the ships of the Carthaginian fleet with iron *corvi* (crows), destroying or capturing some fifty vessels, more than one-third of the whole flotilla. Remarkably enough, this was Rome's first venture on the sea—and a successful one at that, against experienced seafarers. Duilius erected a column in the Roman forum, adorned with the bronze rams of the ships he had captured.

Then in 36 another sea battle off Mylae played a significant role in the civil war between Octavian (the future Augustus) and Sextus Pompeius (son of Pompey the Great), who had seized control of Sicily. For it was beside this coast that Octavian's admiral Agrippa defeated Sextus' officer Demochares, destroying thirty of his ships. Sextus came to Demochares' aid, leaving the Straits of Messana open, and thus enabling Octavian to land three legions on the island. This was not the end of the war, but now that his troops were on Sicilian soil, the conclusion of the campaign was only a matter of a few weeks (*see* Naulochus).

In contrast to the extensive prehistoric remains, traces of the Greco-Roman city are sparse, though a Hellenistic cemetery and Roman mosaic have come to light.

Mylasa (Milas). A city in Caria (southwestern Asia Minor) near the river Cybersus, eight miles from the Aegean coast. Under Persian domination, a town of that name, located at Peçin Kalesi (a hill above the village of Peçin), was the principal non-Greek community of Caria; it was ruled by local dynasts except for a brief interruption during the Ionian Revolt (499–494 BC) which the Mylasans supported. The city was a member of the Delian League led by Athens *c* 450/449, but during the rebellion of Samos against Athens (441–439) Persian control was probably resumed.

In 390 the satrap Hecatomnus established the capital of the new Persian province of Caria at a new settlement of Mylasa, four miles north of Peçin, or this may have been the work of his son Mausolus. Subsequently, *c* 360, Mausolus moved his residence to Halicarnassus (Bodrum). However, Mylasa remained his religious capital, and gave him an additional port at Passala (Küllük). Later, in or after the time of Alexander the Great, a certain Eupolemus issued coins at the city in his own name; during the third century, however, the place belonged successively to the Ptolemies and the Seleucids. After the defeat of the Seleucid monarch Antiochus IV Epiphanes by the Romans (189), Mylasa was exempted from tribute—and spared subordination to the Rhodians, which was the fate of the rest of Caria. Not long afterward it formed a union (*sympoliteia*) with certain of its smaller neighbors.

When a Roman renegade, Quintus Labienus, overran Caria with a Parthian army in 40 BC, the rhetorician Hybreas persuaded his Mylasan people to resist, whereupon the city suffered severely at Labienus' hands. It recovered, however, with the help of Octavian (the future Augustus)—who reaffirmed its freedom in 31—and resumed the issue of coins, which continued until Gordian III (AD 238–44). These pieces depict the famous sanctuary of Zeus Osogos or Osogoas, also known as Zenoposeidon, a combination of Zeus and Poseidon; his emblems were an eagle, crab and trident. Part of the wall of his precinct is still standing, to the southwest of the city. A further important shrine was dedicated to Zeus Stratios or Labraundus (Labrandenus). This, too, was away from the city, in the eastern hills of Labraunda; it is one of the best-preserved sites in Asia Minor (even windows survive). Herodotus and Strabo also mention a temple of Zeus Karios, with which traces at Peçin Kalesi can be identified. A high podium (and one column) still to be seen within Mylasa itself may belong to another temple of the same deity; and another sanctuary on Hisarbaşı hill, reconstructed after Labienus' sack and dedicated to Augustus and Rome, was noted by a visitor in 1675 and has likewise left scanty remains. In addition, there was a holy place of a native divinity Sinuri eight miles southeast of the city. Secular monuments include an arched gateway, now known as Baltalı Kapı, Gate of the Axe, because it is adorned with a relief of the double axe which was the emblem of Mylasan Zeus. Standing at the beginning of a Sacred Way to the Labraunda shrine, the gate was subsequently utilized to support an aqueduct. Elaborate Hellenistic and Roman graves in the neighborhood include a tomb of the second century AD which is modelled on the Mausoleum at Halicarnassus, thus suggesting what that building looked like.

Myra (Kale, formerly Demre or Dembre, derived from *ta myra*). A city near the coast of Lycia (southern Asia Minor), situated above the west bank of the river Myrus (Demre Çayı), which lay in a fertile plain. Its harbor was at Andriace (Kocademre), three miles away. Monuments and inscriptions, including a number in the Lycian language, show that Myra was one of the most important cities of the region from at least the fifth century BC.

In 197 the Seleucid Antiochus IV Epiphanes captured Andriace. After the formation of a Lycian League under Roman auspices (168), Myra became one of its six leading communities and the capital of the district of Mount Massicytes, of which the name appears on the city's coins. In 42 Publius Cornelius Lentulus Spinther, raising funds for the cause of Brutus and Cassius against the Second Triumvirate of Antony, Octavian (the future Augustus) and Lepidus, broke the chain that closed Andriace harbor, and seized Myra's treasures of gold and silver. The city subsequently hailed Augustus (31 BC–AD 14) and Tiberius (AD 14–37) as 'Benefactors and Saviors of the entire Universe.' In AD 60 St. Paul changed ships at its port on his way to Rome. During the second century Myra enjoyed the privileged status of one of the five 'Metropoleis of the Lycian Nation,' and was the recipient of lavish monetary gifts. Its coinage, virtually limited to the reign of Gordian III (238–44), bears the head of the city-goddess Artemis Eleuthera and depicts the archaic image of that deity in her famous local temple, accompanied by a figure of winged Nike (Victory).

Early in the fourth century the Christian bishop of Myra was St. Nicolaus (Nicholas) Orphanos (or of Orphanos) from Patara (Kelemiş), renowned for miraculously saving the lives of travelers and shipwrecked sailors, and for bringing the dead back to life. He was also the protector of prisoners, and gained special fame as the children's patron, Santa Claus: deriving the name of the city from *myrrha* (myrrh), the Byzantine emperor Constantine VII Porphyrogenitus (945–59) wrote of the 'thrice-blessed, myrrh-breathing city of the Lycians, where the mighty Nicolaus, servant of God, spouts forth myrrh.' Theodosius II (408–50) made Myra the capital of an independent province of Lycia.

An acropolis hill rises steeply behind the city, most of which lies buried deep beneath rubble, mud and water at the foot of the cliff. But a Roman theater to its south is well-preserved and has been recently cleared. Of outstanding importance, however, are two groups of nearly a hundred rock tombs dating from the fourth century BC, cut out of the southern and western faces of the cliff. Inscribed, in some cases, in Lycian or Greek, they copy temples and timber-built private houses with curiously detailed realism, and in many cases are adorned with life-size figured reliefs which, according to earlier travelers, were originally covered with vivid paint.

Buildings near the harbor of Andriace include a granary of Hadrian (AD 117–38) of which the front wall contains his bust (together with a head of Antoninus Pius' wife, Faustina the Elder), a relief showing the gods Pluto and Serapis, and an inscription enumerating standard weights and measures.

Mysia. A district (or two districts, Greater and Lesser Mysia) of fluctuating dimensions at the northwestern extremity of Asia Minor, bounded by Lydia to the south, Phrygia to the east, the Troad (sometimes regarded as a Mysian region) to the west, and the Propontis (Sea of Marmara) to the north. Mysia was a country in which mountains, marshes and forests adjoined maritime areas of great fertility; gold, silver and lead were available in abundance, and were said to have been the basis of the riches of Troy. The Mysians, who appear as Trojan allies in the *Iliad,* were said by Strabo to have originated from Thrace (where people bearing that name were still to be found in historical times) and to speak a language that was a mixture of Lydian and Phrygian, an assertion that inscriptional evidence has not been able to confirm.

Greek cities studded the coast, and extended inland. But Mysia came under the control of King Croesus of Lydia (*c* 560–546 BC), and after his downfall belonged to the Persians, until the destruction of their empire by Alexander the Great. The territory subsequently became part of the Seleucid dominions, until the defeat of Antiochus IV Epiphanes at the hands of the Romans (190–188), who transferred it to the kingdom of Pergamum. Mercenary soldiers from the country were in great demand during the Hellenistic period, notably the Mysomacedones who appear to have been a mixed group of Mysian and Macedonians settled there by a Pergamene king.

After the abdication of the last of these monarchs (133), Mysia became part of the Roman province of Asia, and in the later empire became the nucleus of the province of Hellespontus. *See also* Assus, Atarneus, Caicus, Cyzicus, Granicus, Hellespont, Ida, Parium, Pergamum, Troy.

Mytilene, or Mitylene. A Greek city and port in the southeast of the island of Lesbos (*qv*), of which it was the principal city-state. Originally located on another, much smaller island or islet (now joined to Lesbos), Mytilene later expanded onto the territory of the main island. The settlement possessed a fine double harbor, facing toward Asia Minor, and even before 700 it controlled Aeolian cities on the mainland. It was the hometown of Alcaeus (born *c* 620) and perhaps also of Sappho; a local autocrat (tyrant) Melanchros was overthrown by the brothers of Alcaeus, who himself, as a young man, opposed the next rulers Myrsilus and Pittacus (one of the Seven Wise Men), although he had fought under Pittacus' command in a war against the Athenians, contesting the possession of Sigeum (Yenişehir) at the entrance of the Propontis (Dardanelles) (*c* 600).

A period under Persian control was terminated by the battle of Mycale (479), after which Mytilene—by now issuing an extensive coinage of electrum (pale gold)—joined the Delian Confederacy under the leadership of Athens, in the privileged position of an ally contributing ships to the League; and at this time Mytilene controlled almost the whole island of Lesbos, except Methymna. The city's unsuccessful attempt to detach itself from what had now become the Athenian empire in 428/7, during the early years of the Peloponnesian War, provided an opportunity for one of Thucydides' most trenchant analyses. The occasion was a debate in the Assembly at Athens in which the leading Athenian politician Cleon argued for the ruthless annihilation of Mytilene on grounds of imperialistic self-interest. A political opponent named Diodotus prevailed against him with somewhat milder counsels. Yet even these were harsh enough, since they severely penalized the ringleaders, while 2,700 Athenian colonists were brought in to occupy the land of the defeated subject-ally, employing its own citizens as tenant serfs; its fleet, too, was confiscated, the town's fortifications were dismantled, and its possessions on the mainland (Peraea) detached, with disastrous financial results for Mytilene.

It rebelled again, briefly, in 412—once more incurring dire punishment—but then remained a strong point for the Athenians until their final defeat at Aegospotami (405). Thereafter, with interruptions, Spartan and Athenian domination twice alternated, until the Persians established control in 357. After further vicissitudes, however, they were expelled by Alexander the Great (322), who declared the newly liberated Mytilene a free and independent ally, and enlarged its territory. Meanwhile Aristotle had taught for a short time at the city (344/3).

In Hellenistic times, although retaining autonomous institutions, it successively came under the suzerainty of Antigonus I Monophthalmos, Lysimachus, the Ptolemies and the Seleucid monarch Antiochus III the Great. During Antiochus' war with the Romans (190) it supported their cause (subsequently forming a League with three other Lesbian cities), but when Mithridates VI of Pontus fought against Rome, it took his side (owing to excessive taxation), and was destroyed after a siege (80–79). However, the historian Theophanes of Mytilene, who was one of Pompey the Great's chief advisers, persuaded him to restore the city's freedom (within the province of Asia), which was confirmed by Augustus (31 BC–AD 14), suspended by Vespasian (AD 69–79), and restored by Hadrian (117–38). In these imperial times, Mytilene became a favorite holiday resort. Its local coinage, which continued until the time of Gallienus (253–68), depicted an interesting series of local notables, heroes and benefactors, including Pittacus, Alcaeus, Sappho, the deified Theophanes and a philosopher of the Augustan epoch named Lesbonax, as well as his son who was described as a new Dionysus. In the later empire, Mytilene belonged to the province of Insulae (the Islands).

A recently completed architectural survey of its acropolis has revealed the remains of walls and traces of at least eighteen identifiable buildings. The almost completely circular shape of the theater, now excavated, shows it to be one of the oldest in Greek lands; Pompey the Great was said to have imitated its plan when he built the first stone theater at the capital. The area beside the Mytilenean theater has yielded discoveries of mosaic pavements of the third century BC, which depict scenes from the plays of the Athenian New Comedy dramatist Menander. The outskirts of the city display remains of the Roman aqueduct that brought water from a lake (now drained).

N

Nabataea. A kingdom in northwestern Arabia, bordering on Syria, Judaea and Egypt. The Nabataeans derived wealth from their position on trade routes linking Egypt, the Red Sea and southern Arabia; and their monopoly of the caravan trade linking the interior of Arabia to the Mediterranean coast proved particularly lucrative. Their principal divinities were Dusares, a vegetation god, and Allat, a warrior goddess. The inscriptions of Nabataeans are Aramaic in language and script, though most of the population probably spoke a dialect related to Arabic.

In 312 BC Antigonus I Monophthalmos tried unsuccessfully to seize their capital, Rekem (Petra). An expedition sent by Ptolemy II Philadelphus (285–246) occupied the Nabataean port Aelana (Elath) on the Gulf of Akaba, but peaceful relations developed between the two states subsequently. In the third and second centuries the Nabataeans extended their frontiers to the north and east at the expense of the weakening Seleucids, in addition to expanding down the east coast of the Red Sea; investigations have revealed hundreds of settlements extending over a huge area. Early in the first century they occupied the Hauran (Auranitis) east of the Jordan, and temporarily held Damascus, but Pompey the Great's reorganization of the east made them clients of Rome.

The relations of the Nabataeans, however, with another Roman client, Herod the Great of Judaea (37–4 BC), were very uneasy; Antony sent him to attack their king Malchus I (31–30), but after Malchus' death, Herod found Syllaeus, the clever and forceful chief minister of Obodas III (30–9), difficult to deal with. Finally Herod marched into Nabataean territory and opened hostilities, incurring the anger of his patron Augustus; and shortly afterward the Nabataeans enraged him too, when an enemy of Syllaeus, Aretas IV (9 BC–AD 39), seized the throne without seeking his permission. During the first century AD the Nabataeans became increasingly settled, prospering from agriculture.

In 106 Trajan forcibly abolished their kingdom (106), transforming it into the Roman province of Arabia (*c* 11), with its capital at Bostra (Busra Eski-Sham). In the later empire this province was subdivided into Arabia and Palaestina Tertia (Salutaris). *See also* Arabia, Bostra, Oboda, Petra.

Nahr El-Asi (River) *see* Orontes

Naissus (Niš). A city in Moesia (Serbia, Yugoslavia) on the river Nišava, nine miles from its junction with the Margus (Morava), a southern tributary of the Danube. The name of the place was Thracian, and its pre-Roman inhabitants belonged to the Thracian tribe of the Dardanians. First occupied by Roman troops in 75–72 BC, Naissus later became part of the province of Moesia and then the capital of Upper Moesia (*c* AD 85/6), deriving strategic importance from its position as a center where five roads met. It became a *municipium* under Marcus Aurelius (161–80) or later, and was the scene of a decisive Roman victory over the Goths in the last year of the reign of Gallienus (268); although later historians claimed that the victor was instead his successor Claudius II Gothicus, because they wanted to do Claudius honor as the alleged ancestor of Constantine I the Great.

Constantine was born at Naissus (*c* 285), which subsequently became part of the province of Dardania (and then of Dacia Mediterranea); he frequently returned to the city during his reign (306–37), enriching it (according to the Anonymus Valesianus) with splendid buildings and adding an additional palace quarter (Mediana) three miles outside the walls. The city also became an episcopal see.

Constantine's sons stayed in Naissus, and as Julian (the Apostate) prepared to attack one of them, Constantius II, in 361, it was there that he established his headquarters. In 365 Valentinian I and Valens met at the Mediana palace to share out their generals between the western and eastern empires. Constantius III, joint emperor of the west in 421, was born at Naissus. During this later imperial epoch it contained important arms factories. In 441 it was destroyed by the Huns, but later partially restored.

Portions of the imperial residence at Mediana, with mosaic floors, are now excavated, and in another suburb (Jagodin Mahala), four early Christian churches have been uncovered. A bathing establishment and part of the city wall can also be seen.

Namurtköy *see* Cyme

Naousa *see* Mieza

Napata *see* Aethiopia

Napoca (Cluj, Klausenburg, Kolosvar). A settlement in Dacia (Rumania), which was incorporated in Trajan's conquered province of that name (105), and under Hadrian (117–38) became capital of the province of Upper Dacia and later of Dacia Porolissensis, with the rank first of *municipium* and then of Roman colony (under Commodus, 180–92). Surrounded by fertile agricultural territory and situated on Dacia's main north-south road, Napoca prospered as a commercial and industrial center until the abandonment of the province by Aurelian (271). Thereafter, Roman coins still continued to arrive as late as the reign of Theodosius II (408–50).

The city walls, reflecting the rectangular shape of the original camp, enclosed an area of eighty acres. Roman remains have been found under St. Michael's church, in the large square known as the Piaţa Libertatii, which was probably the ancient forum. Inscriptions bearing dedications to the gods indicate the presence of Thracian, Illyrian, Celtic, Syrian, Carian and Galatian cults and communities.

Naqa *see* Aethiopia

Narbo (Narbonne). A city in southern Gaul (France), twelve miles from the Mediterranean coast, near the outlet of the river Atax (Aude) into Lake Rubresus, a sea lagoon, which provided the place with one of its harbors. The name of Narbo, recorded by Hecataeus (*c* 500 BC), originally denoted the hill fort of Montlaurès (three miles northwest of the later city), which was the capital of the tribe of the Elisycii and became the center of a Celto-Iberian kingdom, issuing coins inscribed NERONC (Avienus called the place Naro). In the third century the town was annexed and destroyed by the tribe of the Volcae Tectosages, but was subsequently rebuilt, serving them as a harbor, and trading in tin from south Britain.

In 118, according to Velleius Paterculus (although some favor a date a few years later), the Romans—despite reluctance among their senators to embark on such a foundation outside Italy—established the colony of Narbo Martius in the plain beneath the hill fort, after annexing the strip of southern Gaul of which it became the capital, so that the province was now known as Gallia Narbonensis. The colony, which issued a short-lived but varied series of Roman *denarii,* stood on the Via Domitia (121) which ran from the river Rhodanus (Rhône) to Spain, forming the main street of the town.

About 69, Cicero spoke of Narbo as a 'watchtower and bulwark' of the Roman people, with reference to its role as a defence against the still unconquered Gallic tribes in the hinterland. After Julius Caesar had reduced these tribes to subjection, he settled veterans of the Tenth Legion in the city (45), which was renamed Colonia Julia Paterna Narbo Martius Decumanorum; it constituted the eastern terminal of a cross-country route to Tolosa (Toulouse) and Burdigala (Bordeaux). In 27 Augustus presided at Narbo over a general assembly drawn from the whole of Gaul. Claudius enlarged the colony, which took his name. It possessed a number of commercial corporations and exported large quantities of pottery from Condatomagus (La Graufesenque). Damage by fire in AD 145, which contributed to the transfer of the provincial capital to Nemausus (Nîmes), started a slow process of decline accentuated by the city's remoteness from the main Rhône-Rhine channel of communications. Nevertheless, in the fourth and fifth centuries Ausonius and Sidonius Apollinaris described Narbo as still flourishing. The Visigoths entered the city in 413 and their king Ataulf married the imperial princess Galla Placidia there in the following year, but they were expelled soon afterward and allotted territories further to the west. In 462, however, their descendants took the city again, thanks to the treachery of the imperial governor Agrippinus.

The main topographical outline of ancient Narbo can be reconstructed by studying the plan of the medieval town. Its very large Capitol, raised high on a lofty podium, was surrounded by a colonnaded precinct, of which one side adjoined the colonnade of the forum. Also bordering on the forum was a large underground grain silo, constructed in the time of Augustus; it contained a hundred and twenty-six rooms, opening on to vaulted corridors. Another group of buildings, on the outskirts of the city, included an amphitheater (one-third of the size of the Colosseum) and public baths dating from about the time of Vespasian (AD 69–79), in whose reign a priest of the province's imperial cult is mentioned on an inscription. A residential district lying between this complex and the principal urban center was burned down and abandoned in the third century, after which new walls were built enclosing a diminished perimeter. A Christian basilica of the age of Constantine I the Great (306–37) was destroyed by invasions, but replaced by a new building in 442/5.

Narnia (Narni). A city in Umbria (central Italy) situated high above the gorge of the river Nar (Nera), beyond which the Sabine country began. Indeed, Narnia itself, before belonging to Rome, was a Sabine town, called Nequinum. In 299 BC it was captured by the consul Marcus Fulvius Paetinus and made into a Latin colony with the new name of Narnia (after the river) since the former designation Nequinum seemed too close to *nequam* ('worthless').

Located in a position strengthening the northern defences of the Roman homeland, Narnia gained greatly in importance in 220 when it became a station on the Via Flaminia from Rome to Ariminum (Rimini). Shortly afterward, however, during the Second Punic War, it was one of the twelve Latin colonies that claimed in 209 that they could fight for the Roman cause no longer, owing to their exhausted condition. After the war, in 199, Narnia received a thousand new colonists.

The emperor Nerva (AD 96–98) was born in the city *c* 30, and it had a moment of historical importance during the Civil Wars of 69 when Vitellius planned to utilize this powerful site in order to make a stand against the invading force of Vespasian's general Marcus Antonius Primus. Losing confidence, however, Vitellius returned to Rome. When he did so, he left behind a strong force of praetorian troops and cavalry at Narnia; but they surrendered to his enemies shortly afterward.

The topography of the ancient city is little known, since modern buildings have overlaid it, but there are traces of the difficult engineering work that was needed to bring the Via Flaminia through this point. It was carried across the Nar by one of the most remarkable of Roman bridges—the hundred-and-fifty-foot high Ponte di Augusto—which spanned a distance of nearly five hundred feet. The first of its four arches still survives; the second, a hundred feet wide, was one of the largest of any Roman bridge. The Nar was navigable in ancient times, and Virgil refers to the whitish turbidity of its waters, due to its content of sulphur and lime.

Nassica *see* Calagurris

Naucratis, Naukratis (in Egyptian Piemro, now Kom Gieif). A Greek city in Egypt, on the Canopic (western) branch of the river Nile (about forty miles southeast of the later Alexandria). The Egyptian Saite pharaoh Psammetichus (Psamtik) I (664-610 BC)—while settling Greek mercenaries at Daphne (Defenneh), on the eastern branch of the Nile—apparently allowed traders from Miletus to establish a market at Naucratis, which developed under Amasis (Ahmose, 570-526) into a major treaty port and commercial link with the west.

Various other Greek states also received concessions from the Egyptian monarch at Naucratis. The most important of these zones, the Hellenium, was held jointly by Chios, Clazomenae, Teos and Phocaea (Ionian), Rhodes, Halicarnassus, Cnidus and Phaselis (Dorian), and Mytilene (Aeolian). Aegina, Samos and Miletus possessed separate sanctuaries and probably concessions of their own. This was said by Herodotus to be the only port in Egypt to which Greek merchants were allowed to sail and in which they could live (although archaeological discoveries elsewhere now render this doubtful). They brought with them wine, oil and silver; and grain, papyrus and linen were among the wares that they took back. Some of the traders stayed on to become permanent residents, but it may have been a long time before the Egyptians granted them a civic organization. After the Persian invasion (525), the place continued to prosper although on a lesser scale.

When Alexander the Great conquered Egypt (332), he appointed Cleomenes, a former resident of Naucratis, as governor of the whole country. But Cleomenes was swept away by Ptolemy I Soter, under whom, moreover, the city was eclipsed by recently founded Alexandria as the principal Egyptian marketplace. Nevertheless, Naucratis continued to possess territory of its own and to function as an important trading station; it was the chief port of call on the inland voyage from Memphis to Alexandria to the frontier-post of Pelusium. During the earliest Ptolemaic epoch, for a short time, it issued its own local coinage, an exceptional phenomenon in Egypt.

Inscriptions show that buildings were erected under the first two Ptolemies. One of Ptolemy II's foundations was an Egyptian (not Greek) temple, reflecting a native element in the city—which remained separate, since Greek citizens were not permitted to marry Egyptian women. The 'Damanhur Stele,' an inscription of Ptolemy V Epiphanes (205-180) reproducing the hieroglyphic text of the Rosetta Stone, was found at Naucratis; and he himself went to the place to inspect a party of mercenary soldiers brought there by his eunuch-minister Aristonicus.

Under Roman rule, the city steadily declined, but was allowed to retain its own Greek constitution (which served as the model for Hadrian's foundation of Antinoopolis). Naucratis had formerly belonged to the Saite nome (district) but was now the capital of a nome bearing its own name. The site is now covered by lush vegetation.

Naulochus, Naulochoi. An anchorage or small harbor in northeastern Sicily, east of Mylae (Milazzo)—perhaps in the region of Venetico Marina. It was in these waters in 36 BC that the fleet of Octavian (the future Augustus), led by his admiral Agrippa, won the decisive naval battle in the Civil War against Sextus Pompeius, the son of Pompey the Great. Both sides were reported by Appian to have mustered three hundred ships (though Sextus at least is unlikely to have possessed such a large number), while the troops of the two armies watched from the shore. Thanks, for the most part, to Agrippa's invention of the *harpax* (grapnel shot from a catapult), Sextus was crushingly defeated. Twenty-eight of his ships were sunk, most of the rest ran aground or were captured or burned. Only seventeen escaped to Messana. From there he fled to Asia Minor, where he was put to death in the following year at Miletus in Ionia.

Naulochus, Naulochon *see* Priene

Naupactus, Naupaktos (Nafpaktos, Lepanto). A Greek port, and the most important town of Western (Ozolian) Locris, on the north coast of the Gulf of Corinth, of which it commands the narrow entrance. Naupactus possessed an acropolis and a good harbor adjacent to a small coastal plain of Hylaethus (Mornos), cut off from the hinterland by Mount Rigani. According to a legend, perhaps derived from the city's name (meaning 'ship construction'), its harbor had been the shipyard and starting point of the invading Dorians when they originally crossed over to the Peloponnese. The most eminent native of the place, although only dimly known, was Carcinus, probably author of the *Naupactia,* a catalog of famous women.

Naupactus was colonized by settlers from Opus in Eastern (Opuntian) Locris and from Chaleum in Western (Ozolian) Locris. The decree regulating its foundation has been preserved in an inscription, tentatively dated to *c* 500/475, which confirms that from the outset the new settlement was a separate city-state, although interchanges of population with the mother communities were envisaged. In 456 the Athenians settled Messenian refugees at Naupactus, and employed it as their principal western naval base during the Peloponnesian War, sending Phormio in 430 to hamper Corinthian trade and confront the enemy fleet, which he routed in the following year. Sparta subsequently expelled the Athenians and Messenians from Naupactus, but after the eclipse of Spartan power it passed briefly into the hands of the Achaeans across the gulf (367). Philip II of Macedonia, however, captured the port, and gave it to the Aetolian League (338), which it served as an important center during the third and second centuries; a peace congress was held there in 217. In 191 the city may have been besieged by the Romans. In 14 Augustus presented it to his newly founded colony of Patrae (Patras) in Achaea.

Parts of the walls of Naupactus are to be seen incorporated in the later Venetian fortifications. Thucydides mentions a temple of Apollo, and Pausanias, in the second century AD, saw a sanctuary of Poseidon (on the sea), another dedicated to Artemis Aetole, a ruined shrine of Asclepius, and a grotto of Aphrodite. There is also inscriptional evidence for the worship of Dionysus and Serapis. Recent excavations have uncovered part of a very large, apparently five-aisled, early Christian basilica, probably destroyed by an earthquake in 551. In later times the Venetians knew the place as Lepanto, but the famous naval battle against the Turks that goes by that name (1571) was fought farther to the west, at the entrance to the Gulf of Patrae.

Navarino *see* Pylos

Naxos. The largest and most fertile island of the Cyclades group in the Aegean, south of Delos and east of Paros. During the third and second millennia BC it was densely populated and became a highly productive center of 'Cycladic' statuary, made of white marble and smoothed by emery, both of which materials were available on the island. According to tradition, its early inhabitants were Carians, Thracians, and Cretans. In the later Bronze Age Naxos figured prominently in the Mycenaean civilization; and it was the location of many Greek myths. Bearing the alternative or additional name of Dionysia (also Dia), it was one of the rival claimants to the birthplace of the god Dionysus, who was also believed to have found Ariadne on the island—after her abandonment by Theseus—and to have married her there. The twin giants Otus and Ephialtes were said to have died on Naxos, where they were honored by a cult.

It continued to have an active life in the early first millennium, and its artists played a leading part in the emergence of Greek sculpture and architecture. During the Lelantine War between Chalcis and Eretria, (*c* 700?), the mother island took the side of the Chalcidians, who had given its name to the earliest Greek colony in Sicily (*see* next entry). At the same period the continuous hostility of Aegean Naxos to Paros turned into open warfare. Naxos was ruled by an aristocratic government until squabbles about the absorption of the island's growing wealth caused it to be superseded by the autocrat ('tyrant') Lygdamis (*c* 540), who was overthrown *c* 524 by the Spartans. The coinage of Naxos in this period displays a wine cup and grapes, celebrating the famous wines of the island and their patron deity Dionysus. A democratic régime subsequently came into power and, according to Herodotus, the Naxians exercised control over a number of other islands.

In 499, however, its exiles persuaded the Persians (who were egged on by Aristagoras, the ruler of Miletus) to attack the island, which they failed, however, to capture either by surprise or by siege: instead precipitating the Ionian Revolt, after the failure of which the town of Naxos was burned by the Persians on their way to Marathon (490). When the Persian Wars were over, Naxos joined the Delian League sponsored by Athens, which subjugated a rebellion and installed colonists (470, 450). Regaining their independence after the Peloponnesian War, the Naxians again became subject to Athens in 376, and again revolted. In the third century their island became a member of an Islanders' Confederation; after the victory of Antony and Octavian (the future Augustus) over Brutus and Cassius (42), it was briefly placed under the control of Rhodes. During the Roman Principate Naxos was sometimes employed as a place of exile for disgraced notables. Local coinage was issued under Antoninus Pius (138-61) and Septimius Severus (193-211). In the later empire, Naxos was attached to the province of Insulae, the islands.

The ancient city stood on a hill overlooking the harbor; its acropolis was under the modern town, and a Hellenistic agora has been identified inland. Traces of several sanctuaries are to be seen, including a shrine on a hill above the harbor entrance (dating from Lygdamis' time and subsequently converted into a Christian basilica—which was also the destiny of another temple near the village of Sangri). Beside a quarry at the northern end of the island, in a sancturary dedicated to Apollo, stands a statue of the god, nearly thirty feet high, dating from the sixth century BC; in front of the precinct is a row of massive stone lions.

Naxos (Punta di Schisò, near Giardini Naxos). The earliest Greek colony in Sicily. It was situated on a low-lying lava peninsula north of Mount Actna (Etna), above a small bay that could be used as an anchorage, adjoining the mouth of a stream (Santa Venera). The small Alcantara river is less than a mile away; one or the other of these streams is the Assinos personified on the city's coinage (named as Acesines by Thucydides and Asines by Pliny the Elder).

Naxos was founded on a site of earlier Neolithic, Bronze Age and Sicel habitation by settlers from Chalcis in Euboea, under the leadership of a certain Theocles. The foundation, which was named after Chalcis' ally, the Aegean island of Naxos, took place in 734 BC according to Thucydides, whose date is confirmed by archaeological evidence. Theocles also established an altar of Apollo the Founder or Archegetes on which all Sicilian travelers to Greece offered sacrifice before their departure, so that the altar became the common religious center for the Greek cities on the island. Only five years later Theocles left to found a second colony at Leontini (Carlentini near Lentini), while his compatriot Euarchus simultaneously established a settlement at Catana (Catania). Subsequently a further colony was planted at Callipolis, at an unknown location in the interior. These activities were the major achievement of Sicilian Naxos, which otherwise remained undistinguished.

The town was seized by Hippocrates of Gela *c* 495/4 and its inhabitants deported by Hiero I to Leontini (and replaced by Dorians) in 476, but ten years later they returned. Their coins of the ensuing period, with heads of Dionysus and figures of Silenus, are of especially beautiful style. During the Peloponnesian War, Naxos supported the Athenian expeditions against Syracuse (427–424, 415–413), whose later monarch Dionysus I took revenge by destroying the city, dispersing its inhabitants, and handing the site over to native Sicels (403). The descendants of the deported Naxians founded Tauromenium (Taormina) on the hill above, but Naxos, too, continued to enjoy a limited existence, resuming coinage under the name of Ncopolis (unless this was the place where a further batch of emigrants settled, at Mylae [Milazzo]).

Naxos still displays accurately constructed early polygonal walls, which are rare in western Greek cities. Phases of urban development dating from the initial foundation and from the reconstruction of *c* 466 can be traced. Remains of a large sanctuary near the adjacent stream may perhaps be identifiable with a temple of Aphrodite mentioned by Appian. A trapezoidal enclosure contains the foundations of further shrines of *c* 600 and *c* 525. The altar of Apollo Archegetes is not yet located. A potter's quarter, including a complex of three kilns, has been explored; it produced distinctive wares reminiscent of Euboean and Cycladic models, especially during the early years of the city's existence.

Nea Paphos *see* Paphos

Neapolis (Napoli, Naples). A Greek city in Campania (southwestern Italy), on the northern section of the Gulf of Cumae or 'Crater' (Bay of Naples). To its west stretched the fertile area of the Phlegraean Fields (*see* Puteoli). According to legend, the earliest settlement had been known as Parthenope, after the siren of that name who had been washed ashore there after failing to lure Odysseus (Ulysses) to his death.

The city was founded from Cumae (Cuma) in 650 BC along what is now the port area, including the small island of Megaris (the Castel dell'Ovo) in the harbor (where there may have been an older Rhodian trading settlement). Further colonists came from Chalcis in Euboea, from Pithecusae (Ischia) beside the Gulf of Cumae, and from Athens. An extension of the city toward the northeast, constructed according to a rectangular grid plan, was given the name of Neapolis; it soon began to issue a famous long-lived coinage with the type of a man-headed bull. After the creation of Neapolis, the original foundation assumed the name of Palaeopolis or Palaepolis (Old City). About 327/6, the hostile attitude of the Palaeopolitans provoked the Roman general Quintus Publilius Philo to attack and capture their town, which thenceforward ceased to exist; whereas Neapolis, on the other hand, became a close ally of the Romans, issuing bronze coins inscribed (in Greek) with their name, and furnishing help in their hostilities against Pyrrhus or Epirus (280–275) and against Hannibal (the Second Punic War, 218–201).

In 82, however, during the Civil War between Sullans and Marians, the Neapolitans were treacherously massacred by Sulla's troops, and suffered the loss of their fleet. Nevertheless, the city recovered to become a prosperous *municipium,* exporting agricultural products, wine, chestnuts, quinces, rose oil, sulphur and coral. Lucius Licinius Lucullus possessed a magnificent house at Neapolis (in addition to his villa at Misenum, *qv*), which may well have stood on the island of Megaris (on which the Castel dell'Ovo was later built). The city also resumed its position as a renowned center of Greek culture, where Virgil studied under the Epicurean philosopher Siro, subsequently (before 41) inheriting his villa, in which he often resided, writing a large part of the *Georgics* in the house; his (unauthentic) tomb is still shown in the city. Games were founded in honor of the emperor Augustus at Neapolis, and celebrated every four years in the Greek fashion; in the last year of his life (AD 14) Augustus attended them. At first these festivals featured athletic and equestrian events. But then, perhaps in 18, musical competitions were added; and it was from here that Greek contests of various types spread to other parts of Italy.

Nero (54–68), who loved Hellenistic Neapolis, was particularly attracted by the Games; and it was here that he made his personal stage début (64), thus creating a precedent that must have alarmed many senators. It was also here that he received the visiting Armenian monarch Tiridates (66), and subsequently, after his successes in the Great Games of Greece, made a triumphant entry into the city in a chariot drawn by white horses, entering through a breach in the wall after the custom of Greek athletes. Returning to Neapolis yet again after a brief visit to Rome (68), he learned the news of the rebellion of Vindex in Gaul, which set off a chain of circumstances leading to his downfall—though for eight days thereafter he continued to make daily visits to the gymnasium.

Neapolis was the birthplace of Statius (45–96), and the frequent residence of his fellow poet Silius Italicus (d. *c* 101). The city was damaged by the eruption of Mount Vesuvius in AD 79, after which it seems to have received colonial rights from Titus; they were later confirmed by Septimius Severus (193–211) or Caracalla (211–17), by which time the Games had come to be described as the Italica Romaia Sebasta Isolympia. Valentinian III strengthened the city's defences against the menace of Vandal invasion from the sea (*c* 439).

The Neapolitan mansion of Lucullus was also converted into a castle (the *castrum Lucullanum*) guarding the coastline against Vandal incursions. This palace-fortress also housed, in retirement, the last western Roman emperor to reign in Italy, Romulus Augustus ('Augustulus') (475–76). His father, Orestes, military commander in Italy, had placed him on the throne of Ravenna, but was defeated and killed by the German general Odoacer, who thereupon dismissed Romulus with his whole family from the imperial palace, announced his abdication and sent him (with a substantial allowance) to live in Campania, where according to Jordanes he was granted the former residence of Lucullus. As was mentioned above, this may have been the edifice later converted into the Castel dell'Ovo.

It has been possible to reconstruct the outline of the ancient city's walls (including portions going back to the days of Palaeopolis), and the directions of some of its streets have been traced. Remains of Greek and Roman houses have also been found. Beneath the church of San Paolo Maggiore was a Roman temple of the Dioscuri (Castor and Pollux), going back to the time of Tiberius (14–37) but replacing an earlier building.

Neapolis Scythica (near Simferopol). A city in the interior of the Tauric Chersonese (Crimea). From the third century BC it was the capital of the Royal Scyths, a military people whose King Palacus is shown on horseback on a relief; another monarch, Scylurus, is mentioned on a Greek inscription. This and other archaeological evidence indicates that the Scythians underwent a considerable degree of Hellenization—under the influence of their frequently hostile neighbor, the state of the Cimmerian (Crimean) Bosphorus; indeed, the presence of a permanent Greek settlement in the town seems probable.

Before 200 it was surrounded by powerful stone, mortar-bonded walls, of which the main gate was flanked by towers. Remains within the perimeter of these fortifications include a double-colonnaded tile-roofed edifice, and a number of prosperous Hellenistic houses with courtyards and painted and stuccoed walls. The city's cemeteries are monumental and varied. Particularly notable is a mausoleum that contains seventy-two lavishly furnished tombs, probably belonging to members of the royal house who lived between the second centuries BC and AD. Another necropolis contains small chamber tombs furnished with niches and adorned with wall paintings depicting Scythian houses and hunting scenes. The city, like the Royal Scythian kingdom itself, ceased to exist in the third century AD, when the Tauric Chersonese was overrun by Sarmatians, Alans and Goths.

Nea Potidaia *see* Potidaea

Nedvigovka *see* Tanais

Nemausus (Nîmes) in southern Gaul (Gallia Narbonensis; Gard, France). Situated in the plain not far from the right (west) bank of the river Rhodanus (Rhône), at the foot of Mont Cavalier—beside a healing spring which was dedicated to a god bearing the same name as the town—Nemausus was the site of Chalcolithic (Copper) and Bronze Age settlements, and later became the capital of the Celtic tribe of the Volcae Arecomici. The town came within the sphere of influence of Massilia (the Greek Massalia [*qv*], now Marseille), which profited from its position on the old road from Italy to Spain, improved by the Romans before 124 BC and further reconstructed as the Via Domitia (121). It was at this stage that the province of Gallia Narbonensis was created, and Nemausus passed under Roman control.

At some date between 51 and 37, it became a Latin colony (i.e. a city in which the annually elected officials received Roman citizenship). Its authorities began *c* 28 to produce the most abundant bronze coinage ever issued by any colonial community in the Roman world, displaying the heads of Octavian (soon to become Augustus) and Marcus Agrippa (whom fragmentary inscriptions link with Nemausus) and, on the reverse side (in front of a palm tree) a crocodile, which appeared on imperial gold and silver issues of the same period and referred to the recent annexation of Egypt (30) after the defeat of Antony and Cleopatra VII at Actium in the previous year. The repetition of this design on the coins of Nemausus apparently refers to the settlement of Egyptian soldiers and sailors from Antony's forces. These issues continued for a considerable time and enjoyed an enormous circulation in the west, playing a major part in the token coinage of the western Roman world.

Nemausus flourished especially under Antoninus Pius (AD 138–61), whose father's family were among its citizens, and when the capital of the province, Narbo Martius, was destroyed by fire, he transferred the provincial capital of Gallia Narbonensis to Nemausus. From the mid-fourth century onward, however, a considerable part of the former habitation area was evidently uninhabited. Nevertheless, in 396, the city was the meeting place of a Christian synod.

It contains monuments of outstanding importance. Not much of the Augustan wall remains, but a gate (the Porte d'Auguste) and a complex octagonal structure (the Tour Magne, commanding Mont Cavalier) are still to be seen. The forum was dominated by a temple, now known as the Maison Carrée, which is perhaps the best preserved religious building in the entire Roman world. It was dedicated (not, as was thought until recently, rededicated after an earlier Augustan foundation) to Augustus' grandsons Gaius and Lucius Caesar in AD 2–5. The amphitheater of Nemausus, again remarkably well-preserved, dates from toward the end of the first century AD. The area of the local spring was adorned in the second or third century by a series of buildings, including a curved double colonnade, a temple of Diana (or of Rome and Augustus), a theater, a dormitory for pilgrims (?), a shrine of the water-god Nemausus, and a *nymphaeum* (fountain house). Since the spring did not provide the city with a sufficient flow of water, however, Agrippa brought a further supply from Uzès, fifteen miles away, by an aqueduct, of which the span crossing the river Vardo (Gardon), known as the Pont du Gard, is the most famous and one of the best-preserved structures of its kind in the Roman empire.

Nemea. A city on the northern border of the Argolid (northeastern Peloponnese, southern Greece) at the head of an open valley (the word means 'pasturage') and river of the same name, eleven miles from the Gulf of Corinth. A prehistoric site at Tsoungiza was nearby, and Mycenaean and Early Iron Age objects have also come to light beneath the town itself, north of the sacred area. In Greek mythology, Nemea was the scene of Heracles' First Labor, the killing of the monstrous Nemean Lion, which, after the hero's arrow had bounced harmlessly off its skin, he strangled with his bare hands.

The Nemean Games, according to one account, were founded by Heracles after he had killed the lion; though a rival tradition ascribed their establishment to Adrastus of Argos, when he led the Seven against Thebes—the theme of Aeschylus' tragedy of that name. Conducted in the sanctuary of Zeus, these Games originally possessed little more than local significance, and were under the control of the neighboring city-state of Cleonae. But in 573 BC the festivals were raised to Pan Hellenic status, and thenceforward took place in alternate years. Their prizes consisted of crowns of wild celery. By *c* 450 the Games were presided over by Argos, which transferred them to its own city early in the following century.

At Nemea in 394 on the outset of the Corinthian War, the Argives and Corinthians encountered a Spartan army that inflicted heavy losses on them, preventing any further offensive. Aratus of Sicyon, presiding over the Achaean League, tried unsuccessfully (according to Plutarch) to restore the Games to Nemea, a transfer that was successfully accomplished by the Roman general Lucius Mummius Achaicus (145) after his destruction of the League; although later in the Roman period Argos housed these contests once again.

Pausanias, in the second century AD, found the precinct of Zeus at Nemea in a state of total ruin. In the fourth and fifth centuries AD a Christian basilica and baptistery were built out of its stones; they suffered serious destruction from Slav invasions in the 580s. Recent excavations, however, on the site of the shrine have uncovered large amounts of pottery dating back to the eighth and seventh centuries BC. The sanctuary evidently suffered violent destruction in the later fifth century, followed by elaborate restoration. Buildings from the fourth to the second centuries north and south of the temple have now been excavated. Finds of decomposed organic material nearby may have come from a grove of cypress trees seen by Pausanias.

The adjoining open space (*plateia*) was bordered by a Xenon (guest house) and by a line of at least nine buildings (including the treasuries of cities participating in the Games); two of these structures were taken over by a bronze sculptors' workshop not long after 450. A hero's shrine (Heroon) has also been lately identified. A votive pit was found to contain a lead jumping weight, two iron javelin points and a very heavy iron discus, buried in 550/525. Much of the stadium, dating from 325/300, is also exposed; the clearing of its eastern side has recently been continued. A bathing establishment supplied with water through a reservoir system, with large holding troughs, is from about the same period.

Nemorensis (Nemi), Lake. In Latium (Lazio, western Italy), fourteen miles southeast of Rome. Lake Nemorensis was an extinct subsidiary crater in the outer ring of Mount Albanus, east of the lake of the same name. Lake Nemorensis took its name from the grove (*nemus*) of Diana (it was also known as her *speculum,* mirror) which adjoined her famous shrine, a principal sanctuary of the Latin League, dedicated to her, according to Cato the Elder, by the Latin dictator Egerius Baebius of Tusculum (*c* 500 BC?). From *c* 338 the sanctuary formed part of the territory of Aricia (Ariccia).

The worship of Diana had originally been accompanied by human sacrifices. Its priest, 'the king of the grove' (*rex Nemorensis*), was an escaped slave who gained this office by fighting and killing his predecessor after a formal challenge, which took the form of plucking a mistletoe branch from one of its trees. According to ancient tradition, the branch was the Golden Bough (the title of Sir James Frazer's famous book centering on the legend) which, at the Sibyl's bidding, Aeneas took from a tree before he commenced his perilous journey to the underworld. When Diana was equated with the Greek Artemis, her consort Virbius was identified with Hippolytus, and it was explained that he had been brought back from the dead by Asclepius and transported to Diana's Nemorensian shrine. A goddess, probably a water-deity, worshipped in association with Diana at her shrine, was Egeria, reputed to have been the consort of the second of Rome's legendary kings, Numa Pompilius.

The sanctuary was wealthy, and Octavian (the future Augustus) borrowed money from it in 31 BC. The rule of priestly succession by the sword continued to be observed. The emperor Gaius (Caligula, AD 37–41), thinking that the current priest had held office too long, was said to have hired someone to slay him. In the second century the single combats still continued.

The earliest objects found in the area date from the eighth century BC, but there is no evidence for buildings before *c* 300. The platform of the precinct can still be seen to the northeast of the lake, and the temple itself was unearthed, but has now been covered over again. Two large pleasure barges of the first century AD, located during the fifteenth century, were raised in the 1920s from the bottom of the lake when it was partially drained; but they were destroyed by fire during the Second World War (1944). Models of the vessels, together with fine bronze objects forming part of their decoration, are preserved in the local museum.

Nemrud Dağı *see* Commagene

Nemrud Kalesi *see* Aegae

Neocaesarea, Neokaisareia, earlier (according to a disputed but probable interpretation) Cabeira; then Diospolis and Sebaste (now Niksar). A town in the interior of eastern Pontus (northeastern Asia Minor), in the valley of one of the several rivers called Lycus (Kelkit Çayı), commanded by a citadel on a spur of the Paryadres range (Kanık Dağları). It was a stronghold, treasury and hunting lodge of King Mithridates VI Eupator of Pontus (120–63 BC), under whom it issued local coinage.

Mithridates made Cabeira his headquarters in his Third War against the Romans under Lucius Licinius Lucullus, who after an initial reverse captured the fortress in 72. In 64 the place was reorganized by Pompey the Great as a city with the name of Diospolis. In 37/36 Antony presented it, with the rest of Pontus, to King Polemo I (son of the rhetorician Zeno of Laodicea in Phrygia), after whose death it became the royal residence of Polemo's widow and successor Pythodoris (8 BC–*c* AD 22), assuming the new name of Sebaste (i.e. Augusta). When Nero annexed the kingdom of Pontus Polemoniacus in AD 63/4 and attached it to Galatia (united with Cappadocia from *c* 72), he refounded Cabeira-Diospolis-Sebaste as Neocaesarea, under which designation it coined, on its own behalf and for the Assembly of Pontus (Koinon Pontou) of which it was the metropolis, from Trajan (98–117) to Gallienus (253–68). Under Hadrian (117–38) it assumed yet another name, Hadriane.

The city's local monetary issues, under the family of Septimius Severus (193–211), display a temple depicted with a unique diversity of detail. This sanctuary was apparently dedicated to the supreme Pontic goddess Ma (*see* Comana), associated with the worship of Zeus and the imperial cult; the temple serfs were segregated in a separate quarter (Ameria), adjoining the principal seat of worship of a male deity, Men Pharmakou. The shrines of Ma and Men have not survived, because severe earthquakes in 344 and 499 destroyed most of the city. But parts of the walls may be Pontic or Roman, and a rock-cut tunnel is of pre-Roman date.

During the later empire Neocaesarea was capital of the province of Pontus Polemoniacus.

Neopolis *see* Naxos

Nequinum *see* Narnia

Neronias *see* Sepphoris

Neuss *see* Novaesium

Nicaea (İznik). A Greek city in Bithynia (northwestern Asia Minor), situated on level and fertile ground beside the eastern shore of Lake Ascania (İznik Gölü) and the small river Sagaris (Deli Çay). According to mythology, the founders were the god Dionysus and the nymph Nicaea. The original, pre-Greek name of the place is recorded as Ankore or Elikore.

During the Succession Wars after the death of Alexander the Great, it was refounded as Antigoneia by Antigonus I Monophthalmos (316) and again by Lysimachus (301) who gave it his wife's name Nicaea, (although Dio Chrysostom and Nonnus preserved alternative traditions that it owed this name to colonists from a small town named Nicaea near the Sinus Maliacus [Gulf of Lamia] in northeastern Greece). In 282/1 (the inaugural date of a new civic era), it came under the monarchs of Bithynia, whom it often served as a royal residence, profiting from its position as a major communications center. The astronomer Hipparchus was born at Nicaea (*c* 190).

In 75/74, when Nicomedes IV bequeathed Bithynia to Rome, the city passed with the rest of his state into Roman hands. Pompey the Great, organizing the province of Bithynia—Pontus in *c* 63, assigned Nicaea an extensive territory, and it competed with the provincial capital Nicomedia (İzmit) as the principal city of the country. In 29 Octavian (soon to be known as Augustus) authorized the Romans in Bithynia to dedicate a shrine at Nicaea to Rome and the deified Julius Caesar. Pliny the Younger, as Trajan's special representative in Bithynia (*c* AD 110–12), consulted the emperor about expenses incurred in connection with the city's gymnasium and theater. Hadrian came on a visit in 123; a triumphal arch and monumental gateway commemorate the occasion. The Goths inflicted severe damage in 256/8. At the first of two Church Councils at Nicaea (425; the second was in 787) under Constantine I the Great, the Nicene Creed was formulated by an assemblage of three hundred bishops. Ammianus Marcellinus tells how, in 364, Valentinian I was acclaimed emperor at Nicaea, 'the metropolis of Bithynian cities.'

Its local coinage under the Principate, extending from Augustus to Quietus (260/61), is notable for the large number of honorific titles on which the city prided itself, and for the vigorous celebration of its Games, often named after emperors (Commodus, Severus, Valerian, Gallienus); another piece declares that 'under the rulership of Commodus (180–92) the world is happy.' Further types depict the nymph Nicaea, Homer, Theseus, Alexander the Great, Julius Caesar (on his supposedly human-footed horse, *hippon brotopoda*!), the river-god Sagaris, and Caracalla (211–217) accompanied by the Egyptian deity Serapis on a ship. There is also a rich series of coins depicting local architectural features, including a two-storeyed arcade or colonnaded gate (first under Claudius, 41–54), and at least four different temples (including shrines of Asclepius, Dionysus and Agathe Tyche). On a further issue, the entrance court of what looks like another sanctuary is depicted, containing figures of Septimius Severus (193–211) and his sons Caracalla and Geta, the former as the New Dionysus.

Nicaea was famous for the regularity of its plan. The remains of the gymnasium and theater (with which Pliny the Younger was concerned) can still be seen; the excavation of the latter building, which was frequently modified, has continued during a number of seasons. An aqueduct and the twin moles of the lake harbor are also traceable. Massive remains of the city's double concentric fortifications, of various dates, are still standing. Gates were built under Vespasian and Hadrian, and figure imposingly on coins of Gallienus (253–68). The destruction of the walls by the Goths necessitated a rebuilding program, recorded by an inscription celebrating the erection of a monumental gate by Claudius II Gothicus (268–70). New superstructures were added to the fortifications shortly before or after 400. During the fifth century the first Cathedral of Holy Wisdom (Aya Sophia) was erected, in the form of a three-aisled basilica. Recent discoveries at Nicaea have included twenty male skeletons, all exhibiting signs of wounds; they apparently belong to two distinct ethnic groups, which have been classified as north European and Anatolian.

Nicaea *see* Corsica

Nicephorium, Nikephorion, later known as Callinicum (Kallinikon) and then Leontopolis (now Raqqa) in northwestern Mesopotamia (now Syria). Situated less than a mile north of the river Euphrates, near the point where it is joined by its northern tributary the Bilechas (Balikh), the fortress was founded by Alexander the Great (d. 323 BC) according to Isidore of Charax and Pliny the Elder, or by the founder of the Seleucid kingdom Seleucus I in the (more probable) version of Appian: presumably in honor of some military success, as the place-name 'victory-bearing' suggests. Dio Cassius describes its population as 'colonists of the Macedonians and the Greeks who served with them.'

During the Roman Principate, Nicephorium gained considerable and increasing importance as a frontier stronghold of the province of Mesopotamia (*qv*), bordering on the Parthian kingdom. In 165 Avidius Cassius, the leading general of Lucius Verus (the colleague of Marcus Aurelius), crossed the Euphrates and stormed Nicephorium, opening the way for a southern advance (which failed, however, to materialize owing to an outbreak of plague among his troops). After the more formidable Sassanian Persians had replaced the Parthians as the Roman empire's neighbors, it was from Nicephorium that Severus Alexander set out to attack them in 232. In 296 Galerius Caesar, the junior colleague (Caesar) of Diocletian, again crossed the Euphrates at Callinicum—as the place was now called, after a sophist named Callinicus who had been killed there—prior to suffering a severe mauling by the enemy, between that city and Carrhae (Haran); a setback which he was able to redress, however, by a victory in the following year. Thereafter the frontier province was divided into two, Mesopotamia and Osrhoena, of which Callinicum guarded the latter (another province, Euphratensis, lay south of the Euphrates).

Julian the Apostate, in 363, invaded the Persian empire by way of Callinicum, which Ammianus described, at that time, as a powerful fortress deriving wealth from its trade. After his successor Jovian's loss of Nisibis (Nusaybin) in an unfavorable treaty with the Persians a little later, the place seems to have gained something like a monopoly of Roman trade with Persia, as we learn from an edict of Theodosius II (408/9). Under Leo I (457–74) it became a city under the name of Leontopolis, which was taken and demolished by the Persians in 542.

Nicomedia (İzmit). A city of Bithynia (northwestern Asia Minor) at the head of the Gulf of Astacus (the name of an Athenian colony meaning 'crayfish,' that lay further south), now the Gulf of İzmit. Another Greek colony named Olbia had earlier been established (by the Megarians) on the hilly site later occupied by Nicomedia—rather than at Astacus, as has been sometimes supposed.

In 265/4, however, according to Memnon and Strabo, King Nicomedes I of Bithynia (not, probably, his father Zipoetes, as Pausanias believed) refounded Olbia under the name of Nicomedia, making it his capital in place of Zipoetium—which has not been located—and demolishing Astacus to supply the new settlement with its population. Nicomedia soon became an active port, prospering from its extensive and fertile territory and its situation on the principal route between Europe and the east. After the Bithynian kingdom had been bequeathed to the Romans (74), Nicomedia was the capital of their province of Bithynia-Pontus; and in 29 it became the headquarters of the provincial assembly and its imperial cult, when Octavian (Augustus) permitted the Greek population to dedicate a temple to Rome and to himself.

Nicomedia became an important naval headquarters, and Dio Chrysostom, in the later first and early second century AD, depicts a resplendent and flourishing city, although its community was by no means free of social discontents. Pliny the Elder (110-12) frequently consulted Trajan about problems affecting the maintenance of its buildings; and he also wanted to build a canal from the Propontis (Sea of Marmara) to the Euxine (Black) Sea via Nicomedia, but the project never materialized. A Roman imperial monetary issue celebrates Hadrian (117-38) as 'Restorer of Nicomedia,' the only city to be singled out in this series of 'restoration' coinages, which otherwise only name provinces and regions. A Nicomedian festival was known as the Severeia, after Septimius Severus (193-211). His son Caracalla spent the winter of 214/15 at the city, organizing his army for war against Parthia and entertaining himself and the inhabitants with Games and other shows. Elagabalus, too, spent the first winter after his proclamation (218/19) at Nicomedia, where his bizarre religious rituals caused widespread alarm. In 256/8 the city was captured and sacked by the Goths, but its inhabitants were able to get much of its wealth away.

When Diocletian (284-305) established the tetrarchic system of four rulers presiding over separate capitals and courts, he himself, the senior emperor, chose Nicomedia as his residence—because of its convenient location between the Danube and Euphrates frontiers. It is described as a colony in an inscription of 294/5 and it was then that the city's great period of magnificence began; it also became one of the major mints of the empire. It was at Nicomedia, too, that Diocletian formally abdicated in 305, in the presence of his soldiers. After the persecution of the Christians, initiated during his reign, had been reversed (311), Maximinus II Daia cancelled the reversal, in compliance with an appeal from the pagan community at Nicomedia. After his defeat by Licinius in 313, however, he professedly reconfirmed religious toleration by an edict from the same city, shortly before his death later in the same year. One of the most remarkable issues of its mint honored Licinius' puppet colleague Martinian in 324, just before both were suppressed by Constantine I the Great.

It was at Nicomedia that Constantine died in 337, but the eclipse of its preeminence had already been heralded by his foundation of Constantinople (324-30), destined to replace it as capital. Moreover, Nicomedia had often been afflicted by seismic disturbances, and an earthquake in 358 inflicted particularly serious damage; Ammianus Marcellinus, in the course of a vivid account, describes how the destruction was completed by a fire that raged for five days and five nights. Julian the Apostate, when he visited Nicomedia four years later, was distressed by the heap of ashes which was all that remained of the city. But he took steps to initiate its reconstruction; and it subsequently enjoyed something of a revival under Theodosius II (408-50).

Its local coinage, from Claudius (41-54) to Gallienus (253-68), emulated the issues of its rival Nicaea (İznik) in its insistence on honorific civic titles. Among the more unusual designs is a figure of Argus, the builder of the Argonauts' vessel the Argo. Representations of other ships also appear. The architectural remains of the city are disappointing. A shrine of Demeter stood within a large rectangular precinct on a hill linked to the harbor by a colonnaded street (of which a few fragments were once visible). A temple of Isis, an agora and a theater are also recorded, and there is numismatic evidence for the worship of Hera

Lanoia (Juno of Lanuvium). The city's water supply, to which Pliny the Younger gave attention, is represented by the remains of three aqueducts, imposing drains (which were still in use until half a century ago), a large fountain building (*nymphaeum*), and a large domed cistern. This structure is of late imperial date, and so are stretches of brick and stone walls. But otherwise what must have been Diocletian's resplendent capital—including palace, mint, arms factories and new shipyards—has so far yielded scarcely a trace.

Niconium *see* Tyras

Nicopolis, Nikopolis (Pürk, from *pyrgos,* tower). A city in northeastern Asia Minor (eastern Pontus, though frequently placed by ancient writers in Armenia Minor [Lesser Armenia]), near the left bank of the river Lycus (Kelkit). Originally created by Seleucus I Nicator (perhaps under the name of Seleucia), Nicopolis was refounded by Pompey the Great in 66 BC to celebrate his final suppression of Mithridates VI of Pontus in the Third Mithridatic War; retired and wounded soldiers and natives were moved into this 'City of Victory' as settlers. It was attached to the client kingdom of Armenia Minor, becoming its only city and its capital. In 47 BC the Pontic king Pharnaces II defeated Julius Caesar's general Cnaeus Domitius Calvinus near Nicopolis, prior to his own defeat by Caesar at Zela (Zile).

Incorporated, during the first century AD, in the province of Bithynia-Pontus, and serving as an important station on the frontier road system, Nicopolis flourished under the Principate, inaugurating a new era in the reign of Nero (AD 64) and issuing coinage under Trajan (98–117) and Hadrian (117–38), whose name the city assumed as an additional designation. By the third century it held the rank of a colony, with special privileges (*ius Italicum*). During the later empire it became the capital of the province of Armenia Prima.

Nicopolis, Nikopolis, 'Victory City' (Paleopreveza) in Epirus (northwest Greece), on the hilly isthmus of a promontory closing the Ambracian Gulf (Gulf of Arta) from the north. The town, sometimes also known as Actia Nicopolis, was founded by Octavian (the future Augustus) in 31 BC to celebrate his decisive naval victory over Antony and Cleopatra VII of Egypt off Actium at the entrance to the Gulf. By means of the largest of such amalgamations (synoecisms) ever recorded, Nicopolis was forcibly settled by people brought in from the decaying towns and villages of Ambracia, Amphilochia, Acarnania, Leucas (just outside the Gulf) and Aetolia, and statues and marble decorations were also removed from these places to embellish the new city.

The place where his headquarters had stood during the battle was consecrated by Octavian to Apollo and Mars, according to Strabo and Dio Cassius, but in Suetonius' version, the selected deity was Neptune, to whom a fragmentary inscription refers; and Octavian also dedicated *rostra* (the beaks of Antony's captured ships) and set them in a wall, which has now been cleaned and studied. In addition, Nicopolis was the location of the emperor's Actian Games in honor of Apollo, which are frequently mentioned on the city's coinage. It describes him as Leucates (on the Roman series he is called Actian Apollo), and the city pronounces itself, on subsequent local coinage, as *nauarchis,* mistress of the fleet; it enjoyed the rights of a free and federated community.

Situated on the main sea route between Rome and its eastern provinces, Nicopolis possessed harbors on either side of the isthmus and developed plentiful fisheries; for two centuries it was the principal city of western Greece. In the time of Nero (?) it became the capital of the new province of Epirus. St. Paul spent a winter there, during which he wrote his *Epistle to Titus,* inviting him to stay. The stoic philosopher Epictetus, expelled from Rome by Domitian (AD 89), established his residence at Nicopolis, attracting a great number of followers. A coin describes Trajan (98–117) as 'Savior of the City,' owing to some benefaction. Another piece, from the reign of Hadrian (117–38), who is named as 'Pan-Hellenic,' depicts a handsome fountain; and an issue in memory of Antoninus Pius' wife Faustina the Elder (*c* 141) illustrates a two-storeyed hero's shrine (*heroon*).

These buildings have not survived, and only fragments of Neptune's temple are visible, but remains of other ancient buildings are spread over a very extensive area. They include an unusually shaped stadium, rounded at both ends—in which the Games were held—in addition to a fairly well-preserved theater, a small theater (Odeum)—which was originally of Augustan date, later underwent alterations, and has now been largely restored—and an aqueduct traversing the isthmus. Part of the paved road leading to the city's western port on the Ionian Sea (Komato) has also been recently unearthed, and excavations have revealed a rectangular burial enclosure.

Nicopolis continued to coin until the time of Gallienus (253–68). In the later empire it was the capital of the province of Old Epirus (Epirus Vetus). The emperor Julian the Apostate (361–63), inspired by pagan fervor, renovated the city and revived the Actian festival; however, Christianity was strongly established, and a number of early churches are to be seen. During the first decade of the fifth century the passage of Alaric and his Visigoths left a trail of destruction, but the place was refortified in the course of the sixth century, although with a smaller perimeter.

Niksar *see* Neocaesarea (Pontus)

Nile (River) *see* Aegyptus

Niš *see* Naissus

Nisibis (Nusaybin). The chief town of Mygdonia (northeastern Mesopotamia, now southeastern Turkey), at the foot of a range (Tur Abdin) on the bank of the river Mygdonius (Çağağa Suyu), a tributary of the Chaboras (Khabur), which is itself a northern tributary of the Euphrates. Situated in a fertile plain at a point where important roads meet, Nisibis, at the beginning of the first millennium BC, was the capital of an Aramaic state (Hanigalbat) which after 900 fell successively into Assyrian and Babylonian hands. Seleucus I Nicator (d. 281) settled Macedonian colonists on the site, and under a later Seleucid, Antiochus IV Epiphanes (175–163), the city coined briefly under the name of Antioch in Mygdonia.

In 129, like the rest of Mesopotamia, it was annexed to the Parthian empire, but was captured *c* 80 by Tigranes I of Armenia and then in 68 by the Roman general Lucius Licinius Lucullus. After Crassus' defeat by the Parthians at Carrhae (Haran) in 53, Nisibis was lost to the Romans, and was presented by the Parthian king Artabanus III (AD 12–*c* 38) to a client prince, Izates of Adiabene. Trajan's occupation of the place—together with the rest of northern Mesopotamia—proved short-lived (114–16), but Roman control was reasserted as a result of the campaigns of Marcus Aurelius' colleague Lucius Verus (162). As a reward for its support of Septimius Severus during his civil war with Pescennius Niger (193/4), Nisibis obtained colonial rank, with the title of Septimia, and became the capital of Rome's Mesopotamian province. During the subsequent wars between the Romans and Sassanian Persians, it proved to be a continuous bone of contention.

Its local coinage was apparently resumed under Elagabalus (218–22). A siege by the Sassanian (Persian) monarch Artaxerxes (Ardashir) I was relieved by Severus Alexander (234)—who bestowed on the city the title of metropolis—but in the reign of Maximinus I (235–38), according to Zonaras, it fell into the hands of the Persians, who were driven out, however, by Gordian III (238–44). It adopted the title Julia in honor of his successor Philip the Arab (244–49), whose full name was Marcus Julius Philippus. A further period of Persian occupation by Shapur (Sapor) I (241–72) was terminated in 262 after an eleven-year seige by Odenathus of Palmyra, Gallienus' (virtually independent) representative in the east. According to Diocletian's treaty with Narses in 298, all trade between Rome and Persia was to be directed through Nisibis, which became a powerfully fortified frontier strong point. Its first Christian bishop, Babu, was appointed *c* 300.

When war was resumed during the reign of Constantius II, Shapur II three times failed to capture the fortress (*c* 338, 346 and 350). But the unfavorable treaty of Jovian (363) handed Nisibis over to the Persians. Many of its inhabitants were now expelled or departed; among them was St. Ephraim, who had inaugurated a historic school of Syriac literature in the city, but now migrated to Edessa (Urfa). Nisibis never belonged to the Romans again.

Nocera *see* Nuceria Alfaterna

Nola. A city in Campania (southwestern Italy), situated at the southeastern extremity of its plain, twenty miles east of Neapolis (Naples) and seventeen miles southeast of Capua (Santa Maria Capua Vetere). Hecataeus (*c* 500 BC) knew Nola as a settlement of the Italic (Oscan-speaking) tribe of the Aurunci ('Ausonians'), and there was a dubious tradition of settlement from Chalcis in Euboea, but Cato the Elder (234–149) regarded the town as an Etruscan foundation (*c* 471), and it was probably colonized or occupied by Etruscans coming from Capua. Local cemeteries have yielded a remarkable wealth of pottery going back to the early centuries of the first millennium but especially rich in Athenian black- and red-figure vases of the sixth and fifth centuries. Nola was an important station on the inland road from Etruria to the southern regions of Campania.

At the end of the fifth century BC it was also on friendly terms with Neapolis, to judge from its fourth-century coinage, which was inscribed in Greek and imitated Neapolitan types. Nola fell to the Romans *c* 313 and remained loyal to them during the Second Punic War (218–201), during which Hannibal experienced his first rebuff before its walls. It served as a station on the Via Annia *c* 131, an extension of the Via Appia from Capua onward to Rhegium (Reggio di Calabria). However, during the Social War between Rome and its allies the city became a stronghold of the rebels, and succumbed after two sieges (88–80) to Sulla, who established a colony of ex-soldiers there, with the surname of Felix. It employed Pompeii as its harbor.

In 73 Nola was plundered by the slave leader Spartacus, but subsequently received a further draft of colonists from Augustus, who died there in AD 14 on a family property which, according to Dio Cassius, Tiberius subsequently converted into a temple. Vespasian (69–79) and Nerva (96–98) reportedly sent further retired soldiers as colonists. In the later empire it was often the residence of the governor of the province or district of Campania. St. Paulinus became bishop of Nola for the last twenty-two years of his life, making it a leading monastic center (409–31) and reportedly inventing church bells, which were known as *campanae* or *nolae*. However, the city was plundered by Alaric's Visigoths in 410, and largely destroyed by the Vandals of Gaiseric in 455. It partially recovered, but never regained its former importance. The ancient town possessed twelve gates, and traces can be seen of an amphitheater and theater, faced with brick and marble respectively.

Noreia. A city in Noricum (Austria), identifiable with the Magdalensberg mountain in Carinthia (Kärnten), rather than, as has also been suggested, with Neumarkt in Styria (Steiermark). The city stood on the summit of the mountain that rises more than 3,000 feet above the plain of the Zollfeld. Hecataeus (*c* 500 BC) mentions the 'Celtic City Nyrax,' which may well be Noreia. At all events, by the second century, it was the principal settlement of the tribe of the Norici and the capital of their kingdom of Noricum (*qv*). It was here, in 113 BC, that the Roman consul Cnaeus Papirius Carbo suffered a resounding defeat at the hands of migrating German peoples, the Cimbri and Teutones, who thereupon, however, fortunately proceeded to move westward instead of pressing on into Italy. When the Romans annexed Noricum in 15, Noreia passed into thier hands.

Important excavations have revealed a pre-Roman stronghold with an enclosed area of more than two square miles. Before the end of the second century Roman merchants were installed in a quarter of their own, grouped round a commercial forum. About 40–20, a colonnaded, terraced villa (one of a number on the site) was equipped with a bathing establishment and embellished with elegant wall paintings, such are also to be seen in the remains of a local inn. A Roman replica of a Greek statue of Mars (the Helenenberg Youth, now in Vienna) belongs to about the same time. Roman annexation prompted the construction of many new buildings, including a large temple of Rome and Augustus flanked by the governor's tribunal, and a three-halled, three-storeyed meeting place for the provincial council of Noricum, known as the Repräsentationshaus; it contained thirteen niches for statues personifying the tribes of the province. Fragments of inscriptions, dating between 11 and 2 BC, record tributes from eight of these Noric tribes, and honor the family of Augustus. The lower rooms of new or rebuilt houses were stores and workshops, some of which were engaged in working the iron and gold found nearby; and the walls of two cellars (containing niches for statues of Mercury) were found to be covered with more than three hundred graffiti, of which the contents include references to extensive financial and commercial transactions. When, however, the provincial capital was transferred by Claudius (AD 41–54) to Virunum, the position of Noreia declined, and eventually its site became deserted and desolate.

Noricum. A state, and then a Roman province, south of the Danube, between Raetia and Pannonia; comprising central Austria and parts of Bavaria, though the Celtic federal kingdom, which developed from *c* 200 BC, extended further into present-day Hungary and Yugoslavia. The kingdom established control over an earlier Illyrian population and, although the principal Celtic tribe of the region were the Taurisci, took its name from the Norici round the hilltop center of Noreia (Magdalensberg).

The Norican state, of which Noreia was the capital, derived wealth from abundant iron but also from gold, of which a discovery in Tauriscan territory *c* 140, according to Strabo, led to a Roman gold rush and a thirty-three per cent fall in the price of the metal in Italy; Roman interest, from this period onward, is reflected by the issue of coinage with Latin inscriptions. In the following century the importance of the kingdom was illustrated by Julius Caesar's acceptance of its aid in his Civil War against Pompey the Great in 49. About 35, to secure the northern frontier of Italy, suzerainty was established over the Taurisci, and *c* 15 the kingdom was abolished, apparently without bloodshed—and possibly by the ruler's bequest.

During a subsequent intermediate period the territory did not rank as a fully fledged province and may have retained a degree of nominal independence (under a prince of the royal house), the seat of administration remaining at Noreia—where the tribes of the country offered honorific dedications. But full provincial status was acquired under Claudius, when the capital was moved to Virunum (*c* AD 45), which stood in the plain on the main road from Italy to the Danube, and together with four other towns obtained municipal rank. Stable cultural development ensued. Horace praised the swords of Noricum, and in Petronius' *Satyricon,* Trimalchio impressed his guests by giving them Norican knives. Moreover, the Romans were attracted by the availability of slaves in the country. After severe destruction by the Marcomanni and Quadi under Marcus Aurelius (*c* 169), recovery and refortification soon followed, and a Roman legion was stationed in the province, first at Albing and then (before 191) at Lauriacum (Lorch); the provincial capital was moved to Ovilava (Wels), though the Roman financial administrator (procurator) remained at Virunum.

From *c* 310/11 the province—now forming part of the administrative diocese of Illyricum (Pannoniae)—was divided into two, Noricum Ripense and

Noricum Mediterraneum, with their capitals at Ovilava and Virunum respectively. Soon afterward, Christian penetration reached important dimensions. But the frontier was repeatedly overrun: in 357 by Juthungi, in 395 by Marcomanni and Quadi, in 405 by Ostrogoths, and in 407 by Visigoths. During the fifth century Teurnia (St. Peter im Holz) replaced Virunum as the capital of Noricum Mediterraneum. In 431 the Roman general Aetius bloodily put down a provincial uprising, but although the Huns passed through Noricum Ripense two decades later, that province was not lost to the Romans until *c* 472–88 when Alamanni, Thuringians and Heruli broke in. Noricum Mediterraneum remained under the control of the Italian kingdoms, ruled first by Odoacer the Herulian and then by Ostrogoths, until its annexation by the Franks *c* 535. *See also* Lauriacum, Noreia, Ovilava, Virunum.

Notium *see* Colophon

Novae (Stăklen). A fortified city at the southernmost point of the Danube, in Moesia (now northern Bulgaria). Perhaps founded *c* AD 30—near an ancient Thracian site—and taking its name from the tributary stream Noas or Novas (Noes), it became the headquarters of a legion in the time of Claudius (45) and then of another (replacing it in 69), retaining this garrison until the end of the empire. When Moesia was divided by Domitian (81–96), Novae belonged to the Lower province. Situated on a great riverside thoroughfare (the Via Danubiana) and forming the terminal of roads from eastern and western Thrace, it was also a port of the Danube fleet; in 101 Trajan, during his first war against Dacia (Rumania), probably disembarked there after moving down the river with a naval force. A civilian settlement developed round the fortress, and under Marcus Aurelius (161–80) Novae became a *municipium*. It imported abundant pottery from the western provinces, and reexported a considerable amount to central Europe.

In 251 the Goths under Kniva stormed the city, but were driven off by Trebonianus Gallus, governor of the two Moesias, who owed his subsequent call to the purple (after the death in battle of the emperor Trajanus Decius) to this success. Archaeological evidence points to destruction during the first civil war between Constantine I the Great and Licinius (*c* 316). Impressive economic and cultural recovery followed, but violent attacks were again experienced in 376/8—this time at the hands of the Visigoths—and the early fifth century once more provides evidence of devastation. After Attila the Hun had invaded the Danubian cities of Moesia Secunda (to which Novae now belonged), a peace treaty was concluded in 448 by which the south bank of the river as far as Singidunum (Belgrade) should be left as an uninhabited border region. In the early 470s Theoderic the Ostrogoth, when he led his people from their Pannonian homes to Lower Moesia, seems, according to the Anonymus Valesianus, to have established his residence at Novae. During the fifth century it became an episcopal see.

Novae may be the most intensively studied Roman camp town in eastern Europe. Excavations during the past decade have revealed much of the legionary base. A rectangular stone fortress is of early second-century date. Comprehensive rebuilding took place under the dynasty of Septimius Severus (193–211), and after the damage inflicted in 251 the city's perimeter was enlarged. Following the further disaster of *c* 316, in which the *principia* (military administrative headquarters) were demolished, the original stronghold was not revived, although the civilian settlement entered on a new lease on life, protected by reinforced defences, of which large sections are now cleared. Christian basilicas of the fifth and sixth centuries have also come to light. Recent reports record the discovery of an important peristyle structure, of uncertain significance, outside the walls.

Novaesium (Neuss). A Roman stronghold and town on the left bank of the river Rhenus (Rhine) in Lower Germany, north of Colonia Agrippinensis (Köln, Cologne). The troops of Augustus established a military fort, and almost certainly a legionary fortress, *c* 12 BC, at the outset of his generals' campaigns across the river. After the defeat and death of Varus in the Teutoburg Forest (9 BC), and during the campaigns conducted by Germanicus (AD 14–17), the camp was enlarged to accommodate more than one legion.

The garrison fell into deep disgrace during the Gallo-German revolt led by Civilis (69), when it took an oath of allegiance to the 'empire of the Gauls' and murdered the governor of Upper Germany, Hordeonius Flaccus; moreover, not long afterward a Roman deserter sent by Civilis assassinated the legionary commander Dillius Vocula, likewise at Novaesium. Burned down in the course of the revolt, it was rebuilt and again housed a legion until after 104, and then possessed a garrison of auxiliary troops in the second and third centuries, while a civilian settlement grew up on the outskirts. The city was destroyed by a German incursion under Constantius II (350), but his commander-in-chief in the west, Julian (the Apostate), refortified it in 359 as a major granary and storehouse for provisions. Novaesium is mentioned for the last time in 388. At the end of the empire it came into the hands of the Franks, under the name Niusa.

Nearly a dozen successive phases of the construction of the camp have been identified, starting from buildings and walls of wood and earth and continuing with the enlarged base after AD 69, in which a forum, commander's residence, billets for officers and other ranks, and colonnaded streets were surrounded by stone ramparts. Part of the civilian settlement lies under the modern Neuss.

Noviomagus Regnensium (Chichester). A town in southern Britannia (Sussex, England), on the coastal plain at the foot of a spur of the South Downs, beside the river Lavant about a mile from its debouchment into an inlet and harbor (at Bosham). In pre-Roman times the district belonged to the tribe of the Reg(i)-ni or Regnenses. Following Iron Age occupation from the fourth to third centuries BC, revealed by recent excavations, the site became a military fort after the Roman landings in AD 43, which led to the establishment of the province of Britain. The local rule, however, of the tribal client king Tiberius Claudius Cogidubnus (*c* 43–75/80) was confirmed by the Romans, and it was at Noviomagus that he established his capital, with the titles of Great King and Imperial Legate.

From *c* 45 onward, when the Roman army evacuated the place, it began to take on an urban appearance, which has been partly reconstructed by observation of the service trenches dug through the main streets of the modern town prior to the creation of pedestrian precincts. A series of early structures, of military style, have come to light (in the North-West Quadrant). There is evidence of a tidier street plan from *c* 75/85 onward. In the later second century an earthen defence wall was added, with masonry gates and two outside ditches; after 200, masonry was also incorporated in the wall. This township was about a hundred acres in size. Buildings included a forum, basilica, a temple of Neptune and Minerva (erected as an inscription records, in honor of the imperial house, by Cogidubnus' permission), in addition to a bathhouse and an amphitheater. Finds make it clear that the city developed a pottery industry. After naval assaults in 367 its fortifications were strengthened, but it is unknown to what extent it survived the withdrawal of the garrison *c* 385 and 407.

Noviomagus is chiefly remarkable for the great building complex and villa (or palace) of Fishbourne which stands at the head of the harbor. This site was first occupied *c* 43 to provide the military granaries and storehouses required by the Roman invasion force. But these structures were soon superseded by a private residence, at first made of wood and consisting of two separate buildings. Its occupation began *c* 50, while at about the same time work started on a handsome villa in the immediate vicinity, which was ready in the early 60s. It included a bathing establishment, an athletics room (*palaestra*), a colonnaded garden, and slaves' quarters, and the living rooms were decorated with wall paintings, mosaic floors (*opus sectile*) and marble veneers.

Soon after 75, however, the first steps were taken to replace this residence by the much larger palace that we see today, covering an area of ten acres. Its principal portion consisted of four wings enclosing an extensive central garden. The south wing, which lies beneath modern houses and a main road but apparently contained private apartments, was flanked by another garden extending down to the sea, where wharves and jetties were constructed to make a small private harbor. The east wing of the mansion, containing luxurious residential apartments, was entered through a colonnaded entrance hall, approached by visitors from Noviomagus across a small bridge. The west wing, at a slightly higher level, contained large public rooms with mosaic pavements, leading to a square, apsed audience chamber which was originally roofed by a stucco vault. The north wing consisted of an arrangement of twenty-three rooms (probably guest accommodation) round two colonnaded gardens.

The owner of this residence cannot be identified with certainty, but its grandeur strongly suggests that it was built for Cogidubnus himself. By the end of the first century, however (when his client princedom had been fully incorporated in the province), the building was split up into separate units, for which new polychrome mosaics were laid and new bath suites constructed. By the end of the third century another remodelling was under way; but at this juncture the whole complex was destroyed by fire.

Novum Comum *see* Comum

Nuceria Alfaterna (Nocera Superiore, Inferiore). A town in Campania (southwestern Italy) lying seven miles inland in fertile territory, near the foot of the peninsula of Surrentum (Sorrento). Originally a settlement of the Aurunci (known also as Ausonians), it stood at a crossroads on the highway from Etruria to southern Campania (later probably known as the Via Annia, *c* 131 BC), commanding an important pass. The headwaters of the Sarnus (Sarno) were nearby. In the Second Samnite War, Nuceria, which at this time exercised some control over neighboring towns, supported the Samnites against Rome (316), but fell to the Romans in 308. Nevertheless, in the third century it enjoyed the privilege of issuing its own silver coinage, inscribed 'Nuvkrinum Alafaternum' in Oscan. Fine-grained grey tufa quarried in the neighborhood was employed for the construction of houses at Pompeii, which it used as its port.

During the Second Punic War, Nuceria was destroyed by Hannibal (216), but was subsequently reconstructed. In the Social War between Rome and its allies (91–87), its suburbs were burned by the Samnite general Papius Mutilus, although after hostilities were over it may have received, in compensation, part of the lands of the obliterated city of Stabiae (Castellamare di Stabia). Spartacus' revolted slaves destroyed Nuceria again in 73. One of its products was a wealthy knight and adventurer named Publius Sittius, whom Julius Caesar rewarded with a principality in North Africa. About 41, during the Second Triumvirate, Nuceria was made a Roman colony—bearing the surname of Constantia—and was subsequently recolonized with drafts of ex-soldiers by Augustus and again by Nero (AD 57). Nero's settlement is recorded by Tacitus, who also describes a fight between the people of Nuceria and Pompeii two years later (depicted on a Pompeian painting). The Nucerian fans were visiting a gladiatorial show in the amphitheater of Pompeii, and came off worse in the struggle; many of their wounded and mutilated citizens had to be taken to Rome for treatment. In 62 their city was damaged by the earthquake that destroyed most of Pompeii. Seven years later occurred the short-lived reign of the emperor Vitellius, whose family came from Nuceria. In 79 the town must have been seriously affected by the eruption of Vesuvius.

The ancient center lay between the modern towns of Nocera Inferiore and Nocera Superiore, but little is known of its plan; shrines of Sarnus, Juno Sarrana and the Dioscuri (Castor and Pollux) are recorded. The cemetery has yielded rich material, going back to the sixth century BC. The circular church of Santa Maria Maggiore (or della Rotonda) at Nocera Superiore is built over a baptistery of the fifth century AD; the dome of the church collapsed during the eruption of Vesuvius in 1944.

Numantia (Numancia). A fortress-city five miles north of the modern Soria in the interior of northeastern Spain, within the territory of the Celtiberian tribe of the Arevaci; it is situated on a steep hill (the Muela de Garray) two hundred feet above sea level, at the junction of the upper Durius (Duero, Douro) and its tributaries, the Tera and Merdancius (Merdancho). After Neolithic, Copper and Iron Age settlements, the Arevaci reconstructed the strong point *c* 300 BC, and it played a leading part in the resistance of the Spaniards to Rome's establishment in 197 of its province of Nearer Spain (Hispania Citerior, later Tarraconensis).

This resistance was undertaken in two stages. The first stage, starting immediately after annexation, involved an unsuccessful attack by Cato the Elder on Numantia (195), and terminated in a peace treaty in 180. Then followed the Great Insurrection, from 154 to 151 and from 143 to 137. In 153 and 142 Quintus Fulvius Nobilior and Quintus Caecilius Metellus again failed to capture Numantia, in which tribesmen had taken refuge, and in 137, toward the conclusion of the Third Celtiberian (Numantine) War, the Roman senate refused to recognize a peace agreement made by Gaius Hostilius Mancinus, who was left by his compatriots kneeling, naked and shackled before the walls of Numantia. Finally, in 134, Publius Cornelius Scipio Aemilianus (Africanus the Younger) blockaded the fortress and its population of 10,000 people—4,000 of whom were under arms—and after a nine-month siege (134/3) the Numantians were forced by hunger to capitulate. When, however, Scipio insisted on unconditional surrender, most of them killed themselves after burning Numantia down. Its destruction (witnessed by Gaius Gracchus, Gaius Marius, and the Numidian prince Jugurtha) meant the end of all organized resistance to Rome in Spain. However, a Roman army came to the ruined stronghold again in the civil war between Sertorius and Pompey the Great (75/4). It was reinhabited, on a small scale, under Augustus (31 BC–AD 14), as a staging point on the road between Caesaraugusta (Zaragoza) and Asturica (Astorga).

The Celtiberian town has been uncovered on the top of the hill, overlaid by the Roman streets above a red, burned layer of ashes and debris. Remains of a Roman amphitheater (or theater), a bathing establishment and large houses can also be seen. Outside Numantia, the outlines of no less than eleven Roman camps are now visible, including six constructed by Scipio Aemilianus, in addition to the circumvallation over five miles long, consisting of wall and towers and moat, by which he sealed off the fortress.

Numidia. A country in north Africa. The name was at first applied loosely to the extensive zone occupied by the nomadic tribes of the Numidae, a territory which was, at times, roughly equivalent to the modern Algeria. Subsequently, however, the western part of this territory (notably the land of the Masaesyli) was thought of as belonging to Mauretania instead, and the name of Numidia was restricted to its eastern section—including the tribal area of the Massyli—which bordered upon the possessions of Carthage.

In the later third century BC, during the Second Punic War, Syphax, chief of the Masaesyli, overran part of the territory of Masinissa of the Massyli, and supplemented his capital at Siga (Tafna) by a second residence at Cirta (Constantine). The Roman victory in the war (201), however, eliminated Syphax and reestablished Masinissa as monarch of an enlarged Numidia, which he continued to rule until 148. Divided between his sons after his death (except for its western, Masaesylian, portion, which was assigned to Mauretania at this time: *see* above), the country was forcibly reunited by his grandson Jugurtha (118), who after a long war against the Romans was finally given up to them in 105 and executed in the following year. Sallust's *Jugurthine War* tells the story; and he indicates that there were many Italian businessmen in Numidia at this time.

Jugurtha's grand-nephew Juba I (60) sided with Pompey the Great in his civil war against Julius Caesar, and died after the latter's victory at Thapsus (Ed-Dimas, 46). At this juncture Numidia became the Roman province of Africa Nova (of which Sallust was the first governor) and its famous marble quarries at Simitthu (Chemtou) were taken over by the state. However, the country reverted to the status of a client kingdom under the late monarch's son Juba II (30), until the latter was transferred to Mauretania (25). Thereupon Africa Nova was merged with the original province of Africa (Vetus).

Under Tiberius, the Numidian Tacfarinas led a serious insurrection (AD 17–24). In the time of Trajan (98–117) the Third Legion (Augusta) was moved from Africa Vetus to Lambaesis (Tazzoult, Lambèse) in Numidia, which Septimius Severus made into a separate province (197/8), with that stronghold as its capital. During these first two centuries of the Principate the population and agricultural wealth of Numidia had substantially risen. Military colonies were founded, and the slave trade with the Sahara increased, although the majority of the population were little affected by Romanization.

In 305 Numidia was divided into two provinces, Cirtensis and Militiana, with their capitals at Cirta and Lambaesis respectively; though this arrangement only lasted until 312, when Constantine I the Great reunited the two areas. Christianity had already spread rapidly by this time, and in the fourth century Numidia became the center of the fanatically puritanical Donatist heresy. After the Vandals under Gaiseric had crossed over to north Africa (429), they entered Numidia in the following year, and the western Roman emperor Valentinian III recognized their occupation of part of the country in 435. Soon afterward, its remaining areas, too, fell into their hands, with the exception of southern districts, which were overrun by Saharan raiders and Berber tribesmen. *See also* Cirta, Cuicul, Hippo Regius, Lambaesis, Thamugadi.

Nusaybin *see* Nisibis

Nuvla *see* Nola

Nymphaeum, Nymphaion (near Geroevka). A Greek city, with a good harbor, on the east coast of the Tauric Chersonese (Crimea), eleven miles south of Panticapaeum (Kerch): situated on the Cimmerian Bosphorus (*see* Bosphorus) which linked the Euxine (Black) Sea with Lake Maeotis (the Sea of Azov). Occupying the site of an earlier Scythian settlement on a small hill, Nymphaeum was founded by Greek colonists in the first half of the sixth century, and was probably incorporated in the kingdom of the Cimmerian Bosphorus not long after 500, but *c* 444 became the principal Athenian outpost on the eastern shore of the Tauric Chersonese, before reverting to the Bosphoran kingdom after the defeat of Athens in the Peloponnesian War (404).

The city of Nymphaeum, protected by walls, enriched itself from a large-scale grain trade. Investigations of wealthy fifth-century burials have uncovered abundant material (clothing ornaments, arrow heads, horses and harness) that has led to the conclusion that the Scythian nobility partook actively in the life of the Greek community: finds include not only Greek imported ceramics (and brightly colored plaster ornaments) but also extensive local handmade pottery of native style.

The continuation of active life during the fourth century, despite destruction (*see* below), is confirmed by the excavation of a wine-pressing plant—the earliest so far known in the northern Black Sea area—which recalls that the short-lived issue of coinage by Nymphaeum, at a slightly earlier date, had depicted not only the head of a nymph (personifying the place-name) but also a vine branch.

Excavations have traced levels of habitation from the sixth century, when a shrine of Aphrodite on the acropolis was probably founded, in addition to a temple of Demeter near the harbor; a sanctuary of the non-Greek Cabiri was also erected in the same seaside area before 400. All these buildings were demolished in the course of the fourth century. Parts of a third (?) century edifice, however—which now lies underwater, like much of the ancient city and port—have been explored, as well as a large structure of about the same period which was made of rose marl (a mixture of clay and calcium carbonate). Large portions of the city were reoriented and reconstructed in the second century BC, and again in the first century AD, but subsequent epochs witnessed widespread destruction and abandonment, presumably as a result of attacks from natives in the interior.

Nysa *see* Scythopolis

O

Oberhausen *see* Augusta Vindelicorum

Odessus, Odessos (Varna, Bulgaria). A Greek colony on the west coast of the Euxine (Black) Sea, founded by settlers from Miletus in Ionia (western Asia Minor) *c* 600/575 BC. Odessus stood at the head of a bay (the Gulf of Varna) at the point where the river Panysus (Provadiyska) passes out of Lake Devna into the sea; the name of the town has been interpreted as signifying 'waters.' Pottery of the colony's early years, as excavations reveal, was imported from many parts of the Greek world. Inscriptions show Thracian names among its citizens from the third century, when local prosperity is illustrated by finds of splendid gold jewelry.

The city became a member of the League (*koinon*) of Greek cities along the same coast known as the Pontic Pentapolis (Pontus=Euxine Sea). In due course, too, it formed close links with the kingdom of Pontus (northern Asia Minor). In 72 BC Odessus surrendered to the Roman general Lucius Licinius Lucullus and *c* 50 was destroyed, perhaps by the Dacian king Burebista. Attached, during the Roman Principate, to the province of Moesia and then Lower Moesia—in which it was the coastal terminal of a road traversing the whole province—it benefited from the fall of its rival Marcianopolis (Rekna Devnia) to the Goths (238). In the later empire Odessus belonged to the province of Moesia Secunda.

The first coins of the city, in *c* 200 BC, had honored 'the Great God of the Odessians.' Then follows an isolated, apparently unique, piece of Augustus (27 BC–AD 14), which seems to have been issued to celebrate the reorganization of the Pentapolis as a Hexapolis, of which Odessus assumed the presidency (later relinquished to Tomis [Constanţa]). A subsequent imperial monetary series, from Trajan (AD 98–117) to Gallienus (253–68), depicts Hades, Asclepius, Demeter and Nemesis, and a temple of Tyche (Fortune). Statuettes of the second and third centuries AD reveal the existence not only of Greco-Roman cults but also of the worship of Isis and Thracian deities (a shrine of the Thracian rider-god had apparently been destroyed by Burebista). Off the nearby shore (at

Lazurny Bereg), a ship containing three hundred amphoras has been found.

Oea (Trablus, Tarabulus al-Gharb, Tripoli). A town of Tripolitania in north Africa, situated on a rocky promontory between the Lesser Syrtes (Gulf of Gabes) (part of Libya) and Greater Syrtes (Gulf of Sirte). It was one of the three cities (*treis poleis*) which gave rise to the modern name of Tripoli, the others being Lepcis Magna and Sabrata. Situated in a fertile coastal oasis, and possessing a small natural harbor, Oea stood at the meeting place not only of roads along the coast but also of routes into the interior of the continent.

The settlement was founded as a trading station by the Carthaginians (under the name of Wy't). After passing into the Roman province of Africa (146 BC) it issued coinages inscribed with the names of its civic officials (suffetes). Two of these issues bear heads of Augustus and apparently celebrate his confirmation of Oea's status as a free community *c* 12–7 BC; and the series continued under Tiberius (AD 14–37), showing attributes of Apollo and Athena and depicting the empress Livia as Ceres (Demeter). In 70, Oea became involved in a war with Lepcis Magna, caused by the stealing of crops by peasants on both sides. The Oeans, outnumbered, enlisted the help of the brigand tribe of the Garamantes, who ravaged the territory of Lepcis Magna, but were driven off by a Roman force under Valerius Festus. Oea became a Roman colony under Trajan (98–117), perhaps receiving a settlement of veterans. About 155 the novelist Apuleius was accused of securing the affections of a rich widow of the city by bewitchment, and his *Apologia* is a defence against this charge. The place was a Christian episcopal see by 256, and in the later empire became part of a new province of Tripolitana—governed from Lepcis Magna—until the region was occupied by the Vandals *c* 450. Oea is the only one of the 'three cities' to have survived until today (as the capital of the Libyan state).

Two ancient streets converged at right angles near the harbor, at a point where a well-preserved four-faced triumphal arch was dedicated to the emperors Marcus Aurelius and Lucius Verus in 163. Nearby are the remains of a temple dedicated to the Genius of the Colony (183/4). The city walls, demolished in 1913, incorporated long stretches of the ancient fortifications. Three miles outside the town the grave of a female devotee of Mithras has been found; at the time of discovery it displayed the painted figure of a lioness, inscribed 'a lioness lies here,' i.e. the woman buried in the tomb was an initiate of the 'Lion' grade of the Mithraic hierarchy.

Oenone *see* Aegina

Oescus (Ghighen). A fortress-city and river port in Moesia (northern Bulgaria). Situated at the point where the river Oescus (Iskăr) debouched from the south into the Danube (which has now changed course, and is three miles away).

During the early Principate a legion was stationed at Oescus; it has lately been argued that this headquarters dates back to Augustus (31 BC–AD 14), and an inscription confirms its existence under Claudius (AD 41–54). When Domitian divided Moesia into two provinces (85/6), Oescus became a stronghold of the Lower province, strategically placed at the meeting point of the riverside road with another road leading to the south. Under Trajan who annexed Dacia across the Danube (105), the place was raised to the rank of a Roman colony, though its legionary garrison was removed. The troops returned shortly before Aurelian evacuated Dacia (271), and when this happened, Oescus became a frontier station once again—receiving expanded fortifications—within the new province of Dacia Ripensis south of the river. Gothic invasions inflicted severe damage. Constantine I the Great (306-37) built a bridge across the Danube just north of the city. In the fifth century the Huns brought further destruction.

The ancient main street of Oescus has been located, as well as a large three-aisled public building north of the forum, and another east of the forum, stated by an inscription to be 'for use during the winter.' The Capitolium probably dates from the time of Hadrian (117-38). The west gate of the city, poorly preserved, has received examination. Outside the walls, an apsidal bath with subterranean galleries is now unearthed, and the remains of two aqueducts can be seen. Ceramic and metalworks have been traced, and a floor mosaic represents a scene from an unknown comedy of Menander, *The Achaeans.* Inscriptions bear witness to a mixed population, including ex-soldiers and other residents from Asia Minor, north Italy and Gaul. Among a varied array of cults the worship of Mithras was prominent.

Oetaea *see* Doris

Ofanto (River) *see* Aufidus

Olba, Olbe (Uğura or Ura). A city in Cilicia Tracheia or Aspera (Rough Cilicia) in southeastern Asia Minor, situated thirteen miles inland at a height of about 3,000 feet, west of the river Lamus.

In the sixth century Olba was probably the capital of a local state, Pirindu; later it became associated with a powerful shrine of Zeus Olbios (heir to a native weather-god) which lay at what was later known as Diocaesarea and perhaps earlier as Prateana (Uzuncaburç), both centers having been founded, according to tradition, by the Trojan war hero Ajax, son of Telamon and brother of Teucer. By the first century BC, Olba possessed a city organization (and local coinage) under the supervision of princely high priests (toparchs). This dynasty, in which the first known ruler was Taracyaris (Teucer), suffered temporary displacement from a certain Zenophanes. He was deposed, however, in 41 by Antony and Cleopatra in favor of his own daughter Aba, whose husband had belonged to the ruling house; later, she, too, was removed, but according to Strabo her descendants continued to reign.

Coinage was issued by the high priest and toparch Ajax, son of Teucer (from *c* AD 10/11), who describes his subjects as the people of Cennatis (a region to the west of Olba) and Lalassis (which probably lay further north). Subsequently, perhaps from the reign of Claudius (41-54), a certain Marcus Antonius Polemo—who was perhaps the son of Julius Polemo, King Polemo I of Pontus, though Dio Cassius confuses the men bearing this name—coined as 'dynast' of the people of sacred Olba and of the Cennateis and Lalasseis; and this may be the Polemo who describes himself as king (*basileus*) on coins naming the League (*koinon*) on the Lalasseis and Cennateis, and on other pieces bearing the head of Galba (68–69). Later coinage of Olba, after its principality had been incorporated by Vespasian in his new province of Cilicia (*c* 72), invested the city with the titles of Hadriane and Antoniniane, and described it as the metropolis of Cennatis and of Cetis, a district in the interior of Rough Cilicia which was understood to include Olba and part of the coast.

The remains of Olba include a theater and *nymphaeum* (fountain house) of the second century AD and a section of an aqueduct dated to 199–211, that brought water from the upper Lamus and spanned one of the ravines, riddled with rock-cut graves, that surround Olba's hill. A coin of the early second century AD depicts a crenellated tower, of a type still to be seen at the place; some of these strong points guarded the approaches of the city, and others served as tombs in its cemeteries.

When Vespasian abolished and annexed the priestly state of Olba he raised the adjacent sanctuary of Diocaesarea (of which the Turkish name Uzuncaburç means high tower) to the status of an independent city, and it issued coinage on which it describes itself as Hadriane and the metropolis of Cennatis or the Cennateis, in addition to identifying itself with Olba's heritage by the depiction of a personification of 'Olbos' (prosperity). Coins of Septimius Severus (193–211) show his temple and altar. The site of this Hellenistic shrine—one of a number to be seen in the city—has been identified and its platform cleared. Beside it stand the remains of an ornamental gateway, which may be the arch (surmounted by statues) displayed on a coin of Otacilia Severa, wife of Philip the Arab (244–49). Other buildings to be seen on the site include a theater (with an inscription of 164/5) and a long rectangular Roman gymnasium (?). A triple-arched second-century gate in the city wall records repairs (of the gate or wall) in the joint reign of Arcadius and Honorius (395–408).

Olbia, Olbiopolis (Olvia, near Parutino). A Greek city on the coast of the Ukraine (Soviet Union). Olbia was situated at the northwestern extremity of the Euxine (Black) Sea, on the right (west) bank of the river Hypanis (Bug), near the entrance of its great estuary gulf (*liman*), twenty-three miles west of the estuary gulf of the Borysthenes (later Danapris, now Dnieper)—which at that time had a different course. Colonists from Miletus in Ionia (western Asia Minor) and from other Greek cities established Olbia in the first half of the sixth century BC—claiming Apollo as their leader, because of a Delphic oracle—and it soon controlled a state (originally named Borysthenes, personified on its early coinage) comprising numerous other settlements and markets (*emporia*) on the shores of the two gulfs (for one of them, Berezan, *see* below).

The Olbians possessed important fisheries, and issued curious fifth-century bronze coins shaped like a dolphin, as well as exceptionally large circular pieces. They also traded deep into eastern and central Europe, to which they exported not only abundant wine but also weapons and other metal objects, since their territory and contacts provided supplies of iron, copper, quartzite and gold. But their most significant enterprise was the resale and exportation to Greece of wheat grown in the inexhaustibly fertile 'Black Earth' region of the Scythian hinterland. Although this activity did not reach its height, at least as far as Athens was concerned, until relatively late, the commerce of Olbia was already strongly thriving in the middle of the fifth century, when Herodotus visited the place. He writes of a Scythian King Scyles who had imbibed philhellenic tastes from his Greek mother, and indulged them by frequent periods of residence in Olbia (where he had a house and a Greek wife), until these visits were discovered by his compatriots and led to his death. The story of this royal connection suggests that Olbia, which was not located on an easily defensible site, only existed through Scythian acquiescence and protection.

In the middle or later 320s the city was besieged by the Macedonian general Zopyrion, during his northern expedition from Thrace. Through the centuries that followed, it suffered from increasingly menacing incursions by the Scythians and Sarmatians (whom one rich citizen, according to an inscription, bribed to keep away). It was sacked by the Dacian king Burebista *c* 60. Its buildings were restored and reconstructed, but toward the end of the first century AD Dio Chrysostom, although noting that some of its inhabitants expressed a keen admiration of Homer, nevertheless found it impoverished and semi-barbarous. However, it continued to issue an extensive coinage at least until the reign of Severus Alexander (222–35), and a Roman garrison, installed by Antoninus Pius (138–61), did not leave until Gothic attacks in the reign of Philip the Arab (244–49).

The city consisted of an upper town on a plateau about a hundred and twenty feet above sea level, and a lower town bordering the estuary gulf of the Hypanis. The latter area is now partly underwater, owing to a rise in the sea level, but four zones have been recently excavated, prompting the suggestion that the population rose from an original figure of about 6,000 to approximately 10,000. The public buildings of the upper town seem to have been erected in the second half of the sixth century BC. One region includes the agora, adjoined by a huge colonnade, a court house (*dikasterion*), a gymnasium (of the late fourth and third centuries BC), and sacred enclosures containing temples of Zeus and Apollo Delphinios, separated from the agora by a spacious portico. North of the agora, private dwellings have also been uncovered. Some of these attained considerable size and wealth—in contrast to forty Greek huts and semi-huts from the mid-sixth to the early fifth century that have likewise been excavated.

Workshops and storage pits have also come to light. In an early residential district at the western end of the city (overlooking the gorge of 'Zayach'ya Balka [Hare's Ravine]), further inscriptions suggest the presence of a temple of Zeus Eleutherios and indicate the existence of a seven-man committee entrusted with the construction and repair of walls. Across the ravine lay the suburb (*proasteion*) in which Scyles left his Scythian followers behind when he visited the city. An inscription refers to a theater, and another, recently discovered, records the builders of the city's defences, in connection with the siege by Zopyrion (for Scyles and Zopyrion, *see* above). The varied graves around the city include trench tombs and underground vaults, later lined to form chambers.

The heavily populated territory of Olbia, covering an area nearly forty miles wide and thirty deep, has likewise been the subject of intensive recent investigation, revealing a complex of no less than seventy communities, linked by an elaborate intercommunications system that almost amounts to an entire second Greece; although the view that the peoples occupying these centers were wholly or even mainly Greek has been contested, in confirmation of Herodotus' reference to two mixed racial groups (the term Mixellenes, 'mixed Greeks,' was employed, at least at a later date); archaeological evidence bears witness to strong Thracian elements.

Excavations at Berezan have proved particularly important. Berezan, now on an island but originally perhaps a peninsula or promontory—of which the ancient name is unknown—lies at the entrance of the combined mouths of the Hypanis and Borysthenes, twenty-three miles west-southwest of Olbia. Eusebius placed the foundation of the Greek settlement, or market (*emporion*), of Berezan about a century before the establishment of Olbia itself. If that early dating is correct (as is disputed), the center of the original settlement at Berezan may have been transferred to Olbia when the latter came into existence *c* 575; although, if so, Berezan was reoccupied shortly afterward (perhaps in a form of union [synoecism] with Olbia). Much light has been thrown on its economic conditions *c* 500 by the discovery of a private letter (written on lead, rolled into a scroll), the earliest preserved business letter in Greek history.

During the fifth century Berezan possessed a temple, built of bricks on a stone foundation. The town also contained thatched houses that were set low in the ground to afford protection in winter, and possessed fireplaces and storage—or refuse—pits. The island of Berezan has yielded an enormous number of finds at various points and from various periods, and discoveries on the eastern shore, where the only landing place is to be found, extend to the Roman and medieval epochs.

As for the Olbian territory as a whole, archaeological probings have confirmed a series of sharp political and economic vicissitudes. Settlements were abandoned in the fifth century BC, revived in the fourth, and abandoned again in the early third, but regained their prosperity in the first and second centuries AD, and remained in existence until the fourth.

Olbia *see* Nicomedia, Sardinia

Olisipo *see* Tagus (River)

Olympia. Situated in Pisa (Pisatis), a region adjoining Elis (western Peloponnese, southern Greece), seven-and-a-half miles from the Ionian Sea, at the point where the rivers Alpheus and Cladeus meet at the foot of the hill of Cronus (405 feet), before they break out into the fertile coastal plain. Strabo ascribes the initial fame of Olympia to an oracle of Gaia (Earth), and archaeological evidence indicates continual habitation from *c* 2800 to *c* 1100 BC. Olympia was the scene of the most important athletic festival in the world (one of the Great Four, the others being the Pythian, Isthmian and Nemean); it was held there every fourth year in August and September (between the grain harvest and collection of the grapes and olives), for more than a thousand years.

According to Pindar, whose splendid Odes immortalized the victors, the Olympic Games were founded by Heracles; and this was the tradition maintained at Elis. But local traditions of Olympia ascribed their establishment to the legendary Pelops, son of Tantalus—from whom the Peloponnese took its name—after he had killed Oenomaus, king of Pisa, thus acquiring the dead man's daughter Hippodameia as his bride. Tumulus graves ascribed to Pelops and Hippodameia go back to the later years of the second millennium BC, and so also (unless they are earlier still) do cults of Cronus, Gaia, Eileithyia and Themis, round the foot of the hill of Cronus. The worship of Olympian Zeus—who gave the place its name—must have been introduced at the time of the immigrations or invasions ascribed to the Dorian Greeks around the turn of the first millennium. A local athletic contest was held at Olympia at least by *c* 900, and gradually attracted competitors from farther afield and developed their renown. The traditional date of the first recognized Olympiad is 776—the earliest important event in Greek history to which a date can be attributed, though its author (Hippias of Elis) had no sound reason for its choice. After a series of disputes the control of the Games passed, already in 776 according to Strabo but more probably *c* 572, from Pisa to the larger unit of Elis, with which it remained, though in 365 the Arcadian League temporarily gained possession of Olympia.

In their final form the Games lasted for five days. The first day was one of preparation and of sacrifices and prayers to the Gods. On the second day were held the chariot race, horse race and 'Five Events' (*pentathlon*). Since the third day always coincided with the full moon, it was the occasion of further religious functions, leading up to a procession to the altar of Zeus, followed by sacrifices and a feast. In the afternoon came the three juniors' or boys' events. The fourth day witnessed the three senior (men's) running events, and the wrestling, all-in wrestling (*pankration*) and boxing (at a later date also the men's race in armor). The fifth and last day was devoted to farewell celebrations, including a banquet for the winners, the dedication of thank-offerings, and a final set of sacrifices. Women were excluded from Olympic (as from the other leading) Games, but supplementary running races, in honor of Zeus' wife Hera, were added for female competitors.

Entries were by individuals—who had to be free-born Greeks—and not, as now, by states; and the only prizes awarded were wreaths made from the branches of a sacred olive tree in the precinct of Zeus. But this moderation did not suffice to foster a wholly amateur spirit; for one thing, an Olympic victor might well be rewarded and honored by his city-state for the rest of his life. Three heralds sent out from Elis declared a sacred truce for the duration of the Games, and no war between Greek cities ever prevented these festivals from being held; if states engaged in wars did not lay down arms for the period of the truce, a stiff fine was imposed, calculated according to the numbers of soldiers involved.

Alexander the Great (d. 323) refused to take part in the festival 'unless his opponents were kings.' Four centuries later, however, in AD 67, the emperor Nero made a personal appearance. First he had unprecedentedly postponed the Olympic Games for two years, so that he could have an opportunity to perform in all the 'Big Four.' Then, when the Olympic festival was eventually held, he introduced a series of new musical and dramatic contests—and won them himself. In the chariot competition, too, he rode a team of ten horses; during the race he fell out, but was nevertheless allotted the prize. After his death in the following year the Neronian Games were deleted from the record.

Thereafter the Olympic Games continued to reign supreme, despite more than three hundred rival and imitative series of contests throughout the empire. The Games continued at least until 267 (when Herulian Germans sacked Olympia) and probably thereafter until 393, when Theodosius I banned all pagan cults. In 426 the Olympian sanctuary, the Altis, was burned down. Christian churches were built on the site, and in the sixth century it was overwhelmed by earthquakes and floods. Its partial rediscovery in 1766, 1829 and especially 1875–81 helped to inspire Baron Pierre de Coubertin to resuscitate the Games in 1896, when the first of the revived series was held at Athens.

The Altis precinct formed a rectangle measuring about six hundred and fifty by five hundred feet. It has yielded discoveries of huge numbers of dedicated objects, going back to early dates. The most ancient architectural remains are those of a shrine of Hera (*c* 600 BC)—probably the first monumental temple on the Greek mainland—containing statues of herself and Zeus; only the head of Hera has been found, but the building yielded the outstanding Hermes by the fourth-century sculptor Praxiteles, preserved in the Olympia museum. Also to be seen in the museum are the pediment sculptures of the temple of Zeus (*c* 460)—a monument of self-assertion of the new democratic government at Elis—which depicted, at its east end, the chariot race of Pelops and Oenomaus, and at the west end a battle between the Lapiths and Centaurs (at the wedding of Pirithous and Deidamia) quelled by a superb central figure of Apollo; these sculptured groups have been recently reconstructed, with the addition of over three hundred fragments. Most of the original four hundred and fifty column drums of the peristyle have also been identified and measured. Within the temple was an enormous chryselephantine (gold-plated and ivory) seated statue of Zeus by the fifth century Athenian sculptor Phidias. Although his workshop has been located, the statue has vanished, and its appearance can only be inferred from literary descriptions and coins, notably of Elis under Hadrian, (AD 117–38). Of the great adjoining Altar of Zeus scarcely any trace remains.

At a corner of the Altis stood the office of the functionary presiding over the Games, the *prytaneum*, with a dining room for notables and victorious athletes. Other buildings in the sanctuary included a row of Treasuries of various Greek states erected in the sixth and fifth centuries BC—mostly by cities in south Italy and Sicily—as well as a Metroon (temple of the Mother of the Gods) of about 400, a circular monument (the Philippeum) in honor of King Philip II of Macedonia (d. 336), a portico of a later date within the same century, and an apsed *nymphaeum* (fountain house) put up by the wealthy Athenian sophist Herodes Atticus (*c* AD 107–77) to provide Olympia with its first piped supply of water, which had hitherto been supplied by wells.

The early stadium, where the running and the discus- and javelin-throwing competitions were held, had been partly within the boundaries of the Altis, extending along the slope in front of the treasuries; but in the mid-fourth century it was moved to a position wholly outside the precinct, occupying a flat piece of land measuring about 660 by 250 yards. Further south was the Hippodrome where the chariot and horse races were held. Likewise, outside the Altis, near the workshop of Phidias, stood a series of other buildings: a Bouleuterion (Council House or Seat of the Olympic Senate) consisting of a pair of apsidal chambers (later linked by a central hall); a southern portico; a hotel for distinguished visitors (known as the Leonidaeum after its architect of the later fourth century BC, and adapted in the second century AD as a residence for the Roman governor of Achaea); an athletics school (*palaestra*) of the fourth or third century BC, and a gymnasium of the second. Accommodation for the thousands of spectators was, by modern standards, makeshift, being restricted to standing room only—although seats were provided for a few important personages. Except for these, everyone slept in the open air or in tents.

Olympus, Olympos (Mount). The highest mountain in Greece (9,570 feet); situated in the northeastern part of the country (Pieria), on the border between Thessaly and Macedonia. Olympia was early believed to be the abode of the gods, who owe their name of Olympians to this location; the mountain was chosen by tradition as their home either because immigrants to Greece (*c* 1700 BC) had come from the region, or because it stood on the edge of the known world. Since the gods were also, alternatively, believed to dwell in the sky (envisaged as a solid vault), there was confusion between the mountaintop and the heavens, and this dilemma is apparent in Homer's *Iliad* and *Odyssey*.

In historical times the extensive massif of Olympus, extending a long distance inland from the coast, served to protect Greece from invaders, who had to skirt the mountain either by forcing the narrow pass of Tempe to its east (with Mount Ossa [*qv*] beyond it) or by attempting to penetrate the high passes to its west. Lions survived in the district down to the time of Herodotus. (There were other mountains of the same name in Arcadia, Cyprus, Elis, Euboea, Laconia, Lesbos, Mysia and the Troad).

Olynthus, Olynthos (near Miriofita or Neos Olynthos). A city in northern Greece on the Macedonian promontory of Chalcidice, situated on a double hill a mile and a half north of the head of the Gulf of Torone. Late Neolithic and early Iron Age settlements have been identified. Olynthus belonged to the Thracian tribe of the Bottiaeans until 479 BC, when the Persian general Artabazus, after escorting Xerxes I to the Hellespont (Dardanelles), slew the local inhabitants and handed the town over to Greeks from Chalcidice. From 454 it formed part of the Delian League under Athenian control, but in 433/1, instigated by King Perdiccas II of Macedonia, it revolted and received a great increase of population from other city-states of Chalcidice, becoming the center (and later mint) of their new Chalcidic (or Olynthian) League, a pioneer example of ancient federalism.

During the Peloponnesian War Olynthus formed the base for a Spartan expeditionary force under Brasidas (433/2). Concluding a treaty with Macedonia (390), the Chalcidic League issued coins of great artistic distinction at the city. But the growing and considerable territorial expansion of this confederacy aroused the hostility of Sparta, which disbanded it after a successful two-year siege of Olynthus (379). Following the eclipse of Sparta at the hands of Thebes (371), however, the League recovered. When war broke out between Philip II of Macedonia and Athens (357), it sided first with the former (a fragmentary copy of the treaty has been found) and then with the latter: but despite the Athenian orator Demosthenes' brilliant *Olynthiac Speeches*, urging support for the city, it fell to Philip by treachery and was razed to the ground (348).

Its population may have reached a figure of about 15,000. The principal urban area was laid out on a regular 'Hippodamian' design (named after the Milesian town planner Hippodamus, *c* 500). More than a hundred house plans have been traced at Olynthus, including fifty in five complete blocks and others located outside the city (forming an extension on the grid plan); these discoveries have made a major contribution to our knowledge of Greek domestic architecture. The standard house, of prosperous appearance, possessed a court (sometimes colonnaded) with rooms on three sides. Above the principal suites on the north side were upper storeys. Kitchens with flues, and bathrooms with terracotta tubs, have also been uncovered. Walls were constructed of mud brick with stone bases, inner walls were painted (often so as to imitate masonry), and the pebble floor mosaics—occurring mainly in the dining rooms (*andrones*) but also in other parts of the houses—amount to the most extensive and impressive group of late fifth-and early fourth-century examples of this art found anywhere in the Greek world. The mosaics in the 'Villa of Good Fortune' include notable mythological scenes of Dionysus in a chariot, and Thetis bringing armor to Achilles. A group of inscriptions unearthed in these dwellings provides information about their sales, rentals and mortgages.

Few official buildings have so far been found, though traces of a portico and council house can be seen beside an open space. Shops and artisans' houses were located in a separate quarter. Olynthus was provided with water brought by terracotta pipes from a spring ten miles away. Near the city, according to Strabo, was a hollow known as Cantharolethron ('Beetle-Death'), because the beetles which are ubiquitous in the area died when they entered it.

Onchestus *see* Haliartus

Ophiussa *see* Tyras

Opis *see* Seleucia on the Tigris

Oplontis (Torre Annunziata). Situated on the coast of Campania (southwest Italy), beside the Gulf of Cumae (Bay of Naples), about three miles west of Pompeii. Oplontis is the site of a magnificent villa overwhelmed by the eruption of Mount Vesuvius in AD 79, which buried the mansion under six feet of ash and pumice and then fifteen feet of volcanic mud.

Excavations of this residence during the past two decades have produced outstanding finds, comprising the greater part of the main residential block, together with its slave accommodation, and portions of an extensive farming complex (*villa rustica*). The principal block, containing a projecting atrium flanked by a series of rooms, faced a garden on the north side, and opened up, toward the south, onto a continuous colonnade, which stood on a terraced platform and in ancient times apparently looked out directly over the sea. Although the villa, it would seem, was undergoing and awaiting modernization at the time of the eruption, five rooms retain a remarkable series of wall paintings of *c* 40 BC belonging to what is known as the 'Second Style' (*see* Pompeii) which excelled in the depiction of airy, theatrical architectural vistas. Subsequent artistic styles are also represented, for example in a bedroom which exceptionally preserves its painted ceiling.

There is some evidence, based on inscriptions, that this palatial dwelling was at one time owned by Nero's second wife Poppaea Sabina, who came from a leading Pompeian family and is known to have possessed property in the neighborhood. She died in AD 65 and Nero in 68, and it seems that thereafter the villa remained unoccupied (except for the slave quarters) until the eruption of 79. The name Oplontis (sometimes appearing as Eplontis) is only found on two itineraries of late date and on a late Roman map (the Peutinger Table), on which the place is indicated as a station on the road between Pompeii and Herculaneum. Since such lists are often based on outdated information, this allusion to Oplontis could mean that a habitation center (still buried) had adjoined the villa before both were destroyed by Vesuvius. Alternatively, however, the compilers of the itineraries and map may be referring to a settlement that only appeared after the eruption.

Opus *see* Locris

Orange *see* Arausio

Orbetello *see* Calusium

Orchomenus, Orchomenos, or (on nearly all its coins) Erchomenos (recently renamed Orchomenos, combining two modern villages). A city in Boeotia (central Greece), beside the western shore of Lake Copais (now drained), at the eastern end of the rocky ridge of Mount Akontion ('javelin'; now Dourdouvana), above the principal spring of the river Melas (Mavropotamos). A little to the south, another river, the Cephisus, likewise debouches into Lake Copais.

Palaeolithic remains have been found in the neighborhood, and Orchomenus was inhabited in Neolithic times. During the Bronze Age it was one of the most powerful palace centers in the country, founding (according to tradition) the huge island fortress of Glal, and becoming, in the second half of the second millennium BC, the principal city of Boeotia and the capital of the Minyans, half-legendary immigrants from Thessaly under the leadership of Minyas; the Treasury of the Minyans, according to Pausanias, was 'a wonder second to none either in Greece or elsewhere.' The name of Orchomenus, supposedly derived from a son of Minyas, appears in the Catalog of Ships in Homer's *Iliad.* The poem also refers to the wealth of the place, which was reflected in a number of personal names incorporating the word 'gold' (*chrysos*). The Orchomenians were said to have been strong enough to impose tribute on Thebes, the later capital of Boeotia. Many other stories also centered on their city, notably those relating to the fabulous buildings of its architects Trophonius and Agamedes, sons of King Erginus (though the father of Trophonius was also asserted to have been the god Apollo); while other stories tell of the first drainage systems of the shorelands of Lake Copais (temporarily destroyed, according to tradition, by Heracles, who was said to have put Erginus to death.) The Orchomenians of the Bronze Age produced handsome grey and yellow 'Minyan' pottery, and prehistoric drainage works have been tentatively identified two miles east of the city.

In about the eighth century Orchomenus, according to an unexpected statement by Strabo, belonged to a grouping of cities known as the Amphictyony of Calauria (the island of Poros), which was based on the worship of Poseidon and drew the rest of its membership from the Argolid. Within Boeotia itself the city's position was gradually eclipsed by the Thebans. Its first coins (*c* 530), however, suggest that it was still independent of the Theban-controlled Boeotian League at that date, since the design of a buckler that characterized the federal issues does not appear. But Orchomenus joined the League soon after the Persian Wars (if not earlier), playing a prominent part—under the leadership of exiles expelled by the Athenians—in the reconstituted federation in 447/6. After a severe earthquake in 427/6, a further group of exiles from the city hatched an unsuccessful plot with the Athenians to hand them over Chaeronea (424), which at that time was an Orchomenian possession. Allied with Sparta against Thebes in the battles of Coronea and Haliartus (395, 394), Orchomenus was destroyed by the Thebans in 364 and again (after Phocian restoration) in 349. Reconstructed by Philip II of Macedonia and Alexander the Great, it became—following the latter's destruction of Thebes (335)—the leading member of a new Boeotian Confederation. In 86 it was the scene of a victory by Sulla's Roman army over Archelaus—a general of Mithridates VI Eupator of Pontus—which was followed by the plundering of the city. In Roman times it seems to have been wholly insignificant.

Throughout the ancient centuries a number of settlements rose successively at different sites on the eastern slopes and foot of Mount Akontion. A seventh-century BC wall, round the lowest terrace, is poorly preserved, but the complex fourth-century ramparts provide one of the finest specimens of ancient Greek fortification in existence. They are unified by three transverse walls, of which one marks the boundary of the fourth century hilltop acropolis, a thousand feet above the plain. On an intermediate terrace stood a temple of Asclepius, while a theater (*c* 300) has been recently excavated at the foot of the hill. The source of the river Melas was the Acidalia or spring of the Graces (Charites), who were celebrated at Orchomenus by worship and festivals (the Charitesia). Pausanias also refers to shrines of Dionysus and Heracles. (There were other towns with same name of Orchomenus in Arcadia and Phthiotis [Thessaly]).

Oreus *see* Histiaea

Orléans *see* Cenabum

Orontes (River), also known as Axius (now Nahr Al-Asi). The principal river of western Syria, the Orontes rises north of Heliopolis (Baalbek) in the Bekaa valley between Mounts Libanus (Lebanon) and Anti-Libanus in Phoenicia (Lebanon), flows north - northeast past Emesa (Homs), north-northwest past Apamea (Qalaat el-Mudik), and finally southwest past Antioch (Antakya in the Hatay, Turkey), to enter the sea at Seleucia in Pieria.

Strabo, recording that this lowest stretch was navigable, quotes a myth indicating that the river was named after the man who first bridged it, and refers to a locality where in ancient times it flowed underground (hence its additional names Draco and Typhon, a dragon that was struck by lightning and fled beneath the earth); he also praises the fertility of the river valley. In antiquity, as later, the Orontes served as the principal route followed by traders and armies moving between Egypt and the north.

Oropus, Oropos (Skala Oropou, Oropos). A Greek town in the coastal territory (named Oropia after it) beside the mainland shore of the Euripus, the strait facing the island of Euboea.

Oropus was strategically important because its harbor and the adjacent 'Sacred Harbor' of Delphinium (Kamaraki) offered easy access to Euboea and the opportunity for customs tolls—which gave the inhabitants a reputation for avarice. The town also possessed a direct road link to Athens by way of Deceleia, which facilitated supplies of grain and cattle. Nevertheless, Oropus was only occasionally independent. More often, its control oscillated between Boeotia—of which it had originally formed part—and Athens; during the Peloponnesian War it was occupied by a force from the principal Boeotian city, Thebes (412). Ten years later, according to Diodorus, the Thebans moved the population three miles inland, to the site of the modern village of Oropos. There are sparse ancient remains in the area. The coinage of this new city, during a period of freedom in the second or first century BC—before permanent attachment to Athens ensued—displays a dolphin (a play on the name of the port of Delphinium), and a head that appears to represent Amphiaraus.

He was the mythical Argive warrior and seer who joined the expedition described in Aeschylus' *Seven against Thebes,* and was carried away by Zeus during the battle. His oracular shrine, the Amphiaraeum, stood in a wooded glen beside a ravine two miles north of Oropus, and was the city's principal claim to fame. Established perhaps in the sixth century BC, its oracle was consulted by King Croesus of Lydia, and by the later fifth century and especially in Hellenistic times (with the help of benefactions from Ptolemaic monarchs) it had developed extensively as a source of divination by the interpretation of dreams, a place were cures were effected, and the site of the quinquennial festivals of the Amphiaraea, which continued to be celebrated with increasing splendor in Roman times.

On the north side of the ravine are the remains of the Temple of Amphiaraus, beside a holy spring at the place where, according to Pausanias, the seer was believed to have risen to heaven; an adjacent portico was probably employed as a place of incubation, until a larger replacement was created nearby *c*350. There is also a line of stone bases, on which thank-offering dedications were erected; a small Hellenistic theater is still in excellent condition, and ruins of a bathing establishment are to be seen. The south side of the ravine bears extensive but ill-preserved traces of the various residential accommodations required by priests and pilgrims and the sick.

Ortaklar *see* Magnesia on the Maeander

Ortygia *see* Syracuse

Orvieto *see* Volsinii

Osca (Huesca). A city in northeastern Spain; situated on the slopes of a hill overlooking the Rio Isuela, a northern tributary of the river Iberus (Ebro), in territory ascribed by Ptolemy to the tribe of the Ilergetes (though Pliny the Elder and Strabo mention the names of other peoples). Roman occupation reached Osca by 208 BC, and it is mentioned by Livy as a major source of silver in 185. These abundant supplies of the metal—which were sent to Rome—are confirmed by plentiful second-century issues of silver coinage, displaying a bearded head and the figure of a horseman. In the 70s BC Osca was the capital and mint of Quintus Sertorius in his civil war against the governmental authorities; it was the meeting place of his 'senate,' and the location of an academy where the sons of Spanish chiefs wore Roman clothing and were given a classical education. However, it was at Osca that Sertorius was murdered by his own lieutenant Perperna (72).

In 39 BC Cnaeus Domitius Calvinus, the governor of Nearer Spain appointed by Octavian (the future Augustus), issued *denarii* with the old Iberian types, bearing the name of the city of Osca (in Latin), during or after his successful campaign against the tribe of the Cerretani. Subsequent issues with the head of Octavian, describing the city as Urbs Victrix, appear to refer to its elevation to the rank of *municipium* in 28. This coinage continued, at intervals, until the reign of Gaius (Caligula, AD 37-41). From the middle of the third century AD, the city contained a strong community of Christians, to one of whose number the Festa of San Lorenzo bears witness. At Fraga, not far from Osca, was a palatial Roman villa, owned at one time by a certain Fortunatus.

Osijek *see* Mursa Major

Osrhoene. A territory or country of northwestern Mesopotamia (now in southeastern Turkey, but at its widest extension also including parts of northeastern Syria), bounded on the west by the river Euphrates and on the north by Mount Masius, and commanding two major routes from western to central Asia.

Osrhoene (called Orrhoene by Pliny the Elder) took its name from Urha, the Syriac name for Edessa (now Urfa) its capital, which in turn may be derived from the name of Orhai (Osroes), an Iranian who more or less openly broke away from the Seleucid empire and founded an autonomous state in *c* 130 BC. The population of Osrhoene was mainly Aramaic, with Greek and Parthian (Iranian) components; its later rulers were generally Arabs. Their kingdom played a prominent part as a buffer between the Roman and Parthian empires, and was claimed as a dependency by both. In 53 BC Abgar (Ariaramnes) II betrayed Crassus to the Parthians, but in AD 116 and 123 Roman clients came into power, under the protection of Trajan and Hadrian respectively: though Hadrian had evacuated Trajan's short-lived Roman province of Mesopotamia, to which Osrhoene must have been loosely attached.

When the province was revived by Lucius Verus (162-65) and Septimius Severus (197-99), Osrhoene resumed its position as a client state, until Caracalla abolished the kingdom in 216 and incorporated it in a revived Mesopotamian province. Later in the same century, the Sassanian Persians, after they had overthrown the Parthians, coveted and frequently overran the territory. During the later Roman empire a separate province of Osrhoena was established, and became conspicuous not only as a key region in the frontier defence system, but as a center of Christian learning and controversy. *See also* Carrhae, Edessa, Mesopotamia, Nisibis.

Ossa, Mount. A mountain rising to a height of 6,489 feet at the northern end of Magnesia, the coastal district of Thessaly (northeastern Greece) facing the Aegean. At the southern extremity of the same range stands Mount Pelion, and across the Vale of Tempe from Ossa rises Olympus. All three mountains figure in a famous myth recounting how twin giants, Otus and Ephialtes, planned to climb up to heaven by piling Ossa on Olympus and Pelion on Ossa; but according to a tradition preserved by the *Odyssey*, they were killed by Apollo.

Osteria d'Osa *see* Collatia

Ostia. A city on the coast of Latium (Lazio), western Italy, at the mouth of the river Tiber, sixteen miles from Rome. When the Romans began a modest enlargement of their territory in the regal period, they seem to have expanded as far as the coast, establishing the port of Ostia at the mouth of the Tiber in order to exploit adjoining salt beds. This event was attributed to the semi-legendary King Ancus Marcius (traditionally 642-617 BC), but may instead be tentatively ascribed to Servius Tullius (*c* 578-535). Archaeological investigations have so far failed to reveal any trace of so early a settlement, but that may only be because the habitation center in question was located on ground which it has not been possible to explore.

At the time when the Romans broke up the Latin League *c* 338, they also regularized and strengthened whatever settlement they already possessed at Ostia, founding one of their very first colonies on the site. Its three hundred Roman citizen families inhabited a rectangular fort covering five acres, designed like a camp with two geometrically planned intersecting main streets and a strong stone wall, which the male settlers were numerous enough to man if they stood six feet apart. The colony's primary function was to defend the Tiber mouth from maritime enemies and pirates, thus removing the need for a permanent Roman fleet. But although the harbor at the mouth of the delta-forming river was still very inadequate, Ostia also supervized the collection of salt (see above), regulated trade, exacted customs dues, and stored grain and other foodstuffs for transportation by road or river up to Rome.

The First and Second Punic Wars (264-241, 218-201) caused Rome to develop its fleet, so that Ostia became an important naval base. When the wars had been successfully concluded, the impetus to maintain such a navy weakened, but the growth of Rome's population caused Ostia to retain its importance as a supply port for purchases from overseas, especially grain. By 100 BC the original small stronghold had become a substantial town, possessing an improved harbor and surrounded by walls enclosing a much increased perimeter. During the civil wars between Marius and Sulla, the former, returning from Africa, captured Ostia before marching on Rome (83).

The earliest surviving temple in the town, dedicated to Hercules, dates from about this time, but its important cult was dedicated to Vulcan, whose priest was the principal religious authority of the city. Ostia was plundered by pirates *c* 68, and during the wars between Octavian (the future Augustus) and Sextus Pompeius (concluded in 36) the place was imperilled by Sextus' command of the Tyrrhenian sea. Its revival under the Augustan peace is reflected by Agrippa's construction of a permanent theater, adjoined by a commercial meeting place. At the end of the forum a Capitolium was built, and cults of the Dioscuri (Castor and Pollux), Venus, Ceres, Fortuna and Spes (Hope) are of Augustan or earlier origin.

Since, however, the harbor was too small to handle all the ships that now sought entry and the larger of them could not pass the sand bar at the river mouth, Claudius (AD 41–54) constructed a large artificial port two miles to its north, equipped with a towering lighthouse and linked to the Tiber by two canals. Since, however, it soon became clear that this new harbor did not provide sufficient shelter against sudden storms (one of which sank two hundred ships in 62; and now a number of merchant vessels have been found on the seabed), Trajan (98–117) added an inner hexagonal basin, excavated from the coastline, which solved the problem and caused Ostia's activity and prosperity to reach its peak.

A direct result of this efflorescence was a major reconstruction of the city. The most remarkable feature of this new urban development was the type of private housing required to meet the increase in population. The characteristic dwellings of second century Ostia (superseding atrium houses similar to those at Pompeii and Herculaneum, though villas of that type continued to be built on the seashore) were apartments normally four and sometimes five storeys high. They were built of concrete-cored brick; stone was employed to decorate windows and doors, and external architectural details were sometimes picked out with red paint. The exteriors also displayed balconies or continuous terraces, projecting over timber or stone corbels. Roofs were generally sloping and tiled, though occasionally flat. Occupied, in certain cases, by more than one family, the apartments often comprised five or six rooms, with the largest at the end, served by a corridor overlooking the street. Each apartment had its own separate staircase of travertine or brick, with wooden treads, rising either from the street (between ground-floor shops) or from interior courtyards. Walls and ceilings in the apartments were sometimes attractively painted, and floors had mosaic pavements. Yet selenite (glass) was only rarely used in windows, for which wooden shutters were usually the only coverings; and although by this time, in the Roman world, water was piped to many private houses, it did not reach these blocks. Certain groups of them, however, shared a communal bath house, and possessed a garden in common.

The city also obtained three new sets of public baths (one of which was paid for by Hadrian [117–38] and Antoninus Pius [138–61]) and a theater. Other aspects of Ostian life were represented by bars and wineshops, bakeries, new types of shops including impressive business premises, and public warehouses (*horrea*) used for the storage of larger quantities of grain (sometimes in huge sunken jars) before transportation upstream to Rome. Meanwhile the commercial quarter of the city, adjoining the theater, was transformed into what has been interpreted—despite some dissent—as the Square of the Guilds (Piazzale del Corporazioni) containing, according to this interpretation, seventy offices of commercial associations, ranging from workers' guilds to corporations of foreign representatives from all over the ancient world. Religious buildings included a new Capitolium, probably erected by Hadrian. But by this time foreign cults, notably those of Cybele, the Great Mother, and then the Egyptian Isis and Serapis, had taken deep root, and in the latter half of the second century Mithraism also became popular, eventually possessing no less than fifteen chapels. A large synagogue, too, has now been discovered.

In the following century emphasis shifted to the harbor quarter inaugurated by Claudius and Trajan, which under Constantine I the Great (306–37) assumed an autonomous entity of its own under the name of Portus, or Civitas Flavia Constantiniana Portuensis. Meanwhile the city of Ostia itself had become much more a residential center than a trading town; the big apartment houses were allowed to go to ruin, but the construction of lavish new private houses went ahead. Christianity was battling forcibly with Mithraism, and Constantine was said to have endowed an Ostian basilica dedicated to St. Peter and St. Paul. The building tentatively recognized as this church is in reality a guesthouse, but a smaller church and Christian hall have come to light; the latter shows signs of violent destruction. St. Augustine stayed at Ostia with his mother Monica before returning to north Africa.

Portus was sacked by Alaric's Visigoths in 408. Yet *c* 425 a new marble colonnade was built, extending for two hundred yards along the canal; it was known as the Porticus Placidianus (after Placidius, one of the names of Valentinian III). In the following century, however, not only was Ostia chronically vulnerable to marauding enemies, but its harbor was silting up; and, besides, overseas grain was no longer needed for Rome's greatly reduced population.

Osuna *see* Urso

Ö-Szöny *see* Brigetio

Othrys, Mount, in eastern Thessaly (northeastern Greece). An offshoot of the Pindus range, north of the Malian gulf. According to the Greek tale of the Flood, it was on Othrys that Deucalion, king of the adjoining region of Achaea Phthiotis, landed his ship when the waters receded; though other mythologists name Mounts Parnassus, Acte or Aetna instead. Deucalion then offered sacrifice at a sanctuary of Themis, throwing stones behind his back—according to the instructions of Zeus—from which a new race of human beings was born. The son (or brother) of Deucalion was Hellen, after whom the Hellenic (Greek) people were said to have been named.

Oubili *see* Volubilis

Ouranopolis *see* Uranopolis

Ovilava or Oviliabis (Wels). A Roman fortress-city in northwest Noricum (Upper Austria), a little south of the Danube, at a crossing point of its tributary the Traun. Formerly a Celtic settlement, Ovilava was occupied in 16 BC, in the course of Augustus' annexation of Noricum (*qv*). Situated at a meeting point of roads from the south and west, and of two additional thoroughfares that led to the banks of the Danube, Ovilava was destined to become an important supply center for the Roman frontier.

It was raised to the rank of *municipium* by Hadrian (AD 117-38), with the title Aelium, after the name of his family. Then, during the Marcomannic Wars of Marcus Aurelius (161-68), when the garrison of the province was moved to nearby Lauriacum (Lorch) from Virunum, it was at Ovilava that the center of provincial government was installed. Under Caracalla (211-17) it became a Roman citizen colony (*colonia Aurelia Antoniniana*), and was probably provided with fortifications at the same time. Six towers belonging to this defensive system have been brought to light; its approaches were protected by four rings of trenches. In the later empire Ovilava became the capital of the province of Noricum Ripense.

Oxus *see* Bactria

Oxyrhynchus, Oxyrhynchos (Bahnasa). A town in Egypt, two hundred and twenty miles south-southeast of Alexandria, situated at the western edge of the Nile valley, on the shortest route from the valley to the Bahariya oasis. In a local shrine the ancient Egyptians venerated a fish with a sharp nose, from which the Greeks gave the place its name. Under the Ptolemies Oxyrhynchus was the capital of the Oxyrhynchite nome (district), and retained this position when Egypt became a Roman province (30 BC). During the difficult times of the third century AD there were signs of collapse, despite bombastic references to the 'most illustrious city.' During the later empire it was a walled, gated and colonnaded town belonging to the province of Arcadia (after the emperor Arcadius, AD 395-408) within the administrative diocese of Aegyptus. From the later fifth century, like neighboring villages, it became a fief of the immensely rich Apion family.

The place owes its fame to the discovery of an extraordinary number of papyri, extending in date from *c* 250 BC to AD 700 and constituting the most productive single source of this kind of literary and historical material in the world. Among these documents are catalogs and notes of payments to scribes, and imported or locally copied texts (in certain cases previously unknown or incomplete) of ancient Greek writers including Homer, Alcaeus, Sappho, Bacchylides, Pindar, Aeschylus, Sophocles, Euripides, Aristotle, Menander, Callimachus, Cercidas, and a number of orators and historians (including the so-called 'Oxyrhynchus Historian' who narrated events between 409 and 334 BC). Other papyri include a variety of religious texts including the pagan *Miracles of Serapis,* copies of the New Testament (including what was, at the time of discovery, the earliest surviving manuscript of St. John's Gospel), non-canonical Christian writings such as the *Sayings of Jesus* (*Logia Iesu,* part of the Gospel of Thomas); and portions of several other apocryphal Gospels.

Further papyri refer to numerous buildings of the city, including a Temple of Serapis, public baths, gymnasium, hippodrome, theater (of which a small portion survives) and numerous Christian churches. Many other aspects of the life of the community also receive illustration, including the activities of its Council, business affairs, racing, schooling, poetry competitions, the military service of citizens of Oxyrhynchus abroad, and, under the later empire, the importance of the place as a monastic center; although, at the same time, figured sculpture almost wholly pagan in character continued to be produced as late as the fifth and sixth centuries AD.

P

Padua (Padova) *see* Patavium

Padus, Greek Eridanus (Po), River. Italy's longest river, four hundred and five miles long, receiving numerous tributaries both from the north and south and dividing Cisalpine Gaul (north Italy) into northern (Transpadane) and southern (Cispadane) portions. *See also* Atria, Augusta Taurinorum, Brixellum, Cisalpine Gaul, Clastidium, Cremona, Placentia, Spina, Trebia.

Paestum *see* Posidonia

Pagasae *see* Demetrias

Palaiopharsalos *see* Pharsalus

Palaipaphos *see* Paphos

Palea-Navarino *see* Pylos

Paleochora *see* Carystus

Paleokastro *see* Pylos

Paleopolis *see* Lemnos, Samothrace

Paleopreveza *see* Nicopolis

Palermo *see* Panormus

Palestrina *see* Praeneste

Palinurus (Palinuro). The name of a cape in Lucania (southwest Italy), extending into the Tyrrhenian Sea. In Roman mythology, this was the burial place of Palinurus, the helmsman of Aeneas, who was overcome by the god of sleep and fell overboard, but reached the shore where he was murdered by Lucanians. When Aeneas, according to Virgil's *Aeneid,* visited the underworld, he met Palinurus' ghost and promised him a proper burial, a promise which he duly carried out. Caves beside the ruined castle of Molpa have yielded prehistoric remains, and the adjacent necropolis has produced finds of the sixth and fifth centuries BC, now preserved in a local antiquarium.

The waters off Cape Palinurus were the scene of two important naval events. In 253, during the First Punic War, the fleet of the two Roman consuls, returning from north Africa, encountered a storm off the cape, and suffered considerable damage; Polybius estimated their losses at a hundred and fifty ships. In 36, during his civil war against Sextus Pompeius, a substantial fleet recently constructed by Octavian (the future Augustus) in the vicinity was wrecked and scattered in the region by a violent sirocco, and shortly afterward another of his flotillas suffered damage from a similar storm, thus briefly delaying his eventual victory.

Palmyra (formerly Tadmor). A city in the Syrian desert, that derived prosperity from its position in an oasis—containing two wells—on the principal route between Syria and Mesopotamia; the place also had access to an adjacent winter tributary of the Euphrates. Occupied since Palaeolithic times, Tadmor had assumed urban proportions by *c* 2300 BC, and was subsequently mentioned in early Assyrian texts and Babylonian documents from Mari.

The township, containing a mixed Amorite, Aramaean and Arab population, rose to prominence once again in the third century, policing the desert road and presiding over caravan traffic. Antony reputedly attempted to capture Palmyra in 41, but it was not incorporated into the Roman province of Syria until Germanicus took this step in AD 14–17, granting the city, at the same time, numerous privileges. Vespasian built a road linking the oasis to Sura on the Euphrates in 75, and Palmyra, occupied by a strong Roman garrison, received the name of Hadriana from Hadrian (129). A tax law of 137 has survived in Greek and Palmyrene texts. The city was awarded the status of Roman colony by Caracalla (211), after it had become part of Severus' new province of Syria Phoenice. Henceforward many of its famous formations of mounted archers were stationed not far from their own city, constituting important elements in the imperial forces that lined the Parthian frontier.

When Parthia was superseded by the more formidable Sassanian Persian power (223/6), the role fulfilled by Palmyra in the imperial defence system became even more indispensable, and under a local Arab prince, Septimius Odenathus, it played a major part on the world stage. When the Sassanian monarch Sapor (Shapur) I overran Rome's eastern provinces and captured the emperor Valerian (260), Odenathus (after his initial approach to the invader had been rebuffed) supported the Romans, inflicting a severe defeat on Sapor and twice threatening his capital Ctesiphon. These successes confirmed Odenathus' virtually autonomous control of Rome's eastern armies and provinces. Valerian's son Gallienus rewarded him with the titles of Corrector of the Whole Orient, Leader (*dux*) of the Romans, and Imperator: and as a challenge to the Persians, he even permitted him to call himself King of Kings, or turned a blind eye when he did so.

After Odenathus and his eldest son had been murdered in 267, his talented and learned widow Septimia Zenobia, employing the Greco-Syrian scholar Cassius Longinus as her chief minister, set out to establish a totally independent Palmyrene empire. Seizing Egypt (late in 270) and most of Asia Minor, she ruled over territories extending from Mesopotamia almost as far as Europe. She also bestowed the rank of Augustus upon her son Vaballathus Athenodorus (who had inherited his father's title of Corrector), and herself assumed the title of Augusta, as coins and inscriptions show. But efforts to reconcile Aurelian to this situation failed, and the emperor moved east, recapturing Asia Minor and Egypt and defeating the queen's leading general Zabdas outside Antioch and Emesa (Homs) in 272. Palmyra itself fell into his hands, rebelled, and was captured again in the next year, and Zenobia walked in golden chains in his Triumph, subsequently obtaining a Roman pension and a villa at Tibur (Tivoli). Her city Palmyra was devastated, and relapsed into a desert village, until Diocletian (284–305) restored its role as an important fortified base in his province of Phoenice Libanensis.

The culture of Palmyra formed a bridge between west and east. Certain of the trappings of its architecture and costume assumed a Greco-Syrian character, whereas its vigorous styles of painting and sculpture were most closely oriented toward Parthian and Sassanian Babylonia. Local cults were almost entirely Semitic. The city's principal temple, dedicated to Bel, dating from AD 32 and rebuilt in the course of the second century, was a curious asymmetrical building standing in a huge precinct following a traditional Syrian plan of which extensive remains survive. The shrine of Baalshamin, dedicated in 132, replaced a temple constructed a century earlier. Recent excavations have also revealed many features of a temple of Allat that was reconstructed in the second century and restored after suffering damage in Aurelian's capture of the city. A copy of Phidias' statue of Athena Parthenos has been found on this site. A sanctuary of a deity named Nabo, begun in the later first century, was still under construction in 146.

A wide colonnaded street (150 of its former 375 columns are still standing), linked most of the monuments, and terminated in a funerary temple outside the city gate. The street was spanned by triumphal and four-way arches and adjoined by shops, an apsed *nymphaeum* (fountain house), a banqueting hall, and a grand *exedra* (semicircular portico). A large agora or caravanserai, dating from the later years of the first century, was adorned by more than two hundred statues. The theater, of similar date, was surrounded by a semicircular colonnaded court; beside it stood the senate house, with seats likewise arranged in a semicircle. A second avenue runs below the so-called Camp of Diocletian, which has now been revealed as a huge colonnaded military complex dating from that emperor's reign. Beyond this group of buildings, arranged round a courtyard, is a further group of imposing edifices, identified as sections of the royal palace—which were subsequently, it would seem, rearranged and reconstructed by resident Roman commanders to suit their own needs. Other third-century houses have revealed impressive mosaic pavements.

Diocletian's ramparts, replacing earlier walls and enclosing an eight-mile perimeter, were furnished with rectangular and semicircular bastions. Cemeteries surrounding the city display numerous burial places, both overground and underground. Graves of the former type imitate towers and houses; an underground tomb is reconstructed in the local museum.

Paltus, Paltos (Tell Sukas, Balda, Bulda). A commercial station on the Syrian coast (forty-five miles south of its larger counterpart Al Mina). After earlier traces of Mycenaean trade, archaeologists have revealed a first phase of occupation extending from *c* 850 BC to destruction *c* 675, signalized by the use of Greek pottery which mainly originated in Euboea and the Cyclades, and suggests that the Euboean cities Chalcis and Eretria used Paltus as a trading base; it provided access to the inland Syrian kingdom of Hamath.

A second level of habitation can be dated between *c* 675 and *c* 498; the end of the seventh century was marked by an increase in imports from eastern Greece (in contrast to Al Mina), interrupted by further destructions *c* 588 and, on a still graver scale, *c* 552, perhaps at the hands of the Babylonians. Paltus contained a sanctuary of Greek design, and *c* 600 a Greek woman left proof of her presence by inscribing her name on a loom weight.

Pamphylia. A region of southern Asia Minor, bounded on the west by Lycia, on the east by Cilicia, on the north by the Taurus (Toros) mountains, and on the south by the Mediterranean; its coastline covered seventy-five miles or (in earlier times) more, and the country extended about thirty miles inland. It included an alluvial plain watered by four rivers, one of which was the Eurymedon (*qv*). According to Pliny the Elder, Pamphylia's original name was Mopsopia, after Mopsus who, according to legend, colonized its territory after the Trojan War, in conjunction with Amphilochus and Calchas (*see* Mopsuestia). The Greek settlers who, in fact, arrived in the area, were said to have spoken a Greek dialect like Arcadian or Cypriot, though according to Arrian they forgot this form of speech.

The Pamphylians, who, although resembling the non-Greek Cilicians in their way of life, intermixed with these Greek settlers—and were known to Plato, whose Myth of Er is about one of them—belonged successively to the empires of Lydia and Persia until they surrendered to Alexander the Great (333). Subsequently they were subject to Ptolemy I Soter and II Philadelphus of Egypt, and then to the Seleucids. One of the Seleucid monarchs, Antiochus III the Great, ceded the country to the Romans (190/188), who transferred a strip of the Pamphylian coast to Eumenes II of Pergamum.

The maritime cities, however, engaged extensively in piracy. During the first century BC the Romans battled against these activities, and gradually established control over Pamphylia, which was first loosely connected and then formally attached (*c* 44) to the province of Asia. In 36 Pamphylia was given by Antony to Amyntas, king of Galatia, but then successively belonged to Rome's new Galatian province (25), to the province of Lycia-Pamphylia (AD 43), to Galatia again (under Galba), and then to Lycia again (under Vespasian), while nevertheless retaining a separate federal organization (*koinon*) of its own. In the later empire Pamphylia became a separate province. *See also* Aspendus, Attaleia, Perga, Side.

Pamukkale *see* Hierapolis (Phrygia)

Panamara *see* Stratonicea

Pandateria (Ventotene). An islet in the Tyrrhenian Sea off the northwest coast of Campania, between Pontia (Ponza) and Pithecusae (Aenaria, Ischia). The place of banishment of Julia the Younger by her father Augustus (2 BC–AD 4), of Agrippina the Elder by her uncle Tiberius (AD 29–33, when she starved herself to death), of Octavia by her husband Nero (62; she was killed there), and of Flavia Domitilla by her uncle Domitian (95).

Pangaeum, Pangaion, Pangaios, Mount. A mountain 'with bulbous spurs and knobbly summits' in southwestern Thrace (northeastern Greece), between the Angites (a tributary of the Strymon [Struma]) and the seacoast. Pangaeum was closely associated with myths of the Thracian Dionysus, and it was said that Orpheus (whom he supposedly killed) had climbed the mountain every day to greet the sun-god. Strabo also recorded that the wealth of the Phoenician Cadmus came from the mines of Pangaeum; and the same story was told of the Homeric hero Rhesus. For although the mountain itself is made of crystalline white marble, its vicinity contained important gold and silver deposits which were exploited, notably at Scaptosyle, by the Thracian princedoms and by immigrants and businessmen from the island of Thasos.

There are few traces of mines, but the gold was washed down mountain streams. As a recent coin-find shows, the Thraco-Macedonian tribes joined up at the end of the sixth century BC to use Pangaean silver for a common monetary system. The Athenians, too (like many others), took an interest in the metals from the same period, and gained control of their production after the reduction of Thasos (463). In 382 the Greeks of Chalcidice sought to negotiate with the tribes of western Thrace with a view to obtaining these gold mines. But the major exploitation of the metal followed the Macedonian king Philip II's annexation of the area, including the adjacent Thasian mining town of Crenides, which he seized from a Thracian prince (*c* 357) and resettled under the name of Phillippi. Philip at once began to produce gold on a very large scale, deriving as much as a thousand talents a year from this source; the forests of the area gave him abundant timber for ship building.

At the beginning of the second century the Thracian leader Abrupolis tried to gain possession of the mines, but was driven away by King Perseus of Macedonia, whose action was later cited by the Romans as a pretext for making war on the Macedonian kingdom and wiping it out of existence. In subsequent centuries, however, the mines did not play a major part. Pangaeum was also famous for its roses.

Panionion *see* Mycale

Panium, Panion *see* Caesarea Philippi

Pannonia. The land of the Pannonii, a group of partially Celticized Illyrian peoples living south and west of the Middle Danube in territories which now form parts of eastern Austria, western Hungary, and northern Yugoslavia. The southern part of the country included the valleys of the Savus (Save) and Dravus (Drave), tributaries of the Danube.

In 119 BC the Romans made war on the Pannonii, capturing Siscia (Sisak). The same fortress was occupied once again, and garrisoned, by Octavian (the future Augustus) when he received the submission of the local tribes (35/33). A Pannonian invasion of Istria (16 BC) led to further operations in which Marcus Agrippa and Marcus Vinicius penetrated the Save and Drave valleys, which were incorporated into the province of Illyricum. In 12–9 Tiberius completed the conquest of the country as far as the Danube, but in AD 6 the Pannonian tribes, led by the Breuci who dwelt between the Save and the Drave, broke into a serious revolt (supported by the Dalmatians), which was regarded as the gravest threat to Italy since the Second Punic War, and took Tiberius three years to subdue.

When he had done so, Illyricum was divided into the two provinces of Pannonia and Dalmatia. In 106 Trajan subdivided the former into Upper (western) and Lower (eastern) Pannonia, with their capitals at Carnuntum (Petronell) and Aquincum (Budapest) respectively.

Pannonian society displayed a strong military bias, and city councillors were comparatively unimportant, most of the work being done by the town clerks. Outside the urban area, Roman Pannonia had been notable for its splendid villas, of which there were large concentrations in the regions of Lakes Pelso (Balaton) and Neusiedel (in the Leitha valley), and in the territories between the Danube and Savus (Save) and between the Danube and the Dravus (Drave). Important first- and second-century villas include those at Baláca, Tac-Fövenypuszta and Eisenstadt-Gölbesacken.

By the time of Antoninus Pius (138–61), the Danube forts were becoming fossilized into a permanent barrier, and it was they that constituted the principal bases for the Marcomannic Wars of Marcus Aurelius, who died in 180 in the legionary camp of Vindobona (Vienna), after creating, or following, a historic precedent by the settlement of numerous defeated tribesmen in the two provinces. Caracalla (211–17) revised the borders of the provinces so as to enlarge Lower Pannonia. But then followed a period of repeated barbarian attacks, during which Trajanus Decius (249–51), one of a line of Danubian emperors, celebrated the Pannonias on his coinage. It was also in this region, however, that Ingenuus and Regalianus (260/1) and Marcus Aurelius Julianus (284/5) attempted to usurp the throne.

Both these administrative areas were further subdivided by Diocletian (284–305), the upper province into Pannonia Prima (capital Savaria [Szombathely]) and Ripariensis or Savia (capital Siscia), and its lower counterpart into Valeria (capital Sopianae [Pécs]) and Secunda (capital Sirmium [Sremska-Mitrovica], which became an imperial residence). During a period when these territories again suffered greatly from barbarian invasions, Constantine I the Great drove back the Sarmatians and Quadi (322, 332/3), bishops Valens of Mursa Major (Osijek) and Ursacius of Singidunum (Belgrade) joined the Arian 'heresy,' Vetranio briefly claimed the purple (350), and Constantius II defeated another pretender Magnentius at Mursa Major (351) before resuming warfare against the tribesmen.

Valentinian I (364–75), himself a Pannonian, restored and strengthened the frontier, and was dealing with a new irruption when he died at Brigetio (Ö-Szöny). After the defeat and death of his brother Valens at Hadrianopolis (Edirne) (376), Alans and Ostrogoths and Huns were admitted to the Pannonias as federates, and henceforward the structure of Roman life in this area gradually shrank; Carnuntum and Aquincum, for example, ceased to be major centers. Theodosius I used fighting men from all the non-Roman groups in Pannonia to defeat the usurpers Magnus Maximus (383–88) and Eugenius (392–94). In 405 the incursion of Radagaisus with a host of Ostrogoths caused numerous Romans to flee from the territory to Italy. Alaric the Visigoth sought the assistance of the Pannonian tribes with varying success; by 420/23, parts of the country were under the domination of the Huns. In 423, however, the Romans reached an agreement with the Hun prince Rua, and the western emperor Avitus made an appearance in Pannonia as late as 455; but subsequent movements of the Goths and Heruli altered the political map. However, Roman urban culture endured in the southwest (Savia); and Pannonia Secunda, in the southeastern corner of the territory, was held by the Byzantine empire until the sixth century. *See also* Aquincum, Bononia Malata, Brigetio, Carnuntum, Cibalae, Danube, Dravus, Emona, Mursa Major, Poetovio, Savaria, Savus, Singidunum, Siscia, Vindobona.

Panormus, Panormos (Palermo). A coastal city in northwestern Sicily, founded by the Phoenicians in the seventh century BC, and later the principal administrative, military and naval base of the Carthaginian zone in the west of the island. The position of Panormus, adjoining a fine harbor and fertile hinterland (the Conca d'Oro), explains why, according to Polybius, it was the most important city of Carthage's overseas dominions. The Greek character of its name, Pan-Hormos ('harbor for all'), suggests—and finds of Corinthian vases confirm—early contact with Greek settlements, and local coins, from the fifth century onward, bear Greek as well as Punic inscriptions.

Apart from a short-lived occupation by King Pyrrhus of Epirus (276), the city remained in the hands of Carthage until the First Punic War, when it was occupied by the Romans (254), and Carthaginian efforts to get it back failed (250, 247–244). Panormus subsequently became one of the five 'free and immune' communities of the Roman province of Sicily, and maintained a flourishing maritime trade. After Caesar had granted the Sicilians Latin rights (conferring Roman franchise on the principal city officials), Antony, after Caesar's death (44), proposed to confer full Roman citizenship on Panormus, which issued a bronze coinage as a *municipium*, displaying the caps of the Dioscuri (Castor and Pollux) and a dolphin (44/43). From the same mint also (as overstrikings demonstrate) come pieces with the inscription (like similar coins issued at Syracuse) 'Of the Spaniards' (HISPANORVM), evidently issued in the name of Spanish immigrants imported by Sextus Pompeius after his occupation of the island in 43/2, in defiance of the central Roman authorities. Panormus became a Roman colony under Augustus (*c* 20), continued to coin under Tiberius, and was recolonized by Vespasian (AD 69–79).

In 440 it underwent a siege by Gaiseric the Vandal—who had been invited to the island by Maximinus, bishop of its Arian (anti-Catholic) communities—but in 477 passed with most of the rest of the island into the hands of Odoacer (who had recently became king of Italy). The habitation center of Panormus, bounded by two inlets of the sea, was divided into an Old City to the north and a New City to the south, and enclosed by walls of which a few (repaired) stretches remain. The large necropolis has yielded material of great variety and a wide range of dates.

Panticapaeum (Kerch). A city at the eastern extremity of the Tauric Chersonese (Crimea), situated on the Cimmerian Bosphorus (Strait of Kerch) linking the Euxine (Black) Sea with Lake Maeotis (the Sea of Azov). Founded in *c* 600 BC by Greek colonists from Miletus in Ionia (western Asia Minor), on the site of an earlier settlement (Panti Kapa) which possessed an excellent location and a strong acropolis (Mount Mithridates), Panticapaeum became the most important of the many Greek colonies of the Bosphoran area, benefiting from its proximity to the best Crimean grainfields. Soon after 480 its rulers of the Archaeanactid dynasty created the kingdom of the Cimmerian Bosphorus (*qv*)—in order to confront Scythian pressure—and it remained the capital of their successors of the Spartocid house (from 438). Panticapaeum is probably the place named Kremnoi by Herodotus, and described as a market (*emporium*) in the land of the 'Free Scythians' (it may also have been known as Apollonia before Spartocid times). Fifth-century silver coinage was followed, after 400, by pieces made of gold obtained from the Ural or Altai mountains.

The earliest houses, of early sixth-century date (found on Mount Mithridates), square buildings with a single room each, were supplemented in the fifth century by larger residences with painted stucco walls. Traces of an Ionic temple and walls date from *c* 400. In the neighborhood are monumental tumulus graves ranging in date from the fourth century BC to the second century AD; they were found to contain massive treasures, indicating the wealth of the city's leading inhabitants. Objects from many Greek centers have come to light, including a good deal of material from Athens, which manufactured a special type of bowl ('Kerch Ware') for Panticapaeum; and local production imitated a wide range of such imported pottery. The third century inaugurated the construction of houses with painted stucco and terracotta friezes and colonnaded courtyards, and there is a large official building (*prytaneum*) of second-century date.

Panticapaeum became the headquarters of the south Russian possessions of King Mithridates VI of Pontus (in northern Asia Minor) *c* 115, but subsequently resumed its role as capital of the kingdom of the Cimmerian Bosphorus. Cisterns for wine production and potters' kilns date from the first centuries of the Christian era. During the period, the city was strongly influenced by non-Greek cultures. In the third century it was sacked by Sarmatians and Goths.

Paphlagonia. A territory (of fluctuating dimensions) in northern Asia Minor on the (Euxine) Black Sea—between Bithynia to the west, Pontus to the east and Galatia to the south. The country's fertile coastal plains, famous for horses and containing abundant pasturage for sheep, rise to rugged mountains, clothed with dense forests that furnished abundant boxwood. A Paphlagonian chieftain Pylamenes (the name also of later kings of the country) appears in the *Iliad*, and the coastland was occupied, at an early date, by Greek colonies, notably Sinope (Sinop).

More or less conquered by Croesus of Lydia (d. 546 BC), these cities contributed a contingent to the Persian army of Xerxes I in 480. After submission to Alexander the Great (333), they were assigned, following his death, to Eumenes of Cardia, but remained under native princes until most of the country was absorbed by the kingdom of Pontus from the early third through the early second centuries. Mithridates VI Eupator (120–63) strengthened his hold over the coast and interior alike, but after his defeat by the Romans, Pompey the Great incorporated the maritime region into the province of Bithynia Pontus (63/2), while the rest of the country was entrusted to various client princes—of whom the last was Deiotarus Castor Philadelphus (*c* 31–6)—and then attached to the Roman province of Galatia, which had been established in 25.

In the later Roman empire, however, a small province of Paphlagonia was created, with its capital at Gangra (now also known as Germanicopolis), though a certain amount of former Paphlagonian territory was detached and assigned to the provinces of Honorias and Helenopontus, to the west and east of the province given the name of Paphlagonia. *See also* Abonutichus, Amastris, Sinope.

Paphos, Palaipaphos (Kouklia). A city on the west coast of Cyprus. The temple of the Paphian fertility goddess, associated with sacred doves and probably also with temple prostitution, was identified by the Greeks with the cult of Aphrodite, and became her most celebrated shrine in the ancient world; it stood on the place where she was believed (despite alternative claims) to have first come ashore after her birth from the sea foam. Homer refers to her sacred grove and altar at Paphos, where her tomb was also later shown. According to one legend, this temple and the city itself were founded by Agapenor, king of Tegea in Arcadia. Another version, however, maintained that their founder was Cinyras, king of Paphos and all Cyprus, who was reported in the *Iliad* to have sent Agamemnon a breastplate for the war against Troy, and whose descendants the Cinyradae remained priest kings of the city down to Ptolemaic times.

There is archaeological evidence for the existence of Paphos in the Later Bronze (Mycenaean) epoch (*c* 1200), and early Iron Age tombs have been found at the Village of Skales. A local monarch (Eteandros) is mentioned on an Assyrian document of 673/2 BC, and the sequence of many later reigns is determined by coins and inscriptions. Parts of the early city defences have been cleared on a hill 3,000 feet above sea level, and excavations of siege and counter-siege works (including numerous objects taken from a nearby sanctuary to serve as building materials) point to heavy fighting at the time of the Ionian revolt against the Persians (498/7). Paphos later became a mint of Alexander the Great. Nicocles, the last of the Cinyrad line, transferred his capital to New Paphos *c* 312 (*see* below), but the old town, or at least its temple, continued to flourish in Roman times, remaining a place of pilgrimage for people from all parts of Cyprus.

Although most of the extensive site is still unexcavated, the outline of the shrine's great rectangular precinct, situated on the edge of a plateau overlooking a fertile plain and the sea, has been partially uncovered; it shows signs of ancient restoration, after damage by earthquakes. The complex tripartite building, depicted on coins and gems of New Paphos during the Roman imperial epoch, contained a tower that was fronted by a semicircular courtyard and surmounted by a sacred conical stone crowned by a star and crescent at its apex.

New Paphos (Nea, Kato Paphos) lies ten miles to the northwest of Old Paphos, and one mile from the sea. Its foundation by the last Cinyrad Nicocles (*c* 312) followed Ptolemy I's destruction of Marion (Polis), of which the inhabitants were transferred by his order to the new city as a reward for the local king's loyalty to the Ptolemaic cause. New Paphos grew in importance, maintaining autonomous institutions, a mint, and a shipbuilding industry utilized by Ptolemy II Philadelphus (289/8–246). By 200 it had taken the place of Salamis as the capital of the island, a position it retained under Ptolemaic princes who at times ruled Cyprus independently, and thereafter following annexation by the Romans.

Following a serious earthquake in 15, New Paphos was restored by Augustus and renamed Sebaste (Augusta). The *Acts of the Apostles* describe a visit by St. Paul to the proconsul Sergius Paulus in AD 45, and the emperor Titus visited New Paphos in 69. During the fourth century, however, the city lost its position as the provincial capital to Salamis, perhaps as a result of severe earthquakes in the fourth century, and especially, it has now been argued, in 365. The place was eventually rebuilt, but on a reduced scale, although it served as an episcopal see.

The breakwaters of its ancient harbors are still to be seen, and the outline of the city wall is traceable. Various religious cults are recorded, and the sites of various public buildings have been identified; one of them, a structure of late imperial date possessing a colonnaded courtyard, is now excavated, revealing polychrome floor mosaics of fine quality. Other such pavements of substantial dimensions have been uncovered in a number of private houses. At one of these, the 'House of Dionysus,' a mosaic of third-century date overlays a 'pebble' mosaic floor of the fourth century BC. Another very large residence, the 'House of Theseus'—which owes its name to a mosaic of Theseus fighting the Minotaur—was constructed on top of an early imperial layout, and is currently under excavation. Its dimensions invite comparison with the palatial villa near Philosophiana (*qv*) in Sicily, which also has a central apsed room in one wing and a long room with rounded ends at the entrance to another.

A large and small theater (Odeon) have also been located at New Paphos; and the latter has now been partially restored. Outside the city walls are the remains of a sanctuary of Apollo Hylates of the later fourth century BC, and a necropolis of the Ptolemaic princes of the island, which contains tomb chambers cut into the rock to flank colonnaded courtyards. A recently discovered mansion known as the 'House of Hercules' displays evidence of the earthquakes of AD 365.

Paradisus *see* Triparadisus

Paris *see* Lutetia Parisiorum

Parium, Parian (Kemer). A city of Mysia (or Hellespontine Phrygia), in northwestern Asia Minor, upon the Asian coast of the Hellespont (Sea of Marmara) near its entrance to the Propontis (Dardanelles). It was founded *c* 709 BC by a team of colonists from Miletus, Erythrae (Ildırı) and Paros, from which it probably took its name (rather than, as was alternatively suggested, from the mythological Parilarians, or from Parios, one of the Ophiogeneis, who were changed from snakes to human beings and whose descendants cured snake bites by stroking).

Parium began producing electrum (pale gold) coinages before 500. During the fifth century, gaining importance from its strategic and maritime location, it became a member of the Delian League under Athenian sponsorship. In 302, during the wars between the successors of Alexander the Great, the city was seized by Demetrius I Poliorcetes from Lysimachus. Annexed to the Pergamene kingdom, it was permitted to enlarge its territory at the expense of neighboring Priapus. Incorporated in the Roman province of Asia (133), Parium received a draft of ex-soldiers and became a Roman colony (*Colonia Gemina Julia Pariana*) at the beginning of the Second Triumvirate (42/41), coining for the occasion and again for Octavian (the future Augustus) and Marcus Agrippa *c* 29, when the colony was apparently reconstituted. It was again refounded by Hadrian, assuming the name Hadriana.

Its colonial coinage displays figures of Aesculapius (Asclepius) the Helper (AESC*ulapio* SVB*venienti*), Diana Lucifera, and Cupid (DEO CVPIDINI: showing a statue of the god Eros made for the city by Praxiteles). An issue of Gallienus (253–68) depicts an elaborate triple gateway crowned by an elephant-chariot group and a statue of Parios whose head (as alleged founder) appears on other coinages, and whose tomb was said to exist in the city. The best-known building at Parium, however, was a colossal altar (shown on coins *c* 300 BC) which a certain Hermocreon built of stones taken from a large oracular temple of Apollo Actaeus and Artemis that had stood on the neighboring plain of Adrasteia. But little is now to be seen on the site of Parium, except fragments of a theater and of a Roman aqueduct.

Parnassus, Parnassos, Mount. A barren limestone mountain in Phocis (central Greece), rising to the peaks of Tithorea (Gerondovrachos) and Lycorea (Liakoura, 8061 feet above sea level). In ancient times Parnassus was sacred to Dionysus, the Corycian nymphs, and Pan, and later to Apollo, whose sanctuary at Delphi (*qv*) stood on a projecting shelf west of the Castalian spring beneath two cliffs, the Phaedriades (shining ones, now Elafokastro). According to Anaxandrides of Delphi, the hero Parnassus was the first Delphic prophet. The Castalian spring was believed to be a source of poetic inspiration, but the replacement of Mount Helicon by Parnassus as the home of the Muses is a product of Roman poetry. After the Great Flood, according to Greek mythology, Deucalion's boat ran aground on Parnassus.

A sanctuary of Artemis, with a statue by Praxiteles, stood near Anticyra on a high rocky part of the mountain. The two-chambered Corycian (Sandavli) cave on its north face was used as a hiding place from the Persians (480) and Gauls (279), whose invading force suffered severely from huge landslides on the slopes. There were stories of lions on Parnassus in early times, and wolves were seen on the mountain only twenty winters ago.

Paropamisus (Hindu Kush). Mountains in central Asia, meeting the Karakoram range near the point where, today, China borders on Pakistan and Afghanistan. The Paropamisus range was called Parnassus by Aristotle, and identified with the Caucasus by writers about Alexander the Great: hence the name of Alexandria Beside Caucasus (*qv*), founded south of the Paropamisus on the west bank of the united Panjshir-Ghorband rivers. The capital of the people known as the Paropamisadae was at Kapisa, on the opposite shore, but their lands extended into the valley of the river Cabura (Kophen, Kabul).

These territories came under Seleucid and then Indian rule, from which an expedition of Antiochus III the Great (212–206), culminating in his crossing of the range, failed to detach them. Subsequently, however, in the mid-second century, the region was returned to Greek control by the Indo-Greek monarchs, one of whom, Strato I (*c* 130–75), coined at Alexandria beside the Caucasus and Gardez (south of Cabura), while another, Amyntas (*c* 100–75), employing the mint of Kapisa, issued the largest silver piece to have survived from the ancient world, describing himself as Nicator (Conqueror), like Seleucus I, the founder of the Seleucid empire, before him. The Indo-Greek principalities succumbed to Indo-Scythians and Yuëh-Chih invaders before the end of the first century BC.

Paros. An island in the Aegean sea, the second largest of the Cyclades, four miles west of the largest island, Naxos, which was its traditional enemy. Famous for its white marble (from Mount Marpessa), Paros was an important centre of Cycladic sculpture in the third and second millennia BC. According to mythology, the island was colonized by the Cretan king Minos and his sons, who were said to have been expelled by Heracles. Other stories recorded settlement first by Arcadians and then by Ionians, although the harbor of Paros only admits small ships and has a dangerous entrance.

Its most famous native was the iambic and elegiac poet Archilochus, who recounted the myths and history of the island and took part in the later stages of his father's colonization of another island, Thasos (*c* 650), which—together with its gold mines on the Thracian mainland—became a source of the wealth and power of the Parians. They apparently had a share in the settlement of Parium in Mysia (northwestern Asia Minor), and, allied with Eretria in Euboea, took an active part in the Lelantine War between that city and Chalcis, which was associated with Naxos (*c* 700). In 655 experts from Paros were called upon to arbitrate between Chalcis and Andros, and late in the sixth century they were summoned by Miletus in Ionia (western Asia Minor) to sort out its political troubles. Shortly afterward, however, Paros seems to have been, for a time, a dependency of Naxos.

In 490 Paros took the side of the Persian king Darius I against the Greeks, and contributed a ship to his fleet at Marathon, thus provoking an Athenian punitive expedition under Miltiades, whose siege, however, proved unsuccessful. When the Persian Wars were resumed in 480, the Parians attempted to play a double game, but after the invasion was over, joined the Delian League under Athenian leadership; owing to the wealth they derived from the continued widespread employment of their marble for construction and a distinctive school of sculpture, they were able to pay the League a higher tribute than any other island. During the Peloponnesian War they tried to revolt against Athens, but in vain. In 385, in association with Dionysius I of Syracuse, they colonized the island of Pharos (Hvar) off the Dalmatian coast. In 378 Paros was a member of the Second Athenian Confederation. During the Hellenistic epoch it possessed a flourishing culture, but became successively subject to the Ptolemies, the Macedonians (202/1), and then the Romans. A bishopric is attested in the fourth century AD.

The ancient city of Paros (now Parikia), situated at the northwest of the island, was dominated by an acropolis which stood on a low peak overlooking the modern jetty, and contained a large Ionic temple of Athena, of which the eastern end is preserved. A sixth-century *Heroon* (hero's shrine) of Archilochus, restored three centuries later, has yielded a marble stele (the *Marmor Parium*) inscribed with the Parian Chronicle, a historical survey extending from mythical times to 264/3; biographical inscriptions about Archilochus have also come to light. There are also remains of temples of Asclepius, Apollo and other Delian gods, notably Artemis, Zeus Kynthios and Athene Kynthia—whose head appears on local coins under Marcus Aurelius (AD 161–80). The principal temple of Paros, however, dedicated to Demeter Thesmophoros, has left no trace. One sanctuary bore the inscription 'Entry forbidden to Dorian aliens.' There were shrines of Zeus Hypatos, Aphrodite and Eileithyia (goddess of childbirth) on Kounados hill to the east of the city. Recent surveys of the harbors in the bays of Parikia and Naoussa (on the north side of the island) have revealed substantial buildings.

Parotino *see* Olbia

Parthenope *see* Neapolis

Parthia. According to its original and limited meaning, this was a territory roughly corresponding to the modern Iranian province of Khurasan southeast of the Caspian Sea; in a wider sense the name referred to the later Parthian empire, extending from the Euphrates to Soviet Turkmenistan (where Nisa has yielded important finds) and Afghanistan.

Before and after 300 BC the Parni or Aparni, members of a confederacy of three semi-nomad Indo-European (Scythian) tribes, moved from central Asia into Parthia (in its earlier and restricted sense). There, *c* 247, their chieftain Arsaces I rebelled against the Seleucid governor Andragoras (himself in revolt from Antiochus II Theos); Seleucid efforts to reconquer the country by Antiochus III the Great (223–187) proved of no avail. The Arsacid Parthians spoke the Pahlavi dialect of middle Persian—better known through research on Manichaean fragments from Turfan in Sinkiang (western China)—and adopted the Iranian religion of Mazdaism. Their monarch Mithridates I (*c* 171–138) conquered Media (northern Iran) and Babylonia (Mesopotamia), to which the gravity of the empire shifted; the kings established their winter residence at Ctesiphon, opposite the Greek city of Seleucia on the Tigris. The loosely organized dominions of the Parthians included not only provinces administered by their own nobility, but also numerous vassal principalities, contributing their quotas of troops (especially heavy cavalry) to the royal forces.

The history of the Parthian empire was a tale of intermittent wars with the Romans—on whose frontiers they constituted the only major rival power. Their greatest military success was at Carrhae (Haran) in 53 BC, when Crassus was defeated and killed; but they also survived large-scale offensives by Trajan (AD 115), Lucius Verus (165) and Septimius Severus (198). In 224–29, however, the Parthian monarchy was overthrown by the more centralized and formidable régime of the Sassanian Persians. *See also* Babylonia, Bactria, Carrhae, Ctesiphon, Ecbatana, Hatra, Media, Mesopotamia, Seleucia on the Tigris.

Patara *see* Lycia, Xanthus

Patavium (Padova, Padua). A city of the Veneti (the modern Veneto) in Cisalpine Gaul (northeastern Italy), at the eastern extremity of the Padus (Po) plain. Strabo indicates that it was served by the river Medoacus or Meduacus (probably the Bacchiglione, although a branch of the Brenta—which has changed course—has also been suggested); there are also ancient references to streams named Etron or Reton and Togisonus which flowed through marshes to debouch into a large maritime harbor.

According to a myth current in Roman times, the founder of Patavium was Antenor of Troy, who after the Trojan War was said to have brought the Eneti (Veneti) from Paphlagonia (northern Asia Minor) and to have settled them in Venetia, at the head of the Adriatic; festivals held at Patavium every year, at which tragedies were performed, were also ascribed to Antenor's initiative. But it was, in fact, the local Veneti—possibly a people of Illyrian extraction—who founded the city; and in *c* 350 BC, or a little later, it replaced Ateste (Este) as their principal settlement.

In 302/3 Patavium successfully resisted an attack from the Spartan Cleonymus, preserving his body in a temple of Juno and celebrating the victory thereafter in an annual regatta. In the early third century the Patavians became allies of Rome, maintaining their loyalty in the Second Punic War (218–201), which earned them a treaty (*foedus*) conferring autonomy. However, a rising had to be put down in 174. The city gained importance from its position on a number of roads, including the Via Annia (*c* 153 which continued the Via Flaminia and Via Popillia to Aquileia). During the civil war between Caesar and Pompey the Great (49), despite the receipt of favors from the former, Patavium took the side of Pompey, thus earning Cicero's praise.

It had become a *municipium* by *c* 41, when its inhabitants suffered oppression from Gaius Asinius Pollio, governor of Cisalpine Gaul, who later criticized his fellow historian Livy, the region's greatest son (b. 54), for provincialism which he labelled 'Patavinitas.' Strabo alluded to the quantities of clothing and other goods Patavium sent to the Roman market: it specialized in wool for rough cloaks and carpets. He also commented on the unparalleled number of its Roman knights (*equites*)—totalling no less than five hundred—and pronounced the city to be the greatest in northern Italy, a primacy which it lost shortly afterward, however. Pliny the Younger referred to its wine, of which the bouquet recalled the smell of willow trees, and he and Martial stressed the strait-laced morality of its citizens and propriety of its women. Thrasea Paetus, an upright Republican who met his death under Nero (AD 66) came from Patavium, and so did the historian and literary critic Asconius (d. 76).

The structures of the river port have been identified, as well as meagre traces of an amphitheater and theater. Air photography has recently revealed the territorial divisions (centuriation) and military installations of Patavium's territory. Light has also been cast on the blend of Venetian and Roman elements in the funerary art of the city. It owned the medicinal springs dedicated to the local deity Aponus (Abano; who figures prominently in Patavian inscriptions) at the foot of the Euganean hills; according to Suetonius, the emperor Tiberius (14–37) was advised to throw gold coins into the springs.

Patrae, Patrai (Patras). A city in Achaea (northwestern Peloponnese), outside the narrows of the Corinthian Gulf, situated not, like the modern city, directly on the sea, but on a low hill overlooking the shore. According to mythology, the first name of the place was Aroe (from *aroein,* to plough), because Triptolemus taught agriculture to its King Eumelus. A second foundation was called Antheia, reputedly after Eumelus' son Antheias, and a town founded between the two settlements was known as Mesatis. After an alleged Ionian colonization from Attica, the Spartan Patreus was credited with amalgamating (synoecizing) these and four other settlements into a single city at some unknown but early date.

Patrae supported Athens in the Peloponnesian War (building long walls in 419 on the recommendation of Alcibiades), and after the death of Alexander the Great was first occupied by Aristodemus, a general of Antigonus I Monophthalmos (314), and then belonged to Demetrius I Poliorcetes (307–303). Together with Dyme (Kato Akhaia), it took the lead in expelling the Macedonians and forming an Achaean League (280), but suffered severe losses from invading Gauls in the following year, and again from the Aetolians during the First Macedonian War (215–205). Rome's abolition of the League (146) brought even more widespread destruction. Nevertheless, Patrae still remained a convenient harbor town. It was there that Antony spent the winter of 32/31, while its mint depicted Cleopatra wearing the headdress of Isis, before their defeat by Octavian (the future Augustus) in the battle of Actium.

Augustus planted a group of ex-soldiers in the town *c* 14 BC, granting it the rank of a Roman colony under the name of Colonia Aroe Augusta Patrensis. Neighboring Achaean towns were included in its territory, and a famous statue of Artemis Laphria was transferred from Aetolia; later the image appeared on local coinage, and her worship was commemorated by festivals. The half-centenary of the colony was celebrated by a semi-medallic issue, for which special permission was obtained 'by the indulgence of' Gaius (Caligula AD 37–41); and Nero (54–68), who landed at the harbor of Patrae for his Greek tour, endowed the city with the name of Neronia. Hadrian (117–38) and Antoninus Pius (138–61) added further honors, and the harbor was improved in imperial times. The *Metamorphoses* of Apuleius, written in the second century AD, are based on a lost novel of which a certain Lucius of Patrae was either the author or the narrator. Diocletian (284–305) was a benefactor. Bishops are attested from 347.

Pausanias gives details of the topography of ancient Patrae, but little of what he records now remains, though an Odeon (small theater), agora and temples of Zeus and Demeter (on the sea) can be tentatively located, and remains of streets, baths and workshops have been traced; an important Roman public building has also come to light. In 1973/4 alone nearly eighty investigations were conducted in the ancient town and its cemeteries, revealing an extensive array of houses (some with lead water mains and terracotta piped drainage), winepresses and funeral monuments, and an early Christian basilica. More recently a rich young girl's tomb of the later second century BC, containing gold and silver jewelry, has been discovered, and the wheel-rutted remains of a Roman bridge. A coin of Domitian (AD 81–96) illustrates a fountain (surmounted by a statue of Hercules) with water cascading from lion's head spouts down through a series of catchment basins. Another issue, of the reign of Commodus (180–92), depicts the harbor from the sea, with temples behind; and a coinage of Geta (198–212) offers a view across the harbor from the jetty.

Pavia *see* Ticinum

Pedasus *see* Mothone

Peiraeum *see* Corinth

Pelion. A mountain 5,300 feet high in eastern Thessaly (northeastern Greece), overlooking the Gulf of Pagasae (Volos) at the beginning of the Magnesian peninsula. Palaeolithic elephant tusks, and a bone brooch with a head, have been found on its crags. The mountain possessed rich mythological associations. The giants Otus and Ephialtes were said to have piled it on Mount Ossa, a more northerly Thessalian mountain, in an effort to scale Olympus and reach the heavens. It was on Pelion that Apollo surprised the huntress Cyrene, while she was wrestling with a lion; and the legendary Peleus married Thetis on the mountain, which was named after him.

It was also the home of the centaurs, notably Chiron, who educated many heroes in a cave on its upper slopes. Jason came from Iolcus, which lay in the shelter of Pelion, and the ship Argo, of his Argonauts, was reputed to have been built of timber from its trees. On its summit stood an altar of Zeus Actaeus, beside which festivals were held.

Pella. A city of Bottiaea (Macedonia, northern Greece), twenty-four miles northwest of Thessalonica (Salonica), situated on a slope beside a lake formed by the river Lydias, which was navigable from this point to its mouth in the Thermaic Gulf of the Aegean Sea. Stephanus of Byzantium states that the original name of the place was Bounomos or Bounomeia (cattle pasture); or this may be identifiable with Phakos three miles to the south, which was a prehistoric site (and later a royal treasury). Known to Herodotus and Thucydides, Pella replaced Aegae (Vergina-Palatitsa) as the capital of King Archelaus of Macedonia (*c* 413–399); he was laughed at by Greeks for his presumptuousness in constructing a palace, but invited the painter Zeuxis and the poet Timotheus, in addition to Euripides who wrote his *Archelaus* at his court and died in Macedonia. Xenophon described Pella *c* 369 as the largest city in the country.

Alexander the Great was born there in 356, and taught by Aristotle, and subsequently the place became one of his major mints. It reached its zenith under Antigonus II Gonatas (274–239). The Romans, following their defeat of the last Macedonian king Perseus at Pydna (168), took possession of the town, making it the capital of one of the regions into which the destroyed kingdom was divided, but in the subsequent province of Macedonia (146) Thessalonica became the capital instead. Nevertheless, Pella's position on the Via Egnatia (130), linking the Adriatic coast to Byzantium, increased its importance, and it was made a Roman colony by Octavian (the future Augustus) after the battle of Actium (31); the double title *colonia Julia Augusta* suggests that there may have been two successive settlements or settlement plans. But stagnant waters (now eliminated by drainage) subsequently provided a fertile breeding ground for malaria.

Archaeological soundings have revealed many remains in the area between the modern villages of Palea (Old) Pella and Nea (New) Pella and Phakos. The acropolis proves to have occupied a pair of hills. Recent excavations on the westerly hill have revealed a very large palace complex with a peristyle court of the time of Philip V (221–179). A palace of Philip II (?) is now being uncovered, and the area also includes a sanctuary, perhaps identifiable with a temple of Athena Alcidemus mentioned by Livy. In the central area of the ancient city the whole of a huge porticoed agora (traversed by the main street) has now been uncovered, following on the excavation of half-a-dozen symmetrical residential blocks containing Hellenistic houses of the late fourth and early third centuries BC, which are sometimes two storeys high, and possess colonnaded courtyards.

The houses also display black and white pebble mosaic pavements which show that this art, the precursor of tessellated mosaic, attained previously unsuspected heights of distinction and refinement. One mosaic depicts the naked Dionysus riding a bounding panther. Others show two men with swords and spears fighting a lion, and a stag hunt inscribed 'Gnosis made it.' Further scenes illustrate a gryphon killing a deer, a male and female centaur, a battle with Amazons, and the rape of Helen by Theseus. Another mosaic decorates the floor of a circular building.

Pella (Fahl). A city of Galaaditis (Gilead) now in the state of Jordan, on the east bank of the river of that name and the south slopes of Mount Gilead. The locality possessed a famous spring, and, as recent finds have shown, was occupied from the Neolithic epoch onward. Known from Egyptian texts as Pihilum of Pehal, the place flourished in the Bronze Age and survived for most of the Iron Age as well.

During or shortly after the time of Alexander the Great (d. 323 BC), it was colonized by his ex-soldiers and designated Pella, which was the name of his Macedonian birthplace and also bore a resemblance to the earlier name of the settlement. Pella belonged to the Ptolemies until 218, when it was captured, as Polybius recounts, by the Seleucid Antiochus III the Great. It became known as a center of Greek culture, but after its conquest and partial destruction by the Jewish (Hasmonaean) monarch Alexander Jannaeus (83/80), many of the inhabitants, refusing conversion to Judaism, abandoned the city. In 63 it was taken over by Pompey the Great, who made it a member of a league of towns known as the Decapolis; Pella reckoned a new chronological era from this event. The governor of Syria, Lucius Marcius Philippus (61–59 BC), merited the construction of a local Philippeion (honored on a coin of Commodus, AD 180–92), and another governor, Aulus Gabinius (57–4 BC), rebuilt the city.

The Decapolis retained a measure of self-government under Herod the Great (37–4 BC) and then subsequently in the Roman province of Judaea (from AD 6). When the First Jewish Revolt broke out in AD 66, tradition maintained that the entire Jewish Christian church of Jerusalem, led by its chief Simeon (a relative of Jesus), fled to Pella, although this account probably presents a simplified version of what seems to have been a piecemeal exodus. Incorporated, under the later empire, in the province of Palaestina Secunda, Pella became the seat of a bishopric, and attained the zenith of its prosperity in the fifth and sixth centuries.

There are ruins of a massive, uncompleted Seleucid fortress one and half miles east-southeast of the town; within the habitation area itself, impressive remains dating from the later second and early first centuries BC display marks of Alexander Jannaeus' destruction. A coin of Commodus (180–92) offers a remarkable view of the acropolis, crowned by an enormous temple terrace, and a monumental *nymphaeum* (fountain building) appears on an issue of Elagabalus (218–22). Geological, zoological, botanical and anthropological investigations of the site have continued.

Pella *see also* Apamea

Peloponnese, Peloponnesos. The extensive and largely mountainous peninsula of southern Greece, separated from the rest of the mainland by the isthmus of Corinth. The Greeks interpreted its name as *Pelopos nesos,* the island of the mythological Pelops, whose family, the Pelopids (including Agamemnon), were believed to have been kings of Mycenae or Argos. Homer sometimes appears to use the name 'Argos' to signify the whole peninsula, whereas the word 'Peloponnesos' appears in the Cypria, a poem of the later Epic Cycle, and in the Homeric Hymn to Apollo.

The principal divisions of the territory were Achaea, Elis, Arcadia, the Argolid, Messenia, and Laconia; the capital of Laconia, Sparta, was the strongest town in the peninsula, so that its historic war against Athens, narrated by Thucydides, was known as the Peloponnesian War. (In the later Middle Ages the Peloponnese was called the Morea, the Greek word for mulberry, originally applied to mulberry-growing Elis).

Pelusium (Tell Farama). A city in Egypt on the easternmost (Pelusiac) mouth of the Nile; the Egyptians probably called the place Sainu and Per-Amun, 'House of Amon,' after its principal deity, whose name was also later preserved in the Coptic name of the place, Peremun, and perhaps in the modern Tell Farama. Pelusium was famous for its flax. In later Pharaonic times it replaced Sile as the key fortress and customs post on Egypt's frontier with Judaea.

Cambyses, the Achaemenid king of Persia, defeated the Egyptians at Pelusium in 525 BC on his way to conquer their country, which regained its independence by 404. In 374 a further attack on the stronghold (with Athenian assistance) was frustrated by floods, but in 343 it fell to Artaxerxes III Ochus. After the death of Alexander the Great Pelusium was an important customs station of the Ptolemies. The Seleucid monarch Antiochus IV Epiphanes captured it in 170/169, but was obliged by the Romans to return it to Ptolemy VI Philometor.

Antony, as a twenty-five-year-old cavalry officer of Aulus Gabinius, occupied the fortress in 55, while restoring Ptolemy XII Auletes to the Egyptian throne. Then in 30 Octavian (the future Augustus), after defeating the fleet of Antony and Cleopatra VII at Actium, took Pelusium by storm as a prelude to invading and annexing Egypt: whereupon Cleopatra put the wife and children of its defeated garrison commander Seleucus to death; the assertion that she deliberately betrayed the town was hostile propaganda. In Roman times it was a station on the route to the Red Sea. Its population venerated Isis as goddess of sea voyages, as well as her drowned foster son Pelusius, whom they regarded as their founder. They also regarded onions as sacred, thus giving rise to Christian assertions that breaking wind was their religion. Under the later empire Pelusium belonged to the province of Augustamnica.

Peñalba de Castro *see* Clunia

Pente Komai *see* Samaria

Pentelicus, Pentelikon, formerly Brilessos or Brilettos (the name Pentelicus does not appear until Pausanias in the second century AD). A mountain, 3,638 feet above sea level in Attica (eastern Greece), ten miles northeast of Athens. The name is derived from the district (*demos*) of Pentele at the foot of the southwestern slopes. The mountain was famous for its white marble, which was first worked shortly before 500 BC and thereafter was used for most of the chief buildings and sculptures of Athens. The ancient quarries, which can still be seen, are mostly on the south side; their modern counterparts lie both to the south and the north. Another product of the mountain was honey. A sanctuary of Athena stood on the summit, and a cave dedicated to the Nymphs has been discovered lower down.

Perachora *see* Corinth

Perga, Perge (Murtana near Aksu). A city in Pamphylia (southern Asia Minor), six miles from the sea, at the junction of the river Cestrus (Aksu Çayı) with the smaller Catarrhactes. According to tradition—which may possess a certain factual basis—it was founded by a 'mixed' population, which immigrated after the Trojan War under the leadership of Amphilochus, Mopsus and Calchas.

Subsequently colonized from the Argolid and by the Spartans in the seventh century BC, the place derived importance from its close proximity to the river Cestrus, at the mouth of which it possessed a port, seven miles from the city. After periods of Lydian and then Persian control, Perga paid tribute to Athens during the Peloponnesian War (431–404). In 334/3 it supplied guides to Alexander the Great, and served as his base for operations in Pamphylia. The greatest citizen of Perga was the mathematician Apollonius (second only to Archimedes in renown), who worked in the later third century. The Seleucids exercized domination until their garrison was expelled by the Roman Cnaeus Manlius Vulso in 188. Subsequently the place became part of the Pergamene kingdom, and then of the successive Roman provinces to which Pamphylia (*qv*) belonged. Perga was twice visited by St. Paul, and became very prosperous in the second century AD. In the following century it acquired the honorific distinction of *asylia* (inviolability) and the status of metropolis.

The coins of Perga are remarkable for the number of deities that they depict. The city's special pride was a shrine of Artemis Pergaia or Anassa (princess; Vanassa Preiia in the local speech); like 'Diana of the Ephesians' she seems to have been a native goddess of Asia Minor identified with Artemis by the Greeks. The temple, containing an image (perhaps originally a meteoric stone) behind a barrier that was decorated with bands of dancing figures, is depicted on coins, for example of Lucius Verus (161–69) and Tacitus (275–276); but it has never been discovered. The original town, in which it was presumably located, stood on a flat-topped acropolis at the northern end of the site. But a lower town also came into existence, and was fortified by the Seleucids. The wall still stands today (with Byzantine extensions), including a gate of the reign of Hadrian (120–22), which is Perga's most impressive surviving monument; it is flanked by two round towers and opens onto an elliptical interior courtyard. An elaborate triumphal arch across the inner end of the courtyard was one of the many lavish benefactions of Plancia Magna, priestess of Artemis Pergaia, who is mentioned in numerous inscriptions.

Beyond the courtyard starts the city's colonnaded main street, lined by porticoed shops and column bases. Beside the street is a recently excavated, irregularly shaped agora, a *palaestra* (athletics school)—comprising an open courtyard—at the foot of the acropolis, and a *nymphaeum* (fountain building), from which water issued from behind a reclining figure of the river-god Cestrus to flow down a channel in the middle of the street. A second, smaller, *nymphaeum* is flanked by large baths, recently excavated. To the southwest of the city lie a theater and a stadium, both excellently preserved, with seating capacities for 14,000 and 12,000 spectators respectively.

The Christian martyr Nestor died at Perga during the persecution of Trajanus Decius (251), and the line of its bishops known by name goes back to the fourth century.

Pergamum, Pergamon (Bergama). A city in Mysia (northwestern Asia Minor), situated on a ridge fifteen miles from the Aegean Sea (on which it was served by the port of Elaea [Kazıkbağları]) at a strategic point commanding the rich agricultural valley of the river Caicus (Bakir Çayı), of which two tributaries, the Selinus (Bergama Çayı) and the Cetius (Kastel Çayı), flanked the habitation area on either side.

Pergamum began to be important under Philetaerus, a eunuch of Macedonian (?) and Paphlagonian parentage who, after serving under two of Alexander the Great's successors, deserted to a third, Seleucus I Nicator, with an enormous treasure (282) and ruled the town under Seleucid overlordship for nineteen years, gaining prestige from his resistance to Gaulish invaders whom he propelled onward to their future homes in the central part of Asia Minor. Eumenes I (263–241), with Ptolemaic help, threw off Seleucid sovereignty. Attalus I Soter (241–197), who assumed the title of king and gave the Attalid dynasty its name, won a famous victory over the Galatians (230), and cooperated with Rome in its second war against Philip V of Macedonia (200–197).

Eumenes II Soter (197–160/159) vigorously continued his predecessors' efforts to create a magnificent, highly cultured capital (of which the sculpture, in particular, influenced the entire Greek world), and exploited his country's resources of silver, grain, woollen textiles and parchment. He also secured large territorial gains from the Romans after their victory over the Seleucid Antiochus III the Great (190–9), but subsequently lost the favor of Rome; although his brother Attalus II Philadelphus (160/159–138) contrived to regain its goodwill.

The last, eccentric, Attalid monarch, Attalus III Philometor (138–133), bequeathed his kingdom to the Romans, whereupon, putting down a formidable revolt by Aristonicus (133–130), they converted the whole territory into the province of Asia, thus transforming their own economy by its great wealth. The city Pergamum was declared free, but in 88 became, for a time, the headquarters of the hostile king Mithridates VI of Pontus. In 29 Octavian (the future Augustus) authorized the Pergamene Greeks to dedicate a temple to Rome and to himself, and Aristides (AD 117/129–81) employed glowing terms to describe the grandeur and cultural renaissance of the city (bracketed with the other two capitals of the province, Smyrna [İzmir] and Ephesus).

Pergamum owed much of this renown to its Asclepieum, the sanctuary and hospital of the god of healing, Asclepius (Aesculapius) the Savior, and associated deities. The early structures of this building, of which little remains, include halls and incubation rooms, where sick people expected the god to bring them healing dreams at night; while three adjoining springs provided medicinal waters. But most of the principal buildings date from the second century AD, when the reputation of the shrine attained unique heights. Its central feature, belonging to the reign of Hadrian (117–38), was the round temple of Asclepius, a smaller but resplendent version of the Roman Pantheon. This was adjoined by an even more elaborate circular 'Pump Room,' with six radiating apses and an intricate underground water system linked to the largest of a number of springs by a vaulted channel extending for a hundred yards. Approached by a Sacred Way and a monumental gateway (Propylaeum), the colonnaded precinct also contained consulting rooms, a library, a theater and a latrine with forty seats. The great physician of Pergamum, Galen (129–*c* 199), started his career in the Asclepieum as a doctor for gladiators.

Three miles to the northeast of the sanctuary towers the acropolis; it was here that Philetaerus constructed fortified barracks and an arsenal, in which stone catapult-balls have been found. Attalus I erected a great triumphal monument for his Galatian victories (of which the *Dying Gaul* survives in Rome's Capitoline Museum), and Eumenes II greatly enlarged the defended area. On the summit of the acropolis, built up into tiers of arcaded terraces, a royal palace was added to the barracks and arsenal. On a lower terrace stood a temple of Athena and the great Pergamene library, second only to its prototype at Alexandria (its books were made of the local product of parchment, instead of papyrus). Eighty feet below stood the huge Altar of Zeus, reconstructed, with its frieze of Gods and Giants, in the Staatliches Museum of East Berlin. Lower down again were the (Upper) Agora and a temple of Trajan; and below them the city's spectacular theater was constructed on the side of the hill. Its auditorium faced a long terrace supported by arches built into the rock. Beneath, occupying three levels in the Philetaireia quarter, was to be seen the largest gymnasium in the Greek world (several times altered and extended)—one of five gymnasia so far discovered in the city. Beside it are temples of Demeter and Hera, and (according to epigraphic evidence) a shrine known as the Diodoreion, after a benefactor of the early first century BC, Diodorus Pasparus. Excavations also indicate the existence of a dining room belonging to a Dionysiac association. A Lower Agora, too, has been unearthed, and the identification of Hellenistic houses has considerably increased our knowledge of Greek domestic architecture. Pergamum possessed a number of water conduits (now comprehensively surveyed), of which the Hellenistic Madradağ example shows the oldest and boldest construction. The largest aqueduct of the Aksu conduit was evidently destroyed by a powerful earthquake.

As a result of all these discoveries, it is now possible to draw a plan of the Hellenistic city as a whole. Moreover, local coinages throw much light on its appearance during the Principate, not only illustrating various aspects of the Asclepieum but also depicting a wide range of temples dedicated to the imperial cult and other worships, particularly under Caracalla (AD 211–17) who came for a cure. In addition to all these pagan cults, however, the city had already possessed a Christian bishop since the previous century, presiding over one of the seven earliest churches in Asia Minor; and after Constantine I the Great's conversion, a Christian altar was established in the temple of Asclepius, and a baptistery in the gateway to its precinct.

Perinthus, later Heraclea (Marmaraereğlisi, Ereğli). A city in Thrace (now European Turkey), on the coast of the Propontis (Sea of Marmara), founded by the hero Heracles (according to myth) and in fact by colonists from Samos in *c* 602 BC, who overcame attempts by Megarian settlers in the area to prevent this initiative. The colony lay along an elevated peninsula in the shape of an amphitheater, densely packed with high houses. It suffered harassment by Paeonians, a Thracian tribe from across the Strymon (Struma); Herodotus recounts legendary traditions relating to these attacks. Following the European expedition of King Darius I (513), Perinthus refused to accept Persian domination, but was nevertheless captured by Megabyzus, as a first step toward his conquest of Thrace.

After the Persian wars, the city became a member of the Delian League headed by Athens, but in 411, during the Peloponnesian War, it broke away, only to be recovered by Alcibiades in the following year; although this phase, too, proved only temporary, since the final defeat of the Athenians (404) brought the imposition of Spartan control. In the same period the Perinthians suffered from a serious epidemic, described by a medical writer of the school of Hippocrates. In 377 they adhered to the Second Athenian Confederacy, thus gaining support against threats from the Thracian king Cotys I (365), but joined Byzantium in its subsequent rebellion (357), securing autonomy. Both communities formed an alliance with Philip II of Macedonia (352), but failed to support his hostilities against Athens (341/340), during which Perinthus, though its walls were breached, successfully resisted a famous siege with Byzantine, Athenian and Persian help.

During the third century Perinthus and Byzantium formed a united federal union; but this came under the control of the Macedonian king Philip V (202), until his defeat at the hands of the Romans enabled the two cities to regain their freedom (196). Perinthus next became subject to the kingdom of Pergamum, and after its dissolution (133) was attached to the Roman province of Macedonia, retaining importance as a major communications center owing to its position on the Via Egnatia linking the Adriatic to Byzantium (*c* 130); and it was also the terminal of a highway leading inland. Perinthus subsequently became part of the new province of Thrace (AD 46)

During the civil war between Septimius Severus and Pescennius Niger (193–94) the latter, after securing the allegiance of Byzantium, planned to capture Perinthus; but Severus' advance guard prevented him from occupying the city, in which Severus then proceeded to establish his headquarters, while one of his generals defeated Niger's commander-in-chief outside the walls. The victorious Severus later punished Byzantium by making it tributary to Perinthus (195/6).

Coins of Perinthus issued during the Principate honor Heracles as 'founder of the Ionian Perinthians.' Other pieces display Samian Hera (and the emperor Severus) standing in a ship's prow, offer a number of depictions of Egyptian deities and astrological types, and refer to Games described as the Actia, Pythia, Philadelphia and Severeia Prota.

The name of Perinthus was changed *c* 300 to Heraclea, after its mythical founder, and in honor of the emperor Maximian whose patron deity was Hercules. At the same time the place became the capital of Diocletian's province of Europa (eastern Thrace), and an imperial mint. During the civil war between Lucinius and Maximinus II Daia (312–13), Heraclea-Perinthus capitulated to the latter when he invaded Europe, but he was ejected soon afterward. The foundation of Constantinople by Constantine I the Great (324–30) caused a decline in the fortunes of the city, although it partially recovered in the Byzantine epoch.

Perusia (Perugia). A city in Umbria (central Italy), situated upon a hill 1620 feet above sea level overlooking the fertile valley of the upper Tiber. The region had at one time been inhabited, according to Servius, by the Sarsinates, one of the tribes of the Umbrians (speaking an Indo-European Italic dialect), from whom Pliny the Elder records that the Etruscans seized three hundred towns. Perusia was among them, founded, apparently, by Clusium (Chiusi), which had only become a city in the sixth or fifth century BC. The place was largely responsible for the spread of the cultural influence of the Etruscans across the Tiber into Umbria, importing for example, their alphabet in the fourth century BC. The inhabitants of Perusia retained pretentious foundation legends that conceal the comparatively late date of its foundation, but testify to its importance in the subsequent epoch, when the stories were devised. In particular, these traditions tell of legendary northern expansion by the Perusians—asserting that their city was founded by Aulestes, the father or brother of Ocnus and mythical founder of Felsina (Bononia) and Mantua: the purpose of such tales was to eclipse the more authentic achievements of Clusium (Chiusi), at a time when the Perusians had thrown off its suzerainty. The artistic influence of Clusium is still to be seen in their sarcophagi of *c* 475–450 when they also produced important bronze work, including bizarre elongated statuettes that have appealed to modern sculptors.

After 400, Perusia, by now independent, became the most powerful Etruscan center in the upper Tiber valley. During the fourth century, however, after military operations *c* 310, it became officially bound to the Romans by a treaty which—following an attempted revolt in 295—was replaced by a truce. Thereafter the town remained loyal, notably in the Second Punic War (218–201).

During the Second Triumvirate, by now possessing the rank of *municipium,* it underwent a brief period of lurid and disastrous notoriety, known as the Perusine War. The eviction by Octavian (the future Augustus) of many Italian farmers from their properties had aroused protests that were backed by Antony's wife Fulvia and by his brother Lucius Antonius, without the knowledge of Antony himself (41). Forced out of Rome, these homeless men were driven into Perusia, where starvation compelled them to surrender after a harrowing siege. The city was given up to the victorious soldiers to be plundered and burned, and Octavian inflicted such merciless treatment that the designation of 'Perusian altars' for human sacrifice became proverbial. However, he later reconstructed the city, with the title of Augusta. A later emperor, Trebonianus Gallus (AD 251–53), was a native of the place, and promoted it to the status of a Roman colony.

Long stretches of walls of the later second century BC, built of travertine stone, can still be seen, and the Arco Etrusco or di Augusto and Porta Marzia—two of seven identified gates—contain materials of the same epoch, and remain in use today. Appian and Dio Cassius record temples of Juno, the tutelary diety of the city, and a shrine of Vulcan that stood outside the walls and escaped destruction in the conflagration of 40 BC. Among numerous graves surrounding its perimeter, the most conspicuous is the Tomb of the Volumnii (*c* 100), some three miles from the city, constructed in the form of a house centered on an *atrium.*

Pessinus (Ballıhisar, Balhisar). A temple city in Galatia (central Asia Minor), near the borders of that country with Phrygia, to which the place had earlier belonged; it stood beside a stream—now scarcely visible—in the Upper Sangarius (Sakarya) valley, beneath Mount Dindymus. The foundation of Pessinus was attributed to the mythical Ilus, son of Tros (the founder of Troy), or alternatively to Midas of Phrygia. Pessinus owed its fame to its great shrine of the mother goddess (Meter Dindymene) Agdistis (identified with Cybele), whose cult stone was said to have fallen from heaven, so that Greek etymologists fancifully derived the place-name from *piptein,* to fall. The eunuch priests of the goddess, according to Strabo, had at one time been very powerful, owning dominions of considerable size, and an active market town grew up around the precinct.

When the Gauls began to reach Galatia in the 270s BC, Pessinus came under their suzerainty, and became the capital of one of their tribes, the Tolistobogii (Tolostoagii); but the sanctuary retained its autonomy, cultivating the friendship of Pergamum against Galatian aggressors. In 205, probably through the mediation of its King Attalus I, the sacred stone of the goddess (whom the Romans knew as the Great Mother [Magna Mater]) was transported to Rome in pursuance of an alleged Sibylline oracle, and enshrined on the Palatine Hill. When Cnaeus Manlius Vulso, with Pergamene support, invaded Galatia in 189, the priests of Pessinus met him in procession, forecasting Roman victory in the name of their deity. Eumenes II of Pergamum (197–160/159) in his last years—despite the cooling of his relations with the Romans, who discouraged his influence in Galatia—wrote a series of letters to the Pessinuntine priest-king as an ally and an equal, endowing a new temple, assuring him of aid in a proposed attack on some 'holy place,' and promising assistance against his brother's embezzlements; and Attalus II (160/159–138) continued this policy of friendship to the priestly state.

In 25 BC, as its coinage shows, Pessinus inaugurated a new era dating from the foundation of the Roman province of Galatia in that year. The Christianization of the empire in the fourth century AD deprived the priests of most of their power, although the shrine enjoyed a temporary revival in 362 when Julian the Apostate came and propitiated the goddess with victims and vows. In 365 the eastern emperor Valens visited and garrisoned Pessinus as a prelude to his operations against the usurper Procopius.

Excavations have now taken place, revealing a temple dating from the time of Augustus (31 BC–AD 14). The shrine of the mother goddess probably lay a little distance away: its location can perhaps be determined from the presence of a trough (attached to an ancient canal) which was maybe used for the ceremonial washing (*lavatio*) of the holy stone, conducted in front of a large assemblage of pilgrims. In the theater a dedication to Hadrian (AD 117–38) has been found. Discoveries in the necropolis include Roman tombs with door façades resembling those of Phrygian graves. On the summit of Mount Dindymus a sacred grotto and a number of early Christian funerary inscriptions have come to light.

Petra (formerly Rekem, or Selah, in Jordan). A city east of the Wadi Arabah, south of the Dead Sea. 'It lies,' as Strabo observed, 'on a site which is otherwise smooth and level, but is fortified all round by a rock [which is the meaning of Selah]; the outside parts of the site being precipitous and sheer, and the inside parts having springs in abundance.' The only access is by narrow gorges. Formerly the capital of the Edomites, and then a possession of the north Arabian kings of Dedan (Kebar)—whose expansion into the area drove the Edomites away—Petra became the capital of another Arabian kingdom, that of the Nabataeans (*qv,* by 312 BC), maintaining a flourishing caravan trade, which was maintained after their monarchs became clients of Rome.

Germanicus, nephew of the emperor Tiberius, presumably visited the city in AD 18, when we hear of a banquet given in his honor by the Nabataean king. Before the end of the first century, however, Petra had lost much of its commercial importance, owing to the exploitation of sea routes to Egyptian ports and the discovery of the monsoon in the Indian Ocean; and when Trajan annexed the Nabataean state in 106, he established the capital of his new province of Arabia (112) at Bostra (Busra Eski Sham) instead. However, Petra, adopting the additional name Hadriana in honor of a visit by Hadrian (130/31), remained an important intellectual and religious center. During the reign of Gallienus (253–68), according to Suidas, it became the capital of the province of Palaestina Tertia or Salutaris, and a local philosopher and physician of the late fifth century are mentioned by the same source.

Petra's elegant, eleborately decorated pink sandstone buildings ('a rose-red city half as old as time' [J.W. Burgon]) are among the most impressive monuments of the ancient world. At the end of the Siq gorge, which is a mile and a half long and at some points only ten feet wide, appears the spectacular façade of what is known as the Khazneh (treasury), cut out of the rock; it resembles a Roman temple or palace, but contains a huge cross-shaped chamber which suggests that it should be regarded, instead, as the mausoleum of a Nabataean king, probably Aretas IV (9 BC–AD 39). Near the end of the valley, into which the gorge opens, the largest of Petra's theaters is to be seen; constructed during the second century, it has now been cleared, and provides significant information regarding the technological methods of the region during that period. Beyond the theater are the remains of the city itself, constructed on a series of hill terraces above a Roman colonnaded main street, which followed the course of a river bed (the Wadi Musa) and was spanned by a triple archway. South of the arch can be seen the ruins of the principal temple (the Qasr Firaun), dedicated to the most important Nabataean god, Dusares (Dhu Shares, identified with Dionysus); it contained, according to Suidas, a gold-plated sacred stone or baetyl, and its great monumental approach, on a rising series of walled platforms, has now been cleared and opened up. Nearby, a shrine of the god's consort Atargatis (Al-Uzza) has also been excavated, and farther to the west lies a further sacred precinct containing a temple (the Qasr el-Bint) that can be dated to the later first century BC.

The surrounding hills contain traces of Nabataean houses, but are chiefly notable for a remarkable number of rock tombs and shrines connected with the cult of the dead, including the burial places of the Nabataean dynasty. The façades of these structures range in style from various blends of Egyptian, Assyrian, Parthian and Greek motifs to sophisticated designs of a purely Greco-Roman character. One such tomb of the first century AD, shaped like a tall Doric urn, was converted into a Christian cathedral in 446.

Petronell *see* Carnuntum

Pettau *see* Poetovio

Phanagoria, Phanagoreia, Phanagorium (near Sennaya). A Greek city on the Taman peninsula and gulf, beside the Cimmerian Bosphorus (Straits of Kerch) opposite the Tauric Chersonese (Crimea). Situated on an island formed by Lake Maeotis (the Sea of Azov), Lake Corocondamitis and a branch of the river Anticeites (sometimes known as the Hypanis, like the larger Bug), Phanagoria was settled by colonists from Teos (Sığacık) in Ionia (western Asia Minor) *c* 545 BC. From *c* 480 it belonged to the Archaeanactid (later Spartocid) kingdom of the Cimmerian Bosphorus, eventually becoming the capital of the eastern part of the state, though it retained its autonomous civic institutions, and began to issue local coinage in the fourth century, when the place reached the height of its prosperity.

During the late second century Phanagoria was conquered by King Mithridates VI Eupator of Pontus (120–63), against whom, however, its population, under the leadership of a certain Castor, revolted after his final defeat, thus earning the status of a free community from the Romans. In the time of Augustus (31 BC–AD 14), the city assumed the names of Agrippia Caesarea, which are to be seen, after the emperor's death, on coins bearing the head of his widow Julia Augusta (Livia). Their contemporary Strabo described Phanagoria as a market for goods brought down from Lake Maeotis and from the barbarian country beyond, and pottery kilns and wine-making establishments indicate that it became and remained a manufacturing and industrial center. Destroyed by the Huns in the fourth century AD, it had recovered by the end of the century, and was still an important city in medieval times.

The Greek colony extended over two terraces, comprising an acropolis and a lower city; most of the latter has now been submerged by the sea (this movement, locating a depth of between three and thirty feet, is known as the 'Phanagorean Regression'). The town walls, constructed of unhewn blocks, are partly preserved. On the upper plateau four early houses have been recently discovered, including one that apparently dates from the foundation of the settlement. A necropolis on the outskirts testifies to the importation of Ionic pottery at the same period, followed by wares from Attica, Chios and Thasos; and various

Greek models were also imitated locally, from the sixth century BC onward. Important inscriptions have been discovered, as well as a large temple of *c* 400; there is evidence of the worship of Apollo, Dionysus (in whose likeness a Syrian glass vessel of the second century AD is fashioned), Demeter, Persephone (Kore) and Aphrodite Urania or Apaturus—allegedly from *apate,* treachery, since she was said to have used deception to hand over to Hercules the giants who had attacked her.

The remains of a gymnasium of the third century BC and of a hero's shrine (*heroon*) adorned by paintings are preserved, as well as numerous pieces of sculpture of second and first-century date, and an abundance of terracotta, marble and limestone reliefs, which bear witness to Phanagoria's cultural activity. Outside the city, to its southwest and south, imposing chamber tomb complexes are to be seen; they have yielded rich grave gifts, including saddlery and harnesses of gold and gilded bronze that accompanied the burial of horses.

Pharos, later Pharia (Starigrad). A city and port on the island of the same name (now Hvar, formerly Lesina), forty-two miles long, that lies off the Adriatic coast of Dalmatia (Yugoslavia). The island was extensively inhabited since Neolithic times; a terracotta fragment of the fourth millennium BC, found in the Gabrak cave, shows a representation of a ship. The city of Pharos, situated in a position of natural strength within a deep and narrow bay at the head of a valley, was founded in 385 BC—with the help of Dionysius I of Syracuse in Sicily—by settlers from the island of Paros in the Cyclades, after which the new settlement took its name, with an initial *phi* instead of *pi* (compare the Pharian 'Phersephone' for 'Persephone': the variant took root because Pharos also meant lighthouse).

Shortly after their arrival the colonists were attacked by native Illyrians, reinforced by others from the mainland, who were defeated, however, by a fleet sent by Dionysius from his colony at Issa (Vis). However, in the third century Pharos—like all the Greek settlements of the area except Issa—became a dependency of the rising, unified Illyrian kingdom under Agron (d. 229) and his widow Teuta. Her regent on the island was a Greek, Demetrius of Pharos; yet when she became involved in war against the Romans he went over to their side, receiving additional islands and mainland territories as a reward (228). But in 220 he decided to challenge their authority by unauthorized acts of aggressive expansion, and the Romans, after secretly disembarking in a remote part of the island, took the capital by storm and partially destroyed it, bringing an end to all local autonomy. The town was subsequently rebuilt, under the name of Pharia, and ex-soldiers were settled in the neighborhood. Parts of the walls are still preserved, as well as Roman mosaics and farming complexes (*villae rusticae*) in the countryside. The present town of Hvar is built on the site of a second Greek settlement, Demos.

Pharsalus, Pharsalos. A city of Phthiotis (eastern Thessaly, northeastern Greece). Possessing an impressive acropolis that overlooked a lower city (the modern Pharsalos) at the eastern corner of the more westerly of Thessaly's two plains, it stood at the foot of Mount Narthakion (Kassidiari) about three miles south of the left bank of the Riber Enipeus (Mavrolongos). Abundant evidence of Neolithic and especially Bronze Age occupation has come to light. Although Homer's Phthia, legendary birthplace of Peleus the father of Achilles, had been a principality and not a town, the ancients often believed that it was a town, and the Pharsalians claimed to be its successors. They maintained hero cults of Peleus, Thetis, Achilles, Chiron and Patroclus, in whose honor Games were celebrated.

The city became an important communications center and its aristocratic rulers, the Echecratidae, who sought to rival Larissa for the leading position in Thessaly, were allies of Athens after the Persian Wars; but when they were ejected by their own countrymen in 457 BC, an Athenian siege failed to restore them. During the Peloponnesian War (431–404), however, Pharsalus was allied to Athens. In 395 it came into the hands of Medius of Larissa, but was later dominated by the autocratic rulers (tyrants) of Pherae (Velestinou). Their downfall at the hands of Philip II of Macedonia made Pharsalus the strongest city in Thessaly, controlling the important harbor of Halus (Almiros; before 346). Pharsalian cavalry served in Alexander the Great's expedition to Asia, but in the Lamian War after his death, their city declared against the Macedonians, and was captured by Antipater (322).

During the period that followed it was no longer of great importance. The town apparently belonged to the Aetolian League *c* 228 but was occupied not long afterward by Philip V of Macedonia, and again by the Seleucid Antiochus III the Great (192), from whom it was taken in the following year by the Roman general Manius Acilius Glabrio. Its territory was the scene of one of the decisive battles of history during the civil war between Julius Caesar and Pompey the Great (48), when, according to Plutarch, 'the flower and strength of Rome met in collision with itself'. Moving inland from the Adriatic coast, Caesar had marched eastwards into the grain land of Thessaly. Pompey followed, and camped his army opposite Caesar's on higher ground near Pharsalus; the battle that followed was said to have taken place near the town of Palaiopharsalos (Old Pharsalus). But the exact whereabouts of this place is disputed; it has recently been suggested that the engagement took lace near Driskoli, on the north bank of the Enipeus. At all events, Pompey finally decided to move to the attack. But he was defeated with very heavy losses and fled to Egypt, where he was killed.

Pharsalus was described as a free city by Pliny the Elder (d. AD 79), and in the later empire became an episcopal see. Its outstanding remains today are city walls, including polygonal masonry of *c* 500 BC and enlargements and reinforcements of mid-fourth-century date, notably a recently excavated tower. An inscription refers to a temple of Zeus Thaulios, and foundations of a colonnaded building of *c* 300 have come to light. Cemeteries have yielded material of various epochs.

Phaselis (Tekirova). A city on the east coast of Lycia in southern Asia Minor (subsequently, for a time, it was considered to belong to Pamphylia). Phaselis possessed a flat-topped, rectangular acropolis on a ninety-foot high promontory projecting into the sea. The place was reputedly founded in 690/688 BC by colonists from Lindus on the island of Rhodes, and Herodotus regarded its population as of Dorian origin (like the Rhodians) although the tradition is confused. The colonists were said to have presented a local shepherd with some fish in payment for the land.

In the sixth century the Phaselians are named among the Greek communities participating in the market of Naucratis in Egypt. After a period of Persian suzerainty, the town was detached from this allegiance, against its will, by an Athenian expedition under Cimon (468), who enrolled it in the Delian League. When Mausolus of Halicarnassus (Bodrum) occupied Lycia, Phaselis helped him against the Lycians and concluded a treaty with him (*c* 360), of which passages still survive. The city surrendered without a fight to Alexander the Great, who resided there for a time in 333. After his death it belonged to Antigonus I Monophthalmos, from whom Ptolemy I Soter captured it following a siege (309).

During the third century Phaselis became the most important harbor town in the area. The Seleucid Antiochus III the Great took it over in 197, but after his defeat by the Romans (190/88) it was given to Rhodes, and then liberated to become a member of the free Lycian League (169). Early in the first century, however, the city came under the control of the pirate Zenicetes until his suppression by Publius Servilius Vatia Isauricus—who allowed it to be sacked (177/76). Resuming coinage, which resembled that of the League but lacked the phrase 'of the Lycians' (for Strabo recorded that it was no longer a League member), Phaselis was twice visited by Hadrian (AD 129, 131), and briefly revived its monetary issues under Gordian III (238–44).

Strabo records its three harbors, which have now been carefully examined. On the north slope of the acropolis stands a theater, and traces of houses, streets and cisterns can be seen. The town center, lying at the foot of the headland, contained a paved avenue linking two of the harbors and terminating in a triple-arched gateway commemorating one of Hadrian's visits. Not far away is one of three marketplaces, the Rectangular Agora (identifiable by an inscription), into which a small early Christian church was subsequently inserted. A detailed modern description of the fortifications, sea walls and harbor works is now available. North of the city lies an extensive marsh, identifiable with a lake recorded by Strabo (though Livy had already recorded that its swampy nature caused smells and disease). On an adjoining hill there was a spring, now dried up, from which aqueducts (of late and poor construction) led into the city; a Hellenistic fortress rose nearby.

Phasis (Simagre?). A Greek city in Colchis south of the Caucasus mountains (now in the Soviet Republic of Georgia). The place was named after a river of the same name (the modern Rioni), which was navigable (according to Strabo) as far as narrow defiles presided over by a large fortress named Sarapana; the Glaucus and Hippius, which issued from the neighboring mountains, were the tributaries of this river, and it was spanned by a hundred and twenty bridges. The city of Phasis, a market colony settled by immigrants from Miletus, lay somewhere near the mouth of the river, but because of extensive silting the site has not yet been determined. It was evidently close to the modern town of Poti, at which, however, the earliest settlement so far known is of the second century AD (and the adjacent Patara Poti area does not seem to have been occupied until three hundred years later).

Eleven miles upstream, however, there are signs of Greek occupation going back to the sixth century BC, notably at Simagre on the south bank of the river, where large timber buildings were erected upon a mound; they were destroyed *c* 450, but replaced by later houses extending down to the second century. It has been thought that this may have been the location of the city of Phasis. An alternative claim, however, might be made for another settlement, *c* 450–400 BC, of which remains have now been found some four and a half miles away, spanning the river; although these buildings, more probably, were country houses in the neighborhood of Phasis, whether that was at Simagre or elsewhere.

Pherae (Velestinou). A city of Pelasgiotis (eastern Thessaly, in northeastern Greece). The acropolis of Pherae was situated on a flat-topped spur of Mount Chalkedonion flanked by the Maluka and Makalo ravines. The town lay close to important land routes, and dominated the eastern end of the pass leading to Pharsalus. In Greek mythology, it was the home of Admetus, whose wife Alcestis was willing to sacrifice herself on his behalf (as in Euripides' play named after her); their son Eumelus was named as a participant in the Trojan War. These traditions correspond with recent archaeological evidence confirming the richness and importance of Pherae in the Middle and Late Bronze Age.

It issued its own coins from the early fifth century BC onward, and was in control of the port of Pagasae (Volos) before 500, thus becoming the only Thessalian city to enjoy access to the Aegean Sea and benefit from the recent growth of a grain export trade by way of the Pagasaean Gulf. During the Peloponnesian War (431–404) Pherae was an ally of Athens. Thereafter, for half a century, it became the capital of one of the strongest states in Greece. The groundwork for this rise to power was apparently laid by a local leader Lycophon, who defeated the nobles of Larissa and other cities (404), forming an alliance with Sparta. Then *c* 378 Jason of Pherae became master of most of Thessaly and extended his influence throughout northern Greece, as far as Macedonia and the Adriatic. His assassination (370) was followed by the rule of his nephew Alexander, who was defeated by the Theban Pelopidas in 364 and murdered by Jason's sons six years later.

After a brief usurpation by Alexander's brothers-in-law (including Tisiphonus, who issued the city's last coins), Philip II of Macedonia first detached Pagasae from the Pheraean kingdom, and then established a Macedonian garrison in Pherae itself (344). After the defeat of Philip V by the Romans (197), however, Pherae assumed some importance in the Thessalian League, despite a siege and temporary occupation by the Seleucid Antiochus III the Great (192/91). But thereafter it vanishes from the historical record.

From the Kastraki crag overlooking the city, the famous fountain Hypereia gushed forth; it is depicted on the coinage as a stream of water flowing from the mouth of a lion's head. Coins also show the heads of Artemis Ennodia and Hecate (goddess of the crossroads), whose associated worships formed the city's principal cult; although the Pheraean ruler Alexander also devoted special attention to the cult of Dionysus at Pagasae. Remains of a temple of the later fourth century (perhaps that of Artemis Ennodia) have been found on the site of a sixth-century building and of an eighth-century necropolis. The city wall, of which traces are visible at various points, has been shown, by recent test excavations, to extend over a larger area than had been supposed (including the adjoining hill of Ayios Athanasios).

Philadelphia, Philadelpheia (Alaşehir). A city in Lydia (inland western Asia Minor), occupying a plateau on the lower slopes of Mount Tmolus (Boz Dağ). The site commanded the fertile valley of the river Corgamis (Sarıkız Çayı) and a route linking the valleys of the Hermus (Gediz) and Maeander (Büyük Menderes). Although the appearance of a Macedonian shield on the coinage suggests amalgamation with an earlier Seleucid (Greco-Macedonian) foundation—probably a colony at Bebekli, seventeen miles to the northeast—the city of Philadelphia was established by King Attalus II Philadelphus of Pergamum (159–138 BC). Under subsequent Roman rule it enjoyed the favor of Augustus (31 BC–AD 14), because one of its citizens, Gaius Julius Dionysius, had taught him Greek and became his friend.

However, Philadelphia was so frequently subject to seismic disturbances that few of the inhabitants, according to Strabo, lived within its walls. After a particularly damaging earthquake in AD 17 the town was reconstructed with the aid of the emperor Tiberius and assumed the additional name of Neocaesarea, to which Flavia was added in honor of Vespasian (69–79). In the third century the city received additional honors. In imperial times its commercial life was organized through a series of trade guilds.

The coins issued at Philadelphia from the time of its foundation, and particularly under the Roman Principate, throw light on its religious cults and celebrations, which brought numerous pilgrims and much revenue to the city. Festivals were held in honor of Zeus Helios (also described as Lydios and Koryphaios) and of Asclepius, and under the emperor Gaius (Caligula, 37–41) a local official (archon) describes himself as priest of a shrine erected in memory of Gaius' father Germanicus. Remains of a temple were at one time visible outside the city walls. Portions of these fortifications, surrounding the three small spurs of an acropolis, are preserved, and traces of a theater and perhaps a gymnasium and stadium can be seen. Philadelphia was one of the Seven Churches of Asia in the *Book of Revelation,* but its Christian population suffered numerous martyrdoms.

Philadelphia, Philadelpheia (Amman, capital of the state of Jordan). A city east of the river Jordan, beside the source of its tributary the Jabbachos (Jabbok, Wadi Zerka). Settlements go back at least as far as the Bronze Age, from which fortress walls are preserved, and a fortified settlement existed in the time of the patriarchs. Early Iron Age finds have also attained a notable scale, dating from a period when the place, under the name of Rabbath Ammon, was the capital of the Ammonites, whose royal house, speaking a language akin to Canaanite, was in power from at least the tenth century BC. Subsequently the town received a Macedonian colony and the name of Philadelphia from Ptolemy II Philadelphus (285–246), and then passed into the hands of the Seleucid Antiochus III the Great (218). Pompey the Great made it a member of the autonomous group of cities known as the Decapolis (*c* 63). In AD 106–12 it was detached to form part of the new Roman province of Arabia.

A long steep hill contained the acropolis, on which fine ancient fortifications survive, in addition to remains of a three-terraced citadel and of a lofty temple of Heracles dating from the time of Marcus Aurelius (161–80). Beneath the acropolis, a long colonnaded avenue ran along the north bank of a seasonal stream (*wadi*)—which was vaulted as it flowed inside the walls. The city was entered through a monumental three-bayed gate. Near the crossroads of the avenue and another major thoroughfare stood the public baths, adjoined by a large five-apsed *nymphaeum* (fountain building) displaying two tiers of niches and a columnar façade (the apse of an adjacent building was reemployed to form part of a Christian church). On the south side of the *wadi* is a theater of the second century AD, that possessed a seating capacity of 6,000 spectators and is the city's most impressive ancient structure, now restored. There is also a smaller theater (Odeum). The coinage of this and the following century, which sometimes describes Philadelphia as forming part of Coele Syria ('Hollow Syria') in its looser sense (*see* Syria), stresses the cult of Tyrian Heracles, and portrays Thea Asteria, who was identified with Heracles' mother.

Philae *see* Syene

Philippi, Philippoi, formerly Crenides (Krenides). A city in eastern Macedonia, nine miles from the Aegean Sea, overlooking the proverbially fertile inland Datos plain. The site, known as Crenides ('Springs'), was inhabited by Thracians until 360 BC, when colonists from Thasos, led by an exiled Athenian politician Callistratus, founded a new settlement under the name of Daton, which was captured, recolonized and fortified four years later by Philip II of Macedonia. Possessing an acropolis 1,020 feet above sea level, and enjoying access to the sea at the port of Neapolis (Cavalla), Philippi—as it was henceforward called—became a center for the king's gold-mining activities on the adjacent Mount Pangaeum (*qv*), which gained him a massive revenue.

About 130, under Roman rule, the city gained new importance as a station (together with Neapolis) on the Via Egnatia which linked the Adriatic to Byzantium; the road ran through the middle of Philippi, and constituted its main street (*decumanus maximus*). Two miles away, in 42, one of the decisive battles of history was fought during the Roman civil wars that followed the death of Julius Caesar. For it was here that Antony and Octavian (the future Augustus), who had recently formed the Second Triumvirate with Lepidus, confronted Caesar's assassins Brutus and Cassius. In the first of two successive engagements, each army captured the other's camp, whereupon Cassius, under the mistaken impression that the battle and the war were lost, committed suicide. After a pause of twenty days the army of Antony and Octavian, which had by now run out of food, renewed the attack, and in the face of defeat, Brutus sought death at the hands of a friend. The Roman world was now in the hands of the Triumvirs—until Octavian asserted his supremacy eleven years later. After the battle, Antony established a settlement for ex-soldiers at Philippi, under the name of Colonia Victrix, and its administration issued coins with his portrait. Further coinages under the name of Augusta Julia testify to a refoundation by Augustus; their reference to a praetorian cohort indicates the unit in which the veteran colonists had served.

Parts of the wall of Philip II, together with later sections, survive, mainly on the acropolis but also round the city below. Cut into the hillside is a theater, dating back to the same period and reconstructed and enlarged in Roman times; it could accommodate about 8,000 spectators. Also to be seen are remains of temples of Apollo Komaios and Artemis (dated by inscription to the later fourth century BC), two *heroa* (shrines in honor of heroes) of the second century BC, and open air shrines of Artemis Bendis, Cybele, Bacchus and Silvanus. A sanctuary of a group of Egyptian gods, too, is cut into the rock of the acropolis hill. Beside the principal street (Via Egnatia), the imposing architectural complex of the forum, dated by inscriptions to the reign of Marcus Aurelius (AD 161–80), has now been cleared, and its detailed plan reconstructed. A market, athletics school (*palaestra*), small amphitheater and large underground lavatory are also uncovered, while a structure of *c* AD 250 containing a bathing establishment has been found to be a much larger building (with a colonnaded courtyard) of which the baths only form a part.

St. Paul's visit to Philippi in AD 49, and his subsequent *Letter to the Philippians* written from his prison at Rome, bore ample fruit much later in the importance of local Christianity after the empire's conversion by Constantine I the Great (306–37). The bishop of Philippi was housed in elaborate and imposing premises, in which three phases of construction have now been identified, and four important early churches are identifiable. The oldest, an apsed basilica, was apparently destroyed, and replaced by a huge sixth-century enclosed building. It has also been discovered that an octagonal shrine enclosed within a square exterior in the mid-fifth century, and further altered in the sixth, is superimposed on a smaller church that was in turn built over a demolished basilica of St. Paul, dating from Constantine's epoch. A further edifice, containing elaborate water installations, has yielded reliefs bearing numerous Christian symbols. The fortunes of Philippi during this whole later period evidently underwent fluctuations. Coin finds show a high level of prosperity during the fourth and fifth century AD, interrupted perhaps by an earthquake and by barbarian incursions in the 370s, and again in *c* 474 under Theoderic the Ostrogoth. Meanwhile, however, the industrial revival persisted, until it was brought to an end by Slav invasions *c* 600.

Philippopolis, formerly Pulpudeva and also known as Eumolpia and Trimontium (Plovdiv). A city in Thrace (Bulgaria), situated on three rocky hills overlooking the right banks of the river Hebrus (Maritza, Meriç) and one of its tributaries, and commanding the principal route from Macedonia to the Euxine (Black) Sea and the Thracian Bosphorus. A settlement and probably the royal capital of the Thracian people of the Odrysians, with the name (according to Jordanes) of Pulpudeva, the place was refounded in 342 BC by Philip II of Macedonia as a northern outpost of his kingdom, and renamed Philippopolis, receiving a mixed collection of settlers which earned it the appellation of 'Poneropolis' (Crookstown). Thereafter it passed again under Thracian control, which was only temporarily interrupted when Philip V reoccupied the city in 183. Thereafter Philippopolis resumed its existence as a royal Thracian capital, while at the same time remaining, despite its varied population, an outpost of Hellenism in alien territory; and it survived a siege in AD 21 when the Odrysians and other tribes revolted against King Rhoemetalces II of western Thrace.

Under the subsequent rule of the Romans, who sometimes gave the city the additional name of Trimontium because of its three hills, it became the capital of their province of Thrace (46). Issuing coins from the time of Domitian (81-96) onward, it was divided into four artificially constituted tribes. Philippopolis was granted Roman colonial status, and fortified by the Roman emperor Philip the Arab (244-49). In 250, during the reign of Trajanus Decius, his provincial governor Titus Julius Priscus, besieged by the Goths, allowed himself to be proclaimed emperor and joined the besiegers' side, although this did not save the city from extensive destruction, imprisonments and butcheries. However, a further German siege of the city, recorded by Dexippus and perhaps attributable to the year 268, proved unsuccessful. In the later empire it was the capital of one of the five provinces (Thrace) into which the administrative diocese of the same name was divided. An episcopal see since the fourth century, Philippopolis was destroyed by fire before 400, captured by Attila the Hun in 441, and ravaged *c* 473 by the Ostrogoth Theoderic Strabo ('squinter').

Its coinage during imperial times, before elevation to colonial status, depicts Mount Rhodope (which lay to its south) and two river-gods recumbent beneath three mountain peaks. Coins also mention the provincial assembly (*koinon*) of the Thracians, which met at the city, and stress the Games that this assembly conducted, including festivals known as the Alexandreia Pythia—revived in the cities of Thrace by Caracalla (211-17), who adopted Alexander the Great as his model—and the Kendreiseia Pythia, named after a Thracian god Kendreisos, identified with Apollo. A coin of Elagabalus (218-22) depicts a temple, or its model, held in the hands of Apollo and the emperor. The site of the city itself contains the ruins of a temple of Asclepius. Recent excavations have also revealed successive town plans of the mid- and late second century, and have uncovered a stadium, an amphitheater, the outline of the fortress, and the city's forum in which three successive phases of construction are detectable; the first stage was pre-Roman, and the others were Roman before and after the devastations of 250.

Philippopolis (Shahba). A city of Trachonitis (El-Leja in southwestern Syria), south of Damascus and west of the Sea of Galilee. It was the birthplace (*c* AD 204) of the Roman emperor Philip the Arab (244-49). He gave it the titles of *colonia metropolis*, and its mint issued coins, with Greek inscriptions, bearing his head and the portraits of his wife, Otacilia Severa, his son Philip the Younger, and his father Marinus, a local chieftain who now achieved deification. The remains of the city display a Philippeion, a temple of the imperial family, another shrine, a theater constructed of basalt blocks, large public baths, and houses containing extensive polychrome mosaic pavements. The two principal streets, the *decumanus maximus* (on a steep slope) and *cardo maximus* (which carried most of the traffic), can also be seen.

Philosophiana (Filosofiana, Sofiana). A Roman market center in central Sicily, five miles south-southeast of the modern town of Piazza Armerina, in a fertile valley on the inland route from Catana (Catania) to Agrigentum (Agrigento). The *massa Philosophiana* was one of the most extensive Roman estates on the island. Within the town, a large series of edifices of the early fourth century AD, including a bath installation, have been uncovered. Built over Augustan structures, they in turn were at least partly superseded *c* 400, when a small Christian basilica was inserted in the hot room of the baths; another apsed and three-naved church has been found nearby.

Three miles north-northeast of Philosophiana, in the region of Casale, lies the palatial late Roman villa which is known by the name of the adjacent town of Piazza Armerina. This mansion stood on the site of a villa of unknown dimensions of the second century AD. The building that replaced this second century dwelling is one of the largest habitations known in the ancient world—although two only slightly less luxurious villas have been recently discovered elsewhere in Sicily, on the river Tellaro and at Marina di Patti. The palace at Philosophiana was constructed according to an unsymmetrical but unified plan, *c* AD 300, during the period of the tetrarchy. The principal emperors at the time were Diocletian and Maximian, who both abdicated in 305; there has been a theory that the villa was one of Maximian's places of retirement (or that it belonged to his son Maxentius), but it seems more probable that the villa was the property of a millionaire landowner-senator (or provincial procurator) of Roman or Sicilian origin—perhaps the proprietor of the Philosophiana estate described above.

A monumental triple archway leads northward into an irregular D-shaped colonnaded courtyard; its right side contains an entrance to the spacious central colonnaded courtyard round which the principal living accomodation was arranged. At the northwestern corner of the courtyard, set at an oblique angle, is an elaborate bathing establishment, including an octagonal *frigidarium* (cold room). A group of apartments along the northern side of the courtyard has been tentatively identified as the day quarters of the servants on duty. On the east side is a transverse corridor more than two hundred feet long, terminating in an apse at either end. Beyond stands an enormous apsed audience hall ('Basilica'), flanked by two suites of rooms of which one, centered on its own semicircular court with a fountain, appears to have comprised the private residential quarters of the owner and his family. A further complex, on the south side of the central courtyard, consists of a huge three-apsed room, probably a banqueting hall, fronted by a colonnaded court with three rooms on either side.

This huge residence was formerly adorned with statues, and its walls were covered with paintings and rare and precious marble inlays. But its outstanding and unique feature is the large number of enormous mosaic pavements, which originally covered nearly a whole acre; they were probably executed by master artists from North Africa, where comparable achievements are to be seen. Although the mosaics depict a wide range of themes (some charmingly intimate, such as a design of girl gymnasts, wearing bikinis—superimposed on an earlier geometric pattern—and a picture of the lady of the house with her attendants) there is constantly recurrent emphasis on the massive carnage of hunting wild beasts, notably in the vast Great Hunt mosaic in the transverse corridor (on which the owner of the house himself appears to be portrayed), and in the Small Hunt in the north wing; this concentration on such themes has caused some to suppose that the proprietor drew his income from the importation of animals from Africa for gladiatorial shows. The entire floor of the banqueting hall is covered by a mosaic glorifying the Labors and slaughters of Hercules which displays quite a different artistic style, and is unmistakably the work of other designers, favoring huge, boldly foreshortened masses of flesh and drapery, which twist and heave in ferocious contortions. Certain of these mosaics indicate alterations to the original plan of the mansion, perhaps introduced *c* 320. There are signs that the building suffered severe damage from an earthquake, perhaps in 365, when other parts of Sicily are also known to have been afflicted. Subsequently the mosaics were covered by rubbish and earth, and the wealthy owners were replaced by squatters—perhaps *c* 470, or half a century later. About 1000 the ruins became the nucleus of a village named Platia (*palatium*), abandoned in 1161 when the town of Piazza Armerina was founded. The principal excavations took place in 1950–54 although important work was also done before and since.

Phlegraean Fields *see* Puteoli

Phlius, Phleious. The principal city of Phliasia in the Peloponnese (southern Greece), situated beside the upper waters of the river Asopus, near the point where the lands of the Argolid, Achaea, Arcadia and Corinthia meet; its fortified acropolis (Trikaranon) commanded one of the subsidiary roads that led to Corinth.

In the Persian Wars Phlius contributed two hundred men to the battle of Thermopylae (480) and a thousand to Plataea (479). The town, which possessed its own Pythagorean school and provided the setting for Plato's *Phaedo,* was an ally of its fellow Dorians the Spartans, whom it served as a counter weight against Argos. In 383, however, it incurred their displeasure—fomented by returned political exiles who had gained their ear—and succumbed to Agesilaus II (379) after a twenty-month siege; whereupon he appointed a committee 'to determine who should live and who should die'. In 366/65 the new régime at Phlius loyally supported Sparta in spite of incessant attacks from Argos, Sicyon and Arcadia, to which it lost part of its territory; but after Spartan supremacy had been destroyed the Phliasians took an active part in the general treaty that followed (362/61). In the later third century they passed for a time under the rule of autocrats ('tyrants'), after whose abdication Phlius became a member of the Achaean Confederacy (278); though it was temporarily detached by Cleomenes III of Sparta in 225. In the Roman age Pausanias described Phlius as a large and flourishing town, although its coinage (which mostly dates from much earlier times) was only resumed briefly under Septimius Severus (AD 193–211).

The place contained a sacred stone, the *omphalos* (navel), since its inhabitants, disregarding geographical facts, declared it the center of the Peloponnese. Its principal deity was Hebe, and a temple of Asclepius is mentioned; it has been identified, although controversially, with a building occupying a terrace upon the slopes of the acropolis. Traces of the acropolis walls have been found, as well as those of the city below, where a rectangular structure with an interior colonnade of the fifth century BC (known as the Palati) and a theater (Roman in its present form) are to be seen.

Phocaea, Phokaia (Foça). A coastal city of Ionia (western Asia Minor), situated on a bay near the end of a headland flanked by a harbor on either side (Naustathmos and Lampster), beside the northern entrance to the Gulf of Smyrna (Izmir). A small river, the Smardus, flowed into the gulf nearby, and Phocaea commanded the valley of the Hermus (Gediz Çayı). It was the northernmost of the Ionian towns, and indeed, at the time of the earliest Greek settlements, had more properly belonged to Aeolis than to Ionia, since its Ionian colonists—under Athenian leadership, according to ancient authors—had been ceded land by the people of Aeolian Cyme (Namurt Limanı). Pottery found on the site of Phocaea suggests that their occupation took place not later than 800 BC.

Nevertheless, they still lacked good arable soil; so instead they exploited the potentialities of an excellent harbor, and became some of the most skillful and enterprising of all Greek sailors. They provided a port for the Lydian interior, traded with Naucratis (Kom Gieif) in Egypt, and founded Lampsacus (Lapseki) at the northern entrance to the Hellespont (Dardanelles) and in association with Miletus Amisus (Samsun) on the Euxine (Black) Sea. But the historic achievement of the Phocaeans lay in the west. Already in the later seventh century their seamen had passed outside the Straits of Gibraltar to Tartessus, establishing friendly relations that secured them a large share in the tin and bronze market. They also established numerous colonies in the western Mediterranean, of which the most famous—later one of the leading cities of the ancient world—was Massalia (Massilia, Marseille) on the southern coast of Gaul, which in turn created settlements along the same coast and on the Mediterranean shores of Spain, while other Phocaeans colonized Alalia (Aleria) in Corsica (*c* 565–560).

In the sixth century Phocaea inaugurated an extensive and widely circulating electrum (pale gold) coinage, displaying the punning type of a seal (*phoce,* from the shape of some islands adjoining the city). About 540, however, threatened by a besieging Persian army, many of its inhabitants migrated to its Mediterranean colonies, and, in particular, to Alalia, from which later on (after a historic battle *c* 535 against Etruscans [from Caere, now Cerveteri] and Carthaginians), they were obliged to move instead to Elea (Velia, Castellamare di Bruca) in Lucania (southwest Italy). An important Phocaean sculptor, Telephanes, however, worked for the Persian court; and some of the emigrants eventually returned home. Their city joined the Ionian revolt against the Persians, but was only able to send three ships to the disastrous battle of Lade (495), although owing to their naval skill the supreme Ionian command was given to one of their citizens, Dionysius; he fled to Sicily after the defeat. After the Persian

Wars the Phocaeans became members of the Delian League directed by Athens, but rebelled in 412, during the Peloponnesian War, and left the League. Following the death of Alexander the Great (323) their city was eclipsed by the revival of Smyrna, and came successively under the domination of the Seleucids, the Ptolemics and the Attalids of Pergamum. When the last named kingdom was bequeathed to Rome, Phocaea joined Aristonicus' unsuccessful rebellion against the Romans (132), but after its suppression was saved from destruction by the intervention of Massalia. Pompey the Great granted Phocaea the status of a free community *c* 63.

Thereafter it resumed the issues of coinage, from the time of Augustus (31 BC–AD 14) to Philip the Arab (AD 244–49). The designs on these pieces included a figure of Poseidon (Neptune) with his foot on a prow, and the contest of Poseidon with Athena. A temple of that goddess, mentioned by Xenophon and Pausanias, is probably identifiable with a shrine at the tip of the headland, which was erected *c* 575–550, was evidently restored after its destruction by the Persians, and has now been excavated. Adjacent graves carved out of the rock, somewhat resembling tombs in Lycia, Lydia and Phrygia, probably include the burial places of local autocrats who had ruled the city under Persian suzerainty.

Phocis, Phokis. A territory of central Greece including the valley of the river Cephisus to the north and the plain of Crisa on the Corinthian Gulf to the south, linked by passes across the slopes of Mount Parnassus. According to legend, the Phocians took part in the Trojan War, and subsequently fought against the Thessalians. In early days, they controlled Delphi—which lay on Parnassus' southern flank—until a coalition of Greek states brought the oracle under the control of a council of 'dwellers round about' (*Amphictyones*) *c* 596. According to Strabo, the largest town of the region was Elataea.

During the Persian Wars, according to Herodotus, Phocis was compelled to join the Persians, but deserted in time to serve on the Greek side at Plataea (479). Checked by the Spartans from expanding at the expense of its neighbor Doris (458/7), Phocis, with Athenian aid, was nevertheless able to recapture Delphi, but lost it again, and once more regained it (in the Second Sacred War) through the good offices of the Athenian Pericles (448), who hoped to encircle the Thebans in Boeotia. From 447, however, the Phocians allied themselves with Sparta, continuing to support its cause during the Peloponnesian War (431–404) and in the early fourth century, until they were obliged to enroll in the Boeotian (Theban) confederacy (*c* 380).

In 356 Phocian separatists seized Delphi in defiance of Thebes and the Amphictyony, but in the Third Sacred War that broke out in the following year, their leader Philomelus lost his life (354) and his successor Onomarchus was defeated and killed by Philip II of Macedonia (352), to whom the exhausted Phocians eventually had to surrender (346). An indemnity was exacted, they were deprived of their votes in the Delphic Amphictyony to Philip, and their towns were split up into villages. But reconstruction began, with Athenian and Theban support (359), and the Phocians fought against Philip at Chaeronea (338) and against Antipater in the Lamian War (323), in both cases without success.

In 279 they helped to defend Thermopylae against the invading Gauls, but later became subject to Macedonia again. Subsequently, they were attached to the Aetolian League (196), until its dissolution by the Romans (189). Thereupon the conquerors established a new Phocian Confederation; and this, despite participation in the Achaean revolt suppressed in 146, continued to exist. Augustus (31 BC–AD 14) restored its votes on the Delphic Amphictyony, and there is evidence for its survival until the time of Septimius Severus (AD 193–211). Not far from Daulis, which was the federal center, Pausanias records a large building named the Phokikon, containing statues of Zeus, Athena and Hera; it was here that the delegates assembled. *See also* Delphi.

Phoenicia, Phoinikia. The territory approximately corresponding to the modern Lebanon (with adjoining portions of Syria and Israel), comprising Mounts Libanus (Lebanon) and Anti-Libanus (ranges that were rich in shipbuilding timber), the productive Bekaa valley between them, and no less fertile seaboard between the river Eleutherus (Nahr el Kebir) to the north and Ptolemais Ace (Akko, Acre) to the south.

The Phoenicians regarded themselves as Canaanites (*Kena'ani*). The term 'Phoenician' is derived from an Egyptian word (*fenkhw*) meaning an Asiatic in general, and is believed to appear in the Greek Bronze Age (Linear B) script as a word indicating a color and describing part of a chariot. The appearance of 'Phoinikes' in the Homeric poems (a name which some scholars believe to indicate Minoan Cretans) was interpreted to mean 'red-skins', from *phoinos*, blood-red; though the people of the Phoenician coast may have owed this designation to the color of the purple dye derived from the *murex* (rock whelk) which gave them their prosperity. According to Greek mythology, however, they derived their name from Phoenix, the son of Agenor who was also the father of Cadmus, Cilix and Europa, and was variously described as King of Tyre (Es-Sur) and Sidon (Saida).

Following the very ancient example of Byblus (Jebel), these two cities, and especially Sidon—which was known to the Homeric poems—replaced the Mycenaeans as the principal seafaring and trading powers of the eastern Mediterranean from the tenth century onward. Tyre, which lay south of Sidon beyond the river Lita (Litani) is not mentioned by Homer; but it took the lead from *c* 750–700, and the Tyrian colony of Carthage (*qv*) in north Africa may have been established in the same period (though its foundation is traditionally attributed to 814 BC). Subsequently the fleets of the Phoenician city-states, serving under their own kings, formed the nucleus of the navies of the Achaemenid Persian monarchs. However, they surrendered readily to Alexander the Great, except Tyre, which was only captured after a prolonged and famous siege (332).

Thereafter the country was hotly disputed between the Ptolemies and the Seleucids from 274 onward, falling definitively to the latter kingdom under Antiochus III the Great in 200. From 63 BC the cities of Phoenicia, displaying various degrees of Hellenization, shared the fortunes of the Roman province of Syria, and then of Syria Phoenice (created by Septimius Severus in AD 194). During the later empire the coastal strip became a separate province of Phoenice, with its capital at Berytus (Beirut), while the interior of the country was attached to

Augusta (or Libanensis), governed from Damascus. *See also* Aradus, Berytus, Byblus, Dora, Ptolemais Ace, Sidon, Tripolis, Tyre.

Phrygia. A territory in the interior of Asia Minor, comprising the western part of the peninsula's central plateau. The name was at one time understood to embrace a much larger area, extending far inland; while the northwestern corner of Asia Minor was sometimes known as Phrygia Minor or Hellespontine Phrygia. But the real core of the country lay south of Bithynia and the river Sangarius (Sakarya), comprising the upper course of the Maeander (Büyük Menderes) and extending southward to the boundaries of Lycia and Pisidia (of which the northern part was at times described as Pisidian Phrygia). Phrygia's other neighbors were Mysia, Lydia and Caria to the west, and Galatia and Lycaonia to the east.

Herodotus writes of an early migration of the Phrygians from Macedonia, where he says that they had been known as Briges (elsewhere he writes of a Thracian tribe of Brygi) but changed their name when they emigrated. Another historian, Xanthus, on the other hand, while agreeing that the Phrygians originated from Europe, stated that they came from the western side of the Euxine (Black) Sea, under the leadership of Scamandrius.

At all events, by the early first millennium BC, the Phrygians, of Asia Minor, speaking an Indo-European language, had formed a great imperial state, with its centers at Gordium (Yassıhüyük) and 'Midas City' (Yazılıkaya). But this empire was overthrown *c* 700 by the Cimmerians (invaders from beyond the Caucasus), whereupon the Lydians became dominant in the peninsula instead, absorbing Phrygia and its former possessions. After the destruction of the Lydian state by the Achaemenid Persians (546), Phrygia became part of the Persian empire until its occupation by Alexander the Great, who entered Gordium in 333.

After his death the territory was a battleground among his successors, but became a possession of the Seleucids in 301. Regions east of the Sangarius, loosely regarded as Phrygian, fell to the Gauls *c* 275 and became part of Galatia, while western Phrygia passed out of Seleucid control into the Attalid kingdom of Pergamum. When the Romans took over the Pergamene state, Phrygia was disputed between the monarchs of Bithynia and Pontus, until the greater part of the territory was absorbed in Rome's province of Asia *c* 129 and 116 (Cibya becoming incorporated in 84).

Before AD 259 a separate province of Phrygia and Caria existed, and during the later Roman empire there were provinces of Phrygia Prima (southwest) and Secunda (northeast), which became known in the fifth century as Pacatiana and Salutaris respectively; they were administered from Laodicea on the Lycus (Gonçalı) and Synnada (Suhut). Phrygian inscriptions show the survival of the native tongue until the third century, when attempts were made to restore it as a written language. The Greeks and Romans believed that they owed the Phrygians important musical innovations, supposedly introduced by Olympius *c* 900 BC. *See also* Apamea, Cibyra, Gordium, Hierapolis, Laodicea.

Piacenza *see* Placentia

Piazza Armerina *see* Philosophiana

Picentia (Pontecagnano). An Etruscan and Roman city in Campania (southwestern Italy) six miles east-southeast of Salernum (Salerno). The modern town is on the left bank of the river Picentino, two miles from the sea. The site of the ancient settlement is unknown, but discoveries in the large cemeteries of thc region confirm the assertion of Pliny the Eldcr that the territory (the Ager Picentinus) oncc belonged to the Etruscans; and indeed these finds reveal that it was one of their most important Campanian centers—although its Etruscan name is unknown.

The earliest Iron Age graves, going back to the ninth century BC, bear a strong similarity to burials at Tarquinii (Tarquinia), which may, therefore, have been the Etruscan city-state responsible for the colonization of Picentia—possibly superseding or transforming an earlier, perhaps indigenous, community on the site. The Etruscans must have been attracted by the fertility of the region, and by the strategic location of Picentia on a major highway to the interior and the south; it may be conjectured, too, that there was a harbor in the vicinity, through which maritime links with Etruria were established. Objects found in the tombs offer the entire chronological sequence familiar from the Etruscan homeland itself, right down to the sixth century. Among the finds are princely graves of *c* 700, resembling tombs at Cumae (a generation earlier) and Praeneste (Palestrina; contemporary), a seventh-century silver-gilt Phoenician bowl, faience scarabs, and pottery from Greece.

It has been suggested that the subsequent decline of this Etruscan center at Pontecagnano was due to the rise of the Greek colony established at Posidonia (Paestum), on whose products the scanty fourth-century material uncovered at the site shows evident dependence. Thereafter the town disappeared, but partially revived *c* 268 under its new Roman name of Picentia, which was owed to a group of people from Picenum (Marche, Abruzzo) in eastern Italy, transplanted to the area. But during the Second Punic War, after the Roman defeat at Cannae (216), these Picentini rebelled and joined Hannibal, with the result that in 197/94 the Romans took away part of their land for a new colony at nearby Salernum (Salerno), which was equipped with a garrison to keep watch over their future loyalty.

Picenum (Marche, Abruzzo). A region of eastern (Adriatic) Italy extending between Ancona and the region of the Senones to the north—the early Iron Age Picenes had dwelt north of this border as well—and the river Sagrus (Sangro) and the Vestini to the south. Rich inhumation cemeteries from the ninth to the sixth centuries BC have come to light. At the end of this period, in an area centered on Cupra Maritima (Cupra Marittima), large bronze rings found in women's tombs seem to relate to the worship of a mother goddess, the Dea Cupra. The inscriptions in the area fall into two categories: a southern ('Old Sabellic') group—which like the material culture of the region displays close affinities with the Illyrians across the Adriatic, attested, for example, by a type of brooch known as the 'spectacle fibula'—and a northern group which displays links with the overland traffic (including amber) arriving at the head of the Adriatic from central Europe. Picenum underwent conquest by the Romans in 268, and was distributed among Roman settlers by the Flaminian Law (232).

It was at Asculum (Ascoli Piceno) that the Italian insurrection against Rome known as the Social War broke out in 90. After the war, Picenum, like the rest of Italy south of the Padus (Po), received Roman citizenship. Cnaeus Pompeius Strabo, who had put down the rebellion in Picenum, was a native of the territory, in which his family possessed great estates and numerous adherents. This influence (*clientela*) was inherited by his son Pompey the Great, who was, therefore, greatly disappointed when at the outset of the Civil War in 49 Picenum went over to his enemy Julius Caesar without a blow.

Under Augustus it constituted one of the regions of Italy, but *c* 200 AD was joined to northeast Umbria (Flaminia) to form the district or province of Flaminia et Picenum, later divided into two parts, Annonaria and Suburbicaria, assigned respectively to the two administrative dioceses of Italy that bore those names. *See also* Ancona, Asculum, Firmum.

Pichvnari *see* Colchis

Piemro *see* Naucratis

Pieria *see* Olympus, Seleucia in Pieria

Pietrabbondante *see* Samnium

Pillars of Hercules *see* Gades

Pinnata Castra (?). This (or Victoria?) may have been the ancient name of Inchtuthil, a Roman military post in Caledonia (Scotland), on the north bank of the river Tava (Tay), northwest of Carpow. The building of the stronghold of Inchtuthil was begun by Cnaeus Julius Agricola, probably in AD 83, and abandoned before completion in 86 or 87, after Domitian had decided not to proceed with the conquest of Scotland, which that general had envisaged.

The principal feature of the complex is a square legionary fortress, in which it is possible to trace an administrative building (*principia*), officers' quarters, two bathhouses, sixty-four large barracks for soldiers, six substantial granaries (four more were left uncompleted), a porched and aisled drill hall (*basilica exercitatoria*), colonnaded storerooms, a shrine, and a military hospital containing sixty wards. Underneath a construction workshop, no less than twelve tons of unused nails were found; they had evidently been buried when the fortress was evacuated. A temporary camp has also been identified.

Piraeus, Peiraieus. The port of Athens, four miles from the city. The irregular coastline of a promontory or peninsula (Acte) provided three natural harbors, Cantharus, or the 'great harbor,' to the west, and the small round harbor of Zea and inlet of Munychia to the east. The adjacent town occupied the promontory itself, together with the rocky hill of Munychia, the ground dividing it from the promontory and a small spit of land known as Eetioneia.

Athens' autocratic ruler 'tyrant' Hippias (527–510) fortified Munychia, but it was Themistocles who created a strongly fortified port (apparently from *c* 493/92) in order to provide the growing Athenian fleet with an effective base to supersede the open anchorage of Phaleron. In 461–456 (with additions in 445) the Long Walls were built to connect Athens with both Piraeus and Phaleron; the two parallel walls to the Piraeus were about two hundred yards apart. These fortifications made Athens and its ports into a single isolated fortress in which their populations could live on seaborne provisions during a war. About 450 the architect Hippodamus of Miletus designed the town of the Piraeus, farther inland, according to a systematic plan corresponding closely to the center of its modern counterpart; the place had exploded from a medium-sized village to a large planned town, the biggest port in Greece.

After the final Athenian defeat in the Peloponnesian War (431–404), which the Long Walls and the fortifications at the Piraeus had been unable to prevent, these defences were destroyed by the Spartan general Lysander to the accompaniment of flute music. But with Persian help the walls were rebuilt by Conon in 393, following a slightly different course, on which recent excavations have thrown light. Fourth-century inscriptions record the existence of one hundred and ninety-six ship sheds at Zea (the principal naval harbour), ninety-four at Cantharus (devoted mainly to commerce), and eighty-two at Munychia. A number of the Zea sheds and water installations at Cantharus have now been found.

When Athens sided with Mithridates VI Eupator of Pontus against the Romans, Sulla's siege (87–86 BC) inflicted severe damage on the Piraeus, and this time the walls were not rebuilt. Strabo found the town reduced to a small habitation area round the harbors and a temple of Zeus Soter. This temple, of which the site has not been discovered, was bracketed by Pausanias with a shrine of Athena Soteira among the local sights worth seeing. Numerous other temples, however, are also attested; the names of their deities often bear witness to the presence of foreign sailors, notably the Thracian Bendis and a healing hero named Serangos, to whom a bathing establishment may have been dedicated. Remnants of a shrine attributed to Aphrodite Euploia (at the north end of Eetioneia) and of a colonnaded enclosure of the votaries of Dionysus are tentatively identified. According to Pausanias, Piraeus had two agoras, one in the inland town (the Hippodameia) and the other beside the sea, and it seems that certain of the public buildings were correspondingly duplicated. Remains of a large theater built into the western slopes of Munychia, and of a smaller but better-preserved counterpart west of the Zea Harbor, are still to be seen.

Pirene *see* Corinth

Pisa (Pisatis) *see* Olympia

Pisae (Pisa). A coastal city just beyond the northwestern extremity of Etruria. It stood on the right (north) bank of the river Arnus (Arno) at the point where this was joined by the Auser (Serchio). Today the two rivers remain entirely separate, but in ancient times they apparently merged into a single large basin from which their waters debouched together into the Tyrrhenian Sea; the basin formed one of those large protected sea lagoons and harbors which were features of the Etruscan coastline in antiquity. According to Servius, 'Pisae' means 'harbor.'

The appearance of the place-name in a list at Pylos (southwestern Peloponnese) in the later second millennium BC may signify the existence of a Mycenaean market and trading post at Pisae, of which, however, the traces have not yet come to light. The antiquity of the site, however, is also suggested by ancient tales claiming foundation by various Greeks (the sons of Pelops, or people from the Peloponnesian land of Pisa), but these accounts are probably fictitious. Servius records a Celtic King Pisus as another reputed founder, and the obscure tribe of the Teutani also seem to be mentioned in this connection. The Ligurians, who spoke a non-Indo-European language and pervaded northwest Italy, may have had a hand in the origins of Pisae; a male skeleton recently found at Vecchiano and objects discovered at Poggio di Mezzo (San Rossore) seem to belong to this prehistoric phase. An alternative tradition, indicating that it was the Etruscans who played the major part, is recorded by Cato the Elder and confirmed by the discovery of Etruscan or Etruscanizing objects at least as early as *c* 500 BC. The Etruscans possessed the expertise needed to drain the extensive swamps round the coastal lagoons. Pisae may have been an outlying dependency of the Etruscan city-state of Volaterrae (Volaterra).

In later times, according to Strabo, the place was a frequent target for Corsican raiders. In 225 it served Rome as a frontier base against the Ligurians, but after their suppression, when Luna (Luni)—farther north—became a Roman citizen colony (*c* 177), Pisae did not, so that its importance was diminished. Its position, however, on an extension of the Via Cassia from Rome to Arretium (Arezzo, 154–125), and on the Via Aemilia Scauri linking the capital to the north (109), exercised a restorative effect, and after gaining the rank of a *municipium,* like other Italian cities, in 90/89, Pisae achieved colonial status either under Julius Caesar (whose father had died there in 85) or more probably under Octavian (Augustus). Thereupon it assumed the names of Colonia Obsequens Julia.

An inscription of the patriotic city council praised the virtues of Augustus' grandson Gaius Caesar in glowing terms and at voluminous length, obviously believing him to be the heir apparent, though in fact he did not live to succeed to the throne. After the death of Augustus himself in 14, the same body pronounced him 'Guardian of the Roman Empire and Governor of the Whole World.' Inscriptions found at Pisae indicate the existence of a corporation of shipwrights (*fabri navales*), who derived their timber from the thick forests that at that time existed nearby.

In 409 the place witnessed an engagement, in which three hundred Huns, fighting in the imperial army, were said to have slain eleven hundred of Ataulf's Visigoths, losing only seventeen men themselves. By this time the silting up of the coastline had removed the city far from the sea, with the result that San Piero a Grado, four miles to the west, took over its position as a river harbor; and Santo Stefano farther south, near the later Livorno, became known to the *Itineraries* as the Portus Pisanus. Nevertheless, Pisae returned to fame in the Middle Ages, as a leading maritime Republic.

As regards its ancient port before these developments took place, the vast subsequent hydrographical changes have meant that even the location of these harbor installations is still disputable. The sites of the forum and a section of the Via Aemilia Scauri have been tentatively identified (in the Piazza dei Cavalieri and Vie Ulivo-Faggiola or Via Roma), and walls apparently belonging to a house of Roman imperial date—later destroyed by fire—have now been unearthed in the Piazza del Duomo.

Pisidia. An inland territory of southern Asia Minor, bounded by Phrygia on the northwest (the Hellenized northern region of Pisidia was sometimes called Phrygia Pisidica), Lycaonia to the northwest, Lycia to the southwest, and Isauria and Cilicia to the southeast. Although Pisidia included fertile plateaus and valleys, the country was mostly composed of the rugged Taurus (Toros) mountains; it sheltered a lawless population, with a language of its own, which vigorously resisted successive Hellenistic would-be conquerors. Etenna (unidentified) and Selge (Serik) coined from about the fourth century BC onward; but otherwise no coinage was issued in the area before 100.

In 25 BC, on the death of King Amyntas of Galatia, Augustus incorporated Pisidia in his new Galatian province, conducting a long process of pacification and establishing military colonies at four fortress cities, in addition to two others in Lycaonia. The most important of these Pisidian settlements, Antiochia (Yalvaç), was designed to become an important communications center, although at first the progress of Greco-Roman culture was slow. In AD 74 Vespasian divided the country between the provinces of Lycia-Pamphylia and Cappadocia. After 100 urbanization and prosperity advanced more rapidly, so that coinages were issued in the name of thirty-two cities during the second century AD and twenty-eight cities early in the third; the epoch that followed witnessed a considerable decline, although some cities, unusually, continued to coin until Aurelian (270–75). One of the latter was Cremna (Girme), an Augustan colony which in the later empire became the capital of a separate province of Pisidia, within the administrative diocese of Asiana.

Pithagorion *see* Samos

Pithecusae, Pithekusa, Inarime, Arime, the Roman Aenaria (Ischia). A fertile island seven miles from the mainland of Campania (southwest Italy) (the name Pithecusae was also sometimes extended to the neighboring island of Prochyta [Procida]) off the northwest tip of the Gulf of Cumae, which was known also as the Crater, and is now the Bay of Naples. Recent excavations have shown that pottery from Greek lands was present on the island during the later Bronze (Mycenaean) Age (*c* 1400 BC). It has been found on the lofty defensible promontory of Monte Vico above Heraclium (Lacco Ameno) at the northwestern corner of the island, where a flat lofty headland possesses sheltered harbors on either side and is adjoined by a strip of fertile territory. An early Iron Age village has been uncovered at Castiglione, on the north coast some two and half miles east of Monte Vico.

A Greek trading post was also established on Monte Vico itself, where objects from Greece discovered in the cemetery go back to at least 775/770 BC. The founders of the settlement came from the Euboean cities of Chalcis and Eretria, these being the states that were in the forefront of the new expansion of Hellenism—although the Eretrian merchants may have been exiles from their city. These traders were joined in the enterprise by a contingent from Cyme (that is to say, a small town on the same island of Euboea, and not, apparently, the more famous city in Aeolis [western Asia Minor] which took its name).

So one early pot found at Pithecusae displays an inscription in the Chalcidian form of the Greek alphabet. Another vase, significantly, depicts a shipwreck; for the trading post of Pithecusae was established in order to make maritime contact with Etruria, of which the metals, particularly iron and copper, were eagerly sought by the Greeks (and the contact could be facilitated by Etruscan settlements that have recently been identified in Campania itself). Thus a piece of iron in its natural state (haematite) which has now been unearthed at the earliest levels of Pithecusae has been proved to originate from the Etruscan island of Ilva (Aethalia, Elba); and remains of Pithecusan iron-workings have survived. What tempted the leaders of the Etruscan city-states to supply these Euboean visitors with the metals they required, was above all, the gold that they received in return and which brought them the great wealth displayed by their own eighth-century tombs. The Euboeans at Pithecusae, for their part, had obtained this gold from Greek commercial markets at Al Mina and Posidium (Ras-el-Bassit) in northern Syria, which possessed access to the gold mined in various near-eastern lands. In consequence, scarabs (beetle-shaped seals or gems) of Egypto-Phoenician design—both imports and copies—have been found on the island, as well as a locally fabricated amphora with an Aramaic inscription (the place-name Pithecusae, as Pliny the Elder points out, is derived from the local clay deposits).

Having gained confidence and contacts by establishing this island post, the Euboeans moved over to the mainland (*c* 750–725), where they established a second market which became the great city of Cumae. The eclipse of Pithecusae, which this development initiated, was completed by a volcanic eruption of Mount Montagnone (a secondary crater of Epomaeus [Epomeo], an active volcano in ancient times) at about the end of the sixth century. In 474 Hiero I of Syracuse, enlisted by Cumae to repel the Etruscans, occupied Pithecusae and planted a garrison (on the Castello island at Ischia Ponte on the east coast of the island), which fled, however, in 470 when another eruption occurred. Pithecusae was subsequently occupied by settlers from Neapolis (Naples), and then taken over by the Romans (326/322).

Sulla destroyed its settlements in 82 and obliterated its name in favor of Aenaria, under which name the principal habitation center became a large industrial and harbor town. In AD 6 Augustus restored the island to Neapolis in exchange for Capreae (Capri). Its climate and medicinal waters made it a favorite resort for Roman holiday makers. Beneath the church of Santa Restituta at Heraclium are the remains of a Christian basilica of fourth or fifth century date.

Pityus, Pityous (Pitzunda, Bichvint). The northernmost Greek settlement on the eastern Euxine (Black) Sea coast at the foot of the Caucasus mountains, in the tribal area of the Heniochi (now part of the Abkhazian Autonomous Republic attached to Georgia, in the Soviet Union). Pityus may have been settled from Miletus in Ionia (western Asia Minor) in about the sixth century BC, but it is uncertain whether it was a Greek city (*polis*) or a trading market attached to the neighboring state of Colchis (*qv*).

A Roman fortress and extramural settlement dating from the first century until after 500 AD have come to light, in addition to Byzantine churches embellished with mosaics. Evidence of constant peril from tribes in the interior is provided by successive destruction levels of the third, fourth and sixth centuries.

Pityussa *see* Salamis

Pitzunda *see* Pityus

Placentia (Piacenza). A city of Cisalpine Gaul (northern Italy) on the west bank of the river Trebia (Trebbia), near its confluence with the Padus (Po). Finds suggest Etruscan settlement, on what had formerly been a native habitation site. After *c* 400 BC the place was occupied by the Gauls (Anares, Boii) who gave their name to Gallia Cisalpina. The outset of the Second Punic War (218) witnessed the establishment of a Latin colony, despite opposition from the Boii (who captured the colonial commissioners and handed them over to Hannibal). After the defeat of the Roman army at the Trebia in the same year, the new colony sheltered its refugees. Subsequently the morale of the Placentians cracked, and some of them fled. Yet in 207 they successfully resisted the Carthaginian relieving force of Hasdrubal.

Ravaged by the Boii in 200, and menaced by Ligurians who reached its walls in 195, the town was rebuilt in the following year and received new colonists in 190, although the dramatist Plautus described it as a dangerously exposed outpost. It possessed a river harbor, and became the first terminal of the Via Aemilia (187) from Ariminum (Rimini), which opened up the region. In 154 Placentia served Quintus Opimius as a base for his military operations against the Ligurians. In 90/89, like other Italian cities, it became a *municipium,* and seven years later, during the civil war between Sulla and the Marians, its citizens successfully withstood a Marian blockade until Sulla's supporter, Marcus Licinius Lucullus, beat off the besiegers. In 48, during another civil war, in which Julius Caesar confronted Pompey the Great, Placentia momentarily took the center of the historical stage when four of Caesar's legions, who were stationed there, threatened to mutiny, but his prompt action dissuaded them from this action.

Raised to the rank of a Roman colony by Augustus (31 BC–AD 14)—possibly as a sequel to a slightly earlier conferment of the same status—the city again played an important part in the civil war between Otho and Vitellius (AD 69), when the latter's general Caecina, after delivering a formidable assault, failed to take the stronghold by storm. The subsequent suicide of Otho caused many members of the garrison to follow his example. Nevertheless, its inhabitants, according to Pliny the Elder, were generally famous for their longevity. Orestes, the father of the last western emperor to rule in Italy, Romulus Augustulus, was executed at Placentia in 476. The remains of the ancient city lie deep in alluvial mud.

Planctae *see* Symplegades

Plasi *see* Aetolia

Plataea, Plataiai. A small city in Boeotia (central Greece) near its border with Attica, between Mount Cithaeron and the river Asopus. There are traces of Bronze Age (Mycenaean) habitation. Plataea is mentioned in Homer's *Iliad.* It obtained the protection of Athens against Thebes, which was bent on its annexation, *c* 519 BC. During the Persian Wars Plataeans joined the Athenian army at Marathon (490). In 480 their city, like Athens, was destroyed by the Persians, although its inhabitants escaped and fought at Salamis. In the following year Plataea was the scene of the final land battle of the wars. The Persian general Mardonius had moved down from Thessaly and invaded Attica with a force of some 300,000 men, hoping to persuade the Athenians to make peace. When this diplomatic attempt failed, he fell back to Boeotia, and severely harassed an advancing allied army of some 39,000 heavy infantry (hoplites) and 70,000 light infantry. During a retreat to higher ground near Plataea, the Spartan general commander-in-chief Pausanias was attacked by the Persians, but won a total victory, in which the Spartan hoplites played the major part. Mardonius was killed, and the remnants of his severely damaged army evacuated Greece.

After the outbreak of the Peloponnesian War between the Athenians and Spartans, Plataea was attacked by Sparta's ally Thebes, and its civilians were evacuated to Athens (431); but after a long siege by the Spartans (429–427), in which part of the garrison escaped, the remaining defenders were starved out and put to death, and their city was razed to the ground. Rebuilt with Spartan help (*c* 380)—whereupon it issued its only silver coinage—Plataea was again destroyed *c* 373, this time by the Thebans. Its surviving citizens found refuge in Athens until Philip II of Macedonia repatriated them after the battle of Chaeronea (338). His son Alexander the Great reconstructed the city, and Hadrian (AD 117–38) granted it freedom. Plutarch, who died after AD 120, records that in his time the Eleutheria, a festival in memory of the Persian War, was still celebrated. In late imperial and Byzantine times Plataea was a bishopric.

There are traces of walls going back to the fifth century BC, and more elaborate remains of successive fortifications erected *c* 385 and dating from the reigns of Philip II of Macedonia and Alexander the Great (?). A temple of Hera, whose cult was famous from the sixth century BC onward, contained a statue of the goddess by Praxiteles. A large hostel for pilgrims (Katagogion) was built by the Thebans after the city's destruction in 427; the hostel was pulled down and replaced by the city's agora in Roman times. But the temple of Athena Areia, which was enriched by Athens after the Persian War and contained a statue by Pheidias and wall paintings by Polygnotus, has not been located. Efforts to discover the graves of those who fell in 479, and to identify the site of a famous altar of Zeus, have recently been resumed.

Pleuron *see* Aetolia

Plovdiv *see* Philippopolis (Thrace)

Poetovio (Ptuj, Pettau). A city on both banks of the river Dravus (Drave, Yugoslavia) at an ancient crossing point, on the borderland between Celtic and Illyrian territory. Bronze Age and Iron Age settlements have been uncovered on the citadel hill, above the north (left) bank of the river, and in pre-Roman times a habitation center continued to exist beneath the citadel. In the course of his conquest of Pannonia (16 BC), however, it was on the south (right) bank that Augustus established a military camp, garrisoned by a legion. This fortress was attached first to the province of Illyricum (11 BC) and then, after its subdivision, to Pannonia (AD 9).

When the original legion was sent elsewhere *c* AD 43/45, it was replaced by another. Its headquarters provided the scene of an important meeting in 69, when the generals of Vespasian planning to overthrow Vitellius met to discuss their plan of campaign. Dividing the Pannonian province into two (*c* 103), and assigning Poetovio to Upper Pannonia, Trajan detached the legion but established a colony of veterans at the city, under the name of Coionia Ulpia Trajana. The reign of Hadrian (117–38) witnessed the building or rebuilding of a bridge over the Drave, of which parts have been found in the bed of the river; the camp's former civilian quarter (*canabae*) beside the southern end of the bridge became a satellite town, under the name of Vicus Fortunae, developing alongside the main town. In the course of the second century, too, a river customs station (*statio publici portorii Illyrici*) was established at Poetovio. An inscription records that during the wars of Marcus Aurelius (161–80) against the Germans a cavalry officer named Valerius Maximianus was rewarded for slaying Valao, the chieftain of the tribe of the Naristae, with his own hands.

In the time of Diocletian (284–305) the city was transferred to the province of Noricum Mediterraneum; it was during this period that its first Christian bishop Victorinus was martyred. In 352 the pretender Magnentius was defeated by the forces of Constantius II before the walls of Poetovio, and it was there, also, two years later, that one of Constantius' senior officers, Barbatio, arrested the imperial deputy (Caesar) Constantius Gallus, whom the emperor suspected of plotting against him and subsequently put to death. After the defeat and death of the eastern emperor Valens at Hadrianopolis (Edirne) at the hands of the Visigoths (378), Poetovio fell briefly into their hands. In 388 it was the scene of the decisive battle in which Theodosius I crushed the usurper Magnus Maximus. Sacked by Attila the Hun in 448, the place disappeared from history; though returning briefly to notice in the time of the last Roman emperor in Italy, Romulus Augustulus (475–76), because his mother had been born there.

The south bank had its own forum and an industrial district. Centers for the cults of oriental Gods—including two shrines of Mithras—and subsequent places of Christian worship have been located on both sides of the river, and fortifications and remains of a sanctuary of Jupiter, in addition to another well-preserved Christian church, are to be seen on the citadel hill. Recent excavations have revealed that the Zgornji Breg quarter was the seat of the administration and army in the third and fourth centuries, and it has been shown that the Visigothic occupation of 378 was followed by coinsiderable building activity.

Poggio Civitate *see* Murlo

Poggio Sant'Angelo *see* Ecnomus

Poitiers *see* Limonum Pictonum

Pojani *see* Apollonia (Illyricum)

Policoro *see* Heraclea (Lucania)

Polis *see* Marion

Politiko *see* Tamassos

Politorium (identifiable with Castel di Decima; although according to another view the latter is Laurentum [see Lavinium]). An early settlement in 'Old' Latium (Lazio, western Italy), Castel di Decima is ten miles south of Rome, and four miles south of the Tiber. It was one of a dense line of Bronze and Iron Age settlements on the route from Rome to the river-mouth port of Ostia (another, likewise recently unearthed, is Ficana [on Monte Cugno, near the modern Acilia, nearer to the river]).

Excavations at Castel di Decima have revealed a prosperous town with many fine tombs dating from the last decades of the eighth century BC. Among the discoveries are artifacts of Etruscan appearance, including a bronze statuette providing the earliest known Italian representation of the myth of Aeneas, which was so prominent in Etruria and later in Rome, and became the theme of Virgil's *Aeneid.* Settlers may have come to the place from one of the city-states of Etruria, for example Caere (Cerveteri) or Veii (Veio), which were both near at hand; or, alternatively, a flourishing community of the Etruscan type may have arisen at Politorium without such overt intervention, by means of commercial and cultural contacts.

The residential center beside the tombs at Castel di Decima reveals a differentiation between the social grades of the dead which testifies to at least the preliminary stages of urbanization. The tombs stop *c* 630–20, as at other centers in the region. Yet, as recent finds have indicated, habitation continued in the sixth century and later.

Polytobria *see* Aenus

Pompeii (Pompei). A city in Campania (southwest Italy) on the Gulf of Cumae (known also as the Crater; now the Bay of Naples), fourteen miles southeast of Neapolis (Naples). Pompeii was situated on an isolated volcanic ridge a hundred and twenty feet above sea level, produced by a prehistoric flow of lava down the slopes of Vesuvius, five miles away. The cliff-like termination of this lava flow to the south overlooked the river Sarnus (Sarno), which in ancient times was navigable for a considerable distance, making Pompeii a seaport for the communities of the fertile hinterland.

Strabo indicates that Pompeii had formerly been inhabited by Oscans (prehistoric inhabitants of southern Italy), and it is likely enough that at one time a native Italian fishing and agricultural village occupied the site. But, if so, it was later supplemented by a settlement or trading post established by Greeks, who probably came from Cumae at the northern end of the Gulf; their identifiable buildings date from before 500. Long before this time, however, the Etruscans (based on Capua [Santa Maria Capua Vetere]) had already begun to extend their domination over most of the Campanian plain, and although their attempts to capture Cumae itself (524,474) failed, there is archaeological evidence pointing to the destruction of Pompeii at about the former of those dates, and it seems probable that for a time the Etruscans exercised a measure of control over Pompeii, where black vases with fragmentary Etruscan inscriptions have been found.

But it was not long before Campania was invaded by Samnites—otherwise known as Sabellians—from the interior (whose Indo-European language became known as Oscan after the earlier inhabitants of the region). Capturing Capua in 423 and Cumae in 421/420, they also gained possession of Pompeii. These Samnite immigrants soon formed a partially Hellenized league of their own, which appealed to Rome for assistance against invasions by their own former compatriots form the interior; and in the Second and Third Samnite Wars (327–304, 298–290) the Romans brought Pompeii under their own suzerainty. During Hannibal's invasion in the Second Punic War (218–201) the town, unlike Capua, remained loyal to the Romans, but in the Italian revolt against Rome known as the Social War, it joined the rebels, and succumbed to a siege by Sulla (89).

Like other Italian communities Pompeii obtained the Roman franchise when the war was over, but *c* 80 it received a large draft of Sulla's retired soldiers, under the leadership of his nephew, and Cicero records friction between the old citizens and the new colonists. During the reign of Nero (AD 54–68), whose second wife Poppaea Sabina belonged to a Pompeian family, a riot in the amphitheater between factions representing Pompeii and Nuceria Alfaterna (Nocera Superiore) caused the loss of a number of lives. In 62 an earthquake inflicted severe damage on the city; and in 79 it was destroyed by an eruption of Vesuvius, described in a remarkable letter of Pliny the Younger. Overwhelmed by a series of boiling lava torrents (*nuées ardentes* or pyroclastic flows), the city was buried under pumice, ash and eventually a layer of earth as well, and it was not until the eighteenth century that its rediscovery began, with profound effects on the taste and interior decoration of Europe. This task of excavation, which for all its difficulties has been facilitated by the remarkable preservation of many of the buildings and objects trapped beneath the superimposed mass, has continued, with only short intervals, ever since, with the result that Pompeii became and remained the most spectacularly informative archaeological site in the world.

The town, which housed a population of about 25,000 persons, was surrounded by a wall dating from the third and second centuries BC. The remarkably abundant public buildings of Pompeii are concentrated in three principal areas. The earliest of these is the Triangular Forum, occupying a tall southward-facing spur on which the Greeks built a Doric temple during the sixth century BC. Beside it is a theater (second century BC, with additions), a portico converted into a gladiatorial school, a small covered theater or Odeon, and a temple of Isis. Near the southwestern gate of the city (the Porta Marina) is the second principal zone, centered upon the large main forum, which was flanked by two-storeyed colonnades, temples of Jupiter (Capitolium) and Apollo (of which remains survive), of Venus Pompeiana (now vanished) and of the Genius of the Emperor, as well as by a notably early basilica (public meeting place, *c* 125 BC), the Aedificium Eumachiae (described conjecturally as a kind of cloth hall) and four buildings connected with civic and administrative life. At the southeastern extremity of the city (not far from the Porta di Sarno) a third region contains the oldest existing Roman amphitheater (*c* 80–70 BC), of which the exterior displays an arcade of massive vaults. Beside it is a large colonnaded sports and athletic ground (*palaestra*). Pompeii also possessed at least four public baths, the remains of which cast remarkable light on ancient hydraulic arrangements. The city derived its water supply first from wells and cisterns (for rain) and later from an aqueduct which delivered most of its flow to baths and public fountains but was also piped into some private houses.

These dwellings, greatly varying in size and arrangement, constitute the most famous feature of Pompeii. The largest examples, dating from the third century BC, are grouped round an *atrium*—Etruscan in origin—of which the roof contained an aperture (*impluvium*). Often, a colonnaded peristyle (taken from Greek models) served as a garden; but there were also many other types of gardens, of which our knowledge has been greatly increased by recent research.

The interiors of the houses are dominated by their wall paintings (most of the best are now in the National Archaeological Museum at Naples), divided traditionally into four successive or overlapping styles (*see also* Herculaneum): although this classification seems somewhat inadequate—especially in relation to the extremely diversified 'Fourth Style,' nearly all of which dates from the extensive rebuilding of the city after the earthquake of AD 62. These paintings are of extraordinary value not only as technical, and sometimes artistic, achievements in their own right but also because they are frequently copies of important Greek originals that have not survived.

The floors of the houses were covered with the mosaic decoration which is one of the most characteristic achievements of Rome art, ranging from massive 'carpet' designs covering an entire floor—notably a picture of Alexander the Great defeating the Persian Darius III Codomannus at Issus (333 BC), copy of a lost Greek original—to smaller 'rug' designs, of which some of the most delicate were intended not for the adornment of a floor, but for insertion in a metal frame to be set on a table. On the other hand, tables and other furnishings (except beds, of which the rich coverlets, described by Pollux, are lost) were scanty, since if present in any abundance they would have seemed to the Romans and Pompeians—as canvases hung on the walls would also have seemed—to interfere with the architectural design of the house, of which the wall paintings and floor mosaics formed an integral part.

Pompeiopolis *see* Soli

Pontecagnano *see* Picentia

Pontus, Pontos ('Sea'). A region of northern Asia Minor comprising the well-watered, fertile, wooded territory along the south coast of the Euxine (Black) Sea between Bithynia and the river Halys (Kızıl Irmak) to the west and Colchis to the east, and extending southward through mountains, rich in timber and metals, into Cappadocia and Lesser Armenia. At first Pontus was regarded as part of Cappadocia, but then, in order to distinguish it from inland Cappadocian territory, it was called Pontic Cappadocia, and subsequently just Pontus. The people living in its villages, who spoke twenty-two different tongues, were dominated by a feudal Iranian nobility. But Pontus also contained the powerful, autonomous temple states of Comana (Gümenek), Cabeira-Diospolis (Niksar) and Zela (Zile). Moreover, along the coast, apparently in the seventh century BC, Miletus in Ionia (western Asia Minor) established colonies at Amisus (Samsun) and Sinope (Sinop)—which in turn established settlements on its own account.

The kingdom of Pontus took shape under King Mithridates I Ktistes ('the Founder,' 301–266), a partially Hellenized Persian who claimed royal descent and asserted himself against the Seleucids, establishing his capital at Amasia (Amasra; replaced in the early second century by Sinope). A later member of the Mithridatid house, the philhellenic Pharnaces I (186–169), planned a state extending all around the Euxine coast, and Mithridates V Euergetes (*c* 150–120) became the most powerful king in Asia Minor. Then the brilliant Mithridates VI Eupator, who came to the throne in 120, increased his dominions to an enormous extent, overrunning the Asian province of the Romans, to whom, in a protracted series of wars, he laid down the most perilous challenge they had ever received from the east.

When he was finally defeated by Pompey the Great (66–63), the core of his kingdom was incorporated in the Roman province of Bithynia and Pontus. Antony and Cleopatra VII of Egypt entrusted large areas of Pontus to client princes, including Polemo I (37/36) whose dynasty remained in control of the eastern part of the country (with his capital at Cabeira-Diospolis-Neocaesarea) until AD 64, when the kingdom was reannexed by the Romans under the name of Pontus Polemoniacus. The western region of Pontus, centered on Amasia, had been attached to the province of Galatia in 3/2 BC.

In AD 72 the entire Pontic region became part of Vespasian's greatly enlarged province of Galatia-Cappadocia, and remained in association with Cappadocia from Trajan (98–117) until Diocletian (284–305), who detached it from this union and subdivided it into the two provinces of Pontus Polemoniacus and

Diospontus (subsequently Helenopontus), within the administrative diocese of Pontica. *See also* Amasia, Amisus, Comana, Sebasteia, Trapezus, Zela.

Pontus *see* Tomis

Populonia (the Etruscan Pupluna). A town on the coast of northern Etruria, located on and around a defensible promontory that was at that time a peninsula and virtually an island, and served as an acropolis. Already inhabited in the Bronze Age, the site came to be occupied by two villages that from early times presided over, or were associated with, a maritime market based on a harbor (Porto Baratti), which, although vulnerable to west winds, possessed a spacious site on an extensive bay.

Imposing chamber tombs of various types, utilizing Sardinian models, made their appearance in *c* 800 BC, and soon reflected an increasing degree of lavishness, thanks to the enormously rich supplies of metal (copper, iron, lead, tin) available in the nearby hills of the Campigliese and on the adjacent island of Ilva (Aethalia, Elba). Traces of smelting are found at Populonia from at least *c* 750. These metals attracted the Greek markets of southern Italy (first Pithecusae [Ischia] and Cumae [Cuma]), and it was through the sale or exchange of these valuable products that Populonia soon became the largest importer of Greek artifacts in northern Etruria. Phoenician and other near-eastern objects are found in its tombs, and it is possible that Fufluns, the Etruscan deity after which the place was called, owed his name to the Phoenician city Byblos (Jebeil). These Phoenician influences may have come either indirectly through the Greeks or through direct trading with Phoenicia.

In the later seventh century, the two constituent villages and markets of Populonia amalgamated, inaugurating a new growth in power and prosperity; both the acropolis—where public buildings and other structures have now been found—and the city below were equipped with fortified circuit walls. To judge from a passage of Servius, however, the place did not at once become a city-state on its own account, but remained for a time a dependency of Volaterrae (Volterra)—although this link, for geographical and cultural reasons alike, is improbable, and its master was more probably Vetulonia.

However, Populonia seems to have been one of the very first Etruscan centers to issue coinage, although probably not before 500. Early in the fourth century—escaping the economic recession that afflicted much of Etruria—it seems to have broken away from its suzerain and to have become an independent city-state. By this time, apparently, the Populonians had begun to increase their iron-smelting industry by taking over a large proportion of the activity formerly undertaken at Ilva, where wood coal was no longer available in sufficient quantities. Thus although at Populonia, as elsewhere in Etruria, the Romans increasingly gained control, the city continued to flourish as late as the third century BC. Rock-cut chamber tombs are datable to Hellenistic times, and although there is evidence of subsequent decline—accelerated by Sulla's sack in 82—covered graves of the later Roman period are also to be seen.

Porolissum (near Moigrad and Jac). A Roman fortress-city in northwestern Dacia (northern Rumania). After the Roman conquest and annexation of Dacia by Trajan (AD 105), the province was divided by Hadrian (118/119) into Lower and Upper Dacia; and part of the latter was then detached to form a separate province of Dacia Porolissensis (124). Its capital was Napoca (Cluj), but it possessed a northwestern frontier station and customs post at Porolissum (on the site of a Dacian settlement), which received a strong military force as its garrison, the most northerly in eastern Europe. Four military diplomas found on the site date from 106. Because of its geographical position Porolissum was an important center for trading with central Europe; and it served as the terminal of a road that led right through Dacia down to the Danube. Under Septimius Severus (193-211), the civilian settlement (*canabae*) on the terraces beside the camp—inhabited chiefly by ex-soldiers—was elevated to the rank of a *municipium*. Finds of coins bear witness to continued occupation even after Aurelian had evacuated Dacia (271).

The original garrison of auxiliary troops, including units from Palmyra, Britain and Gaul, had been divided into two camps. One of these, of very large dimensions, which stood on Pomet hill, has now been uncovered; it was rebuilt under Caracalla (who paid a visit to Porolissum in 213), and then again, hastily, shortly after the middle of the century. The other camp, smaller in size, lay seven hundred yards to the north, on Citera hill. Both camps possessed defences, initially made of earth and then of stone; the Citera wall was furnished with square and trapezoidal towers. The civilian town was likewise fortified. Excavations at Porolissum have revealed an amphitheater (first of wooden construction, and then rebuilt of stone in 157), a *palaestra* (athletics school), baths, private houses, and a temple of the eastern god Bel, who was identified with the Roman Liber Pater.

Porto Baratti *see* Populonia

Porto Clementino *see* Graviscae

Porto Germano *see* Aegosthena

Portugal *see* Lusitania

Portus (Augusti, Romae) *see* Ostia

Portus Itius *see* Bononia

Portus Julius *see* Avernus, Lucrinus

Portus Lemanis *see* Lemanis

Poseidion, Posidium *see* Mycale

Posidium, Poseidion (Ras-el-Bassit). A town on the north Syrian coast, beside Cape Bassit (Poseidion is often a Greek name for a cape), south of the river Orontes (Nahr el-Asi)—as Strabo indicates—and some thirteen miles from Al Mina (with which Posidium has been mistakenly identified). Excavations have revealed traces of late Bronze Age settlement, including Mycenaean fragments, and subsequent habitation from the ninth or eighth to the fourth century BC (with a break *c* 700).

In the early part of this period the place was evidently a marketing center for Greek traders, and in particular, like Al Mina, served the merchants of Chalcis and Eretria in Euboea as an eastern base for the acquisition of gold and other valuables that they could then transport to their Campanian markets (Pithecusae [Ischia], Cumae [Cuma]), to be exchanged with Etruscan copper and iron. By the third century Posidium had diminished into a mere fortress; apart from its garrison, the population may have been transferred to its new neighbor Seleucia in Pieria. The ruins of Posidium were still conspicuous in the nineteenth century of our era.

Posidonia, Poseidonia, later Paestum. A city beside the west coast of Italy, at the northern extremity of Lucania (now southeastern Campania), seven hundred and fifty yards behind the Bay of Salernum (Salerno). The site was inhabited in Palaeolithic, Neolithic and Chalcolithic times. According to Strabo, the Greek town was founded by colonists from Sybaris (Sibari) in southeastern Italy; pottery finds suggest a date of *c* 625–600 BC. Their settlement succeeded an earlier fort by the sea, perhaps at Agropoli four miles to the south.

Posidonia was Sybaris' most important colony, but to judge from its coinage, it did not depend on the mother city very closely. When, however, Sybaris was destroyed (510), many of the survivors apparently took refuge in Posidonia. Its favorable position for trading, together with the fertility of the surrounding plain of the Silarus (Sele), brought considerable prosperity until the Lucanians, coming down from the hills in the hinterland, captured the city, which they renamed Paiston (Paestum). After a brief period of liberation by the invading King Alexander I the Molossian (from Epirus, 332–326), the Romans established a Latin colony (i.e. including settlers drawn from other Latin peoples as well as from Rome), in order to watch over recent and potential enemies and guard the vulnerable coastline.

During the Second Punic War Paestum vigorously resisted Hannibal. A *municipium,* like other Italian communities, since 90/89 BC, it was unique among them because of its issue of an abundant local bronze coinage under Augustus (31 BC–AD 14) and Tiberius (AD 14–37). It has been suggested that some of these pieces could refer to the elevation of the city to the rank of Roman colony, although this interpretation has been questioned. However, an inscription does confirm that Paestum attained or renewed this status in *c* AD 71, when it received, at the hands of Vespasian, a settlement of former sailors from the fleet at Misenum. However, Paestum was not destined for a prosperous future. Strabo already noted the silting up of the Silarus, and the site gradually became more and more unhealthy and malarial. During the Middle Ages a few Christians were worshipping in the ruins, but thereafter all traces of Paestum were obliterated by woods and swamps.

Still standing, however, beside the ancient habitation center is one of the most impressive groups of Doric temples from the ancient world. The southernmost of these shrines is the so-called 'Basilica' (*c* 550 BC), which was, it is now believed, a temple dedicated to Zeus and Hera. Adjoining it is the 'Temple of Poseidon' (*c* 450?), in reality another shrine of Hera or Zeus, one of the best-preserved of all Greek religious buildings (remains of other, smaller temples of Hera are to be seen nearby). To the north stands a building of *c* 500 known as the 'Temple of Ceres' although, to judge from finds of clay statuettes, it was dedicated to another goddess Athena (and in medieval times to the Virgin Mary). These two precincts, of Hera and Athena, flank the agora, which later became the Roman forum. It was adjoined by a Capitolium, the local senate house, baths, a gymnasium, and a small amphitheater; a larger counterpart is to be seen nearby. The city was surrounded by impressive Greek, Lucanian and Roman walls, of which large portions survive; they were equipped with round and square towers and a bridged moat. The street of the Roman city leading from north to south, the *cardo maximus,* replaced the Greek Sacred Way. Beside the street is an underground shrine (*hypogeum*) of Hera (*c* 500).

Excavations have now been resumed on an extramural sanctuary at the Località Santa Veneria, probably dedicated to the Roman Good Goddess (Bona Dea). An adjacent rectangular hall, originally constructed *c* 400 (and later fronted by a cultic basin), has also come to light, and the development of the city toward the south can be reconstructed. A necropolis in this direction included the 'Tomb of the Diver,' named after a remarkable wall painting of early fifth-century date (and perhaps Etruscan affinities) which is now in the local museum. It also contains a rich variety of fourth-century paintings (some from lately uncovered tombs), and many important vases.

In the same museum are extensive reliefs, of the early and late sixth century BC, from temples of the famous sanctuary of Argive Hera, seven and a half miles from the city at the mouth of the Silarus (Foce di Sele), where a settlement preceding Posidonia had existed (according to pottery finds) from before 600.

Posidonia, Poseidonia *see also* Troezen

Potamos tou Kambou *see* Soli (Cyprus)

Potidaea, Poteidaia, later Kassandrea, Kassandreia (Nea Poteidaia). A city in Macedonia (northern Greece), situated at a strategic point on the isthmus of Pallene, the westernmost of the three prongs of the Chalcidice promontory. Potidaea was founded by King Periander of Corinth *c* 600 BC, under the leadership of his son, in order to serve the Macedonian end of the trans-Balkan route to Illyria (rich in silver) and the Adriatic; it was also in a position to facilitate northeastern trade. The inhabitants issued coinage about a century later, depicting Poseidon (after whom the city was named, and whose statue it contained) carrying his trident, and riding on a horse.

A strongly fortified port, Potidaea resisted a siege by the Persian general Artabazus (480–479) and subsequently joined the Delian League under Athenian control. Its revolt in 432, to which Corinth unofficially sent help, was one of the contributory causes of the Peloponnesian War, and led to the city's reduction by the Athenians in 430, after a terrible siege during which its inhabitants ate human flesh before they surrendered. Athenian colonists occupied the site until the end of the war (404), when Potidaea became independent, joining the Chalcidian League. Recovered and recolonized by Athens (363–361), it was captured in 356 by Philip II of Macedonia, who merged the town with Olynthus and sold its inhabitants into slavery (except the Athenians, whom he sent back to Athens).

About 316 the Macedonian Cassander, one of the successors of Alexander the Great, founded a new city on the site, under the name of Cassandrea, and endowed it with a very large surrounding territory. A short-lived autocratic régime ('tyranny') led by Apollodorus (279–276) was followed by a renewal of Macedonian rule under Antigonus II Gonatas, whose dynasty converted Cassandrea into one of the most important and strongly fortified strongholds of his kingdom. Under Roman rule, it was made a Roman colony in 44/43 by Quintus Hortensius Hortalus, acting on behalf of Brutus, and the colony was renewed (perhaps on two successive occasions) after the battle of Actium (31 BC), coining in the early Principate under the title of Colonia Julia Augusta Cassandrensis. In AD 269 it repulsed an attack by the Goths, but survived (becoming the see of a bishop) until its destruction by the Slavs in 539.

The remains of a temple attributed to Poseidon have been uncovered in Potidaea, and a bilingual inscription recording the construction of a gymnasium has been found.

Pozzuoli *see* Puteoli

Praeneste (Palestrina). A city of Latium (Lazio), twenty-three miles east of Rome, commandingly situated on an isolated ledge of Monte Ginestro (an outcrop of the Apennines), 1,350 feet above sea level. But this was only a second foundation, since the original hill-town and citadel (now Castel San Pietro) had stood 1,200 feet higher, dominating the plain uniting the Anio (Aniene) and Trerus (Sacco) valleys, which provided the main landward route toward the south. Legends variously ascribed the city's foundation to Caeculus the son of Vulcan, Praenestes the son of Latinus, and Telegonus the son of Ulysses (Odysseus).

Excavations have now shown that a major cultural advance, involving urbanization and extensive eastern imports, took place in the later eighth century BC, and played a large part in the creation of a 'Latian civilization' which, although incorporating Italian traditions, displayed an intimate relationship with developments in southern Etruria; thus the rich contents of the Barberini and Bernardini tombs closely resemble finds in the cemeteries of Caere (Cerveteri). (Serious doubts have now been cast on the authenticity of a Latin inscription on a seventh-century Praenestine brooch).

After becoming one of the original members of the Latin League, Praeneste, according to Livy, formed a close association with the Romans, just before the battle they fought against the Latins at Lake Regillus (*c* 499). During the fifth century the city was repeatedly attacked by the tribe of the Aequi who had established themselves in the adjacent Alban Hills. It was also very often at war with the Romans until the dissolution of the Latin League (338); thereafter, despite a loss of territory, its independence was guaranteed by a treaty with Rome. In 198 a slave uprising had to be put down. Becoming a *municipium* (90/89) in common with other Italian communities, Praeneste sheltered Marius the Younger (Marcus Marius Gratidianus) in his civil war against Sulla who, after a siege lasting many months, sacked the town (82), executed 12,000 of its inhabitants, transplanted the remainder to a new location on a lower ledge, and established a colony for ex-soldiers upon a third site on the plain below. This settlement was reinforced by additional settlers in imperial times, when Praeneste became a favorite retreat from the heat of summer for wealthy Romans.

The original hill-town citadel was defended by polygonal walls, of which the surviving portions are datable to the mid-fourth century BC; they extended to the second town below. The sanctuary of Fortuna Primigenia, one of the largest and most famous shrines of the ancient world, belonged to this second town, but spread up the hillside above. The priests of the sanctuary pronounced oracles, the *sortes Praenestinae,* inscribed on pieces of oak wood and greatly revered.

The philosopher Carneades was impressed by the renown of the Temple of Fortuna Primigenia when he visited Rome in 156/5. Its present form, however, is owed to Sulla, whose builders displayed a masterly use of concrete that amounted to an architectural revolution. The Sullan precinct contained two groups of buildings. The lower complex comprised three main structures, a partly natural and partly artificial 'cave of the *sortes*' (paved with a colorful mosaic of fish and other marine subjects), an apsidal hall (containing the famous Barberini mosaic of Nile scenes that is now in the Palazzo Barberini Museum on the site), and a colonnaded edifice that may have been a pagan basilica. The upper sanctuary comprised a series of terraces (to the multiplicity of which Praeneste apparently owed its names 'Polystephanos,' many-wreathed, and 'Stephane'), ascending steeply, by ramps, to a huge enclosure flanked by roofed porticos and terminating in steps that led up to a semicircular colonnade. This colonnade enclosed a theater (employed for religious performances), and fronted the round temple of Fortuna at the summit of the entire complex—which was so extensive that it later housed the entire medieval town.

Inscriptions refer to a wide range of other public buildings at Praeneste, many of which were no doubt located at the foot of the hill, in Sulla's third town. Remains of a so-called Villa of Hadrian (AD 117–38), with stucco decoration, are to be seen not far away.

Pratica di Mare *see* Lavinium

Priene, later Naulochon (Turunçlar). A city in Ionia (western Asia Minor). The original settlement is believed to have stood on a crag 1250 feet above sea level (the Teloneia), overlooking a harbor, or a pair of harbors, beside the mouth of the river Maeander (Büyük Menderes). According to tradition Priene was founded in the eleventh century BC by Aepytus, grandson of the legendary Athenian King Codrus, in association with the Theban Philotas. Dominating a local native population—the Pedieis, who became serfs like the Spartan helots—the town was a member of the Ionian League, and, at most times, controlled the common sanctuary of Ionian cities, the Panionion (see Mycale). The city suffered serious damage from the Cimmerians, Lydians and Persians; but the wisdom of its sixth-century leader Bias earned him a place among the Seven Sages. It supplied twelve ships to the Ionian rebellion against Persia, terminating disastrously in the battle of Lade (495). After the Persian Wars it became a member of the Delian League led by Athens, which intervened in 441 during a war between Miletus and Samos, in which the issue at stake was the control of Priene.

Later the place faded into comparative insignificance at the expense of the harbor town of Naulochus (three miles to the southwest). But it seems to have been in the time of Alexander the Great that Priene was reconstructed on a different site; he himself was a visitor *c* 334, and it was then that the transfer occurred, accompanied, according to an inscription, by an exemption from tribute. The new city occupied a series of terraces on the steep slope of Mount Mycale, facing Miletus and overshadowed by its acropolis on the Teloneia hill, where the garrison was stationed. This revived Priene produced leading authorities on agriculture, and its citizens gained a reputation as experts in boundary litigation. Its subsequent prosperity, however, was gradually hampered by the silting of the river mouth, which by the time of Strabo had already caused the sea to recede five miles (it has now withdrawn three miles further). Nevertheless local coinage of Roman imperial date—on which the wise Bias figures prominently—continued until the time of Valerian (AD 253-60).

This second Priene, of the fourth and later centuries BC, is a model of urban planning and the best surviving example of a town of this period. With its walls extending across a broad spur, sloping down from the precipitous face of the Teloneia toward what must have been the estuary of the Maeander, the new foundation displayed a systematic, symmetrical grid layout designed for a population of perhaps 5,000. The most conspicuous building, towering above a lofty terrace, was a sanctuary of Athena Polias, designed, according to Vitruvius, by Pytheus, the architect of the Mausoleum at Halicarnassus; it was first dedicated to Alexander the Great (although not completed at that time), and later rededicated to Athena and Augustus. The shrine was adorned with a number of different sculptural groups, ranging in date from the later fourth century BC to the early second century AD—and recently reexamined, after the rediscovery of excavation records of AD 1868/9. In front of the temple stood a monumental altar designed by the renowned Hermogenes of Priene (*c* 150 BC), of which little has survived.

The city's water supply was elaborate and long-lived. Its colonnaded agora contained numerous monuments and was flanked by public offices, including the council or assembly chamber. A theater is also to be seen (the manner in which its proscenium was employed is much disputed). There is also a large gymnasium, incorporating a *palaestra* (athletics school) and stadium. But Priene is especially noteworthy for the survival, in varying degrees of completeness, of four hundred private houses, many or most as early as the third century BC. The usual plan of these dwellings comprises an entrance with a vestibule and open courtyard leading to an antechamber and principal living room.

Roofs were tiled, and the walls of the rooms plastered in imitation of marble. External windows seem to have been few, small and high. A few remains of staircases exist but no second storeys are preserved. A three-aisled episcopal basilica dates from the Byzantine epoch.

Primis *see* Aethiopia

Prusias on the Hypius, formerly Cierus, Kieros (Üsküb). A city of Bithynia (northwestern Asia Minor), situated on a defensible hill at the foot of Mount Hypius overlooking the small plain of a river, likewise called Hypius (Düzce). Originally known as Cierus, and colonized from central Greece (as the local designations of surviving tribal divisions, Megaris and Thebais, bear witness), the place was bought from the Bithynian monarchy by Heraclea Pontica (Ereğli) but recaptured by King Prusias I (*c* 230–182) and given his name.

It was an important station on the road from Nicomedia (İzmit) in Bithynia to Amastris (Amasra) in Paphlagonia. Coinage of Roman imperial times, which seems to have started under Vespasian (AD 69–79) and continued until Gallienus (253–68), depicted a figure engaging in sacrifice, identified as Caracalla (211–17), who visited the city (like Elagabalus [218–22] after him). By the early fourth century it was the seat of a bishopric.

The surviving remains of Prusias include a colonnaded street, fortifications embodying a gate, a theater of the second century AD, and a three-arched bridge which remained intact until recent inundations. Floor mosaics depicting mythical scenes have been found outside the walls. (The city has to be distinguished from Prusias on the Sea [formerly Cius, now Gemlik] and Prusa [Bursa, Brusa], which were likewise in Bithynia).

Psoi *see* Ptolemais Hermiou

Ptolemais (Tolmeta). A coastal city of Cyrenaica (Cirenaica, Libya), located in front of a narrow plain beneath the lower spurs of the Jebel-el-Akhdar beside the more ancient port town of Barca. In about the 560s BC Arcesilaus II the Cruel of Cyrene quarrelled with his brothers, who withdrew and founded or refounded Barca, about seventy-five miles to the southwest of Cyrene and sixteen miles inland. Persian domination of Egypt and Cyrenaica (*c* 525) at first left Barca a certain autonomy, which came to an end in 483, when the city was plundered. However, it recovered, and later in the century, as Herodotus shows, it ranked, together with Cyrene, as one of the leading centers of Cyrenaica.

Its port, containing a main and secondary harbor sheltered by a promontory and offshore islands (of which the largest was called Ilus), was refounded by Ptolemy III Euergetes of Egypt (246–221) under the name of Ptolemais, to which Barca was henceforward attached. Ptolemais passed into the hands of Rome in 96 and subsequently became part of the province of Cyrenaica (74) and then of the combined province of Crete and Cyrenaica (67). It served as a mint of Antony's officer Marcus Licinius Crassus *c* 37–34, displaying the Egyptian type of a crocodile in honor of Cleopatra VII's infant daughter Cleopatra Selene, to whose dominions Antony had awarded Cyrenaica. Restored to direct Roman rule in 31, Ptolemais probably became, during the later empire, capital of the province of Upper Libya or Pentapolis, although it subsequently declined, and was supplanted by Apollonia (Sozusa). According to Procopius, Ptolemais remained uninhabited for many years because the aqueduct fell into disrcpair.

The Hellenistic city, of which the fortifications (later rebuilt) are still, in part, to be seen, had possessed a regular layout centering upon a main street which was given a triumphal arch and colonnade in the fourth century AD. Ptolemais also possessed an amphitheater, a hippodrome and three theaters, and its agora has been located. The Villa of the Columns, a pre-Roman house enlarged in the first century AD, possessed two spacious halls (*oeci*), built round a large colonnaded courtyard. Another mansion, built *c* 400, has a mosaic pavement depicting Orpheus singing to the wild beasts. A remarkable urban water supply is attested not only by an aqueduct of the second century AD (brought by a bridge across a gully to a point outside the city), but also by a group of seventeen vaulted cisterns in a colonnaded enclosure, supplemented by two open reservoirs. Both harbors of Ptolemais are now underwater. Numerous chamber tombs, with inscriptions, have been found on either side of the inhabited area. An apsed and aisled Christian basilica is solidly constructed and equipped with defences. Another fortified building, probably of fifth-century date, has been plausibly identified as the residence and headquarters of the provincial governor.

Ptolemais *see also* Arsinoe

Ptolemais Ace, formerly Ace and Antiochia in the Ptolemaid, later Germanicia (Akko, Acre). A coastal city in southern Phoenicia (now northern Israel), with an acropolis overlooking the mouth of the river Naaman (Belos), which contained sand employed in the manufacture of glass. The place (Akka) is mentioned as a commercial center in Egyptian documents of the 15th/14th century BC, and in the fourth century an Athenian trading community at Ace is mentioned by Demosthenes and Isaeus.

It served Alexander the Great as a mint, and its importance as a strategic site prompted its refoundation by Ptolemy II Philadelphus *c* 261, under the name of Ptolemais, although the population remained, for the most part, Phoenician. Taken by the Seleucids, Ptolemais Ace became their main base against the separatist Maccabean (Hasmonaean) Jewish régime, and coined as Antiochia in the Ptolemaid from *c* 175 until *c* 44, when the name Ptolemais was revived. In 33/32 BC an issue bore the heads of Antony and Cleopatra VII of Egypt. Under Claudius (AD 41–54) the city coined as Germanicia in the Ptolemaid—still in Greek—but then became a Roman colony for the settlement of ex-soldiers from four legions, under the designation of Colonia Felix Stabilis Germanica Ptolemais (52/54).

Coins show the river-god Belos or Bel, and an array of Greco-Roman and Egyptian deities. Other coin types include a flat-roofed shrine of the Semitic god Hadad with carry-bars (Macrinus, 217–18), and elaborate views of buildings on the acropolis, as well as a sketch of the colonnaded harbor (Elagabalus, 218–22).

The representation of a *nymphaeum* (fountain building), fronted by a pavement, on another of his coins, recalls a story in the *Mishnah* recounting that the rabbi Gamaliel saw no objection to bathing in the city's public baths beneath a statue of Aphrodite. A gymnasium built by Herod the Great of Judaea (37-4 BC) cannot be traced. For the successive provincial allegiances of the city, *see* Phoenicia.

Ptolemais Hermiou (El-Manshah). A city in Upper Egypt on the Nile, 328 miles south of Cairo. Founded for Greek and Macedonian military veterans on the site of an Egyptian village Psio (of which the name has survived in Coptic and Arabic) by Ptolemy I Soter (323-283/2 BC)—his sole foundation in Egypt—Ptolemais was the metropolis of the Thinite district (nome) and the center of Hellenism in Upper Egypt throughout the Greco-Roman period. Strabo described it as a city equal in size to great Memphis, possessing its own autonomous Greek constitution and institutions, and this account is confirmed by papyri and inscriptions. Ptolemais possessed temples of Isis and of the Ptolemies, and is often believed to have been the birthplace of the astronomer, mathematician and geographer Ptolemy (second century AD).

During the reign of Probus (276-82) its inhabitants revolted, in alliance with the southern tribe of the Blemmyes, and attacked Coptos (Kuft), but the rebellion was suppressed. In the later empire, when Egypt was divided into several provinces, Ptolemais was attached first to the Thebaid (Thebais), and then—when that too was subdivided—to the Upper Thebaid. It retained its pagan character longer than the surrounding territory. (Ptolemais Hermiou is to be distinguished from other Egyptian cities of the same name, for example Ptolemais Euergetis [Arsinoe] beside Lake Moeris [Fayum], Ptolemais Hormos ['Harbor'] on the edge of the Fayum; Ptolemais Theron or Epitheros ['Of the Hunts,' Aquiq, Trinkitat] is on the Red Sea in what is now the Sudan).

Ptuj *see* Poetovio

Pumbeditha *see* Mesopotamia

Punicum *see* Caere

Punta di Schiso *see* Naxos (Sicily)

Puteoli, formerly Dicaearchia, Dikaiarchia (Pozzuoli). A coastal city of Campania (southwestern Italy) in the bay of the same name forming the northwestern part of the Gulf of Cumae or Crater (Bay of Naples); Neapolis (Naples) lies seven miles to its west. Dicaearchia, 'city where justice reigns,' was said by some writers to have been founded *c* 521/0 by Samian refugees who had moved on from Cyme (Cumae, five miles to the west), of which, according to Diodorus and Strabo, it became a dependent port. It was also intended to serve as an outpost against Neapolis; but the town fell to the Samnites in 421, and then became a dependency of the Romans (*c* 338/4).

In 215, during the Second Punic War, it successfully resisted the invading army of Hannibal, receiving a Roman citizen colony (situated on the promontory of Rione Terra) in 194. Puteoli now became the principal harbor of the Romans, channelling their massive and varied trade with Egypt and the east. Indeed, according to Festus, it ranked second only to Delos as a Mediterranean maritime center, becoming especially active after Delos had been granted the status of a free port in 166. Puteoli, too, gained civic privileges, which were later confirmed and enlarged. Sulla and Cicero were among many Romans who became proprietors of villas in the fashionable surrounding area, and Augustus (31 BC–AD 14) added new drafts of veteran colonists, naming the city Julia Augusta (as a recently discovered wax tablet records).

After the emperor Claudius created the port of Ostia (AD 42), which lay so much closer to Rome, Puteoli nevertheless retained major importance, attested, for example, by a plan of Nero (54–68) to link it to the Tiber by a canal; moreover, he promoted the 'old town' (*vetus oppidum*), that is to say, Dicaearchia, to colonial status. The designation of Flavia Augusta is subsequently found. St. Paul visited the port in *c* AD 61, encouraging the early development of Christianity. Domitian built the Via Domitiana (completed 95, and partly superseding the old Via Campana or Via Consularis Capuam Puteolis) linking Puteoli with the Via Appia and Rome, and Hadrian (117–38) possessed a residence in the neighborhood. By the time of Septimius Severus (193–211) ownership of land had replaced overseas trading as the source of the most substantial local incomes at Puteoli. Signs of stagnation began to appear in the later fourth century. Thereafter, devastations by Alaric the Visigoth (410), Gaiseric the Vandal (455) and Totila (Baduila) the Ostrogoth (545) contributed to the final downfall of the city, compelling its inhabitants to move elsewhere.

Puteoli was divided into a lower and upper town. The lower town in which bradyseism (a series of slow, gradual, earth tremors) has caused alarming falls and rises of the land level in relation to the sea—very recently, the land again fell twenty-four feet, and then rose three feet in 1984 alone—displays the remains of a food market (Macellum, wrongly known as the Serapeum) comprising a two-storeyed colonnaded courtyard, surrounded by an enclosure. On a low acropolis nearby (the Rione Terra quarter on the Castello hill), the remains of a temple of Augustan date, overlaying a shrine of the second century, have been uncovered beneath the cathedral; and the Capitolium—until recently regarded as a temple of Augustus—was brought to light by an earthquake in 1980. The port, of which little remains, was famous for the clay, *pulvis Puteolanus* (*pozzolana*), employed for the epoch-making Roman innovation of concrete. An Augustan breakwater (*opus pilarum*), leading out from a colonnaded quay on fifteen huge masonry piers, was surmounted by a lighthouse, a triumphal arch, statues on columns, and a carving of a ship's prow.

The upper town contained an amphitheater of the time of Vespasian (adjoining, it has now been discovered, a smaller Augustan forerunner) that accommodated at least 40,000 spectators and was the third largest of such buildings in Italy, after Rome and Capua. A circus and a bathing establishment (incorporating the wrongly named 'Temples' of Neptune and Diana) are also to be found in this district, in addition to several spacious cisterns served by a pair of aqueducts. Opulent tombs clustered thickly around the roads leading out of the town.

Above Puteoli, extending between Neapolis and Cumae, is the volcanic region known as the Phlegraean Fields (Campi Flegrei, from the Greek *phlegein,* to burn; also known to the Romans as the Campi Leborini). The eruptive activities of the area have left their mark in thirteen low craters, some of which still emit jets of steam (*fumarole*). To the ancients, the subterranean rumblings from the hot and viscous ground suggested the underworld horrors of Tartarus, and prompted many mythological tales (*see* Avernus). The Campi Phlegraei have yielded remarkable finds of ancient plaster casts, which were the débris from the workshop of a sculptor engaged in copying Greek statues for the Roman market.

Pydna (Makrygialos, Kitros). A Greek city in Pieria (southern Macedonia, northeastern Greece), beside the Thermaic Gulf. The original settlement was on the shore, situated on a hill south of the modern Makrygialos. According to Thucydides,the town belonged to King Alexander I of Macedonia (*c* 495–450 BC). In 432, just before the beginning of the Peloponnesian War, it was besieged by the Athenians. About 411/410 the Macedonian King Archelaus besieged and captured Pydna and transplanted it two or three miles inland, to a location described as Citrum (the modern Kitros) by Strabo. The site, of which a large part has now fallen into the sea, possessed an acropolis—protected by cliffs on all four sides—and a harbor (now the Touzla [salt] marsh) at the mouth of river Karagats.

After Archelaus' death (399), however, the inhabitants moved back to the former location of their city, which shortly afterward issued its first coinage as an independent member of the Chalcidian League (see Chalcidice, Olynthus). The place came under Athenian influence in 364/3, but was captured by Philip II of Macedonia in 356, whereupon the activity of its mint ceased. In 317/316 Cassander, one of Alexander the Great's successors, blockaded Alexander's mother Olympias in Pydna, which held out until her elephants all died and her mercenaries were compelled to resort to cannibalism: at that juncture the city surrendered, and Olympias was killed by revengeful relatives of men she had murdered.

In 168, 'the plain before Pydna' was the scene of the decisive battle in the war between King Perseus of Macedonia and the Romans. At a locality below four flat-topped ridges—which has now been identified with the valley area of Ayios Demetrios and Ayios Yeoryios—Perseus' left wing was routed by the allies of the Roman commander Marcus Aemilius Paullus; and then the phalanx in the Macedonian center, after making initial progress, was thrown into disarray by broken ground, and suffered destruction. The whole action was over within an hour, and Pydna was sacked by the victorious Romans. The engagement had decisively displayed the superiority of their legions over the phalanx. Its other result was the abolition of the Macedonian kingdom, the first of the great Hellenistic states to be obliterated by Rome.

Pylae *see* Thermopylae

Pylos. According to Greek mythology, Neleus (from Thessaly, attacked by Heracles) and his wise and aged son Nestor (visited by Telemachus) were kings of a powerful kingdom in the southwestern Peloponnese; and it is clear that this kingdom existed in the Bronze Age. But what is disputed is whether its capital was (1) at the place subsequently known as Messenian Pylos (in medieval times Avarinos or Navarino, later Paleokastro or Palco Navarino)—on the rocky acropolis headland of Coryphasium (traditionally associated with Hermes' theft of Apollo's cattle) facing the Bay of Pylos (Navarino: of which the northern part has now silted up) and separated by a narrow channel from the island of Sphacteria (Sfagia)—or (2) at Ano (or Epano) Anglianos on a ridge seven miles north of Coryphasium, three miles inland, where a Mycenaean palace complex, including a remarkable array of inscriptions ('Linear B'), has been uncovered. Pylos is described by Homer as *emathoeis,* generally translated as sandy, though Strabo offers alternative interpretations.

The place returned to the forefront of ancient history in 425 BC, when it witnessed one of the outstanding events of the Peloponnesian War. The Athenian general Demosthenes landed troops at Coryphasium, which he hastily fortified; whereupon the Spartans attacked his encampment vigorously by sea and land, but suffered a repulse, as a result of which four hundred and twenty of their elite citizen soldiers (Spartiates), together with their helot dependants, were blockaded by Demosthenes' colleague Cleon—who had arrived with reinforcements—on Sphacteria. After a seventy-two day siege, the two hundred and ninety-two survivors, including one hundred and twenty Spartiates, had to lay down their arms, and were taken to Athens, an event which profoundly impressed the Greek world, accustomed to regarding a Spartan surrender as unthinkable.

The Peace of Nicias (421) provided for the return of Pylos to the Spartans, but this was only achieved when they recaptured the stronghold in 409. A late classical town stood on the north slopes of Coryphasium; and on its crest, traces of Greek fortifications and masonry can still be seen, embodied in a medieval castle. Below, there are the remains of an ancient breakwater. Athena Coryphasia appears on Pylian coins; her sanctuary is mentioned by Pausanias, but has not been located. (This Messenian Pylos is to be distinguished from places of the same name in Elis and Triphylia [western and eastern Peloponnese respectively], of which the rival claims to identification with the Homeric Pylos are discussed at length by Strabo).

Pyrgi *see* Caere

Quinto Fiorentino *see* Artemium

R

Raetia or Rhaetia. A Roman province comprising parts of western Austria, eastern Switzerland and southern Bavaria and Württemberg. The Raeti were Illyrians, under strong Celtic influences, whereas Livy's indication that they were of Etruscan origin is only true in so far as their language contained Etruscan elements.

In the reign of Augustus, after a preliminary campaign by Publius Silius Nerva (16 BC), the emperor's stepsons Tiberius and Nero Drusus (Drusus senior) overran the country, together with the lands of the Vindelici to the north, extending as far as the Danube. Then the province of Raetia, with its capital—and for a short time a legionary garrison—at Augusta Vindelicorum (Augsburg, Oberhausen) was formally created not later than the reign of Claudius (41–54), who completed the Via Claudia Augusta from Italy to Augusta Vindelicorum and the Danube (AD 47), and protected the Danube boundary with a line of forts. Traces of burning during the civil wars of AD 69 have been found in Raetian military and civilian settlements alike. Under Vespasian (69–79) and Domitian (81–96) the western part of the frontier was pushed beyond the Danube into the Agri Decumates. During the campaigns of Marcus Aurelius against the German Marcomanni a newly raised legion was stationed at Castra Regina (Regensburg) on the Danube (before 178).

From *c* 233 the Alamanni were pressing strongly against the frontier, of which the western sector was withdrawn to the south of Lake Brigantinus (Lake Constance, Bodensee) *c* 259/260. Heavy fighting continued in the border areas, and under Diocletian the province was divided into two, Raetia Prima to the south (with its capital probably at Curia [Chur in Switzerland]) and Raetia Secunda to the north (with its capital at Augusta Vindelicorum), where the military commander for both provinces (the *dux Raetiarum*) possessed his headquarters. Under increased pressure from the Alamanni and Juthungi (who broke into eastern Raetia in 357) the Lake Brigantinus-Danube frontier line was gradually abandoned *c* 383–88, 395 and 401; and despite the presence of a Roman commander Generidus in 409, and a partial recovery of territory by Aetius *c* 430, the whole plain had passed out of Roman hands by *c* 450; the last outposts on the Danube were evacuated in 475–82. *See also* Agri Decumates, Augusta Vindelicorum.

Raphia (Rafah). A coastal town at the southwestern extremity of Judaea (on the southern boundary of the Gaza strip, administered by Israel, bordering the Sinai peninsula, now returned to Egypt). A station on the coastal road (Via Maris, Ways of Horus) already heard of in the second millennium BC, although according to Diodorus it afforded no anchorage and was subject to shoals. In 720 an Egyptian force that had come to the aid of Gaza was defeated at Raphia by the Assyrian King Sargon II.

In 217 it was again the scene of a major battle, when very large forces of the Seleucid Antiochus III the Great and Ptolemy IV Philopator clashed in the neighborhood. After the Egyptian right wing had routed its opponents, and the Seleucid right wing had done the same, the battle was decided by the two great masses by heavy infantry at the center, fighting on both sides with their flanks uncovered; the Egyptians proved victorious, and Antiochus fled to Raphia and thence to Antioch, his imperialistic plans checked. But the battle also had long-term effects on the stability of the Ptolemaic monarchs, since it was their native Egyptian troops who had won the battle, so that this ethnic element henceforward felt able to assert itself as a political force.

The Jewish (Hasmonaean) monarch Alexander I Jannaeus (103–76) annexed Raphia to his kingdom. As Josephus records, the city was liberated by Pompey the Great in 64 and rebuilt by Aulus Gabinius in 58, when it inaugurated a new era. The geographer Ptolemy (*c* AD 100–78) described it as a city of Judaea (Syria Palaestina). Local coinage, sometimes describing the place as 'holy' (*hiera*), extends from Marcus Aurelius (161–80) to Philip the Arab (244–49). In the later empire the city was an episcopal see of Palaestina Prima, on its border with Palaestina Tertia (Salutaris).

Raqqa *see* Nicephorium Callinicum

Ratiaria (Arčar). A fortress city and legionary base in Moesia (northwestern Bulgaria), on the south (right) bank of the Danube, where a major route from Macedonia and Dalmatia reached the river. Ratiaria was also a station on another important military road running alongside the river, constructed by Tiberius (AD 33/4) and renewed by Domitian, who divided the province into two, allocating Ratiaria to Upper Moesia (*c* AD 85/86). Its river port harbored a flotilla of the Roman Danube fleet. Trajan, after his annexation of Dacia (Rumania; 105), removed the legionary garrison but gave the place the rank of a Roman colony. It received consignments of copper, lead and silver—brought by river—and profited from productive agriculture. When Aurelian evacuated Dacia (271) and created the province of Dacia Ripensis on the southern bank of the Danube, Ratiaria became the provincial capital and resumed the role of a legionary garrison. In 442/3 it was captured, plundered and damaged by Attila the Hun when he overran the Danubian cities of the eastern empire. Its final destruction took place *c* 586. New excavations are uncovering remains of the ancient city.

Ravenna. A city in northeastern Italy (Cisalpine, Cispadane Gaul) on the river Bedesis (Montone); close to the sea in ancient times (it is now seven miles away), and almost surrounded by streams, canals and marshes. There were traditions of foundation by the Thessalians (under the name of Rene), Sapinates (Umbrians) and Veneti. But the name of Ravenna comes from the Etruscans, who left signs of their habitation (notably bronze statuettes of the sixth to fourth centuries BC); but hill people from Umbria took the town over, together with its harbor. Following on the occupation of northern Italy by the Gauls, Ravenna came within the territory of the Boii.

After Roman control had been subsequently established, it became a station on the Via Popillia (132), linking Atria (and later Aquileia) with Ariminum (Rimini). Presumably receiving Roman citizenship as a *municipium* along with other Cispadane communities *c* 90/89 (Cicero's reference to 'treaty' status in 56 is obscure), during the civil war between Sulla and the Marians the city was captured from the latter by Quintus Caecilius Metellus Pius in 82. During Julius Caesar's civil war against Pompey the Great it was the base from which he started his march across the Rubicon into Italy (49); he also established a gladiatorial school in the city.

In the time of Octavian (the future Augustus) it became the headquarters of his Adriatic fleet (*c* 38), a four-mile canal (the Fossa Augusta) being built to carry the waters of a small tributary of the Padus (Po) to a new harbor established at the coastal suburb Classis, two miles away on the ancient coast (of which the contours have now greatly changed). Ravenna seems to have possessed a unique constitution; although receiving new settlers it did not become a colony, while an inscription records a 'controller' (*magister*) of its *municipium,* who was probably more or less subordinate to the fleet commander. The place became a prosperous center of maritime commerce, conducted by a cosmopolitan population consisting largely of sailors from Dalmatia and Thrace, and engaged mainly in shipbuilding, but also promoting the manufacture of linen, and the export of wine, fish, timber and asparagus brought down the Po. The poet Martial remarked that the wine of Ravenna was cheap, but he disliked the taste of its water.

Under Tiberius (AD 14–37) the city was selected for the internment of Arminius' son and Maroboduus, of the tribes of the Cherusci and Marcomanni respectively. In 69 the defection of the Ravenna naval base to Vespasian played a part in the downfall of his rival Vitellius. Ravenna belonged to the district of Aemilia, and in the later empire was capital of the district or province of Flaminia et Picenum Annonarium; its port still housed a fleet, despite silting. In 404, because of its defensibility—strengthened by this silting process—the city was selected by Honorius to replace Mediolanum (Milan) as the capital (and a principal mint) of the western empire, retaining this position until the abdication of Romulus Augustulus (476), the last emperor in Italy, and thereafter under Kings Odoacer the Herulian and Theoderic the Ostrogoth and the Byzantine governors who followed (540–751). It was a town crisscrossed with canals, according to Sidonius Apollinaris (467), where paradoxically 'walls fall flat and waters stand, towers float and ships are seated'—and frogs are citizens. But the almost impregnable situation of the habitation center guaranteed seccessive rulers the security they needed.

Ancient sources refer to temples of Jupiter, Apollo and Neptune, and indicate the existence of a theater, amphitheater, circus and lighthouse. But although parts of the street grid are detectable, only very few traces of the earlier imperial epoch are still to be seen, apart from the foundations of a twenty-mile aqueduct erected by Trajan (98–117). The period, however, after Ravenna's subsequent conversion into the western imperial residence produced buildings of very distinguished architectural and artistic quality. This transformation of the city into a capital worthy of the name was initiated in the reign of Valentinian III (425–55) by his mother Galla Placidia (d. 450). Her Church of the Holy Cross (*c* 425), cruciform in accordance with its name, is only known from excavations. Beside its ruins, however, stands the edifice known as the mausoleum of Placidia, which combines the features of an imperial tomb and martyr's chapel and contains not only her own remains but also those of her husband Constantius III (421) and her half brother Honorius (395–423). The Baptistery of the Orthodox is an octagonal building that was constructed or reconstructed *c* 400, but given its dome during the bishopric of Neon (*c* 449–60) for whom it is sometimes named. Both these monuments contain richly colored, brilliantly imaginative decoration created by the leading artists of Constantinople, or under their influence.

The other principal churches of Ravenna, which are of sixth-century date and therefore fall outside the scope of this book, include San Vitale (famous for its portrait mosaics of Justinian I and Theodora) and Sant'Apollinare Nuovo, in which mosaics depict the palace of Theoderic (his mausoleum is also to be seen in the city) and views of the cities of Ravenna and Classis. Air photographs and excavations of Classis have helped to define the postion of its fort and harbor basin and beyond its habitation center the sixth century church of Sant'Apollinare in Classe is still to be seen.

Razgrad *see* Abrittus

Reate (Rieti). A city in central Italy (northern Lazio), the chief town of the Sabines. Reate was situated at the foot of Mount Terminillo, at a point where the ancient Via Salaria from Rome (forty-five miles to the southwest) crossed the river Avens (Velino) and extensions of the road led to the north and northeast. Finds show that the place existed in the early Iron Age.

Manius Curius Dentatus brought Reate under Roman administration in 290 and it obtained full citizenship in 268. Its upland plain was subject to flooding by the Avens and its tributary the Tolenus, so that drainage and flood control played an important part in the history of the town. Dentatus' draining of the Veline river and lake, now the diminished Lago di Piediluce—which he discharged into the Nar (Nera), thus creating the famous Falls of Terni—was intended to prevent the plain of Reate from being flooded, but proved the cause of recurrent quarrels with Interamna Nahars (Terni), its neighbor along the Via Curia. Thus disputes arose in 54 BC, when Cicero supported the Reatines' complaint, and again in AD 15 when they made a further protest, before the emperor Tiberius, on the grounds that a proposed damming of the lake would burst its banks into the surrounding fertile country (the *Rosea* or *Rosulana rura,* allegedly from *ros,* dew, or humidity, now Le Roscie).

Reate was the birthplace of the great encyclopedic scholar Marcus Terentius Varro (116 BC) and of Vespasian (AD 9), founder of the Flavian dynasty, who planted a settlement of ex-soldiers in the city, although it remained a *municipium* without elevation to the rank of *colonia.* The place was also well-known for its mules. Remains of bridges across the Avens, and traces of another carrying the Via Salaria over a small stream, have come to light, and large rectangular blocks survive from the ancient fortifications.

Reggio di Calabria *see* Rhegium

Regillus, Lake (now the volcanic depression of Pantano, drained in the seventeenth century). South of Gabii (Castiglione) in Latium (Lazio); fourteen miles east of Rome. Lake Regillus was the scene of a battle between the Romans and Latins which, although apparently a historical event (*c* 496 BC), became overlaid by many myths. According to tradition, the last of Rome's kings, Tarquinius Superbus, after his expulsion from the city, took refuge with his son-in-law, who persuaded the Latins to take up arms on his behalf beside the lake (*c* 496 BC). It is doubtful, however, whether Tarquinius was the cause of the battle, since this seems to have been primarily a conflict between the Romans and the Latin League, to which Rome did not belong. The Roman victory that reputedly ensued was attributed to the intervention of the divine Dioscuri (Castor and Pollux), who were afterward seen watering their horses at the spring of Juturna, where they announced the victory and vanished; whereupon a temple in their honor was built on the spot. The engagement does not, however, appear to have been the glorious triumph into which Roman saga transformed it. Nevertheless, it resulted in a memorable treaty between Rome on the one hand and the thirty Latin cities on the other—an agreement that lasted until the Latins were absorbed into the Roman state in 338.

Regina, Fossa *see* Allia (River).

Regium *see* Rhegium

Reims *see* Durocortorum

Rekem *see* Petra

Reşadiye *see* Cnidus

Reşca Dobrosloveni *see* Romula-Malva

Rhaetia *see* Raetia

Rhegium or Regium, Rhegion (Reggio di Calabria). A city in Bruttii (now Calabria) on the toe of the Italian peninsula, bordering the Sicilian (Messina) Strait. Situated in an area named Pallantion, on a sloping plateau that extended between two ridges and overlooked a harbor near the mouth of the river Apsias (Calopinace), Rhegium was founded in the later eighth century BC, and may have been the first Greek colony in the far south of Italy. The information regarding its settlement, however, is conflicting. According to the historian Antiochus of Syracuse, the people of Zancle (Messana, now Messina) sent for colonists from Chalcis in Euboea, and appointed Antimnestus as their leader (*oikistes*). Alternatively, however—or in addition—a part was played in the foundation by Messenians (from the southwestern Peloponnese), who were refugees from their first war with Sparta (*c* 743-720?). The geographical position of the city facilitated its commercial relations with the Greek colonies in Sicily, and it possessed vines and fisheries.

In the sixth century Rhegium was the birthplace of the lyric poet Ibycus and center of a confraternity based on the teachings of Pythagoras. After a period of government by an oligarchic regime borrowing its laws from Charondas of Catana (Catania)—who probably lived in the same period—followed by the settlement of additional colonists *c* 540 by Phocaeans from Ionia in western Asia Minor (who subsequently colonized Elea [Velia] from Rhegium)—the city came under the autocratic rule of Anaxilas (494-476); seizing Zancle, he fortified the straits against Etruscan incursions, but supported the Carthaginians against Syracuse at the time of their defeat at Himera (Imera) in 480. The sons of Anaxilas were driven out of Rhegium in 461, and its new administration joined a refounded 'Achaean League'. But the Syracusans, for their part, offered support to Locri Epizephyrii, the rival of Rhegium, which Dionysius I destroyed in 387/6, dismantling the walls and building a palace.

Reconstructed under the name of Phoebia (358) and liberated from Dionysius II, the city allied itself with his successor Timoleon (d. 334). Later it fell temporarily into the hands of the Mamertini (280), Campanian mercenaries who had seized Messana; but it successfully resisted native Bruttians, and after requesting and receiving a Roman garrison (282) resisted the invading army of King Pyrrhus of Epirus (276). During the Second Punic War Rhegium again stood firm against the Carthaginians under Hannibal, apparently providing the mint at which Rome's earliest silver *denarii* were struck (*c* 211). In 132/131 it was linked by a road (probably a Via Annia, named after Titus Annius Rufus) to Rome, and like other Italian cities was granted the rank of *municipium* in *c* 89. In 36 it received a settlement of marines, adopting the name of Regium Julium, and continued to prosper throughout the imperial epoch.

The acropolis was probably on the higher part of the site occupied by the modern town, whereas the agora corresponds with what is now the Piazza Italia. A large, early, sacred precinct has been identified to its northeast, and inscriptions bear witness to a temple of Apollo and another shrine dedicated to Isis and Serapis. A sanctuary of Artemis, mentioned by Thucydides, has been located outside the walls toward the sea. There is now reason to believe that a category of black-figure vases of the later sixth century BC, hitherto known as 'Chalcidic,' may have been products of Rhegium. The museum at Reggio di Calabria contains the Riace Bronzes, two superb male statues of fifth-century date recently found in the sea some miles to the north.

Rheims *see* Durocortorum

Rhenus (Rhine), River. The Rhine became the Roman frontier in Julius Caesar's time, and retained this position, although short-lived attempts were made to advance the boundary of the empire to the Albis (Elbe) by Augustus (until Varus' disaster in the Saltus Teutoburgiensis in AD 9) and then again by Tiberius' nephew Germanicus (AD 14–17). Subsequently the Agri Decumates, in the reentrant between the right (east) bank of the Upper Rhine and the left (north) bank of the Upper Danube, were occupied under Vespasian (69–79) and Domitian (81–96), and remained in Roman hands until the early 260s. The military regions of Lower and Upper Germany bordering the Rhine were converted by Domitian *c* 90 into the provinces of the same names, and the latter was divided by Diocletian (284–305) into Germania Prima and Maxima Secundorum, while Lower Germany became Germania Secunda. The most important tributaries of the Rhine were the Luppia (Lippe) and Moenus (Main). *See also* Argentorate, Augusta Rauricorum, Basilia, Borbetomagus, Germania, Haltern, Moguntiacum, Noviomagus, Vetera, Vindonissa.

Rhoas *see* Laodicea (Phrygia)

Rhodanus (Rhône), River. Starting in the Alps, this is the principal river flowing into the Mediterranean. The mouths of its delta (variously described by anciant writers as two, three and five in number) were adjoined by a sea-water marsh, the Stamalimne, containing abundant oysters and fish. The commercial access that the Rhône afforded to central and northern Gaul became important following the foundation, to the east of its delta, of Massalia (Massilia, Marseille, *c* 600 BC), of which the trade up the river contributed to the evolution of the Celtic La Tène culture. After southern Gaul became a Roman province (Gallia Narbonensis, *c* 121), Gaius Marius dug a canal (Fossae Marianae, Bras Mort, 104/3) to escape the silt that impeded access to the river from the sea, leading from the main stream (above the bar) to a point on the coast (west of Fos). Traces of the canal have been found by underwater exploration. It provided the Massalians, to whom it was handed over, with lucrative tolls, but above all it inaugurated the importance of Arelate (Arles), just above the Rhône delta. In the later empire the river was the boundary between the provinces of Narbonensis Prima and Viennensis. Its tributaries included the Druentia (Durance), Isara (Isère) and Arar (later Sauconna, now Saône). *See also* Arausio, Arelate, Carpentorate, Lugdunum, Massalia, Nemausus, Valentia, Vienna.

Rhodes, Rhodos. The principal island of the Dodecanese (now belonging to Greece), measuring fifty by twenty-two miles, off the coast of Caria (southwestern Asia Minor).

According to Pindar, Rhodes had emerged from the sea to comprise the special possession of Helios, the sun-god, who became the principal local deity, celebrated in the annual Halieia festival, and whose grandsons, together with the nymph Rhodos the daughter of Aphrodite, were the mythical founders of the island's three cities, Ialysus and Camirus on the west and Lindus on the east coast. Already in early times Rhodes was a stepping stone to other islands and mainland centers, as Mycenaean finds at all three centers (especially Ialysus) testify, and many legendary traditions suggest. Thus the Telchines, magical metalworkers, came from Crete via Cyprus; Danaus and Cadmus stopped at Rhodes; and Tlepolemus the son of Heracles, whose Dorian followers, according to Homer, had settled in the island (perhaps in the thirteenth century BC), was said to have commanded a Rhodian flotilla in the Trojan War.

By *c* 900 many other Dorians had arrived on the island, whose three towns, joining three others (Cos, Cnidus, Halicarnassus) to form a confederation (Hexapolis), became prosperous from about 700, and gained fame for their seamanship. In the sixth century Lindus was ruled for many years by Cleobulus, one of the Seven Sages and author (with his daughter) of a famous collection of riddles. Among colonies founded by Lindus—acting on behalf of the whole island community—were Gela in Sicily, Rhode (Rosas) in northeastern Spain and Phaselis (Tekirova) in Lycia (southern Asia Minor). In the later sixth century the Rhodian communities were subject first to Battus III of Cyrene and then to the Persians, and after the Persian War they became members of the Delian League under the direction of Athens.

They broke, however, with the Athenians in 412/11, during the Peloponnesian War; and the hostilities that followed brought about the amalgamation, in 408, of the island's three cities into a single state with the new federal capital of Rhodes (Rhodos), on the northern tip of the island. In 394 this returned to Athenian sponsorship, and joined a local maritime league. A series of internal political upheavals resulted in the establishment of a moderate democracy, temporarily suspended during a period of Persian rule 355–333). Successfully withstanding one of the most famous of all sieges, at the hands of Demetrius I Poliorcetes 'the Besieger' (305–304), Rhodes now became preeminent in Greek commerce and especially in the grain-carrying trade; it was protected against pirates by a highly efficient fleet, and renowned for the imaginative institutions of its welfare state. The most destructive of several earthquakes, in 227 BC, elicited financial relief from far and wide.

Collaborating with Rome in its wars against Philip V of Macedonia (200–197) and the Seleucid Antiochus III the Great (191–188), the Rhodians were rewarded with territory in Caria and Lycia on the mainland of Asia Minor (the Rhodian Peraea). Their equivocal conduct, however, in the subsequent hostilities against the Macedonian king Perseus (171–168) earned the displeasure of the Romans, whose elevation of Delos to become a rival free port may have crippled Rhodian commerce (although this has lately been contested). After successfully resisting a siege by Mithridates VI of Pontus in 88, Rhodes was reduced to ruins by Julius Caesar (against whom it had sided with Pompey the Great) and then suffered pillage and capture in 42 from Caesar's assassin Cassius, who also destroyed the greater part of its fleet.

Throughout this period Rhodes had become and remained one of the principal cultural centers of Hellenism. Its hundred-and-ten-foot high statue of the sun-god Helios, which was created by Chares of Lindus in 292/280 to commemorate the repulse of Demetrius, did not span the harbor, as legend suggested, but exemplified new bronze-casting skills and ranked as one of the Seven Wonders of the World. It was destroyed by the earthquake of 227, but the dynamic group of the Laocoon, the work of three Rhodian sculptors of second-century BC date (or of copyists of the first century AD) has survived, in the Vatican museum. The leading Stoic philosopher Panaetius (*c* 185–109) was a Rhodian, and his encyclopedic pupil Posidonius of Apamea (*c* 135–51/50) became a member of the same eminent school, which was attended by Cicero and many other leading Romans. In the reign of Augustus, his stepson Tiberius retired to Rhodes for eight years (6 BC–AD 2). A coin of Antoninus Pius (AD 138–61) depicts Poseidon Asphaleois, the god who presided over the safety of ships and harbors. Further disastrous earthquakes devastated the city in AD 345 and 515, but Rhodian maritime law still remained authoritative in Byzantine times.

The city of Rhodes possessed four harbors, and was surrounded by famous walls, of which portions have been identified. According to Strabo, its 'grid' design was the work of the great town planner Hippodamus of Miletus, although, if so, he must have been over ninety at the time of the city's foundation. It comprised both a lower and upper town. The former, beside the harbors, contains remains of temples of Aphrodite and Dionysus, and of ship sheds. In the upper town or acropolis, located on a plateau about three hundred feet above sea level, a shrine of Zeus and Athena, a precinct of Pythian Apollo, a stadium (displaying three phases of construction), and a small theater have been located. Although recently discovered pebble mosaics of the fourth century are of the finest quality, there is relatively little left to justify the superlative terms in which Strabo describes the city's 'harbors and roads and walls and arrangements in general,' or the even more glowing testimonies of Aristides and Lucian. Extensive cemeteries lie outside various sectors of the walls.

The even more scanty traces of Ialysus, of which the commanding acropolis (Mount Philerimos) served as an observation post and fortress, include several temples and a *nymphaeum* (fountain building) of the fourth century BC. Not far away, at Kastonioi (Tholos), are the ruins of a temple of Apollo Erethimios. The upper and lower towns of Camirus display temples, a sacrificial area, a long colonnade, aqueducts, cisterns and drains, and bear witness to comprehensive Hellenistic town planning. Lindus possessed two harbors overlooked by a precipitous acropolis, on the summit of which stood a famous sanctuary of Athena Lindia, founded by Danaus according to Greek mythology but mainly represented today by remains of the fourth century BC. The complex precinct in which the shrine was set displayed an elaborate series of colonnades at different levels, of which the longest opened onto a great terrace extended on vaulted substructure. An inscription of 99 BC, the Temple Chronicle, lists notable dedicated objects (many of which were destroyed in a fire of 348) and miraculous interventions of the goddess. A small theater was built into the slope of the same hill, and monumental tombs are to be seen in the neighborhood. Two ancient wrecks have recently been found off Lindus, one of which apparently dates to *c* 500 BC.

Riace *see* Rhegium

Rieti *see* Reate

Rimini *see* Ariminum

Rioni, Rhioni (River) *see* Phasis

Rome (Roma). A city in Latium (Lazio), western Italy, fifteen miles from the Tyrrhenian Sea, on the south (left) bank of the Tiber at the lowest of its practicable crossing points. The early history of Rome is thickly overlaid by the myths so eloquently recounted by Livy, Virgil and many other writers, telling the stories associated with the city's foundation by Romulus in 753 BC (or alternative dates) and relating to the line of kings that constituted Rome's regal period and came to an end, according to the traditional chronological calculation, in *c* 510. Excavations suggest that early villages on the Palatine, Quirinal and Esquiline Hills had united by the eight century, and that Rome became a strong city-state (dominating Latium) two centuries later, under Etruscan immigrants from Tarquinii (Tarquinia) named Tarquinius Priscus (*c* 616–579) and Tarquinius Superbus (535–510); between their names the king list includes the evidently powerful and innovative Servius Tullius, who appeared in one version as a Roman or Latin but was probably another Etruscan.

The expulsion of Tarquinius Superbus was followed by the establishment of a Republic, governed by annually elected consuls and praetors and other functionaries—all members of the senate—to whose offices plebeians (non-patricians) were gradually admitted after prolonged pressure and friction. This internal strife was accompanied by the equally gradual expansion of Roman domination in Italy. Under the menace of external foes (Volsci, Aequi, Etruscans) Rome formed an alliance with the Latins (*see* Regillus), and a century later, *c* 396, took a decisive step toward breaking Etruscan power by the conquest of Veii (inconveniently close, only just across the Tiber) after a prolonged siege. Invading Gauls routed the Roman army on the river Allia *c* 387 and occupied the capital itself, but Rome recovered and after warfare against the Latins (340–338) dissolved their League, instituting a patient and ingenious system of alliances in its place. A foothold in Campania was strengthened, and finally the whole of the mountainous central region of the peninsula was brought under control by three Samnite Wars (343–290); victory over the Boii, Gaulish occupants of northern Italy (Cisalpine Gaul), soon followed (283/2). Thurii (near Sibari) in the southeast appealed to Rome against the invading King Pyrrhus of Epirus, whose evacuation of Italy (275), followed by the reduction of Tarentum (Taras, now Taranto) three years later, meant that the whole of Italy up to the river Padus (Po) was under Roman rule.

A clash with the other major western Mediterranean power, Carthage, was now inevitable, and materialized when an appeal by Messana (Messina) to Rome was treated by the Carthaginians as a hostile act. In the three Punic Wars that followed the Romans were victorious. The First (264–241), in which they made themselves a naval power, gave them their first provinces, Sicily and Sardinia (with Corsica). The Second War (218–201), comprising the traumatic invasion of Italy by Hannibal but leading to his final defeat at Zama in north Africa, placed Spain in their hands.

The Romans also became deeply involved in the affairs of the Hellenistic east, fighting Illyrian and Macedonian Wars that culminated in victory over the Macedonian monarch Philip V (197). The Seleucid Antiochus III the Great was likewise overcome (190–188), and the defeat of Perseus of Macedonia (168) resulted in the destruction of his kingdom, which was annexed (with Achaea [Greece]) in 146. In the same year, Rome terminated the Third Punic War by the obliteration of Carthage and the creation of the province of Africa, followed by the institution of another great province, Asia (the former kingdom of Pergamum), in 133–129.

Attempts by the brothers Tiberius and Gaius Sempronius Gracchus, occupying the traditionally popular office of the tribunate, to develop a more socially equitable society ended in their deaths (133,122). Transalpine Gaul (southern France) was annexed shortly afterward. Marius, victor in a war against Jugurtha in Numidia (107–104), transformed the Roman citizen militia into an army that depended on its commander for rewards. The civil wars fought by him and his successors against Sulla resulted in the latter's dictatorship (82–80). Then Pompey the Great, by his wars against the Marian Quintus Sertorius in Spain, against pirates in the Mediterranean, and against Mithridates VI of Pontus (followed by large-scale eastern reorganization and annexation), established a powerful position, resisted, however, by determined opponents, notably Cato the Younger.

In 60 Pompey, Julius Caesar and the wealthy Crassus formed the unofficial First Triumvirate. Thereafter Pompey ruled in Italy (with representatives in Spain), and Caesar conquered central and northern Gaul (and reconnoitred Britain), but in 53 Crassus was defeated by the Parthians at Carrhae (Haran) and lost his life. The ensuing civil war between Caesar and Pompey (49) led to the defeat of Pompey at Pharsalus and his subsequent death (48)—followed by the overthrow of his adherents (46/5)—which left the dictator Caesar in absolute control. Further civil strife after his death eliminated his assassins Brutus and Cassius at the battle of Philippi (42), won by their enemies Antony and Octavian (Caesar's grandnephew and adoptive son), who had formed the Second Triumvirate with the high priest Lepidus. In 31 Octavian defeated Antony and his ally and mistress, Caesar's former mistress Cleopatra VII of Egypt, at Actium, and they committed suicide in the following year.

Augustus, as Octavian now called himself (27), ruled the entire Roman world under the guise of a restored republic, performing gigantic feats of permanent reorganization and adding Egypt, the Danubian provinces (Noricum, Pannonia, Moesia) and central Asia Minor (Galatia) to the empire, although he failed to retain Germany beyond the Rhenus (Rhine) and up to the Albis (Elbe). His work was continued by the remaining emperors of his Julio-Claudian dynasty (Tiberius, Gaius, Claudius [who annexed Britannia (England)] and Nero), on whose regimes—characterized by the growing power of the praetorian guard—Tacitus and Suetonius cast a lurid light. The prolonged and complex civil wars in the Year of the Four Emperors finally awarded the purple to Vespasian (AD 69–79), who founded the Flavian dynasty and was succeeded by his sons Titus and Domitian—whom the army loved but senators hated, replacing him by Nerva.

The emperors who ruled for most of the second century (Trajan, Hadrian, Antoninus Pius, Marcus Aurelius) gained their thrones by merit and adoption. Trajan (98–117) conquered Dacia (Rumania) and temporarily overran Mesopotamia (Iraq). Hadrian entertained wider cosmopolitan ideas, and Marcus Aurelius (161–80, author of the *Meditations*) repeated Augustus' failure to annex large parts of Germany. After ferocious civil wars Septimius Severus (193–211), from North Africa, reorganized the empire on more overtly military lines, and his son Caracalla (211–17) completed a gradual process of status unification by conferring Roman citizenship on all provincials.

For most of the rest of the century Rome faced terrible external problems, under an unprecedented dual threat from much-strengthened Germans from the north and formidable Sassanian Persians from the east—a threat greatly exacerbated by continuous violent changes of emperor imposed by the provincial armies. Against all apparent probability, however, external security and internal unity were restored by a succession of soldier emperors, one of the greatest of whom, Aurelian (270–75), built a new wall round Rome. Diocletian (284–305), an administrator and reformer on the scale of Augustus, regularized the permanent regimentation of the populace that such military efforts seemed to necessitate, and established a tetrarchy under which the empire was ruled by two Augusti and two Caesars. His western colleague Maximian located his capital at Mediolanum (Milan) instead of Rome, and Constantine I the Great (306–37), who directed the triumph of Christianity, chose Constantinople (Byzantium).

When Valentinian I (364–75) divided the empire into western and eastern sections, their capital cities remained Mediolanum and Constantinople respectively, while at Rome the power of the increasingly autonomous Popes became more and more evident. However, after Honorius had moved his capital to the more defensible Ravenna (404), the Rhine frontier was permanently breached (406) and Rome itself was temporarily occupied, and sacked, by the Visigoth Alaric (410) and the Vandal Gaiseric (455). In 476 the last western emperor to rule in Italy, Romulus Augustulus, was deposed by Odoacer the Herulian, who ruled as king of the Germans in the peninsula (although a western emperor, Julius Nepos, remained in Dalmatia until 480) and was succeeded by Theoderic the Ostrogoth (493–518). (The eastern emperors continued to reign in Constantinople, with an intermission during the thirteenth century, until 1453; *see* Byzantium.)

Postholes for early Iron Age huts, in the shape of urns, have been found on the Palatine, where Romulus, according to patriotic myth, had founded his city in 753 BC. The marshy depression that was subsequently transformed into the Forum served as a burial ground for the surrounding settlements, until it was drained by the Cloaca Maxima and served as the public square of a gradually unified city. Although unification was under way by the eighth century BC, the completed development was associated with Tarquinius Priscus (616–579), whose successor Servius Tullius was also said to have further enlarged the city, incorporating the Esquiline, Quirinal and Viminal hills, building fortifications (although the 'Wall of Servius Tullius' is of later date; *see* below) and dividing the new town into four regions. The last kings of Rome built the Temples of Jupiter, Juno and Minerva on the Capitol and a shrine of Diana on the Aventine. Other buildings of the monarchic period included the Regia (house of the *pontifex maximus* [chief priest], recently reexcavated), the Temple of Vesta, Curia (senate house), Volcanal—holy place of the god Vulcan (Hephaestus), with which the sacred area containing an inscribed 'Black Stone' of *c* 575–550 has now been identified—and Forum Boarium (cattle market; in which recent excavations carry back the sacred area of Sant'Omobono to successive phases in *c* 600–575).

During the Republic, Rome underwent further continuous expansion. The Forum, which was now the hub of civic life, witnessed the construction of temples of Saturn (*c* 497), the Dioscuri (Castor and Pollux, *c* 484) and Concordia (*c* 336)—all still to be seen, in rebuilt forms. The Aventine Hill became the center of plebeian activity. After its sack by the Gauls (*c* 387) the perimeter of the city was surrounded by the 'Wall of Servius Tullius,' of which portions survive. Appius Claudius Caecus, during his censorship (312), built the first aqueduct and the Via Appia leading southeastward to Campania. Other aqueducts followed, and several basilicas (meeting places for judicial and commercial purposes) were erected in the second century, during which the influx of wealth and booty gave a new impetus to public building. Further encouragement was provided by the revolutionary discovery and initial exploitation of concrete, already displayed in a warehouse, the Porticus Aemilia (193–174), part of a recently excavated river harbor system. As censor in 1984 Cato the Elder improved the sewage arrangements of the city.

A fashionable and relatively luxurious residential quarter developed on the Palatine, and the urban area was extended northward into the Campus Martius (Field of Mars). The remains of a number of temples of Republican date have survived in the Largo Argentina and elsewhere. Quintus Lutatius Catulus (78) built the Tabularium (Record Office) beside the Forum, backing onto the Capitoline Hill, on which he also reconstructed and rededicated the Temple of Jupiter (69), destroyed in the civil war between the Marians and Sulla. Pompey the Great put up the first permanent theater, and Caesar built a forum of his own, thus launching the series of 'Imperial fora' that supplemented the increasingly inadequate dimensions of the crowded Forum Romanum. By this time the population of the capital was between half a million and a million.

The even larger Rome of imperial times displayed a sharp contrast between squalid slums and magnificent public buildings erected by successive emperors. According to Suetonius, Augustus boasted 'I found Rome a city of bricks, and left it a city of marble.' He equipped the temple of Apollo Medicus (Sosianus, 32 BC) with pedimental sculptures—dating from the fifth century BC, and probably transported from Eretria—which have now been restored; their commemoration of the victory of Theseus over the Amazon Hippolyta echoes the Roman ruler's own triumphs over Cleopatra. He also built the great forum named after him, centering round a temple of Mars the Avenger (Ultor), while his deputy Marcus Agrippa repaired the old aqueducts, built new ones, and erected many public buildings in the Campus Martius, notably the Pantheon or Temple of the Olympic Gods (no longer extant in its original form: *see* below). Measures were also taken to protect the city from Tiber floods—also from fires, but in vain, since the Great Fire of AD 64 inflicted enormous damage, though this was repaired by Nero's energetic reconstruction program (including the building of his own Golden House [Domus Aurea]). Vespasian and Titus created the Colosseum (dedicated in 80). The earliest of the surviving Triumphal Arches was set up in honor of Titus (those of Septimius Severus and Constantine I the Great can also still be seen); Vespasian and Nerva and Trajan designed new fora—the latter included a great basilica and market—and Titus and Trajan constructed baths on an unprecedented scale. Then Hadrian erected an enormous Temple of Venus and Rome, and the superb circular, domed Pantheon with its rectangular porch, on the site of Agrippa's earlier shrine.

The epoch that followed witnessed the culmination of the gigantic imperial thermal establishments, represented by the Baths of Caracalla (206–17) and Diocletian, the latter the work of his colleague Maximian (298-305/306). Maximian's son Maxentius started to build the Basilica known by his name, of which three arches still stand; unlike earlier flat-roofed basilicas it possessed mighty vaults, resembling those of the huge halls of the public baths. Maxentius' basilica was altered and completed by Constantine I the Great, whose Basilica Constantiniana (S. Giovanni in Laterano; initiated *c* 320 on the site of a building of about 270) and first Basilica of St. Peter's (the Vatican church) were later overbuilt. The church of SS. Marcellino and Pietro (from 325) and Santa Costanza (*c* 350) housed the mausolea of his mother Helena and his daughter Constantina respectively. Of the first Basilica of St. Paul Outside the Walls (385), little remains, but much of the original structure of S. Maria Maggiore, the work of a great builder Pope Sixtus III (432–44) still survives.

Romula *see* Hispalis

Romula-Malva (Reşca Dobrosloveni). A Roman city in Dacia (Rumania), on the rivers Teslui and Aluta (Olt), a northern tributary of the Danube that ran closer to the town in antiquity than it does today. The Dacian township Malva, which means 'bank,' was annexed and renamed Romula when Dacia was conquered by Trajan in AD 101–105, and Hadrian, dividing the captured territory into two provinces, probably made the place the capital of Lower Dacia (later Malvensis), of which the Aluta at first formed the eastern boundary. Romula-Malva was settled by ex-soldiers, and became a *municipium,* subsequently receiving the rank of a Roman colony under Septimius Severus (193-211). The finding of a hoard of 8,000 coins dating from 180 to 222, suggests insecurity, and the city suffered severe damage from invasions by the Carpi (245-47). Its colonial rank was reconfirmed by the emperor Philip (d. 249), but thereafter incursions continuing down to the time of the evacuation of Dacia by Aurelian (271) seem to have destroyed the town altogether.

Two rectangular camps, housing (according to inscriptions) auxiliary cohorts and legionary detachments, have been located; their fortifications date from the first years of the settlement and embody three phases of construction, of which the last, surrounding both the military and civilian quarters, belonged to the reign of Philip; a palatial villa has now been found outside these walls. Excavations have also revealed a luxurious, marble-veneered bathing establishment served by a three-mile-long aqueduct. A large structure containing three halls, a portico and underground heating appears to be the local senate house. The patron goddess of the city was Fortuna, and numerous dedications to Roman gods bears witness to rapid Romanization, but there is also (as a result of recent excavations) epigraphic evidence for a remarkable array of Danubian and eastern deities, reflecting the origins of the colonists and garrison.

Romula-Malva had two cemeteries, one for the Dacian poor and the other of a much more impressive character, containing sarcophagi of wood, lead and stone (including the tomb of a local official whose remains were adorned with a gold wreath and a bronze medallion, and glass-studded shoes). This prosperity came from local agricultural wealth, and especially vines; these products paid for luxury imports, to which earthenware jars from Italy, Gaul and Spain, as well as Greek amphoras containing wines superior to the local variety bear witness. Weaving and spinning were household industries, but the special craft of Romula-Malva was the carving of intaglio designs on semiprecious stones, notably jasper, carnelian, onyx, sardonyx and rock crystal.

Roselle *see* Rusellae

Roxolanskoye *see* Tyras

Rubicon, Rubico (Fiumicino), River. A small stream in eastern Italy (Romagna)—a little to the north of Ariminum (Rimini)—forming the boundary, in Roman Republican times, between Italy and Cisalpine Gaul. The civil war between Julius Caesar and Pompey the Great was launched by Caesar in 49 BC when he and his army crossed the Rubicon, since this departure outside Cisalpine Gaul (which formed part of the appointed territory of his governorship), in order to effect an unauthorized entry into the homeland with an armed force, was an unconstitutional and illegal act. After horses had been set free as a religious offering—so as to dispel fears of sacrilege—Caesar sent the only legion he had at his disposal across the stream, and, after himself crossing over with his staff, divided this force into two columns that rapidly moved southward, thus inducing his enemies to evacuate Rome (and subsequently Italy).

Rusellae (Resala in Umbrian; the modern Roselle). A city of Etruria on a plateau that in ancient times overlooked the navigable sea lagoon Lake Prilius and the agriculturally rich valley of the river Ombrone, which flowed into the lagoon near the town. The original villages on the plateau amalgamated on a new site in the seventh century BC.

Already before 600 the new settlement was protected, at least in one sector, by a wall with stone foundations and with upper portions of unfired brick, comprising one of the oldest fortifications that have hitherto come to light in Etruria. This wall was replaced not long afterward by another of impressive dimensions, reaching a height at some points of over twenty feet and a breadth of eight or nine. The wall surrounded a perimeter of almost two miles, although the area thus enclosed was never completely filled by buildings. Traces of the habitation center have come to light on a most unusual scale for Etruria, where cemeteries usually provide most of the information. In these buildings, from *c* 550, unfired brick was being supplemented by baked brick, and subsequently stone came into use. Both public and private edifices have been identified. The former were set side by side in a central valley separating the two main portions of the urban area, in which the private houses were located, including some small dwellings that cast unusual light on the lives of the Etruscan poor.

The original amalgamation of the villages, that is to say the foundation of Rusellae, was probably carried out by the Etruscan city-state of Vetulonia, nine miles away on the other side of Lake Prilius (though some attribute the initiative to Vulci instead). It is a reasonable conjecture, however, that in the later sixth century Vetulonia was eclipsed and perhaps partly destroyed by Rusellae. Even before this, the Rusellans are likely to have had access to the rich mining resources of the Massetano, and the elimination of Vetulonia may have given them control over the metal supplies of the Campigliese and of the island of Ilva (Aethalia, Elba). A heap of selected tin has been found at Rusellae, and the firs beside the Umbro basin provided charcoal for smelting.

The city possessed a port or ports on Lake Prilius (at or near Terme di Roselle), one of which could have issued some of the earliest Etruscan silver coins, inscribed Thezi or Thezle. Another of Rusellae's harbors, farther away, may have been Telamon (Talamone) on the river Osa, from which remarkable pedimental terracotta sculptures illustrating the myth of the Seven Against Thebes (*c* 180)—from a temple destroyed *c* 80—have now been reconstructed. The important Etruscan town of Heba (Magliano), seven miles inland, may also have been taken over from Vetulonia by Rusellae.

It was stormed by the Romans in 294, after prolonged struggles. During the Second Punic War it provided Rome with grain and ships' timber (205). As Pliny the Elder records, it became a citizen colony, either in the Second Triumvirate or subsequently during the reign of Augustus (31 BC–AD 14). A Roman forum, flanked by a basilica and a center of the imperial cult, was laid out in the central valley, and the city provided Roman consuls in AD 89 and 98. Excavations have yielded a remarkable collection of sculptures of the second and third centuries AD, comprising the memorials of a single local family, and now to be seen in the museum at Grosseto.

'We put in at the mouth of the Umbro,' wrote Rutilius Namatianus (416). 'It is a large river with a safe entrance for the tired and frightened sailor who comes there.' There were bishops of Rusellae in the fifth century, but barbarian devastations, and the subsequent silting up of Lake Prilius (to form the present Grosseto plain), marked the end of the city's use.

S

Saalburg (ancient name unknown). A Roman fortress (north of Bad Homburg) on the northern border of the Agri Decumates, the reentrant territory between the Upper Rhine and Upper Danube annexed by Vespasian (AD 69–79) and Domitian (81–96). Constructed during Domitian's war against the Chatti (83–85), Saalburg formed part of the frontier defence system (*limes*) along the Taunus ridge. In 125/139 the original small wooden fort was replaced by a larger structure, built of stone and wood, to house an auxiliary unit (a Raetian cohort). Following destruction by the Alamanni (*c* 185/187), a stronger rampart was built, and flanked by a trench; it was subsequently strengthened, and then replaced by massive walls of stone and mortar (209/213). After further devastation, and the retraction of the frontier, the fortress was abandoned between 251 and 260.

Excavations have revealed barracks, stables, workshops and a bathing establishment. But Saalburg is principally notable because its fortifications and principal buildings have now been reconstructed to present a unique picture of a Roman auxiliary fortress. Outside the gates, remains of a civilian settlement (*canabae*) have been uncovered, including shrines of Jupiter Dolichenus, Mithras, Cybele and Gallic deities (Sucellus, Nantosvelta, the Matronae).

Sabastiya *see* Samaria

Sabaudia, Sapaudia (Savoie, Savoy). A territory extending from the middle Isara (Isère) valley (southeastern Gaul) up as far as Lake Brigantius (the lake of Geneva), comprising the modern departments of Haute-Savoie and Savoie; although the name Sabaudia was also sometimes applied to a more limited area). After Aetius, the general of the western emperor Valentinian III— with the aid of his allies the Huns—had destroyed the Burgundian kingdom based on Borbetomagus (Worms) farther north (436), he assigned the surviving Burgundians territory in Sabaudia (443), from which they gradually expanded to the north and west, and attempted to expand to the south.

Sabratha (Sabrata). A coastal city of Tripolitana (Tripolitania, Libya) in north Africa, the westernmost of the three cities (*treis poleis*) that gave the territory its name (Lepcis Magna and Oea were the others). Traditonally founded by the Phoenicians, Sabratha possessed a small harbor—partly screened by a reef—and was employed as a trading post by the Carthaginians, who established a permanent settlement there in the fourth century BC, making a living from grain and olives and perhaps also from tunny fishing.

After the fall of Carthage (146), the town passed in due course under the control of the Roman province of Africa, forming the meeting point of the coastal thoroughfare and a road running south-southwest to Cydamus (Gadames), which controlled the Trans-Saharan caravan route, bringing gold, semi-precious stones, slaves, wild animals and ivory from the interior (there is a mosaic of an elephant in the office of the traders of Sabratha at Ostia). Sabratha was probably declared a free city by Augustus, in common with the other two cities of the Tripolis, which had gained new importance as the road head of food supplies to the Roman armies fighting the rebellious tribe of the Marmaridae in the south. To celebrate the occasion Sabratha issued a coinage bearing Roman and Phoenician inscriptions (*c* 7/6).

Flavia Domitilla, the wife of Vespasian (AD 69–79) came from the place. Elevated to the rank of a Roman colony—together with its associated cities—perhaps by Trajan (98–117), it reached the peak of its prosperity in the second century. The novelist Apuleius stood trial for witchcraft at Sabratha *c* 155; his defence, the *Apologia*, has survived. The city possessed a Christian bishop from 253. Attached to the province of Tripolitana in the later empire, it was sacked and gravely damaged by the southern tribe of the Austuriani (363/5), but subsequently rebuilt, although in the following century it decayed rapidly under Vandal occupation.

On the landward side of the original Phoenician town—beside the harbor, of which extensive later installations have been uncovered—stood the forum, superimposed on earlier constructions during the first century AD (and later realigned). Of the same period are temples of Liber Pater and Serapis, a tribunal adorned with imperial statues, and an internally colonnaded basilica. The whole area, however, underwent remodelling and transformation in the second century AD, when a Capitolium, senate house and public baths were added; while a new quarter, containing temples of Hercules and Isis (of earlier origin), was dominated by a theater, of which the restoration presents a unique impression of a Roman stage, rising to a height of three orders and enriched by numerous sculptures. Many shops and storerooms (often revealing signs of upper storeys) and private residences (some with find mosaics) have also come to light.

After the sack by the Austurians the entire forum area was redesigned, including the basilica, which was again reconstructed in the fifth century to serve as one of the city's several churches (there is also a catacomb). On the outskirts of Sabratha are villas, an amphitheater, remains of an aqueduct, and tombs.

Sadagh, Sadak *see* Satala

Saguntum (Sagunto). A township near the coast of Hispania Citerior (later Tarraconensis; eastern Spain), on the river Udiba or Uvida (Palancia) south of the Iberus (Ebro), in the territory of the Edetani or Arsetani. The name of the Iberian town, Arse ('high fortress'), prompted Livy and Silius Italicus to put forward the fictitious idea that its founder city had been Ardea in Italy, whereas Strabo and Pliny no less erroneously assumed that the name of Saguntum came from colonizers from the Ionian (Adriatic) island of Zacynthus (Zante).

The fortress (Castillo) stood on a plateau dominating coastal and inland roads. The town enjoyed trading relations with Massalia (Massilia, Marseille), but only briefly took the center of the historical stage during the third century BC, when it provided the immediate cause of the Second Punic War between Carthage and Rome. The Carthaginians had built up a powerful empire in Spain; and in 226 Hasdrubal came to an agreement with the Romans. As far as can be discerned through the subsequent fog of propaganda, he agreed not to march north of the Ebro on the condition that the Romans should not cross to its south—where Saguntum was situated. When, however, the Saguntines felt threatened by Hasdrubal's brother-in-law Hannibal, they appealed to Rome, which took the fateful step of responding favorably and sending delegates to Hannibal. But he pressed on with the blockade of the city, which fell to him after a savage eight months' siege (219). The Romans' demand to the Carthaginian government that he should be handed over to them was inevitably refused, and the sequel was the Second Punic War (218–201).

Cnaeus and Publius Cornelius Scipio (the uncle and father of the elder Scipio Africanus) moved against Saguntum in 217, and it fell to them some five years later, thereupon initiating a coinage inscribed (in Iberian) ARS(-A,-ESKEN), subsequently replaced by bilingual pieces which also bear the name of Saguntum in Latin. During the civil war between the rebel Quintus Sertorius and the governmental forces of Quintus Caecilius Metellus and Pompey the Great, Saguntum was one of the few eastern centers to resist the insurgent forces; when, however, Pompey, forcing the Ebro, marched down to its walls, Sertorius defiantly occupied the place (75), until his murder two or three years later.

Under Augustus Saguntum became a citizen *municipium,* issuing coins with this designation in the time of Tiberius (AD 14–37), if not earlier. The city was noted for its grain, a brand of fig, and a type of pottery (including *amphorae* found stacked on a vast refuse heap [the Monte Testaccio] in Rome). The German invasions of the fifth century left its buildings mostly in ruins, to which it owed its medieval name Murbiter, Murviedro (*murum vetus,* old wall).

Excavations on the slope of the fortress have uncovered traces of a forum and theater (of the first century AD), accommodating 10,000 spectators; a circus (of second-century date) between the hill and the river had similar accommodation. There are also remains attributed to Temples of Diana and Venus, and sections of an aqueduct. The Roman inscriptions discovered in the city have now been collected.

Saida *see* Sidon

St. Albans *see* Verulamium

Saint-Bertrand-de-Comminges (Lugdunum Convenarum) *see* Lugdunum

Saint-Denis-lès-Martel *see* Uxellodunum

Saint Remy-de-Provence *see* Glanum

Salamis. A rocky island of thirty-six square miles in the Aegean Sea between the west coast of Attica and the east coast of the Megarid, enclosing the wide, lagoon-like bay of Eleusis that is linked with the Saronic Gulf by narrow straits on either side. Neolithic and Bronze Age (Mycenaean) remains have been found. Salamis, according to Homer, was the birthplace of the heroes Ajax and Teucer, the sons of Telamon.

In early times the island was controlled first by Aegina, lying to its south, and later by Megara (*c* 600?). Soon afterward Solon, in a famous poem, urged his Athenian countrymen to capture Salamis, which they had apparently held briefly and lost, or had failed to take. Plutarch's assumption, however, that Solon's crusade was crowned by success seems erroneous, since the same writer reports elsewhere that the war continued until the intervention of five Spartan arbitrators, who decided in Athens' favor (560s?). It appears likely, however, that Athenian rule over the island was only established on a firm basis by Pisistratus, some decades later. The Athenians sent a batch of colonists. Hitherto the principal town had been on the west of the island, but these settlers built a new capital on a promontory at the base of Cape Tropaea (Kamatero [Punta] peninsula) on the east coast facing Attica; its harbor in Ambelaki Bay, overlooked by an acropolis, became vital for Athenian defence and commerce alike.

In 480 the water off Salamis was the scene of one of the historic battles of the Persian Wars. The fleet of the allied Greeks, under the command of the Spartan Eurybiades (advised by Themistocles the Athenian), lay off the island's chief town, while the fleet of the Persian king Xerxes I (including powerful Phoenician and Greek [Ionian] squadrons) was stationed at Phaleron, one of the ports of Athens which he had occupied. Apparently closing the western strait by the stationing of a flotilla (although recent research has questioned this, suggesting that it was too narrow and shallow at the time to provide an escape route), the Persians landed troops under cover of darkness on the island of Psyttaleia (Ayios Yeoryios or Lipsokoutali) near the eastern end of the strait, and moved in their fleet through the narrows at dawn; it is disputed, however, whether the subsequent battle was precipitated by the Persians making this move, or by the Greeks coming out to a position across the channel entrance. Although more than a thousand ships strong, the Persian fleet was worsted by the three hundred and eighty vessels of the Greeks, whose ramming cast it into disarray in the cramped space; the Phoenician ships which constituted such an important element in the Persian force, being lighter than those of their enemies (contrary to a subsequent Greek tradition), would have fared better in the open sea. A decisive victory had been won by the Greeks; the first prize for valor was awarded to the Aeginetans and the second to the Athenians. What was left of the Persian fleet—though it still remained numerically superior—was ordered to return to the Hellespont (Dardanelles), where Xerxes joined it by land. Although the land battle of Plataea was still to come in the following year, the Persian fleet did not attempt to reverse the outcome of Salamis at sea.

In 318 the Macedonian Cassander, one of the successors of Alexander the Great, took the island from the Athenians and planted settlers. Demetrius I Poliorcetes (the Besieger) won it back for Athens and drove out the colonists in favor of Athenians, but Salamis retained a Macedonian garrison until 230/29, when Aratus of Sicyon, on behalf of the Achaean League, returned it to Athens for renewed colonization. The modern capital has been moved back to the western side of the island at Koulouri.

Trophies for the famous victory were set up on the islands of Salamis and Psyttaleia. Walls of the principal Athenian town of Salamis (on its east coast) have survived, enclosing the agora at the head of the harbor in Ambelaki Bay (where the sea level has risen five feet since ancient times). Small forts are to be seen along the coast. There were sanctuaries of Artemis, Ajax, Athena Sciras (after a hero named Scirus) and the divine hero Cychreus—who killed or bred a serpent, or was a serpent himself. In connection with these shrines, according to Strabo, the island capital had at one time been called both Sciras and Cychreia, as well as bearing the name Pityussa, from *pitys,* pine tree.

Salamis. The principal city of the island of Cyprus, situated beside its east coast (five miles north of the modern Famagusta), where an acropolis standing on a plateau overlooked a wide sandy bay containing a natural harbor—now wholly silted up—at the mouth of the river Pediaeus or Pedias (Pidias). This town succeeded an important Bronze Age (Mycenaean) settlement at Enkomi (a mile and a half inland but connected to the estuary at that time by a navigable channel), at about the end of the first quarter of the eleventh century BC, to which finds of a tomb and fragments of pottery can be dated. According to Greek mythology, the founder of the city was Teucer, son of Telamon, king of the island of the same name off the coast of Attica; the first settlers are believed to have been Mycenaean refugees.

Magnificent finds from royal tombs of the mid- and later eighth and seventh centuries BC strongly recall Homeric burial descriptions, and probably owe this character to the knowledge of the *Iliad* which was spreading at the time. A place bearing the name of Sillua or Sillume, mentioned among tributaries of the Assyrian King Esarhaddon (672), seems to be identifiable with this Salamis. Its King Euelthon (*c* 560–525) claimed to be the ruler of the entire island, and inaugurated the issue of Salaminian coinage, inscribed with his name in syllabic script.

After Cyprus had come under the control of the Persians (545), Euelthon's grandson Gorgos refused to join the Ionian revolt (499/8) and was overthrown by his brother Onesilus, whose defeat outside the city (497), as Herodotus recounts, enabled Persian domination to be restored. In the waters off Salamis, and on land nearby, the Athenians won a double victory over Persia's Phoenician and Cilician forces in 450/449. The most powerful of all the city's kings was Euagoras I (410–374); he inaugurated a Hellenic revival and, although compelled to submit to Persia, remained a friend of the Athenians, whose orator Isocrates devoted a speech to his posthumous praise (*c* 365). Salamis provided ships to Alexander the Great at the siege of Tyre (332) and served as his mint. In 306 it was the scene of a great naval battle between his successors Demetrius I Poliorcetes (the Besieger) and Ptolemy I Soter of Egypt, in which the former was victorious, although not long afterward the island passed into Egyptian hands.

At first Salamis was the capital of this Egyptian Cyprus, but in 200, owing to the silting of its harbor, the seat of government was moved to Paphos instead. Nevertheless Salamis continued to flourish, and still did so after Roman annexation (58), despite initial difficulty (recorded by Cicero) in repaying a Roman loan with an annual interest rate of 48 percent. A Christian community was founded by St. Paul and Barnabas, himself a Cypriot, whose reputed tomb is to be seen in the neighborhood. Under Vespasian (AD 69–79) an earthquake severely damaged the city, which also suffered severe devastation in the time of Trajan, during a large-scale revolt organized by the large local Jewish community (116–17) and forming part of a wider rebellion of the Diaspora.

Partially destroyed by further earthquakes in 332 and 342, Salamis was rebuilt by Constantius II, and under the name of Constantia resumed its position as capital of Cyprus, serving as its metropolitan episcopal see.

Remains of earlier Salamis are so far lacking. But an unusually elaborate, multiple system of later fortifications has come to light. Within these walls, the remains of a Greco-Roman agora display rows of shops behind two long colonnades; the agora is flanked by a temple of Olympian Zeus, who is depicted on coins of an Augustan proconsul (*c* 15 BC). Beside the sea, a colonnaded gymnasium of Hellenistic date, remodelled on a grandiose scale in Roman times, was shattered in the earthquakes of the fourth century AD, and subsequently rebuilt as a bathing establishment, of which the installations, including large halls with niches decorated with mosaics, are well preserved. Much of the stone work employed for this purpose came from the theater, which, twice remodelled, had possessed accommodation for 15,000 spectators. An extensive reservoir was supplied by a thirty-mile-long aqueduct. In the neighborhood are the remains of a large basilica, with three aisles on either side of its nave, which St. Epiphanius started to build during his bishopric (376–403) but left uncompleted at the time of his death.

Salduba *see* Caesaraugusta

Salernum *see* Picentia

Salonae, later Salona (Solin). A coastal city of Dalmatia (Yugoslavia). Salonae was an important, partially Hellenized, fortress of the tribe of the Delmatae, based on a harbor in Manios (Kaštelanski) Bay. Occupied by the Romans, it served as a base for Lucius Caecilius Metellus (later Delmaticus) in his operations against the Delmatae (118–117 BC) but subsequently, after the establishment of the province of Illyricum, had to be recaptured by Gaius Cosconius in 78/77.

A local community of Roman traders (*conventus civium Romanorum*) sided with Julius Caesar in his civil war against Pompey the Great, whose admiral Marcus Octavius they defeated (48), gaining promotion to the status of a Roman veteran colony, under the titles of Martia Julia, either shortly afterward or after the Dalmatian campaigns of Octavian (the future Augustus) in 33; there may, at one time, have been two adjacent sister communities. When the province of Illyricum was divided into Lower and Upper provinces, Pannonia and Dalmatia, in *c* AD 9, Salonae became the capital of the latter, prospering rapidly as the focal point of a communication system which included not only roads parallel to the coast and but also routes leading into the interior. The colony was probably reinforced by Claudius (41–54). During the Marcomannic Wars of Marcus Aurelius (*c* 170) its fortifications were rebuilt by legionary detachments.

Under Diocletian (284–305), who was born in the vicinity, and built a palace for his retirement nearby (*see* below), the city flourished as never before, and gained even greater importance in the years that followed, when it became a leading Christian episcopal center. After the empire had been divided into eastern and western halves, Dalmatia belonged to the latter, but on the death of the western emperor Honorius (423) the eastern government of Theodosius II occupied Salonae, and in the following year dispatched an army from its port to place the infant Valentinian III on the western throne at Ravenna. Subsequently it became the capital of the semi-independent princedom of Marcellinus (454, 461), inherited after his murder (468) by his nephew Julius Nepos, who after a brief tenure of the purple at Ravenna (in 474–75, when he sent away his imperial predecessor Glycerius to become bishop of Salonae), retreated to the same city in his turn, and lived on there for five years, during the last four of which he was the last reigning Roman emperor in the west (although his suzerainty over Italy was only nominal). After his death, Salonae passed into the hands of the *de facto* ruler of Italy, the Herulian (German) King Odoacer.

The ancient city possessed an elongated shape referred to by the poet Lucan. Remains of the forum, pagan basilica, local senate house (*curia*), several public baths, a theater and an amphitheater (built into the defensive perimeter) can be seen. The city also contained early Christian churches of considerable size and grandeur, including a three-aisled cathedral built *c* 400 by bishop Sympherius and his nephew Hesychius, and another basilica of about the same date at Manastirine outside the city, which also possessed three aisles and incorporated several earlier memorial chapels.

Diocletian, after his abdication, lived for his remaining eleven years, at the huge mansion-fortress he had built at Spalatum (Split, Spalato), situated on a promontory three miles from Salonae (Solin is now a suburb of Split). This remarkable blend of civilian and military architecture combined the public rooms of an imperial palace, the personal quarters of a grandiose Dalmatian villa or commander-in-chief's residence, and the defences of a stronghold encircled by a wall studded by towers. A large avenue passes through a colonnaded atrium (flanked by an octagonal mausoleum) to a domed vestibule leading onward to the throne room (Aula Palatina), of which the three-bayed, pedimented, arched columnar facade is still to be seen. The south front of the Aula, flanked by two square towers, consisted of a huge windowed gallery overlooking the Adriatic Sea. Under the threat of Avar and Slav invasions in the seventh century the population of Salonae retreated within the walls of the palace, which became the nucleus of the medieval town of Spalato.

Salonica *see* Thessalonica

Samaria— from Shmer, 'watchtower'—later Sebaste (Shomeron, Sabastiya). A city of Samaritis (Samaria, now attached to Israel). Originally an unfortified village, following the division of Solomon's empire into two kingdoms (Israel and Judah) Samaria was refounded by Omri (*c* 882–871) as capital of his Israelite state. It stood on an isolated summit that descended steeply on three sides, but possessed access to a spring. The site overlooked the main inland highway from north to south, and served as an observation port to keep watch over the plains of Sharon and Jezreel (Esdraelon).

After sharing the vicissitudes of the rest of the country, Samaria was captured by Alexander the Great (332) and settled by numerous Macedonian colonists who employed the hilltop as their acropolis, whereupon much of the former population, comprising heterodox Jews known as Samaritans, emigrated to Shechem. Following further changes of ownership Samaria was conquered and destroyed by the Jewish (Hasmonaean) ruler John I Hyrcanus (108), annexed by Pompey the Great (63), rebuilt by Aulus Gabinius (57), and subsequently reunited with the Judaean kingdom of Herod the Great.

In 27 Herod began its reconstruction on a massive scale, under the name of Sebaste (i.e. Augusta, after his patron Augustus). The work was completed in 25, the year from which the city dated a new era. Its ruling class was Hellenized, and prospered from the fertile surrounding district, famous for its fruit; nearby Herod founded the Five Villages (Pente Komai, Fondaqumia), settled by 6,000 colonists who could be called up when needed, for military service. Although overshadowed by Vespasian's foundation Neapolis (Shechem), Sebaste became a Roman colony in the time of Septimius Severus (193–211)— from whom it adopted the titles Lucia Septimia—and continued to coin for a time thereafter. During the later empire it formed part of the province of Palaestina Prima.

Its principal gateway was flanked by two towers, which still survive; and additional circular towers marked the two-and-a-half-mile perimeter of Herod's fortifications. Inside the walls were a forum (served by an aqueduct), a basilica of the second century AD (built over a Gabinian or Herodian structure), and colonnaded streets; and traces of a stadium and theater have been uncovered on the slopes.

On the western end of the summit stood a temple of Rome and Augustus (rebuilt under Septimius Severus) over the debris of an Israelite palace and Hellenistic acropolis. Traces of a temple of Persephone (Kore) have been located nearby, and her rape by Hades is depicted on the city's coinage.

Samarobriva or Samarabriva, later Civitas Ambianorum or Ambiani (Amiens). A city in Gallia Belgica (Somme, northern France). The Celtic name of the town means 'bridge over the Samara' (Somme); it was the principal township of the tribe of the Ambiani. In 55 BC, during his Gallic War, Julius Caesar held a council of leading Gauls at Samarobriva, and during the following year left Marcus Crassus and a legion in charge of the hostages, grain, archives and heavy baggage that were stored there, himself spending the winter of 54/53—with three legions—in neighboring camps, which he subsequently employed as bases for operations against the Nervii and Menapii.

The location of the original settlement of the Ambiani is uncertain. But during the first century AD, if not earlier, a Roman town was built on flat ground beside the left (south) bank of the river; later it was extended in size, and became an important communications center at the meeting point of four roads. After a German invasion (AD 256), it was equipped with a wall surrounding a considerably diminished perimeter, and in the fourth century, attached to the province of Belgica Secunda, the place became an important military fortress behind the threatened Rhine frontier, under the name of Civitas Ambianorum or Ambiani. Cloth and armaments industries flourished. It was beside one of the city gates that St. Martin of Tours, an officer of the military garrison, encountered the beggar to whom, according to a famous story, he gave his cloak. Ambiani was the birthplace of the usurper Magnentius (350–53), who set up a new mint in the city, and it was there also that Valentinian I proclaimed his son Gratian emperor in 367. The fortifications succumbed to another German assault in 407.

It has now been possible to reconstruct the main features of the town plan of Roman Samarobriva-Ambiani. It contained at least ten major streets running from north to south, and nine or more from east to west. Substructures of an amphitheater of the first century AD have also come to light, as well as a bathhouse and traces of river harbor installations. Dedications reflect the cults of local deities, including Veriugodumnus, and the *Passion of St. Firmin*—who brought Christianity to the city—mentions temples of Jupiter and Mercury. Three of the gates of the third century rampart can be located with a measure of certainty.

Samnium. A mountainous region in the southern Apennines of central Italy. Its inhabitants, known to the Greeks and Romans as the Samnites, probably called themselves by a name based on the root 'Safin'—and were regarded as an offshoot of the Sabines. The longest inscription of their Oscan language (of Indo-European structure) is the Tabula Agonensis, a list of deities found near Bovianum Vetus (Boiano?—not, as was once thought, Pietrabbondante, where a large town has been uncovered). A warlike and relatively primitive people, they dwelt in towns and villages grouped in four tribal units or cantons; the cantons were loosely linked together in a confederation, which appointed a commander-in-chief in time of war.

Common fear of the Gauls brought the Samnites into an alliance with Rome in 354 BC, but three unsuccessful wars against its armies soon followed. The First (343–341), of which the historical authenticity has been treated with undue scepticism, gave the Romans control of northern Campania. The Second (326–304), despite a lull after a massive victory by the Samnites at the Caudine Forks (321), finally eliminated them altogether from southern Campania, Lucania and Apulia. The Third War (298–290), despite a Samnite alliance with Gauls and Umbrians, was virtually won in 295 by the Romans' success at Sentinum (near Sassoferrato); this engagement decided the fate of all peninsular Italy. Nevertheless the Samnites were able to offer some help to the invasions of King Pyrrhus of Epirus (280–275) and Hannibal (in the Second Punic War 218–201), and played a prominent part in the Italian rebellion known as the Social War (91–87). Subsequently, they supported the successors of Marius in their civil war against Sulla, who butchered them during and after his victory at the Colline Gate (82).

But their name was perpetuated at Rome through the gladiators known as 'Samnites,' who were generally regarded as the prototypes of all types of Roman gladiators. They wore a heavy, magnificent armor that was said to have been derived from a uniform worn by Samnite warriors during their Second War against Rome, after large quantities of this equipment had been captured by the Capuans, allies of the Romans, in 308 BC; and then gladiators at Rome wore the same armor when the first Games of this type were instituted there in 264. *See also* Beneventum, Venusia.

Samos. A mountainous island measuring twenty-seven by fourteen miles, less than two miles from Cape Mycale at the southern extremity of Ionia (western Asia Minor). According to Strabo the earliest population belonged to the same race as the inhabitants of Caria (southwestern Asia Minor), and gave the island the name of Parthenia. It was occupied in Neolithic times and during the Bronze Age, and at about the end of the first millennium received Ionian colonists—supposedly from Epidaurus in the Argolid, under the leadership of a certain Procles. Their Samian settlement, now Pithagorion, situated beside a cove on the south side of the island, later became one of the twelve cities of Ionia.

Deriving rapidly increasing importance—in rivalry with Miletus—not only from the fertility of their land (which thus gained the admiring names of Anthemousa or Anthemis, Phyllas, Melamphylus and Dryoussa) but also from their position as the terminal of the all-weather Aegean crossing—which provided access to the trade routes across Asia Minor—the Samians constructed a fleet of warships (*c* 704), gained control of a strip of mainland territory, and sent an explorer Colaeus to make a pioneer voyage through the Straits of Gibraltar into the Atlantic (*c* 638). Samos possessed a trading quarter at Naucratis (Kom Gieif) in Egypt, and its colonies extended from the Aegean islands to Thrace, southeast Asia Minor, and southwest Italy.

After the removal of the tyrant Demoteles during the sixth century, the island was ruled by a landed aristocracy, but *c* 540 this in turn was overthrown by the exceptionally forceful Polycrates, who gave the city a new deep-sea harbor, designed according to advanced engineering ideas, and converted his state into a major expansionist naval power. The philosopher Pythagoras (who left it, *c* 531) was a native of Samos, the poets Ibycus and Anacreon made it their home, and it produced outstanding architects, sculptors, ivory workers and gem engravers.

The Samian enginner Mandrocles bridged the Thracian Bosphorus for Darius I of Persia (513). Later, however, Samos joined the Ionian revolt against the Persians; but its ships deserted the rebel cause at Lade (495), and fought for Xerxes I at Salamis. Thereafter, it joined the Delian League under Athenian control, as a privileged independent ally contributing ships, but seceded in 441/440 when the Athenians backed Miletus in a quarrel between the two cities and was suppressed by an Athenian fleet after a long siege. Nevertheless, throughout the Peloponnesian War, Samos was one of the Athenians' strongest supporters, sheltering their democrats during Athens' oligarchic revolution (411); this loyalty earned it Athenian citizenship in 405, but the island fell to Lysander the Spartan in the following year. After a further brief period of Athenian occupation (394–390) it returned to Persian rule (386), but was recaptured in 365 by the Athenians, who planted colonists.

During the Hellenistic period Samos belonged in turn to different successors of Alexander the Great, and then, in succession, to the Ptolemies (who used it as a naval base), the Seleucids (259–246), the Ptolemies again, Philip V of Macedonia, the Rhodians, and the kingdom of Pergamum (189), subsequently joining the revolt of Aristonicus (132) and campaigns of Mithridates VI of Pontus (88) both directed against Rome. The Samians suffered from the plundering of the Roman governor Verres (82), from raids by pirates (*c* 70–67), and from thefts by Antony (39). But their autonomy and works of art were restored by Octavian (Augustus), who spent the winter of 31/30 on the island and in 21/20 announced its 'freedom.' This privilege was terminated by Vespasian in AD 70. Nevertheless, local coinage continued until Gallienus (253–68); some of the pieces bear inscriptions boasting that the Samians were the 'first of Ionia.'

The coins lay special stress on the goddess Hera and throw varied light on the appearance of her sanctuary (the Heraeum), famous throughout the Greek world, which stood four miles west of the island capital, on marshy ground at the mouth of the river Imbrasus (formerly Parthenius); the goddess was believed to have been born on the riverbank. The temple is much better understood after recent comprehensive excavations. On its site, eight successive strata of prehistoric remains (from *c* 2500 BC) have been distinguished. A tenth-century altar was followed by seven more down to 700, when the festal area to the south was flooded by a branch of the Imbrasus. A temple of eighth century date—the first to have been surrounded by columns—was followed, after a second and worse flood of *c* 660 had destroyed the building and its altar, by a larger structure, the earliest to display a double row of columns across the front. Next, in *c* 540/530, the creation of a new, colossal shrine measuring 290 by 150 feet, the earliest, as far as we know, to employ the Ionic architectural order, was said to have been entrusted to the architects Rhoecus and Theodorus (the hollow casting of statues in bronze was also believed to be their invention). In front of the building stood a stepped altar with a sculptured parapet adjoining the sacred *lygos* ('chaste') tree, and the precinct was approached by a monumental statue-lined Sacred Way.

Thirty years later, after the temple had been burned down in a Persian raid, a replacement was projected (it is possible that this, rather than the earlier edifice, was the project with which Rhoecus was connected). It was to be 365 feet long and 179 feet wide, the largest sacred building ever seen in Greek lands, but although work continued down to Roman times, the task was never completed. A lately discovered coin of *c* 180 BC displays the earliest known representation of an antique formless image of Hera which stood in these successive shrines, and still survived in the time of Pausanias (second century AD). Every year, to celebrate the marriage of the goddess to Zeus, this image was ceremonially bathed and carried out of the town by an armed escort—an occasion which had enabled Polycrates, in the sixth century BC, to carry out his coup while the population were engaged in this procession.

The ancient city of Samos nearby lay beneath an acropolis (the prehistoric Astypalaea) which contained Polycrates' fortified palace. This no longer survives, though a seated statue of his father Aiaces has now been found at the main ascent. A wall of the same period enclosed the city and harbor, of which the ancient 400-yard mole still serves as the foundation of the modern pier. A water supply from the Agiades spring reached the port by way of a tunnel 1,140 yards long; this masterpiece of ancient engineering and surveying was designed for Polycrates by Eupalinus of Megara.

Beside the harbor was a Hellenistic agora, and on the hillside the remains of a small theater can be seen. The Roman city stood a little to the southwest. A circular building with a cruciform interior may be a baptistery or martyr's shrine belonging to an adjacent Christian basilica. Another basilica (*c* AD 500) replaced the ruinous shrine of Hera, and there are remains of a Christian funerary building with a vaulted roof; partly cut out of the rock. Unlike the ancient chief town of the island, the modern capital Vathy is on the north coast.

Samosata, Samosate (Samsat). A city on the west (right) bank of the Euphrates in Commagene, on the northern border of Syria (now southeastern Turkey). The place guarded an important crossing of the river on a principal thoroughfare from west to east, and was a station on another route running from Damascus, Palmyra and Sura up to Lesser Armenia and the Euxine (Black) Sea.

Samosata was inhabited from the sixth millennium BC onward. When Commagene became independent in 162, the town was founded by King Samos as his royal capital (*c* 150). After the Roman annexation of the kingdom by Tiberius (AD 17), Strabo comments on the fertile, though limited, territory of the city, and indicates that it possessed a bridge over the Euphrates (which now flows five hundred yards away). The kingdom was revived (38) but reannexed by Vespasian (72), whereupon Samosata, compelled to acquiesce, assumed the name of Flavia, inaugurated a new civic era, and became the capital of an autonomous Commagenian religious union (*koinon*) within the Roman province of Syria. It was the birthplace of one of the leading authors of the age, the popular philosopher and satirist Lucian (*c* 120–*c* 180), who wrote in Greek, though his mother tongue was probably Aramaic.

When the eastern empire was overrun by the Sassanian Persian Sapor (Shapur) I, Samosata's garrison was withdrawn (*c* 256) and the city was plundered, but then Valerian chose it as his headquarters and place of refuge before falling into Persian hands (260). After his capture, the quartermaster general Macrianus lodged himself and his staff there in an attempt to rally and reorganize the army, setting up his sons Macrianus the Younger and Quietus as emperors. During the later empire Samosata was capital of the province of Euphratensis.

The eastern side of the town is dominated by a mound that is largely of prehistoric origin. Soundings elsewhere have located a city gate; and halls, storerooms and baths are revealed by excavations. A coin shows the figure of a seated city goddess (Tyche) within a temple.

Samothrace, Samothrake. A mountainous island in the northeastern Aegean, already inhabited in the Neolithic and Bronze Ages. According to one Greek mythological tale Dardanus, son of Zeus and Electra and ancestor of the Trojans, came from Samothrace. It owed its name, however, to colonization from Samos in the later sixth century BC, although an earlier Greek settlement (*c* 700) from Aeolis (northwestern Asia Minor) has also, less plausibly, been suggested. The settlers joined a native Thracian population, which—to judge from Greek inscriptions employing a non-Greek language—seems to have been peacefully absorbed. The Greek foundation (Palaeopolis) occupied the shoulder of a ridge, beside a river mouth, on the north coast of the island. A naval power possessing territory on the mainland, Samothrace sent a contingent of ships to the battle of Salamis (480), and then formed part of the Athenian Leagues in the fifth and fourth centuries BC. During the Hellenistic period it frequently changed hands. After the battle of Pydna (168) King Perseus of Macedonia sought refuge on the island in vain. It was recognized by the Romans as 'free.'

Remains of the archaic (polygonal) and Hellenistic wall of the principal town are still to be seen. But Samothrace was above all renowned for its sanctuary and Mysteries of the Great Gods, extending between the three streams of the river in the neighborhood of the city, from which, however, it appears to have been independent. The Greeks, on their arrival, found fertility worship already established—venerating Axierus, Mother of the Rocks—which they took over and developed on their own lines, giving her the name of Demeter. She had a subordinate mate, Cadmilus (Hermes), and was assisted by twin fertility gods of Phrygian (?) origin, the Cabiri (Dioscuri), who were little mentioned because their wrath was considered implacable; they were underworld deities, like Axiocersus (Hades) and Axiocersa (Persephone) who were likewise associated with the cult. To judge from the numeous lamps that have been unearthed, the elaborate initiation ceremonies evidently took place by night.

Pilgrims from all parts of the Greek world attended the Mysteries, which first gained significant importance in the fourth century. Lysander of Sparta (d. 395) was among those who were initiated. Plato and Aristotle mention the Samothracian rites, and it was while attending them that Philip II of Macedonia first had a sight of his future wife Olympias, the mother of Alexander the Great. But the great days of the shrine came under the Hellenistic monarchs, who endowed it with lavish gifts and buildings. Alexander's successor Lysimachus, and then Ptolemies and Seleucids, joined the ranks of the initiates, and so did the learned Varro and Julius Caesar's father-in-law Piso; for the Romans were specially interested in the alleged Samothracian origin of Dardanus, the mythical ancestor of the Trojans, since they claimed Trojan descent for themselves. Another visitor to the sanctuary was Hadrian (AD 117–38). It suffered from an earthquake *c* 200, and its long life was brought to an end after the empire had become Christian (375).

In the heart of the precinct was a walled enclosure with a monumental entrance (*propylon*), of which details have now been published. Recent excavations have clarified the construction, in five sections, of the religious zone. A pre-Greek rock altar to the Great Mother was situated in a sector that later contained the Initiation Hall (Anaktoron, *c* 500). Beside the hall is a Rotunda presented by Queen Arsinoe II, wife of Ptolemy II Philadelphus of Egypt, the largest known circular building anywhere in the Greek world (289–281). Further up the river bank was the unroofed Altar Court (Temenos), dedicated by Alexander's half-brother Philip III Arrhidaeus (330); beside it can be seen a Hall of Votive Offerings and a large building, the Hieron, *c* 325 BC, remodelled AD 200, probably employed for the final stages of the initiation rites. Nearby on a hillside are the traces of a theater, above which stood the sculptured figure of the Victory of Samothrace, a Hellenistic masterpiece (*c* 190 BC?) now in the Louvre. The sacred area was approached from the south by a monumental, triple decorated entrance and façade (Propylon), which was the gift of Ptolemy II Philadelphus and has now been described in detail; and at the northern extremity of the precinct a stuccoed, two-aisled, limestone portico (Stoa), 330 feet long, dating at least in part from the later fourth century BC, provided accommodation for visitors.

Samsun *see* Amisus

Samsun Dağı *see* Mycale

San Pantaleo *see* Motya

Santa Maria Capua Vetere *see* Capua

Santa Maria di Falleri (Falerii Novi) *see* Falerii Veteres

Santa Marinella *see* Punicum

Santa Severa *see* Pyrgi

Santiponce *see* Italica

Santorin(i) *see* Thera

Şar *see* Comana (Cappadocia)

Saragossa *see* Caesaraugusta

Sardes, Sardeis (Sart). The principal city of Lydia (western Asia Minor), forty-two miles inland at the foot of Mount Tmolus (Boz Dağ), of which a spur constitutes its acropolis; this overlooks the plain of the river Hermus (Gediz) and its tributary the Pactolus (Sart Çayı), which flows down from the mountain.

Considerable finds of late Mycenaean, Sub-Mycenaean and early Greek pottery (*c* 1200–900 BC) do something to corroborate Herodotus' assertion that Greek immigrants (descendants of Heracles) established a dynasty at Sardes.

Thereafter, according to Callisthenes, it was occupied by two successive waves of Cimmerian invaders and then by Lycians, and subsequently became the capital of the powerful Lydian Kingdom (*c* 680–547/4)—whose monarchs issued the world's earliest coinage there, made of pale gold (electrum) washed down by the Pactolus. After the downfall of Croesus, Sardes became the principal city of the territories of Asia Minor dominated by his conquerors the Persians, whom it served as the terminus of their Royal Road from Iran to the Aegean; a nearby 'Pyramid Tomb' is almost certainly the monument of a Persian. The town was captured and burned by the Ionian Greeks (with the help of Athenian and Eretrian troops) during their revolt (498), but after its recovery by the Persians, Xerxes I assembled his troops there before crossing into Europe (480). The Spartan Agesilaus defeated the Persian governor Tissaphernes outside Sardes (395), but it was there, too, that the Persian monarch Artaxerxes II Memnon dictated the King's Peace (Peace of Antalcidas) in 387. Both the Lydian and Persian periods of Sardes have yielded important and varied archaeological discoveries, especially on the acropolis and in residential quarters and cemeteries.

In 334 the city was occupied by Alexander the Great, who employed it as a mint; and in 282 it became part of the empire of Seleucus I Nicator. After the usurper Achaeus had proclaimed himself king at Sardes (214), Antiochus III the Great besieged and destroyed it in the following year, but reconstruction on Greek lines followed. The Sardians passed to the kingdom of Pergamum *c* 180, and then, in 133, to the Roman province of Asia. Despite a serious earthquake in AD 17—in which their city suffered worse than any other—it increased in size and prosperity, serving first as the capital of a district (*conventus*) and then, in the later empire, as capital of a new province of Asia. After possessing a Jewish community from at least the fifth century BC (which may have numbered between 5,000 and 10,000 in imperial times), it was listed in the *Book of Revelation* as an important Christian center and one of the Seven Churches of Asia. Its coins under the Principate celebrate the Asian Games and (under Septimius Severus and his sons, AD 193–217) other public Games described as the Philadelpheia, Chrysanthina and Koraia Aktia. Other pieces honor a number of heroes, and Queen Omphale of Lydia, in addition to Zeus Lydius (whose great altar is shown), Men Askenus, Apollo Lycius; while the temples of Aphrodite Paphia and Artemis-Persephone (Kore) appear not only on the city's coinage but on other issues bearing the name of the League of Ionian Cities.

It was in the third century BC that work had been begun on this lofty temple of Artemis in the Pactolus valley; it was converted to the Roman imperial cult when the twin shrines (*cellae*) into which it had become divided were dedicated to Antoninus Pius and Faustina the Elder (*c* AD 140). At the foot of the acropolis—of which a marble bastion dates from the time of Antiochus III the Great (223–187)—are remains of a theater and stadium dating back to early Hellenistic times. After the earthquake in AD 17 imperial funds were made available for a comprehensive replanning of the city, which took place over a period of many years. The central unit of an ambitious combined gymnasium, athletics school (*palaestra*) and bathing establishment was completed in 166 and dedicated to Lucius Verus. These baths included an elaborately decorated, two-storeyed marble court, dedicated in 211 (and now restored). A building that was originally a pagan basilica (of the first century AD) was later modified and employed as a synagogue from *c* 200 to 616.

A painted underground tomb contained the remains of Flavius Chrysanthius, described as a 'painter from life' and director of the local munitions factory under Diocletian (284–305) or Constantine I the Great (324–37). A replanning of the city in 400 involved the construction of new fortifications surrounding a more restricted perimeter; these walls, and a gate and towers, have now been studied, and so has a fortified bridge across the Pactolus. A Christian church of the same date, with two apses, has also been almost completely preserved, as well as a much larger church erected during the sixth century. A row of buildings beside the gymnasium included restaurants and paint-and hardware-shops, apparently owned, in some cases, by Jews and Christians. Recent excavations have uncovered two large residential complexes that testify to an upper-class community at the peak of its wealth in the years before 500.

Sardinia, in Greek Ichnussa, from *ichnos* footstep; because of its shape (suggests Pausanias) or, according to a recent theory, because it was a stepping-stone on early trade routes. Sardinia is the second largest island in the Mediterranean, less mountainous and more fertile than its northern neighbor Corsica (but also more unhealthy). Recent research has carried back the island's history to the Lower Palaeolithic Age. As regards Neolithic times (from the sixth millennium BC)—among other spectacular discoveries—neutron activation analysis has confirmed the presence of Sardinian obsidian in northern Italy and southern France. In the Bronze Age, Sardinia was fully in touch with mainstreams of eastern Mediterranean progress—as fragments of one hundred and fifty Mycenaean vases at a single site (Antigori, Sarroch) now suggest—and entered on a particularly brilliant phase, during which its role as a leading element in contemporary culture was displayed by nearly 7,000 stone towers (*nuraghi*) and highly individual bronzework. Reaching their peak at a later period, in the ninth and eighth centuries BC, these artistic achievements exercized an influence—of which the full magnitude is only now beginning to be appreciated—on the rising cities of northwestern Etruria.

The Sardinians also gained great prosperity from the interest in their metals, and especially in their copper, displayed by the Phoenicians, and their inheritors the Carthaginians. Remarkable evidence of Phoenician-Carthaginian settlement has recently come to light on the island of Sant'Antioco off the southwestern shore of the island, where more thatn 1,500 stone steles, ranging in date between the sixth and first centuries BC, have been discovered.

The Greeks sought to rival the Carthaginian presence by an abortive settlement of Ionians and Messenians at Olbia on the northeast coast (Hellenized earlier, according to Greek mythology, by Iolaus, to whom the nuraghic culture was misleadingly attributed; other mythical visitors included Sardus the son of Heracles, Norax the son of Hermes, Daedalus, Aristaeus, and various Trojans). In *c* 550 the Carthaginian commander Malchus, despite vigorous native opposition, annexed the more productive parts of Sardinia, which were held until 238. But then the Romans, fresh from their victory in the First Punic War, took advantage of a rebellion of Carthaginian mercenaries to annex the island, converting it into a province (after bloody campaigns against the tribesmen) in combination with Corsica (227).

The Romans, who disliked the Sardinians' character, exacted considerable supplies of grain and tribute from the island, despite repeated uprisings and brigandage (which 4,000 Jewish ex-slaves were sent to put down in AD 19, allegedly in the hope that the climate would put an end to them). There were Roman *municipia* at Caralis (Cagliari) and Uselis. The latter city was the probable mint of a coin portraying 'Sardus Pater' and Marcus Atius Balbus, the uncle of Octavian (Augustus). Under Hadrian (AD 117–38) the place became a colony, although this rank had first been conferred on Turris Libisonis (Porto Torres, probably *c* 46–40 BC). The iron and silver mines of the island continued to be worked, and it was used by the imperial government as a place of exile.

In the later empire Sardinia and Corsica became separate provinces. In AD 429 Sardinia was occupied by the Vandals, while they were crossing over from Europe to north Africa. When the eastern emperor Leo I and his western colleague Anthemius organized an expedition against the Vandals in 468, it was reoccupied by Marcellinus, but after the failure of the campaign the Vandals returned. *See also* Caralis.

Sarmizeget(h)usa. The name of a Dacian township and then a Roman city (on a different site) in western Transylvania (Rumania). Sarmizegethusa Regia was one of the principal fortresses (and probably the capital) of Decebalus, king of Dacia, who fought against Domitian (AD 85–89) and was conquered by Trajan in two wars (101/2, 105). This stronghold was at Grădiştea Muncelului in the Hateg valley, within the heart of the Sebesului Mountains (Transylvanian Alps), about five miles east of the Iron Gates Pass. Constructed upon four terraces rising to a citadel 3,937 feet above sea level, Sarmizegethusa Regia contained a huge calendrical sanctuary, which was employed to calculate an eighty-four year cycle, based on a three-hundred-and-sixty-day year. After the destruction of the place in Trajan's First Dacian War, and its subsequent garrisoning by a Roman legion, it was rebuilt by its inhabitants, but suffered final devastation in the same emperor's Second War, after which a legionary detachment was settled on the site as its garrion.

Subsequently in 108/110, Trajan founded the earliest Roman colony in Dacia, some thirty miles to the southwest, under the name of Colonia Dacica Sarmiget(h)usa, attested by an inscription. Settled by ex-soldiers, the new town became a customs station and the capital of the Roman province of Dacia. When Hadrian subdivided the province (118/19), it served as the capital of Upper Dacia, under the additional names of Ulpia Trajana Augusta. When Marcus Aurelius reunified all Dacian territory as a single unit and military command (168/9), Sarmizegethusa became the seat of its governor-general and the meeting place for the Council of the Three Dacias. Shortly afterward, however (*c* 170), the town was destroyed by the German tribe of the Marcomanni. Later, under Severus Alexander (222–35), it assumed the title 'metropolis,' indicating its position as the political, cultural and religious center of the country, which it retained thoughout the period of Roman occupation. Even after the evacuation of Dacia by Aurelian (271), the life of the former colony continued on a reduced scale, until an attack by the Huns (or perhaps an earthquake) caused its obliteration in the middle of the fifth century.

Trajan's town wall, flanked by two moats, stood between twelve and fifteen feet high. The governor's palace—where excavation continues—was adorned with wall paintings and grouped round two colonnaded courtyards, one of which contained an altar dedicated to Rome and the emperor. The office of the Augustales, the priests of the imperial cult—erected in the mid-second century, and reconstructed in the third—was modelled on the headquarters building of a legionary camp. A stone-paved forum, of which the walls have survived in places to a height of ten feet, was adjoined by a marble-faced basilica at the end of which a flight of steps led up to a heated room which was probably the city's council chamber (*curia*).

Outside the wall, excavations have revealed shrines of Nemesis, Mithras and the Syrian gods. The total number of temples at the place, of which traces survive, amounts to more than a dozen, including sanctuaries of Aesculapius (with Salus) and Liber Pater (Bacchus) revealed by recent investigations. An inscription—one of a great many that have been found at Roman Sarmizegethusa—invokes Jupiter Optimus, Maximus, Minerva, Mars Pater Gradivus, and probably Juno Regina, as well as other deities; it was found in an amphitheater of second-century date, with seating for 5,000 spectators. A gladiatorial school has also been identified. An imposing private mausoleum of the second century AD belonged to the Aurelii, a leading local family. Roman farms (*villae rusticae*) in the vicinity have yielded a rich assemblage of finds.

Sassoferrato *see* Sentinum

Satala (Sadak). A Roman stronghold on the Sadak Çayı, a tributary of the Lycus (Kelkit)—of which Satala is near the headwaters—within the territory of Orsene in Lesser Armenia (northeastern Turkey), which was incorporated by Vespasian into the province of Cappadocia (AD 72). The fortress of Satala stood on the sloping floor of a low-lying plain, surrounded by lofty hills. During his eastern wars Trajan, in 114, advanced to Satala, where he was joined by troops from Galatia, Paphlagonia and the Danubian area, and was brought gifts by monarchs, including the king of the Heniochi at the eastern end of the Black Sea. Roads from Satala led westward, northward and eastward and Trajan posted a legion there to control the northern sector of the imperial frontier.

A city which grew out of the civilian settlement (*canabae*) beside the legionary camp is first attested in 372, but probably dates back to before *c* 200, when it seems to have been granted the status of a colony and apparently possessed extensive territory. During the later empire Satala was the capital of the province of Armenia Prima and the seat of a bishopric. Portions of its massive rectangular walls survive, and traces of an aqueduct.

Satricum (Borgo Montello, Casale di Conca). A town in the coastal plain of Latium (Lazio, western Italy), nine miles inland from Antium (Anzio). As a strongly Etruscanized city—with particularly close connections, excavations suggest, with Caere (Cerveteri)—it was of importance from the sixth century BC, although Dionysius' mention of the place as an ally of the Latins against the Romans at the battle of Lake Regillus (*c* 499) is probably apocryphal. As the keypoint between Antium (Anzio) and the Alban Hills, Satricum became a Latin colony, jointly settled by Romans and Latins, in *c* 385. However, *c* 377, according to Livy, it was the scene of a battle in which the Romans defeated a combined force of Antians and Latins, whereupon the latter, deserted by their Antian allics, sct firc to the town. Legend recorded that only thc famous Temple of Mater Matuta was saved, after a miraculous voice from the interior of the shrine commanded the removal of the flaming firebrands. A similar story was told again in connection with events of *c* 346, two years after Antium—a possession of the Volscians at the time—had established a colony of its own at Satricum. Thereafter no more is heard of the center, except that the temple continued to attract pilgrims.

The sanctuary of Mater Matuta was excavated in 1896, but the detailed results were never published, and it is only during the last few years that further investigations have indicated its full importance. The first temple, it now appears, was built *c* 550—over the remains of an oval hut centered on a circular hearth containing charcoal, bone and pottery fragments of the eighth and seventh centuries—and the second shrine dates from *c* 500. Its excavation has yielded an extraordinary wealth of ornamental terracotta sculptures. An inscription found in this second temple (the Lapis Satricanus) mentions a certain Poplios Valesios who may perhaps be the Publius Valerius Publicola included by tradition among the first consuls of the Roman Republic (510/509); the inscription also refers to his *suodales (sodales)*, or body of young dependent warriors. Parts of an ancient fortification without stone facing have been destroyed during the past quarter of a century by agricultural machinery.

Satyrion *see* Taras

Savaria *see* Pannonia

Savaria (Szombathely). A Roman city in Pannonia (Hungary), situated on the amber route that led from Aquileia at the head of the Adriatic to the Baltic Sea (by way of Scarbantia [Sopron] and Carnuntum [Petronell] on the Danube). Savaria also stood at a point where additional routes branched northeastward and eastward to other Danubian river ports.

Earlier belonging to the kingdom of Noricum, it became attached—after the abolition of that state by Augustus—to the Roman province of Pannonia. Romanization was developed by businessmen of Emona (Ljubljana) who, according to an inscription, were represented by agents in the territory of Savaria. A legion may also, for a time, have been stationed there and the emperor Claudius made the town into a Roman citizen colony, settled by veterans (AD 43). It possessed an Altar of Augustus, serving the imperial cult of the province of Pannonia and then, after the subdivision of that province by Trajan (103), of Upper Pannonia; the town also contained an office of the imperial customs (*portorium*).

During the wars of Marcus Aurelius (161–80) against the Quadi and Marcomanni, Savaria suffered severely, and its rural dependencies were destroyed in Gothic invasions of the 260s, when hoards of coins and jewels were buried at

Rábakovács and Balozsameggyes. Under further partitions in the later empire, however, it became the capital of the new province of Pannonia Prima. During Diocletian's persecution of the Christians its Christian bishop Quirinus was executed (309); the *Passion of St. Quirinus* describes his martyrdom. Savaria was the birthplace of St. Martin of Tours (316). Edicts were issued there by Constantine I the Great (306–37), Constantine II (337–40) and Valentinian I, who used it as a winter residence (375), although, according to Ammianus Marcellinus, the place 'was then weak and had suffered from repeated misfortunes': an owl was said to have perched on the top of the imperial bath-house prophesying the emperor's death, and no marksman could bring it down; he died shortly afterward. Subsequently the neighborhood was occupied by Germans and Huns. Savaria was destroyed by an earthquake in 455.

The street plan of the early colony, and its Capitolium and local senate house (*curia*), have been identified. Before and after 100, suburbs and their cemeteries grew up to the north and south of the original Roman town, and toward the end of the second century they were enclosed within a new wall. The same period witnessed rebuilding and enlargement. A large bathing establishment was constructed; a temple of Isis (now on show) dates from before 188; and a nearby shrine of Jupiter Dolichenus was important, according to inscriptions, in the time of Caracalla (211–17). A theater (mentioned in the *Passion of St. Quirinus*) stood on a hill to the west of the city. A granary was rebuilt by Constans I (337–50). Toward the end of the empire the rulers who visited Savaria stayed in the principal municipal building. A catalog of inscriptions and sculptures found in the locality has been published, and air photographs have thrown light on the size and distribution (centuriation) of landed properties in the surrounding countryside.

Savoy *see* Sabaudia

Savus (Save). A river in Pannonia (Yugoslavia); a tributary of the Danube. *See* Emona, Sirmium, Siscia.

Scamander, Skamandros, River (Menderes Suyu). A river in the Troad (northwestern Asia Minor) sixty miles long, rising in Mount Ida and flowing into the Hellespont (Dardanelles). According to Greek mythology, the river-god Scamander was a son of Oceanus and Tethys and father of Teucer, the first king of Troy. In the *Iliad*, Scamander was angered during the Trojan War after the death of Patroclus when his river was filled with Trojan corpses by Achilles, whom he would have drowned if the god Hephaestus had not dried up his stream with a great flame.

Scilla *see* Scylla

Scingomagus *see* Segusio

Scodra (Shkodër, Scutari). A city in Illyricum (now Albania), seventeen miles inland from the Adriatic Sea. Originally situated at the foot of a citadel on an isolated rock past which the river Kiri flows into the Buenë, at the southeastern end of Lake Shkodër, the town gradually extended to the north, abandoning the plain, which was liable to floods. Occupied by the Illyrian state that arose in the middle of the third century BC, and becoming its capital, Scodra subsequently came under the control of Philip V of Macedonia (211–197), to whose reign its earliest bronze coinage, depicting a Macedonian shield, belongs. After his expulsion by the Romans, the city passed into the possession of the Illyrian King Genthius (197–168), who coined at its mint and built its walls; but after joining the Macedonian King Perseus, he was defeated in the neighborhood and captured.

In the Roman province of Illyricum Scodra became a colony under the title of Colonia Claudia. During the late empire it was capital of the province of Praevalitana.

Scotland *see* Caledonia

Scutari *see* Chrysopolis

Scylla, Skylla (Scilla). At the toe of Italy, in Bruttii (now Calabria), at the northern end of the Sicilian Strait (Straits of Messina). The rock of Scylla, towering up two hundred and thirty-nine feet sheer from the sea, was identified with the sea monster of the same name, which, together with Charybdis beside the opposite shore, terrorized mariners who were attempting to pass through the narrows. Scylla, the daughter of Phorcys and Cratais, was said to have had six heads, each with a triple row of teeth, and a dozen feet; and Virgil recorded a tale that she had a girdle of dog's heads around her loins. From her lair within a cave she devoured whatever came within her reach, and seized six of Odysseus' companions. There were stories that she had once been of human shape, but was changed by magic into a monster: this transformation was attributed to Circe (or Amphitrite), jealous of the sea god Glaucus (or of Poseidon), who had been in love with Scylla. A very fine black and white mosaic depicting her (fourth century AD) has recently been found at Paphos in Cyprus.

Scyros, Skyros. The easternmost and largest of the Northern Sporades archipelago in the Aegean, seventeen miles long (with a deeply indented coastline) and twelve miles from the coast of Euboea. It was here, according to Greek mythology, that Achilles, disguised as a girl, was sent by his mother Thetis to the court of Lycomedes, so that he could avoid going to fight in the Trojan War; but Odysseus lured him to Troy, where he eventually met his death. Achilles' son Neoptolemus or Pyrrhus, who had been brought up on Scyros, was also taken to Troy by Odysseus. It was on this island, too, that Lycomedes was said to have killed Theseus king of Athens, who had sought refuge at his court, by treacherously pushing him off a cliff.

Traces of Neolithic and Bronze Age habitation have now been found, and tombs of the tenth, ninth and eighth centuries BC have yielded plentiful jewelery; Scyros was on the fringe of the territory to which the Protogeometric style of pottery, developed at Athens, was able to penetrate. The island also became notorious for its piracy, but in 476 the Athenian Cimon conquered and enslaved its inhabitants, and planted Athenian settlers; he also discovered the alleged bones of Theseus, of heroic dimensions, which he ceremoniously conducted to Athens and installed in the Theseum. In 322 the Macedonians took Scyros from the Athenians, but in 196 their King Philip V was forced by Rome to give it back to them. Strabo comments on the island's valuable goats, and its variegated marble was also prized and exported.

The capital, Scyros, was on the northeast coast, on a high terrace dominated by an acropolis (Castro) which recalls Homer's epithet for the city, 'steep,' and was identified with the cliff from which Theseus was hurled. The substructures of the medieval Venetian castle, and a few sections of the town wall, date from the fifth century BC. (The poet Rupert Brooke, who died off Trebuki Bay on board a French hospital ship, while on his way to fight at Gallipoli in 1915, is buried a mile from the shore.)

Scythia, Skythia, was the name loosely given by the Greeks to the entire area between the Carpathians and the river Tanais (Don), or even extending as far as the Caspian. The term 'Scythian,' sometimes used loosely (*see* below), can be applied, in a stricter sense, to the Indo-European-speaking peoples who penetrated into eastern Europe and the Caucasus after 1000 BC and by *c* 650 controlled northwestern Iran and northeastern Turkey. Expelled by the Medes, many of these Scythians moved into the Kuban basin and then expanded northwestward into other southern regions of what is now the Soviet Union; their graves in these areas abound in gold, mostly dating from the seventh to the fifth centuries BC.

The Royal Scyths, who were at first centered on the lower reaches of the Borysthenes (Dnieper), and maintained close though not invariably cordial relations with the Greek colonies on their coasts, were governed *c* 589 by King Saulius, whose brother Anacharsis (the subject of many legends) was sent to Greece as his envoy and became famous there for 'Scythian eloquence.' In 513 the Achaemenid Persian King Darius I crossed the Danube in order to attack a later Scythian monarch, Idanthyrsus, and pursued him deep into the Ukraine, but could not force a decisive engagement and had to turn back, abandoning his sick and wounded as he went. Idanthyrsus' son Arapeithes successively married a Greek, a Scythian and a Thracian, and his son Scyles (according to Herodotus) was murdered by his brother because of his Greek way of life (inherited from his mother, a Greek from Istrus).

King Ateas was killed in 339 at the age of ninety, while fighting against Philip II of Macedonia, but the Scythians, owing to the exceptional horsemanship of their mounted archers, defeated Alexander the Great's general Zopyrion in 325, although they were fought off by Paerisades I (349/8–311/310), king of the Cimmerian Bosphorus (Crimea).

From this time onward, the Royal Scyths were subjected to attacks from the Sarmatians, who had appeared on the Tanais; and this pressure increased until the second century, when the Scyths, as a political power, found themselves limited to the Tauric Chersonese (Crimea). In that peninsula their King Scylurus established himself at the largely Hellenized city of Neapolis (Simferopol). Greek inscriptions record his name, and a relief shows his son Palacus on horseback. The Royal Scyth kingdom survived until its destruction by the Goths in the third century AD. In the later empire the Dobrogea or Dobruja, the region known as Scythia Minor, became the Roman province of Scythia.

The dismissal of the Scythians, by a work ascribed to Hippocrates, as lazy, fat, jolly and sexually impotent is shown up as a xenophobe myth by the historical facts. The emperor Caracalla (211–17) would scarcely have recruited them, along with Germans, as his bodyguard if they had been as easygoing as all that. In recent years, a dozen books on their civilization and its importance have come from Russian writers, partly prompted by the discovery of splendid Scythian treasures at Haimanova Mogila (1969/70) and Tolstaya Mogila (1971).

As was mentioned above, the name 'Scythian' is often attributed, in a looser sense, to related peoples who instead of migrating to eastern Europe remained in central Asia, notably the nomad Sacae and others who invaded Seleucid territories in Iran before and after 300 BC (including a confederacy of three tribes of which one, the Parni, evolved into the Parthians); and the various peoples against whom the Greek monarch of Bactria (Afghanistan) Euthydemus I Theos (*c* 235–200) probed deep into Sogdiana and Sinkiang were also sometimes described as Scythians. In the later second century the Sacae overran the Greek (Indo-Greek) communities of central Asia and captured their stronghold Gardez (south of Kabul, *c* 75), whereupon Azes I (*c* 57–35), known as an 'Indo-Scythian,' overthrew the last Greek ruler at Taxila beyond the Indus.

Scythopolis, Skythopolis, formerly Beit-shan ('House of [the god] Shan') or Beit-shean ('House of Security') and later Tell el-Husn, 'the Mound of the Fortress.' A city of Judaea (now Israel) at the northern border of Samaria, occupying a strong and fertile site on the bank of the Harod watercourse near the right (west) bank of its mother stream, the Jordan, at the beginning of the Jezreel (Esdraelon) valley. After a long and significant history going back to the Chalcolithic Age and attaining its zenith in the Late Bronze Age and Biblical epoch, Beth-shan formed part of the territories conquered from the Persians by Alexander the Great.

It was then taken over by the Ptolemies, under whom it assumed the designation of Scythopolis, either owing to a similar local Semitic place-name (Succoth?) or because Scythians were settled there by Ptolemy II Philadelphus (289/8–246 BC). But it also claimed (like nearly a dozen other towns listed by stephanus of Byzantium) to be the legendary Nysa, where the infant god Dionysus had been nursed by the nymphs (according to the elder Pliny it was Dionysus who settled the Scythians there!); he and Astarte (Ashtoreth) were the principal divinities of the city. In 198 it passed under Seleucid control as a result of the conquests of Antiochus III the Great. However, the Jewish (Hasmonaean) prince John Hyrcanus I secured possession of the place in 107 either through betrayal or by force of arms (according to contradictory accounts by Josephus); given the choice of converting to Judaism or leaving, most of the inhabitants left. After the conquest of Judaea by Pompey the Great (63), Scythopolis was rebuilt as a pagan city by Aulus Gabinius (57), becoming a member of an autonomous League of Ten Cities or Decapolis (loosely attached to the province of Syria and later Judaea), of which the other nine lay across the Jordan, so that Scythopolis served as the League's indispensable trade-link with the west.

At the outset of the First Jewish Revolt against the Romans (AD 66), the local Jewish community claimed to support the Greek administration of the city against the rebels (or were compelled to take up arms against them: Josephus again gives divergent accounts), but were nevertheless ordered out of their homes and then massacred by its Greek leaders to the number of more than 13,000. Later Scythopolis was successively attached to the provinces of Syria Palaestina and Palaestina Secunda. Over a quarter of all the inscribed milestones in Israel have been found along the road to Legio Maximianopolis (near Megiddo). The scene of Christian martyrdoms in the later third and early fourth centuries, Scythopolis was an episcopal see, and both its Jewish and Christian communities enjoyed great prosperity in the later Roman and Byzantine epochs.

A Christian church was built on the site of a Hellenistic temple (earlier a Canaanite shrine), and outside the town a villa of mid-fifth century date has revealed mosaics indicating the name of the owner, Kyrios Leontis; they depict the Jewish Menorah (seven-branched candlestick), and display Greek mythological and Nilotic scenes. The principal earlier surviving monument is a theater of *c* 200 with accommodation for some 5,000 spectators, restored under Julian the Apostate (361-63) and abandoned by *c* 450; between the theater and the mound are remains of a colonnaded avenue and a bridge.

Sebaa Biar *see* Zama Regia

Sebaste *see* Neocaesarea, Samaria

Sebasteia, formerly (despite modern doubt) Megalopolis (in or near Sivas). A city of Pontus (northern Asia Minor). Megalopolis was founded on the river Halys (Kızıl Irmak) by Pompey the Great (64 BC) in the interior of the former kingdom of the Pontic King Mithridates VI Eupator. A communications center linked to Amaseia (Amasya) and Melitene (Eski Malatya) by important roads, it possessed a large territory, part of which was temporarily transferred by Antony to Comana Pontica and to the Galatian chieftain Ateporix (37/36). Under Augustus the city belonged for a time to Queen Pythodoris of Pontus (in or after 8 BC), but was annexed by the emperor's grandson Gaius Caesar to the Roman province of Galatia *c* 2/1 BC or AD 1/2, adopting the new name of Sebasteia ('Augusta') to which the title of *metropolis* was added in AD 161-65 when local coinage began under Lucius Verus (continuing until Valerian, 253-60). During the later empire Sebasteia was the capital of the province of Armenia Prima. Excavations on the citadel (Toprakkale) have revealed nothing Roman, though there are ancient tombs and traces of a Roman bridge outside the city. Farther to the east, on the Upper Halys, were salt mines, which now been reopened.

Sebastopolis *see* Dioscurias

Segesta, in Greek Egesta, later Dicaeopolis (at first near Calatafimi, in northwestern Sicily. This original city stood on and below Mount Barbaro, near the river Gaggera that debouched into the Crimissus (Fiume Caldo, joining the Fiume Freddo). According to Greek myth, the river-god Crimissus, assuming the form of a dog, became the lover of the Trojan maiden Segesta, who gave birth to the city founder Aegestes (all three deities are depicted on Segestan coinage). The early township was the principal center of the non-Greek Elymi, to whose undeciphered language, of Anatolian (?) origin, some locally discovered graffiti have been attributed; and the inscriptions on some Segestan coins seem to show Elymian forms.

Segesta was in continual conflict with Selinus (Selinunte), from at least *c* 580/576 BC. About 480–461, some of its earliest coins refer to an alliance with another Elymian town, Eryx (Erice); but it was considerably Hellenized from this time onward, as the fine style of these monetary issues indicates. Whether, however, as supposed, it formed an alliance with Athens in 454/3 (or 458/7) is now uncertain. But in 424, during the Peloponnesian War, its inhabitants supported the Athenians' first expedition to Sicily, and then in 418/417 they appealed to them for help (by making a fictitious display of their own wealth), thus encouraging the second, disastrous Athenian expedition to the island. Shortly afterward the Segestans asked for Carthaginian assistance, too, which duly brought about the destruction of Selinus and other cities in 409. In 397, as an ally of Carthage, Segesta was besieged by Dionysius I of Syracuse. Thereafter it remained subject to the Carthaginians, until Agathocles of Syracuse seized the city in 307, treating its population very savagely, and changing its name to Dicaeopolis, 'city of the just.' Rebuilt on the same site and reviving its former name, it resumed its dependency on Carthage, except for a brief period under the control of the invading King Pyrrhus of Epirus (276). At the beginning of the First Punic War (264–241), however, Segesta immediately joined the side of the Romans, with whom it shared a claim to Trojan descent; and, surviving a Carthaginian siege (260), its people were rewarded, after the Roman victory, by the status of a free and tax-free city (*civitas libera et immunis*), accompanied by a grant of extensive territory.

During the Roman period the town was transplanted to a new site (near Castellamare del Golfo, in the vicinity of medicinal sulphur springs). Serious damage was caused by the First Slave Revolt of 104–100. An isolated coinage under Augustus (31 BC–AD 14) probably celebrates the acquisition of Latin rights (under which the annually elected officials became Roman citizens). In AD 25, according to Tacitus, the Segestans successfully appealed to Tiberius for the reconstruction of the Temple of Venus (Aphrodite) on Mount Eryx (*qv*), which belonged to them. But thereafter Segesta disappeared from view; the Vandals, in the fifth century, were probably responsible for its final destruction.

The original township was surrounded by a double circuit of walls, of which certain sections, of various epochs, still survive, including towers and a gate. On a small hill to the west stand the columns, six on the facade and fourteen on the sides, of one of the finest of all surviving Doric temples, begun in 430/420 BC and never completed (an alternative theory pronouncing it to have been, not a Greek temple of the usual type but an open peristyle for oriental worship, has been contested). The art historian Bernard Berenson declared the building 'an affirmation of reason, order and intelligence in the midst of the pell-mell, the indifference and the anarchy of nature.'

An earlier shrine has now been discovered underlying the temple, and another has been found at Mango on Mount Barbaro within the ancient walls. The same hill displays a theater of early Hellenistic date, constructed over a prehistoric site and cave and modified in Roman times. Recent examination of a large deposit at Vanella on the same mountainside, consisting perhaps of votive objects tipped down from a sanctuary, has illustrated the penetration of Greek material from *c* 630 to 420.

Segesta, Segestica *see* Siscia

Segusio, Segusium, earlier Scingomagus (Susa). A city in northwestern Italy, on the foothills of the Alps, where roads lead through Monginevro (Mont Genèvre) and Mons Geminus (Moncenisio, Mont Cenis) passes into southern Gaul. Segusio was the capital of the Celto-Ligurian tribe of the Segusini, whose king Marcus Julius Cottius I, son of Donnus, although earlier (according to Ammianus Marcellinus) unfriendly to the Romans, was recognized by Augustus in 9/8 BC as the prefect of the fourteen tribal towns (*civitates*) of the Cottian Alps (Alpi Cozie), whereupon, as an inscription records, he improved the road through the Mont Genèvre pass at his own expense.

His son of the same name regained his father's position under Claudius (AD 41–54), but in the time of Nero (54–68) Segusio, with the rank of *municipium,* became the capital of a new Roman province of the Cottian Alps which in the later empire, as a district or province of Italy, was extended down to the coast. In 312, during the Civil War between Maxentius and Constantine I the Great, Maxentius, who controlled Italy, posted an advance guard at Segusio, but Constantine crossed the Alps by the Mont Genèvre pass and took the stronghold by surprise.

The Arch of Augustus at Segusio was erected in 9/8 BC to commemorate the pact between the emperor and Cottius I. Remains of an amphitheater, constructed in the second century AD over an earlier building, have been found on the fringe of the ancient inhabited zone. Sections of the third century town walls have also been preserved, as well as remains of their two principal gates. An inscription mentions the Baths of Gratianus.

Selah *see* Petra

Selçuk *see* Ephesus

Seleucia (?) (in Tadjikstan, Soviet Union). Excavators are now bringing to light a major Hellenistic city at the confluence of the river Pyandzh—an upstream extension of the Oxus (Amu Darya)—with its northern tributary the Vaksh, halfway between Seleucia (?) on the Oxus (Ai Khanum, sixty-two miles upstream) and Termez. Most of the remains that have so far been discovered are datable to the third and second centuries BC. They include a large treasure of gold and ivory objects, and an altar in a courtyard or sanctuary-precint inscribed 'Atrosok has vowed to consecrate this to the Oxus.'

Seleucia in Pieria, Seleukeia (between Keboussie and Magharadjek). A city on the northern section of the Syrian coast (now in the Hatay, southeastern Turkey), on and below an outlying spur of Mount Amanus (Gavur Dağları) which overlooks a bay at the mouth of the river Orontes (Nahr el-Asi). The settlement was founded *c* 300 BC on a site known as Hydatos Potamoi—'watery rivers,' from two surrounding watercourses that protected the fortress—by Seleucus I Nicator, who probably brought its colonists (eventually comprising 6,000 adult citizens) from the old Greek settlement at Posidium (Ras-el-Bassit). Seleucus also gave the surrounding territory the name of Pieria, after a region of his native Macedonia.

The new foundation, consisting of an acropolis and an upper and lower town, was at first intended to become Seleucus' capital, but this was soon transferred to Antioch beside the Orontes (Antakya), for which the inner and outer harbors of Seleucia thereafter provided a port. Captured by Ptolemy III Euergetes *c* 245, Seleucia was recovered for the Seleucids by Antiochus III the Great in 219.

A decree of 186 shows that the city enjoyed formal autonomy; and *c* 149 it briefly became a member—and the mint—of a League of Four Brother Peoples, in which its partners were Antioch, Apamea (Qalaat el-Mudik and Laodicea on the Sea (Latakia). Seleucia's inauguration of a new civic era in 109/8 reflects the confirmation of its autonomous status by the Seleucids. Subsequently its resistance to Tigranes I of Armenia (who ejected Seleucid rivals, 83–69) earned a further pronouncement of freedom at the hands of Pompey the Great. Retaining this status in the Roman province of Syria, the port of Seleucia became the base of an imperial fleet, the *classis Syriaca.* It was renovated for this purpose by Vespasian (AD 69–79)—whose canal, running partly underground, can still be seen—and again by Constantine I the Great (306–37), at a time when the harbors were suffering from serious silting (they are now completely blocked up). Raiders from Isauria in southern Asia Minor plundered the city in 403, and it was seriously damaged by an earthquake in 526.

Seleucia was famous for a sanctuary of Zeus on Mount Casius at the end of the bay, the scene of annual festivals visited by Hadrian (117–38) and Julian the Apostate (361–63). The sacred stone and shrine of the cult—surmounted by an eagle or enclosed in a temple—are depicted on local coinage; and this also honors Zeus as Keraunios, god of the thunderbolt (*keraunos*), which is displayed on a stool or on the roof of a shrine. Other coins show a temple of the city goddess or Tyche (Fortuna, Ashtoreth, Astarte). One large Doric temple dating from Hellenistic times, of which the foundations still survive, can be seen to have dominated the site. The surrounding ramparts, including bastions and gates, have also been investigated. Roman villas, containing fine polychrome mosaics that have not been removed to museums, were disposed in tiers along the slopes of the upper town. The foundations of a cruciform Christian Martyr's Shrine (Martyrion) on the later fifth century AD—restored in the sixth—are also visible. (This Seleucia should be distinguished from Seleucia by the Belus [Sqelebiya], beside the east bank of the Orontes.)

Seleucia on the Calycadnus, Seleukeia (Silifke). The most important city in Rough Cilicia (Cilicia Tracheia, Aspera; southeastern Asia Minor), on the right (west) bank of the river Calycadnus (Gök Su), which was navigable up to the town in ancient times. Seleucia was built on the only plain of any size on this coast (created by alluvial deposit), at the terminal of a land route leading into the interior. Overlooked by a steep conical acropolis, the settlement (according to Alexander Polyhistor) was created by Seleucus I Nicator in the 290s or 280s BC—on the site of an earlier habitation center variously named as Hermia and Hyria—and was peopled by colonists brought by him from the neighboring port of Holmi (site unknown), whose goddess Athena the people of the new foundation continued to worship, and honored on their coins.

During the later Roman Republic, despite the cession of all the surrounding districts to kings and dynasts, Seleucia remained a free city. Some of its monetary issues bear the names of Xenarchus and Athenaeus, identifiable as eminent local Peripatetic (Aristotelian) philosophers, of whom the former was described by Strabo as a friend of Augustus, and the second as a plotter against his rule, who received a pardon. Strabo also remarks that the city was populous, and 'differed greatly from the ways of the Cilicians and Pamphylians.' It was subsequently attached to the province of Cilicia (AD 72), but declared itself autonomous (from Hadrian, 117–38) and free (from Severus Alexander, 222–35) on its coinage, which continued until the time of Gallienus (AD 253–68). In the later empire Seleucia became the capital of the province of Isauria, and was the scene of a Church Council in 359.

Its ancient remains include a theater (dug out of a terrace below the acropolis), and traces of a temple, a stadium (beside the river bank), and a late Roman house with mosaic pavements. Outside the city, at Meriamlik, are buildings, of dates before and after 500, belonging to a monastery, frequented by pilgrims, where St. Thecla was believed to have lived in the first century.

Seleucia on the Eulaeus *see* Susa

Seleucia on the Euphrates (Seleucia on the Bridge) *see* Zeugma.

Seleucia (?) on the Oxus, Seleukeia. This is the likely ancient name of Aï Khanum, north of the Paropamisus (*qv*, Hindu Kush) mountains on the eastern fringes of Bactria (*qv*); now in Afghanistan, near its frontier with the Soviet Union. The town stands on the bank of the upper river Oxus (Amu Darya) (sixty-two miles upstream from Seleucia (?) in Tadjikistan) at its confluence with the Kikcha, which descends from an area rich in lapis lazuli mines. The site of Aï Khanum was well protected, since this was the only place for miles where the river was too deep to ford.

After a period of rule by the Persians (whose governors' palace has recently been located not far away), the locality may have been visited by Alexander the

Great (who seems to have crossed the Oxus in the neighborhood) and marked out by him for future development. This remains conjectural, and the site cannot be securely identified with any attested Alexandria, though it may have borne that name for a time. Later, however, it was probably settled by Seleucus I Nicator (*c* 300 BC), forming one of a pattern of about a dozen colonial enterprises in the region.

An acropolis, the 'Hill of the Lady,' rising to a height of one hundred and eighty feet, was reinforced by ramparts, especially to the northeast. Extensive public buildings concentrated in the flat area (likewise fortified) between the main street, running in a straight line below the acropolis, and the left bank of the Oxus included a palace complex, a large peristyle courtyard with one hudred and sixteen columns, a treasury where a store of ingots was found, and a sanctuary known as the 'Temple with Indented Niches'—which has yielded finds revealing a remarkable blend of Greek and oriental influences. One of these objects is a silver disc on which the goddess Cybele, in Hellenized form, is accompanied by an oriental priest at a firealtar; a sun-god appears in the sky. There is also a hero's shrine (*heroon*) in which an inscription was found recording how a certain Clearchus—probably Aristotle's pupil of that name—went to copy out the moral maxims of the oracular shrine and bring them back to Seleucia.

Other discoveries include the city arsenal (containing pieces of the armor of a heavy cavalryman [cataphract]), a gymnasium, and a theater. Residential quarters have come to light partly outside the walls, where a necropolis and irrigation channels are also to be seen. Seleucia must have passed from Seleucid control into the hands of the Parthians and then on the Bactrian (or Indo-Greek) rulers who recovered the area for the Greeks. But the end of Greek rule came about 145 BC, and the city was gutted by fire, presumably at the time when the Sacae (Scythians) overran and settled Bactria and the surrounding territories. Whether what remained of the city was included in the shortlived reconquests of the last Indo-Greek imperial ruler Hermaeus Soter (*c* 40–30) is unknown.

Seleucia on the Pyramus *see* Mopsuestia

Seleucia on the Tigris, Seleukeia (Tell Umar), of which the former Babylonian village of Opis became a part. It was situated in Mesopotamia (Iraq) on a natural lake at the narrowest point between the Euphrates and the Tigris, where the Royal (Nahrmalka) Canal united the two rivers just north of the site. In 324 BC Alexander the Great's plans for a new mixed army of Macedonians and Persians caused the former to mutiny at Opis: and it was there that he pronounced his imaginative, spectacular prayer for a union of hearts and a joint commonwealth between the two peoples, holding a feast of reconciliation attended by 9,000 guests of both races.

On this site of Opis, and on the territory around it, Seleucus I Nicator founded the colony of Seleucia (307/300), which replaced Babylon as the principal city of the country, and became a capital of his empire—a function that it shared with the Syrian towns Seleucia in Pieria and then Antioch. It was at Seleucia on the Tigris that the royal heir resided, and a center of the dynastic cult was established; and the new foundation was destined to become the peerless eastern outpost of Hellenism, and one of the greatest cities in the world. Few other places have so effectively dominated the mercantile affairs of half a continent. Serving as an immensely busy port for river shipping down to the Persian Gulf, and as the meeting place for convoys bringing textiles from Persia, silk from China, and a wide variety of goods from India, Seleucia on the Tigris enjoyed a particular outburst of prosperity *c* 175–170, and eventually possessed a population which, according to Pliny the Elder, reached a total of 600,000. Among these inhabitants were not only Greeks but many Babylonians and numerous Jews. However, the city retained its self-governing Greek constitution and administration, even after damage incurred during rebellions instigated by Molon from Media (220) and the satrap Timarchus (164–62) and further destruction during the conquest of Mesopotamia by the Arsacid Parthian Mithridates I (*c* 141), who established a military camp and winter residence at Ctesiphon on the opposite bank of the Tigris.

The leading Stoic philosopher Diogenes 'the Babylonian' (d. *c* 150), an eminent Epicurean of the same name (d. 144), and their younger contemporary the astronomer 'Seleucus the Chaldaean,' all originated from Seleucia: *c* 86 the Athenian rhetorician Amphicrates agreed to go there as a visiting professor, although when he was offered a permanent post he replied that a dolphin would not fit into a stew pan. The place was often the scene of fierce factional strife, and autonomous coinages of 88 BC, 42–38 BC (dated significantly by the Seleucid era) and AD 14/15 seem to bear witness to rebellions against the Parthians, whose King Vardanes I (AD 35–42) subjected the city to a seven-year siege that terminated in its surrender.

Burned down by Trajan's army (116), Seleucia was rebuilt in a less Greek and more Parthian style, but after opening its gates to Avidius Cassius (164/5)—a leading general of Marcus Aurelius and Lucius Verus—its buildings suffered a further bout of destruction at his hands, which accelerated the decline of Hellenism in Babylonia. On this occasion, occupation by the Roman troops (who caught the plague from the local inhabitants) did not last; but it was resumed when Septimius Severus entered the city, finding it deserted by the Parthians (197/8). After Mesopotamia had come under the control of the Sassanian Persians, the site was abandoned and not reinhabited, but their King Ardashir (Artaxerxes) I (224–41) created a new foundation nearby under the name of Veh-Ardashir, which continued to hold a central position in international commerce. In 283, however, the Roman emperor Carus defeated the Sassanian Bahram II and captured Seleucia; but when he died shortly afterward, Persian rule was resumed.

Excavations have revealed sections of defensive canals and ditches, and of stone fortifications built on foundations of baked bricks. A hero's shrine (Heroon) made of the latter material, according to a fragmentary inscription, was apparently dedicated to the Seleucid Demetrius II (145–140). A theater stood on the south side of the town, beside what may have been a porticoed square. Two sanctuaries have been found near the Royal Canal which flowed through Seleucia; and the uncovering of a residential block has thrown much light on the domestic architecture of this remarkable center, at which Greek, Semitic, Iranian and Roman cultures converge.

Seleucia *see* Gadara, Gaulanitis, Nicopolis (Pontus), Tralles

Selge *see* Pisidia

Selimiye *see* Side

Selinus, Selinous (Selinunte: the name means 'wild celery,' the badge of the city). Selinus is on the southwest coast of Sicily, centered on a low hill jutting into the sea between two rivers, the Selinus (Modione) to the west and the Galici (now the Gorgo di Cottone depression) to the east; this pair of streams provided useful small harbors and penetration routes into a fertile inland plain, and the larger river Hypsas (Belice) debouched a few miles to the west. The place was colonized either *c* 650 BC (Diodorus, Eusebius) or more probably *c* 628 (Thucydides) by settlers from Megara Hyblaea in eastern Sicily, under the leadership of Pamillus or Pammilus, who was summoned from the mother city Megara in Greece.

The westernmost Greek city of the island, Selinus immediately adjoined settlements of native Elymians and of Carthaginians, with both of which communities, however—despite apparent participation in a provocative, unsuccessful Greek attempt to colonize Lilybaeum (Marsala, *c* 580)—it generally maintained adquate relations. The dominions of Selinus were considerable, extending between the rivers Mazarus (Mazaro) in the west and Halycus (Platani) to the east. In the latter direction, the Selinuntines established the coastal colony of Minoa, although its seizure *c* 500 by the Spartan Euryleon (who renamed it Heraclea Minoa) eliminated their influence. Nevertheless, they became extremely prosperous, as their remarkable outlay on buildings (*see* below) clearly showed. This wealth was mainly provided by the export of wine and olive oil to Carthage, with which they sided against the Syracusans and other fellow Greeks in the campign of 480 that led to the Carthaginian defeat at Himera (Imera). Nevertheless, after the battle Selinus succeeded in making peace with victorious Syracuse. During the ensuing period, however, the stagnant waters of the surrounding marshlands silted the city's harbors and caused a devastating pestilence, which was allayed by calling in the sage Empedocles of Acragas (Agrigento) to devise drainage operations.

In the Peloponnesian War between Athens and Sparta, Selinus' long-standing enmity with Segesta prompted an appeal by the latter to the Athenians, who launched their second expedition to Sicily (415). The Selinuntines welcomed its disastrous outcome, but in 409 the Carthaginian general Hannibal sacked and destroyed their city, which the Syracusan general Hermocrates subsequently failed to recapture. It was refounded soon afterward, however, by the refugees. But after joining Pyrrhus of Epirus in his attempt to drive the Carthaginians out of Sicily (*c* 276), Selinus suffered further and final destruction during the Second Punic War (*c* 250), when the Carthaginians removed its inhabitants to Lilybaeum. It seems likely that Selinus was never rebuilt, especially as its harbors were now completely silted up and malarial.

The town plan of Selinus shows that the right-angled, grid-iron pattern of urban layout, later known as Hippodamian, was already familiar in early colonial settlements. But the site is famous, above all, for its remarkable array of large Doric temples (in various degrees of preservation), which have provided sculptures of great distinction and testify to a unparalleled building enterprise during the years of the city's greatest prosperity. On the acropolis of the original site, which lay in front of the residential area (situated on Manuzza hill) and in due course was equipped with elaborate defensive walls—the largest fortification complex in Greek Sicily, extending in date from *c* 500 to 300/275—a primitive sanctuary (the 'Megaron') was followed by two others of sixth-century date (one dedicated to Apollo, and the other perhaps to Athena). The earlier of these shrines, at the highest point of the acropolis, was reconstructed in AD 1925/6. Its sculptural friezes of *c* 550–530 BC, reassembled from many fragments, are to be seen—like other remarkable Selinuntine sculptures—in the museum at Palermo. Remains of another temple, of Artemis (?), date from the first half of the fifth century.

A further group of three temples was erected on a hill to the west of the city and acropolis, across the river Galici. One of these buildings, dedicated to Dionysus (?), was constructed in the mid-sixth century and adorned with metopes depicting a duel between gods and giants. A neighboring edifice tentatively ascribed to Olympian Zeus—on which work was begun in the later sixth century, but remained unfinished when the town was sacked in 409—was one of the largest temples in the entire Greek world: so large that its central nave must have been left unroofed. But it was reduced to total ruin by an earthquake of undeterminable date. An early-fifth-century shrine of Hera (?) was also very large, and its vigorous friezes of *c* 460 represent the highest achievement of Selinuntine art. (It will have been seen that the attributions of these temples are all conjectural: they are usually known by letters, Apollo=C, Athena=D, Artemis=A, Dionysus=F, Zeus=G, Hera=E.)

At Gaggera to the west, beyond the river Selinus, are the remains of a large, complex and frequently replanned sanctuary of the fertility goddess Demeter Malophoros, the 'apple bearer,' adjoined by areas sacred to three-headed Hecate and Zeus Meilichios (the protector of those who propitiate him), both of whom were worshipped at the colonists' original home town of Megara in Greece. The Malophoros precinct, which went back to the beginnings of Selinus but was also frequented by other Greek and non-Greek communities of the area, has yielded extensive finds of pottery, and many thousands of terracotta figures representing goddesses or female donors. Extensive cemeteries have also been uncovered to the west and east of the river Selinus. The river-god is shown on beautiful fifth-century coinages, sacrificing to Apollo Alexikakos (the healer) in gratitude for his deliverance of the population from the plague, through the agency of Empedocles; Artemis, in her capacity as Eileithyia (goddess of childbirth), stands behind, for the pestilence had seriously affected pregnancies. Other coins portray the river-god Hypsas and a fountain-nymph Eurymedusa.

Sellasia. A town in Laconia (southern Greece). It lay about eight miles north of Sparta, overlooking the middle valley of the Oenus (Kelephina), a tributary of the Eurotas, and occupying a strategic position on the road leading up into Arcadia. Described by Diodorus as a city (*polis*), though it is unlikely to have possessed that formal status, Sellasia was plundered and burned by the Theban Epaminondas (370), but recaptured by the Spartans five years later.

In 222 it was the scene of one of the decisive battles of the Hellenistic age. In this engagement, the Macedonian monarch Antigonus III Doson confronted King Cleomenes III of Sparta, whose attempted employment of social revolution to serve Spartan expansion had caused great alarm. Although our three sources for the battle are conflicting, it is clear that Cleomenes occupied the river valley (which was suitable for phalanx warfare) and the hills on either side, but was nevertheless outflanked and succumbed to superior numbers and experience. His army was completely destroyed, and Antigonus entered Sparta unopposed. Sellasia itself suffered destruction and its population was reduced to slavery. Its site has not been identified with certainty; two hills, Ayios Konstantinos and the lower Paleogoulas, have been suggested.

Sennaya *see* Phanagoria

Sentinum (Sentino, a mile from Sassoferrato). A town in Umbria, now Marche (central Italy), on the eastern slopes of the Apennines, at the confluence of the rivers Sentinus (Sentino) and Marena, beside a pre-Roman road to the north. It was here, in 295 BC, that the decisive engagement of the Third Samnite War took place. The Romans had failed to prevent the Samnites from joining forces with their allies the Gauls, and were obliged to face their united army, which may also have included Umbrian and Etruscan contingents. In the battle that followed the steadiness of the Roman legions shattered the ranks of the opposing coalition. The Roman commanders were the consuls Quintus Fabius Rullianus, who showed great skill, and the veteran Publius Decius Mus, who according to Livy performed the act of self-sacrifice known as *devotio,* solemnly dedicating himself and his foes to the gods of the underworld and then charging into the enemy ranks to meet his death. The same act was later attributed to his father and son of the same name, but it is most plausibly ascribed to the commander at Sentinum. Although the war dragged on for another five years, this was the decisive victory that made Rome dominant over peninsular Italy.

In 41, during the Perusine War, in which Antony's brother Lucius Antonius rose against Octavian (the future Augustus), the city was captured and destroyed by Octavian's general Quintus Salvidienus Rufus. Its subsequent restoration, however, is demonstrated by walls constructed during the Augustan period, and by surviving remains of an industrial quarter and public buildings, unearthed by excavations. A bath house and other structures of imperial date have yielded important polychrome floor mosaics. Most of these pavements are in the Sassoferrato museum, but another, now at Munich, testifies to a cult of Mithras, to which animal reliefs and inscriptions also bear witness. It would appear from Zosimus that Sentinum ceased to exist at the time of the invasions of Alaric the Visigoth in the early fifth century AD.

Nearby is Civitalba (Civita Alba), where important terracotta sculptural compositions of the late second century BC have been found; they are preserved in the Museo Civico at Bologna. A complicated group illustrating the myth of Ariadne on Naxos, discovered by the companions of Dionysus, adorned the pediment of a temple, while the rout of the Galatians (Gauls), driven back from the sanctuary at Delphi (in 279 BC), was depicted on the long sides; the latter theme was no doubt suggested by the historic defeat of the Gauls at Sentinum more than a century and a half earlier.

Sepeia *see* Argos

Sepphoris, later Autocratoris and Neronias and Irenopolis and Diocaesarea (Zippori). A city of Israel, in the lower Galilean hills four miles north of Nazareth. In the Jewish (Hasmonaean) kingdom, Sepphoris was the capital of Galilee; and an attempt by Ptolemy IX Soter II Lathyrus of Egypt (116–80 BC) to acquire it forcibly from Alexander I Jannaeus proved a failure. After the conquest of Judaea by Pompey the Great, the town became the capital of one of the five districts into which he divided the country. In 38 the youthful Herod the Great retook it from Parthian invaders during a snowstorm.

After his death (4 BC) Sepphoris, with its armory, was seized by the rebel Judas, the son of Ezekias, but was reoccupied and burned to the ground by the Roman governor of Syria, Publius Quinctilius Varus. Herod's son Herod Antipas (4 BC–AD 39), when he became prince (tetrarch) of Galilee and Paraea, built a new city that he endowed with fortifications and a royal palace, and redesignated Autocratoris (Imperatoria); although the name did not last long, and he later established his principal residence at Tiberias instead (AD 19/20). However, Sepphoris regained its position as capital of Galilee under the Jewish prince Marcus Agrippa I, who after the accession of the emperor Nero (54) renamed it Neronias, adding the further appellation of Irenopolis (Peace City) when Nero closed the Temple of Janus at Rome (64) to celebrate empire-wide peace.

During the First Jewish Revolt (63–73), when Sepphoris was described as the largest city of Galilee, it became the headquarters of Josephus, the (unwilling) rebel leader and future historian, who twice subsequently had to reclaim its allegiance by force. At the request of the inhabitants, he provided the city with new fortifications: but they threw him out and admitted a Roman garrison, which was reinforced by the Roman governor of Syria, Cestius Gallus. Then Sepphoris welcomed the imperial general (subsequently emperor) Vespasian, who confirmed and renewed its garrison.

Local monetary issues under Trajan (98–117) celebrated some imperial gift (*edoken*), and in the time of Hadrian the city assumed yet another designation, Diocaesarea (City of Zeus, from 130 at latest). Under his successor Antoninus Pius (138–61), moneyers depicted a temple of Zeus, Hera and Athena—the Capitoline Triad—on its coinage. Meanwhile, as the center of Jewish habitation and religious life moved northward to Galilee, Judah I ha-Nasi 'the Prince' (135–219) transferred his residence from Beth-Shearim to Sepphoris-Diocaesarea, which became a renowned center of Hebrew scholarship. In 252 it served the quasi-independent Roman commander Odenathus of Palmyra as the place of imprisonment for the captured daughters of Mar Samuel, the late head of the Jewish academy at Nehardea on the Euphrates. In the later empire Sepphoris-Diocaesarea remained a military center, and Constantine I the Great (306-37) authorized a Christian convert named Joseph to build a church in the city, which subsequently became an episcopal see. A Roman theater and aqueduct have been found outside the walls.

Serdica, Serdice, or Serda (Sofia). A city in Thrace (now the capital of Bulgaria). The principal center of the Thracian tribe of the Serdi, Serdica was situated at a junction of the routes from Macedonia to Lower Moesia and the Danube (near the source of whose southern tributary the Oescus [Iskăr] the place lay) with another main thoroughfare from Upper Moesia to Byzantium. The Serdi were overrun in 29 BC by Marcus Licinius Crassus, a general of Octavian (Augustus), but their territory remained in the hands of client princes until the creation of the Roman province of Thrace in AD 46. The town was raised to the status of an honorary *municipium* by Trajan (98-117), retaining the tribal name with the added designation of Ulpia, and at intervals issued coinage, with Greek inscriptions, from Marcus Aurelius (161-80) to Gallienus (253-68). Dedications found fifty miles to the west of the town and forty miles to its east show that it controlled an extensive area.

When Aurelian evacuated Dacia (Rumania) in 271, Serdica became the capital of the more southerly of the two new provinces of the same name established south of the river (Dacia Mediterranea), and housed an imperial mint. The Edict of Serdica (311) was Galerius' dramatic death bed cancellation of the Christian persecutions in which he had played the leading part. One of several other emperors who resided and established his headquarters at the city was Constantine I the Great (in 317/18), who announced the appointment of three new Caesars during his stay; it was said that he considered making Serdica the capital of his empire before deciding on Byzantium instead. In 343 it was the seat of a famous Church Council—attended by a hundred and seventy bishops—which condemned the Arian 'heresy.' In the 440s, its buildings suffered destruction from the Huns, but were reconstructed by Justinian I (527-65).

Surviving remains show the use of stone in the second and third centuries and of brick in the third and fourth. Parts of the wall of the fortress, and of one of its towers (made of a brick and rubble core with stone facings), go back to 176/180. A temple of Serapis has also been traced, and a shrine of Asclepius (Aesculapius) appears on local coinage; its conical roof can be seen on a recently published piece. A bathing establishment of third-century date was transformed some two hundred years later into a complex of buildings known as the Church of St. George. The rotunda and apsed chambers of this edifice are now being restored, and excavations are uncovering four successive structures that preceded Justinian's Church of the Holy Wisdom (Sveta Sophia), which has been in continuous use from the fifth century until now, and gave its name to the modern city.

Serra Orlando *see* Morgantina

Sesamus *see* Amastris

Sestus, Sestos (Akbaşı). A city of the Thracian Chersonese (Gelibolu [Gallipoli] peninsula, European Turkey) on the Hellespont (Dardanelles), situated on a low plateau beside the southern shore of a bay that provided the best harbor on the strait, less hampered by wind and current than Abydus on the opposite coast. Sestus is mentioned in the catalog of ships in Homer's *Iliad.* Its original Greek population consisted of Aeolians from the island of Lesbos.

The Athenian interest in Sestus, because of its importance for grain shipments from the Euxine (Black) Sea, began with the control of the Chersonese by the two Miltiadeses (*c* 555, 524). The Achaemenid Persian King Darius I returned from his Scythian expedition (512 BC) by way of this port, and it was from Apobathra, nearby, that Xerxes I, on his way to Greece (480) crossed the Hellespont on a bridge of boats, after an earlier bridge had been destroyed by a storm. Sestus became the first town to be liberated from Persia by the Athenians—who remained in the area during the winter of 479/8 to conduct the siege—and was the principal naval base for their operations against the Spartans during the later phases of the Peloponnesian War (411-404). When the war was over, the base came under Spartan control until 393/386, but subsequently reverted to Athens (365); its rebellion in 357 only led to recapture, enslavement and recolonization (353/2). The historian Theopompus (born *c* 378) described Sestus as small but well fortified, and protectively linked with its harbor by a double wall. It was from here, in 324, that Alexander the Great launched his conquering expedition into Asia. During the Hellenistic age, the place changed hands a number of times, issuing coinage, which continued (with a gap from *c* 300 to *c* 150 BC) until the third century AD.

Issues of Roman imperial date show Leander swimming, lighted on his way by Hero in her tower, and by Eros from above. This refers to the myth (recounted by Musaeus Grammaticus, fifth century AD), according to which Leander, who lived across the strait at Abydus, fell in love with Hero, the priestess of Aphrodite at Sestus, and swam by night across the Hellespont to see her, until, one night, a storm put out the light by which she guided him across, and he was drowned: whereupon she threw herself into the sea after him.

Sétif *see* Sitifis

Seuthopolis (two miles from Koprinka). A city in Thrace (southeastern Bulgaria), situated on a terrace surrounded on three sides by the river Tonzus (Toundja) and one of its tributaries. Although unmentioned in the literary sources—its name is only known from inscriptions—Seuthopolis appears to have been the capital of the powerful and wealthy Thracian (Odrysian) King Seuthes III, who built it on the site of an earlier settlement during his breakaway from Macedonian rule (330-324), and established a royal mint at the new foundation.

Surviving remains include powerful city walls, towers and gates, in addition to a walled precinct encircling the monarch's residence. This palace (*tyrsis*) contained a finely decorated throne room and was linked to a sanctuary—with a large cult fireplace—dedicated to the Cabiri and the other Great Gods of Samothrace; the shrine is mentioned in a recently discovered inscription, which also records a temple of Dionysus. Constructed according to a rectangular (Hippodamian) street plan, the town included spacious noblemen's houses—sometimes of Greek types—built round courtyards and revealing traces of colonnades, upper storeys and systems of drainage. The site of Seuthopolis casts much new light on the urban history of the Thracians in the early Hellenistic age. It suffered destruction, however, at the end of the fourth century BC and was not rediscovered until the 1940s.

Kazanluk, five miles away, displays a number of domed tombs designed for the burial of Thracian princes before and after 300 BC. In the most important of these graves, the dome is decorated with wall paintings, executed by a Greek artist. The central group displays the dead man, holding a cup (*phiale*), symbolic of divinity; seated at a laden table, he is flanked by his wife and a servant girl, sitting and standing respectively. A procession of women, too, is shown bringing gifts to the royal bride. The artistic concepts of these designs are Greek, but the character of the procession, and the difference in size between the figures—indicative of their hierarchic status—are suggestive of eastern influences.

Sevastopol, Sebastopol *see* Bosphorus (Cimmerian)

Seville *see* Hispalis

Shahat *see* Cyrene

Shahba *see* Philippopolis

Shahr-i-Kohna *see* Arachosia

Sheikh Ibada *see* Antinoopolis

Shkodër *see* Scodra

Shomeron, Shomron *see* Samaria

Shush *see* Susa

Sibari *see* Sybaris

Sicily, Sicilia, Sikelia, Sikanie, originally Trinacria or Thrinacia, a name derived from its triangular shape. Separated from the Italian peninsula by the narrows which bore its name (now the Strait of Messina), Sicily is the largest island in the Mediterranean, with an area of 9,830 square miles. Its long and varied prehistory is extensively illustrated by the contents of Sicilian museums. Ancient writers distinguish between three main pre-Greek peoples, Siculi or Sicels in the east (supposedly late comers from Italy, from whom the name of Sicily was derived), Sicans in the west-center (hence the island's name Sikanie in the *Odyssey*), and Elymians to the west (credited with a Trojan origin).

In the later second millennium BC, during the Bronze Age, Mycenaean traders visited Sicily; and from *c* 735 extensive Greek colonization was undertaken, beginning with Naxos (Capo Schiso; from Chalcis in Euboea) and Syracuse (Siracusa; from Corinth). Meanwhile the Phoenicians settled in the western portion of the island, often in alliance with the Elymians. Although the Carthaginians, who succeeded their Phoenician forebears, maintained the defence of this territory (*c* 580, *c* 510), they were decisively defeated by Gelon (who had moved his capital from Acragas [Agrigento] to Syracuse) and Theron of Acragas at Himera (Imera) in 480.

During the Peloponnesian War the Athenians twice intervened against Syracuse (427–24, 415–413), on the second occasion with the disastrous results immortalized by Thucydides. Following two successive Carthaginian invasions of the island (409, 406), Dionysius I of Syracuse (406–367) resumed hostilities against Carthage in no less than four successive wars. They were ultimately indecisive, but Dionysius maintained control over most of the island, and so did other Syracusan leaders after him, Timoleon (d. 334) and Agathocles (317–289). An invasion by Pyrrhus of Epirus (278/76) proved abortive, and after the First Punic War (264–241) the greater part of Sicily became Rome's first overseas province, with the exception of Syracuse under Hiero II (275–215), which was however, incorporated in the province after his death (211) and became its capital (one of the two financial officers [quaestors] resided at Lilybaeum [Marsala]).

Immensely important to Rome as a source of grain, Sicily was ravaged by two slave rebellions (135/32, 104–100) and plundered by the governor Gaius Verres (73–71), who was attacked by Cicero in a series of famous speeches. Julius Caesar granted the island Latin rights (according to which the annually elected civic officials became Roman citizens), but it became a battlefield after his death (43) when Sextus Pompeius seized Messana (Messina) and cut off the grain supply of Rome. Then he was finally defeated in 36 off Naulochus [Venetico Marina?] by Octavian (the future Augustus), who subsequently established a number of Roman colonies; but the language of the island as a whole remained Greek. In AD 126 Hadrian climbed Mount Aetna (Etna) to see the sunrise.

During the later empire Sicily became a province of the administrative diocese of Italia Suburbicaria. Under Gaiseric (428–77) the Vandals raided and invaded the island from north Africa over a period of four decades, until in 476 they were obliged to relinquish the greater part of its territory to Odoacer the Herulian—who was now king of Italy—against the payment of an annual tribute; though this was discontinued by Odoacer's Ostrogothic successor Theoderic in 491. *See also* Acragas, Aegates Islands, Aetna (Mount), Camarina, Catana, Centuripae, Drepanum, Ecnomus (Cape), Enna, Eryx, Gela, Leontini, Lilybaeum, Lipara (Island), Megara Hyblaea, Metapontum, Morgantina, Motya, Mylae, Naxos, Panormus, Philosophiana, Selinus, Syracuse, Tauromenium.

Sicyon, Sikyon or Sekyon ('town of the cucumbers'), originally, it was said, called Aegiale or Aegialeia—after *aigialos,* 'shore land,' and the mythical Aegialeus—and then later Mecone, and subsequently for a time Demetrias (now Basiliko, two and a half miles from Sikonia). A Greek city in the northern Peloponnese, about eleven miles northwest of Corinth. The original town lay at the foot of two wide plateaus, one of which constituted its acropolis, two miles from the Corinthian Gulf—on which it possessed an artificial port (Kiato)—at the junction of deep ravines cut by the rivers Asopus and Helisson (Elisson). Inhabited in the Mycenaean Late Bronze Age, Sicyon appeared in Greek legend as a dependency of Agamemnon of Mycenae, and as the royal capital of Adrastus while he was a refugeee from Argos.

A long period of subordination to the Argives was ended in *c* 655 BC by the local dynasty of the Orthagorids, whose most powerful monarch Cleisthenes (*c* 600–570) established impressive commercial connections abroad, married his daughter into the great Alcmaeonid family of Athens, supported Delphi in the First Sacred War against Cirtha (*c* 590), and sponsored flourishing schools of painting, pottery, and bronze sculpture; of which the lastnamed art was allegedly developed by Dipoenus and Scyllis, pupils of the legendary (?) Cretan Daedalus, and culminated toward the end of the sixth century in the bronze caster Canachus, famous for his statue of Apollo Philesius at Didyma.

During the following century Sicyon was the most active Peloponnesian mint. When the Spartans eliminated the city's autocratic dynasty, it became a member of their League—to which it remained loyal, despite Athenian harrassment, during the Peloponnesian War (431–404). In 367 it briefly resumed autocratic rule, under Euphron who was described in hostile terms by Xenophon and Diodorus, because he supported the poor against the upper classes. At this juncture Epaminondas had made Sicyon the headquarters of Theban power in the Peloponnese. Subsequently, dictatorial government was established yet again with the help of Philip II of Macedonia (359–336). During this period the place attained a second zenith as an artistic center: Pamphilus (who conducted courses lasting twelve years) taught Apelles painting there, and Sicyonian sculpture culminated in the outstandingly famous and innovative Lysippus, the portrayer of Alexander the Great.

Alexander maintained a major mint in the city. After his death, it was captured by Demetrius I Poliorcetes (the Besieger, 303), who transplanted its inhabitants to the plateaus overlooking the previous site, at a new settlement named Demetrias. Under the sponsorship of Aratus this community joined the Achaean League (251), the destruction of which by the Romans in 146 brought it additional territory and, for a time, the presidency of Corinth's Isthmian Games. Sicyon was so deeply in debt *c* 58 BC, however, that it had to sell its works of art, and during the Principate it was eclipsed by the restoration of Corinth and Patrae; after devastation by an earthquake (*c* AD 140), Pausanias found its site half-ruined and almost deserted. Nevertheless, what remained of the town was the seat of a bishopric in early Christian and Byzantine times.

Remains of walls encircling the habitation center and separating the acropolis from the other (lower) terrace are still to be seen. Pausanias and other writers, and local coins, record temples dedicated to a considerable variety of deities, including Fortune (Tyche Akraia) and the Dioscuri (Castor and Polydeuces

[Pollux]). These two shrines were situated on the acropolis, and the seats of a stadium and a theater—one of the largest on the Greek mainland—were cut into its slopes. Excavations have uncovered a gymnasium with a colonnaded courtyard, and, beside the agora, a portico (Stoa) with traces of a double colonnade, a council chamber (Bouleuterion) of the third century BC—later transformed into a Roman bathing establishment (of which another, larger example exists elsewhere in the city)—and an early temple renovated in Hellenistic times and subsequently converted into a Christian church. A further Christian basilica has been excavated on a low hill beside the ancient port.

Side (Selimiye or Eski Antalya). A city in Pamphylia (southern Asia Minor), on the river Melas (Manavgat) five miles from its mouth, situated on a narrow promontory terminating in an almost wholly artificial harbor (now silted up).

Eusebius (*c* AD 260–240) attributed the foundation of Side to 1405 BC; its claim to Greek origins was put forward in the fourth century *Periplus* (*Round Trip*) of Pseudo-Scylax. According to Strabo and Arrian, the first Greek settlers came from Cyme (Namurt Limanı) in Aeolis (western Asia Minor). This may have occurred some time before 600, but the authenticity of the tradition is doubtful. Arrian adds, quoting the Sidetans themselves, that they forgot their Greek speech and spoke an alien tongue (not resembling their native neighbors' speech), which was presumably the language of the pre-Greek inhabitants and can be seen—though not yet deciphered—on coins issued from *c* 500 with a punning type of a pomegranate (*side*), as well as a few local inscriptions.

Although problems of entering and dredging made the phrase 'a harbor of Side' a proverbial expression of difficulty, the place became the most important city in Pamphylia. It was occupied in 333 by Alexander the Great. After his death it passed successively under the control of Antigonus I Monophthalmos, the Ptolemies (301–218) and the Seleucids, whose naval commander the famous exiled Carthaginian Hannibal, employed by Antiochus III the Great, suffered a naval defeat offshore at the hands of the Rhodians (190). But bad relations with neighboring Aspendus (Belkis) were debilitating; moreover, Side was eclipsed by the foundation of Attaleia (Antalya), and pirates used its port as a principal dockyard and slave market, until their suppression by Pompey the Great in 67.

The city seems to have remained autonomous within the Roman provinces of Cilicia, and then Galatia (a client kingdom whose monarch Amyntas issued coins at the local mint), and subsequently Lycia-Pamphylia. In the second and early third centuries AD it enjoyed a second period of considerable prosperity. While stressing heartfelt loyalty to Rome, the local coinage also celebrated a remarkable variety of civic festivals, and—despite irruptions by Scythians and Isaurians (268/270)—issues continued up to the time of Aurelian (270–75). During the later empire Side became the capital of the province of Pamphylia and then, in the fifth century, of Pamphylia Secunda. It was also the seat of a bishopric.

Parts of the city wall date from the second century BC, but its subsequent course reflects a shrinking of perimeter amid the perils of the later third century AD. At the center of the Agora, of which only the foundations remain, stood a round building of the second century AD, probably a temple of Tyche (Fortune). The theater of about the same period, replacing a Hellenistic building, is one of the largest known in the Greco-Roman world, accommodating 13,000 spectators; it was built on large arches and adorned with lavish decorations. An adjacent complex of buildings of considerable size, comprising a peristyle court and three large halls (which have yielded a large series of statues) has been identified as a gymnasium; but it may have been a second agora instead. A monumental *nymphaeum* (fountain-house) comprised three semicircular half-domed niches. An extensive late imperial bathhouse was fed by a second-century aqueduct twenty miles long.

Two sanctuaries standing side by side on a platform overlooking the harbor were probably dedicated to Apollo and Athena-Roma, the principal deities of the city. Both of these buildings appear on local coinage of imperial date, the temple of Apollo being shown in association with two temples of the imperial cult (Trebonianus Gallus, 251–53). Other issues show models of the shrines of Apollo and Athena-Roma held in the hand of Tyche, whereas a piece issued in the name of Salonina, the wife of Gallienus (253–68), illustrates a temple of Tyche, with an arched lintel and conical roof crowned by a pomegranate. Other coins of the same period display the arcaded harbor and a crenellated gate of the town. Beside the harbor, a large, three-aisled Christian basilica was erected before or after 500.

Sidi Ali bou Djenoun *see* Banasa

Sidon ('the fishery'; now Saida). A coastal city of Phoenicia (Lebanon). Built along the north slope of a headland a little distance from the shore, near the river Bostrenus (Nahr el-Awali), Sidon possessed two harbors, comprising an exposed bay to the south and a more protected northern basin formed by a low line of rocks (strengthened by a wall) extending from the end of the promontory towards the mainland. Excavations have revealed remains dating from the Palaeolithic Age onward.

In the hands of the Phoenicians (who spoke a Semitic language), the people of Sidon freed themselves from Egyptian control and rose to great prosperity as a maritime power *c* 990–980 BC, exporting timber from the Libanus (Lebanon) mountains, and clothing and textiles dyed purple from the *murex* (rock-whelk) caught in baskets off the coast; while their ships also traded in the silver and copper brought from Cilicia (southeast Asia Minor) and Cyprus respectively. According to Greek myth, Agenor was the king either of Sidon or of Tyre (Es-Sur); his daughter was Europa, and one of his sons was Phoenix, founder of the Phoenician people. Homer's *Iliad* refers to the skillful metalwork of the Sidonians, and Strabo praised the astronomical and mathematical expertise they derived from their navigational needs. Sidon was known as the 'mother' of its neighbor Tyre, whose King Hiram was for a time the ruler of both cities.

Successive periods of Assyrian, Babylonian and Persian suzerainty followed, under local kings who depict war galleys on their coinages, sometimes drawn up before the walls of the city. One of these monarchs was Strato I, whose friendly attitude to the Athenians earned him honors from their Assembly (*c* 367?). At some time before the later fourth century, Sidon joined forces with Tyre and Aradus (Arvad) to found the city of Tripolis (Tarabulus esh-Sham, Tripoli). Sidon was conquered by Alexander the Great in 333. Employing the city as a mint, he gave its kingship to Abdalonymus (a gardener by profession), for whose remains one of a number of sarcophagi from the adjacent Ayaa cemetery, the 'Alexander Sarcophagus' (now at Istanbul), was designed; it displays tinted reliefs of battle and hunting scenes in the finest contemporary Greek style.

After a phase of Ptolemaic overlordship, the Sidonians were for the most part under Seleucid domination. They abolished their monarchy in favor of a republic *c* 270/250, and reckoned a new autonomous civic era from 111. This self-government was recognized by Pompey the Great (64/63), and after temporary suspension by Augustus in 20 was reconfirmed *c* 6/5 BC by the same emperor, who also gave the city a large tract of additional territory, extending up to Mount Hermon. During the course of the same century Sidon produced a series of distinguished Greek philosophers, enumerated by Strabo. The discovery of glass-blowing proved very profitable; the signatures of many of its blowers have been preserved on surviving specimens. When St. Paul was taken to Rome, his ship put in at the port, where, according to the *Acts of the Apostles*, he was kindly treated by the centurion Julius.

Under Elagabalus (AD 218–22) Sidon became a Roman colony. Coins issued immediately after his conferment celebrate the imperial donation (*aeternum beneficium*) and local Games, and offer a remarkable picture of a temple of Astarte-Tyche (assimilated to Europa, whom other local pieces frequently depict riding on her bull) behind a courtyard entered between two decorated columns; further issues depict a ceremonial chariot, containing her sacred stone (baetyl). Also honored on the coinage is Dido, temptress of Aeneas in the *Aeneid* of Virgil, who calls her 'Sidonia' although legend declared her to be the daughter of the king of Tyre. In the Bostrenus valley are to be seen the massive walls and other remains of a shrine of the healing god Eshmun (Asclepius, Aesculapius), ranging from Persian to Byzantine times, and surrounded by a network of canals supplying a *nymphaeum* (fountain-house) and sacred and therapeutic pools.

Sığacık *see* Teos

Sigeum (near Yenişehir). A town in the Troad (northwestern Asia Minor), located beside fertile land in a strategic position on the south side of the entry to the Hellespont (Dardanelles); the site controlled the grain route from the Euxine (Black) Sea and Propontis (Sea of Marmara). Sigeum was the first colony of the Athenians, who appear to have settled there at the end of the seventh century BC, under the leadership of Phrynon, an Olympian victor. This colonization involved prolonged warfare with Mytilene (Lesbos)—whose ruler Pittacus killed Phrynon in a duel—and, although the conflict was adjudicated in Athens' favor by the Corinthian autocrat Periander, it appears that firm Athenian control was only established by Hegesistratus, son of the 'tyrant' Pisistratus, probably *c* 546—by which time another Athenian, Miltiades the Elder, had also occupied the Thracian Chersonese (Gelibolu [Gallipoli] peninsula) across the strait.

After 510 Sigeum became the residence of Pisistratus' exiled son Hippias. During the fifth century it was a member of the Delian League under Athenian control, and in 451/450 its settlers were commended for their services by the Athenians, and promised protection against any enemy in Asia. The town was captured, despite resistance, by Alexander the Great's successor Lysimachus (*c* 302), whose capital Lysimachia had been founded on the neck of the Chersonese. There is inscriptional evidence for a guild of coppersmiths at Sigeum, working metal that was mined in the central Troad and the mountains north of Pergamum. The place was destroyed in the second century (?) by the people of Ilium (Troy).

Sikiona *see* Sicyon

Silifke *see* Seleucia on the Calycadnus

Silistra *see* Durostorum

Silvan *see* Tigranocerta

Simagre *see* Colchis, Phasis

Simferopol *see* Scythia

Singara (Balad Sinjar). A city in northern Mesopotamia (Iraq) beside the watercourse Mygdonius, west of the Tigris, on the southern slope of the Jebel Sinjar range. The settlement was of considerable antiquity, and is mentioned in Assyrian records.

A recently discovered milestone of AD 116 testifies to its conquest from the Parthians by Trajan's general Lusius Quietus, some two years earlier. Evacuated after the emperor's death in 117, it was reoccupied by the generals of Lucius Verus (162–65) and became a key military base in the frontier province of Mesopotamia reestablished by Septimius Severus (187–89). Occupying an important strategic and commercial position on routes toward the north (Trajan built a road to Nisibis [Nusaybin]), southwest (Chaboras [Khabur] valley) and southeast (Hatra), Singara was raised to the rank of a colony, under the name of Colonia Aurelia Septimia Severiana, and coined (in Greek) between the reigns of Severus Alexander (222–35) and Philip the Arab (244–49). The Jebel Sinjar mountains fulfilled an important role in the frontier defences established for protection against the Sassanian Persians (who had superseded the Parthians). In 360, however, as Ammianus Marcellinus records, Singara was captured—through the use of a large battering ram—by the Persian Sapor (Shapur) II from Julian the Apostate, with the loss of its whole garrison; and the fortress was ceded to him by Julian's successor Jovian in 363.

The outer and inner walls of the late Roman city, with their ditch and salient towers, can be traced (although much damaged) over a large part of their circumference. The nucleus of this town, and probably the site of the original settlement, is a steep-sided hill to the east of the Mygdonius, on which the Romans built a fortified citadel, including springs, on lower-lying ground within its perimeter. Remains of the south gate, through which the road from the Chaboras valley entered the city, can also be seen.

Singidunum (Belgrade, Beograd). A Roman frontier city at the northwestern extremity of Upper Moesia (now the capital of Yugoslavia), at the confluence of the river Savus (Save) with the Danube. Singidunum was the scene of a battle in which the German Cimbri were defeated by the Scordisci (*c* 115 BC).

The Roman camp, located on the site of Neolithic and Celtic settlements, dates from the first century AD; a legion was stationed there from *c* 9. A squadron of the Danubian fleet, too, was transferred to the local river harbor from Viminacium (Kostolac). Singidunum became a Roman *municipium,* probably in the time of Caracalla (211–17), and was elevated to the rank of a Roman colony under Gordian III (*c* 238/9). It suffered from Gothic and Hun invasions in the fourth and fifth centuries respectively, and was occupied by the Slavs shortly before 600. Foundations and walls of the legionary camp are to be seen below the medieval and modern fortress of Kalemagdan, on a high limestone rock overlooking the junction of the two rivers. The topography of the city that lay below is unclear, but a Roman temple, cisterns and cemetery have been excavated, and extensive discoveries from prehistoric times onward are preserved in the National Museum, including a fine bronze head of Constantine the Great (306–37).

Sinnaca *see* Carrhae

Sinope (Sinop). A city of Paphlagonia (northern Asia Minor), occupying the isthmus of a peninsula or promontory on the south coast of the Euxine (Black) Sea, at the point where the crossing to the Tauric Chersonese (Crimea) is shortest.

After earlier habitation by native Paphlagonians, probably with a Phrygian admixture—in addition (according to Greek mythology) to settlement by Autolycus the Argonaut companion of Jason or by Asopus father of the nymph Sinope—this was believed to be the earliest of the many colonies founded by Miletus in Ionia (western Asia Minor). But it is disputed whether Pseudo-Scymnus was right in implying a foundation before 756 BC or whether Eusebius' date of 631 is more nearly correct; perhaps some Greeks arrived at the earlier date but the Milesians came in 631.

The promontory was fertile and well-watered, the mountainous hinterland produced ample supplies of timber, luxury woods, and nuts, and the city's two deep-water harbors (the best on an otherwise rocky coast) provided not only opportunities for excellent tunny fishing but access to the neighboring silver-and iron-mining regions (known loosely under the name of the Chalybes) that supplied one of the principal motives for Greek colonization in the area.

Sinope commanded the maritime Black Sea commerce (producing numerous amphoras that have attracted recent study), and established not only trading stations but also a number of colonies along the coast, including Trapezus (Trabzon, Trebizond). The place also dominated land routes communicating with the interior of Asia Minor—by which 'Sinopic earth' (red ochre, cinnabar) was brought out from Cappadocia for shipment—and began to issue coinage before 450. In about 437 Sinope was liberated by Pericles the Athenian from the rule of local autocrats (Timesilaus and his brothers) and received a colony of settlers from Athens. Diogenes (*c* 400–325), the founder of the Cynic sect of philosophers, was born at the city.

With brief intervals of occupation by the Persian satraps Datames and Sysinas (*c* 364–353), and by the Cappadocian monarch Ariarathes I (*c* 330), its Greek citizens retained their freedom. Mithridates III of Pontus was repulsed, with Rhodian help, in 220, but in 183 Sinope was captured by one of his successors, Pharnaces I, and became the capital of the Pontic kingdom. During Rome's Third War against Mithridates VI Eupator, who was born (and buried) at Sinope and accorded the place special honors, it was declared a free city by Marcus Licinius Lucullus (70), but reconquered by Mithridates' son Pharnaces II (48/47), who inflicted severe damage. Julius Caesar attempted to remedy this by the dispatch of ex-soldier settlers, under the direction of the proconsul Publius Sulpicius Rufus, to form a Roman citizen colony (45) which coined under the title of Colonia Julia Felix (although, for a time at least, the Greek community maintained a separate existence).

Strabo describes the town as powerfully walled, enjoying the produce of varied market-gardens, and 'splendidly adorned with gymnasia and market-place and colonnades.' Few traces of these buildings have so far been found, though the remains of a Hellenistic temple, within a colonnaded precinct, are visible, and coins show shrines of Apollo and Nemesis. The cult of Poseidon Heliconius, god of the Ionian Federation (to which Miletus belonged), is also attested by an inscription. Greek vases from the site are to be seen in several Turkish museums, and a corpus of Sinopic inscriptions is now being published.

Siracusa *see* Syracuse

Sirkap *see* Taxila

Sirmio (Sirmione). A peninsula, two and a half miles long and in places only one hundred and thirty yards wide, at the southern end of Lake Benacus (Garda) in Cisalpine Gaul (north Italy), near the road from Brixia (Brescello) to Verona. A favorite Roman summer residence (containing sulphur springs, which rise in the lake) Sirmio was praised for its beauty in a famous poem of Catullus (*c* 84–54), who describes himself as its 'master,' indicating that he owned a villa there. This residence has been identified, though without any firm evidence, with the 'Grottos of Catullus,' comprising remains of a building of about the mid-first century BC, on which a larger villa, with a garden, portico, fountains and fine wall paintings, was superimposed in the middle or second half of the following century.

Sirmium (Sremska Mitrovica). A Roman city in Pannonia (Yugoslavia) situated at the junction of the river Bacuntius with the Savus (Save), west of its junction with the Danube. Originally a settlement of the Amantini tribe, the place was occupied by the Romans during their conquest of Pannonia (12–9 BC). Attached at first to the province of Illyricum, it received mention during the widespread revolt of AD 6–9, after which separate provinces of Illyricum (Dalmatia) and Pannonia were created, and Sirmium thereafter belonged to the latter.

In the subsequent years of the same century it became an important military base, and, when its legionary or auxiliary garrison left, was probably elevated to the rank of a Roman colony (Colonia Flavia) by Vespasian (69–79)—although an important role was retained by the native population. When Pannonia was divided into two provinces by Trajan (*c* 103), Sirmium found itself assigned to the Lower province, in which it derived great importance from its fleet station on the Save, and from its position at the junction of roads linking Italy, Dalmatia and the Danube. Trajan himself visited the city, and so did Marcus Aurelius, Septimius Severus, Maximinus I and Gallienus, on one of whose coinages appear the letters S.P., interpreted as Secunda Pannonia, the name of the late imperial province of which Sirmium became the capital.

The emperors Trajanus Decius, Aurelian, Probus, Maximian, Gratian and Constantius II were all born in the vicinity of the city. Under the Tetrarchy of Diocletian and Maximian, and especially from the time of Galerius (305–11), it became one of the principal centers and strongholds of the Roman world, and the military and governmental headquarters of many rulers, including Constantine I the Great, the founder of a major mint at Sirmium (320–26) which resumed activity during the middle and later part of the same century. Sirmium was the capital of the praetorian prefect of Illyricum (one of the principal administrators of the empire), and housed important arms factories. It was also of great ecclesiastical significance, becoming the location of several Church Councils. But the Huns destroyed or severely damaged its buildings, and as a result (a law of Justinian I records) the praetorian prefecture of Illyricum was moved to Thessalonica (Salonica) *c* 441/42. Sirmium was finally destroyed by the Avars before 582.

During the later empire it must have possessed a great imperial palace, of which recent excavators claim to have at last revealed traces, together with the remains of a Constantinian barracks and hippodrome, attached to the palace; the hippodrome was later reconstructed. Parts of the Baths of Licinius (308–24) have also been uncovered, as well as a large warehouse or granary of the same period, a row of shops, rich private houses—one of which, containing geometric floor mosaics of the fourth or fifth century, lies under the present Sremska Museum—and sections of the city wall, comprising successive structural phases of the third and early fourth centuries AD.

Sirsukh *see* Taxila

Sisak *see* Siscia

Siscia (Sisak). A Roman city in Pannonia (Yugoslavia) on the island of Segesta or Segestica (after which it was sometimes named) at the junction of the rivers Colapis (Kupa) and Odra with the Savus (Save). A former Iron Age and Celtic stronghold, supplied with wine and oil from Aquileia in the second century BC in exchange for cattle, hides and slaves, the place was probably captured by Roman forces in 119 and definitively occupied in 35, after a thirty-day siege by Octavian (the future Augustus), who established a legionary garrison there. During the Illyrian (Pannonian) rebellion of AD 6–9 this camp was the base for Tiberius' large army, including a legion that subsequently remained in the fortress until 42 (except for a brief interval in 20–24). With the assistance of a canal constructed by Tiberius across the confluence, Siscia also served as a fleet and customs station, and was a meeting place of five important roads.

It became a Roman colony in the time of Vespasian (69–79)—unless Augustus had granted it this rank previously—under the name of Colonia Flavia, receiving marines discharged from the Ravenna fleet as colonists. The city became part of Trajan's new province of Upper Pannonia *c* 103, and was redesignated Colonia Septimia during the reign of Septimius Severus (193–211). An outstandingly important military headquarters and center of arms manufacture (based on adjacent iron mines that supplemented an earlier bronze industry) Siscia inaugurated its career as one of the greatest and historically most informative imperial mints under Gallienus (*c* 262). At one point (284–85), it coined for the usurper Marcus Aurelius Julianus, for whom it issued pieces inscribed 'the emperor's Pannonias' (PANNONIAE AVG[usti]).

When, shortly afterward, these two provinces were subdivided into four, Sisca became the capital of Pannonia Savia or Ripariensis, continuing to issue extensive coinages, as well as medallions in honor of the sons of Constantine the Great (337). It was also a mint of the pretender Vetranio (350), and finally of the joint emperors Valens (364–78) and Valentinian II (375–92), before falling into the hands of the Ostrogoths at the beginning of the fifth century. The most eminent of its early Christian bishops was St. Quirinus. Bath buildings have been found near the river Colapis, of which the bed has yielded numerous important finds.

Sirte (Gulf) *see* Lepcis Magna

Sitifis (Sétif). A city in the interior of the Roman province of Mauretania Caesariensis (Algeria), not far from its border with Numidia. Situated at a height of more than 3,000 feet, south of the Kabylie mountains where a road between Lambaesis (Tazzoult) and the coast joins another route leading to Cirta (Constantine), Sitifis received a settlement of ex-soldiers from Nerva (AD 96–98), under the title of Colonia Nerviana Augusta Veteranorum. In the later empire it became the capital of the province of Mauretania Sitifensis. After witnessing the execution of the governor Ruricus, accused of sending false reports to Valentinian I (370), the town played a prominent part during the ensuing rebellion of the Mauretanian Firmus, becoming the headquarters of the governmental forces of Theodosius the Elder (father of the future emperor of the same name). According to Ammianus Marcellinus, Theodosius tortured and burned alive the supporters of his own unsatisfactory former general Romanus; and then, after Firmus had killed himself, he made a ceremonial entry into the city, amid enthusiastic applause. Together with the rest of Mauretania, Sitifis fell to the Vandals under Gaiseric in 429.

The center of the Roman town was probably under a subsequent Byzantine fortress, which in turn was partially demolished in the nineteenth century. Remains of houses dating from the foundation of the colony were destroyed when a large temple (of which the foundations can still be seen) was built before or after AD 200. A new northwestern quarter, in which the regular streets, houses, shops and a bathing establishment have been partly uncovered, was added at the beginning of the fourth century, and especially toward its end, and it was at this time that a hippodrome was built and an earlier amphitheater underwent a second restoration (361–63). Two Christian basilicas with funerary inscriptions were erected side by side not long afterward, and have been carefully investigated. They contained nineteen inscriptions dated from 378 to 429 (and one of 471). The layout of city walls of late imperial date have been established from nineteenth-century drawings, supplemented by recent excavations.

Sıvas *see* Sebasteia

Skhimatarion *see* Tanagra

Skripou *see* Orchomenus

Smyrna (İzmir). A Greek city in Ionia (western Asia Minor) at the head of the gulf that bears its name, into which flowed the river Hermus (Gediz). The original city, Old Smyrna, stood on a hilly peninsula (Haci Mutso) on the northeastern coast of the gulf (east of Bayraklı, two-and-a-half miles north of modern İzmir). This settlement existed since Neolithic times but its founders, according to legend, included Amazons, Leleges and Tantalus of Phrygia.

In 1050/950 BC (as pottery finds indicate), the site was occupied by Aeolian Greeks (mainly from Lesbos) and then by Ionians (from Colophon [Değirmendere]), and excavation has shown the presence of a stout fortification wall skillfully built *c* 850, and repaired and thickened a century later. Before 700 Old Smyrna seems to have contained four or five hundred houses, and a population of about two thousand Greeks (other than slaves), with perhaps another thousand living in an extramural suburb. According to a local tradition perpetuated by later coinage but disputed by Chios and other cities, Homer had been a native of Smyrna; and it was the birthplace of the elegiac poet and musician Mimnermus. During the seventh century the city was remodelled, with parallel streets flanked by regularly constructed, spacious houses and containing a large temple of Athena; the uncovering of this building, and of the previous settlement has provided us with a unique picture of an early Greek city, indicating that a rectangular gridiron street plan was already in use at an early date. Rare electrum (pale gold) coinages of this period (depicting the open-jawed head of a lion—the emblem of the mother-goddess Cybele) are attributed to Smyrna. The town provided an export outlet for the agricultural products of the interior.

In 600/575, however, it was captured by King Alyattes of Lydia, by means of a siege-mound that enabled him to overrun its massive defences. This disaster resulted in very severe damage, which was repeated *c* 545 by the Persians when they destroyed the temple of Athena.

After a prolonged period in which, according to Strabo, the inhabitants had retreated to villages—though inscriptions and housing quarters dating from the early fourth century show that the destruction at the hands of the Lydians and Persians had not been total, or, if so, had been partially repaired—Smyrna was rebuilt on its present site around and on Mount Pagos (Kadife Kale), five miles along the bay to the south, beside the river Meles (Kemer Çayı). This refoundation was attributed to Alexander the Great, and it was probably he who drew up the plan; but it was carried out by his successors Antigonus I Monophthalmos (d. 301) and Lysimachus (d. 281). Protected by an acropolis on the hilltop and by walls running down to a crescent-shaped harbor, this new Smyrna became one of the greatest centers of Asia Minor. After periods of Seleucid and Pergamene overlordship, during which spasmodic resumptions of coinage in the course of the fourth and third centuries were followed by substantial issues in the second, the city subsequently possessed 'free' status within the Roman province of Asia (133), and sided with Rome against Mithridates VI of Pontus. In 43, however, it was the scene of the treacherous murder of Gaius Trebonius—Julius Caesar's assassin, who had become governor of Asia—at the hands of Publius Cornelius Dolabella.

During the Principate Smyrna prospered greatly from the production and export of wine, clothing, perfumes and prawns. In AD 26 Tiberius allowed its citizens to build a temple in his honor, and they benefited from the munificence of Hadrian (117–38, whose beloved Antinous was commemorated on local medallions), Marcus Aurelius (following an earthquake in 178), and Caracalla (211–17). Local coinage celebrates 'alliances' with many other cities of the region, boasts of holding the 'First Games of Asia,' displays a varied array of deities, and depicts a temple of Tiberius and Hadrian and Rome, as well as shrines of Tyche (Fortune) and the two Nemeses (symbolized by griffins). It was these Nemeses, according to a legend, who had appeared to Alexander the Great in a dream and directed him to build the city on Mount Pagos, on which he is shown, by coins of several imperial epochs, sleeping beneath a palm tree on the occasion when this message was delivered.

Smyrna was centered, however, on flat ground beside the harbor, where a temple of Cybele and a gymnasium were situated. Strabo also mentions a Homereion, and records that the two principal streets, the Sacred Way and the Golden Road, ran from east to west, so that the wind coming from the sea cooled the town. Traces of these streets, with a roofed-over sidewalk, have been unearthed. But the most impressive monument of New Smyrna is provided by the remains of its huge rectangular agora, which has likewise now been partially excavated. It was flanked on three sides by colonnades and on the fourth by an aisled, two-storeyed basilica, terminating in a tribunal and possessing an unusual vaulted basement. A theater and a stadium have also been identified. Christianity had come early to Smyrna, and it was one of the 'Seven Churches of Asia' in the *Book of Revelation*.

Sofia *see* Serdica

Sogdiana. A region of Central Asia between the Upper Oxus (Amu Darya) and Upper Jaxartes (Syr), taking its name from the river Sogd which, passing near Samarkand and Bokhara, loses itself in sand before approaching the Oxus. Sogdiana comprised parts of the present Soviet Republics of Tajikistan and Uzbekistan. The extensive ruins of the capital Maracanda (Samarkand) in the fertile valley of the Polytimetus (Zeravshan) testify to an important prehistory during the early first millennium BC. The Sogdian language has only left slender remains (notably in documents of the seventh century AD).

A satrapy of the Achaemenid Persian King Darius I (521–486 BC), Sogdiana was conquered in 328/7 by Alexander the Great, who, after capturing its fortresses including the chieftain Oxyartes' supposedly impregnable 'Sogdian Rock' (or Rock of Oxus or Ariamazes), married Oxyartes' daughter, Roxane, at the fortress of another leader Chorienes, thus bringing Sogdian resistance to an end; whereupon Alexander founded Alexandria Eschate ('the farthest') on the Jaxartes (*qv*).

Sogdiana, which controlled an important trade route to China, was subsequently incorporated into the Seleucid empire, and probably formed part of the territory of its governor Diodotus I Soter when he revolted (*c* 256/5) and created a virtually (later wholly) independent Bactrian state. Early in the reign of the Greek monarch Strato I (*c* 130–75), however, the central Asian Yüeh-Chih (Tochari) occupied and annexed Sogdiana and divided it into five principalities. This alienation from the Greek world proved to be permanent, although the country remained a prosperous center of population, and indeed only attained its cultural zenith a millennium later, under Islamic rule.

Soli, Soloi, later Pompeiopolis (Mezitli). A coastal city in southeastern Asia Minor, on the borders of Smooth Cilicia of the Plain (Pedias, Campestris) and Rough Cilicia (Tracheia, Aspera), about five miles west of the modern Mersin. A harbor township from before 2000 BC, Soli was colonized in the later eighth century by settlers from Lindus (Rhodes), and perhaps also from Argos (though the contribution of the Argives may be fictitious). Subsequently Soli came under the control of the Persians, and when occupied by Alexander the Great in 333 was so prosperous that he was able to fine its people a very large sum for having taken the Persian side. He subsequently remitted a part of the fine—in exchange for naval assistance—gave the citizens a new constitution, provided them with Games, and sacrificed to Asclepius (to celebrate his capture of Halicarnassus [Bodrum]).

The Stoic philosopher-poet Aratus (d. 240/239) and the leader of the Stoic school Chrysippus (d. 208) both came from Soli, which nevertheless gave its name to the term *soloikismus* (solecism) owing to the bad Greek spoken by its inhabitants (an alleged, but unlikely, alternative suggested reason for their punishment by Alexander). Soli came under the rule of the Seleucids until occupied by Ptolemaic troops (*c* 246), but was brought back under Seleucid control by Antiochus III the Great in 197. After the establishment of the Roman province of Cilicia, it was captured and almost depopulated in the late eighties or seventies by Tigranes I of Armenia, who removed most of the population to his new city of Tigranocerta (Silvan).

In 67/6, however, Soli was revived by Pompey the Great, who settled a colony of former pirates in the place, and renamed it Pompeiopolis. His head appears on subsequent local coinage. In AD 260 Soli Pompeiopolis was besieged by the Sassanian Persian Sapor (Shapur) I, but was relieved by Callistus, a general of Valcrian, who on the strength of this success—after hearing of Valerian's capture by the Persians—set up two rival emperors on his own account (Macrianus the Younger and Quietus).

The city's monetary issues of imperial date show busts of Aratus and Chrysippus, depict numerous deities and a fountain nymph named Sounia, and under Antoninus Pius (138–61) present a view of the harbor, containing a reclining personification of Oceanus. This harbor is now silted up, but its two parallel moles with curving sides can still be seen, as well as remains of the long colonnaded avenue (probably of the second century AD) leading down to the seafront. Traces of a theater were noted in the nineteenth century, but have now almost completely disappeared.

Soli, Soloi (Potamos tou Kambou, west of Karavostasi). Situated beside the river Kambos in Morphou Bay, on the northwest coast of Cyprus, the city comprised an acropolis and a lower town adjoining the harbor. There were various conflicting Greek legends about its foundation. One story ascribed this even to the mythical Athenian hero Acamas, son of Theseus, accompanied by Phalerus who was also the supposed founder of Phaleron. According to another version, the Athenian statesman Solon advised Philocyprus, the king of Aipeia (three miles to the northwest) to move his people to the coast, which he did, naming the new foundation after his counsellor.

These stories of Soli's Greek origin, however, are Athenian chauvinistic fictions; it is rather to be identified with the pre-Greek town of Sillu, of which the king was an ally of the Assyrian monarch Esarhaddon in 672. Passing under the control of the Achaemenid Persians, it was recaptured by their forces during the Ionian revolt, after a five months' siege (496). Subsequently Soli formed part of the dominions of Evagoras of Salamis (411–374/3). Later, however, it had kings of its own; one of them, Pasicrates, helped to defray the expenses of dramatic performances celebrating the capture of Tyre by Alexander the Great (311), whose friend (and Asian governor) Stasanor belonged to Pasicrates' family. After Alexander's death Pasicrates sided with Ptolemy I Soter of Egypt (321), so that Soli was the only kingdom in Cyprus to escape abolition at his hands, and Pasicrates' son and successor Eunostus married Ptolemy's daughter, Irene. Nevertheless, he was apparently the last king of the city, which thereafter seems to have adopted a Republican constitution. Well-known for its copper mines, and for its position as the main center of Hellenism in the western part of Cyprus (as Salamis was in the east), Soli continued to prosper and became the seat of a bishopric, first occupied for fifty years (*c* AD 52–103), according to legendary tradition, by St. Auxibius, who had been baptized and ordained by St. Mark the Evangelist.

The city wall can be traced along the ridge of the acropolis, and presumably came down to the coast on both sides of the harbor. Among remains of every epoch in the tower town, a large paved street and glass and dyeing factories have been uncovered; and a theater cut in the rock, accommodating 3,500 spectators and overlooking the sea, has now been partially reconstructed. An archaic temple has been excavated on the acropolis, and a sacred precinct at Cholades outside the city, in which inscriptions testify to the worship of a considerable number of deities. One of the cemeteries goes back to an early period in the city's life. An early Christian basilica has come to light, and there are remains of a palatial fifth-century residence five miles west of the town of Vouni.

Solin *see* Salonae

Sophianae *see* Pannonia

Sousa *see* Susa

Sparta, Sparte, or Lacedaemon. A city of Laconia (Peloponnese, southern Greece), at the northern end of the fertile Eurotas valley, protected by spectacular mountain barriers (Taygetus and Parnon) on either side. Prehistoric remains are few, although in the late Bronze (Mycenaean) Age there were habitation centers at Amyclae, three miles to the south of the later Sparta, and Therapne two miles to the southeast of the city. The Therapne settlement stood beside a sanctuary dedicated to a nature goddess and her helpers, later identified with Helen, her brothers the Dioscuri (Castor and Polydeuces [Pollux]) and her husband Menelaus; he and Helen were believed to have been buried there, and the shrine was known as the Menelaion. According to Homer's *Iliad,* Menelaus was the King of Sparta or Lacedaemon (a name used also, as Strabo points out, for the whole of Laconia and Messenia), whose wife's abduction by Paris supposedly caused the Trojan War.

During the tenth century BC Dorian invaders or immigrants settled in four or five villages around the acropolis, and these later coalesced into a town. Early Spartan history is a deeply obscure and profoundly disputed subject, owing to the propagandist efforts of later writers keenly interested in the city's constitution, of which certain details were preserved by Plutarch in a document known as the Great Rhetra, dating back to the eighth or (perhaps most probably) mid-seventh century. By this time there were two royal families of Sparta, the Agiads and Eurypontids—both claiming descent from Heracles—whose autocracy was modified by annual appointed officials (ephors), eventually five in number, and by a Council of Elders (*gerousia*) which prepared business for an assembly (*apella*), of which all Spartiates (free-born Spartans) over thirty years of age were members. The First Messenian War (*c* 740/720?) partially achieved the conquest of Messenia—adjoining Laconia to the west—and grouped the Messenians with the other Dorian or pre-Dorian serfs (helots) who were subjected to the Spartiates. Another section of the population, better off although not enjoying full rights, consisted of the *perioeci,* 'dwellers round about.' A group of Spartans founded Taras (Tarentum) in south Italy *c* 706. Although Sparta was badly defeated by Argos at Hysiae *c* 669, a prolonged Messenian rebellion (the Second Messenian War (*c* 650–620?) was successfully crushed; it prompted or encouraged the development at Sparta of a 'new model' army of heavy infantry (hoplites) manned by Spartiates, supplemented by *perioeci*.

During this century Sparta excelled in the arts of bronze work and ivory carving, and was also the principal home of Greek choral lyric poetry, composed by Tyrtaeus—military commander in the Second Messenian War—and Alcman and Thaletas, who immigrated from Lydia (?) and Gortyna (Crete) respectively (unless Alcman was a native Spartan). During the sixth century Stesichorus of Himera and Theognis of Megara resided at Sparta, and potters and painters produced wares of excellent quality. A great bronze mixing bowl of *c* 550 found at Vix in the interior of France is believed by some to be of Spartan origin.

But those of the craftsmen and artists who were natives must have been not Spartiates but *perioeci*. For by the late seventh or sixth century BC the rigorously austere, communal and totalitarian Spartiate socio-military institutions associated with the name of the semi-legendary Lycurgus had been introduced, with the aim of holding down the subject populations. This comprehensive reform was accompanied by a gradual elimination of exports and imports (in a society which was self-sufficient in essential food-stuffs), and eventually put an end to most cultural life.

By the end of the sixth century the Spartans presided over a League comprising most of the Peloponnese, and extending beyond its borders. Their success was partly due to their most famous ephor, Chilon, one of the Seven Sages. They suffered one serious defeat in *c* 550 when their troops failed to reduce Tegea in Arcadia to subject status, but even Tegea became a member of their League shortly afterward; and according to Herodotus their other wars of the period proved successful. Sparta was not acknowledged as the leading power in Greece. It became the ally of King Croesus of Lydia, and gained a name for action against autocratic governments in other city-states. Thus a Spartan force helped to attack Polycrates of Samos, and Cleomenes I overthrew Hippias at Athens (510). His two subsequent interventions there were unsuccessful, but he won a complete victory over Argos at Sepeia (*c* 494).

In the Persian War of 480–479 Sparta fought at Thermopylae (where King Leonidas I conducted his heroic defence), at Salamis (where another Spartan Eurybiades was, at least nominally, the allied commander), and at Plataea (under the regent Pausanias). After the wars, however, the Spartans were obliged to acquiesce in the naval hegemony of Athens, especially when weakened by a Third Messenian War (*c* 469 or *c* 464) and an earthquake (464). But then came the first outbreak of hostilities against the Athenians (460–446), terminated by the Thirty Years' Peace which implicitly recognized the Athenians' right to their empire. Despite many vicissitudes the Peloponnesian War against Athens (431–404), fought in alliance with Corinth and Thebes, resulted in the total victory of the Spartans, after the final naval victory of Lysander at Aegospotami (405). The active Spartan imperialism that followed, including a war conducted against the Persians by Agesilaus II (396/5), at first received encouragement from the King's Peace (or Peace of Antalcidas) imposed by the Persians in 387, but was then abruptly brought to an end by defeat at the hands of the reorganized Boeotian (Theban) League at Leuctra (371).

By this time there were only 2,000 Spartiates, in contrast to 8,000 in 480, and a period of isolation and decline followed. Agis III led a movement against Alexander the Great while the latter was in Asia, but was defeated and killed by Antipater at Megalopolis (331). Until this time, it was said, Sparta had used bars of iron as money; its first coinage, depicting the archaic statue of Apollo of Amyclae, belonged to the reign of King Areus (*c* 312–265). Remarkable moves by Agis IV (244–241) and Cleomenes III (235–222) to restore Spartan power, by means of a new heady blend of traditionalism and social revolution, ended in Cleomenes' overthrow by the Macedonians and Achaeans at Sellasia. A further attempted revolutionary revival by Nabis (207–192) terminated in his defeat by the Roman general Flamininus, once again joined by the Achaeans, whose League Sparta was thereupon compelled to join.

After the abolition of the Achaean League by the Romans, Sparta was loosely attached to their province of Macedonia-Achaea (146). The Spartan Lachares was executed by Antony for piracy, but his son Eurycles fought against Antony at Actium (31), on the side of Octavian (the future Augustus), who rewarded him with Roman citizenship and with an enlargement of Spartan territory. Eurycles displayed on his coinage a bust of Sparte, the mythical daughter of Eurotas and wife of Lacedaemon. He was succeeded (before 2 BC) by his son Gaius Julius Lacon—who was demoted by Tiberius, restored by Gaius (Caligula), and still in power under Claudius (AD 41–54). Thereafter Sparta reverted to the position of a free city associated with the province of Achaea, enjoying a remarkable revival in the second century and issuing coinage until the reign of Gallienus (253–68). During his reign, however, it was subjected to a destructive raid by the German Heruli (267), and following reconstruction (according to a new town plan) suffered further severe damage from the Visigoth Alaric (395).

Thucydides remarked of Sparta that one cannot judge the importance of a city by its architecture. Our principal evidence for the early settlement comes from excavations of the Sanctuary of Orthia (later assimilated to Artemis) in the village of Limnae on the west bank of the Eurotas. An earthen altar was replaced *c* 725 BC by a simple stone temple within a walled precinct, and in *c* 570 the entire sanctuary was redesigned, perhaps as a result of the flooding of the Eurotas. Numerous small bronze figures (especially of animals) and more then 10,000 lead figurines have been found on the site. It was here that the 'Contest of the Whips' was held, in which Spartan youths were flogged in an initiation rite to prove their virility; this ordeal was revived in Roman times as an advertisement of Sparta's historic past and in order to attract tourists, for whose benefit seating accommodation was constructed.

The site of the temple of Athena Poliouchus on the acropolis, also known as the Bronze House (Chalcioecus) from the bronze sheeting with which it was decorated, has yielded material from the early first millennium BC, and was rebuilt in the sixth century. An inscription of *c* 403/400 (?) records a racing stable owned by a certain Damonon. A theater of Hellenistic date, built into the western slope of the acropolis, is well preserved, and at the citadel's southeastern end are traces of an agora and portico (*stoa*). Below the hill was a small temple, popularly known as the 'Tomb of Leonidas,' though this structure, too, is not to be dated earlier than the third century BC. South of the modern bridge over the Eurotas a building complex of no less than six phases has come to light. Substantial remains of late Roman fortifications have survived, and traces of porphyry quarries can be seen on Spartan territory (at Krokeai). The first stone shrine in the neighborhood dating from *c* 700, was the Menelaion at Therapne (*see* above), and Pausanias writes of a number of other temples on the roads leading out of the city.

Spasinou Charax *see* Charax

Sphacteria *see* Pylos

Sousse *see* Hadrumetum

Sozusa *see* Apollonia

Spain *see* Hispania

Spalatum *see* Salonae

Spina. A city on the Adriatic coast of northeastern Italy (Emilia-Romagna) four miles west of the modern town of Comacchio, where the mouth of a branch of the delta of the river Padus (Po) formed a harbor in a sea lagoon. The name Spina antedates the Etruscans and Greeks, and presupposes a period of previous occupation by the tribe of the Veneti. According to Greek legends, however, the founders were variously described as Pelasgians (a vague term for aboriginal peoples) or Thessalians, but the origins of the place were also ascribed to the Greek hero Diomedes, who, according to epic myth, came to Italy after the Trojan War.

About 520-500 BC, the villages already existing on the site became united to form the port of Spina. Covering an extent of more than seven hundred acres on a line of dunes between the lagoon and the coast (which has receded since then), and thus possessing useful natural defences against attackers from the mainland—with which it was only connected by narrow tongues of ground—Spina enjoyed good fishing facilities in the lagoon and owned riverside grain fields.

The place derives special interest from its apparently friendly joint habitation by Greeks and Etruscans—at the very time when, in Campania on the other side of Italy, relations between the two peoples were becoming increasingly hostile. The abundance of Greek pottery at Spina, reaching its climax in 475/450—and revealing a greater number of fine Athenian vases than any other known site—might seem to suggest Greek predominance, as could Spina's unusual distinction of possessing its own sanctuary at Delphi; it has been suggested, therefore, that the port may have been a Greek foundation, which admitted Etruscan families, however, from neighboring centers. But archaeological evidence indicates that, in this early fifth century, the Etruscans were in fact the dominant partners, since Spina, with its extensive marine and river communications, served as the principal source of overseas supplies for their leading north Italian city-state of Felsina (Bononia). On balance, therefore, it would seem probable that the Greek settlement was a trading colony lodged within, or adjacent to, a community that possessed a basically Etruscan character.

Spina may have been founded to attract Greek goods in competition with a second mixed foundation, Atria (Adria), at the northern end of the Po delta. Nevertheless, the two cities were linked by a navigable canal, and perhaps collaborated with one another to ensure the policing of the Adriatic. In this task Spina was helped by the Veneti, who also provided merchants with horses for export. But well before the middle of the fourth century, like other parts of north Italy, the place had fallen to the Gauls, and by the time of Strabo it was merely an insignificant village far from the sea. As the early church of Santa Maria in Padotevere testifies, however, habitation continued.

As land reclamation and air photography have shown, the marshy site of Spina, protected by complex palisades and earthern ramparts, was centered on a long canal, a hundred feet across. This was constructed to widen the channel between the sea and a lagoon that lay behind the coastline; and it received the influx of many lesser waterways crossed by bridges and flanked by wooden houses, constructed on piles according to a rectangular grid plan. Among recent discoveries on the floors of these houses are the remains of a straw basket. The principal cemeteries of Spina lay to the north, in the Trebba and Rega valleys, beside the middle branch of the river delta (the Old Po). The extensive finds of Greek pottery and other objects that the site has yielded are to be seen in the Museo Archeologico di Spina at Ferrara.

Sremska Mitrovica *see* Sirmium

Stabiae (Castellamare di Stabia). A harbor town of Campania (southwestern Italy), just below the Lactarii (Lattari) mountains, at the southern end of the Gulf of Cumae (Bay of Naples), three miles south of Pompeii. A necropolis in the neighborhood testifies to habitation from the eighth century BC. After the occupation of Campania by the Sabelli (Samnites) during the fifth century, Stabiae became the port employed by Nuceria Alfaterna (Nocera Inferiore) until that city fell to the Romans in the Second Samnite War (308). Silius Italicus records the presence of a trireme manned by Stabians in the Roman fleet during the Second Punic War (218–201). In the rebellion of the Italians against Rome in the Social War Stabiae was occupied by the insurgent leader Papius Mutilus in 90 but suffered destruction at the hands of Sulla in the following year. It is possible that traces of walls and buildings in the area known as Fontana Grande represent the remains of the town which he demolished.

Subsequently, however, the habitation center was transferred from the coast to the hill of Varano, where a lavish and fashionable residential and curative resort was established (Galen records a 'milk cure'). Four letters of Cicero written to his friend Marcus Marius, at the latter's Stabian Villa, have survived. But the place was obliterated by the eruption of Vesuvius in AD 79, when Pliny the Elder, investigating the phenomenon, spent the night at the residence of his friend Pomponianus at Stabiae before falling dead on the shore on the following day.

At least twelve of these dwellings, varying from palatial residences to *villae rusticae* concentrating on agricultural production, have been identified in the area since excavations began in 1749 and were actively resumed in the 1950s. Constructed at different levels, they display a series of winding arched ramps giving access to the beach. The Villa of the Cupid Seller (Villa della Venditrice di Amori; so called after a wall painting adapted by J.-M. Vien in 1763, but also sometimes known as the Villa of Ariadne because of a wall painting in its large dining room, which represents her sleeping form), is aligned with the face of the hillside. Its extensive open colonnaded terrace was equipped with large windows offering superb panoramas of the bay. Another splendid mansion, the Villa of Obsidian Vases, is now seen to have comprised three principal units, built on a series of terraces. One of these complexes is centered on a peristyle with spiral columns. Another set of rooms surrounds a further large colonnaded garden containing an extensive swimming pool; and the third unit is grouped round an atrium with four columns.

The wall paintings of this villa are remarkable and varied. The cold room (*frigidarium*) of its Baths is decorated with gymnasts, battling Cupids and a resting boxer, and other themes include Perseus, Europa, winged Fortune, a hermaphrodite, trees and fantastic shields; while the dining room and its mock gate display winged sea horses and centaurs, peacocks, flying swans and a Nereid riding a sea bull executed in the Third Style (*see* Pompeii). Moreover, one artist at this mansion produced a series of highly individual portraits, painted in a vigorous and emotional manner that makes emphatic use of shading. Another Stabian picture offers a charming sunlit view of the local harbor. But the imperial Julio-Claudian house, which claimed descent from the Trojan Aeneas, may not have appreciated a painting portraying him, and his father and son, with the heads of dogs and apes. The villas of Stabiae also provide an ample range of graffiti.

There is evidence that the inhabitants of the place obtained oil from the south of Spain, but they also possessed their own farms, of which one, at Gragnano nearby, made wine and cheese, and has yielded the best and most scientific grain mill which has so far been discovered. After the disastrous eruption Stabiae alone, among the shattered towns, managed to recover on a considerable scale, profiting from mineral springs in the area, and taking over the trade routes which had previously been controlled by Pompeii. Excavation finds are divided between a local Antiquarium and the Museo Archeologico Nazionale at Naples.

Stagirus, Stageiros, later Stageira (near the modern Stayira). A small Greek town in a gold- and silver-mining area toward the eastern end of the peninsula of Chalcidice in Macedonia, founded *c* 655 BC by people from the island of Andros. After the Persian Wars (490, 480–79) Stagirus belonged to the Delian League under Athenian leadership, but during the Peloponnesian War its inhabitants revolted from Athens (424) in favor of the Spartan commander Brasidas, and successfully defended themselves against the Athenian Cleon. During the Olynthian War, in which Philip II of Macedonia invaded and annexed Chalcidice, he destroyed Stagirus (349), but it was rebuilt owing to the good offices of Aristotle, whose birth there in *c* 384 had endowed the place with its principal, or only, claim to fame. His modern statue now stands at Stayira amid the ruins of a Byzantine fortress. Traces of ancient buildings are also to be seen.

Staklen *see* Novae

Stara Zagora *see* Beroe Augusta Trajana

Starigrad *see* Pharos

Stobi (Stoboi, Stoloi). The principal city of Paeonia (northern Macedonia, southeastern Yugoslavia), on a low ridge beside the left bank of the river Erigon (Crna Reka) at its junction with the Axius (Vardar), of which the valley provided an important route between the Mediterranean and the middle reaches of the Danube. At Stobi this thoroughfare crossed another road coming from the southwest and leading to a lower stretch of the river (in Lower Moesia). Thus the town was an important communications and commerical center. After its Illyrian inhabitants had come under Macedonian rule during the fourth century BC, it played a significant part in the northern campaigns of Philip V shortly before 200.

Under subsequent Roman rule, Stobi coined as a *municipium* from the time of the Flavian dynasty (AD 69–96) to Elagabalus (218–22), issuing pieces that depicted a personification of the city standing between two river-gods. It became a Roman colony during the third century, and in the later empire was the capital of the province of Macedonia Salutaris (Secunda). In Christian times the town became a major ecclesiastical center, and its bishop attended the Council of Nicaea in 325. Theodosius I the Great (379–95) resided there briefly, and it was the birthplace of the influential and encyclopedic anthologist Johannes Stobaeus, who seems to have lived in the early fifth century. In 479 Malchus records destruction by the Ostrogothic King Theoderic the Great, and the process was completed by an earthquake in the following century.

The city wall has been almost completely destroyed, and temples of Asclepius and Dionysus depicted on the coinage have not been traced. But there are extensive remains of a colonnaded street and a bath and a second-century theater, subsequently converted for employment as a gladiatorial arena. A third-century complex included a substantial residence (one of a number in the city) and a Jewish synagogue, and other large buildings have also been explored beneath the flood level of the Erigon river. But most of the monuments revealed by excavations date between the fourth and sixth centuries. They include portions of a river bridge and remains of some half-a-dozen churches, including an elaborately decorated two-storeyed basilica of Bishop Philip, constructed over an earlier building with geometrical wall paintings, and comprising three aisles that were increased to five shortly before or after 500. Beside and below the basilica was a quatrefoil, externally rectangular baptistery, adorned with further wall paintings and with floor mosaics depicting animals in paradise. The extensive episcopal palace can also be seen. Finds are preserved in a museum on the site and at Belgrade and Skoplje.

Strasbourg *see* Argentorate

Stratonicea, Stratonikeia (Eskihisar). A city in the interior of Caria (southwestern Asia Minor). A Carian town named Chrysaoris and then Idrias was said to have first stood on the site; Apollonius of Aphrodisias indicated that Chrysaoris was the first city founded by the Lycians (the southeastern neighbors of the Carians), and Idrias—in the form of Edrieis—appears in the tribute lists of the Delian League presided over by Athens in the fifth century BC.

The Macedonian colony of Stratonicea was founded and lavishly endowed by the Seleucid king Antiochus I Soter (281-261), who named the new settlement after Stratonice, his stepmother and later his wife. The temple of Zeus Chrysaoreus—believed to have been near the city—was the meeting place of the Chrysaoric League, a religious and political federation of Carians; as Strabo records, Stratonicea, although it had no federal vote itself (not being Carian any longer, despite its claim to be 'autochthonous'), controlled the votes of the Carian villages under its ownership. A second important temple, dedicated to Hecate, was at Lagina (Lakene, Leina) nearby, and a sanctuary of Zeus Panamarios stood on a lofty eminence at Panamara twelve miles southeast of the town.

Stratonicea was presented by one of the first three Antiochi to the Rhodians, who later lost but then recovered the city (197). However, its inhabitants were declared free, with the rest of Caria, by the Romans in 167; local coinage seems to have begun at that date. In 130 it was the scene of the final surrender of Aristonicus, who had revolted against the bequest of the kingdom of Pergamum to the Romans, and in 81 the Roman senate recognized its valiant resistance to their late enemy Mithridates VI Eupator of Pontus by a grant of freedom and substantial increase of territory. In 40 Stratonicea repelled an attack by the renegade Labienus and his Parthian troops. In the reign of Antoninus Pius (138-61) it suffered severely from an earthquake, and received imperial aid. The city's monetary issues, which continued for the first three centuries of the Principate, name it Philosebastos ('lover of the emperor') under Titus (79-81) and describe Caracalla's wife Plautilla (d. 205) as Nea Thea Hera, the new goddess Hera (Juno).

A terrace on the slope of the walled acropolis displays remains of a small temple dedicated to the imperial cult, beneath which stands a spacious theater. Below is the ruined shrine of the Egyptian god Serapis (*c* 200). The single-arched principal town gate can also be seen, and a large fortress at the northeastern extremity of the habitatian center. (Stratonicea-Hadrianopolis, also known as Indi-Stratonicea, is a different place, situated in Lydia, although Stephanus of Byzantium wrongly identifies it with the Carian city).

Stratus, Stratos. The most important town and federal center of Acarnania (northwestern Greece), situated on a low bluff commanding the right bank of the broad river Achelous as it enters the plain. Local coinage, inaugurated during the fifth century, depicts the river-god and his daughter the nymph Callirhoe, mother of Acarnan, the mythical ancestor of the Acarnanian people.

During the Peloponnesian War the Spartan general Cnemus besieged Stratus in vain (429), and three years later his colleague Eurylochus passed beneath its walls without venturing to attack. In 391 another Spartan, King Agesilaus II, failed to capture the city, but in 314 it passed into the hands of Alexander's successor Cassander, who organized its amalgamation (synoecism) with Sauria and Agrinium. In 263/260, when Acarnania was partitioned between Actolia and Epirus, Stratus was assigned to the Aetolian League, and after the reduction of the Aetolians to Roman subject status (189) its Roman garrison withstood Philip V and Perseus of Macedonia. Before imperial times the place had lost all its importance.

The city wall enclosed an extensive perimeter, including four parallel ridges with intervening depressions. At the northern extremity of one of the central ridges stood the acropolis, presiding over a fourth-century agora of which the western colonnade was constucted above a row of subterranean chambers. To the west rose a temple of Zeus and to the east a theater, both erected at about the same time.

Strymon (Struma), River. The best-known river of the Balkan peninsula, rising in the Scombrus (Witoša) mountains of Thrace (western Bulgaria) and debouching into the Aegean east of the Chalcidice peninsula (northern Greece). According to Greek mythology, the god after whom the river was named was the father of the Thracian King Rhesus by either Calliope or Euterpe. In the time of Philip II of Macedonia (359–336 BC) the Strymon was the frontier between Macedonia and Thrace, although in the Roman epoch the borderline lay farther to the east. *See also* Amphipolis, Eion.

Stymphalus, Stymphalos. A town in northeastern Arcadia (Peloponnese); its acropolis rose on a promontory overlooking a lake, river and mountain of the same name. Stymphalus stood at the intersection of a number of important roads.

But it owed its renown to the Sixth Labor of Heracles, who was said to have driven out the monstrous birds—as menacing as lions or leopards, according to Pausanias—that infested the lake; the hero employed a bronze rattle to frighten them into flight, and then shot many of them on the wing. According to a further series of Greek myths, Stymphalus owed its name to a monarch, the son of Elatus and Laodice, who was treacherously murdered by Pelops during his conquest of the Peloponnese; though a rival version attributed its foundation to a certain Temenus (which was also the name of a legendary king of Argos, a historic ally of Stymphalus); he was believed to have established the important cult of Hera, of which Stymphalus claimed to be the earliest home. The place is mentioned by Homer's *Iliad* as an Arcadian town.

After 400 BC it began to issue coins, probably during the festivals of Artemis Stymphalia, whose head some of the pieces display, while others show the head and neck of a Stymphalian bird springing from the calyx of a flower with two poppy heads. Pausanias noted that the ceiling of Artemis' ancient temple (of which the site has been tentatively identified, not far from the lake) was adorned with wooden reliefs of birds; and at the back of the shrine stood marble statues of virgins with birds' legs.

At the time when these coins were issued Stymphalus had increased in size, owing to amalgamation (synoecism) with other communities (*c* 375–350), and belonged to the Arcadian League. But in 315 the town was captured by one of Alexander the Great's successors, Cassander. Subsequently it belonged to the Achaean League (issuing federal coins). In 219/218 the forces of Sparta, Aetolia and Elis, under Euripidas, were decisively defeated in the neighborhood by Philip V of Macedonia. By the time of Strabo Stymphalus had become insignificant, but came to attention again in the time of Hadrian (AD 117–38), who built an aqueduct (of which traces survive) to conduct the waters of its local spring to Corinth.

A topographical survey of the ancient buildings, recently completed with the aid of novel computing techniques, suggests that their urban plan dates from the fourth-century synoecism. A tower on the acropolis is partly preserved, and remains of the city wall are still visible. On the slope is a small temple of Athena Polias, and traces of other structures suggest the possible location of the agora. There are also ruins of a theater with its auditorium cut out of the rock; a Hellenistic shrine and *palaestra* (athletics school) and portico are submerged in the lake.

Styx, River. A river in Arcadia (central Peloponnese) which plunges from a snow-fed spring down a black rock on the northeast flank of Mount Chelmos (Aroania), and then flows through a wild gorge to join another river, the Crathis. Herodotus recounts that King Cleomenes I of Sparta (519–490 BC) caused the members of his projected Arcadian League to swear an oath by the Styx. Its name means 'hateful,' because according to tradition its waters were so poisonous that they would dissolve any jar or vessel into which they were poured—unless it was made of a horse's hoof. There was also a legend that Alexander the Great was poisoned by drinking Styx water.

During the classical period this Arcadian watercourse was identified with the Styx, which was one of the traditional nine rivers of the underworld. In Homer and Hesiod the gods swear by the water of this infernal stream, which make the perjurer insensible for a whole year; and the latter poet personifies Styx as the daughter of Ocean and ally of Zeus in his struggle with Cronos.

Subiaco *see* Anio (River)

Succosa *see* Cosa

Sugolin (Zliten; the identification is almost certain). An important villa (on the site of Dar Buk-Ammarah), over twenty miles east of Lepcis Magna in the Roman province of Africa (now in Libya). The villa terminates in a long colonnaded terrace overlooking the sea, behind which lies a series of rooms; while another group of apartments, together with baths, is to be seen at the eastern extremity of the complex.

Its abundant mosaic floors comprise exceptionally fine specimens of *opus tessellatum* (consisting of squared and smoothed *tesserae* of marble, stone and tile, employed to cover broad spaces), *opus sectile* (relatively large, thin, shaped pieces of colored marble, forming geometric or floral patterns) and *opus vermiculatum* (subtly cut and curved for three-dimensional effects). Agricultural and Nilotic scenes are depicted, and representations of the Four Seasons are also to be seen. The four borders of one floor are decorated with pictures of activities in the amphitheater, while the pavement of a small chamber in the form of a quarter circle displays designs of numerous different animals, fishes and mythological sea beasts. The chronology of the various mosaics is much disputed; dates varying between Flavian times (AD 69–96) and the Severan dynasty (193–235) have been proposed. The problem is complicated by the long history of the villa, during which its rooms were repaired and restored on a number of occasions; no less than five superimposed layers of plaster have been distinguished on some of the walls.

Sukhumi *see* Dioscurias

Sulmo (Sulmona). A town of the tribe of the Paeligni in central Italy, situated on a plateau near the confluence of the rivers Gizio and Vella. It resisted Hannibal during the Second Punic War (211) and, after becoming a *municipium* like other Italian cities, *c* 90/89, supported Julius Caesar in his civil war against Pompey the Great (49). Sulmo is chiefly famous, however, as the birthplace of the poet Ovid (43), who came from an old family of equestrian (knightly) rank. He describes the area as 'rich in ice-cold streams.' It also possessed grain, grapes and olives. The plan of the ancient habitation center can be deduced from the rectangular design of the medieval street plan preserved by the central section of the modern town.

Three and a half miles north of Sulmo, on the slopes of Mount Morrone, a large sanctuary of Hercules Curinus (known locally as the 'Villa of Ovid') has been excavated; it was one of the great Italian religious precincts associated with the name of the dictator Sulla (d. 78). On the highest of three terraces, supported by a massive polygonal wall, stands Hercules' temple. The middle terrace displays a colonnade and is linked by a monumental stairway to the third and lowest terrace, which is built of concrete and supported by massive vaults. It contained shops, constructed to serve the festivals associated with the sanctuary, and to provide materials for the sacrifices that accompanied these gatherings.

Sunium, Sounion, Cape. A precipitous headland at the southeastern extremity of Attica in eastern Greece, joined to the mainland by a low isthmus. The sight of the cape welcomed Athenian seamen returning home from their Aegean voyages, and a narrow creek on its eastern side afforded a sheltered anchorage for mariners unable to weather the promontory owing to strong westerly winds. According to Homer's *Odyssey* it was off Sunium that Apollo struck down Menelaus' pilot Phrontis; and the place probably contained a sanctuary of Phrontis in historic times.

The western part of Cape Sunium was crowned by a Doric temple of Poseidon built by Pericles *c* 444 BC near the edge of the cliff, on the foundations of a shrine that had been built shortly before 490 and was destroyed by the Persians soon afterward; and its precinct was entered by a monumental gateway (Propylaea). Some of the temple's columns have now been reerected. A low hill commanding the isthmus on the north displays the remains of a small temple of Athena Sounias, to which an Ionic colonnade was added *c* 460/450 along the sides of an earlier structure.

At the head of the bay stood the town of Sunium, proverbial for its prosperity in ancient times. After the battle of Salamis (480) the Athenians dedicated a captured Phoenician ship there. The harbor was a port of call for grain ships from Euboea to the Piraeus, and for their safety the entire headland was enclosed in 413—during the Peloponnesian War against Sparta—by a double fortification wall, strengthened by square towers. This acropolis-fortress was involved in third-century wars; however, the Roman comic dramatist Terence, in the second century, described the place as a haunt of pirates, while its inhabitants had a reputation for harboring and enfranchising runaway slaves. During a revolt of the slave mine workers at Laurium (104/100), Sunium was seized by a gang of slaves who devastated the neighborhood.

Sura *see* Mesopotamia

Susa, earlier Shushan, Shush (later Seleucia on the Eulaeus), the capital of Susiana (Elymais, formerly Elam), now in southwestern Iran. Susa lay at the foot of the Zagros mountains near the river Choaspes or Eulaeus (of which part was known as the Pasitigris from at least *c* 400 BC; precise identifications with the courses of the modern rivers Karkheh [or Kercha, *see* Charax], Ab-i-Diz, Khersan and Karun are impossible owing to hydrographic changes). The place served as the chief residence of the Achaemenid Persian monarchs since Darius I (521–486), and after the suppression of their kingdom by Alexander the Great it provided the mint for a victory coinage issued by Seleucus I Nicator (*c* 304). The city was refounded as Seleucia on the Eulaeus by a Seleucid monarch; this colony is first heard of under Antiochus III the Great (223–187), but is probably earlier.

In about the middle of the second century Susiana achieved independence under a dynasty whose kings bore the name of Kamnaskires. The first of these monarchs, surnamed Nicephorus, struck silver coins imitating Seleucid mintages. Kamnaskires II (*c* 82) struck pieces with the busts of himself and his queen Anzaze, while a seated Zeus holding a figure of Nike appears on the reverse. Abundant bronze coinages, issued from the time of Kamnaskires IV (*c* 72) onward, bear the portraits of Parthian kings after the first century AD. Their inscriptions are in barbarously formed Greek letters or in Chaldaeo-Pahlavi script.

However, Susa-Seleucia long retained a Greek constitution and the rank of a city state, as inscriptional evidence of AD 21 confirms. Its local decrees were framed in Greek, and its citizens produced a number of poems, including a lyric ode of the first century BC addressed to Apollo. But the poet gives him his Syrian title of Mara; and the city goddess was the Elamite Nanaia, equated with Artemis. Traces of Persian, Babylonian, Syrian, Jewish, and Anatolian elements can be detected in records of the ancient population.

Susa *see* Segusio

Susah *see* Hadrumetum

Sybaris, earlier Lupia, later Thurii, Thourioi (or more properly Thuria, the version given by Thucydides), and subsequently Copia (near the modern Sibari). A Greek city in Bruttii (the modern Calabria), situated on the Gulf of Taras (Tarentum, Taranto), the 'instep' of Italy. Originally known as Lupia (according to Pausanias), Sybaris was perhaps founded *c* 720 BC (by Is of Helice, according to a doubtful reading of Strabo); its colonists came from Achaea in the northern Peloponnese, but Aristotle adds that settlers from Troezen, in the northeastern part of the same peninsula, also participated. The town occupied a large, flat, low-lying site extending over an area of four miles between the rivers Sybaris (Coscile) and Crathis (Cratis) and bordering the seacoast.

The Sybarites became very powerful—and notoriously luxurious—by expanding their territory throughout the adjoining fertile alluvial plain, a process that was assisted by a pact with the local native tribe of the Serdaioi. Local silver (incuse) coinage, which may have been issued as early as *c* 550, bore the type of a bull, which perhaps personified the Crathis, or, more generally, symbolized the wealth Sybaris derived from cattle. It dispatched colonists to the Tyrrhenian coast at Laus (Lao) and Scidrus, and a further settlement at Posidonia (Paestum) enabled its merchants to conduct profitable trading with the states of Etruria. In 510, however, internal dissensions enabled Croton (Crotone), a longstanding rival, to capture Sybaris and blot it out of existence by diverting the course of the Crathis to flow over the city, which has remained buried and unknown until prolonged searches resulted in the identification of the site in 1968. The use of pumps, magnetometers and drilling borings have disclosed the foundations of sixth-century buildings and have uncovered roof tiles, pottery and a pottery kiln of the same epoch. An area paved with large stones has been identified as a shipyard beside the ancient harbor (from which the sea has now receded two miles).

After the destruction of their dwellings the Sybarite refugees seem to have received asylum in their former city's colonies. But they returned home in 453, and with the help of the people of Posidonia built a new settlement near the former habitation center, celebrated by coins which celebrate both cities in conjunction. Five years later, however, the Crotoniates once again moved to the attack, and razed this revived Sybaris to the ground. Shortly afterward its the inhabitants, again expelled and in exile, prevailed on the Athenian leader Pericles to assist them in a further attempt to reestablish themselves, and this time the project resulted in the creation, on the ancient site, of the city of Thurii, as it soon came to be called (after a local spring named Thuria), following initial designation as Sybaris. The change of name came about because the Sybarites in the new colony, though greatly outnumbered by settlers from other Greek cities, made themselves so unpopular that they were obliged, it appears, to depart, retiring to a third site at the mouth of the river Teuthras or Traeis (Trionto). According to another view, however, the Teuthras settlement belongs to an earlier stage; in any case it never achieved any success.

Thurii, on the other hand, was an ambitious Pan-Hellenic foundation, reputedly joined by the historian Herodotus and the orator Lysias, a Syracusan who had settled at Athens. Designed on rectangular lines by the great Milesian town-planner Hippodamus, Thurii initiated the south Italian production of vases, directed by potters with Athenian training. Already in 426, during the Peloponnesian War between the Athenians and Spartans, the city's harbor was regarded as important; and the Thurians were beginning at this time to issue coins of outstanding artistic quality, depicting Athena (and later Hera) and the bull that had already been a feature of the earlier coinage of Sybaris (*thourios* means a butting bull, and that is how the animal is now represented).

Aristotle, who died in 322, refers in his *Politics* to an excessively limited and oppressive oligarchic government at Thurii, which provoked violent revolution. Its people were treated with hostility by its fellow Greeks at Syracuse and Taras (Tarentum, Taranto) and by the non-Greek peoples of Lucania and Bruttii. In 282 Thurii voluntarily received a Roman garrison, and opposed the invasions of Pyrrhus of Epirus (280–275) and the Carthaginian Hannibal (in the Second Punic War, 218–201). To revive the city after Hannibal's depredations (204), the Romans augmented its population by the establishment of a Latin colony, which they named Copia, in 193, just a quarter of a millennium after Thurii had been founded. Gaining Roman citizenship, like other Italian cities, *c* 90/89, it suffered occupation by Spartacus during his slave revolt (72) and was the place where Marcus Caelius Rufus, attempting an insurrection against Julius Caesar, was captured and executed (48). In 40 Thurii was besieged by Sextus Pompeius. Antony maintained, mockingly, that the great-grandfather of Octavian (the future Augustus) was an ex-slave and rope maker from the neighborhood and the emperor himself, according to Suetonius, was happy to admit that he had previously been known as Thurinus.

Soundings and excavations have brought to light various structures of the Roman colony, including a theater, the city wall (built over Hellenistic foundations), a road and a villa. In spite of its strategic importance, however, Thurii-Copia had become insignificant, according to Dio Chrysostom, in the second century AD, and there is evidence that at least parts of the site were abandoned before 400, although it still secured a mention from Proclus in the sixth century.

Sybota. A coastal town of Elinia in Epirus (northwestern Greece), and the name of a group of small islands off its shore, opposite the southern extremity of Corcyra (Corfu). Off these islands, in 433 BC, was fought a naval battle between Corinth and its former colony Corcyra (Corfu), which had recently formed a 'defensive' alliance with Athens, an action regarded by Corinth as hostile to itself. A Corinthian fleet of one hundred and fifty ships confronted a Corcyraean flotilla one hundred and ten strong, supplemented by a squadron of ten Athenian triremes. The Corcyraeans suffered an initial setback, but the Corinthian commander, instead of following up his success, backed water, for he had caught sight of a second Athenian squadron approaching through the dusk, and probably feared that it might be the main battle fleet of Athens.

The Corinthians sailed home, after setting up a trophy to celebrate their victory, while the Corcyraeans set up another trophy for the victory they would have won if the engagement had continued. This clash at Sybota, according to Thucydides, was the first grievance leading to Corinth's alliance with Sparta against Athens in the Peloponnesian War (431–404), because the Corinthians complained that the Athenians had fought against them although there was technically no state of war between the two cities.

Syene (Aswan). A city in Upper Egypt, on the right (east) bank of the Nile, below the First Cataract. It was already a trading town in the fourth millennium BC, quarrying red granite, the famous Syenite stone. Under the Ptolemies Syene replaced Elephantine (formerly Abu, an adjoining river island, seat of the worship of the god of the cataract Khnum, and of a sixth-century Jewish community) as the frontier and customs outpost; while Elephantine also gradually lost its significance as an Egyptian religious center to another island, Philae just above the cataract. The astronomer Erastosthenes visited Syene *c* 250, and it was there that, by comparing the size of the sun's shadow with Alexandria, he was able to estimate the circumference of the earth.

After the Roman annexation of Egypt (30) the place stood at the northern extremity of the boundary zone known as the Dodecaschoenus (*see* Aegyptus); it was freed from invaders from Meroe (*see* Aethiopia), and provided with a garrison, in 25, retaining or resuming its position as a customs station. In the later empire, when Syene formed the frontier post of the province of the Thebaid (and subsequently the Upper Thebaid), it became vulnerable to attacks from the southern tribe of the Blemmyes, until an agreement was reached under the eastern emperor Marcian (451).

In addition to its ancient Pharaonic monuments, the site displays the granite gateway of a temple of Alexander the Great's posthumous son Alexander IV (d. *c* 310), the remains of shrines of Isis (fourth century BC) and Trajan (AD 98–117), and an early Coptic church. At Elephantine a Nilometer mentioned by Strabo is still to be seen—a steeply graded staircase plunging down the side of the island into the river. The principal monuments of Philae, threatened with submersion by the Aswan High Dam and Lake Nasser (1964), have been moved to the nearby island of Agilkia. They include a Ptolemaic restoration of the Kiosk of Nectanebo I (380–362 BC), a much-reconstructed Ptolemaic and Roman temple of Isis (including the Birth House of Ptolemy VI Philometor [180–145], later restored, containing twenty-two rooms and a crypt decorated with scenes of the Birth of Horus), temples of Horus the Avenger and Hathor and Augustus (31 BC–AD 14), a four-sided portico known as the Kiosk of Trajan or 'Pharaoh's Bed,' and a gateway built by Diocletian (AD 284–305). It was not until AD 557 that Bishop Theodorus was able to convert part of the temple of Isis into a church.

Symplegades, the 'Clashing Rocks.' Two rocks on either side of the northern entrance of the Thracian Bosphorus, leading into the Euxine (Black) Sea. Also known as the Cyanean (Blue) Rocks, they were believed to have clashed together, from time to time, with enormous force when driven by the wind. According to Greek myth, they prevented ships from entering the Euxine Sea until the Argo, the vessel of the Argonauts, made the passage successfully, with the help of the goddess Athena and the Thracian King Phineus, who had advised them to test the rocks by seeing if a dove could fly between them before their moment of impact. The dove got through, and so did the Argo. Thereafter the Symplegades remained stationary for evermore.

A similar story was told of the Planctae (Wandering Rocks), which were sometimes identified with the Symplegades and may have been their older name. According to Homer's *Odyssey,* on the other hand, Odysseus encountered Planctae in another region altogether, that is to say north of Sicily—the poet had Strongyle (Stromboli) and Strombalicchio in mind, according to a modern suggestion—and chose, on Circe's advice, to steer clear of them, preferring to brave the terrors of Scylla and Charybdis instead; while Apollonius Rhodius describes the Argo as passing between *both* the Symplegades (of the Bosphorus) *and* the Planctae (off Sicily), with the assistance not of Athena but of Hera.

Syracuse, Syrakousai (Siracusa). A city on the southeast coast of Sicily, based originally on the offshore island of Ortygia, which had been occupied since Palaeolithic times. The island was colonized *c* 733 BC by Corinthians under the leadership of Archias; its location beside the mainland created two excellent harbors, one of which, the Great Harbor, to the south, is very large. Ortygia also possessed an abundant freshwater spring, Arethusa, named after the nymph who, according to Greek mythology, had escaped from Greece to avoid the attentions of the river-god Alpheus; but she fled in vain, since he flowed under the Ionian Sea and rejoined her.

On the adjacent Sicilian mainland the plain of the river Anapus (Anapo) was very favorable to agriculture; and the Corinthian settlers of Syracuse, gained control of a wide surrounding territory. Forming an aristocratic government, they expelled some of the native Sicels, retained others as helot-slaves (Kyllyrioi), and founded some colonies at Helorus (*c* 700), Acrae (Palazzo Acreide, *c* 663), Casmenae (Monte Casale, *c* 643) and Camarina (*c* 598), which is on the south coast of the island. Autocratic rule was established by Gelon (485–478), formerly 'tyrant' of Gela, who in alliance with Theron of Acragas (Agrigento) overwhelmed the Carthaginians at Himera (Imera, 480) and made Syracuse the greatest power in the entire Greek world. The victory may have been celebrated by the production of large and magnificently executed silver pieces known as Demarateia, for they were said to have been struck from the proceeds of a gift presented to Gelon's wife Demarate by the Carthaginians in gratitude for her intervention on their behalf in the peace negotiations; although some scholars prefer to ascribe the issue to *c* 465.

Gelon's brother Hiero I (478–467/6) defeated an Etruscan fleet, mainly derived from Caere (Cerveteri), in a battle off Cumae (Cuma, 474), which ensured Syracusan control of the southern Mediterranean basin. Arts, letters and philosophy flourished; the mime writer Sophron and comic dramatist Epicharmus came from Syracuse, and poets who visited the city included Aeschylus, Simonides and Pindar. In 466/5 its autocratic government gave way to a more or less democratic administration that gained further successes against the Etruscans and compelled the nationalist Sicel leader Ducetius to become a suppliant (*c* 453). In 445 victory over Acragas rightly seemed to Diodorus to mark the recognized hegemony of the Syracusans in Sicily.

During the Peloponnesian War between Athens and Sparta the Athenians, fearing Syracusan intervention against them, accepted an appeal from Leontini (Lentini) and sent a first expedition to the island (427–424), followed by their massive intervention against Syracuse (415–413), immortalized by Thucydides, which resulted in total Syracusan triumph. The victory was celebrated by an issue of the most famous of all Greek coins, the decadrachms with the head of Arethusa and a four-horse chariot signed by the artists Cimon and Euaenetus. However, Hermocrates, the statesman and general who had led the successful resistance, was exiled in 412 and killed when he returned in 408.

During the ensuing epoch Syracuse, after two Carthaginian invasions of the island (409,406), came under the autocratic rule of Dionysius I (406–367). Dionysius conducted four ferocious wars against the Carthaginians, without ultimately changing the *status quo,* but greatly extended his domination in the island, intervened extensively in south Italy, and equipped his city with powerful fortifications, so that he became the most powerful personage in the entire Greek world. Plato's three visits to his court and that of Dionysius II (366/5, 361)—sponsored by the young king's uncle Dion—proved ineffective. Following a subsequent period of decline, the Corinthian Timoleon (345–334) restored the situation, introducing (as far as the sources, biased in his favor, enable us to determine) a moderate oligarchic government; but this was overthrown by Agathocles (317–289), who ruled tyrannically (as his bitter enemy the historian Timaeus perhaps overemphasized), assuming the new title of king (*c* 306), but gained control of the greater part of the island and made incursions into south Italy and north Africa.

After another autocrat, Hicetas (288–278), had been defeated by the Carthaginians, they were fended off by the invading Pyrrhus of Epirus, whose lieutenant Hiero II seized power at his native city Syracuse (275) and retained it for half a century, failing, however, to offer patronage to the Syracusan pastoral poet Theocritus (*c* 275/4), who left for Cos and Alexandria. During the First Punic War Hiero quickly changed sides from Carthage to Rome (263), remaining its prosperous, protected ally until his death during the second of those wars (215). Thereupon, however, his grandson Hieronymus chose to support the Carthaginians instead, and after a long siege (213–211), in which the great mathematician and engineer Archimedes was said to have played a leading part among the defenders, Syracuse was sacked by Marcus Claudius Marcellus.

Incorporated into the Roman province of Sicily, the city became its capital, but suffered depredations from the governor Verres (73–71). It was apparently enfranchised in 44, and then issued coinage for the breakaway administration installed by Sextus Pompeius in 43/42); these pieces, like issues of Panormus (Palermo), were inscribed HISPANORVM, in honor of Sextus' Spanish immigrant partisans. Under Augustus, Syracuse became a Roman colony in 21 BC. St. Paul stopped there for three days on his journey to Rome, staying with the Christian community. Although ravaged by the Franks in *c* 280, the city continued to enjoy prosperity, until disturbances in the fifth century, created by Vandal incursions, caused a large part of its population to flee into the interior.

On the island of Ortygia one-roomed houses belonging to the first generation of Greek colonists have lately been found. There are also remains of temples of Apollo and Athena, dating from the early or mid-sixth (?) and early fifth centuries respectively; the latter, which adjoined a mid-sixth century Ionian edifice, is incorporated into the medieval cathedral. Traces of a temple of Olympian Zeus (the Olympieium), slightly later than the shrine of Apollo, are to be seen two miles outside the town, above what used to be the marshes of Lysimelia. The original city on Ortygia underwent expansion (starting from a very early date, as recent excavations have shown) into the mainland quarters, first Neapolis (social), and then Tyche (residential), Achradina (administrative and commercial) and Epipolae (sparsely populated, on high ground). Neapolis contains a well-preserved theater replacing a former structure where Aeschylus' *Persians* and *Women of Etna* were performed. Its present appearance dates from a reconstruction by Hiero II, whose two-hundred-yard-long altar, intended for celebrating public sacrifices at the Feast of Zeus Eleutherios, is adjacent. Nearby, too, is one of the largest amphitheaters in the world (second century AD), as well as cavernous stone quarries—notably the so-called 'Ear of Dionysius'—resembling those (in the Tyche quarter) where 7,000 Athenian prisoners were incarcerated in 413. Achradina contains the ruins of a small theater of Roman imperial date, inaccurately known as the Roman Gymnasium. At the western end of the Epipolae ridge stands the Euryalus castle built to guard the approaches to the town from the northwest, and forming part of an elaborate defensive system. Planned at the end of the fifth century BC, this was to a large extent the creation of Dionysius I (whose wall round Ortygia has now also been uncovered), but was gradually completed in the fourth and third centuries, and adapted and transformed in the Byzantine period.

Early Christianity is represented by extensive catacombs (large areas of which have been methodically explored), including those named after St. John the Evangelist, beside his church in which St. Marcian, the first bishop, martyred under Valerian (AD 253–60), is believed to have been buried. St. Lucia, the city's patron saint, died in the persecutions of Diocletian (*c* 305). Bishop Chrestus of Syracuse was the one Sicilian representative at the Church Council of Arelate (Arles, 314). The small church of St. Peter the Apostle originally dated from *c* 400.

Syria. In ancient times—although definitions fluctuated—this was the designation of the whole fertile strip between the eastern Mediterranean coast and the desert of northern Arabia (with which the borders of the modern state of Syria do not coincide). After an important previous history of many millennia, involving dependence on successive great powers—punctuated by the rise, from time to time, of independent local states (especially the Phoenician cities [Byblus, Tyre, Sidon] and Damascus), and the presence in the early first millennium BC of Greek trading-stations (Al Mina, Posidium [Ras-el-Bassit])—Syria became a satrapy of the Achaemenid (Persian) empire *c* 539 BC, under the name of 'Beyond the River' (that is to say the Euphrates, in distinction from 'Syria Between the Rivers,' which was Mesopotamia; the terms 'Syria' and 'Assyria' are sometimes confused).

Alexander the Great conquered the country from the Persians in 332. After his death, following the battle of Ipsus (301), it was partitioned between Seleucus I Nicator in the north (Syria Seleucis) and Ptolemy I Soter in the south (Coele Syria, 'Hollow' Syria, a term properly applied to the territory between Mounts Libanus [Lebanon] and Anti-Libanus, but widely extended), with the boundary between these two regions on the river Eleutherus (Nahr el-Kelb). The Seleucids founded many cities and military colonies, including their capital Antioch by Daphne (Antakya), whereas the Ptolemies, while respecting existing local autonomies, imported the bureaucratic arrangements of Egypt.

This division remained substantially unchanged for a century, in spite of three wars. In 217 Antiochus III the Great was decisively defeated by Ptolemy IV Philopator at Raphia (Rafah), but in 200 he won a victory over Ptolemy V Epiphanes at Panium (Panias, Banyas) and annexed his Syrian possessions. Later his position as a Mediterranean leader was undermined by defeat in a war against the Romans (190–188). Antiochus IV Epiphanes (175–163) stimulated Hellenization and civic autonomy; but his attempt to Hellenize Judaea caused an insurrection followed by secession.

After his death, Seleucid Syria disintegrated further, as not only Judaea, but also Ituraea, Nabataean Arabia, and Commagene increasingly asserted their independence. In 83 Tigranes I of Armenia occupied the country until his defeat by Pompey the Great, who made Syria into a Roman province with supervisory powers over city-states and client kingdoms (64/63). The Parthians invaded Syria in 40, but were repelled by Antony's general Publius Ventidius in the two following years. Antony gave Cleopatra VII large parts of the country, which returned, however, to Roman control after Antony's defeat by Octavian (the future Augustus) in 31/30. During the early Principate the province stretched northeast to the upper Euphrates, included Smooth Cilicia of the Plain (Pedias, Campestris) until AD 73, and gradually absorbed the various local client states. Trajan's father Marcus Ulpius Trajanus, during his governorship (73/4–76/77), played a leading part in reorganizing the province. Its cities, led by Antioch, were magnificent, luxurious and cultured, deriving great prosperity from natural products, local industries and caravan trading.

In 175 the Roman governor Avidius Cassius led a three-month revolt against Marcus Aurelius, whom he may have mistakenly believed to be dead. After suppressing Pescennius Niger, another governor who had made a bid for the purple (193–95), Septimius Severus divided the province into two, Syria Coele and Syria Phoenice. His influential wife, Julia Domna, was a Syrian, and in 218 her sister Julia Maesa led a successful revolt against Macrinus, setting her grandson Elagabalus, high priest of Emesa (Homs), on the throne; he was succeeded by his cousin Severus Alexander (222–35). Jotapianus, related to the former royal house of Commagene, rebelled against Philip the Arab in 248/9. During a chaotic period of Sassanian Persian invasions the Emesan high priest Uranius Antoninus asserted his freedom from Valerian's control (253/4). From 260 to 267 Odenathus, a nobleman of Palmyra, was entrusted by Gallienus with a virtually independent command in the eastern provinces. His widow Zenobia and her son Vaballathus Athenodorus assumed the purple *c* 270; but they were crushed by Aurelian three years later.

In the later empire Syria was further subdivided into the provinces of Syria Prima (containing Antioch, one of the major imperial capitals of the time), Syria Salutaris (Coele), Euphratensis (Augusta), Phoenice, and Phoenice (or Augusta) Libanensis. During the campaigns of Constantius II (337–61) and Julian the Apostate (361–63), the country again became the base of operations against the Persians, and the target of their invasions. From the middle of the fifth century religious controversies among the Christian churches, for which the Antiochene patriarchate was particularly famous, assumed a political, secessionist turn with the growth of the Monophysite heresy (declaring that Christ only had one nature), which became a subject of fierce differences among Syrian churchmen. *See also* (with references) Al-Mina, Antioch (Antiochia by Daphne), Apamea, Beroea, Chalcis Beneath Lebanon, Commagene, Damascus, Gerasa, Heliopolis, Heiropolis Bambyce, Laodicea, Orontes, Palmyra, Posidium, Raphia, Seleucia in Pieria.

Syria Palaestina *see* Judaea

Syria Phoenice *see* Phoenicia

Szombathely *see* Savaria

Szöny *see* Brigetio

T

Tabennisi. An island in the upper Nile, near Tentyra (Dendera) in the Thebaid province of Egypt, where St. Pachomius (*c* 292–346) brought together a community of ascetics in what may claim to have been the first monastery (*c* 320). Its occupants, who soon numbered 1,400, were expected to undertake a strenuous program of manual labor and meditation under strict discipline. Before he died Pachomius had founded nine such monasteries and two convents, with a total of 7,000 monks and nuns; every institution was directed by a Superior, and each of these received orders from Pachomius as Abbot-General.

Tac-Fövenypuszta *see* Pannonia

Taganrog *see* Tanais

Tagus (Tejo, Tajo) River. The longest river in the Iberian peninsula, the Tagus rises in Nearer Spain (Hispania Citerior, Tarraconensis)—at a location a hundred miles from the Mediterranean coast—and flows out into the Atlantic at Olisipo (Lisbon) in Lusitania (Portugal). This was an ancient site with a natural deep harbor, surrounded by a strategic semicircle of seven hills, which was fortified by Decimus Junius Brutus in 138 BC and under Julius Caesar or Octavian (the future Augustus) became known as Olisipo Felicitas Julia. *See also* Lusitania.

Takhti-Sangin *see* Bactria

Tamansk *see* Hermonassa

Tamassus, Tamassos (Politiko). A town in central Cyprus, on the left bank of the river Pediaeus. The settlement existed from an early date owing to the proximity of mines, which produced, according to Strabo, sulphate of copper and copper rust, useful for their medicinal properties. (This place may be the Temese mentioned in Homer's *Odyssey*, although recent studies support an alternative view, quoted by Strabo, that Temese was in south Italy). King Pasicyprus of Tamassus in Cyprus sold his kingdom *c* 340 to Pumiathon of Citium (Larnaca), and retired to the city of Amathus; soon afterward however, Alexander the Great took Tamassus away from Pumiathon and gave it to Pnytagoras, king of Salamis. Tamassus was stated by Hierocles to have possessed both the first Christian community in Cyprus and its earliest bishop, a certain Heraclidius.

A sanctuary of Apollo, of which the existence is suggested by inscriptions, has been provisionally identified at a site northeast of the town, where a bronze statue of the god (the Chatsworth Apollo, now in the British Museum) was discovered. Beside an industrial quarter, traces of a temple of Aphrodite are also to be seen. Dating from the archaic period, the building was frequently damaged and reconstructed, notably on the occasion of the Ionian revolt against the Persians (499/8), and again in the times of Alexander the Great and Ptolemy I Soter (d. 283/2). At some date during the Hellenistic Age an earthquake appears to have shattered the shrine. Two large altars have been discovered beside it; the earlier of these was constructed *c* 500, but votive objects in the area date back to the seventh century. Excavations have also revealed two imposing royal tombs; recent finds in one of them included numerous bronze objects, including a horse blinker with a magic ivory eye.

Tanagra (three miles from the modern Tanagra and from Schimatarion). The principal center of eastern Boeotia (central Greece), situated on a round terraced hill at the eastern extremity of Mount Ceryceium, overlooking the left (north) bank of the river Asopus—one of a number of Greek rivers of that name—where it is joined by the Laris (Lari). A fertile plain, famous for its fowls, extends in the vicinity.

The city claimed to have been founded by Poemandrus, who was also credited with the foundation of another Boeotian town, Poemandria. Tanagra fulfilled an active artistic role in the Mycenaean (late Bronze) Age, and at some date in the early first millennium BC was believed by Pausanias to have fought a war against the Eretrians of Euboea. In about 550 its citizens joined Megara in colonizing Heraclea Pontica (Ereğli) on the Euxine (Black) Sea, and later in the same country began to issue coins depicting a Boeotian shield (later inscribed BOI), which indicate that Tanagra had by this time become a member of the Boeotian League. In 457 the Athenians and their allies were defeated by a Spartan army near the town, but sixty-one days later they won a decisive victory over the Boeotians at Oenophyta which was probably nearby.

After a period of Spartan occupation (386–374/2), Tanagra still possessed substantial territory of its own. From *c* 350/330 its workshops, which had made votive objects for centuries, began to produce the famous 'Tanagra' terracotta statuettes, which offer lively and graceful reflections of everyday life, and constitute the city's principal claim to fame; they are habitually named after Tanagra because many specimens were found in an extensive local cemetery, although their principal center of production was probably Athens, anticipated by Taras (Tarentum, Taranto) in southern Italy. Tanagra was the birthplace of the lyric poet Corinna, who probably lived in the third century. In 145 Rome granted the city freedom and immunity from taxes, and in the first century AD, according to Strabo, Tanagra and Thespiae were the only fairly prosperous cities that still existed in Boeotia. Tanagra continued to coin at least until the time of Commodus (180–92).

Its ancient walls (*c* 385 BC), together with towers and gates, have been traced and partly uncovered. A large theater is visible, and (beneath a ruined chapel) the foundations of a temple: it is tentatively identified as a shrine of Dionysus mentioned by Pausanias and depicted on the coinage of Antoninus Pius (138–61). Pausanias also inspected a pickled corpse identified as a sea monster or Triton who had been caught while ambushing cattle or, according to an alternative version, while attacking the women of Tanagra as they swam in the sea before performing Dionysus' secret rites; an expert on marine monsters, Damostratus, reported that the object had rough, hard scales and stank. Hundreds of Tanagran inscriptions are preserved in the walls of local buildings in the museums at Schimatarion and Thebes.

Tanais. A site now under water near Taganrog (in the province of Rostov, southern Russia), on the gulf of that name in the northern part of Lake Maeotis (the Sea of Azov) west of the mouth of the river Tanais (Don), has yielded Greek pottery from the seventh century BC and later. These discoveries have suggested to some (though the conclusion is disputed) that this was the site of an archaic market town or fishing settlement that was known as Tanais and was perhaps colonized from Miletus in Ionia (western Asia Minor) *c* 625–600. It has alternatively been suggested, however, that the name Tanais should rather be applied to the island settlement of Alopecia (?) (Elisavetovskaya), beside the main southern branch of the Don delta, where excavations have cast abundant light on commercial interchanges between Greeks and Scythians between the fifth and third centures BC.

At all events, *c* 300/275 a new city of Tanais was founded by the kings of the Cimmerian (Crimean) Bosphorus (the ancient name of the Straits of Kerch)—perhaps with the participation of other Bosphoran cities, notably Phanagoria (Fanagori)—near Nedvigovka on the right (north) bank of the Mertvy Donets, the northernmost branch of the Don delta. This foundation became, as Strabo describes, a major cosmopolitan market town, the 'common emporium, partly of the Asiatic and the European nomads, and partly of those who navigated the lake from the Bosphorus, the former bringing slaves, hides and such other things as nomads possess, and the latter giving in exchange clothing, wine and the other things that belonged to civilized life.'

After maintaining its autonomy under the Bosphoran kings Pharnaces II (63–47) and Asander (47/44–16), this market city was destroyed by Polemo I of Pontus *c* 9 BC during his attempt, with Roman assistance, to take over the kingdom of the Bosphorus. Subsequently, however, Tanais recovered, and was flourishing by the end of the first century AD. After further destruction *c* 240/250, probably at the hands of the Goths, it again experienced a partial revival from *c* 350 to *c* 400: but thereafter the place ceased to exist.

The town of Tanais was encircled by two walls, one of earth and one of stone. Potters' kilns and traces of local glass production have been uncovered. A cemetery outside the wall comprised inhumation burials and a few cremations, and contained numerous Greek objects.

Tangier *see* Tingis

Taormina *see* Tauromenium

Tarabulus (Trablus) Al-Gharb *see* Oea

Tarabulus (Trablus) Esh-Sham *see* Tripolis (Syria)

Taras (Tarentum, Taranto). A city in Calabria (as the southeastern [not, as now, the southwestern] section of Italy was called in ancient times), in the Tarantine gulf of the Ionian Sea constituting the Italian 'instep.' Taras stood on a promontory or peninsula—virtually an island in ancient times—crowned by an acropolis, between an inland tidal lagoon (Mare Piccolo) to the east (serving as an inner harbor) and the main outer harbor (Marina Grande) to the west; this outer harbor was protected from the sea by two small islands, and formed the safest and most spacious port on any Italian coast. The neighboring waters contained large clusters of *murex* mussels, from which purple was extracted for dyeing, with a specially favored tint (*tarantinon* or *tarantinidion*), the wool derived from flocks in the fertile hinterland, a territory that also produced pears, figs, grapes, chestnut and famous horses.

The town had a prolonged and active Neolithic and Bronze Age (Apennine, Mycenaean) prehistory. It took its Greek name from the mythical founder of its native (Iapygian), pre-Greek settlement, Taras, whose father the god Poseidon, was said to have sent a dolphin to save his son from shipwreck. The traditional date for the Greek foundation, according to Eusebius, was 706 BC. These colonists were supposedly people from Sparta named Parthenians, who were described as the illegitimate offspring of Spartan women and helots (serfs), though this story was soon contested by rival versions and is now regarded with scepticism. The leader of the group was believed to have been a certain Phalanthus, whose relegation to the mythical status of a local sea-god seems unjustified; it is further recorded that he was soon expelled by his former followers, and took refuge with the natives of Brentesion (Brundusium, Brindisi).

The first Greek colonists settled at Satyrion (Leporano), seven miles southeast of Taras, to which they soon moved, joining a mixed population of Iapygians and Cretans. At the end of the sixth century the ruler of Taras was Aristophilides, whose kingship was apparently based on Spartan models. Soon after 500 the Tarantines won a series of victories over adjacent Italian (Messapian) tribes—who had posed a continuous threat to their territory and agriculture—but *c* 475/473 they suffered a severe defeat from a Messapian confederacy, as a result of which the aristocratic government of the city was superseded by a democracy.

The decline of Croton (Crotone) in the middle of the century left Taras as the leading Greek center in south Italy, and it was now that a famous new silver coinage was initiated—repeating an earlier type of the mythical founder Taras on his dolphin, with a horse and rider on the reverse—that was to last for more than two hundred years. In 433/2 Taras founded a colony at Heraclea (Policoro) in Lucania that became the headquarters of a League of Italiot Greeks, in which the Tarantines played a leading part. The Apulian school of pottery was probably centered at Taras from *c* 420. This was during the Peloponnesian War between Athens and Sparta, in the course of which its citizens allied themselves with Syracuse—invaded by the Athenians (415-413)—and provided ships for its fleet. Under the rule of the Pythagorean philosopher Archytas, in the early fourth century, Taras reached the height of its power and prosperity.

Subsequently, however, it came under renewed pressure from the tribes in the interior, and called in foreign mercenary leaders to repel their incursions. King Archidamus II of Sparta was defeated by the Lucanians (338), but Alexander I got the better of them, although, in the process, he fell out with the rulers of Taras (334). After the death of Alexander the Great (323), the sculptor Lysippus of Sicyon arrived at the city and made huge statues of Zeus and Heracles to symbolize its leadership of the local Greek federation. At this period Taras also produced splendid gold jewelry (collected in a recent exhibition), as well as limestone architectural sculptures with human figures, and charming terracotta figurines (developed from an earlier craft), the precursors of those of Athens and Tanagra. In 303 Cleonymus of Sparta repeated the failure of his compatriot Alexander I against the Lucanians. Meanwhile the government of Tarentum (as it was henceforward called in Latin sources), anxious about the Romans' southward expansion, had persuaded them to agree not to send warships into the gulf (*c* 334): which they did, nevertheless, in order to protect Thurii from Lucanian raiders (282; *see* Sybaris). At this juncture the Tarentines called in King Pyrrhus of Epirus to help them, but after initial successes he withdrew (275), so that they were compelled to surrender to Rome three years later. Livius Andronicus came to Rome as a Tarentine prisoner of war and played a dominant part in the creation of Latin literature. Rhinthon of Tarentum, the son of a potter, gave a novel and more sophisticated form to local popular farces (*phlyakes*), which took their material from daily life or from mythology and are depicted on the contemporary local vases.

During the Second Punic War Hannibal captured the city by treachery (213) and then built a cross wall between the harbors as a protection from Roman attacks. But it was recaptured and looted four years later by Quintus Fabius Maximus. In 133 Gaius Gracchus attempted to arrest the decline of Tarentum by the establishment of a Roman colony, thus transforming the place into an Italian town. It was here that Antony and Octavian (the future Augustus) met in 37 to renew the failing Second Triumvirate. Horace describes 'Lacedaemonian (Spartan) Tarentum' as a suitable holiday place for a tired business man. Nero seems to have settled legionary veterans in the city (AD 60). During the later empire it was the capital of the district or province of Apulia and Calabria.

A Doric shrine of Poseidon (Neptune) on the acropolis (*c* 575 BC) has now been restored. A frieze of the first century may come from a Temple of Eirene (Pax, Peace), and an altar perhaps belonged to a sanctuary of Aphrodite (Venus). Thirty thousand terracottas dating from between the sixth and third centuries were found in a precinct that seems to have housed cults of Persephone (Kore, Proserpina) and Dionysus (Bacchus), and a huge number of additional terracottas, many representing the reclining heroes Taras and Phalanthus, have been recovered near the Mare Piccolo: they are dedications by arriving and departing voyagers.

According to Strabo, the acropolis was walled, yet no trace of these fortifications have survived; but remains of defences encircling the city are to be seen below the present waterline. Neither of the two recorded theaters has been uncovered. Like the Spartans from whom they were descended, the Tarentines buried their dead within the walls, and thousands of graves, dating from the seventh to the second century BC, have been found. Ruins of two Roman baths, two aqueducts and a villa have also come to light.

Tarquinii (Etruscan Tarchnal, modern Tarquinia). A town in southwestern Etruria (now in Lazio) five miles from the Tyrrhenian Sea. By tradition Tarquinii was the oldest Etruscan city in Italy, founded by Tarchon the brother of Tyrsenus who supposedly (although this view is untenable) led the Etruscans from Lydia in western Asia Minor toward the end of the second millennium BC, shortly after the fall of Troy. Tages, who allegedly rose from the ground of Tarquinii, was believed to have taught Etruria the rules governing the relations between gods and men.

Excavations confirm that this was the earliest Etruscan center to attain metallic wealth and political power, so that the tenth and ninth centuries have been defined, with some justice, as the period of a 'Tarquinian civilization.' A number of adjoining villages were distributed over most of the Pian di Civita plateau, which is nearly surrounded by the river Marta and its tributaries. These villages rose to importance by working in bronze made from the copper of Mount Tolfa, ten miles away. In the second half of the eighth century, they coalesced into the nucleus of a city and city state. This foundation formed close links with the Greek markets of Pithecusae (Ischia) and Cumae (Cuma) in Campania, and was apparently the first place in Etruria to acquire pottery from those centers and to make painted vases on its own account.

It was believed that in the early seventh century a Greek, Demaratus, emigrated from Corinth with his whole family, settling at Tarquinii and bringing with him three *fictores* or modelers, that is to say terracotta sculptors; and he was said to have brought up one of his sons with a Greek and one with an Etruscan education. And indeed, even if these stories contain a certain measure of oversimplification, it can be seen that from *c* 675 local chamber tombs—of which nearly 7,000 have been found in Tarquinian cemeteries during the last quarter of a century alone, and a hundred are still visible—testify to a new and climactic phase of prosperity. In these graves the mid-sixth century inaugurated an extraordinary efflorescence of wall painting (such as is only very rarely to be found in Greek lands), combining Greek and Etruscan characteristics; about twenty examples, extending over a period of three hundred years, are reasonably well preserved. Stretches of the tufa city wall, enclosing a perimeter of five miles, are also extant, and the first systematic excavations of the urban center have now begun.

Although much or most of Tolfa, it appears, had been lost to Caere (Cerveteri) not long after 700, Tarquinii still controlled a wide and fertile surrounding area. These territories comprised the Marta and Mignone basins; inland, Tuscania (replacing Visentium [Bisenzio] on Lake Volsiniensis [Bolsena]) was under the control of Tarquinii; and on the coastland of the Tyrrhenian Sea it possessed three ports, later known as Graviscae (Porto San Clementino), Martanum and Rapinum, which made possible not only increased commerce with the Greeks—who had their own trading post at Graviscae until the 470s—but also the growth of a considerable Tarquinian sea power.

These widespread tentacles of the city gave rise to the story that Tarchon, after founding Tarquinii, went on to establish all the Etruscan centers in north Italy. This is a chauvinistic Tarquinian fiction; but what appears to be broadly true is that a dynasty originating from Tarquinii was established at Rome (the traditional date is 616) by Tarquinius Priscus and lasted until the expulsion of Tarquinius Superbus from that city (*c* 510). Incidental light is cast on the subsequent history of Tarquinii by a group of Latin *elogia* (statements recounting official careers) of the first century AD, honoring the family of the Spurinnas: Velthur Spurinna I, we are told, led an army to Sicily, thus becoming the first Etruscan leader to take troops overseas—either *c* 474, it would seem, or *c* 307. He also appears to have commanded a force against Caere (Cerveteri), while his son Aulus, we are told, expelled Orgolnius, the Caeretan king, and intervened forcibly at Arretium (Arezzo), probably during social disturbances at that city; he is also said to have captured nine 'Latin towns.'

During Rome's decisive war against Etruscan Veii, however, Tarquinii did not do enough to save its compatriots from their downfall (*c* 396), and subsequently encountered Roman hostility on its own account (*c* 358–351, 314–311/308), suffering defeat and the imposition of stern conditions that virtually put an end to its independent existence. The Romans founded a colony at Castrum Novum *c* 264 (?), on land captured from Tarquinii, and in 181 established another settlement at Graviscae. A third-century temple, known as the Ara della Regina, has provided the city's most famous work of art, a terracotta pair of winged horses, once yoked to a chariot. During the imperial epoch Tarquinii was the headquarters of a Roman priesthood of sixty diviners (*haruspices*).

Tarracina, formerly Anxur (Terracina). A city in Latium (Lazio), on the border of Campania, sixty-five miles south of Rome, situated on a high hill beside the sea. The site was occupied in prehistoric times. The legend of a Spartan foundation is fictitious. Strabo derives the name from *trachys* (rough), but it is rather to be connected with Tarquinii, denoting Etruscan settlement, or with the Tarquins, indicating influence exerted by the Etruscan royal dynasty at Rome. However, the town was subsequently taken over by an Italian people, the Volsci, who named it Anxur and built fortifications against the Romans. Nevertheless, the Romans captured the stronghold *c* 406, captured it for a second time after a rebellion, and established a citizen colony in 329, designed to defeat the coast and hold the Lautulae pass that ran between the Ausonian mountains and the sea. A decisive battle against the Latins was won in the neighborhood fifteen years later.

Tarracina became a station on the Via Appia from Rome to the south (312), and received munificent attention from the dictator Sulla in the early first century. The emperor Galba was born there in 3 BC. During the civil wars of AD 69 Vitellius' brother Lucius crushed a naval rebellion at the port, and massacred the rebels. Trajan (98–117) and Antoninus Pius (138–61) revived earlier attempts to drain the nearby Pomptine (Pontine) Marshes, expanding the lower town of Tarracina—which became the southern terminal of the canal constructed for this purpose—and enlarging its harbor.

The early Roman settlement was a quadrangular camp defended by a powerful wall with round towers and a strongly fortified gate, with barracks on three sides. Below the open south flank of the fortress Sulla added a monumental arcaded terrace for the temple of Jupiter Anxur, enlarged by cutting into the hill at the back. Situated on the edge of a lofty cliff overlooking the sea, this was one of the greatest shrines in Italy. Its pseudo-peripteral exterior (i.e. with a continuous outer ring of columns, some of which were engaged) displayed six columns on the front above the steps, and two on either side of the porch.

The town lay west of the temple on the remaining part of the hilltop. The original Via Appia served as the main longitudinal street. The edge of the forum, facing the sea, is supported by a huge substructure of arches. A triple Capitolium dates from *c* 40 BC, replacing a much earlier building. Trajan brought the Via Appia down into the lower town, which mostly dates from the second and third centuries AD, although the amphitheater is somewhat earlier. Two bathing establishments have been uncovered, three aqueducts have left traces, and there are remains of numerous villas in the neighborhood; some of these mansions are equipped with a multiplicity of terraces, and date from the second century BC. A sanctuary of the goddess Feronia (visited by Horace) stood at the foot of Mount Leano three miles from the city.

Tarraco (earlier Cissa or Cissis [Cese] and Callipolis, now Tarragona). A city on the northeast coast of Spain, beside the river Tulcis (Francoli). In the pre-Roman period it was the principal center of the tribe of the Cessetani. In 218–209, during the Second Punic War, it served as the headquarters of Cnaeus and Publius Cornelius Scipio (the uncle and father of Scipio Africanus the Elder), who constructed fortifications.

After Roman annexation (205–197), Tarraco became the most prolific local mint in the new province of Nearer Spain (Hispania Citerior), and was employed as a landing place by Roman generals setting out to suppress the tribes of the interior, notably Tiberius Sempronius Gracchus (father of the Gracchi) in 180, and Scipio Aemilianus in 134. During the Civil War between the Pompeians and Julius Caesar, the local inhabitants changed sides from the former to the latter, who established a civilian colony under the name of *Colonia Julia Victrix Triumphalis* (45). Augustus employed this settlement as his headquarters during his Spanish wars (26–24)—withdrawing there to recuperate from a serious illness—and arranged for it to replace Carthago Nova (Cartagena) as the capital of the province, which later, in consequence, came to be known as Hispania Tarraconensis. The population of Tarraco at this time has been estimated at 30,000; Strabo considered it the most important city in Spain, and it was famous for its wine.

During Galba's revolt against Nero (68), it sided with the former. Hadrian spent the winter of 121 there, convening a meeting of representatives from all the towns of the province. Tarraco was sacked by the Franks *c* 264, but was still regarded as one of the principal Spanish townships by Ausonius (*c* 370), although his praise may be partly nostalgic, since by his time the place had been eclipsed by Barcino (Barcelona). In 410 the Roman commander-in-chief in Spain, Gerontius (of British origin), set up a puppet emperor, Maximus, at Tarraco, but he fled shortly afterward. In 473/476 the city was captured by Euric the Visigoth, but later recovered and became an important Visigothic center.

Tarraco has provided the earliest Roman inscription in Iberia, consisting of a dedication by Manius Vibius to Minerva (200–190 BC). The ancient walls, enclosing a three-mile circuit, are still, in parts, to be seen, dating from the sixth and third centuries BC and from Roman times; the six surviving gates date from the earliest period. The upper city included the forum, a Temple of Jupiter (beneath the cathedral), and at the highest point an altar dedicated to Augustus, which was replaced in AD 15 by a temple in his honor, illustrated on coins of its founder Tiberius. A lower city stood beside the port. There are remains of numerous houses including the governor's palace (known also as the Torréon de Pilatos, because Pontius Pilate was believed, according to an unfounded tradition, to have come from the city) and Tarraco also possessed a theater, amphitheater and circus, as well as both a pagan and later a Christian basilica. The latter was erected over the tombs of Fructuosus, Augurius and Eulogius, who were martyred in the persecutions of Valerian (253–60).

The great two-tiered, two-hundred-and-fifty-foot high aqueduct known as the 'Devil's Bridge,' bringing water from the river Gaya, traversed a lateral valley of that river. On its bank, a cemetery contains two hundred tombs dating from the third to the sixth century. Four miles to the northwest of the city is the mausoleum of Centcelles, which has been carefully restored; and four miles to the east is a square tower of the first century AD, fancifully known as the Tower of Scipio. The province of Tarragona contains a number of important Roman villa-farms, notably at Els Munts (with three bathhouses), El Vilarene and Calafell.

Tarsus, Tarsos, later Antiochia on the Cydnus, Juliopolis, Antoninoupolis (*see also* below). The most important city of Cilicia (southeastern Asia Minor), in its eastern, 'Smooth' region (Pedias, Campestris), within the alluvial plain of the river Cydnus (Tarsus Çayı), at the mouth of which, some four miles distant, lay the port of Tarsus, Rhegnia, now covered by a eucalyptus forest planted to drain the swampland of the silted river estuary. Tarsus later claimed Heracles, Perseus and Triptolemus (together with Argives) as its founders, while other traditions assigned its foundation to the Assyrian kings Ashurbanipal or Sennacherib (705–680 BC), telling of a Greek landing party repulsed by the Assyrians.

Under the Persian empire Tarsus enjoyed autonomy under its own rulers (who were known as *Synnesis*), issuing coins before 400 with the city name but Persian designs. During the fourth century the names of Persian satraps appear—in addition to a temple of the god Anu, and a scene of a lion attacking a bull beside the city walls—until Tarsus was captured by Alexander the Great

(333), becoming one of his major mints. After his death, its possession was disputed between the Ptolemies and Seleucids, whose monarch Antiochus I Soter (293/2–261) or Antiochus II Theos (261–246) renamed the place Antiochia on the Cydnus, though it soon reverted to its original name. A coin of Demetrius II (129–125) depicts a shrine of Sandan.

Following further vicissitudes, Tarsus was occupied by Pompey the Great during his campaign against the pirates (67), though during his subsequent civil war against Julius Caesar (49–48) it sided with the latter, temporarily assuming the name of Juliopolis. In 41 Cleopatra VII of Egypt was summoned to the city by Antony, and made her regal progress up the Cydnus for their historic meeting, described by Plutarch and Shakespeare. Although at that time Tarsus was the center of famous philosophical and rhetorical schools, its inhabitants, according to Strabo, had a tendency to emigrate. Shortly after the beginning of the Christian era it was the birthplace of Saul (later St. Paul), whose family belonged to the local Jewish (Pharisee) community. His father was a tentmaker; Pliny the Elder and Athenaeus also refer to perfume industries in the city.

In AD 72 it became the capital of a new Roman province of Cilicia (separated from Syria). Dio Chrysostom (*c* 40–after 112) refers to a boundary dispute with Mallus (Kızıltahta), and rebukes the Tarsians for their aggressive, litigious spirit. In 260 their city was temporarily captured by Spates, a general of the Sassanian Persian King Sapor (Shapur) I. In 276 the armies of the rival emperors Florian and Probus confronted each other outside its walls, but Florian's troops murdered him before a battle could be fought. Maximinus II Daia succumbed to an illness there in 313. In the later empire the province of which Tarsus served as capital was Cilicia Prima, comprising the western part of the plain. Tarsian linen is mentioned in third- and fourth-century documents.

Until the time of Gallienus (253–68) the local mint produced an immensely varied coinage, including a number of silver issues. Honoring a succession of emperors—in fierce competition with other cities that had begun to compete with its rank—Tarsus described itself on these pieces as Commodiane, Severiane, Antoniniane (or Antoninoupolis), Macriniane and Alexandriane, and as 'the first, the greatest and most beautiful' and 'the free city presiding over the three provinces.' The same series records the 'free' Cilician Assembly (*koinon, eleutherion koinoboulion*), and Ciliciarchs who served as its presidents. Other coins bear witness to a variety of local festivals—including the Games held to celebrate Septimius Severus' victory over Pescennius Niger (194)—and illustrate a wide range of mythological scenes, with special relation to the city's traditional founders. A temple of Hadrian's youthful friend Antinous, described as the New Dionysus (*Neos Iakchos*), also appears, and under Caracalla (211–17) an elaborately ornamented gateway is depicted. The only certain ancient monument still surviving in the city is a concrete podium known as the 'Frozen Stone,' but numerous local finds are exhibited in Adana museum.

Tartessus, Tartessos. A region and kingdom of southwestern Spain, centered on the lower and middle reaches of the river Baetis (itself sometimes known as the Tartessus, now the Guadalquivir); although the name was also, on occasion, loosely applied to the whole of Spain, and even to western Europe in general.

The kingdom's commercial relations with the Phoenicians and Carthaginians (notably by way of Sardinia, Sicily and Cyprus), and the procurement of tin from Callaecia (Galicia, northwest Spain) and perhaps also from Galicia, Brittany and Britain (Scilly Islands, Cornwall), contributed to its proverbial wealth: and excavations have been specially directed to the Ría de Huelva, where metals were mined. The capital of the state of Tartessus was a city bearing the same name. Numerous attempts have been made to locate its site, both in ancient times—as recounted by Strabo—and more recently, but without success. It probably lay near the river mouth.

This town was the principal outlet for the rich silver mines of southwestern Spain. The civilization of the kingdom seems to have been created by the impact of Greece and Phoenicia on its indigenous populations. About 640/630 BC Colaeus of Samos traveled to its port, and took home silver, tin, bronze. But it was another group of Ionians, from Phocaea (Foca), who *c* 600 established relations with King Arganthonius of Tartessus, stated by Herodotus to have reigned for eighty years; and he gave them money to erect a wall around Phocaea for its defence against the Persians. The names of other Tartessian kings are known, and many legends gathered around their personalities and careers. One, Habis, was said by Justin to have taught his people agriculture, and attributions of Geryon's mythical cattle to the region illustrate one of the sources of its wealth. Habis, who allegedy proclaimed himself a god, was believed to have been a legislator, and local legends recorded that the laws of Tartessus were 6,000 years old and had been written in verse. The traditions of the kingdom took the fancy of the poets Stesichorus (5th–6th centuries) and Anacreon (born *c* 570).

Although strong arguments to the contrary have been put forward, it may perhaps be identifiable with the Biblical Tarshish (Tarsisi in Assyrian inscriptions), of which the ships, as early as King Solomon's time (tenth century), were said to have traveled as far afield as the Red Sea. At first Tarshish was only dimly localized; by the seventh century, however, it is already set in the western Mediterranean, being named in an early Phoenician dedication found at Nora in Sardinia. In the following century the Jewish prophet Ezekiel wrote of the silver, iron, tin and lead that came from Tarshish to Tyre (Es-Sur) in Phoenicia, and Jeremiah described the 'silver, beaten into plates, that is brought from Tarshish': this silver had been exported to Greek lands from *c* 630 BC.

Tartessus exerted a powerful influence—notably through its transmission of Greek pottery—on the civilized native populations throughout a wide area of southern and southeastern Spain. In particular, the chieftain burials of Lower Andalusia seem to reflect the world of the Tartessian monarchs. Their trading activities also extended to the less advanced peoples of the center and north of the peninsula. In about 500, however, the capital was probably destroyed by the Phoenicians, whose expansion it had hindered.

Tartus *see* Aradus

Tauris *see* Chersonese (Tauric)

Tauromenium (Taormina). A town near the east coast of Sicily, on the slopes of Mount Taurus (Tauro), above the stream Tauromenius (Selina). The settlement was established in 396 BC, on the site of a small previous habitation center, by the Carthaginian Himilco. According to Diodorus (although the course of events is obscure), Himilco populated his new foundation with Sicels who had been settled by Dionysius I of Syracuse at Naxos (Punta di Schiso—ten miles to the south, on the coast below), but had subsequently abandoned his cause (and Naxos was destroyed). In 394/3, however, Dionysius besieged Tauromenium and, under an agreement with the Carthaginians, occupied the place, dispossessing most of the Sicel settlers in favor of his own ex-soldiers. In 358 some of the survivors from the destruction of Naxos were gathered together and settled at Tauromenium by Andromachus, father of the historian Timaeus (*c* 356–260) who was the town's most distinguished citizen. A powerful opponent of tyrants, Andromachus supported Timoleon, the Corinthian who put an end to autocratic rule at Syracuse (344).

When this autocracy was revived, however, by Agathocles, the Tauromenians, too, came under his domination (316). Subsequently they were ruled by a local autocrat Tyndarion (*c* 285), who facilitated the invasion of Sicily by Pyrrhus of Epirus and allowed him to land at his harbor (278). Later Tauromenium formed part of the dominions of King Hiero II of Syracuse—by agreement with the Romans (263)—and when Syracuse passed into Roman hands Tauromenium went with it (211), obtaining the rank of a federated state (*civitas foederata*). During the First Slave Revolt it was occupied by the rebels, but recaptured in 132. In 36 Sextus Pompeius inflicted a serious naval defeat on Octavian (the future Augustus) off the shore of Tauromenium, but when, shortly afterward, Octavian had won the final victory, he established a Roman colony of ex-soldiers at the town, which subsequently prospered during the imperial epoch, largely because of its choice wines.

The Greek agora then became the Roman forum. A large bathhouse of the first or second century AD has been excavated to the north of this space, and to its west is a small theater or Odeon. A hundred yards to the east is the principal surviving ancient monument, a spacious theater, which was erected in about the second century AD on the site of a Hellenistic building, and subsequently adapted for use as an amphitheater. Below the forum is a brick wall (known as the Naumachia) which formed the outer wall of a large cistern, brick built and stuccoed and divided into two aisles, is to be seen in the Giafari district not far away. The temple of Apollo Archegetes, shown by local coinage to have been the city's principal patron, has not been located.

Taurus (Toros) Mountains. The principal mountain range of Asia Minor, extending through the southwestern part of the peninsula, along the coast of Lycia, and through Pisidia and Isauria to the borders of Cilicia and Lycaonia. The offshoots of the range include Antitaurus (Cappadocia, Armenia) and Amanus (at the junction of northwestern Syria and Asia Minor). The Taurus massif, regarded by the ancients as the backbone of Asia, was also loosely enlarged by their geographers to include the mountains of Mesopotamia and Armenia and northern Iran and even the Paropamisus (Hindu Kush) and Imaus or Emodus (Himalayas), and was extended, by rumor, as far as the unexplored Eastern Ocean.

Tava, from the river Tavesis (Tay), may have been the name of the Roman fortress at Carpow in Perthshire (Caledonia, Scotland), which lies on the south bank of that river. Carpow was occupied by the sixth legion (which stamped its tiles with the words 'Britannica Pia Fidelis') during Septimius Severus' British campaigns of 208–11. The defences consisted of an eighteen-foot-wide earth bank, with two stone gates, and a double ditch. Near the center of the camp was the administrative headquarters (*principia*), made of stone, and a bathing establishment apparently attached to the commander's residence (*praetorium*). Aerial photography has also revealed the legionary barracks, and a large temporary encampment; traces of a military hospital (*valetudinarum*) are also to be seen. An unusual find of scale armor, still attached to its original backing, has recently come to light. A bridge of boats depicted on coins and medallions of Severus and his son Caracalla (208)—labelled TRAIECTVS ('crossing') on the latter's issues—may refer to a Tay bridge at Carpow (but a first Forth Bridge has been alternatively suggested). In any case, the Carpow stronghold was abandoned when Caracalla evacuated Caledonia after Severus' death (211).

Tavium *see* Galatia

Taxila (Bhir mound, Sirkap, Sirsukh, near Rawalpindi, now in the western Punjab, northeastern Pakistan). The capital of a kingdom extending between the rivers Indus and Hydaspes (Jhelum) or Acesines (Chenab), east of Gandhara and the Paropamisus (Hindu Kush) range. Strabo praises the region's fertile soil and excellent laws. After a period of attachment to the Achaemenid (Persian) empire, the local king Omphis (Ambhi)—one of a series of monarchs who controlled Gandhara, and were known to the Greeks as Taxiles—welcomed Alexander the Great, out of fear of a southeastern neighbor Porus (Parvataka, Parvatesha) whom Alexander (with Omphus' help) defeated (326), but subsequently reinstated. Alexander was impressed by Indian sages whom he encountered at Taxila, according to the historian Aristobulus of Cassandrea, who also described curious local marriage customs. At first Omphis was placed under a Macedonian governor Philippus, but after Philippus' assassination, he was confirmed as joint ruler of Taxila and resumed virtual independence. Toward the end of the century, however, his kingdom became part of the Mauryan empire of Chandragupta (Sandracottus).

The former capital Taxila (one of a number of towns of that name) was refounded as a Greek city by one of the Indo-Greek monarchs, either Demetrius I (*c* 200–185) or one of his successors (who were probably his sons) Pantaleon and Agathocles Dikaios, both of whom issued coins at the local mint. Eucratides I 'Maharajasa,' the Great (*c* 170/165–*c* 155), who eventually gained control of a united Indo-Greek kingdom extending from Taxila to Margiana (Merv). His general Menander Soter Dikaios, who subsequently became the most renowned of the Indo-Greek monarchs (*c* 155–140/130), was born at Sacala (Sialkot) near Taxila. Taxila was one of the mints of Strabo I Epiphanes Soter Dikaios (*c* 130–75), who, for a time, maintained or revived Indo-Greek unity.

Not long afterward Indo-Scythian invaders moved up the Indus to capture the city, where their ruler Azes I (*c* 57–35) overthrew the diminished Greek regime. According to a later legend one of his successors, Gondophares (*c* AD 19–45), welcomed St. Thomas to his court, impressed by the saint's ability as a builder. Subsequently, however, Taxila became a dependency of the Parthians, whom it served as a regional metropolis, commercial entrepôt, and communications center.

Excavations have revealed successive habitation centers. The Greek town lies between twelve and fifteen feet beneath Indo-Scythian and Parthian buildings, but its general, mainly symmetrical plan has now been reconstructed. Houses were built of rubble masonry and grouped round central courtyards, and sections of a city wall enclosing a three-and-half mile perimeter have survived. Excavations reveal a rich transit trade to and from further Asia, and the sculptural figures that have been uncovered, mostly carved in green schist, offer an important contribution to our understanding of later Gandharan art. In particular, a considerable quantity of stylized stucco sculpture, which was founded in monasteries destroyed by the White Huns during the later fifth century AD, displays a characteristic blend of eastern and western influences.

Tazzoult *see* Lambaesis

Tegea. A city in southeastern Arcadia (Peloponnese, southern Greece), on the route between Sparta and the Gulf of Corinth. The founder-hero Tegeates was said to have been the father of Gortys (see Gortyna). According to another myth, however, Tegea was established by Arcas' grandson Aleus, whose daughter Auge, ravished by Heracles, became the mother of Telephus, the future king of Mysia and Pergamum. There was also a story that another of Heracles' sons, Hyllus, was killed by Echemus, the king of Tegea. The town is mentioned in the catalog of ships in Homer's *Iliad*.

At an uncertain date before 600 BC (although some place the event considerably later) the villages of the valley basin, which contained good arable land, amalgamated to become a single town and city. About 560/550, after fighting that may have lasted for twenty years, its citizens induced Sparta to come to terms and form an alliance, and Tegea became a member of the Peloponnesian League. Its heavy (hoplite) infantry was renowned, and in the Persian Wars it provided the second strongest Peloponnesian contingent after that of Sparta, with which it shared the burden of the battle of Plataea (479). In 476/5 the Spartan king Leotychidas II took refuge at Tegea, which in *c* 471 revolted against the Spartan alliance and joined Argos, but suffered a decisive military setback in the neighborhood. In 468 it revolted once more, supported by all the Arcadian cities except Mantinea, but was again heavily defeated at Dipaea (*c* 466). During the Peloponnesian War, however, between Athens and Sparta, Tegea sided with the Spartans, out of hostility toward Mantinea, which took the Athenian side (420). At this period the Tegeans began to issue their own coins.

Their history during the fourth and third centuries continued to abound in vicissitudes. In 370 Mantinea helped the Tegean democrats to seize power within their own city and to form an Arcadian League, which soon entered into alliance with Elis and Argos; and in 362 Tegea fought alongside the Thebans at the battle of Mantinea, to break Spartan supremacy. In 316 it resisted a siege by Alexander the Great's successor Cassander. In 267 the Tegeans left the Arcadian League and rejoined Sparta, but subsequently became members of the Aetolian (*c* 240) and then the Achaean Confederacy (229/8) before returning to Spartan allegiance. In 223 the city was captured by Antigonus III Doson of Macedonia and restored to the Achaeans, but was taken again by Sparta in 218 and 210. In 207, however, the Achaean leader Philopoemen reoccupied Tegea as a base for his operations against the Spartans.

In Roman times the city maintained its position better than other Arcadian communities. The emperor Hadrian was a visitor in AD 124, a date from which Tegea reckoned the commencement of a new civic era. Later in the century Pausanias offered a detailed description of its monuments. Local coinage was revived for a brief period under the dynasty of Septimius Severus (193–217). Many buildings were destroyed by Alaric's Visigoths *c* 395, but there were still inhabitants in early Byzantine times.

Remains of an early temple of Artemis Knakeatis include column capitals very close in style to those of the Mycenaean past. But the most sacred building in Tegea was a large shrine outside the city dedicated to Athena Alea (345/335 BC), whose statue—together with the tusks of the Calydonian Boar—was removed by Octavian (the future Augustus) after his victory over Antony and Cleopatra VII at Actium (31 BC). This temple—the building in which the Spartans Leotychidas II and Pausanias had sought asylum—was burned down in 395/4 but replaced *c* 350/340 (?) according to the designs of Scopas, who also created its elaborate sculptures (of which fragments survive in the museums of Tegea and Athens). The Tegeans, according to Pausanias, also possessed a sanctuary of their special protector Athena Poliatis. According to tradition, Athena had vowed to Aleus' son Cepheus that the city should never fall, cutting off some of the hairs of the Gorgon Medusa (bronze snakes) as a guarantee, and giving them to Sterope, the daughter of Aleus, to be kept in a bronze jar.

The protagonists in this myth all appear on local coinage; but the temple, which stood on the acropolis hill (Phylactris or Acra, now Ayios Sostis), has not been found. Nor have other holy places mentioned by Pausanias, e.g. a second shrine of Artemis, who supposedly caused a tyrant of Arcadian Orchomenus, Aristomelidas or Aristocleides (of doubtful historicity), to be murdered, because he had fallen in love with a Tegean girl and had kept her in confinement. The colonnaded agora of the city, however, has been located, and there are remains of Christian basilicas of the fifth century AD; one of them was found to possess a mosaic pavement showing the seasons and the rivers Tigris and Euphrates.

Telamon *see* Rusellae

Tell Aphek *see* Antipatris

Tell Arqua *see* Arca

Tell el-Husn *see* Scythopolis

Tell Farama *see* Pelusium

Tell Sandahana *see* Marissa

Tell Sukas *see* Paltus

Tell Umar *see* Seleucia

Tempe. A narrow valley, between five and six miles long and from thirty to fifty-five yards wide, in northern Thessaly (northeastern Greece), through which the river Peneus breaks through to the coast between Mounts Olympus and Ossa. The vale of Tempe provided the principal road between Thessaly and Macedonia and could be held by a few troops, though there were also mountain routes further inland. According to Greek mythology, the defile had been cut by Poseidon's trident.

During the Persian Wars, in 480, the Greeks sent a force 10,000 strong to hold Tempe against Xerxes I, but withdrew this contingent soon afterward to Thermopylae, thus abandoning Thessaly to the invader. In 336 Alexander the Great, faced by Thessalian hostility, turned Tempe without a fight by cutting steps ('Alexander's ladder') up the slopes of Ossa. Rome's Second Macedonian War ended with an armistice between Flamininus and King Philip II at Tempe (197). In the Third Macedonian War Perseus fortified the valley against Quintus Marcius Philippus (170), but two years later Lucius Aemilius Paullus penetrated into Macedonia over another pass. After Roman rule had been established (146), the civil war of 48 between Julius Caesar and Pompey the Great prompted the construction of a road through the valley, undertaken by Caesar's general Lucius Cassius Longinus.

At the eastern entrance to Tempe stood an ancient shrine of Apollo, from which, every eight years, a procession conducted a sacred laurel branch to Delphi, in memory of the branch planted there by Apollo—after he had killed the serpent Python, and had purified himself in the waters of the Peneus, plucking a laurel branch from its bank. The Thessalians, according to Herodotus, attributed the creation of Tempe to convulsions produced by the god Poseidon, a story echoed in the myths of the War of the Gods and Giants.

Tenos. An Aegean island belonging to the Cyclades group, between Andros (one mile distant) and Myconos. The region now known as Kardiani has yielded material dating back to the Neolithic period, as well as finds of the early first millennium BC. During the latter period Tenos made its own pottery with relief decorations, mainly between 750 and 650. Not long afterward, it began to issue its own coins—displaying, at first, the design of a bunch of grapes. The island was famous for the abundance of its springs.

During the Persian Wars its ships were enrolled in the fleet of Xerxes I (480), but before the battle of Salamis one of these vessels succeeded in deserting to the Greeks, whom its crew then informed of the Persians' plans. Subsequently Tenos was honored for thus joining the victorious Greek side. It became a member of the Delian League, under the leadership of Athens, and during the Peloponnesian War sent vessels to take part in the Athenian expedition against Syracuse (415-413). Tenos was overrun by Alexander of Pherae of Thessaly (369-358). During the third century it became one of the principal members of an Island League—with recognized rights of asylum—and after 200 came under the protection of Rhodes. Its inhabitants suffered seriously from piracy, but regained prosperity during the Principate—when their rights of asylum were confirmed by Tiberius (AD 14-37)—and resumed coinage in the second century AD. In the later empire Tenos became part of a new province of the Aegean Islands (Insulae).

Its principal settlement, in the southwestern district, seems to have lain beneath the modern town (though this is disputed: *see* below). Remnants of its wall and towers have survived, dating from the fifth and third centuries BC. Tenos owed its fame, however, to a sanctuary of Poseidon and Amphitrite at Kionia to the west of the city, much frequented, according to Strabo, by people from the neighboring islands; its attribution to the fourth and early third centuries BC has been confirmed by discoveries on the site. A recently excavated portico parallel to the beach, five hundred and fifty feet long, is the largest known in Greece; erected and then redesigned before 100 BC, it suffered destruction in the following century—no doubt as a result of piratical raids—and was never wholly reconstructed. A colonnaded refectory has been identified nearby. The museum contains huge jars of the seventh century BC, ornamented with friezes; and there is also a sundial, attributed to Andronicus Cyrrhestes. Further north, at the foot of Mount Xambourgo, another ancient fortified center, containing a public building and a temple, has left traces below the Venetian castle. According to some scholars this, rather than the more southerly center, was the ancient city of Tenos.

Tentyra, Tentyris (Dendera). A city in Egypt, on the left (west) bank of the Nile, thirty-seven miles north of Thebes. It was one of the oldest Pharaonic cult-centers of the goddess Hathor, whose great temple, however, was only begun by the late Ptolemies, and enlarged under Tiberius (AD 14-37). Behind the temple is a shrine of Isis built by Augustus (31 BC-AD 14); he rebuilt the whole sanctuary, surrounding it with a wall which also enclosed the Birth House of Nectanebo I (380-362 BC). This latter building was replaced by another Birth House, surrounded by an ambulatory displaying reliefs of the emperor Trajan (AD 98-117) offering sacrifices to Hathor. A zodiac map of the sky found on the site is now in the Louvre.

Strabo remarks that the people of Tentyra differed from all other Egyptians because they hated and dishonored crocodiles—which were revered elsewhere—and sought to destroy them. In the early second century AD the satirist Juvenal wrote of an ancient and extremely violent feud, of religious origin, between the populations of Tentyra and Ombi (Kom-Ombo). During the later empire Tentyra formed part of the province of the Thebaid. In the fifth century, north of Nectanebo's Birth House, a Christian church was built of sandstone blocks taken from the pagan precinct.

Teos (Sığacık). A city in Ionia (western Asia Minor), on the coast north of Ephesus and southwest of Smyrna (İzmir), situated on the isthmus of a peninsula, with harbors lying both to the north and to the south (the latter is now silted up).

According to tradition, Teos was founded by the god Dionysus (known as Setaneus), or alternatively by the prehistoric tribe of the Minyans, coming from Orchomenus in Boeotia (central Greece), who were subsequently joined by Ionians and Athenians, led by the sons of the Athenian King Codrus (attributed to the eleventh century BC). Teos became one of the twelve cities of the Ionian League, and began to issue its own coins in the sixth century, with the type of a seated griffin. After the Persian occupation of Ionia, its citizens, including the lyric poet Anacreon, emigrated to Thrace and founded Abdera (*c* 545); but many came back soon afterward. During the Ionian Revolt against the Persians, seventeen Teian ships took part in the disastrous battle of Lade (495). After the Persian Wars the city became a member of the Delian League under Athenian leadership, but revolted during the Peloponnesian War after the defeat of the Athenian expedition to Syracuse (413). Under the King's Peace (Peace of Antalcidas) in 387, Teos returned to Persian rule.

In 303 Antigonus I Monophthalmos proposed to strengthen the city, which had become poor, by incorporating the whole population of another Ionian town, Lebedus (Kimituria, Kısık), but the plan was not carried out, and in the following year Lysimachus captured both centers and transferred many of their inhabitants to his new foundation at Ephesus (Arsinoeia). Teos later belonged to Attalus I of Pergamum (241-197), becoming a major cultural center and headquarters of the Asian corporation of the Artists of Dionysus, but, after dissensions this organization was moved to Ephesus half a century later. In 204 Teos passed into the hands of the Seleucid monarch Antiochus III the Great (who remitted Attalus' taxes and received civic honors). Subsequently, however, it was the scene of a battle in which Antiochus was defeated by the Romans and Rhodians (189). The subsequent Treaty of Apamea returned the city to Pergamene control, and it later became part of the Roman province of Asia (133). A recently published inscription describes the synoecism (amalgamation) of Teos with the hitherto unknown community of Cyrbissus.

Teian coinage of imperial date depicts an early temple of Augustus (31 BC–AD 14), who was given the title of 'Founder'—perhaps after an earthquake. But the issues concentrate mainly on representations relating to the cult of Dionysus Setaneus, to whom, from at least *c* 200 BC, the city and its territory were regarded as sacred; his temple of local blue limestone was designed by Hermogenes at that time and restored by Hadrian (AD 117–38). The remnants of a theater, Odeum, gymnasium and quays are also to be seen, beneath the walled acropolis.

Termessus (Major), Termessos. A city in Pisidia (southern Asia Minor), twenty-two miles northwest of Attaleia (Antalya) and nineteen miles from the modern Korkuteli. Situated in a narrow valley 3,500 feet above sea level, on the western flank of Mount Solymus (Güldere or Güllük Dağı), and with another mountain to its east, Termessus was only approachable from the northern interior overlooking and controlling a vital pass (the Yenice Boğazı) leading in that direction. Its people called themsleves Solymians in inscriptions (the name is also recorded in Homer's *Iliad*), and at one period, according to Strabo, they spoke a language or dialect bearing that designation, but later, except for personal names, this form of speech died out.

In 334 Alexander thc Great forced the pass, but decided, according to Arrian, that the fortress was too strong to attack, and moved on. In 319 his former officer Alcetas (the brother of Perdiccas), defeated by Antigonus I Monophthalmos, took refuge in Termessus, but committed suicide in order to avoid capture; his body was handed over to Antigonus, but the Termessians fought to secure its recovery, and gave it a hero's burial. In 189 they besieged neighboring Isinda (Kışla), but were compelled to withdraw by the Roman general Cnaeus Manlius Vulso, whom they dissuaded, however, from further hostilities by a large monetary gift. In the same period they engaged in a war against the Lycian League, and formed an alliance for mutual defence with the Pisidian city of Adada (Karabavlı).

In 91 and 70 they also concluded a treaty with the Romans, and from the latter date onward issued local coinage dated by a new civic era. The issues were temporarily suspended under the rule of Amyntas (39), later ruler of Galatia, but resumed after Termessus became part of Rome's Galatian province. Zeus Solymeus and many other deities are represented on these pieces, which describe the city as autonomous, free and 'Major' (*meizon*, to distinguish it from its colony Termessus Minor [Beside Oenoanda] in Lycia, founded in the third century BC). Termessus Major was still very prosperous, and the recipient of extensive endowments *c* AD 200. By this time, or a little later, it formed part of the province of Pamphylia, but two new towns, Jovia and Eudocias, created by Diocletian (284–305) and Theodosius II (408–50 respectively), were carved out of its extensive territory.

Although the site is heavily overgrown, numerous buildings can still be identified. There is an agora, flanked by stoas (porticos) erected by the Pergamene King Attalus II Philadelphus (160/59–138) and by a certain Osbaras. Adjoining the agora are a theater and Odeum—both in a good state of preservation—and the ruins of a large residence (known as the Founder's House). Remnants of a gymnasium lie farther north, not far from a colonnaded street. At least five temples have been located, including two dedicated to Artemis and a smaller building that has been conjecturally identified as the shrine of Zeus Solymeus. Considerable traces of an upper and lower city wall are also to be seen.

During the second century BC the Termessians built a wall, blocking the mountain pass. Since its ten towers are situated on the western side of the wall, they would have halted a hostile force only after it had passed below the city, and were probably, therefore, designed to collect tolls rather than for purposes of military defence.

Terni *see* Interamna

Terracina *see* Tarracina

Teurnia *see* Noricum

Teutoburgiensis, Saltus. A forest in western Germany, possibly between the modern Osnabrück and Detmold, although the site has been the subject of much inconclusive discussion (and the modern 'Teutoburger Wald' is a seventeenth-century guess). The Saltus witnessed a major Roman military disaster during the reign of Augustus. His stepsons Tiberius Nero Drusus (Drusus the Elder) had overrun 'free' Germany from the Rhenus (Rhine) to the Albis (Elbe), but the territory had not seemed ready for conversion into a Roman province. In AD 9 Publius Quinctilius Varus, who had married the grandniece of the emperor, was appointed commander of the Rhine armies, with control over this recently annexed area. During the latter part of the year he began to withdraw his three legions westward from their advanced summer camps far in the depths of Germany toward their winter quarters on the Rhine. But as he was marching through the dense Teutoburgian Forest, Arminius, the chief of the Cherusci, who was a Roman citizen, knight and auxiliary officer, and a personal friend of Varus, launched a sudden ambush attack on his force. The three legions were virtually annihilated, Varus committed suicide, and Germany east of the Rhine was lost—as it turned out, forever. It has been argued that the last Roman stand, located by Tacitus *in medio campi,* took place 'on the parade-ground' within the camp itself, after the main ramparts had been stormed.

Six years later Tiberius' nephew Germanicus, conducting further operations in Germany, led his troops to this site, where he buried the remains of Varus' massacred soldiers. But this action was censured by the emperor. 'He may have felt,' suggested the historian, 'that the sight of the unburied dead would make the army too respectful of its enemies, and reluctant to fight—nor should a commander belonging to the antique priesthood of the Augurs have handled objects belonging to the dead.'

Tevarya *see* Tiberias

Thamugadi (Timgad). A city of Numidia in the Roman province of Africa (Algeria), founded as a colony of ex-soldiers by Trajan, under the name of Colonia Marciana Trajana (AD 100). Situated in a fertile countryside where the east-west road from Theveste (Tebessa) to the garrison town of Lambaesis (Tazzoult, Lambèse) crossed a route leading northward to Rusicade (Skikda) on the coast, Thamugadi was one of a series of centers strategically located just north of the Aurès mountain range, in order to block the passes. Irrigation made agriculture possible in the neighborhood, and the town served as a market for a large district.

It attained great prosperity under the dynasty of the north African Septimius Severus (193–211). In the fourth century it was the center of the puritanical Donatist schism, which—aided by bands of militant itinerant harvesters (Circumcelliones)—became the majority church of Africa until *c* 400, when a series of imperial rescripts (culminating in the decisions of the Council of Carthage,

411) imposed sanctions and persecutions. These lasted until occupation by the Vandals (see Numidia), under whom Thamugadi underwent plundering by raiders from the Aurès mountains at the end of the fifth century.

With the single exception of Lepcis Magna, Thamugadi displays the most complete Roman remains in Africa, and they have been thoroughly excavated. The original town was designed according to a regular camp-like grid plan, with one hundred and eleven more or less equal blocks; its main streets met at an intersection where the colonnaded forum, an apsed basilica, a fine library, the local senate-house (*curia*), and a row of shops were all situated. Behind the forum a street climbs to the theater, of which the construction was begun *c* 160. A Roman house (known as the Maison des Jardinières) has been plausibly identified with the residence occupied by the legionary commander and governor of Numidia on the occasion of his visits to Thamugadi. More than a dozen bathing establishments have also been located, and numerous temples.

But as the habitation area began to outgrow its original rectangle—shortly after the mid-second century—an imposing new Capitoline temple was built outside the walls. Under Septimius Severus, when the size of the city had been magnified fourfold, parts of these defences and their gates were pulled down, to make room for houses and for a finely decorated three-bayed triumphal arch, now restored. Beside the arch a local citizen, Marcus Plotius Faustus Sertius, constructed a new marketplace at his own expense; his enormous house, too, has come to light, in addition to the 'House of the Hermaphrodite,' one of a number of residences possessing pavements which display the original, talented, varied and intricate work of a local school of mosaicists. A medicinal spring, the Aqua Septimia Felix, was associated with a temple of water divinities, which contained three shrines filled with statues and interlinked by terraces and stairs, and was further adorned with colonnaded gardens and other enrichments in the time of Severus' son Caracalla (211–17). Another sanctuary was dedicated to Saturn, identified with a local deity.

At the beginning of the fourth century new buildings were added, including two additional, palatial sets of Baths. Two Christian basilicas seem to have been the Catholic and Donatist cathedrals (*see* above), the latter forming part of an elaborate precinct; a house was found to contain an inscription bearing the name of Optatus, the Donatist leader from 388 to 398.

Thapsus, Thapsos (Ed-Dimas). A town in the Roman province of Africa (Tunisia), on the west coast of Syrtis Minor (the Gulf of Gabes), approached by two corridors of land on either side of a large lagoon. Its name comes from the Carthaginian *tapsah,* transit, since the town not only possessed this anchorage but was also situated on the coastal road. In 310 BC Thapsus was briefly captured from the Carthaginians by Agathocles of Syracuse. During the Third Punic War (149–146) it sided with the Romans against Carthage, and was rewarded, after the destruction of that city, with the status of a free community (*civitas libera*).

In 46 the decisive African battle of the Civil War between Julius Caesar and the Pompeians took place in the neighborhood. Caesar laid siege to the town and contrived to tempt the Pompeian leader, Quintus Caecilius Metellus Scipio, into the western corridor of the lagoon. There Metellus Scipio stood and fought; but his line was quickly broken by Ceasar's troops, whose victory turned into a massacre. Metellus Scipio committed suicide, and Cato killed himself, at Utica (Bordj ben Chateur); Africa was lost by the Pompeians, whose surviving leaders escaped to Spain.

Under Augustus and Tiberius coinage issued at Thapsus describes the city as Colonia P(ia?) Julia, indicating the city's promotion to colonial rank, apparently before 27 BC. The god Mercury is depicted, and in the reign of Tiberius, that emperor's mother Livia appears in the roles of Ceres Augusta and Juno Augusta; three proconsuls are named (AD 21–24). Remains of an amphitheater and cisterns have survived.

Thasos. An island in the northern Aegean Sea, sixteen miles in diameter, situated five miles from the mouth of the river Nestos, which (at one time) formed the boundary between Macedonia and Thrace. Although mountainous, Thasos contained fertile valleys and was well provided with water. Before the arrival of the Greeks it had borne the name of Odonis and had been occupied by the Sintes, a Thracian people, whose settlements have been identified on Mount Kastri (near Theologos, in the south of the island)—occupied since late Neolithic times—as well as on the site of the later Greek city, which lay on the northern coast.

Thasos was colonized *c* 650 BC from Paros, one of the Cyclades archipelago, under the leadership of Telesicles, whose enterprise was sanctioned by a surviving Delphic oracle. The Parian iambic and elegiac poet Archilochus was one of the original or early settlers on Thasos. They rapidly gained control of the whole island; and within two or three decades, as pottery finds indicate, they had also planted townships on the mainland opposite, at Neapolis (Kavalla), Oesyme and Galepsus, in order to dominate the gold mines of Mount Pangaeum (the tradition that there were gold mines on Thasos itself, earlier worked by Phoenicians, has been doubted). In a more easterly sector of the mainland coast, opposite Samothrace, they disputed the control of Stryme with Maronea. One of the most important colonies of the northern Aegean, Thasos was a rampart of Hellenism against the mainland Thracians, whose island township at Kastri was brought to an end; although a tomb set up in the Thasian agora by 'the sons of Bendis' testifies to the continuance of a mixed population.

The sixth and fifth centuries were the times of the island's greatest prosperity, when it sold ships' timber abroad and began to export a famous wine; and its mines on the mainland were very productive. There was a flourishing local school of sculpture, and from *c* 500 local coins were issued with the design of a sexually excited satyr carrying off a nymph. In 491 the Thasians yielded to Persian demands, and gave up their fleet. After the Persian Wars they joined the Delian League under the leadership of Athens (477), but a dispute over the mainland mines provoked an attempted secession from the Athenians who crushed them after a siege lasting for more than two years (465/63). The great fifth-century painter Polygnotus was a Thasian, though he became an Athenian citizen. In 411, during the Peloponnesian War, the island tried to break away from Athens once again, issuing a gold coinage and calling for the help of the Spartans, whose general Lysander, after prolonged civil strife on Thasos, massacred the Athenian partisans (404). During the next century, however, the state joined the Second Athenian Confederacy, until it was overrun by Philip II of Macedonia (340). During the subsequent epoch, its income from the mainland mines was much diminished, but this loss was counterbalanced by very large exports of wine, confirmed by widely distributed discoveries of Thasian wine-jars in the Balkan area, where the island's coinage also enjoyed a huge circulation, and was frequently imitated by the tribal peoples of Thrace. In 196 Thasos was liberated from Macedonia with the support of the Romans, who subsequently, after their annexation of the Balkan peninsula (146), granted Thasos the status of a free and friendly city, as a reward for its loyalty in the war against Mithridates VI Eupator of Pontus (80). During the Roman Principate, Thasian marble and oil gained a widespread reputation. Local coinage was resumed in the second and early third centuries AD, but during the later third century there are signs of destruction at the hands of invaders. In Christian times, there were bishops of the island.

One of the two harbors of its principal city was protected by a breakwater and the other was enclosed within the city's fortifications. These were reconstructed after demolitions in 491 and 464/3 and again in 411 (the well-preserved Gate of Silenus can still be seen). The agora displays, near its center, a sacred enclosure and an altar of Zeus Agoraios, and was flanked by colonnades on three sides and by public buildings on the fourth. The principal temple of Thasos, expanded into a building with five chambers, was dedicated to Heracles, whose cult may have been derived from the Phoenician Melkart. That sanctuary stood in the lower town; and this area also contained shrines of Poseidon, Dionysus and foreign deities, whose presence testifies to the various ethnic origins of the inhabitants. There is also a precinct of Artemis, which has been thoroughly examined in recent years. It seems to have been destroyed and rebuilt in the third century AD, and remodelled in the fifth. North of the great altar of this shrine, however, votive objects dating from *c* 500 BC have been found. A so-called 'Monument of Thersilochus,' which has likewise been reinvestigated, was completely destroyed in late antiquity and subsequently buried by the alluvium of continual flooding. Residential quarters have also come to light. At the western extremity of the city stood a well-preserved theater, and at its eastern end was a stoa (portico) of the fourth century BC, converted into a Christian basilica some nine hundred years later.

The steep acropolis, four hundred and fifty feet above sea level—which was one of twin summits overlooking the town—housed temples of Pythian Apollo and Pan, and a shrine of Athena Poliouchos that was conspicuously visible from the waterfront; nearby, too, an ancient iron and copper mine, operating between the sixth and fourth centuries BC, has been discovered. Fifty-eight inscriptions of the late fifth century, expressing pederasts' admiration of their boys, have been found at the bottom of Kalami Bay. Greco-Roman remains have come to light at Cape Pyrgos, Coinyra, and Aliki. There are numerous towers intended for defence against pirates; the densest concentration is in the region of Astris.

Thebaid *see* Egypt, Thebes

Thebes, formerly Waset, also known as Diospolis Megale or Magna (Luxor and Karnak). A city on the Nile in Upper Egypt, four hundred and forty-six miles south of Cairo. The capital of the Pharaonic empire in the second millennium BC—replacing Memphis—Thebes was later praised for its wealth in Homer's *Iliad.* It still remained important during the Ptolemaic epoch, but was severely damaged during and after rebellions against Ptolemy V Epiphanes (206) and Ptolemy IX Soter II Lathyrus (88).

Following the annexation of Egypt by Octavian (the future Augustus), the city was sacked by his first provincial governor, the poet Gaius Cornelius Gallus (30/29), and Strabo only found a group of villages on the site. During the Principate, however, Thebes became a major touristic attraction; among its visitors were Hadrian and his wife Sabina (AD 130). Finds include many papyri and inscribed ostraca (pottery fragments) mostly relating to finance and taxation. During the early Christian epoch, the western part of the city became a monastic center, and most of the temples were converted into churches. At this period Thebes was the capital of a separate Roman province of the Thebaid (and later of the Upper Thebaid).

A sanctuary at Karnak on the east bank of the river commemorates the coronation of Alexander the Great's half-brother Philip III Arrhidaeus (323 BC). In the great Precinct of Amon, the Kiosk of Taharka (690–664) and Second Pylon were restored by the Ptolemies, who also added gateways in front of the temples of Ptah, Mut and Montu, and a chapel to the west of the last-named building. Within the ancient temple at Luxor a shrine was devoted to Alexander himself. Across the river, in Thebes West, stand two colossal seated figures of Amenhotep III (*c* 1386–1349), of which the figure to the north was supposed by the Greeks to represent Memnon, a mythical king of Aethiopia believed to have fought for the Trojans in the Trojan War; this statue became one of the principal objects of Greek and Roman sightseeing, because of the sound it emitted everyday. To the west of these statues, at Medinet Habu, the great mortuary temple of Rameses (*c* 1185–1152) was adjoined by a sanctuary restored by Thothmes III (*c* 1505–1450) containing the 'Barque Chapel' of Amon, which Ptolemy VIII Euergetes II (170–116) redecorated; a pylon dedicated by Shabaka (713–698) likewise reached its final form in the Ptolemaic period, and a columnar portico and courtyard were begun by Antoninus Pius (AD 138–61) but never completed. A dedication by Domitian (81–96) is also to be seen. To the south of Medinet Habu, Antoninus completed a temple begun by his predecessor Hadrian. To the north, at Deir-el-Medina, stood a small Ptolemaic shrine surrounded by an enclosure.

Thebes, Thebai (Thivai). The principal city of Boeotia (central Greece), on the southern edge of its fertile eastern plain. The acropolis (Cadmeia) stood on an elongated plateau, half-a-mile long and a quarter-mile wide, flanked by the rocky gullies of the rivers Dirce and Ismenus and overlooking a lower city to the north and east.

The mythology of Thebes was exceptionally rich, inspiring an epic poem, the *Thebais,* sometimes inaccurately attributed to Homer. After occupation by a people known as Ectenians, whose king was Ogyges, the town was said to have been founded either by Zeus' son Amphion, who could charm stones into movement with his lyre, or by Cadmus who came from Tyre (Es-Sur) to establish a Phoenician enclave before the end of the Bronze Age (or, according to another theory, he originated from Minoan Cretan legend), and sowed dragon's teeth producing a harvest of armed warriors: five of these were said to have become the ancestors of the Theban aristocracy (who were known as Spartoi, 'sown men'). Heracles, although elsewhere ascribed to Argos or Tiryns, was also stated, according to an alternative version, to have been born, and to have undertaken his early enterprises, at Thebes. It was also the scene of the sagas of the House of Oedipus and of the *Seven Against Thebes* immortalized by Sophocles and Aeschylus respectively.

During the Bronze (Minoan, Mycenaean) Age and earlier, Thebes was a princely palace stronghold, rivalling Mycenae for thc supremacy of Greece; it owed its strength to the productivity of its soil, and to its position on routes between Attica and central Greece and leading down to the Corinthian gulf. This Bronze Age center, however, as archaeological evidence indicates, was sacked, burned and abandoned during the thirteenth century BC. The epic tradition attributes the destruction to the *Epigoni*, the sons of the Seven. The Catalog of Ships in Homer's *Iliad* only mentions Hypothebae, 'the place below Thebes.'

After the Boeotians, as Thucydides reports, had arrived from Thessaly, some of them before and some after the Trojan War, Thebes outstripped its rival Orchomenus, and from the seventh century grouped a dozen towns of the region in the Boeotian League under its leadership. The coinage of this confederation, displaying a Boeotian shield, began early in the sixth century. The hostility of Thebes to the Athenians dates from about 519, when Plataea, by now the only Boeotian town south of Lake Copais to have evaded its domination, appealed for and received the protection of Athens in face of a Theban threat. The Thebans sided against their Greek compatriots in the Persian War (480–479)—a policy accepted by the Boeotian poet Pindar, though without enthusiasm—and in consequence lost their leadership of the Boeotian League. In 457 a war with Athenians began with an indecisive engagement at Tanagra and ended with a decisive Boeotian defeat at Oenophyta, which led to the replacement of oligarchic government by a democracy, at Thebes as well as other Boeotian cities. In 447, however, victory at Coronea restored the ascendancy and oligarchy of the Thebans, who sided with Sparta against Athens in the Peloponnesian War (431–404), absorbing Plataea (after a long siege, 429–427) and Thespiae (423).

Discontented with the peace at the end of hostilities, Thebes joined Athens and Argos in the Corinthian War against Sparta (395) but was defeated at Coronea in the following year. The King's Peace (Peace of Antalcidas) of 387 enabled Sparta to isolate Thebes from the other Boeotian towns, which garrisoned its citadel; but it reasserted itself in 382. The famous Sacred Band of one hundred and fifty couples, the elite Theban frontline infantry corps, was formed by Gorgidas in 378. In 371 a proposed treaty collapsed because the Thebans tried, in vain, to insist on signing for all the Boeotian cities. War broke out again, and at Leuctra a Theban army defeated the Spartans and drove them out of central Greece, thereafter enjoying a unique nine years of power and glory, under the brilliant leadership of Epaminondas and Pelopidas. But the former's death in his last victorious battle of Mantinea (362) marked the beginning of decline.

Thebes was occupied by Philip II of Macedonia in 338, after victory at Chaeronea, and razed to the ground after its citizens revolted from his son Alexander the Great two or three years later. Reconstructed by Cassander (316), the city was captured in 290 by Demetrius I the Besieger (Poliorcetes) and then by the Macedonian King Antigonus II Gonatas, but from *c* 280 it resumed an independent but modest place in the revived Boeotian League, forming successive links with the Aetolians, Macedonians, Romans (197) and Seleucids, and then with the Romans (who captured the place in 173) and Macedonians (171–168) once again. In 146 Thebes' participation in the Achaean revolt earned it destruction from Lucius Mummius, who annexed the country, and in 86 it was again sacked and dismembered, this time by Sulla, because it had welcomed Mithridates VI Eupator of Pontus. Strabo described the surviving buildings as a village hardly worth mentioning, but it retained city status, although habitation was restricted to the Cadmea; coinage was occasionally revived, notably under Galba (AD 68–69). In AD 248 and again in 396 Thebes was taken by the Goths, but spared from devastation (by Alaric) on the latter occasion. During the late imperial and Byzantine periods it resumed its position as the most important town of central Greece.

After its Bronze Age preeminence—confirmed by excavations of the Mycenaean palace—the site of classical Thebes, in view of its repeated destructions, does not have a great deal to show. Thus only traces of its two ramparts can be seen. The temple of Apollo Ismenius, however, has been uncovered; a wood and brick shrine of *c* 800 BC was replaced in the sixth century by a stone building, where Herodotus saw tripods inscribed with 'Cadmean' (Mycenaean?) writing. The colonnaded agora, Fountain of Oedipus, and sanctuaries—including a shrine that allegedly contained the funeral pyres of the Seven—lay to the east of the Cadmea, and an eminence to its north displayed the tombs of Amphion and his brother Zethus, roofed by a stepped pyramid. South of the agora was a precinct of Heracles, in whose honor Thebans celebrated the Herakleia, a festival including gymnastic contests. In the cemetery chapel of St. Luke are fragments of a sarcophagus locally venerated as the Evangelist's, although its inscriptions refer to the family of a Roman official named Cosimus.

Within a few miles of the city was another temple of Heracles (Hippodetes), as well as another in honor of the oracular Amphiaraus, who during the attack by the Seven was swallowed up in a cleft made by Zeus' thunderbolt (this shrine is distinct from the more famous Amphiaraon on the north coast of Attica). There were also sanctuaries dedicated to Demeter Cabiraia and Persephone (Kore)—no traces of this survives—and to the Cabiri, underworld deities of non-Hellenic origin, whose precinct, which has been carefully investigated, was evidently the scene of ritual dining and drinking. Its successive strata display a history of many centuries, reaching a climax in the first century BC.

Theline *see* Arelate

Theodosia (Feodosya). A Greek city on the east coast of the Tauric Chersonese (Crimea), with an acropolis overlooking the western end of the Bay of Theodosia, near the beginning of the Panticapaeum (Kerch) peninsula extending into the Cimmerian Bosphorus (Straits of Kerch). Theodosia seems to have been colonized by settlers from Miletus in Ionia (western Asia Minor) between 575 and 500 BC, apparently on the site of an earlier native settlement. Strengthened, it would seem, by a further draft of colonists from Heraclea Pontica (Ereğli), it became a trading rival of Panticapaeum, and by the late fifth century (according to one view) had started to issue its own coins, with the curious Greek inscription *Theodeo* (or *Theu*).

With the help of the recently founded town of Chersonesus (another colony of Heraclea), it resisted encroachment from the Bosphoran monarchy until 389/8, when it was captured by King Leucon I and incorporated into his state. During the fourth and third centuries, under Bosphoran rule, Theodosia was at the height of its prosperity as a commercial entrepôt collecting huge quantities of grain from the peninsula's Scythian hinterland for export to Greece. In 107 the city fell temporarily into Scythian hands and was then convulsed by a slave insurrection, put down by the intervention of Mithridates VI Eupator of Pontus, against whose suzerainty, however, Theodosia later revolted. It was apparently destroyed in the second century AD, but had recovered by the third, survived the collapse of the Bosphoran Kingdom in the fourth, and became one of the principal cities of the Chersonese in early Byzantine times.

Sixth-century BC potsherds have been unearthed on the site, including Attic black figure vases dating back to the earliest days of the colony; among later finds are amphoras bearing the marks of Heraclea and Sinope (Sinop). A considerable quantity of pottery of the fourth and fifth centuries BC has come to light on the acropolis. Outside the town, cemeteries have been excavated, and remains of a fortified fourth-century farm are to be seen.

Thera (Santorini). An Aegean island in the southern Cyclades, one of the nearest to Crete. Forming part of the cone of an ancient volcano, Thera was diminished to its present shape by a series of violent seismic disturbances; among these were earthquakes of *c* 1550 and 1520/10 and an eruption of *c* 1460 BC, which convulsed the brilliant Bronze (Minoan) Age prosperity of cities near Akrotiri, in the south of the island, and in the region of Therasia (which was detached from its northern flank by another eruption in 236).

Thera, according to Callimachus, was originally known as Calliste, 'most beautiful.' Fanciful stories identified it with Scheria, the home of the mythical Phaeacians in the *Odyssey*, or with lost Atlantis, described by Plato. The island was also said to have been settled by the Phoenician Cadmus—during his search for Europa—and then by Achaeans, Minyans and Dorians, the branch of the Greek race to which the later inhabitants belonged. According to a tradition preserved by Herodotus, these Dorians came from Sparta, apparently in the later tenth century. They settled on a sheltered rocky peninsula joined by a narrow ridge (Messa Vouno) to the southeast part of the island, seven-and-a-half miles from Akrotiri and about the same distance from the modern town of Thira or Fira.

About 640, however, oppressed by drought and consequent famine, the inhabitants obeyed the counsel of the Delphic oracle (after their King Grinnus had earlier ignored a similar injunction) and dispatched two hundred men in two ships to colonize Cyrene in north Africa, under the leadership of a Theran nobleman Aristoteles, who took the royal Libyan name of Battus. The island was famous for its wine. Although linked to the Spartans by their Dorian blood, the population attempted to remain neutral during the Peloponnesian War between Sparta and Athens (431–404), but were compelled by the Athenians to pay tribute. During the third and second centuries their city became an important naval base. In early Christian times there were bishops at Thera, which formed part of a Roman province of the Islands.

The Dorian colonists introduced the cult of Apollo Carneius, the surviving foundations of whose temple perhaps date from the seventh century BC. Beside the shrine lay the terrace on which the god's festivals were celebrated, including dances by naked gymnasts; early erotic graffiti are scratched on the rock nearby. The most important local remains, however, date from Ptolemaic times. They include a number of temples and a twin-naved, colonnaded royal basilica (*stoa basilike*), later containing busts of the family of Marcus Aurelius (AD 161–80), under whom the city briefly resumed coinage. There was also a temple of Apollo (later converted into a church), an area sacred to the Ptolemaic deities Isis, Serapis and Anubis, and a shrine of the Ptolemies (Ptolemaion), which Octavian (the future Augustus), after his victory over Antony and Cleopatra at Actium (31 BC), converted to the cult of the deified Julius Caesar (Kaisareion).

The northern end of the city displays an archaic grotto-shrine of Hermes and Heracles (later enlarged), together with a gymnasium for young men, while the southern extremity shows the remains of a sanctuary of Demeter and Kore (Persephone), and a precinct of the third century BC dedicated to a number of divinities by Artemidorus of Perga, a Ptolemaic admiral. In the theater four distinct building periods can be discerned, ranging between the late Hellenistic epoch and the reign of Tiberius (AD 14–37); nearby is a colonnaded house, conjecturally identified with the residence of one of Ptolemy III Euergetes' sons, who was brought up at Thera (*c* 260 BC). The cemetery on the northeast slope of the hill has yielded rich material down to Hellenistic times.

Therme *see* Thessalonia

Thermopylae, Thermopylai ('Hot Gates,' after its sulphur springs); also known as Pylai ('Gates'). A defile in eastern Greece, between the steep north side of Mount Kallidromon and the south side of the Aegean Sea's Gulf of Malis. Early in the first millennium BC the temple of Demeter at Anthela near Thermopylae was the meeting place of the famous Amphictyony ('dwellers round about'), a religious confederacy consisting of small Greek tribes of the vicinity (which later transferred their center to the shrine of Apollo at Delphi). Thermopylae belonged to Phocis—which fortified the pass—but by the early fifth century BC had come to form part of Malis instead.

It was the principal point of entrance into Greece for any large body of troops, along a road which passed between steep cliffs and the sea. But there is easy ground above, and the pass could be outflanked, so that, in the words of Edward Gibbon, Thermopylae 'seemed to protect, but had so often betrayed, the safety of Greece.' The Thessalians overpowered the Phocian fortification in the sixth century BC, and it was here, in 480, that the Spartan King Leonidas offered his heroic resistance to the invading Persian army of Xerxes I. Against an enemy force estimated at 300,000, Leonidas—owing to the unwillingness of his fellow-Spartans to fight north of the Corinthian isthmus—was only able to muster between 7000 and 8000 armored men, including the Spartan royal guard of 300 men (each accompanied by seven helots [serfs], of whom perhaps three apiece were armed), 2,120 Arcadians, 680 from the Argolid, 1,100 Boeotians, and contingents from Phocis and Locris. When it was learned that the Greek position, on the advice given to Xerxes by Ephialtes of Malis, had been turned—by an outflanking route that has recently been identified—Leonidas (according to a tradition that soon became distorted from patriotic motives) ordered his Peloponnesian troops to leave him, so that they could fight another day; and some of the Boeotians allegedly surrendered, although seven hundred from Thespiae stood firm. After a final ferocious stand on the semi-isolated Colonus hill, in which two of Xerxes' young brothers perished, all the Greeks who remained fell fighting, including the entire body of Spartans and about nine hundred helots. Their grave mound is pointed out, but its attribution is dubious.

In 323, during the Lamian War between Alexander the Great and the Greeks, Thermopylae was seized by the Macedonian general Leosthenes. In 279 it was evacuated by its garrison, and abandoned to invading Gauls. In 191, 10,000 soldiers of the Seleucid King Antiochus III the Great failed to hold the pass against 40,000 Roman legionaries. By this time, the silting of the river Spercheius had already begun to cause the sea's recession (it is now nearly three miles away). In AD 257 the defile was successfully manned against the Goths, but succumbed without resistance to Alaric the Visigoth in 395. Remains can be seen of its numerous defences, culminating in a strong wall erected by the Byzantine emperor Justinian I (539/540). Traces of the Pylaean Sanctuary of Demeter, where the Amphictyonic Council held its meetings, have been discovered at Anthela. The shrine itself has not yet been located, but a stoa (portico) and stadium, which were apparently attached to it, can be identified.

Thermum, Thermon, Thermos (Thermon, formerly Kephalovrisi). A quasi-urban center of Aetolia in west-central Greece. Situated on a long terrace of an upland valley above marshy ground, surrounded by fields, beside the north-eastern shore of Lake Trichonis, Thermum dominated the central Aetolian plain. Settlement took place in the later Bronze Age (from which houses survive), and traces of occupation in the early first millennium BC have come to light. The principal center of worship of the Aetolian people, Thermum also became the meeting place for their League when this was established in the fourth century BC. During the Lamian War, in which the Greek city-states rebelled against Macedonian rule, Thermum fell into the hands of the Macedonian generals Antipater and Craterus (323); and it was twice subsequently sacked by Philip V (218, 206), who destroyed most of the local collection of 2000 statues. But the town was rebuilt and remained in existence until eclipsed by the foundation of Nicopolis by Octavian (the future Augustus) after the battle of Actium (31).

It was here that the Aetolians elected their federal officials, holding a large Fair and athletic games to celebrate the cult of Apollo Thermius. His precinct, at the foot of Mount Mega Lakkos, included a temple which goes back to a rudimentary three-chambered structure of the early first millennium BC. This was replaced by a Doric shrine of unusually early date (*c* 630–600), with metope plaques displaying mythological paintings, which was remodelled in the later sixth century—when architectural decorations (antefixes) displaying bearded men and Sileni were added—and again shortly before 200, after the damage inflicted by Philip V. At this juncture the sanctuary was surrounded by a rectangular fortification protected by square towers. Nearby is a smaller, equally early temple of Apollo Lyseius, from which painted terracotta metopes have been recovered. There are also remains of another small shrine of the same epoch, which is believed to have been devoted to the worship of Artemis. Traces of three stoas (porticos) mark the site of the agora. A fountain with several spouts, dating from about the third century, is still in operation.

Thespiae, Thespiai or Thespeia. The chief town of southern Boeotia (central Greece), situated between Thebes and Mount Helicon, at the foot of twin hills beside the right bank of the river Thespius (Kanavari). Its ports Creusis, Siphae (Aliki) and Chorsiae (Paralia) stood on the Corinthian Gulf. Inhabited since Neolithic times, Thespiae was an important commercial center in the Late Bronze (Mycenaean) Age. According to conflicting traditions it was named after Thespia, daughter of the river-god Asopus, or (as the Athenians maintained) after Thespius, son of their monarch Erechtheus.

Hesiod, *c* 700 BC (?), complains of the greed and corruption of the 'kings' (aristocracy) of Thespiae. It was the scene of a crushing defeat *c* 540 of the Thessalians by a Theban army, which put an end to Thessalian encroachments in central Greece. In 506, according to Herodotus, Thebes—which was only fifteen miles away—cited the Thespians among their loyal allies. In 480 seven hundred of them helped (unlike most other Boeotians) to defend Thermopylae to the end against the Persian king Xerxes I: who in consequence razed their city to the ground.

Its subsequent reconstruction by the Athenians was resented by Thebes. Yet Thespiae played an important part in the restored Boeotian Confederacy (446), exercising control over the Sanctuary of the Muses on Mount Helicon. During the Peloponnesian War one hundred and two Thespians, listed on inscriptions, fell fighting against the Athenians—on the Theban side—at Delium (424). Nevertheless, its fortifications were destroyed by the Thebans in the following year. But they were rebuilt in 382 by Sparta, which employed the city as a base for its anti-Theban policy. In 371, Epaminondas degraded Thespiae to the status of a Theban village, but after his death it revived, and figured prominently in the resuscitated Boeotian League (338). Richly endowed by the Attalids of Pergamum, its citizens also enjoyed good relations with the Macedonians and then with the Romans—although Lucius Mummius Achaicus took away all their statues (except those that were consecrated) in 146.

Under Roman rule Thespiae was granted freedom and immunity from taxes (47) and survived as one of the principal Boeotian cities, organizing Pan-

Hellenic festivals in honor of the Muses (locally known as the Thespiadae, whose temple has been located on the acropolis) and to celebrate the principal civic patron-deity Eros, of whom an archaic image, as well as statues by Lysippus and Praxiteles, were to be seen; the masterpiece of Praxiteles, according to Cicero, 'is what people go to Thespiae to see, for there is no other reason to go there.' Pausanias records that the statue was removed by the emperor Gaius (AD 37–41), returned by Claudius, removed again by Nero and later destroyed by fire. He also refers to a sanctuary of Heracles and Black Aphrodite, who appears on the local coinage as a moon-goddess. The traces of a temple of Apollo, dating from the fifth century BC, have been discovered; he appears as Citharoedus (Lyre-Player) on an isolated local coinage of imperial date under Domitian (81–86). The demolition of what remained of the ancient walls yielded more than three hundred and fifty inscriptions.

Thessalonica, Thessalonike (Salonica). A city and port in Macedonia (northern Greece), at the head of the Thermaic Gulf. After earlier settlement of the area by the Thracian tribe of the Mygdones, the city was founded on the site of their township Therme (Sedes) *c* 316 BC by one of Alexander the Great's successors, Cassander, who named it after his wife, Thessalonice, the sister of Alexander. The new foundation was the product of the amalgamation (synoecism) of twenty-six small towns and villages. It owed its importance to its location at the meeting-point between the highway to central Europe (by way of the rivers Axius [Vardar] and Margus [Morava]) and the east-west route—the later Via Egnatia—leading from Byzantium (İstanbul) to the Adriatic.

Protected by the peninsula of Chalcidice, the open anchorage of Thessalonica replaced Pella (where the harbor had silted up) as Macedonia's principal port. When Pyrrhus of Epirus invaded the country, the Macedonian king Antigonus II escaped to Thessalonica (274). Following the Roman victory over Perseus of Macedonia at Pydna, it underwent a long siege that resulted in its capitulation; but the Romans made it the capital first of the Second Macedonian Region and then of their new province of Macedonia-Achaea (146). During the civil war between Pompey the Great and Julius Caesar (49), Thessalonica served as the former's base, but during the Philippi campaign (42) it chose the winning side of Antony and Octavian (the future Augustus), issuing coinage with both their heads and receiving confirmation of its free status (*libertas*). In AD 49/50 (and again in 56) St. Paul visited the city, whose Christian community he addressed in his *Epistles to the Thessalonians.*

The prosperity of Thessalonica in imperial times was illustrated by abundant monetary issues, on which special attention was devoted to the local Pythian (Victory, Caesarean, Cabirian) Games, intended to compete with the festivals of its rival Beroea. Under Trajanus Decius (249–51) it became a Roman colony, striking coins that display four temples connected with the imperial cult (neocorate); but these issues continued to employ Greek, rather than Latin, inscriptions until they ceased under Gallienus (253–68). At this period the city had to repel repeated attacks by the Goths. During the tetrarchy introduced by Diocletian (284–305), however, it entered on a new period of brilliant life as one of the major imperial capitals, in which his Caesar Galerius resided; from now onward it was also one of the principal mints of the Roman world. In 324 Constantine the Great mustered his fleet at its port before launching his victorious campaign against Licinius.

Theodosius I the Great (379–95) employed Thessalonica as his base for operations against the Germans. In his reign, its important ecclesiastical vicariate became a standing institution. His Edict that bore its name (380) attacked pagans and supporters of the Arian Church. In 390, after his military commander, the Visigoth Butheric, had been lynched for failing to control outrages by his troops, Theodosius invited the population to a special performance in the hippodrome, where he had between seven and fifteen thousand of them massacred—an action for which he was compelled to do penance by St. Ambrose, Bishop of Mediolanum (Milan). In 441/2, in replacement of threatened Sirmium (Sremska Mitrovica), Thessalonica was made the headquarters of the praetorian prefect of Illyricum—one of four such officials who administered the eastern and western empires—and subsequently rose to become the second city of the Byzantine empire.

Certain discoveries go back to the period of Mygdonian (Thracian) habitation. Thus a temple of *c* 500 BC has been located at Therme, the township that preceded Thessalonica. Moreover at Sindos, a suburb of the modern city, investigations below thick alluvium from the river Echedorus (Gallicos) have revealed an inhumation cemetery of *c* 540–470 BC that contained rich material including five gold face-masks, and seems to have been the burial center of the adjacent Thracian settlement of North Anchialos (the ancient Sindos or Chalastra or Strepsa).

The later city of Thessalonica, rising from its bay in the form of an amphitheater on the slopes of Mount Khortiatis, was designed according to a regular plan; a Hellenistic temple of Serapis and a gymnasium have been identified. There was also extensive building activity during the later second and early third centuries AD, including the construction of a colonnaded agora and houses with large mosaic floors. The presence of Galerius during the tetrarchy prompted the creation of a magnificent new palace quarter *c* 300. Two large halls that formed part of his residence have been uncovered. One is an octagonal building with apsed niches, and the other, a rectangular structure, forms the vestibule of a colonnaded processional street, flanked by the hippodrome (the scene of Theodosius' massacre), which has recently been reexamined. The crossroads at which this street began is surmounted by the triple, domed Arch of Galerius, adorned with reliefs illustrating his victory over the Persians. The street led up to a precinct enclosing Galerius' sumptuously decorated circular mausoleum (though he was eventually buried at his birthplace Romulianum instead, because Licinius would not permit the removal of his body to Thessalonica). When the empire became Christian, this rotunda was transformed into a church, which, like several others inside and outside the walls, may go back as early as the fourth century AD.

The selection of Thessalonica as the capital of one of the four imperial prefectures in 441/2 instigated a further lavish phase of development. A new palace was built for the prefect, new walls were constructed (incorporating marble seats taken from the hippodrome), and traces of baths and private dwellings of the same date are to be seen. There was also a remarkable array of Christian churches. A two-aisled basilica, known from the later Middle Ages as the Akheiropoietos ('made without hands,' after an ikon believed to have been miraculously painted), was dedicated to the Theotokos (Virgin Mary) soon after her recognition by the Third Ecumenical Council of Ephesus in 431, and completed *c* 470; it is the only major pre-Byzantine basilica hall-church in Greece that still remains in use. The cupola of the Church of St. George, of the same century, was adorned by a mosaic that, although largely destroyed, can be partly reconstructed. The more or less contemporary Basilica of St. Demetrius, a martyr of Galerius' persecutions, possessed four aisles and transepts, and is the largest church in Greece. The small chapel of Hosios David (an obscure hermit), alternatively known as Panayia tou Latomou, seems to date back to the late fifth century, and is perhaps the earliest church in Europe to exhibit the Syrian cross-in-square grand plan; it contains a remarkable apse mosaic of the beardless Christ between Ezekiel and Habakkuk, discovered beneath a plaster coating. An edifice at Monolaki Kyriakou displays Roman, early Christian, Byzantine and Islamic constructional phases. A severe earthquake in 1978 has necessitated extensive conservation and restoration work in the city.

Thessaly, Thessalia. A region of north-eastern Greece, bordering on the Aegean Sea, south of Macedonia and east of Epirus. It consists of two large plains watered by the river Peneus and its tributaries, and surrounded by mountains. Because of this extensive plainland—the most spacious in Greece, originally a lake, as Herodotus states—Thessaly was richer in horses, cattle and grain than any other district of Greece. After an extensive Neolithic culture and gradual participation in the Late Bronze (Mycenaean)Age—reflected in the appearance of a network of little kingdoms in the *Iliad*'s catalog of the Achaeans—the tribe of the Thessali immigrated from Thesprotia (southern Epirus) toward the end of the second millennium BC. According to Greek mythology, as reported by Strabo, the country was at one time called Pyrrhaea, after Pyrrha the wife of Deucalion, and was also known as Haemonia after another legendary figure called Haemon, before taking the name of Thessalia from Haemon's son Thessalus. Jason, leader of the Argonauts, came from Iolcus on the Gulf of Pagasae. Achilles and his Myrmidons were also credited with Thessalian roots.

From the tenth to the eighth centuries the clays and marls of the higher ground were preferred to the alluvial plain for settlements. From the seventh century at latest, within the four cantons of the Thessalian tribal state, dynastic families such as the Aleuadae of Larissa and the Scopadae of Crannon dominated the fertile lowlands—reducing the previous population to the status of serfs (Penestae) or driving them into the hills—and organized a Thessalian Confederacy under an elected military leader (*tagos*). Its members attended regular celebrations at the sanctuary of Athena Itonia near Pharsalus. The League's political power and centralization was evidently spasmodic, but at some period during the sixth century it became the major power of northern Greece. It is possible, but not certain, that the 'Thessalians' who successfully participated in the First Sacred War (between Delphi and Cirrha, *c* 595–590) were a federal army, and there is uncertain evidence pointing in the same direction relating to the 560s and 540s. However, the earliest firm evidence for a joint council or assembly dates from 511, when 'by common decision,' according to Herodotus, the Thessalians sent a force to help the Athenian autocrat Hippias.

By this time the Thessalians dominated Boeotia and Phocis. Nevertheless, despite generous patronage of the poets Simonides and Anacreon and Pindar, their country remained isolated and backward; Simonides said they were the only people he had never cheated, because they were too stupid. Moreover, the rivalry of their noble houses—and their adherence, for the most part, to the cause of the invaders during the Persian Wars, when the Tempe pass had to be abandoned as a line of defence (480)—caused a decline that was accelerated by social unrest. From the 420s the main external influence came from Sparta, which founded the colony of Heraclea (in Trachis) on Thessaly's southern borders (426).

Toward the end of the century a powerful state was created by the autocratic rulers of Pherae, who, emerging from prolonged struggles with other Thessalian groups, led by the Aleuadae temporarily unified the country. But it fell easily under the domination of Philip II of Macedonia (359–336), who reorganized the League under his own leadership (as its *archon*, 'ruler'), while conceding its members nominal independence. In 196 the Romans established a new Thessalian confederacy—detached from Macedonian influence, and empowered to issue its own federal coinage—and in 146 associated it loosely with their new province of Macedonia-Achaea. When Achaea was detached by Augustus (31 BC–AD 14) to form a separate province, Thessaly became incorporated in its territory, but in the second century AD was transferred to the province of Macedonia instead. Diocletian (284–305), however, created a separate province of Thessaly, with its capital at Larissa. *See also* Demetrias, Gonnus, Iolcus, Lamia, Larissa, Magnesia, Olympia, Ossa, Pelion, Pharsalus, Pherae.

Thezi, Thezle *see* Rusellae

Thrace, Thrakia. The country of the Thracians, who spoke an Indo-European language and possessed a warlike reputation. At one time peoples and principalities of wholly or partly Thracian stock (including the Getae) extended over most of the northern Balkans as far as the Danube, but in later times Thrace was defined as a more limited territory comprising southeastern Bulgaria and European Turkey, with its western border generally thought of as the river Nestus. Imposing megalithic tombs dating from between the twelfth and sixth centuries BC point to southeastern Thrace as a center of advanced civilization. The southern coastal plain was a major center of horse-breeding.

From the eighth century onward these coastlands, including the Thracian Chersonese (Gallipoli peninsula), were extensively colonized by Greeks, whose settlements became independent city-states. However, the Thracians in the hinterland resisted Greek influence. Herodotus described the huge population of the country, and its 'potential power, unrealizable owing to disunity.' Nevertheless, in the fifth and fourth centuries BC the tribe of the Odrysae, centered on a densely inhabited region along the rivers Tonzus (Tunca) and Hebrus (Maritza), controlled an empire of considerable size. It was developed by King Teres I. In 513 Darius I of Persia, in the course of his expedition into Europe, annexed a large part of Thrace and converted it into a Persian satrapy. After the evacuation of the area by his successor Xerxes I following the Persian Wars (480/479), Teres conquered its eastern region, between Salmydessus (Midye) and the Bosphorus, dying at the age of ninety-two.

The most powerful of the Odrysian kings, however, was his son Sitalces, who ruled at Cypsela (Ipsala) on the Hebrus, reorganized the entire state—describing himself as 'King of the Thracians'—and increasingly sought to encroach upon the Aegean coastal cities, to the alarm of the Athenians, who nevertheless concluded a treaty with him (431) in order to bring pressure on Macedonia; though his campaigns against the Macedonians, from 429, did not bring any lasting territorial gain. His son Seuthes I, who succeeded him in 424, was credited by Thucydides with unprecedented financial prosperity. A subsequent Odrysian monarch, Cotys I (*c* 382–358), made war on Athens; but, according to Plutarch, he expressed a desire to share his bed with Athena.

After his death the kingdom split into three parts, so that although his son Cersobleptes made peace with the Athenians (357), Philip II of Macedonia was able to annex the whole of Thrace (342) and plant Greek and Macedonian colonies. Nevertheless, Lysimachus, one of the successors of Alexander the Great, had to reconquer the country, creating a new capital Lysimachia (308), although he met determined resistance from Seuthes III, who founded the city of Seuthopolis. In 279 Celtic (Gallic) invaders swept through the interior, but toward the end of the century their kingdom was destroyed by the Thracians, whose tribal states, however, were overthrown by Philip V of Macedonia (201–200); and Philip V also occupied the Greek coastal cities. But he was compelled to evacuate these conquests when he had been defeated by the Romans (197), and the invasion of Thrace in the following year by the Seleucid king Antiochus III came to nothing when he, too, succumbed to Roman arms.

After Rome's subsequent destruction of the Macedonian kingdom (168), Thrace west of the Hebrus was incorporated into the puppet zones of Macedonia, and the Odrysian king Cotys II became an ally of the Romans. In 149 a Macedonian pretender, Andriscus, launched his revolt from Thracian territory, which was traversed, however, in 130 by Rome's Via Egnatia, extending between the Adriatic and Byzantium (İstanbul). The tribe of the Bessi (extending eastward from Mount Rhodope) came into conflict with Marcus Licinius Lucullus in 72 and Gaius Octavius (the father of Augustus) in 60, but were later described by Cicero as loyal. Rhescuporis, king of the Sapaei (in the part of the country annexed to Macedonia) sided with Pompey the Great against the victorious Julius Caesar (49–48) and with Brutus and Cassius against the equally successful Antony and Octavian (43–42), but nevertheless survived, and assumed the royal title. His son Cotys became the father-in-law of another Cotys, prince of the Astae (ruling at Bizye [Vize], whose son Rhoemetalces I (*c* 11 BC–AD 12) ruled a united kingdom of Thrace.

After Rhoemetalces' death the Romans divided his territories into a western and eastern state, and when the last king of the latter, Rhoemetalces III, was murdered in AD 46 the entire country was converted by Claudius into the Roman province of Thrace, with its capital at Perinthus-Heraclea (Marmaraereğlisi). The country was economically dependent on mining and agriculture. A colony was founded at Apri or Aprus in Caenice (southeastern

Thrace), to which others were added by the Flavian dynasty (81–96) at Develtus or Deultum (Develt, at the head of the Gulf of Burgas) and Flaviopolis (perhaps also known as Aphrodisias). Trajan (98–117) and Hadrian (117–38) developed urbanization in various parts of the country. A provincial Thracian assembly is first attested under Antoninus Pius (138–61). Its seat was at Philippopolis (Trimontium, Plovdiv), which Philip thc Arab promoted to colonial rank (248) at a time when the region was subject to barbarian invasions.

The later empire witnessed the creation of an administrative diocese that bore the name of Thrace, and comprised the (Thracian) provinces of Thracia, Rhodope, Europa and Haemimontus, and the (Moesian) provinces of Moesia Secunda and Scythia. *See also* Abdera, Aegospotami, Beroe Augusta Trajana, Bizye, Byzantium, Cardia, Chersonese (Thracian), Hadrianopolis, Haemus, Lysimachia, Perinthus, Philippopolis, Sestus, Seuthopolis.

Thrinacia *see* Sicily

Thronium *see* Locris

Thugga (Dougga). A hill-town in north Africa (Tunisia), overlooking the Wadi Khaled, a tributary of the Bagradas (Medjerda), beside an ancient road from Carthage to Theveste (Tebessa). Inhabited in Neolithic times, and situated in the center of rich agricultural territory, Thugga passed under strong Carthaginian influence, but in the late third or early second century BC—when it had already attained appreciable size—was dependent on one of the Numidian princes, on the walls of whose mausoleum a bilingual inscription (in Berber and Punic) has survived.

When the Roman province of Africa was established in 146, Thugga came just within its borders. Italian settlers were planted nearby by Gaius Marius, after his African campaigns (107–105), and subsequently this immigrant community (*pagus*) depended on Julius Caesar's colony at Carthage (45). Under Septimius Severus (AD 205) the *pagus* was united with the native town to become a Roman *municipium* (with the titles of Septimium Aurelium), which was elevated by Gallienus in 261 to the rank of a Roman colony (Colonia Licinia Septimia Aurelia Alexandriana). In Christian times the place became an episcopal see; but it was abandoned *c* 600.

Thugga has been described as perhaps the richest city of the African province after Carthage and its remains are among the most striking in Roman North Africa; they exemplify the fusion of Libyan, Punic and Roman cultures. The Capitolium, dedicated to Jupiter, Juno and Minerva in the time of Marcus Aurelius and Lucius Verus (AD 166–67), stands out impressively, beside the forum and market ('Place of the Winds'). There are also temples of Mercury, Fortuna, Pietas Augusta, Concordia, Hades (Pluto), Frugifer, Liber Pater or Bacchus (the largest of all), Saturn-Baal (dominating the valley below and adjoining a theater built in 168/9), and Juno-Caelestis-Tanit (constructed in 222–35 within an extensive precinct). Thermal establishments include the towering Licinian Baths and the Cyclops Baths. The latter building was given this name after the mythological theme of one of its floor-mosaics, which were also a feature of numerous private houses; but most of these pavements have now been taken to the Bardo Museum in Tunis. A triumphal Arch of Septimius Severus (205) stands astride a street descending the hill. A noteworthy feature of Thugga is the considerable age attained by many of the people buried in its cemeteries; probably the town was a favorite place of retirement.

Thule. A northern land first mentioned by the Greek explorer and geographer Pytheas of Massalia (Massilia, Marseille) at the end of the fourth century BC. He describes it as an inhabited but relatively infertile territory adjoining a mass that was 'neither land, nor sea, nor air' (freezing fog?), six days' sail from the north of Britain. Spoken of by Virgil as 'farthest Thule,' the northernmost place in the world, it has been variously located in Iceland or Norway (a peninsula near Trondhjem?): the 'land of Thule' which, according to the historian Tacitus, was sighted by the fleet of his father-in-law Agricola, may have been one of the Shetland islands, but Procopius in the sixth century AD uses the name for Scandinavia, the 'island' that was the old home of the Goths.

Thurii *see* Sybaris

Thysdrus (El Djem). A town in north Africa (Tunisia). Its name suggests Berber rather than Carthaginian origins. A small 'free' city in the Roman province of Africa, Thysdrus figured prominently in the civil war between Julius Caesar and the Pompeians in 46 BC, when the latter employed it for the storage of large quantities of grain—and Caesar could not get a siege under way, owing to the scarcity of water in the neighborhood. Toward the end of the second century AD the town became a Roman *municipium*, deriving importance from its position on the road from Carthage to Hadrumetum (Sousse)—with which it competed for the position of second city in the province after Carthage—as well as on a route toward the hinterland; and large profits, too, were derived from the intensive production and export of olive oil. In 238 Thysdrus was the scene of the *coup d'état* of Gordianus I Africanus, proconsul of Africa, and his son of the same name, who launched a short-lived rebellion against Maximinus I. After the collapse of this revolt Thysdrus seems to have been ravaged and burned, though it attained colonial rank in *c* 240–50 or later and continued to receive mention in fourth- and fifth-century documents.

Two amphitheaters are to be seen on the site; the larger, dating from the mid-third century and capable of accommodating about 50,000 spectators, is the best-preserved of such monuments in Africa, the largest Roman building of the continent, and the third largest amphitheater in the entire Roman world. Despite modern restoration, its interior only remains a skeleton, but beneath the floor lies a cruciform system of cellars with vaulted compartments. A spacious hippodrome has been revealed by aerial photography. Thousands of yards of fine floor mosaics, especially of Antonine and Severan times, have been uncovered at a large bathing establishment. They are now to be seen at the museums of Tunis (Bardo) and El Djem. An elegantly decorated mansion has also been partially excavated beside two temples. Behind these shrines lies an industrial quarter that housed potteries and foundries and even workshops manufacturing hairpins.

Tiber (Tiberis, Tevere), River. The longest river in the Italian peninsula, two hundred and fifty-two miles in length. The Tiber rises in the Etruscan Apennines not far from Arretium (Arezzo), flows south past Volsinii (Orvieto)—below which it is joined by the Pallia (Paglia) from the west and by the Nar (Nera) from the east—and then continues beyond its confluence with the Anio (Aniene) through Rome to its mouth at Ostia, where its delta was much altered, over the centuries, by silting and by imperial canals and harbors. In its lower reaches the river was the boundary between Latium and Etruria (the border between modern Lazio and Tuscany lies farther north), so that it was sometimes known by the names of Tyrrhenus and Lydius (Etruscan). Navigation, although hazardous, was practicable as far as Horta (Orte), and up to Narnia (Narni) on the Nar. Floods were frequent at all periods; Augustus (31 BC–AD 14) created a permanent river commission (*curatores riparum et alvei Tiberis*). *See also* Allia, Anio, Fidenae, Narnia, Ostia, Perusia, Politorium, Rome.

Tiberias (Tevarya, Tebarya). A city of Galilee in Judaea (Israel), on the western shore of the lake named after it, which was also known as Lake Gennesaret and the Sea of Galilee. The town was founded *c* AD 18—taking its name from the reigning emperor Tiberius—by Herod Antipas, ruler of Galilee and Peraea, on the site of an earlier settlement's cemetery, so that, although the new foundation was settled by Jews, strict Jewish opinion deemed it unclean. Nevertheless, Tiberias was equipped with civic status and institutions, and became Antipas' capital and mint, subsequently passing into the hands of other Jewish princes, Agrippa I (41–44) and II (*c* 53–93), and assuming the name of Claudio-Tiberias. During the First Jewish Revolt (66–73), although the city's populace as a whole did not share the pro-Roman views of its ruling class, it surrendered to Vespasian and was spared; an account of what happened, hostile to the historian Josephus, was provided by Justus, a native of the place. After the Second Revolt (132–35), Tiberias was paganized by Hadrian, whose temple the Hadrianeum, containing a figure of Jupiter, is depicted on its coinage.

Nevertheless, the place subsequently became the headquarters of the Jewish patriarchate established by the Romans to control his co-religionists' affairs. The patriarch Judah II Nessiah (*c* 230–86) moved his residence there from Sepphoris-Diocaesarea (Saffuriyeh), and Tiberias became the capital of world Jewry; it contained thirteen synagogues—including one each for people from Babylon, Antioch and Tarsus—and possessed a preeminent theological college, under the direction of Rabbi Johanan bar Nappaha (d. 279). It was at Tiberias that the Mishnah and Jerusalem or Palestine Talmud (Gemara) were edited.

The city remained well-known in the fourth century, according to Eusebius, and was frequently mentioned by Byzantine writers. Excavations have revealed a Roman basilica and bath, and a synagogue of the early third century AD, replaced soon after 300 by a four-aisled building that was adorned with floor-mosaics of outstanding quality, including a representation of a Torah shrine flanked by Menorahs.

Tibur (Tivoli). A city of Latium (Lazio) in western Italy, eighteen miles east-northeast of Rome, perched above gorges and waterfalls of the Anio (Aniene) at the point where that river leaves the Sabine hills. According to legend Tibur was founded four centuries before Rome; its founders were variously described as Arcadians (under Catillus) or as Siculi, who were later expelled either by Tiburnus, the son of Amphiaraus, or by Amphiaraus' grandsons Tiburtus, Catillus and Cetas. Remains of an important early Iron Age village have come to light. Diodorus described the place as a colony of Alba Longa.

Subsequently, it became one of the principal members of the Latin League, dominating several dependent towns, and in the fourth century frequently fought against Rome, suffering defeats in 360 and 354 and losing much of its territory in 338. Thereafter, however, it remained independent until 90, when it became a Roman citizen community. It was notable (as now) for its building stone the *lapis Tiburtinus* (travertine), and earned revenue from the sale of its fruits. Tibur's cults of Hercules, Vesta and Sibyl Albunea (among various other deities) were celebrated by major poets, and the place became a fashionable resort. The poet Catullus and the emperors Augustus and Hadrian (*see* below) owned villas in or near the town, and one such mansion was allocated to Zenobia, queen of Palmyra, after she had been taken prisoner by Aurelian (AD 273).

The forum, on the hillside, was supported by a vaulted arcade that may have served as a covered street-market. To the southwest, likewise resting upon a vaulted substructure, was a two-storeyed colonnaded terrace, on which stood a temple of Hercules Victor, adjoined by a place of assembly. The temple probably dates from the early first century BC, like two picturesque shrines, the round so-called 'Temple of Vesta' (perhaps, in fact, dedicated to Hercules) and a rectangular 'Temple of the Sibyl' (more probably Tiburnus), that rise aloft above the Anio at the northern end of the town. At the southern extremity of the habitation center are traces of an amphitheater, rebuilt in the second century AD. To the west stands a well-preserved circular building of fourth-century date (the Tempio della Tosse). Four of Rome's aqueducts passed beside Tibur, and traces of their bridges across the neighboring valleys are still to be seen.

About three miles southwest of the city rise the enormous but fragmentary remains of Hadrian's Villa, erected in the 120s and 130s AD, on and around the site of an earlier mansion. The group of loosely related or independent edifices that constituted this palatial complex was intended to recall the localities and buildings that the emperor had admired on his empire-wide travels; but this was only a modest pretext for a massive display of adventurous design and virtuosity (best discernible from a model at the entrance). The inventions of some talented experimental architect, prompted and stimulated by the emperor's own enquiring, restless mind, these structures ingeniously exploit the potentialities of an uneven terrain, displaying impressive mastery of their concrete, brick-faced material. Nothing, anywhere, is straight or obvious; curvilinear shapes, of abundant diversity, prevail on every side.

At the entrance to the Villa is the Poikile, a gigantic version of the Painted Porch of Athens. Beyond it is a round, artificial island (known misleadingly as the 'Teatro Marittimo'), surrounded by a moat and by a colonnaded circular promenade. The residential quarters of the palace, flanked by large colonnaded squares (the Piazza d'Oro, and 'Court of the Libraries'), lie in ruins, but enough can be seen of two sets of baths to appreciate their surprising, asymmetrical design. The Canopus is a complex of pool- and stage-architecture, designed to imitate a famous sanctuary of Serapis near Alexandria; it was overlooked, at one end, by a *nymphaeum* or fountain-building (commonly known as the Serapeum), in which numerous sculptures were discovered; many of them are now in the Capitoline and Vatican museums, but there is also a small local antiquarium.

Ticinum (Pavia). A city of Cisalpine Gaul (northern Italy) near the confluence of the rivers Ticinus (Ticino) and Padus (Po). At the outset of the Second Punic War Hannibal defeated the Romans in the neighborhood (218 BC), but the town remained unrecorded until the epoch of the Principate. An inscription bears witness to an Arch of Augustus.

In later imperial times Ticinum became a vitally important fortress within the northern Italian defence system, and began a long career as a major issuer of official coinage when Aurelian, in 274, installed an imperial mint, transferred from Mediolanum (Milan). It was at Ticinum in 408 that the military mutiny broke out that brought down Honorius' great general Stilicho. In 452 the garrison attempted to buy off the Huns led by Attila, but the fortress suffered partial destruction at their hands. In 489/90 the stronghold was the winter headquarters of Theoderic the Ostrogoth during his invasion of Italy. The crypt of the church of San Pietro in Ciel d'Oro contains the remains of the Roman poet and statesman Boethius, whom Theoderic executed for treason (524). The place owes its modern name to the Lombards, who captured it *c* 570 and made it their capital, under the designation of Papia.

Tigranocerta, later Martyropolis, in Armenian Maepheracta (now, it would appear, Silvan, formerly Farkin or Mayafarkin, in southeastern Turkey; although other locations have also been suggested for Tigranocerta). Silvan stands on the site of a very ancient settlement not far from the river Nymphius (Batman Suyu), a northern tributary of the Tigris, in the district that was known as Sophanene or Sophene, south of the Anti-Taurus mountains. Shortly after 100 BC Tigranocerta was founded—on the site of an earlier settlement—by Tigranes I the Great, as his southern capital, to balance Artaxata (Artashat) in the north. Tigranes increased the population of his new foundation by compulsorily introducing colonists from twelve cities of Cappadocia and other territories that he had conquered. However, the fortifications of the town were still not complete in 69, when it succumbed to the Roman army of Lucius Licinius Lucullus. Thereupon the Cappadocian settlers returned to their original homes, but Tigranocerta remained an important center and fortress. In AD 52 it fell into the hands of king Vologeses I of Parthia, but was captured by Cnaeus Domitius Corbulo seven years later, during one of Rome's recurrent attempts to establish a puppet monarch in Armenia.

In the course of the wars of the Sassanian Persian king Sapor (Shapur) II (309–79) against the Romans, the stronghold suffered destruction, thanks to the siege-skills of Sapor's Greek prisoners. Numerous Christians who refused to accept the monarch's Zoroastrian religion met their deaths; as a consequence, Tigranocerta, restored to Roman control in 387, was refounded under the name of Martyropolis by Bishop Marutha, who built a famous Church of the Martyrs in which he collected the relics of Sapor's victims. The restored fortress became the capital of the province of Sophanene (later Gentes) and then of Armenia Quarta under Justinian I (527–65), who granted the place the status of a city.

Tigris. One of the two principal rivers of Mesopotamia, 1,180 miles long, following roughly parallel to, and northeast of the, Euphrates (from which, at Seleucia, it is only eighteen miles distant). Rising in Armenia (eastern Turkey) it continued its course, collecting tributaries from the north and east, through Babylonia (Iraq) to the Persian Gulf; its course has greatly changed throughout the centuries. From AD 197 to 237 the Tigris north of Mosul formed the frontier between Roman Mesopotamia and Parthian Adiabene, and the stronghold of Amida (Diyarbakır) figures prominently in fourth-century wars between the Romans and the Sassanian Persians. During the later empire the river marked the border between the Roman provinces of Sophanene (later Gentes, then Armenia Quarta) and Mesopotamia. *See also* Amida, Assyria, Charax, Ctesiphon, Seleucia on the Tigris.

Tingis, Tingi, earlier Tinx (Tangier). A coastal city of western Mauretania (Morocco), beside the Straits of Gibraltar, Tingis was situated at the end of a broad bay which afforded a moderate degree of shelter. According to Greek mythology, it was founded by Antaeus, the son of Poseidon and Gaia (Earth). From the fifth century BC onward the populations of the area—as their cemeteries indicate—were in close touch with the Carthaginian traders of southern Spain; and it has been suggested that Tingis itself may have received a Phoenician or Carthaginian settlement.

After passing into Roman hands it was seized by Quintus Sertorius (in rebellion against the central government) in 81. At this period, if not earlier, the town was issuing coins with Neo-Punic (Carthaginian) inscriptions, apparently as an autonomous community, although it no doubt owed loose allegiance to the kings of western Mauretania. One of these monarchs, Bogud—after invading Spain—lost his dominions *c* 38 to Bocchus II (or III), formerly ruler of the eastern part of the country; whereupon Octavian (the future Augustus) confirmed Bocchus' seizure, but granted Tingis Roman citizenship as a *municipium.* In this capacity it issued a number of coins (imperfectly preserved and recorded) with the names of local officials and the heads of Baal and a goddess, as well as others bearing the portraits of Augustus and Agrippa, and later (under Tiberius or Gaius) those of Nero Caesar and Drusus Caesar, the sons of Germanicus. Another coin of one of these reigns, claiming the title of *colonia,* is unconfirmed, and its acquisition of this rank is usually attributed to Claudius, who made Tingis the capital of his new province of Mauretania Tingitana (before AD 44).

The place provided a useful naval station, and was connected by military roads with Sala (Chella) and Volubilis (Ksar Pharaoun)—which later replaced Tingis as the provincial capital. During the later empire, however, it became the capital of the much smaller province of Tingitana or Tingitania—attached to the administrative diocese of the Spains—until North Africa was overrun by the Vandals (429). Funerary inscriptions bear witness to a Christian community from the fourth or fifth century onward, and there is evidence of a bishopric in the sixth. The limits of the ancient town are marked out by the cemeteries surrounding its walls, and traces of baths and of a Christian basilica have been noted. Remains of farming estates and brick factories have come to light in the neighborhood.

Tipasa. A coastal city of Mauretania Caesariensis (eastern Mauretania, now Algeria), adjoining a bay in which its port was protected by small islands. At least as early as the sixth century BC Tipasa was a Phoenician or Carthaginian town, or at least possessed close relations with Carthage, as its cemeteries show. Later it benefited from its proximity to the Mauretanian capital Iol (Caesarea). The town gained Latin rights (conferring Roman citizenship on its elected officials) or, alternatively, was made a Roman *municipium* (possessing full citizen rights) under Claudius (*c* AD 46), and became a Roman colony, with the name of Colonia Aelia Augusta, in the time of Antoninus Pius, during whose reign it served as a base for warfare against rebellious tribes in the mountainous interior (*c* 144–50); these operations were conducted by troops from the Danubian region, who constructed strong walls around the habitation center.

The seat of a bishopric from the fourth century onward, Tipasa became the scene of violent clashes between Catholics and Puritan fundamentalists of the Donatist persuasion; and it also played an important part in the control of dissident tribesmen in the hinterland. Its defences enabled it to hold out against the usurper Firmus (372–75)—supposedly through the exertions of a leading local Christian, St. Salsa—but the Vandals occupied the town in 429, installing an Arian bishop toward the end of the century.

The remains of Tipasa are noteworthy for their picturesque setting. Excavations, penetrating the silt brought down by floods and blown sand, have revealed a forum—extending across a rocky hillock that juts out over the sea—as well as an amphitheater, theater, *nymphaeum* (fountain-head of the city's water supply), pagan basilica (from which an important floor-mosaic is preserved in the local museum), temples, and spacious private houses, as well as several sectors of the fortifications. Particularly notable is a huge apsed Christian cathedral, with a nave flanked by three aisles on either side; a square baptistery with a circular pool and the bishop's house stand nearby. Outside the walls, to the east, is the church of St. Salsa, surrounded by a large array of sarcophagi that remain in place; and to the west stands the basilica of Bishop Alexander, near a burial-place of martyrs who died in the persecutions of Diocletian (284–305). Underwater diving has discovered port installations.

Tiryns. A town on a rocky hill in the southeast section of the plain of Argos, one mile from the sea. Tiryns had fulfilled an enormously important role in the Bronze Age, displaying massive strength and imposing palatial form during the epoch of adjacent Mycenae from *c* 1400 onward. A lower town, too, has been the scene of significant recent Bronze Age excavations. In Greek mythology, the formidable walls of Tiryns, mentioned by Homer, were said to have been built by the Cyclopes—brought in by the city's monarch Proetus, at war with his brother Acrisius of Mycenae, the grandfather of Perseus. Perseus, too, was believed to have been a Tirynthian king. Moreover, it was from Tiryns that Heracles, himself traditionally believed to have originated from the place, was said to have set out to perform the Twelve Labors for King Eurystheus. Tiryns survived into the Iron Age and classical period, and dispatched a contingent to fight the Persians at the Battle of Plataea (479). But the town was destroyed by the Argives about a decade later, whereupon the survivors emigrated to Halieis (Porto Cheli), where they issued coins in the following century under the name of Tirynthians. By the times of Strabo and Pausanias the site of Tiryns itself was deserted.

Tolfa, Mount *see* Caere, Tarquinii

Tolmeta *see* Ptolemais (Cyrenaica)

Tolosa (Toulouse). A city in southwestern Gaul, on the right (north) bank of the river Garumna (Garonne). In pre-Roman times it was the capital of the Volcae Tectosages: this township was at Vieille-Toulouse, four miles south of the present town, linked to Narbo (Narbonne) by an ancient road, and controlling the route to Burdigala (Bordeaux). Subsequently the Volcae became allies of Rome after the establishment of the Roman province of Gallia Narbonensis (*c* 121).

In 106, however, after a rebellion, the Roman consul Quintus Servilius Caepio sacked this Tolosa, and captured its sacred treasure (*aurum Tolosanum*), which was believed to have been taken by the Gauls at Delphi, and lay under a curse (it subsequently disappeared, however, and he was defeated in the following year by the Germans). Nevertheless, Tolosa, reconstructed on a new site beneath the modern town, recovered and flourished, owing to its export of wine to Italy; and under the Principate it gained Latin rights (conferring Roman citizenship on its elected officials). The most famous native of Roman Tolosa was Marcus Antonius Primus, whose invasion of Italy in AD 69 gained the throne for Vespasian. But the city became chiefly famous for its schools of rhetoric and an advanced literary culture, which earned it the name Palladia, after the goddess Athena. The first Christian bishop of the place suffered martyrdom in the third century.

In 408 Tolosa was one of the few Gallic towns that successfully resisted the German invaders, thanks, it was said, to the energy of its bishop Exuperius. In 413, however, Rutilius Namatianus reports, it was captured by the Visigothic king Ataulf. Soon afterwards the Visigoths were compelled to leave for Spain, but when Constantius (III), the general of Honorius, recalled Wallia in 418 to establish a federated state in southern Gaul he established his capital at Tolosa. It was there, too, in 455, that Avitus was proclaimed western Roman emperor by the Visigoths, on the prompting of their monarch Theoderic. Tolosa was taken in 508 by Clovis the Frank.

The Roman city had been laid down according to a symmetrical grid lay-out, which can still be detected in the surviving street plan. The ancient buildings are buried to a depth of twelve feet, but the theater has been located, and portions of walls, perhaps of second- and fifth-century date, can be seen. Across the Garumna, three miles downstream at Saint-Michel-du-Touch, the ruins of an amphitheater and two large public bathing establishments have been recently excavated, near a sanctuary where the river is joined by its tributary the Touch. The route between Tolosa and Aquae Tarbellicae (Dax) was flanked by the huge villa of Chiragan, the second largest town in Gaul (the largest, at Montmaurin, was only thirteen miles away).

Tolstaya Mogila *see* Scythia

Tomis, Tomi, Tomai, later Constantia (Constanţa). A city of Scythia Minor (Dobrogea) on the Rumanian coast of the Euxine (Black) Sea, colonized by Miletus in Ionia (western Asia Minor) *c* 500–475 BC. Its founder was said to have been a certain Tomos. Built on a promontory protecting a south-facing harbor, and presiding over a trade-route across the neck of the Dobrogea to the Danube, the colony conducted active commerce not only with the rest of the Greek world but also with the Scythian interior, as finds preserved in the local museum confirm.

Nevertheless, it was only in about the third century that Tomis ceased to be overshadowed by its neighbor Istrus (Histria). From the time of Alexander the Great's successor Lysimachus (d. 281) gold and silver coins bearing his name were issued at the local mint. About 262, according to Memnon, the control of the Tomians' merchandise was the issue in a war between Byzantium (İstanbul) and Istrus' ally Callatis (Mangalia), which vainly tried to take over Tomis' port. Occupied by Marcus Licinius Lucullus in 72, the city suffered raids from hinterland tribes until its incorporation in the province of Moesia created by Augustus and Tiberius, within which it became the head of a Federation (*koinon*) of neighboring Pontic (Euxine) cities. Tomis owes its fame to its selection by Augustus as the place of banishment of the poet Ovid (AD 8), who paints a gloomy picture of a superficially Hellenized, spiritually and culturally arid frontier town subject to ferocious tribal attacks and a depressingly bleak climate.

When Domitian divided the province into two (AD 85/86), Tomis became the capital of Lower Moesia. During the third century local prosperity was gravely affected by Gothic invasions. But the city recovered in the later empire, when it became capital of the new province of Scythia, under the name of Constantia (for the Dobrogea rampart, see Axiopolis). When the empire became Christianized, Tomis was the seat of a bishop. During this period shipping and ship-building were major activities.

The town-wall which closed off the promontory in the second century AD, and was rebuilt several times thereafter, has been preserved at a number of points. But the principal monument that excavators have unearthed is the 'Mosaic Building,' a large complex of commercial structures of fourth-century date, designed on three levels and supporting a sixty-foot-high cliff. The edifice opens onto adjacent quays, where warehouses filled with amphorae (employed for storing grain) have been uncovered, in addition to the ruins of a large bathing establishment. Other finds include a cache of twenty-four pieces of pagan sculpture of various dates, including the best known representation of the sheep-headed snake-god Glycon, whose worship was professed by the second-century charlatan Alexander of Abonuteichus or Ionopolis (Inebolu) in Paphlagonia (northern Asia Minor).

Another statue depicts Tyche (Fortuna), accompanied by a small bearded figure of Pontus (standing for the Euxine [Black] Sea coastland, not Pontus in northern Asia Minor), whose presence testifies to an ancient consciousness of the economic and cultural unity of the region. This statuary group also seems to be shown on early third-century coins. Other issues describe Tomis as the 'metropolis of Pontus,' and depict a trophy between captives. In addition, Tomis has yielded more than seven hundred inscriptions. Four early Christian basilicas have come to light, including one, of considerable size, that is built over a huge seven-roomed cruciform crypt.

Torino *see* Augusta Taurinorum

Tornata *see* Bedriacum

Torone. A city on the west coast of Sithonia, the middle of the three peninsulas of Chalcidice (Macedonia, northern Greece). Situated on the northern slope of a rocky promontory, Torone possessed a good harbor (Porto Koufo) to the southeast of the cape, balanced by the Toronean bay to the northwest. After habitation—revealed by cremation and less numerous inhumation burials—since the early first millennium BC, the place was settled by colonists from Chalcis in Euboea before 650, and was the most important foundation of the Chalcidians in these waters.

When the Persians entered Greece in 480, Torone collaborated with the invaders, but after their defeat became a member of the Delian League under the leadership of Athens. In the Peloponnesian War the city was taken by the Spartan general Brasidas in 423, but recaptured in the following year by Cleon, who transported seven hundred of its male population to Athens and sold the women and children into slavery. Before the end of the same century Torone became a member of the Chalcidian Confederacy under Olynthus, but succumbed to Philip II of Macedonia, through treason, in 348. In 169, during the Third Macedonian War between the Romans and Perseus, Eumenes II of Pergamum and Prusias II Cynegus of Bithynia tried to seize the town from the Macedonians without success, but it fell to the Romans in 167. When they abolished the Macedonian kingdom and instituted four puppet Republics, Torone served as the harbor for one of these districts. In Roman and early Christian times it continued to flourish.

Recent studies of its fortification system have thrown interesting light on Thucydides' account of the operations during the Peloponnesian War. During the fourth century an impressive new circuit was constructed, probably after the capture of Torone by Philip II. A number of spacious houses have also been uncovered. One of these dwellings consisted of five units, including a long forecourt, and possessed a tiled roof. Another, containing fine pottery, ceased to be occupied at about the time of the Peloponnesian War. Late Roman burials are both pagan and Christian, and five early Christian basilicas have been located.

Tortona *see* Dertona

Toulouse *see* Tolosa

Tours *see* Caesarodunum

Trablus (Tarabulus) **Al-Gharb** *see* Oea

Trablus (Tarabulus) **Esh-Sham** *see* Tripolis (Syria)

Trabzon *see* Trapezus

Trachonitis (Leja, Safa). A territory at the southern extremity of Syria, south of Damascus, north of the plain of Batanea (Bashan, En-Nukra) and the mountains of Auranitis (Hauran), and east of Gaulanitis (Golan, adjoining the east bank of the upper Jordan). A cracked and crumpled maze of lava ridges and gullies, Trachonitis proved ideal for brigandage. In the pre-classical period it formed part of a region which was constantly disputed between Israelites and Aramaeans. During the second century BC the Ituraeans, a turbulent and warlike race originating from the Libanus (Lebanon) and Anti-Libanus regions, had extended their power over Trachonite territory, which was then conquered, however, by the Jewish (Hasmonaean) state, probably under John Hyrcanus I (134–104).

Subsequently Trachonitis belonged to the tetrarchs Lysanias (40–36) and Zenodorus (30–20) of Chalcis Beneath Lebanon, under the protection of Antony and Octavian (Augustus) respectively. But Zenodorus encouraged the local robber bands for his own profit, and in 23 Augustus transferred Trachonitis, Auranitis and Batanea to Herod the Great, the client-king of Judaea. Herod quickly reduced the local population to quiescence. Moreover, when the brigands resumed operations in 12, they were crushed. Forty of their leaders, however, were given refuge by the ruler of Nabataean Arabia; whereupon Herod invaded Arab territory, and settled 3,000 of his own Idumaean partisans in Trachonitis (supplemented by a military colony of Babylonian Jews in Batanea). His invasion of the Arab kingdom greatly annoyed Augustus, and on learning of this imperial reaction the Trachonite hillsmen renewed their rebellion, massacring many of the new settlers.

After Herod's death Trachonitis became part of the tetrarchy of his son Philip (4 BC–AD 34). Subsequently it belonged to Agrippa I and Agrippa II, under whom two of the territory's chieftains tried to defect to the historian Josephus (unwillingly in command of a rebel force) at the beginning of the First Jewish Revolt (AD 66); but he sent them back home. Following the death of Agrippa

II (before 93/94), Trachonitis belonged to the province of Judaea (soon to be renamed Syria Palaestina). But *c* 295 the territory was transferred to the province of Arabia.

Tralles, Tralleis, later Seleucia, Caesarea (Aydın). A city in western Asia Minor, variously attributed to Caria, Ionia, and Lydia. Its steep acropolis (Laris[s]a) occupied a defensible position above a plateau (now known as Güzel Hisar, 'beautiful castle') that formed a southern spur of Mount Messogis (Cuma Dağı), overlooking the fertile lower valley of the Maeander (Büyük Menderes). The place was believed to have borne, at various times, the names of Euantheia, Polyantheia, Erymna and Charax; it was said to have been founded either by a certain Tralleus or by a mixed group of Argives and Tralleis (a barbarian tribe) from Thrace or Illyria. First mentioned by Xenophon, the town belonged in his time (the fourth century) to the Hecatomnid monarchs of Halicarnassus (Bodrum), and subsequently became a important center in the Seleucid empire, taking the name of Seleucia and initiating its coinage under this title in the late third century.

Following the defeat of Antiochus III the Great by the Romans, the city passed into the hands of Eumenes II of Pergamum (190/188), and after the Pergamene kingdom had been bequeathed to Rome (133) supported Aristonicus' rebellion against Roman rule. During Rome's first war against Mithridates VI of Pontus (88–83), whose portrait appears on the gold coins of Tralles, it was dominated by the sons of Cratippus, who massacred the Italian residents. Roman proconsuls, like the Pergamene monarchs before them, issued silver coinage at the local mint from 58 to 53, and a praetor did the same in 49/8. After serious earthquake damage in 27/26, the city received assistance from Augustus, and adopted the name of Caesarea. Although Strabo described the large number of its wealthy and influential inhabitants, it was refused permission to build a temple of Tiberius (AD 14–37) on the grounds that its resources were inadequate.

The very extensive monetary issues of Tralles during the Principate refer to its Pythian and Olympian Games, to a combined Olympian Augustan Pythian festival, and to numerous deities, of whom Zeus Larasios was the chief (Strabo links his cult, perhaps wrongly, with Larisa three miles to the north on Mount Messogis). Large semi-medallic pieces of Antoninus Pius (AD 138–61) offer a remarkable variety of elaborate mythological scenes, and in the third century the Trallians designate themselves 'the First of Greece' (*protoi Hellados*).

Little is left of their habitation area today. Three high arches, of third-century date, formed part of a gymnasium. There are also remains of a theater at the foot of the acropolis. The last great mathematical physicist of antiquity was born at the place *c* 500. He was Anthemius of Tralles, one of the architects of Aya Sofya at Constantinople (Istanbul).

Trapani *see* Drepanum

Trapezus, Trapezous ('Table Mountain,' Trabzon, Trebizond). A city in Pontus (northern Asia Minor) on the coast of the Euxine (Black) Sea, situated on a coastal ridge at the foot of the Paryadres mountains, and protected on the other side by cliffs descending into ravines. Earlier inhabited by the Mossynoeci, who traded in monstrously fat boys, fed on boiled chestnuts and tattooed with floral designs, Trapezus, according to Eusebius, was founded in 756 BC. It is not certain, however, that the town, or any other Greek settlement on this coast, was founded as a colony before the seventh century (though it might have existed earlier as a trading post or emporium): it is described by Xenophon as a colony of Sinope (Sinop), which is assigned a foundation date no earlier than 631.

Although Trapezus was the northern terminal of a route leading over the Zigana pass from Armenia and the Euphrates and stimulating trade with the metal-workings of the Ararat region, its inadequate harbor and unfriendly neighbors hampered rapid development; and its people were still dependent on Sinope in 400, when the Greek force that had been fighting in Mesopotamia in support of the Persian Cyrus the Younger reached the Euxine at this point, after glimpsing its coast from the mountains above, and crying out *thalatta, thalatta,* 'the sea, the sea.' The long march was described in Xenophon's *Anabasis.*

The earliest coins, issued in the fourth century, bear the type of a table (*trapeza*). One of the products of the neighborhood was 'mad' honey made by bees who have drunk from Pontic azaleas. The city formed part of the Pontic kingdom of Mithhridates VI Eupator (120–63 BC), the Galatian realm of Deiotarus I (died 40), and then again the Pontic state of the Polemos (38 BC–AD 38), of whose royal fleet it became the principal base. When their kingdom was annexed to the Roman province of Galatia as Pontus Polemoniacus (64/65), Trapezus remained a naval base, enjoying the status of free city, and assumed increasing significance as the nearest port to the empire's eastern frontier. But it remained for Hadrian to build a satisfactory harbour (*c* 131); and his governor Arrian, while appreciating the importance of the place, held a low opinion of its culture. Trepezus was sacked by the Goths in 257/260, but was garrisoned by a legion in the later empire, when it became the capital of the province of Pontus Polemoniacus.

Some Hellenistic masonry and two moles of Hadrian's harbor can be seen taday. The church of Panayia Askepastos occupies the site of a probable temple of Mithras, who often appears on the city's coinage of imperial times. The Orta Hisar mosque was formerly the church of the Golden-headed Virgin (Panayia Chrysokephalos), supposedly founded by Constantine's nephew Hannibalianus, whom he made king of Armenia (336); though the present structure dates from the tenth or eleventh century—two or three hundred years earlier than the Byzantine empire of Trebizond which endowed the city with many additional churches and provided a romantic legend: 'still,' wrote Rose Macaulay, 'the towers of Trebizond, the fabled city, shimmer on a far horizon, gated and walled and held in a luminous enchantment.'

Trasimene, Trasumenus. A lake in Etruria, northwest of Clusium (Chiusi), southeast of Cortona, and east of Perusia (Perugia): the largest lake in Italy, with an area of forty-nine square miles. It was the scene of a disastrous Roman defeat by the Carthaginians in 217, early in the Second Punic War. Hannibal, advancing eastward along the north shore, stationed his army in the hills at a point where they came close to the lake (either east or west of Passignano, where the shoreline has now receded), and awaited the approach of the Roman consul Gaius Flaminius, who had marched from Arretium (Arezzo). With the help of a mist, Hannibal successfully ambushed the Roman force, attacking it from the front, rear and flank and killing 15,000 men, including many who jumped into the lake and were drowned. A further 6,000 soldiers, at the head of the Roman column, succeeded in breaking through, but surrendered on the following day. The road to Rome was now open, but Hannibal never captured the city.

Trebia (Trebbia), River, in Cisalpine Gaul (north Italy). A southern tributary of the Padus (Po), which it joins four miles west of Placentia (Piacenza). The Trebia was the scene of a victory won by Hannibal over the Romans in the first year of the Second Punic War (218 BC). The consul Publius Cornelius Scipio (father of the famous Africanus) had advanced across the Ticinus (Ticino), a northern Po tributary, but after a cavalry reverse withdrew south of the Po to a point west of Placentia, not far from the Trebia. There the Carthaginians moved to within a short distance of Scipio's army; but the Roman general, deserted by 2000 Gallic auxiliaries, retreated east of the Trebia, where he was joined by his fellow consul Tiberius Sempronius Longus. Encouraged by their new united strength and by a successful cavalry skirmish, the Romans returned across the Trebia, but Hannibal's outflanking tactics, combined with an ambush, resulted in their total defeat. Most of their soldiers met their death in the river, but 10,000 in the front ranks of the center broke through to Placentia, where they were joined by the cavalry. However, Hannibal was now free to ravage Etruria as he pleased.

Trebizond *see* Trapezus

Treveri, Treviri *see* Augusta Trevirorum

Trier *see* Augusta Trevirorum

Trimontium *see* Philippopolis

Trinacria *see* Sicily

Triparadisus. An uncertain site in northern Syria; possibly identifiable with Paradisus on the upper Orontes (Nahr el-Asi). Triparadisus was the scene of an important conference between the successors of Alexander III the Great in 321 BC. The result of the meeting was that Antipater was made sole guardian and viceroy of the two young kings Philip III Arrhidaeus (Alexander's mentally retarded half-brother) and Alexander IV (Alexander's posthumous son by Roxane), while Antigonus I Monophthalmos, who was Antipater's ally, gained command of the royal Macedonian army in Asia. Seleucus I, later known as Nicator (Conqueror)—who had been friendly with Alexander the Great, but was not one of his prominent generals—became governor of Babylon, and in due course founder of the Seleucid empire.

Tripolis (Tripoli, Tarabulus Esh-Sham). A city in Phoenicia (Lebanon), at the foot of Mount Libanus (Lebanon): the terminal of a route from the Syrian hinterland, situated at the end of a peninsula (in what is now the suburb of Al Mina). As Diodorus and Strabo record, Tripolis was a joint foundation of Tyre (Es-Sur), Sidon (Saida) and Aradus (Tartus); in the fourth century BC if not earlier, their colonists or merchants established separate quarters in the town, which was believed to have derived its designation ('three cities') from this triple enterprise, although an alternative explanation interpreted the name as *tarpol*, new land.

A principal base of the Phoenicians' fleet, Tripolis was also the headquarters of their consultative Council, which revolted against the Achaemenid Persian monarch Artaxerxes III Ochus in 351 BC. After conquest by Alexander the Great (332), the city became a mint of Ptolemy V Epiphanes (188) and subsequently of the Seleucid Antiochus IV Epiphanes (175–164). Tripolis dated a new era of autonomy from 112/111 but continued to coin for the Seleucids until Antiochus X Eusebes Philopator (95–83). Later it came under the control of a local autocrat, Dionysius, whom Pompey put to death in 63, when a further civic era was inaugurated. The local mint subsequently coined for Antony and his wife Fulvia (42/40), and later for Cleopatra VII of Egypt, when yet another era began.

The subsequent coinage of Tripolis under the Principate displays figures of Helios, Selene and the Dioscuri (Castor and Polydeuces [Pollux]), a temple of Zeus Hagios with its sanctuary gate—under Caracalla, AD 211–17—and a tripartite shrine of Astarte under Elagabalus (218–22); in his time the city described itself not only as *neokoros* (an honorific title mainly referring to the imperial cult) but also as *nauarchis* (dominant on the sea). There was also a temple of Isis of the Many Names (Myrionymus), identified with Artemis Orthosia. The territory of Tripolis contained a number of other sanctuaries (at Bziza, Naous and Sfire); and it produced a famous wine.

Tripolis *see* Lepcis Magna, Oea

Tripolitana (Tripolitania). The region of north Africa bordering on the Lesser Syrtes (Gabes) Gulf (now the western section of Libya). Texts deriving from the Map of Agrippa (who died in 12 BC) suggest that the whole territory was at that time included in the Roman province of Crete and Cyrenaica; but, if so, it was detached and assigned to the province of Africa before the death of Augustus (AD 14). The development of the frontier defence system involved frequent (but ill-documented) operations against the nomadic tribes, which led to the establishment by Commodus (180–92) and Septimius Severus (193–211) of outposts on oases beyond the frontier, commanding the caravan routes into the interior.

In the later empire there was a separate province of Tripolitana—within the administrative diocese of Africa—which had to confront dangerous incursions by the tribe of the Austuriani. These attacks required the proprietors of the fortified farms (*burgi*) of the frontier areas to perform military duties, specified in legislation of 409 but probably dating back to the middle of the previous century. *See also* Lepcis Magna, Oea, Sabratha.

Troad, Troas *see* Abydus, Assus, Hellespont, Ida, Ilium, Lampsacus

Troesmis (Igliţa). A Roman city in Scythia Minor (Dobrogea, Rumania), behind the right-angled reentrant of the Lower Danube, fifty-five miles from its mouth. Before Roman occupation, the place was inhabited by the tribe of the Getae, whose king, at the time of the military operations of Marcus Licinius Crassus (29–27 BC), was called Zyraxes. Ovid refers to barbarian attacks in AD 15, provoking Roman countermeasures. Troesmis formed part of the Augustan and Tiberian province of Moesia, though maintaining links with the client kingdoms of Thrace until their annexation in 46.

When Moesia was divided by Domitian (85/86), the town was assigned to the lower province. At a date not later than 112, Trajan moved a legion from Oescus (Ghighen) to Troesmis, where it remained until 167/8; at that time Marcus Aurelius granted one of the two civilian settlements beside the camp the status of a *municipium.* Dedicatory inscriptions honor the dynasty of Septimius Severus, who himself passed through the Dobrogea in 202. During the later part of the third century, however, Troesmis was destroyed by the Goths; but new cities subsequently emerged on the sites of the *municipium* and the camp. Under the administrative reforms of Diocletian (284–305), the city became the headquarters of the council and official worship of the new province of Scythia, and was once again garrisoned by a legion. It became the seat of a bishop, and its fortifications were strengthened in 337–40 and 540–50.

The two centers of this later Troesmis have been excavated. The western settlement stood on a promontory with steep slopes on three sides, and was guarded by semicircular towers. The eastern town, of which much more is known, enjoyed similar protection with the addition of a rampart and ditch; and, it, too, was isolated by cliffs on three sides. This eastern township comprised the acropolis or citadel, which contained military accommodation, the governor's residence, and three sixth-century Christian basilicas.

Troezen, Troizen. A city in the southeastern part of the Argolid (Peloponnese, southern Greece), on the north slope of Mount Phorbantion (Aderes). Formerly, it was said, known as Posidonia, Troezen figured in Greek mythology as the place where Poseidon—who contended with Athena for its land—caused the horses of Theseus' son Hippolytus to take fright and drag their master to death; and it was also the alleged site of Orestes' purification, after he had killed his mother Clytaemnestra (Pausanias was shown the stone on which this rite took place) and had been freed from the Erinyes (Furies) by the verdict of the Athenian Areopagus. Furthermore, Troezen was alleged to have been the birthplace of the Athenian hero Theseus.

In Greek history, the role of the place—although not altogether unimportant, owing to its geographical position—was always secondary. Founded in an ancient habitation area, Troezen is described in the *Iliad* as part of the kingdom of Diomedes based on Argos, though it subsequently became independent enough to gain control of the adjoining islands of Calauria and Hydra, to colonize Halicarnassus (Bodrum) in Caria (southwestern Asia Minor), and to play a part in the settlement of Sybaris (Sibari) in south Italy (*c* 720). Troezen began to issue its own coins in the fifth century, and became a member of Sparta's Peloponnesian League. In 480 it joined other Greek cities that resisted the invasion by the Persians under Xerxes I, and when Xerxes occupied Athens, the Troezenians gave hospitality to its refugees, mindful of their joint mythological traditions. Reference to these events appears on an inscription of the third century professing to describe Themistocles' evacuation plan, although its accuracy is seriously disputed.

In their bid to establish naval supremacy against the Peloponnesian states, the Athenians gained the adherence of Troezen in 457/5, which forfeited its support under the Thirty Years' Treaty (446/5). In 435 its people promised aid to Corinth against Athens' ally Corcyra, and during the Peloponnesian War (431–404) continued to side with Corinth and Sparta. After the defeat of the Greek states by Philip II of Macedonia at Chaeronea (338) Troezen fell briefly under the domination of a local autocrat ('tyrant') Athenogenes. Subsequently, the city belonged to the Macedonian kings Demetrius I Poliorcetes and his son Antigonus II Gonatas (287–239), who lost it to Pyrrhus of Epirus in 272. In 243 Aratus acquired Troezen for the Achaean League, but the place fell to the Spartan King Cleomenes III in 225.

Later it was granted a treaty relationship with Rome, and was described by Pausanias as a very flourishing town. During the later second and third centuries AD its mint resumed coinage, depicting a rich variety of local myths. The designs on these pieces include a statue of Athena Sthenias on the acropolis, and her archaic statue by Callon of Aegina, described by Pausanias. Depictions of Hippolytus, who was said to have founded the temple of Artemis, figure prominently on the issues; and traces of his sanctuary (of the fourth century BC) have been identified on the ground; and so have the remains of a large and complex Asclepieum of slightly later date. Sections of an encircling wall, and of another wall separating the citadel from the habitation area—and paid for, according to Pausanias, by contributions from the citizens—can also be seen. He also refers to an oracular shrine of Apollo Thearios and Artemis Lycia in the agora, and records a precinct of Demeter outside the city (near the modern Damala). A coin of Septimius Severus (AD 193–211) shows the 'fountain of Heracles,' consisting of a figure of a lion from whose mouth water pours down into an elaborate basin.

Tropaeum Augusti Alpium, Alpine trophy of Augustus (La Turbie). A monumental trophy on the eastern border of Gallia Narbonensis (Alpes Maritimes, southern France), dominating the slopes which descend sharply to Monoecus (Monaco) and the sea. Completed in 7/6 BC to celebrate Augustus' pacification of the Alps between 25 and 14, the trophy bore an inscription listing the names of the forty-five Alpine tribes that his armies had subjugated. This inscription was inserted in a marble slab, which was flanked by reliefs of trophies and captives and formed part of a massive square podium. Above the podium rose a second, smaller counterpart, crowned by a huge cylindrical drum providing a base for twenty-four columns. Above their architrave, which was decorated with metope reliefs, rose a conical and (apparently) stepped roof, surmounted either by a statue of Augustus or by the representation of a trophy.

Tropaeum Trajani, Trophy of Trajan (Adamclisi). A town in Scythia Minor, the northeastern region of Lower Moesia (now the Rumanian Dobrogea). Formerly a Getic (Dacian) habitation center, situated on an important crossroads mid-way between Tomis (Constanţa) and Durostorum (Silistra in Bulgaria), the place was converted into a Roman settlement by Trajan, to whom the ex-soldiers and Dacians whom he planted there, under the name of Trajanenses Tropaeenses, dedicated a statue in AD 115/16.

Under Antoninus Pius (138-61), a large legionary detachment swelled the local population. The community was given the rank of a *municipium* by Marcus Aurelius, shortly before 170. Its stronghold was subsequently repaired by Septimius Severus (193-211), and on two further occasions during the first half of the second century; nevertheless, it was subsequently destroyed by the Goths. Rebuilt during the joint reign of Constantine I the Great and Licinius—as a verbose inscription of 316 records—the town continued to exist until the sixth century. Surviving ruins belong to the last two hundred years of its life. They included walls with horseshoe-shaped towers (and one of rectangular form), a colonnaded main street, three aqueducts, a large pagan basilica, and four Christian churches. Finds are divided between the museum at Constanţa and the Archaeological Institute at Bucharest.

On an elevated plateau a mile and a half to the east of the site stands the Trophy of Trajan after which the place was named, erected in 109 to commemorate his victory over the Dacians and their allies (though an alternative attribution to the wars of Domitian, 85-89, has met with some support). The monument is a huge limestone-faced concrete drum, one hundred feet in diameter, standing on a platform reached by nine steps and faced with (originally) fifty-four metopes, averaging five feet high by four feet wide. These metopes are designed in a remarkable artistic style, possessing strong non-classical affinities; they portray battles and Dacian men, women and children, and the emperor, too, is depicted. Above the cornice ran a parapet with twenty-six crenellations: each of which bears a relief depicting a trousered Dacian, Sarmatian or German captive beside a tree, with his hands tied behind his back. The parapet was surmounted by a conical, tiled roof rising to a two storeyed hexagonal pedestal which bore two identical dedications to Mars the Avenger and was crowned by a trophy consisting of a thirty-three-foot-high stone copy of a tree trunk, carved with enemy armor and weapons and flanked by three captives. The fragments of the trophy, metopes and parapet sculptures are preserved beside the drum.

Troy *see* Ilium

Troyes *see* Campi Catalaunii

Turnu Severin *see* Drobeta

Turones *see* Caesarodunum

Turris Libisonis *see* Sardinia

Turunçlar *see* Priene

Tusculum. A city in Latium (Lazio), occupying a site on the outer ring of Mount Albanus (more than 2000 feet above sea level) and dominating the route from the Algidus Pass to Rome (which lay fifteen miles to the northwest). The place-name suggests Etruscan foundation. According to tradition, however, Tusculum was colonized by Latins from Alba Longa (Castel Gandolfo); although an alternative legend named its founder as Telegonus, son of Ulysses (Odysseus) and Circe, whose descendant Octavius Mamilius was believed to have supported the cause of his son-in-law Tarquinius Superbus—the last king of Rome expelled *c* 510/509 BC—and to have died at the head of Rome's Latin enemies at the battle of Lake Regillus (*c* 496).

Subsequently, however, Tusculum, fearing attacks from the tribes of the Aequi and Volsci through the Algidus Pass, became a firm ally of the Romans, and was the first Latin city to obtain their citizenship (381), though friction occasionally followed (340, 323). The Tusculans provided Rome with a number of eminent families (the Cordii, Fonteii, Fulvii, Juventii, Mamilii, Plaetorii, Porcii [family of the two famous Catos] and Servii). During the civil wars in the early years of the first century, Tusculum supported the losing side of the Marians against Sulla. In the late Republic and early Principate, it was a fashionable resort where many wealthy Romans resided and possessed estates, including Lucullus, Cicero (who located the scenario of his *Tusculan Disputation* there), Maecenas and the emperor Tiberius (AD 14–37).

On the acropolis, according to ancient writers, stood temples of Castor and Pollux (the Dioscuri)—the principal divinities of the place—and a sanctuary of Jupiter. But these buildings have not survived. In the remaining part of the town, however, which extended along the ridge of the hill, there are remains of the local senate house (*curia*), a city wall of the early first century AD, a theater, an amphitheater—imaginatively known as the 'School of Cicero'—and buildings bearing the equally conjectural designations of 'Villa of Cicero' and 'Villa of Tiberius.'

Tyana, later Eusebeia (near Kemerhisar). A city in southwestern Cappadocia (eastern Asia Minor), situated on a fortified hill rising from one of the few fertile Cappadocian plains, on the main route across the Taurus (Toros) mountains into Syria. Already an important center in the second millennium BC, it was noted by Xenophon (*c* 400) as a prosperous town, under the name of Dana. With the single exception of Mazaca (the later Caesarea, now Kayseri), Tyana was the only city in Cappadocia. It served as the mint for a loyal dynast called Ariarathes (early third century) and then for King Ariaramnes of Cappadocia (*c* 250–225). Later it assumed the name of Eusebeia, after King Ariarathes V Eusebes Philopator (163–130).

The place was famous as the birthplace of the Neopythagorean sage and wonder-worker Apollonius of Tyana, at about the beginning of the Christian era. Under Caracalla (AD 211–17) it gained the status of a Roman colony, but continued to coin with Greek inscriptions, assuming the titles Antoniniana and Aurelia. In 272 it was the scene of Aurelian's first victory over the forces of the Palmyrene usurper queen, Zenobia. Through the treachery of a certain Heraclammon, Aurelian was able to occupy a height dominating the town, which then surrendered, thus throwing open the Taurus passes for his further advance. His refusal to let his troops plunder Tyana (although he had promised them this privilege) created an excellent local impression, which prompted the Greek cities ahead of his line of march to submit. In 276 Aurelian's successor Tacitus, after repelling the Goths, died at the city—apparently from natural causes—after which his brother or half-brother and praetorian prefect Florian declared himself emperor, but his own men deserted him three months later, in favor of Probus. Under a provincial reorganization by the eastern emperor Valens (371–72), Tyana became the capital of the province of Cappadocia Secunda.

Its principal surviving monument is a well-preserved aqueduct bringing water from a spring (Köşk Pınarı) adjoining a Neolithic settlement.

Typhon, River *see* Orontes

Tyras (Belgorod Dniestrovsky). A Greek city in the Ukraine (Soviet Union), twelve miles up the southwest bank of the Euxine (Black) Sea estuary of the river Tyras (Dniester), at a point where, in ancient times, an island apparently existed between two arms of the river, but was later submerged. Pliny the Elder mentions Ophiussa as an earlier designation of Tyras, but Ophiussa may, instead, have been a separate settlement on the island. The name of Tyras seems to be Thracian; but it was colonized by Miletus in Ionia (western Asia Minor) in the sixth century BC. Finds testify to commercial relations not only with native tribes in the hinterland but with other Euxine Greek cities, and with centers as far afield as Athens.

One of the successors of Alexander the Great, Lysimachus, coined at Tyras toward the end of the fourth century, and the city later began to issue coins of its own, of which our knowledge has been greatly increased by a recently discovered hoard from Dorotskoye; half-a-dozen Greek goddesses are portrayed. Destroyed by the Getae in the mid-first century, Tyras was rebuilt and resumed monetary issues from the later first century AD, with the heads of Roman emperors. In the following century the place formed an advance outpost of the Roman province of Dacia, protected by a garrison of legionary detachments. However, its local coinage came to an end in the reign of Severus Alexander (222–35), when further destruction was suffered at the hands of the Goths.

Although the ancient town is concealed by thick medieval strata, excavations have brought to light stretches of Hellenistic and Roman walls, as well as remains of private dwellings that date from the third century BC onward and include rows of houses of the second century AD, flanking a broad street. On the opposite (northeast) bank of the Dniester estuary stood another town, Niconium (Roxolanskoye), occupied between the fifth and third centuries BC and again in Roman times. Half-a-dozen additional native and Greek sites have been located beside the river mouth.

Tyre, Tyrus, Tyros (Es-Sur). A coastal city of Phoenicia (Lebanon). Tyre lay a few hundred yards from the mainland on the two largest of a chain of rocky islands, which its King Hiram (*c* 970–936 BC) joined together by an embankment and linked to the coast by a mole, thus forming two excellent harbors, offering sheltered anchorage whatever the wind; the northern (Sidonian) harbor was protected by the island chain, and connected by a canal with the other (Egyptian) harbor, which was artificial. At this period Tyre and Sidon (Saida) were the principal agents of the great Phoenician burst of maritime commercial exploration. It was Tyre that founded Carthage, traditionally in 814. Greek mythology honored its monarchs Agenor (alternatively named as a king of Sidon), and his sons Cadmus, Cilix and Phoenix, who supposedly established colonies far and wide (including Thebes in Boeotia); Europa, said to have borne Zeus children in Crete and to have married the island's king, was believed to have been their sister.

The long and complex history of Tyre involved disturbed relationships with the successive dominant near-eastern powers, Assyria, Babylonia and Achaemenid Persia. During the fourth century (at the latest) its people combined with those of Sidon and Aradus (Tartus) to found Tripolis (Tripoli, Tarabulus-Esh-Sham). In 332 Tyre capitulated to Alexander the Great after a famous siege, but was rebuilt and repeopled by his orders, and subsequently became a satellite of the Ptolemies, at first under its own native monarchs, and then (from 274) with a republican constitution. In 210 the city passed into Seleucid hands, and later dated an era of civic autonomy from 126/25. In 64/63 it became part of the new Roman province of Syria.

During the early Principate Tyre, although deprived of its freedom by Augustus, not only possessed a very large territory, but ranked as one of the three or four major imperial Mediterranean ports, becoming the headquarters of Rome's eastern navy and the base of a major merchant fleet that maintained offices at Rome and Puteoli (Pozzuoli). According to a source cited by the geographer Ptolemy, it was trading with Lian-shu in China (by way of Kashgar, and probably through Persian agents) in AD 100. During the civil war beween Septimius Severus and Pescennius Niger (194), hoping to gain an advantage over its rival Berytus (Beirut), Tyre declared for Severus. This prompted Niger to burn many of its buildings, but Severus, after his victory, promoted it to be the capital of his new province of (Syria) Phoenice, drafting in settlers and conferring the rank of Roman colony *c* 201 (which appears to have been temporarily lost during the reigns of Elagabalus [218–22] and Severus Alexander [222–35]). Tyre was a center of philosophical and rhetorical studies (it was probably the birthplace of Porphyry [c. 232/3]), and became the seat of a bishop as early as the second century AD; Origen died there in 254/55.

Coins refer to the festivals of the Actia Heraclia, Heraclia Olympia and Actia Commodiana; and they also illustrate a lavish range of local mythological traditions, as well as depicting temples of Melkart (Heracles) and Ashtoreth (Astarte-Tyche) and portable shrines fitted with carry-bars. The agora of Roman times has been located, in addition to a colonnaded main street, theater and hippodrome; a large triumphal arch of late second-century date has been partly restored, and mosaic pavements of the following century are now to be seen. Air photography and land and underwater investigation have revealed extensive remains of both harbors, and the walls of the city are shown to have possessed towers of considerable size. Recent excavations have uncovered an early Christian chapel containing a bust of the Virgin carrying the infant Jesus.

Tzirallum (Sinekli, Çorlu). A Roman post station in Thrace (European Turkey), north of Heraclea (the former Perinthus, now Marmaraereğlisi), near the river Arzus (Çorlu); during the later empire the place formed part of the province of Europa. In AD 313 it gave its name to a major battle between Licinius and Maximinus II Daia, competing for the control of the eastern provinces (Constantine I the Great dominated the west). Licinius ruled in eastern Europe and Maximinus in Asia. Before the coming of spring, however, Maximinus advanced by forced marches through Asia Minor, leading an army 70,000 strong, and crossed the Thracian Bosphorus, compelling Byzantium (İstanbul) to capitulate.

Thereupon Licinius moved from Mediolanum (Milan) to confront him, and the two armies encamped three miles apart near Tzirallum and Drizipara. Maximinus offered a vow to Jupiter, and Licinius appealed to the 'Highest God,' in terms suggestive of a Christian interpretation. In the subsequent battle, which took place in a district known as Campus Serenus, the numerical superiority of Maximinus' force was cancelled by his soldiers' physical exhaustion, and they suffered a total defeat. He fled, disguised as a slave, and later in the year fell ill and died at Tarsus. The stage was now clear for the encounter between Constantine and Licinius which, eleven years later, placed the whole empire in the hands of the former.

U

Uğura *see* Olba

Ulpia Trajana *see* Sarmizegethusa

Umbria. A region of eastern Italy beyond the Apennines, including most of modern Umbria and extending northward to the Adriatic. It was bounded to the west by Etruria (across the Tiber), to the south by Sabine terrritory and to the east (toward the Adriatic) by Picenum and the Ager Gallicus, a coastal strip settled for a time by the Gauls as an extension of their dominions in northern Italy (Cisalpine Gaul).

The name 'Umbrians' was used very loosely and with a variety of meanings. Pliny the Elder states that they were said to be the most ancient race in Italy, attributing their Greek name *Ombrikoi* ('rainy') to survival from the primeval Flood. Although frequently engaged in hostilities against the Etruscan city-states, the Umbrians were nevertheless subject to strong Etruscan influences, as is evident from their art. Linguistic evidence shows that a non-Etruscan, Indo-European ('Umbrian') dialect was spoken at Iguvium (Gubbio) *c* 400 BC. The Umbrians, who were subdivided into tribes as well as into townships, made only insignificant attempts to help the Samnites against encroachment by the Romans, who built the Via Flaminia through their country in 220, and in 200 gave them part of the reconquered Ager Gallicus. During the Social War (91–87), in which Rome's Italian allies revolted, they were late in assisting the rebels, and quickly made peace with the Romans.

Under Augustus (31 BC–AD 14), Umbria and the Ager Gallicus constituted the Sixth Region of Italy, and in the later empire there was a district or province of Tuscia et Umbria (later Tuscia Suburbicaria), including the western portion of Umbria, while its eastern part belonged to the district of Flaminia et Picenum Annonarium. The principal products of Umbria, grown in its fertile Apennine valleys, were olives, vines and cereals (spelt), while the higher country contained the finest wild boars of the peninsula. *See also* Ager Gallicus, Asisium, Iguvium, Interamna Nahars, Narnia, Sentinum, Spoletium.

Umm Keis *see* Gadara

Uranopolis, Ouranopolis ('City of Heaven'). A Greek town in Chalcidice (Macedonia, northern Greece), on the isthmus leading to the peninsula of Acte (Mount Athos). The site of the settlement is uncertain; but it is known to have been founded *c* 316 BC by Alexarchus, son of Antipater and brother of Cassander, who were among the successors of Alexander the Great.

The settlers, who described themselves as Uranidae, issued a brief series of silver coins depicting the enthroned goddess Aphrodite Urania on one side, and the sun—sometimes associated with the moon and five stars—on the other. Alexarchus assumed the name of 'Helios' (the sun-god), and called his colonists *heliokrateis,* subjects of the sun, evidently under the influence of Utopian conceptions currently emanating from the legends inspired by Alexander's career. Prompted by the spirit of cosmopolitanism that accompanied such ideas, Alexarchus also endeavored to introduce a special language, of which Athenaeus gives examples. The fate of the settlement is unknown. (The modern Ouranoupoli [Prosfori, Pyrgos], founded by refugees from Cappadocia [central Asia Minor] in AD 1923, in a wide bay dotted with wooded islets, appears to stand on the site not of ancient Uranopolis but of another township named Dion.)

Urfa *see* Edessa

Urso, Ursao (Osuna). A city in southern Spain (Baetica), of Iberian origin. During the Second Punic War, the Roman generals Cnaeus and Publius Cornelius Scipio (uncle and father of Scipio Africanus the Elder) spent the winter of 211/210 at Urso and Castulo (Cazlona), and it was at Urso in 145/44 that Quintus Fabius Maximus Aemilianus, during the war against the nationalist Viriathus, concentrated his troops. Three of Urso's citizens were Viriathus' close friends and negotiators, but under Roman influence he put them to death. During the civil war between Julius Caesar and Sextus Pompeius (younger son of Pompey the Great)—whose quaestor Lucius Appuleus Decianus issued coinage at the town—it was stormed by Caesar (45), who planned the replacement of its population by a colony of ex-soldiers, under the name of Colonia Genetiva Julia Urbanorum; the settlement was probably undertaken in the following year, after his death.

The colony of Urso stood at the meeting point of north-south and east-west routes. Five out of an original nine bronze sheets inscribed with Caesar's colonial charter have survived (although the inscriptions themselves date from the Flavian period, AD 69–96), and can be seen at Madrid's Archaeological Museum; they cast exceptionally valuable light on Roman administrative arrangements in Spain. In 309 a bishop of Urso took part in the Council of Illiberis (Elvira). Parts of the city wall survived until 1932, and remains of houses and floor mosaics (including one depicting the Greek river Achelous surrounded by nymphs) have been unearthed.

Uselis *see* Sardinia

Üsküb *see* Prusias on the Hypius

Üsküdar *see* Chrysopolis

Utica (Bordj bou Chateur). A coastal city in north Africa (Tunisia), thirty miles northwest of Carthage. Although now lying six miles inland, in ancient times it stood on a promontory at the mouth of the river Bagradas (Medjerda), and possessed a port. Traditionally the oldest Phoenician settlement in north Africa, it was outstripped by Carthage, but remained the second center of the Carthaginian homeland. At the end of the Second Punic War Utica was besieged by Scipio Africanus the Elder (204), but in the Third War supported the Numidian King Masinissa against Carthage (149). After the fall of Carthage (146), it was rewarded with some of the conquered city's lands, and became the capital of the new Roman province of Africa and the residence of numerous Italian financiers and businessmen.

In 81, during the civil war between Sulla and the followers of Marius, Utica became the base of Pompey the Great's campaign against the followers of Marius in Africa. In 46 it sided with the Pompeians against Julius Caesar and after their defeat was the scene of the famous suicide of the younger Cato, who in consequence was known as *Uticensis.* Although made to suffer severely for this allegiance—and dealt a severe blow by the refoundation of Carthage—the Uticans received the status of a Roman *municipium* from Octavian (the future Augustus) in 36, and under Hadrian (AD 117–38) gained colonial rank, which was confirmed by Septimius Severus (193–211). Their maritime trade suffered from the silting up of their port, but intensified agricultural activities provided partial compensation.

The basic features of the Roman Republican city can be traced, but under the Principate more elaborate development took place. Two theaters were constructed, as well as large baths at the foot of the hill, and extensive cisterns fed by an aqueduct. On the south side of the colonnaded, hundred-and-twenty-foot wide, main street (partly built over a Carthaginian cemetery, and bordering the Roman forum), extended a residential district containing a number of important houses erected in the time of Severus and frequently altered and restored in later periods. Shops are also to be seen, and the conversion of one of the private dwellings into a grain store, during the fourth century, perhaps indicates a deterioration in the living standards of the local ruling class. The locations of the Capitolium and of temples of Apollo and Jupiter (mentioned by Pliny the Elder and Plutarch respectively) still present problems of identification.

Uxellodunum (generally identified, despite dissenting opinions, with Saint-Denis-lès-Martel and Vayrac). A fortress in Gaul, on the isolated plateau of Le Puy d'Issolu (northern Dordogne), which had been occupied since Neolithic times. Uxellodunum was the scene of the last nationalist stand during Julius Caesar's invasion of Gaul (51 BC). Two thousand men of the Gallic armies, when he had defeated elsewhere, fled south and occupied the hill, which Caesar besieged. One of their leaders, Drappes, starved himself to death, and his colleague Lucterius was betrayed to the Romans, but the blockade dragged on until Caesar succeeded in diverting the single spring from which the members of the garrison derived its water supply. This loss compelled them to surrender, and Caesar ordered their hands to be cut off as a warning to other Gauls who might be contemplating continued resistance.

Uzuncaburç *see* Olba

V

Vaison *see* Vasio Vocontiorum

Valchetta (River) *see* Cremera

Valentia (Valence). A city in Gallia Narbonensis (Drôme, southern France), beside the river Rhodanus (Rhône), just north of its confluence with the Isara (Isère). Formerly a town of the Segovellauni, Valentia became a Roman colony under Julius Caesar or Augustus, and was situated at the point where the road from north to south built by the latter's general Marcus Agrippa was met by a highway leading in an easterly direction toward Italy. In the later empire, when Valentia belonged to the province of Viennensis, its first Christian bishop was Saint Aemilian (AD 362–74).

During the usurpation of Constantine III in the western provinces (407), Sarus, a Gothic general of the western emperor Honorius, besieged but failed to capture the city, which (according to Zosimus) was relieved by another German general, Gerontius, acting on the pretender's behalf. After the fall of Constantine III a further usurper, Jovinus, fled from the Visigoth Ataulf (who at this juncture supported the central Roman government) and took refuge in Valentia, which underwent a second siege and fell, whereupon Jovinus was captured and executed at Narbo (Narbonne). In 440 the western Roman general Aetius, as Prosper records, settled a colony of barbarians (Alans) at Valentia, and in 451 they agreed to admit Attila the Hun within the walls; after his defeat on the Campi Catalaunii, however, he withdrew from the town and from Gaul. In 473/4 Valentia was one of the cities ravaged by King Euric after his declaration of an independent Visigothic state.

The old quarter of the modern town retains the outline of the ancient grid plan, and remains of the walls and of a theater and amphitheater (?) have come to light. A cruciform Christian baptistery, built in the fourth century round an octagonal pool, was adorned with mosaics *c* 500 and subsequently converted into a chapel.

Valentia (Valencia). A city on the eastern coast of Nearer Spain (Hispania Citerior, later Tarraconensis) beside the mouth of the river Turis (Turia). Originally a Greek settlement, Valentia later became Carthaginian. Although alternative locations have been suggested, this is probably the Valentia at which, according to Livy, Decimus Junius Brutus planted the former soldiers of Rome's nationalist enemy Viriathus in 138 BC; whereupon the town issued its own bronze coinage until the following century.

Its citizens subsequently supported Quintus Sertorius in his revolt against the central government. After heavy fighting in the area, the town was captured from his lieutenants by Pompey the Great in 75; but the conquest of the fertile adjoining plain long eluded him. Although the sources are conflicting, Valentia seems to have become a Roman colony, perhaps *c* 60, serving as an important station on the coastal road between Carthago Nova (Cartagena) and Tarraco (Tarragona). The prosperity of the town, however, dates from Augustus, who confirmed its colonial status. In the third century AD it replaced Saguntum (Saguntum) as the most important center between the rivers Iberus (Ebro) and Sucro (Jucar). In 413 it passed into Visigothic hands. Fragments of ancient buildings are incorporated in later churches, and finds of Roman Republican objects appear at a depth of twelve feet beneath the modern surface.

Vani *see* Colchis

Varna *see* Odessus

Vasio Vocontiorum (Vaison-la-Romaine). A city in southern Gaul (Vaucluse, southern France), on a hill beside the left (north) bank of the Ouvèze, a tributary of the Rhodanus (Rhône), thirteen miles from Arausio (Orange). Vasio was the capital of the tribe of the Vocontii, who were defeated by the Roman generals Marcus Fulvius Flaccus and Gaius Sextius Calvinus in 124/23 BC. After incorporation in the province of Gallia Narbonensis (121), a rebellion was harshly put down by Manius Fonteius (74–72), defended by Cicero in one of his speeches. Subsequently, perhaps under Julius Caesar, the town received the privileged rank of a treaty state (*civitas foederata*).

By the initiative of Augustus and Agrippa, the site was transferred from the left to the right bank of the Ouvèze *c* 20/19. The city's most famous son was Nero's tutor and adviser Sextus Afranius Burrus (d. AD 62). Earlier in the same century Mela had described the city as prosperous, since although it was small, and its geographical position peripheral—the religious center (Lucus Augusti) lay further to the north—local production of wine, oil and grain was very abundant. A bishop of Vasio was present at church congresses in 314 and 439, and another is recorded in 475. In 442 a regional council was held in the town.

Roman Vasio, on its picturesque site, has been described as the Pompeii of Provence. Prolonged excavations have been conducted in two quarters, Puymin and La Villasse. Puymin proves to be the site of the military headquarters (*praetorium*), decorated by brightly colored wall paintings; the so-called Portico of Pompey is a garden, about one hundred and seventy square feet, presented to the city by a local official and priest of Rome and Augustus, the grandson of a Gaul who had been granted citizenship by Pompey the Great. A *nymphaeum* (fountain building) is linked by a tunnel to the (extensively restored) theater, which was adorned by a large collection of statues—now in the local museum—including representations of Tiberius (AD 14–37) and members of his family, and of Hadrian (117–38) and his wife Sabina (?), in addition to civic personages and various divinities.

Both Puymin and La Villasse display important remains of private houses, varying from luxurious elegance to more modest proportions, and La Villasse also contained a pagan basilica, with paintings on its walls and a polychrome marble pavement. Recent excavations have uncovered another residence (the Peacock Villa), as well as baths and a business quarter. Eventually some or all of the inhabitants moved back to their original hill.

Vatzindro *see* Buthrotum

Vayrac *see* Uxellodunum

Veii (Veio). A city in southeastern Etruria (now Lazio), situated on a broad plateau consisting of two ridges and a southern outcrop (the acropolis), and surrounded on three sides by steep cliffs descending to the river Cremera (Valchetta, a tributary of the Tiber)—which was still navigable in antiquity—and to one of its tributaries. Although objects of the second millennium BC have been found, permanent settlement only seems to have been established after 1000, when three, four or even five villages existed on the site, each with its own cemetery.

These villages coalesced into a city between 750 and 700. Its creation and development, reaching a climax after 600 when Veii was second only to Rome as an urban center in non-Greek Italy, received a strong stimulus from its geographical location at the southeastern extremity of Etruria, which prompted the Greek traders at Pithecusae (Ischia) and Cuma (Cumae), and elsewhere in Campania, to regard the place as a natural intermediary with other metal-rich Etruscan cities further north. From the seven main gates of Veii an elaborate system of routes radiated outward. The wealth of its agricultural resources provided a massive income, enhanced by extremely skillful irrigation, to which an abundance of artificial, rock-cut arched drainage channels (*cuniculi*) still testifies. Vital revenue was also derived from the highly productive salt beds at the mouth of the Tiber, which, as Dionysius of Halicarnassus records, the Veientines controlled.

Yet this salt was also the cause of eventual friction with Rome, which was far too close for comfort—only just across the Tiber in Latium. Indeed, Veii even had a left-bank outpost of its own, Fidenae (*qv*), only five miles north of Rome itself. During Rome's regal period relations between the two cities were generally friendly, but after the fall of its Etruscan monarchy, their competing claims to salt beds and commercial markets soon led to serious tension. The people of Veii repulsed a Roman attack on Fidenae *c* 477/75, but lost the outpost in 435/425.

Then a new king—who had restored the Veientine monarchy after a brief interruption—strengthened the natural defences of the site; and in the last decade of the century, the Romans moved to the attack. Their siege, conducted with forces of unprecedented dimensions on either side, was believed to have continued for ten years; and it may well, as a matter of historical fact, have lasted for at least six or seven. It concluded with the city's capture by the Roman general Camillus, who may not, indeed, have destroyed the place as completely as tradition records, but abolished its existence as an independent state. The other Etruscan states had done little or nothing to help their compatriots, and within hardly more than a century, they, too, had been reduced to subjection by Rome. The construction of the Via Cassia in the second century passed Veii by; but a small town continued to exist beside a local crossroads.

The tombs adjoining the earliest habitation center had been reached by staircases with niches cut into the walls; the Tomb of the Ducks, of late seventh-century date, is the oldest painted grave that has hitherto come to light in Etruria. In addition to the cemeteries, however, there is also archaeological evidence (which is somewhat scarce in Etruscan cities) from the area in which the Veientines lived. This comprised a number of right-angled main thoroughfares on the Greek model juxtaposed with narrow, crooked streets containing modest houses of sun-dried brick and timber constructed on stone foundations.

The acropolis (Piazza d'Armi), at the southern end of the plateau, displays the remains of the earliest of the five temples so far identified at Veii, dating from the mid-sixth century BC. Of more impressive dimensions is the triple shrine dedicated to Menrva (Athena, Minerva) *c* 520/500, within the Portonaccio sanctuary area outside the walls. On its central beam were perched large terracotta statues, including the famous Apulu (Apollo) of Veii preserved in the Villa Giulia Museum at Rome, based on Greek models but, like all the finest Etruscan sculpture, injecting an element that is alien to Hellenism. At this time Veii was the leading artistic center of southern Etruria. The most famous local sculptor was Vulca, who may have had a workshop in Rome; the Apollo of Veii was perhaps a product of his school.

Inscriptions relating to the diminished Veii of subsequent Roman times bear witness to a theater, a bathing establishment, a building connected with a corporation (*collegium*), and a Porticus Augusta, to which colossal heads of Augustus (31 BC–AD 14) and Tiberius (AD 14–37), now in the Vatican Museum, may have belonged.

Velcha *see* Vulci

Velestino *see* Pherae

Velia *see* Elea

Velitrae (Velletri). An ancient city of Latium (Lazio, western Italy), on a spur of Mount Artemisio, dominating the gap between the Alban Hills—of which it lay on the southern rim—and the mountains of the Volsci: it was they who founded or occupied the settlement, under the name of Velester (although this name has also been believed to suggest an Etruscan link). According to Livy, Velitrae received a Latin colony (founded by the Latin League, to which it belonged, in concert with the Romans) in 494 BC, after its inhabitants' defeat by the consul Publius Verginius; and a further batch of colonists was introduced *c* 404.

After the Romans had defeated the Latins in 338 the town was annexed by the victors, who destroyed its walls, deported its senate, and distributed its lands among new Roman settlers. In the third century, as an inscription indicates, the Volscian language (related to Umbrian) was still spoken at Velitrae; but further settlers followed, under a Lex Sempronia. Wine production flourished at the place. It was the native city of the wealthy knight (*eques*) Gaius Octavius, the father of Augustus, praetor in 61 BC. Velitrae received a new draft of veteran immigrants under Claudius (AD 41–54) and became a Roman colony.

The site has yielded richly decorated terracotta architectural features from an early temple (very similar to other such objects found at Rome and Veii). Shrines of Apollo, Sancus, Fortuna and Diva Declona are recorded, in addition to a basilica, theater and amphitheater. Finds in the neighborhood include a large variety of statues which presumably belonged to the villas of rich Romans. Burials range from the Early Iron Age to the Christian period.

Venosa *see* Venusia

Venta Belgarum (Winchester). A town in southern Britannia (Hampshire, England). Venta was a stronghold of the Belgae before Roman rule, and became (or remained) their capital after annexation (AD 43–48). The Belgic earthworks were replaced by new earth and timber defences *c* AD 70. A street grid was laid out some twenty years later, and the next decade witnessed the construction of a forum and other public buildings. During the centuries that followed, the simple timber houses were replaced by more elaborate dwellings with mosaic pavements. In the latter part of the second century, and again after 200 when Venta Belgarum belonged to the province of Upper Britain, its defences were reconstructed, and further rebuilding followed, probably after the suppression of the usurper Allectus by Constantius I. This is probably the Venta described in the *Notitia Dignitatum* as the location of an imperial weaving works. Soon after the mid-fourth century, finds suggest the immigration of German mercenaries (*foederati*), and a second wave of immigrants appeared after 400; their descendants formed the nucleus of medieval Winchester.

Venta Icenorum (Caistor-by-Norwich, near Caistor St. Edmund). A town in eastern Britannia (Norfolk, England) on the east bank of the river Tas; the capital of the British tribe of the Iceni under Roman rule. The position of their privious capital is unknown, but after the suppression of the revolt of Boudicca (Boadicea) in AD 61 they were resettled *c* 70 at Venta, which became their administrative center and market town.

A grid pattern of streets was laid down, and during the reign of Hadrian, *c* 125, a forum, basilica, public baths and new houses were constructed, and a pottery industry developed. In the third century, when Venta Icenorum came within Septimius Severus' province of Upper Britain, massive town walls were constructed. Twenty feet high and eleven feet thick, they are studded with towers and backed by an earthen bank and ditch; these fortifications, which perhaps date to *c* AD 369, enclosed an area of thirty-five acres, and reduced the size of thc town by about a quarter. Two Romano-Celtic temples of the early third century have been identified. Thirty-six human skulls found with other bones in the ruins of a room burned down at the end of the fourth century have been tentatively associated with an uprising by German immigrants enrolled as mercenary soldiers (*foederati*) of whom there is evidence in a local cemetery.

Venta Silurum (Caerwent). A town in eastern Britannia (Gwent, South Wales). The capital of the British tribe of the Silures, a tribe that resisted Roman annexation until its conquest by Sextus Julius Frontinus in AD 74. The Romans refounded the settlement later in the same century, and a bank and ditch surrounded it before 130. Stone walls were built *c*200 (when the city belonged to the province of Upper Britain) and polygonal bastions added after 340; this is the finest surviving stretch of town defences in Britain. Opposite the forum and pagan basilica stood the principal baths; in addition, there was a second bathing establishment, a late amphitheater, and two Romano-British temples. Numerous houses have also been excavated, ranging from modest dwellings, associated with shops, to courtyard mansions decorated with wall paintings and floor mosaics and equipped with heating arrangements (hypocausts).

During the later empire, Venta Silurum served, together with a late fort at Cardiff, as a strong point in the defence of the Bristol Channel against sea-rovers. It seems to have been some of these raiders, however—probably originating from Hibernia (Ireland)—who were responsible for the destruction of the fortress *c* 440.

Ventotene *see* Pandateria

Venusia (Venosa). A Samnite and then a Roman town in the interior of southern Italy, on the borders of Apulia and Lucania; it was subsequently reckoned as part of Apulia (and is now in Basilicata). Venusia stood on a strong and defensible ridge—surrounded on three sides by deep ravines—and dominated the upper valley of the Aufidus (Ofanto), the largest river in the southern part of the peninsula. Extensive material from Palaeolithic times is preserved in the local museum.

In 292 BC, toward the end of the Third Samnite War, the Romans captured the place, and in the following year established a Latin colony there, so as to split the Samnite tribe of the Hirpini from the related Lucani to their south, while at the same time placing an obstacle in the way of the expansion of the Greek city of Taras (Tarentum, Taranto). Although the colonists at Venusia cannot have been nearly as many as the 20,000 indicated by Dionysius of Halicarnassus, they were numerous, and indeed this was the largest colony in the Roman world. It became a military fortress and an important station on the Via Appia, Rome's principal road to the south. In 280 BC the town provided refuge to survivors from a Roman army after its defeat by Pyrrhus of Epirus at Heraclea (Policoro), and in 216, during the Second Punic War, it performed the same function after Hannibal's victory at Cannae (216). It was also in this neighborhood that Marcus Claudius Marcellus was ambushed and killed in 208, and Hannibal, too, suffered a defeat not far off.

After the war, in 200, the colony was reinforced; but during the Social War (91–87), in which the Italian towns revolted against Rome, the town took the side of the rebels. It was the birthplace of the poet Horace (65), whose father, of slave origin, was a local auctioneer and small farmer. The triumvirs Antony, Octavian (the future Augustus) and Lepidus settled veterans on the site *c* 41. Excavations have revealed a bathing establishment of the time of Hadrian (AD 117–38), an amphitheater (used as a quarry), Jewish catacombs dating from the second to the sixth centuries, and, most recently, a three-naved Christian basilica of the time of Bishop Stephanus (489–504).

Verghina *see* Aegae

Verona A city in Gallia Cisalpina (north Italy), beside the river Athesis (Adige) on the route from the Brenner Pass to the south. The surrounding territory produced abundant wine. The Raetians, together with the Italic tribe of the Euganei, were described as the founders of Verona, and the existence in the region of a community named the Arusnates (possessing a cult of Cuslanus or Culsans) recalls the Etruscan family name Aruzinaie, and thus suggests that Etruscans played a part in the settlement. Celtic foundation by the Gallic tribe of the Cenomani was also claimed. Under Roman rule Verona was a prosperous trading town and station on the Via Postumia running from east to west across Cisalpine Gaul (148 BC).

It was the birthplace of the poet Catullus (*c* 87BC), whose family was of some standing in the region. His description of the city as a 'colonia' refers to the Latin status (conferring Roman citizenship on local officials) that was enjoyed by the Transpadane area in 89 and only replaced by full Roman franchise in 49 (prior to incorporation in Italy seven years later). Verona played a leading part in the civil war of AD 69 between the supporters of Vitellius and Vespasian, when its fortifications were strengthened. In 249 the emperor Philip and his son were killed by the troops of their successor Trajanus Decius in a great battle outside the walls. During the sole reign of Gallienus (260–68) it was elevated to the rank of a Roman colony and incorporated into his new defensive system for the protection of Italy.

In the later empire, the city was part of the province or district of Venetia et Histria within the administrative diocese of Italia Annonaria. When Constantine I the Great invaded Italy in 312 to suppress Maxentius, the latter stationed a force at Verona, under the experienced Ruricius Pompeianus, in order to defend the Brenner Pass in case Licinius should decide to join his colleague Constantine in the invasion; but after a fierce battle Pompeianus was killed, and

Verona capitulated to Constantine. In 403 the Visigothic army of Alaric delivered an attack, but was defeated by the emperor Honorius' general Stilicho, and evacuated Italy for a time. Verona suffered from the invasion of Attila the Hun in 452, and in 489 after the fall of the western empire, was the scene of the decisive victory of Theoderic the Ostrogoth over Odoacer the Herulian, followed by extensive reconstruction of its buildings.

The pre-Roman fortress was later linked with the town by a bridge, which is partly preserved. Well-preserved Roman monuments include a riverside theater, a huge and famous amphitheater (the Arena), partly of the first century AD —preserved because of a thirteenth-century endowment for its maintenance. Portions of the city walls, the base of a Capitolium, a basilica, the first century Arch of the Gavii (a leading local family), and two city gates (the Porta dei Leoni and Porta dei Borsari), have also survived. The Christian basilica of San Zeno Maggiore—the name of Verona's first important bishop—may go back to *c* 400; beneath it, an earlier church has recently been uncovered. The origins of the cruciform, aisleless church of Santo Stefano Maggiore go back to about 450, and the chapel of Saints Tosca and Teuteria beside the Church of the Holy Apostles seems to belong to the same century.

Verulamium (near St. Albans). A town in southeastern Britannia (Hertfordshire, England), situated beside the river Ver; a station on Watling Street, twenty-one miles northwest of Londinium (London). The name Verlamio appears on a coin of Tasciovanus (*c* 20 BC–AD 5), king of the Belgic tribe of the Catuvellauni, whose capital was at Prae Wood, a mile and a quarter to the west of the later city. Even after his son Cunobelinus moved his residence to Camulodunum, Verulamium remained important.

When the Romans established the province of Britannia, a military post was established at the town (*c* AD 43/44), and a civilian settlement was laid out on a regular grid plan, at the unusually early date of *c* 50; Verulamium probably received the rank of *municipium* at this time. It suffered destruction during the revolt of the Iceni under Boudicca (Boadicea), but was restored by Tacitus' father-in-law Cnaeus Julius Agricola (*c* 79). About 155, however, during the reign of Antoninus Pius, it was burned down once more, and again reconstructed, with new fortifications that were renewed at several later dates. St. Alban was executed at Verulamium, probably under Septimius Severus (193–211) or Trajanus Decius (249–51), becoming, according to tradition, the first Christian martyr in Roman Britain.

Verulamium provides our fullest information about urban life in this country. The early Roman earth and timber rampart and ditch, and the defences that were erected at various dates after the second century destruction, can be seen at a number of points. The forum and pagan basilica (completed in 79) lie beneath St. Michael's Church, and a food market (*macellum*) and two temples were added soon afterward. Beside a theater—originally almost circular in form, corresponding with the 'cockpit' or 'theater-amphitheater' tradition of northern Gaul—it has been possible to trace the outlines of early houses and shops, destroyed by Boudicca; timber restorations were undertaken *c* 130, and the conflagration of *c* 155 was followed by rebuilding on a much grander scale.

Decay set in during the middle or later third century, but was followed by a revival soon afterward, at least in the southern residential quarter. The heating system (hypocaust) belonging to the bathing section of one of a number of palatial houses has been preserved, beneath a large mosaic pavement. A late fourth-century mansion, after a number of adaptations, was replaced by a large hall, which in turn collapsed and was cut through by a water pipe. Urban construction was still taking place *c* 370, and perhaps as late as *c* 450.

The first St. Michael's Church was probably erected at the place where St. Alban was believed to have been sentenced, but his principal shrine, the abbey on the opposite hill, marks the site of his execution. Recent excavations have reached the earliest foundations of this building. Saint Germanus, visiting the abbey in 429, found it still in existence, and it was here, after the original Verulamium became deserted not long afterward, that the medieval town of St. Albans sprang up subsequently, in connection with a revival of the martyr's cult.

Vesontio. Visontio, later Bisontii (Besançon). A town in eastern Gaul (Doubs, France), situated in a strong position at the foot of a citadel hill on a bend of the river Dubis (Doubs), a tributary of the Rhodanus (Rhône). Vesontio was the capital of the Celtic tribe of the Sequani. After the Roman conquest by Julius Caesar and subsequent reorganization by Augustus, the town probably came under the military command of Upper Germany, which was at first administratively attached to the province of Gallia Belgica. At Vesontio, the highway from Italy branched into roads leading to Lugdunum (Lyon), Andematunum (Langres) and the Rhine.

In AD 21 the Sequani joined the Gallic revolt of Florus and Sacrovir against Tiberius and in 68, under Nero, they supported the rebellion of Gaius Julius Vindex, who was defeated at Vesontio by Lucius Verginius Rufus, commander in Upper Germany, and committed suicide. Under Domitian, *c* 90, the city became part of an Upper German province, and in the later empire was the capital of the province of Maxima Sequanorum. By the mid-fourth century its fortunes were declining.

An elaborate commemorative arch (the Porte Noire) of about the time of Marcus Aurelius (161–80) marks the entrance of the main road from Italy that became the city's principal street, leading to a forum and Capitolium. Inscriptions and sculptures bear witness to cults of Mercurius Cissonius, the Matronae, and a god carrying a hammer. The remains of baths and of houses with floor mosaics have been uncovered, and beside the road to Lugdunum stood an amphitheater.

Vesuvius *see* Herculaneum, Oplontis, Pompeii, Stabiae

Vetera, Castra Vetera (Xanten). A Roman stronghold near the lower course of the Rhenus (Rhine), opposite its confluence with the Luppia (Lippe). Under Augustus, before 12 BC, a camp (Vetera I) was established for a legion on the Fürstenberg hill near Birten—a mile and a half southwest of the Rhine, and a mile south of Xanten—forming part of the Lower German command, which was at first attached, for administrative purposes, to Gallia Belgica, and later became a separate province.

The camp was reconstructed by Tiberius, Claudius and Nero; these buildings, constructed of stone, housed two legions. In the Gallo-German revolt of AD 69 Vetera was besieged by the rebels; its garrison—after destroying the adjacent civilian quarter to prevent its employment as enemy cover—was starved into surrender and then massacred. The camp was subsequently reconstructed on a site a little to the northeast, nearer the Rhine (Vetera II), which accommodated one legion and remained under occupation until *c* 260/270; it may subsequently have been refortified by Julian the Apostate (361-63), when the region formed part of the province of Germania Secunda.

On the northwestern outskirts of the modern Xanten was a civilian settlement to which Tiberius, before AD 20, had transported the German tribe of the Sugambri from the other (east) bank of the Rhine. This settlement was promoted to colonial rank by Trajan (98-117), under the name of Colonia Ulpia Trajana, and received new buildings. It existed until the fourth or fifth century, when archaeological evidence points to a violent end.

The administrative headquarters (*principia*) of Vetera I, shared by both the legions that were in the camp at the time, has been revealed by excavations and air photography (employing a linear filter). The *principia* were flanked by the residences of the two legionary commanders (*praetoria*); these buildings (one of which is exceptionally well-preserved) were planned around a central court, with a large dining room and offices. The camp hospital (*valetudinarium*) possessed its own bathing establishment, a casualty reception center, and a room equipped with small hearths that may have been used for sterilizing instruments. The main street of the camp was colonnaded.

Vetera II was destroyed by the flooding of a branch of the Rhine in the early Middle Ages. Recent excavations have noted five main phases of timber construction of varying types, dating from Tiberius to Trajan. The Trajanic colony possessed a wall enclosing an area of two hundred and five acres and perforated by at least eight gates or doors. The layout of the town was regular, but not entirely symmetrical. Two temples have been located, in addition to large baths, an extensive wrestling school, warehouses, shops, an amphitheater, and riverside harbor installations.

Vetulonia (in Etruscan, Vetluna or Vatluna). A city in western Etruria. Situated within a bend of the river Bruna and its tributaries, the habitation center stood on a hill 1,130 feet above sea level, protected by steep cliffs on three sides and overlooking a fertile territory. In the ancient epoch Lake Prilius (now drained, but at that time open to the Tyrrhenian Sea through deep, partly man-made entrances), into which the rivers Bruna and Umbro (Ombrone) discharged (unless their link with the lagoon was by means of canals), came very close to the southeastern walls of the settlement. The discovery of two groups of cemeteries indicates that two separate villages had stood on the site in the early first millennium BC, when the area was already densely populated. Another settlement existed on the shores of Lake Accesa (a little to the northwest), which was on the outskirts of the rich copper- and iron-bearing Massetano zone. It was these metals which gave the villages their wealth, and caused them to amalgamate into a city and city-state shortly before 600.

Already by that time Vetulonia possessed a native school of large stone statuary that was rare in Etruria; the sculptors displayed direct or indirect eastern influences. During the century that followed, local craftsmen produced abundant, fine-quality bronze work and magnificent jewelry, made of gold that was mostly imported from Greek Campania in exchange for Etruscan copper. At the same time, too, the city seems to have reached the climax of its political power. To judge from finds, its territory reached, to the southeast, as far as the river Albinia (Albegna)—which was at that time navigable—and included quite important towns on the sites of Marsiliana and Ghiaccio Forte. The river Umbro, together with its tributary the Orcia, opened up contacts not only with Etruscan Clusium (Chiusi) but also with the far north, from which amber of Baltic origin came to Vetulonia while its goods were found from the Baltic to the Danube, and in southeastern France. And the influence of the city spread toward the south as well, for discoveries of its artifacts at Politorium (Castel di Decima) in Latium lend plausibility to Silius Italicus' assertion that the insignia worn by Roman officials had originated from Vetulonia.

Moreover, the objects in its cemeteries showed that its inhabitants possessed not only important land links but a significant overseas maritime commerce as well. In particular, a vital early contact with Sardinia is evident. Vetulonia, on its adjacent hillsides, possessed timber to make ships, and on the sea lagoon Lake Prilius, it had its own harbors at Badiola del Fango and elsewhere. Populonia, too, before becoming a city-state on its own account, seems to have been a dependency of the Vetulonians, providing their links with the mining zone of the Campigliese and the no less metal-rich island of Ilva (Elba).

Vetulonia was also, in all probability, the founder of Rusellae (Roselle), just across the water of Lake Prilius. However, Rusellae also seems to have been the agent of its mother city's eclipse. The first signs of this decline were the destruction of Marsiliana and Ghiaccio Forte, before the middle of the sixth century. Then, between 550 and 500, Vetulonia itself seems to have flagged and succumbed to Rusellae, or at least to have been eliminated from power politics; although its eclipse was not total, as a recently discovered building of third-century date has confirmed. Subsequently the community survived as an insignificant Roman *municipium.*

Within the urban area of Etruscan Vetulonia, a winding ten-foot-wide main thoroughfare, crossed by smaller crooked streets, has come to light, together with the traces of square dwellings of modest and more ambitious dimensions, and a wall of polygonal stones enclosing a two-mile perimeter; while recent discoveries have included terracottas belonging to a sixth-century frieze or pediment. As elsewhere in Etruria, however, investigation of cemeteries has been far more productive than that of the residential zone. Already in the eighth century there were 'interrupted circle' tombs peculiar to the region, consisting of cylindrical pits (less often trenches) dug into the rock and grouped together within rings of stones. Next came 'white stone' tombs (in which the circle was continuous) containing either a single trench or two, one for the burial of the body and the other serving as a receptacle for the valuable objects interred to keep it company.

From *c* 700 the Vetulonian graves begin to be covered with great mounds, perhaps earlier than those found farther south, for example at Caere (Cerveteri). The chambers within these tombs possessed 'false domes,' of the type already seen in Populonia (*qv*), which had apparently borrowed the formula from Sardinia. A Vetulonian gravestone of late seventh- or early sixth-century date bears an incised figure named as Avle Feluske, who strides impressively in his crested helmet, carrying a round shield and brandishing a double axe, the symbol of power in the Mediterranean world since the previous millennium.

Victoria *see* Pinnata Castra

Vicus Fortunae *see* Poetovio

Vid *see* Narona

Vidin *see* Bononia (Upper Moesia)

Vienna (Vienne). A city in southern Gaul (Isère, France) on a bend of the river Rhodanus (Rhône), near its juncture with the Gère and the Gier on its left and right banks respectively, at a meeting point of east-west and north-south highways. The acropolis on the heights of Sainte-Blandine was the capital of the tribe of the Allobroges, whose annexation by Rome in 121 was accompanied by the creation of the province of Gallia Narbonensis; a tribal revolt in 62-61 was severely repressed. Julius Caesar (or as some believe Antony) settled veterans at Vienna, and probably conferred on it the rank of Latin colony (in which the elected officials became Roman citizens), but the city lost its privileges during the disturbances of subsequent years.

Augustus revived its fortunes, and full Roman citizenship, under the title of Colonia Julia Augusta Florentina, was conferred either by him or by Gaius (AD 37-41) or Claudius (41-54), who praised the colony's distinction in a speech to the senate in 47/8. When Vindex rose against Nero in 68, Vienna was the headquarters of the rebellion—in marked contrast to its always unfriendly neighbors, the people of Lugdunum (Lyon), who remained loyal to the emperor—and in the following year the town barely escaped destruction from Vitellius' general Valens during his advance through Gaul into Italy.

During the second century it reached the height of its prosperity, providing Rome with a number of consuls and other high officials. A persecution of the Christian community took place under Marcus Aurelius in 177. Vienna suffered in the German invasions of 275. But in the later empire it became the capital both of the province of Viennensis and of the administrative diocese of the Seven Provinces, to which that province belonged, and was the second city of the entire Gallo-German region after Treviri (Trier, formerly Augusta Trevirorum), until superseded by Arelate (Arles) at the end of the fourth century. The Rhône fleet was at Vienna *c* 440. It was there, in 411, that Constans II, joint usurper with his father Constantine III, was captured by their own former general Gerontius, and put to death. The place was occupied by the Burgundians *c* 460/68 and, according to Ammianus Marcellinus, became one of their principal centers until they succumbed to the Franks (534).

The first of Vienna's walls was built by Augustus *c* 16/15 BC; one of its gates is depicted on a contemporary local coin, behind the prow of a ship. After the German devastations of AD 275 a second wall was erected, enclosing a much smaller perimeter. A well-preserved temple of Augustus and Livia was dedicated in the emperor's lifetime, then rededicated by Claudius, and subsequently modified. Augustus' theater at Vienna (now restored), was the second largest in Gaul, after Augustodunum (Autun), accommodating between eleven and thirteen thousand spectators. Vienna also possessed a smaller, covered theater (Odeon), and a third theater, unique in Gaul, for the performance of Mystery plays in connection with the cult of the Magna Mater (Cybele), associated with a complex of other buildings relating to her worship.

A circus on the banks of the Rhône, south of the walls, was built of masonry soon after AD 100—probably replacing an earlier wooden structure—and is notable for a square-based pyramid constructed after 275 to adorn the center of the axial rib (*spina*). Vienna received water by way of at least ten aqueducts, five parallel to one another on the left (south) bank of the Gère; many traces of these structures still survive. A five-arched bridge linked the official section of the city on the left (east) bank of the Rhône with further zones on the opposite bank, comprising a large residential quarter, a commercial and industrial area, and harbor installations at Saint-Romain-en-Gal, shown by recent excavations to date back to the early first century AD.

Vienna *see* Vindobona

Viminacium (Kostolac). A city in Upper Moesia (Yugoslavia) on the right bank of the river Mlava, a channel of the Danube. Formerly a Celtic settlement, Viminacium became a Roman camp in the early first century AD, not long after the annexation of Moesia. It was garrisoned by a legion from 56/57, served as a base for the Danubian fleet, and became the headquarters of the emperor Trajan during his First Dacian War (102). The civilian settlement (*canabae*) attached to the camp became a *municipium* under Hadrian (117-38) and a Roman colony in 239, under Gordian III.

The strategic and commercial importance of the place at this juncture was indicated by the issue of an exceptionally abundant and widely circulating local coinage, dated by the years of the colony and extending from its foundation in 239 to the year 257, during the reign of Valerian, when disturbed conditions brought about the closure of the mint. In the later empire Viminacium was the capital of the province of Moesia Prima in the administrative diocese of Dacia. Its Christian bishop Amantius attended the Council of Serdica (Sofia) in 343. In 441, according to Priscus, the city was destroyed (or severely damaged) by Attila. Restored by Justinian I, it was obliterated by the Avars in 582.

Vindelicia *see* Raetia

Vindobona (Vienna). A city on the Danube in Pannonia (now the capital of Austria). In pre-Roman times it lay in the territory of a Celtic people, the Boii. After Roman annexation under Augustus, an auxiliary cavalry unit (*ala*) was stationed at Vindobona by Domitian (AD 81–96). At the beginning of Trajan's reign (98/100), a legion was moved to the camp, and later in the same reign was successively replaced by two others; meanwhile Pannonia had been subdivided into two, and Vindobona attached to the upper province. It became an important strong point, especially in the Marcomannic Wars of Marcus Aurelius (161–80), when its buildings were apparently destroyed and reconstructed. Aurelius is believed to have died there. A civilian town (*canabae*) to the southeast of the military settlement became a *municipium* sometime during the third century.

In the later empire, when Pannonia was divided into four provinces, Vindobona belonged to Pannonia Prima. During the fourth century a river fleet station was transferred to Vindobona (from Carnuntum [Petronell]), but *c* 395 part of its fortress was burned down, and early in the fourth century most, or all, of the site was abandoned. The medieval township did not develop from the *municipium,* but grew out of what remained of the earlier camp.

The plan of that camp is still partly recognizable from the configuration of the modern streets, on the plateau of the Hohe Markt. The stronghold was protected by dykes and linked to the military river harbor that lay to its north. The *principia* (administrative center), *praetorium* (commander's residence), barracks, military hospital, and bath buildings have been located. The last repairs were made by Valentinian I (364–75). It is hoped to unearth part of the civilian town in the neighborhood of the Aspang railway station.

Vindolanda (Chesterholm). A fort in northern Britannia (Northumberland, England). Founded by Cnaeus Julius Agricola as part of his (Stanegate) defence system *c* AD 80, Vindolanda was abandoned when the garrison was moved up to Hadrian's new Wall (122–26), but reoccupied under Antoninus Pius (*c* 163). During the reign of Septimius Severus (193–211) a new fort was laid out, facing south. This was completely rebuilt, in the reigns of Diocletian and Maximian, by their deputy (Caesar) Constantius I Chlorus (*c* 300)—who turned the stronghold around, so that it faced toward the north; and there were extensive repairs *c* 369. The garrison in the late first century may have been a part-mounted Dalmatian cohort, but in the third century it was furnished by a Gallic unit, which probably remained at Vindolanda for most of the fourth century as well.

The visible remains, covering three and a half acres, date from Constantius' reconstruction. In his *principia* (administrative headquarters) the *tribunal* and stone screens have been uncovered, as well as a pit for the storage of the military pay chests. During the late fourth century these *principia* were adapted to provide living accommodation and storehouses. In a substantial civilian settlement that grew up outside the walls of the fort, an inn for travellers (*mansio*) and a large bathing establishment have been uncovered; the baths were supplied with water by a stone conduit.

But the most important discoveries at Vindolanda are portions of wooden writing tablets found in 1973 on the pre-Hadrianic floor of a large wooden building, perhaps the *praetorium* (commander's residence). When photographed under infrared light, these pieces of wood revealed traces of writing. Some were thin slices inscribed with a quill or reed pen, dipped into a carbon-based ink; but most of the tablets were evidently thicker, and hollowed out to take a wax surface, on which the texts were written with iron stylus pens. The texts include both military documents—records of stores ordered or issued—and private correspondence, between the years 90 and 110: thus providing historical information about a place and period for which no literary evidence exists.

The soil conditions of Vindolanda have also enabled large quantities of leather to survive, including marching boots, sandals, women's slippers, whips, purses, hats and fragments of aprons, laces, the sides of tents, and horse harnesses—as well as the tools of the leather workers.

Vindonissa (Windisch). A Roman legionary camp in Upper Germany (now Switzerland), nine miles south of the river Rhenus (Rhine), at the confluence of the Aare, Reuss and Limmat. Its name indicates the presence of a pre-Roman town. Standing at a point where four roads met, Vindonissa housed a small Roman fort under Augustus, and was garrisoned by a legion from the reign of Tiberius (shortly after AD 16), which was replaced by another from 45/46 to 69 and then by a third until 101.

Thereafter, since the frontier had by this time been moved northward, only a legionary detachment remained, and the settlement assumed a civilian character, comprising a pair of communities (a *vicus* and *canabae*) that had grown up to the west and southeast of the camp respectively; for the protection of these two expanding centers the fortress was reconstructed *c* 260, under pressure from attacks by the Alamanni. In the later empire Vindonissa belonged to the province of Maxima Sequanorum. During the fourth century a smaller fortress was constructed just west of the earlier stronghold, on the spur between the Aare and the Reuss. The *Notitia Galliarum* describes this Castrum Vindonissense as a suffragan episcopal see (it later became a full bishopric). At this period, *c* 401, the garrison departed. But the civilian settlement continued to flourish.

The existence of a military center as early as the time of Augustus has been confirmed by recent excavations. Because of the nature of the ground, the subsequent legionary camp was of irregular, heptagonal shape. After two earlier periods of wooden construction, it was rebuilt in stone in 45/46–69. The remains of the ten-foot-thick walls, which were equipped with six towers, mostly date from after *c* 260, although one of the two main gates goes back to the later second century. These fortifications were flanked by double ditches. The rectangular *principia* (administrative headquarters), erected in 47 at an angle between the main streets, consists of two open courts divided by a wall. A basilica, barracks, officers' quarters, granary, storehouses and bathing establishment—adorned with wall paintings and floor mosaics—have also been located, as well as other buildings of which the identification is less certain. Outside the walls were a forum and amphitheater. From an adjoining refuse dump, employed by the garrison from *c* 30 to 100, materials such as wood, leather, ink and plants have survived in a good state of preservation (and can now be seen in the Vindonissa museum at Brugg). Thereafter, few new buildings dating from before the later empire are to be seen. The fourth-century fortress was surrounded by three concentric ditches, twenty-five feet in width. Numerous tombs of late imperial date, belonging to its occupants, have been found at Windisch-Oberburg.

Vinkovci *see* Cibalae

Vipaca, Vipacco (River) *see* Frigidus

Viroconium Cornoviorum (Wroxeter). A town in Britannia (Shropshire, western England), situated on the north-south highway, Watling Street, at the point where the river Sabrina (Severn) emerges from the foothills of Wales and turns southward toward its estuary in the Bristol Channel. On the summit of adjoining Wrekin Hill stood an important Iron Age fortress. After Roman annexation, Viroconium was strategically placed for operations against Caratacus, who had raised the Welsh tribes in revolt, and may have been occupied *c* 50 AD by Publius Ostorius Scapula, appointed to suppress him. A little later a legion was moved there, to constitute a garrison, and was replaced by another in 69.

Army units remained until *c* 90, when they departed (although perhaps a small detachment stayed on), whereupon Viroconium became a civilian city and the capital of the Cornovii. Benefiting from a visit in 122 by Hadrian (who upgraded the frontier towns), it formed one of the most important towns in Britain during the ensuing decades. At the time of the usurpation of Carausius (*c* 286), or shortly afterward, its buildings suffered destruction by fire; but life continued vigorously, in new forms and conditions, until the end of the western empire, or later; a tomb of the Irish chieftain Cunorix—presumably a mercenary employed to repel marauders—is dateable to the late fifth century. Soon afterward, the site was abandoned in favor of a smaller and more easily defensible location.

A stone rampart dates from the time of the legionary fortress (*c* 85). After the departure of the legion, work was begun on the construction of a large bathing establishment shortly before 100. But it was swept away in the time of Hadrian, and replaced by a spacious forum, surrounded by an aisled basilica and shops; an inscription records the dedication of the forum by the Cornovii in 129/130. After the middle of the century, perhaps following a fire (although the exact chronology is disputed), more elaborate new public baths, an enlarged shopping quarter, and a temple were constructed. Air photography has also shown a number of substantial private houses and an aqueduct. The latest excavations have concentrated on the site of a *macellum* (provision market). At the same time, it has become clear that the bath block and basilica were disused from the end of the second century, and later demolished in stages; although an earth rampart of later second century date, enclosing a perimeter of about two hundred acres, was augmented soon after 200 by a stone wall. About 400 all the flimsy timber structures of the area were destroyed, and massive new timber buildings, often of two storeys, were erected: it has been suggested that this drastic clearing and replanning operation, conducted in two successive phases, may have been organized by some chief seeking to establish his local power in the disturbed circumstances of the time.

Virunum (Zollfeld). A city in southern Noricum (Austria), near the river Glan, a tributary of the Drave. Strategically placed at the crossing of north-south and east-west routes, Virunum has a Celtic name but became a city of Roman type when Augustus abolished the kingdom of Noricum (*c* 15 BC). Under Claudius, who organized the territory into a province, Virunum replaced Noreia (on the Magdalensberg) as its principal town (AD 45), becoming the provincial capital and a *municipium,* in possession of extensive territory in Middle and Lower Carinthia. When Marcus Aurelius (161–80) established a legionary fortress at Lauriacum (Lorch) to deal with the Marcomanni, the capital was transferred to Ovilava, though the imperial finance agent (procurator) maintained his office at Virunum. Archaeological evidence suggests German devastation in the time of Gallienus (260–68).

After the province had subsequently been divided into two, Virunum became the capital of Noricum Mediterraneum. Afterward it held the rank of an episcopal see. But renewed and repeated German incursions followed, and *c* 408 the Visigothic King Alaric probably maintained his headquarters in the town. Not long afterward the provincial capital was moved to Teurnia or Tiburnia (near Spittal), although Virunum continued to survive until the Slav invasions at the end of the sixth century.

Its forum was situated toward the eastern end of the urban grid plan, flanked at the eastern extremity by a Capitol in the center of an open rectangular space, and enclosed on the other three sides by a double colonnade. A basilica was added later at the opposite end of the forum; it is now in fragmentary condition. Excavations nearby have revealed a residential block and a multi-purpose complex including baths (from which numerous marble copies of Greek statues have been extracted) and a meeting place of adherents of Dionysus, adorned with a floor mosaic depicting the god and his followers. A temple of Jupiter Dolichenus and another, double, shrine have been uncovered. The town also possessed a theater (in which a bust of Hadrian [117–38] has been discovered) and a building resembling a curiously elongated amphitheater, or a stunted circus.

An abundant water supply was provided by a canal, fountains, and water pipes, and sewage was carried in pipes beneath the main road. A hill north of the town (Grazer Kogel) contained rectangular and apsidal churches and was eventually fortified.

Vis *see* Issa

Vize *see* Bizye

Volaterrae, the Etruscan Velathri (Volterra). An inland city in northwestern Etruria, situated on a precipitous hill between the river Era—a southern tributary of the Arnus (Arno)—and the river Caecina (Cecina), of which the valley was rich in metals, exploited, it would appear, by Volaterrae as early as the second millennium BC.

After 1000, Iron Age cemeteries lying on the flanks of the hill suggest that a group of villages existed nearby; they evidently made small bronze figures. These villages amalgamated into a single city shortly before 600—rather late, since Mediterranean influences took some time to percolate so far north—although a huge landslide (Le Balze) has concealed most of the evidence of this process from our inspection. A relief on a gravestone, perhaps of *c* 500, displays a figure of a certain Avle Tite, wearing an elaborate hairstyle in the near-eastern manner and carrying a long spear and bow or short sword. It was during the Hellenistic period, however, that Volaterrae reached the height of its prosperity, under the guidance, it would seem, of the Ceicna (Caecina) clan, which owned extensive lands and clay pits and salt beds, and lent its name to (or took its name from) the adjoining river, of which the metal-rich valley, containing important burial places (Casale Marittimo, Montescudaio) gave Volaterrae access to the sea; where the city evidently possessed harbors, though their locations (Vada Volterrana, Castiglioncello, or at the mouth of the Fine stream?) still remain conjectural.

Toward the north, it is possible that a chain of further ports possessed Volaterran allegiance, extending upward from Pisae (Pisa) at the Arno estuary. But Volaterrae was particularly noteworthy for its landward expansion into the interior, up the Arno's tributaries the Era and Elsa, and along the Arno itself—where finds at Artemium (Artimino), Quinto Fiorentino and Faesulae (Fiesole) display strong Volaterran influence—and beyond the Arno in the fertile Mugello valley, and even as far north as the basin of the Po, where Misa (Marzabotto) and Felsina (Bononia, Bologna) received its imports, and two horseshoe-shaped gravestones at the latter city are inscribed with the name of the Caecina family.

Like other Etruscan cities, however, the Volaterrans gradually lost their independence to Rome. In 298 they joined the Latins against the Romans, whose consul defeated them and celebrated a triumph. In 205, during the Second Punic War, Livy records their contribution of ships' timber and grain to the Roman cause. After slave revolts at the beginning of the second century, reforms benefiting the middle class gave the city a new lease on life. In common with communities elsewhere in the peninsula, it gained the Roman franchise as a citizen *municipium* (90/89). After holding out, however, on behalf of the followers of Marius against Sulla (82–80), it was demoted to Latin status (according to which only the elected officials were Roman citizens). But Cicero, who, according to his *Letters,* enjoyed close links with Volaterrae, defended a native of the town against this loss of rank (63), and its restoration to full Roman citizenship was confirmed by Julius Caesar four years later. The Caecina house still remained rich enough to dedicate a large theater at Vallebona, north of the city. Volaterrae was the birthplace of the poet Persius (AD 34–62). It remained an important township after the beginning of the Middle Ages.

The overwhelming Balze landslide has removed the early buildings. But even before the villages coalesced into a single urban habitation, they reveal trench tombs of north Italian type; and burials between the seventh and fifth centuries have yielded fragmentary discoveries. The characteristic art form of Volaterrae, however, was represented by its great series of funerary urns—receptacles for ashes, since cremation persisted in northern Etruria—of which more than six hundred are to be seen in the local museum. Decorated with lively reliefs depicting scenes from Greek mythology (often portrayed with an Etruscan twist), and originally embellished with brilliant polychrome coloring and gilding, these cremation urns first made their appearance *c* 400 BC, but mostly date from a century or two later, when the local material of alabaster—a granular form of gypsum—came into extensive use. Volaterrae also retained its reputation as an important center of bronze work, and in the same epoch produced a characteristic type of red-figure pottery, which enjoyed widespread distribution.

The gate known as the Porta dell'Arco or Arco Etrusco, incorporated in the ancient walls, comprises a Roman vault rising from piers dating from the years around 200 BC. During the century that followed, a large increase of exports to the Adriatic port of Atria (Adria), near the mouth of the Padus (Po), bears witness to a revival in the fortunes of Volaterrae, apparently under the auspices of a commercial middle class.

Volos *see* Iolcus

Volsinii, the Etruscan Velsu, Velzna (Orvieto, from Latin Urbs Vetus, 'Old City'). Volsinii was situated in the interior of Etruria (now Umbria) on a volcanic plateau protected by formidable cliffs and overlooking the junction of the rivers Clanis (Chiana, now drained) and Pallia (Paglia), tributaries of the Tiber. The Clanis valley provided a route to Clusium (Chiusi), which—to judge from archaeological evidence—was responsible for the amalgamation of a group of villages at Volsinii *c* 500 BC. When, in the later part of the sixth century, the great Lars Porsenna is described by Livy as 'King of Volsinii,' this is probably because, as the monarch of Clusium, he ruled over Volsinii as its dependency.

Volsinii was useful to the Clusines because its river basins provided access to the navigable Tiber. But the city also possessed exceptional religious importance—and claimed antique mythical origins—not only because of its own temles (notably shrines of Nortia and the underworld deities), but also because of the proximity of the greatest of all the sanctuaries of Etruria, the Fanum Voltumnae; to which all the Etruscan states sent representatives every year to perform religious rituals, banding themselves into a Federation for this purpose. It may well have been because of the prestige derived from this holy place (which is now unidentifiable) that Volsinii played a large part in Etruscan expansion beyond the homeland, particulary, it would seem, in Campania, where local coins display the inscription 'Velzu,' which is closely reminiscent of the 'Velsu' on issues of Volsinii itself.

After the eclipse of Clusine power in about 500, Volsinii became an independent city-state. The tombs in its two cemeteries, laid out like miniature houses in straight right-angled streets, attain their wealthiest appearance at this time, though burials range in date from the eighth to third centuries BC (paintings from three graves, formerly kept at Florence, have now been returned to Orvieto). A necropolis in the suburban area of Cannicella, reexcavated in recent years, has been found to include or adjoin an important cult center; the objects unearthed have now been lodged in the Museo della Fondazione Faina. A strip of bronze displays an inscription giving the name of a goddess called Vei. In the surrounding region, the influence of Volsinii is apparent in finds at Acquapendente (above the Pallia), Bomarzo on the river Vezza, Bolsena (*see* below) on Lake Volsiniensis, and elsewhere. During the fourth century BC, however, the Romans saw in Volsinii an obstacle to their own expansion, and the city's natural defences were overcome when the supposedly impenetrable Ciminian Forest to the south was traversed by a Roman consul in 310. Not long afterward, in 294 and 280, other Roman commanders, too, celebrated Triumphs over Volsinii; and in 265-64, according to Zonaras, the Romans intervened to put down an insurrection of the local proletariat, thus strengthening the position of the city's to additional ruling class, whom as usual Rome maintained or installed as its puppets.

Nevertheless, the incident evidently convinced the Romans that the place had no useful future; and so its population was moved to another ancient center henceforward known as New Volsinii (Volsinii Novi; now Bolsena in Lazio), which was a station on the Via Cassia. Excavations at New Volsinii have revealed a town designed according to a rectangular street plan and containing a forum, amphitheater, theater, and baths. Private houses have also been uncovered. Volsinii Novi was the birthplace of Tiberius' praetorian prefect and principal minister Sejanus and of the fourth-century geographical writer Avienus, who belonged to the distinguished local family of the Rufii Festi.

Volsinii Novi *see* Volsinii

Volubilis (Oubili, Ksar Pharaoun). A city in western Mauretania (Morocco), thirteen miles north of the modern Meknès, on a fertile grain-bearing plateau at the foot of Mount Zerhoun, Volubilis was situated between two streams from which it took its name, meaning 'winding' in Berber. After an existence going back to prehistoric times, there is evidence of Phoenician (Carthaginian) and Liby-Phoenician influence from the third and second centuries BC.

Under Juba II, Rome's client king of Mauretania (25 BC–AD 23), the place enjoyed considerable prosperity. When his successor Ptolemaeus was murdered in AD 40 and the Mauretanians revolted against the Romans, Volubilis, under the command of its chief local official and chief priest Marcus Valerius Severus (son of Bostar), took the Roman side, and after Claudius' establishment of two provinces four years later, it became a Roman *municipium* in Mauretania Tingitana. Thereafter the town grew rapidly, especially in the period of the Severi (193–235), and seems to have replaced Tingi (Tangier) as the provincial capital. Inscriptions bear witness to a century-long series of meetings and agreements at Volubilis between the Roman governors (procurators) and the tribe of the Baquates in the interior. About 280/85, however, these tribesmen had become so menacing that the city was evacuated by the imperial administration. Thus it lay outside the province of Tingitana or Tingitania established shortly afterward by Diocletian and Maximian; although a population of Romanized Berbers retaining a semblance of the old organization went on living on the ruins until the Arabs arrived.

Pre-Roman houses have been excavated in the western sector of the habitation center, and traces of somewhat later dwellings can be seen on the south spur of the plateau, on which the early acropolis apparently stood. To the east, an unusual shrine of the epoch of Juba II, erroneously known as the 'Temple of Saturn,' goes back to an oriental tradition that has not been satisfactorily identified. At the city center a large colonnaded forum was built over earlier structures at about the time of Nero (AD 54–68). Then, in the 160s, a city wall perforated by eight gates and equipped with semicircular towers was erected. Major construction, systematization and reorientation took place in the Severan era, which witnessed the rebuilding of the forum, adjoined by a basilica and a capitolium dedicated by Macrinus (217–18).

This period also witnessed the major development of a northeastern quarter, comprising spacious and attractive houses (with which shops and oil presses and grain mills were often associated). It has been disputed whether the character of these dwellings is basically Greek or Roman, but the latter interpretation is now regarded as more probable. The quarter was approached from the south by a monumental colonnaded street, preceded by a monumental arch in honor of Caracalla (211–17) and flanked by the so-called 'Palace of Gordian,' probably the governors' residence and administrative office, rebuilt by Marcus Ulpius Victor under Gordian III (238–44), perhaps on the site of Juba's palace. Second- and third-century housing also provides examples of workmen's two-room dwellings, made of mud-brick. Three sets of baths and a small provision market (*macellum*) have come to light, and inscriptions offer evidence of Mithraic, Egyptian and Syrian cults, bearing witness to the presence of extensive near-eastern elements in the community. A remarkable feature of Volubilis is the quantity of first-class bronzes that have been found among its ruins. They include portraits of Cato the Younger and Juba, and a study of an old fisherman, and are now divided between the Volubilis and Rabat museums.

Vraona *see* Brauron

Vulci, the Etruscan Velcha. A city of southwestern Etruria (now Lazio), standing on a hill protected by steep cliffs, above a loop made by the river Armenta (Fiora) and two of its tributaries, six miles from the sea. The Armenta valley had known human habitation since early in the second millennium BC, and cemeteries at Vulci containing material going back at least as far as the ninth century bear witness to the early existence of approximately five separate villages on the site.

Their inhabitants already produced bronze work, suggesting exploitation of the metals of Mount Amiata, some thirty miles up the river (before Clusium [Chiusi] took over the major part of these mines). The villages at Vulci coalesced into a single city shortly before or after 700, at a time when the metal resources of the local inhabitants may have been increased by the acquisition (jointly with Caere [Cerveteri]) of part of Mount Tolfa—previously owned by Tarquinii (Tarquinia); and perhaps they also gained access to the more northerly Catena Metallifera (Metal-Bearing Chain). As was also the case elsewhere in Etruria, what prompted the Vulci villages to amalgamate was the desire to acquire these metals, and pay well for them, shown by Greek traders and settlers from Campania; and since these Greeks were in close touch with their compatriots at eastern Mediterranean trading posts, early Vulci tombs include gold and ivory objects decorated with various Syrian and other near-eastern motifs, as well as a scarab of the Egyptian pharaoh Psammetichus (Psamtik) I (*c* 663–610).

To judge by the magnificence of one of these graves, the Cuccumella (*see* below), Vulci must have reached the height of its grandeur at the time of its construction (*c* 560–550). The Vulcentines became the principal Etruscan mass-imitators of Corinthian vases, and developed their own attractive black-figure style—misleadingly known as 'Pontic,' owing to an erroneous interpretation—dispatching oil and wine far and wide, and exporting their own agricultural produce as well. Vulci was also the main Etruscan center of stone sculpture, and, in addition, expanded its traditional bronze work into an unequalled industry, of which examples are found in widespread areas far outside Etruria.

The rivers Armenta and Albinia (Albegna, further to the north) were not only the bases of Vulci's hinterland, containing dependent towns such as Suana (Sovana) and Statonia (Poggio Buco) beside the Armenta and Aurinia (the Etruscan Urina, now Saturnia) beside the Albinia, but also provided it with its ports, Regae (or Regisvilla, now Le Murelle: where traces of the Etruscan harbor have now been found) and Calusium (?) (*qv*; Orbetello) respectively. By sea and land alike Vulci possessed intensive connections with more southerly regions of Italy. Wall paintings from the François Tomb (*c* 300) reveal extensive glimpses of a rich historical and legendary tradition, related to the city's wars with the Romans, in which a certain Cneve Tarchunies Rumach—a 'Cnaeus Tarquinius of Rome,' clearly related to the Tarquin dynasty expelled from that city *c* 510—is slain by a Vulcentine; and other links appear on these paintings as well, strongly suggesting that Rome may have been dominated by men not only from Tarquinii (the Tarquins) and probably Clusium (Lars Porsenna), but also from Vulci—where, it should be noted, the Romans' mythical hero Aeneas was greatly revered.

There is also archaeological evidence that men from Vulci—no doubt with Rome as a convenient staging point—were principal agents and pioneers in the Etruscan expansion into Campania. One of its towns was known to the Romans as Volcei or Vulcei (now Buccino) and Campanian coins were inscribed with the name of 'Velecha,' which seems to be of similar derivation; while other pieces from the territory bear the name of Urina, presumably taken from Vulci's dependency Aurinia.

The overthrow of Etruscan interests in Campania by the Samnites, in the fifth century BC, must have been a serious blow to the Vulcentines, but they evidently succeeded in transferring their trading relations to northern Italy instead, where some of the best bronze work and jewelry found at Spina came from Vulci or imitated its techniques; while, conversely, numerous 'red-figure' vases from Greece continued to arrive at Vulci, probably often by way of Spina, until the middle of the same century. Like other Etruscans, the Vulcentines failed to help their compatriots at Veii against the Romans (*c* 396), so that their own turn came later. In 280 BC a Roman consul, Titus Coruncanius, celebrated a Triumph against not only Volsinii (Orvieto) but Vulci—which shortly afterward lost part of its territory to provide land for the new Roman colony at Cosa (Ansedonia). Thereafter its continued existence, although far below the glories of earlier times, received some encouragement from its position on the Via Aurelia, which led into the city over a five-arched bridge (The Ponte Rotto, poorly preserved); there is also a famous Abbadia Bridge of three arches, going back in part to the first century BC.

The hill of Vulci rises above a deserted countryside, and apart from a bare record in geographers' itineraries, Greek and Latin writers have left no account of its history and might. The habitation site has yielded a fourth-century temple and a first-century house. But in contrast to these sparse traces, the finds that have come out of Vulci's cemeteries since the 1820s have been gigantic. In 1842 it was observed that their yield even exceeded the riches of Pompeii and Herculaneum combined: by 1856 more than 15,000 tombs had been excavated and that was only a beginning. Forty per cent of all Athenian black-figure pots found in Etruria, and fifty per cent of all red-figure, come from Vulci's graves. The largest of them, the Cuccumella, of sixth-century date, has already been mentioned: it was a huge mound over two hundred feet in diameter, honeycombed by labyrinthine passages and originally surmounted by two thirty- or forty-foot-high towers of uncemented masonry, one cylindrical and the other conical. A smaller tomb of about the same period, the Cuccumelletta—with a roof carved to imitate woodwork—has recently been restored.

The fourth century witnessed the construction of large graves (culminating in the François Tomb) in which cells were built round a central T-shaped chamber. After 300, further burial places, of more modest dimensions and character, bear witness to the diminished importance of Vulci.

Wandering Rocks *see* Symplegades

Welschbillig *see* Augusta Trevirorum

Winchester *see* Venta Belgarum

Windisch *see* Vindonissa

Wippach (River) *see* Frigidus

Worms *see* Borbetomagus

Wroxeter *see* Viroconium Cornoviorum

Xanten *see* Vetera

Xanthus (Xanthos; in Lycian, Arnña; now Kınık). The principal city in Lycia (southern Asia Minor), presided over by an isolated hill with two summits, rising steeply above the left bank of the river Xanthus (Sirbis or Sirmis in Lycian, now Eşen Çayı), seven miles from the port of Patara (Kelemiş) near the river mouth. The town of Xanthus, mentioned in Homer's *Iliad,* was apparently first settled at the end of the eighth century BC, to which the earliest ceramic finds can be dated.

Herodotus records the Xanthians' heroic but unavailing resistance in 564/65 BC to a siege conducted by the Persian general Harpagus. The city submitted to Alexander the Great in 334/33 and then came under the successive influences of the Ptolemies and the Seleucids (197), whose monarch Antiochus III the Great ostensibly recognized its independence; but after his defeat by the Romans, the Treaty of Apamea (188) transferred it to the territory of Rhodes. Twenty years later Xanthus again had a period of relative independence, in which it was one of the leading cities of the Lycian League (*see* Lycia) and issued both local and federal coinage.

During the Civil Wars following the death of Julius Caesar, however, it was besieged and captured by Brutus, after an obstinate defence, suffering serious destruction and bloodshed (42). According to Appian, Brutus' enemy Antony subsequently encouraged its restoration (while confirming Lycian freedom); and a Temple of Caesar and priesthood of his cult, recorded in an inscription, may signify that Octavian (the future Augustus) provided aid for the same purpose in 30/29. In AD 43 Xanthus was incorporated in the Roman province of Lycia-Pamphylia, as one of the 'Metropoleis of the Lycian Nation.' On one occasion an appeal to the emperor by the representatives of Xanthus and the Lycian League secured the reversal of a governor's ruling.

An extraordinary feature of Xanthus is the abundance of its monumental shrines and heroes' tombs (*heroa*), ranging in date from the sixth century BC to first century AD. These structures generally took the form of a broad square pillar or shaft, or 'tower,' surmounted by a funerary chamber or sarcophagus; and some of the graves were adorned with sculptural reliefs of fine quality. The earliest is the Lion Tomb of *c* 545 BC, of which the reliefs are in the British Museum; so are those of the Tomb of the Harpies (or, more correctly, Sirens), of the early fifth century. A larger number of these monuments date from the period that followed. One remarkable example, dating from *c* 400, possesses a projecting roof that was once surmounted by the statue of the Lycian prince who was evidently buried there; this statue has vanished, but the rest of the tomb is almost completely preserved. The funerary chamber beneath the roof was decorated with reliefs showing the dynast's alleged victories (now in the İstanbul Archaeological Museum), and the monolithic podium was inscribed both in a version of the Lycian script—'Lycian B' or Milyan, still undeciphered—and in Greek. It has recently been established that this inscription describes the ruler who set up the pillar as a certain Kherei, who is also named on coins—issued mainly by mints in the Xanthus valley—that imitate the issues of the Persian satrap Tissaphernes.

The 'Monument of the Nereids' of *c* 400 assumes the appearance of a small Ionic temple, once again set on top of a tall shaft; this edifice, too, probably contained a burial chamber. The Nereid Monument was embellished with abundant carvings (preserved in the British Museum) and took its name from figures of girls with clinging drapery that are set between the columns, with birds and dolphins beneath their feet. Other reliefs on the monument, as elsewhere in Lycia, illustrate themes of local interest; although the idiom of such sculptures is Greek, their general concept is mainly derived from oriental traditions. Another impressive Xanthus tomb, of fourth-century date, still carries an ogival-lidded sarcophagus perching intact on its sturdy pillar.

The twin summits of the hill were occupied by the Lycian acropolis and its Greco-Roman equivalent. These two heights were enclosed by walls forming an irregular oblong shape. Stretches of polygonal masonry date from the fourth century BC, and are adjoined by Hellenistic sections. A city gate was erected *c* 190, and a *nymphaeum* (fountain building) that has now been surveyed combines Hellenistic and Hadrianic phases of construction. Other recent excavations have been directed to the Letoon or temple of Leto (Latona), who had long been the principal goddess of Xanthus, associated with the Nymphs from at least 337/6 BC, the date when a trilingual inscription in Greek, Lycian and Aramaic recorded the establishment of an altar and associated priesthood in her precinct. The temple of Leto, constructed *c* 175–150 but going back to a Lycian building erected (according to an inscribed base that has recently been discovered) by the dynast Arbinas *c* 400, probably developed out of a sanctuary at a spring. When Antiochus III recognized the independence of Xanthus, he formally consecrated the city to Leto and to her children Apollo and Artemis.

The monumental entrance (Propylaeum) of the Letoon, at the termination of a Sacred Way leading from the town, belongs, in its present form, to *c* AD 200, although earlier phases of Hellenistic and imperial construction are detectable. During the Principate, according to an inscription, a local priest of the Augusti staged gladiatorial combats and wild beast fights in the sanctuary. On the north and west sides of the temple terrace, the precinct was enclosed by a large Doric portico, dating back to the third century BC (when it replaced earlier structures), and subsequently modified on several occasions. A triumphal arch is dedicated to the emperor Vespasian (AD 69–79) as Savior and Benefactor of the Universe, and a Roman theater and Roman agora flanked by colonnades and dedicated to the twelve Lycian gods date from *c* 200.

Xanthus (River) *see* Ilium, Xanthus (city)

Xydas *see* Lyttus

Y

Yassıhüyük *see* Gordium

Yavneh *see* Jamnia

Yenişehir *see* Sigeum

Yevpatoriya *see* Cercinitis

Z

Zagora *see* Andros

Zama Regia. A city in north Africa (Tunisia). Its site is still undetermined; Polybius places it five days' journey from Carthage, and Sallust described it as a citadel on flat ground protected by artificial defences. It has been suggested that there were two or even four different Zamas, including a 'Major' and 'Minor' city, of which the former may or may not be the same as the Zama known as 'Regia' (royal). Sites proposed for the locations of one or another of these towns include Sidi Abd-el-Djedidi (or Sidi Amor Djedid) northwest of Kairouan—which is now, however, considered too remote for the more important settlement—Jama (which does not suit Sallust's description), and, more plausibly, Sebaa Biar, not far from the road leading northeast to Carthage.

The final engagement of the Second Punic War (202 BC), in which the army of Hannibal (back from Italy) was destroyed by Scipio Africanus, is known as the battle of Zama. But the location of this battle, too, is uncertain; though there is much to be said for its attribution to the plain of Draa-el-Metnan, about halfway between Sebaa Biar and the place described by Livy as Naraggara (Margaron in Polybius).

While the Numidian kingdom was independent, Zama Regia was one of its royal residences, and after Rome's annexation of Carthage (146) it was left outside the new province of Africa and remained one of the principal cities of the Numidian princes. Loyal to Jugurtha in his war against the Romans, it successfully resisted an attack by Quintus Caecilius Metellus, later known as Numidicus (109). During the civil war between Julius Caesar and the Pompeians, the Zamans supported Caesar after his victory at Thapsus and closed their gates to King Juba I of Numidia (46). Numidia was now converted into the province of Africa Nova, of which Zama Regia became the capital and Sallust the first governor.

According to Strabo, either this Zama or another was 'cast into ruins' by the Romans. It appears possible, however, that Zama Regia was made a Roman *municipium* by Octavian (the future Augustus) with the title of Julia—presumably before Numidia was temporarily allotted to Juba II (30-25 BC)—although the two coins that might seem to justify this supposition only survive in very few and very poorly preserved specimens. An inscription describing Zama 'Major' (or 'Minor,' the text is defective) as a Colonia Augusta may refer to Zama Regia and indicate that the place was elevated to colonial rank by Augustus after its incorporation in the province of Africa in 25. At all events, another inscription shows that a veteran colony was established or reestablished by Hadrian (AD 117-38), under the title of Colonia Aelia Hadriana Augusta.

Zancle *see* Messana

Zaragoza *see* Caesaraugusta

Zariaspa *see* Bactra

Zela (Zile). An inland center of Pontus (northern Asia Minor), situated on a low, isolated hill presiding over a crossroads beside a tributary (the Zile Suyu) of the Iris (Yeşil Irmak). Zela was an ancient autonomous temple domain dedicated to the cult of the goddess Anahita (Anaitis) and to the 'Persian deities' Omanus and Anadatus—to whose worship the annual sacred festival of the Sacaea was devoted—and possessed extensive territory in the adjoining fertile plain, cultivated by temple serfs. The cult, which was especially revered in connection with oaths, was attributed to the legendary Semiramis, queen of Assyria, but seems to have been inaugurated or developed by Achaemenid Persian generals, and continued, in partially Hellenized form, under the protection of the Mithridatid rulers of Pontus.

In 67 BC, during his Third War against the Romans, Mithridates VI Eupator defeated Lucullus' general Gaius Triarius in a swamp near Mount Scotium, three miles from Zela, inflicting a loss of 7000 men. During Pompey's settlement of 64, while he was pausing at Zela to bury Triarius' soldiers, he gave the place a civic constitution, settled many of its inhabitants within the walls (according to Strabo), and increased its territorial possessions. In 47 a narrow valley to the northwest of Zela was the scene of Julius Caesar's victory over the Pontic king Pharnaces II, after a brilliant campaign of five days; Pharnaces rashly launched an uphill attack that proved totally unsuccessful, and at his subsequent Triumph at Rome, Caesar displayed a placard bearing the message 'I came, I saw, I conquered (*veni, vidi, vici*)'.

Under Antony, *c* 40 or 37, Zela gained additional lands (thus possibly recuperating territorial losses inflicted by Caesar), and reverted from urban rank to its previous temple status within the kingdom of Polemo I of Pontus (d. 8 BC), in which it remained, with at least part of its territory, until Roman annexation in AD 64. Thereupon it became a city again, issuing coinage under the family of Septimius Severus (193-217). These issues portrayed the Propylaea on Zela's acropolis, a flaming altar on top of the same hill (?), a temple with a barrier across the entrance, a temple or gate with a curious triple pediment, an altar within a portico, and a gate to an altar court. Most or all of these designs relate to the sanctuary of Anaitis, which now lies beneath Byzantine and Turkish fortifications. On a flank of the acropolis a small theater is partly carved out of the rock.

Zeugma, formerly Seleucia on the Euphrates or on the Bridge (Balkıs). A city in Commagene (northern Syria, now southern Turkey), with a conical acropolis, overlooking the right (west) bank of the Euphrates, at its principal crossing point opposite Apamea (Birecik). The town was founded or refounded by Seleucus I Nicator (301–281 BC), who gave it the name of Seleucia. It was further defined as Seleucia on the Euphrates or on the Bridge—which originally seems to have been a pontoon—and was later known just as the Bridge (Zeugma). In 69 Cleopatra Selene, the daughter of Ptolemy VII Euergetes II, was put to death there by Tigranes I of Armenia, who had occupied the Seleucid territories. Zeugma was included in the client kingdom of Commagene by Pompey the Great (64/63), and subsequently became a strategically important and prosperous stronghold (and probably a legionary garrison) of the Roman province of Syria, guarding its frontier with the Parthian empire.

Pliny the Elder describes it as Zeugma, and its mint issued coinage under that name from the time of Trajan (AD 98–117); a new stone bridge over the Euphrates dates from his reign. Coins issued under Philip the Arab (244–49) depict the temple of Zeus on the acropolis, offering a bird's-eye perspective view of the building, together with its forecourt and portico and the mountain behind. The temple has not survived, but traces of walls and a road can be seen. Fine mosaic floors have also been found, of which parts are preserved at Berlin and Leningrad; one such pavement illustrates the Labors of Hercules, and another depicts a Roman emperor surrounded by personifications of the provinces of the empire. During the later imperial epoch, Zeugma formed part of the province of Euphratensis. Theodoretus (*c* 393–466), listing the hermits who flourished during his youth, mentions the region around Zeugma as one of their favorite habitations, implying that the whole of Euphratensis and Syria Salutaris were divided into large territories belonging to this and other cities.

Zippori *see* Sepphoris

Zliten *see* Sugolin

Zollfeld *see* Virunum

BIBLIOGRAPHY

This bibliography contains only writers mentioned in the text. Those whose work has not survived, or survived only in fragments, are marked thus *.

ANCIENT LITERARY SOURCES

GREEK

Acts of the Apostles. A book of the New Testament, probably written in the late 1st century AD. An account of the early Church, with special reference to St. Paul.

Aeschines, *c* 397 or 389–*c* 322 BC. Athenian orator

Aeschylus, born Eleusis (Attica), 525/524–456 BC. Athenian tragic dramatist

Agathias, born Myrina (Aeolis), *c* 531–80 AD. Byzantine historian

Alcaeus, born Mytilene (Lesbos), *c* 620 BC. Lyric poet*

Alcman, born Lydia (?), lived at Sparta later 7th century BC. Poet*

Alexander of Aphrodisias, born Aphrodisias (Caria), end of 2nd century AD. Peripatetic (Aristotelian) philosopher

Alexander Polyhistor, born Miletus (Ionia), 1st century BC. Encyclopedic compiler*

Anacreon, born Teos (Ionia), *c* 570 BC. Lyric, elegiac and iambic poet

Anaxagoras, born Clazomenae (Ionia), *c* 500–428 BC. Pre-Socratic philosopher*

Anaximander, born Miletus (Ionia), *c* 610–after 546 BC. Pre-Socratic philosopher*

Anaximenes, born Miletus (Ionia), soon after 600–528/525 BC. Pre-Socratic philosopher*

Anthemius, born Tralles (Lydia), 6th century AD. Architect and architectural writer

Antiochus, born Syracuse (Sicily); 5th century BC. Historian*

Anyte, born Tegea (Arcadia), early 3rd century BC. Poet*

Apollodorus of Athens, born Alexandria (Egypt), *c* 180 BC. Writer on mythology, theology and geography

Apollonius of Perga, born Perga (Pamphylia), first half of the 3rd century BC. Mathematician

Apollonius Rhodius, born Egypt, *c* 295–*c* 215 BC. Epic poet (*Argonautica*)

Appian, born Alexandria (Egypt), *c* AD 95–*c* 160. Historian

Aratus, born Soli (Cilicia), *c* 315–*c* 240 BC. Stoic astronomical poet

Archilochus, born Paros, *c* 710–after 648 BC. (?). Poet

Archimedes, born Syracuse (Sicily), *c* 287–212 BC. Mathematician and scientist

Archytas, born Taras (southern Italy), first half of the 4th century BC. Scientist and philosopher*

Aristeas, Letter of, *c* 100 BC or a little earlier. By a Jewish author professing to be a pagan official Aristeas writing to his brother Philocrates.

Aristides, Aelius, born Mysia (northwestern Asia Minor), AD 117–*c* 189. Orator and literary hypochondriac

Aristippus, born Cyrene, 4th century BC. He or his grandson of the same name founded the Cyrenaic philosophical school.*

Aristobulus, born Cassandrea (Macedonia), late 4th century BC. Historian of Alexander the Great*

Aristophanes, 457/445–shortly before 385 BC. Athenian comic dramatist

Aristotle, born Stagirus (Macedonia), 384–322 BC Philosopher and scientist

Arrian, born Nicomedia (Bithynia), *c* AD 95–*c* 175. Historian, geographer and military writer

Artemidorus, born Ephesus (Ionia), *c* 100 BC. Geographer*

Athanasius, St., born Alexandria (Egypt) (?), *c* AD 295–373. Christian theologian

Athenaeus, born Naucratis (Egypt), *c* AD 200. Writer of an encyclopedic symposium

Aurelius, Marcus, AD 121–80. Roman emperor (161–80) and Stoic philosopher

Bacchylides, born Iulis (Ceos), *c* 524/521 (?)–after 452 BC. Poet

Basil, St., born Caesarea (Cappadocia), *c* AD 330–69. Christian bishop and theologian

Callimachus, Cyrene, *c* 310/305–*c* 240 BC. Poet and scholar

Callisthenes, born Olynthus (Macedonia), late 4th century BC. Nephew of Aristotle; historian of Alexander the Great*

Carneades, born Cyrene, 214/13–129/8 BC. Platonist philosopher; founder of the New or Third Academy.*

Cassius Dio *see* Dio Cassius

Cercidas, born Megalopolis (Arcadia), *c* 290–220 BC. Lawgiver, soldier, popular and semi-satirical Cynic poet

Charito, born Aphrodisias (Caria). 2nd century AD. Novelist (*Chaereas and Callirhoe*)

Chrysippus, born Soli (Cilicia), *c* 280–207/6 BC. Head of the Stoic school of philosophy*

Chrysostom, St. John *see* John Chrysostom

Cleanthes, born Assus (Troad), *c* 331–232 BC. Head of the Stoic school of philosophy

Clearchus, born Soli (Cyprus), *c* 340–250 BC. Peripatetic (Aristotelian) philosopher*

Clement of Alexandria, St., born Athens (?), *c* AD 150–211/16. Christian theologian

Ctesias, born Cnidus (Caria), before and after 400 BC. Physician and historian*

Damostratus, probably later 1st century BC. Writer on marine and historical matters*

Demetrius of Phaleron, born Phaleron (Attica), later 4th century BC. Athenian statesman, orator, popular philosopher and critic*

Democritus, born Abdera (Thrace), 460/457 BC. Atomic philosopher*

Demosthenes, 384–322 BC. Athenian orator and statesman

Dio Cassius, born Nicaea (Bithynia), *c* AD 163/4–after 229. Historian and Roman official

Dio Chrysostom (Dio of Prusa), born Prusa (Bithynia), *c* AD 40–after 112. Orator and philosopher

Diodorus Siculus, born Agyrium (Sicily), 1st century (until at least 21) BC. Universal historian

Diogenes of Tarsus, born Tarsus (Cilicia), later 2nd century BC. Epicurean philosopher*

Diogenes the Babylonian, born Seleucia on the Tigris (Mesopotamia), *c* 240–152 BC. Head of the Stoic school of philosophy*

Dionysius of Halicarnassus, born Halicarnassus (Caria), later 1st century BC. Rhetorician, critic and historian

Ecclesiasticus *see* Hebrew writers (Ben Sira)

Empedocles, born Acragas (Sicily), *c* 493–433 BC. Poet, statesman, scientist, physician, mystic

Ephorus, born Cyme (Aeolis), *c* 405–330 BC. Historian*

Epicurus, born Samos, 341–270 BC. Founder of the Epicurean school of philosophy

Eratosthenes, born Cyrene, *c* 275–194 BC. Polymath, geographer and poet*

Eucleides, born Megara, *c* 450–380 BC. Founder of the Megarian school of philosophy*

Eudoxus, born Cnidus (Caria), *c* 390–340 BC. Mathematician, astronomer and geographer*

Euripides, born Phlya (Attica), *c* 485/80–407/6 BC. Athenian tragic dramatist

Eusebius, born Caesarea Maritima (Syria Palaestina), *c* AD 260–340. Christian bishop and ecclesiastical historian; biographer of Constantine I the Great.

Galen, born Pergamum (Mysia), *c* AD 129–*c* 199. Physician, anatomist, physiologist, psychologist, philosopher and critic

Gorgias, born Leontini (Sicily), *c* 483–376 BC. Rhetorician and sophist (itinerant lecturer)

Gospel of Thomas *see* Coptic Writers

Hegesinous or Hegesinos, 3rd century BC. Platonist philosopher; head of the Academy*

Heliodorus, born Emesa (Syria), probably 3rd century AD. Novelist (*Aethiopica*)

Herodes Atticus, born Marathon, *c* AD 101–77. Athenian sophist and Roman senator*

Herodotus, born Halicarnassus (Caria), *c* 480–*c* 425 BC. Historian

Hesiod, born Cyme (Aeolis), migrated to Ascra (Boeotia), late 8th century BC (?). Epic poet (*Theogony, Works and Days*).

Hieronymus, born Cardia (Thrace), *c* mid-4th century–*c* 260/250 BC. Officer, administrator and contemporary historian*

Hipparchus, born Nicaea (Bithynia), *c* 190–after 126 BC. Astronomer and geographer*

Hippocrates, born Cos, 5th or perhaps early 4th century BC. Physician, regarded as the founder of medical science. It is uncertain whether any of the *Corpus Hippocraticum* derives from his authorship.

Homer, born Chios or Smyrna or elsewhere, 8th century BC (?). Epic poet: reputed composer of *Iliad* and *Odyssey*. Various other poems in Epic Cycle and Hymns (*see* next item) are wrongly ascribed to him.

Homeric Hymn to Demeter, late 7th or early 6th century BC. Not by Homer

Hymn to Isis, 2nd century AD. On an inscription found on the island of Andros; prose later reworked into verse.

Hymn to Serapis (Sarapis), *c* 225/200 BC. Inscribed on a column of the Serapeum at Delos

Hypatia, born Alexandria, died AD 415. Mathematician, astronomer and Neoplatonist philosopher*

Iamblichus, born Chalcis Beneath Libanus (Syria), *c* AD 250–306/37. Neoplatonist philosopher and writer on the supernatural

Ibycus, born Rhegium (southern Italy), 6th century BC. Poet*

Ignatius, St., born Antioch (Syria), died AD 107/110. Christian bishop and theologian

Isaeus, born Chalcis (Euboea) (?), *c* 420/15–mid-4th century BC. Athenian author

Isidorus of Charax, born Charax (near mouth of Tigris), early 1st century AD. Geographical writer*

Isocrates, 436–338 BC. Athenian rhetorician and educationalist

John (Johannes) Chrysostom, St., born Antioch (Syria), mid 4th century–AD 407. Christian patriarch and theologian.

John Malalas *see* Malalas

John Stobaeus *see* Stobaeus

John, St., Gospel According To., probably early 2nd century AD. The fourth Gospel in the New Testament. Of uncertain authorship

Josephus, born Jerusalem, AD 37/8–after 94/5. Jewish notable and historian (*The Jewish War, Jewish Antiquities, Against Apion, Life)*

Julian the Apostate, AD 332–63. Roman emperor (361–63) and writer on many themes

Justus, born Tiberias (Galilee), 1st century AD. Jewish notable and historian (opposed to Josephus)*

Lesbonax, born Mytilene (Lesbos), 1st century BC. Philosopher*

Libanius, born Antioch (Syria), AD 314–*c* 393. Greek rhetorician and popular lecturer

Logia Jesu *see* Coptic Writers (Gospel of Thomas)

Longus, born Lesbos (?), early 3rd century AD. Novelist (*Daphnis and Chloe,* a pastoral romance).

Lucian, born Samosata (Commagene), *c* AD 120/25–after 180. Popular philosopher and satirical writer

Lucius of Patrae, born Patrae (Achaea), Uncertain date. Novelist (*Metamorphoses*); source of Apuleius (*see* Latin writers)*

Lysias, born Athens (of Syracusan father), *c* 459 (?)–*c* 380 BC. Speechwriter

Maccabees, First Book of, *c* 125 BC (and subsequent second edition). History of achievements of Hasmonaean (Jewish) dynasty; translation of lost Hebrew original. Canonical to Catholicism and Orthodoxy; part of the Protestant Apocrypha.

Malalas, John (Johannes), born (?) and lived at Antioch (Syria), *c* AD 549–78. Byzantine rhetorician and historian

Marcus Aurelius *see* Aurelius

Marcus the Deacon, *c* AD 420. Life of Pophyrius, Bishop of Gaza. Rewritten in the sixth century

Megasthenes, born Ionia, *c* 350–290 BC. Envoy of Seleucus I Nicator and geographical writer on India (*Indica*)*

Meleager, born Gadara (Syria), *c* 140–*c* 170 BC. Epigrammatic poet and anthologist

Memnon, born Heraclea Pontica (Pontus), early 2nd century AD (?). Historian of his city*

Menedemus, born Eretria (Euboea), *c* 339–265 BC. Philosopher*

Menippus, born Sinope (Pontus) (?), early 3rd century BC. Popular philosopher and satirical writer

Mimnermus, born Colophon or Smyrna (Ionia) or Astypalaea (Sporades), late 7th century BC. Elegiac poet

Musaeus Grammaticus, late 5th or early 6th century AD. Epyllion (miniature epic): *Hero and Leander.*

Mythographi Vaticani, collection of mythological tales formed in 9th or 10th century AD.

Nonnus, born Panopolis (Egypt), 5th century AD (?). Epic poet (*Dionysiaca*)

Origen, born Alexandria (Egypt), AD 185/6–254/5. Christian theologian

Oxyrhynchus Historian, 387/346 BC. Historian. Nine hundred and ninety lines (mainly relating to 396/95 BC) were discovered on papyri at Oxyrhynchus (Egypt).

Panaetius, born Rhodes, 185/80–*c* 109 BC. Head of the Stoic school of philosophy (129)*

Panyassis, born Halicarnassus (Caria), early 5th century–*c* 454 BC. Epic poet*

Parmenides, born Elea (southwest Italy), *c* 515 BC. Pre-Socratic philosopher

Paul, St., born Tarsus (Cilicia), *c* 10/1 BC–AD 64/67 (?). Writer of *Epistles* in New Testament

Pausanias, born near Magnesia Beside Sipylus (Lydia), 2nd century AD. Travel writer

Phaenias, born Eresus (Lesbos), *c* 320 BC. Peripatetic (Aristotelian) philosopher*

Philistion, born Locri Epizephyrii (southern Italy), late 5th and early 4th century BC. Physician

Philistus, born Syracuse, Sicily, *c* 430–356 BC. Historian of Sicily*

Philo of Byblos, born Byblos (Phoenicia), AD 64–141. Writer on Phoenician religion, etc. drawing on Sanchuniathon (*see* Phoenician writers)*

Philodemus, born Gadara (Syria), *c* 110–*c* 40 BC. Philosopher and poet

Philostratus, born Lemnos (?), *c* AD 170–between 244 and 249. Sophist (popular philosopher)

Pindar, born Cynoscephalae (Boeotia), *c* 518–*c* 438 BC. Lyric poet

Plato, *c* 429–347 BC. Athenian philosopher

Plutarch, born Chaeronea (Boeotia), before AD 50–after 120. Biographer and philosopher

Pollux, born Naucratis (Egypt), later 2nd century AD. Rhetorician and scholarly writer (*Onomasticon*)

Polyaenus, born Macedonia, 2nd century AD. Rhetorician and excerpter*

Polybius, born Megalopolis (Arcadia), *c* 200–after 118 BC. Historian

Porphyry, born Tyre (Phoenicia) or Batanea (Syria), Philosopher and writer on religion

Posidonius, born Apamea (Syria), *c* 135–*c* 50 BC. Philosopher, rhetorician and scientist*

Priscus, born Panium (Thrace), 5th century AD. Rhetorician, historian and envoy

Proclus, born Lycia, AD 410/12–485. Neoplatonist philosopher

Procopius, born Caesarea Maritima (Syria Palaestina), *c* AD 500–65. Byzantine historian

Pseudo-Scylax *see* Scylax

Pseudo-Scymnus *see* Scymnus

Ptolemy, born Ptolemais Hermiou (Upper Egypt), *c* AD 100–*c* 178. Astronomer, mathematician and geographer

Pytheas, born Massalia (southern France), end 4th century BC. Explorer and geographer*

Revelation of St. John the Divine (Apocalypse), 2nd century AD. Book of the New Testament. Authorship uncertain.

Rhinthon, born Taras (southwestern Italy), *c* 300 BC. Comic playwright*

Sappho, born Eresus (?) (Lesbos), later 7th century BC. Lyric poet*

Scylax, born Caryanda (Caria), late 5th century BC. Geographer. *Periplus* (Pseudo-Scylax) is of the 4th century BC.

Scymnus, born Chios, *c* 185 BC. Geographer. *Periegesis* (Pseudo-Scymnus) is of *c* 90 BC or earlier

Seleucus the Chaldaean, born Seleucia on the Tigris (Mesopotamia), *c* 150 BC (?). Astronomer*

Semonides, born Samos, but especially associated with Amorgos, 7th–6th centuries BC. Iambic and elegiac poet

Simonides, born Iulis (Ceos), *c* 556–468 BC. Poet

Siro, 1st century BC. Epicurean philosopher at Naples (southern Italy). Teacher of Virgil, to whom he left his home and property*

Sophocles, born Colonus (Attica), *c* 496–406 BC. Atheneian poet and tragic dramatist

Sophron, born Syracuse (Sicily), 5th century BC. Writer of mime*

Stephanus of Byzantium, 6th century AD. Grammarian and compiler who worked at Constantinople.

Stesichorus (originally named Tisias), born Mataurus (southern Italy), lived at Himera (Sicily), *c* 632/29–556/3 BC (?). Choral lyric poet.

Stobaeus, John (Johannes), born Stobi (Macedonia), early century AD. Encyclopedist and excerpter

Strabo, born Amasia (Pontus), *c* 63 BC–at least AD 21. Geographer and historian

Suidas (Suda). A lexicon of the later 10th century AD.

Thaletas, born Gortyna (Crete), lived at Sparta, 7th century BC. Wrote songs and paeans*

Thebais. Poem of Epic Cycle, 7th century BC. Wrongly attributed to Homer

Theocritus, born Syracuse (Sicily), 310/300–260/50 BC. His *Idylls* founded bucolic and pastoral poetry

Theognis, born Megara, mid-6th century BC. Elegiac poet

Theophrastus, born Eresus (Lesbos), *c* 370–288/5 BC. Philosopher and scientist; Aristotle's successor as head of the Lyceum

Theopompus, born Chios, *c* 378/76–after 323 BC. Historian*

Thomas, Gospel of *see* Coptic Writers (Gospel of Thomas)

Thucydides, *c* 460/55–*c* 400 BC. Athenian historian of Peloponnesian War

Timaeus, born Tauromenium (Sicily), *c* 356–*c* 260 BC. Historian*

Timotheus, born Miletus (Ionia), *c* 450–*c* 360 BC. Poet*

Tisias *see* Stesichrous

Tyrtaeus, born (?) and lived at Sparta, 7th century BC. Elegiac poet

Vatican Mythographers *see* Mythographi Vaticani

Xanthus, born Sardes (Lydia), 5th century BC. Historian*

Xenarchus, born early 1st century BC. Lived in Seleucia Beside the Calycadnus (Cilicia), Alexandria, Athens and Rome. Peripatetic (Aristotelian) philosopher*

Xenocrates, born Calchedon (Bithynia), late 4th century BC. Platonist philosopher, head of Academy*

Xenocrates, born Aphrodisias (Caria), later 1st century AD. Physician*

Xenophanes, born Colophon (Ionia), *c* 570 (?)–*c* 476 BC. Pre-Socratic philosopher, scientist, theologian and poet*

Xenophon, *c* 428–*c* 354 BC. Athenian historian, man of letters, public figure and soldier

Zeno, born Citium (Cyprus), 335/4–*c* 262. Founder of the Stoic school of philosophy*

Zeno of Elea, born Elea (southern Italy), *c* 500. Pre-Socratic philosopher*

Zeno of Laodicea, born Laodicea by the Lycus (Phrygia), 1st century BC. Orator, rhetorician and statesman*

Zonaras, 12th century AD. Byzantine historian and theologian

Zosimus, *c* AD 500. Pagan Byzantine historian

LATIN

Aetna, 1st century AD (before 79). Didactic poem of unknown authorship

Ambrose, St., born Gaul, *c* AD 339–97. Christian bishop and theologian

Ammianus Marcellinus, born Antioch (Syria), *c* AD 330. Historian

Anonymus Valesianus (Valesiana Excerpta). Two historical texts about Constantine I the Great (AD 306–37) and the period 474–526

Apuleius, born Madaurus (Numidia), *c* AD 123. Novelist (*Metamorphoses* or *The Golden Ass*), orator and philosopher

Asconius, born Patavium (northeastern Italy), 9 BC–AD 76. Biographer, essayist and critic

Augustine, St., born Thagaste (northern Africa), AD 354–430. Christian bishop and theologian

Augustus (Gaius Octavius, Octavian), 63 BC–AD 14. First Roman *princeps* (emperor) and author of minor literary works. Left political testament (*Res Gestae Divi Augusti* or *Monumentum Ancyranum*)

Ausonius, born Burdigala (Aquitania), *c* AD 310–*c* 395. Poet (*Mosella* etc.)

Avienus, born Volsinii (Etruria), 4th century AD. Geographer and poet

Boethius, *c* AD 480–524. Philosopher and Christian theologian

Caesar, Julius, 100–44 BC. Conqueror of Gaul, dictator: *Gallic War, Civil War*

Cato the Elder ('the Censor'), born Tusculum (Latium), 234–149 BC. Historian (*Origines*), earliest text-book on rhetoric, scientific studies;* *On Agriculture*

Catullus, born Verona (northern Italy), *c* 84–late 50s BC. Poet

Cicero, born Arpinum (Latium), 106–43 BC. Orator, rhetorician, philosopher, letter writer, poet and statesman

Columella, born Gades (southern Spain), *c* AD 65. Writer on agriculture, in prose and verse

Cornelius Gallus *see* Gallus

Curtius, mid-1st century AD or soon after. Historian and biographer

Cyprian, St., born northern Africa, *c* AD 200–58. Christian bishop and theologian

Eugippius, died after AD 533. Abbot of Castellum Lucullanum (near Neapolis, Campania) and writer of *Life of St. Severinus* (d. 482)

Eumenius, born Augustodunum (Gaul), *c* AD 264. Teacher of rhetoric; delivered speech in 298 urging the emperors to help rebuild the local school (no. 9 of *Panegyrici Latini qv*)

Eutropius, born Burdigala (Aquitania) (?), 4th century AD. Historian

Festus, later 2nd century AD. Epitomizer of the Augustan scholar Verrius Flaccus

Frontinus, *c* AD 30–104. Roman official and writer on military subjects and engineering

Gallus, Cornelius, born Forum Julii (southern Gaul), *c* 69–26 BC. First governor of Egypt. Elegiac poet*

Gregory of Tours, St., born Arverna (Gaul), *c* AD 539–94. Bishop of Civitas Turonum (tours) and historian of the Franks

Hieronymus, St. *see* Jerome

Historia Augusta, probably late 4th century AD. Collection of biographies (bearing the names of fictitious authors) of Roman emperors, Caesars and usurpers from AD 117 to 284

Horace, born Venusia (southern Italy), 65–8 BC. Poet: *Odes, Epodes, Satires, Epistles, Art of Poetry*

Hydatius, born Lemica (northwestern Spain), 4th century AD, died after 468. Wrote continuation of St. Jerome's *Chronicle*

Itineraries of the Roman empire include *Itinerarium Antoninianum* (late 3rd century AD), *Bordeaux or Jerusalem Itinerary* (4th century), and itinerary in *Ravenna Cosmography* (*c* 700)

Jerome (Hieronymus), St., born Stridon (northwestern Illyricum), c. AD 348–420. Christian writer: Latin Bible (Vulgate), *Chronicle* (to 378), *Letters* etc.

Jordanes, of Gothic or Danubian origin, mid-6th century AD. Historian of the Goths (*Getica*) and Romans (*Romana*)*

Julius Caesar *see* Caesar

Justin, probably 3rd century AD. Wrote an Epitome of universal history (*Historiae Philippicae*) by the Augustan writer Trogus [*qv*]

Juvenal, born Aquinum (Latium), *c* AD 50–after 127. Satirist

Lactantius, born northern Africa, *c* AD 240/50–*c* 320. Christian theologian

Livy, born Patavium (northeastern Italy), 59 BC–AD 17. History of Rome in 142 books (35 survive)

Lucan, born Corduba (southern Spain), AD 39–65. Epic poet (*Civil War,* known as *Pharsalia*)

Lucretius, *c* 94–55 (?). Philosophical (Epicurean) poet (*On the Nature of the Universe*)

Martial, born Bilbilis (Spain), *c* AD 40–*c* 104. Epigrammatist

Mela, born Tingentera (southern Spain), wrote *c* AD 37/54. Geographer

Monumentum Ancyranum *see* Augustus

Naevius, *c* 270–201 BC. Comic dramatist and epic poet (*Bellum Poenicum*)*

Nonius Marcellus, born Thubursicu (Numidia), early 4th century AD. Lexicographer and grammarian

Notitia Dignitatum, *c* AD 395/414. A description of the administrative system and official posts of the western and eastern Roman empires

Orosius, born Bracara Augusta (Callaecia, northwestern Spain), *c* AD 380–*c* 420. Christian theologian and historian

Ovid, born Sulmo (central Italy), 43 BC–AD 17 (?). Elegiac poet; also *Metamorphoses* (hexameters) and lost tragedy

Pacuvius, born Brundusium (southern Italy), 220–*c* 130 BC. Tragic dramatist*

Panegyrici Latini (XII). Collection of speeches eulogizing the emperor or his representatives, from the times of Trajan (AD 98–117) to Theodosius I (379–95), but mostly of the early 4th century AD. *See also* Eumenius

Passions (Passiones, Martyrdoms). Descriptions of the execution of Christian martyrs, e.g. St. Firmin and St. Quirinus

Patrick, St., born Bannauenta (unidentified, northwestern England), 5th century AD. Patron saint of Ireland. *Confession* and *Coroticus* (letter to Celtic king of Strathclyde)

Petronius 'Arbiter' (perhaps the consul Titus Petronius Niger), died AD 66. Novelist (*Satyricon*; much is lost, but *Dinner of Trimalchio,* etc. survive)

Placidus, Spain (?), 5th/6th century AD. Grammarian and compiler

Plautus, born Sarsina (Umbria), *c* 254–184 BC. Comic dramatist

Pliny the Elder, born Comum (northern Italy), AD. 23/4–79. Writer on military science, language, history.* *Natural History*

Pliny the Younger, born Comum (northern Italy); AD 61/2–before 114. Literary letters and Panegyric of Trajan

Pollio, born Marrucini (central Italy), 76 BC–AD 5. Public figure and historian, orator, critic, grammarian, tragic dramatist*

Prosper Tiro, born Aquitania (southwestern Gaul); 5th century AD. Christian theologian

Prudentius, born Caesaraugusta (?) (northeast Spain), AD 348–after 405. Christian poet

Quintillian, born Calagurris (northern Spain), c. AD 35–c. 100. Educationalist and critic

Res Gestae Divi Augusti *see* Augustus

Rufinus, born Aquileia (northeastern Italy), *c* AD 345–410. Christian translator and writer, and founder of a monastery on the Mount of Olives (Jerusalem)

Rutilius Namatianus, born Tolosa (?) (southwestern Gaul), early 5th century AD. Poet; works include *The Return Home* or *The Gallic Journey*

Scriptores Historiae Augustae *see* Historia Augusta

Seneca the Elder, born Corduba (southern Spain), *c* 55 BC–AD 37/41. Historian,* and writer on rhetoric

Seneca the Younger, born Corduba (southern Spain), *c* 4 BC–AD 65. Statesman, philosopher, literary letter writer, tragic poet and satirist

Servius, born *c* AD 360/65 (?). Commentator on Virgil and grammarian

Sidonius Apollinaris, born Lugdunum (Gaul), AD 430/31–480s. Lived in land of Arverni. Public figure, poet and literary letter writer

Silius Itálicus, born Patavium (?) (northern Italy), AD 25/6–101. Epic poet (*Punica*)

Solinus, early 3rd century AD. Geographical encyclopedist

Statius, born Neapolis (southwestern Italy), *c* AD 45–96. Epic poet (*Thebais, Achilleis*); also *Silvae*

Suetonius, born Hippo Regius (northern Africa), *c* AD 69–140. Biographer (*The Twelve Caesars,* etc.)

Sulpicius Severus, born *c* AD 363. Christian historian and hagiographer (Life of St. Martin of Tours)

Tacitus, born southern Gaul or northern Italy, AD 56/7–before or after 117. Historian (*Histories, Annals*). Biographer of his father-in-law *Agricola.* Descriptive *Germania. Dialogue on Orators*

Tertullian, born Carthage (northern Africa), *c* AD 155/60–*c* 240 (?). Christian writer

Trogus, Pompeius, born in the territory of the Vocontii (southern Gaul), wrote during the age of Augustus. Author of the *Historiae Philippicae,* a universal history in 44 books, epitomized by Justin (*qv.*)

Ulpian, born Tyre (Phoenicia), after mid-2nd century AD–223. Jurist

Valerius Antias, born Antium (Latium), early 1st century BC. Historian*

Valesiana Excerpta *see* Anonymus Valesianus

Varro, born Reate (Latium), 116–27 BC. Encyclopedic scholar and writer, historian and antiquarian.* *On the Latin Language* and *On Farming*

Velleius Paterculus, born Capua (?) (Campania), *c* 19 BC–after AD 31. Officer and historian.

Virgil, born Andes (near Mantua/northern Italy/), 70–19 BC. Epic (*Aeneid*), descriptive and quasi-didactic (*Georgics*) and pastoral poet (*Eclogues*).

Vitruvius, wrote *c* 27/13 BC on architecture and engineering

OTHER WRITERS

Aramaic

Talmud comprises *Mishnah* (*see* Hebrew writers) and *Gemara* ('completion'), but the term is generally applied to the latter (a commentary on the *Mishnah*), comprising (1) the Jerusalem or Palestinian *Talmud,* in western Aramaic (completed 4th century AD), and (2) the Babylonian *Talmud,* in eastern Aramaic (5th century).

Armenian

Mesrop (Mashtotz), St., born Hatzekatz (Taraun, Armenian SSR), *c* AD 362–440. Inventor of the Armenian alphabet and first translator of the New Testament and Proverbs

Coptic

Gospel According to Thomas (*Logia Jesu, Sayings of Jesus*), 2nd century AD (?). Inscribed on a papyrus found at Nag Hammadi (Upper Egypt). Ascribed to 'Didymus Judas Thomas'

German (Middle High German)

Nibelungenlied, *c* AD 1200. Epic poem containing material going back to the 5th century

Hebrew

Ben Sira (Sirach), *c* 190–180 BC Author of *Ecclesiasticus* (or *The Wisdom of Jesus the Son of Sirach*), a non-canonical (deuterocanonical) 'wisdom' book of the Apocrypha, translated from the Hebrew original (of which parts have been found) into Greek by the author's grandson Yeshua (Joshua.)

Damascus Document (or *Zadokite Fragment*), of uncertain date; parts have been found at Cairo and Qumran (Israel), and the Document is analogous to the *Rule* of the Qumran community (founded *c* 140/130 BC)

Ecclesiasticus *see* Ben Sira

Ezekiel, Book of. Part of the Hebrew Bible (Old Testament). The prophet Ezekiel was exiled from Jerusalem to Babylonia in 597 BC and probably composed the greater part of the book

Jeremiah, Book of. Part of the Hebrew Bible (Old Testament). The prophet Jeremiah was active before the fall of the kingdom of Judah (587 BC) and then moved to Egypt. A portion of the (composite) book was probably dictated by the prophet to Baruch.

Joshua, Book of. Part of the Hebrew Bible (Old Testament), 6th century BC (?). An account of Joshua the son of Nun, successor of Moses (early 12th century ?).

Joshua *see also* Ben Sira

Mishnah, reputedly systematized by Patriarch Judah I ha-Nasi (*c* AD 135–219). A massive collection of teachings of the oral Hebrew Law, in Mishnaic Hebrew

Sirach *see* Ben Sira

Song of Songs (*Song of Solomon*). Part of the Hebrew Bible (Old Testament); one of the Megilloth (Rolls). Love poems, much later than King Solomon, indicated as the author in the title.

Zadokite Fragment—*see* Damascus Document.

Syriac

Bardesanes (Bar-Daisan), born Edessa (northern Syria), born AD 154–222. Scholarly treatises, of which *Dialogue of Destiny* (or *Book of the Laws of Nations*) has survived, in the original and partly in Greek translation. Hymns.

Ephraim (Aphrem, Ephraem), St., born Nisibis (Mesopotamia), *c* AD 306–73. Hymns, homiles and biblical commentaries, of which early versions in Greek, Armenian, Coptic, Arabic and Ethiopic are also extant.

II Modern Books

E. Akurgal, *Ancient Civilizations and Ruins of Turkey,* Istanbul, 1983

G. Alföldy, *Noricum,* London, 1974

Arheologiya S.S.S.R., Moscow, 1984

G. E. Bean, *Aegean Turkey,* London, 1966

G. E. Bean, *Lycian Turkey,* London, 1978

G. E. Bean, *Turkey Beyond the Maeander,* London, 1971

G. E. Bean, *Turkey's Southern Shore,* London, 1968

J. Bennett, *Towns in Roman Britain,* Princes Risborough, 1984.

D. Berciu, *Daco-Romania,* Geneva-Paris-Munich, 1978.

W. R. Biers, *The Archaeology of Greece,* Ithaca, 1980

J. Boardman, *The Greeks Overseas,* London, 1980

A. Boethius, and J.B. Ward-Perkins, *Etruscan and Roman Architecture,* Harmondsworth, 1970

F. Boitani, M. Cataldi and M. Pasquinucci, *Etruscan Cities,* London, 1975

L. Bonfante, *Out of Etruria: Etruscan Influence North and South,* Oxford, 1981

K. Branigan (ed.), *The Atlas of Archaeology,* London, 1982

W. Bray and D. Trump, *A Dictionary of Archaeology,* London, 1970

O. J. Brendel *Etruscan Art,* Harmondsworth 1978

Cambridge Ancient History (new ed.), Vol. III, Part I (*The Prehistory of the Balkans*), Part 3 (*The Expansion of the Greek World*), Cambridge, 1982; Vol. VII, Part 1 (*The Hellenistic World*), Cambridge, 1984; Vols. III. 2, IV, V, VII. 2 and VII are due to be published in 1986/7.

G. E. F. Chilver, *Cisalpine Gaul,* Oxford, 1941

G. M. Cohen, *The Seleucid Colonies, Wiesbaden, 1978*

J. M. Cook, *The Greeks in Ionia and the East,* London, 1962

T. Cornell and J. Matthews, *Atlas of the Roman World,* Oxford, 1982

A. Cotterell (ed.), *The Encyclopedia of Ancient Civilizations,* Leicester 1980

J. J. Coulton, *Greek Architects at Work,* London, 1977

E. M. Craik, *The Dorian Aegean,* London, 1979

C. Davaras, *Guide to Cretan Antiquities,* Park Ridge, 1976

B. De Jongh, *Companion guide to Mainland Greece,* London, 1979

C. De Palma, *La Tirrenia antica,* Florence, 1984

J. F. Drinkwater, *Roman Gaul: The Three Provinces 58* BC–AD *260,* Ithaca, 1983

C. J. Emlyn-Jones, *The Ionians and Hellenism,* London, 1978

M. I. Finley (ed.), *Atlas of Classical Archaeology,* London, 1977

M. Frederiksen and N. Purcell, *Campania,* London, 1984

R. Goodburn and P. Bartholomew (ed.), "Aspects of the *Notitia Dignitatum*" (British Archaeological Reports, Supplementary Series 15); Oxford Conference 1974, London, 1976

M. Grant, *From Alexander to Cleopatra,* London, 1982

M. Grant, *The Etruscans,* London, 1980

M. Grant, *The Jews in the Roman World,* London, 1973

P. Grimal (ed. G.M.Woloch), *Roman Cities,* Madison 1983

M. Guido, *Sicily: An Archaeological Guide,* London 1967

M. Guido, *Southern Italy: An Archaeological Guide,* London 1972

N. G. L. Hammond, *A History of Macedonia,* Vols. I & II, Oxford 1972, 1978

N. G. L. Hammond, *Atlas of the Greek and Roman World in Antiquity,* Park Ridge, 1981

N. G. L. Hammond, *Epirus,* Oxford, 1967

N. G. L. Hammond, and H. H. Scullard (ed.), *The Oxford Classical Dictionary,* 2nd ed., Oxford 1970

W. V. Harris, *Rome in Etruria and Umbria,* Oxford, 1971

B. V. Head, *Historia Numorum,* 2nd ed., Oxford, 1911, reprint 1963

R. F. Hoddinott, *Bulgaria in Antiquity,* London, 1975

A. H. M. Jones (ed. P. M. Fraser), *Cities of the Eastern Roman Provinces,* 2nd ed., Oxford, 1971

A. H. M. Jones, *The Greek City,* Oxford, 1940

L. Lepple, *Colonisation and Veteran Settlement in Italy: 47* BC–AD *14,* London, 1983

R. Krautheimer, *Early Christian and Byzantine Architecture,* Harmondsworth, 1965

P. La Baume, *The Romans on the Rhine,* 2nd ed., Bonn, 1972

D. Leekley and N. Efstratiou, *Archaeological Excavations in Central and Northern Greece,* Park Ridge, 1980

D. Leekley and R. Noyes, *Archaeological Excavations in Southern Greece,* Park Ridge, 1976

D. Leekley and R. Noyes, *Archaeological Excavations in the Greek Islands,* Park Ridge, 1975

A. Lengyel and G. Radan, *The Archaeology of Roman Pannonia,* Lexington (Kentucky) and Budapest, 1980

P. Levi, *Atlas of the Greek World,* Oxford, 1980

P. Mackendrick, *Roman France,* New York, 1972

P. Mackendrick, *Romans on the Rhine,* New York, 1970

P. Mackendrick, *The Dacian Stones Speak,* Chapel Hill, 1975

P. Mackendrick, *The Greek Stones Speak,* 2nd ed., New York, 1982

P. Mackendrick, *The Iberian Stones Speak,* New York, 1967

P. Mackendrick, *The Mute Stones Speak,* New York, 1960

P. Mackendrick, *The North African Stones Speak,* New York, 1980

J. C. Mann, *Legionary Recruitment and Veteran Settlement during the Principate,* London, 1983

A. Mocsy, *Pannonia and Upper Moesia,* London, 1974

O. Morkholm and G. K. Jenkins, *Hellenistic Coins,* London, 1985

W. J. Murnane, *The Penguin Guide to Ancient Egypt,* London, 1983

O. Murray, *Early Greece,* London, 1980

R. F. Paget, *Central Italy: An Archaeological Guide,* London, 1973

A. Pauly, G. Wissowa and W. Kroll (ed.), *Realencyclopädie der classischen Altertumwissenschaft,* Stuttgart, 1894

A. G. Poulter (ed.), *International Symposium on Ancient Bulgaria (1981),* Nottingham, 1983

M. J. Price, *Greek Coins under the Roman Empire,* London 1985

M. J. Price and B. L. Trell, *Coins and their Cities,* London, 1977

D. and F. R. Ridgway, *Italy Before the Romans,* London, 1979

M. Robertson, *History of Greek Art,* Cambridge, 1975

S. Rossiter, *Greece (Blue Guide),* 4th ed., London, 1981

E. T. Salmon, *Roman Colonisation under the Republic,* London, 1969

E. T. Salmon, *The Making of Roman Italy,* London, 1982

K. N. Schoville, *Biblical Archaeology in Focus,* Grand Rapids, 1978

H. Schutz, *The Romans in Central Europe,* New Haven, 1985

H. H. Scullard, *Roman Britain,* London, 1979

A. Sherratt (ed.), *The Cambridge Encyclopaedia of Archaeology,* Cambridge, 1980

E. M. Smallwood, *The Jews under Roman Rule,* Leiden, 1976

G. Adam Smith, *The Historical Geography of the Holy Land,* new ed., London, 1966

A. M. Snodgrass, *Archaeology and the Rise of the Greek State,* Cambridge, 1977

R. Stillwell (ed.), *The Princeton Encyclopaedia of Classical Sites,* Princeton, 1976

J. A. Thompson, *The Bible and Archaeology,* Grand Rapids, rev. ed., 1980

V. Velkov, *Roman Cities in Bulgaria,* Amsterdam, 1980

J. Wacher, *Roman Britain,* 2nd ed. London, 1980

G. Williams, *Eastern Turkey: A Guide and History,* London, 1972

R. J. A. Wilson, *A Guide to the Roman Remains in Britain,* 2nd ed., London 1980

Also catalogs of coins and inscriptions

Journals and Archaeological Reports

American Journal of Archaeology

Ampurias

Anatolian Studies

Antike Welt

Antiquaries' Journal

Apulum

Archaeologia Hungarica

Archaeologia Iugoslavica

Archaeologiai Értesito

Archäologische Zeitung

Archaeology

Archaiologia

Archaiologika Analekta ex Athenon

Archaiologike Ephemeris

Archaiologikon Deltion

Archeo

Archeologia (Paris)

Archeologia Classica

Archeologia Viva

Archeologiya

Archivo Español de Arqueologia

Arheološki Vestnik

Atiquot

Berytus

Britannia

Buletin Arkeologjik

Bulletin d'Archéologie Algérienne

Bulletin d'Archéologie Marocaine

Classical Review

Dacia

Das Altertum

Fasti Archaeologici

Gallia

Gazette Archéologique

Germania

Iliria

Illustrated London News

Iraq

Israel Exploration Journal

Jahrbuch des Deutschen Archäologischen Instituts (Archäologischer Anzeiger)

Jahreshefte des Österreichischen Archäologischen Instituts in Wien

Journal of Hellenic Studies (Archaeological Reports)

Journal of Roman Studies

L'Année Epigraphique

L'Année Philologique

Levant

Libyan Studies

Magna Graecia

Mitteilungen des Archäologischen Instituts der Ungarischen Akademie der Wissenchaften

Mitteilungen des Deutschen Archäologischen Instituts (Athenische, Römische Abteilung)

Monumenti Antichi

Notizie degli Scavi

Opuscula Romana

Palestine Exploration Quarterly

Pontica

Pro Austria Romana

Revue Archéologique

Revue des Études Anciennes

Rivista di Archeologia

Saalburg Jahrbuch

Starinar

Studi Etruschi

Studi Romani

Studi şi Cercetàri de Istorie Veche şi Arheologie

Syria

Türk Arkeoloji Dergisi

Also numismatic journals